Lecture Notes in Computer Science 3729

Commenced Publication in 1973
Founding and Former Series Editors:
Gerhard Goos, Juris Hartmanis, and Jan van Leeuwen

Yolanda Gil   Enrico Motta
V. Richard Benjamins   Mark A. Musen (Eds.)

The Semantic Web – ISWC 2005

4th International Semantic Web Conference, ISWC 2005
Galway, Ireland, November 6-10, 2005
Proceedings

  Springer

Volume Editors

Yolanda Gil
University of Southern California
Information Sciences Institute
Marina Del Rey, CA 90292, USA
E-mail: gil@isi.edu

Enrico Motta
The Open University
Knowledge Media Institute
Walton Hall, Milton Keynes, MK7 6AA, UK
E-mail: e.motta@open.ac.uk

V. Richard Benjamins
Intelligent Software Components, iSOCO S.A.
Spain
E-mail: rbenjamins@isoco.com

Mark A. Musen
Stanford University
Stanford Medical Informatics
251 Campus Drive, MSOB X-215, Stanford, CA 94305, USA
E-mail: musen@smi.stanford.edu

© Photograph on the cover: Brian Wall, Galway, Ireland

Library of Congress Control Number: 2005934830

CR Subject Classification (1998): H.4, H.3, C.2, H.5, F.3, I.2, K.4

ISSN	0302-9743
ISBN-10	3-540-29754-5 Springer Berlin Heidelberg New York
ISBN-13	978-3-540-29754-3 Springer Berlin Heidelberg New York

Springer is a part of Springer Science+Business Media

springeronline.com

© Springer-Verlag Berlin Heidelberg 2005
Printed in Germany

Typesetting: Camera-ready by author, data conversion by Scientific Publishing Services, Chennai, India
Printed on acid-free paper   SPIN: 11574620   06/3142   5 4 3 2 1 0

Preface

A little over a decade has passed since the release of the first Netscape browser. In 1995, the World Wide Web was viewed largely as an academic curiosity. Now, of course, the Web is an integral part of the fabric of modern society. It is impossible to imagine science, education, commerce, or government functioning without the Web. We take the Web for granted, and often assume that Internet connectivity is guaranteed to all of us as a birthright.

Although the Web indeed has become "world wide" and has lost a bit of its original aura as a consequence of its ubiquity, a burgeoning community of researchers and practitioners continues to work toward the next generation of the Web—a Web where information will be stored in a machine-processable form and where intelligent computer-based agents will access and automatically combine myriad services on the Internet of the kind that are now available only to people interacting directly with their Web browsers.

It is this vision that attracted several hundred computer scientists, developers, vendors, government workers, venture capitalists, students, and potential consumers of the Semantic Web to Galway, Ireland, November 6–10, 2005, for the 4th International Semantic Web Conference (ISWC 2005). Building on previous successful meetings in Sardinia, Sanibel Island, and Hiroshima, this fourth annual conference demonstrates new research results and technology that are bringing us closer to making the Semantic Web as real as the Netscape browser was in 1995. With increasing participation from industry and mounting evidence that research initiatives are being translated into practical solutions, ISWC 2005 showed that the Semantic Web is taking root.

This volume contains the main proceedings of ISWC 2005, which we are uniformly excited to provide. The tremendous response to our Call for Papers from a truly international community of researchers and practitioners, the careful nature of the review process, and the breadth and scope of the papers finally selected for inclusion in this volume all speak to the quality of the conference and to the contributions made by the papers in these proceedings.

The Research/Academic Track of the conference attracted 217 submissions, an increase over the number of papers submitted to ISWC 2004. This result shows the robustness of the research base in this area, at a time when everyone's conference calendar has become extremely crowded. The review process included three distinct phases. First, all papers were reviewed by members of the Scientific Program Committee; then, in a second phase, each paper and associated reviews provided the basis for a meta-review process, led by an experienced member of the Scientific Program Committee, who had not participated in the earlier review process. This strategy produced a joint recommendation from reviewers and the meta-reviewer to the Program Chairs, who then, in a third phase, analysed each recommendation in detail, in some cases commissioning additional reviews and initiating further discussions. The Program Chairs then made a definitive decision regarding each paper. Such a structured process ensured a high-quality review, but of course required a great deal of effort from the members of the Scientific Program Committee. It is a sign of the health of our community that the Scientific Program Committee responded extremely well to the task and put tremendous work into ensuring a high-quality review process. In total, 54 papers were accepted, out of 217 submissions, a 25% acceptance rate.

The Industrial Track of ISWC 2005 comprised 17 papers, a significant increase compared to ISWC 2004. We are very encouraged to see the growing number of organizations that are applying Semantic Web technology in industrial settings. More than 30 papers were submitted to the Industrial Track, and each paper was reviewed by three referees. All reviewers were recognized researchers, managers, and practitioners from non-academic organizations, enabling us to obtain "industrial" feedback on these contributions. The majority of the papers deal with applications in particular industrial sectors, including automobile manufacturing, law, healthcare, entertainment, public administration, and telecommunications. A second group of papers describes new technology for building applications, including Web services and aggregation technology. Other papers present methodological and feasibility aspects of building industrial applications that incorporate Semantic Web technology.

A unique aspect of the International Semantic Web Conferences is the *Semantic Web Challenge*. The challenge is a competition in which workers from both academia and industry are encouraged to show how Semantic Web techniques can provide useful or interesting applications to end-users. In the three years since the Challenge was first organised, we have seen more than 30 integrated applications built around distributed data sources, which use some kind of semantic descriptions to handle the data. This year, nine applications were submitted to the Challenge. Each submission was reviewed by three different reviewers who have backgrounds in either industry or academia. The reviewers judged the applications on the extent to which they take full advantage of Semantic Web techniques and provide interesting usage scenarios. The submitters of the top five applications were asked to provide short descriptions of their work, which are included in these proceedings. This year's Semantic Web Challenge applications are quite diverse. They include a system that uses ontologies to integrate information from different bio-informatics databases, peer-to-peer systems that exchange ontology meta-data or publication data, an annotation system for conference photos, and a system that visualises the distribution and evolution of research areas. The winner(s) of the challenge were announced at the ISWC and they received 1,000 travel support plus a 250 voucher to purchase books from Springer.

IWSC 2005 was further enriched by four invited talks from prominent scientists: Professor Carole Goble, University of Manchester; Dr. Alfred Spector, IBM Software Group; Daniel J. Weitzner, W3C; and Sir Tim Berners-Lee, W3C. The conference was also enlivened by a large poster and demonstration session, a tutorial program, a doctoral symposium for graduate students, and a rich set of workshops that highlighted new and emerging ideas. We are grateful to Riichiro Mizoguchi (Poster and Demo Chair), Natalya F. Noy (Workshop Chair), R.V. Guha (Tutorial Chair), and Edward Curry and Enda Ridge (Doctoral Symposium Organizers) for ensuring the success of these events. We offer many thanks to Eric Miller, for co-ordinating the production of the semantic mark-up associated with each contribution to the conference.

We would like to thank the Semantic Web Science Association for providing the organizational oversight for ISWC 2005. The meeting would not have been possible without the tireless work of the local organizers at the Digital Enterprise Research Institute in Galway. Christoph Bussler provided executive oversight to an impressive team that included Brian Cummins (local arrangements), Liam Ó Móráin (industrial relations), Brahmananda Sapkota (publications), and Juan Gomez and Tingting Zhu (publicity). We would also like to acknowledge the generous contribution from our sponsors, in particular from Science Foundation Ireland (SFI), and to thank our sponsor chairs, Dean Allemang and York Sure, for their excellent work.

Finally we would like to thank Manos Papagelis, for providing excellent support for the Confious conference system, which was used to manage the review process.

In conclusion, ISWC 2005 was an extremely exciting event, reflecting the high level of energy, creativity, and productivity that permeates the Semantic Web community. This is a great time to be involved in Semantic Web activities and we hope all the attendees found the conference both productive and stimulating.

November 2005   Yolanda Gil and Enrico Motta
                              Programme Co-chairs, Research/Academic Track

                                                   Richard V. Benjamins
                                      Programme Chair, Industrial Track

                                              Michel Klein and Ubbo Visser
                                 Co-chairs, The Semantic Web Challenge

                                                          Mark A. Musen
                                                      Conference Chair

Organising Committee

General Chair: Mark A. Musen (Stanford University, USA)

Research/Academic Track Co-chairs: Yolanda Gil (ISI, University of Southern California, USA)

Enrico Motta (The Open University, UK)

Industrial Track Chair: Richard V. Benjamins (iSOCO S.A., Spain)

Tutorials Chair: R.V. Guha (Google, USA)

Workshops Chair: Natalya F. Noy (Stanford University, USA)

Meta-data Chair: Eric Miller (World-Wide Web Consortium)

Sponsorship Chair: Liam Ó Móráin (DERI, Ireland)

Local Organization Chair: Christoph Bussler (DERI, Ireland)

Publications Chair: Brahmananda Sapkota (DERI, Ireland)

Doctoral Symposium Co-chairs: Edward Curry (National University of Ireland, Galway, Ireland)

Enda Ridge (University of York, UK)

Posters and Demo Chair: Riichiro Mizoguchi (Osaka University, Japan)

Semantic Web Challenge Co-chairs: Michel Klein (Vrije Universiteit Amsterdam, The Netherlands)

Ubbo Visser (Universität Bremen, Germany)

Programme Committee

Karl Aberer (EPFL, Switzerland)

Jose Luis Ambite (ISI, USA)

Lora Aroyo (Eindhoven University of Technology, The Netherlands)

Wolf-Tilo Balke (L3S and University of Hannover, Germany)

Sean Bechhofer (University of Manchester, UK)

Zohra Bellahsene (Université Montpellier II, France)

Richard V. Benjamins (iSOCO, Spain)

Abraham Bernstein (University of Zurich, Switzerland)

Walter Binder (EPFL, Switzerland)

Kalina Bontcheva (University of Sheffield, UK)

Paolo Bouquet (University of Trento, Italy)

Francois Bry (Ludwig-Maximilians-Universität München, Germany)

Liliana Cabral (The Open University, UK)

Diego Calvanese (Free University of Bozen-Bolzano, Italy)

Mario Cannataro (University "Magna Graecia" of Catanzaro, Italy)

Jeremy Carroll (Hewlett-Packard Labs, UK)

Pierre-Antoine Champin (University of Lyon, France)

Vinay Chaudhri (SRI International, USA)

Weiqin Chen (University of Bergen, Norway)
Ann Chervenak (ISI, University of Southern California, USA)
Nigel Collier (National Institute of Informatics, Japan)
Oscar Corcho (University of Manchester, UK)
Isabel Cruz (University of Illinois at Chicago, USA)
Jos de Bruijn (University of Innsbruck, Austria)
Mike Dean (BBN, USA)
Keith Decker (University of Delaware, USA)
Stefan Decker (National University of Ireland, Galway, Ireland)
Thierry Declerck (DFKI, Germany)
Grit Denker (SRI International, USA)
Ian Dickinson (Hewlett-Packard, UK)
Ying Ding (University of Innsbruck, Austria)
John Domingue (The Open University, UK)
Erik Duval (Katholieke Universiteit Leuven, Belgium)
Martin Dzbor (The Open University, UK)
Jerome Euzenat (INRIA, Rhône-Alpes, France)
Boi Faltings (EPFL, Switzerland)
Dieter Fensel (University of Innsbruck, Austria)
Richard Fikes (Stanford University, USA)
Aldo Gangemi (National Research Council, Italy)
Maria Gini (University of Minnesota, USA)
Fausto Giunchiglia (University of Trento, Italy)
Carole Goble (University of Manchester, UK)
Christine Golbreich (University of Rennes, France)
Asun Gomez-Perez (Universidad Politecnica de Madrid, Spain)
Marko Grobelnik (J. Stefan Institute, Slovenia)
Nicola Guarino (National Research Council, Italy)
Mohand Said Hacid (University of Lyon 1, LIRIS-CNRS, France)
Patrick Hayes (Florida Insitute for Human and Machine Cognition, USA)
Jeff Heflin (Lehigh University, USA)
Jim Hendler (University of Maryland, USA)
Masahiro Hori (Kansai University, Japan)
Ian Horrocks (University of Manchester, UK)
Michael Huhns (University of South Carolina, USA)
Jane Hunter (University of Queensland, Australia)
Zachary Ives (University of Pennsylvania, USA)
Anupam Joshi (University of Maryland, Baltimore County, USA)
Rich Keller (NASA Ames, USA)
Carl Kesselman (ISI, University of Southern California, USA)
Roger (Buzz) King (University of Colorado, USA)
Yasuhiko Kitamura (Kwansei Gakuin University, Japan)
Matthias Klusch (DFKI, Germany)
Alfred Kobsa (University of California, Irvine, USA)
Yiannis Kompatsiaris (Informatics and Telematics Institute, Thessaloniki, Greece)

Manolis Koubarakis (Technical University of Crete, Greece)
Ruben Lara (Technologia, Informacion y Finanzas, Spain)
Ora Lassila (Nokia Research Center, USA)
Thibaud Latour (CRP Henri Tudor, Luxembourg)
Georg Lausen (Albert-Ludwigs-Universität Freiburg, Germany)
David Leake (Indiana University, USA)
Domenico Lembo (University of Rome, Italy)
Maurizio Lenzerini (University of Rome, Italy)
Robert MacGregor (Siderean Software, USA)
David Martin (SRI International, USA)
Mihhail Matskin (Royal Institute of Technology, Sweden)
Masaki Matsudaira (OKI, Japan)
Diana Maynard (University of Sheffield, UK)
Brian McBride (Hewlett-Packard, UK)
Luke McDowell (United States Naval Academy, USA)
Deborah McGuinness (Stanford University, USA)
Sheila McIlraith (University of Toronto, Canada)
Vibhu Mittal (Google Research, USA)
Pavlos Moraitis (University of Cyprus, Cyprus)
Boris Motik (FZI Forschungszentrum Informatik, Germany)
Wolfgang Nejdl (L3S and University of Hannover, Germany)
Tim Oates (University of Maryland, Baltimore County, USA)
Bijan Parsia (University of Maryland, USA)
Peter Patel-Schneider (Bell Labs, USA)
Terry Payne (University of Southampton, UK)
Paulo Pinheiro da Silva (Stanford University, USA)
Dimitri Plexousakis (University of Crete, Greece)
Line Pouchard (Oak Ridge National Laboratory, USA)
Chris Priest (Hewlett-Packard, UK)
Chantal Reynaud (University of Orsay – LRI, France)
Mark Roantree (Dublin City University, Ireland)
Marie-Christine Rousset (University of Orsay – LRI, France)
Stefan Rüger (Imperial College London, UK)
Henryk Rybinski (Warsaw University of Technology, Poland)
Norman Sadeh (Carnegie Mellon University, USA)
Fereidoon Sadri (University of North Carolina, USA)
Ulrike Sattler (University of Manchester, UK)
Guus Schreiber (Vrije Universiteit Amsterdam, The Netherlands)
Amit Sheth (University of Georgia, USA)
Wolf Siberski (L3S and University of Hannover, Germany)
Carles Sierra (Spanish Research Council, Spain)
Michael Sintek (DFKI, Germany)
Andrzej Skowron (Institute of Mathematics, Warsaw University, Poland)
Derek Sleeman (University of Aberdeen, UK)
Steffen Staab (University of Koblenz, Germany)

Giorgos Stamou (National Technical University of Athens, Greece)
Lynn Andrea Stein (Olin College, USA)
Heiner Stuckenschmidt (Vrije Universiteit Amsterdam, The Netherlands)
Rudi Studer (University of Karlsruhe, Germany)
Gerd Stumme (University of Kassel, Germany)
Said Tabet (Macgregor Group, USA)
Hideaki Takeda (National Institute of Informatics, Japan)
Herman ter Horst (Philips Research, The Netherlands)
Raphael Troncy (National Research Centre, Italy)
Yannis Tzitzikas (University of Namur, Belgium)
Andrzej Uszok (Florida Institute for Human and Machine Cognition, USA)
Frank van Harmelen (Vrije Universiteit Amsterdam, The Netherlands)
Dan Vodislav (Conservatoire National des Arts et Métiers, France)
Christopher Welty (IBM Watson Research Center, USA)
Steve Willmott (Universitat Politècnica de Catalunya, Spain)
Marianne Winslett (University of Illinois at Urbana - Champaign, USA)
Michael Wooldridge (University of Liverpool, UK)
Guizhen Yang (SRI International, USA)
Yiyu Yao (University of Regina, Canada)
Djamel Zighed (University of Lyon 2, France)

Industrial Track Programme Committee

Chair: Dr. Richard V. Benjamins (iSOCO, Spain)

Technology

Rama Akkiruja (IBM T.J. Watson Research Center, New York, USA)
Dean Allemang (TopQuadrant Inc., USA)
Jose Manuel Lopez Cobos (Atos Örigin, Spain)
Jürgen Angele (Ontoprise, Germany)
Jack Berkowitz (Network Inference, USA)
Vinay K. Chaudhri (SRI, USA)
Jesús Contreras (iSOCO, Spain)
Oscar Corcho (iSOCO, Spain)
Marten Den Uyl (ParaBots, The Netherlands)
Michael Denny (Consultant, USA)
Elmar Donar (SAP, Germany)
Garry Edwards (ISX, USA)
David Ferrucci (IBM T.J. Watson Research Center, New York, USA)
Lars M. Garshol (Ontopia, Norway)
Atanas Kiryakov (Ontotext, Bulgaria)
Chris Preist (HP Labs, Bristol, UK)

Juan Antonio Prieto (Ximetrix, Spain)
Christian de Sainte Marie (ILOG, Franca)
Amit Sheth (Semagix, UK)
Chris van Aart (Acklin, The Netherlands)
Andre Valente (Knowledge Ventures, USA)

Telecom

John Davies (British Telecom, UK)
Alistair Duke (BT, UK)
Shoji Kurakake (NTT DoCoMo, Japan)
Alain Leger (France Télécom, France)

Cultural Heritage

Carlos Wert (Residencia de Estudiantes, Spain)

Knowledge Management

Ralph Traphoener (Empolis, Germany)
Andy Crapo (GE, USA)
Gertjan van Heijst (Oryon, The Netherlands)

Enterprise Systems

Kim Elms (SAP, Australia)

Automotive

Ruediger Klein (DaimlerChrysler, Germany)
Alexander Morgan (General Motors, USA)

Aeronautics

Mike Uschold (Boeing, USA)

Public Administration

Alasdair Mangham (London Borough of Camden, UK)

Pharmaceutics, Biomedicine

Andreas Presids (Biovista, Greece)

Engineering

Richard Watts (Lawrence Livermore National Labs, USA)

Legal

Pompeu Casanovas (IDT, UAB, Spain)

Standards

Jose Manuel Alonso (W3C)
Ivan Herman (W3C)

Local Organising Committee

Chair: Christoph Bussler (DERI, Ireland)
Johannes Breitfuss (DERI, Austria)
Brian Cummins (DERI, Ireland)
Alice Carpentier (DERI, Austria)
Edel Cassidy (DERI, Ireland)
Peter Capsey (DERI, Ireland)
Gerard Conneely (DERI, Ireland)
Brian Ensor (DERI, Ireland)
Christen Ensor (DERI, Ireland)
Hilda Fitzpatrick (DERI, Ireland)
Gearóid Hynes (DERI, Ireland)
Mick Kerrigan (DERI, Ireland)
Edward Kilgarriff (DERI, Ireland)
Sylvia McDonagh (DERI, Ireland)
Fergal Monaghan (DERI, Ireland)
Matthew Moran (DERI, Ireland)
Liam Ó Móráin (DERI, Ireland)
Seaghan Moriarty (DERI, Ireland)
Joseph O'Gorman (DERI, Ireland)
Katharina Siorpaes (DERI, Austria)
Brendan Smith (DERI, Ireland)
Maria Smyth (DERI, Ireland)
Brian Wall (DERI, Ireland)
Ilona Zaremba (DERI, Ireland)

Additional Reviewers

Nik Naila Binti Abdullah (Université Montpellier II, France)
Raja Afandi (University of Illinois at Urbana-Champaign, USA)
Salima Benbernou (Université Montpellier II, France)

Ansgar Bernardi (DFKI, Germany)
Uldis Bojars (National University of Ireland, Ireland)
Roberto Boselli (University of Milano-Bicocca, Italy)
Carola Catenacci (National Research Council, Italy)
Philippe Chatalic (University of Orsay, France)
Wei Chen (University of Delaware, USA)
Timothy Chklovski (USC Information Sciences Institute, USA)
Massimiliano Ciaramita (National Research Council, Italy)
Emilia Cimpian (DERI, Ireland)
Philippe Cudre-Mauroux (Ecole Polytechnique Fédérale de Lausanne,
    Switzerland)
Martine De Cock (Ghent University, Belgium)
Tomasso Di Noia (Politecnico di Bari, Italy)
Jörg Diederich (L3S and University of Hannover, Germany)
Thomas Eiter (Vienna University of Technology, Austria)
Carlos F. Enguix (National University of Ireland, Ireland)
Nicola Fanizzi (University of Trento, Italy)
Cristina Feier (University of Innsbruck, Austria)
Mariano Fernandez-López (Universidad Politecnica de Madrid, Spain)
Stefania Galizia (The Open University, United Kingdom)
Sarunas Girdzijauskas (Ecole Polytechnique Fédérale de Lausanne, Switzerland)
Birte Glimm (University of Manchester, UK)
Francois Goasdoue (University of Orsay, France)
Antoon Goderis (University of Manchester, UK)
Jennifer Golbeck (University of Maryland, USA)
Karthik Gomadam (University of Georgia, USA)
Perry Groot (University of Nijmegen, The Netherlands)
Yuanbo Guo (Lehigh University, USA)
Hakim Hacid (University of Lyon 2, France)
José Kahan (World Wide Web Consortium, France)
Yardan Katz (University of Maryland, USA)
Christoph Kiefer (University of Zurich, Switzerland)
Malte Kiesel (DFKI, Germany)
Jintae Kim (University of Illinois at Urbana-Champaign, USA)
Fabius Klemm (Ecole Polytechnique Fédérale de Lausanne, Switzerland)
Jacek Kopecky (University of Innsbruck, Austria)
Reto Krummenacher (University of Innsbruck, Austria)
Julien Lafaye (Conservatoire National des Arts et Métiers, France)
Holger Lausen (University of Innsbruck, Austria)
Adam Lee (University of Illinois at Urbana-Champaign, USA)
Lei Li (University of Manchester, UK)
Carsten Lutz (Institute for Theoretical Computer Science, Germany)
Francisco Martin-Recuerda (University of Innsbruck, Austria)
Meenakshi Nagarajan (University of Georgia, USA)
Natalya F. Noy (Stanford University, USA)

Table of Contents

Industrial Track

Semantic Web Challenge

Using the Semantic Web for e-Science: Inspiration, Incubation, Irritation
(Extended Abstract)

Carole Goble

School of Computer Science,
The University of Manchester, Manchester, M13 9PL UK
carole@cs.man.ac.uk

We are familiar with the idea of e-Commerce - the electronic trading between consumers and suppliers. In recent years there has been a commensurate paradigm shift in the way that science is conducted. e-Science is science performed through distributed global collaborations between scientists and their resources enabled by electronic means, in order to solve scientific problems. No one scientific laboratory has the resources or tools, the raw data or derived understanding or the expertise to harness the knowledge available to a scientific community. Real progress depends on pooling know-how and results. It depends on collaboration and making connections between ideas, people, and data. It depends on finding and interpreting results and knowledge generated by scientific colleagues you do not know and who do not know you, to be analysed in ways they did not anticipate, to generate new hypotheses to be pooled in their turn. The importance of e-Science has been highlighted in the UK, for example, by an investment of over £240 million pounds over the past five years to specifically address the research and development issues that have to be tacked to develop a sustainable and effective e-Science e-Infrastructure.

The Web has served scientists well. Many data sets and tools are published and accessed using web protocols and web browsers. Sharing data repositories and tool libraries has become straightforward. Widespread collaboration is possible by publishing a simple web page. However, standard web technology is now straining to meet the needs of scientists. The scale of data is one problem thanks to high throughput scientific methods – more data is about to be generated in the next five years than has been generated by mankind hitherto fore. Another problem is that communities can no longer be isolated silos – chemists must share with molecular biologists; earth scientists collaborate with physicists and so on. Yet a Web-based distributed information infrastructure is still a place where the scientists manually: *search* the web for content; *interpret and process* content by reading it and interacting with web pages; *infer* cross-links between information; *integrate* content from multiple resources and *consolidate* the heterogeneous information, while preserving the *understanding* of its *context*. Sound familiar?

It would seem self-evident that the Semantic Web should be able to make a major contribution to the fabric of e-Science [1,2]. The first W3C Semantic Web for Life Science Workshop in 2004 attracted over 100 participants with representation from all the major pharmaceutical and drug discovery players, and leading scientists (http://www.w3.org/2004/07/swls-ws.html). Scientific communities are ideal **incubators** for the Semantic Web: they are knowledge driven, fragmented, and have

Y. Gil et al. (Eds.): ISWC 2005, LNCS 3729, pp. 1–3, 2005.

valuable knowledge assets whose contents need to be combined and used by many applications. The content is diverse, being structured (databases, electronic lab books), semi-structured (papers, spreadsheets) and unstructured (presentations, Web blogs, images). The scale necessitates that the processing be done automatically. There are many suppliers and consumers of knowledge and a loose-coupling between suppliers and consumers – information is used in unanticipated ways by knowledge workers unknown to those who deposited it. People naturally form communities of practice, and there is a culture of sharing and knowledge curation. For a Semantic Web to flourish, the communities it would serve needs to be willing to create and maintain the semantic content. Most scientific communities embrace ontologies. The Life Science world, for example, has the desire for collaboration, a culture of annotation, and service providers that might be persuaded to generate RDF or at least annotated XML. A semantic web is expensive to set up and maintain, and thus is only likely to work for communities where the added value is worthwhile and an "open source data" philosophy prevails.

The Scientific Community has been **inspired** by the results of the Semantic Web initiative already. The inferencing capabilities of OWL have been shown to aid the building of large and sophisticated ontologies such as The Gene Ontology (http://www.geneontology.org) and BioPAX (http://www.biopax.org/). The self-describing nature of RDF and OWL models enables flexible descriptions for data collections, suiting those whose schemas may evolve and change, or whose data types are hard to fix, like knowledge bases of scientific hypotheses, provenance records of *in silico* experiments or publication collections [3]. These are examples where the semantic technologies have been adopted by scientific application. Genuine "Semantic WEB" examples, with the emphasis on Web, are also starting to appear. SciFOAF builds a FOAF community mined from the analysis of authors and publications over PubMed (http://www.urbigene.com/foaf/). Scientific publishers like the Institute of Physics (http://syndication.iop.org/), publish RSS feeds in RDF using standard RSS, Dublin Core and PRISM RDF vocabularies. The Uniprot protein sequence database has an experimental publication of results in RDF (http://www.isb-sib.ch/~ejain/rdf/). YeastHub [4] converts the outputs of a variety of databases into RDF and combines them in a warehouse built over a native RDF data store. BioDASH (http://www.w3.org/2005/04/swls/BioDash/Demo/) is an experimental Drug Development Dashboard that uses RDF and OWL to associate disease, compounds, drug progression stages, molecular biology, and pathway knowledge for a team of users. Correspondences are not necessarily obvious to detect, requiring specific rules. Semantic technologies are being used to assist in the configuration and operation of e-Science middleware such as the Grid [6]. These examples should be an inspiration to the Semantic Web community.

However, there is also **irritation**. There are some problems with the expressivity of OWL for Life Science, Chemical and Clinical ontologies. The mechanisms for trust, security, and context are important for intellectual property, provenance tracing, accountability and security, as well as untangling contradictions or weighting support for an assertion; yet these are immature or missing. Performance over medium-large RDF datasets is disappointing – the CombeChem combinatorial chemistry project generated 80 million triples trivially and broke most of the triple stores it tried (http://www.combechem.org). There is poor support for grouping RDF statements, yet this is fundamental. Semantic web purists claim that the Life Science Identifier [5], for example, is unnecessary, although these critics seem not to have actually developed any applications for life scientists. Sometimes there is irritation that the wrong emphasis is being placed on what is important and what is not by the technologists, leading to a communication failure between those for whom the Semantic Web is a means to an end and those for whom it *is* the end [7].

The Web was developed to serve a highly motivated community with an application and a generous spirit–High Energy Physics. The Semantic Web would also benefit from the nursery of e-Science. In my talk I explore this opportunity, the mutual benefits, give some pioneering examples, and highlight some current problems and concerns: inspiration, incubation, and irritation.

References

[1] James Hendler *Science and the Semantic We*b Science 299: 520-521, 2003

[2] Eric Neumann *A Life Science Semantic Web: Are We There Yet?* Sci. STKE, Vol. 2005, Issue 283, 10 May 2005

[3] Jun Zhao, Chris Wroe, Carole Goble, Robert Stevens, Dennis Quan, Mark Greenwood, *Using Semantic Web Technologies for Representing e-Science Provenance* in Proc 3rd International Semantic Web Conference ISWC2004, Hiroshima, Japan, 9-11 Nov 2004, Springer LNCS 3298

[4] Cheung K.H., Yip K.Y., Smith A., deKnikker R., Masiar A., Gerstein M. *YeastHub: a semantic web use case for integrating data in the life sciences domain* (2005) *Bioinformatics* 21 Suppl 1: i85-i96.

[5] Clark T., Martin S., Liefeld T. *Globally Distributed Object Identification for Biological Knowledgebases* Briefings in Bioinformatics 5.1:59-70, March 1, 2004.

[6] Goble CA, De Roure D, Shadbolt NR and Fernandes AAA *Enhancing Services and Applications with Knowledge and Semantics* in The Grid: Blueprint for a New Computing Infrastructure Second Edition (eds. I Foster and C Kesselman), Morgan Kaufman 2003

[7] Phillip Lord, Sean Bechhofer, Mark Wilkinson, Gary Schiltz, Damian Gessler, Carole Goble, Lincoln Stein, Duncan Hull. *Applying semantic web services to bioinformatics: Experiences gained, lessons learnt.* in Proc 3rd International Semantic Web Conference ISWC2004, Hiroshima, Japan, 9-11 Nov 2004 , Springer LNCS 3298

Semantic Acceleration Helping Realize the Semantic Web Vision or "The Practical Web"

Alfred Z. Spector

Vice President of Strategy and Technology,
IBM Software Group

Abstract. The Semantic Web envisions a future where applications (computer programs) can make sense and therefore more productive use of all the information on the web by assigning common "meaning" to the millions of terms and phrases used in billions of documents. AI and knowledge representation must rise to the occasion and work with decentralized representations, imprecision and incompleteness. Standard web-based representations are an essential enabler and we have made good progress in their design. But we still rely on humans to assign semantics and here there is a big leap of faith: The World Wide Web has grown at startling rates because humans are prolific at producing enormous volumes of unstructured information, that is, information without explicit semantics; on the other hand navigating this mass of information has proven to be both possible and profitable to the point that there is a $6 B search advertising industry. It's is not practical to expect the same will automatically happen for semantically enriched content. And yet we need semantics to better leverage the huge value on the web.

The Practical Web is about confronting this challenge. Its about realizing that we will need to automate the assignment of semantics to unstructured content to ultimately realize the vision of the Semantic Web. If well done the results will be synergistic with the motors of web expansion: user value and commercial value.

Y. Gil et al. (Eds.): ISWC 2005, LNCS 3729, p. 4, 2005.
© Springer-Verlag Berlin Heidelberg 2005

Semantic Web Public Policy Challenges: Privacy, Provenance, Property and Personhood

Daniel J. Weitzner

Co-director, MIT Decentralized Information Group (DIG),
Technology and Society Domain Lead, World Wide Web Consortium (W3C)
http://www.w3.org/People/Weitzner.html

Abstract. The growing inferencing and knowledge linking power of the Semantic Web will, we all hope, make the world a better place: enrich democratic discourse, support more rapid scientific discovery, enable new forms of personal communication and culture, and generally enhance critical analysis of information. However, with this greater inferencing power comes daunting social and public policy questions that must be faced as first class technical design challenges, not just as issues to be resolved in courts and legislatures. How will we maintain fundamental privacy values in the face of inferencing and searching power that can systematically uncover sensitive facts about us even has we try to keep such data secret? Today's Web has enabled a departure from traditional editorial control and historically-trusted information sources. Will attention to provenance on the Semantic Web enable us to develop new mechanisms for assessing the reliability of information? What new challenges to already frayed intellectual property regimes will the Semantic Web bring? Finally, how will we assert and represent personal identity on the Semantic Web? At this early stage of the development of the Semantic Web, it's hard enough to have problems in focus, much less solutions. However, we believe that transparent reasoning and accountability mechanisms will play a critical role in enabling systems and services built on the Semantic Web to be more responsive to social and policy needs.

Y. Gil et al. (Eds.): ISWC 2005, LNCS 3729, p. 5, 2005.
© Springer-Verlag Berlin Heidelberg 2005

Constructing Complex Semantic Mappings Between XML Data and Ontologies

Yuan An[1], Alex Borgida[2], and John Mylopoulos[1]

[1] University of Toronto, Canada
{yuana, jm}@cs.toronto.edu
[2] Rutgers University, USA
borgida@cs.rutgers.edu

Abstract. Much data is published on the Web in XML format satisfying schemas, and to make the Semantic Web a reality, such data needs to be interpreted with respect to ontologies. Interpretation is achieved through a *semantic mapping* between the XML schema and the ontology. We present work on the heuristic construction of *complex* such semantic mappings, when given an initial set of simple correspondences from XML schema attributes to datatype properties in the ontology. To accomplish this, we first offer a mapping formalism to capture the semantics of XML schemas. Second, we present our heuristic mapping construction algorithm. Finally, we show through an empirical study that considerable effort can be saved when constructing complex mappings by using our prototype tool.

1 Introduction

An important component of the Semantic Web vision is the annotation, using formal ontologies, of material available on the Web. Semi-structured data, published in XML and satisfying patterns expressed in DTD or XML Schema form an important subclass of such material. In this case, the annotation can be expressed in a formal way, through a semantic mapping connecting parts of the schema with expressions over the ontology. For example, [1,11] essentially connect paths in XML to chains of properties in an ontology. Such mappings have already found interesting applications in areas such as data integration as well as peer-to-peer data management systems [7].

Mappings from database schemas to ontologies could be as simple as value correspondences between single elements or as complex as logic formulas. In most applications, such as information integration, complex logic formulas are needed. Until now, it has been assumed that *humans* specify these complex mapping formulas — a highly complex, time-consuming and error-prone task. In this paper, we propose a tool that assists users in the construction of complex mapping formulas between XML schemas and OWL ontologies, expressed in a subset of First Order Logic.

Inspired by the success of the *Clio* tool [14,15], our tool takes three inputs: an ontology, an XML schema (actually, its unfolding into tree structures that

Y. Gil et al. (Eds.): ISWC 2005, LNCS 3729, pp. 6–20, 2005.
© Springer-Verlag Berlin Heidelberg 2005

we will call *element trees*), and simple correspondences between XML attributes and ontology datatype properties, of the kind possibly generated by already existing tools (e.g., [4,12,13]). The output is a ranked list of complex formulas representing semantic mappings of the kind described earlier.

In short, the main contributions of this work are as follows: (i) we propose a mapping formalism to capture the semantics of XML schemas based on tree-pattern formulas [3]; (ii) we propose a heuristic algorithm for finding semantic mappings, which are akin to a tree connection embedded in the ontology; (iii) we enhance the algorithm by taking into account information about (a) XML Schema features such as occurrence constraints, `key` and `keyref` definitions, (b) cardinality constraints in the ontology, and (c) XML document design guidelines under the hypothesis that an explicit or implicit ontology existed during the process of XML document design; (iv) we adopt the accuracy metric of schema matching [13] and evaluate the tool with a number of experiments.

The rest of the paper is organized as follows. Section 2 discusses related work, while Section 3 presents formal notations used later on. Section 4 describes some principles, as well as the mapping construction algorithm. Section 5 reports on empirical studies and Section 6 discusses how to refine the results by reasoning about ontologies. Finally, Section 7 summarizes the results of this work and suggests future directions.

2   Related Work

Much research has focused on converting and storing XML data into relational databases [16]. It is natural to ask whether we could utilize the mapping algorithm we have developed in [2] – for discovering mappings from relational schemas to ontologies – by first converting XML DTDs/schemas into relational tables. Unfortunately, this approach does not work. Among others, the algorithms that generate a relational schema from an XML DTD use backlinks and system generated *ids* in order to record the nested structure, and these confuse the algorithms in [2], which rely heavily on key and foreign key information.

The *schema mapping* tool *Clio* [14,15] discovers formal queries describing how target schemas can be populated with data from source schemas, given sets of simple value correspondences. The present work can be viewed as extending *Clio* to the case when the target schema is a ontology treated as a relational schema consisting of unary and binary tables. However, as argued in [2], the chase algorithm of *Clio* would not produce the desired mappings due to several reasons: (i) the chase only follows nested referential constraints along one direction, while the intended meaning of an XML element tree may follow a binary relationship along either direction (see also Section 4.1); (ii) *Clio* does not explore occurrence constraints in the XML schema. These constraints carry important semantic information in searching for "reasonable" connections in the ontology.

The Xyleme [5] project is a comprehensive XML data integration system which includes an automatic mapping generation component. A mapping rule in terms of a pair of paths in two XML data sources is generated based on term matching and structural, context-based constraints. Specifically, terms of paths are first matched syntactically and semantically. Then the structural information is exploited. Our work differs from it significantly in that we propose to discover the mappings between tree structures in XML data and that in ontologies. The discovery is guided by a forward engineering process.

The problem of *reverse engineering* is to extract a conceptual schema (UML diagram, for example) from an XML DTD/schema [8]. The major difference between *reverse engineering* and our work is that we are given an existing ontology, and want to interpret the XML data in terms of it, whereas reverse engineering aims to construct a new one.

Finally, *Schema Matching* [4,12,13] identifies semantic relations between schema elements based on their names, data types, constraints, and structures. The primary goal is to find the one-one simple correspondences which are part of the input for our mapping discovery algorithm.

3   Formal Preliminaries

An OWL ontology consists of classes (unary predicates over individuals), object properties (binary predicates relating individuals), and datatype properties (binary predicates relating individuals with values). Classes are organized in terms of a subClassOf/ISA hierarchy. Object properties and their inverses are subject to cardinality restrictions; the ones used here are lower bound of 1 (marking *total* relationships), and upper bound of 1 (called *functional* relationships). We shall represent a given ontology using a directed graph, which has class nodes labeled with class names C, and edges labeled with object properties p. (Sometimes, when we speak class C, we may mean its corresponding node in the ontology graph.) Furthermore, for each datatype property f of class C, we create a separate attribute node $N_{f,C}$ labeled f and an edge labeled f too from C to $N_{f,C}$ in the graph. We propose to have edge p from C to B, written in the text as $\boxed{C}$ -- p -- $\boxed{B}$, to represent that p has domain class C and range class B. (If the relationship is functional, we write $\boxed{C}$ -- p -->- $\boxed{B}$.) We may also connect C to B by edge labeled p if we find a restriction stating that each instance of C is related to *some (all)* instances of B by p. For the sake of space limitation, graphical examples of ontologies (see [2]) are omitted.

For our purpose, we require that each XML document be described by an XML schema consisting of a set of element and attribute type definitions. Specifically, we assume the following countably infinite disjoint sets: **Ele** of element names, **Att** of attribute names, and **Dom** of simple type names including the built-in XML schema datatypes. Attribute names are preceded by a "@" to distinguish them from element names. Given finite sets $E \subset$ **Ele** and $A \subset$ **Att**, an XML schema over (E, A) specifies the type of each element ℓ in E, the attributes that ℓ has, and the datatype of each attribute in A. Specifically, an element type τ is defined by the grammar $\tau ::= \epsilon \mid \mathsf{Sequence}[\ell_1 : \tau_1, ... \ell_n : \tau_n] \mid \mathsf{Choice}[\ell_1 : \tau_1, .., \ell_n : \tau_n]$, where $\ell_1, .., \ell_n \in E$, ϵ is for the empty type, and $\mathsf{Sequence}$ and Choice are complex types. Each element associates an occurrence constraint with two values: *minOccurs* indicating the minimum occurrence and *maxOccurs* indicating the maximum occurrence. (We mark with * multiply occurring elements.) The set of attributes of an element $\ell \in E$ is defined by the function $\rho : E \rightarrow 2^A$; and the function $\kappa : A \rightarrow \mathbf{Dom}$ specifies the datatypes of attributes in A. For brevity, in this paper we do not consider *simple type elements* (corresponding to DTD's **PCDATA**), assuming instead that they have been represented using attributes. We also assume the Unique Name Assumption (UNA) for attributes, i.e., for any two elements $\ell_i, \ell_j \in E$, $\rho(\ell_i) \cap \rho(\ell_j) = \emptyset$.

For example, an XML schema describing articles and authors has the following specification:

$E = \{article,\ author,\ contactauthor,\ name\}$,
$A = \{@title,\ @id,\ @authorid,\ @fn,\ @ln\}$,
$\tau(article) = \mathsf{Sequence}[(author)* :\tau(author),\ contactauthor:\epsilon]$,
$\tau(author) = \mathsf{Sequence}[name:\epsilon]$,
$\rho(article) = (@title)$, $\rho(author) = (@id)$, $\rho(contactauthor) = (@authorid)$,
$\rho(name) = (@fn, @ln)$, $\kappa(@title) = \mathsf{String}$, $\kappa(@authorid) = \mathsf{Integer}$, $\kappa(@id) = \mathsf{Integer}$, $\kappa(@fn) = \mathsf{String}$, $\kappa(@ln) = \mathsf{String}$, and the element *article* is the root. Note that for the *article* element, *title* and *contactauthor* only occur once, while *author* may occur many times. For the *author* element, *name* occurs once.

The XML Schema Language is an expressive language that can also express key and `keyref` constraints.

An XML schema can be viewed as a directed node-labeled graph called *schema graph* consisting of the following edges: parent-child edges $e = \ell \rightarrow \ell_i$ for elements $\ell, \ell_i \in E$ such that if $\tau(\ell) = \mathsf{Sequence}[...\ell_i : \tau_i...]$ or $\mathsf{Choice}[...\ell_i : \tau_i...]$; and attribute edges $e = \ell \rightarrow \alpha$ for element $\ell \in E$ and attribute $\alpha \in A$ such that $\alpha \in \rho(\ell)$. For a parent-child edge $e = \ell \rightarrow \ell_i$, if the *maxOccurs* constraint of ℓ_i is 1, we show the edge to be functional, drawn as $\ell \Rightarrow \ell_i$. Since attributes are single-valued, we always draw an attribute edge as $\ell \Rightarrow \alpha$. The schema graph corresponding to the XML schema above is shown in Figure 1.

Elements and attributes as nodes in a schema graph are located by path expressions. To avoid regular expressions, we will use a simple path expression $Q = \epsilon | \ell.Q$. In order to do this in a general fashion, we introduce the notion of *element tree*.

An *element tree* represents an XML structure whose semantics we are seeking. A semantic mapping from the entire XML schema to an

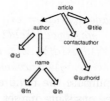

Fig. 1. The Schema Graph

ontology consists of a set of mapping formulas each of which is from an element tree to a conjunctive formulas in the ontology. An *element tree* can be constructed for *each element* by doing a depth first search (DFS). During the DFS, shared attributes are renamed to maintain the UNA, and cycles are unfolded. For the schema graph shown in Figure 2 (a), the element trees for the

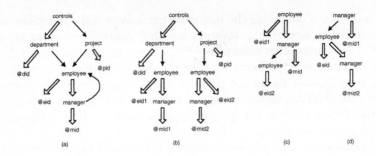

Fig. 2. Schema Graph and Element Trees

elements *controls*, *employee*, and *manager* are shown in Figure 2 (b), (c), (d). For simplicity, we specify each element tree as rooted in the element from which the tree is constructed.

Now we turn to the mapping language describing XML schemas in terms of ontologies. On the XML side, we start with *attribute formulas*, which are specified by the syntax $\alpha ::= \ell | \ell(@a_1 = x_1, .., @a_n = x_n)$, where $\ell \in E$, $@a_1, .., @a_n \in A$, and $x_1, \ldots, x_n$ are distinct variables. *Tree formulas* over (E, A) are defined by $\varphi ::= \alpha | \alpha[\varphi_1, .., \varphi_n]$, where α are attribute formulas over (E, A). For example, $employee(@eid1 = x_1)[manager(@mid = x_2)[employee(@eid2 = x_3)]]$ is the tree formula representing the element tree in Figure 2 (c).

On the ontology side, we use conjunctive formulas, which treat concepts and properties as unary and binary predicates respectively.

A *mapping formula* between an element tree and an ontology then has the form $\Phi(\overline{X}) \rightarrow \Psi(\overline{X}, \overline{Y})$, where $\Phi(\overline{X})$ is a tree formula in the XML schema and $\Psi(\overline{X}, \overline{Y})$ is a conjunctive formula in the ontology. For example, given an ontology containing the class *Employee*, with a datatype property *hasId*, and a functional property *hasManager* (whose inverse is *manages*, which is not functional), the following mapping formula ascribes a semantics of the element tree in Figure 2 (c):
$employee(@eid1 = x_1)[$
    $manager\ (@mid = x_2)[$
        $employee\ (@eid2 = x_3)\ ]] \rightarrow$
$Employee(Y_1), hasId(Y_1, x_1),\ Employee(Y_2), hasId(Y_2, x_2),$
$hasManager(Y_1, Y_2),\ Employee(Y_3), hasId(Y_3, x_3), manages(Y_2, Y_3).$
Since we maintain the UNA assumption, we can drop the variable names x_is, and just use attribute names in the formula. The variables Y_js are implicitly existentially quantified and refer to individuals in the ontology.

Given an element tree T and an ontology O, a *correspondence* $P.@c \leadsto C.f$ will relate the attribute "$@c$" of the element E reached by the simple path P to the datatype property f of the class C in the ontology. A simple path P is always relative to the root of the tree. For example, we can specify the following correspondences for the element tree in Figure 2 (c):
$employee.@eid1 \leadsto Employee.hasId,$
$employee.manager.@mid \leadsto Employee.hasId.$
$employee.manager.employee.@eid2 \leadsto Employee.hasId$

Since our algorithm deals with ontology graphs, formally a correspondence L will be a mathematical relation $L(P, @c, C, f, N_{f,C})$, where the first two arguments determine unique values for the last three.

4 Mapping Construction Algorithm

Before presenting the algorithm, we first explain some principles underlying it.

4.1 Principles

As in the relational case [2], we start from a methodology presented in the literature [6,9] for designing XML DTDs/schemas from an ontology/conceptual model (CM). As with relational schemas, there is a notion of XML normal form (XNF) for evaluating the absence of redundancies and update anomalies in XML schemas [6]. The methodology in [6] claims to develop XNF-compliant XML schemas from CMs. It turns out that these "good" XML schemas are trees embedded in the graph representations of the CMs. Using the term *"element tree"* instead of *"schema tree"* in [6], we briefly describe the algorithm of [6] (called *EM-algorithm*).

Example 1. *For a "binary and canonical hypergraph" H (viz. [6]), representing a CM, EM-algorithm derives an element tree T such that T is in XNF and every path of T reflects a sequence of some connected edges in H. For example, starting from the Department node of the ontology in Figure 3 the following element tree (omitting attributes) T is obtained: Department[(FacultyMember[(Hobby)*, (GradStudent[Program, (Hobby)*])*])*], where we use [ ] to indicate hierarchy and ( )* to indicate the multiple occurrences of a child element (or non-functional edges) in element trees.*

In essence, EM-algorithm recursively constructs the element tree T as follows: it starts from a concept node N in CM, creates tree T rooted in a node R corresponding to N, and constructs the direct subtrees below R by following nodes and edges connected to N in CM. Finally, a

Fig. 3. Sample CM/ontology graph

largest hierarchical structure embedded within CM is identified and an edge of T reflects a semantic connection in the CM. □

A binary and canonical CM can naturally be viewed as an OWL ontology: concepts are classes, binary relationships are object properties, and attributes are datatype properties. So, given an XNF-compliant element tree T, we may assume that there is a *semantic tree S* embedded in an ontology graph such that S is isomorphic to T. If the correspondences between elements and classes were given, we should be able to identify S in terms of the ontology.

Example 2. *Suppose elements in the element tree T of Example 1 correspond to the classes (nodes) in Figure 3 by their names. Then we can recover the semantics* of T recursively starting from the bottom, e.g., for the subtree GradStudent[Program, (Hobby)*], because the edge GradStudent $\Rightarrow$ Program is functional and GradStudent $\rightarrow$ Hobby is non-functional, and GradStudent is the root, we look for functional edges from GradStudent to Program and $1:N$ or $M:N$ edges from GradStudent to Hobby in the ontology graph. Likewise, we can recover the edges from FacultyMember to GradStudent and Hobby. Finally, the $1:N$ edge between Department and FacultyMember is recovered.   □

In an element tree T, attributes are the leaves of T and correspond to the datatype properties of classes in an ontology. There has been much research on schema matching tools [4,12,13] which focus on generating these kinds of correspondences automatically. Given the correspondences from XML attributes to datatype properties of an ontology, we expect to identify the root and the remaining nodes of the semantics tree S and connect them meaningfully.

Example 3. *Suppose the following correspondences:*
$\mathcal{X}$*:GradStudent.@ln*↞↝*$\mathcal{O}$:GradStudent.lastname,*
$\mathcal{X}$*:GradStudent.@fn* ↞↝ *$\mathcal{O}$:GradStudent.firstname,*
$\mathcal{X}$*:GradStudent.Program.@pname*↞↝*$\mathcal{O}$:Program.name,*
are for the element tree GradStudent(@ln, @fn)[Program(@pname)], where we use prefixes $\mathcal{X}$ and $\mathcal{O}$ to distinguish terms in the element tree and the ontology. Then we could identify the class $\mathcal{O}$:GradStudent as the root of the semantic tree and recover it as the edge $\mathcal{O}$:GradStudent --\>- $\mathcal{O}$:Program.   □

The *first principle* of our mapping construction algorithm is to identify the root of a semantic tree and to construct the tree by connecting the root to the rest of nodes in the ontology graph using edges having compatible cardinality constraints with edges in the element tree.

However, identifying the root of the semantic tree is the major obstacle. The following example illustrates the problem for an XML schema which is not XNF compliant. Such a schema can be easily encountered in reality.

Example 4. *for the element tree*
GradStudent[Name(@ln, @fn), Program(@pname)]
with the correspondences
$\mathcal{X}$*:GradStudent.Name.@ln*↞↝*$\mathcal{O}$:GradStudent.lastname,*
$\mathcal{X}$*:GradStudent.Name.@fn* ↞↝*$\mathcal{O}$:GradStudent.firstname,*
$\mathcal{X}$*:GradStudent.Program.@pname*↞↝*$\mathcal{O}$:Program.name,*
the element $\mathcal{X}$:Name corresponds to $\mathcal{O}$:GradStudent by its attributes and the element $\mathcal{X}$:Program corresponds to $\mathcal{O}$:Program. Further, both $\mathcal{X}$:Name and $\mathcal{X}$:Program occur once and are at the same level. Then the question is which one is the root of the semantic tree? $\mathcal{O}$:GradStudent or $\mathcal{O}$:Program? Since the order of nodes on the same level of the element tree does not matter, both are potential roots. Therefore, the mapping algorithm should recover the functional edges from $\mathcal{O}$:GradStudent to $\mathcal{O}$:Program as well as from $\mathcal{O}$:Program to $\mathcal{O}$:GradStudent, if any.   □

This leads to the *second principle* of our algorithm: for each class C in the ontology graph such that C corresponds to a child element E of the root element

R in the element tree T and $R \Rightarrow E$ is functional, C is a potential root of the semantic tree S. Treating an attribute as a subtree, the mapping construction algorithm will recursively recover the semantic tree S in a bottom-up fashion.

Unfortunately, not every functional edge from a parent element to a child element represents a functional relationship. Specifically, some element tags are actually the collection tags containing a set of instances of the child elements. For example, for the element tree: $GradStudent[Name(@ln, @fn),$ $Hobbies[(Hobby(@title))*]]$ with the correspondences
$\mathcal{X}:GradStudent.Name.@ln\leadsto\mathcal{O}:GradStudent.lastname,$
$\mathcal{X}:GradStudent.Name.@fn \leadsto\mathcal{O}:GradStudent.firstname,$
$\mathcal{X}:GradStudent.Hobbies.Hobby.@title\leadsto\mathcal{O}:Hobby.title,$
the element tag $\mathcal{X}:Hobbies$ represents a collection of hobbies of a graduate student. Although the edge $\mathcal{X}:GradStudent \Rightarrow \mathcal{X}:Hobbies$ is functional, $\mathcal{X}:Hobbies \rightarrow \mathcal{X}:Hobby$ is non-functional. Therefore, when $\mathcal{O}:Hobby$ is identified as the root of the semantic tree for the subtree $Hobbies[(Hobby(@title))*]$, $\mathcal{O}:Hobby$ should not be considered as a potential root of the semantic tree for the entire element tree. Eliminating classes corresponding to collection tags from the set of the potential roots is our *third principle*.

In most cases, we try to discover the semantic mapping between an XML schema and an ontology such that they were developed independently. In such cases, we may not be able to find an isomorphic semantic tree S embedded in the ontology graph, or we may find an isomorphic tree that is not the intended one, for a given element tree. For example, for the element tree $City(@cityName)[$ $Country (@countryName)]$ and a ontology with a path $\boxed{City}$ -- locatedIn -->- $\boxed{State}$ -- locatedIn -->- $\boxed{Country}$ (recall -->- indicates a functional property), the intended semantics is the path rather than a single edge. The *fourth principle* for discovering mappings is to find shortest paths in the ontology graph instead of single edges, where the semantics of the paths is consistent with the semantics of the edges in the element tree in terms of cardinality constraints.

Even though we could eliminate some collection tags from the set of potential roots to reduce the number of possible semantic trees, there are still too many possibilities if the ontology graph is large. In order to further restrict the set of potential roots, we can make use of key and keyref definitions in XML schemas.

Example 5. *For the element tree*
$Article[Title(@title), Publisher(@name),$
$ContactAuthor(@contact), (Author(@id))*]$
if the attribute @title is defined as the key *for Article, then we should only choose the class corresponding to @title as the root of the semantic tree, eliminating the classes corresponding to @name and @contact (picked by the second principle). Further, if @contact is defined as a* keyref *referencing some key, we also can eliminate the class corresponding to @contact.* □

So our *fifth principle* is to use key and keyref definitions to restrict the set of potential roots.

Reified Relationships. To represent n-ary relationships in OWL ontologies, one needs to use classes, called *reified relationship (classes)*. For example, an ontology may have class $\mathcal{O}$:*Presentation* connected with functional *roles* to classes $\mathcal{O}$:*Author*, $\mathcal{O}$:*Paper*, and $\mathcal{O}$:*Session*, indicating participants. It is desirable to recover reified relationships and their role connections from an XML schema. Suppose the element tree *Presentation[Presenter(@author), Paper(@title), Session(@eventId)]* represents the above ternary relationship. Then, in the ontology, the root of the semantic tree is the *reified relationship class* $\mathcal{O}$:*Presentation*, rather than any one of the three classes which are role fillers. The *sixth principle* then is to look for *reified relationships* for element trees with only functional edges from a parent to its children that correspond to separate classes[1].

ISA. In [6], ISA relationships are eliminated by collapsing superclasses into their subclasses, or vice versa. If a superclass is collapsed into subclasses, correspondences can be used to distinguish the nodes in the ontology. If subclasses are collapsed into their superclass, then we treat the ISA edges as special functional edges with cardinality constraints $0 : 1$ and $1 : 1$. The *last principle* is then to follow ISA edges whenever we need to construct a functional path[2].

4.2   Algorithm

First, to get a better sense of what we are aiming for, we present the encodeTree(S, L) procedure, which translates an ontology subtree S into a conjunctive formula, taking into account the correspondences L.

Function encodeTree(S, L)
Input subtree S of ontology graph, correspondences L from attributes of element tree to datatype properties of class nodes in S.
Output variable name generated for root of S, and conjunctive formula for the tree.
Steps:

1. Suppose N is the root of S, let $\Psi = \{\}$.
2. If N is an attribute node with label f, find @d such that $L(\_, @d, \_, f, N) = true$, return $(@d, true)$.
3. If N is a class node with label C, then introduce new variable Y; add conjoint $C(Y)$ to Ψ; for each edge p_i from N to N_i:

   (a) let S_i be the subtree rooted at N_i;
   (b) let $(v_i, \phi_i(Z_i))$=encodeTree(S_i, L);
   (c) add conjunct $p_i(Y, v_i) \wedge \phi_i(Z_i)$ to Ψ;

4. return (Y, Ψ).

---

[1] If a parent functionally connects to only two children, then it may represent an M:N binary relationship. So recover it as well.

[2] Thus, ISA is taken care of in the forthcoming algorithm by proper treatment of functional path.

The following procedure constructTree(T, L) generates the subtree of the ontology graph for the element tree after appropriately replicating nodes[3] in the ontology graph.

Function constructTree(T, L)
Input an element tree T, an ontology graph, and correspondence L from attributes in T to datatype properties of class nodes in the ontology graph.
Output set of (subtree S, root R, *collectionTag*) triples, where *collectionTag* is a boolean value indicating whether the root corresponds to a collection tag.
Steps:
1. Suppose N is the root of tree T.
2. If N is an attribute, then find $L(\_, N, \_, \_, R) = true$; return ($\{R\}, R, false$).
   /*the base case for leaves.*/
3. If N is an element having n edges $\{e_1, .., e_n\}$ pointing to n nodes $\{N_1, .., N_n\}$,
   let T_i be the subtree rooted at N_i,
   then compute (S_i, R_i, *collectionTag$_i$*)= constructTree(T_i, L) for $i = 1, .., n$;
   (a) If $n = 1$ and e_1 is non-functional, return ($S_1, R_1, true$);/*N probably is a
       collection tag representing a set of instances each of which is an instance
       of the N_1 element.*/
   (b) Else if $n = 1$ and e_1 is functional return (S_1, R_1, *collectionTag$_1$*).
   (c) Else if $R_1=R_2=...=R_n$, then return (combine($S_1, .., S_n$), $R_1, false$)[4].
   (d) Else let $F=\{R_{j_1}, .., R_{j_m}|$ s.t. e_{j_k} is functional and *collectionTag$_{j_k}$* $=$
       $false$ for $k = 1, .., m$, $j_k \in \{1, ..., n\}\}$ and $NF=\{R_{i_1}, ..., R_{i_h}|$ s.t. e_{i_k} is
       non-functional, or e_{i_k} is functional and *collectionTag$_{i_k}$* $= true$ for $k =$
       $1, .., h$, $i_k \in \{1, ..., n\}\}$, let $ans = \{\}$, /*separate nodes according to their
       connection types to N.*/
       i. Try to limit the number of nodes in F by considering the following
          cases: 1) keep the nodes corresponding to **key** elements located on
          the highest level; 2) keep those nodes which are not corresponded by
          keyref elements.
       ii. If $NF = \emptyset$, find a reified relationship concept R with m roles $r_{j_1}, .., r_{j_m}$
           pointing to nodes in F, let $S=$ combine($\{r_{j_k}\}$, $\{S_{j_k}\}$) for $k = 1, .., m$;
           let $ans=$ $ans\cup(S, R, false)$. If R does not exist and $m = 2$, find
           a non-functional shortest path p connecting the two nodes R_{j_1}, R_{j_2}
           in F; let $S=$ combine(p, S_{j_1}, S_{j_2}); let $ans=$ $ans\cup(S, R_{j_1}, false)$.
           /*N probably represents an n-ary relationship or many-many binary
           relationship (footnote 3 of the sixth principle.)*/
       iii. Else for each $R_{j_k} \in F$ $k = 1, .., m$, find a shortest functional path p_{j_k}
            from R_{j_k} to each $R_{j_t} \in F - R_{j_k}$ for $t = 1, .., k-1, k+1, .., m$; and find
            a shortest non-functional path q_{i_r} from R_{j_k} to each $R_{i_r} \in NF$ for $r =$
            $1, .., h$; if p_{j_k} and q_{i_r} exist, let $S=$ combine($\{p_{j_k}\}$, $\{q_{i_r}\}$,$\{S_1, .., S_n\}$);
            let $ans=ans\cup(S,R_{j_k},false)$. /*pick an root and connect it to other
            nodes according to their connection types.*/

---

[3] Replications are needed when multiple attributes correspond to the same datatype
property. See [2] for details.
[4] Function combine merges edges of trees into a larger tree.

iv. If $ans \neq \emptyset$, return ans; else find a minimum Steiner tree[5] S connecting $R_1, .., R_n$, return $(S, R_1, false)$. /*the default action is to find a shortest Steiner tree.*/

It is likely that the algorithm will return too many results. Therefore, at the final stage we set a threshold N_{thresh} for limiting the number of final results presented. In the following experimental section, this threshold was set to 10.

5   Mapping Construction Experiences

We have implemented the mapping algorithm and conducted a set of experiments to evaluate its effectiveness and usefulness.

Measures for mapping quality and accuracy. We first attempt to use the notions of *precision* and *recall* for the evaluation. Let R be the number of correct mapping formulas of an XML schema, let I be the number of correctly identified mapping formulas by the algorithm, and let P be the total number of mapping formulas returned. The two quantities are computed as: $precision = I/P$ and $recall = I/R$. Please note that for a single input element tree T, which has a single correct mapping formula, the algorithm either produces the formula or not. So the *recall* for T is either 0 or 1, but the *precision* may vary according to the number of output formulas. For measuring the overall quality of the mapping results, we computed the average precision and recall for all tested element trees of an XML schema.

However, precision and recall alone cannot tell us how useful the algorithm is to users. The purpose of our tool is to *assist* users in the process of constructing complex mappings, so that productivity is enhanced. Consider the case when only one semantic mapping is returned. Even if the tool did not find the exactly right one, it could still be useful if the formula is accurate enough so that some labor is saved. To try to measure this, we adopt the accuracy metric for schema matching [13]. Consider the mapping formula $\Phi(\overline{X}) \rightarrow \Psi(\overline{X}, \overline{Y})$ with the formula $\Phi(\overline{X})$ encoding an element tree. The formula $\Psi(\overline{X}, \overline{Y})$ encodes a semantic tree $S = (V, E)$ by using a set of unary predicates for nodes in V, a set of binary predicates for edges in E, and a set of variables, $\overline{Y}$, assigned to each node (there are predicates and variables for datatype properties as well). For a given element tree T, writing the complex mapping formula consists of identifying the semantic tree and encoding it into a conjunctive formula (which could be treated as a set of atomic predicates). Let $\Psi_1 = \{a_1(\overline{Z}_1), a_2(\overline{Z}_2), .., a_m(\overline{Z}_m)\}$ encode a tree S_1, let $\Psi_2 = \{b_1(\overline{Y}_1), b_2(\overline{Y}_2), .., b_n(\overline{Y}_n)\}$ encode a tree S_2. Let $D = \Psi_2 \backslash \Psi_1 = \{b_i(\overline{Y}_i) |$ s.t. for a given partial one-one function $f : \overline{Y} \rightarrow \overline{Z}$ representing the mapping from nodes of S_2 to nodes of S_1, $b_i(f(\overline{Y}_i)) \in \Psi_1\}$. One can easily identify the mapping $f : \overline{Y} \rightarrow \overline{Z}$ by comparing the two trees S_2 and S_1 (recall an ontology graph contains class nodes as well as attribute nodes representing datatype properties) so we consider that it comes for free. Let $c = |D|$. Suppose Ψ_1 be the correct

---

[5] A Steiner tree on $R_1, .., R_n$ is a spanning tree that may contain nodes other than $R_1, .., R_n$.

formula and Ψ_2 be the formula returned by the tool for an element tree. To reach the correct formula Ψ_1 from the formula Ψ_2, one needs to delete $n - c$ predicates from Ψ_2 and add $m - c$ predicates to Ψ_2. On the other hand, if the user creates the formula from scratch, m additions are needed. Let us assume that additions and deletions need the same amount of effort. However, browsing the ontology for correcting formula Ψ_2 to formula Ψ_1 is different from creating the formula Ψ_1 from scratch. So let α be a cost factor for browsing the ontology for correcting a formula, and let β be a factor for creating a formula. We define the accuracy or labor savings of the tool as $labor\ savings = 1 - \frac{\alpha[(n-c)+(m-c)]}{\beta m}$. Intuitively, $\alpha < \beta$, but for a worst-case bound let us assume $\alpha = \beta$ in this study. Notice that in a perfect situation, $m = n = c$ and $labor\ savings = 1$.

Schemas and ontologies. To evaluate the tool, we collected 9 XML schemas varying in size and nested structure. The 9 schemas come from 4 application domains, and 4 publicly available domain ontologies were obtained from the Web and literature. Table 1 shows the characteristics of the schemas and the ontologies; the column heads are self-explanatory. The *company* schema and ontology are obtained from [9] in order to test the principles of the mapping construction. The *conference* schema is obtained from [10]. *UT DB* is the schema used for describing the information of the database group in University of Toronto. *SigmodRecord* is the schema for SIGMOD record. The rest of the schemas are obtained from the *Clio* test suite (http://www.cs.toronto.edu/db/Clio). The KA ontology, CIA factbook, and the Bibliographic-Data are all available on the Web. We have published the schemas and ontologies on our website along with some sample mapping results at the following URL:
http://www.cs.toronto.edu/ ~yuana/research /maponto/testData.html.

Experimental results. Our experiments are conducted on a Dell desktop with a 1.8GHZ Intel Pentium 4 CPU and 1G memory. The first observation is the efficiency. In terms of the execution times, we observed that the algorithm generated results on average in 1.4 seconds which is not significantly large, for our test data.

Table 1. Characteristics of Test XML Schemas and Ontologies

XML Schema	Max Depth (DFS) in Schema Graph	# Nodes in Schema Graph	# Attributes in Schema Graph	Ontology	# Nodes	# Links
Company	6	30	17	Company	18	27
Conference	5	21	12	KA	105	4396
UT DB	6	40	20	KA	105	4396
Mondial	6	214	93	CIA factbook	52	77
DBLP 1	3	132	63	Bibliographic	75	749
DBLP 2	5	29	11	Bibliographic	75	749
SigmodRecord	3	16	7	Bibliographic	75	749
Amalgam 1	3	117	101	Bibliographic	75	749
Amalgam 2	3	81	53	Bibliographic	75	749

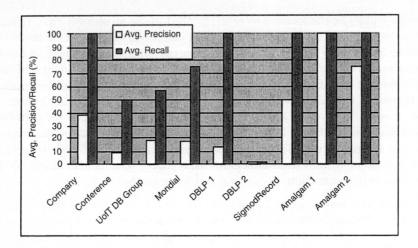

Fig. 4. Average Recall and Precision for 9 Mapping Cases

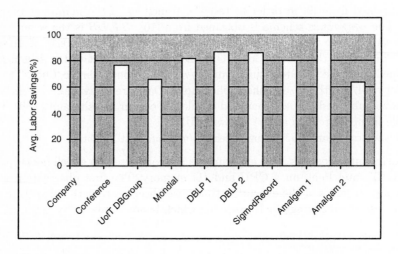

Fig. 5. Average Labor Savings for 9 Mapping Cases

Figure 4 shows the average precision and recall measures of the 9 mapping pairs. For each pair of schema and ontology, the average precision and recall are computed as follows. For the element trees extracted from the schema graph, a set of correct mapping formulas is manually created. We then apply the algorithm on the element trees and ontologies to generate a set of formulas. Next we examine each of the generated formulas to count how many are correct and compute the average precision and recall. The overall average precision is 35% and overall average recall is 75%. Notice that we have limited the number of formulas returned by the tool to 10.

Finally, we evaluate the usefulness of the tool. Figure 5 shows the average values of labor savings for the 9 mapping cases. For each mapping case, the average labor savings is computed as follows. Examine each incorrect formula returned by the algorithm and compute its labor saving value relative to the manually created one. Take the average value of the labor savings of all incorrect formulas. Note that even when the correct formula was identified by the algorithm, we still computed the labor savings for all incorrect ones to see how useful the tool is in case only one formula was returned. The overall average labor savings is over 80%, which is quite promising. Especially in view of the pessimistic assumption that $\alpha = \beta$ in the *labor savings* formula, we take this as evidence that the tool can greatly assist users in constructing complex mappings between XML schemas and ontologies with a proper schema matching tool as a front-end component.

6   Refining Mappings by Ontology Reasoning

Rich ontologies provide a new opportunity for eliminating "unreasonable" mappings. For example, if the ontology specifies that once a Person owns a CellPhone, they do not rent another one, then a candidate semantic formula $Person(X)$, $rents(X,Y)$, $Cell(Y)$, $owns(X,Z)$, $Cell(Z)$ can be eliminated [6], since no objects X can satisfy it. When ontologies, including constraints such as the one about renting/owning, are expressed in OWL, one can actually use OWL reasoning to detect inconsistent semantics by converting semantic trees into OWL concepts, and then testing them for incoherence with respect to the ontology. For example, the above formula can be translated, using an algorithm resembling encodeTree(S,L), into the OWL concept whose abstract syntax is *intersectionOf(Person, restriction(rents someValuesFrom(Cell)), restriction(owns someValues-From(Cell)))*. The ontologies we have found so far are unfortunately not sufficiently rich to demonstrate the usefulness of this idea.

7   Conclusions

In this paper, we have motivated and defined the problem of constructing complex semantic mappings from XML data to ontologies, given a set of simple correspondences from XML attributes to OWL datatype properties. The problem is well-motivated by the needs to annotate XML data in terms of ontologies, to translate XML data into ontologies, and to integrate heterogeneous XML data on the semantic web. We have proposed a tool for semi-automatically constructing complex mappings for users, and we evaluated the tool on a variety of real XML schemas and ontologies. Our experimental results suggest that quite significant savings in human work could be achieved by the use of our tool.

Integrating our tool with schema matching tools which automatically generate schema and ontology element correspondences is an open problem to address in the future. We also plan to develop filters for mappings by making use of instance data to assist users in choosing the correct mapping among a list of possible candidates.

---

[6] Probably some other relationship than $rents(X,Y)$ needs to be used.

Acknowledgments. We are grateful to anonymous reviewers for offering valuable comments, corrections, and suggestions for improvement.

References

1. B. Amann, C. Beeri, I. Fundulaki and M. Scholl. Ontology-Based Integration of XML Web Resources. In ISWC'02.
2. Y. An, A. Borgida, and J. Mylopoulos. Inferring Complex Semantic Mappings between Relational Tables and Ontologies from Simple Correspondences. In ODBASE'05.
3. M. Arenas and L. Libkin. XML Data Exchange: Consistency and Query Answering. In PODS'05, Baltimore, USA.
4. R. Dhamankar, Y. Lee, A. Doan, A. Halevy, and P. Domingos. iMAP: Discovering Complex Semantic Matches between Database Schemas. In SIGMOD'04.
5. C. Delobel, C. Reynaud, and M. Rousset, J. Sirot, and D. Vodislav. Semantic Integration in Xyleme: A Uniform Tree-Based Approach. Data and Knowledge Engineering 44(2003), 267-298, 2002.
6. D. W. Embley and W. Y. Mok. Developing XML Documents with Guaranteed "Good" Properties. In ER'01.
7. A. Halevy, Z. Ives, P. Mork, and I. Tatarinov. Piazza: Data Management Infrastructure for Semantic Web Applications. In WWW'03.
8. M. Jensen, T. Moller and T. Pedersen. Converting XML DTDs to UML Diagrams for Conceptual Data Integration. Data and Knowledge Engineering 44(2003), 323-346, 2002.
9. C. Kleiner and U. W. Lipeck. Automatic Generation of XML DTDs from Conceptual Database Schemas. GI Jahrestagung (1), 2001.
10. D. Lee and W. W. Chu. Constraint-Preserving Transformation from XML Document Type Definition to Relational Schema. In ER'00.
11. L. V.S. Lakshmanan and F. Sadri. Interoperability on XML Data. In ISWC'03.
12. J. Madhavan, P. A. Bernstein, and E. Rahm. Generic Schema Matching with Cupid. In VLDB'01.
13. S. Melnik, H. Garcia-Molina and E. Rahm. Similarity Flooding: A Versatile Graph Matching Algorithm and its Application to Schema Matching. In ICDE'02.
14. R. Miller, L. Haas, and M. Hernandez. Schema Mapping as Query Discovery. In VLDB'01.
15. L. Popa, Y. Velegrakis, R. Miller, M. Hernandez, and R. Fagin. Translating Web Data. In VLDB'02.
16. J. Shanmugasundaram et al. Relational Database for Querying XML Documents: Limitations and Opportunities. In VLDB'99.

Stable Model Theory for Extended RDF Ontologies*

Anastasia Analyti[1], Grigoris Antoniou[1,2],
Carlos Viegas Damásio[3], and Gerd Wagner[4]

[1] Institute of Computer Science, FORTH-ICS, Greece
{analyti, antoniou}@ics.forth.gr
[2] Department of Computer Science, University of Crete, Greece
[3] Centro de Inteligência Artificial, Universidade Nova de Lisboa, Portugal
cd@di.fct.unl.pt
[4] Inst. of Informatics, Brandenburg Univ. of Technology at Cottbus, Germany
G.Wagner@tu-cottbus.de

Abstract. Ontologies and automated reasoning are the building blocks
of the Semantic Web initiative. Derivation rules can be included in an
ontology to define derived concepts based on base concepts. For example, rules allow to define the extension of a class or property based on
a complex relation between the extensions of the same or other classes
and properties. On the other hand, the inclusion of negative information
both in the form of negation-as-failure and explicit negative information
is also needed to enable various forms of reasoning. In this paper, we
extend RDF graphs with weak and strong negation, as well as derivation rules. The *ERDF stable model semantics* of the extended framework
(*Extended RDF*) is defined, extending RDF(S) semantics. A distinctive
feature of our theory, which is based on partial logic, is that both truth
and falsity extensions of properties and classes are considered, allowing
for truth value gaps. Our framework supports both closed-world and
open-world reasoning through the explicit representation of the particular closed-world assumptions and the ERDF ontological categories of
total properties and total classes.

1 Introduction

The idea of the Semantic Web is to describe the meaning of web data in a way
suitable for automated reasoning. This means that descriptive data (meta-data)
in machine readable form are to be stored on the web and used for reasoning.
Due to its distributed and world-wide nature, the Web creates new problems for
knowledge representation research. In [2], the following fundamental theoretical
problems have been identified: negation and contradictions, open-world versus
closed-world assumptions, and rule systems for the Semantic Web. For the time
being, the first two issues have been circumvented by discarding the facilities to

---

* This research has been partially funded by European Commission and by the Swiss
Federal Office for Education and Science within the 6th Framework Programme
project REWERSE number 506779 (www.rewerse.net).

introduce them, namely negation and closed-world assumptions. Though the web ontology language OWL [13], which is based on description logic (DL), includes a form of classical negation through class complements, this form is limited. This is because, to achieve decidability, classes are formed based on specific class constructors and negation on properties is not considered. Rules constitute the next layer over the ontology languages of the Semantic Web and, in contrast to DL, allow arbitrary interaction of variables in the body of the rules. The widely recognized need of having rules in the Semantic Web [10,14] has restarted the discussion of the fundamentals of closed-world reasoning and the appropriate mechanisms to implement it in rule systems, such as the computational concept of *negation-as-failure*.

The RDF(S) recommendation [6] provides the basic constructs for defining web ontologies and a solid ground to discuss the above issues. RDF(S) is a special predicate logical language that is restricted to existentially quantified conjunctions of atomic formulas, involving binary predicates only. Thus, RDF(S) does not support negation and rules. In [18], it was argued that a database, as a knowledge representation system, needs two kinds of negation, namely *weak negation* $\sim$ (expressing negation-as-failure or not-truth) and *strong negation* $\neg$ (expressing explicit negative information or falsity) to be able to deal with partial information. In [19], this point was made for the Semantic Web as a framework for knowledge representation in general. In the present paper we make the same point for the Semantic Web language RDF and show how it can be extended to accommodate the two negations of partial logic [7], as well as derivation rules. We call the extended language *Extended RDF* and denote it by *ERDF*. The model-theoretic semantics of ERDF, called *ERDF stable model semantics*, is developed based on partial logic [7].

In partial logic, relating strong and weak negation at the interpretation level allows to distinguish four categories of properties and classes. *Partial properties* are properties p that may have truth-value gaps and truth-value clashes, that is $p(x,y)$ is possibly neither true nor false, or both true and false. *Total properties* are properties p that satisfy *totalness*, that is $p(x,y)$ is true or false (but possibly both). *Coherent properties* are properties p that satisfy *coherence*, that is $p(x,y)$ cannot be both true and false. *Classical properties* are total and coherent properties. For classical properties p, the *classical logic law* applies: $p(x,y)$ is either true or false. Partial, total, coherent, and classical classes c are defined similarly, by replacing $p(x,y)$ by $rdf{:}type(x,c)$.

Partial logic allows also to distinguish between properties (similarly, classes) that are completely represented in a knowledge base and those that are not. The classification if a property is completely represented or not is up to the owner of the knowledge base: the owner must know for which properties there is complete information and for which there is not. Clearly, in the case of a completely represented (*closed*) predicate p, negation-as-failure implies falsity, and the underlying completeness assumption is also called *Closed-World Assumption (CWA)*. A CWA for p is represented in our framework through the inclusion of the derivation rule $\neg p(?x,?y) \leftarrow \sim p(?x,?y)$ (for a closed class c, the corresponding CWA is $\neg rdf{:}type(?x, c) \leftarrow \sim rdf{:}type(?x, c))$. In the case of an incompletely represented (*open*) predicate p, negation-as-failure is not applicable and explicit negative information has to be supplied along with ordinary (positive) information. In particular, the inclusion of the derivation rule $\neg p(?x, ?y) \leftarrow \sim p(?x, ?y)$ will not affect the semantics of p. Unfortunately, neither classical logic nor Prolog supports this distinction between "closed" and "open" predicates. Classical logic supports only open-world reasoning. On the contrary, Prolog supports only closed-world reasoning, as *negation-as-failure* is the only negation mechanism supported. For arguments in favor of the combination of closed and open world reasoning in the same framework, see [1].

Specifically, in this paper:

1. We extend RDF graphs to ERDF graphs with the inclusion of strong negation, and then to ERDF ontologies (or ERDF knowledge bases) with the inclusion of general derivation rules. ERDF graphs allow to express existential positive and negative information, whereas general derivation rules allow inferences based on formulas built using the connectives $\sim$, $\neg$, $\supset$, $\wedge$, $\vee$ and the quantifiers $\forall$, $\exists$.

2. We extend the vocabulary of RDF(S) with the terms $erdf{:}TotalProperty$ and $erdf{:}TotalClass$, representing metaclasses of total properties and total classes, on which the open-world assumption applies.

3. We extend RDFS interpretations to ERDF interpretations including both truth and falsity extensions for properties and classes. Then, we define *coherent ERDF interpretations* by imposing coherence on all properties. In the developed model-theoretic semantics of ERDF, we consider only coherent ERDF interpretations. Thus, total properties and classes become synonymous to classical properties and classes.

4. We extend RDF graphs to ERDF formulas that are built from positive triples using the connectives $\sim$, $\neg$, $\supset$, $\wedge$, $\vee$ and the quantifiers $\forall$, $\exists$. Then, we define ERDF entailment between two ERDF formulas, extending RDFS entailment between RDF graphs.

5. We define the ERDF models, Herbrand interpretations, minimal Herbrand models, and stable models of ERDF ontologies. We show that stable model entailment on ERDF ontologies extends RDFS entailment on RDF graphs.

6. We show that if all properties are total, classical (boolean) Herbrand model reasoning and stable model reasoning coincide. In this case, we make an open-world assumption for all properties and classes.

The rest of the paper is organized as follows: In Section 2, we extend RDF graphs to ERDF graphs and ERDF formulas. Section 3 defines ERDF interpretations and ERDF entailment. We show that ERDF entailment extends RDFS entailment. In Section 4, we define ERDF ontologies and the Herbrand models of an ERDF ontology. In Section 5, we define the stable models of an ERDF ontology and show that stable model entailment extends RDFS entailment. Section 6 reviews related work and Section 7 concludes the paper.

2   Extending RDF Graphs with Negative Information

In this section, we extend RDF graphs to ERDF graphs, by adding strong negation. Moreover, we extend RDF graphs to ERDF formulas, which are built from positive ERDF triples, the connectives $\sim$, $\neg$, $\supset$, $\wedge$, $\vee$, and the quantifiers $\forall$, $\exists$.

According to RDF concepts [12,6], URI references are used for naming web resources. A URI reference consists of two parts: a namespace URI ns and a local name ln, and is denoted by $ns{:}ln$. A plain literal is a string "s", where s is a sequence of Unicode characters, or a pair of a string "s" and a language tag t, denoted by "s"@t. A typed literal is a pair of a string "s" and a datatype URI reference d, denoted by "s"^^d. A (Web) *vocabulary* V is a set of URI references and/or literals (plain or typed). We denote the set of all URI references by URI, the set of all plain literals by $\mathcal{PL}$, the set of all typed literals by $\mathcal{TL}$, and the set of all literals by $\mathcal{LIT}$.

In our formalization, we consider a set Var of variable symbols, such that the sets Var, URI, $\mathcal{LIT}$ are pairwise disjoint. In the main text, variable symbols are explicitly indicated, while in our examples, variable symbols are prefixed by ?.

Below we extend the notion of RDF triple to allow for both positive and negative information.

Definition 1 (ERDF triple). Let V be a vocabulary. A *positive ERDF triple* over V (also called *ERDF sentence atom*) is an expression of the form $p(s,o)$, where $s, o \in V \cup Var$ are called *subject* and *object*, respectively, and $p \in V \cap URI$ is called *predicate* or *property*.
A *negative ERDF triple* over V is the strong negation $\neg p(s,o)$ of a positive ERDF triple $p(s,o)$ over V.
An *ERDF triple* over V (also called *ERDF sentence literal*) is a positive or negative ERDF triple over V. □

For example, $ex{:}likes(ex{:}Gerd, ex{:}Riesling)$ is a positive ERDF triple, and $\neg ex{:}likes(ex{:}Carlos, ex{:}Riesling)$ is a negative ERDF triple. Note that an RDF triple is a positive ERDF triple with the constraint that the subject of the triple is not a literal. For example, $ex{:}nameOf($"$Grigoris$"$, ex{:}Grigoris)$ is a valid ERDF triple but not a valid RDF triple. Our choice of allowing literals appearing in the subject position is based on our intuition that this case can naturally appear in knowledge representation (as in the previous example). Moreover, note that a variable in the object position of an ERDF triple in the body of a rule, can appear in the subject position of the ERDF triple in the head of the rule. Since variables can be instantiated by a literal, a literal can naturally appear in the subject position of the derived ERDF triple.

Definition 2 (ERDF formula). Let V be a vocabulary. We consider the logical factors $\{\sim, \neg, \wedge, \vee, \supset, \exists, \forall\}$, where $\neg$, $\sim$, and $\supset$ are called *strong negation*, *weak negation*, and *material implication* respectively. We denote by $L(V)$ the smallest set that contains the positive ERDF triples over V and is closed with respect to the following conditions: if $F, G \in L(V)$ then $\{\sim F, \neg F, F \wedge G, F \vee G, F \supset G, \exists x F, \forall x F\} \subseteq L(V)$, where $x \in Var$. An *ERDF formula* over V is an element of $L(V)$. We denote the set of variables appearing in F by $Var(F)$, and the set of free variables[1] appearing in F by $FVar(F)$. □

For example, let $F = \forall?x\ \exists?y\ (rdf{:}type(?x, ex{:}Person) \supset ex{:}hasFather(?x, ?y))$ $\wedge\ rdf{:}type(?z, ex{:}Person)$. Then, F is an ERDF formula over the vocabulary $V = \{rdf{:}type, ex{:}Person, ex{:}hasFather\}$ with $Var(F) = \{?x, ?y, ?z\}$ and $FVar(F) = \{?z\}$.

We will denote the sublanguages of $L(V)$ formed by means of a subset S of the logical factors, by $L(V|S)$. For example, $L(V|\{\neg\})$ denotes the set of (positive and negative) ERDF triples over V.

Definition 3 (ERDF graph). An *ERDF graph* G is a set of ERDF triples over some vocabulary V. We denote the variables appearing in G by $Var(G)$, and the set of URI references and literals appearing in G by V_G. □

Intuitively, an ERDF graph G represents an existentially quantified conjunction of *ERDF* triples. Specifically, let $G = \{tr_1, ..., tr_n\}$ be an *ERDF* graph, and let $Var(G) = \{x_1, ...x_k\}$. Then, G represents the formula $\exists x_1, ...x_k\ tr_1 \wedge ... \wedge tr_n$. Following the RDF terminology [12], the variables of an ERDF graph are called *blank nodes*, and intuitively denote anonymous web resources.

Note that as an RDF graph is a set of RDF triples [12,6], an RDF graph is also an ERDF graph.

3   ERDF Interpretations

In this section, we extend RDF(S) semantics by allowing for partial properties and classes. In particular, we define ERDF interpretations and satisfaction of an ERDF formula. For simplicity, we disregard RDF(S) containers, collections, and reification, as no special semantic conditions are imposed on these, and thus can be included by a straightforward extension.

Below we define a partial interpretation as an extension of a simple interpretation [6], where each property is associated not only with a truth extension but also with a falsity extension allowing for partial properties.

Definition 4 (Partial interpretation). A *partial interpretation* I of a vocabulary V consists of:

- A non-empty set of resources Res_I, called the *domain* or *universe* of I.
- A set of properties $Prop_I$.
- A vocabulary interpretation mapping $I_V : V \cap URI \rightarrow Res_I \cup Prop_I$.
- A property-truth extension mapping $PT_I : Prop_I \rightarrow \mathcal{P}(Res_I \times Res_I)$.
- A property-falsity extension mapping $PF_I : Prop_I \rightarrow \mathcal{P}(Res_I \times Res_I)$.
- A mapping $IL_I : V \cap \mathcal{TL} \rightarrow Res_I$.
- A set of literal values $LV_I \subseteq Res_I$, which contains $V \cap \mathcal{PL}$.

We define the mapping: $I : V \rightarrow Res_I \cup Prop_I$ such that:

---

[1] Without loss of generality, we assume that a variable cannot have both free and bound occurrences in F, and more than one bound occurrence.

- $I(x) = I_V(x)$, $\forall x \in V \cap URI$.
- $I(x) = x$, $\forall\, x \in V \cap \mathcal{PL}$.
- $I(x) = IL_I(x)$, $\forall\, x \in V \cap \mathcal{TL}$. □

Definition 5 (Satisfaction of an ERDF formula w.r.t. a partial interpretation and a valuation). Let F, G be $ERDF$ formulas and let I be a partial interpretation of a vocabulary V. Let v be a mapping $v : Var(F) \to Res_I$ (called *valuation*). If $x \in Var(F)$, we define $[I+v](x) = v(x)$. If $x \in V$, we define $[I+v](x) = I(x)$.

- If $F = p(s,o)$ then $I,v \models F$ iff $p \in V \cap URI$, $s,o \in V \cup Var$, $I(p) \in Prop_I$, and $\langle [I+v](s), [I+v](o)\rangle \in PT_I(I(p))$.
- If $F = \neg p(s,o)$ then $I,v \models F$ iff $p \in V \cap URI$, $s,o \in V \cup Var$, $I(p) \in Prop_I$, and $\langle [I+v](s), [I+v](o)\rangle \in PF_I(I(p))$.
- If $F = {\sim}G$ then $I,v \models F$ iff all URIs and literals appearing in G belong to V, and $I,v \not\models G$.
- If $F = F_1 \wedge F_2$ then $I,v \models F$ iff $I,v \models F_1$ and $I,v \models F_2$.
- If $F = F_1 \vee F_2$ then $I,v \models F$ iff $I,v \models F_1$ or $I,v \models F_2$.
- If $F = F_1 \supset F_2$ then $I,v \models F$ iff $I,v \models {\sim}F_1 \vee F_2$.
- If $F = \exists x\, G$ then $I,v \models F$ iff there exists mapping $u : Var(G) \to Res_I$ such that $u(y) = v(y)$, $\forall y \in Var(G) - \{x\}$, and $I,u \models G$.
- If $F = \forall x\, G$ then $I,v \models F$ iff for all mappings $u : Var(G) \to Res_I$ such that $u(y) = v(y)$, $\forall y \in Var(G) - \{x\}$, it holds $I,u \models G$.
- All other cases of $ERDF$ formulas are treated by the following DeMorgan-style rewrite rules expressing the falsification of compound ERDF formulas:
  $\neg(F \wedge G) \to \neg F \vee \neg G$, $\neg(F \vee G) \to \neg F \wedge \neg G$, $\neg\neg F \to F$, $\neg {\sim} F \to F$,
  $\neg \exists x\, F \to \forall x\, \neg F$, $\neg\forall x\, F \to \exists x\, \neg F$, $\neg(F \supset G) \to F \wedge \neg G$. □

Definition 6 (Satisfaction of an ERDF formula w.r.t. a partial interpretation). Let F be an $ERDF$ formula and let I be a partial interpretation of a vocabulary V. We say that I *satisfies* F, denoted by $I \models F$, iff for every mapping $v : Var(F) \to Res_I$, it holds $I,v \models F$. □

Note that as an ERDF graph represents an existentially quantified conjunction of ERDF triples, the above definition applies also to ERDF graphs. Specifically, let G be an ERDF graph representing the formula $F = \exists x_1, ...x_k\ tr_1 \wedge ... \wedge tr_n$. We say that a partial interpretation I *satisfies* the ERDF graph G ($I \models G$) iff $I \models F$.

We are now ready to define an ERDF interpretation over a vocabulary V as an extension of an RDFS interpretation [6], where each property and class is associated not only with a truth extension but also with a falsity extension, allowing for both partial properties and partial classes. Additionally, an ERDF interpretation gives special semantics to terms from the ERDF vocabulary.

The vocabulary of RDF, $\mathcal{V}_{RDF}$, and the vocabulary of RDFS, $\mathcal{V}_{RDFS}$, are defined in [6]. The *vocabulary of ERDF*, $\mathcal{V}_{ERDF}$, is a set of URI references in the *erdf:* namespace. Specifically, the set of ERDF predefined classes is $\mathcal{C}_{ERDF} = \{erdf{:}TotalClass,\ erdf{:}TotalProperty\}$. We define $\mathcal{V}_{ERDF} = \mathcal{C}_{ERDF}$. Intuitively, instances of the metaclass *erdf:TotalClass* are classes c that satisfy totalness, meaning that each resource belongs to the truth or falsity extension of *c.* Similarly, instances of the metaclass *erdf:TotalProperty* are properties p that satisfy totalness, meaning that each pair of resources belongs to the truth or falsity extension of p.

Definition 7 (ERDF interpretation). An *ERDF interpretation* I of a vocabulary V is a partial interpretation of $V \cup \mathcal{V}_{RDF} \cup \mathcal{V}_{RDFS} \cup \mathcal{V}_{ERDF}$, extended by the new ontological categories $Cls_I \subseteq Res_I$ for classes, $TCls_I \subseteq Cls_I$ for total classes, and $TProp_I \subseteq Prop_I$ for total properties, as well as the class-truth extension mapping $CT_I : Cls_I \to \mathcal{P}(Res_I)$, and the class-falsity extension mapping $CF_I : Cls_I \to \mathcal{P}(Res_I)$, such that:

1. $x \in CT_I(y)$ iff $\langle x, y \rangle \in PT_I(I(rdf{:}type))$, and
   $x \in CF_I(y)$ iff $\langle x, y \rangle \in PF_I(I(rdf{:}type))$.
2. The ontological categories are defined as follows:
   $Prop_I = CT_I(I(rdf{:}Property))$ $Cls_I = CT_I(I(rdfs{:}Class))$
   $Res_I = CT_I(I(rdfs{:}Resource))$ $LV_I = CT_I(I(rdfs{:}Literal))$
   $TCls_I = CT_I(I(erdf{:}TotalClass))$ $TProp_I = CT_I(I(erdf{:}TotalProperty))$.
3. if $\langle x, y \rangle \in PT_I(I(rdfs{:}domain))$ and $\langle z, w \rangle \in PT_I(x)$ then $z \in CT_I(y)$.
4. If $\langle x, y \rangle \in PT_I(I(rdfs{:}range))$ and $\langle z, w \rangle \in PT_I(x)$ then $w \in CT_I(y)$.
5. If $x \in Cls_I$ then $\langle x, I(rdfs{:}Resource) \rangle \in PT_I(I(rdfs{:}subclassOf))$.
6. If $\langle x, y \rangle \in PT_I(I(rdfs{:}subClassOf))$ then $x, y \in Cls_I$, $CT_I(x) \subseteq CT_I(y)$, and $CF_I(y) \subseteq CF_I(x)$.
7. $PT_I(I(rdfs{:}subClassOf))$ is a reflexive and transitive relation on Cls_I.
8. If $\langle x, y \rangle \in PT_I(I(rdfs{:}subPropertyOf))$ then $x, y \in Prop_I$, $PT_I(x) \subseteq PT_I(y)$, and $PF_I(y) \subseteq PF_I(x)$.
9. $PT_I(I(rdfs{:}subPropertyOf))$ is a reflexive and transitive relation on $Prop_I$.
10. If $x \in CT_I(I(rdfs{:}Datatype))$ then $\langle x, I(rdfs{:}Literal) \rangle \in PT_I(I(rdfs{:}subClassOf))$.
11. If $x \in TCls_I$ then $CT_I(x) \cup CF_I(x) = Res_I$.
12. If $x \in TProp_I$ then $PT_I(x) \cup PF_I(x) = Res_I \times Res_I$.
13. If "*s*"^^*rdf:XMLLiteral* $\in V$ and s is a well-typed XML literal string, then
    $IL_I(\text{"}s\text{"}\hat{\ }\hat{\ }rdf{:}XMLLiteral)$ is the XML value of s,
    $IL_I(\text{"}s\text{"}\hat{\ }\hat{\ }rdf{:}XMLLiteral) \in LV_I$, and
    $IL_I(\text{"}s\text{"}\hat{\ }\hat{\ }rdf{:}XMLLiteral) \in CT_I(I(rdf{:}XMLLiteral))$.
14. If "*s*"^^*rdf:XMLLiteral* $\in V$ and s is an ill-typed XML literal string then
    $IL_I(\text{"}s\text{"}\hat{\ }\hat{\ }rdf{:}XMLLiteral) \in Res_I - LV_I$, and
    $IL_I(\text{"}s\text{"}\hat{\ }\hat{\ }rdf{:}XMLLiteral) \in CF_I(I(rdfs{:}Literal))$.
15. I satisfies the *RDF* and *RDFS* axiomatic triples [6], as well as the *ERDF* axiomatic triples:
    $rdfs{:}subClassOf(erdf{:}TotalClass, rdfs{:}Class)$.
    $rdfs{:}subClassOf(erdf{:}TotalProperty, rdf{:}Property)$.   □

Note that the semantic conditions of ERDF interpretations may impose constraints to both the truth and falsity extensions of properties and classes.

Definition 8 (Coherent ERDF interpretation). An ERDF interpretation I of a vocabulary V is *coherent* iff for all $x \in Prop_I$, $PT_I(x) \cap PF_I(x) = \emptyset$. □

Coherent ERDF interpretations enforce the constraint that a pair of resources cannot belong to both the truth and falsity extensions of a property. Since *rdf:type* is a property, this constraint also implies that a resource cannot belong to both the truth and falsity extensions of a class.

In the rest of the document, we consider only coherent ERDF interpretations. This means that referring to an "ERDF interpretation", we implicitly mean a "coherent" one.

According to RDFS semantics, the only source of RDFS-inconsistency is the appearance of an ill-typed XML literal in the RDF graph (possibly causing an *XML clash*, for details see [6]). An ERDF graph can be ERDF-inconsistent[2], not only due to the appearance of an ill-typed XML literal in the ERDF graph, but also due to the additional semantic condition for coherent ERDF interpretations.

For example, let $p, q, s, o \in URI$ and let $G = \{p(s,o),\ rdfs{:}subPropertyOf(p, q),\ \neg q(s,o)\}$. Then, G is ERDF-inconsistent, since there is no (coherent) ERDF interpretation that satisfies G.

The following proposition shows that for total properties and total classes of (coherent) ERDF interpretations, weak negation and strong negation coincide (boolean truth values).

Proposition 1. Let I be an ERDF interpretation of a vocabulary V and let $V' = V \cup \mathcal{V}_{RDF} \cup \mathcal{V}_{RDFS} \cup \mathcal{V}_{ERDF}$. Then,

1. For all $p, s, o \in V'$, such that $I(p) \in TProp_I$, it holds:
   $I \models \sim p(s,o)$ iff $I \models \neg p(s,o)$ (equivalently, $I \models p(s,o) \vee \neg p(s,o)$).
2. For all $x, c \in V'$ such that $I(c) \in TCls_I$, it holds:
   $I \models \sim rdf{:}type(x,c)$ iff $I \models \neg rdf{:}type(x,c)$
   (equivalently, $I \models rdf{:}type(x,c) \vee \neg rdf{:}type(x,c)$).

Definition 9 (Classical ERDF interpretation). A (coherent) ERDF interpretation I of a vocabulary V is *classical* iff for all $x \in Prop_I$, $PT_I(x) \cup PF_I(x) = Res_I \times Res_I$. ☐

A classical ERDF interpretation is close to an interpretation of classical logic, since for every formula F, weak and strong negation coincide.

Proposition 2. Let I be an ERDF interpretation of a vocabulary V and let $V' = V \cup \mathcal{V}_{RDF} \cup \mathcal{V}_{RDFS} \cup \mathcal{V}_{ERDF}$. Then,

1. If $TProp_I = Prop_I$ then I is a classical ERDF interpretation.
2. If I is a classical ERDF interpretation and F is an ERDF formula over V' such that $I(p) \in Prop_I$, for every property p in F, then it holds:
   $I \models \sim F$ iff $I \models \neg F$ (equivalently, $I \models F \vee \neg F$).

The following definition defines ERDF entailment between two ERDF formulas.

Definition 10 (ERDF Entailment). Let F, F' be ERDF formulas. We say that F *ERDF-entails* F' ($F \models^{ERDF} F'$) iff for every ERDF interpretation I, if $I \models F$ then $I \models F'$. ☐

For example, let $F = \forall ?x\ \exists ?y\ (rdf{:}type(?x, ex{:}Person) \supset ex{:}hasFather(?x, ?y)) \wedge rdf{:}type(ex{:}John, ex{:}Person)$, and let $F' = \exists ?y\ ex{:}hasFather(ex{:}John, ?y) \wedge rdf{:}type(ex{:}hasFather, rdf{:}Property)$. Then $F \models^{ERDF} F'$.

The following proposition shows that an RDF graph is RDFS satisfiable iff it is ERDF satisfiable.

---

[2] Meaning that there is no (coherent) ERDF interpretation that satisfies the ERDF graph.

Proposition 3. Let G be an RDF graph such that $V_G \cap V_{ERDF} = \emptyset$. Then, there is an RDFS interpretation that satisfies G iff there is an ERDF interpretation that satisfies G.

The following proposition shows that ERDF entailment extends RDFS entailment from RDF graphs to ERDF formulas.

Proposition 4. Let G, G' be RDF graphs such that $V_G \cap V_{ERDF} = \emptyset$ and $V_{G'} \cap V_{ERDF} = \emptyset$. Then, $G \models^{RDFS} G'$ iff $G \models^{ERDF} G'$.

4   ERDF Ontologies

In this section, we define an ERDF ontology as a pair of an ERDF graph G and a set P of ERDF rules. ERDF rules should be considered as derivation rules that allow us to infer more ontological information based on the declarations in G. Moreover, we define the Herbrand interpretations and the Herbrand models of an ERDF ontology.

Definition 11 (ERDF rule, ERDF program). An *ERDF rule r* over a vocabulary V is an expression of the form: $G \leftarrow F$, where $F \in L(V)$ is called *condition* and $G \in L(V|\{\neg\})$ is called *conclusion*. We assume that no bound variable in F appears free in G. We denote the set of variables and the set of free variables of r by $Var(r)$ and $FVar(r)^3$, respectively. Additionally, we write $Cond(r) = F$ and $Concl(r) = G$.

An *ERDF program P* is a set of ERDF rules over some vocabulary V. We denote the set of URI references and literals appearing in P by V_P.   □

Definition 12 (ERDF ontology). An *ERDF ontology* (or *knowledge base*) is a pair $O = \langle G, P \rangle$, where G is an ERDF graph and P is an ERDF program.   □

The following definition defines the models of an ERDF ontology.

Definition 13 (Satisfaction of an ERDF rule and an ERDF ontology). Let I be an ERDF interpretation of a vocabulary V.

- We say that I *satisfies* an ERDF rule r, denoted by $I \models r$, iff it holds: If there is a mapping $v : Var(r) \rightarrow Res_I$ such that $I, v \models Cond(r)$ then $I, v \models Concl(r)$.
- We say that I *satisfies* an ERDF ontology $O = \langle G, P \rangle$ (also, I is a *model* of O), denoted by $I \models O$, iff $I \models G$ and $I \models r, \forall\, r \in P$.   □

Definition 14 (Skolemization of an ERDF graph). Let G be an ERDF graph. The *skolemization function* of G is an 1:1 mapping $sk_G : Var(G) \rightarrow URI$, where for each $x \in Var(G)$, $sk_G(x)$ is an artificial URI denoted by $G{:}x$. The set $sk_G(Var(G))$ is called the *Skolem vocabulary* of G.

The *skolemization* of G, denoted by $sk(G)$, is the ground ERDF graph derived from G after replacing each variable $x \in Var(G)$ by $sk_G(x)$.   □

---

^{3} $FVar(r) = FVar(F) \cup FVar(G)$.

Intuitively, the Skolem vocabulary of G (that is, $sk_G(Var(G))$) contains artificial URIs giving "arbitrary" names to the anonymous entities whose existence was asserted by the use of blank nodes in G.

Proposition 5. Let G be an ERDF graph and let I be an ERDF interpretation. Then, $I \models sk(G)$ implies $I \models G$.

Definition 15 (Vocabulary of an ERDF ontology). Let $O = \langle G, P \rangle$ be an ERDF ontology. The *vocabulary* of O is defined as $V_O = V_{sk(G)} \cup V_P \cup V_{RDF} \cup V_{RDFS} \cup V_{ERDF}$.   □

Let $O = \langle G, P \rangle$ be an ERDF ontology. We denote by Res_O^H the union of V_O and the set of XML values of the well-typed XML literals in V_O minus the well-typed XML literals.

Definition 16 (Herbrand interpretation, Herbrand model of an ERDF ontology). Let $O = \langle G, P \rangle$ be an ERDF ontology and let I be an ERDF interpretation of V_O. I is a *Herbrand interpretation* of O iff:

- $Res_I = Res_O^H$.
- $I_V(x) = x$, for all $x \in V_O \cap URI$.
- $IL_I(x) = x$, if x is a typed literal in V_O other than a well-typed XML literal, and $IL_I(x)$ is the XML value of x, if x is a well-typed XML literal in V_O.

We denote the set of Herbrand interpretations of O by $\mathcal{I}^H(O)$.
A Herbrand interpretation I of O is a *Herbrand model* of O iff $I \models \langle sk(G), P \rangle$.
We denote the set of Herbrand models of O by $\mathcal{M}^H(O)$.   □

Obviously, every Herbrand model of an ERDF ontology O is a model of O.

5   Minimal Herbrand Interpretations and Stable Models

In the previous section, we defined the Herbrand models of an ERDF ontology O. However, not all Herbrand models of O are desirable. In this section, we define the intended models of O, called *stable models* of O, based on minimal Herbrand interpretations. In particular, defining the stable models of O, only the minimal interpretations from a set of Herbrand interpretations that satisfy certain criteria are considered.

For example, let $p, s, o \in URI$, let $G = \{p(s, o)\}$ and let $O = \langle G, \emptyset \rangle$, Then, there is a Herbrand model I of O such that $I \models p(o, s)$, whereas we want $\sim p(o, s)$ to be satisfied by all intended models of O, as p is not a total property[4] and $p(o, s)$ cannot be derived from O (negation-as-failure).

To define the minimal Herbrand interpretations of an ERDF ontology O, we need to define a partial ordering on the Herbrand interpretations of O.

Definition 17 (Herbrand interpretation ordering). Let $O = \langle G, P \rangle$ be an ERDF ontology. Let $I, J \in \mathcal{I}^H(O)$. We say that J *extends* I, denoted by $I \leq J$ (or $J \geq I$), iff $Prop_I \subseteq Prop_J$, and for all $p \in Prop_I$, it holds $PT_I(p) \subseteq PT_J(p)$ and $PF_I(p) \subseteq PF_J(p)$.   □

---

[4] On total properties and classes, the open-world assumption applies.

The intuition behind Definition 17 is that by extending a Herbrand interpretation, we extend both the truth and falsity extension for all properties, and thus (since *rdf:type* is a property), for all classes.

Definition 18 (Minimal Herbrand Interpretations). Let O be an ERDF ontology and let $\mathcal{I} \subseteq \mathcal{I}^H(O)$. We define $minimal(\mathcal{I}) = \{I \in \mathcal{I} \mid \nexists J \in \mathcal{I} : J \neq I$ and $J \leq I\}$. $\qquad\square$

Let $I, J \in \mathcal{I}^H(O)$, we define $[I, J]_O = \{I' \in \mathcal{I}^H(O), \ I \leq I' \leq J\}$. Additionally, we define the *minimal Herbrand models* of O, as $\mathcal{M}^{min}(O) = minimal(\mathcal{M}^H(O))$.

However minimal Herbrand models do not give the intended semantics to all ERDF rules. This is because ERDF rules are derivation and not implication rules. Derivation rules are often identified with implications. For nonmonotonic rules (e.g. with negation-as-failure), this is no longer the case.

To define the intended (*stable*) models of an ERDF ontology, we need first to define grounding of ERDF rules.

Definition 19 (Grounding of an ERDF program). Let V be a vocabulary and r be an ERDF rule. We denote by $[r]_V$ the set of rules that result from r if we replace each variable $x \in FVar(r)$ by $v(x)$, for all mappings $v : FVar(r) \to V$. Let P be an ERDF program. We define $[P]_V = \bigcup_{r \in P}[r]_V$. $\qquad\square$

Below, we define the stable models of an ERDF ontology based on the coherent stable models of partial logic [7] (which, on extended logic programs, are equivalent [7] to Answer Sets [5]).

Definition 20 (Stable model). Let $O = \langle G, P \rangle$ be an ERDF ontology and let $M \in \mathcal{I}^H(O)$. We say that M is a *stable model* of O iff there is a chain of Herbrand interpretations of O, $I_0 \leq ... \leq I_k$ such that $I_{k-1} = I_k = M$ and:

1. $I_0 \in minimal(\{I \in \mathcal{I}^H(O) \mid I \models sk(G)\})$.
2. For $0 < \alpha \leq k$:
   $I_\alpha \in minimal\{I \in \mathcal{I}^H(O) \mid I \geq I_{\alpha-1}$ and $I \models Concl(r)$, for all $r \in P_{[I_{\alpha-1}, M]}\}$, where
   $P_{[I_{\alpha-1}, M]} = \{r \in [P]_{V_O} \mid I \models Cond(r), \forall I \in [I_{\alpha-1}, M]_O\}$.

The set of stable models of O is denoted by $\mathcal{M}^{st}(O)$. $\qquad\square$

The following proposition shows that a stable model of an ERDF ontology O is a Herbrand model of O.

Proposition 6. Let $O = \langle G, P \rangle$ be an ERDF ontology and let $M \in \mathcal{M}^{st}(O)$. It holds $M \in \mathcal{M}^H(O)$.

On the other hand, if all properties are total, a Herbrand model M of an ERDF ontology $O = \langle G, P \rangle$ is a stable model of O. This is because, in this case $M \in minimal(\{I \in \mathcal{I}^H(O) \mid I \models sk(G)\})$ and $M \in minimal\{I \in \mathcal{I}^H(O) \mid I \geq M$ and $I \models Concl(r)$, for all $r \in P_{[M,M]}\}$.

Proposition 7. Let $O = \langle G, P \rangle$ be an ERDF ontology, such that $rdfs{:}subclass(rdf{:}Property, erdf{:}TotalProperty) \in G$. Then, $\mathcal{M}^{st}(O) = \mathcal{M}^H(O)$.

From Proposition 2, it follows that if $rdfs{:}subclass(rdf{:}Property,$ $erdf{:}TotalProperty) \in G$ then each $M \in \mathcal{M}^H(O)$ is a classical ERDF interpretation. Therefore, the above proposition shows that classical (boolean) Herbrand model reasoning on ERDF ontologies is a special case of stable model reasoning.

Similarly to [5,8,7], stable models do not preserve Herbrand model satisfiability. For example, let $O = \langle \emptyset, P \rangle$, where $P = \{p(s,o) \leftarrow {\sim}p(s,o)\}$, and $p, s, o \in URI$. Then, $\mathcal{M}^{st}(O) = \emptyset$, whereas there is a Herbrand model of O that satisfies $p(s,o)$.

Definition 21 (Stable model entailment). Let $O = \langle G, P \rangle$ be an ERDF ontology and let F be an ERDF formula. We say that O *entails* F under the *(ERDF) stable model semantics*, denoted by $O \models^{st} F$ iff for all $M \in \mathcal{M}^{st}(O)$, $M \models F$. ☐

For example, let $O = \langle \emptyset, P \rangle$, where $P = \{p(s,o) \leftarrow {\sim}q(s,o)\}$ and $p, q, s, o \in URI$. Then, $O \models^{st} {\sim}q(s,o) \wedge p(s,o)$. Let $O = \langle G, P \rangle$, where $G = \{rdfs{:}subclass(rdf{:}Property, erdf{:}TotalProperty)\}$ and P is as in the previous example. Then, $O \models^{st} q(s,o) \vee p(s,o)$, but $O \not\models^{st} {\sim}q(s,o)$ and $O \not\models^{st} p(s,o)$. This is the desirable result, since q is a total property, and thus in contrast to the previous example, an open-world assumption is made for q. As another example, let $p, s, o \in URI$, let $G = \{p(s,o)\}$, and let $P = \{\neg p(?x,?y) \leftarrow {\sim}p(?x,?y)\}$. Then, $\langle G, P \rangle \models^{st} {\sim}p(o,s) \wedge \neg p(o,s)$ (note that P contains a CWA on p). Let $G = \{rdf{:}type(p, erdf{:}TotalProperty), p(s,o)\}$ and let P be as in the previous example. Then, $\langle G, P \rangle \models^{st} \forall ?x\, \forall ?y\ (p(?x,?y) \vee \neg p(?x,?y))$ (see Proposition 1), but $\langle G, P \rangle \not\models^{st} {\sim}p(o,s)$ and $\langle G, P \rangle \not\models^{st} \neg p(o,s)$. Indeed, the CWA in P does not affect the semantics of p, since p is a total property.

Let us now see a more involved example[5]. Consider the following ERDF program P, specifying some rules for concluding that a country is not a member state of the European Union (EU).

(r_1) $\neg rdf{:}type(?x, EUMember) \leftarrow rdf{:}type(?x, AmericanCountry).$
(r_2) $\neg rdf{:}type(?x, EUMember) \leftarrow rdf{:}type(?x, EuropeanCountry),$
              ${\sim}rdf{:}type(?x, EUMember).$

A rather incomplete ERDF ontology $O = \langle G, P \rangle$ is obtained by including the following information in the ERDF graph G:

$\neg rdf{:}type(Russia, EUMember).$	$rdf{:}type(Canada, AmericanCountry).$
$rdf{:}type(Austria, EUMember).$	$rdf{:}type(Italy, EuropeanCountry).$
$rdf{:}type(?x, EuropeanCountry).$	$\neg rdf{:}type(?x, EUMember).$

Using stable model entailment on O, it can be concluded that Austria is a member of EU, that Russia and Canada are not members of EU, and that it exists a European Country which is not a member of EU. However, it is also concluded that Italy is not a member of EU, which is a wrong statement. This is because G does not contain complete information of the European countries

---

[5] For simplicity, the example namespace $ex{:}$ is ignored.

that are EU members (e.g., it does not contain $rdf\!:\!type(Italy, EUMember)$). Thus, incorrect information is obtained by the closed-world assumption expressed in rule r_2. In the case that $rdf\!:\!type(EUMember, erdf\!:\!TotalClass)$ is added to G (that is, an open-world assumption is made for the class $EUMember$) then $\sim rdf\!:\!type(Italy, EUMember)$ and thus, $\neg rdf\!:\!type(Italy, EUMember)$ are not longer entailed. This is because, there is a stable model of the extended O that satisfies $rdf\!:\!type(Italy, EUMember)$. Moreover, if complete information for all European countries that are members of EU is included in G then the stable model conclusions of O will also be correct (the closed-world assumption will be correctly applied). Note that, in this case G will include $rdf\!:\!type(Italy, EUMember)$.

The following proposition shows that stable model entailment extends RDFS entailment from RDF graphs to ERDF ontologies.

Proposition 8. Let G, G' be RDF graphs such that $V_G \cap V_{ERDF} = \emptyset$, $V_{G'} \cap V_{ERDF} = \emptyset$, and $V_{G'} \cap sk_G(Var(G)) = \emptyset$. It holds: $G \models^{RDFS} G'$ iff $< G, \emptyset >\models^{st} G'$.

Below we define the stable answers of a query F w.r.t. an ERDF ontology.

Definition 22 (Stable answers). Let $O = \langle G, P \rangle$ be an ERDF ontology. A *query* F is an ERDF formula. The *(ERDF) stable answers* of F w.r.t. O are defined as follows: $Ans_O^{st}(F) = \{v : FVar(F) \to V_O \mid \forall M \in \mathcal{M}^{st}(O) : M \models v(F)\}$, where $v(F)$ is the formula F after replacing all the free variables x in F by $v(x)$. □

An ERDF ontology $O = \langle G, P \rangle$ is called *simple* if each rule in P has the form $L_0 \leftarrow L_1, ..., L_k, \sim L_{k+1}, ..., \sim L_n$, where each L_i is an ERDF triple (positive or negative). The following proposition shows that the stable answers of a query F w.r.t. a simple ERDF ontology can be computed through Answer Set Programming [5] on an extended logic program (ELP).

Proposition 9. Let $O = \langle G, P \rangle$ be a simple ERDF ontology and let F be an ERDF formula. We can define an extended logic program Π_O and a corresponding formula F' such that: The answers of F' according to the answer set semantics [5] of Π_O coincide with $Ans_O^{st}(F)$.

Intuitively, Π_O is generated as follows: (i) each $[\sim|\neg]p(s,o) \in L(V_O|\{\sim, \neg\})$ is represented by $[\sim|\neg]Holds(s,p,o)$, where $Holds$ is a conventional predicate name and p becomes a term, (ii) $sk(G)$ is represented as a set of facts, and (iii) semantics implicit in the definition of an ERDF interpretation is represented as rules. Π_O is the union of the rules generated in (ii-iii).

6   Related Work

In this section, we briefly review extensions of web ontology languages with rules.

TRIPLE [15] is a rule language for the Semantic Web supporting RDF and a subset of OWL Lite [13]. It is based on F-Logic [11]. Part of the semantics of the RDF(S) vocabulary is represented in the form of pre-defined rules and not as semantic conditions on interpretations. TRIPLE includes a form of negation-as-failure under the well-founded semantics [4]. Strong negation is not used.

Flora-2 [20] is a rule-based object-oriented knowledge base system for reasoning with semantic information on the Web. It is based on F-logic [11] and supports metaprogramming, nonmonotonic multiple inheritance, logical database updates, encapsulation, dynamic modules, and two kinds of weak negation (specifically, Prolog negation and well-founded negation [4]). In Flora-2, anonymous resources are handled through skolemization (similarly to our theory).

Notation 3 (N3) provides a more human readable syntax for RDF and also extends RDF by adding numerous pre-defined constructs ("built-ins") for being able to express rules conveniently (see [17]). Remarkably, N3 contains a built-in (log:definitiveDocument) for making restricted completeness asumptions and another built-in (log:notIncludes) for expressing simple negation-as-failure tests. The addition of these constructs was motivated by use cases. However, N3 does not have any direct formal semantics for these constructs, and does not provide strong negation. In an extended version of this paper we will show how these N3 constructs can be mapped to ERDF.

OWL-DL [13] is an ontology representation language for the Semantic Web, that is a syntactic variant of the $\mathcal{SHOIN}(\mathbf{D})$ description logic and a decidable fragment of first-order logic. However, the need for extending the expressive power of OWL-DL with rules has initiated several studies, including the SWRL (Semantic Web Rule Language) proposal [10]. In [9], it is shown that this extension is in general undecidable. For an overview of (decidable) approaches of combining Description Logics with rules, see [3]. In several of these approaches, entailment on the extended with rules DL is based on first-order logic, that is both the DL component and the logic program are viewed as a set of first-order logic statements. Thus, negation-as-failure, closed-world-assumptions, and non-monotonic reasoning cannot be supported. In contrast in our work, we support both weak and strong negation, and allow closed-world and open-world reasoning on a selective basis.

7 Conclusions

In this paper, we extended RDF graphs to ERDF graphs by allowing negative triples, and then to ERDF ontologies with the inclusion of derivation rules, allowing freely appearance of (meta)properties and (meta)classes in the body and head of the rules, all logical factors $\sim$, $\neg$, $\forall$, $\exists$, $\supset$, $\wedge$, $\vee$ in the body of the rules, and strong negation $\neg$ in the head of the rules. Moreover, the RDF(S) vocabulary was extended with the terms *erdf:TotalProperty* and *erdf:TotalClass*. We have developed the model-theoretic semantics of ERDF ontologies, called *ERDF stable model semantics*, showing that stable model entailment extends RDFS entailment on RDF graphs. We have shown that classical (boolean) Herbrand model reasoning is a special case of our semantics, when all properties are total. In this case, similarly to classical logic, an open-world assumption is made for all properties and classes. Allowing totalness of properties and classes to be declared on a selective basis and the explicit representation of closed-world assumptions (as derivation rules) enables the combination of open-world and closed-world reasoning in the same framework. For simple ERDF ontologies, our semantics can be computed through Answer Set Programming [5]. Future work concerns the support of datatype maps, including XSD datatypes, and the extension of the ERDF vocabulary to other useful ontological categories possibly in accordance with [16].

References

1. A. Analyti, G. Antoniou, C. V. Damasio, and G. Wagner. Negation and Negative Information in the W3C Resource Description Framework. *Annals of Mathematics, Computing & Teleinformatics (AMCT)*, 1(2):25–34, 2004.
2. Tim Berners-Lee. Design issues - architectual and philosophical points. Personal notes, 1998. Available at http://www.w3.org/DesignIssues/.
3. E. Franconi and S. Tessaris. Rules and Queries with Ontologies: A Unified Logical Framework. In *Second International Workshop on Principles and Practice of Semantic Web Reasoning (PPSWR 2004)*, pages 50–60, 2004.
4. A. Van Gelder, K. A. Ross, and J. S. Schlipf. The well-founded semantics for general logic programs. *Journal of the ACM*, 38(3):620–650, 1991.
5. M. Gelfond and V. Lifschitz. Logic programs with classical negation. In Warren and Szeredi, editors, *7th International Conference on Logic Programming*, pages 579–597. MIT Press, 1990.
6. Patrick Hayes. RDF Semantics. W3C Recommendation, 10 February 2004. Available at http://www.w3.org/TR/2004/REC-rdf-mt-20040210/.
7. H. Herre, J. Jaspars, and G. Wagner. Partial Logics with Two Kinds of Negation as a Foundation of Knowledge-Based Reasoning. In D.M. Gabbay and H. Wansing, editors, *What Is Negation?* Kluwer Academic Publishers, 1999.
8. H. Herre and G. Wagner. Stable Models are Generated by a Stable Chain. *Journal of Logic Programming*, 30(2):165–177, 1997.
9. I. Horrocks and P. F. Patel-Schneider. A Proposal for an OWL Rules Language. In *13th International Conference on World Wide Web (WWW'04)*, pages 723–731. ACM Press, 2004.
10. I. Horrocks, P. F. Patel-Schneider, H. Boley, S. Tabet, B. Grosof, and M. Dean. SWRL: A semantic web rule language combining OWL and RuleML. W3C Member Submission, 21 May 2004. Available at http://www.w3.org/Submission/2004/SUBM-SWRL-20040521/.
11. M. Kifer, G. Lausen, and J. Wu. Logical Foundations of Object-Oriented and Frame-Based Languages. *Journal of the ACM*, 42(4):741–843, 1995.
12. G. Klyne and J. J. Carroll. Resource Description Framework (RDF): Concepts and Abstract Syntax. W3C Recommendation, 10 February 2004. Available at http://www.w3.org/TR/2004/REC-rdf-concepts-20040210/.
13. D. L. McGuinness and F. van Harmelen. OWL Web Ontology Language Overview. W3C Recommendation, 10 February 2004. Available at http://www.w3.org/TR/2004/REC-owl-features-20040210/.
14. The rule markup initiative (ruleml). Available at http://www.ruleml.org.
15. M. Sintek and S. Decker. TRIPLE - A Query, Inference, and Transformation Language for the Semantic Web. In *First International Semantic Web Conference on The Semantic Web (ISWC2002)*, pages 364–378. Springer-Verlag, 2002.

16. H. J. ter Horst. Extending the RDFS Entailment Lemma. In *3rd International Semantic Web Conference (ISWC2004)*, pages 77–91, 2004.
17. Tim-Berners-Lee. Notation 3 - An RDF language for the Semantic Web. W3C Recommendation, 1998. Available at http://www.w3.org/DesignIssues/Notation3.html.
18. G. Wagner. A Database Needs Two Kinds of Negation. In *3rd Symposium on Mathematical Fundamentals of Database and Knowledge Base Systems (MFDBS'91)*, pages 357–371. Springer-Verlag, 1991.
19. G. Wagner. Web Rules Need Two Kinds of Negation. In *1st International Workshop on Principles and Practice of Semantic Web Reasoning (PPSWR'03)*, pages 33–50. Springer-Verlag, December 2003.
20. Guizhen Yang and Michael Kifer. Inheritance and Rules in Object-Oriented Semantic Web Languages. In *2nd International Workshop on Rules and Rule Markup Languages for the Semantic Web (RULEML'03)*, pages 95–110, 2003.

Towards a Formal Verification of OWL-S Process Models *

Anupriya Ankolekar, Massimo Paolucci, and Katia Sycara

Carnegie Mellon University,
Pittsburgh, Pennsylvania, USA
{anupriya, paolucci, katia}@cs.cmu.edu

Abstract. In this paper, we apply automatic tools to the verification of interaction protocols of Web services described in OWL-S. Specifically, we propose a modeling procedure that preserves the control flow and the data flow of OWL-S Process Models. The result of our work provides complete modeling and verification of OWL-S Process Models.

1 Introduction

Verification of the interaction protocol of Web services is crucial to both the implementation of Web services and to their use and composition. The verification process can prove important and desirable properties of the control flow of a Web service. At implementation time, a Web service provider will want to verify that the protocol to be advertised is indeed correct, e.g. does not contain deadlocks. A Web service provider may also want to guarantee additional properties, e.g. purchased goods are not delivered if a payment is not received.

Even if the Web service provider verifies the correctness of the programming logic behind its Web services, it will still need to verify the advertised interaction protocol. The mapping from the programming logic of the Web service to the interaction protocol of the Web service is typically lossy. Thus, the Web service provider will need to verify that claims that were true of the Web service program also hold true of the interaction protocol. Furthermore, the interaction protocol may make use of several Web services provided by the same Web service provider or possibly by other third-party providers. In either case, verifying the programming logic of multiple Web services is impracticable. In these cases, verifying the interaction protocol itself is both possible and useful.

During composition and use of Web services, a Web service client may want to verify the Web service provider's interaction protocol to obtain a guarantee that the protocol is correct, e.g. it does not contain an infinite loop, and that it conforms to the client's requirements. For example, the client may want to ensure that whenever a payment is received by the service provider, the goods

---

* This research was funded by the Defense Advanced Research Projects Agency as part of the DARPA Agent Markup Language (DAML) program under Air Force Research Laboratory contract F30601-00-2-0592 to Carnegie Mellon University.

Y. Gil et al. (Eds.): ISWC 2005, LNCS 3729, pp. 37–51, 2005.

are delivered to the client, or that there is the possibility of reimbursement, if the goods are returned.

In this paper, we explore the verification of OWL-S[1] interaction protocols using automatic verification tools, such as the SPIN model-checker [8]. OWL-S is one of the leading standards for the description of Web services on the Semantic Web. The OWL-S Process Model describes the interaction protocol between a Web service and its clients. Such protocols are inherently non-deterministic and can be arbitrarily complex, containing multiple concurrent threads that may interact in unexpected ways. By performing an efficient exploration of the complete set of states that can be generated during an interaction between a Web service and its clients, SPIN is able to verify numerous properties of the OWL-S Process Model.

The work presented in this paper builds on work presented in [2][2]. In particular, we relaxed many of the abstractions in the previous version, added the modeling of loops and enriched the literature review. The rest of this paper is organized as follows. After reviewing related work in section 2, we provide a quick overview of OWL-S 1.1 in section 3, using a running example based on the Amazon Web service. In section 4, we provide an introduction to verification with Spin. In section 5, we then define a mapping of the Amazon example from OWL-S 1.1 to SPIN's PROMELA language, which is used to construct models that the SPIN system can analyze. We then describe the verification of claims on the Amazon Process Model using SPIN in section 6. Finally, in section 7 we will discuss our results and future work.

2   Related Work

Previous work on OWL-S verification is scant. Narayanan et al. [9] proposed a Petri Net-based operational semantics, which models the control flow of a Process Model exclusively[3]. On the basis of this mapping of OWL-S Process Models to Petri Nets, a number of theorems are proven on the computational complexity of typical verification problems, such as reachability of states and discovery of deadlocks. The results show that the complexity of the reachability problem for OWL-S Process Models is PSPACE-complete. This result is not surprising given the complexity of the OWL-S Process Modeling language.

Our approach improves on Narayanan's seminal work in three directions. First, we provide a model of Web service data flow in addition to control flow. As a result, the verification procedure can detect harmful interactions (see section 5.1) between data and control flow that would be undetected otherwise. Second, as part of our modeling methodology, we translate an OWL-S Process Model

---

[1] Our work is based on the OWL-S 1.1 release available at
http://www.daml.org/services/owl-s/1.1/.

[2] The authors are in debt to the participants of the workshop on "Semantic Web Services" at ISWC2004 for their useful comments.

[3] Narayanan's semantics was defined for an earlier version of OWL-S (namely DAML-S 0.5), which did not model data-flow.

into a simpler model that nevertheless preserves all the essential behavior to be verified. Third, we provide initial results on the actual verification of OWL-S Process Models using existing verification tools such as SPIN. The result of our work is a complete procedure for the modeling and verification of OWL-S Process Models.

While we are aware of only one other work on the verification of OWL-S Process Models, there has been a considerable amount of work on the verification of BPEL [1] Models. For example, WSAT (Web Service Analysis Tool) [13,6] provides a formal verification of composite Web services expressed in BPEL and WSDL using guarded automata (GA) to construct the model, and then mapping the GA into PROMELA using SPINas verifier. A different approach to the verification of BPEL is followed by [7], which is based on message sequence charts, while [11] provide a Petri Net semantics and verification model.

Unfortunately, there is no clear mapping between OWL-S and BPEL. BPEL aims to represent the composition of Web services, showing how different services can interact to solve a problem. Consequently, any verification of BPEL compositions aims to check that the different composed services can indeed work together. OWL-S, on the other hand, provides a representation of the Process Model of one single Web service, leaving the composition problem to some other entity, typically a synthetic planner. The focus here is on verifying whether the particular Web service has the properties that the client expects in order to make use of it. It is therefore quite difficult to export the results of work on verifying BPEL to the verification of OWL-S Web services.

3   OWL-S Process Model

The OWL-S Process Model is organized as a workflow of processes. Each process is described by three components: inputs, preconditions and results. Results specify what outputs and effects are produced by the process under a given condition. For example, a process may have different results depending on whether the client is a premium user, or an ordinary user. OWL-S processes describe the information transformation produced by the Web service; while preconditions and effects describe the knowledge state transition produced by the execution of a Web service.

Processes in the workflow are related to each other by data flow and control flow. Control flow allows the specification of the temporal relation between processes. OWL-S supports a wide range of control flow mechanisms including sequentially executed processes, spawning of concurrent processes, synchronization points between concurrent processes, conditional statements and non-deterministic selections of processes. OWL-S distinguishes between atomic and composite processes. Atomic processes are indivisible processes that result in a message exchange between the client and the server. Composite processes are used to describe the control flow relation between processes. Fig. 1 shows a simple fragment of the Process Model adopted by Amazon.com's Web service. The nodes of the tree correspond to composite processes that represent different

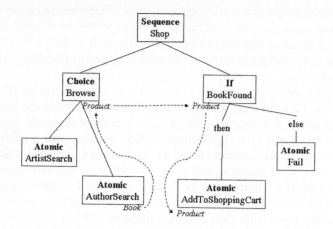

Fig. 1. The Process Model of Amazon.com's Web service

control constructs such as **Choice** for non-deterministic choices, **Sequence** for deterministic sequences of processes, and **If** conditionals. Atomic processes are represented as the leaves of the tree. For example, *Author Search* requires the client to provide information such as the name of an author. It then reports books found written by that author.

Data flow allows the specification of the relation between inputs and outputs of processes. An example of data flow is shown using dashed lines in Fig. 1. An output of the process *AuthorSearch* is a book which is then passed to the parent process, *Browse* and further up until it reaches the input of the process *AddToShoppingCart*. The scope of the data flow is limited to within a composite process. Therefore processes in a composite process can exchange data among themselves or with the parent process, but with no other processes. As the figure shows, data exchanges between two arbitrary processes, as for example *AuthorSearch* and *AddToShoppingCart* result from the composition of data flow links in the whole Process Model.

4   Model Checking with SPIN

OWL-S Process Models are typically verified using human inspection, simulation and testing. However, due to their complex and concurrent nature, OWL-S Process Models are not very amenable to such verification techniques. Instead, we use model checking [5], a method that has been successful in the verification of distributed systems, such as Web services [6,12]. Model checking exhaustively checks all possible executions of a system to verify that certain properties hold. It can thus formally *prove* the correctness of a system.

To construct such proofs, model checking requires two decisions to be made [8]. The first decision is about *what claims to prove*: a claim states invariant properties of the code, e.g. that a variable will always be instantiated or that it will always reach a given value. Typically, two kinds of properties are proven about a given protocol: safety properties, which guarantee that specified undesired states, such as deadlocking states, are never reached; and liveness properties, which specify that desired states are eventually reached.

The second decision relates to *what and how to model*, in other words which aspects of the protocol are relevant to the claims to be verified, and how to ensure that the model of the protocol preserves the behaviors to be checked. Certain aspects of the protocol may be verified better in other ways, for instance type safety can be ensured using a type checker. Moreover, a simplified model of the implementation, one that captures the essentials of the design, but avoids the full complexity of the implementation, can often be verified easily, even when the full implementation cannot. Thus, generating a *verification model* for an interaction protocol entails the translation of the protocol into a formal specification, which encapsulates the modeling decisions and specifies the claims to be verified.

This specification is input to a model checking tool, such as SPIN, to automatically verify that the protocol satisfies the claims. If SPIN verifies that a claim is true in the PROMELA specification, given that the specification captures the relevant behavior of the OWL-S Process Model, we know that the claim is also true in the corresponding Process Model. On the other hand, if the protocol contains an error, a model checker can provide a counter-example, identifying the conditions under which the error occurs. The claim may still hold in the OWL-S Process Model, because the PROMELA specification does not capture the full behavior of the Process Model. In this case, the counterexample that Spin provides can be analyzed and simulated in the actual Process Model. If this does produce faulty behavior, then a bona fide bug has been discovered, else a spurious bug [5] has been identified.

In this work, we use the SPIN model checker, a generic verification system that supports the design and verification of a system of asynchronous processes. SPIN accepts design specifications in PROMELA (a *Process Meta Language*) and correctness claims in LTL (Linear Temporal Logic). PROMELA is akin to a highly concurrent programming language, while LTL enables the representation of formulae about possible execution paths of a process. Due to space limitations, in the rest of the paper we will describe aspects of PROMELA and LTL only as relevant to our work. For a comprehensive discussion of PROMELA and LTL, the readers are referred to Chapters 3 and 6 of [8].

5   Modeling OWL-S Process Models in Promela

The mapping of OWL-S to PROMELA hinges on the decision of which aspects of the OWL-S Process Model are to (and can) be expressed in PROMELA, and on how to perform such a mapping. In the rest of this section, we describe the mapping of OWL-S Process Models to PROMELA models. Throughout this section, the Process Model of the Amazon Web service (Fig. 1) [10] will be used as a running example to illustrate the mapping rules.

```
(1)   proctype Shop () {
(2)     chan syncChan = [1] of { int,mtype };
(3)     chan dataChan = [1] of { int };
(4)     pid x1, x2;
(5)     x1 = run Browse(syncChan, dataChan);
(6)     if
(7)     :: syncChan??eval(x1),done ->
(8)          x2 = run BookFound(syncChan, dataChan);
(9)          if :: syncChan??eval(x2),done -> skip; fi
(10)    fi;
(11) }
```

Fig. 2. The Shop Process

Modeling Composite Processes. OWL-S Processes map naturally onto processes in PROMELA. Processes in PROMELA are introduced by `proctype` and are instantiated with the `run` operator. For example, Fig. 2 shows the result of the translation of the top-level Shop process to PROMELA. Shop, being a top-level process, does not take any arguments. Instantiated processes are inherently concurrent. Thus, Browse and BookFound run concurrently with Shop.

In PROMELA, if processes are to be executed in a particular order, e.g. in a sequence, they must be explicitly synchronized. Each parent composite process, therefore, creates a syncChan, a typed channel for control flow[4], and optionally an additional typed channel for data flow, dataChan, to be used by its child processes. Channels are used to model data flow between processes and can be either globally scoped or locally scoped within a single process. Channels can have a predetermined storage capacity. When the channel capacity has been reached, additional messages sent to the channel will be dropped. Receive statements (lines 7 and 9) that retrieve messages from channels block until a message is present in the channel. Fig. 2 shows the definition of these channels, within the Shop process, in lines 2-3. The channels have a storage capacity of at most one message. They are passed to the processes Browse and BookFound (lines 5 and 8 resp.). The if statement in lines 6-10 is explained later when we discuss the modeling of OWL-S sequences.

The syncChan channel holds tuples consisting of an integer, corresponding to the process id of the sending process, and done. Messages sent to dataChan are integers, representing the data values sent via data flow links (see below). PROMELA supports all the traditional programming language types such as int,

---

[4] An alternative to channels is the use of variables, as follows: a process would set a particular synchronization variable just before it terminates and other processes would wait for the variable to become true before executing. Although this mechanism is attractively simple, it fails when multiple concurrent processes are used. Since PROMELA admits only two kinds of scope, global or local to a single process, any synchronization variable must necessarily be globally defined. However, global variables may be overwritten when multiple instances of processes can be spawned dynamically.

```
(1)    proctype SplitJoin(chan syncChan, dataChan) {
(2)      chan childSync = [2] of { int,mtype };
(3)      pid childA = run A(childSync);
(4)      pid childB = run B(childSync);
(5)      if
(6)      :: childSync??eval(childA),done ->
(7)          if
(8)          :: childSync??eval(childB),done;
(9)          fi
(10)     fi
(11)     syncChan!_pid,done;
(12)}
```

Fig. 3. Implementation of a prototypical SplitJoin statement

char, boolean, arrays and records. In addition, PROMELA supports a form of enumerated type called mtype, which is typically used to describe message types, such as done.

Modeling Split and SplitJoin. Since processes in PROMELA are intrinsically concurrent, Split and SplitAndJoin can be naturally implemented as follows: the counterpart of each construct is a process in PROMELA, which simply spawns all its child processes. At this point, a Split process would immediately terminate, whereas a SplitAndJoin process would wait for the termination of the processes it spawned.

Since there are no Split and SplitAndJoin statements in the Amazon example, Fig. 3 shows a prototypical implementation of a SplitAndJoin in lines 3-4. The process spawns off two processes A() and B() with no data flow link in between. The guards in lines 6 and 8 check whether childSync contains a done message sent by childA or childB, respectively. The entire SplitAndJoin process blocks until the guard becomes true, thus synchronizing the process with the termination of its child processes. Finally, in line 11, the process signals its own termination. The implementation of a Split statement would be identical, but skip lines 5-10, which implement the Join synchronization.

Modeling Sequences. While concurrent processes can be implemented in a relatively straightforward way, the modeling of OWL-S sequences requires explicit synchronization, which is similar to the synchronization proposed for SplitJoin. We implement sequences by first spawning off the first process in the list, blocking until the process terminates, then spawning off the second process. The implementation of the Shop process, a sequence of Browse and BookFound processes is shown in Fig. 2. The PROMELA specification of Shop first spawns the Browse process in line 5. In the if statement, the execution of Shop is blocked (line 7) until it receives a done message from Browse, signaling that the Browse process is complete. Shop then spawns BookFound (line 8) and waits for it to complete before terminating itself.

```
(1)   proctype Browse (chan syncChan, dataChan) {
(2)     chan childSync = [1] of { int,mtype };
(3)     chan childData = [1] of { int };
(4)     pid child; int product;
(5)     if
(6)     :: true -> child =
               run AuthorSearch(childSync, childData);
(7)        if
(8)        :: childData?product -> dataChan!product;
(9)        :: childSync??eval(child),done;
(10)       fi
(11)    :: true -> child =
               run ArtistSearch(childSync, childData);
(12)       if
(13)       :: childData?product -> dataChan!product;
(14)       :: childSync??eval(child),done;
(15)       fi
(16)    fi;
(17)    syncChan!_pid,done;
(18)}
```

Fig. 4. Choice and Conditionals: the Browse Process

Modeling Choices and Conditionals. OWL-S Choices and Conditionals
are both implemented using PROMELA's guarded non-deterministic choice statements if :: fi. A non-deterministic choice in PROMELA is defined by an if
statement, where all guard conditions are true. The implementation of Browse,
shown in Fig. 4, provides an example of a choice between two atomic processes,
AuthorSearch and ArtistSearch. The conditions of the if statement at lines
6 and 11 are both true, so PROMELA non-deterministically chooses one of the
branches for execution. After spawning the chosen process, the execution blocks,
waiting for the process to complete, and then sets the output product.

In OWL-S conditions occur in Result statements and if statements. A
Result condition specifies when a given output or effect is generated, an if
is defined as part of the control construct. OWL-S Result conditions reflect
the state of the server. For example, while interacting with a Web service like
Amazon's, the client may discover that the book being sought is not available.
Similarly, if conditions in OWL-S depend on the knowledge of the agent at
execution time, in particular on the effects of previous steps and their interaction with the agent's knowledge. From the point of view of software verification,
such a condition could be considered a random variable, whose value cannot
be known at verification time and may equally be true or false. We therefore
model Results and if statements as non-deterministic choice. This forces the
verifier to evaluate the correctness of both branches of the Model. An OWL-S
conditional is implemented in a similar way to OWL-S Choice, but with the
if condition as a guard to the then statement and an else guard to the else
statement. According to PROMELA semantics, the else guard is only true, if all
other guards are false.

```
(1) proctype AuthorSearch (chan syncChan, dataChan) {
(2)    if /* implement conditional outputs */
(3)    :: true -> atomic {
(4)       int bookResult= 1;
(5)       dataChan!bookResult;}
(6)    :: true -> skip
(7)    fi;
(8)    syncChan!_pid,done;
(9) }
```

Fig. 5. Atomic process: the `AuthorSearch` Process

Modeling Atomic Processes. Finally, we present the mapping of an *atomic* process, which produces different results, to PROMELA. We model the selection of results with a non-deterministic choice. The implementation of the atomic process `AuthorSearch` is shown in figure 5. The conditional outputs are specified in lines 3 and 6 with a non-deterministic choice. If line 3 is selected, then the variable `bookResult` is assigned to 1 (line 4) and its value is sent out on the data channel (line 5). The other atomic processes, `ArtistSearch` and `AddToShoppingCart` can be specified analogously.

Modeling Data Flow. For a given data flow link that maps outputs to inputs, one would ideally like a guarantee that the class of the input always subsumes the class of the output. Verifying this using SPIN would require the subsumption relations in the ontology of the client to be represented within the PROMELA model. In addition, SPIN would need to be able to compute a subsumption hierarchy of classes. Since this would immediately overwhelm the verifier, we abstract from the actual values of inputs and outputs. Instead, the types of inputs and outputs are modeled as integers and data flow links as channels. Inputs that are not bound by a data flow link are expected to be initialized with some suitable value, usually 0. The evaluation of type subsumption claims are deferred to a pre-processor, such as a type-checker or a reasoner, that can methodically verify the integrity of all data flow links.

The data flow is represented by a variable that represents the output and the `dataChan` channel that transfers data between processes. Different parts of the data flow have been represented in the samples code shown above. For instance, lines 3 to 5 of Fig. 5 represent the output `bookResult` and the transmission of its

```
(1) proctype AddToShoppingCart (chan syncChan, dataChan) {
(2)    int product; dataChan?product;
(3)    assert(product);
(4)    syncChan!_pid,done;
(5) }
```

Fig. 6. Data flow: the `AddToShoppingCart` Process

```
(1)   proctype Repeat-While(chan syncChan, dataChan) {
(2)     int v_1 = v_1_init;
(3)     int v_2 = v_2_init;
(4)     do
(5)     :: c -> p
(6)     :: else -> break
(7)     od
(8)     syncChan!_pid,done;
(9)   }
```

Fig. 7. Implementation of a prototypical `Repeat-While` statement

value on the `dataChan` channel. Lines 8 and 13 of Fig. 4 show how channels are chained in composite processes, where the results of child processes are transmitted as the results of the parent process. This chaining implements the data flow chain, shown in Fig. 1. Finally, the data transmitted across all the links of the chain should reach the input of another atomic process and be consumed there. Line 3 of Fig. 6 shows the implementation of the input `product` and its instantiation with the value coming from `dataChan`. The line `assert(product)` (line 3) specifies a claim on the state reached, namely that the value of product should not be zero, i.e. the input is instantiated to some value.

Modeling Loops. There are two kinds of loops in OWL-S: the `Repeat-While` process and the `Repeat-Until` process. OWL-S loops have a loop condition c, a process p that is executed during every iteration of the loop and a number of variables, v_i that are local to the loop. Some of these variables may be referenced in the loop condition c.

PROMELA supports loops through the guarded `do :: od` statements. As an example of the implementation of loops, the definition of the `Repeat-While` process using `do` is shown in Fig. 7. The process first declares and initialises the loop variables, v_1 and v_2, in lines 2 and 3 respectively. Then, the process enters the `do` loop, checking during each iteration that the condition c is true (line 5). If so, the process p is executed; otherwise, the loop is broken (line 6) and the process signals its termination (line 8). The `Repeat-Until` statement is implemented

```
(1)   proctype Repeat-Until(chan syncChan, dataChan) {
(2)     int v_1 = v_1_init;
(3)     int v_2 = v_2_init;
(4)     p;
(5)     do
(6)     :: !c -> p
(7)     :: else -> break
(8)     od
```

Fig. 8. Implementation of a prototypical `Repeat-Until` statement

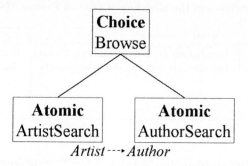

Fig. 9. An example of interaction between data and control flow in OWL-S

analogously (Fig. 8) with two key differences. The loop process p is executed once before checking the loop condition c. Secondly, in the `Repeat-Until` construct, the condition c is a termination condition, such that the loop terminates when c is true. Therefore, in the do loop, the loop process is executed if the condition is not satisfied.

5.1 Verifying Interaction Between Data and Control Flow

Data and control flow can often interact in unexpected ways. The simple process model depicted in Fig. 9 shows one such interaction that may prove harmful. The figure depicts a choice process, named `Browse`, that can be realized by either an atomic process named `ArtistSearch` or by an atomic process named `AuthorSearch`. A data flow link exists between the output of `ArtistSearch` to the input of `AuthorSearch`. Although this Process Model is legal in OWL-S, it is flawed. This is because either `AuthorSearch` or `ArtistSearch` is executed, but not both. Thus, whenever `AuthorSearch` is executed, `ArtistSearch` is not and therefore the input to `AuthorSearch` is never instantiated.

The PROMELA model generated by the mapping described thus far, would detect the harmful interaction between control flow and data flow. The model of the choice statement specifies that one of the two atomic processes will execute, while the `assert` constraint on the input of `AuthorSearch` requires that `ArtistSearch` is always instantiated. Since there does not exist a model where both claims are simultaneously true, SPIN reports an error. The ability to detect such interactions between data flow and control flow in OWL-S Process Models is one of the main contributions of this work, which goes beyond other verification models constructed for OWL-S. Indeed we claim that the model provided by Narayanan et al. [9], would not detect the flaw in the process model described above.

5.2 Summary of the OWL-S Model Construction

This section presented a detailed description of the modeling of OWL-S Process Models in the PROMELA modeling language. A summary of our modeling is

Table 1. Summary of the Modeling of OWL-S Process Models in PROMELA

Full Modeling	Partial Modeling	Out of scope
Processes	Conditions (non-deterministic choice)	Preconditions and Effects
Control Flow	Inputs/Outputs (model assignment)	Data Values
Concurrency		
Data Flow		
Loops		

presented in Table 1, highlighting the OWL-S Process Model features retained, partially modeled and the features out of scope. We already discussed how the checking of data values could be deferred to a type-checker or semantic reasoner. Thus, while we represent inputs and outputs, we do not represent their values or their (ontological) data-type, limiting ourselves to modeling assignment.

Similarly, we do not model OWL-S preconditions and effects. Preconditions to OWL-S processes are essentially warnings, that if the preconditions are not heeded, the execution of the process may fail. If the client is a hard-coded process, then the preconditions and effects serve as warnings or information for the programmer; on the other hand, if the client is an agent, the OWL-S preconditions and effects are for the benefit of the agent's planner. However, there is nothing to prevent a client from ignoring the preconditions, trying to execute the process, and possibly failing. Thus, OWL-S preconditions and effects do not affect execution of the Process Model. Consequently, they do not affect the verification of the Process Model either. Nevertheless, if a client wishes to ensure that the preconditions can be fulfilled in addition to verifying the Process Model, a promising approach might be to use a planner based on model-checking [4].

6   Verification of the Amazon Example

Given a PROMELA specification of an OWL-S Process Model, SPIN constructs a verifier, that can check several claims on the execution of the Process Model. These properties include the values of certain variables at certain points in the code and true statements that can be made about execution states (state properties) or the paths of execution (path properties). In addition, since SPIN searches the entire state space of a verification model, it can also identify unreachable or dead code in a Process Model.

In this section, we present various kinds of verification that can be performed on a PROMELA model generated by the mapping described in the sections above. Using SPIN and the PROMELA specification presented in the previous section, several properties of the execution of the Amazon OWL-S Process Model were verified. These properties were verified as part of five tests described below. For each test, the size of the model constructed by SPIN, the time taken in seconds to construct the model and the time for verification were measured[5].

---

[5] The tests were carried out on a 750MHz Pentium 4 machine with 256MB of memory.

Table 2. Performance of OWL-S verification using SPIN (time in seconds)

	#States	Model Construction Time	Verification Time
Amazon	132	0.20	0.01
Data flow	139	0.35	0.02
Liveness	345	0.15	0.04
Loop-2	654382	0.03	8.77
Loop-3	3902280	0.04	>7200

1. *Simple Amazon*: In the first case, the PROMELA specification of the Amazon.com Web service was checked for basic safety conditions, such as the absence of deadlocks and the correctness of the data-flow within the model which derive directly from the mapping reported in the previous section.
2. *Data flow*: To the simple Amazon model, we added an `assert` statement to verify the data flow between the `Browse` and `ProductFound` processes. The statement specifies that `Browse` must return a product before the product is added to the shopping cart, i.e. before `ProductFound` executes the process `AddToShoppingCart`.
3. *Liveness*: Several interesting liveness claims can be made about the Amazon example. For example, a client may wish to verify that the Amazon Web service will always complete and not execute in an infinite loop, before deciding to use it. In other words, the user would like to express the requirement that "ShopBook process will eventually complete." In LTL this statement is expressed as: $\Diamond$Done_ShopBook. Another liveness claim a client may wish to verify is that if a desired product is found with Amazon, then the client can always add it to the shopping cart. This can be expressed as "in every execution sequence in which a product was found, the next process to be executed is `AddToShoppingCart`." In LTL this statement is expressed as : $\Box$(productAvailable $\rightarrow$ $X(\Diamond$Done_AddToShoppingCart)). In other words, whenever `productAvailable` is true, in the next state, the `AddToShoppingCart` process will eventually complete.
4. *Loop-2 and Loop-3*: In order to test how loops could affect the performance of SPIN, we added a loop to the Promela model, which created multiple concurrent instances of `ShopBook`. In the cases of Loop-2 and Loop-3, two and three concurrent instances of `ShopBook` were created respectively.

The experiment shows that the verification of OWL-S Process Models that do not contain any loops can be done very effectively. This is an important result since we expect that the great majority of Process Models will be loop-free[6]. Narayanan et al. [9] shows that the complexity the verification of the OWL-S Process Model with loops is PSPACE while the complexity of the same model without loops is NP-complete. Consistent with Narayanan's claim, the search complexity increases greatly, when the OWL-S Process Model is augmented with additional loops. However, it should be pointed out that the loops

---

[6] The great majority of e-business sites available on the Web are loop-free. We expect that these sites provide a blue print for e-commerce Web services.

we constructed are among the most difficult to verify since they spin off two concurrent executions of the Amazon's Process Model. Sequential executions of Process Models would certainly exhibit less interaction.

The exponential increase in number of states and verification time, while troublesome, seems to be manageable since checking more than two concurrent instances of ShopBook is superfluous and violates the requirement that the verification model be the minimum sufficient model to perform the verification successfully. Verifying two concurrent instances of ShopBook reveal all the dangerous interaction effects just as well as three concurrent instances do. Therefore, we do not gain in verification power by checking more than two instances. In our future research we will search for a better modeling of loops that will minimize the state explosion that has been revealed by our experiments.

7 Conclusions

In this paper we proposed a procedure for the verification of correctness claims about OWL-S Process Models. We described a mapping of OWL-S statements into equivalent PROMELA statements that can be evaluated by the SPIN model checker. In the process, a number of abstractions were presented for OWL-S Process Models. The abstractions reduce the complexity of verification while producing a model that is sufficiently rich to be able to make useful claims about OWL-S Process Models.

The work presented here is a starting point and we see numerous possible extensions to it. For instance, we intend to relax some of the modeling abstractions to report a richer output. In particular, we would like to specify not only the reachability of states, but also under which conditions a state is reachable. This information is important for a Web service client because it typically needs to know what information must be sought in order to guarantee a correct execution of the Process Model and what kind of commitments it will have to make. To this extent we are currently exploring the use of a different verification system, specifically NuSMV [3] which may allow a natural representation of conditions.

Another extension of this work that we would like to pursue is the automatic generation of liveness claims. Based on the OWL-S markup and an appropriate services ontology, a Web service client should be able to reason about processes in an OWL-S Process Model, generating claims on-the-fly, such as "the Delivery process always executes after the Buy process." These claims can then be verified before the client decides to invoke the Web service. There are multiple sources of liveness claims; in this paper we tested the reachability of one particular state, but the client of a service may also want to verify the correctness with respect to policies that the client has to satisfy.

Finally, this work does not include any modeling of the interaction between the client and the server. We intend to extend the verification to the data mappings specified in the OWL-S Grounding. Such verification may provide guarantees on the data that processes will receive from the Server. In this direction the work proposed in [13,6] is of particular interest since it may provide a representation of the mapping between the XML data that Web services exchange with the OWL based data representation used in the OWL-S Process Model.

References

1. T. Andrews, F. Curbera, H. Dholakia, Y. Goland, J. Klein, F. Leymann, K. Liu, D. Roller, D. Smith, S. Thatte, I. Trickovic, and S. Weerawarana. Specification: Business process execution language for web services version 1.1. http://www.ibm.com/developerworks/library/ws-bpel/, 2003.
2. A. Ankolekar, M. Paolucci, and K. Sycara. Spinning the OWL-S Process Model– Towards the verification of the OWL-S Process Models. Presented at the *Semantic Web Services: Preparing to Meet the World of Business Applications* workshop at the *International Semantic Web Conference (ISWC 2004)*, Hiroshima, Japan, 2004.
3. A. Cimatti, E. M. Clarke, E. Giunchiglia, F. Giunchiglia, M. Pistore, M. Roveri, R. Sebastiani, and A. Tacchella. Nusmv 2: An opensource tool for symbolic model checking. In *Proceeding of International Conference on Computer-Aided Verification (CAV 2002)*, Copenhagen, Denmark, 2002.
4. A. Cimatti and M. Roveri Conformant Planning via Symbolic Model Checking. In *Journal of Artificial Intelligence Research*, 31, pg. 305–338, 2000.
5. E. M. Clarke, O. Grumberg, and D. A. Peled. *Model Checking*. The MIT Press, Cambridge, MA, USA, 2000.
6. X. Fu, T. Bultan, and J. Su. Analysis of interacting bpel web services. In *Proceedings of the 13th International World Wide Web Conference (WWW'04)*, New York, NY, USA, 2004. ACM Press.
7. H.Foster, S. Uchitel, J. Kramer, and J. Magee. Model-based verification of web service compositions. In *Proceedings of the Automated Software Engineering (ASE) Conference 2003*, Montreal, Canada, October 2003.
8. G. J. Holzmann. *The SPIN Model Checker: Primer and Reference Manual*. Addison-Wesley Professional, 2003.
9. S. Narayanan and S. McIlraith. Simulation, verification and automated composition of web services. In *Proceedings of the Eleventh International World Wide Web Conference (WWW-11)*, May 2002.
10. M. Paolucci, A. Ankolekar, M. Srinivasan, and K. Sycara. The DAML-S virtual machine. In *Second International Semantic Web Conference*, Sanibel Island, Florida, USA, 2003.
11. K. Schmidt and C. Stahl. A petri net semantic for bpel4ws - validation and application. In *Proceedings of the 11th Workshop on Algorithms and Tools for Petri Nets (AWPN '04)*, Paderborn, 2004.
12. C. Walton. Model checking multi-agent web services. In *Proceedings of the 2004 Spring Symposium on Semantic Web Services*, Stanford, CA, USA, March 2004.
13. T. B. X. Fu and J. Su. Wsat: A tool for formal analysis of web services. In *Proceedings of the 16th International Conference on Computer Aided Verification*, 2004.

Web Service Composition with Volatile Information

Tsz-Chiu Au, Ugur Kuter, and Dana Nau

Department of Computer Science and Institute for Systems Research,
University of Maryland, College Park, MD 20742, USA
{chiu, ukuter, nau}@cs.umd.edu

Abstract. In many Web service composition problems, information may be needed from Web services during the composition process. Existing research on Web service composition (WSC) procedures has generally assumed that this information will not change. We describe two ways to take such WSC procedures and systematically modify them to deal with volatile information.

The *black-box* approach requires no knowledge of the WSC procedure's internals: it places a wrapper around the WSC procedure to deal with volatile information. The *gray-box* approach requires partial information of those internals, in order to insert coding to perform certain bookkeeping operations.

We show theoretically that both approaches work correctly. We present experimental results showing that the WSC procedures produced by the gray-box approach can run much faster than the ones produced by the black-box approach.

1 Introduction

Most existing research on automated composition of semantic Web services has focused on *Web service composition* (WSC) procedures, i.e., procedures for finding a composition of Web services to accomplish a given task. In order to assemble a composition, a WSC procedure itself may need to retrieve information from Web services while it is operating. Existing works have generally assumed that such information is *static*, i.e., it will never change. For example, the Golog-based [1] and HTN-based [2, 3] approaches both use the Invocation and Reasonable Persistence (IRP) condition. The WSC procedures reported in [4, 5] are even more restrictive: they require that all of the information needed by their procedures is provided by the user as input parameters. We will refer to such procedures as *static-information* WSC procedures.

Clearly there are many cases where the static-information assumption is unrealistic. There are thousands of Web services whose information may change while a WSC procedure is operating: for example, whether a product is in stock, how much it will cost or how much has been bid for it, what the weather is like, what time a train or airplane will arrive, what seats are available for an airplane or a concert, what resources are available in a grid-computing environment, and so forth.

This paper focuses on how to take static-information WSC procedures such as the ones mentioned above, and translate them into *volatile-information* WSC procedures that work correctly when information obtained from Web services may change.

Y. Gil et al. (Eds.): ISWC 2005, LNCS 3729, pp. 52–66, 2005.

Our primary contributions are as follows:

1. We provide a general procedural model for a class of WSC procedures. We model them as trial-and-error search procedures that may try different possible Web service compositions in order to find one that accomplishes the desired task.
2. We describe a *black-box approach* for translating static-information WSC procedures into volatile-information WSC procedures. In particular, we describe a wrapper that can be placed around any WSC procedure, without needing to know how the underlying composition procedure operates.
3. We describe a *gray-box approach* for translating static-information WSC procedures into volatile-information WSC procedures. This approach is based on taking our procedural model mentioned above, and modifying it to deal with volatile information—hence the same modification will work on any WSC procedure that is an instance of our general procedural model. We call this approach a *gray-box* approach because it requires *partial* knowledge about a WSC procedure: namely, that the WSC procedure is an instance of our procedural model.
4. We state theorems saying that both the black-box and the gray-box approaches work correctly on any WSC procedure that is an instance our general model.
5. We provide experimental results demonstrating that the gray-box approach produces volatile-information WSC procedures that may run exponentially faster than the ones produced by the black-box approach. For example, in a set of problems in which there were only seven information items that needed to be retrieved from Web services, the procedure produced by the gray-box approach ran 50 times as fast as the one produced by the black-box approach.

It also would be possible to define a *white-box* approach, namely to take the code for the WSC procedure and rewrite it by hand. But this approach would be labor-intensive and it would only extend a single composition procedure, hence we do not consider it in this paper. Our results show that in comparison with the black-box approach, the gray-box approach already can provide substantial speedups without having to delve into all of the details of the original WSC procedure.

2 Procedural Model of Web Service Composition

Existing approaches for Web Service Composition formulate the problem in different ways, depending mainly on how the developers of those approaches perceive the problem. Examples include the following:

- In [1], the states of the world and the world-altering actions are modeled as Golog programs, and the information-providing services are modeled as external functions calls made within those programs. The goal is stated as a Prolog-like query and the answer to that query is a sequence of world-altering actions that achieves the goal, when executed in the initial state of the world. During the composition process, however, it is assumed that no world-altering services are executed. Instead, their effects are simulated in order to keep track of the state transitions that will occur when they are actually executed.

- In [2], the WSC procedure is based on the relationship between the OWL-S process ontology [6] used for describing Web services and *Hierarchical Task Networks* as in HTN Planning [7]. OWL-S processes are translated into tasks to be achieved by the SHOP2 planner [7], and SHOP2 generates a collection of atomic process instances that achieves the desired functionality.

- [3] extends the work in [2] to cope better with the fact that information-providing Web services may not return the needed information immediately when they are executed, or at all. The ENQUIRER algorithm presented in this work does not cease the search process while waiting answers to some of its queries, but keeps searching for alternative compositions that do not depend on answering those specific queries.

- [4] models Web services and information about the world using the "knowledge-level formulation" first introduced in the PKS planning system [8]. This formulation models Web services based not on what is actually true or false about them, but what the agent that performs the composition actually knows to be true or false about their operations and the results of those operations. A composition is formulated as a conditional plan, which allows for interleaving the executions of information-providing and world-altering services, unlike the works described above.

Despite their differences, the aforementioned approaches have the following features in common:

1. The WSC procedure is given the specification of the Web services written in a formal language such as OWL-S [6], and a goal to be accomplished in the world.
2. The WSC procedure does a trial-and-error search through some space of possible solutions, to try to find a complete solution. A *solution* for a Web service-composition problem is a set of services with ordering constraints such that, when executed, the services achieve the desired functionality required by the input service-composition problem.
3. The WSC procedure does not have a complete knowledge of the state of the world; the missing information must be obtained from information-providing services. The WSC procedures execute the information-providing services to obtain the missing information either during the composition process or during the execution of the composition.
4. The WSC procedure does not execute any Web services that have world-altering effects during the composition process.
5. The information returned from the information-providing services is static. *This is the assumption that our work is intended to overcome.*

We now describe a way to take a class of WSC procedures that have the characteristics mentioned above, and modify them to work with volatile information. We start by defining an *unknown* to be any item of information that a WSC procedure needs to obtain to carry out the composition process. For an unknown u, a WSC procedure sends a *query* q_u to the available information-providing Web services that can provide the *value* v_u for u. The value for u is returned by a Web service to the WSC procedure as

Procedure General-WSC(P)
  $S_0 \leftarrow$ **create-initial-state**(P); OPEN $\leftarrow \{S_0\}$; ANSWERS $\leftarrow \emptyset$
  loop
    insert all new answers for the pending queries (if any) into ANSWERS
    select a node S from OPEN and remove it
    if **solution**($S, P,$ ANSWERS) then return **extract-solution**(S, P)
    issue queries about zero or more unknowns in S that are not in ANSWERS
    OPEN $\leftarrow$ (OPEN $\setminus \{S\}$) $\cup$ **children-of**(S, P)

Fig. 1. The General-WSC procedure is an abstract model of many static-information WSC procedures. It is based on the observation that most existing WSC procedures are trial-and-error search procedures that may try different possible Web service compositions in order to find one that accomplishes the desired task. P is the problem description, and the initial state S_0 is derived from it.

an *answer* for the query q_u. A query issued by a WSC procedure is said to be *pending* if no answers have been received for that query. Otherwise, it is *completed*. A pending query becomes completed if all answers for that query is received.

Our procedural model is the General-WSC procedure shown in Figure 1. This model captures the procedural behavior of most existing service-composition techniques. Examples include [1, 2, 3, 4, 5], and others.

In the General-WSC procedure, each *state* is an abstract representation of a partial solution to the WSC problem. If S is a state, then each child S' of S is obtained by making some kind of refinement to the partial solution represented by S. We assume that whether or not S can be refined to produce S' will depend on some *precondition* $pre(S, S')$, whose value may be *true* or *false* depending on the values of some of the unknowns. If $pre(S, S') = false$ then the refinement cannot be performed, hence S' is a dead end. But if $pre(S, S') = true$ then the refinement can be performed. In the latter case, either S' is a solution to the WSC problem or else it has one or more children of its own. A state is a *terminal* state if it is either a dead end or a solution.

Let S_0 be the initial state of a WSC problem, and let $\langle S_0, S_1, \ldots, S_n \rangle$ be a sequence of states such that each S_{i+1} is a child of S_i and S_n is a terminal node. Then from the above assumptions, it follows that S_n is a solution if and only if

$$pre(S_0, S_1) \wedge pre(S_1, S_2) \wedge \ldots \wedge pre(S_{n-1}, S_n) = true.$$

The variable OPEN is the set of all states that the WSC procedure has generated but has not yet been able to examine. The variable ANSWERS is the set of all answers that have been returned in response to a WSC procedure's pending queries; i.e.,

ANSWERS $= \{(u, v) :$ a Web service has returned the value v for the unknown $u\}$.

General-WSC begins with a set called OPEN that contains only the initial state S_0. Within each iteration of the loop, General-WSC does the following:

- It updates ANSWERS to include any answers that have been returned in response to its queries.
- It selects $S \in$ OPEN to work on next. Which node is selected depends on the particular WSC procedure. For example, in both the Golog-based [1] and SHOP2-based [2] approaches, the search is performed in a depth-first manner. The PKS-based approach reported in [4] can perform either depth-first or breadth-first search.
- It checks whether or not S constitutes a solution (i.e., a composition that achieves the goals of the current WSC problem). In the pseudocode of Figure 1, this check is represented by the solution subroutine. The definition of the solution subroutine depends on the particular instance of General-WSC. For example, in [1, 2, 3], solution checks whether or not the sequence of world-altering services can really be executed given the information collected from the information-providing services during the composition process. In the PKS-based approach of [4], the definition of solution includes (1) checking for the correctness and consistency of the knowledge-level databases that PKS maintains, and (2) checking for whether the current solution achieves the goals of the current WSC problem.
- If S is not a solution, then the procedure has an option to issue queries about the unknowns that appear in S. Then it generates the successors of S, and inserts them into the OPEN set. The children-of subroutine is responsible for this operation, and again the details depend on the particular WSC procedure. In [1], children-of a state is defined through the Trans rules described in that work. A successor state generated by those rules specify the next Golog program to be considered by the composition procedure as well as the current partial composition generated so far. In HTN plannning based approaches as in [2, 3], successor states are computed via task-decomposition techniques.

3   Dealing with Volatile Information

The previous section dealt with *static-information* WSC procedures, i.e., WSC procedures for the case where the values of the unknowns will never change. We now consider *volatile-information* WSC procedures, i.e., WSC procedures for the case where values of the unknowns may change over time.

Figure 2 illustrates the life cycle for the value of an unknown u. Suppose a WSC procedure issued a query q_u to a Web service W at time $t = t_{issue}(q_u)$, asking for the value of u. The answer for this query will arrive at time $t_{return}(q_u) = t_{issue}(q_u) + t_{lag}(q_u)$, where the *lag time* $t_{lag}(q_u)$ includes both the time the information-providing service takes to process the query q_u and the time delay due to network traffic.

In addition to the lag times of queries, we also need to consider (1) the time needed to compute a precondition $pre(S, S')$, and the time needed to perform the refinement $refine(S, S')$ that takes us from the state S to the state S'. Note that if $pre(S, S') = false$, then the time to perform $refine(S, S')$ is zero. If pre and $refine$ refer to unknowns whose values are not currently known, then computing them may require sending queries to Web services, thereby incurring some lag times. We assume that except for those lag times, the time needed to compute pre and $refine$ is negligible.

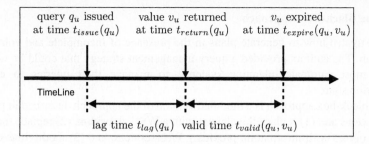

Fig. 2. A typical execution of an information-providing service. Above, $t_{issue}(q_u)$ is the time that a WSC procedure issues a query to a Web service for the value of an unknown u. $t_{return}(q_u)$ is the time at which the value of u is received, and $t_{expire}(q_u, v_u)$ is the time point after which that value is no longer guaranteed to be valid.

Suppose the answer for q_u specified the value v_u for u. Associated with the answer is a *valid time* $t_{valid}(q_u, v_u)$, i.e., the amount of time that the answer is guaranteed to be valid.[1] This means that the value of the unknown u is guaranteed to be v_u between the times $t_{return}(q_u)$ and $t_{expire}(q_u, v_u) = t_{return}(q_u) + t_{valid}(q_u, v_u)$. At $t_{expire}(q_u, v_u)$, the value v_u *expires*; i.e., u's value is no longer guaranteed to be v_u after the time $t_{expire}(q_u, v_u)$.

Since the values of the unknowns change over time, the correctness of a solution composition returned a volatile-information WSC procedure depends on the values gathered during the composition time. In order to guarantee that the returned composition will be executed correctly on the Web, we will define a solution composition to be *T-correct* if it is guaranteed to remain correct for at least some time T after a WSC procedure returns that solution. In order to provide such a guarantee, we assume that a value obtained for an unknown u will remain valid for at least time T.

A static-information WSC procedure is said to be *sound* if whenever it returns a solution to a WSC problem, the solution is a correct one. By analogy, we will say that a volatile-information WSC procedure is *T-sound* if whenever it returns a solution, the solution is T-correct.

In the following subsections, we introduce two approaches for taking static-information WSC procedures and translating them into volatile-information WSC procedures. For both of them, if the original WSC procedure is sound, the translated procedure will be T-sound.

---

[1] Some WSC procedures provide a valid time explicitly. For example, hotel rooms can usually be held without charge until 6pm on the night of arrival; and the web site at our university's concert hall will hold seating selections for several minutes (with a countdown timer showing how much time is left). However, our approach does not actually need a valid time to be given explicitly, as long as there is a mechanism to inform the WSC procedure immediately after an expiration has occurred.

However, in that case, the WSC procedure can no longer guarantee how long the solution will remain valid after it is returned, because expirations may occur anytime after the solution is returned.

3.1   The Black-Box Approach

[9] investigated how to generate plans in the presence of incomplete and volatile information. The authors provided a query management strategy that could be wrapped around most automated-planning systems, to manage their queries to external information sources.

Our black-box approach is a modified version of the approach described in [9]. The modifications are: (1) replace the planner with a WSC algorithm, (2) replace the information sources with information-providing Web services, and (3) modify the strategy to pretend that each unknown u's expiration time is $t_{expire}(q_u, v_u) - T$ rather than $t_{expire}(q_u, v_u)$. The latter modification is necessary to ensure that the solution returned by the WSC procedure is T-correct.

[9] also described two query-management strategies that we can use with the black-box approach:

- In the *eager* strategy, when the information collected from external information sources is expired, the query-management strategy immediately re-issues the relevant query or queries and suspends execution of the underlying WSC procedure until the answers come back.

- In the *lazy* strategy, the query-management strategy does not immediately reissue new queries about the expired information. Instead, it assumes that such information is still valid and continues with the composition process until the underlying WSC procedure generates a solution. At that point, the lazy strategy re-issues queries about all expired information that that solution depends on, and suspends execution of the WSC procedure until all of the answers is received.

If the same answers are received for the re-issued queries as before, these strategies restart the WSC procedure from where it left off. With the lazy strategy, this means the procedure immediately returns the solution and exits. Otherwise, the strategies backtrack the WSC procedure to the first point where it made a decision that depends on an unknown whose value has changed, and restarts the procedure from that point.

The following theorem establishes the correctness of the black-box approach:

Theorem 1. *Let A be a WSC procedure that is an instance of* General-WSC, *and let* A^B *be the modified version of A produced by the black-box approach. If A is sound, then* A^B *is T-sound.*

For a detailed discussion and analysis on the black-box approach, please see [9].

3.2   The Gray-Box Approach

Although the black-box approach described in the previous section is a simple and a general technique to modify WSC procedures to deal with volatile information, it has one drawback: it does not consider the internal operations of the underlying WSC procedures, and therefore, it may not perform very efficiently in some WSC problems. In this section, we describe another technique, called the *gray-box* approach, that takes into account the internals of WSC procedures that are instances of General-WSC in order to generalize them to deal with volatile information.

```
Procedure VI-General-WSC(P, T)
  S₀ ← create-initial-state(P); OPEN ← {S₀}; ANSWERS ← ∅

  loop
    remove some or all expired answers from ANSWERS
    insert all new answers for the pending queries into ANSWERS
    select a node S from OPEN
    if solution(S, P, ANSWERS) then
       if S contains no unknowns whose values have expired or will
          expire within time period T, then
             return extract-solution(S, P)
       else
          remove zero or more values from ANSWERS that have expired or
             will expire within time period T, and re-issue queries about them
          OPEN ← OPEN ∪ {S}
    else
       issue queries about zero or more unknowns in S that are not in ANSWERS
       OPEN ← (OPEN \ {S}) ∪ children-of(S, P)
```

Fig. 3. The VI-General-WSC procedure generalizes the General-WSC to deal with volatile information. It returns a solution to the WSC problem that will remain correct for at least T amount of time after the solution is returned.

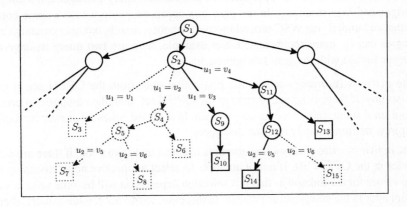

Fig. 4. An example snapshot of a VI-General-WSC search space. There are three unknowns, and their current values are $u_1 = v_3$, $u_1 = v_4$, and $u_2 = v_5$. The squares represent the states in the open list, and the circles represent the states that have already been visited. The label on each edge (S_i, S_j) gives a value $u_h = v_k$ that the refinement $refine(S_i, S_j)$ depends on. For example, $refine(S_{12}, S_{14})$ only works if $u_2 = v_5$, and the state S_{14} is a valid refinement of S_1 only if both $u_1 = v_4$ and $u_2 = v_5$. The solid squares denote active states; these represent valid refinements of S_1. The dashed squares denote inactive states: these once were valid refinements of S_1, but they are not currently valid because some of the information they depend on has expired.

The gray-box approach is based on a modified version of the General-WSC procedure, called VI-General-WSC, that works with volatile information. This procedure is shown in Figure 3. In this approach, we take an instance of the abstract General-WSC service-composition procedure, and translate it into the corresponding instance of VI-General-WSC.

Like General-WSC, VI-General-WSC performs a search in the space of states, but it also keeps track of the *expired* values for the unknowns for which it issued queries previously, and maintains the ANSWERS set accordingly. At each iteration, a state S in OPEN is *active*, if for every unknown u that appears in S we have $(u, v) \in$ ANSWERS, where v is the value of u in S. In other words, a state in OPEN is active at a particular iteration of VI-General-WSC, if all of the information that it depends on is valid at that iteration. Otherwise, S is *inactive*. As an example, in Figure 4, the solid squares are active states and the dashed squares are inactive ones.

The following theorem establishes the correctness of the gray-box approach:

Theorem 2. *Let A be a WSC procedure that is an instance of* General-WSC, *and let* A^G *be the modified version of A produced by the gray-box approach. If A is sound, then* A^G *is T-sound.*

This theorem holds because (1) given a set of unknowns and possible values for them, both A and A^G have the same search traces, and (2) A^G terminates only when the solution satisfies the **solution** function and the values the solution depends on remain valid for time T. Therefore, the solution is T-correct only if A is sound.

Earlier, for the black-box approach, we defined two query-management strategies: the *eager* and *lazy* strategies. In the gray-box approach, since we have some control over the way underlying WSC procedures perform their search, our query-management strategies can be more sophisticated. For example, here are two query management strategies for use with the gray-box approach:

- The *active-only strategy* selects the first active state from the OPEN set, if there exists any. If there is no active state in the OPEN set, then the composition process stops until some states become active again. In this case, when an answer for a query expires, we immediately re-issue that query.

- The *active-inactive strategy* first attempts to select an active node, if there are active nodes in the OPEN list. If not, it attempts to select an inactive node, assuming that the values for the unknowns that this selection depends on will become valid at some point later in the composition process. In this case, we do not reissue a query after its value is expired; instead, we treat the expired values as if they are not expired. When we get to a goal state, we reissue all the queries for all expired values that some goal state in the OPEN set depends on.

4 Implementation and Experimental Evaluation

In our experiments, we used both the black-box and gray-box techniques to generate volatile-information WSC procedures. In particular, we used the static-information WSC procedure described in [2], which is an instance of the abstract General-WSC procedure. This WSC procedure is based on a translation of OWL-S process models into HTN methods and operators for use within the SHOP2 planning system [7].

In our experiments, we assumed that this translation process had already been carried out, hence we started directly with the SHOP2 methods and operators. We implemented the following four volatile-information WSC procedures:

- Eager and Lazy: black-box translations of the static-information WSC procedure using the eager and the lazy strategies, respectively.
- Active-Only and Active-Inactive: gray-box translations of the static-information WSC procedure using the active-only and the active-inactive strategies, respectively.

For our experiments, we used two service-composition scenarios. The first is the Delivery-Company application described in [3]. In this domain, a delivery company is trying to arrange the shipment of a number of packages by coordinating its several local branches. The company needs to query Web services to gather information from its branch offices about the locations and the availability of vehicles (i.e., trucks and planes) and the status of packages. The goal is to generate a sequence of commands to send as Web service calls to the vehicle controllers, such that the execution of these commands will route all of the packages to their final destinations.

Our second service-composition scenario involves a simplified model for grid- and utility-based computing [10]. In our scenario, there are a number of Grid Services for reserving computing resources owned by several different companies on the Web. Some of them are information-providing grid services giving the current workload, memory usage, software license, etc. The WSC procedure's goals are to figure out which computing resources to use for a given computing task, and to generate a composite Grid Service that actually makes the reservation once it is executed. Since the workload and the memory usage of the machines keep changing, it is necessary for the WSC procedure to deal with the change of information during composition.

We randomly created 7 delivery-company problems and 8 grid-computing problems. Then, in the description of each problem, we randomly inserted n number of unknown symbols, for $n = 1, \ldots, 9$. For each number of unknowns, we ran each problem 50 times and averaged the running times. Every time a query was issued, we generated the lag time for that query and the valid time for the answer by choosing numbers at random from the time interval $0.5 \le t \le 2.5$ seconds.

The results are shown in Figures 5 and 6 on Delivery-Company and Utility-Computing problems using an Intel Xeon 2.6GHz CPU with 1GB memory. Each data point is an average of 350 and 400 runs, respectively. Missing data points correspond to experiments where one or more of the runs went for longer than 30 minutes.

In these experiments, the two WSC procedures produced by the gray-box approach (the Active-Only and Active-Inactive procedures) performed much better than the two WSC procedures produced by the black-box approach (the Eager and Lazy procedures). This occurred because the former were able to explore alternative compositions for a problem while awaiting responses from the information-providing services. The improvement in running time was roughly exponential. For example, with 7 unknowns Active-Inactive took roughly 1/50 the time required by the Lazy procedure.

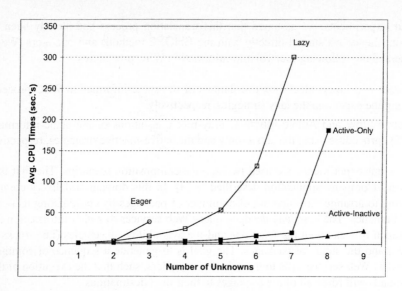

Fig. 5. Average running times of our algorithms on Delivery-Company problems, as a function of the number of unknowns

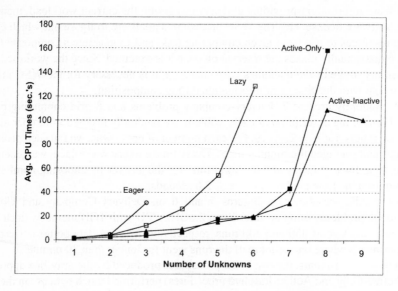

Fig. 6. Average running times of our algorithms on Utility-Computing problems, as a function of the number of unknowns

In addition, the **Active-Inactive** procedure performed much better than the *Active-Only* procedure.[2] The reason is that in the case when there are no active nodes

---

[2] Analogously, Lazy performed much better than Eager. This confirms the results reported in [9].

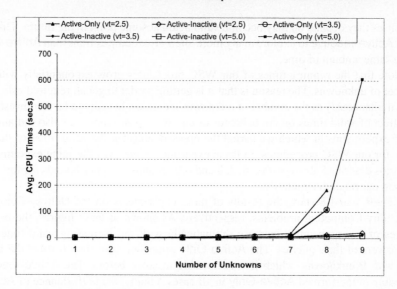

Fig. 7. Average running times of our algorithms on Delivery-Company problems with varying number of unknowns and valid times for the answers of queries. In each case, "vt" denotes the upper bound for the valid times used in the experiments.

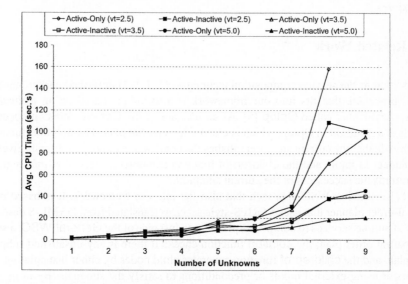

Fig. 8. Average running times of our algorithms on Utility-Computing problems, with varying number of unknowns and valid times for the answers of queries. In each case, "vt" denotes the upper bound for the valid times used in the experiments.

(i.e., when every state in the OPEN set depends on an unknown whose value has expired), Active-Only suspends execution while waiting for responses from Web services, whereas Active-Inactive keeps working: it expands the inactive nodes assuming the responses they depend on may become valid again at some point in the future. This enables Active-Inactive to explore many more alternative compositions than Active-Only in the same amount of time.

Note that the running times of our WSC procedures grow exponentially with the number of unknowns. The reason is that it is getting harder to get all required valid values simultaneously as the number of unknowns increases. In order to further investigate the effect of valid times on the behavior of our WSC procedures, we also did another set of experiments in which we varied the upper bounds for the valid times of the answers for our WSC procedures. In these experiments, we used the same experimental scenarios described above with 2.5, 3, 5 and 5.0 seconds as upper bounds for the valid times in our random simulation.

Figures 7 and 8 show the results of these experiments on the Delivey-Company and Utility-Computing problems, respectively. As shown in these figures, the performances of our procedures increase dramatically with the increasing valid times for the answers of their queries. The Active-Only procedure was able to solve the problems with 9 unknowns, which it was not able to solve before. The Active-Inactive procedure outperformed Active-Only in all cases. Finally, the performance of Active-Inactive increased expoenentially with the increasing valid times. This is because, when the values obtained for the unknowns do not expire very quickly as in our first set of experiments, Active-Inactive quickly finds a solution as it expands inactive states as well as active ones and returns it before any value that that solution depends on expires.

5   Related Work

In addition to the service-composition techniques [1, 2, 3, 4] described earlier, another WSC procedure that fits into our framework is a technique based on an *estimated-regression* planner called Optop [5]. As an instance of the General-WSC procedure, a state is a *situation* in Optop, which is essentially a partial plan. The solution function checks whether the current situation satisfies the conjunction of the goal literals given to the planner as input, and the children-of function computes a regression-match graph and returns the successors of the current situation.

[11] is another WSC approach that also fits into our framework. It is based on a partial-order planner that uses STRIPS-style services translated from DAML-S descriptions of atomic services to compose a plan. As an instance of the General-WSC, a state is a partial-order plan; the solution function checks if there is any unsatisfied subgoal in a plan, and the children-of function generates child nodes by either instantiating operators or using external inputs or preconditions to satisfy the subgoals. By using our approach, the extended procedure might obtain information about the conditions of the subgoals though Web services during planning.

In [12] and [13], a planning technique based on the "Planning as Model Checking" paradigm is described for the automated composition of Web services. The BPEL4WS process models was first translated into state transition systems that describe the dynamic interactions with external services. Given these state-transition systems, the planning algorithm, using symbolic model checking techniques, returns an executable process rather than a linear sequence of actions. It is not immediately clear to us if this approach fits into the trial-and-error framework that our approaches are based on.

6 Conclusions and Future Work

In this paper, we have described two approaches for taking WSC procedures designed to work in static-information environments, and modifying them to work correctly in volatile-information environments.

The black-box approach requires no knowledge of the internal operation of the original WSC procedure. It puts a wrapper around the procedure to deal with the volatile information.

The gray-box approach requires some knowledge of the original WSC procedure, but only partial knowledge: it requires knowing that the original procedure is an instance of our General-WSC. The gray-box approach works by inserting some additional bookkeeping operations at various points in the instances of General-WSC.

Our experimental results show that despite the simplicity of these modifications, the resulting volatile-information WSC procedures can perform much better than the ones produced by the black-box approach. This is because the modifications enable the volatile-information WSC procedure to explore alternative Web service compositions while waiting for its queries to be answered.

This paper is just a first step in the development of WSC procedures for volatile-information environments. There are several important topics for future work:

- There are situations in which some of the valid times are so short that the WSC procedure cannot finish its task due to an overwhelmingly large number of expirations. Furthermore, there are situations in which the WSC procedure can never get hold of valid values of some of the unknowns simultaneously, and thus it is impossible to return a valid solution. We would like to determine what kinds of conditions are sufficient to guarantee that our procedure will terminate with a solution.

- Like most of the previous work on WSC procedures, we have assumed that the WSC procedure does not execute any Web services that have world-altering effects during the composition process—just the information-providing services. We intend to generalize our work to accommodate the execution of services that have information-providing effects, world-altering effects, or both during service composition.

- Even more generally, we are interested in allowing the possibility of interleaving composition and execution—e.g., to allow the WSC procedure to execute a portion of the composition before generating the rest of the composition.

- We believe the gray-box approach can be made even more efficient by extending it to make use of knowledge of what the search space looks like, and what the solutions should look like.

Acknowledgment. This work was supported in part by NSF grant IIS0412812 and AFOSR grant FA95500510298. The opinions expressed in this paper are those of authors and do not necessarily reflect the opinions of the funders.

References

[1] McIlraith, S., Son, T.: Adapting Golog for composition of semantic web services. In: KR-2002, Toulouse, France (2002)

[2] Sirin, E., Parsia, B., Wu, D., Hendler, J., Nau, D.: HTN planning for web service composition using SHOP2. Journal of Web Semantics 1 (2004) 377–396

[3] Kuter, U., Sirin, E., Nau, D., Parsia, B., Hendler, J.: Information gathering during planning for web services composition. In: ISWC-2004. (2004)

[4] Martinez, E., Lespérance, Y.: Web service composition as a planning task: Experiments using knowledge-based planning. In: ICAPS-2004 Workshop on Planning and Scheduling for Web and Grid Services. (2004)

[5] McDermott, D.: Estimated-regression planning for interactions with web services. In: AIPS. (2002)

[6] OWL Services Coalition: OWL-S: Semantic markup for web services (2004) OWL-S White Paper http://www.daml.org/services/owl-s/1.1/owl-s.pdf.

[7] Nau, D., Au, T.C., Ilghami, O., Kuter, U., Murdock, W., Wu, D., Yaman, F.: SHOP2: An HTN planning system. JAIR 20 (2003) 379–404

[8] Petrick, R.P.A., Bacchus, F.: A knowledge-based approach to planning with incomplete information and sensing. In: AIPS. (2002)

[9] Au, T.C., Nau, D., Subrahmanian, V.: Utilizing volatile external information during planning. In: ECAI. (2004)

[10] Foster, I., Kesselman, C., Nick, J.M., Tuecke, S.: The physiology of the grid: An open grid services architecture for distributed systems integration. http://www.globus.org/research/papers/ogsa.pdf (2002)

[11] Sheshagiri, M., desJardins, M., Finin, T.: A planner for composing services described in daml-s. In: AAMAS Workshop on Web Services and Agent-based Engineering. (2003)

[12] Pistore, M., Barbon, F., Bertoli, P., Shaparau, D., Traverso, P.: Planning and monitoring web service composition. In: AIMSA. (2004)

[13] Traverso, P., Pistore, M.: Automated composition of semantic web services into executable processes. In: ISWC. (2004)

A Large Scale Taxonomy Mapping Evaluation

Paolo Avesani[1], Fausto Giunchiglia[2], and Mikalai Yatskevich[2]

[1] ITC-IRST, 38050 Povo, Trento, Italy
avesani@itc.it
[2] Dept. of Information and Communication Technology,
University of Trento, 38050 Povo, Trento, Italy
{fausto, yatskevi}@dit.unitn.it

Abstract. Matching hierarchical structures, like taxonomies or web directories, is the premise for enabling interoperability among heterogenous data organizations. While the number of new matching solutions is increasing the evaluation issue is still open. This work addresses the problem of comparison for pairwise matching solutions. A methodology is proposed to overcome the issue of scalability. A large scale dataset is developed based on real world case study namely, the web directories of Google, Looksmart and Yahoo!. Finally, an empirical evaluation is performed which compares the most representative solutions for taxonomy matching. We argue that the proposed dataset can play a key role in supporting the empirical analysis for the research effort in the area of taxonomy matching.

1 Introduction

Taxonomic structures are commonly used in file systems, market place catalogs, and the directories of Web portals. They are now widespread as knowledge repositories (in this case they can be viewed as shallow ontologies [23]) and the problem of their integration and interoperability is acquiring a high relevance from a scientific and commercial perspective. A typical application of hierarchical classification interoperability occurs when a set of companies wants to exchange products without sharing a common product catalog. The typical solution to the interoperability problem amounts to performing matching between taxonomies. The Match operator takes two graph-like structures as input and produces a mapping between the nodes of the graphs that correspond semantically to each other.

Many diverse solutions to the matching problem have been proposed so far, see for example surveys in [20, 21] and concrete solutions [13, 15, 6, 18, 24, 3, 19, 17, 8], etc. Unfortunately nearly all of them suffer from the lack of evaluation. Until very recently there were no comparative evaluations and it was quite difficult to find two systems which were evaluated on the same dataset. At the same time the evaluation efforts were mostly concentrated either on datasets artificially synthesized under questionable assumptions or on the "toy" examples.

In this paper we introduce a large scale dataset for evaluating matching solutions. The dataset is constructed from the mappings extracted from real

Y. Gil et al. (Eds.): ISWC 2005, LNCS 3729, pp. 67–81, 2005.

web directories and contains thousands of mappings. We have evaluated the dataset using the most representative state of the art solutions to the matching problem. The evaluation highlighted that the dataset has four key properties namely *Complexity*, *Discrimination capability*, *Incrementality* and *Correctness*. The first means that the dataset is "hard" for state of the art matching systems, the second that it discriminates among the various matching solutions, the third that it is effective in recognizing weaknesses in the state of the art matching systems and the fourth that it can be considered as a correct tool to support the improvement and research on the matching solutions. At the same time the current version of dataset contains only "true positive" mappings. This fact limits the evaluations on the dataset to measuring only Recall. This is a weakness of the dataset that we plan to improve. However, as highlighted in [16], the biggest problem in nowadays matching systems is recall, while completeness is much less of an issue.

The rest of the paper is organized as follows. Section 2 summarizes the definition of the matching problem and recalls the state of the art. Section 3 expands more on the notion of mapping evaluation problem. Section 4 illustrates how the large scale dataset has been arranged. Section 5 is devoted to a large scale empirical evaluation on two leading matching systems. Section 6 presents the results of our experiments and argues why the proposed dataset is of interest. Section 7 concludes the paper.

2   The Matching Problem

In order to motivate the matching problem and illustrate one of the possible situations which can arise in the data integration task let us use the two taxonomies A and B depicted on Figure 1. They are taken from Yahoo! and Standard business catalogues. Suppose that the task is to integrate these two taxonomies.

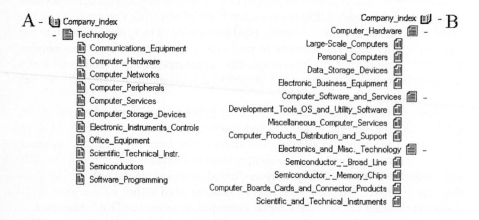

Fig. 1. Parts of Yahoo and Standard taxonomies

We assume that all the data and conceptual models (e.g., classifications, database schemas, taxonomies and ontologies) can be represented as graphs (see [9] for a detailed discussion). Therefore, the matching problem can be represented as extraction of graph-like structures from the data or conceptual models and matching the obtained graphs. This allows for the statement and solution of a generic matching problem, very much along the lines of what done in [15, 13].

The first step in the integration process is to identify candidates to be merged or to have relationships under an integrated taxonomy. For example, $Computer\_Hardware_A$ can be assumed equivalent to $Computer\_Hardware_B$ and more general than $Personal\_Computers_B$. Hereafter the subscripts designate the schema (either A or B) from which the node is derived.

We think of a mapping element as a 4-tuple $\langle ID_{ij}, n1_i, n2_j, R \rangle$, $i = 1, ..., N_1$; $j = 1, ..., N_2$; where ID_{ij} is a unique identifier of the given mapping element; $n1_i$ is the i-th node of the first graph, N_1 is the number of nodes in the first graph; $n2_j$ is the j-th node of the second graph, N_2 is the number of nodes in the second graph; and R specifies a similarity relation of the given nodes. A mapping is a set of mapping elements. We think of matching as the process of discovering mappings between two graph-like structures through the application of a matching algorithm.

Matching approaches can be classified into syntactic and semantic depending on how mapping elements are computed and on the kind of similarity relation R used (see [10] for in depth discussion):

- In *syntactic matching* the key intuition is to find the syntactic (very often string based) similarity between the labels of nodes. Similarity relation R in this case is typically represented as a $[0, 1]$ coefficient, which is often considered as equivalence relation with certain level of plausibility or confidence (see [13, 7] for example). Similarity coefficients usually measure the closeness between two elements linguistically and structurally. For example, the similarity between $Computer\_Storage\_Devices_A$ and $Data\_Storage\_Devices_B$ based on linguistical and structural analysis could be 0,63.
- *Semantic matching* is an approach where semantic relations are computed between concepts (not between labels) at nodes. The possible semantic relations (R) are: equivalence ($=$); more general or generalization ($\supseteq$); less general or specification ($\subseteq$); mismatch ($\perp$); overlapping ($\cap$). They are ordered according to decreasing binding strength, i.e., from the strongest ($=$) to the weakest ($\cap$). For example, as from Figure 1 $Computer\_Hardware_A$ is more general than $Large\_Scale\_Com\text{-}puters_B$

In this paper we are focused on taxonomy matching. We think about taxonomy as a $\langle N, A, F_l \rangle$, where N is a set of nodes, A is a set of arcs, such that $\langle N, A \rangle$ is a rooted tree. F_l is a function from N to set of labels L (i.e., words in natural language). An example of taxonomy is presented on Figure 1. Notice that the distinguishing feature of taxonomies is the lack of formal encoding semantics.

3   The Evaluation Problem

Nearly all state of the art matching systems suffer from the lack of evaluation. Till very recently there was no comparative evaluation and it was quite difficult to find two systems evaluated on the same dataset. Often authors artificially synthesize datasets for empirical evaluation but rarely they explain their premises and assumptions. The last efforts [22] on matching evaluation concentrate rather on artificially produced and quite simple examples than real world matching tasks. Most of the current evaluation efforts were devoted to the schemas with tenth of nodes and only some recent works (see [6] for example) present the evaluation results for the graphs with hundreds of nodes. At the same time industrial size schemas contain up to tenth thousands of nodes.

The evaluation problem can be summarized as the problem of acquiring the reference relationship that holds between two nodes. Given such a reference relationship it would be straightforward to evaluate the result of a matching solution. Up to now the acquisition of the reference mappings that hold among the nodes of two taxonomies is performed manually. Similarly to the annotated corpora for information retrieval or information extraction, we need to annotate a corpus of pairwise relationships. Of course such an approach prevents the opportunity of having large corpora. The number of mappings between two taxonomies are quadratic with respect to taxonomy size, what makes hardly possible the manual mapping of real world size taxonomies. It is worthwhile to remember that web directories, for example, have tens thousands of nodes. Certain heuristics can help in reducing the search space but the human effort is still too demanding.

Our proposal is to build a reference interpretation for a node looking at its use. We argue that the semantics of nodes can be derived by their pragmatics, i.e., how they are used. In our context, the nodes of a taxonomy are used to classify documents. The set of documents classified under a given node implicitly defines its meaning. This approach has been followed by other researchers. For example in [5, 14] the interpretation of a node is approximated by a model computed through statistical learning. Of course the accuracy of the interpretation is affected by the error of the learning model. We follow a similar approach but without the statistical approximation. The working hypothesis is that the meaning of two nodes is equivalent if the sets of documents classified under those nodes have a meaningful overlap.

The basic idea is to compute the relationship hypotheses based on the co-occurence of documents. This document-driven interpretation can be used as a reference value for the evaluation of competing matching solutions. A simple definition of equivalence relationship based on documents can be derived by the F1 measure of information retrieval.

Figure 2 shows a simple example. In the graphical representation we have two taxonomies, for each of them we focus our attention on a reference node. Let be S and P two sets of documents classified under the reference nodes of the first and second taxonomies respectively. We will refer to A_S and A_P as the set of documents classified under the ancestor nodes of S and P. Conversely, we will refer to T_S and T_P as the set of documents classified under the subtrees of S

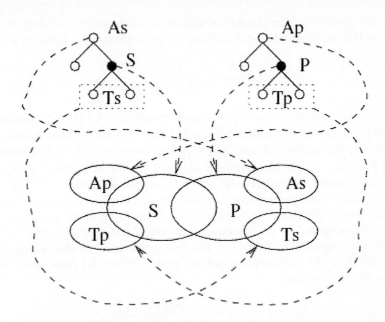

Fig. 2. The pairwise relationships between two taxonomies

and P. The goal is to define a relationship hypothesis based on the overlapping of the set of documents, i.e. the pragmatic use the nodes.

The first step, the *equivalence* relationship, can be easily formulated as the F1 measure of information retrieval [2]. The similarity of two sets of documents is defined as the ratio between the marginal sets and the shared documents:

$$Equivalence = \frac{|M_P^S| + |M_S^P|}{|O_P^S|}$$

where the set of shared documents is defined as $O_P^S = P \cap S$ and $M_P^S = S \setminus O_P^S$ is the marginal set of documents classified by S and not classified by P (similarly $M_S^P = P \setminus O_P^S$). The following equivalence applies $O_P^S = O_S^P$. Notice that "O" stands for "overlapping" and "M" stands for "Marginal set".

We do a step forward because we do not only compute the equivalence hypothesis based on the notion of F1 measure of information retrieval, but we extend such equation to define the formulation of generalization and specialization hypotheses. Generalization and specialization hypotheses can be formulated taking advantage of the contextual encoding of knowledge in terms of hierarchies of categories. The challenge is to formulate a generalization hypothesis (and conversely a specialization hypothesis) between two nodes looking at the overlapping of set of documents classified in the ancestor or subtree of the reference nodes [1].

The *generalization* relationship holds when the first node has to be considered more general of the second node. Intuitively, it happens when the documents classified under the first nodes occur in the ancestor of the second node, or the documents classified under the second node occur in the subtree of the first node. Following this intuition we can formalize the generalization hypothesis as

$$Generalization = \frac{|M_P^S| + |M_S^P|}{|O_P^S| + |O_{A_S}^P| + |O_{T_P}^S|}$$

where $O_{A_S}^P$ represents the set of documents resulting from the intersection between M_S^P and the set of documents classified under the concepts in the hierarchy above S (i.e. the ancestors); similarly $O_{T_P}^S$ represents the set of documents resulting from the intersection between M_P^S and the set of documents classified under the concepts in the hierarchy below P (i.e. the children).

In a similar way we can conceive the *specialization* relationship. The first node is more specific than second node when the meaning associated to the first node can be subsumed by the meaning of the second node. Intuitively, it happens when the documents classified under the first nodes occur in the subtree of the second node, or the documents classified under the second node occur in the ancestor of the first node.

$$Specialization = \frac{|M_P^S| + |M_S^P|}{|O_P^S| + |O_{T_S}^P| + |O_{A_P}^S|}$$

where $O_{T_S}^P$ represents the set of documents resulting from the intersection between M_S^P and the set of documents classified under the concepts in the hierarchy below S (i.e. the children); similarly $O_{A_P}^S$ represents the set of documents resulting from the intersection between M_P^S and the set of documents classified under the concepts in the hierarchy above P (i.e. the ancestors).

The three definitions above allow us to compute a relationship hypothesis between two nodes of two different taxonomies. Such an hypothesis relies on the assumption that if two nodes classify the same set of documents, the meaning associated to the nodes is reasonably the same. Of course this assumption is true for a virtually infinite set of documents. In a real world case study we face with finite set of documents, and therefore, this way of proceeding is prone to error. Nevertheless, our claim is that the approximation introduced by our assumption is balanced by the benefit of scaling with the annotation of large taxonomies.

4   Building a Large Scale Mapping Dataset

Let us try to apply the notion of document-driven interpretation to a real world case study. We focus our attention to web directories for many reasons. Web directories are widely used and known; moreover they are homogeneous, that is they cover general topics. The meaning of a node in a web directory is not defined with formal semantics but by pragmatics. Furthermore the web directories address the same space of documents, therefore the working hypothesis of co-occurence of documents can be sustainable. Of course different web directories don't cover the same portion of the web but the overlapping is meaningful.

The case study of web directories meets two requirements of the matching problem: to have heterogeneous representations of the same topics and to have taxonomies of large dimensions.

We address three main web directories: Google, Yahoo! and Looksmart. Nodes have been considered as categories denoted by the lexical labels, the tree structures have been considered as hierarchical relations, and the URL classified under a given node as documents. The following table summarizes the total amount of processed data.

Web Directories	Google	Looksmart	Yahoo!
number of nodes	335.902	884.406	321.585
number of urls	2.425.215	8.498.157	872.410

Let us briefly describe the process by which we have arranged an annotated corpus of pairwise relations between web directories.

Step 1. We crawled all three web directories, both the hierarchical structure and the web contents, then we computed the subset of URLs classified by all of them.

Step 2. We pruned the downloaded web directories by removing all the URLs that were not referred by all the three web directories.

Step 3. We performed an additional pruning by removing all the nodes with a number of URLs under a given threshold. In our case study we fixed such a threshold at 10.

Step 4. We manually recognized potential overlapping between two branches of two different web directories like

```
Google:/Top/Science/Biology
Looksmart:/Top/Science-and-Health/Biology

Yahoo:/Top/Computers-and-Internet/Internet
Looksmart:/Top/Computing/Internet

Google:/Top/Reference/Education
Yahoo:/Top/Education
```

We recognized 50 potential overlapping and for each of them we run an exhaustive assessment on all the possible pairs between the two related subtrees. Such an heuristic allowed us to reduce the quadratic explosion of cartesian product of two web directories. We focussed the analysis on smaller subtrees where the overlaps were more likely.

Step 5. We computed the three document-driven hypothesis for *equivalence*, *generalization* and *specialization* relationships as described above. Hypotheses of equivalence, generalization and specialization are normalized and estimated by a number in the range [0,1]. Since the cumulative hypothesis of all three relationships for the same pair of nodes can not be higher than 1, we introduce a threshold to select the winning hypothesis. We fixed such a threshold to 0.5.

We discarded all the pairs where none of the three relationship hypotheses was detected. This process allowed us to obtain 2265 pairwise relationships defined using the document-driven interpretation. Half are equivalence relationships and half are generalization relationships (notice that by definition generalization and specialization hypothesis are symmetric).

In the following we will refer to this dataset as TaxME, TAXonomy Mapping Evaluation.

5   The Empirical Evaluation

The evaluation was designed in order to assess the major dataset properties namely:

- *Complexity*, namely the fact that the dataset is "hard" for state of the art matching systems.
- *Discrimination ability*, namely the fact that the dataset can discriminate among various matching approaches.
- *Incrementality*, namely the fact that the dataset allows to incrementally discover the weaknesses of the tested systems.
- *Correctness*, namely the fact that the dataset can be a source of correct results.

We have evaluated two state of the art matching systems $COMA$[1] and $S-Match$ and compared their results with *baseline solution*. Let us describe the matching systems in more detail.

The $COMA$ system [13] is a generic syntactic schema matching tool. It exploits both element and structure level techniques and combines the results of their independent execution using several aggregation strategies. $COMA$ provides an extensible library of matching algorithms and a framework for combining obtained results. Matching library contains 6 individual matchers, 5 hybrid matchers and 1 reuse-oriented matcher. One of the distinct features of the COMA tool is the possibility of performing iterations in the matching process. In the evaluation we used default combination of matchers and aggregation strategy (*NamePath+Leaves* and *Average* respectively).

S-*Match* is a generic semantic matching tool. It takes two tree-like structures and produces a set of mappings between their nodes. S-*Match* implements semantic matching algorithm in 4 steps. On the first step the labels of nodes are linguistically preprocessed and their meanings are obtained from the Oracle (in the current version WordNet 2.0 is used as an Oracle). On the second step the meaning of the nodes is refined with respect to the tree structure. On the third step the semantic relations between the labels at nodes and their meanings are computed by the library of element level semantic matchers. On the fourth step

---

[1] In the evaluation we use the version of $COMA$ described in [13]. A newer version of the system $COMA++$ exists but we do not have it. However as from the evaluation results presented in [10, 11], $COMA$ is still best among the other syntactic matchers.

the matching results are produced by reduction of the node matching problem
into propositional validity problem, which is efficiently solved by SAT solver or
ad hoc algorithm (see [10, 11] for more details).

We have compared the performance of these two systems with *baseline solution*. The pseudo code of baseline node matching algorithm is given in Algorithm
1. It is executed for each pair of nodes in two trees. The algorithm considers a
simple string comparison among the labels placed on the path spanning from a
node to the root of the tree. Equivalence, more general and less general relations
are computed as the corresponding logical operations on the sets of the labels.

Algorithm 1. Baseline node matching algorithm

1: String nodeMatch(Node *sourceNode*, Node *targetNode*)
2: Set *sourceSetOfLabels*=getLabelsInPathToRoot(*sourceNode*)
3: Set *targetSetOfLabels*=getLabelsInPathToRoot(*targetNode*)
4: **if** *sourceSetOfLabels* $\equiv$ *targetSetOfLabels* **then**
5:      *result*="$\equiv$"
6: **else if** *sourceSetOfLabels* $\subseteq$ *targetSetOfLabels* **then**
7:      *result*="$\subseteq$"
8: **else if** *sourceSetOfLabels* $\supseteq$ *targetSetOfLabels* **then**
9:      *result*="$\supseteq$"
10: **else**
11:     *result*="Idk"
12: **end if**
13: **return** *result*

The systems have been evaluated on the dataset described in Section 4.
We computed the number of matching tasks solved by each matching system.
Notice that the matching task was considered to be solved in the case when the
matching system produce specification, generalization or equivalence semantic
relation for it. For example, TaxME suggests that specification relation holds in
the following example:

```
Google:/Top/Sports/Basketball/Professional/NBDL
Looksmart:/Top/Sports/Basketball
```

COMA produced for this matching task 0.58 similarity coefficient, which can be
considered as equivalence relation with probability 0.58. In the evaluation we
consider this case as true positive for *COMA* (i.e., the mapping was considered
as found by the system).

Notice that at present TaxME contains only true positive mappings. This
fact allows to obtain the correct results for Recall measure, which is defined as
a ratio of reference mappings found by the system to the number of reference
mappings. At the same time Precision, which is defined as ratio of reference
mappings found by the system to the number of mappings in the result, can not
be correctly estimated by the dataset since, as from Section 4, TaxME guarantee
only the correctness but not completeness of the mappings it contains.

Table 1. Evaluation Results

	Google vs. Looksmart	Google vs. Yahoo	Looksmart vs.Yahoo	Total
COMA	608	250	18	876 (38,68%)
=	608	250	18	876
⊆	not applicable	not applicable	not applicable	not applicable
⊇	not applicable	not applicable	not applicable	not applicable
S-Match	584	83	2	669 (29,54%)
=	2	5	0	7
⊆	46	19	2	67
⊇	536	59	0	595
Baseline	54	76	0	130 (5,39%)
=	52	0	0	52
⊆	0	76	0	76
⊇	2	0	0	2

6   Discussion of Results

Evaluation results are presented on Table 1. It contains the total number of mappings found by the systems and the partitioning of the mappings on semantic relations. Let us discuss the results through the major dataset properties perspective.

6.1   Complexity

As from Table 1, the results of *baseline* are surprisingly low. It produced slightly more than 5% of mappings. This result is interesting since on the previously evaluated datasets (see [4] for example) the similar baseline algorithm performed quite well and found up to 70% of mappings. This lead us to conclusion that the dataset is not trivial (i.e., it is essentially hard for simple matching techniques).

As from Figure 3, *S-Match* found about 30% of the mappings in the biggest (Google-Yahoo) matching task. At the same time it produced slightly less than 30% of mappings in all the tasks. *COMA* found about 35% of mappings on Google-Looksmart and Yahoo-Looksmart matching tasks. At the same time it produced the best result on Google-Yahoo. *COMA* found slightly less than 40% of all the mappings. These results are interesting since, as from [13, 10], previously reported recall values for both systems were in 70-80% range. This fact turn us to conclusion that the dataset is hard for state of the art syntactic and semantic matching systems.

6.2   Discrimination Ability

Consider Figure 4. It presents the partitioning of the mappings found by *S-Match* and *COMA*. As from the figure the sets of mappings produced by *COMA* and *S-Match* intersects only on 15% of the mappings. This fact turns us to an important conclusion: the dataset is discriminating (i.e., it contains a number of features which are essentially hard for various classes of matching systems and allow to discriminate between the major qualities of the systems).

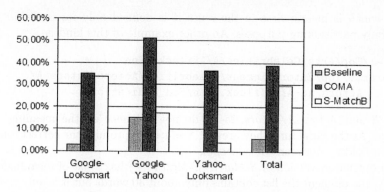

Fig. 3. Percentage of correctly determined mappings(Recall)

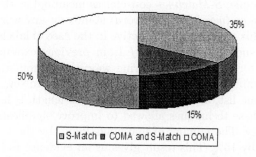

Fig. 4. Partitioning of the mappings found by COMA and S-Match

6.3   Incrementality

In order to evaluate incrementality we have chosen *S-Match* as a test system. In order to identify the shortcomings of *S-Match* we manually analyzed the mappings missed by *S-Match*. This analysis allowed us to clasterize the mismatches into several categories. In this paper we describe in detail one of the most important categories of mismatches namely *Meaningless labels*.

Consider the following example:

```
Google:/Top/Science/Social_Sciences/Archaeology/Alternative/
        South_America/Nazca_Lines
Looksmart:/Top/Science_&_Health/Social_Science/Archaeology/
        By_Region/Andes_South_America/Nazca
```

In this matching task some labels are meaningful in the sense they define the context of the concept. In our example these are *Social_Sciences*, *Archaeology*, *South_America*, *Nazca*. The other labels do not have a great influence on the meaning of concept. At the same time they can prevent *S-Match* from producing the correct semantic relation. In our example *S-Match* can not find any semantic relation connecting *Nazca_Lines* and *Nazca*. The reason for this is *By_Region* label, which is meaningless in the sense it is defined only for readability and taxonomy partitioning purposes. An other example of this kind is

```
Google:/Top/Arts/Celebrities/A/Affleck,_Ben
Looksmart:/Top/Entertainment/Celebrities/Actors/Actors_A/
         Actors_Aa-Af/Affleck,_Ben/Fan_Dedications
```

Here, A and $Actors\_A/Actors\_Aa\text{-}Af$ do not influence on the meaning of the concept. At the same time they prevent S-$Match$ to produce the correct semantic relation holding between the concepts.

An optimized version of S-$Match$ (S-$Match{+}{+}$) has a list of meaningless labels. At the moment the list contains only about 30 words but it is automatically enriched in preprocessing phase. A general rule for considering natural language label as meaningless is to check whether it is used for taxonomy partitioning purposes. For example, S-$Match{+}{+}$ consider as meaningless the labels with the following structure $by \langle word \rangle$, where $\langle word \rangle$ stands for any word in natural language. However, this method is not effective in the case of labels composed from alphabet letters (such as $Actors\_Aa\text{-}Af$ from previous example). S-$Match{+}{+}$ deals with the latter case in the following way: the combination of letters are considered as meaningless if it is not recognized by WordNet, not in abbreviation or proper name list, and at the same time its length is less or equal to 3. The addition of these techniques allowed to improve significantly the S-$Match$ matching capability. The number of mappings found by the system on TaxME dataset increased by 15%. This result gives us an evidence to incrementality of the dataset (i.e., the dataset allows to discover the weaknesses of the systems and gives the clues to the systems evolution).

Analysis of S-$Match$ results on TaxME allowed to identify 10 major bottlenecks in the system implementation. At the moment we are developing ad hoc techniques allowing to improve S-$Match$ results in this cases. The current version of S-$Match$ (S-$Match{+}{+}$) contains the techniques allowing to solve 5 out of 10 major categories of mismatches. Consider Figure 5.It contains the results of

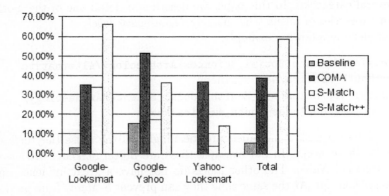

Fig. 5. Percentage of correctly determined mappings(Recall)

comparative evaluation *S-Match++* against the other systems. As from the figure *S-Match++* significantly outperforms all the other systems. It found about 60% of mappings in all the matching tasks, what is twice better than *S-Match* result. This significant improvement would hardly be possible without comprehensive evaluation on TaxME dataset.

6.4   Correctness

We manually analyzed correctness of the mappings provided by TaxME. At the moment 60% of mappings are processed and only 2-3% of them are not correct. Taking into account the notion of idiosyncratic classification [12] (or the fact that human annotators on the sufficiently big and complex dataset tend to have resemblance up to 20% in comparison with their own results), such a mismatch can be considered as marginal.

7   Conclusions

In this paper we have presented a mapping dataset which carries the key important properties of *Complexity, Incrementality, Discrementality* and *Correctness*. We have evaluated the dataset on two state of the art matching systems representing different matching approaches. As from the evaluation, the dataset can be considered as a powerful tool to support the evaluation and research on the matching solutions.

The ultimate step which needs to be performed is to acquire the user mappings for TaxME dataset. We have already arranged such a kind of test and the results though preliminary are promising. Unfortunately at the moment more significant statistics needs to be collected in order to further improve TaxME.

Acknowledgment

We would like to thank Claudio Fontana and Christian Girardi for their helpful contribution in crawling and processing the web directories. We also would like to thank Pavel Shvaiko and Ilya Zaihrayev for their work on S-Match.

This work has been partially supported by the European Knowledge Web network of excellence (IST-2004-507482).

References

1. P. Avesani. Evaluation framework for local ontologies interoperability. In *AAAI Workshop on Meaning Negotiation*, 2002.
2. R. Baeza-Yates and B. Ribeiro-Neto. *Modern Information Retrieval.* Addison Wesley, 1999.
3. S. Bergamaschi, S. Castano, and M. Vincini. Semantic integration of semistructured and structured data sources. *SIGMOD Record*, (28(1)):54–59, 1999.

4. P. Bouquet, L. Serafini, and S. Zanobini. Semantic coordination: a new approach and an application. In Fensel D., Sycara K. P., and Mylopoulos J., editors, *The Semantic Web*, volume 2870 of *LNCS*, Sanibel Island, Fla., 20-23 October 2003.

5. H. Doan, P. Domingos, and A. Halevy. Learning to match the schemas of data sources: A multistrategy approach. *Machine Learning*, 50:279–301, 2003.

6. M. Ehrig and Y. Sure. Ontology mapping - an integrated approach. In Christoph Bussler, John Davis, Dieter Fensel, and Rudi Studer, editors, *Proceedings of the First European Semantic Web Symposium*, volume 3053 of *Lecture Notes in Computer Science*, pages 76–91, Heraklion, Greece, MAY 2004. Springer Verlag.

7. J. Euzenat and P. Valtchev. An integrative proximity measure for ontology alignment. In *Proceedings of Semantic Integration workshop at International Semantic Web Conference (ISWC)*, 2003.

8. J. Euzenat and P. Valtchev. Similarity-based ontology alignment in OWL-lite. In *Proceedings of European Conference on Artificial Intelligence (ECAI)*, pages 333–337, 2004.

9. F. Giunchiglia and P. Shvaiko. Semantic matching. *The Knowledge Engineering Review Journal*, (18(3)):265–280, 2003.

10. F. Giunchiglia, P. Shvaiko, and M. Yatskevich. S-match: an algorithm and an implementation of semantic matching. In Bussler C., Davies J., Fensel D., and Studer R., editors, *The semantic web: research and applications*, volume 3053 of *LNCS*, Heraklion, 10-12 May 2004.

11. F. Giunchiglia, M. Yatskevich, and E. Giunchiglia. Efficient semantic matching. In *Proceedings of the 2nd european semantic web conference (ESWC'05)*, Heraklion, 29 May-1 June 2005.

12. D. Goren-Bar and T.Kuflik. Supporting user-subjective categorization with self-organizing maps and learning vector quantization. *Journal of the American Society for Information Science and Technology JASIST*, 56(4):345–355, 2005.

13. H.H.Do and E. Rahm. COMA - a system for flexible combination of schema matching approaches. In *Proceedings of Very Large Data Bases Conference (VLDB)*, pages 610–621, 2001.

14. R. Ichise, H. Takeda, and S. Honiden. Integrating multiple internet directories by instance-based learning. In *IJCAI*, pages 22–30, 2003.

15. J. Madhavan, P. A. Bernstein, and E. Rahm. Generic schema matching with cupid. *The Very Large Databases (VLDB) Journal*, pages 49–58, 2001.

16. B. Magnini, M. Speranza, and C. Girardi. A semantic-based approach to interoperability of classification hierarchies: Evaluation of linguistic techniques. In *Proceedings of COLING-2004*, August 23 - 27, 2004.

17. D. L. McGuinness, R. Fikes, J. Rice, and S. Wilder. An environment for merging and testing large ontologies. In *Proceedings of International Conference on the Principles of Knowledge Representation and Reasoning (KR)*, pages 483–493, 2000.

18. S. Melnik, H. Garcia-Molina, and E. Rahm. Similarity flooding: A versatile graph matching algorithm. In *Proceedings of International Conference on Data Engineering (ICDE)*, pages 117–128, 2002.

19. Noy N. and Musen M. A. Anchor-prompt: Using non-local context for semantic matching. In *Proceedings of workshop on Ontologies and Information Sharing at International Joint Conference on Artificial Intelligence (IJCAI)*, pages 63–70, 2001.

20. E. Rahm and P. Bernstein. A survey of approaches to automatic schema matching. *VLDB Journal*, (10(4)):334–350, 2001.

21. P. Shvaiko and J. Euzenat. A survey of schema-based matching approaches. *Journal on Data Semantics*, IV, 2005.

22. Y. Sure, O. Corcho, J. Euzenat, and T. Hughes. *Evaluation of Ontology-based Tools.* Proceedings of the 3rd International Workshop on Evaluation of Ontology-based Tools (EON), 2004. http://CEUR-WS.org/Vol-128/.
23. C. Welty and N. Guarino. Supporting ontological analysis of taxonomic relationships. *Data and Knowledge Engineering*, (39(1)):51–74, 2001.
24. L. Xu and D.W. Embley. Using domain ontologies to discover direct and indirect matches for schema elements. In *Proceedings of Semantic Integration workshop at International Semantic Web Conference (ISWC)*, 2003.

RDF Entailment as a Graph Homomorphism

Jean-François Baget

INRIA Rhône-Alpes, 655 avenue de l'Europe,
38334, Saint Ismier, France
jean-francois.baget@inrialpes.fr

Abstract. Semantic consequence (entailment) in RDF is ususally computed using Pat Hayes Interpolation Lemma. In this paper, we reformulate this mechanism as a graph homomorphism known as projection in the conceptual graphs community.

Though most of the paper is devoted to a detailed proof of this result, we discuss the immediate benefits of this reformulation: it is now easy to translate results from different communities (*e.g.* conceptual graphs, constraint programming, ...) to obtain new polynomial cases for the NP-complete RDF ENTAILMENT problem, as well as numerous algorithmic optimizations.

1 Introduction

Simple RDF is the knowledge representation language on which RDF (Resource Description Framework) and its extension RDFS are built. As a logic, it is provided with a syntax (its abstract syntax will be used here), and model theoretic semantics [1]. These semantics are used to define entailments: an RDF graph G entails an RDF graph H iff H is true whenever G is. However, since an infinity of interpretations must be evaluated according to this definition, an operational inference mechanism, sound and complete w.r.t. entailment, is needed. This is the purpose of the interpolation lemma [1]: a finite procedure characterizing entailments. It has been extended to take into account more expressive languages (RDF, RDFS [1], and other languages *e.g.* [2]). All these extensions rely on a polynomial-time initial treatment of the graphs, the hard kernel remaining the basic simple entailment, which is a NP-hard problem.

In this paper, we intend to contribute to the study of this fundamental simple entailment by reformulating it as a graph homomorphism, extensively studied both in mathematics and in graph theory. This will allow the RDF community to import numerous results from related problems: colored homomorphisms [3], conceptual graphs projection [4], or constraint satisfaction problems [5]. The experience acquired during the last 20 years in these different communities can help us to quickly develop efficient algorithms for RDF entailment, as well as understand what are the polynomial cases for this problem.

However, the bulk of the paper presented here is devoted to the reformulation as a graph homomorphism itself. All necessary proofs have been included, independently from the proof of the interpolation lemma [1]. Indeed, we believe

Y. Gil et al. (Eds.): ISWC 2005, LNCS 3729, pp. 82–96, 2005.

that our proof framework can be used as a basis to apply our reformulation to many extensions of simple RDF: in that case, an in-depth understanding of that proof is required.

Section 2 is devoted to the basic definitions and results of [1]. In section 3, we reformulate the interpolation lemma as a directed, multigraph homomorphism. Section 4 provides a standalone proof of this result, via a reformulation of entailment as a directed hypergraph homomorphism. In section 5, we provide a list of results that can be translated to simple RDF entailments. Finally, in section 6, we discuss the advantages and limitations of this approach.

2 Simple RDF: Syntax, Semantics, and Inferences

This section presents *simple RDF*, the basic logic on which RDF and RDFS are built: we recall here definitions and results presented in [1]. We first present the abstract syntax of RDF: note that we distinguish here an RDF *tripleset* (a set of triples) from its associated graph (that will be presented in the next section). The semantics of RDF triplesets allows to formally define the notion of entailment, that is characterized by the interpolation lemma. Note also that though we use here the terms of interpretations, entailment, it refers here without ambiguity to what is called simple interpretation or simple entailment in [1]. These definitions precise our notations, and the examples given introduce the running example used all along this paper. The reader should refer to [1] for more explanations.

2.1 RDF Abstract Syntax

We consider a set of *terms* $\mathcal{V}$ partitioned in three pairwise disjoint sets: a set $\mathcal{U}$ of *URI references* (or *urirefs*), a set $\mathcal{B}$ of *blanks*, and a set $\mathcal{L}$ of literals (itself partitioned into two disjoint sets, the set $\mathcal{L}_P$ of plain literals and the set $\mathcal{L}_T$ of typed literals). Let $V \subseteq \mathcal{V}$ be a subset of $\mathcal{V}$, then we denote by $\mathcal{U}(V)$ (resp. $\mathcal{B}(V)$, $\mathcal{L}_P(V)$, $\mathcal{L}(V)$, $\mathcal{L}_T(V)$) the set of urirefs of V (resp. of blanks of V, of literals of V, of plain literals of V, of typed literals of V). Without loss of generality, and for the sake of simplicity, we have not taken language tags into account here.

Definition 1 (RDF tripleset). *An* RDF tripleset *is a subset of* $(\mathcal{U} \cup \mathcal{B}) \times \mathcal{U} \times \mathcal{V}$. *Its elements are called* RDF triples.

An RDF triple $\langle s, p, o \rangle$ can be read "there is a relation of sort p whose subject is the entity s an whose object is the entity o". Let G be an RDF tripleset. We denote by $\mathcal{V}(G)$ the terms of $\mathcal{V}$ that appear in any triple of G, i.e. $\mathcal{V}(G) = \{v \in \mathcal{V} \mid \exists \langle s, p, o \rangle \in G,\ x = s \text{ or } x = p \text{ or } x = o\}$.

Example 1. Let $V = \{u_1, u_2, b_1, b_2, l\}$ be a set of terms where u_1 and u_2 are urirefs, b_1 and b_2 are blanks, and l is a plain literal. Let us now consider the two following RDF triplesets, used as a running example along this paper:

- $H = \{\langle u_1, u_1, b_1 \rangle \langle u_1, u_1, b_2 \rangle, \langle b_2, u_2, l \rangle, \langle b_1, u_1, b_2 \rangle\}$
- $G = \{\langle u_1, u_1, b_1 \rangle \langle b_1, u_1, b_1 \rangle, \langle b_1, u_2, l \rangle, \langle u_1, u_2, u_2 \rangle \}$

2.2   Interpretations

Definition 2 (Simple Interpretations). *Let V be a set of terms. An interpretation of V is a 5-tuple $\langle I_R, I_P, \iota_{ext}, \iota_s, \iota_l \rangle$ where I_R is a set of resources containing $\mathcal{L}_P(V)$[1], I_P is a set of properties, $\iota_{ext} : I_P \to 2^{I_R \times I_R}$ maps each property to a set of pairs of resources (the extension of the property), $\iota_s : \mathcal{U}(V) \to I_R \cup I_P$ maps each uriref to a resource or a property, and $\iota_l : \mathcal{L}_T(V) \to I_R$ maps each typed literal to a resource.*

Example 2. Let V be the set of terms defined in Ex. 1. We consider the following interpretation $I = \langle I_R, I_P, \iota_{ext}, \iota_s, \iota_l \rangle$ of V defined by:

- $I_R = \{\clubsuit, \heartsuit, l\}$;
- $I_P = \{\clubsuit, \heartsuit\}$;
- $\iota_{ext}(\clubsuit) = \{\langle \clubsuit, \heartsuit \rangle, \langle \heartsuit, \heartsuit \rangle\}$ and $\iota_{ext}(\heartsuit) = \{\langle \heartsuit, l \rangle\}$;
- $\iota_s(u_1) = \clubsuit$ and $\iota_s(u_2) = \heartsuit$.

For the sake of clarity, it has been proposed in [1] to give a graphical representation of an interpretation as shown in Fig. 1.

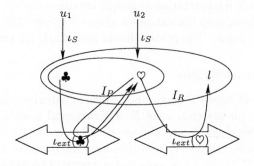

Fig. 1. A Graphical Representation of the Interpretation I

Definition 3 (Models). *Let G be an RDF tripleset, and V be a set of terms that contains the set of terms of G, i.e. such that $(\mathcal{U}(\mathcal{V}(G)) \cup \mathcal{L}(\mathcal{V}(G))) \subseteq V$. An interpretation $\langle I_R, I_P, \iota_{ext}, \iota_s, \iota_l \rangle$ of V is a model of G iff there exists a mapping $\iota : \mathcal{V}(G) \to I_R \cup I_P$ such that:*

1. *for each plain literal $l \in \mathcal{L}_P(\mathcal{V}(G))$, $\iota(l) = l$;*
2. *for each typed literal $l \in \mathcal{L}_T(\mathcal{V}(G))$, $\iota(l) = \iota_l(l)$;*
3. *for each uriref $u \in \mathcal{U}(\mathcal{V}(G))$, $\iota(u) = \iota_s(u)$;*
4. *for each blank $b \in \mathcal{B}(\mathcal{V}(G))$, $\iota(b) \in I_R$;*
5. *for each triple $\langle s, p, o \rangle \in G$, $\langle \iota(s), \iota(o) \rangle \in \iota_{ext}(\iota(p))$.*

---

[1] This inclusion allows to avoid, for the sake of simplicity, the set LV of literal values.

Example 3. Let us show that the interpretation I in Ex. 2 is a model for the RDF tripleset H in Fig. 1. We have $\iota(u_1) = \clubsuit$, $\iota(u_2) = \heartsuit$, and $\iota(l) = l$ (all these values are constrained by the interpretation I). Our only choice is with the blanks: we chose $\iota(b_1) = \iota(b_2) = \heartsuit \in I_R$. It remains now to check that for each triple $\langle s, p, o \rangle$ of H, $\langle \iota(s), \iota(o) \rangle \in \iota_{ext}(\iota(p))$. We will only check the triple $\langle b_2, u_2, l \rangle$: $\iota_{ext}(\iota(u_2)) = \iota_{ext}(\heartsuit) = \{\langle \heartsuit, l \rangle\} \supseteq \langle \iota(b_2), \iota(l) \rangle$. The condition is also verified for the 4 other triples. It follows that I is a model of H. A tenacious reader can now check that I is not a model of G (he has to prove that no mapping ι respects these conditions).

2.3   The Interpolation Lemma

Definition 4 (Satisfiability, Entailment). *Let G and H be two RDF triplesets. We say that G is* satisfiable *if there exists an interpretation that is a model of G. We say that H is a* semantic consequence *of G (we also say that G entails H, and note $G \models H$) if every model of G is also a model of H.*

Example 4. The RDF tripleset H of Ex. 1 is satisfiable since the interpretation I of Ex. 2 is a model of H. Since I is not a model of G (Ex. 1), we can conclude that H does not entail G.

Definition 5 (Instance). *Let G be an RDF tripleset, and let V be a set of terms that contains the set of terms of G. Let us consider an* instance mapping $\alpha : \mathcal{V}(G) \to V$ *mapping each blank of G to a term of V, and each uriref or literal to itself. The RDF tripleset $G_\alpha = \{\langle \alpha(s), p, \alpha(o) \rangle \mid \langle s, p, o \rangle \in G\}$ is called an* instance *of G.*

Example 5. Let us consider the set of terms V and the RDF tripleset G of Ex. 1. We define an instance mapping α as follows: $\alpha(b_1) = b_1$, $\alpha(b_2) = b_1$ (every other element of V is mapped to itself). The instance H_α is the RDF tripleset defined by: $H_\alpha = \{\langle u_1, u_1, b_1 \rangle, \langle b_1, u_2, l \rangle, \langle b_1, u_1, b_1 \rangle\}$ (notice that a second occurence of $\langle u_1, u_1, b_1 \rangle$ has been removed from the set).

Theorem 1 (Interpolation Lemma). *Let G and H be two RDF triplesets. Then $G \models H$ iff there exists an instance H' of H such that $H \subseteq G$.*

Example 6. Since the RDF tripleset H_α of Ex. 5 is a subset of the RDF tripleset G of Ex. 1, then $G \models H$.

3   RDF Triplesets as Directed, Labelled Multigraphs

RDF triplesets are given a standard graphical representation: the drawing of the graph (as a mathematical structure) associated with the tripleset (hence the usual name of RDF graphs). It is generally assumed that most people are more comfortable with this representation than with triples, at least when the graphs involved are not to big. The graphs whose drawings correspond to this representation are directed, labelled multigraphs (there can be many arcs between two nodes, a requirement since two arcs can have different labels). In this section, we reformulate the usual characterization of entailment (the interpolation lemma of [1], expressed on the RDF tripleset) as a graph homomorphism: graphs are no longer only used for a representation purpose, but also for reasonings.

3.1 Standard Graphical Representation of an RDF Tripleset

Definition 6 (Directed, Labelled Multigraphs). *A directed labelled multigraph (or* M-graph*) over a set of terms V is a 4-tuple $G = \langle N, A, \gamma, \epsilon \rangle$ where N is a finite set of* nodes*, A is a finite set of* arcs*, $\gamma : A \to N \times N$ maps each arc to a pair of nodes called its* ends *(the first being the* origin *and the second the* destination*), and $\epsilon : N \cup A \to V$ maps each node and arc to a term.*

Let G be an RDF tripleset. We call *entities* of G the subset of $\mathcal{V}(G)$ that contains the terms appearing either as subject or object in a triple of G, i.e. $ent(G) = \{x \in \mathcal{V}(G) \mid \exists \langle s, p, o \rangle \in G, \ x = s \text{ or } x = o\}$ (it is called the *nodeset* in [2]). The M-graph $\mathcal{M}(G) = \langle N, A, \gamma, \epsilon \rangle$ associated with the RDF tripleset G is built as follows:

1. To each term $e \in ent(G)$ we associate a distinct node $m(e)$. Then $N = \{m(e) \mid e \in ent(G)\}$. Each node is labelled by the element of the set of terms associated to it: $\epsilon(m(e)) = e$.
2. To each triple $t = \langle s, p, o \rangle \in G$ we associate a distinct arc $m(t)$. Then $A = \{m(t) \mid t \in G\}$. The ends of the arc $m(t)$ are the nodes associated with the subject and the object of the triple t: $\gamma(m(t)) = \langle m(s), m(o) \rangle$. The label of the arc $m(t)$ is the property of the triple t: $\epsilon(m(t)) = p$.

Example 7. The M-graph $\mathcal{M}(H) = \langle N, A, \gamma, \epsilon \rangle$ obtained from the graph H of Ex. 1 is defined by: $N = \{1, 2, 3, 4\}$, $A = \{a, b, c, d\}$, $\gamma(a) = \langle 1, 2 \rangle$, $\gamma(b) = \langle 2, 3 \rangle$, $\gamma(c) = \langle 1, 3 \rangle$, $\gamma(d) = \langle 3, 4 \rangle$, $\epsilon(1) = u_1$, $\epsilon(2) = b_1$, $\epsilon(3) = b_2$, $\epsilon(4) = l$, $\epsilon(a) = u_1$, $\epsilon(b) = u_1$, $\epsilon(c) = u_1$, and $\epsilon(d) = u_2$.

The M-graph $\mathcal{M}(G)$ associated with an RDF tripleset G can be drawn as follows: each node labelled by a uriref or a blank is represented by an oval, and each node labelled by a literal is represented by a rectangle. The label of the node is written inside the oval or rectangle associated to it (it is not mandatory to write the label when it is a blank). Each arc a with $\gamma(a) = \langle x, y \rangle$ is represented by an arrow from the figure associated with x to the figure associated with y. The label $\epsilon(a)$ is written next to this arrow.

Example 8. Fig. 2 represents the drawing of the M-graph $\mathcal{M}(H)$ of Ex. 7 (usually conflated with the RDF tripleset H itself).

Note that the complexity in both time and space of the transformation $\mathcal{M}$ is linear in the size of the tripleset if the graph is encoded by an adjacency list, and is quadratic if it is encoded by an incidence matrix.

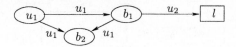

Fig. 2. Drawing of the M-graph associated with an RDF tripleset

3.2   Simple Entailment as a Multigraph Homomorphism

Here we caracterize RDF entailment as a M-graph homomorphism. Graphs homomorphisms have been extensively studied in mathematics as well as in computer science (*e.g.* [3]), though the generalization we use here is more akin to the projection used to caracterize entailment of conceptual graphs (CGs) [4]. Though we have decided not to present our results via a translation to CGs, the reader can refer to [6] or [7] for precise relationships between RDF and CGs.

Definition 7 (Directed, Labelled Multigraph Homomorphism). *Let $G = \langle N, A, \gamma, \epsilon \rangle$ and $G' = \langle N', A', \gamma', \epsilon' \rangle$ be M-graphs over a set of terms V. Let $\leq$ be a preorder over V. A directed, labelled multigraph homomorphism* according to *$\leq$ (or $\leq$-M-morphism) from G into G' is a mapping $\pi : N \to N'$ that preserves the preorder on labels as well as incidence of arcs, i.e.:*

1. *for each $n \in N$, $\epsilon'(\pi(n)) \leq \epsilon(n)$;*
2. *for each $a \in A$ with $\gamma(a) = \langle s, o \rangle$, $\exists a' \in A'$ such that $\gamma'(a') = \langle \pi(s), \pi(o) \rangle$ and $\epsilon'(a') \leq \epsilon(a)$.*

Example 9. Let us consider the M-graphs associated with the triplesets G and H of Ex. 1. Now we define $\leq_1$ as the smallest preorder defined on the set of terms V fulfilling these conditions:

– for each two blanks b_1 and b_2, $b_1 \leq_1 b_2$;
– for each blank b and each uriref or literal c, $c \leq_1 b$.

It implies that urirefs and literals are pairwise non comparable. Then there exists a $\leq_1$-M-morphism from H into G, illustrated by the dashed arrows in FIG. 3.

   It remains now to prove that such a $\leq_1$-M-morphism caracterizes simple RDF entailment.

Theorem 2. *Let G and H be two RDF triplesets defined over a set of terms V. Let $\leq_1$ be the partial order on V defined in Ex. 9. Then $G \models H$ if and only if there is a $\leq_1$-M-morphism from $\mathcal{M}(H)$ into $\mathcal{M}(G)$.*

As proven below, this is a mere reformulation of the interpolation lemma. Next section provides a standalone proof (that can be considered as an another proof for the interpolation lemma). Further sections will be devoted to the advantages of this reformulation (complexity and algorithms).

Proof. We use the interpolation lemma to prove both directions of the equivalence:

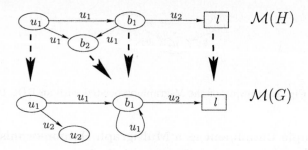

Fig. 3. $\leq_1$-M-morphism from the M-graph $\mathcal{M}(H)$ into the M-graph $\mathcal{M}(G)$

($\Rightarrow$) Suppose $G \models_s H$. Then there exists an instance mapping α such that $H_\alpha \subseteq G$. Let us consider the mapping π from the nodes of $\mathcal{M}(H)$ into the nodes of $\mathcal{M}(G)$ defined as follows: for each node $m(x)$ of $\mathcal{M}(H)$ (i.e. associated with the term x in $\mathcal{V}(H)$), $\pi(m(x)) = m(\alpha(x))$ (where $m(\alpha(x))$ is the node of $\mathcal{M}(G)$ associated with the term $\alpha(x)$). Let us now prove that π is a $\leq_1$-M-morphism from $\mathcal{M}(H)$ into $\mathcal{M}(G)$.

1. We first prove that π preserves the preorder on nodes labels. Let $m(x)$ be an arbitrary node of $\mathcal{M}(H)$. The label of $m(x)$ is x. The label of $\pi(m(x))$ is the label of $m(\alpha(x))$, i.e. $\alpha(x)$. It remains to show that $\alpha(x) \leq_1 x$. If x is a blank, then it is greater than anything else (def. of $\leq_1$). Otherwise, $\alpha(x) = x$. In both cases, $\alpha(x) \leq_1 x$.

2. Finally, we prove that π preserves the incidence of arcs and the preorder on their labels. Let a be an arc of H with $\gamma(a) = \langle m(s), m(o) \rangle$ and $\epsilon(a) = p$. By construction of $\mathcal{M}(H)$, $\langle s, p, o \rangle$ is a triple of H. The interpolation lemma asserts that $\langle \alpha(s), p, \alpha(o) \rangle$ is a triple of G. By construction of $\mathcal{M}(G)$, it contains an arc a' such that $\gamma(a') = \langle m(\alpha(s)), m(\alpha(o)) \rangle$ and $\epsilon(a') = p$. We have $\epsilon(a') = p \leq_1 \epsilon(a) = p$ and, by definition of π, $\gamma(a') = \langle \pi(m(s)), \pi(m(o)) \rangle$. $\square$

($\Leftarrow$) Suppose a $\leq_1$-M-morphism from $\mathcal{M}(H)$ into $\mathcal{M}(G)$. Let us consider the mapping $\alpha : \mathcal{V}(H) \to V$ defined as follows: for every node $m(b)$ in $\mathcal{M}(H)$ labelled by a blank, $\alpha(b) = \epsilon(\pi(m(b)))$, for every node $m(x) \in M(H)$ labelled by an uriref or a literal, $\alpha(x) = x$. The mapping α is an instance mapping. It remains to prove that $H_\alpha \subseteq G$. Let us consider an arbitrary triple $\langle \alpha(s), p, \alpha(o) \rangle \in H_\alpha$. We have to prove that this triple is an element of G. By construction of $\mathcal{M}(H)$, there exists an arc a of $\mathcal{M}(H)$ such that $\gamma(a) = \langle m(\alpha(s)), m(\alpha(o)) \rangle$ and $\epsilon(a) = p$. By definition of an homomorphism, there exists an arc $a' \in \mathcal{M}(G)$ with $\gamma(a') = \langle \pi(m(\alpha(s))), \pi(m(\alpha(o))) \rangle$ and $\epsilon(a') \leq_1 \epsilon(a)$. Since it is an uriref, $\epsilon(a) = \epsilon(a') = p$. See that for every entity $e \in H$, $\pi(m(\alpha(e))) = m(\alpha(e))$. If e is a uriref or a literal, $\alpha(e) = e$, and we have to prove that $\pi(m(e)) = m(e)$. It is true because there is a unique node in $\mathcal{M}(G)$ labelled by e, and the node labelled by e in $\mathcal{M}(H)$ must be mapped into it.[2] If e is a blank, then $\alpha(e) = \epsilon(\pi(m(e)))$ (by definition of α). Then $m(\alpha(e)) = m(\epsilon(\pi(m(e)))) = \pi(m(e))$. It follows that $\gamma(a') = \langle m(\alpha(s)), m(\alpha(o)) \rangle$ and finally, that the triple $\langle \alpha(s), p, \alpha(o) \rangle$ (used to obtain a') is in G. $\square$

---

[2] The reader familiar with conceptual graphs will recognize here the requirement for a normality condition.

A first interest of this reformulation is in a representational point of view: in FIG. 3, not only data is graphically represented, but also inferences (the drawing of the morphism that caracterizes entailment). Experiences in the CG community (*e.g.* [8]) show that these "graphical inferences" are very easy to understand for non-specialists in logics or computer science. We will also show (in Sect. 5) that this reformulation offer great benefits for computational purposes.

4   RDF Triplesets as Directed, Labelled Hypergraphs

But before that, we will focus on another encoding of RDF triplesets (as hypergraphs). A different representation of RDF triplesets (as bipartite graphs) has been proposed in [9]. Its main advantage is its proximity to the tripleset's semantics. Here we use this representation (these bipartite graphs are the incidence bipartites associated with our hypergraphs, so they can be considered as the same mathematical objects) also for a reasoning purpose. Indeed we use a transformation of RDF triplesets into hypergraphs (as in [9]) as well as a transformation of interpretations into the same hypergraphs.

A first result (Lemma 2) shows that an interpretation I is a model for a tripleset G iff there is a morphism from the hypergraph associated with G into the one associated with H. The immediate interests are twofold: it provides us with a clear graphical representation of interpretations (extending the representation in [9] to interpretations), and, in the same way as in the previous section, it is a graphical representation of the proof that an interpretation is a model of a tripleset.

The same morphism, this time between two graphs associated with triplesets, is used to caracterize simple RDF entailment (Theorem 3). It shows how the graphs in [9] can be used for reasonings. Finally, we show the equivalence between this caracterization and the one used in Theorem 2, effectively providing another proof for the Interpolation Lemma.

Let us now discuss about the proof of Theorem 3 itself. It is grounded on a very simple framework. Let us consider a logic $\mathcal{L}$ (here simple RDF). Let us consider a set $\mathcal{E}$ (here the hypergraphs), and a transitive relation $\sqsubseteq$ (here the existence of a morphism) on $\mathcal{E}$. Let us now introduce a transformation $\mathcal{H}$ associating an element of $\mathcal{E}$ to each formula and each interpretation of $\mathcal{L}$. This transformation must satisfy the following criteria:

1. i is a model of f if and only if $\mathcal{H}(f) \sqsubseteq \mathcal{H}(i)$;
2. for every satisfiable formula f of $\mathcal{L}$, there exists a model i of f such that $\mathcal{H}(i) = \mathcal{H}(f)$.

These two criteria are then sufficient to prove that $\sqsubseteq$ is sound and complete w.r.t. entailment of $\mathcal{L}$, *i.e.* that $f \models f'$ iff $f' \sqsubseteq f$. Lemma 2 expresses the first condition, and lemma 3 the second. Theorem 3 reformulates this soundness and completeness result in the case of RDF triplesets.

Note that this framework has been successfully applied for conceptual graphs [10], and remains valid for many extensions of simple RDF: we show in the next section how it can be extended to RDF/RDFS, but it could also be used for the extensions presented in [2]. A Master's thesis is actually devoted in our team, using this framework, to extend RDF entailment to path queries.

4.1   Preliminary Definitions

Definition 8 (Directed, Labelled Hypergraph). *A directed labelled hyper-graph (or H-graph) over a set of terms V is a triple $G = \langle N, H, \epsilon \rangle$ where N is a finite set of* nodes, *$H \subseteq N^+$ is a finite set of* hyperarcs, *and $\epsilon : N \cup H \to V$ maps each node and hyperarc to an element of the set of terms.*

An H-graph can be represented as follows: a node is represented by a rectangle in which we write its label. An hyperarc $\langle x - 1, ..., x_p \rangle$ is represented by an oval in which we write its label. For $1 \leq i \leq p$, we draw a line between the oval and the rectangle associated with the node x_i, and write the number i next to this line to indicate the ordering of this tuple. We have chosen this representation by analogy with conceptual graphs (indeed, the CG semantically equivalent to a tripleset has the same representation as this hypergraph).

We must now update our morphisms to this new structure. The following lemma handles the required transitivity of the binary relation associated with the existence of a morphism.

Definition 9 (Directed, Labelled Hypergraph Homomorphism). *Let $G = \langle N, H, \epsilon \rangle$ and $G' = \langle N', H', \epsilon' \rangle$ be two H-graphs over a set of terms V. Let $\leq$ be a preorder over V. A* directed, labelled hypergraph homomorphism according to $\leq$ (or $\leq$-H-morphism) *from G into G' is a mapping $\pi : N \to N'$ that preserves the preorder on labels as well as incidence of hyperarcs, i.e.:*

1. *for each $n \in N$, $\epsilon'(\pi(n)) \leq \epsilon(n)$;*
2. *for each $h = \langle n_1, \ldots, n_k \rangle \in H$, $\exists a' = \langle \pi(n_1), \ldots, \pi(n_k) \rangle \in H'$ such that $\epsilon'(a') \leq \epsilon(a)$.*

Lemma 1 (Composition). *The composition of two $\leq$-H-morphisms is a $\leq$-H-morphism.*

Proof. Let G_1, G_2, G_3 be three H-graphs over a set of terms V. Let $\leq$ be a preorder on V. Let π_1 (resp. π_2) be a $\leq$-H-morphism according to $\leq$ from G_1 into G_2 (resp. from G_2 into G_3). We prove that $\pi_2 \circ \pi_1$ is a $\leq$-H-morphism from G_1 into G_3.

1. Let n be a node of G_1. We have $\epsilon(\pi_1(n)) \leq \epsilon(n)$ and $\epsilon(\pi_2(\pi_1(n))) \leq \epsilon(\pi_1(n))$ (def. of H-morphism). Since a preorder is transitive, $\epsilon(\pi_2(\pi_1(n))) \leq \epsilon(n)$.
2. Let $h_1 = \langle n_1, \ldots, n_p$ be an hyperarc of G_1. Then there exists an hyperarc $h_2 = \langle \pi_1(n_1), \ldots, \pi_1(n_p) \rangle$ of G_2 with $\epsilon(h_2) \leq \epsilon(h_1)$ (def. of H-morphism). Similarly, there exists an hyperarc $h_3 = \langle \pi_2(\pi_1(n_1)), \ldots, \pi_2(\pi_1(n_p)) \rangle$ with $\epsilon(h_3) \leq \epsilon(h_2)$. We also conclude thanks to the transitivity of $\leq$.   □

4.2   Hypergraph Representation of a Simple Interpretation

Let $I = \langle I_R, I_P, \iota_{ext}, \iota_s, \iota_l \rangle$ be an interpretation of a set of terms V. We associate
to this interpretation an H-graph $\mathcal{H}(I) = \langle N, H, \epsilon \rangle$ built as follows:

1. To each resource $r \in I_R \cup I_P$ we associate a distinct node $h(r)$. Then $N =$
   $\{h(r) \mid r \in I_R \cup I_P\}$. Each of these nodes will be labelled by a subset of V.
   Intuitively, $\epsilon(h(x)) = \{v_1, \ldots, v_k\}$ means that $v_1, \ldots, v_k$ are all the terms of
   V interpreted by the resource or property x in I. Let us now formally build
   this labelling: each node is initially labelled by the emptyset $\{\}$. Then for
   each element x of V:
     – if x is a plain literal in $\mathcal{L}_P(V)$, $\epsilon(h(x)) = \epsilon(h(x)) \cup \{x\}$;
     – if x is a typed literal in $\mathcal{L}_T(V)$, $\epsilon(h(\iota_l(x))) = \epsilon(h(\iota_l(x))) \cup \{x\}$;
     – if x is an uriref in $\mathcal{U}(V)$, $\epsilon(h(\iota_s(x))) = \epsilon(h(\iota_s(x))) \cup \{x\}$;
     – otherwise, if x is a blank in $\mathcal{B}(V)$, do nothing.
2. For each element $p \in I_P$, for each pair $\langle x, y \rangle \in \iota_{ext}(p)$, there exists an
   hyperarc $\langle h(x), h(p), h(y) \rangle$ in H labelled by $\{iext\}$.

Example 10. Fig. 4 shows the representation of the H-graph associated with
the interpretation of Ex. 2. This representation is simpler than the usual one
(Fig. 1), and highlights the structure of the interpretation. However we have lost
information on the set I_P, since a node that is not the second argument of an
hyperarc may belong to I_P or not (though this information is never needed).

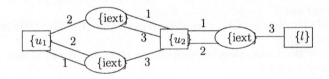

Fig. 4. The H-graph associated with an interpretation

4.3   Hypergraph Representation of an RDF Tripleset

Let G be an RDF tripleset. The directed, labelled hypergraph $\mathcal{H}(G) = \langle N, H, \epsilon \rangle$
associated with G is built as follows:

1. To each element $e \in \mathcal{V}(G)$ we associate a distinct node $h(e)$. Then $N =$
   $\{h(e) \mid e \in \mathcal{V}(G)\}$. As for the hypergraph associated with an interpretation,
   each node h(e) is labelled by a set. This set is the emptyset if e is a blank
   and the singleton $\{e\}$ otherwise.
2. To each triple $t = \langle s, p, o \rangle \in G$ we associate a distinct hyperarc $h(t) =$
   $\langle h(s), h(p), h(o) \rangle$. Then $H = \{\langle h(s), h(p), h(o) \rangle \mid \langle s, p, o \rangle \in G\}$. The label of
   the arc h(t) is $\{iext\}$.

Example 11. Fig. 5 shows the H-graph associated with the RDF tripleset H of
Ex. 1.

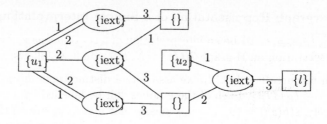

Fig. 5. The H-graph associated with an RDF tripleset

4.4   Simple Entailment as an Hypergraph Homomorphism

Lemma 2. *Let G be an RDF tripleset, and V be a set of terms that contains the set of terms of G. Let $\leq_2$ be the partial order defined by $e \leq_2 e' \Leftrightarrow e' \subseteq e$. An interpretation I of V is a model of G iff there exists a $\leq_2$-H-morphism from $\mathcal{H}(G)$ into $\mathcal{H}(I)$.*

Proof. We successively prove both directions of the equivalence.

$(\Rightarrow)$ Let us consider a model $I = \langle I_R, I_P, \iota_{ext}, \iota_s, \iota_l \rangle$ of G. We have to show that there exists a $\leq_2$-H-morphism from $\mathcal{H}(G)$ into $\mathcal{H}(I)$. Since I is a model of G, there exists a mapping $\iota : V(G) \to I_R \cup I_P$ that respects the 5 conditions listed in Def. 3. We build the mapping π from the nodes of $\mathcal{H}(G)$ into the nodes of $\mathcal{H}(I)$ as follows: if $h(x)$ is a node of G, then $\pi(h(x)) = h(\iota(x))$. It remains to show that π is a $\leq_2$-H-morphism.

1. Let $h(x)$ be a node of x. Let us show that $\epsilon(\pi(h(x))) \leq_2 \epsilon(h(x))$, i.e. $\epsilon(h(x)) \subseteq \epsilon(\pi(h(x)))$.
   - if x is a blank, then by construction $\epsilon(h(x)) = \emptyset$ and is thus a subset of any other set;
   - otherwise, by construction, $\epsilon(h(x)) = \{x\}$. It remains only to check that x is an element of $\epsilon(\pi(h(x))) = \epsilon(h(\iota(x)))$. If x is a plain literal, then $\iota(x) = x$ and the label of $h(\iota(x))$ contains x. If x is an uriref (resp. a typed literal), $\iota(x) = \iota_s(x)$ (resp. $\iota_l(x)$). Then the label of $h(\iota(x))$ also contains x.

2. Let us now prove that for every hyperarc $a = \langle h(s), h(p), h(o) \rangle \in \mathcal{H}(G)$, there exists an hyperarc $a' = \langle \pi(h(s)), \pi(h(p)), \pi(h(o)) \rangle \in \mathcal{H}(I)$. If such an hyperarc exists, it will be easy to check that $\epsilon(a') \leq_2 \epsilon(a)$: all hyperarcs are labelled by $\{iext\}$. Since $a = \langle h(s), h(p), h(o) \rangle \in \mathcal{H}(G)$, then by construction there must be a triple $\langle s, p, o \rangle$ in G. Thus (Def. 3) $\langle \iota(s), \iota(o) \rangle \in \iota_{ext}(\iota(p))$. By construction of $\mathcal{H}(I)$, it contains an hyperarc $\langle h(\iota(s)), h(\iota(p)), h(\iota(o)) \rangle$. And by construction of π, this hyperarc is exactly $\langle \pi(h(s)), \pi(h(p)), \pi(h(o)) \rangle$. □

$(\Leftarrow)$ Now let us consider a $\leq_2$-H-morphism π from $\mathcal{H}(G)$ into $\mathcal{H}(I)$. We build a mapping $\iota : V(G) \to I_R \cup I_P$ as follows: for each node $h(x)$ of $\mathcal{H}(G)$, consider the node $h(y)$ of $\mathcal{H}(I)$ such that $h(y) = \pi(h(x))$. Then $\iota(x) = y$. It remains now to prove that ι satisfies the 5 conditions of Def. 3. For each node $h(x)$ of $\mathcal{H}(G)$, we consider the node $h(y)$ of $\mathcal{H}(I)$ such that $h(y) = \pi(h(x))$.
   - If x is a plain literal, we must prove that $\iota(x) = x$. By construction, $\iota(x) = y$. We know that $h(x)$ is labelled by $\{x\}$. Since π maps $h(x)$ into $h(y)$, $x \in \epsilon(h(y))$ and thus, by construction of $\mathcal{H}(I)$, $x = y = \iota(x)$.

- If x is a typed literal, we must prove that $\iota(x) = \iota_l(x)$. By construction, $\iota(x) = y$. As before, $x \in \epsilon(h(y))$. By construction of $\mathcal{H}(I)$, $\iota_l(x) = y = \iota(x)$.
- If x is an uriref, proceed as for typed literals (replacing ι_l with ι_s).
- If x is a blank, then x is the subject or object of a triple of G. Thus $h(x)$ is the first or third argument of an hyperarc of $\mathcal{H}(G)$. Since π is a H-morphism, $\pi(h(x) = h(y)$ is the first or third argument of an hyperarc of $\mathcal{H}(I)$. By definition of ι_{ext}, $y = \iota(x) \in I_R$.
- Let us now prove that, for every triple $\langle s, p, o \rangle \in G$, $\langle \iota(s), \iota(o) \rangle \in \iota_{ext}(\iota(p))$. If $\langle x_s, x_p, x_o \rangle \in G$, then, by construction of $\mathcal{H}(G)$, there exists an hyperarc $\langle h(x_s), h(x_p), h(x_o) \rangle$ of $\mathcal{H}(G)$. Since π is a H-morphism, the hyperarc $\langle \pi(h(x_s)), \pi(h(x_p)), \pi(h(x_o)) \rangle = \langle h(y_s), h(y_p), h(y_o) \rangle$ is an hyperarc of $\mathcal{H}(I)$. By construction of $\mathcal{H}(I)$, $\langle y_s, y_o \rangle \in \iota_{ext}(y_p)$, i.e.: $\langle \iota(x_s), \iota(x_o) \rangle \in \iota_{ext}(\iota(x_p))$. □

Lemma 3 (Isomorphic Interpretation). *Let G be an RDF tripleset. Then there exists an interpretation I of G such that $\mathcal{H}(I) = \mathcal{H}(G)$.*

Proof. By "reverse engineering" the transformation $\mathcal{H}$, we can build from $\mathcal{H}(G)$ an interpretation I such that $\mathcal{H}(I) = \mathcal{H}(G)$. To each node in $\mathcal{H}(G)$ we associate a resource of I_R (note that we impose $I_P \subseteq I_R$). For each node x, for each term $e \in \epsilon(x)$, we impose the term e to be interpreted (via ι_s or ι_l) by the resource associated with x. Finally, for each hyperarc $\langle s, p, o \rangle$ in $\mathcal{H}(G)$, we add the pair of resources associated with s and o to the extension of the resource asssociated with p. It is immediate to chack that, by applying $\mathcal{H}$ to that interpretation, we obtain the H-graph $\mathcal{H}(G)$ (or more precisely, the H-graph isomorphic to it).

Corollary 1. *Each RDF tripleset is satisfiable.*

Proof. Since there always exists a H-morphism from a graph into itself, we conclude thanks to Lem. 2 that the isomorphic interpretation of any RDF tripleset G is a model of G. Thus G is satisfiable.

Theorem 3. *Let G and H be two RDF triplesets defined over a set of terms V. Then $G \models H$ if and only if there is a $\leq_2$-H-morphism from $\mathcal{H}(H)$ into $\mathcal{H}(G)$.*

Proof. We prove both directions of the equivalence.

($\Rightarrow$) Let us suppose that $G \models H$. It means that every model of G is also a model of H. In particular, the isomorphic interpretation I of G (see Lem. 3), being a model of G, is also a model of H. Thanks to Lem. 2, it means that there exists a $\leq_2$-H-morphism from $\mathcal{H}(H)$ into $\mathcal{H}(I) = \mathcal{H}(G)$. □

($\Leftarrow$) Let us suppose that there exists a $\leq_2$-H-morphism π from $\mathcal{H}(H)$ into $\mathcal{H}(G)$. We have to prove that every model of G is also a model of H. Let us consider an arbitrary model M of G. Thanks to Lem. 2, there exists a $\leq_2$-H-morphism π' from $\mathcal{H}(G)$ into $\mathcal{H}(M)$. We use Lem. 1 to show that $\pi' \circ \pi$ is a $\leq_2$-H-morphism from $\mathcal{H}(H)$ into $H(G)$. Finally, we conclude (Lem. 2) that M is also a model of H. □

4.5   Relationships with Multigraphs

This section finishes with this last theorem, asserting the equivalence of M-morphisms and H-morphisms for RDF simple entailment. Since the proof is immediate, it is left out. It means that we can use indifferently M-graphs or H-graphs for computing entailments, or for checking if an interpretation is a model for a tripleset. It is also the final step providing another proof for the interpolation lemma.

Theorem 4. *Let G and H be two RDF triplesets defined over a set of terms V. Then there is a directed, labelled hypergraph homomorphism from $\mathcal{H}(H)$ into $\mathcal{H}(G)$ according to $\leq_2$ if and only if there is a directed, labelled multigraph homomorphism from $\mathcal{M}(H)$ into $\mathcal{M}(G)$ according to $\leq_1$.*

5   Complexity and Algorithms

It is now well known that SIMPLE RDF ENTAILMENT (deciding whether or not an RDF tripleset simply entails another one) is a NP-complete problem. It has been proven via the equivalence with conceptual graphs [6, 7] or via a reduction to graph colouring [2]. Thus checking if an interpretation is a model for an RDF tripleset is also an NP-complete problem (we have shown here that they were the same problem). The latter author also provides us with a polynomial case for SIMPLE RDF ENTAILMENT: when there is no blank node in the entailee H.

We present here links and guidelines allowing to quickly translate results obtained in other knowledge representation communities (namely conceptual graphs and constraint programming), thanks to our reformulation of entailment as a graph homomorphism.

5.1   Constraint Networks and Polynomial Cases

The relationships between homomorphisms, conceptual graphs projection and constraint satisfaction problems allow to obtain much more interesting polynomial cases. Let us consider here the following equivalences:

1. the RDF tripleset G simply entails the RDF tripleset H
2. there is a $\leq_1$-M-morphism from $\mathcal{M}(H)$ into $\mathcal{M}(G)$
3. there is projection from the conceptual graph $\mathcal{C}(\mathcal{M}(H))$ into $\mathcal{C}(\mathcal{M}(G))$
4. the constraint network $\mathcal{N}(\mathcal{C}(\mathcal{M}(H)), \mathcal{C}(\mathcal{M}(G)))$ is satisfiable.

We do not have the place here to explicit the transformations involved, though it should be done in an extended version of this paper. 1) $\equiv$ 2) is proven in this paper, 2) $\equiv$ 3) is proven in [7], and 3) $\equiv$ 4) is proven in [11]. The interesting point is that these transformations are polynomial, and that the graphs $\mathcal{M}(H)$, $\mathcal{C}(\mathcal{M}(H))$ and $\mathcal{N}(\mathcal{C}(\mathcal{M}(H)), \mathcal{C}(\mathcal{M}(G)))$ have exactly the *same structure*. So every polynomial case based upon the structure of a constraint network or upon the structure of the projected conceptual graph immediately translates into a polynomial case based upon the structure of the entailee in simple RDF.

Both conceptual graphs projection [12] and constraint network satisfiability [13] have been proven polynomial when the graphs are trees. It follows naturally that SIMPLE RDF ENTAILMENT is polynomial when the entailee M-graph is a tree. A lot of work has been produced in the constraint satisfaction community to generalize this result: more general cases (using hypertree decompositions) are listed in [14], all can be directly translated to SIMPLE RDF ENTAILMENT.

5.2 Algorithms

Since the Backtrack algorithm used to solve constraint satisfaction problems rely on the structure of the associated graph, the same algorithm optimizations can be used for the SIMPLE RDF ENTAILMENT. Some of these optimizations have been selected in [10] (in the conceptual graph formalism). The main point is that these optimizations do not require any overhead cost. These algorithms are considered as very efficient outside the phase transition.

6   Conclusion and Perspectives

We have presented here a reformulation of simple RDF entailment as a graph homomorphism. The standalone proof of soundness and correctness is used as a new proof of the interpolation lemma.This proof can be used as a framework to study reasoning engines for extensions of simple RDF. Though we have shown that a benefit of our reformulation was to offer the end-user with a graphical illustration of reasonings, our main interest resides in using the graph structure for an optimization purpose. The links we establish between RDF entailment, graph homomorphism, conceptual graphs projection and constraint satisfaction problems are an important step in that direction.

However, RDF is a language developped for the web. And the specific problem that will be encountered is the huge size of the data. The RDF WEB ENTAILMENT problem should be presented as follows: given a RDF tripleset (a query) Q, is there a set of RDF triplesets $G_1, ..., G_2$ available on the (semantic) web such that they entail Q? Though there is no theoretical problem (we have just to compute whether the merge of $G_1, ..., G_2$ entails Q), it is doubtful that it will be possible to compute the merge of all triplesets available on the web. [15] provides us with an algorithm that remains sound and complete without merging the graphs (in conceptual graphs terms, when the target is not in nortmal form). Moreover, this algorithm is less efficient than the standard backtrack, and do not benefit effectively from the above mentioned optimizations. This example, among other, shows that, though RDF ENTAILMENT can benefit from results obtained in similar formalisms, its new feature (a language designed for the web) leads to particular problems that we should take into account.

References

[1] Hayes, P.: RDF Semantics. W3C Recommendation (2004)
    http://www.w3.org/TR/2004/REC-rdf-mt-20040210/.
[2] ter Horst, H.J.: Extending the RDFS Entailment Lemma. In: Proceedings of the Third International Semantic Web Conference, ISWC'04. Volume 3298 of LNCS., Springer (2004) 77–91

[3] Hahn, G., Tardif, C.: Graph homomorphisms: structure and symmetry. In: Graph Symmetry. Number 497 in NATO Adv. Sci. Inst. Ser. C. Math. Phys. Sci. (1997) 107–166

[4] Chein, M., Mugnier, M.L.: Conceptual Graphs: fundamental notions. Revue d'Intelligence Artificielle **6** (1992) 365–406

[5] Montanari, U.: Networks of Constraints: Fundamental Notions and Application to Picture Processing. Information Sciences **7** (1974) 95–132

[6] Corby, O., Dieng, R., Hebert, C.: A Conceptual Graph Model for W3C Resource Description Framework. In: International Conference on Conceptual Structures. (2000) 468–482

[7] Baget, J.F.: Homomorphismes d'hypergraphes pour la subsomption en RDF/RDFS. In: 10e conférence sur langages et modèles à objets (LMO). Volume 10. (2004) 203–216

[8] Genest, D.: Extensions du modèle des graphes conceptuels pour la recherche d'informations. PhD thesis, Université de Montpellier II (2000)

[9] Hayes, J., Guttiérrez, C.: Bipartite Graphs as Intermediate Model for RDF. In: Proceedings of the Third International Semantic Web Conference, ISWC'04. Volume 3298 of LNCS., Springer (2004) 47–61

[10] Baget, J.F.: Simple conceptual graphs revisited: hypergraphs and conjunctive types for efficient projection algorithms. In: 11th international conference on conceptual sructures (ICCS). Number 2870 in LNCS, Springer (2003) 195–208

[11] Mugnier, M.L.: Knowledge Representation and Reasonings Based on Graph Homomorphism. In: 8th International Conference on Conceptual Structures (ICCS'00). Volume 1867 of LNCS., Springer (2000) 172–192

[12] Mugnier, M.L., Chein, M.: Polynomial algorithms for projection and matching. In: Selected Papers from AWCG'92. Volume 754 of LNAI., Springer (1993)

[13] Freuder, E.: A sufficient condition for backtrack-free search. Journal of the ACM **29** (1982) 24–32

[14] Gottlob, G., Leone, N., Scarcello, F.: A comparison of structural decomposition methods. (1999)

[15] Guinaldo, O., Haemmerlé, O.: Knowledge querying in the conceptual graphs model: the RAP module. In: Proc. of ICCS. 98. LNCS, (Springer) 287–294

RitroveRAI: A Web Application for Semantic Indexing and Hyperlinking of Multimedia News[*]

Roberto Basili, Marco Cammisa, and Emanuale Donati

University of Roma, Tor Vergata, Department of Computer Science,
Via del Politecnico snc, 00133, Roma
{basili, cammisa, donati}@info.uniroma2.it

Abstract. In this paper, a system, RitroveRAI, addressing the general problem of enriching a multimedia news stream with semantic metadata is presented. News metadata here are explicitly derived from transcribed sentences or implicitly expressed into a topical category automatically detected. The enrichment process is accomplished by searching the same news expressed by different agencies reachable over the Web. Metadata extraction from the alternative sources (i.e. Web pages) is similarly applied and finally integration of the sources (according to some heuristic of pertinence) is carried out. Performance evaluation of the current system prototype has been carried out on a large scale. It confirms the viability of the RitroveRAI approach for realistic (i.e. 24 hours) applications and continuous monitoring and metadata extraction from multimedia news data.

1 Introduction

Web services actually tend to offer functional and non-functional requirements and capabilities in an agreed, machine-readable format. The target is the support to automated service discovery, selection and binding as a native capability of middleware and applications. However, major limitations are due to the lack of clear and processable semantics. Multimedia data are even more critical as semantics often depends on multiple and independent aspects: *functional information*, e.g. data format and processing constraints, *application criteria*, e.g. the different commercial constraints that may be applied, as well as *content information*, e.g. the *topics* to which a TV program refer or the *genre* of a song or video clip. In particular audio-visual data suffer from the fact that they are particularly rich in content and the level of semantic description is not easily detected from the different co-operating information (the video content vs. the environment sound as well as speaker's comments) that give rise to a variety of abstraction levels.

Methods of Information Extraction from multimedia data have thus to face specific problems in order to support realistic Semantic Web scenarios:

---

[*] The research work presented in this paper has been partially funded by the PrestoSpace IST Integrated Project, n. IST-FP6-507336.

Y. Gil et al. (Eds.): ISWC 2005, LNCS 3729, pp. 97–111, 2005.

- They must capture *levels of abstraction* able to express content at the visual level as well as at the sound (or speech) level
- Given the richness of the audio-visual information and the usually large size of target archives they must be *efficient* and *scalable*
- They should be as much *adaptable* as possible even in the early development phases in order to afford problems of realistic size. In particular, methods of machine learning for the construction of the required large knowledge bases and rule sets are needed.
- They must be robust with respect to noise and complexity (often incompleteness) of the source data

For the above reasons, extraction of audio-visual semantic metadata is thus a critical problem for a large class of Semantic Web applications. In the PrestoSpace[1] project (IST Integrated Project, n. IST-FP6-507336) the problem of preservation of the huge archives of European audio-visual providers (i.e. BBC, RAI and INA) through systematic digitalisation and restoration techniques has been pursued. In this scenario, the need for making digitised data accessible through intelligent information retrieval interfaces has been approached by the automation of semantic metadata extraction from raw material. Ontological resources are thus also used as a reference model for extraction and ontology-based and multilingual retrieval.

In this paper a system, RitroveRAI, developed for the semantic metadata extraction from TV and radio broadcasted news, is presented. It realizes the semantic extraction component of the overall PrestoSpace solution to preservation and indexing of audio-visual material: it is actually implemented for Italian over the data of the RAI TV channel. The RitroveRAI system makes use of human language technologies for IE over multimedia data (i.e. speech recognition and grammatical analysis of incoming news). News are topically categorised by means of a statistical categorizer. IE results are then exploited to find on the Web texts/pages equivalent (or weakly equivalent) to source news: this aims to extend the metadata derived from news with systematic material available on the aligned Web texts. Finally integration of internal (i.e. expressed by the source news) as well as external (as found on the Web) information produces the final set of metadata published with the digitised news.

The next section will introduce the overall approach by discussion the architecture of the current RitroveRAI prototype. Then advanced aspects like automatic (machine learning driven) categorisation of news, enrichment of broadcasted news via Web alignment and mining, will be discussed. Finally, performance evaluation results over large data sets will be reported to drive the final discussion.

2 An Approach to Metadata Indexing Based on HLT and the Web

The source information in RitroveRAI system have a well identifiable topic related to the content, i.e. the events and participants to which the reported news refer. Methods of extraction can use some visual information (in TV news) but are mainly tight to the

---

[1] URL: http://www.prestospace.org/index.en.html

speaker output. This is captured by a speech recognition system that initiates the processing chain. Some preprocessing focuses on the segmentation of source programs into individual news relying on special content features like the time span of silence intervals, detected changes in the speaker's voice or program schemes (e.g. alternating videos and studio contributions). The approach discussed in this paper refers to all the remaining Information Extraction and Web mining steps up to the final metadata publishing and browsing facilities. Figure 1 reports the overall client-server architecture.

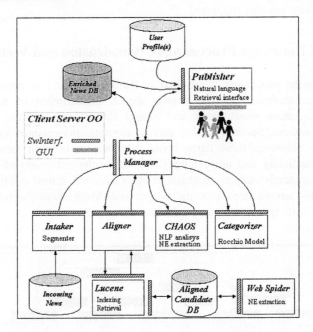

Fig. 1. The RitroveRAI Client-Server Architecture

The workflow processing is organized around a modular client-server architecture coordinated by a glueware module, called the *"Process Manager"*. A second independent server is the *Web Spider*. It is based on the Google's API and retrieves all the documents published by a reference content provider (i.e. a journal) within a time window centered on the day of the news transmission. Finally a linguistic processing server, called *CHAOS* [2,4], makes available grammatical recognition capabilities over both transcriptions and Web pages.

The Information Extraction chain applies first the *Intaker* module. It collects and normalizes the incoming broadcasted news as they are transcribed and segmented by the speech recognition tool. The result of the intaking process is the update of news and segments into an internal DB structure responsible of supporting all the later processing stages. Then, the *Categorization* module is invoked by the Process Manager over the intaken news: it returns the pertinent topical categories (with their associated confidences) according to the RAI internal classification scheme. Concurrently, the *Aligner* module selects the candidates equivalent news from those extracted by the *Web Spider* process. This starts from the transcriptions parsed by the

CHAOS server. Web pages are also parsed[2] and indexed according to traditional IR models. For each news item, the *Alignment* process selects the Web pages from a set of candidate ones, i.e. those made available by the Web Spider, and create direct hyperlinks to them. This also allows to include auxiliary more precise metadata as those associated to the aligned news in order to prune the possibly irrelevant information[3]. Whenever internal and external metadata are made available, customized browsing (i.e. navigation through a user-specific hypertext built over the processed news) is allowed by a specialized *Web browsing interface*. Queries in Natural Language are also supported.

3   Natural Language Processing of Broadcasted and Web News

Natural Language processing is required in RitroveRAI for two purposes. First it enables the extraction from the source speech transcription of a number of phenomena: common nouns, verbs and Named Entities (e.g. person, location and organization names). Second, it also derives semantic information from the Web aligned news. However, these latter, being them written in plain natural language (i.e. not automatically and noisy transcribed) allow the extraction of grammatical relations: for example subject or object relation between named entities and verb. Notice that this has an impact on the system knowledge about the role played by individuals as participants to the target facts of the news.

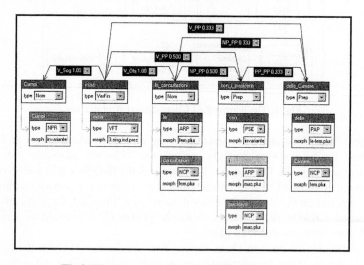

Fig 2. The dependency graph of an Italian sentence

---

[2] The parsing process is different in the two cases as automatic transcriptions follow less rigidly linguistic well-formedness criteria so that specific grammatical and lexical rules are required.
[3] When mistakes made by the speech recognizer over incoming transcriptions affect the quality of the source metadata, external, i.e. Web originated, metadata can be used to validate the former and compensate such errors.

Linguistic extraction is carried out by a Natural language parser called CHAOS [2,4]. Chaos is a server for modular and lexicalized parsing based on a cascade of morphosyntactic recognisers. The main CHAOS modules are: the *Tokenizer*, the *morphological analyzer* (who identifies the possible morphological interpretation of every token), a *part of speech tagger*, a *named entity recognizer*, a *chunker* (who collects possibly multiple tokens to form bigger grammatical and unambiguous units called *chunks*), the *temporal expressions recognizer*, a *verb subcategorization analyzer* (for the recognition of the main verbal dependencies) and a *shallow syntactic analyzer* (for the recognition of remaining and possibly ambiguous dependency, e.g. prepositional modifiers of verbs and nouns).

In Fig. 2, as an example, the dependency graph (called XDG) for the Italian sentence

"Ciampi inizia le consultazioni con i presidenti delle camere"[4]

is reported.

The *eXtended Dependency Graph* (*XDG*) formalism, introduced in [4], represents, the recognized sentence as a planar graph, whose nodes are constituents and arcs the grammatical relationships between them. The constituents are chunks, i.e. kernels of verb phrases (VPK), noun phrases (NPK), prepositional phrases (PPK) and adjectival phrases (ADJK). Examples of PPK and NPK chunks in Fig. 2 are respectively *"con i presidenti"*[5] and *"le consultazioni"*[6]. Relations among the constituents represent grammatical functions among their syntactic heads: logical subject (*lsubj*), logical objects (*lobj*), and prepositional modifiers. More technical details on the CHAOS parser can be found in [4].

3.1 Two Parsing Models for RitroveRAI

The incoming broadcast news set, hereafter called N_I, and the published Web news set, hereafter N_E, must be distinguished, as introduced above, to apply different parsing strategies.

Several difficulties arise when Chaos is applied to the N_I set, due to its noisy nature. First, frequent misspellings characterize elements in N_I. This is very variable depending on the speed, clarity, pronounce of the speaker and by the quality of the signal.

Another problem is that all the misspellings are also correct words of the Italian language. This can lead to errors in the named entities extraction, because semantically odd entities are also introduced in the text.

A third problem is the absence of case information in the transcribed text. Most technologies for NE extraction are actually based on capitalized words.

Finally, text segments are generated automatically during the transcription process. Speeches are translated into "news units" by using time and intensity rules. When the audio signal goes under a specified lower intensity for a sufficient time interval a new

---

[4] *"Ciampi starts the counsels with the presidents of the Chambers"*.

[5] *"with the presidents"*.

[6] *"the counsels"*.

segment is initiated. These heuristics are not error free so that multiple news items may appear in a segment or, dually, a single news can be split into multiple (but less complete) segments. The segmentation process is a special case of the recognition of boundaries between distinct textual units in documents. Errors in this phase impact on the accuracy of all later processing steps in RitroveRAI.

CHAOS has been applied over the broadcasted news only to recognize a subset of grammatical data as wrong POS tagging is the general case: contexts are not reliable enough to trigger POS tagging rules. Here the recognition of basic distinctive information to support categorization and Web alignment is carried out. The transcription's parsing model supports shallow parsing including only the tokenizer and the morphological analyzer based on gazetteer lookup. Evaluation of the adopted design choice (Section "*Performance Evaluation*") confirms that such limited (but reliable) information is sufficient most of the times.

On the other hand, the Chaos full parsing cascade was applied with its full functionalities to the aligned Web news, i.e. the set N_E. This allowed to extract named entities as well as all their verbal relations from the N_E set. In this way Named Entities of the source news are confirmed (as they also appear in the aligned news found in the Web) but their role in the described fact is also captured most of the times. In the previous example we would know that (*Carlo Azeglio*) "*Ciampi*" (current President of the Italian Republic) is the agent initiating the counsels. This results in an higher abstraction level in the derivation of content metadata able to match more specific queries in future retrieval scenarios.

3.2 Recognizing Named Entities from Broadcasted News (NE$_I$ set)

Named Entities in the incoming transcribed segments are herefter called internal named entities , i.e. NE$_I$. As an example, in the following segment "*calling for democracy and freedom, the leaders of iraq's interim government today challenged the country's new national assembly to strive for unity president bush congratulated the people of iraq. "it was a hopeful moment", bush told reporters at the white house*", the following NE$_I$ list is derived: "*Iraq*", "*National Assembly*", "*Bush*", "*White House*". The gazetteers used by CHAOS are here used as a major source of information.

As a segment is to be categorized and then also aligned with other Web pages, it is also useful to recognize common nouns in the text. In the above example "*democracy*", "*leaders*", "*freedom*", "*government*", "*country*", "*people*" and "*reporters*" would be extracted. NE$_I$ and other nouns are a surrogate of the segment transcription useful for categorization and Web mining. We make use of this information to build an efficient search vector for Web retrieval. In order to distinguish the different importance of Named Entities and common nouns, we modified slightly the usual weighting scheme of the IR platform adopted (i.e. Lucene [5]). Common nouns n are given a weight equal to their document frequency (occ_n) (i.e. the default weight in Lucene syntax). Named Entities are instead amplified by a factor w, with a resulting weight of $w \cdot occ_n$. We found that different domains require different ratios w. In all our settings $w=4$ is used.

4   Machine Learning for Broadcasted News Categorization

Text categorization is a traditional supervised machine learning task. In RitroveRAI a the Rocchio model, as a profile based classifier, presented in [3], has been used. Given the set of training document R_i, classified under the topics C_i (positive examples), the set $\overline{R}_i$ of the documents not belonging to C_i (negative examples) and given a document d_h and a feature f, the Rocchio model [8,3] defines the weight Ω_f of f in the profile of C_i as:

$$\Omega^i_f = \max\left\{0, \frac{\beta}{|R_i|}\sum_{d_h \in R_i} \omega^h_f - \frac{\gamma}{|\overline{R}_i|}\sum_{d_h \in \overline{R}_i} \omega^h_f\right\} \tag{1}$$

where ω^h_f is the weight of the feature f in the document d_h. In formula (1), the parameters β and γ control the relative impact of positive and negative examples and determine the weight of f in the i-th profile. In [8], values $\beta=16$, $\gamma=4$ have been first used for the categorization of low quality images. These parameters indeed greatly depend on the training corpus and different settings of their values produce a significant variation in performances.

Notice that, in Equation (1), features with negative difference between positive and negative relevance are set to 0. This is an elegant feature selection method: the 0-valued features are irrelevant in the similarity estimation. As a result, the remaining features are optimally used, i.e. only for classes for which they are selective. In this way, the minimal set of truly irrelevant features (giving 0 values for all the classes) can be better captured and removed.

In [3] a modified Rocchio model is presented that makes use of a single parameter γ_i as follows:

$$\Omega^i_f = \max\left\{0, \frac{1}{|R_i|}\sum_{d_h \in R_i} \omega^h_f - \frac{\gamma_i}{|\overline{R}_i|}\sum_{d_h \in \overline{R}_i} \omega^h_f\right\} \tag{2}$$

Moreover, a practical method for estimating the suitable values of the γ_i vector has been introduced. Each category in fact has its own set of relevant and irrelevant features and Eq. (2) depends for each class i on γ_i. Now if we assume the optimal values of these parameters can be obtained by estimating their impact on the classification performance, nothing prevents us from deriving this estimation independently for each class i. This result in a vector of γ_i each one optimising the performance of the classifier over the i-th class. The estimation of the γ_i is carried out by a typical cross-validation process. Two data set are used: the training set (about 70% of the annotated data) and a validation set (about 30% of the remaining data). First the categorizer is trained on the training set, where feature weights (ω^d_f) are estimated. Then profile vectors Ω^i_f for the different classes are built by setting the parameters γ_i to those values optimising accuracy on the validation set. The resulting categorizer is then tested on separated test sets. Results on the Reuters benchmark are about 85%, close to state-of-art more complex classification models ([3]). In Section "*Performance Evaluation*" the results as measured on the transcribed RAI news will be discussed.

5 Extending Internal Metadata with Web Material

5.1 Collecting External Evidence from the Web: The N_E Set

In RitroveRAI the task of creating a N_E set is achieved by mining several Web sites of news providers. Indexed web pages provide external news sets for each provider N_E^1, N_E^2, ..., N_E^n. Finally, the $N_E = N_E^1 \cup N_E^2 \cup ... \cup N_E^n$ is the union of individual sets.

As a case of study, we considered only the Web site of the Italian newspaper "*La Repubblica*"[7]. It publishes news categorized by legacy metadata (e.g. a set of 8 newspaper categories). Moreover, it is refreshed as new articles are available with news items published in standard HTML and tagged with date information, e.g. "(January, 12, /2003)".

A simple spidering process has been developed, based on the Google's API, to retrieve all the documents published in a date. A temporal window is used. It is centered in the day of publication of the internal news and its symmetrical width is proportional to a parametric time span[8]. Accordingly, the temporal distance between the retrieved news and the source transcribed segment is considered as an inversely proportional ranking score. The main criteria is still the IR relevance score extended as follows.

The task of creating a link between elements in N_I and Web elements in N_E require to assess topical relevance and temporal proximity. Notice that the search vector extracted for internal news is used as a query for retrieval among the N_E set.

It is to be noticed that the IR engine is first run over a superset of the target Web pages in order to get general and reliable statistics for feature weighting (i.e. occ_n scores). Then the ranking function is modeled according to the following properties:

- Document similarity must be maximized
- The time distance D between the source segments and the Web page should be minimal
- The (RAI) topical category C^R of the segments should be coherent with the Repubblica category C^W for the Web news item

A comprehensive scoring model is as follows:

$$S(s,w) = sim(s,w) \cdot \frac{coh(C^R,C^W)}{D+1} \qquad s \in N_I, w \in N_E \qquad (3)$$

where *sim* is the relevance produced by Lucene, and *coh* is a static function (*coherence table*) that measures the topical similarity between different categories (RAI, C^R, and "*La Repubblica*", C^W, respectively). The role of D promotes the alignment of "facts" happened in the same days. The category similarity *coh* refines the score and it is 1 only if the categories are the same, and lower as long as they tend to diverge: for example, it is almost 0 between RAI "*Sport*" and "*La Repubblica*" "*Foreign Affair*".

---

[7] http://www.repubblica.it
[8] Currently a time span of 2 days are used. Web pages outside such [-2,2] range are not considered for alignment.

Given a segment s, the alignment with a Web candidate w is finally accepted whenever the score $S(s,w)$ is above a given acceptance threshold that has to be determined experimentally (see Section "*Performance Evaluation*").

5.2 Selecting Named Entities from Web Material: The NE_E Set

The aligned news provide evidence external to a segment able to trigger the extraction of more correct named entities as additional metadata.

The major problem in this phase is that the two source texts have quite different extensions. Usually Web data are excerpts of texts published on a newspaper and are longer: they discuss a "fact" in a broader way. This "additional" information is a suitable enrichment if:

- Misspellings in the transcriptions prevented the correct recognition of named entities that are alternatively found in the Web text;
- Time constraints in the TV news led to the exclusion of some relevant information (e.g. the name of a person entering into the underlying fact but not mentioned).

On the contrary, several aspects lead to consider carefully the external information:

- Newspaper articles discusses facts and opinions in a lengthy fashion, so that other facts and participants can be mentioned even when they are not directly related to the transcribed segment.
- The Web news are not perfectly aligned or time distance D is not 0: in this case new found named entities may be misleading.

The above observation lead us to apply filtering criteria to the acceptance of external Named Entities. A simple heuristic, based on a word distance metrics, has been developed.

An external Named Entity ne_e can be accepted if one of the following occurs:

- ne_e is also contained into the transcribed segment, i.e. $ne_e \in NE_I$;
- ne_e is repeated more than m times within the external Web news (appears to be central in the fact discussed in the aligned Web news);
- The named entity ne_e is close *enough* to other named entities that are also internal named entities, i.e. it exists one or more $n \in NE_I$ such that in the Web document

$$word\_dist(ne_e, n) < v$$

where v is a positive threshold. In this case the fact involving external and internal named entities is the same.

6 Publishing and Searching Enriched News

The publishing modules is responsible for showing the process results to the users, presenting them with a personalized profiles. The user logs in into the system identifying himself and implicitly declaring a filtering profile. This profile defines the categories of interests for the user.

The browser interface is shown in the following picture:

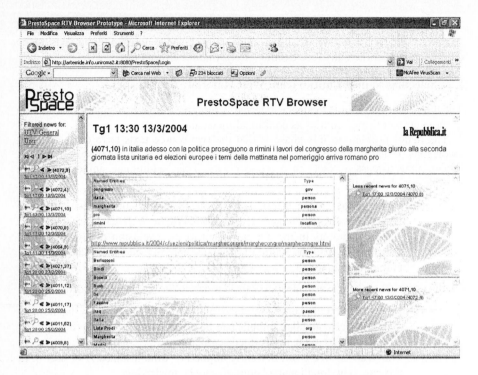

Fig. 3. A snapshot of the RitroveRAI browser

The left frame presents the entire broadcast news collection, with the ability to access to the audio recording. The user can access to the news information selecting its hyperlink. All the data associated to the news are shown in the central frame.

In the upper part of the central frame the transcribed segment is presented. The upper link refers to the best "*La Repubblica*" Web text aligned. The same link is shown in the middle of the bottom central frame (as a full URL).

Categorization is also reported in the bottom central frame as list of categories with their corresponding confidence factors (not visible in Fig. 3). The "legacy metadata" follow the categorization information, i.e. reporting data like the broadcasted segment, the day of recording, the TV channel or the tape IDs.

Finally, semantic metadata are presented (Fig 3, bottom central frame): one table for the internal metadata and one for the external ones. As we discussed before, the internal metadata are extracted using NLP over the broadcast news, and the external are collected using NLP over the aligned web news. These metadata are used to propose links to "related" broadcasted segments: in the right upper and bottom frames links are available to the set of less recent and more recent broadcasted news, respectively. These links are computed over the metadata and are built at run time according to user profiles.

7   Performance Evaluation: The RAI TV News

The RitroveRAI system has been tested on a large set of transcriptions from about one year of TV news (July 2003-June 2004). Segments of news have been used as source information units for metadata extraction. The corpus includes about 20,676 of such units. The validation has been carried out for two independent tasks: news categorisation and Web alignment. Performances in the two cases have been estimated by the standard measures of *recall* and *precision*. *F-measure* as the harmonic mean of the two values as well as the *Break-even Point (BEP)*, as the value for which recall is equal to precision, are also reported.

7.1 Evaluation of the RitroveRAI Text Categorization

The set of manually categorized news (annotated by RAI archivist) includes 1,861 segments. A split of 80% for training and 20% for testing has been imposed by random sampling the data set and balancing the different 26 RAI categories. Categories range from news specific classes (like *"Economics"* and *"Foreign Politics"*) to more general area like *"Health"*. Each news was assigned to one or more classes, so that 2,328 assignments were available with an average rate of 1.25 class per news item. News items are distributed evenly among categories, so that only 11 categories had more than 80 members, an amount sufficient for reliable training. Validation has thus been carried out in two fashions: first by measuring the selection of the system among all the 26 classes, and then by restricting the testing to only the 11 reliable classes. Results (as *BEP* points) are reported in Table 1 for the 11 reliable classes.

Performance of the categorizer are good considering that a small subset of the archived material from RAI has been used for training. In particular small data sets penalize the categories that are more general (i.e. *"Employment/Job"*) although more specific classes require less information to scale up to reasonable performances (e.g. *"Sport"*, *"Life and Religion"*). When enough material is available the performances confirm the results of benchmarking (e.g. *"Politics"*). Notice how these measures are only based on tokens (bag-of-word modeling) of the transcribed news and how this material includes a significant amount of noise. Moreover, real-time categorization is ensured by the Rocchio model that, compared to more sophisticated text categorization techniques (e.g. Support Vector Machines), is much more efficient[9]

Table 1. Results (*BEP*) of the RitroveRAI Text Categorizer

Category	Training Set Size	BEP (26)	BEP (11)
Sport	76	0,83	0,72
Environment	55	0,45	0,56
Life and Religion	59	0,89	0,79
Current Events	172	0,45	0,54
Economics	149	0,60	0,76
Transportation	48	0,68	0,67
Foreign Affairs	518	0,75	0,78
Justice	346	0,61	0,67
Employment/Job	62	0,55	0,52
Politics	437	0,80	0,79
Health	58	0,73	0,46

---

[9] Profile based classification requires a number of scalar products tight to the number of classes that is much lower to the number of documents.

7.2 Evaluation of the RitroveRAI News Alignment

The validation of the Web alignment capability of RitroveRAI has been carried out on a reference set of about 410 news items (i.e. segments in transcriptions) manually annotated. The annotation has been added by a team of three archivists with a judgment about each of the candidate alignment in four classes: *"bad"*, *"fair"*, *"good"* and *"very good"*. *"very good"* expresses an exact correspondence between the event/fact described in the two documents. As the focus of the Web material can be slightly different from the TV news, degrading levels of evaluation express overlaps of decreasing size: *"good"* is a valid correspondence but between a shorter transcribed news than the longer Web document with many more facts. *"fair"* reflects the same specific topic (e.g. *"Iraki war"*) but possibly not the same fact. *"bad"* refers to clear mistakes of the links. In order to study the accuracy of the thresholds imposed to Eq. (3) annotators were presented with all the links receiving a score greater than 0^{10}.

In the evaluation we wanted to focus on news transcriptions of reasonable quality, i.e. significant segments to accurately measure the linking accuracy. We distinguish between *"monothematic"* and *"multithematic"* units, i.e. segments reporting just one or many more facts, respectively. Multithematic segments are usually due to wrong segmentations that groups two or more facts. Annotators found 308 monothematic and 102 multithematic segments. Data reported will refer only to the 1,587 alignments proposed for the monothematic segments.

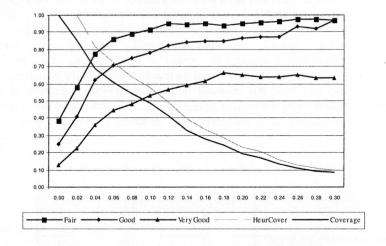

Fig. 4. Precision and Coverage of the RitroveRAI hyperlinking

Two performance indexes have been used: *precision* at the three levels of evaluation and *coverage*. Precision is the ratio between the number of links that received an evaluation equal or better then the level (from "fair" to "very good") and the total number of links proposed by the system. Figure 4 plots the three measures

---

[10] Notice that recall here does not apply: the annotators did not analyse the full "La Repubblica" Web site in the target time windows so that the gold standard set of all Web news valid for the alignment is not available.

according to the thresholds of acceptance imposed to the IR alignment scores (Eq. (3)). As the trends of all the curves suggest, there is a strong correlation between the thresholds and the accuracy. As a contrastive measure we computed the *coverage* as the ratio between the number of segments receiving at least one link and the total number of monothematic segments (i.e. 308). In Fig. 4 we see that coverage decreases smoothly and a kind of breakeven point is reached in the range of 65-75% precision. This is a quite good result if compared with standard performance of IR systems. Of course the constraints imposed on the alignment (in particular, the dates) are quite effective. Moreover, it must be said that not all the segments can be aligned by the system as (1) they may be not present on the "*La Repubblica*" Web site or (2) segments can be too short for significantly express a full fact.

An analysis of the optimal threshold (around 0,03) has been thus carried out. By imposing such a threshold we found that the amount of news not receiving any link is 62 (about 20%). However, among these segments we found 48 segments that are receiving only "bad" links. An analysis of about 20 such segments revealed in fact that there were no Web pages suitable for the alignment on that date (in the adopted source, i.e. "*La Repubblica*"). TV news may be in fact on local or curiosity information and some of them are not even mentioned on newspapers. It is likely that all the 48 segments were not to be linked at all. Correctly, a default threshold of 0.03 would have been prevented all the erroneous links to be proposed. Accordingly, we removed those 48 segments from the testing data set (i.e. the 308 monothematic segments) obtaining a reduced set of segments (302-48=254). This simulates a system with an heuristic threshold that correctly assigns no link to the above 48 candidates. Evaluation of such a system would be focused only on the 254 test segments with an alternative coverage plot ("Heuristic coverage" in Fig. 4) that is slightly higher than the previous. Notice how the precision plots for such a modified system (by imposing every threshold 0.03 or higher) do not change for any acceptance rate.

8   Conclusion and Future Work

In this paper the RitroveRAI system for the extraction of semantic metadata from broadcasted TV and radio news has been presented. Human Language Technologies are here exploited to extract from the news transcriptions grammatical and semantic information and align them with Web documents. Alignment with these latter well-formed texts is used to validate the extracted metadata as well as to complete them with additional information.

The result is a metadata repository that supports querying in plain natural language (e.g. "*Bush commenting Irak elections*") as well as more conceptually motivated languages (e.g. comment(*Bush*:agent, *'Irak elections'*:theme)). In the originating European projects, PrestoSpace, work is in progress to integrate the RitroveRAI language processing functionalties with ontology services, like Named Entity classification and semantic-driven coreference resolution in texts, made available by other partners (the KIM ontology, [11]). As the involved NLP technologies (in particular, the CHAOS parser) support text processing in two languages, Italian and English, the RitroveRAI system already enables extraction of language-neutral semantic metadata and multilingual information access: querying in English can be parsed and normalized by CHAOS so that metadata can be searched in a language neutral manner for cross-lingual reitrieval.

Experimental work presented in this paper has been carried out on a significant scale (hundreds of segments and thousands of links) and demonstrates viability for large scale processing. The client-server Web architecture of the system is currently under testing to process TV broadcasted by RAI, daily. Categorization, although trained over a limited test set, is currently running with an acceptable accuracy. More importantly, the Web alignment method proposed reaches high level accuracy. This opens more space for the extraction of deeper phenomena from Web, like event descriptions with recognition and role assignment to participant of the detected events.

Open problems refer to the improvements needed to deal with noisy input, i.e. wrong news segmentation. All the current RitroveRAI processing is based on the strict assumption that segmentation is provided as a form of preprocessing. After alignment however, more semantic information is available to the system for some analysis of odd segments (e.g. too short or too long): algorithms for a posteriori merging and splitting can thus be made available. This task is close to automatic segmentation of long documents as carried out in text summarization ([1], [10] or [12]). In particular Lexical Chains ([1]) and Latent Semantic Analysis ([8],[6]) can be here applied either to the TV segments or to their alignments on the Web. Integration of these two (independent) information sources will capitalize further the alignment to improve segment detection as well as all the subsequent processing steps.

The browsing capabilities of the RitroveRAI system are already supporting natural language querying and user specific Web browsing (as in Fig. 3). Moreover, as mentioned in the introduction, significant portions of the system are adaptive, including categorization and Web alignment. This makes RitroveRAI a typical example of large scale adaptive Semantic Web application. Its capabilities for IE and automatic Web alignment coupled with its browsing and querying modalities are a feasibility proof of a new generation of multimedia information brokering systems over the Web.

Acknowledgement

The authors want to thank RAI, Centro Ricerche ed Innovazione Tecnologica (CRIT) of Torino (Italy), and in particular the staff involved in PrestoSpace, Giorgio Dimino, Daniele Airola Gnota and Laurent Boch, for having made available the data set for training and testing and for the helpful support to the architectural and application design choices.

References

[1] R. Barzilay, M. Elhadad, *Using Lexical Chains for Text Summarization.* In the Proceedings of the Intelligent Scalable Text Summarization Workshop (ISTS'97), ACL, Madrid, 1997.

[2] Basili, Roberto, Pazienza, Maria Teresa, Zanzotto, Fabio Massimo, *Efficient Parsing for Information Extraction*, Proceedings of the European Conference on Artificial Intelligence (ECAI98), Brighton, UK, 1998.

[3] R. Basili, A. Moschitti, M.T. Pazienza, "*NLP-driven IR: Evaluating performance over a text classification task*", In Proceeding of the 10th "International Joint Conference of Artificial Intelligence" (IJCAI 2001), August 4th, Seattle, Washington, USA 2001.

[4] Basili R., F.M. Zanzotto, Parsing Engineering and Empirical Robustness, 8 (2/3) 97120, Journal of Language Engineering, Cambridge University Press, 2002

[5] F.Y.Y. Choi, P. Wiemer-Hastings and J. Moore. "Latent semantic analysis for text segmentation". In Proceedings of the 6th Conference on Empirical Methods in Natural Language Processing, pp. 109- 117, 2001

[6] Vasileios Hatzivassiloglou, Judith Klavans, and Eleazar Eskin. 1999. *Detecting text similarity over short passages: Exploring linguistic feature combinations via machine learning.*

[7] Otis Gospodnetic. 2003. Advanced Text Indexing with Lucene. http://lucene.apache.org

[8] David J. Ittner and Lewis, David D. and David D. Ahn, *Text categorization of low quality images*, Proceedings of SDAIR-95, 4th Annual Symposium on Document Analysis and Information Retrieval, 1995, Las Vegas, US, 301—315.

[9] Landauer, T. K., Foltz, P. W., & Laham, D., *Introduction to Latent Semantic Analysis.* Discourse Processes, 25, 259-284, (1998).

[10] Daniel Marcu. 1999. *The automatic construction of large-scale corpora for summarization research.* In Proceedings of SIGIR 99.

[11] Borislav Popov, Atanas Kiryakov, Damyan Ognyanoff, Dimitar Manov, Angel Kirilov, Miroslav Goranov. *KIM – Semantic Annotation Platform.* 2nd International Semantic Web Conference (ISWC2003), Florida, USA, 2003.

[12] Hongyan Jing. 2002. *Using hidden Markov modeling to decompose human-written summaries.* Computational Linguistics, 28(4):527–543

Querying Ontologies:
A Controlled English Interface for End-Users

Abraham Bernstein, Esther Kaufmann, Anne Göhring, and Christoph Kiefer

University of Zurich, Department of Informatics,
Winterthurerstrasse 190, 8057 Zurich, Switzerland
{bernstein, kaufmann, goehring, kiefer}@ifi.unizh.ch,
http://www.ifi.unizh.ch/ddis

Abstract. The semantic web presents the vision of a distributed, dynamically growing knowledge base founded on formal logic. Common users, however, seem to have problems even with the simplest Boolean expressions. As queries from web search engines show, the great majority of users simply do not use Boolean expressions. So how can we help users to query a web of logic that they do not seem to understand? We address this problem by presenting a natural language interface to semantic web querying. The interface allows formulating queries in Attempto Controlled English (ACE), a subset of natural English. Each ACE query is translated into a discourse representation structure – a variant of the language of first-order logic – that is then translated into an N3-based semantic web querying language using an ontology-based rewriting framework. As the validation shows, our approach offers great potential for bridging the gap between the logic-based semantic web and its real-world users, since it allows users to query the semantic web without having to learn an unfamiliar formal language. Furthermore, we found that users liked our approach and designed good queries resulting in a very good retrieval performance (100% precision and 90% recall).

1 Introduction

The semantic web presents the vision of a dynamically growing knowledge base that should allow users to draw on and combine distributed information sources specified in languages based on formal logic. Common users, however, were shown to have problems even with the simplest Boolean expressions; the use of the description logic formalism underlying the semantic web is beyond their understanding. Experience in information retrieval, for example, demonstrates that users are better at understanding graphical query interfaces than simple Boolean queries [1]. As queries from web search engines reveal, the great majority of users simply do not use Boolean expressions. Bowen and colleagues even show that people (CS students) who are trained in formulating queries in a logic-based formalism (SQL in their case) are usually inept in composing correct queries in realistically-sized databases rather than the small toy examples used in database classes [2]. *So how can we bridge the gap between the (description) logic-based semantic web and real-world users, who are at least ill at ease and, oftentimes, unable to use formal logic concepts?*

We address this problem by *presenting a natural language interface to the semantic web*. In its current form the interface provides users with a controlled natural

Y. Gil et al. (Eds.): ISWC 2005, LNCS 3729, pp. 112–126, 2005.

language interface to formulate queries. The controlled natural language used, Attempto Controlled English (ACE) [3, 4], is an unambiguous subset of English, which is translated *automatically* into the N3-style[1] triple-based semantic web query language PQL [5] (which can easily be mapped to query languages such as SquishQL [6]). It provides the users with an almost natural language interface to the semantic web. As experience with controlled languages has shown, they are much easier to learn by end-users than formal languages like logic and are sufficient for querying knowledge bases [7]. We, therefore, believe that the approach presented here has great potential in bridging the gap between the semantic web and its end-users as well as becoming a major enabler for the growth of the semantic web.

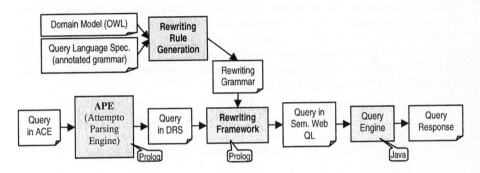

Fig. 1. Overall data flow of the controlled English query interface

The rest of this paper closely follows the data flow of the query interface (Fig. 1). Section 2 introduces Attempto Controlled English (ACE) and the Attempto Parsing Engine (APE). APE translates ACE texts into a discourse representation structure (DRS), a variant of the language of first-order logic introduced by Kamp and Reyle [8]. Section 3 describes the rewriting framework that translates the DRS to the semantic web query language. The translation is based on a rewriting grammar, which was generated using both an OWL-based domain model and a query language specification. The queries are evaluated by a standard query engine not discussed in this paper. Note that we used APE as a black-box component, which uses extended DRSs as internal representations. This allows us to exchange it with another NLP parser should the need arise. Therefore, we did not attempt a direct translation from ACE to N3. In section 4 we provide three evaluations of the approach. We close with a discussion of the current limitations as well as related and future work.

2   Attempto Controlled English as a Query Language

Our query interface automatically processes queries expressed in Attempto Controlled English (ACE), a controlled natural language originally designed for requirements specifications and knowledge representation [3, 4]. ACE is a subset of English meaning that each ACE sentence is correct English, but not vice-versa. ACE's

---

[1] More information about N3 can be found at http://www.w3.org/DesignIssues/Notation3

grammar is specified by a small set of construction and interpretation rules. The construction rules allow users to build simple sentences (e.g., "John sells books."), composite sentences (e.g., "If John sells books and John's business does not fail then he is content."), and queries (e.g., "Which books does John sell?"). The interpretation rules eliminate syntactic and semantic ambiguities, for which natural languages are highly notorious, hereby also reducing the computational complexity of processing ACE sentences. As such, ACE avoids the major disadvantages of full natural language processing, while maintaining the ease of use for end-users and allowing the translation of all ACE sentences to first-order logic.

Though ACE appears completely natural, it is in fact a formal language and its small set of construction and interpretation rules must be learned. As an example, consider the sentence "A man sees a girl with a telescope." In full English this sentence is ambiguous since the prepositional phrase "with a telescope" can either modify the verb phrase "sees", leading to the interpretation that the man has the telescope, or the noun phrase "a girl", meaning that the girl has the telescope. In ACE, however, the sentence is unambiguous since an interpretation rule limits the meaning to the first alternative "sees with a telescope".

DRS	First-order Logic
A B	
customer(A) book(B) buy(A, B)	$\exists$ A B : customer(A) $\wedge$ book(B) $\wedge$ buy(A, B)

Fig. 2. DRS and first-order logic representation of "A customer buys a book."

The Attempto Parsing Engine (APE) – implemented in Prolog as a Definite Clause Grammar – translates a possibly multi-sentence ACE text into a *discourse representation structure* (DRS) that logically represents the information of the text [8]. DRSs are a powerful means to adequately capture linguistic phenomena, for instance anaphoric references. A DRS consists of discourse referents, i.e., quantified variables representing the objects of a discourse, and of conditions for the discourse referents. The conditions can be logical atoms or complex conditions built from other DRSs and logical connectors (negation, disjunction, and implication). As an example, the translation of the sentence "A customer buys a book." is shown in its typical box-styled DRS representation in Fig. 2 on the left. The two discourse referents, A and B, are shown at the top and the three conditions derived from the sentence are listed below. Fig. 2 shows on the right the first-order logic formula equivalent to the DRS.[2]

3   The Rewriting Framework: From DRSs to Queries

The next (and central) step in our natural language semantic web interface is the rewriting of the APE generated DRSs into a semantic web query language (an extension and modification of [9]). To that end we generated a DRS-to-QL rewriting

---

[2] To emphasize the principle of the translation we radically simplified the DRSs in all examples. Real DRSs are much more complex to adequately represent a wide range of linguistic phenomena.

grammar using an ontology-based domain-model (in OWL) and a query language specification (cf. Fig. 1). This section will first succinctly introduce the exemplary domain ontology – the MIT Process Handbook [10] – which will provide the underlying examples throughout the text. Then, it will introduce the rewriting rule generation and the rewriting framework, which has both ontology specific as well as general vocabulary rules.

3.1 An Example Ontology: MIT Process Handbook

As an example ontology we chose the *MIT Process Handbook* [10] which describes organizational processes. The Process Handbook treats a real-world domain that everybody can relate to, has a large number of instances (>5000), and has been used in a number of semantic web projects. Each process (object) of the ontology enters a variety of relationships to attributes, sub-processes, exceptions, etc., and has a detailed textual description (cf. Fig. 3).

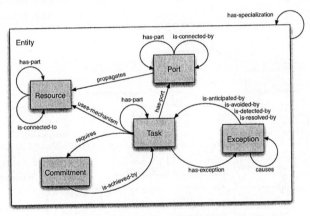

Fig. 3. The Process Handbook Meta-model

Full-text and Keywords	N3-style PQL-Query[3]		
"Find all processes that sell books over the internet."	?process	<#name>	"*sell*" ,
			"*book*" ;
		<#has-mechanism> ?mechanism .	
Keywords:	?mechanism ?var "*internet*" .		
"sell book internet"	?var	<#subpropertyof> <#attribute> .	

Fig. 4. An example full-text query with its corresponding keywords and derived N3-style PQL query

The *process query language* (PQL) presented in [5] allows to pose queries, which are then evaluated against the process ontology. PQL essentially allows the composition of (process) ontology fragments that result in a query-by-example style

---

[3] For the syntax of the triple queries we slightly extended the N3-syntax to allow for substring matching. The literal "book" matches any other literal "book." The literal "*book*" matches any other literal, which contains the substring "book."

specification of the sought-after processes. It can be mapped straightforwardly to any triple-based semantic web query language such as SquishQL [6]. Consequently, none of our findings are limited to the Process Handbook and PQL.

PQL supports two major statement types: the first one queries for the subject and/or the predicate of a given property; the second doesn't make any assumptions about the property but does (mostly) assume that the object is a literal.[4] Fig. 4 shows an example full-text query and its corresponding triple-based query.

3.2   The Rewriting Rule Generation and Framework

In order to translate the DRSs generated by APE into triples and N3-style PQL queries, we developed rewriting rules for the DRS structures. Each linguistic structure is first matched against a set of *ontology-model specific keyword rules* that – when they apply – result in a constraint between objects (i.e., a query statement with a fixed property).

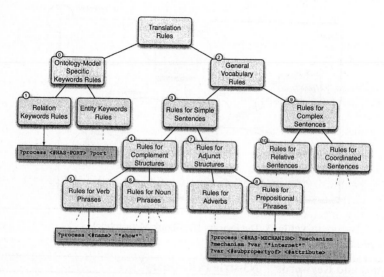

Fig. 5. The translation rules grammar (numbers are referred to in the text)

If none of these rules applies, then a set of *general vocabulary rules* is tried, typically resulting in the comparison with a literal value (i.e., a query statement without a known property). This structure is reflected in Fig 5., which provides a graphical overview of the most important rules of the translation grammar. To further explain this approach we will now discuss each of these two rule types referring to the rules by their numbers in Fig. 5.

3.2.1   Ontology-Model Specific Keyword Rules

The *ontology-model specific keyword rules* apply if one of the keywords of the ontology – including its morphological or syntactic variants – appears in the DRS to

---

[4] Note that we follow the *subject–property–object* designation of triples throughout the paper.

be translated. For example, the expression "has a port" in the query "Which process has a port?" is identified as the ontology-model property HAS-PORT and, hence, translated into the triple-based PQL query in Ex. 1 (firing rules ⓪ and ① in Fig. 5).

ACE: Which process has a port?	
DRS	**N3-style PQL Query**
A B C query(A, which) object(A, process, object) object(B, port, object) predicate(C, state, have, A, B)	`?process  <#has-port>  ?port .`

Ex. 1. Transformation of "Which process has a port?"

A limitation of this approach is the choice of the vocabulary when building the ontology. In some cases we, therefore, had to include synonyms of the ontology-keywords in the rewriting rules.[5]

3.2.2 General Vocabulary Rules

Elements of the DRS not handled by the ontology-model specific keyword rules are passed to the *general-vocabulary rules* (② in Fig 5.). These rules distinguish between *simple* and *complex* sentences. Simple sentences don't contain embedded relative sentences or a coordination of sentences (using connectors such as "and," "or," etc.) whereas complex sentences consist of more than one sentence.

Simple Sentences Rules. If a simple sentence is identified (③ in Fig. 5) the framework differentiates between *complement and adjunct clauses*. Complements correspond to the mandatory elements of a sentence (also called *arguments*). Adjuncts comprise elements of a sentence that are not required by the sentence's main verb. Consider the sentence: "Which service shows the campus restaurants over the internet?" The main verb "shows" calls for the arguments "which service" and "the campus restaurants". The prepositional phrase "over the internet" provides additional, non-mandatory information to the sentence. The motivation for this distinction in our framework derives from the idea that complements contribute more pivotal information to a sentence's meaning than adjunctive structures. Exploiting this aspect for query formulation, we mirror the syntactic structure of an ACE sentence in the query using the ontology model.

ACE: Which service **shows** the campus restaurants?	
DRS	**N3-style PQL Query**
A B C query(A, which) object(A, service, object) **predicate(B, event, show, A, C)** object(C, 'campus restaurant', object)	`?process <#name> "*show*" .`

Ex. 2. Transformation of the sentence's main verb "show"

---

[5] We intend to extend our framework with automated keyword expansion using WordNet.

Complement Structures Rules. Complements consist of verb phrases, noun phrases, prepositional phrases, and adjective phrases. They are interpreted as simple literal values. For example, the verb "show" in the above query "Which service shows the campus restaurants?" is represented in the DRS as "predicate(C,event,show,B,E)". It is treated as a literal value and translated as shown in Ex. 2 (firing rules ④ and ⑤ in Fig. 5).

ACE: Which service shows the menus **of the campus restaurants**?	
DRS	**N3-style PQL Query**
A B C D	

query(A, which)
object(A, service, object)
predicate(B, event, show, A, C)
object(C, menu, object)
relation(C, menu, of, D)
object(D, 'campus`restaurant', object)
	`?process   <#name>    "*show*" ,`
	`                       "*menu*" ,`
	`                       "*campus*" ,`
	`                       "*restaurant*" .`

Ex. 3. Transformation of "Which service shows the menus of the campus restaurants?"

In ACE any noun phrase can furthermore be coordinated (e.g., *menus and drinks*), modified by adjectives (e.g., *the different restaurants*), *of*-prepositional phrases (e.g., *the menus of the restaurants*), and possessive elements (e.g., *the restaurants' menus*). These modifiers are also treated as literal values. Ex. 3 shows a simple sentence consisting of a verb and two complements with a modifying *of*-prepositional phrase in the object complement (firing rules ④ and ⑥). Note that the rewriting framework splits the compound "campus restaurants" into its constituents to improve recall.

Adjunct Structures Rules. If a simple sentence consists of complement elements as well as adjunct elements, the resulting query inherits this linguistic differentiation. Consider the query "Which service shows the menus of the campus restaurants over the internet?". Here, the prepositional phrase "over the internet" indicates that the menus are shown using the internet as an instrument, which is noted in the sentence's DRS. As instruments, or rather their synonym "mechanisms", are included in the Process Handbook ontology-model as the HAS-MECHANISM property, we can translate the phrase "over the internet" into the PQL query in Ex. 4 (firing rules ⓪, ⑦, and ⑧).

ACE: Which service shows the menus of the campus restaurants **over the internet**?	
DRS	**N3-style PQL Query**
A B C D E	

query(A, which)
object(A, service, object)
predicate(B, event, show, A, C)
object(C, menu, object)
relation(C, menu, of, D)
object(D, 'campus restaurant', object)
object(E, internet, object)
modifier(B, location, over, E)
	`?process   <#has-mechanism> ?mechanism .`
	`?mechanism ?var  "*internet*" .`
	`?var   <#subpropertyof>   <#attribute>`[6] `.`

Ex. 4. Transformation of the prepositional phrase "over the internet"

---

[6] The subproperty statement ensures that ?var is only unified to an attribute property preventing the unification with a structure property.

Complex Sentences Rules. Similar to adjunct structures, complex sentences initiate a search in the ontology-model for corresponding relationships indicating that the nested syntactic structures of ACE queries are used to phrase structured queries. Complex sentences are composed of more than one sentence. In the sentence "Which service provides all available pizza couriers that are in the city?" the compound "pizza couriers" is modified by a relative sentence turning the simple sentence "Which service provides all available pizza couriers?" into a complex sentence. The complex syntactic structure is exploited in our translation framework resulting in a query that searches for corresponding relationships in the ontology (rules ⑨ and ⑩) as shown in Ex. 5.

We emphasize the linguistic difference between the main sentence and the embedded relative sentence by searching for the relative sentence's literal values not only in the specific attribute "Name" of the process' subparts but in all attributes of the subparts. The query becomes less restrictive in order to improve recall.

ACE: Which service provides all available pizza couriers **that are in the city?**	
DRS	**N3-style PQL Query**

A B C D E
 	
query(A, which)
object(A, service, object)
object(B, 'pizza delivery', object)
predicate(C, event, provide, A, B)
object(D, city, object)
predicate(E, state, be, B)
modifier(E, location, in, D)
	`?process <#name> "*provide*" ,`
	`            "*pizza*" ,`
	`            "*courier*" .`
	
	`?process <#has-part> ?part .`
	`?part ?var "*city*" .`
	`?var <#subpropertyof> <#attribute> .`

Ex. 5. Transformation of "Which service provides all available pizza couriers that are ..."

If sentences are coordinated by conjunction (*and*) or disjunction (*or*) the result is again a complex sentence. An example is "Which service provides all available pizza couriers over the internet and which service takes orders 24-hours-a-day?" Each coordinated sentence is translated into a separate set of query statements according to the simple sentences rules (③). In addition, the conjunction "and" triggers the translation rules for complex sentences (⑨) which ensure that the overall sentence is translated into one cohesive query.

3.2.3 Post Processing Rules

At the end of the rewriting procedure the framework applies some post processing rules priorizing the fired rewriting rules or simplifying the resulting query. For example: If the search in the ontology-model results in no corresponding relationships, then the structure is simplified by treating the modifiers as literals. The following example illustrates the simplification of the modifier "24 hours a day" in the sentence "Which pizza courier takes orders 24 hours a day?".

Query according to general vocabulary rules:
```
?process <#has-part> ?part .
?part ?var "*24 hours a day*" .
?var <#subpropertyof> <#attribute> .
```

Simplified query according to the post processing rules:
```
?process ?var "*24 hours a day*" .
?var <#subpropertyof> <#attribute> .
```

4 Validation

For the implementation of the validation prototype we combined Prolog and Java components, as APE and the rewriting framework are programmed in SICStus Prolog, and the user interface and the query engine are programmed in Java (see Fig. 1). Currently, ACE queries are entered into the user interface and then passed to APE using the *Jasper* Java-to-Prolog bridge. The resulting DRSs are forwarded to the rewriting framework that generates the semantic web query language queries. These are then evaluated by the query engine that passes the result back to the user interface (Fig. 6).

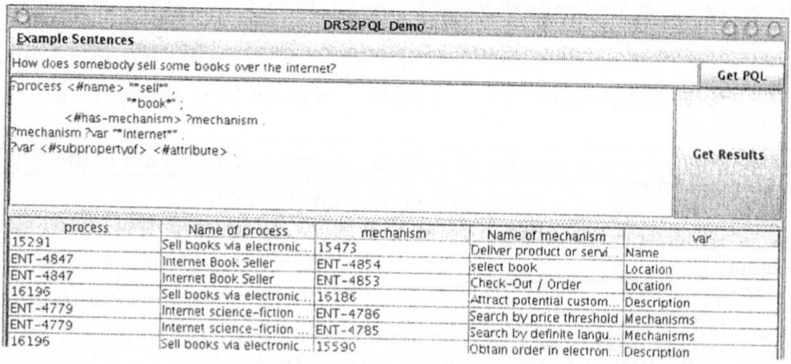

Fig. 6. The user interface of the query engine showing an ACE query, its corresponding N3-style PQL representation, and the results from the database matching the query

We chose this mixed-programming language approach as we used APE as a black-box (indeed we did not make any changes to its source code) and found that the prolog-style data-structures generated by APE where easiest processed in a rewriting framework using the same language.

Using the prototype we validated our approach in three ways. First we tried to generate correct translations for real-world queries. Next, we confronted users with tasks in which they had to retrieve answers from a semantic web database and measured the users' performance as well as utilized a standardized usability test to assess the ease of usage compared to using a formal query language. Additionally, we measured precision and recall of the resulting answers. Last, we compared the retrieval performance of our framework to two different keyword-based retrieval approaches using an exemplary query.

4.1 Validation of the Rewriting Framework with Real-World Queries

To ensure the correct translation of real-world queries we asked masters students to phrase queries, which search for web services that would be of interest to them. We also asked them to enter the queries in a query-by-example-style form. Fig. 7 shows a selection of these queries sorted by increasing syntactic complexity. We received 50 queries, reformulated them in ACE, and ran them through our query interface. All reformulations were very simple (such as adding articles/determiners or using relative sentences instead of certain types of connectors). The system translated all queries correctly taking an average processing time of about 2 seconds (on a standard PC with a 2 GHz Celeron processor and 512 MB RAM).

Which service provides a shoe cleaning service?
Which service helps with the classes and the exams?
Which service provides the summaries of the different courses for free over the web?
Which service provides an internet streaming server that streams the requested tracks over the internet?
Which service provides a car renting and uses a web interface that allows a keyword search?
Which service takes the groceries orders via a website and delivers the food within 24 hours?
Where does somebody enrol to a university and choose the courses and get a personal university scheduler?
Which internet page shows the movies that are on in the city and provides a seat booking?
Where does somebody enter some hardware components and the service returns a list which has a sorting by price?
Which service provides the songs of the different artists and the customers pick the desired songs over the internet?

Fig. 7. A selection of real-world ACE queries for which the query interface generated correct N3-style PQL queries

4.2 Usability and Performance Evaluation in a Retrieval Task

We also wanted to evaluate the *interface's usability in a concrete usability task*. To that end we used the NLP database interface evaluation tasks defined by [11], in which 1770 queries are defined to be run on three different databases. We translated the databases into OWL to make it accessible from our query processor. We then randomly chose 30 questions of varying complexity and asked 20 users to compose queries both using our system as well as a simplified version of SQL. As a preparation, the subjects, whom we recruited from the computer science and computer linguistics departments, read a 2-page instruction on how to construct correct ACE sentences and a ½ page refresher on SQL.

We found that users where significantly faster in writing the ACE queries than the SQL queries (t-test with $p = 2.84E-05$). Using the standardized SUS-test [12] for usability, we found that ACE performed significantly better than SQL in the SUS test questions "I found the various functions of ACE were well integrated", "I think there was too much inconsistency in ACE", and "I would imagine that most people would learn to use ACE very quickly" (at $p = 2.8\%$, 0.4%, and 4.1%). Furthermore, people overall preferred ACE over SQL, barely missing significance at the 5% level (with a t-test result of 5.6%). None of the questions in which SQL performed better on average yielded significant results.

Note that these results are influenced by the subject pool, which is composed of people who are very familiar with both computers and formalized languages. Experiences with logic-based query languages suggest that the average population will experience more problems with a language like SQL and even perform worse than the computer and logic educated subjects we had [1, 2]. Consequently, we have reason to believe that the general population will have an even larger affinity towards ACE, but will also have to climb a slightly steeper learning curve to learn it.

To evaluate the *retrieval performance of the overall system* we executed the 30 queries formulated in ACE by the users and partly corrected to valid ACE sentences on the Mooney Natural Language Learning Data [11]. The retrieved answers achieved a precision of 100% and a recall of 90%.

The performed retrieval task highlights that subjects with no previous familiarity with ACE can translate real-world queries to correct ACE queries (faster than to SQL), which in turn are processed correctly by our rewriting system resulting in a very good retrieval performance.

4.3 Exemplary Validation with a Complicated Query Sentence

We also executed a number of highly complex queries and compared their retrieval performance with two keyword-based retrieval approaches: one using a TFIDF-style ranking [13], the other one searching for the conjunction of keywords. Both of those approaches have a proven track record of being suitable for end-users. We then hand-coded the database to find the correct results for the natural language queries.

For the non-trivial query presented in Ex. 6 the database contained four correct answers. Our NLP query interface found three correct answers, missing one. The TFIDF-ranking found the correct answers at the 2nd, 35th, 47th, and 183rd positions, which provides an overall better recall than our approach but at the cost of an abysmal precision. The simple keyword matcher returned no answers as the conjunction of all keywords overconstrained the query. This example indicates that our approach – while maintaining natural language simplicity – provides a performance akin to logic-based retrieval engines that usually outperform precision and recall of keyword engines.

Summarizing our evaluation results, we have found that ACE can correctly process real-word queries, which are slightly reformulated from students' textual descriptions. Using the standardized usability tests we also found that people prefer ACE-querying over SQL, even though most of the subjects had no ACE but good SQL knowledge before the usability task. Executing the ACE queries with our framework and comparing the retrieved answers with the results of [11], we achieved a very good retrieval performance. Last, a non-trivial exemplary query indicated that ACE-queries also have the potential to be used to compose complex queries that are easily understood by users.

ACE: Which sales process informs its customers over the internet and avoids the unwanted solicitations with an opt-out list?	
DRS	**PQL**
A B C D E F G H	`?process   <#name>   "*sale*"  ;`
query(A, which)	`           <#has-part> ?part  .`
object(A, sales_process, object)	`?part   ?varpart   "*inform*"  .`
object(B, customer, person)	`?varpart <#subpropertyof> <#attribute> .`
predicate(C, event, inform, A, B)	`?part   ?varpart   "*customer*"  .`
object(D, internet, object)	`?varpart <#subpropertyof> <#attribute> .`
modifier(C, instrument, over, D)	`?part   <#uses-mechanism>  ?mechanism  .`
object(E, solicitation, object)	`?mechanism  ?varmech   "*internet*"  .`
property(F, unwanted, E)	`?varmech <#subpropertyof> <#attribute> .`
predicate(G, event, avoid, A, E)	`?part   <#has-exception>  ?exception  .`
object(H, opt_out_list, object)	`?exception  ?varex   "*unwanted*"  .`
modifier(G, instrument, with, H)	`?varex <#subpropertyof> <#attribute> .`
	`?exception  ?varex   "*solicitation*"  .`
	`?varex <#subpropertyof> <#attribute> .`
	`?exception  <#is-avoided-by>  ?handler  .`
	`?handler  ?varhand  "*opt-out*"  .`
	`?varhand <#subpropertyof> <#attribute> .`
	`?handler  ?varhand  "*list*"  .`
	`?varhand <#subpropertyof> <#attribute> .`

Ex. 6. Transformation of a complex query "Which sales process informs its customers over the internet and avoids the unwanted solicitations with an opt-out list?"

5 Limitations of Our Approach and Future Research

We can think of three limitations to the work presented in this paper. First, the use of a controlled language imposes a cost on the user since the language has to be learned. Users might be discouraged from employing a language they have to learn, but experience with ACE – and with other controlled languages such as Boeing Simplified English [14] – has shown that learning a controlled language to phrase statements and queries is much easier than learning logic, and takes only a couple of days for the basics and two weeks for full proficiency, which is beyond what users need to write queries. As our evaluation above shows, educated users (i.e., members of a computer science or computer linguistics department) were able to use ACE querying reasonably well after reading a 2-page explanatory text. Furthermore, some researchers are currently developing query interfaces that will help people to write correct controlled English sentences by guiding them as they write [15]. Last and most importantly, Malhotra [7] has shown that users tend to use a limited language when querying a knowledge base as opposed to conversing with other people indicating that the limitation might not be as grave. Similar results have recently been found by Dittenbach et al. [16] through the implementation of a multilingual natural language interface to a real web-based tourism platform. They show that most natural language queries are formulated in a simple manner and don't consist of complex sentence constructs even when users are neither limited by a conventional search interface nor narrowed by a restricted query language.

Second, our current prototype requires some manual adaptation of the rewrite rules when using it with a new ontology or new knowledge base. Given our experience with hand-adaptation, we found that most of the time an inspection of the meta-model was sufficient. Motivated by the work of Cimiano [17] we believe that the rules can be automatically generated based on the ontology model and intend to investigate this avenue in future work.

Last, the validations shown in this paper are slightly limited by the choice and size of the subject pool from among computer scientists/linguists. We, therefore, intend to extend the evaluation to more subjects with different backgrounds and compare our system's performance with other semantic-web query interfaces allowing us to investigate how people's retrieval performance and affinity to different tools is related to their background.

6 Related Work

We hardly found any other application of controlled natural language querying semantic web content. The most closely related work we encountered is the GAPP project [18], a question-answering system developed for querying the *Foundational Model of Anatomy* (FMA) knowledge base. GAPP takes natural language questions as input and translates them into the structured query language *StruQL*, a database language designed for querying graphs. The system then returns the results of a query as an XML document. Similar to our interface GAPP analyses English questions and divides them into the three elements *Subject*, *Relationship*, and *Object*. Along with pattern-matching and word-combination techniques, which resemble our ontology-model specific keywords rules, GAPP's parser exploits the syntactic structures in order to generate the appropriate structured queries. The results of the evaluation, where the generation of the correct query was considered to be a correct response, show that GAPP provides an intuitive and convenient way for anatomists to browse the FMA knowledge base. The approach differs from ours in that its query construction and, therefore, its overall application are highly restricted to one semantically constrained domain. Furthermore, their model doesn't use a full-fledged rewriting grammar but seems to be limited to a set of domain-specific user-defined pattern matching rules. Another project addressing a similar task is the MKBEEM project [19]. In contrast to our approach it focuses, largely, on adding multilinguality to the process of automated translation and interpretation of natural language user requests.

We also found that work on natural language interfaces to data bases (not ontologized knowledge bases) has largely tapered off since the 80's [20], even though the need for them has become increasingly acute. Accordingly, a few approaches in the area of database interfaces have emerged recently [21-23]. Among them the most closely related approach is the PRECISE project [24] that proposes a natural language interface to relational databases. PRECISE uses a data-base augmented tokenization of a query's parse tree to generate the most likely corresponding SQL statement. It is, consequently, limited to a sublanguage of English, i.e., the language defined by the subject area of the database. In contrast, our approach limits the possible language constructs and not the subject domain. Our interface will not return any useful answers when none can be found in the queried ontology. It will, however, be able to generate an appropriate triple-based statement. We hope to be able to include an empirical comparison between these two approaches in our future work.

7   Conclusions

People's familiarity with natural language might be the key to simplify their interaction with ontologies. Our approach provides exactly such a natural language interface. Following Malhotra's [7] and Dittenbach et al.'s [16] findings, which state that using a subset of English is sufficient to query knowledge bases, we could forgo the need for a full natural language processing machinery avoiding all the computational and linguistic complexities involved with such an endeavor. The result is a simple but adaptive approach to controlled English querying of the semantic web – a potentially important component for bridging the gap between real-world users and the logic-based underpinnings of the semantic web.

Acknowledgements

The authors would like to thank Norbert Fuchs and his Attempto team for providing APE, the MIT Process Handbook project for making available the data on which the evaluation is based, Ray Mooney and his group for having generously supplied the databases, English questions, and corresponding queries to us, and the anonymous reviewers for their helpful comments. This work was partially supported by the Swiss National Science Foundation (200021-100149/1).

References

1. Spoerri, A.: InfoCrystal: A Visual Tool for Information Retrieval Management. Second International Conference on Information and Knowledge Management. Washington, D.C. (1993) 11-20
2. Bowen, P.L., Chang, C.-J.A., Rohde, F.H.: Non-Length Based Query Challenges: An Initial Taxonomy. Fourteenth Annual Workshop on Information Technologies and Systems (WITS 2004). Washington, D.C. (2004) 74-79
3. Fuchs, N.E., et al.: Attempto Controlled English (ACE). (2003) http://www.ifi.unizh.ch/attempto
4. Fuchs, N.E., et al.: Extended Discourse Representation Structures in Attempto Controlled English. Technical Report IfI-2004. University of Zurich, Zurich (2004)
5. Klein, M., Bernstein, A.: Towards High-Precision Service Retrieval. IEEE Internet Computing 8/1 (2004) 30-36
6. Miller, L., Seaborne, A., Reggiori, A.: Three Implementations of SquishQL, a Simple RDF Query Language. The International Semantic Web Conference (ISWC2002). Sardinia, Italy (2002) 423-435
7. Malhotra, A.: Design Criteria for a Knowledge-based English Language System for Management: An Experimental Analysis. Ph.D. MIT Sloan School of Management, Cambridge, MA (1975)
8. Kamp, H., Reyle, U.: From Discourse to Logic: Introduction to Modeltheoretic Semantics of Natural Language. Kluwer, Dordrecht Boston London (1993)
9. Bernstein, A., et al.: Talking to the Semantic Web: A Controlled English Query Interface for Ontologies. Fourteenth Annual Workshop on Information Technologies and Systems (WITS 2004). Washington, D.C. (2004) 212-217
10. Malone, T.W., et al.: Tools for Inventing Organizations: Toward a Handbook of Organizational Processes. Management Science 45/3 (1999) 425-443
11. Tang, L.R., Mooney, R.J.: Using Multiple Clause Constructors in Inductive Logic Programming for Semantic Parsing. 12th European Conference on Machine Learning (ECML-2001). Freiburg, Germany (2001) 466-477
12. Brooke, J.: SUS - A "quick and dirty" Usability Scale. In: Jordan, P.W., et al., Editors: Usability Evaluation in Industry. Taylor & Francis, London (1996)
13. Salton, G., McGill, M.J.: Introduction to modern information retrieval. McGraw-Hill computer science series. McGraw-Hill, New York (1983)
14. Wojcik, R.H.: Personal Communication. Richard H. Wojcik is Manager of the Boing Simplified English Project, (2004)
15. Schwitter, R., Tilbrook, M.: Dynamic Semantics at Work. International Workshop on Logic and Engineering of Natural Language Semantics. Kanazawa, Japan (2004) 49-60
16. Dittenbach, M., Merkl, D., Berger, H.: A Natural Language Query Interface for Tourism Information. 10th International Conference on Information Technologies in Tourism (ENTER 2003). Helsinki, Finland (2003) 152-162
17. Cimiano, P.: ORAKEL: A Natural Language Interface to an F-Logic Knowledge Base. 9th International Conference on Applications of Natural Language to Information Systems (NLDB 2004). Salford, UK (2004) 401-406
18. Distelhorst, G., et al.: A Prototype Natural Language Interface to a Large Complex Knowledge Base, the Foundational Model of Anatomy. American Medical Informatics Association Annual Fall Symposium. Philadelphia, PA (2003) 200-204
19. MKBEEM: Multilingual Knowledge Based European Electronic Market Place. (2005) http://mkbeem.elibel.tm.fr/
20. Androutsopoulos, I., Ritchie, G.D., Thanisch, P.: Natural Language Interfaces to Databases - An Introduction. Natural Language Engineering 1/1 (1995) 29-81

21. Guarino, N., Masolo, C., Vetere, G.: OntoSeek: Content-Based Access to the Web. IEEE Intelligent Systems 14/3 (1999) 70-80
22. Andreason, T.: An Approach to Knowledge-based Query Evaluation. Fuzzy Sets and Systems 140/1 (2003) 75-91
23. Minock, M.: A Phrasal Approach to Natural Language Interfaces over Databases. Umeå Techreport UMINF-05.09. University of Umeå, Umeå (2005)
24. Popescu, A.-M., Etzioni, O., Kautz, H.: Towards a Theory of Natural Language Interfaces to Databases. 8th International Conference on Intelligent User Interfaces. Miami, FL (2003) 149-157

Semantic Browsing of Digital Collections

Trevor Collins, Paul Mulholland, and Zdenek Zdrahal

Knowledge Media Institute, The Open University, UK
{t.d.collins, p.mulholland, z.zdrahal}@open.ac.uk

Abstract. Visiting museums is an increasingly popular pastime. Studies have shown that visitors can draw on their museum experience, long after their visit, to learn new things in practical situations. Rather than viewing a visit as a single learning event, we are interested in ways of extending the experience to allow visitors to access online resources tailored to their interests. Museums typically have extensive archives that can be made available online, the challenge is to match these resources to the visitor's interests and present them in a manner that facilitates exploration and engages the visitor. We propose the use of knowledge level resource descriptions to identify relevant resources and create structured presentations. A system that embodies this approach, which is in use in a UK museum, is presented and the applicability of the approach to the broader semantic web is discussed.

1 Introduction

This paper presents an approach that exploits the use of semantics to create and present online digital collections for museum visitors to explore after their visit. Learning from museums is an example of what has been referred to as "free-choice learning"[1]. Other examples include learning "when watching television, reading a newspaper, talking with friends, attending a play, or surfing the internet" [1]. Characteristically, the learning that occurs is a product of how we choose to spend our playtime rather than the product of a formal education or job activity. As noted in [2] "play is not just mindless entertainment, but an essential way of engaging with and learning about our world and ourselves - for adults as well as children."

1.1 Background

In a survey of visitors to a museum web site Kravchyna and Hastings [3] found that 57% of respondents visited a museum's web site both before and after visiting the museum. Yet, other than the hours of business, admission price and travel advice, little information is tailored to the pre- or post-visit reader. For someone who has never visited the museum, this essential information is very valuable, but for those who have already been, additional information can be made available that enables the visitor to build on their museum experience and in doing so encourage return visits. Falk and Dierking [1] reported finding extensive evidence that showed how visitors are able to draw on their museum experience, long after their visit, to construct new knowledge when they come across applicable situations in their everyday lives.

Y. Gil et al. (Eds.): ISWC 2005, LNCS 3729, pp. 127–141, 2005.

Rather than considering the museum visit as a one off event, the web offers an opportunity for visitors to continue learning when they get home [4].

1.2 Search

Rose and Levinson [5] proposed a hierarchical framework for classifying the goals of search engine users. They suggested that the purpose of an internet search can be broadly categorized as either 'navigational,' 'resource' or 'informational'. A navigational search is to locate to a known web site. Resource searches are used to obtain a resource available on the web. The purpose of informational searches is to learn something new by reading or viewing web pages. Across three samples of approximately 500 Alta Vista queries an average of 13.50% where categorized as navigational, 24.57% as resource, and 61.93% as informational. Although the navigational goal is least common, it is the best supported by traditional search engines [6].

To support exploratory informational searches several researchers have investigated the use of categories for presenting search results [7], [8]. Dumais, Cutrell and Chen [7] found in a series of four experimental studies, each involving between 18 and 20 people, that category interfaces were more effective than list interfaces. From a two month longitudinal study of sixteen users' search behaviors, Kaki [8] found categories were more beneficial that lists when more than one result was sought.

Guha, McCool and Miller [9] make the case that informational searches can significantly exploit the semantic web. Specifically, they showed how semantics can be used to augment the results of traditional information retrieval search techniques and to improve the text retrieval part of a search engine by identifying the context of the concepts denoted in the search phrase. We are particularly interested in identifying information related to a museum visitor's interests that can be drawn together to form a collection of resources for them to explore when they return home.

1.3 Collections and Narratives

An organized collection of objects forms a narrative that expresses relationships across the included items [10]. For example, a curated exhibition of paintings constitutes a narrative that expresses a story across the selected works. Here we are interested in forming a digital collection from a set of resources (according to the knowledge level description of those resources) and creating a series of hypertext presentations to support the reader's exploration of the resources in the collection. Exploring a collection involves the active interpretation of the included objects and the discovery of relationships between them.

Several systems for generating narratives have been developed recently in the cultural heritage domain. For example, Geurts, Bocconi, van Ossenbruggen and Hardman [11] present an ontology-driven approach for producing multimedia presentations. For a given query (such as 'life and work of Rembrandt'), presentation genre (such as 'biographies' or 'curriculum vitae') and presentation medium (such as 'screen' or 'paper'), a multimedia presentation is created through a two step process. A semantic graph, produced in response to the user query, is first of all transformed into a structured progression according to the chosen genre. The media items that represent the concepts identified in the structured progression are then retrieved to produce a multimedia presentation in the chosen medium. Within the Artequakt system [12] information extraction procedures are used to populate a knowledge base. Facts in the knowledge base are then used to fill in a predefined presentation template to produce a narrative. For example, information regarding an artist's place and date of birth and date of death can be used to complete the opening sections of a biographical template.

Rather than building a coherent narrative from relevant facts (taken from a semantic graph or information extraction procedures) we are interested in building collections out of units that are meaningful in their own right, that is, the resources being used are lexia [13]. Examples include textual story passages, meaningful video clips and paintings. This avoids the problem of creating low-level narrative coherence, but raises the challenge of ensuring coherence across a collection of resources. The approach taken in response is to ensure the relationships between the included resources are clear and transparent to the user. The Topia [14] and Noadster [15] systems apply a concept lattice clustering approach to hierarchically group components that share characteristics. In the Topia system this is applied to group media components in order to generate hypermedia presentations. Similarly, we are interested in creating structured presentations that identify groups of related resources and show the relationships between resources in an online collection.

1.4 Summary and Overview

In summary, we are interested in applying semantic web technologies to support free-choice learning. We believe the semantic web offers an opportunity for museums to extend their visitors' museum experience in a rewarding manner that can be used to encourage future museum visits.

The following section explains the ontologies we use for describing heritage resources and our approach for retrieving and presenting resources related to a given set of concepts. Section 3 describes how these approaches were put together to form the Bletchley Park Text system, which is now in daily use at Bletchley Park, a museum in the UK. Several examples of how the system is being used to explore a collection of resources are given in Section 4. The limitations of our approach and its potential application across the semantic web are discussed in Section 5. Section 6 summarizes what we consider to be the primary costs and benefits of adopting a semantic approach to support the exploration of digital collections.

2 Approach

We can explain the approach we took by first describing the context of the work, the ontologies used to represent the museum resources, and the method used to represent the key information taken from the tour guides' presentation. We then describe how a set of resources are retrieved to produce a collection of related resources, and how these are organized into structured presentations to support the exploration of the relationships, which are used to connect concepts across the resource archive and form groups within the visitor's collected set of resources.

2.1 Bletchley Park Museum

This work has been carried out in collaboration with Bletchley Park Museum. The Park was the headquarters of the British Government Code and Cipher School during the Second World War. The Park was closed in 1945 and did not become a museum until the early 1990s after decades of secrecy. Since then the museum has been piecing together much of its hidden history. Several of the original buildings are still there and a number of them have been restored. The museum includes a range of exhibits that seek to explain the life of the people that worked there, the significance of the work they carried out, and how this pioneering work shaped modern computing and communication technologies.

2.2 Representing Resources

Bletchley Park Trust provided us with a set of transcripts of interviews with people that worked in the Park during the Second World War and a set of historical accounts of the activities related to the work of Bletchley Park for each month during the war. The knowledge level description of these resources was created using three distinct ontologies: the CIDOC Conceptual Reference Model (CRM), a Story and Narrative ontology (created as part of the Story Fountain system [16]), and a Bletchley Park domain ontology. CIDOC is the International Committee for Documentation of the International Council of Museums. Their CRM is a high-level ontology for describing cultural heritage objects and events, and is currently being considered as a potential ISO standard [17]. The story and narrative ontology was used to represent the historical accounts and first person interviews that make up a significant portion of the archive. The story and narrative ontology follows structuralist theories of narrative in distinguishing between a story (i.e. the conceptualization of what is told) and a narrative (i.e. how that story is told and what media is used) [18].

An example of the type of metadata used to describe a story is given in Figure 1. A story is represented as having any number of central actors (i.e. the main people or groups in the story), existents (i.e. the main physical objects), themes and events. Each event is described as having actors, existents, locations and a time specification. Depending on the type of event, existing properties were specialized or additional properties added. For example, an interview event had an interviewer and interviewee, and a creation event had a creator and an object of creation. Currently, the archive contains over 400 stories, which refer to over 1,700 distinct concepts, these include approximately: 450 people, 250 groups, 500 places, 200 physical objects, 300 conceptual objects and 50 work roles.

Sample resource:

Margot McNeely and Diana Lauder interview

My name is Margot McNeely; I was 17 and a half a schoolgirl in Burnham when I decided to volunteer for the WRNS that was in 1944. I took my school certificate and done some basic training then had lots of interviews. I don't know how they chose us, we were sent down here not knowing what we were going to be doing. ...

OCML knowledge model:

```
(def-instance margot-mcneely-interview story
    ((describes-event mmc-event)
    (describes-existent bombe)
    (has-associated-narrative margot-mcneely-narrative)
    (has-central-actor margot-mcneely)
    (has-theme life-and-work-in-bletchley-park)))

(def-instance mmc-event bletchley-park-life-experience
    ((has-actor margot-mcneely wrns)
    (has-billeting-location woburn-abbey crawley-grange)
    (has-work-location hut-11)
    (has-working-object bombe)
    (has-working-role bombe-operator p5)
    (is-described-in-story margot-mcneely-interview)))

(def-instance margot-mcneely-narrative cipher-digital-narrative
    ((has-associated-story-object margot-mcneely-interview)
    (has-uri "http:// ... ")))
```

Fig. 1. An extract from a sample resource and an example of the type of metadata used to describe it

2.3 Representing the Museum Tour Experience

While visiting the Park visitors are given a guided tour of the grounds and about told the history of the Park. A knowledge level description of the key facts given in the tour was stored as a set of fact triples in the knowledge base. These facts are not necessarily mentioned in the interviews or historical accounts, but provide useful background knowledge that is helpful when reading the resources.

Within educational hypertext, the concepts of vertical and horizontal navigation are used to describe the types of links within a hypertext [19]. Vertical navigation refers to traversing the hierarchical structure of a hypertext from parent to child and child to parent, whereas horizontal navigation links associated pages across the content hierarchy. Horizontal navigation is particularly beneficial within educational hypertext for referring the reader to related examples, counter examples, and sources of related information.

In our approach the fact triples are used to produce horizontal links that highlight relationships between groups of resources. For example, during the tour of Bletchley Park visitors are told that Alan Turing was the head of Hut 8. This is represented by a fact triple where 'Alan Turing' is an instance of a person, 'was head of' is a relation, and 'Hut 8' is an instance of a place within Bletchley Park. This additional fact is then used to provide a horizontal link between groups of resources relating to Alan Turing and groups relating to Hut 8. These horizontal links provide a navigational aid and serve to reinforce the story of Bletchley Park told by the tour guides.

2.4 Retrieving Related Resources

The visitor to the museum can identify any class, slot or instance as a concept of interest. For example, they may be interested in Alan Turing (an instance of a person), the places where people lived referred to as billeting locations, (an example of a slot), or a broader interest in decryption machines (an example of a class of machine). For a given query such as 'Alan Turing, billeting locations and decryption machines' the relevant stories are those where the knowledge level description refers to the instance Alan Turing, the slot billeting location, or any instance of the class 'decryption machine' (such as the Bombe or Colossus). Logical OR is used to identify all of the related stories. The combined set is referred to as the visitor's collection.

2.5 Identifying Connections Between Concepts

Connections can be found when they exist between any pair of concepts (i.e. instances, slots or classes) by applying a path finding algorithm. The algorithm connects concepts in the archive using the slot values in each story event. For example, if one story explains that Alan Turing invented the Bombe, represented by an event of type 'birth' with a value of Alan Turing in the 'has-actor' slot and a value of Bombe in the 'has-recipient' slot, then this would constitute a connection between Alan Turing and the Bombe decryption machine as explained in that story.

For connections involving more than one story, common slot values are used to connect them. For example, to connect Alan Turing and Block G (one of the locations within Bletchley Park) two stories are required, one story describes that Alan Turing invented the Bombe and another explains that the Bombe machines were used in Block G. In terms of the knowledge level description, the first story includes an event of type 'birth' that identifies Alan Turing as the value of the 'has-actor' slot and the Bombe machine as the value of the 'has-recipient' slot, the second story includes an event of type 'bletchley park life experience' with a value of Bombe in the 'has working object' slot and a value of 'Block G' in the 'has work location' slot.

Within the archive there are over 1,700 concepts, and all concept pairs can be connected within a maximum of seven stories. The most common path length involves just three stories.

2.6 Identifying Categories Within a Collection

To group stories in a collection, categories are formed according to the most frequently used slot-value pairs (see Table 1). Two forms of categories are produced: a flat list of categories and a hierarchical list of categories. A flat list is simply a set of categories ordered by frequency, such as 'has actor Alan Turing (three stories), has actor Winston Churchill (two stories), has actor John Tiltman (two stories), has actor Frank Birch (one story), and billeting location Woburn Abbey (one story)'. The same story can be included in multiple categories. To form a hierarchy of categories the same approach is used recursively within each category, down to a minimum category size. In the example given in Table 1, the category formed for 'has actor Alan Turing' contains three stories (i.e. story 1, 4 and 5), and within this category a sub-category can be formed containing the two stories that include 'has actor Winston Churchill' (i.e. story 1 and 4). The nested category includes stories that contain all of the parent slot-value pairs (i.e. 'has actor Alan Turing' AND 'has actor Winston Churchill').

Table 1. An example of the type of frequency data used to form a set of categories within a collection of stories. In this case the most common category would contain the stories that describe the activities of Alan Turing.

Slot-value pairs		Stories (an illustrative sample of five)					Frequency
Slot	Value	Story 1	Story 2	Story 3	Story 4	Story 5	
has actor	Alan Turing	Y	N	N	Y	Y	3
has actor	Winston Churchill	Y	N	N	Y	N	2
has actor	John Tiltman	N	N	Y	N	Y	2
has actor	Frank Birch	N	Y	N	N	N	1
billeting location	Woburn Abbey	N	Y	N	N	N	1

3 Bletchley Park Text

The knowledge level description of the resources and tour experience were developed using the Apollo knowledge modeling application [20]. The resulting knowledge model was exported as OCML [21] and placed on a Lisp server. A reasoning engine written in Lisp was used to produce story collections for any given set of concepts, generate pathways connecting concepts, and identify categories within a story collection.

Museum visitors express their interests using SMS text messages. Around the museum additional labels have been posted in locations and on exhibits to identify concepts of interest. One or more messages can be sent by a visitor, which are automatically downloaded from a mobile phone and stored in a database using commercially available text messaging software (i.e. SMS Demon available from www.dload.com.au). When a visitor enters their mobile phone number to log onto the web site, the concepts identified in their messages are used to query the knowledge model and identify a collection of related stories. Alternative mobile technologies for recording the visitor's interests, such as Radio Frequency Identification ('RFID') tags and readers, and location tracking Personal Digital Assistants ('PDAs') were also considered. However, the cost to the museum of providing and maintaining these technologies and the effort involved for the visitor to learn how to use them was prohibitive for our purposes.

Bletchley Park Text was built using the Story Fountain system [16]. Story Fountain was designed to support the investigation of questions and topics that require the accumulation, association or triangulation of information across a story archive. The underlying architecture of the Story Fountain is shown in Figure 2 along with the addition of the mobile phone service used to create the Bletchley Park Text application. An Apache web server coordinates the delivery of the site and uses the ModPython and ModLisp modules to access the presentation module (i.e. Python) and the knowledge module (i.e. the OCML knowledge model).

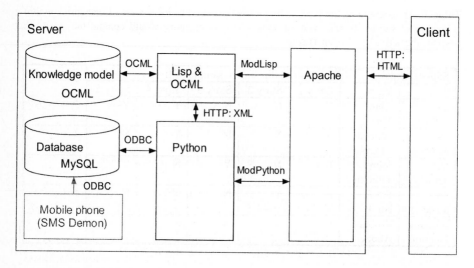

Fig. 2. The system architecture of the Bletchley Park Text application

Following a series of pilot trials the text application has been in daily use by visitors to Bletchley Park since May 2005.

4   Examples

After sending a text message the visitor can access the web site by entering their mobile phone number (see Figure 3, left). Six areas are available for the visitor to explore: stories, connections, categories, hierarchy, spotlight and modify (Figure 3, right). The first five present the collection of stories in different formats, and the sixth enables the visitor to change their selected set of concepts and thereby modify their story collection.

The 'stories' area presents all of the related stories from the archive (see Figure 4, left). In the five presentation areas each story is represented as a preview containing the title, an image (if available) and the first few lines of text (if available). The visitor can view any single story by clicking on its title (see Figure 4, right). The 'stories' area initially presents the collection as a single set, which the user can reduce by choosing one or more of their concepts as a filter. For example, by selecting Alan Turing as a filter concept only the stories relating to Alan Turing will be displayed (see Figure 5, left).

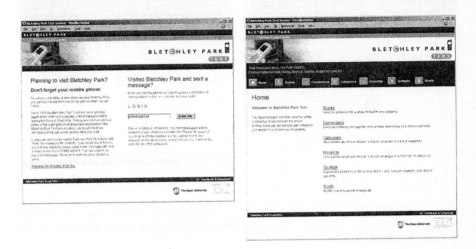

Fig. 3. The Bletchley Park Text login page (left), and the home page (right)

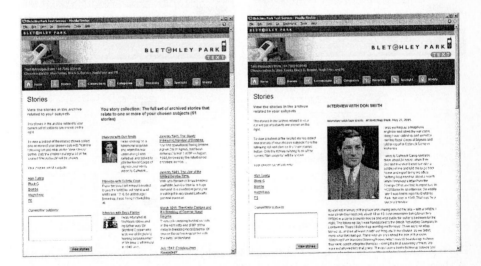

Fig. 4. The 'stories' area showing all of the stories in the archive related to the visitor's chosen set of concepts (left), and a subset of the stories relating to a specific concept, Alan Turing (right)

The 'connections' area allows the visitor to chose two of their concepts as start and end nodes, and presents a connection extracted from the knowledge model (see Figure 5, right). The first two of the visitor's concepts are used initially by default.

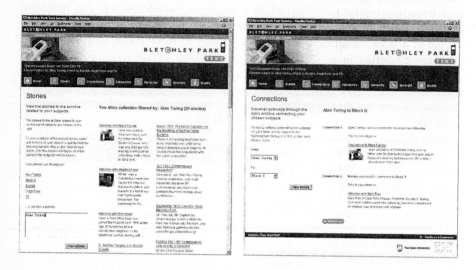

Fig. 5. An example of an interview story being displayed in the stories area (left), and an example of a pathway using two stories to link Alan Turing to Block G shown in the 'connections' area (right)

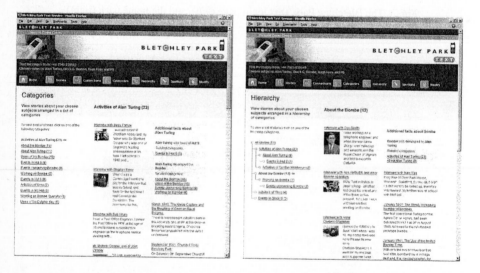

Fig. 6. Examples of the 'categories' (left) and 'hierarchy' (right) areas showing the use of the 'Additional facts' box to provide horizontal links between categories of stories

Along with a preview of the stories used in the connection the semantics from the knowledge model are transformed to produce a natural language description of each part of the connection.

The additional facts, used to represent the key information from the visitor's tour experience, are applied to produce horizontal links in the 'categories', hierarchy' and 'spotlight' presentation areas. The 'category' area shows the visitor's story collection organized in a list of up to 12 categories (see Figure 6, left). The 'hierarchy' shows the same collection in a hierarchically organized list of categories (see Figure 6, right). These categories are formed in a bottom-up fashion from the resources retrieved by the visitor's chosen concepts. Forming groups within a collection of resources based on the underlying semantics enables the visitor to see how the resources can be organized and highlights distinctions between the resources in separate groups.

The 'spotlight' area separates out the list of categories into two sets (see Figure 7). One set contains the five most frequent categories that explicitly mention the visitor's chosen concepts. The other contains the five most frequent categories that do not mention any of the visitor's concepts. Although these categories may overlap those shown in the 'categories' area, the distinction between the directly and indirectly related categories emphasizes the relationship between the concepts used to identify the collection and those closely related according to the knowledge level descriptions. The spotlight metaphor is used here to convey a sense that the visitor's set of concepts illuminate a section of the online archive. Choosing concepts in the indirectly related set of categories will slowly move the spotlight to a nearby section. Conversely, choosing a set of completely unrelated concepts will make the spotlight jump to an entirely new section of the archive.

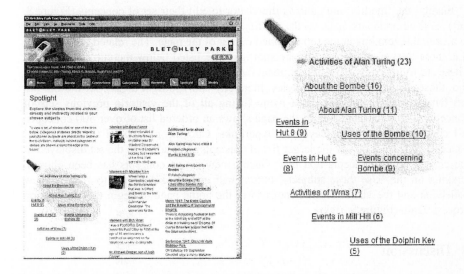

Fig. 7. The 'spotlight' area showing sets of categories directly and indirectly related to the visitor's chosen concepts (left). Directly related categories are shown in the focus of the torch beam, indirectly related categories are shown to the side of the torch beam (right detail).

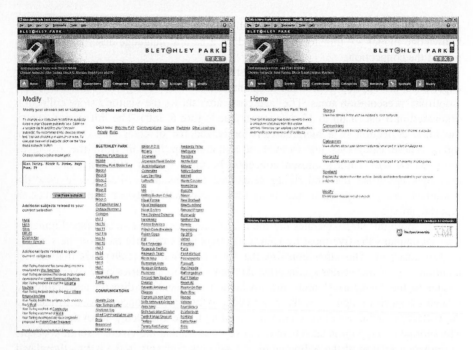

Fig. 8. The 'modify' area where the visitor can edit their chosen set of concepts (left). When the visitor finishes editing their concepts and selects the 'Use these concepts' button, they are taken back to the home page with a new story collection (right).

Finally, the 'modify' area allows the visitor to edit their set of concepts (Figure 8, left). Five components make up the modify page. The current set of concepts is listed in an editable text box at the top left hand corner of the page. The related concepts (i.e. those shown on the edge of the spotlight) are listed below the current concepts. These are followed by a list of additional facts related to the current set of concepts (i.e. those displayed in the categories, hierarchy and spotlight areas). At the bottom left hand corner of the page is a menu listing all of the visitor's previous sets of concepts. The right hand side of the page shows an ordered list of over 500 concepts. All concept labels are displayed as hyperlinks. Clicking on a label (in the related concept, additional fact or the larger list of concepts) will add it to the set displayed in the chosen set of concepts text box. Once a new set of concepts has been chosen, clicking on the 'Use these subjects' button will use these concepts to create a new collection and the visitor will be returned to the home page to begin the exploration process again (Figure 8, right).

5   Discussion

The content of the Bletchley Park Text system is primarily text with illustrative pictures, but the approach is applicable to any media type. Within the current system a single content source and knowledge model is used. However, providing the ontologies are used consistently to describe the resources there is no reason why the content and knowledge model could not be distributed. The Apollo tool used to develop the knowledge model can also export models using the standard RDF and XML syntaxes. The OCML syntax was used in our case because it was directly compatible with a Lisp-based reasoning engine, which offered us a fast and efficient means for retrieving and organizing the resources.

Currently, the Bletchley Park Text system presents the shortest path connecting any pair of concepts. However, we have also been exploring ways of presenting alternative pathways. The choice of connections in a pathway could be biased towards or away from the visitor's current set of concepts. Including the visitor's concepts may highlight the connections between their chosen set of concepts, whereas excluding them would bring the visitor in contact with related but yet unconsidered concepts. Another possibility is to use the pathways as a means to construct time-ordered sequences of events. For example, introducing a particular person the work they carried out at Bletchley Park and where they went afterwards.

The category based presentations currently show the most frequently occurring categories within the visitor's collection. Revealing the complete set of categories within any given collection would provide a more flexible means for exploring the resources. However, this may also provide the visitor with too much information. One solution being considered is to enable the user to select which slots and values are used, or not used, to form categories.

A pilot study involving a group of 35 high school pupils and their teachers was carried out in September 2004 [22]. All of the pupils used their mobile phones to send messages, 20 of them chose to follow up their visit by signing onto the Bletchley Park Text web site. Six of the students were asked to write an essay after their visit and a follow-up interview was carried out with this group. In both the essays and interview the pupils clearly demonstrated that they had drawn on the resources available from the web site, and several of the pupils indicated that they wanted to continue to use the site. As noted earlier, the Bletchley Park Text system is now available to all visitors, and we are currently monitoring the messages received and the changes visitors make to their concepts. Further evaluation studies are being planned to explore visitors' use of the web site and alternate forms of presentation.

6 Conclusion

This paper has explained our approach for using semantics to create structured presentations of personalized collections. The Bletchley Park Text system uses this approach to produce a web site where visitors can read historical accounts and interviews with the people that worked at Bletchley Park.

The cost in effort of providing this (or similar) sites is primarily the annotation of the resources. Identifying and digitizing appropriate content is a relatively small task compared to the development of the knowledge level description. Although considerable advances are being made in the automatic annotation of text resources (as illustrated by the Artequakt system [12]), developing an accurate knowledge model is a difficult and critical aspect of this approach. However, the benefits are clear. The automated identification of pathways connecting concepts and the formation of meaningful categories, as used in the Bletchley Park Text system, are currently not possible without the use of knowledge level descriptions. Furthermore, once produced, the knowledge model can be used to provide a range of services, not just for museum visitors but also museum staff.

The majority of the existing approaches for searching the web have focused on the retrieval of single pages. This form of presentation fails to support the exploration and analysis of web resources. By exploiting the semantics of online resources (such as museum archives) the semantic web is creating an opportunity for us to support people's playful explorations in ways that highlight the connections across web resources and categories within collections of resources.

References

1. Falk, J.H. and L.D. Dierking, Learning from museums: Visitor experiences and the making of meaning. American Association for State and Local History, ed. R. Rodgers. 2000, Walnut Creek, CA: AltaMira Press. 272.
2. Gaver, B., Designing for Homo Ludens, in i3 magazine. 2002. p. 2-6.
3. Kravchyna, V. and S.K. Hastings, Information Value of Museum Web Sites. Fisrt Monday, 2002. 7(2).
4. Anani, N. Enhancing the Heritage Experience. in Museums and the Web. 2005. Toronto, Canada: Archives & Museum Informatics.
5. Rose, D.E. and B. Levinson. Understanding User Goals in Web Search. in WWW. 2004. New York, USA: ACM Press.
6. Yee, K.-P., et al. Faceted Metadata for Image Search Browsing. in CHI. 2003. Fort Lauderdale, Florida, USA: ACM Press.
7. Dumais, S., E. Cutrell, and H. Chen. Optimizing Search by Showing Results in Context. in SIGCHI. 2001. Seattle, WA, USA: ACM Press.
8. Kaki, M. Findex: Search Result Categories Help Users when Document Ranking Fails. in CHI. 2005. Portland, Oregon, USA: ACM Press.
9. Guha, R., R. McCool, and E. Miller. Semantic Search. in WWW. 2003. Budapest, Hungary: ACM Press.
10. Pearce, S.M., On collecting: An investigation into collecting in the European tradition. 1995, London: Routledge.
11. Geurts, J., et al. Ontology-driven Discourse: From Semantic Graphs to Multimedia Presentations. in International Semantic Web Conference. 2003. Florida, USA: Springer Verlag.
12. Alani, H., et al., Automatic Ontology-Based Knowledge Extraction from Web Documents. IEEE Intelligent Systems, 2003. 18(1): p. 14-21.
13. Landow, G., Hypertext: The Convergence of Contemporary Critical theory and Technology. 1992: The John Hopkins University Press, Baltimore, USA.
14. Rutledge, L., et al. Finding the Story - Broader Applicability of Semantics and Discourse for Hypermedia Generation. in Hypertext. 2003. Nottingham, UK.: ACM Press.
15. Rutledge, L., J.v. Ossenbruggen, and L. Hardman. Making PDF Presentable. in WWW. 2005. Chiba, Japan: ACM Press.
16. Mulholland, P., T. Collins, and Z. Zdrahal. Story Fountain: Intelligent support for story research and exploration. in International Conference on Intelligent User Interfaces. 2004. Madeira, Portugal.: ACM Press.
17. CIDOC Conceptual Reference Model. Available from: http://zeus.ics.forth.gr/cidoc/

18. Chatman, S., Story and Discourse: Narrative structure in fiction and film. 1980, New York: Cornell University Press.
19. Brusilovsky, P. and R. Rizzo. Map-Based Horizontal Navigation in Educational Hypertext. in Hypertext. 2002. College Park, Maryland, USA.: ACM Press.
20. Apollo Knowledge Modelling Application. Available from: http://apollo.open.ac.uk
21. OCML: Ontological Conceptual Modelling Language. Available from: http://kmi.open.ac.uk/projects/ocml/
22. Mulholland, P., T. Collins, and Z. Zdrahal. Spotlight Browsing of Resource Archives. in Hypertext. 2005. Salzburg, Austria: ACM Press.

Decentralized Case-Based Reasoning
for the Semantic Web

Mathieu d'Aquin, Jean Lieber, and Amedeo Napoli

LORIA (INRIA Lorraine, CNRS, Nancy Universities),
Campus scientifique, BP 239,
54 506 Vandœuvre-lès-Nancy, France
{daquin, lieber, napoli}@loria.fr

Abstract. Decentralized case-based reasoning (DzCBR) is a reasoning framework that addresses the problem of adaptive reasoning in a multi-ontology environment. It is a case-based reasoning (CBR) approach which relies on contextualized
ontologies in the C-OWL formalism for the representation of domain knowledge
and adaptation knowledge. A context in C-OWL is used to represent a particular
viewpoint, containing the knowledge needed to solve a particular local problem.
Semantic relations between contexts and the associated reasoning mechanisms allow the CBR process in a particular viewpoint to reuse and share information about
the problem and the already found solutions in the other viewpoints.

1 Introduction

This paper presents a research work on the application of case-based reasoning (CBR,
see e.g. [1,2]) within the semantic Web technologies and principles. CBR is a type
of analogical reasoning in which problem-solving is based on the adaptation of the
solutions of similar problems, already solved and stored in a case base. In particular,
knowledge-intensive CBR (KI-CBR [3]) relies on a knowledge base including domain
knowledge and, as well, knowledge units exploited for the retrieval and adaptation operations of CBR.

Ontologies are at the heart of semantic Web technologies and OWL is the standard
language for representing ontologies [4]. An ontology is used for the conceptualization
of a particular domain and for knowledge exchange. The OWL language allows the
use of deductive reasoning mechanisms, such as classification and instantiation. In this
paper, we want to show that the classical deductive reasoning made in the semantic
Web technologies may be completed and enhanced with KI-CBR that may take advantage of domain ontologies and provide an operationalization for reasoning by analogy.
Moreover, the representation of the knowledge used for adaptation in CBR (*adaptation
knowledge*) must be integrated within ontologies.

Usually, the adaptation knowledge is dependent on the application context. For example, a Web service applying CBR for advising customers on computer sales will
consider a male customer as similar to a female customer. However, in a case-based
Web service dedicated to fashion advises, a male and a female customers have to be
considered as dissimilar. In other terms, the knowledge for CBR is dependent on the
considered viewpoint, i.e. on the type of problem that the system has to solve.

Y. Gil et al. (Eds.): ISWC 2005, LNCS 3729, pp. 142–155, 2005.

C-OWL (for context-OWL) is a formalism that has been recently proposed [5] for the representation of mappings between several OWL ontologies for the purpose of ontology alignment. A local ontology in C-OWL is considered as a context, having its own language and its own interpretation. Mappings are made of bridge rules that express semantic relations between classes, properties and individuals of the local ontologies. In this way, aligning ontologies using C-OWL allows the coordinated use of these ontologies, keeping the knowledge contained in each of them in its local context. Moreover, beyond ontology alignment, C-OWL can be used for representing modular ontologies, combining different viewpoints on the same domain, and this is how we use it hereafter.

In this paper, we propose DzCBR (decentralized case-based reasoning), a KI-CBR mechanism that exploits the decentralized knowledge represented in a C-OWL contextualized ontology. Each context of a contextualized ontology is used for representing a particular viewpoint, containing the domain knowledge and the adaptation knowledge needed for solving a particular type of problem. Several DzCBR processes are then distributed among these viewpoints, each one being carried out locally in a context and relying on local knowledge. Collaboration between these multiple local processes is implemented thanks to C-OWL bridge rules and to the associated reasoning mechanisms. In this way, decentralized problem-solving is based both on local knowledge, for a particular viewpoint, and on the combination of several viewpoints. DzCBR is a new paradigm that we have designed and that we currently use in an application in oncology. The roots of decentralized reasoning can be found in pattern recognition and distributed artificial intelligence [6], and we have extended this approach within the C-OWL formalism, to design DzCBR and to enhance problem-solving capabilities for the semantic Web.

The next section presents a motivating application of DzCBR in the domain of oncology. In the section 3, CBR and its integration in the semantic Web framework are detailed. A short introduction to C-OWL follows in section 4. The section 5 details the knowledge and reasoning models of DzCBR, and how problem-solving is carried out by combining several decentralized viewpoints represented by C-OWL contexts. An example of a DzCBR process applied to a breast cancer treatment problem is presented in section 6. Finally, the related work is discussed in section 7, and the section 8 concludes the paper.

2   Motivating Application: Adaptation Within Multiple Viewpoints in Oncology

Oncology is a complex domain where several specialties, e.g. chemotherapy, surgery and radiotherapy, are involved in several treatment phases. In most cases, the adequate therapeutic decision is given according to a protocol that associates standard patient characteristics with a recommended treatment. Even if it is designed to take into account the majority of the medical cases, a protocol does not cover all the situations. Decisions concerning patients out of the protocol are elaborated within a multi-disciplinary expert committee, and rely on the adaptation of the solutions provided by the protocol for similar cases. Specialties in oncology organize their background knowledge and past experiences in different ways. Indeed, a protocol is structured according to the oncology specialties and, during a meeting of an expert committee, each expert from each specialty supplies a personal view on the solution as a part of a collective solution. For each specialty, a particular type of treatment is requested, in a particular treatment phase, and the patient characteristics used to find the solution change from one specialty to another. Thus, oncology specialties provide different viewpoints on oncology, and these viewpoints are related to each other. Information about a problem, e.g. finding a therapeutic decision for a patient, can be shared across specialties, and decisions taken in a particular specialty may influence decisions taken in another one.

A protocol contains the standard knowledge for decision making in oncology. As a standard Web formalism for knowledge representation and exchange, OWL is a well-suited language for Furthermore, reasoning mechanisms associated with OWL, such as classification and instantiation, may be used to provide intelligent access to this knowledge, for the purpose of decision support in oncology. In the perspective of decision support for out of the protocol cases, a KI-CBR mechanism relying on a formalized protocol may be applied. In this way, the knowledge used by expert committees is represented and operationalized in the form of adaptation knowledge to become sharable and reusable. Knowledge representation and reasoning have to take into account the multiple viewpoints involved in the decision, corresponding to oncology specialties. C-OWL provides a formalism for representing several alternative representations of the domain and for relating these local representations to each other. Thus, domain knowledge (contained in a protocol) as well as adaptation knowledge are represented within contextualized ontologies in C-OWL. A KI-CBR mechanism may be used with profit for exploiting such decentralized knowledge. The framework of DzCBR is proposed here for this purpose.

3   Case-Based Reasoning with OWL

3.1   Principles of Case-Based Reasoning

A case is a problem solving episode usually represented by a *problem* pb and a *solution* Sol(pb) of pb. A case base is a (usually structured) set of cases, called *source cases*. A source case is denoted by (srce, Sol(srce)). CBR consists in solving a *target problem*, denoted by tgt, thanks to the case base. The classical CBR process relies on two steps, retrieval and adaptation. *Retrieval* aims at finding a source problem srce in the case base that is considered to be similar to tgt. The role of the *adaptation* task is to adapt the solution of srce, Sol(srce), in order to build Sol(tgt), a solution of tgt. Then, the solution Sol(tgt) is tested, repaired, and, if necessary, memorized for future reuse.

In knowledge intensive CBR (KI-CBR, see e.g. [3, 7, 8]), the CBR process relies on a formalized model of domain knowledge. This model may contain, for example, an ontology of the application domain, and can be used to organize the case base for case retrieval. KI-CBR may also include some knowledge for adaptation, as explained in the following.

3.2   Reformulations: An Approach for Representing Adaptation Knowledge

Reformulations are basic elements for modeling adaptation knowledge for CBR [9]. A reformulation is a pair $(r, \mathcal{A}_r)$ where r is a relation between problems and $\mathcal{A}_r$ is an *adaptation function*: if r relates srce to tgt –denoted by "srce r tgt"– then any solution Sol(srce) of srce can be adapted into a solution Sol(tgt) of tgt thanks to the adaptation function $\mathcal{A}_r$ –denoted by "Sol(srce) $\mathcal{A}_r$ Sol(tgt)"".

In the reformulation model, retrieval consists of finding a *similarity path* relating srce to tgt, i.e. a composition of relations r_k, introducing intermediate problems pb_k between the source and the target problems. Every r_k relation is linked by a reformulation to an adaptation function $\mathcal{A}_{r_k}$. Thus, the sequence of adaptation functions following the similarity path may be reified in an *adaptation path* (see figure 1).

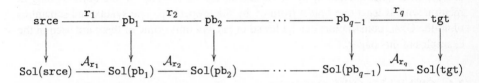

Fig. 1. A similarity path from srce to tgt (first line) and the corresponding adaptation path (second line)

The model of reformulations is a general framework for representing adaptation knowledge. The operations corresponding to problem relations r_k and adaptation functions $\mathcal{A}_{r_k}$ have to be designed for a particular application. Generally, these operations rely on transformation operations such as specialization, generalization and substitution, that allow the creation of the pb_k problems for building the similarity path and of the Sol(pb_k) solutions for the adaptation path: relations of the form pb_1 r pb_2 and adaptation like Sol(pb_1) $\mathcal{A}_r$ Sol(pb_2) correspond to applications of such transformations.

Moreover, the reformulation framework follows the principle of adaptation-guided retrieval [10]. A CBR system using adaptation-guided retrieval retrieves the source cases whose solution is adaptable, i.e. for which adaptation knowledge is available. According to this principle, similarity paths provide a kind of symbolic reification of similarity between problems, allowing the case-based reasoner to build understandable explanation of the results.

3.3   A Brief Introduction to OWL

OWL is the standard formalism for the representation of ontologies for the semantic Web. In OWL, the knowledge about a domain is represented within an ontology. An OWL ontology contains definitions of classes, properties and individuals from the represented domain. An *individual* corresponds to an object. A *property* denotes a binary relation between objects. A *class* represents a set of objects. Formally, the semantics of an OWL ontology is given by an interpretation $\mathcal{I} = (\Delta^{\mathcal{I}}, \cdot^{\mathcal{I}})$, where $\Delta^{\mathcal{I}}$ is a non empty set called the interpretation domain, and $\cdot^{\mathcal{I}}$ is the interpretation function. This function maps a class C into a subset $C^{\mathcal{I}}$ of the interpretation domain $\Delta^{\mathcal{I}}$, a property p into a subset $p^{\mathcal{I}}$ of $\Delta^{\mathcal{I}} \times \Delta^{\mathcal{I}}$, and an individual a to an element $a^{\mathcal{I}}$ of $\Delta^{\mathcal{I}}$.

An OWL *ontology* O is defined by a set of axioms and a set of assertions. Classes are introduced through the use of *axioms* of the form[1] C $\sqsubseteq$ D , C and D being two classes. C $\sqsubseteq$ D is satisfied by an interpretation $\mathcal{I}$ if $C^{\mathcal{I}} \subseteq D^{\mathcal{I}}$. C $\equiv$ D is a notation for C $\sqsubseteq$ D and D $\sqsubseteq$ C. *Assertions* are used to introduce individuals. The two possible types of assertions are C(a) and p(a,b), C being a class, a and b two individuals, and p a property. C(a) is satisfied by an interpretation $\mathcal{I}$ if $a^{\mathcal{I}} \in C^{\mathcal{I}}$ and p(a,b) is satisfied by $\mathcal{I}$ if $(a^{\mathcal{I}}, b^{\mathcal{I}}) \in p^{\mathcal{I}}$. $\mathcal{I}$ is a model of O if it satisfies all the axioms and assertions defining O. OWL provides constructors for building complex classes and complex properties. For example, a class conjunction, C $\sqcap$ D, is interpreted as an intersection ($C^{\mathcal{I}} \cap D^{\mathcal{I}}$), and the existential quantifier, $\exists p.C$, represents the set $(\exists p.C)^{\mathcal{I}}$ of the objects being in relation with at least one object from $C^{\mathcal{I}}$ by the property p. The syntax and semantics of all the OWL constructors can be found in [4], but only some of them are used in the examples of this paper.

3.4   CBR Within OWL Ontologies

In OWL, problems and solutions are represented as instances of the Problem and Solution classes. The link between a problem pb and its solution Sol(pb) is materialized by a property called hasSolution. OWL axioms are used to relate Problem and Solution to classes of the domain knowledge. For example, in the application for breast cancer treatment, the Patient and Treatment classes correspond respectively to the Problem and Solution classes, and thus, the two axioms Patient $\sqsubseteq$ Problem and Treatment $\sqsubseteq$ Solution are added to the ontology. Furthermore, the hasSolution property relates patients to the recommended treatments. Problem relations, adaptation functions and reformulations are also formalized in OWL. The specific underlying mechanisms are made by Web services implementing transformation operations like specialization, generalization and property substitution on OWL individuals.

Given two classes C and D, the *subsumption test* in OWL is defined by C is subsumed by D (C is more specific than D) if, for every model $\mathcal{I}$ of O, $C^{\mathcal{I}} \subseteq D^{\mathcal{I}}$. Based on the subsumption test, *classification* consists of finding for a class C, the most specific classes in the ontology subsuming C, and the most general classes subsumed by C. Classification organizes the classes of the ontology in a hierarchy. Regarding CBR, the class hierarchy is used as a structure for the case base, where a class represents an index for a source problem. Every index is considered as an abstraction of a source problem, containing the relevant part of the information leading to a particular solution.

Instance checking tests whether an individual a is an instance of a class C, i.e. if for every model $\mathcal{I}$ of O, $a^{\mathcal{I}} \in C^{\mathcal{I}}$. It supports the *instantiation* reasoning service that consists of finding the most specific classes of an individual. It is used during the retrieval step of CBR for finding index classes of source problems. A source prob-

---

[1] In this paper, we use the description logic way of writing expressions instead of the RDF/XML syntax and of the abstract syntax of OWL.

lem `srce` is an instance of its index class `idx(srce)`, and its solution `Sol(srce)` is considered to be reusable for any problem pb that is an instance of `idx(srce)`, i.e. `Sol(srce)` can be reused to solve `tgt` whenever `tgt` is recognized as an instance of `idx(srce)`.

Instantiation is used to infer new pieces of information about an individual on the basis of its class membership, and of constraints contained in class definitions. For example, if an individual named `bob` is an instance of the class `Man`, if `Man` is declared to be more specific than `Human` (`Man ⊑ Human`), and if the capability of intelligence is associated with humans (`Human ⊑ ∃capability.Intelligence`), then, `bob` has to be capable of intelligence. The information known about `bob` is automatically completed, thanks to constraints inherited from `Human`. This reasoning service has proved to be useful for CBR in [7], where it is called *instance completion*. Particularly, it is used in the *problem elaboration* operation, to extend the available information on the target problem with respect to the domain knowledge. Moreover, since a particular index `idx(srce)` may lead to a particular solution `Sol(srce)`, this solution can be directly attached to the index class through a *problem-solution axiom* of the form: `I ⊑ ∃hasSolution.S`. This means that, based on instance completion, any instance of the index class `I` is related to an object of the solution class `S` by the `hasSolution` property.

4   An Introduction to C-OWL

4.1   C-OWL: Contextualizing Ontologies

C-OWL is an extension of OWL for representing *contextualized (or contextual) ontologies* [5]. Contextualized ontologies are local representations of a domain, named contexts, that are semantically related with other contexts thanks to mappings. The original motivation for C-OWL is the alignment and coordinated use of ontologies made for different purposes. In our framework, C-OWL is used as a way to formalize and implement several alternative representations of the domain that we call *viewpoints*. In C-OWL, the knowledge about a domain is contained in a set of contexts. Each context O_i is an OWL ontology, with its own language and its own interpretation. Mappings are expressed by bridge rules. A bridge rule from O_i to O_j is a way to declare a correspondence between the interpretation domains of these two contexts. On the basis of these correspondences, a part of the knowledge contained in O_i can be interpreted and reused in O_j.

Formally, a C-OWL *context space* contains a set of contexts $\{O_i\}_{i \in I}$, I being a set of indexes for contexts. The indexes of I are used to prefix the expressions, associating an expression to the context in which it is defined. For example, `i:C`, `i:∃p.C`, `i:a`, `i:C ⊑ D` and `i:C(a)` are expressions of the local language of O_i.

The semantics of a context space is given by a distributed interpretation $\mathfrak{J}$ that contains an interpretation $\mathcal{I}_i$ for each $i \in I$. Each $\mathcal{I}_i$ is composed of a local interpretation domain $\Delta^{\mathcal{I}_i}$ and a local interpretation function $\cdot^{\mathcal{I}_i}$. A context is interpreted with the corresponding local interpretation, i.e. an axiom or an assertion of O_i is satisfied by $\mathfrak{J}$ if it is satisfied by $\mathcal{I}_i$.

A mapping $\mathcal{M}_{ij}$ is a set of *bridge rules* from O_i to O_j. There are different types of bridge rules, occurring between classes, individuals or properties of two contexts. We are only interested here in some particular forms. An *into rule* is a bridge rule of the form $\texttt{i:C} \xrightarrow{\sqsubseteq} \texttt{j:D}$, where $\texttt{i:C}$ and $\texttt{j:D}$ are classes respectively from O_i and O_j. This type of rule means that the class $\texttt{i:C}$ of O_i is considered, from the viewpoint of O_j, as more specific than the class $\texttt{j:D}$ [11]. The *onto rule* $\texttt{i:C} \xrightarrow{\sqsupseteq} \texttt{j:D}$ means that O_j considers the class $\texttt{i:C}$ to be more general than $\texttt{j:D}$. Bridge rules are directional: a bridge rule from O_i to O_j is considered in the viewpoint of O_j, and so, $\texttt{i:C} \xrightarrow{\sqsubseteq} \texttt{j:D}$ is not equivalent to $\texttt{j:D} \xrightarrow{\sqsupseteq} \texttt{i:C}$.

Formally, the distributed interpretation $\mathfrak{I}$ of a context space is associated with a set of *domain relations*. A domain relation $r_{ij} \subseteq \Delta^{\mathcal{I}_i} \times \Delta^{\mathcal{I}_j}$ states, for each object of $\Delta^{\mathcal{I}_i}$, the object of $\Delta^{\mathcal{I}_j}$ it corresponds to. The notation $r_{ij}(\texttt{C}^{\mathcal{I}_i})$ denotes the interpretation of the class $\texttt{i:C}$ of O_i as considered in the interpretation domain of O_j. Then, the semantics of a bridge rule is given with respect to domain relations: $\mathfrak{I}$ satisfies $\texttt{i:C} \xrightarrow{\sqsubseteq} \texttt{j:D}$ if $r_{ij}(\texttt{C}^{\mathcal{I}_i}) \subseteq \texttt{D}^{\mathcal{I}_j}$ and $\mathfrak{I}$ satisfies $\texttt{i:C} \xrightarrow{\sqsupseteq} \texttt{j:D}$ if $r_{ij}(\texttt{C}^{\mathcal{I}_i}) \supseteq \texttt{D}^{\mathcal{I}_j}$.

Another form of bridge rules is used to specify a correspondence between individuals. $\texttt{i:a} \xrightarrow{\equiv} \texttt{j:b}$ means that the individual $\texttt{i:a}$ in O_i corresponds to the individual $\texttt{j:b}$ in O_j. Formally, $\mathfrak{I}$ satisfies $\texttt{i:a} \xrightarrow{\equiv} \texttt{j:b}$ if $r_{ij}(\texttt{a}^{\mathcal{I}_i}) = \texttt{b}^{\mathcal{I}_j}$.

4.2   Global and Local Reasoning with C-OWL

Local reasoning services in C-OWL are the standard OWL reasoning services, performed in a particular context, without taking into account the bridge rules. A *global reasoning service* uses bridge rules to infer statements in a context using knowledge from the other contexts. [11] presents an extension of the standard tableau algorithm for the computation of the global subsumption test. *Global subsumption* uses the principle of subsumption propagation which, in its simplest form, can be expressed as:

if the mapping $\mathcal{M}_{ij}$ contains $\texttt{i:A} \xrightarrow{\sqsupseteq} \texttt{j:C}$ and $\texttt{i:B} \xrightarrow{\sqsubseteq} \texttt{j:D}$
then $\mathfrak{I}$ satisfies $\texttt{i:A} \sqsubseteq \texttt{B}$ implies that $\mathfrak{I}$ satisfies $\texttt{j:C} \sqsubseteq \texttt{D}$.

Intuitively, this means that subsumption in a particular context can be inferred from subsumption in another context thanks to bridge rules.

Similarly, we consider here a *global instance checking* based on an instantiation propagation rule:

if $\mathcal{M}_{ij}$ contains $\texttt{i:C} \xrightarrow{\sqsubseteq} \texttt{j:D}$ and $\texttt{i:a} \xrightarrow{\equiv} \texttt{j:b}$
then $\mathfrak{I}$ satisfies $\texttt{i:C(a)}$ implies that $\mathfrak{I}$ satisfies $\texttt{j:D(b)}$.

Instantiation is extended in order to use global instance checking. Based on bridge rules, information known about an individual in a particular context can be completed using inferences made in other contexts.

5   Decentralized Case-Based Reasoning with C-OWL

5.1   CBR and Contextualized Knowledge

Using C-OWL for DzCBR, a context is used to represent a particular viewpoint on the domain. A global target problem is represented as a set $\{\texttt{i:tgt}\}_i$ of local target problems, with a problem $\texttt{i:tgt}$ in each context O_i. In addition, a bridge rule $\texttt{i:tgt} \overset{\equiv}{\longrightarrow} \texttt{j:tgt}$ is declared for each O_i and O_j of the context space, i.e. $\texttt{i:tgt}$ in O_i is viewed as $\texttt{j:tgt}$ in O_j.

A context O_i includes knowledge and cases that are used to find a local solution $\texttt{i:Sol(tgt)}$ for the local problem $\texttt{i:tgt}$. Thus, a local problem $\texttt{i:pb}$ is solved by a solution $\texttt{i:Sol(pb)}$ inside the context O_i. The adaptation knowledge used for solving a local problem $\texttt{i:tgt}$ is also represented within the context O_i. Local reformulations $\texttt{i:}(\texttt{r}, \mathcal{A}_r)$ are the basic adaptation knowledge units for solving $\texttt{i:tgt}$ in the O_i context.

In a context O_i, there is a class hierarchy where a class represents the index of a source problem to be reused. An index $\texttt{i:idx(srce)}$ is an abstraction of the $\texttt{i:srce}$ problem, retaining the relevant information according to the viewpoint of the O_i context, i.e. $\texttt{i:Sol(srce)}$ can be reused to solve $\texttt{i:tgt}$ whenever $\texttt{i:tgt}$ is an instance of $\texttt{i:idx(srce)}$ (in accordance with the solving schema described in the section 3.4).

Then, in O_i, the instantiation reasoning service is used in a *localized retrieval* process for finding the index $\texttt{i:idx(srce)}$ of the source problem $\texttt{i:srce}$ to be reused. More precisely, the retrieval process consists of finding a similarity path between the target problem $\texttt{i:tgt}$ and the index $\texttt{i:idx(srce)}$ that is composed of relations defined in O_i:

$$\texttt{i:srce} \overset{isa}{\longrightarrow} \texttt{i:idx(srce)} \overset{isa}{\longleftarrow} \texttt{i:pb}_1 \ \texttt{i:r}_1 \ldots \texttt{i:r}_q \ \texttt{i:tgt}$$

where the "isa" arrows mean "is an instance of". In addition, a *localized adaptation* process has to build an associated adaptation path using reformulations and adaptation functions defined in O_i for building $\texttt{i:Sol(tgt)}$. Using contextualized knowledge and cases, the CBR process is then "contained" in a context. A detailed example of this localized CBR process is given at the end of the next section.

5.2   Combining Viewpoints Thanks to Bridge Rules

Decentralized artificial intelligence, as defined by [6], is concerned with the activity of autonomous intelligent agents that coexist and may collaborate with other agents, each of them having its own goals and its own knowledge. In the same way, the DzCBR mechanism is:

1. local to a context in the sense that it is carried out in each context, not in a centralized manner,
2. collaborative in the sense that it relies on knowledge sharing between contexts.

In the following, we present an example of a DzCBR process that is distributed among contexts and that takes advantage of this distribution for building a global solution for a target problem.

Let us introduce three contexts named O_1, O_2 and O_3, where a source problem is represented by its index class, and each association between a problem and its solution is represented by a problem-solution axiom. For example, the expression $1:\text{I1} \equiv \text{Problem} \sqcap \exists \text{p1.C1}$ defines a source problem in the context O_1, and $1:\text{I1} \sqsubseteq \exists \text{hasSolution.S1}$ associates an instance of the solution class $1:\text{S1}$ to an instance of the problem class $1:\text{I1}$. In the same way, the source problems $2:\text{I2}$ and $3:\text{I3}$ are respectively defined in the contexts O_2 and O_3, together with their problem-solution axioms (1st and 2nd lines of the figure 2). Bridge rules have been declared between the three local target problems $1:\text{tgt}$, $2:\text{tgt}$ and $3:\text{tgt}$, making precise the fact that these local problems are three views about a single problem (3rd line of the figure 2). Moreover, bridge rules between classes indicate the subsumption constraints between the contexts (4th line of the figure 2). Finally, a set of assertions is given for the three local target problems (5th, 6th and 7th lines of figure 2).

O_1	O_2	O_3
I1 ≡ Problem ⊓ ∃p1.C1	I2 ≡ Problem ⊓ ∃p21.C21 ⊓ ∃p22.C22	I3 ≡ Problem ⊓ ∃p3.C3
I1 ⊑ ∃hasSolution.S1	I2 ⊑ ∃hasSolution.S21	I3 ⊑ ∃hasSolution.S31
2:tgt $\xrightarrow{\equiv}$ 1:tgt	1:tgt $\xrightarrow{\equiv}$ 2:tgt	2:tgt $\xrightarrow{\equiv}$ 3:tgt
2:∃p21.C21 $\xrightarrow{\equiv}$ 1:∃p1.C1	1:∃hasSolution.S1 $\xrightarrow{\sqsubseteq}$ 2:∃p23.C23	2:∃hasSolution.S22 $\xrightarrow{\sqsubseteq}$
		3:∃hasSolution.S32
Problem(tgt)	Problem(tgt)	Problem(tgt)
	C21(a)	
	p21(tgt, a)	
	Dz1. ∃p21.C21(tgt)	
Dz2. ∃p1.C1(tgt)	Dz4. ∃p23.C23(tgt)	
Dz3. ∃hasSolution.S1(tgt)	Dz5. ∃hasSolution.S22(tgt)	Dz6. ∃hasSolution.S32(tgt)

Fig. 2. A DzCBR example. 1st and 2nd lines define some source problems. 3rd and 4th lines describe mappings associated with the contexts. 5th to 7th lines describe the target problem. 8th to 11th lines show 6 DzCBR inference steps.

When the DzCBR process is run in each context, the three local target problems $1:\text{tgt}$, $2:\text{tgt}$, and $3:\text{tgt}$ are instantiated in their respective contexts.

Dz1. In the O_2 context, $2:\text{tgt}$ is recognized as an instance of the class $2:\exists \text{p21.C21}$.

Dz2. The bridge rules $2:\exists \text{p21.C21} \xrightarrow{\sqsubseteq} 1:\exists \text{p1.C1}$ and $2:\text{tgt} \xrightarrow{\equiv} 1:\text{tgt}$ allow the completion of the instance $1:\text{tgt}$. $1:\text{tgt}$ is recognized as an instance of the class $1:\exists \text{p1.C1}$, and thus of the class $1:\text{I1}$.

Dz3. Through the problem-solution axiom, a solution $1:\text{S1}$ is associated with $1:\text{tgt}$, that in turn becomes an instance of the class $1:\exists \text{hasSolution.S1}$.

Dz4. The instance completion process is run through the bridge rule $1:\exists \text{hasSolution.S1} \xrightarrow{\sqsubseteq} 2:\exists \text{p23.C23}$, and the local target problem $2:\text{tgt}$ is recognized as an instance of the class $2:\exists \text{p23.C23}$.

Dz5. As it is explained below, let us assume that the CBR process in the context O_2 builds a solution that is an instance of $2:\text{S22}$ and that is associated with $2:\text{tgt}$. $2:\text{tgt}$ becomes an instance of $2:\exists \text{hasSolution.S22}$ in O_2.

Dz6. Finally, based on the bridge rule $2:\exists\mathtt{hasSolution.S22} \xrightarrow{\sqsubseteq} 3:\exists\mathtt{hasSolution.S32}$, it can be inferred in O_3 that $3:\mathtt{tgt}$ is an instance of $3:\exists\mathtt{hasSolution.S32}$.

The solution of the target problem, represented by the three local target problems $1:\mathtt{tgt}$, $2:\mathtt{tgt}$, and $3:\mathtt{tgt}$, is a set of local solutions, represented as instances of $1:\mathtt{S1}$, $2:\mathtt{S22}$, and $3:\mathtt{S32}$, that have been built in a decentralized way.

Relying on this example, two main operations may be distinguished in the DzCBR process:

(i) *localized CBR* that applies local knowledge for building a solution to the local problem $\mathtt{i:tgt}$. The steps Dz3. and Dz5. are examples of such a local operation in DzCBR, respectively carried out in O_1 and O_2.

(ii) *case completion* represents the *collaborative* part of DzCBR. It is based on bridge rules and completes the local target case –either the problem or the solution part– thanks to knowledge sharing with the other contexts. The steps Dz2., Dz4. and Dz6. are examples of this collaboration, using bridge rules for combining viewpoints.

These two operations are run in each context, until no more inferences can be drawn. The solution set $\{\mathtt{i:Sol(tgt)}\}_i$ is then delivered.

Details of the localized CBR Process Dz5. The O_2 context contains a reformulation of the form $2:(\mathtt{r}, \mathcal{A}_r)$ that is used in the localized CBR operation in this context (see figure 3). During the retrieval step, the $2:\mathtt{r}$ relation creates an intermediary problem $2:\mathtt{pb}_1$ from $2:\mathtt{tgt}$ such that the difference between these two individuals lies in the fact that $2:\mathtt{pb}_1$ is an instance of $2:\exists\mathtt{p22.C22}$, whereas $2:\mathtt{tgt}$ is an instance of $2:\exists\mathtt{p23.C23}$. Thus, $2:\mathtt{pb}_1$ is recognized as an instance of $2:\mathtt{I2}$, and is associated with a solution $2:\mathtt{Sol(pb}_1)$ from $2:\mathtt{S21}$, as stated by the problem-solution axiom in O_2. The $2:\mathcal{A}_r$ adaptation function is used in the adaptation step for creating the solution $2:\mathtt{Sol(tgt)}$ from $2:\mathtt{Sol(pb}_1)$. $2:\mathcal{A}_r$ is such that the difference between $2:\mathtt{Sol(pb}_1)$ and $2:\mathtt{Sol(tgt)}$ lies in the fact that $2:\mathtt{Sol(pb}_1)$ is an instance of $2:\mathtt{S21}$, whereas $2:\mathtt{Sol(tgt)}$ is an instance of $2:\mathtt{S22}$. Therefore, $2:\mathtt{Sol(tgt)}$, instance of $2:\mathtt{S22}$, becomes a solution of $2:\mathtt{tgt}$.

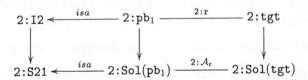

Fig. 3. The similarity path and the adaptation path of the localized CBR process in O_2

6   An Example of Application to Breast Cancer Treatment

The task of finding the right treatment for a patient ill with breast cancer is supported by a protocol. This protocol can be seen as a set of rules $Cond \Rightarrow Ttt$ where $Cond$ is a set of conditions on patients and Ttt is a description of the type of treatments recommended for the patients satisfying *Cond*. Several specialties are involved in this decision, and the protocol is structured according to these specialties. In breast cancer treatment, the surgery specialty is mainly concerned with partial or total breast ablation, the chemotherapy specialty is concerned with the administration of drugs useful to stop or lower the tumor evolution and the radiotherapy specialty treats the patients by irradiation of the potentially infected zones. The global recommendation combines the decisions taken in all the specialties. The protocol rules may be directly applied in 60 to 70 % of the situations (with respect to the characteristics of the patients). In situations not considered by the protocol, the decision is taken by a multi-disciplinary expert committee. This committee adapts the protocol rules to find a solution, taking into account the characteristics of the considered patient.

In our research work, decision support for breast cancer treatment relies on DzCBR, where a problem is a description of the characteristics of a patient, and a solution is a treatment proposition. The case base and the domain model rely on a formalized representation of the protocol in C-OWL. In the following example, three different contexts, namely O_r, O_s, and O_c, standing for the radiotherapy, surgery and chemotherapy viewpoints, are considered. These contexts correspond respectively to the O_1, O_2 and O_3 contexts of the example of section 5.2. A protocol rule $Cond \Rightarrow Ttt$ is represented and implemented as a problem-solution axiom of the form PC $\sqsubseteq$ $\exists$hasSolution.T, where PC and T are classes respectively representing the *Cond* and *Ttt* parts of the protocol rule. For example, O_r contains a problem class corresponding to the patients having a tumor that is smaller than 4cm. For the members of this class, a radiotherapy of the internal mammary chain is recommended. Therefore, the problem solution axiom 1:I1 $\sqsubseteq$ $\exists$hasSolution.S1 of the preceding example is restated as:

r:Patient $\sqcap$ $\exists$tumorSize.lessThan4cm $\sqsubseteq$ $\exists$hasSolution.IntMamChainRadio

In the same way, O_s contains the problem-solution axiom:

s:Patient $\sqcap$ $\exists$hasTumor.($\exists$size.moreThan4cm) $\sqcap$ $\exists$radiotherapy.IntMamChain

  $\sqsubseteq$ $\exists$hasSolution.TotalAblation

meaning that, for patients having a tumor greater than 4cm and for whom a radiotherapy of the internal mammary chain may be applied, a total ablation of the breast is recommended. In O_c, the axiom:

c:Patient $\sqcap$ $\exists$lymphNode.infected $\sqsubseteq$ $\exists$hasSolution.PreSurgicalChemo

means that for patients having infected lymph nodes, some cures of chemotherapy should be applied before the surgical treatment in order to prepare the patient for a partial ablation.

The bridge rules of the example of the section 5.2 are now redefined on the classes of O_r, O_s and O_c:

s:$\exists$hasTumor.($\exists$size.lessThan4cm) $\overset{\sqsubseteq}{\longrightarrow}$ r:$\exists$tumorSize.lessThan4cm

r:$\exists$hasSolution.IntMamChainRadio $\overset{\sqsubseteq}{\longrightarrow}$ s:$\exists$radiotherapy.IntMamChain

s:$\exists$hasSolution.TotalAblation $\overset{\sqsubseteq}{\longrightarrow}$ c:$\neg$$\exists$hasSolution.PreSurgicalChemo

The first one allows the surgery context to share the information about the size of the tumor with the radiotherapy context. Problem-solving in surgery can reuse the solution found in radiotherapy thanks to the second bridge rule. The third bridge rule expresses that, when a total ablation is recommended, a chemotherapy must not be applied before surgery.

Moreover, the O_s context contains some adaptation knowledge in the form of a reformulation $s:(r, A_r)$. The $s:r$ relation holds between an instance of Patient having a little-sized tumor (less than 4 cm) that covers a large part of the breast (more than 60%) and an instance of Patient having a larger tumor (more than 4cm). In other terms, a patient with a small tumor in a small breast is considered *for surgery* to be similar to a patient having a large tumor. The $s:A_r$ adaptation function simply consists in a copy of the solution.

The target problem is represented by three local target problems denoted by r:tgt, s:tgt and c:tgt, that are linked by bridge rules. Each of these individuals is an instance of the patient class, i.e. the assertions r:Patient(tgt), s:Patient(tgt) and c:Patient(tgt) are stated in the O_r, O_s and O_c contexts respectively. Moreover, s:tgt is described as a patient having a small tumor in a small breast, i.e. the assertion s:∃hasTumor.(∃size.lessThan4cm ⊓ ∃cover.MoreThan60%)(tgt) is stated in O_s.

The DzCBR process for solving this problem corresponds to the six steps of the section 5.2 example. The information about the tumor size is first shared between surgery and radiotherapy, and so, a radiotherapy of the internal mammary chain is recommended in O_r. In O_s, the reformulation $s:(r, A_r)$ is applied, considering s:tgt as similar to a patient having a large tumor. According to the problem-solution axiom contained in O_s, the solution for a patient with a large tumor is a total ablation. This solution is copied through A_r for s:tgt. Finally the solution found in surgery, the total ablation, implies that no chemotherapy has to be applied before surgery. It must be remarked that the target problem is treated differently in O_s and O_r. Indeed, it has been considered as a patient with a small tumor for radiotherapy, whereas it has been considered as a patient with a large tumor in surgery.

7   Discussion and Related Work

A CBR system based on the reformulation model has been implemented in the form of a generic Web service manipulating OWL ontologies. This architecture based on Web services is very helpful in the implementation of localized CBR. For global reasoning in C-OWL, we are using the system described in [11] that is currently under development. A complete protocol for breast cancer treatment has also been formalized in C-OWL. This particular representation was made of 4 contexts, each of them containing between 50 and 100 classes, and about 50 bridge rules have been described between these classes. The lesson learned from this experiment is that building and managing multiple contexts that reflect existing viewpoints in the domain appear to be simpler than finding and maintaining a consensual representation for these viewpoints all together. Moreover, even if bridge rules are generally related to domain expertise and have to be built manually, this task can sometimes be semi-automated, on the basis of ontology alignment techniques.

Considering related work, description logics have been used for KI-CBR in several systems (see e.g. [7, 12]). These systems consider a single knowledge model, and take into account a single way of interpreting and using cases. DzCBR combines several viewpoints on the problems and solutions, thanks to multiple inter-related contexts. Some systems use several views on cases to retrieve several local best cases. Generally, a single global case is built from these sub-cases. For example, in [13] a choice is made between cases that are retrieved using different case representations, called perspectives. In [14], several agents retrieve local best cases that are assembled in a global best case thanks to negotiation between agents. Since there is no centralized mechanism in DzCBR, a CBR process is carried out in each context and collaborates with the other contexts through bridge rules. In this way, among contexts, several local source cases are retrieved and used independently for adaptation. If one want to apply our approach to *distributed* CBR, i.e. problem-solving by several agents with the same set of goals (by contrast to *decentralized* CBR), it would be necessary to incorporate in the reasoning process a mechanism for managing conflicts.

Our interest for a DzCBR process exploiting semantic Web technologies and principles has started with the design of a semantic portal for oncology [15]. The goal of this portal is to give an intelligent access to standard knowledge for a geographically distributed community of oncologists. There are many other situations, like adaptive query answering, case-based ontology alignment or flexible Web service invocation, where CBR would be useful for the semantic Web. Some studies have been interested in defining markup languages for case representation, on the basis of XML [16] or RDF [17]. But, to our knowledge, there is no work concerned with the design of CBR systems in the semantic Web framework. Our aim here is not to build a general theory concerning the use of CBR in the framework of the semantic Web. However, we hope that the work presented in this paper will provide a guideline for practitioners to apply such techniques.

8   Conclusion

In this paper, a KI-CBR mechanism that exploits decentralized knowledge represented by contextualized ontologies in the C-OWL formalism has been proposed. This framework, called DzCBR, addresses the problem of adaptive reasoning in the multi-ontology environment of the semantic Web. The process of DzCBR takes advantage of the distribution of knowledge into multiple contexts and of the semantic relations between these contexts for solving problems. The motivation for a decentralized KI-CBR system comes from an application in the multi-disciplinary domain of oncology. Particularly it has been applied for the problem of breast cancer treatment recommendation. In this application, different specialties, like surgery, radiotherapy and chemotherapy, correspond to several viewpoints that must be taken into account and combined. A viewpoint is implemented as a C-OWL context, and semantic mappings between contexts are used for collaboration between viewpoints.

References

1. Lenz, M., Bartsch-Spörl, B., Burkhard, H.D., Wess, S., eds.: Case-Based Reasoning Technology: From Foundations to Applications, LNAI 1400. Springer (1998)
2. Aamodt, A., Plaza, E.: Case-Based Reasoning: Foundational Issues, Methodological Variations, and System Approaches. Artificial Intelligence Communications 7 (1994) 39–59
3. Aamodt, A.: Knowledge-Intensive Case-Based Reasoning in CREEK. In Funk, P., Gonzàlez-Calero, P.A., eds.: Proc. of the European Conference on Case-Based Reasoning, ECCBR'04, Springer (2004) 1–15
4. Bechhofer, S., van Harmelen, F., Hendler, J., Horrocks, I., McGuinness, D., Patel-Schneider, P., Stein, L.A.: OWL Web Ontology Language Reference. W3C Recommendation (2004)
5. Bouquet, P., Giunchiglia, F., van Harmelen, F., Serafini, L., Stuckenschmidt, H.: Contextualizing Ontologies. Journal of Web Semantics 1 (2004) 1–19
6. Demazeau, Y., Müller, J.P.: Decentralized Artificial Intelligence. In Demazeau, Y., Müller, J.P., eds.: Decentralized A.I. – Proc. of the First European Workshop on Modelling Autonomous Agents in a Multi-Agent World, North-Holland (1989) 3–13
7. Gómez-Albarrán, M., Gonzàles-Calero, P., Díaz-Agudo, B., Fernàndez-Conde, C.: Modelling the CBR Life Cycle Using Description Logics. In Althoff, K.D., Bergamnn, R., Branting, L., eds.: Proc. of the International Conference on Case-Based Reasoning, ICCBR'99, Springer (1999) 147–161
8. Lieber, J., Napoli, A.: Correct and Complete Retrieval for Case-Based Problem-Solving. In Prade, H., ed.: Proc. of the European Conference on Artificial Intelligence, ECAI'98, John Wiley & Sons Ltd, Chichester (1998) 68–72
9. Melis, E., Lieber, J., Napoli, A.: Reformulation in Case-Based Reasoning. In Smyth, B., Cunningham, P., eds.: Proc. of the European Workshop on Case-Based Reasoning, EWCBR'98, Springer (1998) 172–183
10. Smyth, B.: Case-Based Design. PhD. thesis, Trinity College, University of Dublin (1996)
11. Serafini, L., Tamilin, A.: Local Tableaux for Reasoning in Distributed Description Logics. In Haarslev, V., Moeller, R., eds.: Proc. of the International Workshop on Description Logics, DL'04. (2004) 100–109
12. Kamp, G., Lange, S., Globig, C.: Related Areas. [1] chapter 13
13. Arcos, J.L., Lopez de Mántaras, R.: Perspectives: a declarative bias mechanism for case retrieval. In Leake, D.B., Plaza, E., eds.: Proc. of the International Conference on Case-Based Reasoning, ICCBR'97, Springer (1997) 279–290
14. Nagendra Prassad, M., Lesser, V., Lander, S.: Retrieval and Reasoning in Distributed Case Bases. Journal of Visual Communication and Image Representation 7 (1996) 74–87
15. d'Aquin, M., Brachais, S., Bouthier, C., Lieber, J., Napoli, A.: Knowledge Editing and Maintenance Tools for a Semantic Portal in Oncology. International Journal of Human-Computer Studies (IJHCS) 62 (2005) 619–638
16. Coyle, L., Doyle, D., Cunningham, P.: Representing Similarity for CBR in XML. In Funk, P., González Calero, P., eds.: Advances in Case-Based Reasoning (Procs. of the Seventh European Conference), LNAI 3155, Springer (2004) 119–127
17. Chen, H., Wu, Z.: CaseML: a RDF-based Case Markup Language for Case-based Reasoning in Semantic Web. In Fuchs, B., Mille, A., eds.: From structured cases to unstructured problem solving episodes for experience-based assistance. Workshop at ICCBR-2003. (2003)

Finding and Ranking Knowledge on the Semantic Web *

Li Ding, Rong Pan, Tim Finin, Anupam Joshi,
Yun Peng, and Pranam Kolari

Department of Computer Science and Electrical Engineering,
University of Maryland, Baltimore County, Baltimore MD 21250
{dingli1, panrong1, finin, joshi, ypeng, kolari1}@cs.umbc.edu

Abstract. Swoogle helps software agents and knowledge engineers find Semantic Web knowledge encoded in RDF and OWL documents on the Web. Navigating such a Semantic Web on the Web is difficult due to the paucity of explicit *hyperlinks* beyond the namespaces in URIrefs and the few inter-document links like rdfs:seeAlso and owl:imports. In order to solve this issue, this paper proposes a novel Semantic Web navigation model providing additional navigation paths through Swoogle's search services such as the *Ontology Dictionary*. Using this model, we have developed algorithms for ranking the importance of Semantic Web objects at three levels of granularity: documents, terms and RDF graphs. Experiments show that Swoogle outperforms conventional web search engine and other ontology libraries in finding more ontologies, ranking their importance, and thus promoting the use and emergence of consensus ontologies.

1 Introduction

As the scale and the impact of the World Wide Web has grown, search engines have assumed a central role in the Web's infrastructure. Similarly, the growth of the Semantic Web will also generate a need for specialized search engines that help agents[1] find knowledge encoded in Semantic Web languages such as RDF(S) and OWL. This paper discusses two important aspects of Semantic Web search engines: helping agents *navigate*[2] the Semantic Web and ranking search results.

The utility of Semantic Web technologies for sharing knowledge among agents has been widely recognized in many domain applications. However, the Semantic Web itself (i.e., the unified RDF graph comprised of many decentralized online knowledge sources) remains less studied. This paper focuses on the Semantic Web materialized as a collection of **Semantic Web Documents** (SWDs)[3] because web pages are well known as the building blocks of the Web.

---

* Partial support for this research was provided by DARPA contract F30602-00-0591 and by NSF awards NSF-ITR-IIS-0326460 and NSF-ITR-IDM-0219649.

[1] The term *agents* refers to programs, tools, and human knowledge engineers that might use Semantic Web knoweledge.

[2] The term *navigation* refers to a process of following a series of links (explicit or implicit) from an initial starting point to a desired information resource.

[3] A *Semantic Web document* is a web page that serializes an RDF graph using one of the recommended RDF syntax languages, i.e., RDF/XML, N-Triples or N3.

Y. Gil et al. (Eds.): ISWC 2005, LNCS 3729, pp. 156–170, 2005.

One advantage of the Semantic Web is that people can collaboratively create ontologies and build common vocabulary without centralized control. One building block of Semantic Web ontologies is a **Semantic Web Term** (SWT)[4], which plays the role of a word in natural languages. SWTs bridge RDF statements with formal semantics defined in RDF(S) and OWL, and are intended to be reused as universal symbols.

We call an SWD that defines a significant number of SWTs a **Semantic Web Ontology**(SWO) to distinguish it from documents that mostly populating and/or asserting class instances[5]. The Semantic Web depends on three "meta ontologies" (RDF, RDFS and OWL) and, according to Swoogle [1], thousands of additional ones developed by institutions (e.g., CYC, WordNet, DC[6], FOAF[7], and RSS) and individuals.

These ontologies often overlap by defining terms on similar or the same concepts. For example, Swoogle finds over 300 distinct SWTs that appear to stand for the 'person' concept. This raises interesting issues in finding and comparing Semantic Web ontologies for knowledge sharing. For example, how can an agent find the most popular domain ontology (currently FOAF is the best choice) to publish a personal profile?

Conventional web navigation and ranking models are not suitable for the Semantic Web for two main reasons: (i) they do not differentiate SWDs from the overwhelming number of other web pages; and (ii) they do not parse and use the internal structure of SWD and the external semantic links among SWDs. Hence, even Google, one of the best web search engines, can sometimes perform poorly in finding ontologies. For example, the FOAF ontology (the most used one for describing a person) is not among the first ten results when we search Google using the phrase "person ontology"[8].

Although we are familiar with surfing on the Web, navigating the Semantic Web is quite different. We have developed a Semantic Web navigation model based on how knowledge is published and accessed. To publish content, information providers need to obtain appropriate domain ontologies by reusing existing ones and/or creating new ones, and then use them to create instances and make assertions. When accessing knowledge, consumers need to search for instance data and pursue corresponding ontologies to fully understand the knowledge encoded. Meanwhile, the navigation model should also acknowledge the context – the Web, which physically hosts RDF graphs in SWDs. Most existing navigation tools (e.g., HyperDAML[9] and Swoop[10]) employ the URL semantics of the URIref to a RDF resource; however, they cannot answer questions like "find instances of a given class" or "list all URIs using the same local name *person*" due to the limited number of explicit links.

The navigation model supports ranking the 'data quality' [2] of Semantic Web knowledge in terms of common case importance. In particular, this paper focuses on

---

[4] A *Semantic Web term* is an RDF resource that represents an instance of rdfs:Class (or rdf:Property) and can be universally referenced by its URI reference (URIref).

[5] Since virtually all documents will contain some definitions and instances, the classification must either be a fuzzy one or depend on a heuristic threshold.

[6] Dublin Core Element Set 1.1,http://purl.org/dc/elements/1.1/.

[7] Friend Of A Friend ontology, http://xmlns.com/foaf/0.1/.

[8] This example is not intended to undermine Google's value; instead, we argue that the Semantic Web is quite different from the Web and needs its own navigation and ranking models.

[9] http://www.daml.org/2001/04/hyperdaml/

[10] http://www.mindswap.org/2004/SWOOP/

ranking ontologies at various levels of granularity to promote reusing ontologies. Rank-ing ontologies at the document level has been widely studied since most ontologies are published through SWOs. Its common approaches include link-analysis [3, 1] and semantic-content-analysis [4]. Document level ontology ranking, however, is not enough. For example, foaf:Person and dc:creator together can describe the author of a web page, and an ontology containing both of the concepts might not be as good as the combination of FOAF and DC. Hence, a finer level of granularity (i.e., ranking at SWT level) is needed especially to encode knowledge using popular terms from mul-tiple ontologies[11], but is seldom investigated in literature. Besides ranking individual SWTs, agents may also rank inter-term relations (e.g., how frequently a property has been used to modify the instances of a class). Such an ontology ranking approach is a special case of ranking sub-graphs of an RDF graph [5, 6].

The remainder of this paper is structured as follows: Section 2 reviews the test-bed (the Swoogle Semantic Web search engine) and related works on navigating and rank-ing Semantic Web knowledge. Section 3 introduces the novel Semantic Web navigation model, which enriches navigation paths and captures surfing behaviors on the Semantic Web on the Web. Sections 4 and 5 describe and evaluate mechanisms for ranking ontolo-gies at different levels of granularity, namely document, term and sub-graph. Section 6 concludes that effective navigation support and ranking mechanisms are critical to both the emergence of common ontologies and the growth of the Semantic Web on the Web.

2   Background and Related Work

2.1   Swoogle

The Swoogle [1] search engine discovers, indexes, and analyzes Semantic Web docu-ments published on the Web and provides agents with various kinds of search services. Its architecture, shown in Figure 1, is comprised of four components.

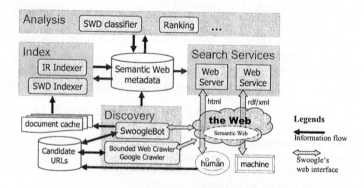

Fig. 1. Swoogle's architecture involves four major components.

---

[11] Importing part of ontologies is especially helpful when using large upper ontologies like CYC.

- The **Discovery** component collects candidate URLs to find and cache SWDs using four mechanisms: (i) submitted URLs of SWDs and sites; (ii) a web crawler that explores promising sites; (iii) a customized meta-crawler that discovers likely URLs using conventional search engines; and (iv) the SwoogleBot Semantic Web crawler which validates and analyses SWDs to produce new candidates.
- The **Indexing** component analyzes the discovered SWDs and generates the bulk of Swoogle's metadata about the Semantic Web. The metadata not only characterizes the features associated with individual SWDs and SWTs, but also tracks the relations among them, e.g., "how SWDs use/define/populate a given SWT" and "how two SWTs are associated by instantiating 'rdfs:domain' relation".
- The **Analysis** component analyzes the generated metadata and hosts the modular ranking mechanisms.
- The **Services** module provides search services to agents, allowing them to access the metadata and navigate the Semantic Web. It is highlighted by the "Swoogle Search" service that searches SWDs using constraints on URLs, the SWTs being used or defined, etc.; and the "Ontology Dictionary" service that searches ontologies at the term level and offers more navigational paths.

2.2 Related Work and Motivation

Random Surfing Model and PageRank. The random surfing model underlying the PageRank [7] algorithm has been widely accepted as the navigation model for the Web. In this model, the surfer begins by jumping to a random URL. After visiting a page, he either (i) with probability d^{12} randomly chooses a link from the page to follow to a new page; or (ii) with probability $1 - d$ jumps to another random URL. This model is essentially a simple random walk modeled by a Markov chain. Based on this surfing model, the basic PageRank algorithm computes the rank (indicating popularity rather than relevance) for each web page by iteratively propagating the rank until convergence.

Variations of PageRank. The basic PageRank algorithm is limited by its assumptions and relaxing them has resulted in several extensions. In Topic-Sensitive PageRank [8], documents are accessed non-uniformly according to their topics. For Weighted PageRank extensions [9, 10, 11], links are followed non-uniformly according to their popularity. Several link-semantics-aware extensions [12, 13] recognize links with different meanings and compute a PageRank weighted by the link semantics.

Navigating the Semantic Web. Navigating the Semantic Web is quite different from navigating the conventional Web. It is currently supported by tools such as browsers (e.g., HyperDAML and Swoop), ontology libraries (e.g., DAML ontology library[13] and SchemaWeb[14]), search engines (e.g., Ontaria[15] and Swoogle), and crawlers (e.g., scutter[16] and SwoogleBot). Most tools only capture navigational paths based on the seman-

---

[12] d is usually a constant except in personalized ranking.
[13] http://www.daml.org/ontologies/
[14] http://www.schemaweb.info/
[15] http://www.w3.org/2004/ontaria/
[16] http://rdfweb.org/topic/Scutter

tics of URIref. Swoogle, however, supports effective navigation by providing additional navigational paths among SWDs and SWTs.

Ranking Semantic Web knowledge. Ranking knowledge can be considered as a problem of evaluating *data quality* [2, 14] which focuses on *data product quality* [15]. It has been studied at various levels of granularity in Semantic Web and database literature.

- Ranking Semantic Web ontologies at the document level has been studied using both content analysis [16, 4] and link-structure-based analysis [3, 1].
- Ranking knowledge at the instance or object level has been investigated by both database and Semantic Web researchers, including ranking elements in XML documents [17]; ranking objects in databases [18] or the Web [19, 11]; and ranking relevant class-instances in domain specific RDF database [20].
- Ranking knowledge at a sub-graph level has been studied using ontology-based content analysis [5, 21, 6] in the context of ranking query results in the Semantic Web, and using context-based trust computation [22, 23].

Ranking Semantic Web ontologies has remained at the document level even though other granularity levels are applicable. For example, SWTs are a special kind of class instances and should be ranked differently from normal instances. Doing so enables a retrieval system to find a set of SWTs drawn from more than one ontologies to cover a collection of target concepts.

Most link-analysis-based approaches have focused on either a particular domain (e.g., bibliographic data) or a small set of SWOs. Swoogle is unique in its ambition to discover and index a substantial fraction of the published SWDs on the Web (currently over 7×10^5 SWDs of which about 1% are SWOs).

3   Semantic Web Navigation Model

In this paper, we consider the Semantic Web materialized on the Web. To navigate such a Semantic Web, a user cannot simply rely on the URL semantics of URIref due to three main reasons: (i) the namespace of a URIref at best points to an SWO, but there are no reverse links pointing back; (ii) although rdfs:seeAlso has been widely used to interconnect SWDs in FOAF based applications, it seldom works in other SWDs; (iii) owl:imports does interlink ontologies, but such relations are rare since ontologies are usually independently developed and distributed. In addition, many practical issues should be addressed in web-scale Semantic Web data access, such as "how two reach the SWDs which are not linked by any other SWDs" and "what if the namespace of a URIref is not an SWD". It is notable that the intended users of this navigation model are both software agents, who usually search SWDs for external knowledge and then retrieve SWOs to fully understand SWDs, and Semantic Web researchers, who mainly search SWTs and SWOs for publishing their knowledge.

3.1   Overview

The navigation model is specialized for publishing and accessing Semantic Web knowledge as shown in Figure 2. Users can jump into the Semantic Web using conventional

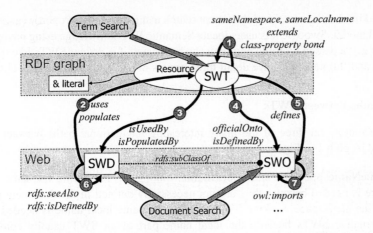

The block arrows link search services to the Semantic Web. Paths 2 and 5 are straightforward since SWTs are referenced by SWDs/SWOs. Paths 6, 7 and part of 4 are supported by most existing RDF browsers. Paths 1, 3 and the rest of 4 require global view of the Semantic Web on the Web, and are currently only supported by Swoogle metadata.

Fig. 2. The Semantic Web navigation model

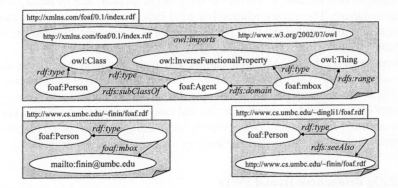

A user can use Swoogle term search to find SWTs having local name 'Person'. If she picks SWT *foaf:Person*, she can jump to the corresponding SWO http://xmlns.com/foaf/0.1/index.rdf by following path 4 via *isDefinedBy*, jump to an SWT *foaf:mbox* by following path 1 via *sameNamespace*, or jump to another SWD http://www.cs.umbc.edu/ dingli1/foaf.rdf by following path 3 via *isPopulatedBy*. From the FOAF SWO, she can pursue OWL ontology by following path 7 via *owl:imports*, jump to SWT *rdfs:domain* by following path 2 via *populates*, or jump to SWT *foaf:Agent* by following path 5 via *defines*. For the SWD to the right, she can jump to another SWD http://www.cs.umbc.edu/ finin/foaf.rdf by following path 6 via *rdfs:seeAlso*.

Fig. 3. A navigation use-case

Web search (e.g., Google and Yahoo) or Semantic Web search (e.g., Swoogle). Users can also navigate the Semantic Web within or across the Web and RDF graph via seven groups of navigational paths. An example is shown in Figure 3.

In addition to conventional document search using document properties and/or bag-of-word model, Swoogle lets users locate Semantic Web knowledge using navigational paths, e.g., "a personal profile ontology can be located if it *defines* SWTs like 'person', 'email' and 'homepage' ". We detail three groups of navigational paths as follows.

3.2   Paths Between SWTs

We concentrate on three of the many interesting navigational paths between SWTs grouped by path 1 in Figure 2 as follows.

1. **sameNamespace** and **sameLocalname**. linking SWTs sharing the same namespace is needed because they are not necessarily defined in the document pointed by the namespace. Linking SWTs sharing the same local name is needed to find alternative SWTs because the local name part of an SWT usually conveys its semantics.

2. **extends**. An SWT $t1$ *extends* another SWT $t2$ when either (i) there exists a triple $(t1, P, t2)$ where P (e.g., *rdfs:subClassOf*, *owl:inverseOf* and *owl:complementOf*) connects two classes (or two properties), or (ii)there exists a triple $(t1, P, LIST)$ where P (e.g., *owl:unionOf*) connects a class $t1$ to a *rdf:List* $LIST$ which has another class $t2$ as a non-nil member. For example, in Figure 3, *foaf:Agent* is extended by *foaf:Person* because it is closer to the concept 'person' and its *mobx* property can be inherit. The *extends* relation is a good indicator for the importance of term because it implies that the term being extended is commonly accepted and well-defined but too general for instantiating the intended concept.

3. **class-property bond**. Although classes and their attributes have been tightly bonded in frame-based systems, the connections between classes and properties are loose in the Semantic Web. For example, Dublin Core defines widely used properties without specifying their domains and ranges. Swoogle links from a class to its instance properties (i.e., class-property bond) using two sources: (i) rdfs:domain assertions in SWOs and (ii) instantiation of such bond in class-instances.

3.3   Paths Between SWDs and SWTs

Swoogle maintains three types of navigational paths across SWDs and SWTs: (i) paths 2 and 5 in Figure 2 can be easily extracted from an SWD by analyzing the usage of SWTs; (ii) paths 3 and 4 are mainly the reverse of paths 2 and 5. Generating such paths requires the global view of the Semantic Web; and (iii) the **officialOnto** relation in path 4 links an SWT to an SWO. It is needed by software agents to locate ontologies defining the encountered SWTs in the absence of explicit import instruction.

1. Swoogle recognizes six types of binary relations between an SWT T in an SWD D as shown in Table 1. They can be further generalized to three groups namely, *defines*, *uses* and *populates*. For example, in figure 3, `http://xmlns.com/foaf/0.1/index.rdf` defines foaf:Person as class and populates rdfs:domain as property. An SWD using or populating an SWT indicates that the publisher is satisfied with the SWT's definition.

Table 1. Six types of binary relations that can hold between an SWD D and an SWT T

Relation	Condition
define-class	D has a triple $(T, rdf\!:\!type, MC)$ where MC is a sub-class of $rdfs\!:\!Class$.
define-property	D has a triple $(T, rdf\!:\!type, MP)$ where MP is a sub-class of $rdf\!:\!Property$.
use-class	D has a triple $(\_, P, T)$ where the range of P is a sub-class of $rdfs\!:\!Class$, or D has a triple $(T, P, \_)$ where the domain of P is a sub-class of $rdfs\!:\!Class$.
use-property	D has a triple $(\_, P, T)$ where the range of P is a sub-class of $rdf\!:\!Property$, or D has a triple $(T, P, \_)$ where the domain of P is a sub-class of $rdf\!:\!Property$.
populate-class	D has a triple $(\_, rdf\!:\!type, T)$.
populate-property	When D has a triple $(\_, T, \_)$.

Table 2. Heuristics for finding official ontologies, and their performance on 4508 namespaces

Type	Percent
The namespace of T;	59%
the URL of an ontology which is redirected from T's namespace (e.g., `http://purl.org/dc/elements/1.1/` is redirected to `http://dublincore.org/2003/03/24/dces`);	0.4%
the URL of an ontology which has T' namespace as its absolute path, and it is the only one that matches this criteria (e.g., `http://xmlns.com/foaf/0.1/index.rdf` is the official ontology of `http://xmlns.com/foaf/0.1/`);	3.4%
N/A, cannot decide	37.2%

2. Swoogle tracks the "official ontology" of an SWT T using heuristics listed in Table 2. The 'percent' column shows the percentage that the heuristics has been successfully applied. It is notable that heuristics 2 and 3 help find some important official ontologies of DC and FOAF even though they have only improved the performance from 59% to 62.8%.

3.4 Paths Between SWDs

Swoogle also supports well-known navigational paths between SWDs.

1. Although not defined explicitly, the triples populating properties *rdfs:isDefinedBy* and *rdfs:seeAlso* are widely used in linking to web pages or even SWDs. In practice, many RDF crawlers use *rdfs:seeAlso* to discover SWDs.
2. Instances of *owl:OntologyProperty* is explicitly defined to associate two SWOs, and owl:imports is frequently instantiated far more than the others. Therefore, Swoogle indexes the usage of the **imports**[17] relation.
3. Inspired by RDF test-case ontology[18], we have developed a class *wob: RDFDocument* (which asserts that a resource is an SWD) to support explicit 'hyperlinks' in

---

[17] An SWO $D1$ *imports* another $D2$ when there is a triple in $D1$ in form of ($D1$, owl:imports, $D2$), and so does *daml:imports*. This relation shows the dependency between ontologies and is complemented by "officalOnto" relation.

[18] http://www.w3.org/2000/10/rdf-tests/rdfcore/testSchema

the Semantic Web. A consequent idea is RDF sitemap which let website publish their SWDs through a special index file[19].

4   Ranking Semantic Web Documents

Since RDF graphs are usually accessed at the document level, we simplify the Semantic Web navigation model by generalizing navigational paths into three types of document level paths (see below) and then applying link analysis based ranking methods with 'rational' surfing behavior.

- An **extension (EX)** relation holds between two SWDs when one defines a term using terms defined by another. EX generalizes the *defines SWT-SWD* relations, the *extends SWT-SWT* relations, and the officialOnto *SWT-SWD* relation. For example, an SWD $d1$ *EX* another SWD $d2$ when $d1$ defines a class $t1$, which is the subclass of a class $t2$, and $t2$'s official ontology is $d2$.
- A **use-term (TM)** relation holds between two SWDs when one uses a term defined by another. TM generalizes the *uses* and *populates SWT-SWD* relations, and the officialOnto *SWT-SWD* relation. For example, an SWD $d1$ *TM* another SWD $d2$ when $d1$ uses a resource t as class, and t's official ontology is $d2$.
- An **import (IM)** relation holds when one SWD *imports*, directly or transitively, another SWD, and it corresponds to the imports *SWD-SWD* relation.

4.1   Rational Surfer Model and OntoRank

Swoogle's *OntoRank* is based on the *rational surfer model* which emulates an agent's navigation behavior at the document level. Like the random surfer model, an agent either follows a link in an SWD to another or jumps to a new random SWD with a constant probability $1 - d$. It is 'rational' because it emulates agents' navigation on the Semantic Web, i.e., agents follow links in a SWD with non-uniform probability according to link semantics. When encountering an SWD α, agents will(transitively) import the "official" ontologies that define the classes and properties referenced by α.

Let $link(\alpha, l, \beta)$ be the semantic link from an SWD α to another SWD β with tag l; $linkto(\alpha)$ be a set of SWDs link directly to the SWD α; $weight(l)$ be a user specified navigation preference on semantic links with type l, i.e., TM and EX; $OTC(\alpha)$ be a set of SWDs that (transitively) IM or EX α as ontology; $f(x, y)$ and $wPR(x)$ be two intermediate functions.

OntoRank is computed in two steps: (i) iteratively compute the rank, $wPR(\alpha)$, of each SWD α until it converges (equations 1 and 2); and (ii) transitively pass an SWD's rank to all ontologies it imported (equation 3).

$$wPR(\alpha) = (1 - d) + d \sum_{x \in linkto(\alpha)} \frac{wPR(x) \times f(x, \alpha)}{\sum_{link(x, \_, y)} f(x, y)} \qquad (1)$$

---

[19] http://swoogle.umbc.edu/site.php

Table 3. OntoRank finds more ontologies in each of the 10 queries

Query	C1:# SWOs by OntoRank	C2:# SWOs by PageRank	Difference (C1-C2)/C2
name	9	6	50.00%
person	10	7	42.86%
title	13	12	8.33%
location	12	6	100.00%
description	11	10	10.00%
date	14	10	40.00%
type	13	11	18.18%
country	9	4	125.00%
address	11	8	37.50%
organization	9	5	80.00%
Average	11.1	7.9	40.51%

$$f(x, \alpha) = \sum_{link(x,l,\alpha)} weight(l) \qquad (2)$$

$$OntoRank(\alpha) = wPR(\alpha) + \sum_{x \in OTC(\alpha)} wPR(x) \qquad (3)$$

4.2 Evaluation: OntoRank vs PageRank

OntoRank is evaluated on a real dataset *DS-APRIL* collected by Swoogle by April 2005. DS-APRIL contains 330K SWDs (1.5% are SWOs, 24% are FOAF documents and 60% are RSS documents) and interlink by 200K document level relations.

The first experiment compares the performance between PageRank and OntoRank in boosting the rank of SWOs among SWDs, i.e., ranking SWOs higher than normal SWDs. In this experiment, we first compute both ranks for SWDs in DS-APRIL[20]; and then ten popular local-names (according to Swoogle's statistics) were selected as the keywords for Swoogle's document search. The same search result for each query is ordered by both PageRank and OntoRank respectively. We compared the number of *strict SWO* (see definition 1) in the first 20 results in either order. Table 3 shows an average 40% improvement of OntoRank over PageRank.

Definition 1. ontology ratio
The ontology ratio *of an SWD refers to is the fraction of its class-instances being recognized as classes and properties. It is used to identify SWOs among SWDs. For example, given an SWD defining a class "Color" and populating the class with three class-instances namely, 'blue', 'green' and 'red', its ontology ratio is 25% since only one out of the four is defined as class. A document with a high ontology ratio indicates a preference for adding term definition rather than populating existing terms. According to Swoogle, an SWD is an ontology document if it has defined at least one term, and it is called a* **strict SWO** *if its ontology ratio exceeds 0.8.*

---

[20] Note this PageRank is computed on the same dataset as OntoRank, which is a preprocessed web of SWDs where no simply hyperlinks but only semantic links are considered.

Table 4. Top 10 SWDs according to OntoRank and their PageRank

URL of Ontology	Ontology Ratio	OntoRank	PageRank
http://www.w3.org/2000/01/rdf-schema	94%	1	1
http://www.w3.org/2002/07/owl	86%	2	5
http://www.w3.org/1999/02/22-rdf-syntax-ns	81%	3	6
http://purl.org/dc/elements/1.1	100%	4	3
http://purl.org/rss/1.0/schema.rdf	100%	5	2
http://www.w3.org/2003/01/geo/wgs84_pos	100%	6	10
http://xmlns.com/foaf/0.1/index.rdf	84%	7	4
http://xmlns.com/wot/0.1/index.rdf	100%	8	29
http://www.w3.org/2003/06/sw-vocab-status/ns	75%	9	7
http://www.daml.org/2001/03/daml+oil	96%	10	11

The second experiment studies the best ranked SWDs using both ranking methods. In table 4, RDFS schema clearly ranks first according to both OntoRank and PageRank. OWL ranks higher than RDF because it is referred to by many popular ontologies. DC and FOAF ontologies rank 4th and 5th by PageRank due to their many instance documents but rank lower by OntoRank due to their narrow domain and fewer references by other ontologies. An interesting case is the web of trust (WOT) ontology which PageRank ranks only 29th since our data set only contains 280 FOAF documents referencing it directly. OntoRank ranks it at 8 since it is referenced by the FOAF ontology, greatly increasing its visibility. We are not expecting OntoRank to be completely different from PageRank since it is a variation of PageRank. OntoRank is intended to expose more ontologies which are important to Semantic Web users in understanding term definition.

5   Ranking for Ontology Dictionary

Ranking ontologies at the term level is also important because SWTs defined in the same SWO are instantiated in quite different frequency. For example, owl:versionInfo is far less used than owl:Class. Users, therefore, may want to partition ontologies and then import a part of an SWO [24, 25]. In addition, users often use SWTs from multiple ontologies together, e.g., *rdfs:seeAlso* and *dc:title* have been frequently used modifying the instances of *foaf:Person*.

These observations lead to the "Do It Yourself" strategy i.e., users can customize ontologies by assembling relevant terms from popular ontologies without importing them completely. To this end, Swoogle's *Ontology Dictionary* helps users to find relevant terms ranked by their popularity, and supports a simple procedure *CONSTRUCT-ONTO* for publishing knowledge using class-instances.

```
CONSTRUCT-ONTO
    1. find an appropriate class C
    2. find popular properties whose domain is C
    3. go back to step 1 if another class is needed
```

Table 5. Top ten classes with 'person' as the local name ordered by Swoogle's TermRank

TermRank	Resource URI	pop(swd)	pop(i)	def(swd)
1	http://xmlns.com/foaf/0.1/Person	74589	1260759	17
2	http://xmlns.com/wordnet/1.6/Person	2658	785133	80
3	http://www.aktors.org/ontology/portal#Person	267	3517	6
4	ns1:Person [1]	257	935	1
5	ns2:Person [2]	277	398	1
6	http://xmlns.com/foaf/0.1/person	217	5607	0
7	http://www.amico.org/vocab#Person	90	90	1
8	http://www.ontoweb.org/ontology/1#Person	32	522	2
9	ns3:Person [3]	0	0	1
10	http://description.org/schema/Person	10	10	0

[1] ns1 - http://www.w3.org/2000/10/swap/pim/contact#
[2] ns2 - http://www.iwi-iuk.org/material/RDF/1.1/Schema/Class/mn#
[3] ns3 - http://ebiquity.umbc.edu/v2.1/ontology/person.owl#

5.1 Ranking Semantic Web Terms

Swoogle uses TermRank to sort SWTs by their popularity, which can be simply measured by the number of SWDs using/populating an SWT. This naive approach, however, ignores users' rational behavior in accessing SWDs, i.e., users access SWDs with non-uniform probability. Therefore, *TermRank* is computed by totaling each SWD's contribution (equation 4). For each SWD α, its contribution to each of its SWTs is computed by splitting its OntoRank proportional to SWTs' weight $TWeight(\alpha,t)$, which indicates the probability a user will access t when browsing α. $TWegiht$ is the product of $cnt\_uses(\alpha,t)$ - t's popularity within α measured by the number of occurrence of t in α and $|\{\alpha|uses(\alpha,t)\}|$ – t's importance in the Semantic Web measured by the number of SWDs containing t (see equation 5).

$$TermRank(t) = \sum_{uses(\alpha,t)} \frac{OntoRank(\alpha) \times TWeight(\alpha,t)}{\sum_{uses(\alpha,x)} TWeight(\alpha,x)} \qquad (4)$$

$$TWeight(\alpha,t) = cnt\_uses(\alpha,t) \times |\{\alpha|uses(\alpha,t)\}| \qquad (5)$$

Table 5 lists top ten classes in *DS-APRIL* having 'person' as the local name ordered by TermRank. For each class, *pop(swd)* refers to the number of SWDs populating it; *pop(i)* refers to the number of its instances; and *def(swd)* refers to the number of SWDs defining it. Not surprisingly, *foaf:Person* is number one. The sixth term is a common mis-typing of the first one, so it has been well populated without being defined. The ninth term has apparently made the list by virtue of the high OntoRank score of the SWO that defines it.

Table 6 lists top ten SWTs in Swoogle's Ontology Dictionary. The *type* of an SWT is either 'p' for property or 'c' for class. *rdfs:comment* is ranked higher than *dc:title* even though the latter is better populated because the former is referenced by many important SWDs. Properties are ranked higher than classes since they are less domain specific.

Table 6. Top ten terms order by TermRank

TermRank	SWT	type	pop(swd)	pop(i)
1	rdf:type	p	334810	8174201
2	dc:description	p	60427	918644
3	rdfs:label	p	12795	197079
4	rdfs:comment	p	4626	137267
5	dc:title	p	60229	1452612
6	rdf:Property	c	4117	52445
7	dcterms:modified	p	11881	25321
8	rdfs:seeAlso	p	55985	1167786
9	dc:language	p	149878	225600
10	dc:type	p	9461	54676

5.2 Ranking Class-Property Bonds

A more specific issue directly related to step 2 in *CONSTRUCT-ONTO* is ranking *class-property bonds* (see definition 2), which helps users choose the most popular properties for a class when they are publishing data with the desire of maximizing the data's visibility. For example, when publishing an instance of *foaf:Person*, we might always supply a triple that populates the most common property *foaf:mbox_sha1sum*.

Definition 2. *A* **class-property bond (c-p bond)** *refers to an* rdfs:domain *relation between property and class. While c-p bonds can be specified in ontologies in various ways, e.g., direct association* (rdfs:domain) *and class-inheritance; we are interested in finding c-p bonds in class instances characterized by the two-triple graph pattern:* $(\_x, rdf : type, class), (\_x, property, \_)$.

To rank c-p bonds, we cannot simply rely on the definition from ontologies because that does not show how well a c-p bond has been adopted in practice. We evaluate c-p bonds, therefore, by ranking the subgraph that instantiates c-p bonds, e.g., the number instance of foaf:person modified by foaf:name. In DS-APRIL, the five highest ranked properties (by the number of SWDs instantiated c-p bond) of *foaf:Person* are (i) foaf:mbox_sha1sum (67,136 SWDs), (ii) foaf:nick (62,266), (iii) foaf:weblog (54,341), (iv) rdfs:seeAlso (47,228), and (v) foaf:name (46,590).

6   Conclusions and Future Work

Swoogle supports two primary use cases: helping human knowledge engineers find ontologies and terms and serving agents and tools seeking knowledge and data. While no formal evaluation has yet been done, we offer some observations that address how well Swoogle meets its goals and informally compare it to the alternatives.

Swoogle's web-based service has been available since Spring 2004 and has received several million hits, supporting hundreds of regular users and thousands of casual ones. Swoogle continuously discovers online SWDs and thus maintains a global view of the public Semantic Web. The results reported here are based on a dataset (DS-APRIL) of over 330,000 SWDs and 4,000 SWOs, about half the size of the current collection. Swoogle has found many more SWDs, most of which are FOAF or RSS documents, that are excluded from the database to make Swoogle's dataset balanced and interesting. Swoogle's ability to search content at various granularity levels and its ranking mechanisms are novel and promote the emergence of consensus ontologies.

There are three alternatives to Swoogle that can be used to find knowledge on the Semantic Web: conventional search engines, Semantic Web repositories, and specialized RDF data collections. Some conventional search engines index RDF documents and can be used to find SWDs and SWTs. However, none understands the content being indexed, recognizes terms as links, or even correctly parses all RDF encodings. Any ranking done by such systems ignores links between SWDs and their corresponding semantic relationships. Some useful SWD repositories are available (e.g., those at www.schemaweb.info and rdfdata.org) but require manual submission and have limited scope. Several crawler-based systems exist that are specialized to particular kinds of RDF (e.g., FOAF, RSS, DOAP, Creative Commons), but their scope and services are restricted. Intellidimention has an experimental crawler based system [21] similar to Swoogle but with abridged coverage.

A formal evaluation of Swoogle's performance on finding and ranking SWDs and SWTs would be based, in part, on measuring the precision and recall for a set of queries against human judgments. This would allow us to compare Swoogle's performance to other systems, to evaluate different ranking algorithms and to evaluate the impact of doing more or less inference. While we intend to carry out such an evaluation, it requires careful design and significant labor to acquire the necessary human evaluations. User studies through questionnaires or surveys on Swoogle ranking results are planned to provide a subjective reference.

By enlarging the test dataset and compensating for biases due to the predominance of FOAF and RSS documents, we expect to refine our evaluation of Swoogle's navigation model and ranking algorithms. We are also improving the ranking algorithms without generalizing the navigation model, motivated by the the success of XML object-level ranking [17, 11]. We are extending class-property bond ranking to a more general issue – tracking the provenance of and ranking arbitrary RDF sub-graphs [26]. This can be used to resolve, for example, a case where multiple RDF triples claim different values for a person's homepage (whose cardinality constraint is one).

References

1. Ding, L., Finin, T., Joshi, A., Pan, R., Cost, R.S., Peng, Y., Reddivari, P., Doshi, V.C., Sachs, J.: Swoogle: A search and metadata engine for the semantic web. In: CIKM'04. (2004)
2. Wang, R., Storey, V., Firth, C.: A framework for analysis of data quality research. IEEE Transactions on Knowledge and Data Engineering 7 (1995) 623–639
3. Patel, C., Supekar, K., Lee, Y., Park, E.K.: OntoKhoj: a semantic web portal for ontology searching, ranking and classification. In: WIDM'03. (2003) 58–61
4. Alani, H., Brewster, C.: Ontology ranking based on the analysis of concept structures. In: Proc. of the 3rd International Conference on Knowledge Capture (K-Cap). (2005)

[21] http://www.semanticwebsearch.com/

5. Stojanovic, N., Studer, R., Stojanovic, L.: An approach for the ranking of query results in the semantic web. In: ISWC'03. (2003)
6. Anyanwu, K., Maduko, A., Sheth, A.: Semrank: Ranking complex relationship search results on the semantic web. In: WWW'05. (2005) 117–127
7. Page, L., Brin, S., Motwani, R., Winograd, T.: The pagerank citation ranking: Bringing order to the web. Technical report, Stanford University (1998)
8. Haveliwala, T.H.: Topic-sensitive pagerank. In: WWW'02. (2002) 517–526
9. Jeh, G., Widom, J.: Scaling personalized web search. In: WWW '03. (2003) 271–279
10. Xing, W., Ghorbani, A.A.: Weighted pagerank algorithm. In: Proc. of the 2nd Annual Conference on Communication Networks and Services Research. (2004) 305–314
11. Nie, Z., Zhang, Y., Wen, J.R., Ma, W.Y.: Object-level ranking: Bringing order to web objects. In: WWW'05. (2005) 567–574
12. Zhuge, H., Zheng, L.: Ranking semantic-linked network. In: WWW'03 Posters. (2003)
13. Baeza-Yates, R., Davis, E.: Web page ranking using link attributes. In: WWW'04 Posters. (2004) 328–329
14. Wand, Y., Wang, R.Y.: Anchoring data quality dimensions in ontological foundations. Communications of the ACM **39** (1996) 86–95
15. Kanh, B.K., Strong, D.M., Wang, R.Y.: Information quality benchmarks: Product and service performance. Communications of the ACM **45** (2002) 184–192
16. Supekar, K., Patel, C., Lee, Y.: Characterizing quality of knowledge on semantic web. In: Proc. of 7th International Florida Artificial Intelligence Research Society Conf. (2002)
17. Guo, L., Shao, F., Botev, C., Shanmugasundaram, J.: XRANK: ranked keyword search over XML documents. In: SIGMOD'03. (2003) 16–27
18. Balmin, A., Hristidis, V., Papakonstantinou, Y.: ObjectRank: Authority-based keyword search in databases. In: VLDB'04. (2004) 564–575
19. Xi, W., Zhang, B., Chen, Z., Lu, Y., Yan, S., Ma, W.Y., Fox, E.A.: Link fusion: A unified link analysis framework for multi-type interrelated data objects. In: WWW'04. (2004) 319–327
20. Rocha, C., Schwabe, D., Aragao, M.P.: A hybrid approach for searching in the semantic web. In: WWW'04. (2004) 374–383
21. Aleman-Meza, B., Halaschek, C., Arpinar, I.B., Sheth, A.: Context-aware semantic association ranking. In: SWDB'03. (2003) 33–50
22. Bizer, C.: Semantic web trust and security resource guide. (http://www.wiwiss.fu-berlin.de/suhl/bizer/SWTSGuide/ (last accessed 08-11-05))
23. Ding, L., Kolari, P., Finin, T., Joshi, A., Peng, Y., Yesha, Y.: On homeland security and the semantic web: A provenance and trust aware inference framework. In: Proceedings of the AAAI Spring Symposium on AI Technologies for Homeland Security. (2005)
24. Volz, R., Oberle, D., Maedche, A.: Towards a modularized semantic web. In: Proceedings of the ECAI'02 Workshop on Ontologies and Semantic Interoperability. (2002)
25. Grau, B.C., Parsia, B., Sirin, E.: Working with multiple ontologies on the semantic web. In: ISWC'04. (2004)
26. Ding, L., Finin, T., Peng, Y., da Silva, P.P., McGuinness, D.L.: Tracking rdf graph provenance using rdf molecules. Technical Report TR-05-06, UMBC (2005)

Choreography in IRS-III – Coping with Heterogeneous Interaction Patterns in Web Services

John Domingue, Stefania Galizia, and Liliana Cabral

Knowledge Media Institute, The Open University, Milton Keynes, UK
{J.B.Domingue, S.Galizia, L.S.Cabral}@open.ac.uk

Abstract. In this paper we describe how we handle heterogeneity in web service interaction through a choreography mechanism that we have developed for IRS-III. IRS-III is a framework and platform for developing semantic web services which utilizes the WSMO ontology. The overall design of our choreography framework is based on: the use of ontologies and state, IRS-III playing the role of a broker, differentiating between communication direction and which actor has the initiative, having representations which can be executed, a formal semantics, and the ability to suspend communication. Our framework has a full implementation which we illustrate through an example application.

1 Introduction

Web services provide a mechanism to connect applications regardless of the underlying software/hardware platform and their location. From an Information Technology (IT) perspective the key features of web services are that, a) they are based on standard XML based protocols which can run over the internet and b) the descriptions of a web service are distinct from the actual implementation. From a business perspective one key feature is that web services can be viewed as implementations of business services. Commercial organizations can thus use web services technology to expose elements of their business processes. For example, Amazon Web Services allows software developers to directly access their technology platform and product data [1].

Interest in web service technology is high. Many of the major IT vendors (e.g. Microsoft, IBM, SAP) now provide web service based solutions. Moreover, current predictions indicate that the market for web service based solutions will be worth $2.9 billion in 2006 growing to $6.2 billion by 2008 [13].

The web service community is now beginning to accept that the majority of the current problems associated with web services are related to the fact that all of the technologies are based on syntactic descriptions such as WSDL [25] and UDDI [21]. Because syntactic level descriptions are not amenable to computer based interpretation, all of the tasks associated with creating applications from web service based components are carried out manually. Requiring IT specialists to discover, compose and deploy web services manually is time-consuming, costly and error-prone. Moreover, as stated by Larry Ellison:

Y. Gil et al. (Eds.): ISWC 2005, LNCS 3729, pp. 171–185, 2005.

> *"Semantic differences remain the primary roadblock to smooth application integration, one which Web Services alone won't overcome....When I pass customer data across [the Web] in a certain format using a Web services interface, the receiving program has to know what that format is. You have to agree on what the business objects look like."* [8]

The most significant task when connecting software components together is not the plumbing (the data and control flow) but coping with the semantic differences. Two main types of communication mismatches can occur. The first is that the data can have different underlying representations. For example, one web service may represent an address as a number followed by a street name and town, whereas another may represent an address as a number followed by a postal code. The second type of mismatch is related to interaction. Each web service will have a specific interaction pattern related to how the underlying processes are implemented. For example, one web service may require credit card details (e.g. card number, card expiry date) to be sent one at a time whereas another may require that all details are sent in a single message.

In this paper we describe how we cope with heterogeneous web service interaction patterns in the context of IRS-III [7]. IRS-III is a framework and implemented infrastructure which supports the creation of semantic web service based applications. IRS-III has been used to teach semantic web services in a number of tutorials [19] and is currently being deployed in a number of application areas in the context of the DIP [6] project. Following the WSMO [17] framework we use the term choreography to denote the IRS-III component which deals with web service interaction. Our primary contributions which we describe in this paper include: a set of design principles for choreography, a formal definition of choreography based on abstract state machines, a well founded set of ontology based choreography specific primitives and a full implementation.

The rest of this paper is structured as follows: in the following section we describe related work, then we present an overview of IRS-III framework. The section 4 describes the choreography within IRS-III outlining the design principles, our formal model, the main primitives and the execution. In section 5 we describe an example application and the final section concludes the paper.

2   Related Work

The existing approaches describing the communication among web services propose different definitions of choreography, and some of them do not clearly distinguish between choreography and message exchange pattern defininitions.

A message exchange pattern (MEP) is a syntactic template that represents a model for the exchange of messages between web services; a choreography should also describe patterns semantically. However, some approaches view choreography as the composition of atomic MEPs [23], without the support of semantics. Actually, the only standard choreography definition, available on the W3C glossary [24], states simply that choreography concerns the interaction of services with their users.

However, the requirements emerging from e-Business necessitate that web services exchange information at the semantic level. Thus, the choreography of a semantic web service should include a communication protocol specification, which represents service interactions at a semantic level.

The Web Service Choreography Description Language (WS-CDL) provides the choreography representation from a global point of view [12]. According to this vision, the choreography describes the behaviour observable from an external point of view, emphasizing the collaboration of parties, where the communication progresses only when jointly agreed ordering rules are satisfied. Furthermore, the model depicted by the WS-CDL working group describes the choreography at three levels of abstraction: abstract, portable and concrete [22]. An abstract choreography definition will contain descriptions of the data types used and the conditions under which a given message is sent. A portable choreography includes descriptions of the physical structure of the information exchanged and of the technologies used. A concrete choreography extends a portable description including destination URLs, and specific rules, such as information about digital certificates to be used for securing messages. When creating a choreography, the chosen level of abstraction would depend on the current context (e.g. the type of organization it was designed for) and the level of reusability and extendibility required.

Another global approach is presented by Dijman and Dumas [5]. They depict both static and dynamic aspects of the global communication among heterogeneous web services using Petri Nets.

The main current approaches to representing web service communication at a semantic level are proposed by the WSMO [17] and OWL-S [16] working groups.

A web service description within WSMO contains an interface definition. An interface includes a definition of orchestration – how a composite web service invokes subsidiary web services - and a choreography. WSMO adopts, furthermore, the Abstract State Machine (ASM) formalism to model the behavioral aspects of the communication.

In contrast OWL-S does not provide an explicit definition of choreography but instead focuses on a process based description of how complex web services invoke atomic web services.

Within IRS-III, our viewpoint is based on the WSMO approach, which is different from the global approaches described above, as it represents the choreography of a single web service. That is, we describe how one web service talks to one other.

We strictly keep to the WSMO vision, in fact, by separating the orchestration and choreography concepts, WSMO emphasizes the difference between communication and cooperation among web services.

There are also other choreography descriptions that follow the WSMO approach, for instance, Arroyo and Duke propose a Conceptual Model for a Semantic Choreography Engine (SOPHIE) [2], where they aim to separate in a clear-cut way the syntactic and the semantic level and adopt the ASM formalism to model the communication.

In the rest of this paper we give a detailed description of choreography in IRS-III.

3   IRS-III Overview

The IRS project has the overall aim of supporting the automated or semi-automated construction of semantically enhanced systems over the internet. IRS-I [4] supported the creation of knowledge intensive systems structured according to the UPML framework [9] and IRS-II [15] integrated the UPML framework with web service technologies. Within IRS-III we have now incorporated and extended the WSMO ontology [17].

IRS-III has three main classes of features which distinguish it from other work on semantic web services.

Firstly, it supports *one-click publishing* of 'standard' program code. In other words, it automatically transforms programming code (currently we support Java and Lisp environments) into a web service, by automatically creating an appropriate wrapper. Hence, it is very easy to make existing standalone software available on the net, as web services.

Secondly, by extending the WSMO goal and web service concepts, clients of IRS-III can directly invoke web services via goals - that is IRS-III supports *capability-driven* service invocation.

Finally, IRS-III services are web service compatible – standard web services can be trivially published through the IRS-III.

The main components of the IRS-III architecture are the IRS-III Server, the IRS-III Publisher and the IRS-III Client, which communicate through the SOAP protocol. The IRS-III server holds descriptions of Semantic Web Services at two different levels. A knowledge level description is stored currently represented internally in OCML [14], an Ontolingua-derived language which provides both the expressive power to express task specifications and service competencies, as well as the operational support to reason about these.

Publishing with IRS-III entails associating a specific web service with a WSMO web service description. When a web service is published in IRS-III all of the information necessary to call the service, the host, port and path are stored within the choreography associated with the web service.

The IRS publishing platform is furthermore responsible for the actual invocation of a web service; additionally, it automatically generates wrappers which turn standalone code into a web service. The platform also copes with the syntactic level differences between the various web service platforms e.g. AXIS and Apache.

IRS-III was designed for ease of use, in fact a key feature of IRS-III is that web service invocation is capability driven. The IRS-III Client supports this by providing a goal-centric invocation mechanism. An IRS-III user simply asks for a goal to be solved and the IRS-III broker locates an appropriate web service semantic description and then invokes the underlying deployed web service.

In the rest of the paper we will use the terms "IRS" and "IRS-III" interchangeably.

4   IRS-III Choreography Model

A choreography is described in IRS-III by a grounding declaration and a set of guarded transitions. The *grounding* specifies the conceptual representation of the operations involved in the invocation of a Web Service and their mapping to the implementation level. More specifically, the grounding definitions include `operation-name`, `input-roles-soap-binding`, `output-role-soap-binding`. The *guarded transitions* are the set of rules, which represent the interaction between IRS-III and the Web Service on behalf of an IRS client. They are applied when executing the choreography. This model is executed at a semantic level when IRS-III receives a request to achieve a goal.

In the rest of this section we list the main design principles which motivate our choreography model.

4.1 Design Principles

Ontology Based. Ontologies form a central pillar of the semantic web. Founding our choreography descriptions on ontologies means that we can refer to relevant domain dependent concepts or relations within guarded transitions.

IRS as a Broker. As we mentioned earlier the IRS acts as a broker for capability based invocation. A client sends a request to achieve a goal and the IRS finds, composes and invokes the appropriate web services. The choreography to the IRS is thereby fixed. We assume that IRS clients are able to formulate their request as a goal instance. This means that we only require choreographies between the IRS and the deployed web services. Our choreography descriptions are therefore written from the perspective of IRS as a client of the web service.

The Predominance of State. Our overall view is that any message sent by IRS to a web service will depend on its current state, which will include a representation of the messages received during the current conversation.

Given the above we decided to adopt the Abstract State Machine (ASMs) model [3] to represent IRS choreography. Additionally, ASMs are also used within WSMO [18] which is the ontology adopted within IRS-III. A further reason for using ASMs is that they combine mathematical rigor with a practical execution model to represent message exchange patterns.

By representing ASM as rules, the sequence of operations and the message pattern instantiations are generated through the evaluation of conditions. A condition is a generic statement on the current situation, for instance, that an error has occurred. The executive part of the guarded transitions (after 'then') updates the state.
The general form of a guarded transition is given below:

"**if** currentstate = s $\wedge$ Cond **then** currentstate = s1 "

Open. The major components of IRS-III are semantic web services represented within the IRS-III framework. This feature enables the main functionalities of the IRS to be redefined to suit specific requirements. Following this the IRS choreography engine is itself a semantic web service.

Communication Representation. We have chosen to classify the communication in IRS choreography according to two dimensions, following the system-client cooperation model proposed in KADS [11], namely:

- The initiative in the communication, and
- The direction of the communication.

The initiative expresses which actor, either IRS or the web service, is responsible for starting the communication, while the direction represents the communication route, which can be from the system to the client or vice-versa.

The reason for preferring this communication model is that in this way we can verify at every state which actor has initiative. Initiative is associated with the actors who in some sense have control of the conversation. For example, only actors with initiative are allowed to start a conversation or update data previously sent.

A message exchange *event* is a kind of transfer task, an elementary executed operation by an actor during a conversation.

From the IRS perspective, and according to Greef and Breuker's communication representation, we consider six kinds of events: *obtain, present, provide, receive, obtain-initiative, present-initiative*. When the IRS does not have the initiative, *receive* and *provide* messages are used. Conversely, *obtain* and *present* events occur when the IRS is in control of the conversation. *Obtain-initiative* and *present-initiative* allow the initiative to be transferred. For detailed event descriptions see [10].

When a client, that can also be a web service, invokes the IRS, in order to achieve a goal, the choreography engine runs. We depict a simple invocation goal scenario below, underlining the events involved during choreography execution.

Figure 1 depicts the event sequence for this typical goal driven web service invocation scenario.

Fig. 1. A typical sequence of choreography events occurring during goal based web service invocation in IRS-III

The client initiates the communication with IRS by requesting that a goal be achieved. Within our model this corresponds to *receive* and *obtain-initiative* events as the client delegates initiative to the IRS to invoke the required service. During a second phase the IRS invokes a web service which returns a response. In this phase the IRS has the initiative and therefore the occurring events are *present* and *obtain*.

Ability to Suspend Communication. There will be some situations where it is necessary to suspend the current dialog and resume it later. For example, either the IRS or the web service may not have some required data or a web service may go offline.

Executable Semantic Descriptions. The semantic representations of choreography should be executable directly or should be able to be compiled to a runnable representation. Our underlying modelling language OCML [14] is operational. Additionally, extensions within the IRS allow us to attach OCML functions to deployed web services. This means that within a guarded transition one can refer to external data, for example, to "today's exchange rate".

Formalization. A formal semantics allows us to reason about the choreography descriptions which is useful if we want to automatically compose web services. For this reason, we adopt ASMs and our formal model is described in the following section.

Easy to use. If we want our system to be used widely, it is important that the components are easy to use. For this purpose we have defined a relatively small set of choreography specific primitives.

4.2 Formal Definition

Our abstract model of choreography is represented by four main entities: *events, states, conditions,* and *guarded transitions.*
We perform the IRS-III choreography through the tuple $\langle E,S,C,T \rangle$, where

- E is a finite set of events;
- S the (possibly infinite) set of states;
- C the (possibly infinite) set of conditions;
- T represents the (possibly infinite) set of the conditional guarded transitions.

The events that can occur are: {*obtain, present, provide, receive, obtain-initiative, present-initiative*} [10]. Every event maps to an operation during the conversation viewed from the IRS perspective.

The states are the possible message exchange pattern instantiations. A state $s_i \in S$ at a given conversation step T_i, is represented by a set of instances. It contains a constant subset, the web service host, port, location, that is invariant whenever the same web service is invoked, and the event instantiation, dependent on the event that occurred at step T_i.

The web service host, port and location are defined during the IRS publishing process – see section 3.1.

A condition $c \in C$ depicts a situation occurring during the conversation.

The guarded transitions, according with WSMO definition [18], express changes of states by means of rules:

A guarded transition $t \in T$, is a function $t : \left(S, 2^C\right) \xrightarrow{E} S$, that associates a couple (s,

$\{c_1, .., c_j\}$ to s', where s and s' $\in S$, and every c_k $(1 \le k \le i) \in C$.
A guarded transition updates the communication state by an event $e \in E$.

4.3 Choreography Primitives

We have defined a set of choreography specific primitives which can be used in guarded transitions. Our primitives provide an easy to use interface to control a conversation between the IRS and a web service. Developers are also able to include any relation defined with the imported ontologies within guarded transition specifications.

Init-choreography. Initializes the state of the choreography. This primitive runs before a web service is invoked by IRS-III. At this step the IRS has the initiative and it is ready to start the communication.

Send-message. Calls a specific operation in the Web service. If no inputs are explicitly given IRS obtains the input values from the original goal invocation.

The type of event which occurs with send-message is "present" since the IRS holds the initiative and the communication direction is from the IRS to the web service (see figure 1).

Send-suspend. Suspends the communication between IRS and the web service, without stopping the choreography executions. This action will occur, for example, when the IRS lacks some data required by a web service. Executing this primitive suspends the dialog and stores the current state so that communication can be resumed later. The event associated to send-suspend is "present" since communication direction is from the IRS to the web service and the IRS has (and keeps) the initiative.

Received-suspend. The communication is suspended by the web service, when for some reason it is not able to respond to an invocation. As with send-suspend the choreography execution is put on hold. The web service is free to resume the dialog when conditions allow. The event occurring here is "receive", because the web service has taken the initiative from IRS and the communication direction is from the web service to IRS.

Figure 2 shows all events which occur when a web service suspends communication. Initially IRS has initiative, but it is handed over to the web service which suspend the communication through the event "receive". When the web service resumes the dialog the associated event is "receive" again, because the web service has the initiative.

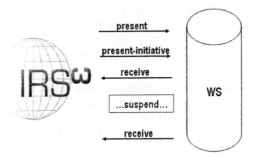

Fig. 2. The occurring choreography events if the web service suspends the communication

Received-message. Contains the result of a successful send-message for a specific operation. In the general case the trigged event is "obtain" as shown in figure 1. If however the web service had previously suspended the communication it will be "receive" (see figure 2). In the both situations the message direction is from the web service to the IRS, but in the former one, IRS has the initiative, and in the latter the web service has control of the dialog.

Received-error. If the execution of a web service causes an error to occur then the received-error primitive is used. The parameters of received-error include the error message and the type of error which occurred. In a fashion similar to received-message, described above, the event taking place is either "obtain" (see figure 1), or "receive" (see figure 2).

End-choreography. Stops the choreography. No other guarded transitions will be executed.

4.4 Choreography Execution

IRS uses a forward-chaining-rule engine to execute a choreography. This means the rules belonging to a choreography are fired according to the state.

Within the IRS there is an internal method which selects one guarded transition when two or more are selected.

One important feature of the execution environment of IRS is that it allows the scope of the choreography to be defined for the set of ontologies involved in the Web Service description.

The IRS server carries out inferences at an ontological level. During communication with a web service the ontological level descriptions need to be mapped to the XML based representations used by the specific web service invoked. We provide two mechanisms which map a) from the ontological level to XML (lower) and b) from XML to the ontological level (lift).

Lift. Lifts an XML string into an ontological construct, represented in OCML. A generic version of this relation is defined within the IRS ontology. SWS developers are free to overwrite this relation inline with the relationship between the results of web service calls and the ontologies used. The lift primitive has the following input parameters: `class-name`, `web-service-class`, `xml-string` and produces an `instance` of `class-name` as output. The semantic developer can thus customize how XML is parsed according the classes within the underlying ontology and the particular web services selected. In order to cope with XML based input the lift primitive utilizes an inbuilt SAX based XML parser.

Lower. Lowers the ontological construct to XML. The input parameters to lower are: `instance-name` and a class `web-service`. The output is `xml-string`. As for the lift primitive the XML generated can be customized according to classes within the ontology and the web service class. For example, the XML generated for instances of a person class may include a full name for one web service and only a family name for another.

5   Virtual Travel Agency Example

Our example application is based on the WSMO Virtual Travel Agency (VTA) application [20]. The overall scenario is to provide a portal where clients can ask for train tickets between any two cities in Europe specifying a departure time and date. The portal maintains a profile for regular users which contains personal preferences.

Our implementation of the VTA includes four web services which can book tickets for specific countries (e.g. Austria, France) and two which can book tickets for travellers with particular profiles (e.g. students and business people). In the rest of this description we will focus on one particular web service – the train ticket service for Germany - and describe its choreography.

German-buy-train-ticket-service-choreography
grounding:

```
normal
  book-german-train-journey
      has-person "sexpr"
      has-departure-station "sexpr"
      has-destination-station "sexpr"
      has-date-and-time "sexpr"
   "string"

first-class-upgrade
  book-first-class-upgrade-german-train-journey
  …..

standard-class
  book-standard-class-german-train-journey
  …..

acknowledge-error
  acknowledge-error-message
      has-acknowledgement "int"
   "string"
```

guarded-transitions:

```
start
  init-choreography
then
  send-message 'normal

accept-first-class-upgrade
  received-message normal ?result
  upgrade-class ?result
  operation-input normal has-person ?person
  accept-upgrade ?person ?accept-upgrade
then
  send-message 'first-class-upgrade
  end-choreography

date-error-transition
  received-error normal ?error-message ?error-type
  date-format-error ?error-type
then
  send-message-with-new-input-role-pairs
      'acknowledge-error (has-acknowledgement 0)
  end-choreography
```

If the traveller booking the train ticket is a gold card member the German train ticket service offers a free upgrade to first class. Travellers can state that they automatically accept these offers within their profile. The choreography definitions below enable the IRS to interact with the web service so that the correct types of bookings are made. The choreography starts with the guarded transition containing `init-choreography` and it ends with the `end-choreography` execution.

The choreography contains two components. The first is a grounding which maps between semantic operations and the implementation level. Above we show the full grounding for the `normal` and `acknowledge-error` operations and only partial definitions for the other operations. After the operation name the next part of the grounding shows the name of the implementing component. In this case it is the name of the Lisp function within the Lisp publishing platform. For a standard web service it would be the name of the operation within the WSDL file and for a Java implementation it would be the name of the Java class and method. The soap bindings for the inputs and output are then specified.

The second part of the choreography contains the set of guarded transitions. Above we show three guarded transitions. `Start` initializes the choreography session and then invokes the deployed service by sending the message associated with the `normal` operation. `Send-message` is a choreography specific relation which takes the values of the input roles from the associated goal instance, transforms the values to an XML representation (using a relation called `lower`), and then invokes the web service. `Accept-first-class-upgrade` uses the choreography specific `received-message` relation. Responses from a web service invocation are first transformed into an ontological representation, using the relation `lift`, and then asserted as (`received-message <operation-name> <lifted-invocation-response>`). The following expressions in the condition check whether the result of the invocation is an offer of an upgrade and whether the traveller's profile states that s/he automatically accepts upgrades. The executive part of the guarded transition sends a message for the `first-class-upgrade` operation and ends the choreography.

The final guarded transition shown, `date-error-transition`, handles errors. If invoking a web service causes an error then an instance of the relation `received-error` is created. The signature of this relation is `<operation> <error-message> <error-type>`. `Error-type` is an instance of a subclass of the `invocation-error` class. The condition for this guarded transition checks to see if the error is a date format error. When this is the case the `acknowledge-error` operation is invoked. Note that because the input-role name and value (`has-acknowledgement` and `0`) are not present in the original goal invocation they are provided here. Hence the use of the relation `send-message-with-new-input-role-pairs`.

Every guarded transition execution updates the choreography state.

German-buy-train-ticket-service-publisher-information
web-service-host: `"137.108.24.227"`
web-service-port: `3001`
web-service-location: `"/soap"`

Once the semantic descriptions have been created we 'publish' the web service through a simple dialog where we state the URL of the appropriate publishing platform. The definition created for the `german-train-ticket-service` is shown above. Host, port and location represent also the invariant part of choreography state when a given web service is invoked.

Before running a set of guarded transitions the IRS creates a new ontology which inherits from the ontology in which the web service is defined. All new assertions are made within the new ontology which is deleted after the choreography completes (with `end-choreography`). This allows the IRS to cope with simultaneous goal driven web service requests. Additionally, the ontology is used to capture the current state of a choreography run when a suspend primitive is invoked.

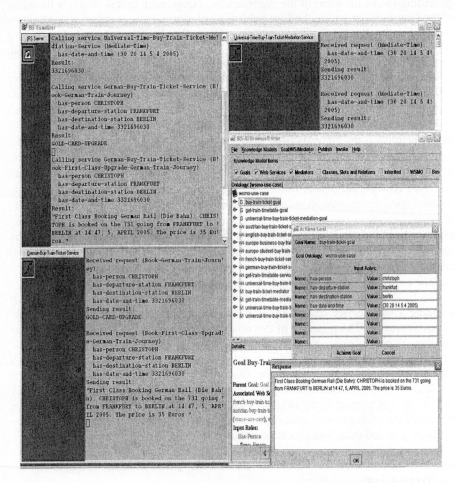

Fig. 3. A screen snapshot showing the VTA running on IRS-III

Figure 3 shows a screen snapshot of the VTA application running in IRS-III. The bottom right of the figure contains three windows. The *Invocation Client* (with title "Achieve Goal") provides a dialog where the client has specified the input role values for the `buy-train-ticket-goal` (Christoph wants to travel from Frankfurt to Berlin at 14:20:30 on the 5th April 2005). Below the *Response* window shows the final result – Christoph has a first class booking on the German rail system at 14:47 for 31 Euros. Behind the Invocation Client and Response window we can see the *IRS-III*

Browser/Editor. The top part displays a list of the goals, web services and mediators defined within the wsmo-use-case ontology. The bottom part shows a detailed description of buy-train-ticket-goal, where every item, classes, relations and instances, can be inspected by clicking on it.

The main window (titled "IRS Visualizer") is a simple visualization system which displays the interactions between the IRS server and the published web services. The top left pane within the visualization (with the label "IRS Server") shows the goal based requests received by the server and the web service invocation requests sent.

The portion of the interaction history shown contains a call to the universal-time-buy-train-ticket-mediation-service, a mediation service which converts the date from (30 20 14 5 4 2005) into 3321696030 format. The german-buy-train-ticket-service is called twice. The first call with the implementation component identifier book-german-train-germany results in the response GOLD-CARD-UPGRADE. This call corresponds to the invocation with the start guarded transition. The second call with the implementation component identifier book-first-class-upgrade-german-train-journey results in the response shown in the Response window. The second call corresponds to the invocation associated with the accept-first-class-upgrade guarded transition.

The pane on the top right of the visualizer (labelled "Universal-Time-Buy-Train-Ticket-Mediation-Service") shows that the mediation service was called twice. As mentioned earlier, during the web service selection process the IRS evaluates the logical expression within the assumption slot of a web service's capability. If the logical expression evaluates to true the corresponding web service is deemed to be selected. Before evaluating the expression the IRS runs the web service's associated mediators to transform the values within the invoked goal instance. The date and time mediation service is run twice because both the German and Austrian rail services within our application use a universal date and time format.

The pane of the bottom left of the visualizer (labelled "German-Buy-Train-Ticket-Service") shows that two invocations were made to the german-buy-train-ticket-service. The first with the component identifier book-german-train-germany and the second invocation with book-first-class-upgrade-german-train-journey. Within the Lisp publishing platform these correspond to a Lisp function name. As mentioned earlier for a standard web service the identifier would correspond to a WSDL operation.

6   Conclusions and Future Work

Enabling heterogeneous software components, available on the internet, to be integrated is a primary aim for research in the area of semantic web services. In this paper we have described how IRS-III is able to handle heterogeneity related to web service interaction patterns through a choreography.

The choreography execution occurs in IRS-III from the client perspective, that is to say, to carry out a web service invocation, the IRS executes the choreography as well as a requester client.

Our underlying design principles are based on the use of ontologies and state, the IRS acting as a broker for capability based invocation, the dimensions of initiative and communication direction, the provision of a formal description, and semantic descriptions which are realised within simple-to-use constructs that can be executed.

We have shown through a detailed example how choreographies can be defined and executed with little effort with our framework. As mentioned earlier a key element of our design is that the choreography component of IRS-III is itself a semantic web service allowing developers to easily replace our choreography execution engine with another if desired.

We have recently used our platform and the choreography execution in various tutorials: at the European Semantic Web Conference (ESWC 2005), the International Conference on Web Engineering (ICWE2005), and the Knowledge Web Summer School (SSSW 2005) and we will continue to evaluate the framework at the European Conference on Web Services (ECOWS 2005) and at this year's International Semantic Web Conference (ISWC 2005).

Additionally, we are currently deploying an IRS-III based application within an e-Government demonstrator in the context of the DIP project.

In relation to future work we plan to semi-automatically generate client choreographies from the choreography descriptions of WSMO-compliant web services.

The IRS-III browser/editor and publishing platforms are currently available at http://kmi.open.ac.uk/projects/irs/. We periodically release executable versions of the server for specific usage contexts.

Acknowledgements

This work is supported by DIP (Data, Information and Process Integration with Semantic Web Services) (EU FP6 - 507483) and AKT (Advanced Knowledge Technologies) (UK EPSRC GR/N15764/01) projects.

References

1. Amazon (2005). Web Services (Available at http://www.amazon.com/gp/browse. html/104-6906496-9857523?%5Fencoding=UTF8&node=3435361).
2. S. Arroyo, S. and A., Duke (2005). SOPHIE - A Conceptual Model for a Semantic Choreography Framework. In proceedings of the Workshop on Semantic and Dynamic Web Processes (SDWP 2005). Orlando, Florida, USA, July 2005.
3. Börger, E. (1998). High Level System Design and Analysis Using Abstract State Machines. In proceedings of the International Workshop on Current Trends in Applied Formal Method: Applied Formal Methods, p.1-43, October 1998.
4. Crubezy, M., Motta, E., Lu, W. and Musen, M. (2002). Configuring Online Problem-Solving Resources with the Internet Reasoning Service. IEEE Intelligent Systems 2002.
5. Dijkman, R. and Dumas, M. (2004). Service-Oriented Design: A Multi-Viewpoint Approach. International Journal of Cooperative Information Systems 13(4): 337-368, 2004.
6. DIP (2005). The DIP Project. http://dip.semanticweb.org/.
7. Domingue, J., Cabral, L., Hakimpour, F., Sell, D. and Motta, E. (2004). IRS III: A Platform and Infrastructure for Creating WSMO-based Semantic Web Services. In proceedings of the Workshop on WSMO Implementations (WIW 2004) Frankfurt, Germany. CEUR Workshop Proceedings, ISSN 1613-0073 II.

8. Ellison, L. (2002). Looking Toward the Next Phase for Web Services. (Available at http://webservicesadvisor.com/doc/09586).

9. Fensel, D. and Motta, E. (2001). Structured Development of Problem Solving Methods. IEEE Transactions on Knowledge and Data Engineering, Vol. 13(6). 913-932.

10. Galizia, S. and Domingue, J. (2004). Towards a Choreography for IRS-III. In proceedings of the Workshop on WSMO Implementations (WIW 2004) Frankfurt, Germany, September 29-30, 2004, CEUR Workshop Proceedings, ISSN 1613-0073. (Available at http://CEUR-WS.org/Vol-113/paper7.pdf).

11. Greef, H. P. and Breuker, J. A. (1992). Analysing system-user cooperation in KADS. Knowledge Acquisition, 4:89–108, 1992.

12. Kavantzas, N., Burdett, D., Ritzinger, G., Fletcher, T. and Lafon, Y. (Eds) (2004). Web Service Choreography Description Language Version 1.0. W3C Working Draft 17 December 2004. (Available at http://www.w3.org/TR/2004/WD-ws-cdl-10-20041217/).

13. Kerner, S. M. (2004). Web Services Market to Explode (Available at http://www.internetnews.com/dev-news/article.php/3413161)

14. Motta, E. (1998). An Overview of the OCML Modelling Language. In proceedings of the 8th Workshop on Knowledge Engineering Methods and Languages (KEML '98).

15. Motta, E., Domingue, J., Cabral, L. and Gaspari, M. (2003). IRS-II: A Framework and Infrastructure for Semantic Web Services. In proceeding of the 2nd International Semantic Web Conference (ISWC2003). Sundial Resort, Sanibel Island, Florida, USA. LNCS 2870, pp. 306–318.

16. OWL-S Working Group (2004). OWL-S: Semantic Markup for Web Services (Available at http://www.daml.org/services/owl-s/1.1/overview/).

17. Roman, D., Lausen, H. and Keller, U. (Eds) (2005). The Web Service Modeling Ontology WSMO, final version 1.1. WSMO Final Draft D2, 2005.

18. Roman, D., Sciluna, D. and Feier, C. (Eds) (2005). Ontology -based Choreography and Orchestration of WSMO Services. Final Draft D14.

19. Stollberg, M. and Arroyo, S. (2005). WSMO Tutorial. WSMO Deliverable (Available at http://www.wsmo.org/TR/d17/)

20. Stollberg, M. and Lara, R. (Eds) (2004). D3.3 v0.1 WSMO Use Case: Virtual Travel Agency.

21. UDDI (2003). UDDI Spec Technical Committee Specification v. 3.0, http://uddi.org/pubs/uddi-v3.0.1-20031014.htm

22. W3C [a] (2004). Web services choreography model overview. W3C Working Draft 24 March 2004 (Available at http://www.w3.org/TR/2004/WD-ws-chor-model-20040324).

23. W3C [b] (2004). Web Services Architecture. W3C Working Draft 11 February 2004 (Available at http://www.w3.org/TR/ws-arch/).

24. W3C [c] (2004). Web Services Glossary. W3C Working Group Note. 11 February 2004 (Available at http://www.w3.org/TR/ws-gloss/).

25. WSDL (2001). Web Services Description Language (WSDL) 1.1, http://www.w3.org/TR/2001/NOTE-wsdl-20010315.

Bootstrapping Ontology Alignment Methods with APFEL

Marc Ehrig[1], Steffen Staab[2], and York Sure[1]

[1] Institute AIFB, University of Karlsruhe
[2] ISWeb, University of Koblenz-Landau

Abstract. Ontology alignment is a prerequisite in order to allow for interoperation between different ontologies and many alignment strategies have been proposed to facilitate the alignment task by (semi-)automatic means. Due to the complexity of the alignment task, manually defined methods for (semi-)automatic alignment rarely constitute an optimal configuration of substrategies from which they have been built. In fact, scrutinizing current ontology alignment methods, one may recognize that most are not optimized for given ontologies. Some few include machine learning for automating the task, but their optimization by machine learning means is mostly restricted to the extensional definition of ontology concepts. With APFEL (Alignment Process Feature Estimation and Learning) we present a machine learning approach that explores the user validation of initial alignments for optimizing alignment methods. The methods are based on extensional and intensional ontology definitions. Core to APFEL is the idea of a generic alignment process, the steps of which may be represented explicitly. APFEL then generates new hypotheses for what might be useful features and similarity assessments and weights them by machine learning approaches. APFEL compares favorably in our experiments to competing approaches.

1 Introduction

Semantic alignment between ontologies is a necessary precondition to establish interoperability between agents or services using different ontologies. Thus, in recent years different methods for automatic ontology alignment have been proposed to deal with this challenge. Thereby, the proposed methods were constricted to one of two different paradigms: Either, *(i)*, proposals would include a manually predefined automatic method for proposing alignments, which would be used in the actual alignment process (cf. [10, 12, 19]). They typically consist of a number of substrategies such as finding similar labels. Or, *(ii)*, proposals would learn an automatic alignment method based on instance representations, e.g. bag-of-word models of documents (cf. [1, 7]).

Both paradigms suffer from drawbacks. The first paradigm suffers from the problem that it is impossible, even for an expert knowledge engineer, to predict what strategy of aligning entities is most successful for a given pair of ontologies. Furthermore, it is rather difficult to combine the multiple different substrategies to behave optimally. This is especially the case with increasing complexity of ontology languages or increasing

Y. Gil et al. (Eds.): ISWC 2005, LNCS 3729, pp. 186–200, 2005.

amounts of domain specific conventions, which should also be included for optimal performance. The second paradigm is often hurt by the lack of instances or instance descriptions, because not in every case an ontology has many instances and in many cases instances exist only for some part of the ontology. Knowledge encoded in the intensional descriptions of concepts and relations is only marginally exploited this way.

Hence, there remains the need to automatically combine multiple diverse and complementary alignment strategies of *all* indicators, i.e. extensional (like similar instances) *and* intensional (like the same position in a taxonomy) descriptions, in order to produce comprehensive, effective and efficient semi-automatic alignment methods. Such methods need to be flexible to cope with different strategies for various application scenarios, e.g. by using parameters. We call them "Parameterizable Alignment Methods" (PAM).

We have developed a bootstrapping approach for acquiring the parameters that drive such a PAM. We call our approach APFEL for "Alignment Process Feature Estimation and Learning". The learnt PAM may be applied to ontologies of specific domains, but also for on-the-fly alignment of arbitrary ontologies.

Bootstrapping with APFEL

APFEL is based on four major considerations. First, at the level of *executing the alignment method*, APFEL is based on the general observation that alignment methods like QOM [10] or PROMPT [19] may be mapped onto a generic alignment process (cf. Section 3). Major steps of this generic process include:

1. Feature Engineering, i.e. select small (also domain-specific) excerpts of the overall ontology definition to describe a specific entity (e.g., the label 'Daimler' to describe the concept o1:Daimler).
2. Search Step Selection, i.e. choose two entities from the two ontologies to compare (e.g., o1:Daimler and o2:Mercedes).
3. Similarity Assessment, i.e. indicate a similarity for a given description of two entities (e.g., $simil_{label}$(o1:Daimler,o2:Mercedes)=0).
4. Similarity Aggregation, i.e. aggregate multiple similarity assessments for one pair of entities into a single measure (e.g., simil(o1:Daimler,o2:Mercedes)=0.5).
5. Interpretation, i.e. use all aggregated numbers, some threshold and some interpretation strategy to propose the equality for the selected entity pairs (align (o1:Daimler)='⊥').
6. Iteration, i.e. as the similarity of one entity pair influences the similarity of neighboring entity pairs, the equality is propagated through the ontologies (e.g., it may lead to a new simil(o1:Daimler,o2:Mercedes)=0.85, subsequently resulting in align(o1:Daimler)=o2:Mercedes).

Second, at the meta level of *representing an alignment method*, APFEL parameterizes each of these steps by maintaining a declarative representation of features engineered Q_F, similarity assessments Q_S for the features, a weighting scheme Q_W for the aggregation of such similarity assessments and a threshold Q_T to feed into the interpretation strategy (see Section 4.1).[1] In principle APFEL can be applied to every approach based on the presented generic process.

Third, such a declarative representation, e.g. of QOM or PROMPT, can be given to a *parameterizable alignment method*, PAM. In fact, we initialize PAM with the representation of a QOM-like strategy, PAM(QOM), before some initial alignments of two given ontologies are generated through it. The alignments are then handed over to the user for validation (cf. Section 4.2).

Fourth, APFEL generates hypotheses of useful features H_F for a domain-specific pair of ontologies and proposes similarity assessments H_S for these hypotheses (cf. Section 4.3). APFEL uses the validated initial alignments for machine learning the weighting scheme. The aggregation scheme recurs to all feature/similarity combinations under consideration, which are represented by $D_F := Q_F \cup H_F$ and $D_S := Q_S \cup H_S$. Finally, it outputs the weighting scheme D_W and the threshold it has learned D_T (cf. Section 4.4).

The APFEL process is summarized in Figure 2 and will be explained in detail in Section 4. The result of APFEL is a representation of an alignment scheme. The scheme then has been optimized by machine learning to consider the indicators initially used for bootstrapping as well as the newly generated domain/ontology-specific indicators. Thus, it may integrate indicators working at the level of intensional *and* extensional ontology descriptions to result in a comprehensive improved alignment method (cf. Section 4.5).

The paper is structured as follows. In the next section we will explain the foundations for our approach, ontologies and alignments. In Section 3 we describe all steps of the general alignment process in detail. Section 4 illustrates our APFEL approach. In the subsequent Section 5, we evaluate APFEL against various alignment methods, in particular QOM. Before we conclude, we contrast APFEL with further approaches.

2   Foundations

2.1   Ontology

The following short definition describes an ontology structure as used here. In the understanding of this paper an ontology consists of both schema and instantiating data.

An ontology O is defined through the following tuple:

$$O := (C, H_C, R_C, H_R, I, R_I, \iota_C, \iota_R, A)$$

Concepts C of the schema are arranged in a subsumption hierarchy H_C. Relations R_C exist between pairs of concepts. Relations can also be arranged in a hierarchy H_R. (Meta-)Data is constituted by instances I of specific concepts. Theses instances are interconnected by relational instances R_I. Instances and relational instances are connected to concepts resp. relations by the instantiations ι_C resp. ι_R. Additionally one can define axioms A which can be used to infer knowledge from already existing knowledge. An extended definition can be found in [20]. Common languages to represent ontologies are RDF(S) or OWL, though one should note that each language offers different modeling primitives.

---

[1] Unlike done in QOM [10], we do not vary the search step selection, as QOM was about the trade-off between efficiency and effectiveness and in this paper we focus on effectiveness alone. Further, we do not vary iteration strategies to limit the exploration space.

The following fragment of an automobile ontology

$$O := (\{automobile, luxury, \ldots\}, \{\ldots\}, \{speed(automobile, INTEGER), \ldots\},$$
$$\{\ldots\}, \{\ldots\}, \{\ldots\}, \{\ldots\}, \{\ldots\}, \{\ldots\})$$

can be represented in OWL as shown in Example 1.

```
<owl:Class rdf:about=''auto:automobile''/>
<owl:Class rdf:about=''auto:luxury''/>
<owl:DatatypeProperty rdf:about=''auto:speed''>
 <rdfs:domain rdf:resource =''auto:automobile''/>
 <rdfs:range rdf:resource=''xsd#INTEGER''/>
</owl:DatatypeProperty>
```

Example 1. Domain Ontology

2.2   Alignment

We here define our use of the term "alignment" similarly to [15]: Given two arbitrary ontologies O_1 and O_2, aligning one ontology with another means that for each entity $e \in \mathcal{E}$ (concept C, relation R_C, or instance I) in ontology O_1, we try to find a corresponding entity, which has the same intended meaning, in ontology O_2. The result are alignments between pairs of entities of the two ontologies. Semantically the alignment returns two entities linked by an identity relation.

Definition 1. *We define an ontology alignment function, $align$, based on the vocabulary, $\mathcal{E}$, of all terms $e \in \mathcal{E}$ and the set of possible ontologies, $\mathcal{O}$, as a partial function:*
   $align : \mathcal{E} \times \mathcal{O} \times \mathcal{O} \rightharpoonup \mathcal{E}$,
   with $\forall e \in \mathcal{E}_{O_1}(\exists f \in \mathcal{E}_{O_2} : align(e, O_1, O_2) = f \vee align(e, O_1, O_2) = \bot)$.
We write $\mathcal{E}_{O_1}$ if all $e \in \mathcal{E}$ are from ontology O_1. Any entity can either be aligned to exactly one other entity or none.

Apart from one-to-one alignment as investigated in this paper one entity often has to be aligned to a complex composite such as a concatenation of terms (first and last name) or an entity with restrictions (a sports-car is a car going faster than 250 km/h). We refer to [4, 6] for first thoughts on complex alignments. Alignment of axioms has to the best of our knowledge not been a topic of research yet.

3   General Alignment Process

We briefly introduce our definition of the generic alignment process that subsumes all the alignment approaches we are aware of (e.g. PROMPT [19], GLUE [7], QOM

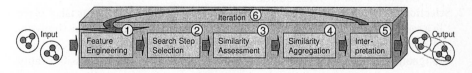

Fig. 1. General Alignment Process in PAM

[10, 11]). This subsumption makes our work a meta-framework valid for many ontology alignment approaches. In this section, we only focus on the definition to the extent that is necessary to understand how APFEL operates on the steps of the generic process. Figure 1 illustrates the six main steps of the generic alignment process. As input, two ontologies are given which are to be aligned. The steps are illustrated through examples where necessary.

1. **Feature engineering** selects only parts of an ontology definition in order to describe a specific entity. Implicitly, [12] made a similar observation. For instance, alignment of entities may be based only on a subset of all RDFS primitives in the ontology. A feature may be as simple as the label of an entity, or it may include intensional structural descriptions such as super- or sub-concepts for concepts (a `sports car` being a subconcept of `car`), or domain and range for relations. Instance features may be instantiated attributes. Further, we use extensional descriptions.

```
<rdf:Description rdf:about=''o1:Daimler''>
    <rdf:type rdf:resource=''auto:automobile''>
    <rdf:type rdf:resource=''auto:luxury''>
    <auto:speed rdf:resource=''auto:fast''>
</rdf:Description>
```

Example 2. Fragment of the First Example Ontology

```
<rdf:Description rdf:about=''o2:Mercedes''>
    <rdf:type rdf:resource=''auto:automobile''>
    <auto:speed rdf:resource=''auto:fast''>
</rdf:Description>
```

Example 3. Fragment of the Second Example Ontology

In our Examples 2 and 3 we have fragments of two different ontologies, one describing the instance `Daimler` and one describing `Mercedes`. Both `o1:Daimler` and `o2:Mercedes` have a generic ontology feature called `type`. The values of this feature are *(i)*, `automobile` and `luxury`, and, *(ii)*, `automobile`, respectively.

Often ontology alignment has to be performed in a specific application of one domain. For these scenarios domain-specific features provide excess value for the alignment process. Returning to our example, the relation `speed` is not a general ontology feature, but a feature which is defined in the automobile domain, e.g. in a domain ontology. Thus it will be important for correctly and only aligning `o1:Daimler` and `o2:Mercedes`.

2. **Selection of Next Search Steps.** The derivation of ontology alignments takes place in a search space of candidate pairs. This step may choose to compute the similarity of a restricted subset of candidate concepts pairs $\{(e, f)|e \in \mathcal{E}_{O_1}, f \in \mathcal{E}_{O_2}\}$ and to ignore others. For the running example we simply select every possible entity pair as an alignment candidate. In our example this means we will continue the comparison of `o1:Daimler` and `o2:Mercedes`.

3. Similarity Assessment determines similarity values of candidate pairs. We need heuristic ways for comparing objects i.e. similarity functions such as on strings [16], object sets [3], checks for inclusion or inequality, rather than exact logical identity. The result lies within a range between 0 and 1. In our example we use a similarity function based on the instantiated results, i.e. we check whether the two concept sets, parent concepts of o1:Daimler (automobile and luxury) and parent concepts of o2:Mercedes (only automobile), are the same. In the given case this is true to a certain degree, effectively returning a similarity value of 0.5. The corresponding feature/similarity assessment (FS2) is represented in Table 1 together with a second feature/similarity assessment (FS1) based on the similarity of labels. For APFEL we refer to them as Q_F/Q_S assessments. According to the classification by [8] the feature/similarity combinations may be referred to as rule-based alignment approaches.

Table 1. Informal and Formal Feature/Similarity Assessment

FS1: if labels are the same, the entities are also the same to a certain degree
FS2: if parent concepts are the same, the instances are also the same to a certain degree

Comparing	No.	Feature Q_F	Similarity Q_S
Entities	FS1	(label,X_1)	string similarity(X_1, X_2)
Instances	FS2	(parent,X_1)	set equality(X_1, X_2)

4. Similarity Aggregation. In general, there may be several similarity values for a candidate pair of entities (e, f) from two ontologies O_1, O_2, e.g. one for the similarity of their labels and one for the similarity of their relationship to other terms. These different similarity values for one candidate pair must be aggregated into a single aggregated similarity value. This may be achieved through a simple averaging step, but also through complex aggregation functions using weighting schemes Q_W. For the example we only have to result of the parent concept comparison which leads to: simil(o1:Daimler,o2:Mercedes)=0.5.

5. Interpretation uses the aggregated similarity values to align entities from O_1 and O_2. Some mechanisms here are e.g. to use thresholds Q_T for similarity [19], to perform relaxation labelling [7], or to combine structural and similarity criteria. simil(o1:Daimler,o2:Mercedes)=0.5$\geq$0.5 leads to align(o1:Daimler)= o2:Mercedes. Semi-automatic approaches may present the entities and the alignment confidence to the user and let the user decide.

6. Iteration. Several algorithms perform an iteration (see also similarity flooding [17]) over the whole process in order to bootstrap the amount of structural knowledge. Iteration may stop when no new alignments are proposed, or if a predefined number of iterations has been reached. Note that in a subsequent iteration one or several of steps 1 through 5 may be skipped, because all features might already be available in the appropriate format or because some similarity computation might only be required in the first round. We use the intermediate results of step 5 and feed them again into the process and stop after a predefined number of iterations.

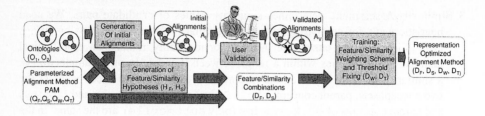

Fig. 2. Detailed Process in APFEL

4   APFEL

In this section it is explained how APFEL works to optimize a given parameterizable alignment method (cf. Figure 2). Data structures are illustrated through white boxes and process steps through colored boxes. We will describe first the data structures, then the process steps. Finally, we show how the PAM resulting from APFEL is applied.

4.1   Data Structures

We here describe the data structures on which APFEL operates. APFEL requires two ontologies O_1 and O_2 as inputs to its processing. Either these are the ontologies for which the further alignment process will be optimized directly. Or, they exemplarily represent a type or domain which requires an optimized alignment method.

Core to APFEL is the representation of the generic alignment process. Relevant data structures for representation include:

(*i*) Q_F: features engineered (e.g. label, instances, domain), (*ii*) Q_S: similarity assessments corresponding to the features of Q_F (e.g. equality, subsumption), (*iii*) Q_W: weighting scheme for an aggregation of feature-similarity assessments (e.g. weighted averaging), and (*iv*) Q_T: interpretation strategy (e.g. alignments occur if similarity is above the fixed threshold).

Such a declarative representation can be given to a parameterizable alignment method, PAM, for execution. In fact, we can initialize PAM with a representation of different strategies. Thus, an initial alignment function, $\mathrm{align}_{\mathrm{init}}$, may be defined by $\mathrm{align}_{\mathrm{init}}$:=PAM(PROMPT) or $\mathrm{align}_{\mathrm{init}}$:=PAM(QOM).

Then, APFEL uses user validations A_V of the initial proposals of $\mathrm{align}_{\mathrm{init}}$. In general, the described input does not explicitly require an ontology engineer. The two ontologies, an arbitrary (predefined) alignment method, and the validation of the initial alignments may be processed by a typical (domain) user as well, as long as she understands the meaning of the aligned entities.

The output of APFEL is an improved alignment method, $\mathrm{align}_{\mathrm{optim}}$, defined as $\mathrm{align}_{\mathrm{optim}}$:=PAM(APFEL($O_1, O_2, Q_F, Q_S, Q_W, Q_T, A_V$)). Parameters characterizing APFEL($O_1, O_2, Q_F, Q_S, Q_W, Q_T, A_V$) constitute the tuple ($D_F, D_S, D_W, D_T$).

Through the optimization step alignment results may change: the result of $\mathrm{align}_{\mathrm{init}}$(o1:Daimler, O_1, O_2) might be '$\perp$' and the result of $\mathrm{align}_{\mathrm{optim}}$(o1:Daimler, O_1, O_2) might be o2:Mercedes.

Table 2. Initial Alignments Returned for Validation

Entity 1	Entity 2	Confidence	User Grade
car	car	0.95	to be rated
auto	automobile	0.8	to be rated
wheel	tire	0.6	to be rated
speed	hasSpeed	0.6	to be rated
driver	gear	0.2	to be rated

4.2   Generation and Validation of Initial Alignments

Machine learning as used in this paper requires training examples. The assistance in their creation is necessary as in a typical ontology alignment setting there are only a small number of really plausible alignments available compared to the large number of candidates, which might be possible a priori. Presenting every candidate for validation makes the process tiring and inefficient for the human user. Therefore, we use an existing parametrization as input to the Parameterizable Alignment Method, e.g. align$_{init}$=PAM(QOM) to create the initial alignments A_I for the given ontologies. As these results are only preliminary, PAM does not have to use very sophisticated processes: very basic features and similarities (e.g. label similarity) combined with a naïve simple averaging and fixed threshold are sufficient in most cases. Resulting proposed pairs are stored starting with the highest probability alignments as shown in Table 2.

This allows the domain user to easily validate the initial alignments and thus generate correct training data A_V. She does not need to understand the complex ontology concepts i.e. does not need to be an ontology engineer, but has to understand the meanings of the aligned entities. If the user further knows additional alignments she can add these alignments to the validated list. Obviously the quality of the later machine learning step depends on the quality and quantity of the validated alignments at this point.

4.3   Generation of Feature/Similarity Hypotheses

As mentioned in the introduction it becomes difficult for the human user to decide which features and similarity heuristics make sense in indicating an alignment of two entities. Our approach therefore generates these feature/similarity combinations automatically.

The basis of the feature/similarity combinations is given by an arbitrary alignment method such as PAM(QOM) with which we have achieved good results.

Further, from the two given ontologies APFEL extracts additional features H_F by examining the ontologies for overlapping features. "Overlapping" means that they occur in both ontologies. Currently this implies the same identifier, but very similar features can also be used. These might be additional features from the ontology model such as OWL primitives or special XML datatypes. But at this point also domain-specific features are integrated into the alignment process such as auto:licensenumber from an upper-level automobile ontology. The features are then combined in a combinatorial way with a generic set of predefined similarity assessments including similarity

$$\left\{ \begin{array}{l} extras \\ licensenumber \end{array} \right\} \times \left\{ \begin{array}{l} equality \\ inclusion \end{array} \right\} \Rightarrow$$

Comparing	No.	Feature H_F	Similarity H_S
Cars	FS1	(extras,X_1)	set equality(X_1, X_2)
Cars	FS2	(extras,X_1)	subset(X_1, X_2)
Cars	FS3	(license no.,X_1)	equality(X_1, X_2)
Cars	FS4	(license no.,X_1)	substring(X_1, X_2)

Fig. 3. Generation of Additional Hypotheses

measures for, e.g., equality, string similarity, or set inclusion. Thus, APFEL derives similarity assessments H_S for features H_F.

Figure 3 illustrates this process for generating hypotheses for feature/similarity combinations. In the given example two domain attributes extras and license number are compared using the equality and the inclusion similarity. All feature/similarity combinations are added for now. Some feature/similarity combinations will not be useful, e.g. FS4, checking whether one license number is a substring of another. However, in the subsequent training step machine learning will be used to pick out those which actually improve alignment results.

From the feature/similarity combinations of (Q_F, Q_S) and of the extracted hypotheses (H_F, H_S) we derive an extended collection of feature/similarity combinations (D_F, D_S) with $D_F := Q_F \cup H_F$ and $D_S := Q_S \cup H_S$.

4.4 Training

After determining the classification of two entities of being aligned or not (A_V), all validated alignment pairs are processed with the previously automatically generated collection of features and similarities. From each FS set a numerical value is returned which is saved together with the entity pair as shown in Table 3. Further the user validation is added to the table.

We can now apply machine learning algorithms to the automatically generated features D_F and similarities D_S using the example training alignments A_V. More specifically, the numerical values of all feature/similarity combinations are the input for the algorithm. The classification of being aligned or not represents the output. Different machine learning techniques for classification (e.g. decision tree learner, neural networks,

Table 3. Training Data for Machine Learning (including user validation and value returned by each feature/similarity combination FS$_i$)

Entity1	Entity2	FS1	FS2	FS3	FS4	User Grade
car	car	1.0	1.0	0.8	0.0	1
auto	automobile	0.7	1.0	0.7	0.0	1
wheel	tire	0.0	1.0	0.8	0.0	0
speed	hasSpeed	0.7	0.0	0.0	1.0	1
driver	gear	0.2	0.0	0.0	0.0	0

or support vector machines) assign an optimal internal weighting D_W and threshold D_T scheme. However, the number of training alignments and feature/similarity combinations need to correlate to return meaningful results. Machine learning methods like C4.5 further capture relevance values for feature/similarity combinations. If they do not have any (or only marginal) relevance they are given a weight of zero and can thus be omitted. In a decision tree they simply are not present.

From this we finally receive the most important feature/similarity combinations (features D_F and similarity D_S) and the weighting D_W and threshold D_T thereof. With this we can set up the final ontology alignment method which we call align$_{\text{optim}}$:= PAM(APFEL($O_1, O_2, Q_F, Q_S, Q_W, Q_T, A_V$)). Depending on the complexity of the alignment problem it might be necessary to repeat the step of test data generation (based on the improved alignment method) and training, especially if the initial method was very simple.

4.5   Application in Alignment Process

The final system is parameterized with D_F, D_S, D_W, and D_T. It allows for fully or semi-automatic alignment of two ontologies — and further uses domain-specific optimization of the alignment system. If training data represented general ontologies, the system can be applied to any pair of ontologies for aligning, not only the domain of training ontologies. Depending on the weighting and threshold scheme this may also include an explanation facility which provides evidence why two entities are aligned.

5   Evaluation

5.1   Implementation

The presented approach has been implemented as part of the FOAM framework of ontology alignment and mapping[2]. It is based on Java using the capabilities of the KAON2-framework [14], which can handle OWL-DL ontologies.

5.2   Evaluation Approach

This paper mainly focuses on an approach to create a method for the alignment of two ontologies. The quality of neither the learning process APFEL itself nor the alignment method PAM can be evaluated directly. Therefore, we evaluate the quality of alignments returned by the learned process. They are compared to the manually created alignment process QOM, which has shown very good results in previous experiments [10]. Additionally we evaluated the effect of different numbers of training examples.

5.3   Measures

We use standard information retrieval metrics to assess the approaches (cf. [5]):

---

[2] http://www.aifb.uni-karlsruhe.de/WBS/meh/foam

$$\text{Precision} \quad p \; = \; \frac{\#correct\_found\_alignments}{\#found\_alignments}$$

$$\text{Recall} \quad r \; = \; \frac{\#correct\_found\_alignments}{\#existing\_alignments}$$

$$\text{F-Measure} \; f_1 = \frac{2pr}{p+r}$$

We consider the f-measure as most relevant for our evaluation since it balances well precision and recall. If the focus were laid more onto precision or recall, as may be necessary for specific use cases, slight changes would be necessary in the parameters of the learning step, but this does not jeopardize the general APFEL process.

5.4   Training and Test Data Sets

We here present two of the different scenarios which have been used to evaluate the machine-learning approach.

The first scenario represents the case where we want to align two ontologies based on general ontology features. We want to prove that a good algorithm for aligning very different ontologies can be learned. We rely on eight different ontology pairs and their respective correct alignments as training data. The data has been provided for the alignment contest I3Con[3]. Students created two test ontologies with the objective to represent the content of two independent travel websites about Russia for evaluation. The ontologies have approximately 400 entities each, including concepts (region, river,...), relations (has_capital, has_mouth,...), and instances (Moscow, Black_Sea,...). The gold standard of 160 possible alignments was assigned by the students manually.

In the second scenario we want to optimize the ontology alignment process for one specific domain. This usage scenario is directly taken from the Bibster application, a peer-to-peer system to exchange bibliographic metadata [13]. Thus, we do not use general training data as in the previous scenario, but data from the same ontology domain. For the evaluation the used training alignments are excluded. We have only one ontology, but want to identify equal entities (duplicates) within it. In terms of the problem structure this scenario doesn't differ from a scenario where we want to find equal objects in two ontologies. In this scenario, the two ontologies describe bibliographical entities, such as articles, books, theses, etc. and their respective authors, editors, or involved organizations. For the 2100 entities, 275 duplicates have been manually identified by a domain expert.

One should be aware that the *correct* alignments are also always subjective to a certain degree. Humans normally do not agree on alignments either, often only to 60%, thus making an evaluation result of 100% an unrealistic goal. Further, it is not possible to compare the absolute evaluation results of the two data sets with each other, as the sets differ considerably. For evaluation only the different strategies' results within one set are expressive and may be interpreted.

5.5   Evaluation Strategies

We pursue seven strategies for evaluating the two scenarios.

---

[3] http://www.atl.external.lmco.com/projects/ontology/i3con.html

Table 4. Results of the Evaluation

Scenario	Strategy (#/name)		No. of FS	Precision	Recall	F-Measure
Russia	1 Only Labels		1	0.990	0.335	0.501
	2 QOM		25	0.618	0.596	0.607
	3a Decision Tree Learner	20	1	0.826	0.475	0.603
	3b	50	1	0.819	0.471	0.598
	3c	150	7	0.723	0.591	0.650
	4 Neural Net	150	7	0.777	0.485	0.597
	5 Support Vector Machine	150	8	0.509	0.572	0.539
Bibliographic	1 Only Labels		1	0.909	0.073	0.135
	2 QOM		25	0.279	0.397	0.328
	3a Decision Tree Learner	20	1	0.047	0.280	0.080
	3b	50	2	0.456	0.246	0.318
	3c	150	7	0.630	0.375	0.470
	4 Neural Net	150	7	0.542	0.359	0.432
	5 Support Vector Machine	150	6	0.515	0.289	0.370

- The first strategy simply aligns based on the equality of labels. This is a strategy used for example in the original PROMPT tool [19].
- The second strategy applies a variety of general ontology alignment feature/ similarity combinations and an aggregation thereof (QOM). They have been exclusively created by an ontology engineer understanding the domain of knowledge modeling with ontologies. Further, the combinations were assigned manual weights and an optimized threshold (see [10]).
- The remaining strategies represent the APFEL approach. The third strategy uses a C4.5 (J4.8 in Weka) decision tree learner. We took a varying number of 20, 50, and 150 training examples from the correct alignments to further investigate the effect of different quantities of training examples. Half of the examples were positives and half were negatives. For all machine learning approaches we use the well-known WEKA machine learning environment[4].
- The next strategy uses a neural net based on 150 examples.
- And the last strategy was to train a support vector machine, with 150 examples.

5.6   Results and Lessons Learned

From several evaluation runs we have obtained the results in Table 4. Although the precision of an approach based on labels only is very high, the very low recall level leads to a low overall f-measure, which is our key evaluation value. Thus, our key competitor in this evaluation, QOM, receives a lot better f-measure with its semantically rich feature/similarity combinations.

To investigate the effectiveness of APFEL, we have first tested the different strategies against each other (with 150 training examples for the different learning methods). In both scenarios the decision tree learner returns results better than the two other machine learning approaches, i.e. neural nets and support vector machines, the decision tree learner delivers the best f-measure. The margin on improvement as compared to

---

[4] http://www.cs.waikato.ac.nz/ ml/weka/

QOM in the Russia scenario (4.3 percentage points) and in the Bibliography scenario (14.2 percentage points) is both times very good. Alignments for the Russia scenario are identified precisely. Similarly as in the manual approach `labels` were given a very high rate, but surprisingly `domain` and `range` differentiate concepts better than the obvious `sub-classes`. In the bibliographic scenario the alignment method can make extensive use of the learned domain-specific features e.g. it identifies the attribute `last_name` as being highly relevant to find identical authors and rates it higher than e.g. the `middle_initial`. Finally, the lower number of feature/similarity combinations (maximum of eight for machine learning vs. 25 for QOM) leads even to an increase in efficiency compared to QOM.

Second, we have considered the learning rate (see 3a-3c in Table 4). Quality increases with the number of training examples rising, somewhat leveling off at a good value. Unfortunately due to the complex structures of ontologies with many possible feature/heuristics combinations, a high absolute number of training examples is required to fully capture their semantic value for alignment. In the research domain of ontology alignment with its current lack of real big examples this is a challenge. However, once learned it can be transferred to ontology alignment problems in the same domain/ontology model without further learning effort.

To sum up, APFEL generates an alignment method which is competitive with the latest existing ontology alignment methods. However, it is important to apply the correct machine learner and a sufficient amount of training data.

6   Related Work

In [8] schema matching approaches for the database community are split into rule-based and learning-based techniques. In this paper we have shown how to apply learning techniques on-top of a rule-based approach. To contrast our approach we use their classification in the following.

The tools PROMPT and AnchorPROMPT [19] use the similarity of labels and to a certain extent the structure of ontologies, creating alignment rules thereof. The concrete algorithm is set through the tool developers manually. Adaptations to new ontological constructs or even domain-specific features can not be incorporated. In their tool ONION [18] the authors use rules and inferencing to execute alignments, but the inferencing is again based on initially manually assigned alignments or simple similarities. An interesting field of future research are complex alignments, which we do not consider yet in this paper. These cover alignments e.g. based on the concatenation of two fields such as "first name" and "last name" to "name" (cf. COMA[6]). [2] finally present an approach for semantic alignment based on SAT-solvers. In their approach an alignment can only be created if there are no inherent semantic rules restricting this, thus making it an approach based on exact semantics rather than on heuristics as in our work. Nevertheless in all these works one faces the difficulty to predict which strategy of aligning entities is most successful for a given pair of ontologies. The optimization strategy APFEL pointed out in this paper could enhance these existing approaches.

[7] use machine learning in their approach GLUE. From all ontology alignment approaches their work is closest to APFEL. However, their learning component is restricted

on concept classifiers for instances based on instance descriptions, i.e. the textual content of web pages, or their naming. From these two learned concept classifiers they derive whether concepts in two schemas correspond to each other, whereas our approach focuses on learning parameters for a general alignment process. The GLUE machine learning approach suits a scenario with extensive textual instance descriptions, but may not suit a scenario focused more onto ontology structures. Further, relations or instances can not be directly aligned with GLUE. The additional relaxation labeling, which takes the ontological structures into account, is again based solely on manually encoded predefined rules. Finally, in [9] the same authors introduce the notion of the use of domain specific attributes, thus restricting their work on databases. However, the inclusion of domain typical structures has not been topic of their work while it is provided by APFEL.

7   Conclusion

High-quality semantic alignment between ontologies is a necessary precondition to establish interoperability between agents or services using different ontologies. Recent work suffers from the problem that it is impossible to predict which strategy of aligning entities is most successful, given an often semantically and structurally rich domain ontology.

Thus, we have developed a method called APFEL ("Alignment Process Feature Engineering and Learning") that applies machine learning for creating an alignment method that produces a better quality than an initial alignment strategy it starts with.

The involvement of users happens in two phases. Initially, users provide domain ontologies and a simple general alignment method for getting started. During the process, users need to evaluate the generated initial alignments. However, there is no requirement for ontology engineers being involved. I.e., users without specific knowledge about ontology engineering are able to use our approach.

APFEL iteratively bootstraps a new alignment method which is optimized for the input ontologies. This process has been presented in detail on the preceding pages. The resulting alignment method can then be used to automatically align ontologies, depending on the training set-up either general arbitrary ontologies or domain-specific ones. From the evaluation results we have obtained, we see that our initial hypothesis of using machine learning to gain a better alignment approach was fulfilled. The machine learned process outperforms the various manual approaches.

Acknowledgements.   Research reported in this paper has been partially financed by the EU in the IST projects SEKT (IST-2003-506826), SWAP (IST-2001-34103), and KnowledgeWeb (EU IST-2003-507482).

References

1. R. Agrawal and R. Srikant. On integrating catalogs. In *Proceedings of the Tenth International Conference on the World Wide Web (WWW-10)*, pages 603–612. ACM Press, 2001.
2. P. Bouquet, B. Magnini, L. Serafini, and S. Zanobini. A SAT-based algorithm for context matching. In *Proc. of the Fourth International and Interdisciplinary Conference on Modeling and Using Context (CONTEXT'2003)*, Stanford University (CA, USA), June 2003. Springer.

3. T. Cox and M. Cox. *Multidimensional Scaling*. Chapman and Hall, 1994.

4. R. Dhamankar, Y. Lee, A. Doan, A. Halevy, and P. Domingos. iMAP: discovering complex semantic matches between database schemas. In *Proceedings of the 2004 ACM SIGMOD International Conference on Management of Data*, pages 383–394, Paris, France, June 2004.

5. H. Do, S. Melnik, and E. Rahm. Comparison of schema matching evaluations. In *Proceedings of the Second International Workshop on Web Databases (German Informatics Society)*, 2002.

6. H.-H. Do and E. Rahm. COMA - a system for flexible combination of schema matching approaches. In *Proceedings of the 28th VLDB Conference*, Hong Kong, China, 2002.

7. A. Doan, P. Domingos, and A. Halevy. Learning to match the schemas of data sources: A multistrategy approach. *VLDB Journal*, 50:279–301, 2003.

8. A. Doan and A. Y. Halevy. Semantic-integration research in the database community. *AI Magazine*, pages 83–94, March 2005.

9. A. Doan, Y., Lu, Y. Lee, and J. Han. Object matching for data integration: A profile-based approach. In *Proceedings of the IJCAI-03 Workshop on Information Integration on the Web*, Acapulco, Mexico, August 2003.

10. M. Ehrig and S. Staab. QOM - quick ontology mapping. In F. van Harmelen, S. McIlraith, and D. Plexousakis, editors, *Proceedings of the Third International Semantic Web Conference (ISWC2004)*, LNCS, pages 683–696, Hiroshima, Japan, 2004. Springer.

11. M. Ehrig and Y. Sure. Ontology mapping - an integrated approach. In *Proceedings of the First European Semantic Web Symposium, ESWS 2004*, volume 3053 of *Lecture Notes in Computer Science*, pages 76–91, Heraklion, Greece, May 2004. Springer Verlag.

12. J. Euzenat and P. Valtchev. Similarity-based ontology alignment in owl-lite. In *Proceedings of the 16th European Conference on Artificial Intelligence (ECAI2004)*, pages 333–337, Valencia, Spain, August 2004.

13. P. Haase et al. Bibster - a semantics-based bibliographic peer-to-peer system. In F. van Harmelen, S. McIlraith, and D. Plexousakis, editors, *Proceedings of the Third International Semantic Web Conference (ISWC2004)*, LNCS, pages 122–136, Hiroshima, Japan, 2004. Springer.

14. U. Hustadt, B. Motik, and U. Sattler. Reducing SHIQ-description logic to disjunctive datalog programs. In *Proceedings of Ninth International Conference on Knowledge Representation and Reasoning 2004*, pages 152–162, Whistler, Canada, June 2004.

15. M. Klein. Combining and relating ontologies: an analysis of problems and solutions. In A. Gomez-Perez, M. Gruninger, H. Stuckenschmidt, and M. Uschold, editors, *Workshop on Ontologies and Information Sharing, IJCAI01*, Seattle, USA, 2001.

16. I. V. Levenshtein. Binary codes capable of correcting deletions, insertions, and reversals. *Cybernetics and Control Theory*, 1966.

17. S. Melnik, H. Garcia-Molina, and E. Rahm. Similarity flooding: A versatile graph matching algorithm and its application to schema matching. In *Proceedings of the 18th International Conference on Data Engineering (ICDE'02)*, page 117. IEEE Computer Society, 2002.

18. P. Mitra, G. Wiederhold, and M. Kersten. A graph-oriented model for articulation of ontology interdependencies. In *Proceedings of the Conference on Extending Database Technology 2000 (EDBT'2000)*, volume 1777, pages 86+, Konstanz, Germany, 2000.

19. N. F. Noy and M. A. Musen. The PROMPT suite: interactive tools for ontology merging and mapping. *International Journal of Human-Computer Studies*, 59(6):983–1024, 2003.

20. G. Stumme et al. The Karlsruhe view on ontologies. Technical report, University of Karlsruhe, Institute AIFB, 2003.

A Strategy for Automated Meaning Negotiation
in Distributed Information Retrieval

Vadim Ermolayev[1], Natalya Keberle[1], Wolf-Ekkehard Matzke[2],
and Vladimir Vladimirov[1]

[1] Dept of IT, Zaporozhye National Univ., Ukraine
eva,kenga,vvlad@zsu.zp.ua
[2] Cadence Design Systems, GmbH, Feldkirchen, Germany
wolf@cadence.com

Abstract. The paper reports on the development of the formal framework to design strategies for multi-issue non-symmetric meaning negotiations among software agents in a distributed information retrieval system. The advancements of the framework are the following. A resulting strategy compares the contexts of two background domain theories not concept by concept, but the whole context to the other context by accounting the relationships among concepts, the properties, the constraints over properties, and the available instances. It contains the mechanisms for measuring contextual similarity through assessing propositional substitutions and to provide argumentation through generating extra contexts. It uses presuppositions for choosing the best similarity hypotheses and to make the mutual concession to the common sense monotonic. It provides the means to evaluate the possible eagerness to concede through semantic commitments and related notions of knowledgeability and degree of reputation.

1 Introduction

Information systems in Distributed Information Retrieval are characterized by the fact that Information Resource Providers (IRPs) and Users who pose queries form an Open System in the sense that:

- **Semantic heterogeneity**: The IRPs are legally and physically autonomous and do not care about establishing the common set of concepts describing their resources. A User's background theory of a domain may as well have various semantic discrepancies with the ontologies describing involved information resources.
- **Resource changes without notice**: IRPs normally do not notify other IRP-s and users about the changes in their resources because they may not even know about these IRP-s and Users. The changes may occur at any time and affect both resource semantics and the terms of use.

An information retrieval system in the mentioned settings should be intelligent in the following aspects. Firstly, it needs to accumulate the common knowledge describing the involved IRPs with their resources and its users with their individual terminological preferences in a uniform and coherent way. Secondly, it should pro-actively cope with the dynamic changes or reconfigurations of its collection of

Y. Gil et al. (Eds.): ISWC 2005, LNCS 3729, pp. 201–215, 2005.

registered resources affecting both semantics and the conditions of resource usage. And, thirdly, it should pro-actively conduct distributed information retrieval by keeping an eye on how different participants of the team obey their commitments to the collaboration convention while performing their parts of the query posed by a user. Normally it is achieved through striking a sort of a contract deal and monitoring contract execution.

In the humans' world mentioned aspects of collaborative intelligent behavior are often arranged through various sorts of negotiation. Hence, if a framework for automating negotiations among autonomous software components in an open information retrieval system is elaborated we'll make a substantial advancement towards solving the abovementioned problems inferred by semantic heterogeneity and dynamic changes of a resource. We'll denote negotiating intelligent software components in an information retrieval system as actors. Actors are naturally implemented by software agents and play different roles. These roles in a system with a centralized or de-centralized mediator are at least:

- a **User** (an agent assisting a human user to formulate his or her queries and to process the results of these queries) – hereafter referred to as Q
- a **Mediator** (an agent or a multi-agent system which, in compliance with [1], provides services to Users through arranging the performance of their queries by available and matching IRPs) – hereafter referred to as M
- An **IRP** (which is often an agent wrapping the Information Resource (IR) and processing queries to this IR if contracted by M) – hereafter referred to as P

It should be noted that Q, M, and Ps take part in two different types of negotiations in this scenario. Negotiations are focused on two aspects: on concept meaning and on the (commercial or contract) terms of the information delivery like the price, the terms of use, the deadline. A variety of papers provide extensive results on negotiation mechanisms dealing with the commercial aspects, e.g. [2], [3], [4]. However, negotiations on the meaning of concepts are not covered well enough in the literature. In this paper we intend to make this white spot narrower.

The reminder of the paper is structured as follows. Section 2 outlines the conceptual framework for negotiations we use in our research. Section 3 describes the example we use to illustrate our framework throughout the paper and introduces the formal notation for knowledge representation. Section 4 contains the high-level description of the proposed strategy for automated multi-issue meaning negotiation. Sections 5, 6, and 7 provide more detailed elaboration of the aspects of argumentation through propositional substitutions and contexts, making presuppositions, measuring semantic similarity of concepts respectively. Section 8 denotes semantic commitment and discusses the problem of concession in negotiation. Section 9 briefly outlines the related work. Section 10 summarizes the results and outlines our future work.

2   Interactions and Negotiations

"... perhaps the most fundamental and powerful mechanism for managing inter-agent dependencies at run-time is *negotiation* — the process by which a group of agents comes to a mutually acceptable agreement on some matter." (c.f. [3]).

Negotiation type and, therefore, the corresponding negotiation mechanism is determined by the goal, the protocol, the negotiation set, and the strategies of the participants [4].

A protocol defines the rules of encounter commonly accepted by all negotiating parties. Different protocols are applicable to different negotiation encounters which may be symmetric or non-symmetric and have different number of parties: one-to-one encounters, one-to-many encounters, and many-to-many encounters. It is evident that one-to-one protocols are easier to implement and require less communication overhead. That is why it is rational (though not always possible) to substitute more complex encounters by the sequences of one-to-one negotiations.

Symmetric negotiation settings occur when the parties of the encounter do not differ neither formally, for example by their role or in the terms of Game Theory by their part of the payoff matrix, nor informally – by their capability to influence the process, for example by their reputation. In our domain symmetric negotiations may occur among the peer-agents in a decentralized mediator (e.g., [5]). Non-symmetric negotiations are more common in practice because their settings reflect real life more adequately. Indeed, even in information retrieval a) an agent within a centralized mediator (e.g., [6]) has different roles in its negotiations with IR providing agents, b) the roles of different parties are also different – a user, a mediator, an IR provider, c) the abilities of different parties to influence the process of negotiation differ as well – a mediator agent should be more conservative in its concessions on the meaning of concepts (Section 8). Of course, the mechanisms for non-symmetric encounters, though more realistic, are more difficult to implement and subsume symmetric ones as singular cases.

A negotiation set stands for the matter or the matters on which the parties try to agree. Negotiations may be single issue and multi issue according to the number of these matters. In the real world settings different matters in multi-issue negotiations are rarely independent. Hence, a multi-issue negotiation mechanism should be capable to account mentioned dependencies among the items in the negotiation set.

A negotiation strategy stands for the set of internal agent's rules it uses to pursue the goal of the encounter. Negotiation goal is often described in the terms of a deal stricken on the successful accomplishment of the encounter.

In our domain the goal of the meaning negotiation is to find the match between the contexts (negotiation set) of the background domain theories of the parties in order to align the domain ontology, and ensure that all parties commit to this common ontology in their subsequent interactions. A deal means a joint agreement and a commitment on the negotiated context and on the mapping of the concepts of the parties to the agreed concept.

In this paper we leave aside the discussion of the possible negotiation protocols and concentrate on the elaboration of the formal framework to design agents' strategies for multi-issue, non-symmetric meaning negotiation, provided that the agents play the aforementioned roles in a distributed information retrieval system.

3   Illustrative Example

Let's consider the following query submitted by a user agent Q to mediator agent M: *"Please retrieve all short papers by Ermolayev published in LNCS series"*. The conceptual graph for this query is presented in Fig. 1a. We implicitly assume here that

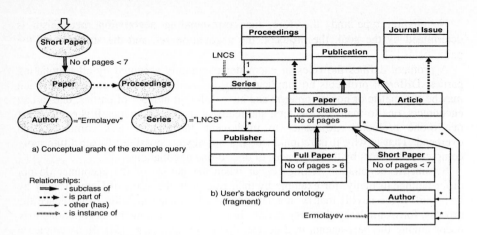

Fig. 1. Example query and corresponding background domain theory

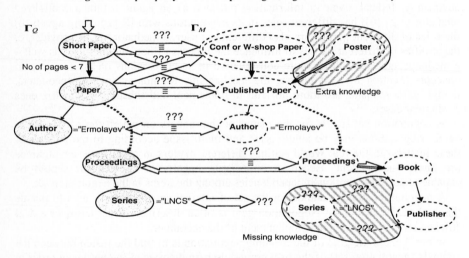

Fig. 2. Searching for the semantic match between Γ_Q and Γ_M

the corresponding background domain theory Γ_Q of Q is the one given in graphical notation in Fig. 1b. Following the approach of [7] we'll encode Γ_Q using the extended formalism of the Type Theory (TT) [8]:

$\Gamma_Q \vdash ShortPaper : \star_s$ (concept (type) *ShortPaper* is in the abstract type of sorts $\star_s$)
$\Gamma_Q \vdash Paper : \star_s$ (concept *Paper* is in the abstract type of sorts $\star_s$)
$\Gamma_Q \vdash Author : \star_s$ (concept *Author* is in the abstract type of sorts $\star_s$)
$\Gamma_Q \vdash Proceedings : \star_s$ (concept *Proceedings* is in the abstract type of sorts $\star_s$)
$\Gamma_Q \vdash Series : \star_s$ (concept *Proceedings* is in the abstract type of sorts $\star_s$)
$\Gamma_Q \vdash ShortPaper.NoOfPages : \star_a$ (property *NoOfPages* of the concept *ShortPaper* is in the abstract type of properties $\star_a$)
$\Gamma_Q \vdash ShortPaper < Paper : \star_s$ (concept *ShortPaper* is subsumed by the concept *Paper*)
$\Gamma_Q \vdash (N < 7) : ShortPaper.NoOfPages \to \star_p$ (proposition ($N < 7$) applied to the property *NoOfPages* of the concept *ShortPaper* holds true – i.e. is in the abstract type of propositions $\star_p$)

$\Gamma_Q \vdash Datatype(N, Integer)$: $Paper.NoOfPages \rightarrow \bigstar_p$ (proposition $Datatype(N, Integer)$ applied to the property $NoOfPages$ of the concept $Paper$ holds true – i.e. is in the abstract type of propositions $\bigstar_p$)
$\Gamma_Q \vdash has(P, Author)$: $Paper \rightarrow \bigstar_p$ (as above)
$\Gamma_Q \vdash is\_part\_of(P, Proceedings)$: $Paper \rightarrow \bigstar_p$ (as above)
$\Gamma_Q \vdash published\_in(R, Series)$: $Proceedings \rightarrow \bigstar_p$(as above)
$\Gamma_Q \vdash Ermolayev$: $Author$ (Instance $Ermolayev$ is of type $Author$)
$\Gamma_Q \vdash LNCS$: $Series$ (Instance $LNCS$ is of type $Series$)

This context of Γ_Q is submitted to M as the negotiation set. M will try to match it to his domain theory Γ_M as graphically outlined in Fig. 2. The task for our paper is to develop the formal framework for the strategy of negotiations between Q and M which will allow them to automatically make this match as precise as possible. The specificity of our settings is that:

- Background theories Γ_Q and Γ_M are not necessarily taxonomies – different types of semantic relationships should be accounted. This may imply various types of dependencies between the elements of the negotiation set.
- Background theories Γ_Q and Γ_M may be poor with instances. This may imply the necessity to use several kinds of semantic similarity metrices (not only instance similarity which proved to be quite precise [9] in comparing ontologies which are rich with instances).
- Background theories Γ_Q and Γ_M can not be disjoint in the sense that there will certainly be at least a partial match between them. The reason for this constraint is that normally a query is posed to the resources in the particular domain and the semantic discrepancies are at most surmountable.
- The cardinality of Γ_Q and Γ_M is moderate enough to allow NP-complete processing algorithms be acceptable. This actually means the constraint on Γ_M only because a query and its underlying domain theory are normally not bulky.

4   A Strategy for Meaning Negotiation

For simplicity reasons we'll further on consider that meaning negotiation occurs between two parties (one to one negotiation) – a query submitter Q and a mediator M agents. We shall build the framework for designing strategies for meaning negotiations trying to provide a mechanism to find the context of a concept in Γ_M closest to the context of a concept in Γ_Q of a query submitted by Q. As Γ_M and Γ_Q are further on formalized as the sets of TT statements we shall build up our definition on the notion of a context given in [7]:

Definition 1 (Context): The context $\mathbf{C}_c$ of a concept $c \in \Gamma$ is the union of the set Γ_i of TT statements $\gamma_i \in \Gamma$ which are the assumptions over c and the set Γ_j of TT statements $\gamma_j \in \Gamma$ which may be explicitly inferred from $\{\Gamma \vdash c : \bigstar_s\} \cup \Gamma_i$ using the rules of the type system [7]:

$$\mathbf{C}_c = \Gamma\big|_c = \Gamma_i \cup \Gamma_j. \qquad (1)$$

To design such a negotiation strategy over Γ_Q we need to address the following problems:

- Which of the parties starts first?
- How to generate argumentation on the semantic discrepancies between Γ_Q and Γ_M?
- How to ensure that the ratio of these semantic discrepancies is monotonically decreasing in negotiation rounds?
- How to assess if the current level of these semantic discrepancies is sufficient to strike the deal?
- How to detect that the movement to the perfect match (no discrepancies) between Γ_Q and Γ_M is no longer possible?

Negotiations are evidently the series of mutually beneficial concessions. In the context of meaning negotiation we also need to denote what a concession is and how to compute the minimal effective concession.

Which of the parties starts first? The answer to this question in our settings is straightforward – the one who initiates negotiation by submitting a query makes the 1-st cry.

Argumentation on the semantic discrepancies and concession. We first need to denote how to formalize and to measure the semantic discrepancies between two contexts Γ_Q and Γ_M and then proceed with argumentation. It is natural to denote semantic discrepancies between two ontological contexts by means of the appropriately defined semantic distance **SD**, which is obviously a kind of a mapping $SD : \Gamma_Q \times \Gamma_M \rightarrow R$ (**R** is the set of real numbers). Suppose this mapping is defined (Section 5), then efficient argumentation should contain the set of presuppositions **PR** over Γ_Q and Γ_M which, if applied to Γ_Q, decreases **SD**. Some of the concepts, concept properties, or propositions expressing relationships from Γ_Q may have no analogy in Γ_M (or Γ_M in Γ_Q). We shall call these elements of Γ (Γ_Q or Γ_M) orphans. Local semantic distance SD_o between an orphan and Γ evidently has the maximal possible value. Argumentation on orphans should provide the counter-party with the information on the possible or anticipated context C_o to check it over his background domain theory and, possibly, find some extra context Δ_o to bridge the gap. If context Δ_o is found it extends the context of the party (Γ_Q or Γ_M). We shall say that a party concedes on the orphan o if $C_o \cap \Delta_o \neq \varnothing$, i.e., if some of the arguments from C_o were accepted to Δ_o. Of course it is rational to make the smallest concession possible in a round because the acceptance of (the part of) C_o may induce the contradictions with another portions of Γ, which may result in harmonization overheads and, which is even more important, violate some of the collective commitments on the elements of Γ. From the other hand the concession should be sound enough for not to concede on the next negotiation round. Details are provided in Section 7.

How to make negotiation converging to a deal? We shall formulate the answer in the terms of the semantic distance **SD** between the contexts Γ_Q and Γ_M. Negotiation will converge to a deal if **SD** will be monotonically decreasing from round to round. A deal may be stricken between the parties if:

- No orphans are left in Γ
- The difference in **SD** in the current round and of the previous round equals to 0 or is less than the commonly agreed threshold

How to detect that further negotiation is useless? Negotiation is useless when all the parties have exhausted their argumentation and the deal is not stricken. In our settings this means that the orphans are still present in Γ, but there were no concessions in the two subsequent rounds. In this case the deal is impossible and the negotiation should result in failure. Practically this means that the party which submitted a query needs to reformulate it in the terms which are more coherent to the common ontology, or to give up.

5 Argumentation Using Propositional Substitutions and Contexts

Let $\mathbf{C}$ be the set of concepts in Γ_Q: $\mathbf{C} = \{c_i\}$. Evidently there may be several hypotheses on concept equivalence for each concept c_i. We'll denote the set of hypotheses on concept equivalence as: $\mathbf{H} = \bigcup_{i=1}^{n} H_i$, where n is the number of concepts defined in Γ_Q, H_i is the set of hypotheses on the equivalence of c_i to the concepts of Γ_M.

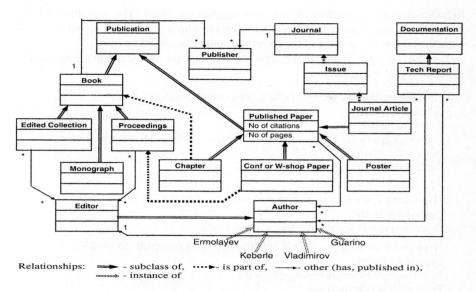

Fig. 3. Background domain theory Γ_M of M

Γ_Q provides a certain portion of facts on each c_i which is communicated by Q to M. For our example the portion of facts on the concept *ShortPaper* : $\star_s$ in TT notation is as follows:

$\Gamma_Q \vdash ShortPaper : \star_s$
$\Gamma_Q \vdash ShortPaper.NoOfPages : \star_a$
$\Gamma_Q \vdash ShortPaper < Paper : \star_s$
$\Gamma_Q \vdash (N < 7) : ShortPaper.NoOfPages \rightarrow \star_p$

M will try to apply this context to Γ_M (Fig. 3) and form hypotheses on the equivalence of c_i to the concepts of Γ_M. While forming these hypotheses M will exploit different applicable kinds of similarity measurement (Section 6) and, particularly, will try propositional substitutions for context similarity assessment.

Let:

- $\left.\Gamma_Q\right|_{c_i} = \left.\{\gamma_1,...,\gamma_n\}_Q\right|_{c_i}$ be the context of c_i in Γ_Q

- $h: c_{i_Q} \xleftrightarrow{\equiv} c_{k_M}$ be a hypothesis on the equivalence of c_i and c_k, $\Gamma_Q \vdash c_i$: $\star_s$,
  $\Gamma_M \vdash c_k$: $\star_s$

We'll say that γ'_j is the propositional substitution of $\gamma_j \in \left.\Gamma_Q\right|_{c_i}$ if it is obtained by the substitution of c_i by c_k in γ_j. We'll say that the similarity asset of γ'_j to the evaluation of the context similarity s_j of γ'_j equals to 1 if $\Gamma_M \vdash \gamma'_j$, otherwise $s_j=0$.

We'll then compute the context similarity of c_i and c_k as $Sim_C = \dfrac{1}{m}\sum_{j=1}^{m} s_j$. If computed $Sim_C < 1$ M may provide Q with some context $\left.\Gamma_M\right|_{c_k}$ to allow Q to make its hypotheses and assessments on the next negotiation round. The soundness of the hypothesis h may then be assessed by the overall similarity Sim_h of c_i and c_k. We'll compute Sim_h as the average of the measured similarities in frame of h.

For our example some of the hypotheses, contexts and similarity assessments generated by M are as follows:

Hypothesis: *Author$_Q$* $\xleftrightarrow{\equiv}$ *Author$_M$*, **Assessment:** *Sim$_h$*= 0.625
Instance similarity:
Ermolayev : *Author$_Q$*
Ermolayev : *Author$_M$*; *Guarino* : *Author$_M$*; *Keberle* : *Author$_M$*; *Vladimirov* : *Author$_M$*;
Author$_Q$ $\equiv$ *Author$_M$*, *Sim$_I$* = 0.25
Lexical similarity:
Author$_Q$ $\equiv$ *Author$_M$*, *Sim$_L$* = 1.0

Hypothesis: *Proceedings$_Q$* $\xleftrightarrow{\equiv}$ *Proceedings$_M$*, **Assessment:** *Sim$_h$*= 1
Lexical similarity:
Proceedings$_Q$ $\equiv$ *Proceedings$_M$*, *Sim$_L$* = 1.0

Hypothesis: *ShortPaper$_Q$* $\xleftrightarrow{\equiv}$ *PublishedPaper$_M$*, **Assessment:** *Sim$_h$*= 0.3
Lexical similarity:
ShortPaper$_Q$ $\equiv$ *PublishedPaper$_M$*, *Sim$_L$*= 0.3
Propositional substitutions:
$\Gamma_M \vdash \neg ((N < 7) : PublishedPaper_M.NoOfPages \rightarrow \star_p)$, $Sim_h = 0$ – orphan constraint
$\Gamma_M \vdash \neg (PublishedPaper_M < Paper_Q : \star_s)$, $Sim = 0$ – orphan subsumption
$\Gamma_M \vdash (Datatype(N, Integer) : PublishedPaper_M.NoOfPages \rightarrow \star_p)$, $Sim = 1$
Context:
$\Gamma_M \vdash PublishedPaper_M < Publication_M : \star_s$
$\Gamma_M \vdash JournalArticle_M < PublishedPaper_M : \star_s$
$\Gamma_M \vdash Chapter_M < PublishedPaper_M : \star_s$
$\Gamma_M \vdash ConfOrW\text{-}shopPaper_M < PublishedPaper_M : \star_s$
$\Gamma_M \vdash Poster_M < PublishedPaper_M : \star_s$
$\Gamma_M \vdash has(P, Author_M) : PublishedPaper_M \rightarrow \star_p$
$\Gamma_M \vdash Datatype(N, Integer) : PublishedPaper_M.NoOfPages \rightarrow \star_p$

Hypothesis: $ShortPaper_Q \overset{=}{\longleftrightarrow} ConfOrW\text{-}shopPaper_M$, **Assessment:** $Sim_h = 0.3$
Lexical similarity:
$ShortPaper_Q \equiv ConfOrW\text{-}shopPaper_M$, $Sim_L = 0,2$
Propositional substitutions:
$\Gamma_M \vdash \neg ((N < 7) : ConfOrW\text{-}shopPaper_M.NoOfPages \rightarrow \star_p)$, $Sim = 0$ – orphan constraint
$\Gamma_M \vdash \neg (ConfOrW\text{-}shopPaper_M < Paper_Q : \star_s)$, $Sim = 0$ – orphan subsumption
$\Gamma_M \vdash (Datatype(N, Integer) : ConfOrW\text{-}shopPaper_M.NoOfPages \rightarrow \star_p)$, $Sim = 1$
$ShortPaper_Q \equiv ConfOrW\text{-}shopPaper_M$, $Sim_C = 0,3$
Context:
$\Gamma_M \vdash ConfOrW\text{-}shopPaper_M < PublishedPaper_M : \star_s$
$\Gamma_M \vdash has(P, Author_M) : ConfOrW\text{-}shopPaper_M \rightarrow \star_p$
$\Gamma_M \vdash is\_part\_of(P, Proceedings_M) : ConfOrW\text{-}shopPaper_M \rightarrow \star_p$

Hypothesis: $ShortPaper_Q \overset{=}{\longleftrightarrow} Poster_M$, **Assessment:** $Sim_h = 0,6$
Lexical similarity:
$ShortPaper_Q \equiv Poster_M$, $Sim_L = 0$
Propositional substitutions:
$\Gamma_M \vdash ((N < 7) : ConfOrW\text{-}shopPaper_M.NoOfPages \rightarrow \star_p)$, $Sim = 1$
$\Gamma_M \vdash \neg (Poster_M < Paper_Q : \star_s)$, $Sim = 0$ – orphan subsumption
$\Gamma_M \vdash (Datatype(N, Integer) : Poster_M.NoOfPages \rightarrow \star_p)$, $Sim = 1$
$ShortPaper_Q \equiv Poster_M$, $Sim_C = 0.6$
Context:
$\Gamma_M \vdash Poster_M < PublishedPaper_M : \star_s$
$\Gamma_M \vdash has(P, Author_M) : Poster_M \rightarrow \star_p$
$\Gamma_M \vdash is\_part\_of(P, Proceedings_M) : Poster_M \rightarrow \star_p$

Hypothesis: $Paper_Q \overset{=}{\longleftrightarrow} PublishedPaper_M$, **Assessment:** $Sim_h = 0$
Lexical similarity:
$Paper_Q \equiv PublishedPaper$, $Sim_L = 0,5$
Propositional substitutions:
$\Gamma_M \vdash \neg (is\_part\_of(P, Proceedings_Q) : PublishedPaper \rightarrow \star_p)$, $Sim = 0$ – orphan meronymy
$\Gamma_M \vdash \neg (has(P, Author_Q) : PublishedPaper_M \rightarrow \star_p)$, $Sim = 0$ – orphan relationship
$Paper_Q \equiv PublishedPaper_M$, $Sim_C = 0$
Context:
$\Gamma_M \vdash PublishedPaper_M < Publication_M : \star_s$
$\Gamma_M \vdash JournalArticle_M < PublishedPaper_M : \star_s$
$\Gamma_M \vdash Chapter_M < PublishedPaper_M : \star_s$
$\Gamma_M \vdash ConfOrW\text{-}shopPaper_M < PublishedPaper_M : \star_s$
$\Gamma_M \vdash Poster_M < PublishedPaper_M : \star_s$
...

Hypothesis: $Series_Q \overset{=}{\longleftrightarrow} \varnothing$, **Assessment:** $Sim_h = 0$ – missing knowledge in Γ_M
We shall measure the semantic distance D_i between c_i and Γ_M as follows:

$$SD_i = 1 - \max_{H_i}(Sim_{h_j}) . \tag{2}$$

We may now compute the overall semantic distance between Γ_Q and Γ_M as follows:

$$\mathbf{SD} = \sum_{i=1}^{n} SD_i . \tag{3}$$

6 Presuppositions

Extending the approach of [7] we'll make presuppositions on the equivalence of the concepts according to the measured Sim_h values. We'll then revise the propositional substitutions for other concept hypothesis and re-compute the corresponding Sim_h values. In result the presupposition set **PR** may be extended as well. Let

$$\mathbf{PR} = \bigcup_{i=1}^{n} PR_i \,,$$ where PR_i is the set of presuppositions on the equivalence of c_i. The

rule for **PR** formation is as follows:

(1) Set up the similarity threshold *minSim* for accepting a hypothesis as the presupposition
(2) For each H_i:
- Choose the hypothesis h with the highest Sim_h value and add it to PR_i as pr iff its Sim_h value is over *minSim*
- Revise propositional substitutions for **H** with respect to pr and re-assess Sim_h values
(3) Repeat (2) until at least one pr is added to **H**
(4) For PR_i delete all pr except the one with the highest Sim_h value

After **PR** is formed we may also drop all the hypotheses in each H_i except the one with the highest Sim_h value. The difference in $\mathbf{SD}_b$ before and $\mathbf{SD}_a$ after the formation of **PR** will show us the efficiency of the formed **PR**: $E_{\mathbf{PR}} = (\mathbf{SD}_b\text{-}\mathbf{SD}_a)/\mathbf{SD}_b$.

For the presented fragment of our example $\mathbf{SD}_b = 2.775$. Presuppositions (*minSim*=0.5) with the highest Sim_h values are:

Proceedings$_Q \equiv$ *Proceedings, $Sim_h = 1$* and *Author*$_Q \equiv$ *Author, $Sim_h = 0.625$*.

By revising propositional substitutions we obtain the following changes in *Sim* values:

Paper$_Q \xleftrightarrow{\;=\;}$ *PublishedPaper, $Sim_h = 1$* (both propositional orphans are eliminated)
Paper$_Q \equiv$ *PublishedPaper, $Sim_h = 1$* may now be added to **PR**

ShortPaper$_Q \xleftrightarrow{\;=\;}$ *Poster, $Sim_h = 1$* (subsumption orphan is eliminated)
ShortPaper$_Q \equiv$ *Poster, $Sim_h = 1$* may now be added to **PR**

ShortPaper$_Q \xleftrightarrow{\;=\;}$ *ConfOrW-shopPaper, $Sim_h = 0.6$* (subsumption orphan is eliminated)
ShortPaper$_Q \equiv$ *ConfOrW-shopPaper, $Sim_h = 0.6$* may now be added to **PR**.
After **PR** is formed $\mathbf{SD}_a = 1.375$ and $E_{\mathbf{PR}} = 1.4/2.775 = 0.505$.

7 Concept Similarity

As it was mentioned before a negotiation set represented by the context of a background domain theory Γ_Q can not be treated as a well-defined rich ontology. Hence, we need to make all the efforts possible to assess its similarity to Γ_M (which is rather rich) through analyzing all facets of its semantics. We may achieve it only by following the advice of Weisberg [10]:

"... I would contend that analysts frequently should not seek a single measure and will never find a perfect measure. Different measures exist because there are different concepts to measure ... It is time to stop acting embarrassed about the supposed surplus of measures and instead make fullest possible use of their diversity."

The reminder of this section outlines the variety of similarity measures which we consider to be applicable for computing semantic distances in presuppositions. Most of these measures are widely used in ontology alignment [17].

Instance Similarity. The rationale behind the instance similarity is that similar concepts have similar instances. Let **D** be the domain, A and B be the concepts in **D**. A is similar to B if $I_A \cap I_B \neq \emptyset$, where I_A and I_B are the sets of instances of **D** and $I_A = \{i_k\} : \forall k, instance\_of(i_k, A)$. We'll follow the approach of [9] and measure Instance Similarity by symmetric Jaccard coefficient:

$$Sim_I(A,B) = \frac{P(I_A \cap I_B)}{P(I_A \cup I_B)},$$ (4)

where $P(I)$ is the probability that a randomly chosen instance of D belongs to I.

Context or Feature Similarity. The rationale behind the contextual similarity is that similar concepts have similar contexts. These contexts may be understood as feature sets. Similarity between feature sets may be measured for example by means of Tversky metrics [11]. However, Tversky metrics works only if there is a well defined and a commonly accepted feature set. This is not true in our case. Therefore we shall measure Context Similarity in frame of a hypothesis h through assessing the propositional substitutions as shown in Section 5: If s_i are the similarity assessments of the respective propositional substitutions γ'_j, then:

$$Sim_C = \frac{1}{m} \sum_{j=1}^{m} s_j .$$ (5)

Datatype and Measurement Similarity. It seems rational to consider that similar concepts have similar properties. However, the problem of determining similarity among properties has the same complexity as measuring the similarity of concepts. Another observation is that the set of properties of a concept is the part of its feature set. Hence, it is worth trying to measure Property Similarity by a Context Similarity metrics. The peculiarity of a property is that there are different types of them: domain properties and referential (slot) properties. While a slot property is the matter reflecting the relationship to another concept (property), a domain property reflects that a concept has the feature which:

- Has a certain datatype (like a *colour*, a *weight*, an *age*, a *string*...)
- Is measured in certain (standard) units (like an *RGB vector*, a *kilogram*, a *year*, an *integer*, ...)
- Has certain constraints on its values expressed as logical formulas, like: $(weight \leq 90) \wedge (age > 30)$

For example, if concept A (a *ShortPaper*) has property a having *integer* datatype and is measured in the *NoOfPages* and concept B (a *Poster*) has property b having *integer* datatype and is measured in the *NoOfPages*, a and b may be considered similar and, this fact may increase the similarity between A and B. The ratio of Sim_A in frame of the hypothesis $A \xleftrightarrow{\equiv} B$ will be increased if a and b have the same constraints. For example, $(a < 7)$ and $(b < 7)$ for a *ShortPaper* and a *Poster* respectively.

As far as Property similarity measurement is also based on the propositional substitutions we do not distinguish Sim_C and Sim_A in the discussion of the example in Section 5.

Lexical Similarity. Considering concepts with the same names (or the same lexical roots) may of course lead to confusion. However, the same root in names may be a good hint in finding a perfect match in a pair of concepts from different contexts like Γ_Q and Γ_M. Human experience says that this heuristics works if supported by other evidence (like instance similarity for $Author_Q$ and $Author_M$ or effective presuppositions based on the acceptance of $Proceedings_Q \xleftrightarrow{\equiv} Proceedings_M$ hypothesis in our example). We use the following lexical measure Sim_L. Let R_A, R_B be the sets of roots of the words which constitute the name of concept A and B respectively, then:

$$Sim_L = \frac{|R_A \cap R_B|}{|R_A \cup R_B|}.$$
(6)

In our example Sim_L of the concepts *Paper* and *PublishedPaper* equals to 0.5. Technically it is quite simple to build the sets of roots as far as the words which constitute a concept name often have capitalized first letters.

8   Concession and Reputation

What is concession with respect to a concepts' meaning in a multi-issue (i.e., multi-concept) negotiation? We'll denote this concession in the terms of concept similarity and satisfiability of the logical formulae describing the background theories of negotiating parties. Let: M be an actor in an information retrieval system, $\mathbb{N} = \{N_i\}$ be the set of its peers with whom M has agreed on the similarity of the concept A from its Γ_M to their concepts B_i from respective Γ_{N_i} in previous negotiations. We denote *Semantic Commitment* of M with respect to A as the set of hypotheses $H_A = \{h_{A,i} = (A \xleftrightarrow{\equiv} B_i, Sim_i)\}$ accepted by M as his beliefs. The strength of this *Semantic Commitment* may be assessed by:

$$S_A = \sum_i Sim_i .$$
(7)

When Q and M detect an orphan A in their negotiation a concession on A means the extension of Γ with $C_A \cap \Delta_A \neq \varnothing$ by one of the parties (Section 4). Adopting this new portion of Γ for a party, say M, may force him to drop some of $h_{X,i}$ in his

Semantic Commitments with respect to the concepts X related to A. It is rational to consider that the party having less strong commitments (7) on the concepts related to A should concede.

A more knowledgeable party, having stronger *Semantic Commitments* may and is actually forced to concede less, i.e., require that the difference in similarity between its initial context and the agreed context is less than of the other party. Concessions of a more knowledgeable party will affect more commitments of the other parties which should of course be re-negotiated. It is therefore clear that negotiation strategy while determining the concession should:

- Avoid conceding on the concepts associated with strong *Semantic Commitments*
- If it is not possible to avoid concession, and there are alternative concepts to concede on – concede on the concept having *Semantic Commitment of* lower strength S_A

And, finally, the reputation of a party may be assessed by evaluating the extent to which its knowledge is really consensual. It is natural to consider a party more reputable if its overall strength of *Semantic Commitments* $\mathbf{S}^M = \sum_A S_A$ is greater than the $\mathbf{S}^N$ of another party. In our example it is evident that $\mathbf{S}^Q < \mathbf{S}^M$. Hence, it will be difficult for Q to convince M to accept the knowledge about *Series* concept (Fig. 2).

9 Discussion

The paper reports on the formal framework to design strategies for software agents engaged in multi-issue non-symmetric meaning negotiation. These agents are thought to be the actors in distributed information retrieval system based on centralized (e.g., [6], [13]) or de-centralized (e.g., [5]) mediator architecture with centralized, decentralized or hybrid ontology representation (please refer to [14] for a survey). In understanding the nature and the conceptual foundation of negotiation among software agents we base our work on the results from DAI and eCommerce domains. We adopt the theoretical basics of [2], [3] and build our conceptual framework on it. While designing a strategy for automated multi-issue meaning negotiation we address the aspects typical to a negotiation strategy in a more general sense (Section4). Speaking in terms of the Game Theoretical approach such a strategy should ideally lead to a deal in a reasonably small no of rounds and, if adopted by all negotiation parties, be in Nash equilibrium. Though it is not formally proved that the proposed strategy will be in the Nash equilibrium with similar strategy of another party, it seems to look like that according to the monotonic nature of similarity measures, the rules for forming presuppositions and concessions.

In the presented framework we used and extended various contributions of other authors in: measuring concept similarity [15], [9], [12], [11], using logical formulae to approximate semantic discrepancies [16], using Type Theory for formalizing argumentation [8], making presuppositions [7]. Sound experimental results of the colleges evaluating these basic contributions allow us to believe that our evaluation planned for the near future will bring positive results.

The advancements of the presented framework are as follows. It results in a strategy which compares the contexts of two background domain theories not concept by concept, but the whole context to the other context by accounting the relationships among concepts, the properties, the constraints over properties, and the available instances. The mechanisms for measuring contextual similarity through assessing propositional substitutions and to provide argumentation through generating extra contexts are also new. One more novelty of our framework is the use of presuppositions for choosing the best similarity hypotheses and to make concession to common sense monotonic. The means for evaluating the possible eagerness to concede through semantic commitments and related notions of knowledgeability and the degree of reputation to our knowledge also have not been reported before.

10 Concluding Remarks

As Tom Gruber said in one of his recent interviews:

> "I find it critical to remember that every ontology is a treaty – a social agreement – among people with some common motive in sharing."[1]

This view may definitely be applied also onto the artificial agents acting on behalf of their human owners. In this paper we have reported on the formal framework which provides strategies to gain such a social agreement automatically among software agents in an open system. These agents, as mentioned in Section 3, also have some common motive in sharing, though the semantics of their individual beliefs or background theories of the domain may well have surmountable discrepancies. We design multi-concept meaning negotiation strategies for software agents in distributed information retrieval which allow dealing on the common sense of a negotiated context and may be implemented in a software. Providing means to agree on the set of matters with respect to their semantics for autonomous intelligent components of an open software system is quite important. Such means will facilitate to making mutual understanding and collaborative work in such software systems more sound and effective.

Our plans for future work are to experiment with the prototype strategies based on the presented framework for multi-agent system in the successor of the RACING[2] project (distributed information retrieval). We also consider the implementation and the experimentation with such strategies in the frame of PSI[3] project. PSI objective is to prototype a multi-agent system which simulates dynamic engineering design processes and assists human designers in their cooperative work on a design project.

---

[1] Interview for the Official Quarterly Bulletin of AIS Special Interest Group on Semantic Web and Information Systems, Volume 1, Issue 3, 2004.
[2] RACING: Rational Agent Coalitions for Intelligent Information Retrieval on the Net, URL: http://www.zsu.zp.ua/racing.
[3] PSI: Productivity Simulation Initiative. Cadence Design Systems, GmbH.

References

1. Wiederhold, G.: Mediators in the Architecture of Future Information Systems. IEEE Computer, 25(3) (1992) 38–49
2. Lomuscio, R., Wooldridge, M., Jennings, N. R.: A Classification Scheme for Negotiation in Electronic Commerce" In: Dignum, F. and Sierra C. (eds.) Agent-Mediated Electronic Commerce: A European Perspective. Springer Verlag, Berlin Heidelberg, New York (2000), 19–33
3. Jennings, N. R., Faratin, P., Lomuscio, A. R., Parsons, S., Sierra, C., Wooldridge, M.: Automated Negotiation: Prospects, Methods and Challenges. Int. J. of Group Decision and Negotiation 10(2) (2001) 199-215
4. Beam, C., Segev, A.: Automated Negotiations: A Survey of the State of the Art. CITM Working Paper 96-WP-1022 (1997). URL: http://haas.berkeley.edu/~citm/wp-1022-summary.html
5. Zhang H., Bruce Kroft W., Levine B., Lesser V.: A Multi-agent Approach for Peer-to-Peer-based Information Retrieval Systems. In: Proc. AAMAS'04, July 19-23, 2004, New York, New York, USA
6. Ermolayev, V., Keberle, N., Kononenko, O., Plaksin, S., Terziyan, V.: Towards a framework for agent-enabled semantic web service composition. Int. J. of Web Services Research, 1(3) (2004) 63-87
7. Beun R.-J., van Eijk R.M., Prüst H.: Ontological Feedback in Multiagent Systems. In: Proc. AAMAS'04, July 19-23, 2004, New York, New York, USA
8. Luo Z.: Computation and Reasoning: A Type Theory for Computer Science. Int. Series of Monographs on Computer Science. Clarendon Press, Oxford (1994)
9. Doan, A., Madhavan, J., Domingos, P., Halevy, A.: Learning to Match Ontologies on the Semantic Web. Int. J. Very Large Data Bases, 12(4) (2003) 303-319
10. Weisberg, H.F.: American Political Science Review 68 (1974) 1638-1655
11. Tversky, A.: Features of Similarity. Psychological Review 84(4) (1977) 327-352
12. Bouquet, P., Magnini, B., Serafini, L., Zanobini, S.: A SAT-based Algorithm for Context Matching. Dept of Information and Communication Technology, Univ of Trento, T.R. # DIT-03-005, Jan. 2003
13. Bergamaschi, S., Castano, S., De Capitani di Vimercati, S., Montanari, S. Vincini, M.: An Intelligent Approach to Information Integration. In: Proc. Int. Conf. on Formal Ontology in Information Systems (FOIS-98), June, 1998.
14. Wache, H. et al.: Ontology-Based Integration of Information - A Survey of Existing Approaches. In: Gomez-Perez, A., Gruninger, M., Stuckenschmidt, H., Uschold, M. (eds.) Proc. of the IJCAI-01 Workshop on Ontologies and Information Sharing, Seattle, USA, August 4-5 (2001) 108-118
15. Lin, D.: An Information-Theoretic Definition of Similarity. In: Proc. Int. Conf. on Machine Learning (1998)
16. Aleksovski, Z., ten Kate, W., van Harmelen, F.: Semantic Coordination: a New Approximation Method and its Application in the Music Domain. In: Proc. ISWC-04 workshop on Meaning Coordination and Negotiation, 8 Nov.2004, Hiroshima, Japan (2004)
17. Euzenat, J. et al.: State of the Art on Ontology Alignment. KnowledgeWeb project deliverable D2.2.3, v.1.2. August 2, 2004. URL: http://knowledgeweb.semanticweb.org/

On Applying the AGM Theory to DLs and OWL

Giorgos Flouris, Dimitris Plexousakis, and Grigoris Antoniou

Institute of Computer Science, FO.R.T.H.
P.O. Box 1385, GR 71110, Heraklion, Greece
{fgeo, dp, antoniou}@ics.forth.gr

Abstract. It is generally acknowledged that any Knowledge Base (KB) should be able to adapt itself to new information received. This problem has been extensively studied in the field of belief change, the dominating approach being the AGM theory. This theory set the standard for determining the rationality of a given belief change mechanism but was placed in a certain context which makes it inapplicable to logics used in the Semantic Web, such as Description Logics (DLs) and OWL. We believe the Semantic Web community would benefit from the application of the AGM theory to such logics. This paper is a preliminary study towards the feasibility of this application. Our approach raises interesting theoretical challenges and has an important practical impact too, given the central role that DLs and OWL play in the Semantic Web.

1 Introduction

One of the crucial tasks towards the realization of the vision of the Semantic Web is the encoding of human knowledge in special structures (ontologies), using certain formal encodings (representation languages), such as DLs [3] and OWL [5]. Simply encoding the knowledge is not enough though; knowledge needs to be updated as well. There are several reasons for that: a piece of knowledge that was previously unknown, classified or otherwise unavailable may have become known; or a mistake may have occurred in the conceptualization of the domain or during the input; or the domain itself may have changed. In all these cases the ontology needs to be updated to accommodate the change. Even the development of an ontology is a highly iterative revision process, in which the ontology passes through several revising steps before reaching its "final" version.

For all the above reasons, developing an automatic, consistent and rational updating method for ontologies is a task of great interest to the Semantic Web community. Despite this fact, the problem of ontology updating has been generally disregarded in the relevant literature [13]. In the current paper, we view this problem as a special case of the general problem of *belief change* (also known as *belief revision*) [8], which deals with the updating of a KB in the face of new information.

The problem of belief change has been extensively studied in the literature, resulting in several interesting results, the most important approach being the work by Alchourron, Gärdenfors and Makinson (AGM for short) in [1], known as the *AGM theory*. In that paper, the authors did not attempt to introduce a new algorithm for belief change; instead, they proposed certain rationality constraints (known as the *AGM postulates*) which should be satisfied by any rational belief change algorithm, thus setting

Y. Gil et al. (Eds.): ISWC 2005, LNCS 3729, pp. 216–231, 2005.
© Springer-Verlag Berlin Heidelberg 2005

the foundations for future research on the subject. The importance of the AGM theory lies in the fact that these postulates were accepted by most researchers as an appropriate condition to determine the rationality of a certain belief change operator.

Unfortunately, the AGM theory is based on assumptions [1] that generally fail for DLs and OWL [7]; thus, the AGM theory cannot be directly applied to the Semantic Web. Moreover, to the authors' knowledge, there has been no attempt towards a general standard of rationality for belief change operators, in the AGM pattern, for several logics outside the AGM framework (such as the logics used in the Semantic Web). One possible way to address this issue would be to introduce several different, language-specific postulates that take into account the peculiarities of each language.

In this work, we opt for a more general approach. We believe that the concept of rationality is largely independent of the underlying knowledge representation scheme, despite the different properties of each language. Thus, it may be possible to use any condition determining the rationality of a belief change operator in several different contexts; this avoids the problem of "reinventing the wheel" for each different logic.

Given the appeal of the AGM model in the belief change literature, we believe that dropping the AGM assumptions and using the theory in a more general context is a reasonable initial choice. Some people may disagree on whether the AGM theory is the best choice for the Semantic Web; only future research can uncover the strengths and weaknesses of this method, as well as of its alternatives. This paper focuses on the AGM theory of *contraction* [1], by determining whether this theory can be successfully generalized to apply to DLs and OWL. This is the first step towards evaluating the feasibility of applying the AGM theory in the context of the Semantic Web.

The idea of using the intuitions behind the AGM theory to develop a more general version was initially pursued by the authors in [6], [7], where this generalization was defined and its properties were studied; the use of belief change techniques to address the problem of ontology updating has also been independently considered in [12], [13], [16]. Such techniques could be useful in automating the third phase of ontology evolution (as defined in [17]), under which the change(s) to be made in the ontology in response to a certain need are determined (Semantics of Change phase).

In the current paper, we extend the work presented in [7]; we study the feasibility of applying the generalized AGM theory of contraction to DLs and OWL, develop conditions under which (the generalized version of) the AGM theory can (or cannot) be applied to DLs and show that the approach fails for OWL. Our focus lies on the theoretical aspects of our approach; practical issues, like implementation, or applications of our method to specific languages are given less weight. Throughout this paper, for uniformity purposes, we will use the term KB to refer to ontologies as well.

2   Preliminaries

2.1   Description Logics (DLs) and the Web Ontology Language (OWL)

The term *Description Logics* [3] refers to a family of knowledge representation languages, heavily used in the Semantic Web [4]. In DLs, *classes* are used to represent basic concepts, *roles* to represent basic binary relations between objects and *individuals* to represent objects. Those primitive notions can be combined using certain *operators* (such as ¬, ⊓, ∃ etc) to produce more complex *terms*. Finally, *connectives* are used to represent relationships between terms, such as inclusion (⊑), disjointness (disj) and others. Each such relationship is called an *axiom*. Axioms dealing with classes and roles form the *Tbox*, while axioms dealing with individuals form the *Abox*. The operators and connectives that a certain DL admits determine the type and complexity of the available axioms, which, in turn, determine the expressive power and the reasoning complexity of the DL. Reasoning in DLs is based on standard model-theoretic semantics. For more details on DLs and their semantics, see [3]. In the following, the term *DL Knowledge Base (DL KB)* will refer to a set of general Tbox and/or Abox axioms representing knowledge regarding a domain of interest.

The Web Ontology Language [5], known as OWL, is a knowledge representation language that is expected to play an important role in the future of the Semantic Web, as it has become a W3C Recommendation. OWL comes in three flavors (or species), namely OWL Full, OWL DL and OWL Lite, with varying degree of expressive power and reasoning complexity. In OWL, knowledge is represented using an RDF-like syntax. OWL contains several features allowing the representation of complex relationships between classes, roles and objects in a pattern very similar to the one used in DLs; this close relationship was verified in [10], where OWL DL and OWL Lite (with their secondary annotation features removed) were shown equivalent to the DLs SHOIN$^+$(D) and SHIF$^+$(D) respectively. On the other hand, OWL Full provides a more complete integration with RDF, containing features not normally allowed in DLs; furthermore, its inference problem is undecidable [10]. For more details on OWL and the differences between OWL Full, OWL DL and OWL Lite, refer to [5].

2.2 The AGM Theory and Its Generalization

The problem of belief change deals with the updating of a KB in the face of new, possibly contradictory, information. Undoubtedly, the most influential work in the area of belief change is the work by AGM [1]. In that paper, three fundamental operations of belief change were defined, namely *expansion*, *revision* and *contraction*, as well as a set of rationality postulates that should apply to each of the above operations.

In the current paper, we restrict our attention to the operation of contraction (denoted by '−') which refers to the consistent removal of a piece of information from a KB when this information is no longer believed. Contraction was chosen for our initial approach because, according to AGM, it is the most fundamental among the three belief change operators [1], [8]. Indeed, the theoretical importance of contraction has been accepted by most researchers, even though revision (which refers to consistent addition of information) is more often used in practical applications.

AGM used several assumptions when formulating their theory. Under these assumptions, a logic is a pair <L,Cn>, where L is a set containing all the expressions of the logic and Cn is a *consequence operator* that satisfies the Tarskian axioms (iteration, inclusion, monotony). Using this consequence operator, we can define the implication relation as: K⊢X ⇔ Cn(X)⊆Cn(K). This is the only assumption that was kept during the generalization of the AGM theory in [7]; AGM additionally assumed that the logic is closed under the standard operators (¬, ∧, etc); they also assumed that the consequence operator includes classical tautological implication, it is compact and it satisfies the "rule of introduction of disjunctions in the premises".

It is easy to see that many AGM assumptions fail for DLs and OWL. For example, a DL is not necessarily closed under the usual operators ($\neg$, $\wedge$, etc); DL axioms are of equational form (e.g., $A\sqcap B\sqsubseteq C$), so the negation of an axiom cannot be defined in general. Furthermore, many DLs are not compact. The same holds for OWL, as well as for many other families of knowledge representation languages [7]. On the other hand, our more general framework engulfs DLs, since, for any given DL, we can take L to be the set of all axioms that can be formed in this DL and $Cn(X)$ the set of all implications of a set of axioms $X\subseteq L$ under the standard model-theoretic semantics of DLs [3]. Similar facts hold for OWL.

Regarding the operation of contraction, AGM assumed that a KB is a set of propositions of the underlying logic (say $K\subseteq L$) which is closed under logical consequence (i.e., $K=Cn(K)$), also called a *theory*. Any single expression $x\in L$ of the logic can be contracted from the KB. The operation of contraction can be formalized as a function mapping the pair (K, x) to a new KB K' (denoted by $K'=K-x$). In [7], the definition of the contraction operator was slightly extended to include cases where both operands are sets of expressions of the underlying logic (i.e., $K'=K-X$, for $K,X\subseteq L$).

The above assumptions allow any binary operator to be a "contraction" operator, which, of course, should not be the case; for this reason, AGM introduced several restrictions on the result of a contraction operation. First of all, the result should be a theory itself. As already stated, contraction is an operation that is used to *remove* knowledge from a KB; thus the result should not contain any new, previously unknown, information. Moreover, contraction is supposed to return a new KB such that the contracted expression is no longer believed or implied. Finally, the result should be syntax-independent and should remove as little information from the KB as possible, in accordance with the *Principle of Minimal Change* [8]. The above intuitions were formalized in a set of six postulates, the *basic AGM postulates for contraction*; these are omitted due to lack of space, but can be found in [1].

As shown by the above analysis, the intuitions that led to the development of the AGM postulates are independent of the underlying knowledge representation language. On the other hand, the formulation of the AGM postulates themselves depends on the AGM assumptions (see [1]). For this reason, in [7], each AGM postulate was reformulated in such a way as to be applicable to all logics in our more general framework, while preserving the original intuition that led to its definition. The resulting postulates can be found in the following list, where the naming and numbering of each postulate corresponds to the original AGM naming and numbering [7]:

(K−1) Closure:	$Cn(K-X)=K-X$	
(K−2) Inclusion:	$K-X\subseteq Cn(K)$	
(K−3) Vacuity:	If $X\nsubseteq Cn(K)$, then $K-X=Cn(K)$	
(K−4) Success:	If $X\nsubseteq Cn(\emptyset)$, then $X\nsubseteq Cn(K-X)$	
(K−5) Preservation:	If $Cn(X)=Cn(Y)$, then $K-X=K-Y$	
(K−6) Recovery:	$K\subseteq Cn((K-X)\cup X)$	

Unfortunately, it soon became clear that not all logics in our wide framework can admit a contraction operator that satisfies the (generalized) AGM postulates. Following this observation, we defined a logic to be *AGM-compliant* iff a contraction operator that satisfies the generalized AGM postulates can be defined in the given logic. This class of logics was characterized using the following proposition [7]:

Proposition 1. A logic <L,Cn> is AGM-compliant iff for all sets K, X⊆L such that $Cn(\varnothing) \subset Cn(X) \subset Cn(K)$ there is a Z⊆L such that $Cn(Z) \subset Cn(K)$ and $Cn(X \cup Z) = Cn(K)$.

With the above postulates, we have succeeded in developing a generalized version of the AGM theory for contraction. The generalized AGM postulates can be used in all logics in our framework; however, for a non-AGM-compliant logic, such an option does not make much sense, as no contraction operator satisfying the postulates (K−1)-(K−6) can be defined. Proposition 1 is the tool that allows us to determine whether this is the case or not.

3 Conditions for AGM-Compliance

3.1 General Intuition and Main Results

In the following, we will refer to a DL as a pair <L,Cn>, where L is the set that contains all the axioms that can be defined in this DL and Cn is the consequence operator under the standard model-theoretic semantics of DLs [3]. Initially, we will consider DLs that allow for the top concept ⊤ and the connective ⊑ (applicable to concept terms, at least), plus an arbitrary number of other connectives and/or operators.

Our approach is based on the following observation: take two sets of DL axioms of the form K={A⊒⊤}, X={B⊒⊤} such that $Cn(\varnothing) \subset Cn(X) \subset Cn(K)$. Set Z={A⊒B}; Z is a good candidate for the set Z required by proposition 1, since $Cn(Z) \subseteq Cn(K)$ and $Cn(X \cup Z) = Cn(K)$. There is a catch though: proposition 1 requires that $Cn(Z) \subset Cn(K)$; in the above approach sometimes it so happens that $Cn(Z) = Cn(K)$. For example, if K={A⊒⊤} and X={¬A⊔∃R.A⊔∀R.⊥⊒⊤} for some role R, then it holds that $Cn(\varnothing) \subset Cn(X) \subset Cn(K)$. If we take Z as above, we get Z={A⊒¬A⊔∃R.A⊔∀R.⊥}, which is equivalent to K={A⊒⊤}, so $Cn(Z) = Cn(K)$. Thus, the constructed Z does not satisfy the conditions set by proposition 1 (example provided by Thomas Studer, personal communication). To deal with this problem, the idea must be somehow refined in order to guarantee that $Cn(Z) \subset Cn(K)$ will hold in all cases. This refinement is described and proved in a more general setting in the following lemma:

Lemma 1. Consider the sets of axioms K={A_j⊒⊤ | j∈J} and X={B⊒⊤}. If $Cn(\varnothing) \subset Cn(X) \subset Cn(K)$ and there is an interpretation I such that $B^I = \varnothing$, then there is a set Z such that $Cn(Z) \subset Cn(K)$ and $Cn(X \cup Z) = Cn(K)$.

Proof. Set Z={A_j⊒B | j∈J} and assume that Z⊨K. Then Z⊨X. By the hypothesis, there is an interpretation I such that $B^I = \varnothing$; for this interpretation, Z is obviously satisfied, while X is not. This is a contradiction, so Z⊭K. On the other hand, K⊨Z; thus, $Cn(Z) \subset Cn(K)$. The relation $Cn(X \cup Z) = Cn(K)$ is obvious by the transitivity of ⊑. □

Lemma 1 guarantees the existence of the set Z required by proposition 1, but only for sets K, X of a special form. This might cause one to believe that it is of limited use; on the contrary, lemma 1 forms the backbone of our theory. Before showing that, we will show that the prerequisites of proposition 1 need to be checked for only a subset of all the possible (K,X) pairs:

Lemma 2. Consider a logic <L,Cn> and two sets K, X⊆L, such that $Cn(\emptyset) \subset Cn(X) \subset Cn(K)$. If there are sets K', X'⊆L such that $Cn(K')=Cn(K)$, $Cn(\emptyset) \subset Cn(X') \subseteq Cn(X)$ and a Z⊆L such that $Cn(Z) \subset Cn(K')$, $Cn(X' \cup Z)=Cn(K')$, then $Cn(Z) \subset Cn(K)$ and $Cn(X \cup Z)=Cn(K)$.

Proof. Obviously $Cn(Z) \subset Cn(K)$. Since $Cn(X') \subseteq Cn(X) \subset Cn(K)$ we can conclude that $Cn(X \cup Z) \supseteq Cn(X' \cup Z)=Cn(K')$, so $Cn(X \cup Z)=Cn(K)$.   □

Now consider any two sets of axioms K, X⊆L of the underlying DL, such that $Cn(\emptyset) \subset Cn(X) \subset Cn(K)$. If K and X are of the form required by lemma 1, then we are done; lemma 1 allows us to find a set Z that satisfies the requirements of proposition 1 for an AGM-compliant logic. If, on the other hand, K or X are not of the desired form, lemma 2 shows the way; all we need is to find two sets K', X' of the desired form such that $Cn(K')=Cn(K)$ and $Cn(\emptyset) \subset Cn(X') \subseteq Cn(X)$. Then, lemma 1 can be applied for K', X' and the resulting set Z can be propagated to K, X using lemma 2. These ideas lead to the main result of this section:

Theorem 1. Consider a DL <L,Cn>, such that:

- For all K⊆L there is a K'⊆L such that $K'=\{A_j \sqsupseteq \top \mid j \in J\}$ and $Cn(K)=Cn(K')$
- For all X⊆L there is a X'⊆L such that $X'=\{B \sqsupseteq \top\}$, there is an interpretation I such that $B^I=\emptyset$ and $Cn(\emptyset) \subset Cn(X') \subseteq Cn(X)$

Then this DL is AGM-compliant.

The important question is, in which DLs do the sets K', X' required by theorem 1 exist? With the aid of table 1, it can be shown that several very expressive DLs allow transformations resulting in these K', X'. Table 1 shows how each of the axiom types commonly used in DLs can be equivalently rewritten in the form $A \sqsupseteq \top$. Using this table, we can generate K', X' as required by theorem 1 as follows: for K', replace each axiom of K with its equivalent in the second column; for X', select one non-tautological axiom of X, replace it with its equivalent from table 1 (say $B \sqsupseteq \top$) and set $X'=\{\forall \top_R.B \sqsupseteq \top\}$.

All the transformations in table 1 can be shown using model-theoretic arguments. Moreover, K' as defined above obviously fulfills the requirements of theorem 1. For X', notice that the axiom selected from X is non-tautological, so there is an interpretation for which $B^I \neq \top^I$; for this interpretation, it holds that $(\forall \top_R.B)^I=\emptyset$. Furthermore, $X \vDash \{B \sqsupseteq \top\} \vDash \{\forall \top_R.B \sqsupseteq \top\}$ and $Cn(X') \neq Cn(\emptyset)$, so X' is of the desired form as well.

Table 1 shows that the necessary transformations are possible for axioms involving concepts, roles and even individuals. Thus, our results apply also to DL KBs that contain a non-empty Abox. In table 1, A, B refer to concept terms, R, S refer to role terms and a, b refer to individuals. All operators subscripted by $\cdot_R$ (in the third column)

Table 1. Transforming axioms into the form $A \sqsupseteq \top$

Axiom	Equivalent axiom of the proper form	Required operators
$A \sqsubseteq B$	$\neg A \sqcup B \sqsupseteq \top$	$\neg, \sqcup$
$R \sqsubseteq S$	$\forall (R \sqcap \neg S). \bot \sqsupseteq \top$	$\bot, \forall, \neg_R, \sqcap_R$
$A \not\sqsubseteq B$	$\exists \top_R.(A \sqcap \neg B) \sqsupseteq \top$	$\neg, \sqcap, \exists, \top_R$
$R \not\sqsubseteq S$	$\exists \top_R.\exists (R \sqcap \neg S). \top \sqsupseteq \top$	$\exists, \top_R, \neg_R, \sqcap_R$
$A \equiv B$	$(\neg A \sqcup B) \sqcap (A \sqcup \neg B) \sqsupseteq \top$	$\neg, \sqcup, \sqcap$
$R \equiv S$	$\forall (R \sqcap \neg S). \bot \sqcap \forall (S \sqcap \neg R). \bot \sqsupseteq \top$	$\bot, \sqcap, \forall, \neg_R, \sqcap_R$
$A \not\equiv B$	$\exists \top_R.[(A \sqcap \neg B) \sqcup (B \sqcap \neg A)] \sqsupseteq \top$	$\neg, \sqcap, \sqcup, \exists, \top_R$
$R \not\equiv S$	$\exists \top_R.\exists [(\neg R \sqcap S) \sqcup (\neg S \sqcap R)]. \top \sqsupseteq \top$	$\exists, \top_R, \neg_R, \sqcap_R, \sqcup_R$
$A \sqsubset B$	$(\neg A \sqcup B) \sqcap \exists \top_R.(B \sqcap \neg A) \sqsupseteq \top$	$\neg, \sqcap, \sqcup, \exists, \top_R$
$R \sqsubset S$	$\forall (R \sqcap \neg S). \bot \sqcap \exists \top_R.\exists (S \sqcap \neg R). \top \sqsupseteq \top$	$\bot, \sqcap, \exists, \forall, \top_R, \neg_R, \sqcap_R$
$A \backslash\!\sqsubset B$	$\forall \top_R.\exists \top_R.(A \sqcap \neg B) \sqcup \forall \top_R.(\neg B \sqcup A) \sqsupseteq \top$	$\neg, \sqcap, \sqcup, \exists, \forall, \top_R$
$R \backslash\!\sqsubset S$	$\forall \top_R.\exists \top_R.\exists (R \sqcap \neg S). \top \sqcup \forall \top_R.\forall (S \sqcap \neg R). \bot \sqsupseteq \top$	$\bot, \sqcup, \exists, \forall, \top_R, \neg_R, \sqcap_R$
$disj(A,B)$	$\neg A \sqcup \neg B \sqsupseteq \top$	$\neg, \sqcup$
$disj(R,S)$	$\forall (R \sqcap S). \bot \sqsupseteq \top$	$\bot, \forall, \sqcap_R$
$A(a)$	$\neg \{a\} \sqcup A \sqsupseteq \top$	$\neg, \sqcup, \{\ldots\}$
$R(a,b)$	$\exists R.\{b\} \sqcup \neg \{a\} \sqsupseteq \top$	$\neg, \sqcup, \exists, \{\ldots\}$
$a=b$	$\neg \{a\} \sqcup \{b\} \sqsupseteq \top$	$\neg, \sqcup, \{\ldots\}$
$a \neq b$	$\neg \{a\} \sqcup \neg \{b\} \sqsupseteq \top$	$\neg, \sqcup, \{\ldots\}$

apply to role terms; the other operators apply to concept terms or individuals, depending on the context. Likewise, connectives apply to concepts, roles or individuals, depending on the context. The symbol $\top_R$ refers to the top role, i.e., the role connecting every individual to every individual and the connective $\backslash\!\sqsubset$ stands for non-proper-inclusion. The symbols $\neg$ and $\exists$ refer to full (rather than atomic) negation and full (rather than limited) existential quantification respectively.

The above analysis shows that, if the DL under question contains the operators necessary for the transformations of table 1, then it is AGM-compliant. The required operators are the constant $\top$ and the connective $\sqsubseteq$ for the basic case (lemma 1), the operators of table 1 for the transformation of K plus the operator $\forall$ and the constant $\top_R$ for the transformation of X. Notice that there is a certain amount of redundancy in table 1; by eliminating this redundancy the following corollary can be shown:

Corollary 1. A DL containing the constants $\top$, $\top_R$, the operators $\neg$, $\sqcap$, $\forall$, $\neg_R$, $\sqcap_R$, $\{\ldots\}$, the concept connective $\sqsubseteq$ plus any connectives from table 1 is AGM-compliant.

3.2 Discussion

Notice that corollary 1 provides one possible application of theorem 1; the family of DLs described by corollary 1 is not the only AGM-compliant one. There are several reasons for that: first of all, the transformations we propose are probably not the only possible ones. Other transformations for K and X would possibly generate a different set of operators required for AGM-compliance.

For example, an alternative for the transformation of X is to take $X'=\{\forall R.B \sqsupseteq \top\}$ for a "fresh" role name R instead of $X'=\{\forall \top_R.B \sqsupseteq \top\}$. The validity of this alternative can be easily shown using model-theoretic arguments. Notice that this requires a fresh role name, so the logic must admit an infinite number of role names. Additionally, this alternative transformation introduces roles which are completely irrelevant to the original KB and the contracted expression; the introduction of new, irrelevant roles during each contraction operation may appear irrational for some applications, despite the fact that it results to an AGM-compliant operation.

Additionally, corollary 1 gives a *minimal* set of operators that are needed to guarantee AGM-compliance. Any additional operators do not bar AGM-compliance (notice however that any additional connectives might). Thus, all logics that contain more operators than the DL described in corollary 1 are AGM-compliant too.

Furthermore, some of the operators could be replaced by others; for example the combination $\{\neg, \forall\}$ is equivalent to the combination $\{\neg, \exists\}$. Similar facts hold for other operators as well. Moreover, the constants $\top$ and $\top_R$ could be removed from the minimal required set of operators, because they can be replaced by $A \sqcup \neg A$ and $R \sqcup \neg R$ respectively. Of course, this requires that there is at least one concept (A) and at least one role (R) in the namespace of the logic, but this is hardly an assumption.

As it is clear by theorem 1, the operators we need to guarantee AGM-compliance are just those that are required to produce the sets K', X'; for example, if we are interested in DL KBs without an Abox, then the operator $\{\ldots\}$ is not necessary, i.e., it could be removed from the minimal set of operators required for AGM-compliance. Similarly, certain logics disallow certain connectives or certain uses of ones. Such restrictions might affect (i.e., reduce) the required minimal operator set (by allowing simpler transformations). Furthermore, in some DLs it might be the case that for all concept terms B there is an interpretation I such that $B^I=\emptyset$; if this is the case, then the last transformation for X ($\forall \top_R.B \sqsupseteq \top$) is not necessary and we could set $X'=\{B \sqsupseteq \top\}$.

In theorem 1 we state that the DL under question must allow for concept hierarchies (connective $\sqsubseteq$). This is a reasonable assumption, since most interesting DLs do satisfy it. However, it turns out that it is also an unnecessary one. To show that, we will use the concept of *equivalence of logics with respect to AGM-compliance* that appeared in [6], where it was shown that equivalent logics have the same status as far as AGM-compliance is concerned. Now, using model-theoretic arguments, we can show the following equivalences: $\{A \sqsupseteq \top\} \Leftrightarrow \{A \cong \top\} \Leftrightarrow \{\neg \forall \top_R.A \sqsubset \top\} \Leftrightarrow \{\neg \forall \top_R.A \not\sqsubset \top\} \Leftrightarrow \{\neg \forall \top_R.A \not\sqsupseteq \top\} \Leftrightarrow \{A \setminus \sqsubset \top\} \Leftrightarrow \{disj(\top, \neg A)\}$. These equivalences are all definable using the minimal set of operators of corollary 1. Using these transformations and proposition 5 in [6], we can show that a DL that contains the operators required by corollary 1 plus any of the usual concept connectives ($\cong$, $\sqsubset$, $\not\cong$, $\not\sqsubseteq$, \\$\sqsubset$, disj(.,.)), but not $\sqsubseteq$, is equivalent to a similar DL that contains the same operators and connectives as well as the connective $\sqsubseteq$. The latter logic (which includes $\sqsubseteq$) is AGM-compliant by corollary 1; thus the original logic (which does not include $\sqsubseteq$) is AGM-compliant too (since the two logics are equivalent). This argumentation shows that the existence of concept hierarchies in the DL under question is not mandatory for corollary 1 to be applicable; any of the usual concept connectives would do.

The AGM-compliance of a certain family of DLs is the primary result of this section; however, the constructive proof employed in theorem 1 has the secondary effect of suggesting one possible contraction operator that satisfies the generalized AGM postulates. Indeed, if $Cn(\emptyset) \subset Cn(X) \subset Cn(K)$, the principal case in an AGM-compliant contraction operation, then by setting $K-X=Cn(Z)$, where Z is the set constructed in the proof of lemma 1, we get an AGM-compliant result for the contraction. This set Z can be constructed in linear time on the number of axioms in K, X (this is obvious; see the proof of lemma 1). We can complete the definition of the contraction operator for the non-principal cases as follows: if $Cn(X) \not\subseteq Cn(K)$, then (K–3) leaves us little choice: $K-X=Cn(K)$; if $Cn(X)=Cn(\emptyset)$ then (K–6) implies $K-X=Cn(K)$; finally, if $Cn(K)=Cn(\emptyset)$ or $Cn(K)=Cn(X)$, then $K-X=Cn(\emptyset)$ is a valid choice. These results can be computed in constant time. Thus, given an oracle that solves the reasoning problem of the underlying DL in constant time, the result of this contraction operator can be computed in linear time on the number of axioms in K, X. So, the computational bottleneck of the above contraction operator is the inference problem of the underlying DL. However, the semantic properties of this operator have not been studied; this is reserved for future work.

Many of the required operators of corollary 1 are standard in most interesting DLs. One exception is the operator $\{...\}$, which is common in many DLs, but could not be classified as "standard". Fortunately, this operator is not necessary for AGM-compliance if we assume an empty Abox in the DL under question. A more important problem is posed by the role operators ($\neg_R$, $\sqcap_R$, $\top_R$), which do not appear in most DLs. These operators are required when role connectives are admitted and for the transformation of X, unless we use the alternative transformation with the fresh role name. Thus, role operators are not necessary if axioms involving roles are not allowed in the DL under question and an alternative transformation for X is available.

One last (but certainly not least) observation that can be made is that theorem 1 and its various corollaries do not provide a complete characterization of AGM-compliant DLs. However, it looks like this characterization is close to being complete: all the AGM-compliant DLs that we have considered fall into one of the theorem's innumerable variations and corollaries; those who don't, eventually turn out to be non-AGM-compliant (see the next sections for some examples). It is part of our future work to determine whether this pattern is simply coincidental or not.

4   Conditions for Non-AGM-Compliance

Unfortunately, many DLs are not AGM-compliant; to show that, we will initially show the following simple lemma, which is applicable in any logic:

Lemma 3. Consider a logic <L,Cn> and a set K⊆L. Set X={x∈L | Cn({x})⊂Cn(K)}. If Cn(∅)⊂Cn(X)⊂Cn(K) then <L,Cn> is not AGM-compliant.

Proof. Take any set Z⊆L such that Cn(Z)⊂Cn(K). Then, obviously Z⊂X, so Cn(X∪Z)=Cn(X)⊂Cn(K). Thus, we can find no Z⊆L as required by proposition 1 for the sets K,X⊆L, which proves that <L,Cn> is not AGM-compliant.   □

Lemma 3 states that, if a logic contains a belief which cannot be deduced by all its proper consequences combined, then this logic is not AGM-compliant. Unfortunately, this is the case for many DLs that admit axioms between role terms but forbid the use of operators $\neg_R$, $\sqcap_R$. Indeed, the axiom R⊑S implies ∃R.A⊑∃S.A, $(\leq_2 R)\sqsupseteq(\leq_2 S)$, etc, but sometimes all such implications combined do not imply R⊑S, as shown below:

Theorem 2. Consider a DL with the following properties:

- The DL admits at least two role names (say R, S) and one concept name (say A)
- The DL admits at least one of the operators ∀, ∃, $(\geq_n)$, $(\leq_n)$, for at least some n
- The DL admits any (or none) of the operators ¬, ⊓, ⊔, $^-$, ⊤, ⊥, {...}
- The DL admits only the connective ⊑ applicable to both concepts and roles

Then this DL is not AGM-compliant.

Sketch of Proof. Set K={R⊑S}, X={x∈L | Cn({x})⊂Cn(K)}, as in lemma 3. We define two interpretations I, I′, as follows:

$\Delta^I=\Delta^{I'}=\{a_1,a_2,b_1,b_2,c\}$
$B^I=B^{I'}=\varnothing$ for all concepts B
$y^I=y^{I'}=c$ for all individuals y
$R_0^I=R_0^{I'}=\varnothing$ for all roles R_0, other than R, S
$R^I=R^{I'}=\{(a_1,b_1),(b_1,a_1),(a_2,b_2),(b_2,a_2)\}$
$S^I=\{(a_1,b_1),(b_1,a_1),(a_2,b_2),(b_2,a_2)\}$
$S^{I'}=\{(a_1,b_2),(b_2,a_1),(a_2,b_1),(b_1,a_2)\}$

Notice that the two interpretations differ only in the interpretation of the role S. An easy induction on the number of operators of a concept term C shows that $C^I=C^{I'}$ for all C in all DLs considered by the hypothesis. Thus, any axiom involving concept terms is satisfied by I iff it is satisfied by I′. Using induction, we can also show that all axioms in X that involve role terms are actually tautological.

Thus, I satisfies K (obviously), so it satisfies X (because K⊨X); since I satisfies X, I′ satisfies X (by the results above), but K is not satisfied by I′ (obviously). Thus Cn(X)⊂Cn(K). To complete the proof, we need to show that Cn(X)≠Cn(∅); this follows from the fact that at least one of the operators ∀, ∃, $(\geq_n)$, $(\leq_n)$ (for some n) exists in the DL. The above, combined with lemma 3, conclude the proof.   □

The above negative result persists if the DL under question admits $\cong$ (applicable to both concepts and roles) instead of $\sqsubseteq$, or if it admits both connectives; the proof is identicsal. The same result can be shown (using the same proof) if we add transitive roles (the axiom Trans(.)), axioms with individuals, functional-only roles and/or qualified number restrictions. This analysis uncovers a rule of thumb regarding DLs: if theorem 1 cannot be applied, then there is good chance that lemma 3 will be applicable for a set of the form $\{R \sqsubseteq S\}$ or $\{R \cong S\}$ (for any two roles R, S). This provides a simple test to determine whether a DL is AGM-compliant, applicable to many DLs.

5   A Case Study: OWL

5.1   OWL DL and OWL Lite Without Annotation Features

One of the corollaries of theorem 2 is that OWL DL and OWL Lite without annotation features are not AGM-compliant. To show this, we will use the result of [10] that identifies OWL DL and OWL Lite (without annotations) as equivalent to $SHOIN^+(D)$ and $SHIF^+(D)$ respectively. $SHOIN^+(D)$ is a very expressive DL allowing for the following operators: $\top$, $\bot$, $\sqcap$, $\sqcup$, $\neg$, $\{\ldots\}$, $\bar{\ }$, $\exists$, $\forall$, $(\geq_n)$, $(\leq_n)$. In addition, it allows a *datatype theory* (D), which is a mapping from a set of datatypes to a set of values plus a mapping from data values to their denotation (see [10] for details). To make datatypes useful, the logic also allows *datatype* (or *concrete*) *roles*, which are binary relationships between individuals and data values, as well as the operators $\exists$, $\forall$, $(\geq_n)$, $(\leq_n)$, $\{\ldots\}$ for datatype roles and data values. The axioms allowed in this logic are concept, role and datatype role hierarchies; individual inclusion, equality and inequality; role transitivity (for object roles only); and a new *concept existence* axiom (see [10]). $SHIF^+(D)$ is just $SHOIN^+(D)$ without the $\{\ldots\}$ constructor and with the at-least and at-most constructors limited to 0 and 1. $SHOIN^+(D)$ and $SHIF^+(D)$ can be shown non-AGM-compliant, so OWL DL and OWL Lite are not AGM-compliant either:

Corollary 2. $SHOIN^+(D)$ and $SHIF^+(D)$ are not AGM-compliant.

Proof. The only difference from the proof of theorem 2 is the existence of datatypes; to remedy this problem, augment the interpretations with a datatype domain $(\Delta_D^1, \Delta_D^{1'})$ and map all datatype roles to the empty set. The rest of the proof is identical. $\square$

5.2   OWL with Annotation Features

But what if annotation features are included? Does this make the situation any better? Unfortunately not: the annotation features are meant to be read by humans, so they carry no special meaning for the system (they imply nothing) and the same negative results apply here. There is one exception though: the owl:imports annotation feature carries some meaning for the parser, making it substantially different from the other annotation constructs. More specifically, owl:imports is a meta-logical annotation property forcing the parser to include another KB (ontology) in the current KB. In effect, the axiom owl:imports(O) has exactly the same implications as O itself. One may believe that owl:imports does not add anything new to the language in terms of expressiveness, because owl:imports(O) can be replaced by the axioms of O themselves.

Unfortunately, there is one problem with this approach: owl:imports must be replaced dynamically at the time when the consequences of a certain KB are calculated (at "run-time"). However, the naïve approach above replaces owl:imports statically, thus losing the connection between our ontology and O. This would work nicely until O is changed; if O is somehow revised, then the correct, dynamic approach should replace owl:imports with the axioms of the new O, while the static approach would leave our KB with the axioms of the old O. Notice that this would not be an issue if we could somehow guarantee that O would remain static and unchanged; however, given the dynamic nature of the Web, such an assumption would be highly unrealistic.

Therefore, the axiom owl:imports(O) is not equivalent to O; rephrasing this fact in the terminology of this paper, we conclude that, for $K=\{owl:imports(O)\}$, it holds that $Cn(K)=Cn(O)\cup K$ and $Cn(O)\subset Cn(K)$, thus making lemma 3 applicable for K. Since owl:imports is allowed in all three flavors of OWL, we conclude that OWL Full, OWL DL and OWL Lite (with annotation features) are non-AGM-compliant. Furthermore, this analysis shows that any fragment of OWL that contains the owl:imports construct and at least one other non-tautological expression is non-AGM-compliant.

6 Discussion and Directions for Future Work

6.1 Application to DLs in the Literature

Our study was kept at a fairly abstract level; we did not focus on any specific DL but dealt with the DL family as a whole, including DLs that have not yet been considered in the literature. This approach allows our results to be of use to researchers who develop new DLs; if the focus is on developing a DL that can be rationally updated, then AGM-compliance should be a desirable feature of the new DL, along with high expressive power, low reasoning complexity etc.

However, theorems 1 and 2 can be applied to several DLs that have already been considered in the literature as well. We provide an indicative (but not necessarily complete) list of DLs for which a definite answer regarding AGM-compliance can be given. For a definition of the logics below, refer to [2], [3], [5], [10], [11], [14].

The following DLs can be shown to be non-AGM-compliant: SH, SHI, SHIN, SHOIN, SHOIN(D), SHOIN$^+$, SHOIN$^+$(D), SHIQ, SHIF, SHIF(D), SHIF$^+$, SHIF$^+$(D); all these logics admit role hierarchies, so these results are actually corollaries of theorem 2. For similar reasons, adding role hierarchies to the AL family leads to non-AGM-compliance; that is, FL_0 and FL^- with role axioms and all DLs between ALH and ALHCIOQ are non-AGM-compliant. This family includes several logics, such as ALHE, ALHNC, etc. None of the three flavors of OWL is AGM-compliant if the owl:imports axiom is included; OWL DL and OWL Lite without their annotation features are non-AGM-compliant either. These facts were proven in section 5.

The addition of role operators to the AL family results in some AGM-compliant DLs, such as ALCO$^{\neg,\sqcap,\sqcup}$, ALC$^{\neg,\sqcap,\sqcup}$ with empty Abox, ALCO$^{(\neg),\sqcup}$ and ALCO$^{(\neg),\sqcap,\sqcup}$

with no axioms involving role terms and $ALC^{(-),\sqcup}$ and $ALC^{(-),\sqcap,\sqcup}$ with empty Abox and no axioms involving role terms. AGM-compliance persists if we add more operators (but not new axiom types) to any of the above logics; for example, all DLs with more operators than $ALC^{\neg,\sqcap,\sqcup}$ and no Abox (such as ALB) are AGM-compliant.

If we have an infinite pool of role names, we can use the alternative transformation introduced in section 3.2 to produce X'; this makes ALC (and all languages with more operators than ALC) AGM-compliant, provided that no axioms involving role terms are included and that the Abox is empty. Similarly, all languages with more operators than ALCO are AGM-compliant if they do not allow axioms involving roles.

As shown by the above results, it is the absence of role operators (role intersection, union and complement) that bars AGM-compliance in most cases. For this reason, we highly encourage research on DLs that admit these operators due to their nice behavior with respect to updates. Unfortunately, very few logics with role operators have been studied in the literature (notable exceptions being [11], [14]), so the computational overhead caused by such operators is largely unknown.

6.2 Role Operators, Negation, the Levi Identity and Ontology Revision

An additional advantage of the use of role operators (especially $\top_R$) is the fact that they allow the definition of an *axiom's negation*. The negation of $A \sqsubseteq B$ is $A \not\sqsubseteq B$, but most logics do not allow axioms with the connective $\not\sqsubseteq$. However, $A \not\sqsubseteq B$ is equivalent to $\exists \top_R.(A \sqcap \neg B) \sqsupseteq \top$ (see table 1), so the negation of $A \sqsubseteq B$ can be defined indirectly using $\top_R$; similar facts hold for other axiom types as well. This concept can be extended to finite sets of axioms by noticing that the set $X = \{A_j \sqsupseteq B_j \mid j \in J\}$ is equivalent to $\{\sqcap_{j \in J}(A_j \sqcup \neg B_j) \sqsupseteq \top\}$, which is a singular set, so it has a negation, as above.

It must be emphasized at this point that not all AGM-compliant DLs are closed with respect to axiom negation. The negation of a set of axioms in an AGM-compliant logic, when available, is a very important concept, because it allows us to use the Levi identity: $K+X=Cn((K-\neg X)\cup X)$ to produce a revision operator from a given contraction operator [8]. This identity says that, in order to revise a KB with some set of axioms X, we can first contract $\neg X$ and then add X. The contraction operation is needed to guarantee that no inconsistency will arise when X is added to the new KB.

Therefore, for these logics, the problem of ontology revision can be solved indirectly through the problem of contraction, which is studied in this paper; this way, the definition of a rational contraction operator is of dual significance. As future work, we are planning to study the problem of revision more thoroughly. Due to the above facts, a related issue is the refinement of the proposed contraction operator for AGM-compliant DLs, to produce an operator that will be based on semantic rather than syntactic considerations, in addition to being AGM-compliant.

6.3 Evaluation of AGM-Compliance

The purpose of this paper is to evaluate the usefulness of applying the AGM theory to DLs and OWL. As the above analysis indicates, OWL does not support the AGM postulates, so the approach is not useful for OWL ontologies. Regarding DLs, the situation is much better: there are certain DLs in which an AGM-compliant contraction operator can be defined, as well as several non-AGM-compliant DLs. Our results do not currently provide a complete characterization of AGM-compliance for DLs; this is an important goal for our future work.

The AGM theory has always been the most influential approach to the problem of belief change, because it properly captures common intuition regarding the concept of rationality and it has several interesting theoretical properties [8]. However, our results showed that there are certain problems regarding its application to certain DLs, for the operation of contraction. On the other hand, as we showed in [6], all logics <L,Cn> admit a contraction operator that satisfies (K−1)-(K−5), i.e., all AGM postulates except the recovery postulate. Coincidentally, the only seriously debated AGM postulate is the postulate of recovery, as some works (e.g., [9]) state that (K−6) is counter-intuitive; for a thorough examination on the theoretical implications of using (K−6) see [15]. It is generally acceptable however that the recovery postulate cannot be dropped unless replaced by some other constraint that would somehow express the Principle of Minimal Change. Given the negative results appearing in this paper and the above facts, we believe it is useful to work on a "replacement" of the recovery postulate, or on some approximation of it, that would properly capture the Principle of Minimal Change in addition to being applicable to non-AGM-compliant DLs.

As far as AGM-compliant DLs are concerned, we believe that research on ontology change should use the feature of AGM-compliance, thus taking advantage of the numerous results that appeared in the literature on belief change and the AGM theory during the past 20 years. For this reason, we plan to continue our research on the application of the AGM theory to the DLs that support it. In this respect, notice that AGM-compliance simply guarantees the existence of a contraction operator that satisfies the basic AGM postulates for contraction; one of our future goals is to determine the relation of AGM-compliance to other results related to the AGM theory, such as the various representation theorems [8], the supplementary AGM postulates [1] etc.

7   Conclusion

The AGM theory is a mature and widely accepted model for belief change with several applications; a further application of this theory in DLs will hopefully indicate rational methods for updating such logics. This paper partly evaluated the applicability and usefulness of this approach by determining whether contracting a DL KB using the AGM model is possible for certain DLs and by providing a roadmap allowing one to check AGM-compliance for DLs not covered by this work. We also described one possible AGM-compliant contraction operator for the DLs that were found to allow one and showed that OWL is incompatible with the AGM theory.

We are hoping that our work will help in uncovering the limitations of the AGM theory with respect to DLs, by verifying the applicability of the method in certain

DLs and forcing us to consider alternative approaches in others. DLs and OWL have an important role to play in the design of the Semantic Web [4], so our research has the potential to find applications in ontology evolution and merging and,consequently, in the automation of the task of ontology maintenance on the Semantic Web.

Acknowledgments

The authors would like to thank Thomas Studer for his example in section 3.1, which resolved a long-standing issue.

References

1. Alchourron, C., Gärdenfors, P., Makinson, D.: On the Logic of Theory Change: Partial Meet Contraction and Revision Functions. Journal of Symbolic Logic 50 (1985) 510-530
2. Baader, F., Sattler, U.: An Overview of Tableau Algorithms for Description Logics. Studia Logica 69 (2001) 5-40
3. Baader, F., Calvanese, D., McGuinness, D., Nardi, D., Patel-Schneider, P. (eds.): The Description Logic Handbook: Theory, Implementation and Applications. Cambridge University Press (2002)
4. Baader, F., Horrocks, I., Sattler, U.: Description Logics as Ontology Languages for the Semantic Web. In Hutter, D., Stephan, W. (eds.): Festschrift in honor of Jörg Siekmann, Lecture Notes in Artificial Intelligence, Springer-Verlag (2003)
5. Dean, D., Schreiber, G., Bechhofer, S., Van Harmelen, F., Hendler, J., Horrocks, I., McGuiness, D., Patel-Schneider, P., Stein, L.A.: OWL Web Ontology Language Reference. W3C Recommendation (2004). Available at URL: http://www.w3.org/TR/owl-ref/
6. Flouris, G., Plexousakis, D., Antoniou, G.: AGM Postulates in Arbitrary Logics: Initial Results and Applications. Technical Report FORTH-ICS/TR-336, April 2004
7. Flouris, G., Plexousakis, D., Antoniou, G.: Generalizing the AGM Postulates: Preliminary Results and Applications. In Proceedings of the 10th International Workshop on Non-Monotonic Reasoning (2004) 171-179
8. Gärdenfors, P.: Belief Revision: An Introduction. In Gärdenfors, P., (ed.) Belief Revision, Cambridge University Press (1992) 1-20
9. Hansson, S. O.: Knowledge-level Analysis of Belief Base Operations. Artificial Intelligence 82 (1996) 215-235
10. Horrocks, I., Patel-Schneider, P.: Reducing OWL Entailment to Description Logic Satisfiability. Journal of Web Semantics, 1(4) (2004) 345-357
11. Hustadt, U., Schmidt, R.A.: Issues of Decidability for Description Logics in the Framework of Resolution. In Automated Deduction in Classical and Non-Classical Logics, vol. 1761, LNAI, Springer, (2000) 191-205
12. Kang, S.H., Lau, S.K.: Ontology Revision Using the Concept of Belief Revision. In Proceedings of the 8th International Conference on Knowledge-Based Intelligent Information and Engineering Systems (2004) 8-15
13. Lee, K., Meyer, T.: A Classification of Ontology Modification. In Proceedings of the 17th Australian Joint Conference on Artificial Intelligence (2004) 248-258, Cairns, Australia
14. Lutz, C., Sattler, U.: Mary Likes All Cats. In Proceedings of the 2000 International Workshop in Description Logics (2000) 213-226

15. Makinson, D.: On the Status of the Postulate of Recovery in the Logic of Theory Change. Journal of Philosophical Logic 16 (1987) 383-394

16. Meyer, T., Lee, K., Booth, R.: Knowledge Integration for Description Logics. In Proceedings of the 7th International Symposium on Logical Formalizations of Commonsense Reasoning (2005)

17. Stojanovic, L., Maedche, A., Motik, B., Stojanovic, N.: User-driven Ontology Evolution Management. In Proceedings of the 13th International Conference on Knowledge Engineering and Knowledge Management, vol. 2473, LNCS, Springer-Verlag, (2002) 285-300

A General Diagnosis Method for Ontologies

Gerhard Friedrich and Kostyantyn Shchekotykhin

Universitaet Klagenfurt, Universitaetsstrasse 65,
9020 Klagenfurt, Austria, Europe
firstname.lastname@ifit.uni-klu.ac.at

Abstract. The effective debugging of ontologies is an important prerequisite for their successful application and impact on the semantic web. The heart of this debugging process is the diagnosis of faulty knowledge bases. In this paper we define general concepts for the diagnosis of ontologies. Based on these concepts, we provide correct and complete algorithms for the computation of minimal diagnoses of knowledge bases. These concepts and algorithms are broadly applicable since they are independent of a particular variant of an underlying logic (with monotonic semantics) and independent of a particular reasoning system. The practical feasibility of our method is shown by extensive test evaluations.

1 Introduction

Ontologies are playing a key role for the successful implementation of the Semantic Web. Various languages for the specification of ontologies were proposed. The W3C Web Ontology working group has developed OWL [1] which is currently the language of choice for expressing Semantic Web ontologies. In fact OWL consists of three languages of increasing expressive power: OWL Lite, OWL DL and OWL Full. For the two decidable languages OWL Lite and OWL DL the strong relation to description logics was shown in [2]. OWL Lite and OWL DL are basically very expressive description logics built upon RDF Schema. Based on these methods efficient reasoning services for OWL Lite can be provided by systems like RACER [3].

Hand in hand with the increase of applications of ontologies and their growing size, the support of ontology development becomes an important issue for a broad and successful technology adoption. In the development phase of ontologies, testing and debugging is a major activity. Testing validates if the actual knowledge base matches the intended meaning of the knowledge engineer. In case of errors, the knowledge engineer has to debug the knowledge base. In this debugging process, the knowledge base must be diagnosed and changed such that all test cases are successfully passed. Consequently, the diagnosis process has to identify sets of axioms (preferable minimal sets) which should be changed in order to match the requirements expressed in tests.

In order to support the debugging process current work focuses on the identification of sets of axioms which are responsible for an incoherent (rsp. inconsistent) knowledge base [4, 5]. We enhance current techniques in several lines.

First, we will provide a general definition of the diagnosis problem employing a broadly accepted theory of diagnosis. On the bases of this theory we introduce test

Y. Gil et al. (Eds.): ISWC 2005, LNCS 3729, pp. 232–246, 2005.

cases which allow the knowledge engineer to formulate application specific requirements. Furthermore, this general theory of diagnosis allows the diagnosis of incoherent and inconsistent knowledge bases which comprise both terminological and assertional axioms. Second, we will show that concepts introduced in [4] are special cases of the proposed diagnosis theory. In addition, we argue that the concept of *minimal diagnoses* should be preferred over *cores*, if the goal is to find minimal changes of the knowledge base. Third, we provide correct and complete algorithms for the computation of minimal diagnoses. These algorithms are independent of a particular variant of a logic with monotonic semantics and work with arbitrary reasoning systems. Forth, we evaluate our algorithms employing standard test libraries showing the feasibility of our methods.

The reminder of the paper is organized as follows: In order to make the paper self contained Section 2 provides a brief introduction to the main concepts of description logic. Section 3 presents an introductory example for the diagnosis of ontologies. The basic concepts and properties of our approach are introduced in Section 4. Section 5 describes the algorithms for the computation of minimal diagnoses and minimal conflicts, followed by the presentation of our evaluation results in Section 6. The paper closes with a discussion of related work.

2 Description Logics

Since the underlying knowledge representation method of ontologies in the Semantic Web is based on description logics we introduce briefly the main concepts. For our investigation we employ the usual definition of description logics as defined in [6, 7]. A knowledge base comprises two components a TBox (terminology $\mathcal{T}$) and a ABox ($\mathcal{A}$). The TBox defines the terminology whereas the Abox contains assertions about named individuals in terms of a vocabulary defined in the TBox. The vocabulary consists of concepts, denoting sets of individuals, and roles, denoting binary relationships between individuals. These concepts and roles may be either atomic or complex. Complex descriptions are obtained by employing description operators. The language of descriptions is defined recursively by starting from a schema $S = (\mathcal{CN}, \mathcal{RN}, \mathcal{IN})$ of disjoint sets of names for concepts, roles, and individuals. Typical operators for the construction of complex descriptions are $C \sqcup D$ (disjunction), $C \sqcap D$ (conjunction), $\neg C$ (negation), $\forall R.C$ (concept value restriction), and $\exists R.C$ (concept exists restriction), where C and D are concept descriptions and $R \in \mathcal{RN}$.

Knowledge bases are defined by a finite set of assertions. Assertions regarding the TBox are called terminological axioms. Assertions regarding the ABox are called assertional axioms. Terminological axioms are expressed by $C \sqsubseteq D$ (Generalized Concept Inclusion) which corresponds to the logical implication. Let $a, b \in \mathcal{IN}$ be individual names then $C(a)$ and $R(a, b)$ are assertional axioms.

Concepts (rsp. roles) can be regarded as unary (rsp. binary) predicates. Roughly speaking description logics can be seen as fragments of first-order predicate logic (without considering transitive closure or special fixpoint semantics). These fragments are specifically designed to assure decidability or favorable computational costs.

The semantics of description terms are usually given denotationally using an interpretation $\mathcal{I} = \langle \Delta^{\mathcal{I}}, (\cdot)^{\mathcal{I}} \rangle$, where $\Delta^{\mathcal{I}}$ is a domain (non-empty universe) of values, and

$(\cdot)^{\mathcal{I}}$ a mapping from concept descriptions to subsets of the domain, and from role descriptions to sets of 2-tuples over the domain. The mapping also associates with every individual name in $\mathcal{IN}$ some value in $\Delta^{\mathcal{I}}$.

An interpretation $\mathcal{I}$ is a model of a knowledge base iff it satisfies all terminological axioms and assertional axioms. A knowledge base is satisfiable iff there exists a model.

A description E is coherent w.r.t. a TBox $\mathcal{T}$, if there exists a model $\mathcal{I}$ of $\mathcal{T}$ such that $E^{\mathcal{I}} \neq \emptyset$. A TBox is incoherent iff there exists an incoherent concept or role.

3   Example

For the debugging of a knowledge base KB, we distinguish two basic operations. The first operation is the deletion of axioms and the second operation deals with the addition of axioms. Changes of axioms can be viewed as combined add/delete operations. Diagnosis deals with the first operation, i.e. the identification of axioms which must be changed (deleted) whereas repair deals with the addition of appropriate axioms.

Knowledge bases are designed in order to provide reasoning services. In classical logical systems such reasoning services assume a satisfiable knowledge base. Consequently, restoring consistency of unsatisfiable knowledge bases is a major goal in debugging. In addition, the coherence of knowledge bases may be required.

Furthermore, knowledge bases may be tested by employing test cases. These test cases are formulated by the knowledge engineer and define requirements for the knowledge base. A test case is a set of test axioms. For example, we may exploit assertional axioms to validate a knowledge base. In the configuration domain we may test the knowledge base if a set of requirements (a set of key components) leads to an intended configuration which assures certain properties.

Let us assume we test the following knowledge base KB_E which is a variant of the example provided by [4].

$ax_1 : A_1 \sqsubseteq \neg A \sqcap A_2 \sqcap A_3$	$ax_2 : A_2 \sqsubseteq \neg D \sqcap A_4$
$ax_3 : A_3 \sqsubseteq A_4 \sqcap A_5$	$ax_4 : A_4 \sqsubseteq \forall s.F \sqcap C$
$ax_5 : A_5 \sqsubseteq \exists s.\neg F$	$ax_6 : A_6 \sqsubseteq A_4 \sqcap D$

In addition, we define a background theory $B_E = \{A_6(w), A_1(u), s(u, v)\}$ which is considered as correct.

In the following we assume that the knowledge engineer formulates requirements (test axioms). The goal of the diagnosis process is to find subsets of axioms which *must* be changed such that all requirements (test cases) can be met. We will characterize these sets of axioms by minimal (irreducible) sets. Of course the knowledge engineer may decide to change supersets of these minimal sets, e.g. because the knowledge base should reflect the mental model of the knowledge engineer as close as possible. However, the incorporation of mental models for generating diagnoses and repairs is out of the scope of this paper. Therefore, we use symbols in our example that have no predefined intended interpretation. The intended interpretation is solely defined by the knowledge base and the test cases.

Let us assume we require a coherent knowledge base (Requirement 1). In our example the knowledge base is incoherent (i.e. A_1 and A_3 are incoherent). The irreducible set of axioms which preserves the incoherence of the knowledge base is $\langle ax3, ax4, ax5 \rangle$[1] (i.e. A_3 is incoherent). It follows that at least one of these axioms must be changed in order to fulfill Requirement 1.

If we in addition require that $KB_E \cup B_E$ is consistent with the assertional test axiom $\neg C(w)$ (Requirement 2) then an additional irreducible set of axioms of the knowledge base which is unsatisfiable with the test axiom is $\langle ax4, ax6 \rangle$. Similar to the previous case, one of these axioms must be changed. In order to achieve satisfiability and coherence with *minimal* changes, we have to change at least either axiom $ax4$ or the axioms $[ax3, ax6]$ or $[ax5, ax6]$.

Let us assume Requirement 3 says that $F(v)$ must be unsatisfiable with $KB_E \cup B_E$. In case where we consider $ax4$ to be faulty, then it is possible to fulfill all the requirements, i.e. we can delete $ax4$ and find an extension of KB_E to satisfy all requirements including Requirement 3. A trivial extension to satisfy Requirement 3 is to add $\neg F(v)$ to KB_E.

However, in the cases where we consider either $[ax3, ax6]$ or $[ax5, ax6]$ to be changed then all 3 requirements could not be satisfied since $KB_E \cup B_E - [ax3, ax6] \models F(v)$ and also $KB_E \cup B_E - [ax5, ax6] \models F(v)$. In order to satisfy Requirement 3 in addition to Requirements 1 and 2 one of the axioms in $\langle ax1, ax2, ax4 \rangle$ and in $\langle ax1, ax3, ax4 \rangle$ must be changed. Consequently, the minimal change in order to satisfy all requirements is to replace $ax4$ (e.g. by $A_4 \sqsubseteq \forall s.\neg F \sqcap \neg C$). All other *minimal* changes involve at least 3 axioms, e.g. $[ax1, ax3, ax6]$.

In the next section we will develop a general theory for the diagnosis of logic-based ontologies.

4   Diagnosis of Ontologies

The goal of the diagnosis process is to identify those axioms which cause faults. Such axioms are considered as the cause of faults iff the knowledge base without these axioms is not faulty. What is regarded as fault depends on properties defined by the knowledge engineer. In knowledge bases which are based on logical descriptions usually satisfiability is a necessary property. In addition the knowledge engineer may specify a test case by a set of axioms. In the following we regard these axioms as correct. Of course the formulation of these test cases is restricted by the expressive power of the underlying language.

Let the set of test cases TST be partitioned in 4 disjoint sets TC^+, TC^-, TI^+, and TI^-. We can distinguish four different scenarios for testing.

1. $KB \cup e^+$ consistent, $\forall e^+ \in TC^+$
2. $KB \cup e^-$ inconsistent, $\forall e^- \in TC^-$
3. $KB \models ne^-, \forall ne^- \in TI^-$
4. $KB \not\models ne^+, \forall ne^+ \in TI^+$

---

[1] According to the terminology used in model-based diagnosis such a set is called a conflict set. For denoting conflict sets (rsp. diagnoses) we use the notation $\langle ... \rangle$ (rsp. $[...]$) employed in model-based diagnosis.

By exploiting negation the third case is equivalent to the second by checking if $KB \cup \neg ne^-$ is unsatisfiable. Likewise, the forth case can be reduced to the first case by checking if $KB \cup \neg ne^+$ is satisfiable. Therefore, (without limiting the generality) we will consider only cases 1 and 2.

Please note that requiring coherence of a knowledge base corresponds to the specification of appropriate test axioms. Formulated in predicate logic this means we require $\{\{\exists X : C(X)\}|C \in \mathcal{CN}\}$ as a set of test axioms contained in TC^+. For presentation purposes we refer to this set of axioms by ax_{co}. For the coherence of roles (e.g. for DLs with role constructors) ax_{ro} is $\{\{\exists X, Y : r(X,Y)\}|r \in \mathcal{RN}\}$.

In the following we will extend the approach of diagnosing configuration knowledge bases presented in [8] to logical knowledge bases. In addition, we will allow the definition of a background theory (represented as a set of axioms) which is considered to be correct. One reason for the introduction of a background theory is, that during the debugging process, the knowledge engineer may define some axioms as correct and therefore these axioms should not be included in any diagnoses.

Definition 1. KB-Diagnosis Problem: *A KB-Diagnosis Problem (Diagnosis Problem for a Knowledge Base) is a tuple (KB, B, TC^+, TC^-) where KB is a knowledge base, B a background theory, TC^+ is a set of positive and TC^- a set of negative test cases. The test cases are given as sets of logical sentences. We assume that each test case on its own is consistent.*

The principle idea of the following definition is to find a set of axioms of the knowledge base which must be changed (respectively deleted) and, eventually, some axioms must be added such that all test cases are satisfied.

Definition 2. KB-Diagnosis: *A KB-Diagnosis for a KB-Diagnosis Problem (KB, B, TC^+, TC^-) is a set $S \subseteq KB$ of sentences such that there exists an extension EX, where EX is a set of logical sentences added to the knowledge base, such that*

1. $(KB - S) \cup B \cup EX \cup e^+$ *consistent* $\forall e^+ \in TC^+$
2. $(KB - S) \cup B \cup EX \cup e^-$ *inconsistent* $\forall e^- \in TC^-$

Note, that an extension may be needed to achieve inconsistency with the test cases of TC^-. If we assume that we are interested in minimal changes of the existing axioms (i.e. it is more likely that an axiom is correct than it is incorrect) then we are especially interested in minimal (irreducible) diagnoses. In addition, these minimal diagnoses are exploited to characterize the set of all diagnoses.

Definition 3. Minimal KB-Diagnosis: *A KB-Diagnosis S for a KB-Diagnosis Problem (KB, B, TC^+, TC^-) is minimal iff there is no proper subset $S' \subset S$ s.t. S' is a diagnosis.*

Definition 4. Minimum cardinality KB-Diagnosis: *A KB-Diagnosis S for a KB-Diagnosis Problem (KB, B, TC^+, TC^-) is a minimum cardinality diagnosis iff there is no diagnosis S' s.t. $|S'| < |S|$.*

In the following we assume the monotonic semantics of standard logic. A diagnosis will always exist under the (reasonable) condition that background theory, positive test cases, and negative test cases do not interfere with each other. The following proposition allows us to characterize diagnoses without the extension EX. The idea is to use the negative examples to define this extension.

Proposition 1. *Given a KB-Diagnosis Problem* (KB, B, TC^+, TC^-), *a diagnosis* S *for* (KB, B, TC^+, TC^-) *exists iff* $\forall e^+ \in TC^+ : e^+ \cup B \cup \bigwedge_{e^- \in TC^-} (\neg e^-)$ *is consistent.*

From here on, we refer to the conjunction of all negated negative test cases as NE, i.e. $NE = \bigwedge_{e^- \in TC^-} (\neg e^-)$.

Corollary 1. S *is a diagnosis for* (KB, B, TC^+, TC^-) *iff* $\forall e^+ \in TC^+ : (KB - S) \cup B \cup e^+ \cup NE$ *is consistent.*

Example: Let $TC^+{}_E = \{\{\neg C(w)\} \cup ax_{co}\}$ and $TC^-{}_E = \{\{F(v)\}\}$. The minimal diagnoses of $(KB_E, B_E, TC^+{}_E, TC^-{}_E)$ are $[ax4]$, $[ax1, ax3, ax6]$, $[ax1, ax5, ax6]$, and $[ax2, ax3, ax6]$.

As a consequence, every superset of a minimal diagnosis is a diagnosis. Therefore, the set of all diagnoses is characterized by the set of minimal diagnoses, i.e. at least the elements of a minimal diagnosis must be changed.

In order to compute minimal diagnoses we exploit the concept of conflict sets.

Definition 5. *Conflict Set: A conflict set* CS *for* (KB, B, TC^+, TC^-) *is a set of elements of the knowledge base* $CS \subseteq KB$ *such that* $\exists e^+ \in TC^+ : CS \cup B \cup e^+ \cup NE$ *is inconsistent.*

Definition 6. *Minimal Conflict Set: A conflict set* CS *for* (KB, B, TC^+, TC^-) *is minimal iff there is no proper subset* $CS' \subset CS$ *s.t.* CS' *is a conflict.*

Example: The minimal conflict sets for $(KB_E, B_E, TC^+{}_E, TC^-{}_E)$ are $\langle ax3, ax4, ax5 \rangle$, $\langle ax4, ax6 \rangle$, $\langle ax1, ax2, ax4 \rangle$, and $\langle ax1, ax3, ax4 \rangle$.

The following proposition (which follows from results of [9]) shows the relation between minimal conflict sets and minimal diagnoses. It is based on the observation that at least one element from each minimal conflict must be changed.

Proposition 2. *Provided that there exists a diagnosis for* (KB, B, TC^+, TC^-). S *is a minimal diagnosis for* (KB, B, TC^+, TC^-) *iff* S *is a minimal hitting set for the set of all minimal conflict sets of* (KB, B, TC^+, TC^-).

For the debugging of incoherent TBoxes without test cases and background theory [4] introduces the concept of *minimal incoherence-preserving sub-TBox (MIPS)* which corresponds to the concept of *conflict sets* (see [9]) of model-based diagnosis.

Definition 7. *Minimal incoherence-preserving sub-TBox [4]: Let* T *be an incoherent TBox. A TBox* $T' \subseteq T$ *is a minimal incoherence-preserving sub-TBox (MIPS) of* T *if* T' *is incoherent, and every sub-TBox* $T'' \subset T'$ *is coherent.*

Let $TC^+{}_{MIPS} = ax_{co} \cup ax_{ro}$.

Proposition 3. *Let $\mathcal{T}$ be the TBox of a knowledge base KB. M is a MIPS of $\mathcal{T}$ iff M is minimal conflict set of $(\mathcal{T}, \emptyset, TC^+{}_{MIPS}, \emptyset)$.*

Based on the concept of MIPS [4] defines the concept of *cores*. Cores are sets of axioms occurring in several of these incoherent TBoxes. The rational is that the more MIPS such a core belongs to, the more likely its axioms will be the cause of contradictions. Similar ideas (however with a different intention) were formulated in [10].

Definition 8. *MIPS-Core [4]: Let $\mathcal{T}$ be a TBox. A non-empty intersection of n different MIPS of the MIPS of $\mathcal{T}$ (with $n \geq 1$) is called a MIPS-core of arity n for $\mathcal{T}$.*

Under the assumption that the correctness of axioms is more likely than their faultiness, we are interested in minimal diagnoses with a small cardinality. These minimal diagnoses define minimal sets of axioms to be changed. Unfortunately elements of cores with maximal arity may not be included in such diagnoses.

Remark 1. Let $CORE$ be a core of $\mathcal{T}$ with maximal arity. Let $MINDIAG$ be the set of minimal cardinality diagnoses of $(\mathcal{T}, \emptyset, TC^+{}_{MIPS}, \emptyset)$. It could be the case that $CORE$ does not contain any element of any minimal cardinality diagnosis, i.e. $CORE \cap S_i = \emptyset$ for all $S_i \in MINDIAG$.

Example: Consider the minimal conflict sets C_1:$\langle a, d\rangle$, C_2:$\langle b, e\rangle$, C_3:$\langle c, f\rangle$, C_4:$\langle a, x\rangle$, C_5:$\langle b, x\rangle$, and C_6:$\langle c, x\rangle$. The arity of core $\{x\}$ is 3 (maximal). All other cores have a lower arity than 3. However, the set of minimal cardinality diagnoses is $\{[a, b, c]\}$. x is only contained in minimal diagnoses with cardinality 4, e.g. $[x, d, e, f]$.
Consequently, cores may point to axioms which need not be changed. In order to discover a minimal number of axioms which must be changed, we therefore propose the computation of minimal diagnoses. Of course the knowledge engineer might decide to change additional axioms based on her design goals (e.g. readability of the knowledge base).

5 Computing Minimal Diagnoses

For the computation of minimal diagnoses one of our major design goal is generality of our methods. In particular, our only prerequisite is a reasoning system which correctly outputs *consistent* (rsp. *inconsistent*) if a set of sentences is consistent (rsp. inconsistent). Consequently, we neither employ any restriction regarding the variant of a knowledge representation language (based on the standard monotonic semantics) nor restrictions on the knowledge bases (e.g. acyclic).

The principle idea of our approach is to employ Reiter's Hitting Set (HS) algorithm [9] for the computation of a HS-tree. However, this algorithm has the drawback that it degrades rapidly if the underlying reasoning system does not output minimal conflict sets. In the worst case some minimal diagnoses may be missed as pointed out by [11] who proposed a DAG-variant of the original algorithm. However, the DAG-variant does not solve the computational problems in case a reasoning system does not output minimal conflict sets (or close approximations of them). Therefore, we apply methods proposed in [12] to compute minimal conflict sets which allow us to use the original (and simpler) variant of Reiter's diagnosis methods.

For the computation of the HS-tree we employ a labeling that is similar to the original HS-tree. See Figure 1 for the HS-tree of our example. Nodes are labeled either by a minimal conflict set or by *consistent* ($\sqrt{}$). Closed branches are marked by ×. If a node n is labeled by a minimal conflict set $CS(n)$ then for each $s \in CS(n)$, edges are leading away from n which are labeled by s. The set of edge labels on the path leading from the root to node n is referred to as $H(n)$. If there does not exist a conflict set, the root is labeled by *consistent*. A node n must be labeled by a minimal conflict set CS if there exists a minimal conflict set CS s.t. $CS \cap H(n) = \emptyset$, otherwise this node is labeled by *consistent*.

The HS-tree is computed as follows by the application of pruning rules. The result is a pruned HS-tree which contains also closed branches. The HS-tree is a directed tree from the root to the leaves.

- If no diagnosis exists stop with exception. I.e. there is a $e^+ \in TC^+$ s.t. $e^+ \cup B \cup NE$ is inconsistent.
- Generate the HS-tree in breath-first order, level by level.
- Try to generate a minimal conflict set CS for the root node. Label the root with this conflict set, if such a conflict set exists. Otherwise, label the root with *consistent*. In this case return no fault was discovered.
- If a node n' (other than the root) has to be labeled:

  1. If a node n is labeled by *consistent* and $H(n) \subseteq H(n')$ close n', no successors are generated.
  2. If node n has been generated and $H(n) = H(n')$ then close n'.
  3. If there exists a node n labeled by $CS(n)$ s.t. $CS(n) \cap H(n') = \emptyset$ then reuse $CS(n)$ to label n'.
  4. Otherwise try to generate a *minimal* conflict set $CS(n')$ for n' s.t. $CS(n') \cap H(n') = \emptyset$. Label n' with this conflict set, if such a conflict set exists. Otherwise, label n' with *consistent*.

The leaf nodes of such a pruned HS-tree are either closed nodes or nodes labeled with *consistent*. Let n be a node labeled with *consistent* then $H(n)$ is a minimal diagnosis. Since the HS-tree is computed in breath-first order, minimal diagnoses are generated with increasing cardinality. Consequently, for the generation of all minimum cardinality diagnoses only the first level of the HS-tree has to be generated, where a node is labeled with *consistent*.

For the generation of minimal conflict sets we employ a simplified variant of QUICKXPLAIN [12] (i.e. no preferences are considered). QUICKXPLAIN takes as inputs two sets of sentences. The first set is a knowledge base (KB) and the second set is a background theory (B). If the knowledge base joined with the background theory is consistent QUICKXPLAIN outputs *consistent*. If the background theory is inconsistent the output is $\emptyset$. Otherwise, the output is a minimal conflict set $CS \subseteq KB$ (w.r.t. a background theory). QUICKXPLAIN operates on a divide and conquer strategy where

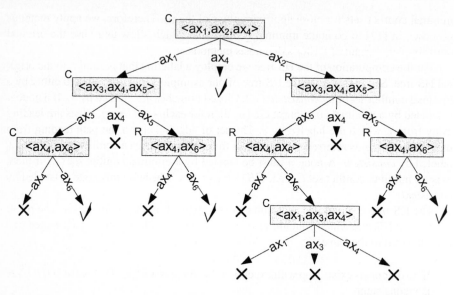

Fig. 1. HS-tree for the example given in Section 3. Closed branches are marked with ×. Computed minimal conflict sets are marked with C. Reused minimal conflict sets are marked with R. Consistent nodes are marked with √.

a sequence of calls to a consistency checker is performed in order to minimize the conflict sets. If this divide and conquer strategy splits the knowledge base in half, QUICK-XPLAIN needs $log_2(n/k) + 2k$ calls in the best case and $2k \cdot log_2(n/k) + 2k$ in the worst case where k is the length of the minimal conflict and n is the number of axioms in the knowledge base.

In order to generate a minimal conflict set for a node n, we have to check if there exists an $e^+ \in TC^+$ s.t. $(KB - H(n)) \cup B \cup e^+ \cup NE$ is inconsistent (i.e. $KB - H(n)$ contains a conflict set). For the calls to QUICKXPLAIN $KB - H(n)$ plays the role of the knowledge base and $B \cup e^+ \cup NE$ is considered as background theory. Note that an e^+ which is consistent with $(KB - H(n)) \cup B \cup NE$ need not be reconsidered for any successor n' of n since $H(n) \subset H(n')$. Therefore, we store for each node n all e^+ which were found to be consistent with $(KB - H(n)) \cup B \cup NE$ in the set $CE(n)$. For the generation of a label for n' we only need to check if there is an $e^+ \in \{TC^+ - \cup_{m \in predecessor(n')} CE(m)\}$ which is inconsistent with $(KB - H(n')) \cup B \cup NE$. The correctness and completeness of the generation of minimal diagnoses follows by the correctness and completeness of the HS-tree algorithm, QUICKXPLAIN, and the consistency checker.

Many factors are influencing the execution time of computing minimal diagnoses. The critical task of computing minimal conflict sets is dominated by the costs of consistency checking which strongly depend on the knowledge representation language as well as the actual content of the knowledge base. Finding a minimal diagnosis corresponds to a depth first construction of the HS-tree and therefore $|MD| + 1$ calls to QUICKXPLAIN are needed where $|MD|$ is the cardinality of this minimal diagnosis.

However, we can construct cases where even the number of minimum cardinality diagnoses grows exponential in the problem size. Therefore, in practice the problem is simplified.

Diagnosis and conflict generation is exploited to guide further discrimination and repair actions. Therefore, only a set of *leading diagnoses* is generated which is a trade off between computational costs and further costs for diagnoses discrimination. Such actions may comprise additional tests, validation of axioms, and incremental repair. The definition of leading diagnoses is problem specific, e.g. a subset of minimal cardinality diagnoses. If necessary, the knowledge engineer can interrupt the generation of minimal diagnoses at any time and exploit the minimal conflicts and (partial) diagnoses found so far for further actions [13].

The execution time strongly depends on the actual diagnosis problem. In particular, computing minimal diagnoses (i.e. the HS-tree construction) significantly depends on the cardinality of the minimal diagnoses, the cardinality of minimal conflict sets, their reuse for constructing the HS-tree, and the actual costs of consistency checking. We therefore conducted various experiments in order to evaluate the execution time behavior for frequently used test ontologies.

6 Evaluation

The algorithms described above are implemented in JAVA (Version 1.5.01). For the consistency (coherence) checks we employed RACER (Version 1.7.23). The tests were performed on a PC (Intel Pentium M 1.8 GHz) with 1 GB RAM. The operating system was Windows XP Prof SP2. The results of our tests are depicted in Table 1. For these tests we employed the test knowledge bases bike2 to bike9, bcs3, galen, and galen3 provided at RACER's download site.[2]

For each test we randomly altered the knowledge bases. The result of each single alteration is an incoherent knowledge base. In order to introduce an incoherency we randomly picked two concepts where one concept subsumes the other (exploiting the taxonomy). In a next step, axioms which define these concepts were extended such that disjointness of these two concepts is enforced. An incoherent concept is the result. Consequently, every alteration will introduce at least one conflict set. However, since the introduction of these conflict sets is randomly performed there might be more but also less *minimal* conflict sets than the number of alterations.

The diagnosis task is to find minimal diagnoses in order to restore coherence. We did not provide a background theory and negative test cases because this corresponds just to additional axioms for consistency checks. The number of axioms (ax) for each knowledge base (including alterations) is stated in Table 1.

In order to provide realistic test cases from an application point of view we define a set of leading diagnoses. This set of leading diagnoses comprises the set of minimum cardinality (MC) diagnoses where we consider at most 10 diagnoses.

Note that in the worst case even the output of a single minimal conflict supports further actions for localizing faulty axioms. However, the generation of additional (minimal) diagnoses reduces the costs of actions for diagnoses discrimination and repair.

---

[2] http://racer-systems.com/products/download/index.phtml

Table 1. Test results for diagnosing faulty knowledge bases. Columns are: number of axioms contained in minimum cardinality diagnoses ($|D|$), number of minimum cardinality diagnoses (# D, at most 10), number of minimal conflict sets computed (# C), cardinality of smallest minimal conflict set (min$|C|$), cardinality of largest minimal conflict set (max$|C|$), number of QUICKX-PLAIN calls (QX), number of coherence checks (# CH), total time for discovering the first minimum cardinality diagnosis (FDT), total time for discovering the first minimal conflict set (FCT), total time for performing coherence checks (COT), total time for computing leading diagnoses (TT). Time is measured in seconds.

KB		$|D|$	# D	# C	min $|C|$	max $|C|$	QX	# CH	FDT	FCT	COT	TT
bike2	min	3	6	4	2	6	10	134	23	7,1	27,4	35
154 ax	avg	3,7	8,7	5	2,1	4	13,7	181	47,5	8,3	44,2	55
	max	4	10	7	2	4	17	284	61,4	10,1	62,3	77
bike3	min	4	10	4	3	3	14	120	16,3	3,4	16,2	19
109 ax	avg	4,5	9,2	5,6	2,6	3	14,9	164	22,4	3,4	25,5	29
	max	4	6	7	2	3	13	202	22,4	4,3	31,7	37
bike4	min	3	10	4	3	4	14	162	52,3	12,5	53,1	58
166 ax	avg	3,6	9,6	5,9	2,6	5	15,5	244	71,1	12,1	76,7	84
	max	4	10	8	3	10	18	358	83,3	13,4	104	115
bike5	min	1	1	3	3	4	4	131	40,6	20,1	56	60
184 ax	avg	2,6	5,9	4,6	2,9	3,9	10,5	193	79,8	22	97,4	105
	max	3	7	6	3	4	13	247	90,7	21,6	135	145
bike6	min	1	1	3	3	4	4	137	54,3	26,3	75	80
207 ax	avg	3	7	5,1	2,8	4	12,1	220	108,5	25,3	127	135
	max	3	7	6	3	4	13	263	111,2	25,5	160	171
bike7	min	1	2	2	3	3	4	84	12,6	11,6	23,1	25
162 ax	avg	2,9	8,3	3,6	2,8	3	11,9	151	40	12,2	49,9	54
	max	3	8	5	2	3	13	186	57,3	12,9	67,7	73
bike8	min	2	4	3	2	3	7	104	33,7	17	50,4	54
185 ax	avg	3,2	8,9	4	2,7	3	12,9	172	59,7	17	72,7	79
	max	4	10	5	3	3	15	216	89,9	16,3	91,5	99
bike9	min	1	1	3	3	4	4	127	50,1	23,3	72,8	78
215 ax	avg	3,1	7,2	4,9	2,7	4	12,1	211	116,2	27,1	131	140
	max	4	10	5	3	4	15	218	242,6	28,5	243	253
bcs3	min	3	4	4	2	3	8	118	16,3	1	15,5	18
432 ax	avg	3,4	7,1	5,7	2	17,1	12,9	276	46,7	1	51,4	61
	max	4	10	9	2	51	19	968	251,7	1,2	232	269
galen	min	2	2	3	2	2	5	86	95,8	30,4	65,4	104
3963 ax	avg	2,3	3,1	3,2	2	2	6,4	104	172,4	41	125	227
	max	3	8	3	2	2	11	116	223,6	39,8	234	366
galen3	min	1	1	2	2	2	3	53	60	49,6	38,2	105
3927 ax	avg	2,2	3,6	3	2	2	6,6	94,7	157	34,4	93,2	203
	max	4	10	4	2	2	14	150	452,1	40,3	421	489

We therefore not only measured the total time for computing leading diagnoses (TT) and the total time for performing coherence checks (COT) but also the total time for discovering the first minimal conflict (FCT) and the first minimum cardinality diagnosis (FDT). Time is measured in seconds. In addition to time information we reported the number of axioms contained in minimum cardinality diagnoses ($|D|$), the number of minimum cardinality diagnoses (# D, at most 10), the number of QUICKXPLAIN calls (QX), the number of coherence checks (# CH), and the number of minimal conflicts (# C) computed by the algorithm in order to compute the leading diagnoses for each test case. Since the cardinality of the minimal conflict sets defines the branching of the HS-tree we reported the minimum cardinality ($\min|C|$) as well as the maximum cardinality ($\max|C|$) of these conflict sets.

For each knowledge base we performed 30 tests. Each test corresponds to 4 random alterations (i.e. 8 changes) in order to evaluate the algorithms for multiple failure scenarios. Table 1 shows the average values of the test results as well as the data for the test case with minimum TT and maximum TT. Note, that for these special test cases the data values may lie above or below the average case.

The algorithm correctly computes the necessary conflicts. As expected each minimal conflict contains two changed axioms (beside others). All computed diagnoses are correct minimum cardinality diagnoses. Furthermore we empirically checked the completeness of the set of minimum cardinality diagnoses. As expected, the execution time greatly depends on the number and costs of the consistency checks. The costs of consistency checks not only depend on the number of axioms but on the content of a knowledge base. E.g. let us compare the maximum time cases of bike9 and bcs3. Although bcs3 is two times larger than bike9 and we require roughly 4 times more coherence checks (# CH) for bcs3 the time spent for these checks (COT) is almost the same.

As mentioned in the previous section the execution time for finding minimal diagnoses depends on the actual diagnosis problem. E.g. knowledge bases with many failures result in deep HS-trees whereas knowledge bases with many dependencies between the axioms result in high cardinality minimal conflict sets. These conflict sets cause broad HS-trees. The generation of conflicts and diagnoses shows no irregularity except for the knowledge base bcs3, where the cardinality of the minimal conflicts may become large, i.e. there are many axioms contributing to an incoherence because of the high cyclical complexity. As expected the overall execution time increases. However, discovering the first minimal conflict takes approximately a second for bcs3. Note, that the output of minimal conflict sets is already a valuable help for debugging the knowledge base. Even for the galen knowledge bases (approximately 4000 axioms) computing the first minimal conflict set takes not longer than 50 seconds.

In addition, we can observe that in the average, discovering the first minimum cardinality diagnosis requires roughly 80% of the total execution time. Therefore, spending some additional computational resources after the discovery of the first minimum cardinality diagnosis may be appropriate. At this stage the reuse of minimal conflict sets saves computational costs significantly.

The execution time behavior of the proposed method can be regarded as very satisfying given the size of the knowledge bases. Without such a support, debugging becomes a very time consuming activity (e.g. locating multiple faults in hundreds or even thousands of axioms). Consequently, our tests show the practical applicability and utility of the proposed methods.

The integration of the consistency checker and QUICKXPLAIN is a source for improvements. If a consistency checker *efficiently* returns a set of axioms (i.e. a conflict, not necessarily minimal) involved in the generation of an inconsistency (incoherence) then this helps QUICKXPLAIN to reduce the number of consistency (coherence) checks. We recommend to implement this feature in consistency (coherence) checkers.

7   Related Work

Diagnosis is strongly related to the generation of explanations. In the description logic community the work on explanations was pioneered by [14] and further enhanced for tableaux-based systems [15]. The intention of this work is to provide the basis for "natural" explanations of subsumption inferences. In particular, their goal is to derive a sequence of rule applications (i.e. proof fragments) which serve as a basis for natural explanations. Our approach is different since we compute minimal diagnoses which can be regarded as sources for unwanted behavior. We think that the work in the area of generating understandable proofs can be excellently integrated in a diagnosis framework for the explanations of conflicts (e.g. why a set of axioms is inconsistent).

In the area of description logics, the work by [4] is most closely related to our methods. However, we generalize and unify their concepts with concepts of the theory of diagnosis. Compared to our approach [4] require unfoldable $\mathcal{ALC}$-TBoxes. Their computation methods are based on the construction of tableaus where formulas are labeled. This label holds the information which axioms are relevant for the closure of branches. In contrast to this approach, our proposal works for arbitrary reasoners. However, provided that the label generation is not too expensive, we can explore this label for limiting the number of consistency (coherence) checks in order to speed up the computation.

In the work of [5] simple debugging cues are proposed which are integrated in an ontology development environment based on Pellet (open-source OWL DL reasoner). The main focus of their work is to improve the interaction between the knowledge engineer and the ontology development systems by debugging features. Regarding diagnosis our approach adds functionality, since we provided a clear definition of diagnosis (which allows the incorporation of test cases) and the correct and complete computation of multi-fault diagnoses.

Additional important work on improving the quality of ontologies is performed by [16] and [17]. The basic idea of these approaches is to find general rules and guidelines which assess the quality of ontologies. Furthermore, properties are expressed which specify conditions which must hold for error free ontologies. Some of these conditions may be formulated as test cases, but there are conditions which require reasoning about the terminology. This is beyond the expressive power of most ontology languages and therefore cannot be specified as tests. However, one possible extension which could be investigated is to generate a logical description of an ontology and to apply the general diagnosis approach to this description.

Since our method deals with the diagnosis of descriptions, the work on model-based diagnosis of hardware designs [13, 18] and software [19] shows some similarities. However, the fundamental difference is that these approaches have to generate a (logical) model of the description whereas in our domain we can exploit the descriptions directly.

8   Conclusions

In this paper we have proposed a general diagnosis theory for a broad range of ontology description languages. These concepts allow the formulation of test cases and the diagnosis of arbitrary knowledge bases containing terminological and assertional axioms. Minimal diagnoses identify minimal changes of the knowledge base such that the requirements specified by test cases can be met. We have provided algorithms which are correct and complete regarding the generation of all minimal diagnoses. Our methods are broadly applicable since they operate with arbitrary reasoning frameworks which provide consistency (coherence) checks. The practical feasibility of our method was shown by extensive test evaluations.

Acknowledgments

We thank anonymous referees for valuable remarks. The research project is funded partly by grants from the Austrian Research Promotion Agency, Programm Line FIT-IT Semantic Systems (www.fit-it.at), Project AllRight, Contract 809261 and the European Union, Project WS-Diamond, Contract 516933.

References

1. Bechhofer, S., Harmelen, F., Hendler, J., Horrocks, I., McGuinness, D., Patel-Scheider, P., Stein, L.: OWL Web Ontology Language Reference. W3C Recommendation, available at http://www.w3.org/TR/2004/REC-owl-ref-20040210/. (2004)
2. Horrocks, I., Patel-Schneider, P.: Reducing OWL entailment to description logic satisfiability. J. of Web Semantics 1 (2004) 345–357
3. Haarslev, V., Möller, R.: High performance reasoning with very large knowledge bases: A practical case study. In: Proc. IJCAI 01, Seattle, WA, USA (2001) 161–168
4. Schlobach, S., Cornet, R.: Non-standard reasoning services for the debugging of description logic terminologies. In: Proc. IJCAI 03, Acapulco, Mexico (2003) 355–362
5. Parsion, B., Sirin, E., Kalyanpur, A.: Debugging owl ontologies. In: WWW 2005, Chiba, Japan, ACM (2005)
6. Borgida, A.: On the relative expressive power of description logics and predicate calculus. Artificial Intelligence **82** (1996) 353–367
7. Baader, F., Calvanese, D., McGuinness, D.L., Nardi, D., Patel-Schneider, P.F., eds.: The Description Logic Handbook: Theory, Implementation, and Applications. Cambridge University Press (2003)
8. Felfernig, A., Friedrich, G., Jannach, D., Stumptner, M.: Consistency-based diagnosis of configuration knowledge bases. Artificial Intelligence **152** (2004)
9. Reiter, R.: A theory of diagnosis from first principles. Artificial Intelligence **23** (1987) 57–95
10. Saraswat, V.A., de Kleer, J., Raiman, O.: Critical Reasoning. In: Proc. IJCAI 93. (1993) 18–23
11. Greiner, R., Smith, B.A., Wilkerson, R.W.: A correction to the algorithm in Reiter's theory of diagnosis. Artificial Intelligence **41** (1989) 79–88
12. Junker, U.: QUICKXPLAIN: Preferred explanations and relaxations for over-constrained problems. In: Proc. AAAI 04, San Jose, CA, USA (2004) 167–172

13. Friedrich, G., Stumptner, M., Wotawa, F.: Model-based diagnosis of hardware designs. Artificial Intelligence **111** (1999) 3–39
14. McGuinness, D.: Explaining Reasoning in Description Logics. PhD thesis, Department of Computer Science, Rutgers University (1996)
15. Borgida, A., Franconi, E., Horrocks, I., McGuinness, D.L., Patel-Schneider, P.F.: Explaining *ALC* subsumption. In: International Workshop on Description Logics, CEUR Workshop Proc. (CEUR-WS.org). Volume 22. (1999)
16. Guarino, N., Welty, C.: Evaluating Ontological Decisions with Ontoclean. Communications of the ACM **45** (2002) 61–65
17. Gómez-Pérez, A., Suárez-Figueroa, M.C.: Results of Taxonomic Evaluation of RDF(S) and DAML+OIL ontologies using RDF(S) and DAML+OIL Validation Tools and Ontology Platforms import services. In: Proceedings of the 2nd International Workshop on Evaluation of Ontology-based Tools, CEUR Workshop Proc. (CEUR-WS.org). Volume 87. (2003)
18. Wotawa, F.: Debugging VHDL designs: Introducing multiple models and first empirical results. Applied Intelligence **21** (2004) 159–172
19. Chen, R., Wotawa, F.: Exploiting alias information to fault localization for Java programs. In: International Conference on Computational Intelligence for Modelling Control and Automation (CIMCA2004), Gold Coast, Australia (2004)

Graph-Based Inferences in a Semantic Web Server for the Cartography of Competencies in a Telecom Valley

Fabien Gandon, Olivier Corby, Alain Giboin, Nicolas Gronnier, and Cecile Guigard

INRIA, ACACIA, 2004 rt des Luciole, BP93, 06902 Sophia Antipolis, France
Fabien.Gandon@sophia.inria.fr
http://www-sop.inria.fr/acacia/

Abstract. We introduce an experience in building a public semantic web server maintaining annotations about the actors of a Telecom Valley. We then focus on an example of inference used in building one type of cartography of the competences of the economic actors of the Telecom Valley. We detailed how this inference exploits the graph model of the semantic web using ontology-based metrics and conceptual clustering. We prove the characteristics of theses metrics and inferences and we give the associated interpretations.

1 Semantic Annotation of Competencies

In knowledge-based solutions, user interfaces have the tricky role of bridging the gap between complex knowledge representations underlying collective applications and focused views tuned to day-to-day uses. For this reason, we believe that interface design and knowledge representation must be tackled in parallel. In this paper, we describe and analyze an experience in simulating the inferences done by economists and management researchers in building a cartography of the competences of the economic actors of a region. The implementation is now part of a public semantic web server maintaining annotations about the actors of a telecom valley. This paper will explain how we designed such an inference using ontology-based metrics defined above the graph structure of the semantic web annotations statements, but before we go in such details we need to introduce the overall project: the Knowledge management Platform (KmP[1]) of the Telecom Valley of Sophia Antipolis[2].

The goal of KmP was the elaboration of a public repository supporting three application scenarios: (1) promoting the Scientific Park of Sophia Antipolis and its international development by providing the local institutions with a pertinent and up-to-date snapshot of the park. (2) facilitating partnerships between different industrial firms of the park. (3) facilitating collaboration on projects between industrial partners and the different research institutes. This platform is available online[3] and relies on a semantic web server publicly available for all the actors of the value chain of the Telecom Valley of Sophia Antipolis. The steering committee of KmP is composed of eleven pilot companies involved in the specifications of the application and the

---

[1] http://www-sop.inria.fr/acacia/soft/kmp.html
[2] http://www.sophia-antipolis.org/index1.htm
[3] http://beghin.inria.fr/

Y. Gil et al. (Eds.): ISWC 2005, LNCS 3729, pp. 247–261, 2005.
© Springer-Verlag Berlin Heidelberg 2005

population of the ontologies: Amadeus, Philips Semiconductors, France Telecom, Hewlett Packard, IBM, Atos Origin, Transiciel, Elan IT, Qwam System and Cross Systems.

KmP is a real world experiment on the design and usages of a customizable semantic web server to generate up-to-date views of the telecom valley and assist the management of competencies at the level of the organizations (companies, research institute and labs, clubs, associations, government agencies, schools and universities, etc.). This platform aims at increasing the portfolio of competences of the technological pole of Sophia Antipolis by helping companies, research labs and institutions express their interests and needs in a common space in order to foster synergies and partnerships. The platform implements a public knowledge management solution at the scale of the telecom valley based on a shared repository and a common language to describe and compare the needs and the resources of all the organizations.

Ontologies were built from models provided by domain experts [Lazaric & Thomas, 2005] and end-users: models of competencies, models of the telecom domains (networks, computer science, etc.), task models, value chain of the telecom valley, etc. The implementation merges the frameworks of the semantic web (RDF, RDFS), the classic web (HTML, CSS, SVG) and the structured web (XML, XSLT) to integrate data coming from very different sources, allow queries from different viewpoints, adapt content to users, analyze, group, infer and render indicators of the Telecom Valley situation. KMP relies on the integration of multiple components: databases for back-end persistence, web servers with JSP and servlets to provide front ends, and the CORESE semantic web server [Corby et al, 2004] to provide semantic web processing capabilities. Databases are used to store the different ontologies (e.g. ontology of technologies, of actions, of deliverables, of markets, of cooperation, etc.), the models (e.g. value chain of a telecom valley), and the users' data (e.g. descriptions of firms, research centers, competences, projects, etc.). Direct accesses and modifications of ontologies and other data are managed directly at the database level. Wrappers extract the relevant and authorized data from the databases and export them in RDF/S to feed CORESE as needed.

The platform integrates contributions coming from whole the Telecom Valley:

- several ontologies are populated and validated by multiple actors using interviews and brainstorming sessions animated by the local government administration[4].
- several sources of data are integrated: models provided by practitioners and researchers in management, descriptions of firms using industrial and economic markets vocabulary, description of research institutes using academic terms, etc.

The whole system relies on RDF, RDFS, and production rules [Corby et al, 2004] to describe the models and actors of the Telecom Valley. Exploiting this semantics the platform is able to:

- apply rules to enrich the different contributions and bridge the different viewpoints allowing a broad variety of queries and analysis to be run e.g. a set of rules generalize and group identical competences detailed in the profiles of the actors to provide statistics to researchers in management;

---

[4] http://www.telecom-valley.fr/index.php4?lang=ang

- exploit underlying models to propose graphic views of the Telecom Valley using XSLT to produce SVG rendering and combining on-the-fly models defined by the economists with data entered by the different actors; e.g. figure 1 shows an SVG interface to browse the value chain of the Telecom Valley and obtain statistics on the exchanges by clicking on the arrows. To each arrow is attached a query that CORESE solves against the RDF/S annotations of the Telecom Valley. For instance the screenshots shows statistics on the exchanges between two segments of the value chain (8b and 6a) and the distribution of these exchanges over the disjoint sub-classes of exchanges.
- apply complex query constructors to find partners, build consortiums, extract indicators, build statistics, sort and group results, find approximate answers, etc.
- apply clustering algorithms and produce graphic representations in SVG to allow institutional and industrial actors to get abstract views of the cartography of competences in the Telecom Valley;

	4	1	7b	2b	2a	8b	7a	5a	9	3	8a	6a	5b	6b	0
7b				3							3				
8b	14	1	7	5	6	19	7	7	3	6	19	12	18	11	8
9						1		1	26			1			1
8a			11					11	1	3	1	1	11	11	2
6a						4			1			16			4
5b									1		1				5

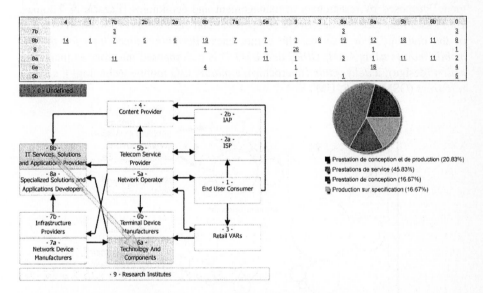

Fig. 1. SVG view of exchanges on the value chain of the Telecom Valley of Sophia Antipolis

In this article we focus on one inference supported by the graph models underlying this semantic web repository: an ontology-based conceptual clustering providing a customizable and up-to-date cartography of competences available in the telecom valley. Section 2 briefly introduces an extract of the domain models and the users' requirements. Section 3 details the inferences underlying this representation, in particular the ontology-based metrics exploiting the semantic web graph structures. Section 4 concludes with the evaluation of this representation.

2   Model-Based Automated Cartography of Competencies

The first requirement and scenario of KmP is "*to acquire and give a broader visibility of the community of the technological pole*". As part of its answers, the platform provides a dynamic up-to-date cartography of the competencies available in the technological pole and grouped in clusters.

In KmP, the overall design methodology was oriented toward use and users. We relied on participatory design involving end-users, domain experts, information management experts and knowledge modeling experts. A large part of the specifications relied on mock-ups of interfaces built from the visual representations the users are used to. In particular, figure 2 shows a draft made by users when making explicit their notion of competences; it shows what they called a "*readable representation of the clusters of competencies in the technological pole*".

The first consequence of such a readability requirement is a set of expressivity requirements on the ontology. The current model used in the project relies on an ontology that consists of more than a thousand concept types and a hundred relations. Central to the modeling is the concept of "competence" used by the organizations when describing their profiles or the profile of the partners they are looking for. The model proposed by researchers in management and economics [Lazaric & Thomas, 2005] uses four facets to describe a competence and each facet is formalized in a part of the ontology. For instance, the competence "*designing microchips for the 3G mobile market using GSM, GPRS and UMTS*" is decomposed into four elements: an *action* (design); a *deliverable* (microchip); a *market* (3G mobile technology); a set of *resources* (GSM, GPRS, UMTS).

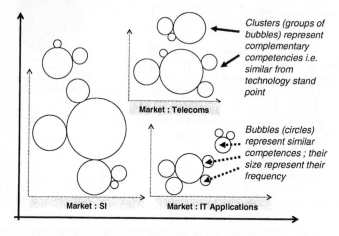

Fig. 2. Draft of a representation of clusters of competences

The second consequence of the readability requirement is the ability to simulate the inferences mobilized by the users when building this representation. The branch or the level of the ontology used to describe the situation is not always the same as the one used to display inference results. For instance, different users (e.g. industrialists vs. economists) may enter and use knowledge at different levels. In simple cases, we use rules close to Horn clauses to bridge these gaps. For the inferences behind the representation in Figure 2, the algorithm is much more complex and is a matter of conceptual clustering usually performed by economy and management analysts:

1. Analysts chose a market to which the analysis will be limited; all sub-types of this market will be considered, all ancestors or siblings will be discarded.
2. In this market, analysts group competences according to the *similarity* of their resources; a competence may have several resources (e.g. java, c, c++, project management) and one is chosen as the most representative (e.g. programming). This first grouping represents a *cluster*.
3. In each cluster, analysts group competences according to the *similarity* of their action (e.g. design) to form *bubbles*.

On the one hand we use ontology-based modeling to provide meaningful and dynamic representations (clusters as core competences of the technological pole) and on the other hand we need ontology-based inferences to automate this clustering (clusters as emergent structures in knowledge analysis). Questions associated to this problem include: what are the inferences underlying this representation? How can they be linked to semantic web models of the valley? How can we ensure that the clustering will be meaningful to the users?

In literature, the work on the formal side of the semantic web is largely influenced by the fact that logic-based languages are the most frequently used implementation formalisms. However, entailment is not the only product one should expect from a knowledge-based system, and the conceptual structures of the semantic Web can support a broad variety of inferences that goes far beyond logical deduction evening its simplest forms (RDF/S). Let us take the example of the class hierarchy which is considered to be the backbone of the RDFS schemata. The interpretation of the subsumption link is that the extension of a concept type (e.g. laptop) is a subset of the extension of another concept type (e.g. computer). What this logical implication hides is a graph structure that links the concept types through their *genus* and *differentia*. The graph structure of the semantic web formalisms supports inferences that go far beyond the set inclusion. The rest of this article shows how we designed such inferences to recreate the representation drafted in Figure 2 and how this specific example illustrates the richness of the underlying graph model of the semantic web.

3   Semantic Metrics to Visualize Knowledge

3.1   Semantic Metrics on the Ontological Space

The idea of evaluating conceptual relatedness from semantic networks representation dates back to the early works on simulating the humans' semantic memory [Quillian, 1968] [Collins & Loftus, 1975]. Relatedness of two concepts can take many forms for instance, functional complementarity (e.g. nail and hammer) or functional similarity (e.g. hammer and screwdriver). The latter example belongs to the family of semantic similarities where the relatedness of concepts is based on the definitional features they share (e.g. both the hammer and the screwdriver are hand tools). The natural structure supporting semantic similarities reasoning is the concept type hierarchy where subsumption links group types according to the characteristic they share. When applied to a semantic network using only subsumption links, the relatedness calculated by a spreading algorithm gives a form of semantic distance e.g. the early system of [Rada et al., 1989] defined a distance counting the minimum number of edges between two types.

We can identify two main trends in defining a semantic distance over a type hierarchy: (1) the approaches that include additional external information in the distance, e.g. statistics on the use of a concept; see for instance [Resnik, 1995] [Jiang & Conrath, 1997] (2) the approaches trying to rely solely on the structure of the hierarchy to tune the behavior of the distances [Rada et al., 1989][Wu & Palmer, 1994]. Including external information implies additional costs to acquire relevant and up-to-date information and furthermore, this information has to be available. Thus in a first approach we followed the second trend.

In the domain of Conceptual Graphs [Sowa, 1984], where the graph structure of knowledge representation is a core feature, a use for such a distance is to propose a non binary projection, i.e. a similarity $S:C^2 \rightarrow [0,1]$ where 1 is the perfect match and 0 the absolute mismatch. We used the CORESE platform provided by [Corby et al, 2004] to build our system. It is provided with an implementation of a depth-attenuated distance allowing approximate search. The distance between a concept and its father is given in (1):

$$dist\,(t,\,father\,(t)) = \left[\frac{1}{2}\right]^{depth\,(father\,(t))} \tag{1}$$

where $depth(t)$ is the depth of t in the ontology i.e. the number of edges on the shortest path from t to the root. In the rest of the article we will only consider tree structures (not latices in general) and therefore there will be one and only one directed path between a concept and one of its ancestors; thus the distance is:

$$dist(t_1,t_2) = \frac{1}{2^{depth(LCST(t_1,t_2))-2}} - \frac{1}{2^{depth(t_1)-1}} - \frac{1}{2^{depth(t_2)-1}} \tag{2}$$

where $LCST(t_1,t_2)$ is the least common supertype of the two concept types t_1 and t_2.

3.2 Ontological Granularity and Detail Level

The representation in Figure 2 shows that the way market analysts usually group the competences correspond to what is called a monothetic clustering algorithm i.e. the different features of the competence are not combined in one distance but considered sequentially: first they chose the market sector they will limit their analysis to; second they chose the level of details at which the competences are to be grouped based on the resources they mobilize and form clusters; finally they chose a level of details for the actions and in each of the clusters previously obtained they group competences by types of actions to form bubbles in the clusters.

Limiting the competences to a given market sector is directly done by using the graph projection algorithm provided by CORESE: when one projects a query graph with a given market sector, by subsumption, only those competences with this market sector or a subtype of it will be retrieved. However the two other features (resources and action) require the ability to cluster competencies and to control the level of details of this clustering. The field of Data Clustering [Jain et al., 1999] studied this problem in great details and the typical structure built to control clustering details is a dendrogram: cutting a dendrogram at a given height provides a clustering at a corresponding granularity.

We already have a tree structure (the hierarchy of concepts) and a similarity measure (semantic similarities). However, the construction of a dendrogram relies on an ultrametric and the similarity measure defined between the classes does not comply with the definition of an ultrametric. Indeed, an ultrametric is a metric which satisfies a strengthened version of the triangle inequality:

$$dist(t1,t2) \leq max(dist(t1,t'), dist(t2,t')) \quad \text{for any } t'$$

Figure 3 gives a counter example where the distance defined in (2) violates this inequality.

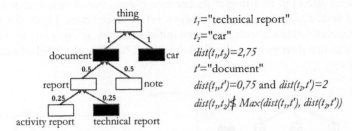

t_1="technical report"
t_2="car"
$dist(t_1,t_2)=2,75$
t'="document"
$dist(t_1,t')=0,75$ and $dist(t_2,t')=2$
$dist(t_1,t_2) \nleq Max(dist(t_1,t'), dist(t_2,t'))$

Fig. 3. Counter example the metric defined in (2) to be an ultrametric

The problem we then considered was a transformation of the ontological distance that would provide an ultrametric and transform the ontological tree into a dendrogram used to propose different levels of details in clustering the semantic annotations on competencies. A simple transformation would be to use a maximal distance that would only depend on the least common supertype of the two types compared:

$$dist_{MH}(t_1,t_2) = \max_{\forall t < LCST(t_1,t_2)} (dist(t, ST(t))) = \left[\frac{1}{2}\right]^{depth(LCST(t_1,t_2))} \tag{3}$$

where $ST(t)$ is the supertype of t.

As shown in Figure 4, this transformation provides a dendrogram with levels of clustering that directly correspond to the levels of the ontology and therefore brings no added value compared to the direct use of the ontology depth to control the level of detail. In order to provide the users with a better precision in choosing the level of

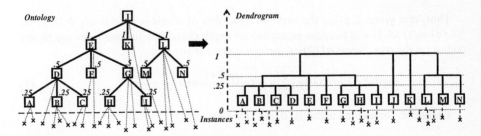

Fig. 4. Simple transformation using depth of LCST

details we needed a criterion to differentiate the classes and order their clustering. The distance given in (4) takes into account the depth of the hierarchy below the least common supertype.

$$dist_{CH}(t_1,t_2) = \max_{\forall st \leq LCST(t_1,t_2)} \left(dist\left(st, LCST(t_1,t_2)\right)\right) \text{ when } t_1 \neq t_2$$

$$dist_{CH}(t_1,t_2) = 0 \text{ when } t_1 = t_2 \tag{4}$$

where $st \leq LCST(t_1,t_2)$ means that st is a subtype of the least common supertype of t_1 and t_2.

Doing so, it allows us to differentiate between classes that already gather a number of levels of details and classes with a shallow set of descendants. Figure 5 shows the result of this transformation using the same initial ontology as Figure 4; we see a new level appeared that differentiates the classes L and E based on the level of details they already gather.

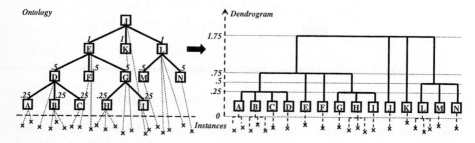

Fig. 5. Improved transformation using depth of descendants

To be precise, $dist_{MH}$ takes its values in (5):

$$E_{MH} = \left\{\frac{1}{2^n}; 0 \leq n < D\right\} \cup \{0\} \tag{5}$$

where D is the maximal depth of the ontology.

Therefore the maximum number of levels in the dendrogram of $dist_{MH}$ is $Card(E_{MH})=d+1$. In comparison, $dist_{CH}$ takes its values in (6):

$$E_{CH} = \left\{\sum_{i=m}^{n} \frac{1}{2^i}; 0 \leq m \leq n < D\right\} \cup \{0\} \tag{6}$$

Thus, at a given depth d the maximum number of levels is recursively defined by $NL(d) = NL(d-1) + d$ because an additional depth possibly adds one more arc to any path from the root. Since $NL(0)=1$, we can deduce that:

$$Card(E_{CH}) = NL(D) = \left(\sum_{n=1}^{D} n\right) + 1 = \frac{D(D+1)}{2} + 1 = \frac{D^2}{2} + \frac{D}{2} + 1 \tag{7}$$

Therefore, for a given maximal depth D we have

$$Card(E_{CH}) - Card(E_{MH}) = \frac{D^2}{2} - \frac{D}{2} = \frac{D}{2}(D-1) > 0 \text{ since } D > 1 \tag{8}$$

Thus $dist_{CH}$ generates more levels than $dist_{MH}$ and the difference is upper-bounded by the square of D. Now we need to prove that $dist_{CH}$ is an ultrametric:

(a) By definition $dist_{CH}(t,t) = 0$ see (4)

(b) Let us show that $dist_{CH}(t_1,t_2) = dist_{CH}(t_2,t_1)$

$$dist_{CH}(t_1,t_2) = \max_{\forall st \leq LCST(t_1,t_2)} (dist(st, LCST(t_1,t_2))) = \max_{\forall st \leq LCST(t_2,t_1)} (dist(st, LCST(t_2,t_1))) = dist_{CH}(t_2,t_1)$$

This is because $LCST(t_1,t_2) = LCST(t_2,t_1)$ i.e. the least common supertype of t_1 and t_2 is also the least common supertype of t_2 and t_1.

(c) Let us show that $dist_{CH}(t_1,t_2) = 0 \Rightarrow t_1=t_2$: if $t_1 \neq t_2$ we have

$$dist_{CH}(t_1,t_2) = \max_{\forall st \leq LCST(t_1,t_2)} (dist(st, LCST(t_1,t_2))) \geq dist(t_1, LCST(t_1,t_2)) + dist(t_2, LCST(t_1,t_2)) > 0$$

So the only way to have $dist_{CH}(t_1,t_2) = 0$ is when $t_1=t_2$

(d) Let us show that $\forall t'$ $dist_{CH}(t1,t2) \leq max(dist_{CH}(t1,t'), dist_{CH}(t2,t'))$ (strengthened triangle inequality)

If $t_1=t_2$ then $dist_{CH}(t_1,t_2) = 0$ and the inequality is verified.

If $t' \leq t_1$ and $t_1 \not\leq t_2$ and $t' \not\leq t_2$ then

$$dist_{CH}(t',t_2) = \max_{\forall st \leq LCST(t',t_2)} (dist(st, LCST(t',t_2))) = \max_{\forall st \leq LCST(t_1,t_2)} (dist(st, LCST(t_1,t_2)))$$

since if $t' \leq t_1$ then $LCST(t',t_2) = LCST(t_1,t_2)$ or more generally the least common supertype for t_1 and t_2 is the same as the one of the subtypes of t_1 and t_2 since we are in a tree.

If $t' \leq t_2$ and $t_2 \not\leq t_1$ and $t' \not\leq t_1$ the same reasoning applies *mutatis mutandis*.

If $t_1 \leq t_2$ and $t' \leq t_2$ then $LCST(t',t_2)=t_2$ and $LCST(t_1,t_2) = t_2$ so $dist_{CH}(t_2,t')= dist_{CH}(t_1,t_2)$. If $t_2 \leq t_1$ and $t' \leq t_1$ the reasoning is, mutatis mutandis, the same.

If $t' \not\leq t_2$ and $t' \leq t_1$ then $LCST(t_1,t_2) \leq LCST(t',t_1)$ or $LCST(t_1,t_2) \leq LCST(t',t_2)$ otherwise we would have $LCST(t_1,t_2) > LCST(t',t_1)$ and $LCST(t_1,t_2) > LCST(t',t_2)$ and since $t_1 \neq t_2$, $t' \leq t_2$ and $t' \leq t_1$, it would require t' or one of its ancestors to have two fathers which is impossible in a tree. So if $LCST(t_1,t_2) \leq LCST(t',t_1)$ then $dist_{CH}(t_1,t_2) \leq dist_{CH}(t_1,t')$ since $\{st \; ; \; st \leq LCST(t_1,t_2)\} \subset \{st \; ; \; st \leq LCST(t',t_1)\}$. Likewise if $LCST(t_1,t_2) \leq LCST(t',t_2)$ then $dist_{CH}(t_1,t_2) \leq dist_{CH}(t_2,t')$ since $\{st \; ; \; st \leq LCST(t_1,t_2)\} \subset \{st \; ; \; st \leq LCST(t',t_2)\}$. Thus, in both cases the inequality is verified. Therefore, we covered all the cases and $dist_{CH}$ is an ultrametric that can be used to produce a range of levels of details exploitable in widgets for interfaces.

The maximal distance $dist_{Max}$ between two sister classes of depth d in an ontology of maximal depth D is

$$dist_{Max}(d,D) = \sum_{i=d-1}^{D} \left[\frac{1}{2}\right]^i = \frac{1}{2^{d-1}} \sum_{i=0}^{D-d+1} \frac{1}{2^i} = \frac{1}{2^{d+1}} \times \frac{1 - \frac{1}{2^{D-d+2}}}{\frac{1}{2}} = \frac{1}{2^{d-2}}\left(1 - \frac{1}{2^{D-d+2}}\right) = \frac{1}{2^{d-2}} - \frac{1}{2^D}$$

The minimal distance between two sister classes of depth d is $dist_{Min}(d) = 1/2^{d-1}$. Therefore $dist_{Max}(d+1) < dist_{Min}(d)$ i.e. the clustering of classes respects the ontology hierarchy and a class cannot be clustered before its descendants. However between two sister classes, the children of a shallow class will be grouped before the children of a class with a deep descendant hierarchy. Finally since the clustering follows the class hierarchy, a name can be given to every cluster Cl and it is very important to produce a meaningful clustering: $Name(Cl) = Name\ (LCST(\{t\ ;\ type\ t \in Cl\}))$

3.3 Ontology-Based Queries to Form Clusters

Using our transformation of an ontological distance into an ultrametric, we create two dendrograms respectively for the ontology of resources and the ontology of actions. Each dendrogram supports a widget (e.g. scrollbar) allowing the user to chose a clustering levels detail respectively for resources and actions.

To choose a level to cut the dendrograms amounts to select a number of classes that can be used to differentiate competences during the clustering: every class visible at this level may be used to describe a competence. Therefore the two levels of detail chosen for resources and actions result in two sets of classes of resources and actions that have to be considered. Based on these sets and the market sector the user chose, we generate all the combinations of queries that cover all the combinations of resources and actions; thus each one of these queries corresponds to a potential bubble, and the bubble will be shown if there is at least one answer to this query. To consider a competence once and only once, the queries exclude the subclasses that have not been collapsed *i.e.* the subclasses that are above the detail level and for which there will be a dedicated query. Each query is submitted to the CORESE search engine to retrieve and count instances of competences falling in the corresponding bubble.

As we mentioned, there might be several resources for a competence and the analyst chooses the most representative one. For each competence, this inference is simulated by considering the classes of resources available at the chosen level of details and by sorting them according to the number of instances of resources they cover for this competence. For instance if a competence uses *java*, *c*, *c++*, and *project management* as resources and the level of details include classes like *management theory*, *programming language* and *mathematic models*, these classes will be sorted as follows: *programming language* (3 instances), *management theory* (1 instance), *mathematic models* (0 instance). Therefore the most representative resource type picked will be *programming language* and this competence will be counted in a cluster on *programming language*. This process is illustrated in figure 6.

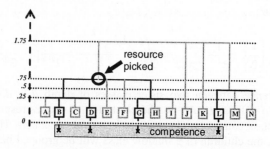

Fig. 6. Choosing the most representative resource

The final result is a list of bubbles grouped in clusters. The last problem is the display of these bubbles and clusters in an intelligent and intelligible fashion.

3.4 Conceptual Classification and Spatial Grouping

Users are interested in two aspects when comparing clusters: their size and the type of resource they use. They combined these two dimensions to obtain what they called a "radar view" of the technological pole that they draft in Figure 2. The radar view uses angular coordinates: the angle is derived from the place of the resource classes in the ontology and the radius from the size of the cluster. Figure 7 shows two opposite approaches in using the ontology for angular positions: a top-down division where the children equally share the angle allocated to their parent (left part of the figure); a bottom-up merging where leaves equally share the available angle and parents 'inherit' the sum of the angles of their children (right part of the figure).

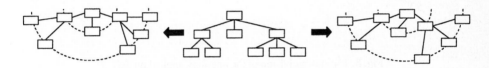

Fig. 7. Using the ontology for angular positions

Here the initial angle was 180°. On the left (top-down division) it was divided into three for the first level of children (60° each) and then the first and last thirds were respectively divided into two (30°) and three (20°) for the second descendants. On the right (bottom-up merging), the 180° were divided into 6 for the leaves of the tree (30° each) then the nodes of the first level are respectively allocated angles of 60°, 30° and 90°. The top-down division maintains the equality between brothers and favors the structure of the upper modules while the bottom-up merging maintains the equality between leaves and favors the detailed branches.

In our case the top-down division was more interesting since it divides the space equally between the main domains of resources and, as shown in Figure 8, the ontology is much more detailed in some parts (e.g. the computer resources) than in some others (e.g. management resources). On such an ontology, bottom-up merging would bias the view while the top-down division applied on 360° in Figure 8 maintains an equal angle for brothers; this is used to have an egalitarian positioning of the clusters based on their representative resource. Figure 9 shows the result of this approach applied to the list of clusters obtained with the inference previously described: the angular position is given by the place of the representative resource in the ontology, and the radius corresponds to the size of the cluster. As a result we can see that the activity of the technological pole is primarily focused in a given sector on which Figure 10 provides a partial zoom.

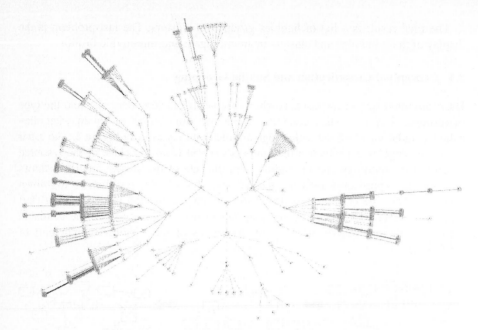

Fig. 8. Top-down division of the ontology applied on 360°

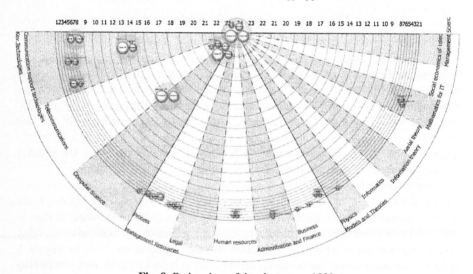

Fig. 9. Radar view of the clusters on 180°

Fig. 10. Zoom on the Radar view in figure 8

4   Evaluation and Conclusions

The two types of evaluations were carried out: (1) usability and ergonomics; (2) complexity and real time. The usability and ergonomic evaluation triggered several evolutions of the interfaces (including two major reengineering) and some tests are still being carried out using different techniques (thinking aloud, video analysis, questionnaires, etc.). We are currently carrying out the second iteration of the usability and ergonomics studies. Needs for redesign have already been recorded, for instance: (a) a need to provide simple widgets to select the levels of details (b) a need to use statistics on the instances instead of the ontology, to calculate the angular position, thus accounting for the effective use of concepts rather than a theoretical importance (c) a need to have an idea of the time it will take to compute a clustering view. One of the major points is that the acceptance of KmP was so effective that we are now moving from a group of 20 pilot user companies to a park of 70 user companies and more and more public research centers are describing themselves, while the project is entering an industrialization phase. We also abstracted a methodology to involve users and keep them involved in the design of an ontology-based application [Giboin et al, 2005].

Concerning complexity and real time, there are two phases in the inference we detailed here: the initialization of the dendrograms and tree of angles (which is done once) and the calculation of the clusters and their position (which is done each time a user submits a query). The complexity of the algorithm for the initialization of the dendrograms and tree of angles breaks down as follows, where n and m are the number of classes respectively in the ontologies of resources and actions:

- Parsing the schema to build the tree: $O(n+m)$
- Initializing the depth and angular distribution: $O(n+m)$
- Sorting the dendrogram: $O(n{\times}log(n)+ m{\times}log(m))$

The size of the set of queries produced to build the clusters depends on the level of details chosen by the users. For two levels of details n' and m' respectively chosen in the dendrograms of resources and actions we have to solve $n'{\times}m'$ queries and so the worse case is $n*m$ queries. We carried out a number of real time tests using a small configuration (Pentium 4 M / 1.7GHz / 512 Mo running MS Windows):

- The average minimum time (for $n'=1$ and $m'=1$ and thus 1 query/potential cluster) is 86 milliseconds.
- The average maximum time ($n'=596$ and $m'=118$ thus 70 328 queries/potential clusters) is 11 minutes.
- The average typical time ($n'=109$ and $m'=9$ thus 981 queries/potential clusters) is 9 298 milliseconds i.e. roughly 9 seconds.

The notion of typical query is due to the fact that the level of details used by users of the radar view is much lower than the level of details provided by the ontology and used by the end-user companies to describe themselves. For instance when market analysts are interested in activities of the telecom valley that involve programming in general, they do not want to differentiate between java, c++, c#, *etc.*

Figure 11 shows the behavior of the response time against the level of details provided by the possible combinations of n' and m' and Figure 12 shows the behavior of the response time against the actual value of $n'\times m'$ that is to say the number of generated queries. The linear regression of Figure 12 approximately corresponds to $y= x \times 8.42+89.24$ and it has two very useful applications: (a) it provides a very simple and rapid way to foresee and warn the users about the time a clustering request will take to be solved before they actually submit it, and (b) it predicts the level of details above which it is better to rely on a reporting functionality that prepares a set of views in batch mode at night rather than relying on a real-time calculation; typically above 15 seconds of response time *i.e.* above $n'\times m'=2000$ in our case.

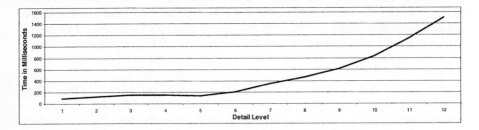

Fig. 11. Response time against detail level

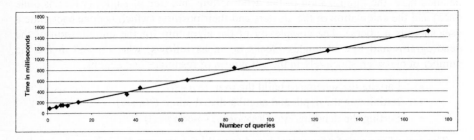

Fig. 12. Response time against number of queries

KmP now includes a set of views and analysis tools as the radar view we detailed in this article. This semantic Web portal provides indicators for institutional organizations to understand the landscape of the technological pole, and for actors to find opportunities, niches, partners, *etc.* By detailing the work done on one RDFS-based graph inference, we showed how the graph structure of semantic web formalisms can be exploited in new inferences to support intelligent interfaces in bridging the gap between the complexity of these underlying conceptual models and the ergonomic constraints of end-users' interfaces and daily concerns. The inferences at play here can be reused to support other functionalities and of course other inferences exist on these graph structures; in fact the algorithm has already been reused to produce other clustering view such as the identification of competency poles. Here, we proved the characteristics of the metrics and inferences we proposed and we illustrated the interpretation that can be associated to their results. In parallel we are conducting an experiment to evaluate and compare these simulated metrics with the ones humans naturally use in handling information [Gandon et al., 2005].

References

[Collins & Loftus, 1975] Collins, A., Loftus, E., A Spreading Activation Theory of Semantic Processing. *Psychological Review*, vol. 82, pp. 407-428, 1975

[Corby et al, 2004] Corby, O., Dieng-Kuntz, R., Faron-Zucker, C., Querying the Semantic Web with the Corese Search Engine, In Proc. of *European Conference on Artificial Intelligence*, IOS Press, pp.705-709, 2004

[Gandon et al., 2005] Gandon F., Corby O., Dieng-Kuntz R., Giboin A., Proximité Conceptuelle et Distances de Graphes, To be published in Proc. Raisonner le Web Sémantique avec des Graphes, Nice, Journée thématique de la plate-forme AFIA, Nice, 2005

[Giboin et al, 2005] Giboin A., Gandon F., Gronnier N., Guigard C., Corby, O., Comment ne pas perdre de vue les usage(r)s dans la construction d'une application à base d'ontologies ? Retour d'expérience sur le projet KmP, To be published in Proc. Ingénierie des Connaissances, plate-forme AFIA, p133-144, 2005

[Jain et al., 1999] Jain, A.K., Murty, M.N., and Flynn, P.J. (1999): Data Clustering: A Review, *ACM Computing Surveys*, Vol 31, No. 3, 264-323.

[Jiang & Conrath, 1997] Jiang, J., Conrath, D., Semantic Similarity based on Corpus Statistics and Lexical Taxonomy. In Proc. of *International Conference on Research in Computational Linguistics*, Taiwan, 1997

[Lazaric & Thomas, 2005] Lazaric N., Thomas C., "The coordination and codification of knowledge inside a network, or the building of an 'epistemic community': The 'Telecom Valley' case study" in "Reading the Dynamics of a Knowledge Economy », to be published in 2005 by Edward Elgar Publishing.

[Quillian, 1968] Quillian, M.R., Semantic Memory, in: M. Minsky (Ed.), *Semantic Information Processing*, M.I.T. Press, Cambridge, 1968.

[Rada et al., 1989] Rada, R., Mili, H., Bicknell, E., Blettner, M., Development and Application of a Metric on Semantic Nets, *IEEE Transaction on Systems, Man, and Cybernetics*, vol. 19(1), pp. 17-30, 1989.

[Resnik, 1995] Resnik, P., Semantic Similarity in a Taxonomy: An Information-Based Measure and its Applications to Problems of Ambiguity in Natural Language. In *Journal of Artificial Intelligence Research*, vol 11, pp. 95-130, 1995

[Sowa, 1984] Sowa., J.F., *Conceptual structures: Information Processing in Mind and Machine*. Addison-Wesley, Reading, Massachusetts, 1984

Ontology Design Patterns for Semantic Web Content

Aldo Gangemi

Laboratory for Applied Ontology, ISTC-CNR, Rome, Italy
a.gangemi@istc.cnr.it

Abstract. The paper presents a framework for introducing design patterns that facilitate or improve the techniques used during ontology lifecycle. Some distinctions are drawn between kinds of ontology design patterns. Some content-oriented patterns are presented in order to illustrate their utility at different degrees of abstraction, and how they can be specialized or composed. The proposed framework and the initial set of patterns are designed in order to function as a pipeline connecting domain modelling, user requirements, and ontology-driven tasks/queries to be executed.

1 Introduction

The lifecycle of ontologies over the Semantic Web involves different techniques, ranging from manual to automatic building, refinement, merging, mapping, annotation, etc. Each technique involves the specification of core concepts for the population of an ontology, or for its annotation, manipulation, or management [7][9][10][11][14][19]. For example, an OWL ontology of gene expression for bioinformatics can be manually built by encoding experts' conceptual patterns [20], or can be automatically learnt e.g. out of a textual corpus by encoding natural language patterns, then refined according to conceptual patterns provided by experts [3], and finally annotated with meta-level concepts for e.g. confidence measurement, argumentation, etc.

Throughout experiences in ontology engineering projects[1,2] at the Laboratory for Applied Ontology (LOA)[3], typical conceptual patterns have emerged out of different domains, for different tasks, and while working with experts having heterogeneous backgrounds. For example, a simple *participation* pattern (including objects taking part in events) emerges in domain ontologies as different as enterprise models [11], legal norms [30], sofware management [17], biochemical pathways [9], and fishery techniques [10]. Other, more complex patterns have also emerged in the same disparate domains: the *role<->task* pattern, the *information<->realization* pattern, the *description<->situation* pattern, the *design<->object* pattern, the *attribute parametrization* pattern, etc.

Those emerging patterns are extremely useful in order to acquire, develop, and refine the ontologies from either experts or documents. Often it's even the case that a community of expertise develops its own conceptual pattern, usually of an informal

---

[1] For example, in the projects *IKF*: http://www.ikfproject.com/About.htm,
  FOS: http://www.fao.org/agris/aos/, and *WonderWeb*: http://wonderweb.semanticweb.org.
[2] http://www.loa-cnr.it
[3] http://dolce.semanticweb.org

Y. Gil et al. (Eds.): ISWC 2005, LNCS 3729, pp. 262–276, 2005.

diagrammatic sort, which can be reengineered as a specialization of the mentioned patterns, for the sake of an ontology project. In some situations, experts do not grasp the utility of ontologies until they realize that an ontology can encode effectively a domain conceptual pattern. Once experts realize it, they usually start discussions on how to improve their own rational procedures by means of ontology engineering techniques!

Following this evidence, for two years a set of conceptual patterns has been used for practical, domain ontology design while still being based on a full-fledged, richly axiomatic ontology (currently DOLCE and its extension s[4] [14][15]). A major attention has been devoted to patterns that are expressible in OWL [18], and are therefore easily applicable to the Semantic Web community.

Independently, in 2004 the W3C has started a working group on Semantic Web Best Practices and Deployment, including a task force on Ontology Engineering Patterns (OEP) [21], which has produced some interesting OWL design patterns that are close, from the logical viewpoint, to some of the ontology design patterns that the LOA has been developing.

In this paper a notion of pattern for ontology design is firstly introduced, contrasting it to other sibling notions. Then a template to present ontology design patterns that are usable to assist or improve Semantic Web ontology engineering is sketched, focusing on patterns that can be encoded in OWL(DL). Some distinctions are drawn between patterns oriented to individuals, to classes or properties, to logical primitives, and to argumentation. Some content-oriented patterns are discussed in order to illustrate that notion at different degrees of abstraction, and how they can be composed. Finally, some conclusions are provided.

2 Some Bits of History

The term "pattern" appears in English in the 14th century and derives from Middle Latin "patronus" (meaning "patron", and, metonymically, "exemplar", something proposed for imitation).[5] As Webster's puts it, a pattern has a set of senses that show a reasonable degree of similarity (see my italics): «a) a *form* or *model* proposed for *imitation*, b) something *designed* or used as a *model* for *making things*, c) a *model* for making a *mold*, d) an artistic, musical, literary, or mechanical *design* or *form*, e) a natural or chance *configuration*, etc., and, f) a *discernible coherent system* based on the *intended interrelationship* of component parts».

In the seventies, the architect and mathematician Christopher Alexander introduced the term "design pattern" for shared guidelines that help solve design problems. In [1] he argues that a good design can be achieved by means of a set of rules that are "packaged" in the form of patterns, such as "courtyards which live", "windows place", or "entrance room". Design patterns are assumed as archetypal solutions to design problems in a certain context.

Taking seriously the architectural metaphor, the notion has been eagerly endorsed by software engineering [2][6][13], where it is used as a general term for formatted guidelines in software reuse, and, more recently, has also appeared in requirements

---

[4] Cf. Online Etymology Dictionary: http://www.etymonline.com)

[5] In software engineering, formal approaches to design patterns, based on dedicated ontologies, are being investigated, e.g. in so-called *semantic middleware* [17].

analysis, conceptual modelling, and ontology engineering [12][20][21][24][29]. Traditional desing patterns appear more like a collection of shortcuts and suggestions related to a class of context-bound problems and success stories. In recent work, there seems to be a tendency towards a more formal encoding of design patterns (notably in [2][12][13][19]). [24] also addresses the issue of ontology design patterns for the Semantic Web, taking a foundational approach that is complementary with that presented here.

2.1 The Elements of a Design Pattern from Software to Ontology Engineering

For space reasons, a review of the existing literature, and how this proposal differs from it, is not attempted here. Instead, the typical structure of design patterns in software engineering is presented, and contrasted with typical patterns in ontology engineering and with the so-called *content* patterns.

The mainstream approach in Software Engineering (SE) patterns is to use a template that can be similar to the following one (adapted from [22]), used to address a problem of form design in user interfaces:

Slot	Value
Type	UI form
Examples	• Tax forms • Job application forms • Ordering merchandise through a catalog
Context	The user has to provide preformatted information, usually short (non-narrative) answers to questions
Problem	How should the artifact indicate what kind of information should be supplied, and the extent of it?
Forces	• The user needs to know what kind of information to provide. • It should be clear what the user is supposed to read, and what to fill in. • The user needs to know what is required, and what is optional. • Users almost never read directions. • Users generally do not enjoy supplying information this way, and are satisfied by efficiency, clarity, and a lack of mistakes.
Solution	Provide appropriate "blanks" to be filled in, which clearly and correctly indicate what information should be provided. Visually indicate those editable blanks consistently, such as with subtle changes in background color, so that a user can see at a glance what needs to be filled in. Label them with clear, short labels that use terminology familiar to the user; place the labels as close to the blanks as is reasonable. Arrange them all in an order that makes sense semantically, rather than simply grouping things by visual appearance

The slots used here follow quite closely those suggested by Alexander: given an *artifact type*, the pattern provides *examples* of it, its *context*, the *problem* addressed by the pattern, the involved *"forces"* (requirements and constraints), and a *solution*.

In ontology engineering, the nature of the artifact (ontologies) requires a more formal presentation of patterns.[5] For example, the pattern for "classes as property values" [16] produced by the OEP task force [21] can be sketched as follows (only an excerpt of the pattern is shown here):

Slot	Value
General issue	It is often convenient to put a class (e.g., Animal) as a property value (e.g., topic or book subject) when building an ontology. While OWL Full and RDF Schema do not put any restriction on using classes as property values, in OWL DL and OWL Lite most properties cannot have classes as their values.
Use case example	Suppose we have a set of books about animals, and a catalog of these books. We want to annotate each catalog entry with its subject, which is a particular species or class of animal that the book is about. Further, we want to be able to infer that a book about African lions is also a book about lions. For example, when retrieving all books about lions from a repository, we want books that are annotated as books about African lions to be included in the results.
Notation	In all the figures below, ovals represent classes and rectangles represent individuals. The orange color signifies classes or individuals that are specific to a particular approach. Green arrows with green labels are OWL annotation properties. We use N3 syntax to represent the examples.
Approaches	Approach 1: Use classes directly as property values In the first approach, we can simply use classes from the subject hierarchy as values for properties (in our example, as values for the dc:subject property). We can define a class Book to represent all books.
Considerations	• The resulting ontology is compatible with RDF Schema and OWL Full, but it is outside OWL DL and OWL Lite. • This approach is probably the most succinct and intuitive among all the approaches proposed here. • Applications using this representation can directly access the information needed to infer that Lion (the subject of the LionsLifeInThePrideBook individual) is a subclass of Animal and that AfricanLion (the subject of the TheAfricanLionBook individual) is a subclass of Lion.
OWL code (N3 syntax)	default:BookAboutAnimals a owl:Class ; rdfs:subClassOf owl:Thing ; rdfs:subClassOf [a owl:Class ; owl:unionOf ([a owl:Restriction ;

Slot	Value
	owl:onProperty dc:subject ; owl:someValuesFrom default:Animal] [a owl:Restriction ; owl:onProperty dc:subject ; owl:someValuesFrom [a owl:Restriction ; owl:hasValue default:Animal ; owl:onProperty rdfs:subClassOf]])]

As evidenced from the examples, an ontology engineering pattern includes some formal encoding, due to the nature of ontological artifacts. OEP slots seem to "merge" some SE slots: examples and context are merged in the "use case", while the slot "forces" is missing, except for some "considerations" related to the "solution" slot (called "approach" in OEP).

In this paper, a step towards the encoding of *conceptual*, rather than *logical* design patterns, is made. In other words, while OEP is proposing patterns for solving design problems *for OWL*, independently of a particular conceptualization, this paper proposes patterns for solving (*in OWL* or another logical language) design problems for the domain classes and properties that populate an ontology, therefore addressing *content* problems.

3   Conceptual Ontology Design Patterns

3.1   Generic Use Cases

The first move towards conceptual ontology design patterns requires the notion of a "Generic Use Case" (GUC), i.e. a generalization of use cases that can be provided as examples for an issue of domain modelling. Differently from the "artifact type" slot in SE patterns and from the "issue" slot in OEP patterns, a GUC should be the expression of a recurrent issue in many domain modelling projects, independently of the particular logical language adopted. For example, this is a partial list of the recurrent questions that arise in the modelling practice during an ontology project:

- Who does <u>what</u>, <u>when</u> and <u>where</u>?
- Which objects <u>take part in</u> a certain event?
- What are the <u>parts</u> of something?
- What's an object <u>made of</u>?
- What's the <u>place</u> of something?
- What's the <u>time</u> frame of something?
- What <u>technique, method, practice</u> is being used?
- Which <u>tasks</u> should be executed in order to achieve a certain goal?
- Does this behaviour <u>conform</u> to a certain rule?
- What's the <u>function</u> of that artifact?
- How is that object <u>built</u>?

- What's the <u>design</u> of that artifact?
- How did that phenomenon <u>happen</u>?
- What's your <u>role</u> in that transaction?
- What that information <u>is about</u>? How is it <u>realized</u>?
- What <u>argumentation model</u> are you adopting for negotiating an agreement?
- What's the <u>degree of confidence</u> that you give to this axiom?

Being generic at the use case level allows us to decouple, or to refactor the design problems of a use case, by composing different GUCs. Ideally, a library of GUCs should include a hierarchy from the most generic to the most specific ones, and from the "purest" (like most of the examples above) to the most articulated and applied ones (e.g.: "what protein is involved in the Jack/Stat biochemical pathway?").

The intuition underlying GUC hierarchies is based on a methodological observation: ontologies must be built out of domain tasks that can be captured by means of *competency questions* [11]. A competency question is a typical query that an expert might want to submit to a knowledge base of its target domain, for a certain task. In principle, an accurate domain ontology should specify *all and only* the conceptualizations required in order to answer all the competency questions formulated by, or acquired from, experts.

A GUC can thus be seen as the preliminary motivation to build the pipeline connecting modelling requirements, expected queries (semantic services), and ontology population. Following the distinction between tasks, problem-solving methods, and ontologies that underlies recent architectures for Semantic Web Services [26], GUCs can be used to access at a macroscopic level (partly similar to "use-case diagrams" in UML) the profile (or registries) for a service, the available ontology design patterns (see next section), as well as existing ontologies and knowledge bases. GUC taxonomy is not addressed here for space reasons.

3.2 Features of Conceptual Ontology Design Patterns

A GUC cannot do much as a guideline, unless we are able to find formal patterns that encode it. A formal pattern that encodes a GUC is called here a *Conceptual* (or *Content*) *Ontology Design Pattern* (CODeP).

CODePs are characterized here in a twofold way. Firstly, through an intuitive set of features that a CODeP should have; secondly, through a minimal semantic characterization, and its formal encoding, with the help of some examples.

- A CODeP is a template to represent, and possibly solve, a modelling problem.
- A CODeP "extracts" a fragment of either a *foundational* [14] or *core* [8] ontology, which constitutes its background. For example, a connected path of two relations and three classes (Ax ∧ By ∧ Cz ∧ Rxy ∧ Syz) can be extracted because of its domain relevance. Thus, a CODeP lives in a reference ontology, which provides its taxonomic and axiomatic context. A CODeP is axiomatized according to the fragment it extracts. Since it depends on its background, a CODeP inherits the axiomatization (and the related reasoning service) that is already in place.
- Mapping and composition of patterns require a reference ontology, in order to check the consistency of the composition, or to compare the sets of axioms that are to be mapped. Operations on CODePs depend on operations on the reference ontologies. However, for a pattern user, these operations should be (almost) invisible.

- A CODeP can be represented in any ontology representation language whatsoever (depending on its reference ontology), but its intuitive and compact visualization seems an essential requirement. It requires a critical size, so that its diagrammatical visulization is aesthetically acceptable and easily memorizable.
- A CODeP can be an element in a partial order, where the ordering relation requires that at least one of the classes or relations in the pattern is specialized. A hierarchy of CODePs can be built by specializing or generalizing some of the elements (either classes or relations). For example, the *participation* pattern can be specialized to the *taking part in a public enterprise* pattern.
- A CODeP should be intuitively exemplified, and should catch relevant, "core" notions of a domain. Independently of the generality at which a CODeP is singled out, it must contain the central notions that "make rational thinking move" for an expert in a given domain for a given task.
- A CODeP can be often built from informal or simplified schemata used by domain experts, together with the support of other reusable CODePs or reference ontologies, and a methodology for domain ontology analysis. Typically, experts spontaneously develop schemata to improve their business, and to store relevant know-how. These schemata can be reengineered with appropriate methods (e.g. [10]).
- A CODeP can/should be used to describe a "best practice" of modelling.
- A CODeP can be similar to a database schema, but a pattern is defined wrt to a reference ontology, and has a general character, independent of system design.

4 Examples of CODePs

4.1 Some Foundational and Core Patterns

Some examples of CODePs are shown here, but many others have been built or are being investigated. Due to space restrictions, the presentation is necessarily sketchy.

As proposed in the previous section, a CODeP emerges out of an existing or dedicated reference ontology (or ontologies), since it needs a context that facilitates its use, mapping, specialization, and composition.

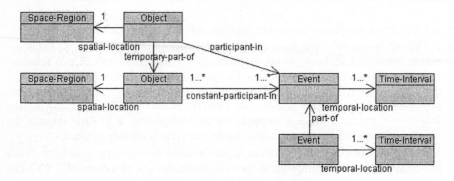

Fig. 1. The basic DOLCE design pattern: participation at spatio-temporal location

A first, basic example (Fig. 1) is provided by the *participation* pattern, extracted from the DOLCE [14] foundational ontology, developed within the WonderWeb Project [5]. It consists of a "participant-in" relation between *objects* and *events*, and assumes a time indexing for it. Time indexing is provided by the temporal location of the event at a *time interval*, while the respective spatial location at a *space region* is provided by the participating object.

Some inferences are automatically drawn when composing the participation CODeP with the *part* CODeP (not shown here, see [14]). For example, if an object *constantly participates in* an event, a temporary part of that object (a part that can be detached), will simply *participate in* that event, because we cannot be sure that the part will be a part at all times the whole participates. For example, we cannot infer for each member of a gang that she participated in a crime, just because she is a member.

An alternative CODeP (Fig. 2) for time-indexed participation can be given by reifying the participation relation (in OWL a ternary relation cannot be expressed conveniently). The *reified participation* pattern features a kind of "situation" (see next example), called *time-indexed-participation*, which is a setting for exactly one object, one event, and one time interval. This simple reification pattern can be made as complex as needed, by adding parameters, more participants, places, etc.

A third, more complex example, is the *Role<->Task* CODeP (Fig. 3). This CODeP is based on an extension of DOLCE, called D&S (Descriptions and Situations) [9][15], partly developed within the Metokis Project [4]. D&S provides a vocabulary and an axiomatization to type-reified [27] classes and relations ("concepts" and "descriptions"), and to token-reified [27] tuples ("situations"; for a semantics of D&S, see [28]).

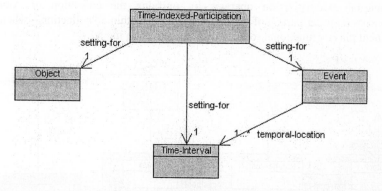

Fig. 2. A pattern for reification of time-indexed relations (in this case, *participation*): a situation (like *time-indexed participation*) is a *setting for* an event, the entities participating in that event, and the time interval at which the event occurs

In practice, the *Role<->Task* pattern allows the expression, in OWL(DL), of the temporary *roles* that objects can play, and of the *tasks* that events/actions allow to execute. The reified relation specifying roles and tasks is a *description*, the reified tuple that satisfies the relation for certain individual objects and events is called *situation*. Roles can have assigned tasks as *modal targets*. This CODeP is very expressive, and can be specialized in many domains, solving design issues that are quite hard without reification. For example, the assignments of tasks to role-players in a workflow can be easily expressed, as well as plan models [28].

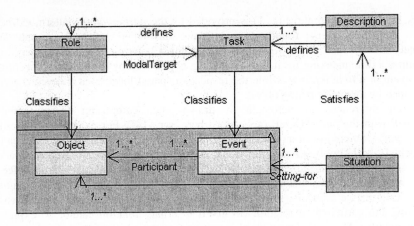

Fig. 3. A pattern for roles and tasks defined by descriptions and executed within situations

By composing the *Role<->Task* pattern with the *Collection<->Role* pattern (not shown here), and specializing such composition to the domain of material design, we obtain the so-called *Design<->Artifact* CODeP (Fig. 4). This pattern is very expressive and quite complex. Starting from *Role<->Task*, and *Collection<->Role*, and specializing objects to *material artifacts*, descriptions to *designs, situations to design materialization*, and substituting tasks with *functions*, we can conceive of a *functional unification* relation holding between a design model and a material artifact. The internal axiomatization operates by unifying the collection of "relevant" components ("proper parts") of the material artifact within a "collection", where each component plays a functional role defined by the design model.

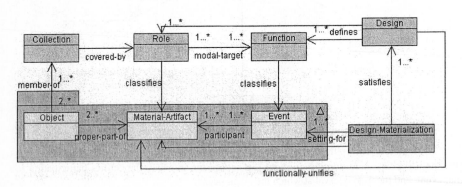

Fig. 4. A pattern for talking about relations between design models and material artifacts

The design materialization keeps together the actual physical components of an individual material artifact. This CODeP can be easily specialized for manufacturing, commercial warehouses, etc.

The previous CODePs are *foundational*. An example of a *core* CODeP is instead provided here with reference to the NCI ontology of cancer research and treatment [23] (Fig. 5). It specializes the foundational *Role<->Task* CODeP (Fig. 3).

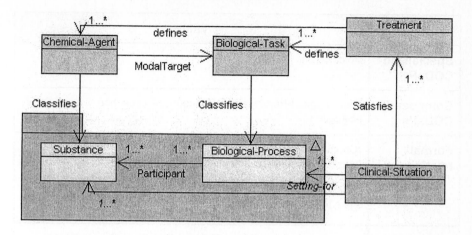

Fig. 5. A *core* pattern for chemotherapy, specializing the *Role<->Task* CODeP

4.2 How to Introduce a CODeP

A template can be used to annotate CODePs, to share them in pre-formatted documents, to contextualize them appropriately, etc. Here the following frame is proposed, and presented through the previous example from the NCI ontology [23]:

Slot	Value
Generic use case (GUC)	Chemicals playing roles in biological processes for chemotherapy.
Local use case(s)	Various chemical agents, mostly drugs, are used to control biological processes within a chemotherapeutical treatment. When talking about drugs and processes, there is a network of senses implying a dependence on roles and functions (or tasks) within a clinical treatment. Intended meanings include the *possible* functional roles played by certain substances, as well as the actual administration of amounts of drugs for controlling actually occurring biological processes. Therefore, both class- and instance-variables are present in the maximal relation for this pattern.
Logic addressed	OWL, DL species
Reference ontologies	DOLCE-Lite-Plus, NCI Ontology

Slot	Value
Specialized CODeP	Role<->Task
Composed CODePs	Time-Indexed-Participation, Concept<->Description, Description<->Situation
Formal relation	rChemical_or_Drug_Plays_Role_in_Biological_Process(ϕ,ψ,x,y,t, c_1,c_2,d,s), where ϕ(x) is a chemical agent class, ψ(y) is a biological process class, t is a time interval, c_1 and c_2 are two reified intensional concepts, d is a reified intensional relation, and s is a reified extensional relation.
Sensitive axioms	rChemical_or_Drug_Plays_Role_in_Biological_Process(ϕ,ψ) $=_{df}$ $\forall$x,y,t(ϕ(x) $\wedge$ ψ(y) $\wedge$ participates-in(x,y,t) $\wedge$ Chemical-Agent(x) $\wedge$ Biological-Process(y) $\wedge$ Time-Interval(t)) $\leftrightarrow$ $\exists c_1,c_2$,d(CF(x,c_1,t) $\wedge$ MT(c_1,c_2) $\wedge$ CF(y,c_2,t) $\wedge$ DF(d,c_1) $\wedge$ DF(d,c_2) $\wedge$ $\forall$s(SAT(s,d)) $\leftrightarrow$ (SETF(s,x) $\wedge$ SETF(s,y) $\wedge$ SETF(s,t))
Explanation	Since OWL(DL) does not support relations with >2 arity, reification is required. The Description<->Situation pattern provides typing for such reification. Since OWL(DL) does not support classes in variable position, we need reification for class-variables. The Concept<->Description pattern provides typing for such reification. Similarly, since participation is time-indexed, we need the time-indexed-participation pattern, which is here composed with the previous two patterns (time indexing appears in the setting of the general treatment situation).
OWL(DL) encoding (abstract syntax)	Class(Chemical_Plays_Role_in_Bio_Process complete Description restriction(defines someValuesFrom(Chemical-Agent)) restriction(defines someValuesFrom(Biological-Task))) Class(Chemical-Agent complete Role restriction(defined-by someValuesFrom(Chemical_Plays_Role_in_Bio_Process)) restriction(classifies allValuesFrom(Substance)) restriction(modal-target someValuesFrom(Biological-Task))) Class(Biological-Task complete Task restriction(classifies allValuesFrom(Biological-Process)) restriction(modal-target-of someValuesFrom(Chemical-Agent))) Class(Chemical-in-Biological-Process_Situation complete

Slot	Value
	Situation restriction(satisfies someValuesFrom(Chemical_Plays_Role_in_Bio_Process)) restriction(setting-for someValuesFrom(Substance)) restriction(setting-for someValuesFrom(Biological-Process)) restriction(setting-for someValuesFrom(Time-Interval)))
Class diagram	

The CODeP frame consists of:

- Two slots for the *generic use case*, and the *local use cases*, which includes a description of context, problem, and constraints/requirements.
- Two slots for the addressed *logic*, and the *reference ontologies* used as a background for the pattern.
- Two slots for -if any- the *specialized* pattern and the *composed* patterns.
- Two slots for the *maximal relation* that encodes the case space, and its intended *axiomatization*: a full first-order logic with meta-level is assumed here, but the slot can be empty without affecting the functionality of a CODeP frame.
- Two slots for *explanation* of the approach, and its *encoding* in the logic of choice.
- A last slot for a *class diagram* that visually reproduces the approach.

The frame for introducing CODePs can be easily encoded in XSD or in richer frameworks, like semantic web services (e.g. [25]) or knowledge content objects [26], for optimal exploitation within Semantic Web technologies. The high reusability of CODePs and their formal and pragmatic nature make them suitable not only for isolated ontology engineering practices, but ideally in distributed, collaborative environments like intranets, the Web or the Grid.

CODePs can also be used to generate intuitive, friendly UIs, which can present the user with only the relevant pattern diagram, avoiding the awkward, entangled graphs currently visualized for medium-to-large ontologies.

5 Conclusions

Conceptual Ontology Design Patterns (CODePs) have been introduced as a useful resource and design method for engineering ontology content over the Semantic Web. CODePs are distinguished from architectural, software engineering, and logic-oriented design patterns, and a template has been proposed to describe, visualize, and make operations over them.

The advantages of CODePs for ontology lifecycle over the Semantic Web are straightforward: firstly, patterns make ontology design easier for both knowledge engineers and domain experts (imagine having a menu of pre-built, formally consistent components, pro-actively suggested to the modeller); secondly, patterned design makes it easier ontology integration - perhaps the most difficult problem in ontology engineering. For example, the *time-indexed participation* presented in this paper requires non-trivial knowledge engineering ability to be optimally represented and adapted to a use case: a CODeP within an appropriate ontology management tool can greatly facilitate such representation.

The CODeP examples and the related frame and methods introduced in this paper have been applied for two years (some of them even before) in several administration, business and industrial projects, e.g. in fishery information systems [10], insurance CRM, biomedical ontology integration [9], anti-money-laundering systems for banks [30], service-level agreements for information systems, biomolecular ontology learning [3], legal norms formalization, and management of digital content [26].

Current work focuses on building a tool that assists development, discussion, retrieval, and interchange of CODePs over the Semantic Web, and towards establishing the model-theoretical and operational foundations of CODeP manipulation and reasoning. In particular, for CODePs to be a real advantage in ontology lifecycle, the following functionalities will be available:

- Categorization of CODePs, based either on the use cases they support, or on the concepts they encode.
- Pattern-matching algorithms for retrieving the pattern that best fits a set of requirements, e.g. from a natural language specification, or from a draft ontology.
- Support for specialization and composition of CODePs. A CODeP p_1 *specializes* another p_2 when at least one of the classes or properties from p_2 is a sub-class or a sub-property of some class resp. property from p_1, while the remainder of the CODeP is identical. A CODeP p_1 *expands* p_2 when p_1 contains p_2, while adding some other class, property, or axiom. A CODeP p_1 *composes* p_2 and p_3 when p_1 contains both p_2 and p_3. The formal semantics of these operations is ensured by the underlying (reference) ontology for the patterns, and will be given in an extended version of this paper.
- Interfacing of CODePs for visualization, discussion, and knowledge-base creation
- A rich set of metadata for CODeP manipulation and exploitation within applications.

References

1. Alexander, C.: The Timeless way of building. Oxford University Press, New York (1979).
2. Baker, N., A. Bazan, G. Chevenier, Z. Kovacs, T Le Flour, J-M Le Goff, R. McClatchey, S. Murray: Design Patterns for Description-Driven Systems.
3. Ciaramita, M., Gangemi, A., Ratsch, E., Rojas, I., Saric, J.: Unsupervised Learning of Semantic Relations between Concepts of a Molecular Biology Ontology. To appear in the proceedings of the Nineteenth IJCAI, Edimburgh, Scotland (2005).
4. EU FP6 Metokis Project: http://metokis.salzburgresearch.at
5. EU FP5 WonderWeb Project: http://wonderweb.semanticweb.org

6. Gamma, E., Helm, R., Johnson, R. and Vlissides, J.: Design Patterns: Elements of Reusable Object-Oriented Software. Addison-Wesley, Reading, MA (1995).
7. Gangemi, A., Navigli, R., Velardi, P.: ML: The OntoWordNet Project: extension and axiomatisation of conceptual relations in WordNet. International Conference on Ontologies, Databases and Applications of SEmantics (ODBASE 2003), Catania, (Italy), (2003).
8. Gangemi, A., Borgo, S. (eds.): Proceedings of the EKAW*04 Workshop on Core Ontologies in Ontology Engineering. Available from:
   http://sunsite.informatik.rwth-aachen.de/Publications/CEUR-WS//Vol-118/ (2004).
9. Gangemi, A., Catenacci, C., Battaglia, M.: Inflammation Ontology Design Pattern: an Exercise in Building a Core Biomedical Ontology with Descriptions and Situations.D.M. Pisanelli (ed.) Ontologies in Medicine, IOS Press, Amsterdam (2004).
10. Gangemi, A., F. Fisseha, J. Keizer, J. Lehmann, A. Liang, I. Pettman, M. Sini, M. Taconet: A Core Ontology of Fishery and its Use in the FOS Project, in [8] (2004).
11. Gruninger, M., and Fox, M.S.: The Role of Competency Questions in Enterprise Engineering. Proceedings of the IFIP WG5.7 Workshop on Benchmarking - Theory and Practice, Trondheim, Norway (1994).
12. Guizzardi, G., Wagner, G., Guarino, N., van Sinderen, M.: An Ontologically Well-Founded Profile for UML Conceptual Models. A. Persson, J. Stirna (eds.) Advanced Information Systems Engineering, Proceedings of16th CAiSE Conference, Riga, Springer (2004).
13. Maplesden, D., Hosking, J.G. and Grundy, J.C.: Design Pattern Modelling and Instantiation using DPML, Proceedings of the Tools Pacific 2002, Sydney, CRPIT Press (2002).
14. Masolo, C., A. Gangemi, N. Guarino, A. Oltramari and L. Schneider: WonderWeb Deliverable D18: The WonderWeb Library of Foundational Ontologies (2004).
15. Masolo, C., L. Vieu, E. Bottazzi, C. Catenacci, R. Ferrario, A. Gangemi and N. Guarino: Social Roles and their Descriptions. Procedings of the Ninth International Conference on the Principles of Knowledge Representation and Reasoning, Whistler (2004).
16. Noy, N.: Representing Classes As Property Values on the Semantic Web. W3C Note, http://www.w3.org/2001/sw/BestPractices/OEP/ClassesAsValues-20050405/ (2005).
17. Oberle, D., Mika, P., Gangemi, A., Sabou, M.: Foundations for service ontologies: Aligning OWL-S to DOLCE. Staab S and Patel-Schneider P (eds.), Proceedings of the World Wide Web Conference (WWW2004), Semantic Web Track, (2004).
18. OWL Web Ontology Language Overview, D. L. McGuinness and F. van Harmelen, Editors, W3C Recommendation, 10 February 2004, http://www.w3.org/TR/2004/REC-owl-features-20040210/ (2004).
19. Rector, A.L., Rogers, J.: Patterns, Properties and Minimizing Commitment: Reconstruction of the GALEN Upper Ontology in OWL, in [8] (2004).
20. Reich, J.R.: Ontological Design Patterns: Modelling the Metadata of Molecular Biological Ontologies, Information and Knowledge. In DEXA 2000 (2000).
21. Semantic Web Best Practices and Deployment Working Group, Task Force on Ontology Engineering Patterns. Description of work, archives, W3C Notes and recommendations available from http://www.w3.org/2001/sw/BestPractices/OEP/ (2004-5).
22. Tidwell, J.: COMMON GROUND: A Pattern Language for Human-Computer Interface Design. http://www.mit.edu/%7Ejtidwell/interaction_patterns.html (1999).
23. Golbeck, J., G. Fragoso, F. Hartel, J. Hendler, B. Parsia, J. Oberthaler: The national cancer institute's thesaurus and ontology. *Journal of Web Semantics*, 1(1), (2003).

24. Svatek V.: Design Patterns for Semantic Web Ontologies: Motivation and Discussion. In: 7th Conference on Business Information Systems, Poznań (2004).
25. Motta, E., Domingue, J., Cabral, L., Gaspari, M. (2003) IRS-II: A Framework and Infrastructure for Semantic Web Services. 2nd International Semantic Web Conference (ISWC2003) 20-23 October 2003, Sundial Resort, Sanibel Island, Florida, USA (2003).
26. Behrent, W., Gangemi, A., Maass, W., Westenthaler, R.: Towards an Ontology-based Distributed Architecture for Paid Content. To appear in A. Gomez-Perez (ed.), Proceedings of the Second European Semantic Web Conference, Heraklion, Greece (2005).
27. Galton, A.: Reified Temporal Theories and How To Unreify Them. Proceedings of the International Joint Conference on Artificial Intelligence (IJCAI), 1991.
28. Gangemi, A., Borgo, S., Catenacci, C., Lehmann, J.: Task Taxonomies for Knowledge Content. Deliverable D07 of the Metokis Project. Available at http://www.loa-cnr.it.
29. Soshnikov, D.: Ontological Design Patterns in Distributed Frame Hierarchy. In Proceedings of the 5th International Workshop on Computer Science and Information Technologies, Ufa, Russia, 2003.
30. Gangemi A, Pisanelli DM, Steve G,: An Ontological Framework to Represent Norm Dynamics. In R Winkels (ed.), Proceedings of the 2001 Jurix Conference, Workshop on Legal Ontologies, University of Amsterdam, 2001.

Guidelines for Benchmarking the Performance of Ontology Management APIs

Raúl García-Castro and Asunción Gómez-Pérez

Ontology Engineering Group, Laboratorio de Inteligencia Artificial,
Facultad de Informática, Universidad Politécnica de Madrid, Spain
{rgarcia, asun}@fi.upm.es

Abstract. Ontology tools performance and scalability are critical to both the growth of the Semantic Web and the establishment of these tools in the industry. In this paper, we present briefly the benchmarking methodology used to improve the performance and the scalability of ontology development tools. We focus on the definition of the infrastructure for evaluating the performance of these tools' ontology management APIs in terms of its execution efficiency. We also present the results of applying the methodology for evaluating the API of the WebODE ontology engineering workbench.

1 Introduction

The lack of mechanisms to evaluate ontology tools is an obstacle to their use in companies. Performance is one of the critical requirements requested for ontology tools and the scalability of these tools is a primary need.

To the best of our knowledge, no one has evaluated ontology development tools according to their performance. Some general evaluation frameworks for ontology tools have been proposed by: Duineveld et al. [1], the deliverable 1.3 of the OntoWeb project [2] and Lambrix et al. [3]; and the EON workshops series [4, 5, 6] focus on the evaluation of ontology tools but they have not dealt with their performance yet.

The evaluation of the performance of ontology development tools is tightly related to the evaluation of their scalability. To this end, the tools must be evaluated according to different workloads, paying special attention to the effect of high workloads on the tool performance. Magkanaraki et al. [7] and Tempich and Volz [8] performed structural analyses of ontologies in order to define these workloads. Workload generators such as OntoGenerator [2] and the Univ-Bench Artificial data generator [9] produce ontologies for performing experiments in an automatic way and according to some parameters.

In this paper, we present an approach and a realization of a benchmarking methodology with regard to the performance and the scalability of ontology development tools. The advantage of using a benchmarking methodology rather than an evaluation one is that developers will be able to obtain both a continuous improvement in their tools and the best practices that are performed in the area, supporting the industrial applicability of ontology tools.

As we will see in the next section, experimentation is a key part of any benchmarking methodology. This paper presents a general infrastructure to evaluate

Y. Gil et al. (Eds.): ISWC 2005, LNCS 3729, pp. 277–292, 2005.

the performance and the scalability of ontology development tools by assessing the performance of the methods of their ontology management APIs in terms of their execution efficiency.

It also presents the results of applying the proposed infrastructure for evaluating the performance and the scalability of the ontology management API of the WebODE ontology engineering workbench. WebODE [10] provides services for editing and browsing ontologies, for importing and exporting ontologies to classical and semantic web languages, for evaluating ontologies, for mapping ontologies, etc. As we need a tool for generating ontologies in WebODE's knowledge model, we have developed the WebODE Workload Generator that generates synthetic WebODE ontologies according to a predefined structure and to a load factor.

The contents of this paper are the following: Section 2 presents the benchmarking methodology for ontology tools. According to this methodology, Section 3 presents the benchmarking goal and the metrics to be used for evaluating the performance of the ontology management APIs of ontology development tools; Section 4 presents a detailed definition of the infrastructure needed for evaluating the performance of these APIs and an explanation of how this infrastructure was instantiated for evaluating WebODE's API. Sections 5 and 6 present the evaluation of WebODE's API and the analysis of the results of this evaluation, respectively. Finally, Section 7 presents the conclusions obtained and the related future work.

Out of the scope of this paper are other evaluation criteria like stability, usability, interoperability, etc. as well as the evaluation of the performance of other ontology development tool functionalities such as user interfaces, reasoning capabilities when dealing with complex queries, or ontology validators.

2 Benchmarking Methodology for Ontology Tools

In the last decades, the word benchmarking has become relevant within the business management community. One of the definitions widely known was given by Spendolini [11] who defines benchmarking as a continuous, systematic process for evaluating the products, services, and work processes of organisations that are recognised as representing best practices for the purpose of organisational improvement.

The Software Engineering community does not have a common benchmarking definition. Some authors, like Kitchenham [12], consider benchmarking as a software evaluation method. For her, benchmarking is the process of running a number of standard tests using a number of alternative tools/methods and assessing the relative performance of the tools in those tests. Other authors, like Wohlin et al. [13], adopt the business benchmarking definition, defining benchmarking as a continuous improvement process that strives to be the best of the best through the comparison of similar processes in different contexts.

This section summarizes the benchmarking methodology developed by the authors in the Knowledge Web Network of Excellence [14]. The benchmarking methodology provides a set of guidelines to follow in benchmarking activities over ontology tools. This methodology adopts and extends methodologies of different areas such as business community benchmarking, experimental software engineering and software measurement as described in [14].

At the time of writing this paper, this methodology is being used in Knowledge Web for benchmarking the interoperability of ontology development tools.

Fig. 1 shows the main phases of the benchmarking methodology for ontology tools, which is composed of a benchmarking iteration that is repeated forever.

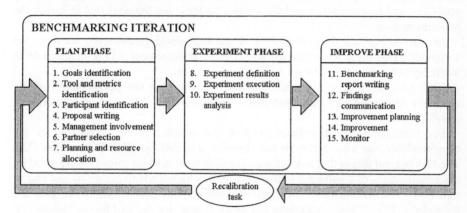

Fig. 1. Knowledge Web benchmarking methodology [14]

Each benchmarking iteration is composed of three phases (*Plan*, *Experiment* and *Improve*) and ends with a *Recalibration* task:

- **Plan phase.** Its main goal is to produce a document with a detailed proposal for benchmarking. It will be used as a reference document during the benchmarking, and should include all the relevant information about it: its goal, benefits and costs; the tool (and its functionalities) to be evaluated; the metrics to be used to evaluate these functionalities; and the people involved in the benchmarking. The last tasks of this phase are related to the search of other organisations that want to participate in the benchmarking with other tools, and to the agreement on the benchmarking proposal (both with the organisation management and with the other organisations) and on the benchmarking planning.
- **Experiment phase.** In this phase, the organisations must define and execute the evaluation experiments for each of the tools that participate on the benchmarking. The evaluation results must be compiled and analysed, determining the practices that lead to these results and identifying which of them can be considered as best practices.
- **Improve phase.** The first task of this phase comprises the writing of the benchmarking report, and this must include: a summary of the process followed, the results and the conclusions of the experimentation, recommendations for improving the tools, and the best practices found during the experimentation. The benchmarking results must be communicated to the participant organisations and finally, in several improvement cycles, the tool developers should perform the necessary changes to improve their tools and monitor this improvement.

While the three phases mentioned before are devoted to the improvement of the tools, the goal of the *Recalibration* task is to improve the benchmarking process itself using the lessons learnt while performing it.

3 Plan Phase

In this section we present the most relevant tasks from the *Plan* phase of the methodology. We will focus on those related to the identification of the benchmarking goals, the tool functionalities and the metrics; as these are the ones that influence the experimentation.

In order to evaluate the performance of ontology development tools, we make the assumption that these tools provide an ontology management API with methods to insert, update, remove, and query ontology components.

Therefore, our goal in the benchmarking is to **improve the performance of the methods provided by the ontology management APIs of the ontology development tools**.

For identifying the tool functionalities and metrics to be considered in the benchmarking, we have followed the Goal/Question/Metric (GQM) paradigm [15]. The idea beyond this is that any software measurement activity should be preceded by the identification of a software engineering goal, which leads to questions and that in turn lead to actual metrics. The questions and metrics derived from our goal are presented in Fig. 2. These questions and metrics show that the tool functionalities that are relevant in the benchmarking are the **methods** of the ontology management APIs, and that the metric to use is the **execution time** of the methods over incremental load states. After performing the experiments, the analysis of their results will provide answers to these questions.

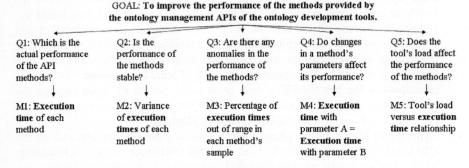

Fig. 2. Questions and metrics obtained through the GQM approach

4 Experiment Phase

This section presents the infrastructure needed when defining and executing experiments to evaluate the performance of the ontology management APIs of ontology development tools. We also identify the variables that influence the execution time of the methods and, in consequence, the evaluation results.

The **evaluation infrastructure** contains the different modules needed to achieve the benchmarking goal. Fig. 3 presents the main modules and the arrows represent the information flow between them.

These modules are described in the next sections, showing the main decisions taken regarding their design and implementation and giving examples according to the instantiation of the infrastructure for the WebODE ontology engineering workbench. In order to have a portable infrastructure, we have implemented it in Java, using only standard libraries and with no graphical components.

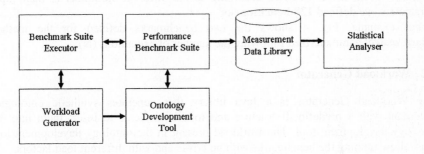

Fig. 3. Evaluation infrastructure

4.1 Performance Benchmark Suite

The Performance Benchmark Suite is a Java library that provides methods for executing each of the benchmarks that compose the benchmark suite. This benchmark suite should be developed taking into account the desirable properties of a benchmark suite [16, 17, 18, 19], that is, accessibility, affordability, simplicity, representativity, portability, scalability, robustness, and consensus.

In order to perform an evaluation of the complete system, every method in the ontology management API is present in the benchmark suite. For each of these methods, different benchmarks have been defined according to the changes in the methods' parameters that affect the performance.

The execution of the benchmarks is parameterised accordant with the parameter **number of executions** (N), which defines the number of consecutive executions of a method in a single benchmark whose execution times are measured. Moreover, the method is executed a certain number of times before starting the measurement so as to stabilise the ontology development tool.

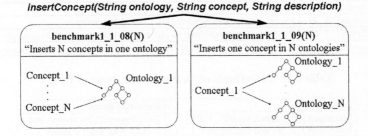

Fig. 4. Benchmarks defined for the method *insertConcept*

A benchmark executes just one method N times consecutively and stores in a text file the wall clock times elapsed in the method executions. The other operation performed by a benchmark is to restore the load state of the tool in case it changes during the benchmark execution.

In the case of WebODE, its ontology management API is composed of **72 methods**. From these methods, according to the different variations in their input parameters, we defined **128 benchmarks**[1].

For example, Fig. 4 shows the two benchmarks defined for the method *insertConcept* parameterized following the number of executions (N).

4.2 Workload Generator

The Workload Generator is a Java library that generates synthetic ontologies accordant with a predefined structure and to a load factor to insert them into the ontology development tool. The workload present in the ontology development tool must allow running the benchmarks with no errors and with different load factors.

The structure of the workload has been defined according to the execution needs of the benchmarks in order to run their methods a certain number of times (N) with no errors. For example, if a benchmark inserts one concept in N ontologies, these N ontologies must be present in the tool for a correct execution of the benchmark. Therefore, the execution needs of all the benchmarks in the benchmark suite define all the ontology components that must exist in the ontology development tool in order to execute every benchmark with no errors.

To define the workload independently of the number of executions of a method in a benchmark (N), we use a new parameter that defines the size of the ontology data. This is named the **load factor** (X) of the ontology development tool. With this load factor, we can define workloads of arbitrary size, but it must be taken into account that to execute the benchmark with no errors the load factor must be greater or equal to the number of executions of a method in a benchmark.

Hence, the workload used when executing all the benchmarks has the same structure as the execution needs of all the benchmarks but is parameterised to a load factor instead of to the number of executions of a method in a benchmark.

Table 1. Execution needs of the benchmarks whose methods insert and remove concepts

Benchmark	Operation	Execution needs
benchmark1_1_08	Inserts N concepts in an ontology	1 ontology
benchmark1_1_09	Inserts a concept in N ontologies	N ontologies
benchmark1_3_20	Removes N concepts from an ontology	1 ontology with N concepts
benchmark1_3_21	Removes a concept from N ontologies	N ontologies with one concept

Table 2. Execution needs of the benchmarks shown in Table 1

Benchmarks	Execution needs
benchmark1_1_08, benchmark1_1_09, benchmark1_3_20, and benchmark1_1_21	1 ontology with N concepts and N ontologies with1 concept

---

[1] http://kw.dia.fi.upm.es/wpbs/WPBS_benchmark_list.html

In the case of WebODE, Table 1 shows the execution needs of each of the four benchmarks whose methods insert and remove concepts in an ontology, being N the number of times that the method is executed. Table 2 shows the execution needs for executing the four benchmarks abovementioned with no errors.

4.3 Benchmark Suite Executor

The Benchmark Suite Executor is a Java application that controls the automatic execution of both the Workload Generator and the Performance Benchmark Suite.

This module defines the values of the variables that influence the evaluation: the one related to the infrastructure, that is, the ontology development tool's load factor (X); and the execution parameter of the benchmarks, that is, the number of executions (N).

The Benchmark Suite Executor guarantees that the load present in the ontology development tool allows executing the benchmarks with no errors (e.g. if a benchmark deletes concepts, these concepts must exist in the tool).

During the evaluation, the Benchmark Suite Executor performs two steps:

1. **To prepare the system for the evaluation.** It uses the Workload Generator for generating ontologies according to the load factor, and inserts them into the tool.
2. **To execute the benchmark suite.** It executes all the benchmarks that compose the benchmark suite. Each benchmark first stabilises the system by executing its corresponding method an arbitrary number of times, and then executes the method N more times, measuring the execution time. These N measurements of the execution time of the method are stored in a text file in the Measurement Data Library.

4.4 Measurement Data Library

The Measurement Data Library stores the results of the different benchmark executions. As the benchmarks provide their results in a text file, we do not propose a specific implementation for the Measurement Data Library.

/EvaluationXX/fYYYY/nZZZ/

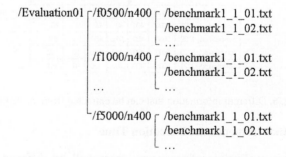

Fig. 5. Structure of the Measurement Data Library

The files with the results are stored in a hierarchical directory tree to be accessed easily. The structure of the tree, shown in Fig. 5, is the following:

- A first level with the number of the evaluation (XX).
- A second level with the ontology development tool's load factor (YYYY).
- A third level with the number of executions of the benchmark (ZZZ).

4.5 Statistical Analyser

Any statistical tool can be used for analysing the results of the benchmarking. Nevertheless, a tool capable of automating parts of the analysis process, like report and graph generation, would facilitate the analysis of the results to a large extent.

As can be seen in Fig. 6, from the results of a benchmark stored in the Measurement Data Library, we can obtain different information that can be used to evaluate the ontology development tools:

- **Graphs** that show the behaviour of the execution times.
- **Statistical values** worked out from the measurements.

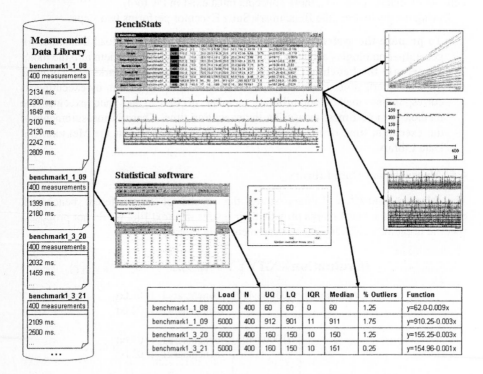

Fig. 6. Different information that can be extracted from the results

4.6 Variables that Influence the Execution Time

According to this evaluation infrastructure, there will be different variables that influence the execution time of a method. Some of them will be related to the features of the computer where the evaluation is performed (hardware configuration, software configuration and computer load) and one will be related to the infrastructure proposed (the load of the ontology development tool). To compare the results of two benchmarks, they must be executed under the same conditions. The definitions of these variables are the following:

- **Hardware configuration.** It is the configuration of the hardware of the computer where the ontology development tool is running.
- **Software configuration.** It is the configuration of the operating system and of the software needed to execute the ontology development tool.
- **Computer load.** It is the load that affects the computer where the ontology development tool is running.
- **Ontology development tool load.** It is the amount of ontology data that the ontology development tool stores.

5   Evaluating WebODE's Ontology Management API

The *Experiment* phase of the benchmarking methodology comprises the evaluation of the tool once the evaluation infrastructure has been defined and implemented. According to the infrastructure presented in section 4, we defined the benchmark suite and implemented the necessary modules regarding WebODE and its ontology management API, and we performed the evaluation on WebODE.

From the different variables that affect the evaluation, we only considered changes in the tool's load variable, to know its effect in WebODE's performance. The other three variables took fixed values during the evaluation so they did not affect the execution times. Furthermore, to avoid other non-controlled variables that may affect the results, the computer used for the evaluation was isolated: it had neither network connection nor user interaction. Then, we defined the values that these variables took during the evaluation:

- **Hardware configuration.** The computer was a Pentium 4 2.4 Ghz monoprocessor with 256 Mb. of memory.
- **Software configuration.** Each software's default configuration was used: Windows 2000 Professional Service Pack 4; SUN Java 1.4.2_03; Oracle version 8.1.7.0.0 (the Oracle instance's memory configuration was changed to: Shared pool 30 Mb., Buffer cache 80 Mb., Large pool 600 Kb., and Java pool 32 Kb.); Minerva version 1 build 4; and WebODE version 2 build 8.
- **Computer load.** This load was the corresponding to the computer just powered on, with only the programs and services needed to run the benchmarks.
- **Ontology development tool load.** The benchmark suite was executed ten times with the following load factors: (X=500, 1000, 1500, 2000, 2500, 3000, 3500, 4000, 4500, and 5000). As with a load factor of 5000 we obtained enough data to determine the methods' performance, the benchmarks have not been executed with higher load factors.

When running all the benchmarks in the benchmark suite:

- The method was first executed 100 times to stabilise the system before taking measures and to avoid unexpected behaviours in WebODE's initialisation.

- The **number of executions** (N) of a method in a benchmark was 400. With the aim of checking that 400 executions is a valid sample size, we have run several benchmarks with higher and lower number of executions and we have confirmed that the results obtained are virtually equivalent. We have not used a higher sample because the slightest precision improvement would mean a much higher duration of the benchmark suite execution.

After executing the 128 benchmarks of the benchmark suite with the 10 different load factors, we obtained 1280 text files, each with 400 measurements.

The source code of the infrastructure implemented for WebODE is published in a public web page[2], so anyone should be able to replicate the experiments and to achieve the same conclusions. The web page also contains the results obtained in this evaluation and all the statistical values and graphs worked out from them.

6 Analysis of the Evaluation Results

We have regarded the results of executing the benchmark suite with the maximum load factor used (X=5000) to be able to clearly differentiate the execution times. When analysing the effect of WebODE's load in the execution times of the methods, we have considered the results of executing the benchmark suite from a minimum load state (X=500) to a maximum load state (X=5000). In every case, we have considered a number of executions (N) of 400.

A first rough analysis of the results of the benchmark suite execution showed two main characteristics:

- Observing the graphs of the execution times measured in a benchmark, we saw that execution times are mainly **constant**. This can be seen in Fig. 7 that shows the execution times of running the method *removeConcept* 400 times with a load factor of 5000 in benchmark1_3_20.
- After running normality tests over the measurements, we confirmed that the distributions of the measurements were non-normal. Therefore, we could not rely on usual values such as mean and standard deviation for describing them and thus we used **robust statistical values** like the median, the upper and lower quartiles, and the interquartile range (upper minus lower quartile).

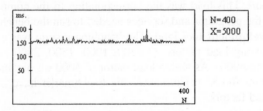

Fig. 7. Execution times of *removeConcept* in benchmark1_3_20

---

[2] http://kw.dia.fi.upm.es/wpbs/

The next sections show the specific metrics used for analysing the performance of the methods and the conclusions obtained from the execution results, that answer the questions previously stated in Fig. 2.

6.1 Metric for the Execution Time

The metric used for describing the execution time of a method in a benchmark has been the **median** of the execution times of the method in a benchmark execution.

Fig. 8 shows the histogram of the medians of the execution times of all the API methods. These medians range from 0 to 1051 milliseconds, with a group of values higher than the rest. The medians in this group belong to 12 benchmarks that execute 8 methods (as different benchmarks have been defined for each method). These 8 methods, with a median execution time higher than 800 ms, have been selected for the improvement recommendations. The rest of the median execution times of the methods are lower than 511 ms, being most of them around 100 ms.

Bearing in mind the kind of operation that the methods carry out (inserting, updating, removing, or selecting an ontology component), we did not find significant differences between the performances of each kind of method.

Taking into account what kind of element of the knowledge model (concepts, instances, class attributes, instance attributes, etc.) a method manages, in the slowest group almost every method that manages relations between concepts are present. Methods that manage instance attributes also have high execution times, and the rest of the methods behave similarly; the methods that stand out are those that manage imported terms and references since they are the ones with lower execution times.

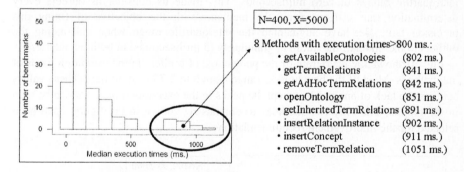

Fig. 8. Histogram of the medians of the execution times

6.2 Metric for the Variability of the Execution Time

The metric used for describing the variability of the execution time of a method in a benchmark has been the **interquartile range** (IQR) of the execution times of the method in a benchmark execution.

Fig. 9 shows the histogram of the IQRs of the execution times. Almost every method has an IQR from 0 to 11 ms, which is a low spread considering that the granularity of the measurements is 10 milliseconds. The only exceptions are the three methods shown in the figure. The method *getAvailableOntologies* has been selected for the improvement recommendations because of its atypical IQR value.

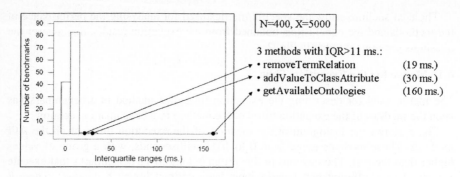

Fig. 9. Histogram of the interquartile ranges of the execution times

6.3 Metric for the Anomalies in the Execution Time

The metric used for describing the anomalies in the execution time of a method in a benchmark has been the **percentage of outliers** in the execution times of the method in a benchmark execution.

The traditional method for calculating the outliers is to consider as potential outlier values the measurements beyond the upper and lower quartiles and to add and subtract respectively 1.5 times the interquartile range [20]. As the Java method used for measuring time (*java.lang.System.currentTimeMillis()*) in the Windows platform has a precision of tens of milliseconds, in the results we frequently encountered interquartile ranges of zero milliseconds. This made us consider as outliers every determination that differed from the median. With the objective of fixing this precision fault, we have augmented the interquartile range when calculating the outliers to include half the minimal granularity (5 milliseconds) in both boundaries.

Fig. 10 shows the histogram of the percentage of outliers in the execution times of the methods. Most of the benchmarks range from 0 to 3.75% of outliers. These values confirm the lack of anomalies except the peaks in the execution times that can be seen in the graphs. The only two methods to emphasize, shown in the figure, have been selected for the improvement recommendations.

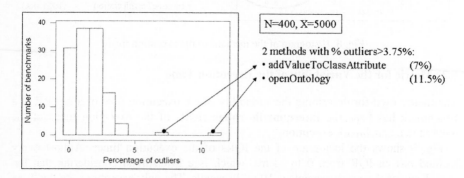

Fig. 10. Histogram of the percentage of outliers of the execution times

6.4   Effect of Changes in the Parameters of a Method

To analyse if changes in the parameters of a method affect the method performance, we compared the medians of the execution times of the benchmarks that use the same method.

The performance of 21 methods varies when its input parameters are changed, but this variation is lower than 60 milliseconds except in the five methods shown in Fig. 11, that have been selected for the improvement recommendations. Fig. 11 also shows the comparison of the execution times of the method *insertConcept* in benchmark1_1_08 and in benchmark1_1_09.

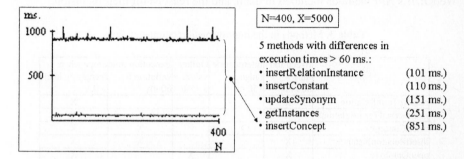

Fig. 11. Execution times of *insertConcept* in benchmark1_1_08 and benchmark1_1_09

6.5   Effect of Changes in WebODE's Load

To analyse the effect of WebODE's load in the execution times of the methods, we studied the medians of the execution times of the methods from a minimum load state (X=500) to a maximum load state (X=5000). We estimated the function that these medians define by **simple linear regression** and considered its **slope** in order to examine the relationship between the load and the execution time of the methods.

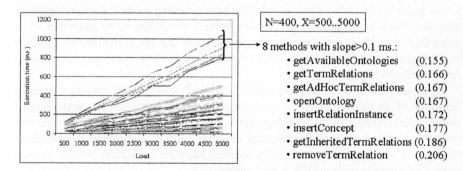

Fig. 12. Evolution of the execution times when increasing WebODE's load

Fig. 12 shows, for every benchmark, the functions defined by the median execution times with the different load factors. The slopes of the functions range from 0 to 0.1

except in 8 methods. The 8 methods whose execution times are higher than the rest are also the methods whose performance is more influenced by the load, and have been selected for the improvement recommendations.

6.6 Improvement Recommendations

From the analysis of the results, we produced a report stating the recommendations to improve WebODE's performance. These recommendations include the methods of the WebODE ontology management API identified in the previous sections.

Table 3 shows a summary of the improvement recommendations with 12 of the 72 WebODE's API methods included in them, and the reasons for their inclusion.

Table 3. Methods in the improvement recommendations

	Execution time > 800 ms	Interquartile range > 150 ms	Outlier values > 3.75%	Execution time variation > 60 ms	Slope when increasing load > 0.1
removeTermRelation	X				X
getInheritedTermRelations	X				X
insertConcept	X			X	X
insertRelationInstance	X			X	X
openOntology	X		X		X
getAdHocTermRelations	X				X
getTermRelations	X				X
getAvailableOntologies	X	X			X
addValueToClassAttribute			X		
insertConstant				X	
updateSynonym				X	
getInstances				X	

7 Conclusions and Future Work

In this paper we provide an overview of the benchmarking methodology for ontology tools developed by the authors in Knowledge Web. We define some guidelines when using this methodology to improve the performance and the scalability of ontology development tools by evaluating the performance of their ontology management APIs' methods.

To support the experimentation tasks of the methodology, we provide a detailed definition of an infrastructure for evaluating the performance and the scalability of ontology development tools' ontology management APIs. We have instantiated this infrastructure for evaluating the ontology management API of the WebODE ontology engineering workbench and the results obtained after the evaluation provide us with precise information on WebODE's performance.

The evaluation infrastructure can be instantiated for evaluating other ontology development tools that provide ontology management APIs. Taking as a starting point the methods of the ontology management API of a certain tool, the following tasks should be performed:

- Benchmarks that evaluate these methods should be defined, and the Performance Benchmark Suite module should be implemented for executing them.
- The Workload Generator should also be implemented to generate workload according to these methods' needs.
- The rest of the modules (Benchmark Suite Executor, Measurement Data Library and Statistical Analyser) already instantiated for WebODE could be used for another tool with minimal or no changes.

To obtain all the benefits of the benchmarking, like the extraction of best practices, other ontology development tools should participate in it. In this case, there are other tasks of the methodology that should be considered and that are not covered by this paper such as the search of other organisations and tools for participating in the benchmarking, the planning of the benchmarking, and the improvement on the tools. To perform a benchmarking like this, the evaluation infrastructure must be the same for every tool. Therefore:

- The Workload Generator should be modified in order to generate workloads independent of the tool, and thus the same workload can be used for every tool.
- The Performance Benchmark Suite should be modified to include only the methods common to all the tools or to use a common ontology management API such as OKBC [21].

Although the benchmark suite execution is automatic, the evaluation infrastructure would benefit significantly if some automatic analysis and summary of the results could be carried out, as there are plenty of them.

The WebODE Workload Generator could be improved and could generate ontologies with other structure or characteristics. In consequence, this module could be employed in other kind of evaluations and, thanks to the WebODE export services to different formats and languages (like RDF(S) or OWL); these ontologies could be used in evaluations performed over other tools, not just over WebODE.

Acknowledgments

This work is partially supported by a FPI grant from the Spanish Ministry of Education (BES-2005-8024), by the IST project Knowledge Web (IST-2004-507482) and by the CICYT project Infraestructura tecnológica de servicios semánticos para la web semántica (TIN2004-02660). Thanks to Rosario Plaza for reviewing the grammar of this paper.

References

1. A.J. Duineveld, R. Stoter, M.R. Weiden, B. Kenepa, and V.R. Benjamins. Wondertools? a comparative study of ontological engineering tools. In Proceedings of the 12th International Workshop on Knowledge Acquisition, Modeling and Management (KAW'99), Banff, Canada, 1999. Kluwer Academic Publishers.
2. Ontoweb deliverable 1.3: A survey on ontology tools. Technical report, IST OntoWeb Thematic Network, May 2002.

3. P. Lambrix, M. Habbouche, and M. Pérez. Evaluation of ontology development tools for bioinformatics. Bioinformatics, 19(12):1564-1571, 2003.
4. J. Angele and Y. Sure (eds.). Proceedings of the 1st International Workshop on Evaluation of Ontology-based Tools (EON2002), Sigüenza, Spain, September 2002.
5. Y. Sure and O. Corcho (eds.). Proceedings of the 2nd International Workshop on Evaluation of Ontology-based Tools (EON2003), Florida, USA, October 2003.
6. Y. Sure, O. Corcho, J. Euzenat, T. Hughes (eds.). Proceedings of the 3rd International Workshop on Evaluation of Ontology-based Tools (EON2004), Hiroshima, Japan, November 2004.
7. A. Magkanaraki, S. Alexaki, V. Christophides, and D. Plexousakis. Benchmarking RDF schemas for the semantic web. In Proceedings of the First International Semantic Web Conference, pages 132–146. Springer-Verlag, 2002.
8. C. Tempich and R. Volz. Towards a benchmark for semantic web reasoners - an analysis of the DAML ontology library. In Proc. of the 2nd International Workshop on Evaluation of Ontology-based Tools (EON2003), Florida, USA, October 2003.
9. Y. Guo, Z. Pan, and J. Heflin. An evaluation of knowledge base systems for large OWL datasets. In Proceedings of the 3rd International Semantic Web Conference (ISWC2004), pages 274.288, Hiroshima, Japan, November 2004.
10. J.C. Arpírez, O. Corcho, M. Fernández-López, A. Gómez-Pérez. WebODE in a nutshell. AI Magazine. 24(3), Fall 2003, pp. 37-47.
11. M. Spendolini. The Benchmarking Book. AMACOM, New York, NY, 1992.
12. B. Kitchenham. DESMET: A method for evaluating software engineering methods and tools. Technical Report TR96-09, Department of Computer Science, University of Keele, Stanfordshire, UK, 1996.
13. C. Wohlin, A. Aurum, H. Petersson, F. Shull, and M. Ciolkowski. Software inspection benchmarking - a qualitative and quantitative comparative opportunity. In Proceedings of 8th International Software Metrics Symposium. 118-130, 2002.
14. R. García-Castro, D. Maynard, H. Wache, D. Foxvog, and R. González-Cabero. D2.1.4 Specification of a methodology, general criteria and benchmark suites for benchmarking ontology tools. Technical report, Knowledge Web, December 2004.
15. V.R. Basili, G. Caldiera, D.H. Rombach. The Goal Question Metric Approach. Encyclopedia of Software Engineering, 2 Volume Set Willey, pp 528-532, 1994.
16. J.M. Bull, L.A. Smith, M.D. Westhead, D.S. Henty, R.A. Davey. A Methodology for Benchmarking Java Grande Applications. EPCC, June 1999.
17. B. Shirazi, L. Welch, B. Ravindran, C. Cavanaugh, B. Yanamula, R. Brucks, E. Huh. DynBench: A Dynamic Benchmark Suite for Distributed Real-Time Systems. IPDPS Workshop on Embedded HPC Systems and Applications. S. Juan, Puerto Rico, 1999.
18. S. Sim, S. Easterbrook, and R. Holt. Using benchmarking to advance research: A challenge to software engineering. In Proceedings of the 25th International Conference on Software Engineering (ICSE'03), pages 74-83, Portland, OR, 2003.
19. F. Stefani, D. Macii, A. Moschitta, and D. Petri. FFT benchmarking for digital signal processing technologies. In 17th IMEKOWorld Congress, Dubrovnik, June 2003.
20. W. Mendenhall and T. Sincich. Statistics for Engineering and the Sciences, 4th Edition. Englewood Cliffs, NJ. Prentice Hall, 1995.
21. V.K. Chaudhri, A. Farquhar, R. Fikes, P.D. Karp, J.P. Rice. The Generic Frame Protocol 2.0. Technical Report, Stanford University, 1997.

Semantically Rich Recommendations in Social Networks for Sharing, Exchanging and Ranking Semantic Context

Stefania Ghita, Wolfgang Nejdl, and Raluca Paiu

L3S Research Center, University of Hanover,
Deutscher Pavillon, Expo Plaza 1, 30539 Hanover, Germany
{ghita, nejdl, paiu}@l3s.de

Abstract. Recommender algorithms have been quite successfully employed in a variety of scenarios from filtering applications to recommendations of movies and books at Amazon.com. However, all these algorithms focus on single item recommendations and do not consider any more complex recommendation structures. This paper explores how semantically rich complex recommendation structures, represented as RDF graphs, can be exchanged and shared in a distributed social network. After presenting a motivating scenario we define several annotation ontologies we use in order to describe context information on the user's desktop and show how our ranking algorithm can exploit this information. We discuss how social distributed networks and interest groups are specified using extended FOAF vocabulary, and how members of these interest groups share semantically rich recommendations in such a network. These recommendations transport shared context as well as ranking information, described in annotation ontologies. We propose an algorithm to compute these rankings which exploits available context information and show how rankings are influenced by the context received from other users as well as by the reputation of the members of the social network with whom the context is exchanged.

1 Introduction

This paper explores how we can use communication in social networks to share and extend context information and how semantically rich recommendations between members of interest groups in such settings can be realized. We will build upon FOAF networks, which describe personal and group information, based on the FOAF vocabulary to describe friends, groups and interests. We will focus on how to share context in such a network, how to use these shared metadata to connect the information of different peers in the social network and how to use it for social recommendations.

The next section describes a motivating scenario that shows how context and rankings are exchanged inside a research group. Section 3 discusses how to describe contexts and their corresponding metadata by means of appropriate ontologies and how to use these metadata for extended desktop search with appropriate ranking of search results. Section 4 describes how we exchange context and importance information among the members of an interest group defined through an extended FOAF vocabulary introduced in section 4.1. Section 4.3 presents the algorithm used for the rank computation, together with the results we get after applying the algorithm on a user's context metadata before and after she receives additional resources and context from another group

Y. Gil et al. (Eds.): ISWC 2005, LNCS 3729, pp. 293–307, 2005.

member. We discuss the influence of user trust upon ranking results and comment the results of some experiments. Section 5 gives an overview of related work. We then conclude and sketch some future research issues.

2   Motivating Scenario

As our motivating scenario, let us consider our L3S Research Group context and within this group, Bob and Alice as two members who exchange information. One important task in a research group is exchanging and sharing knowledge, which we will focus upon in this paper. Unfortunately, the most widely used infrastructure for this purpose, email, is poorly suited to support this exchange. When we exchange documents by email, no context is shared (for example which are the interesting follow-up papers, or which are the interesting references for a paper) and any comments about the documents that are included in the email are lost as soon as the attached documents are stored in some directory.

The following example shows how such a sharing scenario can be supported in a more efficient manner. We assume that Bob mails Alice a document which he sent to the DELOS Workshop, with the title "I know I stored it somewhere - Contextual Information and Ranking on Our Desktop". Bob is one of the authors and therefore he already has all the important context for this paper including the cited papers stored on his computer. In this first email, Alice will therefore not only receive the paper but also its immediate context relevant for the research group, containing information about all papers that are referenced in the DELOS paper, information about important authors for this topic or which conferences are relevant. In other words, whenever we send a paper, the metadata associated to that paper will also be sent. From the five references included, Alice decides that "ObjectRank: Authority-Based Keyword Search in Databases" and "Activity Based Metadata for Semantic Desktop Search" are of particular interest for her and she sends back an email to Bob requiring additional information about those. As an answer, she receives from Bob the context information associated with these papers, containing the references that Bob has already downloaded. So the context information will be exchanged progressively, from the immediate context to the more distant one.

Figures 1 and 2 present the context created on Alice's desktop as result of her metadata exchange with Bob. Figure 1 contains only the *cites* relationship among the various resources, while in Figure 2 we represent additional relationships, like *presented_at*, *downloaded_from*, *author*, or *same_session*. Note that the context networks created on the users' desktop are not separated, but just visualized separately in these figures.

By examining the context graph in figure 2, we see that all the papers labeled from **G** to **Q** were presented at different WWW Conferences, in different years, and all were downloaded from the ACM Portal. Papers **A**, **C** and **K** all share the same author, *Bob*, and have been downloaded from the L3S Publication page. Similarly, the publication labeled **B** and the other two papers which were presented at the same session at the VLDB conference were downloaded from the VLDB web site.

All this information is taken into account when computing the importance of the resources on Alice's desktop. For example, when computing the importance of the

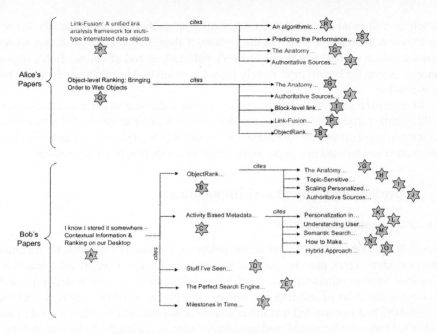

Fig. 1. Publications Context Example - Part 1

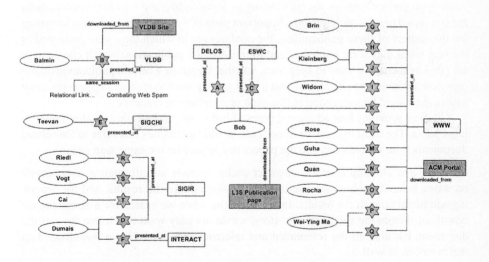

Fig. 2. Publications Context Example - Part 2

conferences, the WWW Conference will be more important than other conferences, since Alice already has a lot of important publications which have been presented there. The number of papers from the same author Alice has already downloaded also influences how important she considers that author. This means that certain authors are more important than others, based on the publications used and cited in the L3S Research

Group, as well as on general citation information about these authors. The fact that Alice knows Bob and Bob is one of the authors of three publications Alice has on her desktop influences the importance of Bob's publications and of course, Bob's importance as author. So he will be definitely more important to Alice than other authors not known to her.

In order to be able to compute the rankings of their documents Alice and Bob have to build a context around the resources they have stored on their desktops. The next section presents in more detail how this context information is created and then describes how this context can be used in computing rankings of search results on the desktop.

3   Representing Context and Importance

3.1   Representing Context

Generally speaking, context information describes all aspects important for a certain situation: ideas, facts, persons, publications, and many more. Context information includes all relevant relationships as well as interaction history. Current desktop search prototypes fall short of utilizing any desktop specific information, especially context information, and just use full text index search. In our scenario we clearly need to use additional context information, and specifically want to exploit the following contexts:

CiteSeer context. The most important aspects we want to record from the CiteSeer context are the publications we are viewing or downloading and how these publications are connected to other publications. Important parts of the available context information are the authors of these publications, the conferences in which they were presented or the year when they were published and even more, the publications which cite them or are cited by them. We want to keep track whether we saved a certain publication on our own desktop in order to be able to find it later and we want to receive suggestions about papers that might be interesting in the same or overlapping contexts.

CiteSeer provides four additional types of links that can be followed after identifying a paper. The most expressive in our case would be the ones that refer to the related documents from co-citations and the papers that appear on the same web site.

Browsing and Desktop context. Browser caches include all information about user's browsing behavior, which are useful both for finding relevant results, and for providing additional context for results. In our scenario, when we search for a document we downloaded from the CiteSeer repository, we do not only want to retrieve the specific document, but also all the referenced and referring papers which we downloaded on that occasion as well.

In general, we view documents stored from emails and from web sites as our personal digital library, which holds the papers we are interested in, plus all relevant contextual information. When we store documents, we can then retrieve them efficiently and restore the original context we built up when storing these documents. Personalized search and ranking on the desktop takes this contextual information into account as well as the preferences implicit in this information. [6] discusses how people tend to associate things to certain contexts. So far, however, search infrastructures neither collect nor use this contextual information.

Scenario specific annotation ontologies. Figure 3 presents our current prototype on-tology, used for implementing our motivating scenario. It specifies context metadata for the CiteSeer context, files and web pages, together with the relations among them (described in more detail in [2]). Conceptually, the elements in the rectangles represent classes, circles represent class attributes. We use classes whenever we want to attach importance / rank on entities, attributes otherwise.

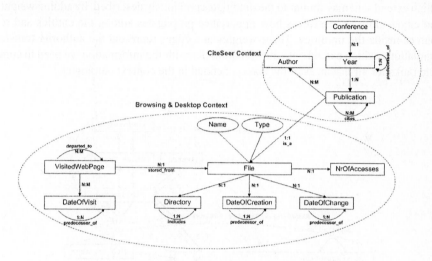

Fig. 3. Context ontology for our prototype

For the browsing and desktop context, we annotate each page with additional infor-mation about its basic properties (URL, access date, etc), as well as more complex ones such as in- and out-going links browsed [2]. The user's behavior as the pages or publica-tions he browsed or downloaded provide useful additional information. Files, which are stored from web pages, reside in certain directories, which in turn can include other di-rectories. The creation or change date of a file together with the number of accesses are some other important indicators which have to be taken into account when describing the desktop context. An extended publication ontology makes use of additional knowl-edge about how CiteSeer pages are connected and what they represent. Publications are referenced by other publications and can cite others, they can have a publication date / year associated with them, as well as a conference or journal. Publications have authors and are stored as documents on the desktop.

Other ontologies describe contexts like conferences, including reviewers, papers, meetings, authors, or private contexts like birthdays, including persons, locations, etc.

3.2   Representing Importance

In addition to the information which resources are included in a specific context, we also want to know how important or valuable these resources are. We therefore have to develop a mechanism which allows us to express this information and use it for ranking search results.

Authority transfer annotations. Annotation ontologies describe all aspects and relationships among resources which influence the ranking. The identity of the authors, for example, influences our opinion of documents so "author" should be represented explicitly as a class in our publication ontology. We then have to specify how these aspects influence each other's importance.

ObjectRank [1] has introduced the notion of authority transfer schema graphs, which extend schemas similar to the ontologies previously described, by adding weights and edges in order to express how importance propagates among the entities and resources inside the ontology. These weights and edges represent the authority transfer annotations, which extend our context ontologies with the information we need to compute ranks for all instances of the classes defined in the context ontologies.[1]

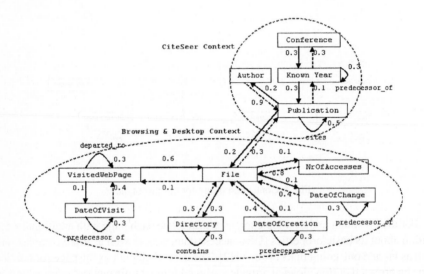

Fig. 4. Authority transfer annotations, including external ranking sources

Figure 4 depicts our context ontology plus its authority transfer annotations. The ontology representing our browsing and desktop context says that a visited web page is important if we arrived at the current one from an important page, if the file under which it is stored is important, or if the date when the page was visited is important. For the CiteSeer context, publications transfer part of their authority to other papers they cite, to their authors, to the files under which they are stored, and to the year when the paper was published. As we can see, citing important papers doesn't make a paper important. As suggested in [1], every edge from the schema graph is split into two edges, one for each direction. This is motivated by the observation that authority potentially flows in both directions and not only in the direction that appears in the schema - if we know that a particular person is important, we also want to have all emails we receive from this person ranked higher. The final ObjectRank value for each resource is calculated based on the PageRank formula.

---

[1] In contrast to ObjectRank, we do not compute a keyword-specific ranking, but a global one.

Personalized Preferences and Ranking. Different authority transfer weights express different preferences of the user, translating into personalized ranking. The important requirement for doing this successfully is that we include in a user ontology all concepts, which influence our ranking function. For example, if we view a publication important because it was written by an author important to us, we have to represent that in our context ontology.

4   Sharing Context and Importance

4.1   Interest Groups

Interest groups in our context are specialized social networks that have a stated common interest which connects the members of the group. One important reason for creating interest groups resides in increasing the efficiency of the information flow inside that group. All members of the same interest group share the same domain of interest and the social relationships are woven around this type of information sharing. They are all possibly part of the same professional group, just as we described in the motivating scenario, Alice and Bob being in the same research group, the L3S Research Group.

We chose to represent interest groups based on an extension of FOAF in order to describe the social network of participants and we will describe all contexts as RDF metadata, as presented in [2]. Being based on RDF, FOAF inherits some of its benefits, like the ease of aggregating and harvesting it, or combining it with other vocabularies, thus allowing us to capture a rich set of metadata. The basic FOAF vocabulary itself is pretty simple, pragmatic and designed to allow simultaneous deployment and extension. It is identified by the namespace URI 'http://xmlns.com/foaf/0.1/' and described in more detail at the FOAF project page [9].

FOAF terms represent information which can be grouped in the following five broad categories: FOAF Basics, Personal Information, Online Accounts/ IM, Projects and Groups, Documents and Images. The most important for us is the *Projects and Groups* category, which allows us to talk about groups and group membership among others. Groups are represented with the aid of the **foaf:Group** class, which represents a collection of individual agents. The **foaf:member** property allows us to explicitly express the membership of agents to a group. Since the **foaf:Person** class is a subclass of the **foaf:Agent** class, persons can also be members of a group. One can specify the interests of the group members by using specific properties, like **foaf:interest**, **foaf:topic_interest**, or **foaf:topic**, even though it is not yet clear how to use them correctly.

A notable omission in the basic FOAF vocabulary is the inability to express anything related to information sharing in a group. Even though being in a group or social network usually means that we want to share information within this social network, there is no vocabulary to express this in FOAF. The assumption we make in this paper is that people belonging to a common interest group will share a specific set of metadata. In our scenario these are the contextual metadata defined by appropriate annotation ontologies, as discussed in the previous section. When members of an interest group express that they want to share a certain set of metadata, they will agree on an appropriate ontology defining this set. We therefore suggest to extend the FOAF vocabulary with a new property **foaf:shared_context** which takes as its value the annotation ontology describing the metadata to be shared. Based on this, the FOAF description of the L3S Research interest group and its members Bob and Alice as presented in our motivating scenario looks as follows:

$< foaf : Group >$
$\quad < foaf : name > L3SResearchGroup < /foaf : name >$
$\quad < foaf : member >$
$\quad\quad < foaf : Person >$
$\quad\quad\quad < foaf : name > Alice < /foaf : name >$
$\quad\quad\quad < foaf : homepage\ rdf : resource = "http : //www.l3s.de/ \sim alice"/ >$
$\quad\quad < /foaf : Person >$
$\quad < /foaf : member >$
$\quad < foaf : member >$
$\quad\quad < foaf : Person >$
$\quad\quad\quad < foaf : name > Bob < /foaf : name >$
$\quad\quad\quad < foaf : homepage\ rdf : resource = "http : //www.l3s.de/ \sim bob"/ >$
$\quad\quad < /foaf : Person >$
$\quad < /foaf : member >$
$\quad < foaf : shared\_context$
$\quad rdf : resource = http : //www.l3s.de/isearch/citeseerContext.rdf/ >$
$\quad < foaf : shared\_context$
$\quad rdf : resource = http : //www.l3s.de/isearch/browsingDesktopContext.rdf/ >$
$< /foaf : Group >$

4.2   Exchanging Context Within Interest Groups

Sharing context in an interest group is useful and necessary because not only do we want to publish our own work but we also want to find out about additional new resources related to our work and get suggestions about possible further developments in that area. Recommendation then means suggesting additional related information to given items. In our motivating scenario, we have as interest group a set of researchers, and a set of ontologies defining which metadata are shared between them. The contextual metadata corresponding to those ontologies as discussed in section 3 represent the context information we have available on our desktop.

These context metadata are generated locally by a set of metadata generators [2], which record user actions as well as interactions and information exchanges between members of a group. These metadata generators create RDF annotation files for each resource whose context they describe, so for each relevant resource on the desktop (e.g. a specific publication) we will have this additional RDF information available.

For the experiments described in this paper, we have implemented a metadata generator, which deals with publications, and crawls one's desktop in order to identify and annotate all papers saved as PDF files. For each identified paper, it extracts the title and tries to match it with an entry into the CiteSeer publications database. If it finds an entry, the application builds up an annotation file, containing information from the database about the title of the paper, the authors, publication year, conference and other CiteSeer references to publications. All annotation files corresponding to papers are then merged in order to construct the RDF graph of publications existing on one's desktop.

In our scenario, whenever Bob sends a publication to Alice, who is member of the same interest group, he wants to attach the appropriate context information, i.e. the publication context we have discussed in the scenario. A second (email) helper application therefore checks who is the recipient of the email, which group she belongs to, and therefore which context information/ metadata to attach. On Alice's side, the helper application has to integrate the newly received annotation files into the existing publication graph.

4.3   Sharing Importance

Ranking of Resources - General Algorithm. In our distributed scenario, each user has his own contextual network / context metadata graph and for each node in this network the appropriate ranking as computed by the algorithm described in section 3.2. The computation of rankings on one's desktop is based on the link structure of the resources as specified by the defined ontologies and the corresponding metadata. When sharing information within the group / network we exchange not only contexts but also rankings. So exchanging context information has also an impact on the ranking of results of the desktop search. These values are then recomputed according to the rankings received together with the context from other persons.

Ranking of resources is calculated based on the PageRank formula:

$$r = dAr + (1 - d)e \qquad (1)$$

applying the random surfer model and including all nodes in the base set. Parameter d in the equation represents the dampening factor and is usually considered to be 0.85. The random jump to an arbitrary resource from the data graph is modeled by the vector e. A is the adjacency matrix which connects all available instances of the existing context ontology on one's desktop. The weights of the links between the instances correspond to the weights specified in the authority transfer annotation ontology. Thus, when instantiating the authority transfer annotation ontology for the resources existing on the users' desktop, the corresponding matrix A will have elements which can be either 0, if there is no edge between the corresponding entities in the data graph, or they have the value of the weight assigned to the edge determined by these entities, in the authority transfer annotation ontology, divided by the number of outgoing links of the same type. According to the formula, a random surfer follows one of the outgoing links of the current page, with the probability specified by d, and with a probability of $(1-d)$, he jumps to a randomly selected page from the web graph. The r vector in the equation stores the ranks of all resources in the data graph. These rankings are computed iteratively until a certain threshold is reached.

To make these details clear, let us look at the following example: we consider the authority transfer annotation ontology for a publication ontology, as depicted in Figure 5 and then instantiate it. A subset of this data graph is shown in Figure 6.

Fig. 5. Authority transfer annotation ontology for a publication ontology

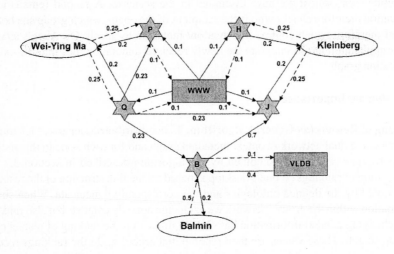

Fig. 6. Data Graph

Table 1. The A matrix

$$A = \begin{pmatrix}
 & Y.Ma & & & & & & & & & & VLDB \\
YingMa & - & - & - & 0.2 & 0.2 & - & - & - & - & - \\
Kleinberg & - & - & - & - & - & 0.2 & 0.2 & - & - & - \\
Balmin & - & - & - & - & - & - & - & 0.2 & - & - \\
P & 0.25 & - & - & - & 0.23 & - & - & - & 0.1 & - \\
Q & 0.25 & - & - & - & - & - & - & - & 0.1 & - \\
J & - & 0.25 & - & - & 0.23 & - & - & 0.7 & 0.1 & - \\
H & - & 0.25 & - & - & - & - & - & - & 0.1 & - \\
B & - & - & 0.5 & - & 0.23 & - & - & - & - & 0.4 \\
WWW & - & - & - & 0.1 & 0.1 & 0.1 & 0.1 & - & - & - \\
VLDB & - & - & - & - & - & - & - & 0.1 & - & -
\end{pmatrix}$$

The instantiation of our matrix A from Equation 1 is depicted in Table 1:

According to Figure 6, the authors transfer 0.5 units of importance divided by the number of "authors" links, to their own publications (Wei-Ying Ma to publications P, Q, Kleinberg to H and J and Balmin to B). Publications transfer 0.7 units of importance divided by the number of "cites" links to other papers they cite, 0.1 units to the conferences where they were accepted and 0.2 units of importance divided by the number of "author" links to their authors. Since the papers can be presented to only one conference, the 0.1 units of importance remain undivided.

The values in the matrix are grouped in blocks, formed by considering the cartesian products *Author* × *Author, Author* × *Publication*, etc. The elements from one block can be either 0, if there is no edge between the corresponding entities in the data graph, or they have the value of the weight assigned to the edge between the entities which determine the block, from the authority transfer annotation ontology.

The e vector, modeling the random jump in the PageRank formula, contains an entry for each resource appearing in the data graph. In the original PageRank/ ObjectRank formula, the probability of reaching a certain resource through a random jump is evenly distributed among the resources, and therefore, the e vector has only 1 values:

$$e = (1\ 1\ 1\ 1\ 1\ 1\ 1\ 1\ 1)^T \qquad (2)$$

Ranking of Resources on Alice's Desktop. We computed the ranking values for the resources existing on Alice's desktop (see Figure 1 for the labels of resources). The results are presented in Table 2. Note that these values represent Alice's personal rankings according to the context existing around her resources and are not necessarily related to external sources of ranking like CiteSeer or Google.

How Ranks Change When Bob Sends Something. After receiving via email the context existing on Bob's desktop, as we described in Section 2, Alice's ranks change as presented in Table 3. By comparing the values in the two tables, we can see that some of the rankings increase, because existing resources are referenced by the newer ones. For example, the rank of the "ObjectRank" paper, labeled **B**, increases from 0.295982 to 0.301975 since it is now referenced by the paper labeled **A**. As a consequence, all the rankings for the resources which have an incoming link from **B** will increase. This process of rank propagation is an iterative one, according to the links in the data graph, and continues until the rank difference between two iterations is less than a certain threshold. Alice receives not only context from Bob, but also resources, so that she will also have rank values for these new resources.

The context which is received from other members of the interest group is used for building the user's own context, which means that it is also taken into account when creating the adjacency matrix A. In order to include the rankings of other users into the computation of the user's own ranking, we work on the vector e, which models the random jump. So, if a resource is highly ranked according to the received rankings and the user wants to take this into account, she will have to assign a higher value for the corresponding element in the vector which simulates the random jump.

Of course, even if two users exchange all of their context metadata, they still will not have the same rankings, as local usage information such as number of accesses etc., which influences rankings, always stays local and is not exchanged. Note that in our data graph, group members usually appear as instances of authors or as senders of emails [2], so we can use their rank as one possible indicator of their trustworthiness.

How Alice's Trust in Bob Influences the Rankings. Even inside an interest group, we have to take into account different reputations. If somebody, whom I trust and who is important for me, sends his recommendations, I want his suggestions to be higher ranked than the ones received from a more untrusted person. These different reputations can be represented by influencing the dampening factor. The higher the trustworthiness

Table 2. Alice's personal rank values

Resource	Rank
B	0.295982
G	0.260644
J	0.260644
S	0.248796
R	0.248796
T	0.244728
P	0.185268
SIGIR	0.181705
WWW	0.176995
Balmin	0.175207
Brin	0.172292
Kleinberg	0.172292
Riedl	0.171261
Vogt	0.171261
Cai	0.170888
Q	0.170745
VLDB	0.162604
W. Y. Ma	0.159406

Table 3. Alice's personal ranking values after receiving context information from Bob

Resource	Rank	Resource	Rank
B	0.301975	P	0.181859
E	0.297845	K	0.178391
G	0.287298	Bob	0.175816
I	0.253764	Teevan	0.175459
WWW	0.245065	Brin	0.174496
S	0.244723	Widom	0.171624
R	0.244723	Riedl	0.170860
N	0.242694	Vogt	0.170860
M	0.242694	Rocha	0.170683
L	0.242694	Quan	0.170683
O	0.242694	Guha	0.170683
F	0.242280	Rose	0.170683
T	0.240779	Cai	0.170521
J	0.232862	Q	0.167610
C	0.228117	SIGCHI	0.162730
A	0.210174	INTERACT	0.160311
H	0.200576	W. Y. Ma	0.159224
D	0.191779	Balmin	0.158563
SIGIR	0.189280	VLDB	0.154282
Dumais	0.186942	ESWC	0.152771
Kleinberg	0.186882	DELOS	0.152553

of someone in my interest group, who sends me her own context and rankings, the higher should be the probability to reach the resources in that set.

In our example, we considered there is only one user Alice exchanges context with. In the previous table, Table 3, the rankings are computed as if Alice is fully trusting Bob, so that she does not make any difference between the resources she already has and the ones she receives from him. This translates into a vector e having all elements 1. If Alice doesn't trust Bob 100%, she will have to bias the PageRank on her resources, that is assign values less than 1 to the elements in the e vector corresponding to the resources coming from Bob. This means that the probability of reaching the resources she receives from Bob through a random jump is less than the probability of jumping to one of her own resources. In our experiments we computed Alice's rankings for different levels of trust she has for Bob, and the results are presented in Table 4. A detailed study about the influence of different trust distributions upon the ranking of resources is presented in [3].

As we would expect, the rankings decrease, as trust decreases. Originally highly ranked resources still have a high rank and for example paper **B** in the case of a trust biasing rank computation of 90% or 70% even acquires a higher rank than before the resource exchange takes place. That is because for these resources Alice already has her own ratings and they will increase due to the fact that they are referenced by some of the received resources. For the newly received resources, (Teevan, Dumais, etc.) for a trust level of 1%, the rankings are quite small compared to the rankings of the originally

Table 4. Alice's ranking values after receiving context information from Bob for different trust levels

Resource Label	PageRank					
	90% Trust	70% Trust	50% Trust	30% Trust	10% Trust	1% Trust
B	0.300138	0.296501	0.292864	0.289226	0.285589	0.283952
G	0.286867	0.286448	0.286029	0.285610	0.285191	0.285003
J	0.232428	0.231741	0.231054	0.230366	0.229679	0.229370
S	0.244652	0.244613	0.244574	0.244534	0.244495	0.244477
R	0.244652	0.244613	0.244574	0.244534	0.244495	0.244477
T	0.240721	0.240683	0.240644	0.240606	0.240567	0.240550
P	0.181833	0.181793	0.181754	0.181714	0.181674	0.181656
SIGIR	0.188384	0.186783	0.185181	0.183579	0.181978	0.181257
WWW	0.238370	0.225374	0.212379	0.199383	0.186388	0.180540
Balmin	0.158504	0.158401	0.158298	0.158195	0.158092	0.158046
Brin	0.174403	0.174367	0.174332	0.174296	0.174261	0.174245
Kleinberg	0.185509	0.182843	0.180177	0.177511	0.174845	0.173645
Riedl	0.170800	0.170796	0.170793	0.170790	0.170786	0.170785
Vogt	0.170800	0.170796	0.170793	0.170790	0.170786	0.170785
Cai	0.170465	0.170461	0.170458	0.170455	0.170452	0.170450
Q	0.167588	0.167551	0.167514	0.167478	0.167441	0.167425
VLDB	0.154252	0.154201	0.154149	0.154098	0.154046	0.154023
W. Y. Ma	0.159220	0.159222	0.159218	0.159216	0.159214	0.159213

existing ones. The probability of jumping to one of these resources is 0.01, in contrast to the probability of 1.0 of executing a random jump to the ones Alice already has on her desktop.

5 Related Work

[4] presents a class of model-based recommendation algorithms for creating a top-N list of recommendations. In their approach, they first determine the similarities between the various items and then use them to identify the set of items to be recommended. [4] also addresses the key steps of this class of algorithms: which are the methods used to compute the similarity between items and which are the methods used to combine these similarities, in order to compute the similarity between a basket of items and a candidate recommender item. Opposed to this, in our approach the recommended items are based on user preferences and explicit context information.

Tapestry [5] is a recommender system which, in a sense, is similar to our approach. Tapestry is an e-mail filtering system, designed to filter e-mails received from mailing lists and newsgroup postings. Each user can write a comment / annotation about each email message and share these annotations with a group of users. A user can then filter these email messages by writing queries on these annotations. Though Tapestry allows individual users to benefit from annotations made by other users, the system requires an individual user to write complicated queries. We extend the idea in Tapestry by annotating not only emails but other resources on the user's desktop. In addition, exchange of annotations is handled (semi-) automatically.

The first system that generated automated recommendations was the GroupLens system [8]. The system, like in our case, provides users with personalized recommendations by identifying a neighborhood of similar users and recommending the articles that this group of users finds interesting.

The most interesting work for recommendation infrastructures, which does not require a central recommender server is PocketLens, [7]. The paper discusses on how to preserve privacy in such an infrastructure. In contrast to our work, they do not exploit semantic connections between items, such as we have for citation relationships.

Compared to the usual recommender systems, including the commercial ones such as Amazon.com, which usually suggest single items, we have the potential to make semantically rich suggestions that are represented as parts of a semantic network which we exchange. Additionally we also provide to the user information about other users' rankings. While most recommender systems define groups by relying on the overlap among preferred items, we rely on an explicit group membership denotation based on FOAF metadata.

6   Conclusions and Future Work

FOAF is a nice vocabulary to describe social networks, but most of the current applications are centered around describing social networks and not how to use them. This paper explores how to build upon FOAF and rich semantic web metadata to exchange and recommend context information and resources in a social network. These contextual metadata are described by appropriate annotation ontologies, and are exchanged within FOAF groups as specified by the group members. The exchange of metadata is done by means of additional attachments for each document exchanged via email, extending email exchange from pure document exchange to an exchange of both document and relevant context information. We presented how the computation of ranking is accomplished and how this computation is influenced by the context exchange as well as by the reputation of persons involved in the exchange process.

There are quite a few interesting issues to be investigated in future work, including privacy and security issues. This is especially important if we exploit peer-to-peer infrastructures instead of email attachments to implement a knowledge sharing infrastructure as described in this paper. It is also worthy to note that the ranking we compute for different resources can be compared to the ratings which are used in recommender systems. We can therefore not only share resources which are semantically connected to the ones we are exchanging, but also resources which are ranked / rated highly by peers in our community. An additional interesting aspect is to explore dynamic social networks, where groups are not statically defined from the beginning but dynamically based on the exchange of context metadata. In this case users can initially choose which pieces of metadata information they want to append to a document for certain recipients, and common exchange patterns then determine common interest groups and allow automatic exchange of metadata based on these previous interactions.

Acknowledgements

We want to thank Andrei Damian for his contribution to the publication metadata generator and Paul Chirita for many good discussions on topics related to this paper.

References

1. A. Balmin, V. Hristidis, and Y. Papakonstantinou. Objectrank: Authority-based keyword search in databases. In *VLDB*, Toronto, September 2004.
2. P. Chirita, R. Gavriloaie, S. Ghita, W. Nejdl, and R. Paiu. Activity based metadata for semantic desktop search. In *Proceedings of the 2nd European Semantic Web Conference*, Crete, May 2005.
3. A. Damian, W. Nejdl, and R. Paiu. Peer-sensitive objectrank-valuing contextual information in social networks. In *L3S Technical Report*, 2005.
4. M. Deshpande and G. Karypis. Item-based top-n recommendation algorithms. In *ACM Transactions on Information Systems*, January 2004.
5. D. Goldberg, D. Nichols, B. M. Oki, and D. Terry. Using collabarative filtering to weave an information tapestry. In *ACM Press*, December 1992.
6. Teevan J., Alvarado C., Ackerman M. S., and Karger D. R. The perfect search engine is not enough: A study of orienteering behavior in directed search. In *CHI*, Vienna, April 2004.
7. B. N. Miller, J. A. Konstan, and J. Riedl. Pocketlens: Toward a personal recommender system. *ACM Trans. Inf. Syst.*, 22(3):437–476, 2004.
8. P. Resnick, N. Iacovou, M. Suchak, P. Bergstrom, and J. Riedl. Grouplens: an open architecture for collaborative filtering of netnews. In *CSCW '94: Proceedings of the 1994 ACM conference on Computer supported cooperative work*, pages 175–186. ACM Press, 1994.
9. The foaf project. http://www.foaf-project.org/.

On Partial Encryption of RDF-Graphs

Mark Giereth

Institute for Intelligent Systems, University of Stuttgart,
70569 Stuttgart, Germany
giereth@iis.uni-stuttgart.de

Abstract. In this paper a method for Partial RDF Encryption (PRE) is proposed in which sensitive data in an RDF-graph is encrypted for a set of recipients while all non-sensitive data remain publicly readable. The result is an RDF-compliant self-describing graph containing encrypted data, encryption metadata, and plaintext data. For the representation of encrypted data and encryption metadata, the XML-Encryption and XML-Signature recommendations are used. The proposed method allows for fine-grained encryption of arbitrary subjects, predicates, objects and subgraphs of an RDF-graph. An XML vocabulary for specifying encryption policies is introduced.

1   Introduction

Giving information a well-defined meaning is on one hand the basis for intelligent applications in an emerging Semantic Web, but on the other hand can have profound consequences when considering privacy, security, and intellectual property rights issues. In the Semantic Web vision agents automatically gather and merge semantically annotated data, infer new data and re-use the data in different contexts [6]. However seemingly harmless pieces of data could reveal a lot of information when combined with others. In the Semantic Web there will also be the need of integrating data which is sensitive in some contexts.

Therefore, methods for specifying *who* is allowed to use *which* data are important in the next step towards the Semantic Web. There are two approaches to achieve this. The first is to specify access rights, to control the data access and to secure the communication channel when the data is transferred. The second attempt is to use cryptographic methods to protect the sensitive data itself.

There has been a considerable amount of work about access control for the Web [4, 26]. However, all these approaches need trustworthy infrastructures for specifying and controlling the data access. If sensitive data is stored in (potentially) insecure environments, such as public web-spaces, shared desktop systems, mobile devices, etc. the only way to do this is to locally encrypt the data before uploading or storing it. The ability to merge distributed data and to re-use the data have been important design aspects for the Semantic Web. From that perspective, partial encryption – where only the sensitive data are encrypted while all other data remain publicly readable – is desirable.

A common practice for encrypting sensitive data in an RDF-graph is to cut the data from the original graph, store the data in a separate file, encrypt the file

Y. Gil et al. (Eds.): ISWC 2005, LNCS 3729, pp. 308–322, 2005.

and finally link the encrypted file to the original graph [12]. This approach has some shortcomings: (1) the original RDF-graph is separated into different physical resources, (2) the encrypted files are not RDF-compliant and therefore could not be consistently processed by common RDF frameworks, (3) the linking has to be done manually, and (4) no rules are given for re-integrating the data into the RDF-graph after decryption. Another practice for encrypting RDF-graphs is to serialize them in XML and to use XML-Encryption [13] and XML-Signature [14] based security frameworks. One problem with this approach, is the structural difference between the tree-based XML Information Set data model [11] and the graph-based RDF Abstract Syntax data model [16]. Another problem is that this approach only allows to handle XML serializations of RDF-graphs.

To address these problems, we propose a method for *partial RDF encryption (PRE)* which allows for fine-grained encryption of arbitrary fragments of an RDF-graph without creating additional resources. Both encrypted data and plaintext data are represented in a single RDF-compliant model together with the metadata describing the encryption parameters. PRE uses the XML-Encryption and XML-Signature standards to represent the encryption metadata.

The rest of this paper is organized as follows. In the next section a brief introduction to RDF-graphs is given. Section 3 gives an overview of the partial encryption process for RDF-graphs. The subsequent sections look at important realization aspects: encryption and decryption of RDF fragments (section 4), description of graph transformations necessary to keep encrypted graphs RDF-compliant (section 5), a graph-pattern based method for dynamic selection fragments to be encrypted and a notion of encryption policies (section 6). The last section summarizes and gives an outlook to future work. In the appendix the namespaces used in the examples are listed.

2 Triple Sets and Graphs

RDF is an assertional language. Each assertion declares that certain information about a resource is true. An assertion is modeled as a $\langle s, p, o \rangle$-triple where s (subject) identifies the resource the assertion is about, p (predicate) is a property of the resource, and o (object) is the value of p. A triple is an element of $(U \cup B) \times U \times (U \cup B \cup L)$, where U denotes the set of URIs [5], B denotes the set of blank node identifiers, and L denotes the set of RDF literals [16]. A triple set can be interpreted as a Directed Labeled Graph (DLG) with the subjects and objects as nodes and node labels, the triples as arcs, and the predicates as arc labels ($\boxed{s} \xrightarrow{p} \boxed{o}$). A subgraph is a subset of the corresponding triple set. In this paper the term *RDF-graph* is used as a synonym for the term *triple set*. A triple set (or any subset) can be serialized in different languages, such as RDF/XML, N-Triples, N3, etc. The result is a sequence of words over an alphabet defined by the particular RDF serialization language.

A DLG encodes two different types of information: structural information and label information. Encrypting structural information means to hide the topology of the graph, whereas encrypting the label information means to hide individual node and arc values. With regard to RDF-graphs, label information is encoded by the URI-references and literals of subjects, predicates and objects. Structural information is encoded in terms of triples. It should be noted that blank nodes only provide structural information but no label information.

RDF-graphs can be interpreted as restricted DLGs having the following properties: (1) structural and label information of nodes are both encoded in terms of URI-references and literals – changing a node label also changes the structure of the graph; (2) node labels can be distributed over several triples. Thus, changing a node label can cause several triples of an RDF-graph to be changed; (3) all nodes are connected by at least on arc – there are no isolated nodes. Thus, the encryption of a triple, can cause the encryption of the connected subject and object nodes if they are only connected by that triple; (4) RDF makes the constraint, that subject and predicate labels have to be URIs. Encrypted labels are not words of the URI language. Therefore, encrypted labels have to be represented as objects which can have arbitrary literal values. As a consequence, graph transformations have to be performed in order to keep an encrypted graph RDF-compliant.

The following three encryption types for RDF-graphs can be distinguished: (1) encryption of subjects and objects (= encryption of node labels) (2) encryption of predicates (= encryption of arc labels) (3) encryption of triples (= encryption of nodes, arcs and subgraphs. An arc is represented by a single triple, a node by a set of triples having the node label either as subject or object, and a subgraph can be any subset of a triple set).

3   Partial RDF Encryption

Partial RDF Encryption (PRE) is a transaction which is composed of the six steps showed in Fig. 1. We will briefly describe each step.

1. **Fragment Selection:** The first step is the selection of the RDF fragments to be encrypted. RDF fragments can either be subjects, predicates, objects, or triples. The selected fragments are called *encryption fragments* and the remaining fragments are called *plaintext fragments*. Selection can be done, for example, by explicitly enumerating the encryption fragments (static selection), by specifying selection patterns which check specific properties (dynamic selection), by random selection, etc. This step is described in more detail in section 6.

2. **Encryption:** In this step, each encryption fragment is serialized and encrypted. The result of this step is a data structure containing both, encrypted data and encryption metadata. We will call this structure an *Encryption Container (EC)*. An encryption container can be serialized and represented as literal value. This step is described in more detail in section 4.

3. **Encryption Transformations:** All encryption fragments are replaced by their corresponding encryption containers. The result is a single self-describing RDF-compliant graph containing three different kinds of components: (1) encrypted data, (2) encryption metadata and (3) plaintext fragments. In order to fulfill RDF well-formedness constraints – in particular

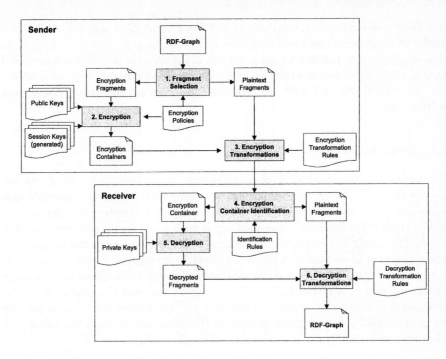

Fig. 1. Partial Encryption Process

the constraint that literals are only allowed as the object of a triple – graph transformations have to be performed. This step is described in more detail in section 5.

4. **Encryption Container Identification:** Encryption containers and encryption metadata are identified and extracted. This can be done by using an RDF query language.
5. **Decryption:** In this step, the encryption containers are decrypted according to the parameters specified in the encryption metadata. If a receiver does not have an appropriate decryption key, the decryption fails.
6. **Decryption Transformations:** The last step is the re-construction of the RDF-graph by replacing the encryption containers with the corresponding decrypted values. Graph transformations have to be performed which are inverse to the encryption transformations in step three. If a recipient has the keys to decrypt all encryption containers, then the re-constructed RDF-graph is identical to original RDF-graph. In the case that keys are missing, there will be remaining encryption containers in the RDF-graph.

4   Encryption of RDF Fragments

A cryptosystem can formally be described as a tuple (P, C, K, E, D), where P is a set of plaintexts, C is a set of ciphers, K is a set of keys, $E = \{e_k : k \in K\}$

is a family of encryption functions $e_k : P \to C$ and $D = \{d_k : k \in K\}$ is a family of decryption functions $d_k : C \to P$. For all $k_e \in K$ there is a $k_d \in K$ so that $d_{k_d}(e_{k_e}(p)) = p$ holds for all $p \in P$. A cryptosystem is called symmetric if $k_e = k_d$. It is called asymmetric if $k_e \neq k_d$. Examples of symmetric cryptosystems are Triple-DES [20] and AES [21]. An example of an asymmetric cryptosystem is RSA [24].

4.1   Encryption Schemes

For secure key transport and in consideration of performance, plaintexts are usually encrypted by using a session-key scheme which combines symmetric and asymmetric encryption (Fig. 2). The sender encrypts a plaintext m using a symmetric encryption function f parameterized with a randomly generated session key k. The result is a cipher c_m. To transmit the session key to the recipient in a secure way, k is encrypted with an asymmetric encryption function g parameterized by the public key pub of the recipient. The result is a cipher c_k. Then the ciphers c_m and c_k are transmitted. The recipient recovers the session key k by decrypting c_k using the decryption function g^{-1} parameterized with its private key $priv$. Finally, the recipient computes the plaintext m from c_m using f^{-1} parameterized with k.

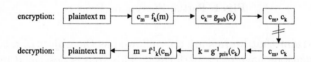

Fig. 2. Session-Key Scheme

We can extend the above session-key scheme to be able to encrypt a set of messages for a set of recipients. Let $M = \{m_1, \ldots, m_m\}$ be a non-empty set of messages to be encrypted, $P = \{pub_1, \ldots, pub_n\}$ be a non-empty set of public keys, and $P_i \subseteq P$ be a non-empty set of public keys representing the recipients of message $m_i \in M$. For each message m_i a new session key k_i is generated. m_i is encrypted using the symmetric function f paramerized by k_i. Then k_i is encrypted $|P_i|$-times using the asymmetric functions g parameterized by $pub_i \in P_i$ (Fig. 3). The encryption of M takes $|M|$ symmetric and $\sum_{i=1}^{|M|} |P_i| \leq |M| \cdot |P|$ asymmetric encryption function calls.

For each message, the extended session-key scheme creates a set of key ciphers $c_{k_1}, \ldots, c_{k_n}$ of which at the most one can be correctly decrypted using a given private key. A naive approach would be to decrypt sequentially each key cipher and to check the integrity of the decrypted values. Providing additional information about the public keys used for encryption (such as finger prints, certificate serial number, etc.) helps to identify the corresponding private key in advance. Thus, key information is an important class of encryption metadata.

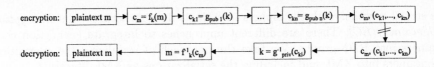

Fig. 3. Extended Session-Key Scheme

4.2 Digests

When using cryptosystems, a method to ensure the data integrity is needed. A common approach for this problem, is to use one-way hash functions, for example SHA-1 [19] or MD5 [23]. A hash or digest is a sequence of bytes that represents the input in a unique way and usually is smaller than the input. The sender computes the digest d_m of a message m using a one-way hash function h. Both, the digest d_m and the cipher c_m are transferred to the recipient. The recipient decrypts the cipher (let m' be the decrypted cipher) and computes the digest $d_{m'} = h(m')$. If $d_{m'} = d_m$ then $m' = m$ holds.

An important idea in PRE is using hash values for merging RDF-graphs, similar to the inverse functional property *mbox_sha1sum* defined in the FOAF vocabulary [9]. *mbox_sha1sum* contains the digest of an email to prevent publishing the email but to allow for merging based on the email. Partially encrypted fragments of an RDF-graph can be used for merging, if they (1) are object fragments, are inverse functional, and provide a direct hash value and (2) are subject fragments and provide a direct hash value.

There are cases in which it is not secure to use direct hash values. For example when the range of a property only contains few values. When using a direct hash for a 4-digit bank account PIN, it takes less than 1000 tests to know the correct PIN by comparing the hash values. In this case a randomization of the value before computing the digest is necessary. Randomized hash values provide a higher security. They still can be used for testing the data integrity but cannot be used for merging. So it is a trade-off between security and data integration.

For the representation of randomized values, we use a simple XML-based method. The original fragment serialization is embedded as the content of a `FragmentValue` element and can be retrieved using a simple XPath expression. `FragmentValue` is a child of `RandomizedValue` which contains randomly generated bytes as text. The structure is described by the following schema fragment.

```
<xs:complexType name='RandomizedValue' mixed='true'>
 <xs:choice><xs:element name='FragmentValue' type='xs:string'/></xs:choice>
</xs:complexType>
```

4.3 Encryption Metadata

To allow for a abstract definition of the encryption process, encryption metadata has to be specified, such as the encryption algorithms and their parameters, the computed hash values, key information for public key identification, canonicalization methods, transformation to be performed, etc. The encryption metadata is stored together with the ciphers in a single data structure – the *Encryption Container (EC)*. There are different approaches to integrate encryption containers into RDF-graphs. We take the approach of serializing the encryption containers into XML and including the serializations as XML literals.

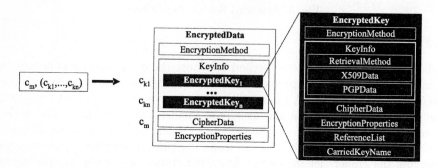

Fig. 4. Overall Encryption Container Structure

The general EC structure is shown in Fig.4. The key ciphers $c_{k_1}, \ldots, c_{k_n}$ are each stored in an *EncryptedKey* slot and the message cipher c_m is stored in an *EncryptedData* slot. Both, *EncryptedKey* and *Encrypted Data* have a similar structure. The XML-Encryption recommendation [13] provides a detailed description about the structure. The *EncryptionMethod* slot specifies the encryption algorithm. Each algorithm has a unique URI (cf. [13]). The *KeyInfo* slot provides information about the key used for encrypting the cipher. When using the extended session-key scheme, the *KeyInfo* slot inside *EncryptedData* contains a sequence of *EncryptedKey* slots, whereas the *KeyInfo* slot inside *EncryptedKey* contains information about the public key, for example a certificate or a certificate reference. The *CipherData* slot stores the concrete cipher value computed by the encryption function as Base64 encoded string. The *EncryptionProperties* slot contains additional information such as the digest value, the digest algorithm, data type information, the language used for serializing the data, etc.

Example 1: Alice has annotated the resource `http://www.xy.de/alice.htm` in RDF. To access the resource, a username and password is needed. Alice wants to store the access data together with other annotations in the same RDF-graph, so that only Bob and Chris can read the access data while all other annotations are publicly readable. Alice has the X.509 certificates of Bob and Chris and wants to encrypt the following RDF triples. AES (with 128-bit key size), RSA and SHA-1 is to be used.

```
<http://www.xy.de/alice.htm> <http://xy.de/schema#username> "alice" .
<http://www.xy.de/alice.htm> <http://xy.de/schema#password> "secret" .
```

First, the triples are serialized using an RDF language (N-Triples [15] in this example). Second, the SHA-1 digest is computed. Then, the data is AES encrypted (in CBC mode) with a generated 128-bit session key k. Then k is RSA encrypted twice using the RSA public keys contained in the X.509 certificates of Bob and Chris. Finally, the ciphers, the digest, the certificate, and the algorithm names and parameters are combined in an encryption container. An XML-Encryption and XML-Signature conforming serialization looks like:

```
<xenc:EncryptedData>
  <xenc:EncryptionMethod Algorithm="&xenc;#aes128-cbc"/>
  <ds:KeyInfo>
    <xenc:EncryptedKey>
      <xenc:EncryptionMethod Algorithm="&xenc;#rsa-1_5"/>
      <ds:KeyInfo>
        <ds:X509Data>
          <ds:X509Certificate>MIICQjCCAasCBE...</ds:X509Certificate>
        </ds:X509Data>
      </ds:KeyInfo>
      <xenc:CipherData>
        <xenc:CipherValue>rrOC4FYSNogKsi...</xenc:CipherValue>
      </xenc:CipherData>
    </xenc:EncryptedKey>
    <xenc:EncryptedKey>encrypted key of Chris...</xenc:EncryptedKey>
  </ds:KeyInfo>
  <xenc:CipherData>
    <xenc:CipherValue>37++haErMYLidG...</xenc:CipherValue>
  </xenc:CipherData>
  <xenc:EncryptionProperties>
    <xenc:EncryptionProperty>
      <ds:DigestMethod Algorithm="&ds;#sha1"/>
      <ds:DigestValue>/84Cdz6BdYd6kY9zSa6sT1IjLoo=</ds:DigestValue>
    </xenc:EncryptionProperty>
  </xenc:EncryptionProperties>
</xenc:EncryptedData>
```

5   Transformations

Since in RDF only the objects can represent literal values, encrypted subjects and predicates cannot directly be replaced by their corresponding encryption container serializations. Instead, graph transformations have to be performed. An overview of the transformations for integrating the encrypted content is given in Fig. 5 (literals containing the encryption container serialization are marked with a 'lock' icon). We will briefly describe each transformation.

1. *Subject Transformation:* In order to encrypt a subject S, a new triple $\langle B, renc:encNLabel, EC_S \rangle$ is added to the graph. EC_S contains the XML serialization of the encryption container of S. All references to S are replaced by references to B. Therefore all triples containing S either as object or subject have to be changed.

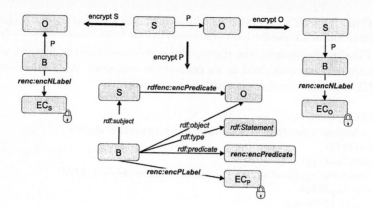

Fig. 5. Subject, Object and Predicate Transformations

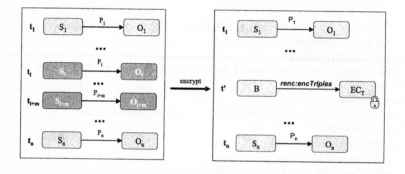

Fig. 6. Triple-Set Transformation

2. *Object Transformation*: Objects could directly be replaced by their encryption container serializations. But this would also change the datatype into `rdf:XMLLiteral`. Therefore, a blank node is introduced which replaces the original object node. A new triple $\langle B, renc:encNLabel, EC_O \rangle$ is added to the graph. EC_O contains the XML serialization of the encryption container of O including the original datatype information. All references to O have to be replaced by references to B.

3. *Predicate Transformation*: Since in RDF only URI references are allowed as predicates, blank nodes cannot be used for bridging between arcs and their encrypted label data. Instead a RDF reification [18] based approach is used. The transformation is carried out in three steps. First, the predicate P of the original triple t is replaced by the URI reference `renc:encPredicate`. Second, a new reification quad is added for identifying t. Finally, a new property $renc:encPLabel = EC_P$ is added to the reification quad stating that the real predicate of t is encrypted in EC_P.

4. *Triple-Set Transformation*: The encryption of a non-empty triple set $T_{enc} = \{t_i, \ldots, t_{i+m}\}$ takes the following steps. First, T_{enc} is serialized into a string s

using an RDF serialization language. Second, an encryption container EC_T is constructed containing the encrypted string s together with the encryption metadata. Third, a new triple $\langle B,\ renc{:}encTriples,\ EC_T \rangle$ is added to the graph. Finally, all triples in T_{enc} are removed from the graph. The transformation for triple sets are showed in figure 6.

5.1   Handling of Blank Nodes

The described transformations can be directly applied to RDF-graphs that do not contain blank nodes (ground graphs). As noted earlier, a blank node identifier is not regarded as node label and thus cannot be encrypted. However blank nodes may be contained in triple sets that are to be encrypted. Blank node identifiers have to be unique in one RDF-graph. They are not required to be globally unique and may be changed to some internal representation by RDF frameworks. In order to be able to encrypt triples containing blank nodes, additional information is needed to uniquely identify the blank nodes after decryption, since their identifiers might have changed.

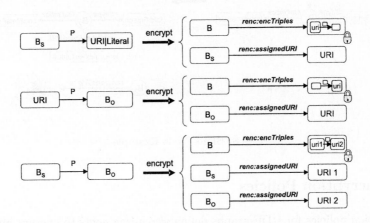

Fig. 7. Graph Transformations for Blank Nodes

Therefore, a unique UUID [17] is generated for each blank node contained in a triple to be encrypted. The UUID is assigned to the blank node as URI value of the `renc:assignedURI` property. The blank nodes of the triples to be encrypted are then replaced by the generated URIs. During decryption, the generated URIs are used for identifying the original blank nodes. Blank nodes can occur as the subject of a triple, as the object of a triple or both. Fig. 7 gives an overview and shows the corresponding transformations.

Example 2: Alice wants to encrypt the `foaf:knows` relation between her and Bob expressed by triple t_{enc}. Since persons have no adequate URI representation, blank nodes are used for bundling properties about the person which are the email addresses in this example. Fig. 8 shows the result of the encryption. The triple t_{enc} is removed. Three new triples are added: two triples for identifying the blank nodes (t_1 and t_2) and one triple containing the encrypted data (t_3). The blank node identifiers for B_1 and B_2 are replaced by the generated UUIDs ($uri1$ and $uri2$) before the encryption. During decryption the t_3 is decrypted, parsed, and removed. Let T_{dec} denote the decrypted triples. In a second step, the objects of all triples having an renc:assignedURI predicate are tested against the subject and object URIs of the triples in T_{dec}. If a correspondence is detected (the object of t_1 with $uri1$ and the object of t_2 with $uri2$), the URI references are replaced by the corresponding blank nodes and the identification triples (t_1, t_2) are removed.

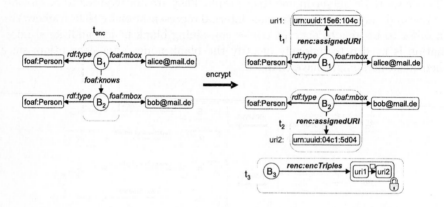

Fig. 8. Blank Node Example

6   Encryption Policies

Encryption policies for RDF-graphs define *which* fragments to encrypt and *how* to encrypt them. The *PRE Policy Language (PRE-PL)* uses a graph pattern based approach that allows for dynamic selection of encryption fragments. PRE-PL uses the RDQL [25, 2] query language. The result of a query can be interpreted as a set of fragments which are instances of the same 'category' defined by the search pattern. Each category is encrypted in the same way (the same keys, algorithms, etc.). RDQL mainly defines a list of triple patterns which are mapped to concrete triples in an RDF-graph. A triple pattern generally has the form

```
TriplePattern ::= '(' (Var|URI) (Var|URI) (Var|Const) ')'
```

where Var are variables, URI are URI references and Const are URI references or (typed) literals. The result of a query is a set of bindings, in which the variables are bound to concrete RDF items (subjects, predicates or objects).

RDQL has been adapted in a way that it returns a set of triples bound to each triple pattern instead of returning variable bindings. Based on the ordered triple pattern sequence, the encryption fragments are identified by using the markers *s*, *p*, *o*, or *t*. The marker *s* (*p*, *o*) will cause the encryption of the subjects (predicates, objects) of the bound triple set. The marker *t* will cause the encryption of each triple in the set. This mechanism allows the encryption of fragments which are not bound to variables, e.g. named values. Additionally, it has to be specified how to encrypt the selected fragments, i.e. which encryption method, keys, parameters, etc. to use. PRE-PL is described in more detail in on the RDF Encryption Project site [3]. We will give a short example here.

Example 3: The rule *„encrypt the email addresses of all persons"* using Triple-DES as block cipher algorithm and the RSA keys provided in the certificates of Bob and Alice can be formulated in PRE-PL as follows:

```
<pre:PREPolicy>
  <ds:KeyInfo>
    <ds:X509Data id="alice">...</ds:X509Data>
    <ds:X509Data id="bob">...</ds:X509Data>
  </ds:KeyInfo>
  <pl:DefaultEncryptionScheme>
    <pl:Symmetric>
      <xenc:EncryptionMethod Algorithm="xenc:tripledes-cbc"/>
    </pl:Symmetric>
    <pl:Asymmetric>
      <xenc:EncryptionMethod Algorithm="xenc:rsa-1_5"/>
    </pl:Asymmetric>
    <pl:Digest type="pl:directDigest">
      <ds:DigestMethod Algorithm="ds:sha1"/>
    </pl:Digest>
    <pl:RDFLanguage name="pl:N-Triples"/>
    <pl:DefaultKeys><pl:KeyRef id="alice"/></pl:DefaultKeys>
  </pl:DefaultEncryptionScheme>
  <pl:GraphPattern>
    <pl:TriplePattern subj="?x" pred="rdf:type" obj="foaf:Person"/>
    <pl:TriplePattern subj="?x" pred="foaf:mbox" obj="?y">
      <pl:Encryption target="o"><KeyRef id="bob"/></pl:Encryption>
    </pl:TriplePattern>
  </pl:GraphPattern>
</pl:PREPolicy>
```

Each `PREPolicy` has a `KeyInfo` section for key definition. Each child element provides key material which is referenced in the `GraphPattern` sections. Note, that the external keys can be referenced using the XML-Signature reference mechanism [14]. Each PRE policy also defines one `DefaultEncryptionScheme` section which defines the default encryption parameters: the symmetric and asymmetric algorithms, the digest algorithm and additional randomization, the RDF serialization language for triples and the default keys for each fragment. Additional encryption schemes can be defined which can be referenced in `Encryption` elements. Each `GraphPattern` section has a list of triple patterns and optional constraints which are mapped to an RDQL query. For each `TriplePattern` it can be defined how to encrypt the bound fragments. In the above example, the object of the second triple pattern (the email address) is encrypted using the default encryption scheme and the additional key with the ID 'bob'.

7   Conclusions and Future Work

A method to partially encrypt RDF-graphs has been presented. It differs from other approaches in that the result is a single self-describing RDF-compliant graph containing both, encrypted data and plaintext data. The method allows for fine-grained encryption of subjects, objects, predicates and subgraphs of RDF-graphs. Encrypted fragments are included as XML literals which are represented using the XML-Encryption [13] and XML-Signature [14] recommendations. Graph transformations necessary to keep the encrypted RDF-graph well-formed have been described. The proposed method is adoptable for different algorithms and processing rules by using encryption metadata. We have motivated the usage of randomized digests for high-sensitive data (such as credit card number, passwords, etc.) and direct digests for low-sensitive data (such as email, phone number, etc.) in order to allow a trade-off between security and application integration needs. We have also introduced the idea of encryption policies for RDF and the PRE-PL policy language which uses RDQL queries for dynamic selection of encryption fragments. In future work we will integrate SPARQL [22] concepts, such as optional pattern matching, in PRE-PL. A prototypical implementation of PRE, PRE4J [3], is available under LGPL for the Jena Framework [2].

PRE heavily relies on a public key infrastructure or on a web of trust. There are RDF vocabularies, such as the Semantic Web Publishing Vocabulary [10, 7] or the WOT Vocabulary [8], for integrating certificates into the Semantic Web and in particular into FOAF [9] profiles. Therefore, it is planned to extend FOAF enabled browsers, such as the Foafscape browser [1], to be able to use the certificates provided in profiles.

As with all partial encryption methods, encrypted data has a certain context which can be used for 'guessing' the corresponding plaintext data. Semantic Web applications also typically make use of ontologies. An ontology formulates a strict conceptual scheme about a domain containing the relevant classes, instances, properties, data types, cardinalities, etc. This information can be used for attacks or even inferring encrypted content. Property definitions for example can dramatically reduce the search space for 'guessing' the plaintexts and can be used for systematically checking the hash value provided in the encryption container. Concerning the confidentiality of encrypted data, it is also crucial to know if the data to be encrypted is inferable. This topic has not been evaluated in detail, yet.

References

1. Foafscape Project Homepage. http://foafscape.berlios.de.
2. Jena Semantic Web Framework. http://jena.sourceforge.net.
3. RDF Encryption Project Homepage. http://rdfenc.berlios.de.
4. L. Bauer, M. Schneider, and E. Felten. A general and flexible access-control system for the web. In *Proceedings of the 11th USENIX Security Symposium*, San Francisco, CA, Aug 2002.
5. T. Berners-Lee, R. Fielding, and L. Masinter. *RFC 2396 – Uniform Resource Identifiers (URI): Generic Syntax.* IETF, August 1998. http://www.isi.edu/in-notes/rfc2396.txt.
6. T. Berners-Lee, J. Hendler, and O. Lassila. The Semantic Web. *Scientific American*, pages 34–43, May 2001.
7. C. Bizer, R. Cyganiak, O. Maresch, and T. Gauss. TriQL.P - Trust Architecture. http://www.wiwiss.fu-berlin.de/suhl/bizer/TriQLP/.
8. D. Brickley. WOT RDF Vocabulary, 2002. http://xmlns.com/wot/0.1/.
9. D. Brickley and L. Miller. FOAF Vocabulary Specification, 2005. http://xmlns.com/foaf/0.1/.
10. J. Carroll, C. Bizer, P. Hayes, and P. Stickler. Named Graphs, Provenance and Trust. Technical report, HP Laboratories Bristol, 2004. HPL-2004-57R1.
11. J. Cowan and R. Tobin, editors. *XML Information Set (Second Edition).* W3C Recommendation, February 2004. http://www.w3.org/TR/xml-infoset/.
12. E. Dumbill. PGP Encrypting FOAF Files, 2002. http://usefulinc.com/foaf/encryptingFoafFiles.
13. D. Eastlake and J. Reagle, editors. *XML Encryption Syntax and Processing.* W3C Recommendation, December 2002. http://www.w3.org/TR/xmlenc-core/.
14. D. Eastlake, J. Reagle, and D. Solo, editors. *XML-Signature Syntax and Processing.* W3C, February 2002. http://www.w3.org/TR/xmldsig-core/.
15. J. Grant and D. Beckett, editors. *RDF Test Cases.* W3C Recommendation, http://www.w3.org/TR/rdf-testcases/, February 2004.
16. G. Klyne and J. Carroll, editors. *Resource Description Framework (RDF): Concepts and Abstract Syntax.* W3C Recommendation, http://www.w3.org/TR/rdf-concepts/, February 2004.
17. P. Leach, M. Mealling, and R. Salz. A Universally Unique IDentifier (UUID) URN Namespace, July 2005.
18. F. Manola and E. Miller, editors. *RDF Primer.* W3C Recommendation, http://www.w3.org/TR/rdf-primer/, February 2004.
19. National Institute of Standards and Technology (NIST). Secure Hash Standard (SHA-1). Technical report, April 1995. http://www.itl.nist.gov/fipspubs/fip180-1.htm.
20. National Institute of Standards and Technology (NIST). Data Encryption Standard (DES). Technical report, October 1999. http://csrc.nist.gov/publications/fips/fips46-3/fips46-3.pdf.
21. National Institute of Standards and Technology (NIST). Advanced Encryption Standard (AES). Technical report, November 2001. http://csrc.nist.gov/publications/fips/fips197/fips-197.pdf.
22. E. Prud'hommeaux and A. Seaborne, editors. *SPARQL Query Language for RDF.* W3C Working Draft, October 2004. http://www.w3.org/TR/rdf-sparql-query/.
23. R. Rivest. The MD5 Message-Digest Algorithm, RFC 1321. Technical report, April 1992. http://www.faqs.org/rfcs/rfc1321.html.

322   M. Giereth

24. R. Rivest, A. Shamir, and L. Adleman. A Method for Obtaining Digital Signatures and Public-Key Cryptosystems. *Communications of the ACM 21,2*, 1978.
25. A. Seaborne, editor. *RDQL - A Query Language for RDF*. W3C Member Submission, January 2004. http://www.w3.org/Submission/2004/SUBM-RDQL-20040109/.
26. D. Weitzner, J. Hendler, T. Berners-Lee, and D. Connolly. Creating a policy-aware web: Discretionary, rule-based access for the world wide web. Hershey, PA (forthcoming), 2004.

Appendix: Namespaces

Prefix	Namespace
ds	http://www.w3.org/2000/09/xmldsig#
foaf	http://xmlns.com/foaf/0.1/
pl	http://rdfenc.berlios.de/pre-pl#
renc	http://rdfenc.berlios.de/pre#
rdf	http://www.w3.org/1999/02/22-rdf-syntax-ns#
xenc	http://www.w3.org/2001/04/xmlenc#
xs	http://www.w3.org/2001/XMLSchema

Seven Bottlenecks to Workflow Reuse and Repurposing

Antoon Goderis, Ulrike Sattler, Phillip Lord, and Carole Goble

School of Computer Science, University of Manchester, UK
{goderis, carole, sattler, plord}@cs.man.ac.uk

Abstract. To date on-line processes (*i.e.* workflows) built in e-Science have been the result of collaborative team efforts. As more of these workflows are built, scientists start sharing and reusing stand-alone compositions of services, or *workflow fragments*. They *repurpose* an existing workflow or workflow fragment by finding one that is close enough to be the basis of a new workflow for a different purpose, and making small changes to it. Such a "workflow by example" approach complements the popular view in the Semantic Web Services literature that on-line processes are constructed automatically from scratch, and could help bootstrap the Web of Science. Based on a comparison of e-Science middleware projects, this paper identifies seven bottlenecks to scalable reuse and repurposing. We include some thoughts on the applicability of using OWL for two bottlenecks: workflow fragment discovery and the ranking of fragments.

1 Towards a Web of Science

As more scientific resources become available on the World Wide Web, scientists increasingly rely on Web technology for performing *in silico* (*i.e.* computerised) experiments. With the publication of scientific resources as Web and Grid services, scientists are making a shift from traditionally copying and pasting their data through a sequence of Web pages offering those resources, to the creation and use of distributed processes for experiment design, data analysis and knowledge discovery. Research councils in various countries have set out to build a global infrastructure to support this under the banner of *e-Science*. e-Science translates the notion of virtual organisations into a customised Grid middleware layer for scientists, thereby aiming to increase collaboration within and between scientific fields [1]. Workflow techniques are an important part of *in silico* experimentation, potentially allowing the e-Scientist to describe and enact their experimental processes in a structured, repeatable and verifiable way. For example, the ^{my}Grid (www.mygrid.org.uk) workbench, a set of components to build workflows in bioinformatics, currently allows access to over thirteen hundred distributed services and has produced over a hundred workflows, some of which orchestrate up to fifty services. These resources have been developed by users and service providers distributed throughout the global biology community. Figure 1 shows an example of a ^{my}Grid workflow which gathers information about genetic sequences in support of research on Williams Beuren syndrome (WBS) [2].

Y. Gil et al. (Eds.): ISWC 2005, LNCS 3729, pp. 323–337, 2005.

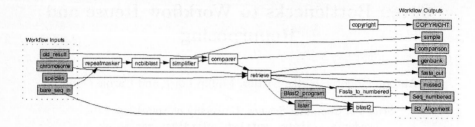

Fig. 1. Part of a ^{my}Grid workflow to annotate genetic sequences as presented by the ^{my}Grid Taverna workbench. The diagram shows the typical fanning out behaviour of a bioinformatics pipeline, producing lots of data from a limited number of inputs (the left and right boxes) based on a set of distributed services (the middle boxes).

We are now witnessing how scientists have started reusing and propagating *in silico* experiments as commodities and "know-how" in their own right. To cater for the reuse of *in silico* experiments on the scale of the Web of Science [3], the e-Science infrastructure will need to expand its current handling of the workflow life cycle. The goal of this paper is to investigate how reuse and re-purposing of *in silico* experiments would work. We see reuse and repurposing as a way of bootstrapping the Web of Science by stimulating the dynamics of sharing and reusing experimental components in the scientific community. Section 2 highlights the benefits of workflow reuse, distinguishes between workflow reuse and repurposing, and analyses the relationship with related work. Section 3 goes bottom up, showcasing different types of reuse based on case studies from e-Science middleware projects. From this survey, we obtain the following seven bottlenecks to reuse and repurposing, which are presented in Section 4. For bottlenecks 5 and 7, we consider how reasoning over ontologies in the Web Ontology Language (OWL) [4] could widen them.

1. Restrictions on service availability
2. Rigidity of service and workflow language definitions
3. Intellectual property rights on workflows
4. Workflow interoperability
5. Lack of a comprehensive discovery model
6. The process knowledge acquisition bottleneck
7. Lack of workflow fragment rankings

The bottlenecks belong to two broad categories. First, some bottlenecks hinder establishing a critical mass for bootstrapping the Web of Science. Bottlenecks 1-4 identify reasons why we do not have as many workflows available for reuse as we might expect. Provided that this set of bottlenecks can be suitable addressed, the available pool of workflows then still needs to be easily searchable and adaptable. Bottlenecks 5-7 identify barriers that keep people from effectively processing the available workflow knowledge.

Bottlenecks 4-7 are closely related to challenges for the Semantic Web, cited in [5] and marked up in italics below. In particular, to maximise the available base of workflows, one would need to resolve workflow language interoperability issues. Workflow interoperability in essence seeks to interoperate different conceptualisations of control flow, a special case of *reconciling different conceptualisations* of a domain. The *tradeoff in Knowledge Representation* between expressivity and tractability relates to the current lack of a comprehensive model for discovering fragments. The building and populating of a comprehensive model is subject to the process *knowledge acquisition bottleneck*. Finally, to fully exploit the resulting model and its contents, the reuse infrastructure should support *unpredictable use of knowledge*, *e.g.* through rankings for fragments dependent on a user's context.

2   Reuse and Repurposing in e-Science

e-Scientists are driven by a desire to set up and run *in silico* experiments which complement the work done in the laboratory. As more workflows are built, scientists start sharing and reusing stand-alone compositions of services, or *workflow fragments*, within and between research projects. As a result, scientists are adopting a "workflow by example" style of workflow construction by reusing and repurposing existing experience. This complements the vision that experiments could be composed automatically, *e.g.* the Robot Scientist [6].

2.1   Why Workflow Reuse?

Workflow reuse in e-Science is intrinsically linked to a desire that workflows be shared and reused by the community as best practice scientific protocols or know-how. It has the potential to: reduce workflow authoring time (less re-inventing the wheel); improve quality through shared workflow development (two heads are better than one, or leveraging the expertise of previous users); and improve experimental provenance at the process level through reuse of established and validated workflows (analogous to using proven algorithms or practices rather than inventing a new, and potentially error-prone, one yourself). Concretely, the research group who produced the Williams' syndrome workflow [2] have already seen a dramatic drop in workflow authoring time through the ability to repurpose *workflow fragments* from previous experiments.

A *workflow fragment* is a piece of an experimental description that is a coherent sub-workflow that makes sense to a domain specialist. It is a snippet of workflow code written in a workflow orchestration language which typically carries annotation to facilitate its discovery. Each fragment forms a useful resource in its own right and is identified at publication time.

2.2   Reuse and Repurposing

We distinguish between *reuse*, where workflows and workflow fragments created by one user might be used as is, and *repurposing*, where they are used as a starting point by others.

- A user will reuse a workflow or workflow fragment that fits their purpose and could be customised with different parameter settings or data inputs to solve their particular scientific problem.

- A user will repurpose a workflow or workflow fragment by finding one that is *close enough* to be the basis of a new workflow for a different purpose and making small changes to its *structure* to fit it to its new purpose.

Repurposing requires techniques to provide a user with suggestions as to what are the relevant pieces of workflow for their experiment, like "Based on the services and structure of your workflow, it looks like you are building a gene annotation pipeline. Other users have found this collection of fragments useful for that." The techniques work off a knowledge base of existing workflows (either a central registry or a peer to peer setting). The end result, a repurposed workflow, is contributed back to the pool of available know-how.

Of the workflows produced by the projects surveyed in Section 3, many model simple pipelines like the one in Figure 1 but some also model complex concurrent control flows. Based on frequent interaction with domain scientists, we adopt the *working hypothesis* that a *scientist* thinks about her workflow primarily as data flow, transforming scientific data sets, and ignores what might be going on under the hood in terms of complex control flow. As a result, a scientist is interested in making queries that involve discovery of fragments based on data, services, and at most involve simple ordering, choice points and loops. We have collected a set of practical reuse and repurposing queries Q1-Q7 for domain scientists. The use of semantics seems relevant to solve queries Q1-Q5; we revisit them in Sections 4.5 and 4.7. For reasons of scope we leave aside Q6 and Q7 in this paper.

Q1 Given a data point, service, fragment or workflow, where has this item been used before?

Q2 Show the common data, services, and compositions of services and data between two workflows or fragments.

Q3 Given a set of data points, services, or fragments, have these been connected up in an existing base of workflows? If not, what are the closest available alternatives for doing so? How do these alternatives rank?

Q4 As more workflows become available, fragments are reused and repurposed in a variety of workflows. How can one systematically keep track of these interrelationships?

Q5 Since the design and implementation of a workflow can extend over long periods of time (months, even years), one might want to store even partially described workflows. Which are the available workflows in progress?

Q6 Show the differences between two workflow versions.

Q7 Show the evolution of a workflow over time.

Conversely, an advanced *workflow developer* typically implements complex distributed processes involving concurrency and has little affinity with scientific jargon. Developers might also ask queries like the above, but these would not involve jargon. In those cases where developers build *complex control flows*, they typically work by example, and as such might issue queries for examples of implemented complex flows. Typically there would be interaction between the two user roles during workflow construction, as part of a collaborative effort.

2.3 Repurposing, Discovery and Composition

How does repurposing relate to service discovery and composition? We answer this by first outlining the different aspects of the service life cycle and then characterising repurposing in these terms. Web-enabled services, whether published as Web, Grid or peer to peer services can be *described* by means of their input and output, and/or based on their behaviour, *e.g.* via pre- and postconditions or Finite State Automata [7]. Based on such descriptions, services can be *discovered, composed, configured, verified, simulated, invoked* and *monitored.* Of these, discovery and composition are the most relevant for repurposing.

- Discovery is the process of finding, ranking and selecting *existing* services. Discovery can be exact or inexact, and operates over descriptions of atomic or composite services which consist of atomic services.
- Composition is the process of combining services into a *new* working assembly. It is performed either manually, semi-automatically or automatically. Composition typically combines service discovery with service integration. If either activity involves manual intervention from a human, composition becomes non-automated.

Mapping repurposing to this classification yields the following distinctive set of features:

Workflow fragments, not services on the Web. Workflow fragments orchestrate services located on the Web. Fragments are not Web-enabled services, however, in the sense that they can be readily invoked over the Web. Instead they require a workflow engine for execution. At an abstract level, fragments can be regarded as composite services, which means some of the formal language machinery being developed for Web-enabled services is still applicable.

Behavioural service descriptions. Fragments are snippets of code published in a workflow language which typically carry annotation to facilitate their discovery. Fragments can describe sophisticated forms of control flow between services.

Design level discovery over composite services. In general, the literature on discovering composite services/ processes is investigating discovery at three levels. For each level, an example of queries is shown for which techniques are available.

Design level discovery. Scientists may ask questions that comprise simple structural elements, such as relating to parts of a process, *e.g.* [8], or loops and choice points *e.g.* [9], whereas developers may pose queries relating to complex control flow, such as dealing with constraints on messaging behaviour *e.g.* [10] or distributed execution models [11].

Enactment level discovery. For instance, based on feedback on the behaviour of particular components during the run of a process, a user may select a new, similar process that is more likely to achieve the stated goal [12].

Post-enactment level discovery. Process languages sometimes allow for great flexibility in the execution path a user can choose. Several authors consider process mining, which seeks to discover from the enactment data of workflow runs, which path users actually follow in practice *e.g.* [13].

With respect to fragment discovery, we are only concerned with design level discovery in order to retrieve snippets of workflow code.

Exact and inexact discovery. Lacking a sufficient set of answers based on exact discovery, repurposing techniques can progress to inexact discovery techniques, which find the closest available alternatives (for a human to then look at). Sections 4.5 and 4.7 discuss some available options based on OWL. A distinctive feature of repurposing techniques is the inclusion of a measure of *integration effort* in the rankings of returned fragments.

Semi-automatic composition. Composition combines service discovery and service integration. Repurposing a workflow based on workflow fragments relies on automated support for the *discovery* part, which generates clues as to what would be the best fragments for a human to consider based on the *existing* workflows. The actual integration part is left up to the workflow developer. Hence a newly repurposed workflow is the result of semi-automatic *composition*. Repurposing techniques in this sense are to be seen as *composition-oriented discovery* techniques and sit in between automated discovery and automated composition. We draw on the observation made in [14] that scientists in general are reluctant to relinquish control over the construction of their experiments. We aim to support scientists' activities, not replace them.

2.4   Abstract and Concrete Workflows

Various authors in the scientific workflow literature use the notion of abstract and concrete workflows [15]. The notion is useful for repurposing as it helps to create a view over aspects of a workflow that either a domain scientist or a developer are interested in. *Abstract* workflows capture a layer of process description that abstracts away from the task and behaviour of a *concrete* workflow. The kinds of abstraction performed are a modelling decision and depend on the application. Generally speaking, abstractions can generalise over:

1. Workflow and service parameters (task, parameters, data, component services): these abstract workflows have also been called *workflow templates* [15]. Templates are un-invocable, un-parameterised workflows whose services are unbound to a specific end point.
2. Control constructs: such abstract workflows can be organised based on *workflow patterns* [16] and distributed execution models [11].
3. Domain specificity: abstract workflows like these focus on capturing problem-solving behaviour and are the subject of *Problem-Solving Methods* research [12].

The distinction between abstract and concrete workflows is useful for at least three types of applications. Firstly, abstract workflows can guide the *configuration* of generic pieces of workflow into concrete workflows. The end result is a concrete workflow like the one depicted on Figure 1. Secondly, the notion of abstract workflows is useful for *dynamic bindings for scheduling and planning*, where service availability changes frequently and one queries for run-time instantiations of service classes. Thirdly, one can use the abstract-concrete distinction to support queries for *repurposing*. In particular, the first type of abstraction layer, over workflow parameters can be used to support queries Q1-Q5 (see [17] for details). The second type of abstraction layer, over control constructs, serves to answer developer's queries for complex control flow.

3   Scientific Workflow Reuse in Practice

After defining reuse and repurposing and contrasting it with related work, we now take a bottom up approach. We ask the question how far off we are at the current time from a Web of Science enabled by reuse and repurposing. As more scientists start to construct workflows, opportunities for cross-fertilisation are likely to arise. We present the results of a survey on how reuse and repurposing occurs in practice.

3.1   Case Studies in Workflow Fragment Reuse

We take a cross-section of middleware projects from the e-Science programme in the United Kingdom, which was the first of its kind [1]. To collect case studies of reuse, we have collaborated with biologists and developers in the ^{my}Grid project and interviewed core developers from the UK-based InforSense (the commercial collaborator of the DiscoveryNet e-Science project [18]), Geodise [19], Triana [20] and Sedna projects. We also interviewed people from the USA-based Kepler project [21]. The following case studies arose from the interviews.[1]

- In ^{my}Grid, around 200 users have built 100 workflows from over 1300 services. Workflow fragments have been repurposed between different research groups in Manchester, Newcastle and Liverpool investigating Williams' syndrome [2], Graves' disease [22] and Trypanosomiasis (sleeping sickness) in cattle, respectively (see Figure 2). New reuse of fragments from the Williams workflow is planned to support research on the Aspergillus fungus.
- In Triana, the GEO power spectrum, a small composition of Java classes aimed at the direct detection of gravitational waves, has been shared between different research groups in the same department at Cardiff University.
- Clients of InforSense, a commercial enterprise, have been building scientific workflows for several years. They exchange and extend workflows based on corporate intranet servers and e-mail lists. Given that these workflows are based on proprietary technology and often contain trade secrets, sharing with external parties has been very limited.

---

[1] The survey form is available from www.cs.man.ac.uk/~goderisa/surveyform.pdf

- The Kepler project so far has around 30 users which have built 10 workflows from a registry of 20 services. They have seen the redeployment of GRASS services for geospatial data management developed in one project (SEEK) to form a new pipeline for another project (GEON). This redeployment required a slight adaptation of the control flow.
- Geodise relies on the Matlab software environment for the orchestration of local Matlab functions which wrap distributed Grid resources. It offers access to some 150 functions, based on which 10 workflows were built to date. It reuses both configurations and assemblies of Matlab functions (*i.e.* scripts) described by various authors.
- The Sedna project at University College London has built a compute intensive workflow for chemistry, generating up to 1200 service instances concurrently. No reuse of this workflow has occurred. Sedna is notable as it is the only project in our sample to use BPEL (Business Process Execution Language), which is considered a *de facto* standard for business workflows.

3.2   Three Kinds of Workflow Reuse

From these use cases, three categories of workflow reuse surfaced, which are based on the person doing the reuse: reuse by third parties who the workflow author never met, reuse by collaborators, and personal reuse.

Reuse by third parties. Third-party reuse is the kind of reuse envisaged by the e-Science vision for inter-disciplinary scientific collaboration. None of the interviewees could report reuse of this kind.

Reuse by collaborators. Scientists are typically part of a research group and various research projects, inside of which they exchange knowledge. Figure 2 shows the reuse of fragments between research groups active in the same project (from Graves to Williams), as well as reuse between affiliated research projects (from Williams to Trypanosomiasis). The Williams bioinformaticians were keen to extend their workflow with a protein annotation pipeline, as well as to introduce microarray analysis functionality. In turn, the Williams workflow itself became the subject of reuse for the Trypanosomiasis workflow, in particular the microarray analysis and gene prediction fragments shown on the figure. In case of the microarray fragment, in effect one sees the emergence of workflow fragment *propagation*.

Personal reuse. Building large workflows can be a lengthy process, sometimes taking years of time. This results in different versions of workflow specifications that co-exist in one location. Manually keeping track of the relationships is a challenging task, so versioning support is required. Versioning can be seen as a case of "personal reuse". In the case of the Graves workflow, the workflow took more than a year to create. During the process of building it, 56 bits of workflow were created, most of which are overlapping versions and used in one shape or other in the other versions. The largest of these bits contains 45 elements, not counting the links between the data and services.

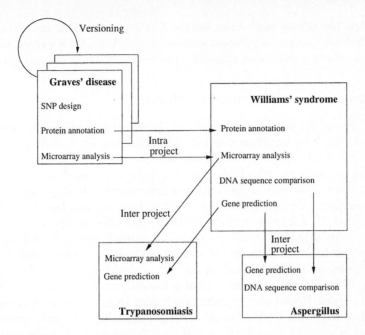

Fig. 2. Different types of workflow reuse illustrated by a scenario from bioinformatics

The picture for the bioinformatics use case in Figure 2 does not do justice to the difficulty it took to reuse the various fragments. Discovery of fragment functionality happened by word of mouth, and comparing and integrating fragments took extensive discussions between the workflow authors. Repurposing the workflow to investigate a different species meant the structure had to be adapted: certain services had to be replaced (for example, some gene prediction services are species-specific), others removed and still others added.

One can conclude that reuse and *manual* repurposing of workflows and fragments of workflows is already happening. It is clear however that reuse becomes harder as the conceptual and physical distance between parties increases. If reuse and repurposing is to happen on a wide scale, a large set of workflows where people can draw from is key. In addition, detailed documentation and ways to search and *compare* the documentation of different workflows are needed. All of the above middleware projects offer a search mechanism to look for available services; none however allow for the possibility to compare workflows descriptions.

4   Seven Bottlenecks to Reuse and Repurposing

Based on the comparison of e-Science middleware projects, we can identify seven bottlenecks to scalable reuse and repurposing. The bottlenecks belong to two broad groups: those preventing the collection of a large pool of workflows, and those that prevent discovery of workflow fragments in that available pool of knowledge. Identifying and addressing the first group is critical to establishing a Web of Science: without a substantial pool of workflows, there cannot be a Web of Science as there will be no scientific components to annotate and query for.

4.1 Restrictions on Service Availability

Restrictions on the availability of services (as a workflow's building blocks) creates a bottleneck for workflow creation and availability. First, domain users have strong opinions about the particular services that they wish to use. For them to be willing to create workflows, they need to have access to their favourite tools and databases from within the workflow environment. If these are not available as services *accessible within the workflow environment*, they will use other technologies. All workflow projects except Sedna offer access to types of services which are other than plain Web services. Second, service availability is also hampered by issues of *authentication, authorisation, accounting* and *licensing*. Third, the incorporation of *local services in a workflow*, be it as local components or Web services deployed behind a firewall, render a service unavailable for third parties. Repurposed workflows will need to replace those local services, unless they are either (i) Web-enabled upon publishing, (ii) made available for download in a public repository, or (iii) their functionality is made part of the workflow specification.

4.2 Rigidity of Service and Workflow Language Definitions

Services on the Web typically are outside the control of a workflow developer. The presented *service interface defines the limit* to which one can reuse the service: if the service interface does not support particular functionality, even though the underlying implementation of the service may, it is out of a developer's reach. This is a standard problem in object-oriented programming, where the solution has been to design objects with reuse in mind by providing rich interfaces.

Workflow specifications can be hard to reuse too, depending on the available support for *workflow evolution and adaptation* in the language. Workflows change as a result of (i) continuous process improvement, (ii) adaptations to changes in the workflow's environment, and (iii) customisation of a workflow to the needs of a specific case [23]. The workflow evolution literature typically considers (i) and (ii), and where (iii) is studied this is done from the perspective of a single organisation, and does not consider unpredictable reuse by third parties.

4.3 Intellectual Property Rights on Workflows

Scientists invest a lot of time in building workflows and are often *hesitant to release workflows* without formal Intellectual Property Rights agreements. We have seen this with the Williams, Graves and InforSense workflows. Science has dealt with this problem before in the context of sharing experimental data. Scientists can publish in a journal when they release their data in public databases, with the inclusion of metadata. The submitted data is then anonymised to the extent that it is of no use for the direct competition or an embargo is imposed over the data, to ensure the original authors enough time to exploit the data. Authors of *in silico* experiments might publish their workflows in the same way.

4.4   Workflow Interoperability

The saying "The nice thing about standards is that you can choose" also holds for scientific workflow languages. Each of the projects in the survey uses its own language for orchestrating resources. This diversity reflects the different demands of the application areas and computer skills of users. For repurposing, it is desirable to have access to as wide a pool of workflows as possible. Libraries of workflow *patterns* for control flow [16] have been developed and used to compare commercial workflow software for business processes. To our knowledge, this work has not been applied to compare and inform interoperation between scientific workflow systems. Also, these patterns do not address how combinations of patterns result into distributed execution models. In particular, developers would want to know how such models *compare* and can be *combined*. Kepler for instance have built workflows for environmental modelling that combines different distributed execution models (called "Directors" [11]) in one specification.

4.5   Lack of a Comprehensive Discovery Model

Designing representations for *in silico* experiments that can capture what is being done, why, and what has been tried before but failed, is a big challenge. Here we focus on the kind of information needed in such a representation to support discovery of fragments.

We have noted in Section 2.4 that different abstraction layers can be used to discover workflow fragments. Our *hypothesis* is that workflow fragment discovery requires the use of control flow constructs. How rich the control flow query support should be depends on the envisaged user (as explained in Section 2.2).

Unfortunately no one formalism can be expected to support all the desired control flow queries. We reflect on whether the Web Ontology Language OWL [4] could be used for searching workflow fragments. We consider this expressive Description Logic (DL) because of: (i) it being a standardised KR language; (ii) the support it offers for classifying a large collection of instances, *e.g.* workflow fragments; (iii) the potential to describe and query for workflows at a level of abstraction suited for a domain scientist through query languages; (iv) the support for representing incomplete workflows. OWL should be well suited to formulate data flow queries pertaining to inputs and outputs of services. DL ontologies in general are limited to modelling simple control flow constructs, however. Other formalisms provide a better fit for querying for complex control flow (*e.g.* process algebras). Though ideally one would like to be able to combine complex data flow queries with complex control flow queries, given the complexity of the task, we will first try to combine the outcome of querying different formalisms and present this in a uniform manner to the user.

Could we use OWL annotation to answer the data flow queries Q1-Q5 of Section 2.2? Various authors have experimented before with *service* discovery using DL reasoning, typically based on the OWL-S upper ontology *ServiceProfile* section, *e.g.* [24] or the Web Service Modeling Ontology (WSMO) *Capability* descriptions, *e.g.* [25]. We, however, are dealing with the discovery of *workflow fragments*, and the difference between atomic services and workflows indeed makes a difference to the discovery task. In service discovery, *ServiceProfile* or *Capability* descriptions are used, which do not include control flow information and thus cannot be considered for workflow discovery purposes. Even though detailed control flow information clearly is present in OWL-S and WSMO ontologies through the *ServiceModel* and *Orchestration* descriptions, respectively, these parts of the ontologies are neither intended nor (to our knowledge) currently used to support discovery. We are now designing a workflow ontology which uses service orderings, conditionals and loops to represent and query workflow fragments. So far, based on OWL Lite (using `hasSuccessor`, `hasDirectSuccessor` and `partOf` roles, the last two of which are transitive), we can retrieve workflows based on Q1-Q2 for fragments in the Williams workflow (more detail can be found in [17]).

4.6   The Process Knowledge Acquisition Bottleneck

The question is then how to get annotations for workflows based on such a model. Scientists are reluctant to manually populate any model of an experiment. Techniques to address the process knowledge acquisition bottleneck are therefore needed. With respect to populating that part of the experimental model that supports repurposing, techniques from service ontology learning and automated service annotation are promising. One could extend such work to address the identification and classification of workflow fragments, by taking into account the structure of fragments when applying the machine learning techniques. Techniques from Web page usability mining also promise to assist in capturing the behaviour of scientists as they construct a workflow, make mistakes and then take corrective actions.

4.7   Lack of Workflow Fragment Rankings

Once workflows and annotations based on the workflow model are created, one can query these for relevant fragments (Q3). As workflow fragment discovery is about retrieving those fragments that are "close enough" to a user's context, the notion of rankings and similarity is inherently present. Fragment rankings are the result of applying a series of *metrics* to workflow annotations based on a *query mechanism*. Challenges lie ahead in both developing suitable metrics for workflow similarity and generating rankings based on these metrics with query mechanisms.

Domain-dependent metrics relate processes on domain-specific issues. For instance, the choice of gene prediction fragments in Figure 2 depends on what species one is interested in. Given the evolutionary similarity between human and cattle, the prediction techniques used for these species (present in the Williams and Trypanosomiasis workflows) are more closely related to each other than to the techniques needed for the Aspergillus fungus. *Domain-independent metrics*, on the other hand, work over features such as data and control flow, calculating for instance how many services are to be moved, removed, added, replaced, merged or split to relate different fragments. This in effect would provide a measure of the *integration effort* involved to transform one piece of workflow into another.

In case one would like to produce rankings based on OWL ontologies, a mechanism will be needed to measure (dis-)similarity between fragment representations. For descriptions in OWL (Lite and DL), we need to retrieve those cases where two fragments are similar but happen to fall outside a strict subsumption relationship, *e.g.* the structure of two fragments is the same, except there are two services which are not in a subsumption relationship.

Three approaches have been proposed over the years to deal with the notion of similarity in DLs. The first is *feature-based*, and builds on the analogy of DL concepts and roles as pieces of conceptual knowledge, where some of the pieces (features) can be shuffled around. Feature-based approaches and implementations relying on structural algorithms have been developed for $\mathcal{FL}^-$ in using shared roles and role values for matching, and by counting shared parent concepts [26]. In [27] a structural algorithm based on abduction and contraction is presented for a fragment of $\mathcal{ALC}$. A tableaux algorithm for abduction and contraction based matching in $\mathcal{ALN}$ is presented in [28]. This approach stays within the first-order logic paradigm. Two alternative approaches for similarity in DL bring in elements from other paradigms, thereby creating a hybrid formalism. The *vector-based* approach adopts normalised vectors and the cosine measure from information retrieval, *e.g.* [29], whereas the *probability-based* approach tries to merge Bayesian inference with DL reasoning, *e.g.* [30]. The theory and practical implications of these alternative approaches are less understood.

We have tried to apply the feature-based approach for ranking fragments but, so far, have been unable to, given the expressive constructs used in our workflow ontology (details in [17]). If no abduction algorithm for OWL Lite can be devised, approximation [31] might offer a way out by simplifying the ontology in a non trivial way to the level of expressivity the abduction algorithm can handle. Another option is to stay within OWL Lite and devise query relaxation strategies for a query manager, treating the reasoner as a black box.

5   Conclusions

The vision for the Web of Science fits well with the vision for the Semantic Web [3]. We see reuse and repurposing as a way of bootstrapping the Web of Science by stimulating the dynamics of sharing and reuse of experimental components in the scientific community. In this paper we investigated what it would mean for scientific problem-solving knowledge, captured in workflows, to be found and adapted, *i.e.* repurposed. We presented evidence that e-Science is an area where workflows are already actively shared, reused and repurposed.

We identified seven bottlenecks for repurposing and related some of these to challenges for the Semantic Web. We considered whether two of the identified bottlenecks, workflow fragment discovery and the ranking of fragments, can be tackled by reasoning based on OWL. We found that the existing OWL-based service description frameworks and querying technology would need extending for doing so. In light of the evidence of reuse, we believe that e-Science offers an appealing test bed for further experiments with Semantic Web discovery technology.

Acknowledgements

This work is supported by the UK e-Science programme EPSRC GR/ R67743. The authors would like to acknowledge the ^{my}Grid team. Hannah Tipney developed the Williams' syndrome workflow and is supported by The Wellcome Foundation (G/R:1061183). We thank the survey interviewees for their contribution: Chris Wroe, Mark Greenwood and Peter Li (^{my}Grid), Ilkay Altintas (Kepler), Vasa Curcin (InforSense), Ian Wang (Triana), Colin Puleston (Geodise) and Ben Butchart (Sedna). Sean Bechhofer provided useful comments on an earlier draft.

References

1. T. Hey and A. Trefethen. The uk e-science core program and the grid. In *Int. Conf. on Computational Science*, volume 1, pages 3–21, 2002.
2. R. Stevens, H. Tipney, C. Wroe, et al. Exploring Williams Beuren Syndrome Using ^{my}Grid. *Bioinformatics*, 20:303–310, 2004.
3. J. Hendler. Science and the semantic web. *Science*, January 23 2003.
4. I. Horrocks, P. Patel-Schneider, and F. van Harmelen. From $\mathcal{SHIQ}$ and RDF to OWL: the making of a web ontology language. *Journal of Web Semantics*, 1(1):7–26, 2003.
5. F. van Harmelen. How the semantic web will change kr: challenges and opportunities for a new research agenda. *The Knowl. Eng. Review*, 17(1), 2002.
6. R. King, K. Whelan, F. Jones, et al. Functional genomic hypothesis generation and experimentation by a robot scientist. *Nature*, 427(6971), 2004.
7. R. Hull, M. Benedikt, V. Christophides, and J. Su. E-services: a look behind the curtain. In *22nd Symposium on Principles of database systems PODS*, 2003.
8. C. Wroe, R. Stevens, C. Goble, A. Roberts, and M. Greenwood. A suite of daml+oil ontologies to describe bioinformatics web services and data. *Intl. J. of Cooperative Information Systems*, 12(2):197–224, 2003.
9. D. Berardi, G. De Giacomo, M. Lenzerini, M. Mecella, and D. Calvanese. Synthesis of underspecified composite e-services based on automated reasoning. In *2nd Int. Conf. on Service Oriented Computing ICSOC*, pages 105–114, 2004.
10. A. Wombacher, P. Fankhauser, B. Mahleko, et al. Matchmaking for business processes based on choreographies. *Int. J. of Web Services*, 1(4), 2004.
11. E. Lee. Overview of the ptolemy project. Technical Memorandum UCB/ERL M03/25, University of California, Berkeley, July 2 2003.
12. Annette ten Teije, Frank van Harmelen, and Bob Wielinga. Configuration of web services as parametric design. In *EKAW'04*, 2004.

13. W. van der Aalst, A. Weijters, and L. Maruster. Workflow mining: Discovering process models from event logs. *IEEE TKDE*, 16(9):1128–1142, 2004.
14. P. Lord, S. Bechhofer, M. Wilkinson, et al. Applying semantic web services to bioinformatics: Experiences gained, lessons learnt. In *ISWC*, 2004.
15. E. Deelman, J. Blythe, Y. Gil, et al. Mapping abstract complex workflows onto grid environments. *Journal of Grid Computing*, 1(1), 2003.
16. W. van der Aalst, A. ter Hofstede, B. Kiepuszewski, and A. Barros. Workflow patterns. *Distributed and Parallel Databases*, 14(1):5–51, 2003.
17. A. Goderis, U. Sattler, and C. Goble. Applying descriptions logics for workflow reuse and repurposing. In *DL workshop 2005*.
18. S. Al Sairaf, F. S. Emmanouil, M. Ghanem, et al. The design of discovery net: Towards open grid services for knowledge discovery. *Int. J. of High Performance Computing Applications*, 2003.
19. F. Tao, L. Chen, N. Shadbolt, et al. Semantic web based content enrichment and knowledge reuse in e-science. In *CoopIS/DOA/ODBASE*, pages 654–669, 2004.
20. S. Majithia, D. Walker, and W. Gray. Automated web service composition using semantic web technologies. In *Int.l Conf. on Autonomic Computing*, 2004.
21. I. Altintas, C. Berkley, E. Jaeger, et al. Kepler: An extensible system for design and execution of scientific workflows. In *16th Intl. Conf. on Scientific and Statistical Database Management(SSDBM)*, 2004.
22. P. Li, K. Hayward, C. Jennings, et al. Association of variations in I kappa B-epsilon with Graves' disease using classical methodologies and ^{my}Grid methodologies. In *UK e-Science All Hands Meeting*, 2004.
23. G. Joeris and O. Herzog. Managing evolving workflow specifications. In *3rd Int. Conf. on Cooperative Information Systems (CoopIS98)*, pages 310–319, 1998.
24. K. Sycara, M. Paolucci, A. Ankolekar, and N. Srinivasan. Automated discovery, interaction and composition of semantic web services. *Web Semantics: Science, Services and Agents on the WWW*, 1(1):27–46, 2003.
25. U. Keller, R. Lara, A. Polleres, et al. Wsmo web service discovery. WSML Working Draft D5.1 v0.1, University of Innsbruck, 2004.
26. S. Bechhofer and C. Goble. Classification Based Navigation and Retrieval for Picture Archives. In *IFIP WG2.6 Conference on Data Semantics, DS8*, 1999.
27. A. Cali, D. Calvanese, S. Colucci, et al. A description logic based approach for matching user profiles. In *DL workshop 2004*.
28. S. Colucci, T. Di Noia, E. Di Sciascio, et al. A uniform tableaux-based approach to concept abduction and contraction in aln. In *DL workshop 2004*.
29. C. Meghini, F. Sebastiani, U. Straccia, and C. Thanos. A model of ir based on a terminological logic. In *116th ACM SIGIR*, pages 298 – 307, 1993.
30. D. Koller, A. Levy, and A. Pfeffer. P-classic: A tractable probabilistic description logic. In *AAAI 1997*, pages 390–397, Rhode Island, August.
31. S. Brandt, R. Küsters, and A.-Y. Turhan. Approximation and difference in description logics. In *KR2002*, pages 203–214, San Francisco, USA, 2002.

On Logical Consequence for Collections of OWL Documents

Yuanbo Guo and Jeff Heflin

Computer Science & Engineering Dept.,
Lehigh University, Bethlehem, PA18015, USA
{yug2, heflin}@cse.lehigh.edu

Abstract. In this paper, we investigate the (in)dependence among OWL documents with respect to the logical consequence when they are combined, in particular the inference of concept and role assertions about individuals. On the one hand, we present a systematic approach to identifying those documents that affect the inference of a given fact. On the other hand, we consider ways for fast detection of independence. First, we demonstrate several special cases in which two documents are independent of each other. Secondly, we introduce an algorithm for checking the independence in the general case. In addition, we describe two applications in which the above results have allowed us to develop novel approaches to overcome some difficulties in reasoning with large scale OWL data. Both applications demonstrate the usefulness of this work for improving the scalability of a practical Semantic Web system that relies on the reasoning about individuals.

1 Introduction

To fully exploit the power of the Semantic Web, it is crucial to reason, in an efficient and scalable way, with its data, e.g., those described in the OWL language [4]. Representative OWL reasoners of today such as FaCT [12] and Racer [9], implemented upon the most advanced reasoning mechanisms, have seen some successful applications. However, the scalability of those systems is still far from satisfactory in the context of the Semantic Web, which represents much larger problem sizes than those traditionally found in artificial intelligence. For instance, as Haarslev and Möller [10] pointed out, the scale of data that Racer could appropriately handle is still rather limited (only up to 30,000 individuals in their experimental setting) given non-naïve ontologies and instances. Hence, a great challenge remains in order to implement a practical Semantic Web system that is capable of reasoning on large scale data.

In this paper, we investigate a specific issue in this regard. We consider the situation when a system needs to reason over a large collection of OWL documents in order to answer queries against them. If scalability was not an issue, we could load the entire set of documents into a contemporary OWL reasoner and then issue queries in a normal fashion. However, this will not work in practice considering the large number of documents the system has to deal with. For instance, practical reasons such as memory limitations might simply prevent the system from processing a document collection in its entirety.

Y. Gil et al. (Eds.): ISWC 2005, LNCS 3729, pp. 338–352, 2005.

This work explores ways for improving the scalability of the system in performing the above kind of task. Note, here we assume we have access to a powerful OWL reasoner and we are not concerned with the implementation or optimization of the reasoner per se. Instead, we consider how large problems that cannot typically be solved by the reasoner can be reduced into problems that can be solved.

Specifically, we have the following considerations. First, given a set of documents, it might be the case that, only a subset of the documents is needed in order for a specific statement to be true. In other words, we do not need to combine the whole set and perform expensive reasoning on it in order to guarantee a correct inference with respect to that statement. Furthermore, if we could show that a set of documents, when combined, would not form any conclusions that are not supported by any of the documents individually, then we may adopt a divide-and-conquer approach for the related reasoning tasks on those documents.

The above considerations have led us to research on what we call dependence and independence relationships among OWL documents. Now that the notions apply to general logical knowledge bases, we define them in general as follows:

Def. 1.1. *Let K be the set of knowledge bases $\{\mathcal{K}_1,...,\mathcal{K}_n\}$ (n>1). The members of K are **logically dependent on each other with respect to a sentence α** iff K is a minimal set such that $K \vDash \alpha$.*

Def. 1.2. *Let K be the set of knowledge bases $\{\mathcal{K}_1,...,\mathcal{K}_n\}$ (n>1). The members of K are **logically independent of each other** iff for every sentence α, there are no members of K that are logically dependent on each other with respect to α.*

What we shall look into in this work is the logical (in)dependence relationships among OWL documents with respect to OWL assertions. Here, we refer to an OWL document as an RDF/XML-syntax document that conforms to the specification by the OWL reference [4: Section 2]. In addition, to clarify the meaning of "K ⊨α" in the above definitions when applied to OWL, we say a set of OWL documents entail an assertion α iff α is entailed by the union of the imports closure[1] of every document in the set. Note that this is different from the notion of entailment defined in ongoing research on distributed description logics [2], which focuses on preventing the propagation of inconsistency.

This work will focus on OWL Lite and OWL DL, the two decidable sublanguages of OWL. Since OWL Lite and OWL DL are logically equivalent to DL $\mathcal{SHIF}(\mathbf{D})$ and DL $\mathcal{SHOIN}(\mathbf{D})$ respectively [13], throughout the discussion, we will regard an OWL document as a description logic (DL) knowledge base consisting of a TBox $\mathcal{T}$ (equivalent to the parse result of the ontology) and an ABox $\mathcal{A}$ (equivalent to the parse result of the instance data committing to the ontology). We use $(\mathcal{T}, \mathcal{A})$ to denote such a knowledge base. To facilitate the discussion, we shall use the following terms, which are not conventionally used in the literature:

---

[1] Imports closure of an OWL document is the information in the document unioned with the information in the imports closure of documents that are imported by that document [19].

An OWL DL knowledge base (resp. an OWL DL TBox, an OWL DL ABox) is the result of parsing an OWL DL document (resp. the ontology part of an OWL DL document, the instance data part of an OWL DL document) into a DL knowledge base (resp. a DL TBox, a DL ABox). Similarly for OWL Lite knowledge base, OWL Lite TBox, and OWL Lite ABox. In the subsequent discussion, for brevity, "DL" will be omitted without confusion.

As a final remark, as the first step of the work, we consider OWL documents that commit to a common ontology. Additionally, we will concentrate on ABox reasoning, in particular the inference of concept assertions and role assertions. This is motivated by the expectation that the instance data will greatly outnumber the ontologies on the Semantic Web.

2   Identifying the Logical Dependence

In this section, we examine the dependence relationship among OWL documents. Specifically, we attempt to define a systematic way to identify what documents, when combined together, may affect the inference of a specific assertion. We base our approach on the identification of the relevant assertion set to a given assertion, as defined below. Again, we first define the notions in general. Then, we give a specific account of the notions for ABox assertions.

Def. 2.1. *A set S of sentences is a **relevant sentence set** to the logical entailment of a sentence α, denoted Rel(S, α), iff $S \vDash \alpha$.*

Def. 2.2. *A set S of sentences is a **minimal relevant sentence set** to the logical entailment of a sentence α, denoted MinRel(S, α), iff S is a minimal set such that Rel (S, α).*

Def. 2.3. *Given a consistent TBox $\mathcal{T}$, a set S of ABox assertions is a **relevant ABox assertion set** to the logical entailment of an ABox assertion α, denoted $Rel_{\mathcal{T}}(S, \alpha)$, iff $<\mathcal{T},S> \vDash \alpha$.*

Def. 2.4. *Given a consistent TBox $\mathcal{T}$, a set S of ABox assertions is a **minimal relevant ABox assertion set** to the logical entailment of an ABox assertion α, denoted $MinRel_{\mathcal{T}}$ (S, α), iff S is a minimal set such that $Rel_{\mathcal{T}}(S, \alpha)$.*

Now we are able to establish a relationship between relevance and dependence for OWL knowledge bases with the same TBox, i.e., they commit to the same ontology.

Proposition 2.1. *Let K be the set of OWL knowledge bases $\mathcal{K}_1=(\mathcal{T}, \mathcal{A}_1),..., \mathcal{K}_n=(\mathcal{T}, \mathcal{A}_n)$ (n>1), wherein $\mathcal{T}$ is consistent. The members of K are logically dependent on each other with respect to an ABox assertion α iff K is a minimal set such that there exist $\alpha_1,...,\alpha_m$ such that $MinRel_{\mathcal{T}}(\{\alpha_1,...,\alpha_m\}, \alpha)$ and for every $\alpha_i (i=1,...,m)$ there exists $\mathcal{A}_j$ (j=1,...,n) such that $\alpha_i \in \mathcal{A}_j$.*

The above proposition, in effect, indicates a way of determining the dependence among a set of OWL knowledge bases with respect to a given assertion, i.e., by looking for relevant assertion sets to that assertion. Therefore, the remaining question is how to identify those relevant sets. We begin by identifying a set of inference rules for an OWL Lite knowledge base, as shown below.

R1) If $\alpha \in \mathcal{A}$ then $\mathcal{A} \vdash \alpha$

R2) If $\mathcal{T} \vDash C_1 \sqcap \cdots \sqcap C_n \sqsubseteq C$ and $\mathcal{A} \vdash a:C_1,\ldots,a:C_n$, then $\mathcal{A} \vdash a:C$

R3) If $\mathcal{T} \vDash R_1 \sqsubseteq R_2$ and $\mathcal{A} \vdash <a,b>:R_1$ then $\mathcal{A} \vdash <a,b>:R_2$

R4) If $\mathcal{T} \vDash U_1 \sqsubseteq U_2$ and $\mathcal{A} \vdash <a,v>:U_1$ then $\mathcal{A} \vdash <a,v>:U_2$

R5) If $\mathcal{A} \vdash <a,b>:R$ then $\mathcal{A} \vdash <b,a>:R^-$

R6) For $R \in \mathbf{R}_+$, if $\mathcal{A} \vdash <a,b>:R$ and $<b,c>:R$ then $\mathcal{A} \vdash <a,c>:R$

R7) If $\mathcal{A} \vdash <a,b>:R$ and $b:C$ then $\mathcal{A} \vdash a: \exists R.C$

R8) If $\mathcal{A} \vdash <a,v>:U$ and $v \in D$ then $\mathcal{A} \vdash a: \exists U.D$

R9) If $\mathcal{A} \vdash a: \forall R.C$ and $<a,b>:R$ then $\mathcal{A} \vdash b:C$

R10) If $\mathcal{A} \vdash <a,b>:R$ then $\mathcal{A} \vdash a:\geq 1R$

R11) If $\mathcal{A} \vdash <a,v>:U$ then $\mathcal{A} \vdash a:\geq 1U$

R12) If $\mathcal{A} \vdash a:\leq 1R$, $<a,b_1>:R$, and $<a,b_2>:R$ then $\mathcal{A} \vdash b_1=b_2$

R13) If $\mathcal{A} \vdash a=b$ then $\mathcal{A} \vdash b=a$

R14) If $\mathcal{A} \vdash a=b$ and $a:C$ (resp. $<a,c>:R$, $<c,a>:R$, $a=c$) then $\mathcal{A} \vdash b:C$ (resp. $<b,c>:R$, $<c,b>:R$, $b=c$)

R15) If $v_1=v_2$ and $\mathcal{A} \vdash <a,v_1>:U$ then $\mathcal{A} \vdash <a,v_2>:U$

We have defined the above rules by referring to the work of Royer and Quantz [20, 21] with several extensions and adaptations. They described a generic approach to deriving, via Sequent Calculus, complete inference rules for description logics. They also provided the result for a specific description logic, which is generally more expressive than OWL Lite if we ignore datatypes and equality. We extend those rules by taking into account datatypes and equality[2]. Moreover, we handle the inference involving subsumption differently. They provided over 100 rules for subsumption. We chose not to include them since our focus is on ABox assertions and those rules greatly complicate the derivation of the relationship we are looking for. Instead, we remedy the absence of those subsumption rules by relying on the entailment of the TBox, as Rules 2 to 4 show. From the implementation point of view, this means we resort to the reasoner for checking subsumptions. We consider this as a reasonable method especially when the application involves a large amount of instance data over a relatively small number of ontologies.

As some other remarks, in defining the rules we only consider a consistent knowledge base.[3] Also, for simplicity we assume no untyped data values in the knowledge

---

[2] OWL supports the expression of equality. Also the language does not make the unique names assumption.

[3] These rules may easily be extended to support the inconsistent case and then we consider they could potentially be exploited for other kinds of tasks such as debugging inconsistencies. However, that is beyond the interest of this paper.

base. In addition, we rely upon the reasoner to reason about the data values such as deciding if they belong to a specific datatype and their equality (refer to Rules 8 and 15). Moreover, in the rules and also the subsequent discussion, we assume that every assertion $a:C_1 \sqcap \cdots \sqcap C_n$ is represented as $a:C_1,\ldots,a:C_n$. Finally, our rule set is incomplete for OWL DL, which additionally supports *oneOf*. As Royer and Quantz pointed out, taking account of enumerated classes would greatly complicate the resultant rule set. Thus they did not give a complete set of rules with respect to reasoning about enumerated classes, and neither did we. We leave this as an open issue.

The above rule set may not be suitable for implementing a practical reasoner due to its special handling of TBox related inferences. However, these natural deduction-style inference rules can facilitate the identification of the relevant assertion sets to a given assertion, as shown in Proposition 2.2. The proposition is obvious by following the rule firing relations (refer to the right column for the corresponding rules).

Proposition 2.2. *In OWL Lite, given a consistent TBox $\mathcal{T}$, a consistent set S of ABox assertions, and a concept or role assertion α, $Rel_{\mathcal{T}}(S, \alpha)$ iff S is at least one of the following sets:*

For any α:
- $\{ \alpha \}$ (R1)

If α is $a:C$:
- $S_1 \cup \cdots \cup S_n$ *wherein* $Rel_{\mathcal{T}}(S_1, a:C_1)$, ..., $Rel_{\mathcal{T}}(S_n, a:C_n)$, $\mathcal{T} \vDash C_1 \sqcap \cdots \sqcap C_n \sqsubseteq C$ (R2)
- $S_1 \cup S_2$ *wherein* $Rel_{\mathcal{T}}(S_1, b: \forall R.C)$, $Rel_{\mathcal{T}}(S_2, <b,a>:R)$ (R9)
- $S_1 \cup S_2$ *wherein* $Rel_{\mathcal{T}}(S_1, a=b)$, $Rel_{\mathcal{T}}(S_2, b:C)$
  (R14)

If α is $a: \exists R.C$:
- $S_1 \cup S_2$ *wherein* $Rel_{\mathcal{T}}(S_1, <a,b>:R)$, $Rel_{\mathcal{T}}(S_2, b:C)$ (R7)

If α is $a: \exists U.D$:
- S *wherein* $Rel_{\mathcal{T}}(S, <a,v>:U)$, $v \in D$ (R8)

If α is $a: \geq 1R$:
- S *wherein* $Rel_{\mathcal{T}}(S, <a,b>:R)$ (R10)

If α is $a: \geq 1U$):
- S *wherein* $Rel_{\mathcal{T}}(S, <a,v>:U)$ (R11)

If α is $<a,b>:R$:
- S *wherein* $Rel_{\mathcal{T}}(S, <a,b>:T)$, $\mathcal{T} \vDash T \sqsubseteq R$ (R3)
- S *wherein* $Rel_{\mathcal{T}}(S, <b,a>:R^-)$ (R5)
- $S_1 \cup S_2$
  wherein $Rel_{\mathcal{T}}(S_1, <a,c>:R)$, $Rel_{\mathcal{T}}(S_2, <c,b>:R)$, $R \in R_+$ (R6)
- $S_1 \cup S_2$
  wherein $Rel_{\mathcal{T}}(S_1, a=c)$, $Rel_{\mathcal{T}}(S_2, <c,b>:R)$, or   (R14)
         $Rel_{\mathcal{T}}(S_1, b=c)$, $Rel_{\mathcal{T}}(S_2, <a,c>:R)$ (R14)

If α is $<a,v>:U$:
- S *wherein* $Rel_{\mathcal{T}}(S, <a,v>:V)$, $\mathcal{T} \vDash V \sqsubseteq U$ (R4)
- S *wherein* $Rel_{\mathcal{T}}(S, <a,w>:U)$, $v=w$ (R15)

If α is a=b:

- $S_1 \cup S_2 \cup S_3$
  wherein $Rel_{\mathcal{T}}(S_1, c{:}{\le}1R)$, $Rel_{\mathcal{T}}(S_2, <c,a>{:}R)$, $Rel_{\mathcal{T}}(S_2, <c,b>{:}R)$ (R12)
- S wherein $Rel_{\mathcal{T}}(S, b{=}a)$ (R13)
- $S_1 \cup S_2$ wherein $Rel_{\mathcal{T}}(S_1, c{=}a)$, $Rel_{\mathcal{T}}(S_2, c{=}b)$ (R14)

Since determining Min$Rel_{\mathcal{T}}$is straightforward given the information of $Rel_{\mathcal{T}}$, Propositions 2.1 and 2.2 have rendered us a systematic way of identifying the dependent knowledge base set with respect to a specific assertion. Next, we show an application of the approach.

Application I

In another work [8], we aim at developing a query answering system for a repository of OWL documents. One important functionality of the system is to answer a user's query about the minimal subsets of documents in the repository that entail a specific assertion. Currently we only consider queries about concept instances on OWL Lite documents. In order to improve query time, the system performs preprocessing of the documents during loading and records which new assertion is entailed by which minimal subsets of documents. To that end, it enumerates the subsets of the documents in the order of their sizes, i.e. single document first, and then the combinations of two documents, and so on, and performs reasoning on those consistent combinations in sequence.

Obviously, processing the document combinations in this fashion is inefficient since the potential number of combinations the system has to handle increases exponentially in the number of documents. Given Propositions 2.1 and 2.2, we are able to employ a different strategy: we perform reasoning on the whole union of the documents immediately after processing every individual document. Then for each inferred concept assertion α from the union, we directly identify, according to those propositions, the minimal document sets (containing more than one document) that entail α, in other words, the sets of documents that are dependent on each other with respect to α.

Although an efficient implementation of the propositions is still a remaining issue, we consider that, with a proper mechanism for indexing and searching the assertions, the complexity of identifying the dependent subsets among a collection of documents will be no more than that of performing reasoning on the union of the entire set. Thus, we can expect prominent performance improvement in cases where new assertions that are entailed by more than one document are relatively few.

To give readers a flavor of this, we introduce an initial evaluation---the system is still under development. We used 100 small OWL Lite documents (committing to the same ontology). These documents are adaptations from the test data of the Lehigh University Benchmark [7], which simulates a realistic domain. We conducted reasoning on the union of the entire document set. Then, we tried to identify the dependent subsets of documents with respect to each of the concept assertions entailed by the union. As a result, we pinpointed 43 subsets each containing two documents from 16 assertions, which were new entailments by the union than the individual documents. Note, in this case, none of those assertions captured 3 or more documents. This is a significant improvement considering that, before the strategy is adopted, the system had to handle the level of 2^{100} document combinations in order to completely find those subsets.

3 Detecting the Logical Independence – Special Cases

Hereafter, we will switch our focus to the detection of independence. Unlike dependence, the notion of independence is not defined with respect to a specific statement. Instead, we are interested in more general relationships such as independence with respect to all ABox assertions of certain forms. The result in the previous section provides an indirect way for determining this kind of independence between a set of OWL knowledge bases K, i.e., by showing that, for every applicable assertion, there are no members of K that are mutually dependent with respect to that assertion. However, this is obviously a very inefficient approach since we have to enumerate and test all possible assertions. In the following two sections, we explore some faster ways. We begin with special cases, in which we demonstrate that, under certain conditions, two OWL documents are independent of each other with respect to the assertions of specific forms.

First, we introduce the following notation:

Ind($\mathcal{K}$): The set of individual names in the OWL knowledge base $\mathcal{K}$.

The following theorem reveals the independence relationship between two OWL knowledge bases with disjoint sets of individual names.

Theorem 3.1. *Let $\mathcal{K}_1=(\mathcal{T}, \mathcal{A}_1)$ and $\mathcal{K}_2=(\mathcal{T}, \mathcal{A}_2)$ be two OWL knowledge bases. If $Ind(\mathcal{K}_1) \cap Ind(\mathcal{K}_2)=\varnothing$, then $\mathcal{K}_1$ and $\mathcal{K}_2$ are logically independent of each other with respect to any concept assertion, role assertion, or equality assertion[4].*

Proof. Let $\mathcal{K}=(\mathcal{T}, \mathcal{A}_1 \cup \mathcal{A}_2)$. This is equivalent to proving that for every assertion α being any form of a:C, <a,b>:R, <a,v>:U or a=b, $\mathcal{K} \vDash \alpha$ iff either $\mathcal{K}_1 \vDash \alpha$ or $\mathcal{K}_2 \vDash \alpha$.

(<=) It is trivially true because OWL is monotonic.

(=>) Since $\mathcal{K} \vDash \alpha$, every model $\mathcal{I}$ of $\mathcal{K}$ satisfies α (1). If either $\mathcal{K}_1$ or $\mathcal{K}_2$ is inconsistent, since everything can be deduced from an inconsistent knowledge base, the theorem is proved. In case both $\mathcal{K}_1$ and $\mathcal{K}_2$ are consistent, suppose $\mathcal{K}_1 \nvDash \alpha$ and $\mathcal{K}_2 \nvDash \alpha$ (2). Then there must exist a model $\mathcal{I}_1 = (\Delta^{\mathcal{I}1}, \cdot^{\mathcal{I}1})$ (resp. $\mathcal{I}_2 = (\Delta^{\mathcal{I}2}, \cdot^{\mathcal{I}2})$) of $\mathcal{K}_1$ (resp. $\mathcal{K}_2$) that does not satisfy α. We assume that $\Delta^{\mathcal{I}1}$ and $\Delta^{\mathcal{I}2}$ are disjoint (3). We could make the assumption because if that is not the case, we can always replace $\mathcal{I}_1$ with another interpretation $\mathcal{I}_1$' such that 1) $\Delta^{\mathcal{I}1'}$ and $\Delta^{\mathcal{I}2}$ are disjoint, and 2) every domain object in $\Delta^{\mathcal{I}1'}$ has a counterpart in $\Delta^{\mathcal{I}1}$ and stands in the same place in $\cdot^{\mathcal{I}1'}$ as its counterpart does in $\cdot^{\mathcal{I}1}$, and vice versa.

Now define an interpretation $\mathcal{I}=(\Delta^{\mathcal{I}}, \cdot^{\mathcal{I}})$ for $\mathcal{K}$ wherein,

- $\Delta^{\mathcal{I}} = \Delta^{\mathcal{I}1} \cup \Delta^{\mathcal{I}2}$
- For every concept C, $C^{\mathcal{I}} = C^{\mathcal{I}1} \cup C^{\mathcal{I}2}$

---

[4] This does not hold for inequality. For instance, if $\mathcal{T}$ claims the concepts C_1 and C_2 as disjoint whereas $\mathcal{A}_1$ and $\mathcal{A}_2$ assert $a:C_1$ and $b:C_2$ respectively, then we can infer that $a \neq b$ from the union of $\mathcal{K}_1$ and $\mathcal{K}_2$.

- For every (object and datatype) role R, $R^{\mathcal{I}} = R^{\mathcal{I}1} \cup R^{\mathcal{I}2}$
- For every individual a:[5]
  If $a \in \mathrm{Ind}(\mathcal{A}_1)$, $a^{\mathcal{I}} = a^{\mathcal{I}1}$; otherwise, $a^{\mathcal{I}} = a^{\mathcal{I}2}$
- For every data value v, $v^{\mathcal{I}} = v^{\mathbf{D}}$
- The concrete domain $\Delta_{\mathbf{D}}{}^{\mathcal{I}} = \Delta_{\mathbf{D}}{}^{\mathcal{I}1} = \Delta_{\mathbf{D}}{}^{\mathcal{I}2}$

Next we prove that $\mathcal{I}$ is a model of $\mathcal{K}$. As it has been shown that OWL DL entailment is reducible to DL $\mathcal{SHOIN}(\mathbf{D})$ satisfiability [13], we will show that $\mathcal{I}$ is a model of $\mathcal{K}$ based on the semantics of $\mathcal{SHOIN}(\mathbf{D})$ (cf. Fig. 3 of [13]).[6]

First, it is straightforward to show from the definition of $\mathcal{I}$ that $\mathcal{I}$ satisfies the semantics relating to atomic concept, datatype, role, individual, data value, inverse role, top/bottom concept, disjunction, oneOf, concept inclusion, and role inclusion. For example,

$$(C_1 \sqcup C_2)^{\mathcal{I}} = (C_1 \sqcup C_2)^{\mathcal{I}1} \cup (C_1 \sqcup C_2)^{\mathcal{I}2} = (C_1^{\mathcal{I}1} \cup C_2^{\mathcal{I}1}) \cup (C_1^{\mathcal{I}2} \cup C_2^{\mathcal{I}2})$$
$$= (C_1^{\mathcal{I}1} \cup C_1^{\mathcal{I}2}) \cup (C_2^{\mathcal{I}1} \cup C_2^{\mathcal{I}2}) = C_1^{\mathcal{I}} \cup C_2^{\mathcal{I}}$$

Moreover, based on the definition of $\mathcal{I}$ plus the assumption (3), we can show that $\mathcal{I}$ satisfies the semantics relating to conjunction, negation, retrictions, and transitive role. For instance,

$$(\exists R.C)^{\mathcal{I}} = (\exists R.C)^{\mathcal{I}1} \cup (\exists R.C)^{\mathcal{I}2}$$
$$= \{x \mid \exists y.<x,y> \in R^{\mathcal{I}1} \text{ and } y \in C^{\mathcal{I}1}\} \cup \{x \mid \exists y.<x,y> \in R^{\mathcal{I}2} \text{ and } y \in C^{\mathcal{I}2}\}$$
$$= \text{via (3)} = \{x \mid \exists y.<x,y> \in R^{\mathcal{I}1} \cup R^{\mathcal{I}2} \text{ and } y \in C^{\mathcal{I}1} \cup C^{\mathcal{I}2}\}$$
$$= \{x \mid \exists y.<x,y> \in R^{\mathcal{I}} \text{ and } y \in C^{\mathcal{I}}\}$$

Lastly, for every ABox assertion β in $\mathcal{K}$, we can show $\mathcal{I}$ satisfies β based on the definition of $\mathcal{I}$ and the fact that β is originally from either $\mathcal{K}_1$ or $\mathcal{K}_2$ and thus either $\mathcal{I}_1$ or $\mathcal{I}_2$ satisfies β. For example, if $a{:}C$ is from $\mathcal{K}_1$ and therefore satisfied by $\mathcal{I}_1$, then $a^{\mathcal{I}} = a^{\mathcal{I}1}$. Since $a^{\mathcal{I}1} \in C^{\mathcal{I}1}$ and $C^{\mathcal{I}1} \subseteq C^{\mathcal{I}}$, $a^{\mathcal{I}} \in C^{\mathcal{I}}$. Thus $\mathcal{I}$ satisfies $a{:}C$.

So far, we can conclude that $\mathcal{I}$ is a model of $\mathcal{K}$. Next we show $\mathcal{I}$ however does not satisfy α. If α is of the form $a{:}C$, according to the definition of $\mathcal{I}$, $a^{\mathcal{I}}$ equals to either $a^{\mathcal{I}1}$ or $a^{\mathcal{I}2}$. Since neither $\mathcal{I}_1$ nor $\mathcal{I}_2$ satisfies α, $a^{\mathcal{I}1} \notin C^{\mathcal{I}1}$ and $a^{\mathcal{I}2} \notin C^{\mathcal{I}2}$. In addition, given the assumption of (3), we have $a^{\mathcal{I}1} \notin C^{\mathcal{I}2}$ and $a^{\mathcal{I}2} \notin C^{\mathcal{I}1}$. Hence, $a^{\mathcal{I}} \notin C^{\mathcal{I}1} \cup C^{\mathcal{I}2}$ and thus $a^{\mathcal{I}} \notin C^{\mathcal{I}}$, which means $\mathcal{I}$ does not satisfy α. With similar arguments, we can show that $\mathcal{I}$ does not satisfy α of the form $<a,b>{:}R$, $<a,v>{:}U$ or $a=b$ either.

In conclusion, $\mathcal{I}$ is a model of $\mathcal{K}$ but $\mathcal{I}$ does not satisfy α. This is contradictory to (1), which means assumption (2) does not hold. Therefore, either $\mathcal{K}_1 \models \alpha$ or $\mathcal{K}_2 \models \alpha$.

The theorem below considers the independence between OWL knowledge bases in terms of deriving inconsistency.

Theorem 3.2. *Under the same precondition of Theorem 3.1, $\mathcal{K}$ is inconsistent iff either $\mathcal{K}_1$ or $\mathcal{K}_2$ is inconsistent.*

---

[5] Note that for every enumerated class $\{o_1,\ldots, o_n\}$, since $\mathrm{Ind}(\mathcal{K}_1)$ and $\mathrm{Ind}(\mathcal{K}_2)$ are disjoint, $o_1,\ldots, o_n$ could not occur in both knowledge bases.

[6] For simplicity, we ignore the translation of OWL DL into $\mathcal{SHOIN}(\mathbf{D})$ since it maintains the satisfaction of theorem's precondition.

Proof. Again the (<=) part is obvious. (=>) That $\mathcal{K}$ is inconsistent means $\mathcal{K}$ has no models. Suppose both $\mathcal{K}_1$ and $\mathcal{K}_2$ are consistent and thus have a model respectively, we could find a model $\mathcal{I}$ for $\mathcal{K}$ as we do in the proof of Theorem 3.1. Therefore, $\mathcal{K}_1$ and $\mathcal{K}_2$ could not be both consistent.

Corollary 3.1. *Theorem 3.1 (and also Theorem 3.2) still holds if every individual $a \in Ind(\mathcal{A}_1) \cap Ind(\mathcal{A}_2)$ appears only in those assertions shared by $\mathcal{A}_1$ and $\mathcal{A}_2$.*

Proof. (<=) It is trivially true again. (=>) Define $\mathcal{K}_2'=(\mathcal{T}, \mathcal{A}_2')$ by removing from $\mathcal{A}_2$ all the assertions that are also in $\mathcal{A}_1$. In this way, $\mathcal{K}_1 \cup \mathcal{K}_2'$ still equals to $\mathcal{K}$, but $Ind(\mathcal{K}_1)$ and $Ind(\mathcal{K}_2')$ become disjoint. Therefore according to Theorem 3.1, for every ABox asser-tion α except the inequality assertion, $\mathcal{K} \vDash \alpha$ implies either $\mathcal{K}_1 \vDash \alpha$ or $\mathcal{K}_2' \vDash \alpha$. Since $\mathcal{K}_2$ subsumes $\mathcal{K}_2'$, based on monotonicity, we have $\mathcal{K} \vDash \alpha$ implies either $\mathcal{K}_1 \vDash \alpha$ or $\mathcal{K}_2 \vDash \alpha$. In a similar fashion, we can prove the cases for Theorem 3.2.

Next, we will consider a different situation by removing the disjointness require-ment on individual names while imposing another restriction: we look at OWL docu-ments that contain only RDF(S) [23] features. We look at the RDF(S) fragment of OWL considering oftentimes applications do not need the full expressivity of OWL and the fact that RDF-style documents occupy a considerable portion of the Semantic Web we have seen so far.

Theorem 3.3. *Let $\mathcal{K}_1=(\mathcal{T}, \mathcal{A}_1)$ and $\mathcal{K}_2=(\mathcal{T}, \mathcal{A}_2)$ be two OWL knowledge bases. If both knowledge bases are limited to the RDF(S) fragment, then $\mathcal{K}_1$ and $\mathcal{K}_2$ are logically in-dependent of each other with respect to any assertion α of the form of a:C or $<a,b>$:p.*

Proof. It is equivalent to proving that $\mathcal{K}_1 \cup \mathcal{K}_2 \vDash \alpha$ iff either $\mathcal{K}_1 \vDash \alpha$ or $\mathcal{K}_2 \vDash \alpha$.(<=) Once again it is obvious. (=>) Table 3.1 illustrates how we can transfer an RDF(S) statement into a FOL rule. As can be seen, if a knowledge base contains only FOL rules mapping to RDF(S) statements, it will fit into Horn Logic. This means we could apply a simple forward chaining reasoning on that knowledge base (in this case $\mathcal{K}_1 \cup \mathcal{K}_2$) to get a sound and complete inferencing.

Table 3.1. Correspondence between OWL and DL and between DL and FOL (RDF(S) frag-ment) [22]

OWL Fact/Axiom	DL Syntax	FOL Rule
a type C	a:C	$C(a)$
$a\ P\ b$	$<a,b>$:P	$P(a,b)$
rdfs:subclassOf	$C_1 \sqsubseteq C_2$	$\forall x.C_1(x) \rightarrow C_2(x)$
rdfs:subpropertyOf	$P_1 \sqsubseteq P_2$	$\forall x,y.P_1(x,y) \rightarrow P_2(x,y)$
rdfs:domain	$\top \sqsubseteq \forall P.C$	$\forall x,y.P(x,y) \rightarrow C(x)$
rdfs:range	$\top \sqsubseteq \forall P.C$	$\forall x,y.P(x,y) \rightarrow C(y)$

Furthermore, since every rule presented in the above table has only one antecedent, any proof tree generated on the knowledge base actually reduces to a chain-like struc-ture, starting from a fact in the input till the goal fact. In other words, no proof trees for a new fact involve more than one fact from the input: for two input facts to be used in a proof, there must be a step in the proof that involves two facts that are respectively either the input facts themselves or facts derived from the input facts. However, this is impossible given the above mentioned structure of the proof tree. Thus the theorem is proved.

Application II

Next, we will show an application of the above results. In yet another work [7], we are conducting benchmarks of OWL knowledge base systems with respect to queries upon the instance data. To facilitate evaluating the query completeness and soundness of the systems under test, we intended to use Racer to generate the answer set as a basis for comparison. However, a big problem was that Racer at the current stage is incapable of handling the dataset used in the benchmark in our experimental environment. The smallest dataset used in the benchmark consists of 15 OWL documents. However, as shown in [11], due to Racer has to perform consistency check before answering queries, it could only load up to 5 of the documents (9555 individuals).

Nevertheless, we were able to overcome this problem by virtue of Corollary 3.1. In the benchmark, a dataset consists of multiple OWL Lite documents that commit to the same ontology (also in OWL Lite). We have found out that these documents meet the precondition in Corollary 3.1 with a handful of exceptions[7]. Furthermore, by focusing on those exceptional assertions we have figured out without difficulty that they will not lead to any inferences or inconsistencies across multiple documents. Therefore, we could conclude that these documents are independent of each other with respect to the kind of inference we need, i.e., concept and role instance retrieval. This means we could let Racer do such reasoning on one document from the test set at a time and still guarantee a sound and complete inference by taking the union of the results on every individual document later on. In this way, we have found a solution the above problem.

4   Detecting the Logical Independence – The General Case

In the previous section, we introduced several ways of quickly detecting the independence of OWL knowledge bases in some special cases. Now we look at the general case, i.e., for arbitrary knowledge bases. We have realized that this is a challenging task. Here we present our initial results. The algorithm below is responsible for checking the independence between two OWL knowledge bases.

```
1 procedure CHECK-INDEPENDENCE(K₁, K₂)
2 input: OWL knowledge bases K₁=(T, A₁) and K₂=(T, A₂)
3 output: indicate if K₁ and K₂ are independent with
    respect to any concept assertion or role assertion
4 begin
5   I:= Ind(A₁) ∩ Ind(A₂); //overlap in individual names
6   if I = ∅ then return true;
```

---

[7] These documents have few overlap in individual names because they are dedicated to the description of different organizations (i.e. academic departments) and their affiliated persons.

```
7   if CHECK-AND-REALIZE(A₁)=false then return true;
8   if CHECK-AND-REALIZE(A₂)=false then return true;
9   𝒪 := { a:C ∈ A₁∪A₂|a ∈ I } ∪ {<a,b>:R ∈ A₁∪A₂|a ∈ I or b ∈ I }∪
        { a:C ∈A₁∪A₂| ∃b∈I. <a,b>:R ∈ A₁∪A₂ or <b,a>:R ∈ A₁∪A₂ };
10  A𝒪₁ := A₁∪𝒪;  //Combine A₁ and 𝒪
11  if CHECK-AND-REALIZE(A𝒪₁)=false then return false;
12  if new assertions have been added to A𝒪₁ then return
    false;
13  A𝒪₂ := A₂∪𝒪;  //Combine A₂ and 𝒪
14  repeat 11-12 for A𝒪₂;
15  return true;
16end
17procedure CHECK-AND-REALIZE (A)
18  Check consistency of A;
19  if A is inconsistent then return false;
20  Perform ABox reasoning on A and update A accordingly,
    i.e.,
    A = A ∪
    {a:C | A ⊨ a:C and C is among the most specific con-
    cepts that a is an instance of} ∪
    {<a,b>:R | A ⊨ <a,b>:R and R is among the most spe-
    cific roles that <a,b> is an instance of};
21  return true;
22end
```

Fig. 4.1 illustrates the key operations in the algorithm.

A_1 (after realization)	A_2 (after realization)	I	$\mathcal{O}$
{ $o_1{:}C_1$,	{ $o_1{:}C_1$,	{ o_1}	{ $o_1{:}C_1$,
$o_2{:}C_2$,	$o_4{:}C_2$,		$o_2{:}C_2$,
$o_3{:}C_3$,	$o_5{:}C_3$,		$o_4{:}C_2$,
$<o_2, o_1>{:}R_1$,	$<o_1, o_4>{:}R_1$,		$<o_2, o_1>{:}R_1$,
$<o_2, o_3>{:}R_2$ }	$<o_4, o_5>{:}R_3$ }		$<o_1, o_4>{:}R_1$ }
$A\mathcal{O}_1$(before realization)	$A\mathcal{O}_2$(before realization)		
{ $o_1{:}C_1$,	{ $o_1{:}C_1$,		
$o_2{:}C_2$,	$o_2{:}C_2$,		
$o_3{:}C_3$,	$o_4{:}C_2$,		
$o_4{:}C_2$,	$o_5{:}C_3$,		
$<o_2, o_1>{:}R_1$,	$<o_1, o_4>{:}R_1$,		
$<o_2, o_3>{:}R_2$,	$<o_4, o_5>{:}R_3$,		
$<o_1, o_4>{:}R_1$ }	$<o_2, o_1>{:}R_1$ }		

Fig. 4.1. Illustration of the algorithm CHECK-INDEPENDENCE. For instance, if R_1 is a transitive role, the algorithm will detect a new inference in $A\mathcal{O}_1$ and thus determine that $\mathcal{K}_1$ and $\mathcal{K}_2$ are not independent.

Proposition 4.1. *CHECK-INDEPENDENCE is sound and complete in determining the independence of two OWL knowledge bases $\mathcal{K}_1=(\mathcal{T}, \mathcal{A}_1)$ and $\mathcal{K}_2=(\mathcal{T}, \mathcal{A}_2)$, wherein T is inconsistent, with respect to the logical entailment of any concept assertion or role assertion.*

Proof (sketch).   The algorithm returns true when both knowledge bases do not overlap in individual names, which is supported by Theorem 3.1. (Lines 5-6)   In   case   the overlap does exist, the algorithm conducts reasoning on $\mathcal{A}_1$ and $\mathcal{A}_2$ respectively (Lines 7-8). If either ABox is found inconsistent, $\mathcal{K}_1$ and $\mathcal{K}_2$ are obviously independent since any assertion can be entailed by the single inconsistent knowledge base. If both ABoxes are consistent, the algorithm performs the realization on each of them and updates them accordingly. Next it calculates $\mathcal{O}$ and combines it with $\mathcal{A}_1$ and $\mathcal{A}_2$ respectively (Lines 10-14). If either $\mathcal{AO}_1$ or $\mathcal{AO}_2$ is found inconsistent, we can immediately decide that $\mathcal{K}_1$ and $\mathcal{K}_2$ are not independent (with respect to any assertion). Otherwise, we check if there are any new inferences in $\mathcal{AO}_1$ and $\mathcal{AO}_2$. All the concept assertions and role assertions that have one or more individuals from I are contained in $\mathcal{O}$. Hence $\mathcal{A}_1\backslash\mathcal{O}$ and $\mathcal{A}_2\backslash\mathcal{O}$ are disjoint in individual names, and according to Theorem 3.1, $\mathcal{A}_1\backslash\mathcal{O}$ and $\mathcal{A}_2\backslash\mathcal{O}$ are independent. Therefore, if both $\mathcal{K}_1$ and $\mathcal{K}_2$ are necessary for the inference of a concept or role assertion (and thus are dependent), there have to be some new inferences of concept or role assertion in either $\mathcal{AO}_1$ or $\mathcal{AO}_2$. This can be justified by considering the inference rules described in Section 2[8]. We can assume that the reasoning is carried out by applying those rules. After the reasoning is done on $\mathcal{A}_1$ and $\mathcal{A}_2$, no more rules are applicable to each ABox. Then, by virtue of the forward chaining style of the rules, we can show that, suppose new inferences occur after combining $\mathcal{A}_1$ and $\mathcal{A}_2$, there must first be some inferences (of concept or role assertions) that involve the assertions in $\mathcal{O}$.

The advantage of the above algorithm lies in that, in case two knowledge bases are independent, it allows us to skip the reasoning on the combination of both knowledge bases by doing extra reasoning on two smaller ABoxes (i.e. $\mathcal{AO}_1$ and $\mathcal{AO}_2$ in the algorithm). This is practically useful, for example, when the reasoning performance degrades significant as the size of the knowledge base increases.

5   Related Work

Logical reasoning is usually complex and expensive. Tons of effort has been made to speed up the reasoning, especially for a large knowledge base. Among this is the research on relevance, i.e., the study of what is the relevant part of the knowledge base to a given reasoning task, e.g., a query. Most of the work is oriented towards a specific logical formalism, reasoning task (e.g. entailment, diagnosis, or abduction), and application domain. As a result, a variety of notions of (ir)relevance have emerged, under different names such as (ir)relevance, (in)dependence, irredundancy, influence-ability, novelty, separability, and interactivity [6, 17, 14, 15].

---

[8] Although the rule set given in Section 2 is incomplete for OWL DL, it does not influence the proof here since we can assume the generation of a complete rule set via applying a similar approach to that used in Section 2.

We compare several of those notions that appeared similar to the (in)dependence we defined in this paper. Darwiche [3] and Lang et al. [14] study the notion of conditional independence between propositions. Although they use the same term, their notion of independence is different from ours. The conditional independence they consider is the logical counterpart to probabilistic independence. Therefore, informally speaking, they look at such a relationship between two sets of propositions X and Y that, given some prior information (i.e., the condition), the addition of information about X (i.e., the truth values for the propositions in X) will not lead to the conclusion of any new information about Y. Levesque [16] and Lang et al. [14] introduce a notion of formula separability, which roughly is a relationship between a set S of sentences with respect to a specific sentence α such that every member of S can entail α individually. If we apply this concept to a set S of knowledge bases with respect to the entailment of a statement a, it would become a relationship that says the members of S are separable because every one of them entails a. We believe that this is unrelated to the independence relationship we defined, but we plan to look at this more closely in the future.

In the DL literature, Tsarkov and Horrocks [22] discuss the use of the relevant information in a TBox to compute a subsumption with respect to that TBox. They define relevance as the transitive closure of the following depends relation: A concept or role expression depends on every concept or role that occurs in it, and a concept or role C depends on a concept or role D if D occurs in the definition of C. In addition, a concept C depends on every general conception inclusion in the TBox. Unlike their work, we focus on the relevance between ABoxes and ABox assertions. Therefore, both works are complementary to each other.

Elhaik and Rousset [5] work on identifying the relevant subpart of an ABox (relative to a fixed TBox) to an update, i.e., those facts that may lead to new entailments together with the newly added fact. Among other differences, their work requires all the entailments to be explicitly recorded in the ABox (they encode and store the ABox using a database), moreover, they deal with a rather restricted DL language called core-CLASSIC with the constructors $\sqcap$, $\forall$, $\geq nR$, $\leq nR$ and $\neg$ (on atomic concept only).

Amir and McIlraith's work on partition-based logical reasoning [1] provides algorithms for reasoning with partitions of related logical axioms in propositional and first-order logic. Like our work in Section 2, they are concerned with reasoning on multiple knowledge bases with overlap in content. However, they are concerned with the overlap in predicates (or propositions) while we look at the overlap in individual names.

McGuinness and Borgida's approach [18] to the explanation of DL reasoning also bases on the use of the natural deduction-style inference rules. Since we have obviously different goals, we face different issues. They work on offering understandable and efficient explanations of subsumption reasoning based on the rules while we derive the dependence relationship between OWL documents in terms of individual reasoning and try to use only a small portion of the rules without those for subsumption.

Distributed Description Logics [2] extends the formalism of DL with the ability to handle complex mappings between domains via the use of so-called bridge rules. Although its semantics is different from that of tradition DL, it could be possible that the future results of this research turn out to be useful to our work.

6   Conclusion and Future Work

Scalability is crucial for the success of the Semantic Web. Great effort has been made on the development of scalable reasoning mechanisms. In this work, we have assumed the use of the reasoner as a black box and taken a different perspective to investigate how to improve the performance of a system that requires reasoning with large scale data. We studied the (in)dependence relationships among OWL documents with respect to the logical consequence of their collections. For most of the work, we have focused on documents that commit to a common ontology, and the inference about concept assertions and role assertions. First, we described a way of identifying those documents that are necessary for the inference of a given assertion. We introduced a notion of relevant ABox assertion set to a given ABox assertion and a systematic approach to identify those sets. Secondly, we revealed two special cases in which two documents are independent of each other with respect to the entailment of assertions of specific forms: when they contain disjoint sets of individual names; and when they contain only RDF(S) statements. Finally, we introduced an algorithm for automatically detecting the independence in the general case. To the best of our knowledge, no prior work has been done to examine OWL documents (or DL knowledge bases) against the relationships of (in)dependence as defined in this paper.

We also described two applications wherein we have developed novel approaches using the above results to solve specific problems. In the first application, we exploit the dependence to help pinpoint from a repository of documents the minimal subsets that have caused the inference of a specific assertion. In the other, we harness the independence to overcome a problem in using the reasoner against large OWL instance data. Both examples demonstrate the potential use of this work in improving the scalability of a Semantic Web system which relies on the reasoning about individuals.

For future work, we intend to extend all the work to the OWL DL language, and to the case in which documents commit to different ontologies. Also, we plan to further improve the algorithm for detecting the independence. At the same time, we intend to implement the approaches in different applications wherein we will conduct empirical evaluations.

Acknowledgement

This material is based upon work supported by the National Science Foundation under Grant No. IIS-0346963.

References

1. Amir, E. and McIlraith, S. Partition-Based Logical Reasoning for First-Order and Propositional Theories, Artificial Intelligence journal, 2003.
2. Borgida, A and Serafini, L. Distributed Description Logics - Assimilating Information from Peer Sources. Journal of Data Semantics (1), 2003.
3. Darwiche, A. A logical notion of conditional independence: properties and applications. Artificial Intelligence 97 (1-2) (1997) 45–82.

4. Dean, M. and Schreiber, G. (Eds). OWL Web Ontology Language Reference, W3C Recommendation 10 February 2004. http://www.w3.org/TR/2004/REC-owl-ref-20040210/

5. Elhaik, Q. and Rousset, M-C. Making an ABox persistent. In Proc. of the 1998 Description Logic Workshop (DL'98).

6. Greiner, R., Pearl, J., Subramanian, D. (Eds.), Artificial Intelligence 97 (1–2) (1997), Special Issue on Relevance.

7. Guo, Y., Pan, Z., and Heflin, J. An Evaluation of Knowledge Base Systems for Large OWL Datasets. In Proc. of the 3rd International Semantic Web Conference (ISWC2004).

8. Guo, Y. and Heflin, J. An Initial Investigation into Querying an Untrustworthy and Inconsistent Web. In ISWC2004 Workshop on Trust, Security and Reputation on the Semantic Web.

9. Haarslev, V. and Möller, R. Racer: A Core Inference Engine for the Semantic Web. In Workshop on Evaluation on Ontology-based Tools, ISWC2003.

10. Haarslev, V. and Möller, R. Optimization Techniques for Retrieving Resources Described in OWL/RDF Documents: First Results. In Proc. of Ninth International Conference on the Principles of Knowledge Representation and Reasoning (KR2004).

11. Haarslev, V., Möller, R., and Wessel, M. Querying the Semantic Web with Racer + nRQL. In Proc. of the Workshop on Description Logics 2004 (ADL2004).

12. Horrocks, I. The FaCT System. In Automated Reasoning with Analytic Tableaux and Related Methods International Conference (Tableaux'98).

13. Horrocks, I. and Patel-Schneider, P. F. Reducing OWL entailment to description logic satisfiability. J. of Web Semantics, 1(4):345-357, 2004.

14. Lang, J., Liberatore, P., and Marquis, P. Conditional independence in propositional logic. Artificial Intelligence Journal, Volume 141(1), October 2002, pp79–121.

15. Lang, J., Liberatore, P., and Marquis, P. Propositional independence: formula-variable independence and forgetting, Journal of Artificial Intelligence Research 18(2003) 391-443.

16. Levesque, H. A completeness result for reasoning with incomplete knowledge bases. In Proc. of KR-98, Sixth International Conference on Principles of Knowledge Representation and Reasoning, 1998.

17. Levy, A.Y., Fikes, R.E., and Sagiv, Y. Speeding up inferences using relevance reasoning: a formalism and algorithms. Artificial Intelligence 97 (1-2) (1997) 83-136.

18. McGuinness, D.L. and Borgida, A. Explaining Subsumption in Description Logics. In Proc. of the 14th International Joint Conference on Artificial Intelligence, 1995.

19. Patel-Schneider, P.F. (Eds). OWL Web Ontology Language Semantics and Abstract Syntax. http://www.w3.org/TR/owl-semantics/

20. Royer, V. and Quantz, J.J. Deriving Inference Rules for Terminological Logics. In Proc. of Logics in AI, European Workshop (JELIA'92).

21. Royer, V. and Quantz, J.J. Deriving Inference Rules for Description Logics: a Rewriting Approach into Sequent Calculi. KIT REPORT 111, Dec. 1993.

22. Tsarkov, D. and Horrocks, I. DL reasoner vs. first-order prover. In Proc. of the 2003 Description Logic Workshop (DL2003).

23. W3C RDF. Resource Description Framework (RDF). http://www.w3.org/RDF/

A Framework for Handling Inconsistency in Changing Ontologies

Peter Haase[1], Frank van Harmelen[2], Zhisheng Huang[2], Heiner Stuckenschmidt[2], and York Sure[1]

[1] Institute AIFB, University of Karlsruhe, Germany
{haase, sure}@aifb.uni-karlsruhe.de
[2] Department of Computer Science, Vrije Universiteit Amsterdam, The Netherlands
{frankh, huang, heiner}@cs.vu.nl

Abstract. One of the major problems of large scale, distributed and evolving ontologies is the potential introduction of inconsistencies. In this paper we survey four different approaches to handling inconsistency in DL-based ontologies: consistent ontology evolution, repairing inconsistencies, reasoning in the presence of inconsistencies and multi-version reasoning. We present a common formal basis for all of them, and use this common basis to compare these approaches. We discuss the different requirements for each of these methods, the conditions under which each of them is applicable, the knowledge requirements of the various methods, and the different usage scenarios to which they would apply.

1 Introduction

Ontologies in real-world applications are typically not static entities, they evolve over time. One of the major problems of evolving ontologies is the potential introduction of inconsistencies as a result of applying changes. Previous related work includes the definition of evolution strategies to handle inconsistencies for evolving ontologies in a centralized setting (*cf.* [14]) and for the handling of ontology changes in a distributed setting (*cf.* [9]). However, such approaches rely on different assumptions, including different ontology models (in particular they do not consider DL-based ontologies), use different notions for ontology change and inconsistency and typically cover a specific use case.

When dealing with changing ontologies we found four major use cases which require methods for dealing with inconsistencies. First, changing an initially consistent ontology potentially introduces inconsistencies. This typically occurs in settings where one is in control of changes and needs support for maintaining consistency during evolution. Second, re-using ontologies in open settings such as the Web might include the retrieval of inconsistent ontologies that should be fixed before usage. While these use cases typically occur during the development of ontologies, handling of inconsistencies is also relevant during runtime of ontology-based applications as illustrated in the following. Third, in some cases consistency cannot be guaranteed at all and inconsistencies cannot be repaired, still one wants to derive meaningful answers when reasoning. Often this is the case when schema-level and instance-level of ontologies are evolved separately without synchronizing the changes continuously. Fourth, when applying an

Y. Gil et al. (Eds.): ISWC 2005, LNCS 3729, pp. 353–367, 2005.
© Springer-Verlag Berlin Heidelberg 2005

ontology one faces the challenge to decide whether the usage of other, e.g. newer, versions of this ontology might lead to inconsistencies in an application, or, in other words, whether the versions are compatible with respect to certain aspects. While the former use cases typically occur during the development of ontologies, the latter ones illustrate the handling of inconsistencies during the runtime of ontology-based applications.

In this paper we define a framework for combining currently separate methods for inconsistency-handling in changing ontologies. This framework is based on formally defined notions including *ontology change* and *inconsistency* for DL-based ontologies, thus being in line with the state-of-the-art representation formalism for ontologies OWL [10]. To meet the requirements of the above mentioned use cases our framework consists of the following main components: *consistent ontology evolution* guarantees the continuous consistency of ontologies in the presence of changes by applying evolution strategies; *repairing inconsistencies* fixes ontologies that are already inconsistent; *reasoning with inconsistent ontologies* returns meaningful query results for queries to inconsistent ontologies; finally, *multi-version reasoning* considers not only the latest version of an ontology, but all previous versions as well to deal with inconsistencies that arise from the interaction of the ontology with its environment in terms of instance data and applications.

Core decisions which had to be taken during the definition of our framework include syntactic vs. semantic definitions for ontology changes, functional vs. non-functional notion of change, language dependent vs. language independent definitions and whether one only considers logical properties or also other forms like structural, data, etc.

The main benefit of our framework consists of the identification of typical kinds of problems one actually has when having to deal with inconsistent ontologies and the provision of methods and implementations to deal with the problems. The framework has been implemented (to large extents) as part of the EU project SEKT[1].

The paper is structured as follows. In the next Section 2 we present a general overview of the framework and describe the core decisions which had to be taken during the design of our framework. In Section 3 we describe basic definitions underlying the framework such as the notion of ontology change. The following Section 4 then describes on top of these definitions each of the components for handling of inconsistencies in detail. We compare the different approaches to help identifying which component can be applied in which situation. Before concluding we present related work.

2 General Overview

The study of ontology change management covers a very broad spectrum [11,9,14]. It encompasses methods and techniques necessary to support modifications to ontologies. One important aspect that must be dealt with in a comprehensive treatment of ontology change is handling of inconsistencies. While we may distinguish various forms of inconsistencies (c.f. [2], in this work, we consider ontologies as logical theories. We therefore focus on *logical inconsistencies* in ontologies. We discuss four different approaches to ontology change, and the different implications each of these has for the management of inconsistencies arising from the changing ontologies:

[1] http://www.sekt-project.com/

Consistent Ontology Evolution is the process of managing ontology changes by preserving the consistency of the ontology with respect to a given notion of consistency. The consistency of an ontology is defined in terms of consistency conditions, or invariants that must be satisfied by the ontology.

Repairing Inconsistencies involves a process of diagnosis and repair: first the cause (or: a set of potential causes) of the inconsistency needs to be determined, which can subsequently be repaired.

Reasoning with Inconsistent Ontologies does not try to avoid or repair the inconsistency (as in the previous two approaches), but simply tries to "live with it" by trying to return meaningful answers to queries, even though the ontology is inconsistent.

Ontology Versioning manages the relations between different versions of an ontology, and a notion of compatibility with such versions. One such compatability relation is inconsistency: even though two versions of an ontology may each be consistent in themselves, they might derive some opposite conclusions, and would then be mutually inconsistent.

In order to find a common ground for these different approaches to dealing with inconsistencies in changing ontologies, a number of choices have to be made concerning this common ground. We outline the most important of these choices here.

Syntactic or semantic. An obvious essential question is what we count as a change in an ontology? Do we count every syntactic modification to an ontology, or only those syntactic modifications that affect the semantics of the ontology. A simple example to illustrate the difference is to consider the ontology (using DL syntax, c.f. Section 3):

$$C1 \sqsubseteq C2, C1(x), C2(x)$$

Removing the third statement is clearly a syntactic change, but not a semantic one (the set of models of the ontology does not change, since the removed statement is also implied by the remaining two). This choice boils down to that of defining an ontology as a set of axioms (a syntactic object), or as a set of models (a semantic object, typically captured by finite set of axioms). In this paper, we have chosen to define an ontology as a set of axioms, allowing us to capture any syntactic modification to an ontology. We consider the syntactic approach most suitable as the same logical theory can be encoded by different sets of axioms that have different computational properties that are also important in applications (e.g. many ontologies that are formally in OWL-Full can be rephrased into an equivalent ontology in OWL-DL). The syntactic approach enables us to distinguish between these two encodings. This choice is in line with other studies of changing ontologies, e.g. [9,11,14].

Language dependent vs. language independent. A second important choice is the restriction of our definitions to a specific ontology language. It is now commonly accepted that any ontology language should have its foundation on logic. While the approaches we present are in general applicable to any ontology language based on a (monotonic) logic, we pay special attention to the OWL ontology language. As the OWL ontology language has been standardized by the W3C consortium, we will adhere to the underlying OWL ontology model. In particular, we consider the language OWL-DL (which includes sublanguages such as OWL-Lite). OWL-DL is a syntactic variant of the $\mathcal{SHOIN}(\mathbf{D})$ description logic [5]. In the following we will therefore use the more compact, traditional description logic syntax.

Functional or non-functional change. A final important decision is whether we regard ontology change as a deterministic or non-deterministic operation: does any operation on an ontology result in a single well-defined result, or in a set of possible outcomes. Our earlier choice for a syntactic view of ontology change makes it plausible to limit change to a deterministic, functional operation.

3   Basic Definitions

This section describes the basic definitions which involve ontology change and inconsistency processing. Some of these basic definitions may be so obvious or well-known that they may be considered to be trivial. Those terminologies are usually found under different contexts and theories with different meanings and implications. In this paper, we would like to provide a unique framework to define those definitions formally, which can serve as a solid foundation for the theory of ontology change to avoid unnecessary ambiguities on the definitions and minimize the disagreement among the researchers.

In general, an ontology language can be considered to be a set that is generated by a set of syntactic rules. Namely, an ontology can be viewed as a formula set, alternatively called axioms, which involves a set of vocabulary.

Definition 1 (Ontology). *We use a datatype theory* $\mathbf{D}$*, a set of concept names* N_C*, sets of abstract and concrete individuals* N_{I_a} *and* N_{I_c}*, respectively, and sets of abstract and concrete role names* N_{R_a} *and* N_{R_c}*, respectively.*

The set of $\mathcal{SHOIN}(\mathbf{D})$ *concepts is defined by the following syntactic rules, where* A *is an atomic concept,* R *is an abstract role,* S *is an abstract simple role,* $T_{(i)}$ *are concrete roles,* d *is a concrete domain predicate,* a_i *and* c_i *are abstract and concrete individuals, respectively, and* n *is a non-negative integer:*

$$C \rightarrow A \mid \neg C \mid C_1 \sqcap C_2 \mid C_1 \sqcup C_2 \mid \exists R.C \mid \forall R.C \mid \geq n\,S \mid \leq n\,S \mid \{a_1, \ldots, a_n\}$$
$$\mid \geq n\,T \mid \leq n\,T \mid \exists T_1, \ldots, T_n.D \mid \forall T_1, \ldots, T_n.D \mid \top \mid \bot$$
$$D \rightarrow d \mid \{c_1, \ldots, c_n\}$$

A $\mathcal{SHOIN}(\mathbf{D})$ *ontology* O *is a finite set of axioms of the form*[2]*: concept inclusion axioms* $C \sqsubseteq D$*, transitivity axioms* $\mathsf{Trans}(R)$*, role inclusion axioms* $R \sqsubseteq S$ *and* $T \sqsubseteq U$*, concept assertions* $C(a)$*, role assertions* $R(a, b)$*, individual (in)equalities* $a \approx b$*, and* $a \not\approx b$*, respectively.*

The semantics of the $\mathcal{SHOIN}(\mathbf{D})$ description logic is defined via a model-theoretic semantics, which explicates the relationship between the language syntax and the model of a domain: An interpretation $I = (\triangle^I, \cdot^I)$ consists of a domain set $\triangle^I$, disjoint from the datatype domain $\triangle_\mathbf{D}^I$, and an interpretation function $\cdot^I$, which maps from individuals, concepts and roles to elements of the domain, subsets of the domain and binary relations on the domain, respectively[3]. An interpretation $\mathcal{I}$ satisfies an ontology O, if it satisfies each axiom in O. Axioms thus result in semantic conditions on the interpretations. Consequently, contradicting axioms will allow no possible interpretations. This leads us to the definition of a consistent ontology:

---

[2] For the direct model-theoretic semantics of $\mathcal{SHOIN}(\mathbf{D})$ we refer the reader to [6].

[3] For a complete definition of the interpretation, we refer the reader to [5].

Definition 2 (Consistent Ontology). *An ontology O is consistent iff O is satisfiable, i.e. if O has a model.*

To be able to define queries against ontologies, we rely on the notion of entailment:

Definition 3 (Entailment). *Given a logical language $\mathcal{L}$, an entailment $\models$ states a relation between an ontology O and an axiom $\alpha \in \mathcal{L}$. Namely, an entailment is a set of pairs $\langle O, \alpha \rangle$. We use $O \models \alpha$ to denote that the ontology O entails the axiom α. Alternatively, we say that α is a consequence of the ontology O under the entailment relation $\models$. The entailment relation is said to be a standard one iff α always holds in any model in which the ontology O holds, i.e., for any model M, $M \models O \Rightarrow M \models \alpha$.*

Usually we use $\models$ and $\approx$ to denote a standard entailment and a non-standard entailment respectively if it does not cause any ambiguity. A standard entailment is explosive, namely, any formula is a consequence of an inconsistent ontology. Namely, if an ontology O is not consistent, then for any axiom α, $O \models \alpha$.

A general goal of the approaches proposed in this paper is to obtain consistent query answers. Thus, we have the following definitions.

Definition 4 (Query). *A query with respect to an entailment relation $\models$ is a pair of an ontology O and an axiom α, written '$O \models \alpha$?'.*

Definition 5 (Query Answer). *An answer to a query '$O \models \alpha$?' is a value in the set $\{true, false\}$ as $O \models \alpha$ and $O \not\models \alpha$ respectively.*

When we talk about inconsistency, we usually assume that the existence of a negation operator $\neg$ which can be used to denote the negation of an axiom[4].

Definition 6 (Consistent Query Answer). *For an ontology O and an entailment relation $\approx$, an answer '$O \approx \alpha$' is said to be consistent if $O \not\approx \neg\alpha$.*

Proposition 1 (Consistent Ontology and Consistent Query Answer). *For a consistent ontology O, its query answer is always consistent under a standard entailment. Namely, the consequence set $\{\alpha : O \models \alpha\}$ is consistent.*

To be able to deal with inconsistent ontologies, the following two definitions are useful:

Definition 7 (Maximal consistent subontology). *An ontology O' is a maximal consistent subontology of O, if $O' \subseteq O$ and O' is consistent and every O'' with $O' \subset O'' \subseteq O$ is inconsistent.*

Intuitively, this definition states that no axiom from O can be added to O' without losing consistency. In general, there may be many maximal consistent subontologies O'.

Definition 8 (Minimal inconsistent subontology). *An ontology O' is a minimal inconsistent subontology of O, if $O' \subseteq O$ and O' is inconsistent and every O'' with $O'' \subset O'$ is consistent.*

---

[4] In the considered description logic, there exists no universal negation operator. However, negation can be simulated, e.g. to express the negation of the role assertion $\neg R(a, b)$ we can write $\neg(\exists R.\{b\})(a)$.

Finally, we formalize changes to ontologies. As we have argued in the previous section, in the paper we will focus on functional ontology changes. Thus, we have:

Definition 9 (Ontology Change Operation). *An* ontology change operation *oco is a function oco* : $\mathcal{O} \rightarrow \mathcal{O}$.

There might exist many different ontology change operations. In this paper, we will not discuss a list of possible ontology changes. Instead, we consider the two atomic change operations of adding and removing axioms. Other change operations can be defined in terms of those two atomic change operations with different sequences of the executions. The semantics of the sequence is the chaining of the corresponding functions: For some atomic change operations $oco_1, ..., oco_n$ we can define $oco_{composite}(x) = oco_n \circ ... \circ oco_1(x) := oco_n(...(oco_1))(x)$.

As we have argued in the previous sections, in this paper, we consider only functional and syntactic-based change operations. Accordingly we define the semantics of the change operations: $O \dot{+} \alpha := O \cup \{\alpha\}$ and $O \dot{-} \alpha := O \setminus \{\alpha\}$.

4   Handling Inconsistencies of Changing Ontologies

In Section 2 we have already presented a general overview of the different strategies for handling the problem of inconsistencies in changing ontologies. In the following, we describe these different strategies in terms of the notions introduced in the previous section and provide a comparison.

4.1   Consistent Ontology Evolution

The goal of consistent ontology evolution is to maintain the consistency of ontology in the presence of changes. There are strong forms of guaranteeing consistency that strictly forbid change operations that can lead to an inconsistent ontology. A radical approach is to forbid the use of logical operators that potentially introduce inconsistency (i.e. negation, but also other constructs). The drawback is a substantial loss of expressive power. The strategy that we consider here is to define a semantics of change that ensures consistency by (1) detecting potential inconsistencies caused by changes and (2) generating additional changes for a transition into another consistent state [2]. We can summarize the approach of consistent ontology evolution as follows: For a consistent ontology O and a change operation *oco*, the task of consistent ontology evolution is to generate a change operation *oco'* such that $O' = oco'(oco(O))$ results in a consistent ontology O'.

Please note that because of the monotonicity of the considered logic, an ontology can only become logically inconsistent by adding axioms: If a set of axioms is satisfiable, it will still be satisfiable when any axiom is deleted. Therefore, we only need to check the consistency for ontology change operations that add axioms to the ontology.

Effectively, if $O \cup \{\alpha\}$ is inconsistent, in order to keep the resulting ontology consistent some of the axioms in the ontology O have to be removed. In this sense, the add-operation and the remove-operation are similar to the belief revision operation and the belief contraction operation in the theories of belief revision [1].

In the following, we will present strategies to ensure logical consistency. The goal of these strategies is to determine a set of axioms to remove to obtain a logically consistent ontology with "minimal impact" on the existing ontology, e.g. based on Definition 7 of a maximal consistent subontology. The main idea is that we start out with the inconsistent ontology $O \cup \{\alpha\}$ and iteratively remove axioms until we obtain a consistent ontology. Here, it is important how we determine which axioms should be removed. This can be realized using a *selection function*. The quality of the selection function is critical for two reasons: First, as we have potentially have to search all possible subsets of axioms in O for a maximal consistent ontology, we need to prune the search space by trying to find the *relevant* axioms that cause the inconsistency. Second, we need to make sure that we remove the *dispensable* axioms.

The first problem of finding the axioms that cause the inconsistency can be targeted by considering that there must be some "connection" between these problematic axioms. We formalize this notion with the following definition.

Definition 10 (Connectedness). *A connection relation C is a set of axiom pairs, namely, $C \subseteq \mathcal{L} \times \mathcal{L}$.*

A very simple, but useful connection is that of the direct structural connection relation:

Definition 11 (Direct Structural Connection). *Two axioms α and β are directly structurally connected – denoted with connected(α, β) –, if there exists an ontology entity $e \in N_C \cup N_{I_a} \cup N_{I_c} \cup N_{R_a} \cup N_{R_c}$ that occurs in both α and β.*

In the following, we present an algorithm (c.f. Algorithm 1) for finding (at least) one maximal consistent subontology using the definition of structural connectedness (c.f. Definition 11): We maintain a set of possible candidate subontologies Ω, which initially contains only $O \cup \{\alpha\}$, i.e. the consistent ontology O before the change and the added axiom α. In every iteration, we generate a new set of candidate ontologies by removing one axiom β_1 from each candidate ontology that is structurally connected with α or an already removed axiom (in $O \setminus O'$), until at least one of the candidate ontologies is a consistent subontology.

The properties of the algorithm (efficiency, completeness) will depend on the properties of the connectedness relation. The above definition of structural connectedness provides good heuristics to efficiently find a maximal consistent subontology, but is not complete for the case where axioms causing an inconsistency are not structurally connected at all.

Algorithm 1. Determine consistent subontology for adding axiom α to ontology O

$\Omega := \{O \cup \{\alpha\}\}$
repeat
   $\Omega' := \emptyset$
   for all $O' \in \Omega$ **do**
      for all $\beta_1 \in O' \setminus \{\alpha\}$ **do**
         if there is a $\beta_2 \in (\{\alpha\} \cup (O \setminus O'))$ such that connected(β_1, β_2) **then**
            $\Omega' := \Omega' \cup \{O' \setminus \{\beta_1\}\}$
         end if
      end for
   end for
   $\Omega := \Omega'$
until there exists an $O' \in \Omega$ such that O' is consistent

---

Example 1. We will now show how Algorithm 1 can be used to maintain consistency. As a running example, we will consider a simple ontology modelling a small research domain, consisting of the following axioms:
$O_1 = \{Employee \sqsubseteq Person,\ Student \sqsubseteq Person,\ PhDStudent \sqsubseteq Student,$
$Employee \sqsubseteq \neg Student,^5\ PhDStudent(peter)\}$.

Now consider a change operation oco_1 that adds the axiom $\alpha = PhDStudent \sqsubseteq Employee$. $oco_1(O_1)$ results in an inconsistent ontology.

Algorithm 1 starts with $O_1 \dotplus \alpha$ as element of the set of potential ontologies. In the first iteration, a set of new potential ontologies is created by removing one of the axioms that are structurally connected with the α. These axioms are: $PhDStudent(peter)$, $Employee \sqsubseteq \neg Student$, $PhDStudent \sqsubseteq Student$ and $Employee \sqsubseteq Person$.

The removal of either $PhDStudent(peter)$, $PhDStudent \sqsubseteq Student$ or $Employee \sqsubseteq \neg Student$ will result in a maximal consistent subontology. For the decision which axiom should be removed from the ontology, one can rely on further background information indicating the relevance of the axioms, or on interaction with the user. For the following examples, we assume that the resulting ontology O_2 is created by removing the axiom $Student \sqsubseteq \neg Employee$, i.e. $O_2 = O_1 \dotplus PhDStudent \sqsubseteq Employee \dotminus Student \sqsubseteq \neg Employee$.

4.2 Repairing Inconsistencies

The most straightforward approach to inconsistencies is to repair them when they are detected [13]. Repairing an inconsistency actually consists of two tasks: Locating Inconsistencies and Resolving Inconsistency. The task of repairing inconsistencies can thus be defined as: For an inconsistent ontology O we generate a change operation oco such that $O' = oco(O)$ results in a consistent ontology O'.

Locating Inconsistencies As a first step, the source of the inconsistency has to be detected. Normally, the source is a set axioms that when being part of the model at the same time make it inconsistent.

An algorithm to find a subontology which leads to an unsatisfiable concept (adopted from [13]) can use similar ideas like those for consistent ontology evolution. The main difference is that the latter assumes that the intended minimal inconsistent ontologies would contain an added axiom α, whereas the former has no such requirement but starting with an unsatisfiable concept C for the connection checking[6]. Algorithm 2 uses the increment-reduction strategy to find a minimal subontology for an unsatisfiable concept. Namely, the algorithm finds a subset of the ontology in which the concept is unsatisfiable first, then reduces the redundant axioms from the subset.

Based on those detected subsets for all unsatisfiable concepts, we can find minimal subsets of the ontology O which leads to all unsatisfiable concepts[13]. That can be used for knowledge workers to repair the ontology to avoid all unsatisfiable concepts.

---

[5] Stating that employees cannot be students.

[6] In order to do so, we extend the directly structral connection relation on concept sets, so that we can say something like an axiom β is connected with a concept c, i.e., $connected(\beta, C)$. It is easy to see that it does not change the definition.

Algorithm 2. Localize a minimal subset of O in which a concept C is unsatisfiable

---

$\Omega := \emptyset$
repeat
  for all $\beta_1 \in O \setminus \Omega$ **do**
    if there is a $\beta_2 \in \Omega$ such that $connected(\beta_1, \beta_2)$ or $connected(\beta_1, c)$ **then**
      $\Omega := \Omega \cup \{\beta_1\}$
    end if
  end for
until c is unsatisfiable in Ω
for all $\beta \in \Omega$ **do**
  if c is unsatisfiable in $\Omega - \{\beta\}$ **then**
    $\Omega := \Omega - \{\beta\}$
  end if
end for

Resolving Inconsistency Once the source of an inconsistency has been found, the conflict between the identified set of axioms has be to resolved. This task again is difficult, because in most cases there is no unique way of resolving a conflict but a set of alternatives. Often, there are no logical criteria selecting the best resolution. A common approach is to let the user resolve the conflict after it has been located.

Example 2. We again use the running example introduced in Example 1. Assume that we start out with the inconsistent ontology $O_3 = \{Employee \sqsubseteq Person, Student \sqsubseteq Person, PhDStudent \sqsubseteq Student, Employee \sqsubseteq \neg Student, PhDStudent \sqsubseteq Employee, PhDStudent(peter)\}$.

In this example the concept $PhDStudent$ is unsatisfiable. Starting with this unsatisfiable concept the algorithm finds the connected set $O_{31} = \{PhDStudent \sqsubseteq Student, PhDStudent \sqsubseteq Employee, PhDStudent(peter)\}$. The concept $PhDStudent$ is still safisfiable in O_{31}. Extending O_{31} with the connection relation the algorithm gets O_3. Reducing the redundant axioms, the algorithm finds the set $O_{32} = \{PhDStudent \sqsubseteq Student, Employee \sqsubseteq \neg Student, PhDStudent \sqsubseteq Employee\}$. Since $PhdStudent$ is the only unsatisfiable concept in this example, the knowledge workers can focus on the set O_{32} to repair O_3.

The approach proposed in this subsection is similar those in diagnosis[12]. There is a relativly well studied method for diagnosis, with a straightforward definitions: diagnosis is the smallest set of axioms that need to be removed to make the ontology consistent. These diagnoses can be calculated relatively easily on the basis of the minimal inconsistent subontologies. So, this covers the two parts of localizing and repairing inconsistencies (repairing an incoherent model by removing the minimal diagnoses).

4.3   Reasoning with Inconsistent Ontologies

In some cases it is unavoidable to live with inconsistencies, if consistency cannot be guaranteed and inconsistencies cannot be repaired. Nevertheless, there is still a need to reason about ontologies in order to support information access and integration of new information. We can summarize the task of reasoning with inconsistent ontologies: For a possibly inconsistent ontology O and a query q, the task of inconsistency reasoning is to return a meaningful query answer.

As shown above, the standard entailment is explosive, namely, any formula is a logical consequence of an inconsistent ontology. Therefore, conclusions drawn from an inconsistent ontology by classical inference may be completely meaningless. For an inconsistency reasoner it is expected that is able to return meaningful answers to queries, given an inconsistent ontology. In the case of a consistent ontology O, classical reasoning is sound, i.e., a formula ϕ deduced from O holds in every model of O. This definition is not preferable for an inconsistent ontology O as every formula is a consequence of O using a standard entailment $\models$. However, often only a small part of O has been incorrectly constructed or modelled, while the remainder of O is correct. Therefore, we propose the following definition of meaningfulness:

Definition 12 (Meaningfulness). *A query answer to a query $O \approx\!\!\!\mid\, \alpha$? is meaningful iff the following two conditions are satisfied:*

1. soundness: *the answer is a consequence of a consistent subontology of O under the standard entailment $\models$,*
2. consistency: *the answer is a consistent query answer under the entailment $\approx\!\!\!\mid$.*

Algorithm 3. Linear extension strategy for the evaluation of query $O \approx\!\!\!\mid\, \alpha$

$\Omega := \emptyset$
repeat
    $\Omega' := \{\beta_1 \in O \setminus \Omega : \text{there exists a } \beta_2 \in \Omega \cup \{\alpha\} \text{ such that } connected(\beta_1, \beta_2)\}$
    if $\Omega' = \emptyset$ **then**
        return $O \not\approx\!\!\!\mid\, \alpha$
    end if
    $\Omega := \Omega \cup \Omega'$
    if Ω inconsistent **then**
        $\Omega'' := maximal\_consistent\_subontology(\Omega)$
        if $\Omega'' \models \alpha$ **then**
            return $O \approx\!\!\!\mid\, \alpha$
            else return $O \not\approx\!\!\!\mid\, \alpha$
        end if
    end if
until $\Omega \models \alpha$
return $O \approx\!\!\!\mid\, \alpha$

The general strategy for processing inconsistent ontologies is: given a connection/relevance relation (c.f. Definition 10), we select some consistent subontology from an inconsistent ontology. Then we apply standard reasoning on the selected subontology to find meaningful answers. If a satisfying answer cannot be found, the relevance degree of the selection function is made less restrictive thereby extending the consistent subontology for further reasoning. If an inconsistent subset is selected, we call the over-determined processing(ODP)[8]. One of the ODP strategies is to find the set of the maximal consistent subontologies of the selected set. If there exist contradictory answers from those maximal consistent subontologies, the algorithm will return 'unknown'. A linear extension strategy with an ODP for the evaluation of a query '$O \approx\!\!\!\mid\, \alpha$?' is described in Algorithm 3. We can prove the following property[8]:

Proposition 2 (Meaningfulness of Linear Extension Strategy). *The answers which are obtained by the linear extension strategy are meaningful.*

Example 3. Consider the inconsistent ontology $O_3 = \{Employee \sqsubseteq Person,$ $Student \sqsubseteq Person, PhDStudent \sqsubseteq Student, PhDStudent \sqsubseteq Employee,$ $Employee \sqsubseteq \neg Student, PhDStudent(peter)\}$.

Assume now we wanted to ask the query $O_3.\ \approx Student(peter)?$. Using standard entailment we would obtain no meaningful answer, as both $Student(peter)$ and $\neg Student(peter)$ are entailed by the ontology. By the linear extension on the connection relation with $Student(peter)$, the algorithm will construct the ontology $\Omega = \{PhDStudent(peter), PhDStudent \sqsubseteq Employee, PhDStudent \sqsubseteq Student\}$. This ontology Ω is consistent, and $\Omega \models \alpha$. Thus, the algorithm concludes that $O_3 \approx Student(peter)$.

4.4 Multi-version Reasoning

Multi-version reasoning is an approach that tries to cope with possible inconsistencies in changing ontologies by considering not only the latest version of an ontology, but all previous versions as well. This approach mostly applies in cases where the problem is not so much an inconsistency in the ontology itself, but inconsistencies that arise from the interaction of the ontology with its environment in terms of instance data and applications. We consider the sequence of ontologies $O_1 \prec \cdots \prec O_n$ where the ordering relation is defined as:

$$O_i \prec O_j \Leftrightarrow \exists oco_{composite} : oco_{composite}(O_i) = O_j$$

Intuitively, O_n is the current version of the ontology. $O_1, \cdots, O_{n-1}$ are older versions of the same ontology that have been created from the respective previous ontology in terms of a composite change action. We can assume that each of the ontologies is consistent. Further, we assume that an application expresses its requirements for compatibility as an expectation α, for which there is an ontology O_i in the sequence such that $O_i \cup \{\alpha\}$ is consistent.

Based on these assumptions, the task of ensuring consistency reduces to the task of finding the right version O_i of the ontology in the sequence of versions. This task requires the ability to determine the satisfiability of certain expressions across the different versions of the ontology. This can be done using an extension of the ontology language called $\mathcal{L}+$ with the operator **PreviousVersion**ϕ, which is read as 'ϕ holds in the previous version', the operator **AllPriorVersions**ϕ, which is read as 'ϕ holds in all prior versions', and the operator **SomePriorVersion**ϕ, which is read as 'ϕ holds in some prior versions'.

Using these basic operators, we can define a rich set of query operators for asking specific questions about specific versions of the ontology and relations between them. In the case where $O_n \cup \{\alpha\}$ is inconsistent, we can for example check whether the previous version can be used (**PreviousVersion** α) and whether there is a version at all that can be used instead (**SomePriorVersion** α). For the formal semantics of these operators we refer the reader to [7].

Example 4. Consider we have an ordered relation of ontologies $O_1 \prec O_2$, using the ontologies from Example 1. Now assume a compatibility criteria that has to fulfilled for compatibility: $\alpha = Employee(peter)$, i.e. a knowledge base in which Peter is an employee. The latest version O_2 is compatible with the compatibility criteria α as $O_2 \cup \{\alpha\}$ is consistent. However, O_1 does not meet the compatibility requirements, as $O_1 \cup \{\alpha\}$ is inconsistent (It still contained the axiom stating the disjointness of students and employees). In fact, it holds that **AllPriorVersions** $\neg Employee(peter)$.

5 Comparison and Evaluation

We are going to compare the four approaches dealing with inconsistency, and make an evaluation on them. By the evaluation, we want to suggest several guidelines for system developers to know under which circumstance which approach is more appropriate.

5.1 Different Functionality

A first major difference that is revealed by the formal analysis in the previous section is the fact that the different methods for dealing with inconsistent ontologies actually have very different functionality (their input/output-relations are rather different). Consequently, they solve rather different tasks, and are suited for different use-cases. The situation is summarised in Table 1.

Table 1. Comparison of Approaches

Approach	Applied At	Input	Output
Consistent Evolution	Development	Consistent Ontology, Change	Consistent Ontology
Inconsistency Repair	Development	Inconsistent Ontology	Consistent Ontology
Inconsistency Reasoning	Runtime	Consistent Ontology, Query	Meaningful answer
Multi-version reasoning	Runtime	Versions of Ontologies, Query	Consistent Answer

Dependence on query. First, this table shows that two of the methods depend on which user-query is given to the ontology (reasoning with inconsistency and multi-version reasoning). Consequently, these two methods are only applicable at *runtime*, when a user interacts with the ontology. The other two methods (ontology evolution and inconsistency repair) are independent of user-queries, and can thus already be applied at ontology *development time*.

Known or unknown change. The two methods that are applicable at ontology development time are actually very similar (as is apparent from sections 4.1 and 4.2). A crucial difference is that the first of these (ontology evolution) requires knowledge of the change that caused the ontology to become inconsistent: algorithm 1 requires the change α to be known, which is not the case with 2. This is clearly a restriction on the applicability of ontology evolution, which comes in exchange for the benefit of a simpler algorithm.

Known or unknown history. The two query-dependent approaches also differ in their respective input-requirements: multi-version reasoning requires a *history* of ontology-versions to be available, which is a very strong demand, often not feasible in many settings, in particular in combination with its runtime usage.

5.2   Other Aspects

Heuristics. Another difference between the various approaches is the extent to which they employ heuristics: in reasoning with inconsistency, one heuristically chooses a consistent subontology that is good enough to answer the query (it need not be minimal, just small enough to be consistent, and large enough to answer the query). In contract, both Evolution and Repair aim at the *smallest* impact on the inconsistent ontology.

Efficiency. Finally, one would expect the various approaches to differ drastically in their computational efficiency. Some observations can be made immediately: the Evolutionary approach exploits the knowledge about the cause of the inconsistency, and can therefore be more efficient then Repair, which does not have access to this information. However, the cost of all of the algorithms described in this paper are dominated by untractable operations such as checking the unsatisfiability of a concept or the inconsistency of an entire ontology. Consequently, worst-case complexity analysis is not going to tell us anything interesting here. Instead, work will have to be done on average-case complexity analysis and experiments with realistic datasets to gain more insight into the relevative costs of each of the approaches.

Knowledge Requirements. Finally, the approaches differ in the knowledge that is required to operate them:

- the repair approach requires the ontology developers to have sufficient domain knowledge to decide which part of the ontology should be removed to recover consistency. On the other hand, once done, it needs no additional expertise from the ontology users.
- Reasoning with inconsistencies on the other hand emposes no knowledge requirements on the developers, but requires some (weak) knowledge from the users to determine whether a query answer is acceptable.
- Ontology versioning places again a heavy knowledge requirement on the user in order to decide which version is most suitable for their application.

6   Related Work

The evolution of ontologies has been addressed by different researchers by defining change operations and change representations for ontology languages. Change operations have been proposed for specific ontology languages. In particular change operations have been defined for OKBC, OWL [9] and for the KAON ontology language [14]. All approaches distinguish between atomic and complex changes. Different ways of representing ontological changes have been proposed: besides the obvious representation as a change log that contains a sequence of operations, authors have proposed to represent changes in terms of mappings between two versions of an ontology [11].

The problem of preserving integrity in the case of changes is also present for ontology evolution. On the one hand the problem is harder here as ontologies are often encoded using a logical language where changes can quickly lead to logical inconsistency that cannot directly be determined by looking at the change operation. On the other hand, there are logical reasoners that can be used to detect inconsistencies both within the ontology and with respect to instance data. As this kind of reasoning is often costly, heuristic approaches for determining inconsistencies have been proposed [9,15]. While deciding whether an ontology is consistent or not can easily be done using existing technologies, repairing inconsistencies in ontologies is an open problem although there is some preliminary work on diagnosing the reasons for an inconsistency which is prerequisite for a successful repair [13].

The problem of compatibility with applications that use an ontology has received little attention so far. The problem is that the impact of a change in the ontology on the function of the system is hard to predict and strongly depends on the application that uses the ontology. Part of the problem is the fact that ontologies are often not just used as a fixed structure but as the basis for deductive reasoning. The functionality of the system often depends on the result of this deduction process and unwanted behavior can occur as a result of changes in the ontology. Some attempts have been made to characterize change and evolution multiple versions on a semantic level [3,4]. This work provides the basis for analyzing compatibility which currently is an open problem.

7 Conclusion

Unlike work in traditional knowledge engineering, knowledge intensive applications on the Web will not be able to ignore the issue of inconsistent knowledge in general, and of inconsistent ontologies in particular. This has been recognised in various contributions to the literature that propose different ways of dealing with inconsistent ontologies. These approaches differ both in the machinery they use, and in the way they propose to deal with inconsistent ontologies, ranging from avoiding inconsistencies, to diagnosing and repairing the inconsistencies, to trying to reason in the presence of the inconsistencies, and to tracking the inconsistencies over the development history of an ontology.

In this paper, we have rephrased four existing approaches to dealing with inconsistent ontologies in terms of a set of elementary definitions. This allowed us to compare these rather different approaches on an equal footing. This comparison revealed among other things that what originally seemed to be different approaches to the same problem (namely dealing with inconsistent ontologies) are actually solutions that apply in very different settings: at ontology-development time or at ontology-use time, and requiring different pieces of information (the cause of the inconsistency, or the history of the ontology changes). For the respective approaches, we provide implementations, which are available at http://www.aifb.uni-karlsruhe.de/WBS/pha/owlevolution/.

Acknowledgements. Research reported in this paper has been partially financed by EU in the IST projects SEKT (EU IST-2003-506826) and Knowledge Web (EU IST-2003-507482).

References

1. Giorgos Flouris. Belief change in arbitrary logics. In *HDMS*, 2004.
2. P. Haase and L. Stojanovic. Consistent evolution of OWL ontologies. In *Proceedings of the Second European Semantic Web Conference, Heraklion, Greece, 2005*, MAY 2005.
3. J. Heflin. *Towards the Semantic Web: Knowledge Representation in a Dynamic, Distributed Environment*. Phd thesis, University of Maryland, 2001.

4. J. Heflin and J. Z. Pan. A model theoretic semantics for ontology versioning. In *Third International Semantic Web Conference*, pages 62–76, Hiroshima, Japan, 2004. Springer.
5. I. Horrocks and P. F. Patel-Schneider. Reducing OWL Entailment to Description Logic Satisfiability. *Journal of Web Semantics*, 1(4), 2004.
6. I. Horrocks, U. Sattler, and S. Tobies. Practical Reasoning for Very Expressive Description Logics. *Logic Journal of the IGPL*, 8(3):239–263, 2000.
7. Z. Huang and H. Stuckenschmidt. Reasoning with multiversion ontologies: a temporal logic approach. In *Proceedings of the 2005 International Semantic Web Conference (ISWC'05)*, 2005.
8. Z. Huang, F. van Harmelen, and A. ten Teije. Reasoning with inconsistent ontologies. In *Proceedings of the International Joint Conference on Artificial Intelligence(IJCAI'05)*, pages 254–259, 2005.
9. M. Klein. *Change Management for Distributed Ontologies*. Phd thesis, Vrije Universiteit Amsterdam, 2004.
10. D. McGuinness and F. van Harmelen. OWL Web Ontology Language. Recommendation, W3C, 2004. http://www.w3.org/TR/owl-features/.
11. N.F. Noy and M.A. Musen. The prompt suite: Interactive tools for ontology merging and mapping. *International Journal of Human-Computer Studies*, 59(6):983–1024, 2003.
12. R. Reiter. A theory of diagnosis from first principles. *Artif. Intelligence*, 32(1):57–95, 1987.
13. S. Schlobach and R. Cornet. Non-standard reasoning services for the debugging of description logic terminologies. In *Proceedings of the International Joint Conference on Artificial Intelligence - IJCAI'03*, Acapulco, Mexico, 2003. Morgan Kaufmann.
14. L. Stojanovic. *Methods and Tools for Ontology Evolution*. Phd thesis, University of Karlsruhe, 2004.
15. H. Stuckenschmidt and M. Klein. Integrity and change in modular ontologies. In *Proceedings of the International Joint Conference on Artificial Intelligence - IJCAI'03*, Acapulco, Mexico, 2003. Morgan Kaufmann.

Preferential Reasoning on a Web of Trust

Stijn Heymans, Davy Van Nieuwenborgh*, and Dirk Vermeir**

Dept. of Computer Science, Vrije Universiteit Brussel, VUB
Pleinlaan 2, B1050 Brussels, Belgium
{sheymans, dvnieuwe, dvermeir}@vub.ac.be

Abstract. We introduce a framework, based on logic programming, for preferential reasoning with agents on the Semantic Web. Initially, we encode the knowledge of an agent as a logic program equipped with call literals. Such call literals
enable the agent to pose yes/no queries to arbitrary knowledge sources on the
Semantic Web, without conditions on, e.g., the representation language of those
sources. As conflicts may arise from reasoning with different knowledge sources,
we use the extended answer set semantics, which can provide different strategies for solving those conflicts. Allowing, in addition, for an agent to express its
preference for the satisfaction of certain rules over others, we can then induce a
preference order on those strategies. However, since it is natural for an agent to
believe its own knowledge (encoded in the program) but consider some sources
more reliable than others, it can alternatively express preferences on call literals.
Finally, we show how an agent can learn preferences on call literals if it is part of
a web of trusted agents.

1   Introduction

The current WWW is a gigantic pool of data, where one can easily imagine two web
sites saying the opposite. Human users are capable of deciding which sources they find
trustworthy or not (irrespective of the fact whether they actually are or not). Semantic
Web software agents [18] on the other hand would have an equally vast amount of data
at their disposition, but a far more difficult time differentiating between good and bad
information.

In this paper, we will gradually build a (abstract) software agent, i.e. an entity on
a web of trust that can reason with a diverse pool of (possibly mutually inconsistent)
knowledge sources. The basic underlying reasoning framework we use for such an agent
is *answer set programming (ASP)* [13, 3], a logic programming paradigm with a stable
model semantics for negation as failure. A *logic program* corresponds to knowledge one
wishes to represent, or, more specifically, to an encoding of a particular problem, e.g.
a planning problem [24, 9]; the *answer sets* of the program then provide its intentional
knowledge, or the solutions of the encoded problem, e.g. a plan for a planning problem.

---

* Supported by the FWO.
** This work was partially funded by the Information Society Technologies programme of the
European Commission, Future and Emerging Technologies under the IST-2001-37004 WASP
project.

Y. Gil et al. (Eds.): ISWC 2005, LNCS 3729, pp. 368–382, 2005.

A traditional logic program has a limited view on the world; it restricts itself to its own knowledge and does not allow calls to external sources. In a first phase, to construct suitable Semantic Web agents, we thus introduce *call literals* in rules, e.g., a rule tr_1 : $\neg train \leftarrow geo1.300km(brussels, madrid)$, where $geo1.300km(brussels, madrid)$ is a call literal and $\neg train$ a normal literal. The rule reads "if according to the *geo1* ontology Brussels is more than 300 km away from Madrid, one should not go by train". The word "ontology" is slightly misleading, since *geo1* can be anything: an OWL DL [4] knowledge base, an SQL database, RDF data, another agent, anything. In order to establish a suitable semantics for such call literals, we associate with each call literal in a program an instance of a decision problem, e.g., satisfiability checking in OWL DL, checking whether a tuple is in the database, ... An evaluation function then assigns **true** or **false** to the call literal, depending on the corresponding instance. Technically, programs with calls are a subclass of logic programs with generalized quantifiers Q_C [10], where a generalized quantifier Q_C checks whether a relation defined by the program is in a class of structures C. In the proposed setting, every call literal corresponds to a class of structures C that is a singleton set containing some literal if the instance of the decision problem associated with that call literal returns **true**.

In contrast with approaches as in [5, 17, 25, 23, 19] where one attempts to reduce reasoning in description logics (DLs) [2] to logic programming or approaches biased more towards the integration of description logics and logic programming reasoning [8, 29, 11], the proposed framework does not restrict itself to DLs, knowledge can be represented in any language with associated reasoning procedures; agents that want to use the knowledge only have to know how to call those procedures.

Besides making calls to sources, agents have to be able to cope with conflicts, e.g., add to the above train rule that if Brussels and Madrid are not divided by water, one should take the train: tr_2 : $train \leftarrow not\ geo2.dividedwater(brussels, madrid)$. If the call to *geo1* returns **true**, claiming that Brussels is indeed more than 300 km away from Madrid, and that the call to *geo2* returns **false** (and is thus faulty), this leads to a conflict since tr_1 deduces $\neg train$ and tr_2 deduces *train*. The normal answer set semantics has no answer sets for this program, which is not feasible on the Semantic Web – we do not want an agent to stay indecisive on different contradicting sources. The extended answer set semantics and its notion of *defeat* loosens up the normal answer set semantics by allowing rules to remain unsatisfied provided there is a competing rule (i.e. a rule with opposite head) that is applied (both the head and body are true). The above program results then in the two *extended answer sets* $\{train\}$ and $\{\neg train\}$, representing the possible alternatives for the conflict, where tr_1, respectively tr_2, is defeated.

The agent can then choose among those possible solutions based on a preference on the satisfaction of rules, e.g., $tr_1 < tr_2$, indicates that the agent prefers to satisfy tr_1 over tr_2. This preference naturally induces an order on its extended answer sets:$\{\neg train\} \sqsubseteq \{train\}$. A wide variety of applications of agents with preferences are imaginable, e.g. to guide service discovery on mobile devices [31].

In the context of the Semantic Web, a preference on call literals seems more natural than an order on the agent's own rules: an agent generally assumes its own rules are correct, whereas the uncertain part, and hence the part that may introduce conflicts, are the external calls. Based on criteria such as authority or reliability the agent can then express its preference for certain calls. Furthermore, we show a translation of an order on call literals to an order on the rules of the agents.

What if the agent does not know which calls are more reliable than others; can it still make an educated guess regarding its preferences? The *web of trust* [14, 16, 15, 28, 7] provides an architecture on which preferential reasoning for agents without (or with incomplete) preferences can be realized.

In [28], a web of trust is essentially a graph of agents where edges have a weight in $[0, 1]$, indicating the amount of trust an agent has in its direct neighbors. Moreover, every user can have a belief, a number in $[0, 1]$, in logical statements. The *merged belief* in a logical statement, i.e. taking into account the beliefs in that statement of trusted agents, can be computed in a large number of ways, e.g., one can demand that the amount of trust between users is at most the minimal trust weight on a path between them or that the further away an agent is, the lower the trust in that agent should be [16]. In the TRELLIS system [14] users rate information sources and, assuming different users rate common sources, TRELLIS rates sources averaging over the ratings of different users.

Relating this to our approach, the beliefs in statements correspond to preferences on call literals. Furthermore, in order to construct agents on top of any web of trust, we do not presuppose any conditions on the trust metric, i.e. the method to calculate the merged trust given a web of trust, but one: it must be possible to associate with every agent a sequence of trusted agents ordered according to trustworthiness. Given, for each agent, such an ordered sequence, we then complete the preferences of an agent by considering its own preferences and adding further preferences according to its trusted agents.

The remainder of the paper is organized as follows. In Section 2, we define the preferred answer set semantics. Section 3 extends the preferred answer set semantics with the possibility to define call literals and their accompanying calls. In Section 4, we define a preference order on literals and a method for constructing this order based on a web of trust. Finally, Section 5 contains conclusions and directions for further research. Due to space restrictions, proofs have been omitted but can be found in [20].

2   Preliminaries: Preferred Answer Set Programming

We introduce the extended answer set semantics as in [30]. A *literal* is an atom a or a classically negated atom $\neg a$; an *extended literal* is a literal l or a literal preceded with the *negation as failure* symbol *not*: $not\ l$. A *program* is a finite set of rules $\alpha \leftarrow \beta$ where α, the *head*, is a set of literals with $|\alpha| \leq 1$, i.e. α is empty or a singleton, and β, the *body*, is a finite set of extended literals. We usually denote a rule as $a \leftarrow \beta$ or $\leftarrow \beta$, and we call the latter a *constraint*. The positive part of the body is $\beta^+ = \{l \mid l \in \beta, l \text{ literal}\}$, the negative part is $\beta^- = \{l \mid not\ l \in \beta\}$, e.g. for $\beta = \{a, not\ \neg b, not\ c\}$, we have that $\beta^+ = \{a\}$ and $\beta^- = \{\neg b, c\}$. For a set of literals α, $not\ \alpha = \{not\ a \mid a \in \alpha\}$, and $\alpha^* = \alpha \cup not\ \alpha$.

The *Herbrand Base* $\mathcal{B}_P$ of a program P is the set of all atoms that can be formed using the language of P. Let $\mathcal{L}_P$ be the set of literals that can be formed with P, i.e. $\mathcal{L}_P = \mathcal{B}_P \cup \neg \mathcal{B}_P$. For a set X of literals, we take $\neg X = \{\neg l \mid l \in X\}$ where $\neg\neg a$ is a; X is *consistent* if $X \cap \neg X = \emptyset$. An *interpretation* I of P is any consistent subset of

$\mathcal{L}_P$. For a literal l, we write $I \models l$, if $l \in I$, which extends for extended literals $not\ l$ to $I \models not\ l$ if $I \not\models l$. In general, for a set of extended literals X, $I \models X$ if $I \models x$ for every extended literal $x \in X$. A rule $r : a \leftarrow \beta$ is *satisfied* w.r.t. I, denoted $I \models r$, if $I \models a$ whenever $I \models \beta$, i.e. r is *applied* whenever it is *applicable*. A constraint $\leftarrow \beta$ is satisfied w.r.t. I if $I \not\models \beta$. The set of satisfied rules in P w.r.t. I is the *reduct* P_I.

For a program P without negation as failure, an interpretation I is a *model* of P if I satisfies every rule in P, i.e. $P_I = P$; it is an *answer set* of P if it is a minimal model of P, i.e. there is no model J of P such that $J \subset I$. For programs P containing *not*, the *GL-reduct* w.r.t. an interpretation I is P^I, where P^I contains $\alpha \leftarrow \beta^+$ for $\alpha \leftarrow \beta$ in P and $\beta^- \cap I = \emptyset$. I is an *answer set* of P if I is an answer set of P^I. A rule $a \leftarrow \beta$ is *defeated* w.r.t. I if there is a *competing* rule $\neg a \leftarrow \gamma$ that is applied w.r.t. I, i.e. $\{\neg a\} \cup \gamma \subseteq I$. An *extended answer set* I of a program P is an answer set of P_I such that all rules in $P \backslash P_I$ are *defeated*.

Consider a program P indicating that one wants to take the train (t_1), that if the distance to the destination is more than 300 km, one does not want to take the train (t_2), and that the distance is actually more than 300 km (t_3).

$$t_1 :\quad train \leftarrow \qquad t_2 : \neg train \leftarrow 300km$$
$$t_3 : 300km \leftarrow$$

This program no answer sets and two extended answer sets $M_1 = \{300km, train\}$ and $M_2 = \{300km, \neg train\}$: there is no competing rule for t_3 such that it must be satisfied and every extended answer set must contain $300km$. The rule t_2 is not satisfied in M_1 (the body is true while the head is not), but it is defeated since the competing rule t_1 is applied in M_1. In M_2, t_1 is defeated by the applied t_2.

Resolving conflicts by defeating rules thus leads to different alternative extended answer sets. Usually however, a user may have some particular preferences on the satisfaction of the rules. As in [30], we impose a strict partial order[1] $<$ on the rules in P, indicating these preferences, which results in an *ordered logic program (OLP)* $\langle P, < \rangle$. This preferential ordering will induce an ordering $\sqsubseteq$ among the possible alternative extended answer sets as follows: for interpretations M and N of P, M is "more preferred" than N, denoted $M \sqsubseteq N$, if $\forall r_2 \in P_N \backslash P_M \cdot \exists r_1 \in P_M \backslash P_N \cdot r_1 < r_2$. Intuitively, for every rule that is satisfied by N and not by M, and which thus appears to be a counterexample for M being better than N, there is a better rule that is satisfied by M and not by N, i.e. M can counter the counterexample of N. We have that M is "strictly better" than N, $M \sqsubset N$, if $M \sqsubseteq N$ and not $N \sqsubseteq M$. An extended answer set is a *preferred answer set* of $\langle P, < \rangle$ if it is minimal w.r.t. $\sqsubseteq$ among the extended answer sets.

Considering the extended answer sets for the train example, we have that $P_{M_1} = \{t_1, t_3\}$ and $P_{M_2} = \{t_2, t_3\}$. If we prefer going by train over not going by train, i.e. $t_1 < t_2$, we have that $M_1 \sqsubseteq M_2$ since for every rule in $P_{M_2} \backslash P_{M_1} = \{t_2\}$, there is a better one in $P_{M_2} \backslash P_{M_1} = \{t_1\}$. Since $M_2 \not\sqsubseteq M_1$, we have that $M_1 \sqsubset M_2$, making M_1 the only preferred answer set of the program.

For reference later on in the paper, we briefly restate the complexity results from [30] for the preferred answer set semantics. Checking whether a program has an extended answer set containing a particular literal is NP-complete, while checking whether

---

[1] A strict partial order on X is an anti-reflexive and transitive relation on X.

an ordered program has a preferred answer set containing a particular literal is Σ_2^P-complete. Recall that NP represents the problems that are nondeterministically decidable in polynomial time, while Σ_2^P is NP^{NP}, i.e. the problems that are nondeterministically decidable in polynomial time using an NP oracle, where an NP oracle is a subroutine capable of solving NP problems in unit time. For an arbitrary complexity class C, the class P^C represents those problems that are deterministically decidable in polynomial time with an oracle for problems in C. Finally, we mention the complexity class EXPTIME (NEXPTIME) of problems deterministically (nondeterministically) decidable in exponential time. A language L is called complete for a complexity class C if both L is in C and L is hard for C. Showing that L is hard is normally done by reducing a known complete decision problem to a decision problem in L. More on complexity in general can be found in, e.g., [27].

3 Preferred Answer Set Programming with Calls

We extend preferred answer set programming with call literals. Take, for example, a program with facts declaring $kine$ to be a movie theater, $pizzi$ and $ilpast$ restaurants, and times 8 P.M. and 10 P.M.

$$\begin{array}{ll} movies(kine) \leftarrow & time(8pm) \leftarrow \\ rest(pizzi) \leftarrow & time(10pm) \leftarrow \\ rest(ilpast) \leftarrow & \end{array}$$

We have a rule p that produces a plan for a night out to a restaurant $Rest$ and a movie theater $Movies$ at respective times $Time1$ and $Time2$.

$$p : plan(Rest : rest, Time1 : time, Movies : movies, Time2 : time) \leftarrow$$
$$Rest.res(Time1), geo.near(Rest, Movies), Time1 \neq Time2,$$
$$not\ otherpl(Rest, Time1, Movies, Time2)$$

The *call literal* $Rest.res(Time1)$ represents a query to a restaurant's knowledge to check whether one can reserve at a time. The call literal, $geo.near(Rest, Movies)$, queries some knowledge source geo in order to ensure that the restaurant and the movie theater are located in each other's vicinity. The inequality $Time1 \neq Time2$ expresses that dinner time must be different from the movie's time. We used syntactic sugar for typing arguments, e.g. $Rest : rest$ indicates that the variable $Rest$ is of type $rest$. Formally, we define a rule with typing $p(T : t, x) \leftarrow \beta$ as the rule $p(T, x) \leftarrow t(T), \beta$. The extended literal $not\ otherpl(Rest, Time1, Movies, Time2)$ ensures that there is only one plan in each result: $o_1 : otherpl(Resta, Time1a, Moviesa, Time2a) \leftarrow plan(Restb, Time1b, Moviesb, Time2b), Resta \neq Restb$, and similar o_2, o_3, and o_4, with inequalities on the $Time$ and $Movies$ variables.

Furthermore, we want a classification of theaters that screen romantic movies. We query two repositories that are able to verify whether a movie theater has romantic movies programmed: $moviedb1.roman(Movies)$ and $moviedb2.roman(Movies)$.

$$r_1 : \quad roman(Movies : movies) \leftarrow moviedb1.roman(Movies)$$
$$r_2 : \neg roman(Movies : movies) \leftarrow not\ moviedb1.roman(Movies)$$
$$r_3 : \quad roman(Movies : movies) \leftarrow moviedb2.roman(Movies)$$
$$r_4 : \neg roman(Movies : movies) \leftarrow not\ moviedb2.roman(Movies)$$

Finally, the night out might be a date or not (rule d, where a rule of the form $a \vee \neg a \leftarrow$ is shorthand for the rules $a \leftarrow not\ \neg a$ and $\neg a \leftarrow not\ a$), and we have a constraint indicating that a plan for a date should involve a movie theater where romantic movies are screened:

$$d : date \vee \neg date \leftarrow$$
$$c : \qquad\qquad\qquad \leftarrow plan(Rest, Time1, Movies, Time2), date, \neg roman(Movies)$$

In the following, we assume, as is usual in logic programming, that programs are *grounded*: each variable is replaced by all possible constants. In the presence of call literals, we further generalize this such that every word starting with a capital letter is replaced by all possible constants. The rule p thus yields, among others,

$$plan(pizzi, 8pm, kine, 10pm) \leftarrow$$
$$pizzi.res(8pm), geo.near(pizzi, kine), not\ otherpl(pizzi, 8pm, kine, 10pm)$$

We grounded the words $Rest$ and $Time1$ in $Rest.res(Time1)$ by $pizzi$ and $8pm$ respectively. Additionally, grounding takes into account inequalities and subsequently removes them from the rules: $Time1$ and $Time2$ are grounded by different constants. Grounding does not care for semantics, e.g., the literal $8pm.res(kine)$ is a valid, albeit nonsensical, grounding for $Rest.res(Time1)$.

Syntactically, a ground program with calls does not differ from a ground program without calls: a literal is only a call literal if it is explicitly associated with a particular instance of a decision problem.

Definition 1. *A* call semantics *for a program R is a mapping $\sigma : \mathcal{C}_R \subseteq \mathcal{L}_R \to Inst$ from a designated set of* call literals $\mathcal{C}_R$ *in R to instances $Inst$ of decision problems D.*

We relate every instance in $Inst$ to its decision problem by a mapping $d : Inst \to D$ such that $d(Inst) = D$. A call semantics is *well-defined* if every decision problem $d \in D$ is decidable and has an associated complexity $comp(d)$. The *call complexity* $comp(\sigma)$ of a well-defined σ is the complexity class $\bigcup\{comp(d) \mid d \in D\}$. For the grounding R of the above program, we define the call literals $\mathcal{C}_R = \{pizzi.res(8pm),$ $pizzi.res(10pm), ilpast.res(8pm), ilpast.res(10pm), geo.near(pizzi, kine),$ $geo.$ $near(ilpast, kine), moviedb1.roman(kine), moviedb2.roman(kine)\}$, with σ as in Table 1. Thus, e.g., $\sigma(pizzi.res(8pm))$ is an instance of *instance checking* for OWL DL ontologies, $\sigma(moviedb1.roman(kine))$ is an instance of the problem that involves checking whether there is an answer set of a program containing a certain literal, and, $\sigma(geo.near(pizzi, kine))$ is some other unspecified instance of a decidable problem. Assuming the complexity of the latter is polynomial, we have, with the NEXPTIME complexity for instance checking in OWL DL [22] and NP complexity for the answer set programming problem [6], that $comp(\sigma) = \text{NEXPTIME} \cup \text{NP} \cup \text{P} = \text{NEXPTIME}$. The particular dot notation $(Rest.res(Time))$ has thus no particular meaning in itself, apart

Table 1. Call Semantics σ

$\sigma(pizzi.res(8pm))$ = 'is $res(8pm)$ in model of OWL DL ontology $pizzi$'
$\sigma(pizzi.res(10pm))$ = 'is $res(10pm)$ in model of OWL DL ontology $pizzi$'
$\sigma(ilpast.res(8pm))$ = 'is $res(8pm)$ in model of OWL DL ontology $ilpast$'
$\sigma(ilpast.res(10pm))$ = 'is $res(10pm)$ in model of OWL DL ontology $ilpast$'
$\sigma(geo.near(pizzi, kine))$= 'is $pizzi$ near $kine$ according to geo DB'
$\sigma(geo.near(ilpast, kine))$= 'is $ilpast$ near $kine$ according to geo DB'
$\sigma(moviedb1.roman(kine))$ = 'exists answer set of $moviedb1$ containing $roman(kine)$'
$\sigma(moviedb2.roman(kine))$ = 'exists answer set of $moviedb2$ containing $roman(kine)$'

from hinting that it might be a call of res to the object $Rest$. The identification of call literals and their semantics is the responsibility of the call semantics only.

In the following, we assume all call semantics are well-defined, and thus have an associated call complexity. Evaluating call literals amounts to evaluating the corresponding instance of the decision problem.

Definition 2. *Let σ be a call semantics for a program R. The evaluation of σ is a mapping* $\mathrm{eval}_\sigma : \mathcal{C}_R \cup not\, \mathcal{C}_R \to \{\textbf{true}, \textbf{false}\}$ *such that, for a call literal l,* $\mathrm{eval}_\sigma(l) = \textbf{true}$ *if $\sigma(l)$ evaluates to true and* $\mathrm{eval}_\sigma(l) = \textbf{false}$ *if $\sigma(l)$ evaluates to false. For a not $l \in not\, \mathcal{C}_R$, we define* $\mathrm{eval}_\sigma(not\, l) = \neg\mathrm{eval}_\sigma(l)$. *For a set of extended call literals X,* $\mathrm{eval}_\sigma(X) = \{\mathrm{eval}_\sigma(l) \mid l \in X\}$.

Definition 3. *A program with calls (LPC) is a pair $P = \langle R, \sigma \rangle$ where R is a program and σ is a call semantics for R.*

The semantics of LPCs is defined by a reduction to the extended answer set semantics for programs without calls. For a LPC $\langle R, \sigma \rangle$, we evaluate all call literals in R by means of σ. Since all call literals are interpreted as instances of decidable decision problems, such an evaluation returns either true or false for each call literal. Similar to the GL-reduct, the *call-free reduct* is then the original program R with call literals removed according to their evaluation: a call literal in the body that evaluates to false amounts to the removal of the rule since the rule can never contribute to an answer set; if a call literal in the body evaluates to true, one just removes it from the body. The same reasoning applies to call literals in the head. If such a call literal is true, the rule is automatically satisfied and one can omit it, otherwise, the call literal is removed from the head.

Definition 4. *The* call-free reduct $^\sigma P$ *of a LPC $P = \langle R, \sigma : \mathcal{C}_R \to Inst \rangle$ are the rules* $(\alpha \backslash \mathcal{C}_R^*) \leftarrow (\beta \backslash \mathcal{C}_R^*)$ *where $\alpha \leftarrow \beta \in R$ and $\bigwedge \mathrm{eval}_\sigma(\beta \cap \mathcal{C}_R^*) = \textbf{true}$ and $\bigvee \mathrm{eval}_\sigma(\alpha \cap \mathcal{C}_R^*) = \textbf{false}$.*[2]

For the call semantics from Table 1, assume the evaluation of σ is as in Table 2. One can thus reserve at both 8 P.M. and 10 P.M. in $pizzi$, while only at 8 P.M. in $ilpast$. Furthermore, $pizzi$ is near the movie theater, and $ilpast$ is not. According to $moviedb1$, $kine$ features romantic movies, contradicting $moviedb2$. The call-free reduct of the example contains, among others, rules

---

[2] If a set X is empty, we assume $\bigwedge X = \textbf{true}$ and $\bigvee X = \textbf{false}$.

Table 2. Evaluation of σ

$\text{eval}_\sigma(pizzi.res(8pm)) = \mathbf{true}$	$\text{eval}_\sigma(geo.near(pizzi, kine)) = \mathbf{true}$
$\text{eval}_\sigma(pizzi.res(10pm)) = \mathbf{true}$	$\text{eval}_\sigma(geo.near(ilpast, kine)) = \mathbf{false}$
$\text{eval}_\sigma(ilpast.res(8pm)) = \mathbf{true}$	$\text{eval}_\sigma(moviedb1.roman(kine)) = \mathbf{true}$
$\text{eval}_\sigma(ilpast.res(10pm)) = \mathbf{false}$	$\text{eval}_\sigma(moviedb2.roman(kine)) = \mathbf{false}$

$$plan(pizzi, 8pm, kine, 10pm) \leftarrow not\ otherpl(pizzi, 8pm, kine, 10pm)$$
$$plan(pizzi, 10pm, kine, 8pm) \leftarrow not\ otherpl(pizzi, 10pm, kine, 8pm)$$

originating from rule p, and rules $roman(kine) \leftarrow$ and $\neg roman(kine) \leftarrow$, originating from, respectively, r_1 and r_4.

Definition 5. *An* interpretation *of a LPC* $P = \langle R, \sigma \rangle$ *is an interpretation of* $^\sigma P$. *An interpretation* M *of* P *is an* extended answer set *of* P *if* M *is an extended answer set of* $^\sigma P$.

We have 6 different extended answer sets of the example LPC:

$$M_1 = \{plan(pizzi, 8pm, kine, 10pm), date, roman(kine)\}$$
$$M_2 = \{plan(pizzi, 8pm, kine, 10pm), \neg date, roman(kine)\}$$
$$M_3 = \{plan(pizzi, 8pm, kine, 10pm), \neg date, \neg roman(kine)\}$$
$$M_4 = \{plan(pizzi, 10pm, kine, 8pm), date, roman(kine)\}$$
$$M_5 = \{plan(pizzi, 10pm, kine, 8pm), \neg date, roman(kine)\}$$
$$M_6 = \{plan(pizzi, 10pm, kine, 8pm), \neg date, \neg roman(kine)\}$$

For the two possible plans – pizza at 8, movie at 10, or vice versa – the night out may be a date or not. If it is a date, one defeats $\neg date \leftarrow$ by the applied rule $date \leftarrow$. Furthermore, by constraint c, we need to have $roman(kine)$ if $date$ is in the answer set, which requires defeating $\neg roman(kine) \leftarrow$ by $roman(kine) \leftarrow$. Consequently, although two different sources ($moviedb1$ and $moviedb2$) yield contradictory information regarding the romantic nature of movies at a movie theater, a situation bound to occur frequently on the Semantic Web, the extended answer set semantics solves this by allowing for both solutions to coexist. The particular defeat mechanism makes sure this happens in a sensible way: a rule can be left unsatisfied if there is a competing applied rule.

Adding calls to programs, or, from a different perspective, wrapping different reasoners together using a logic program, amounts to reasoning that is not much worse than its worst call to a reasoner. It can be done in $P^{comp(\sigma)} \cup NP$: either in polynomial time with an oracle of complexity the call complexity of the call semantics or in NP.

Theorem 1. *Let* $P = \langle R, \sigma \rangle$ *be a LPC and* l *a literal in* R *that is not a call literal. Checking whether there is an extended answer set of* P *containing* l *is in* $P^{comp(\sigma)} \cup NP$.

Given the NEXPTIME call complexity for the night out example, checking whether there is an extended answer set containing a literal is in $P^{NEXPTIME} \cup NP = P^{NEXPTIME}$, i.e. it can be done in polynomial time with an oracle in NEXPTIME (corresponding to the complexity of OWL DL instance checking).

Theorem 2. *Let* $P = \langle R, \sigma \rangle$ *be a LPC and l a literal in R that is not a call literal. Checking whether there is an extended answer set of P containing l is* $(\text{comp}(\sigma) \cup \text{NP})$-*hard.*

Approaches where input from the program can be send to the external source are not expressible in this framework, e.g. in [11] atoms calculated in the program can influence reasoning in a DL knowledge base (semantically, by adding them to the DL knowledge base). Our approach does allow for parametrized calls to sources, but the parameters must be known at compile-time before starting the computation of the answer set.

The extended answer set semantics enables resolution of conflicts. However, usually, some resolutions are more preferred than others. E.g., a particular user preference is that one rather has a quiet night out instead of a stressful date: $\neg date \leftarrow \ < date \leftarrow$. Moreover, not being on a date, there is no need to endure Hollywood's romantic ideals[3]:

$$
\begin{array}{c}
roman(kine) \leftarrow moviedb1.roman(kine) \\
roman(kine) \leftarrow moviedb2.roman(kine) \\
\hline
\neg roman(kine) \leftarrow not\ moviedb1.roman(kine) \\
\neg roman(kine) \leftarrow not\ moviedb2.roman(kine)
\end{array}
$$

The preference between rules in the LPC, induces a natural preference relation on the rules in the call-free reduct: $\neg roman(kine) \leftarrow \ < roman(kine) \leftarrow$. Formally, for an order $<$ on the rules in a LPC $P = \langle R, \sigma : C_R \to Inst \rangle$, we define, for rules $r_1 : (\alpha_1 \backslash C_R^*) \leftarrow (\beta_1 \backslash C_R^*) \in {}^\sigma P$ and $r_2 : (\alpha_2 \backslash C_R^*) \leftarrow (\beta_2 \backslash C_R^*) \in {}^\sigma P$,

$$
r_1{}^\sigma < r_2 \text{ iff } \alpha_1 \leftarrow \beta_1 < \alpha_2 \leftarrow \beta_2 .
$$

Definition 6. *An ordered program with calls (OLPC) is a pair* $P = \langle R, < \rangle$ *where R is a LPC and $<$ is a strict partial order on the rules in R. An extended answer set of P is an extended answer set of R. An extended answer set of P is preferred if it is a preferred answer set of the OLP* $\langle {}^\sigma R, {}^\sigma < \rangle$.

Note that $\langle {}^\sigma R, {}^\sigma < \rangle$ is indeed an OLP, more specifically, ${}^\sigma <$ is a strict partial order on the rules in ${}^\sigma R$. The OLPC $\langle R, < \rangle$ defining the night out example, yields the preferred answer sets M_3 and M_6, corresponding to the preference for nights out devoid of date and romantic movie. The complexity of reasoning with OLPCs again mostly depends on the call complexity.

Theorem 3. *Let* $P = \langle R, < \rangle$ *be an OLPC and l a literal in R that is not a call literal. Checking whether there is a preferred answer set of P containing l is in* $\text{P}^{\text{comp}(\sigma)} \cup \Sigma_2^P$.

Theorem 4. *Let* $P = \langle R, < \rangle$ *be an OLPC and l a literal in R that is not a call literal. Checking whether there is a preferred answer set of P containing l is* $(\text{comp}(\sigma) \cup \Sigma_2^P)$-*hard.*

Even though the night out example did not feature it, the heads of rules may contain calls as well. This allows a form of ontology alignment in the sense that one can enforce that ontologies should agree on some facts. E.g., $moviedb2.roman(kine) \leftarrow$

---

[3] The notation in modules indicates that all rules in one module, divided by a horizontal line, are more preferred than all the rules in the module above.

moviedb1.roman(kine) enforces that if *kine* is a theater screening romantic movies according to *moviedb1* then *moviedb2* should agree. Calls in the heads of rules can, however, always be replaced by their negation in the body.

Theorem 5. *Let $\langle R, \sigma \rangle$ be a LPC with a $\leftarrow \beta \in R$ and a call literal a . Then, M is an extended answer set of $\langle R, \sigma \rangle$ iff M is an extended answer set of $\langle R', \sigma \rangle$ where $R' = (R \backslash \{a \leftarrow \beta\}) \cup \{ \leftarrow not\ a, \beta\}$.*

A similar theorem does not hold for heads that are not call literals: $a \leftarrow$ has the extended answer set $\{a\}$ while its shifted version $\leftarrow not\ a$ has no extended answer sets (one cannot motivate a since there no rules with a in the head, although the constraint demands the presence of a).

4   Preferential Reasoning on a Web of Trust

Often, the user has its particular knowledge, in the form of a program, and a sense of which calls he believes more than other calls, e.g. because (part of) one source of information is more reliable than (part of) another one. Take the LPC $\langle S, \sigma \rangle$ with S the program[4]

$$stock(lmby) \leftarrow \qquad buy(S) \leftarrow ft.buy(S), nyt.buy(S)$$
$$stock(wtww) \leftarrow \qquad \neg buy(S) \leftarrow not\ pdh.buy(S)$$

with a call semantics $\sigma(ft.buy(lmby)) = $ 'buy stock *lmby* according to Financial Times' and similarly for the grounded call literals involving *nyt* (New York Times) and *pdh* (analyst Paul D'Hoore) with the stock *wtww*. Assume the evaluation of σ is as follows

$$\text{eval}_\sigma(ft.buy(lmby)) = \textbf{false} \qquad \text{eval}_\sigma(nyt.buy(wtww)) = \textbf{true}$$
$$\text{eval}_\sigma(ft.buy(wtww)) = \textbf{true} \qquad \text{eval}_\sigma(pdh.buy(lmby)) = \textbf{false}$$
$$\text{eval}_\sigma(nyt.buy(lmby)) = \textbf{true} \qquad \text{eval}_\sigma(pdh.buy(wtww)) = \textbf{false}$$

such that both the Financial Times and Paul D'Hoore discourage buying *lmby*, the Financial Times suggests buying *wtww*, while Paul would not buy *wtww*, and the New York Times suggests buying both stocks. The call-free reduct of this LPC is then

$$s_1 : stock(lmby) \leftarrow \qquad b_f : \quad buy(wtww) \leftarrow$$
$$s_2 : stock(wtww) \leftarrow \qquad b_{p_1} : \neg buy(lmby) \leftarrow$$
$$b_{p_2} : \neg buy(wtww) \leftarrow$$

such that we have two extended answer sets

$$N_1 = \{stock(lmby), stock(wtww), \neg buy(lmby), buy(wtww)\}$$
$$N_2 = \{stock(lmby), stock(wtww), \neg buy(lmby), \neg buy(wtww)\}$$

where b_f defeats b_{p_2}, and b_{p_2} defeats b_f respectively, corresponding to the two strategies of resolving the conflicts caused by b_f and b_{p_2}. In order to deduce the most preferred answer, we allow the user to express its belief in certain calls:

$$\{not\ pdh.buy(lmby), not\ pdh.buy(wtww)\} <$$
$$\{ft.buy(lmby), ft.buy(wtww), nyt.buy(lmby), nyt.buy(wtww)\}\ ,$$

---

[4] As usual, we identify the program with its grounding.

which signifies that every extended call literal in the set on the left-hand side of $<$ is more believed than any extended call literal in the set on the right-hand side, i.e. the opinion of Paul D'Hoore is valued more than the opinion of the Financial Times or the New York Times. Intuitively, this order on calls induces an order on rules. E.g. take the ground rules b_1 : $buy(wtww) \leftarrow ft.buy(wtww), nyt.buy(wtww)$ and $b_2 : \neg buy(wtww) \leftarrow not\ pdh.buy(wtww)$. We can order those rules based on the order on the call literals: we consider b_2 more preferred than b_1 since for every extended call literal in the body of b_1 that is not in the body of b_2 we have a more believed extended call literal in the body of b_2 that is not in the body of b_1. Put otherwise, for every call that b_1 needs to make in order to deduce $buy(wtww)$ and that b_2 does not make to deduce $\neg buy(wtww)$, b_2 makes a more credible call that b_1 does not make. The order on extended call literals thus induces the order $b_2 < b_1$, and a similar ordering for the grounding with $lmby$, which in turn leads to the order $\neg buy(wtww) \leftarrow <$ $buy(wtww) \leftarrow$ in the call-free reduct. Consequently, the example LPOC has the preferred answer set N_2. Things get more complicated, however, if we replace, e.g., b_1 by $b_1^1 : buy(wtww) \leftarrow tmp$ and $b_1^2 : tmp \leftarrow ft.buy(wtww), nyt.buy(wtww)$. Obviously, one still prefers b_2 over b_1^1, but, now, a direct comparison based on the order on the call literals in their respective bodies does not makes sense. Instead, we look at the *trace* of both bodies, i.e. those extended call literals that must be evaluated as true in order to make the extended literals in the body true. The trace of a set of extended literals thus identifies those calls that are responsible for the truth of those literals in an extended answer set, and on which we can base the induced order on rules.

Definition 7. *Let* $\langle R, \sigma \rangle$ *be a LPC with call literals* C_R, $c \in C_R^*$, *and* $l \in \mathcal{L}_R^* \backslash C_R^*$. *Then* $c \in tr(l)$ *iff for every evaluation* $eval_\sigma$ *of* σ: *if* M *is an extended answer set of* $\langle R, \sigma \rangle$ *(w.r.t.* $eval_\sigma$) *such that* $M \models l$, *then* $eval_\sigma(c) = \textbf{true}$.

Furthermore, $tr(c) = \{c\}$ *and* $tr(\beta) = \bigcup \{tr(b) \mid b \in \beta\}$.

The trace of tmp is then $tr(tmp) = \{ft.buy(wtww), nyt.buy(wtww)\}$, i.e. in order make tmp true one needs the truth of the call literals in $tr(tmp)$. The trace of the body of b_2 is $\{not\ pdh.buy(wtww)\}$. Such that, based on those traces and the order on the call literals, we can deduce that b_2 is more preferred than b_1^1.

Definition 8. *A* program with ordered calls (LPOC) *is a pair* $P = \langle R, \prec \rangle$ *where R is a LPC with call literals* C_R *and* $\prec$ *is a strict partial order on the (extended) call literals in* C_R^*. *An* extended answer set *of P is an extended answer set of R. An extended answer set of P is* preferred *if it is a preferred answer set of the OLPC* $\langle R, < \rangle$, *where, for conflicting rules* $r_1 : a \leftarrow \beta_1$ *and* $r_2 : \neg a \leftarrow \beta_2$ *in R,* $r_1 \leq r_2$ *iff* $\forall c \in tr(\beta_2) \backslash tr(\beta_1)$. $\exists c' \in tr(\beta_1) \backslash tr(\beta_2) \cdot c \prec c'$, *and, for arbitrary rules* $r, s \in R$, $r < s$ *iff* $r \leq^* s \wedge s \not\leq^* r$ *where* $\leq^*$ *is the transitive closure of* $\leq$.

The preference order $<$ is a strict partial order such that $\langle R, < \rangle$ is indeed a LPOC.

Note that one can immediately reduce an order on knowledge sources – knowledge source Σ_1 has more authority than Σ_2 – to an order on extended call literals by grouping call literals concerning the same sources together, as we did in the stock example. An order on extended call literals instead of on sources allows for a finer granularity as it makes it possible to prefer sources for certain types of knowledge while preferring others for other types of knowledge: calls to the sports paper *L'Equipe* regarding tennis could be considered more reliable than tennis-related calls to *Le Monde*, while the opposite may be true for political subjects.

A Semantic Web agent may not always have preferences on the sources it is reasoning with, but if there is a network of agents it trusts available, it can easily learn preferences from those trusted agents. We model the Semantic Web as a pair $\langle \mathcal{K}, \mathcal{A} \rangle$ where $\mathcal{K}$ is a set of knowledge sources K and $\mathcal{A} = (V, E)$ is a directed graph with agents V and edges E between them. Each agent in V is defined as a LPOC, i.e. an agent has reasoning capabilities through a logic program with calls and can express preferences on its calls. Denote with $R(A)$ the sequence of agents that are reachable from A via a path in E, and assume $R(A)$ is ordered according to the trust A has in them. Thus $R(A)$ is a sequence of agents $A_1, A_2, \ldots$, such that each A_i is trusted more by A than A_{i+1} is. We thus assume that the agent resides on a web of trust, with a suitable trust metric that allows for the construction of $R(A)$ for every agent A.

For our convenience, we identify the set of sources $\mathcal{K}$ with the set of all instances of decidable decision problems d that have an associated complexity $\mathrm{comp}(d)$. E.g., the identification of a particular description logic knowledge base $\Sigma \in \mathcal{K}$ includes the set of all satisfiability checking problems w.r.t. Σ.

Take an agent $A = \langle P, \prec \rangle$ with P a simplified version of the stock example, $b_1 : buy \leftarrow ft.buy, nyt.buy$, and $b_2 : \neg buy \leftarrow not\ pdh.buy$, with call literals $ft.buy$, $nyt.buy$, and $pdh.buy$, evaluated as **true**, **true**, and **false** respectively. We assume that the agent has no preference on the two extended answer sets $\{buy\}$ and $\{\neg buy\}$ of this program, i.e. $\prec$ is empty, such that both extended answer sets are preferred. Due to the empty preference, the agent has to choose between 2 equally preferred, but contradicting, strategies. Assuming the agent is part of network of agents it trusts, it can try to find out what the trusted agents think of its call literals. E.g., assume that agent A is connected to agents $A_1 = \langle P_1, \prec_1 \rangle$, $A_2 = \langle P_2, \prec_2 \rangle$, and $A_3 = \langle P_3, \prec_3 \rangle$ with preferences defined as follows:

$$not\ pdh.buy \prec_1 ft.buy \qquad\qquad not\ pdh.buy \prec_3 nyt.buy$$
$$lat.buy \prec_1 ft.buy \qquad\qquad ft.buy \prec_3 lat.buy$$
$$ft.buy \prec_2 not\ pdh.buy$$

Thus, agent A_1 prefers Paul D'Hoore's advice as well as the Los Angeles Times's advice over that of the Financial Times, agent A_2 holds an opposite view and prefers the Financial Times over Paul D'Hoore, and agent A_3 prefers Paul's advice over the New York Times's and has more believe in the Financial Times than in the Los Angeles Times. We do not specify the programs of those agents since we are only interested to learn preferences for agent A from the preferences its trusted agents have – for A it does not matter how the trusted agents deploy those preferences.

In order to let agent A construct its preferences based on this web of agents, we assume its reachable agents are ranked according to trustworthiness: $R(A) = A_1, A_2, A_3$, such that A_1 is the agent that A trusts the most and A_3 the agent that it trusts the least. Considering the preference of A_1, A only retains $not\ pdh.buy \prec_1 ft.buy$: combining this preference with A's own preference, a strict partial order on the call literals of P can be constructed. The other preference of A_1 involves $lat.buy$ which is of no concern to agent A since it is not a call literal in P.

Moving to agent A_2, second in the line of trust, A ignores $\prec_2$: it contradicts the order already constructed in A with the more trusted agent A_1. Finally, A ignores the preference in $\prec_3$ involving $lat.buy$, but it updates its preference with $not\ pdh.buy \prec_3 nyt.buy$. This results in an updated agent $A' = \langle P, \prec' \rangle$ with $not\ pdh.buy \prec' ft.buy$, and $not\ pdh.buy \prec' nyt.buy$. This order on call literals induces then the order $b_2 < b_1$ such that $\{\neg buy\}$ is the preferred answer set of the updated agent A'.

Definition 9. *For an agent* $A = \langle P, \prec \rangle$ *in* $\mathcal{A}$, *let* $R(A) = \langle P_1, \prec_1 \rangle, \langle P_2, \prec_2 \rangle, \ldots$ *The updated agent of* A *is* $A' = \langle P, \prec' \rangle$ *where* $\prec' = (\prec \cup \bigcup_{i=1} B_i)^*$ *with*

1. $B_i \subseteq \prec_i$,
2. $\forall c_1 \prec_i c_2 \in B_i \cdot c_1, c_2 \in C_P^*$,
3. $(\prec \cup \bigcup_{j=1}^i B_j)^*$ *is a strict partial order,*
4. B_i *is a maximal set satisfying* 1., 2., *and* 3.

Intuitively, the agent updates its own preference $\prec$ with maximal subsets of preferences of trusted agents, and this according to the order of trust. Condition 2. ensures that only preferences on call literals of the agent's own program P are considered, and condition 3. ensures that only those preferences of $\prec_i$ are retained that, when added to the accumulated preference and transitively closing the result, one still has a strict partial order. The latter only amounts to checking irreflexivity since transitivity is entailed by taking the transitive closure. Condition 4. forces $\prec'$ to consider as much preferences as possible from each preference $\prec_i$.

The updated $\prec'$ is a strict partial order on call literals such that the updated agent A' is a LPOC, and we can compute preferred answer sets of an agent by computing the preferred answer set of its updated version that takes into account the web of trust.

Definition 10. *Let* A *be an agent in* $\mathcal{A}$. *The preferred answer set of* A *is the preferred answer set of the updated* A'.

In order to be able to compute the updated agent for an agent A, we assume that $R(A)$ is finite. Since the Semantic Web with software agents is finite this sounds like a reasonable restriction. However, due to the sheer amount of envisaged agents on the Semantic Web, it is unlikely that feasible reasoning with all connected agents is possible. A possible strategy in overcoming this problem is to add a bound on the number of trusted agents in the sequence $R(A)$.

In considering an agent as a logic program, we neglected a lot of the machinery involved in agent definitions. E.g., in the IMPACT System [1] an agent consists of two parts: software code and a semantic wrapper consisting of a message manager, an action module, and a meta-knowledge module. In [12], the theory and implementation of the action module is described, with, among others, code call atoms that are able to call software, and agent programs that express the choices for actions. E.g., $\mathbf{O}(send\_note(Person)) \leftarrow \mathbf{Do}(run\_audit(Person))$, indicates that if one is executing the audit run, one is obliged to send a note. Conflict resolution in [12] amounts to allowing defeat of the meta-rule "if $\mathbf{O}\alpha$ then $\mathbf{Do}\alpha$", which says that if action α is obliged then one should execute it. This type of behavior can be simulated under our extended answer set semantics by introducing the ordered rules $\mathbf{Do}(\alpha) \leftarrow \mathbf{O}(\alpha) < \neg\mathbf{Do}(\alpha) \leftarrow \mathbf{O}(\alpha)$, thus minimizing defeat of the meta-rule. Moreover, our preference relation between rules allows for more fine-grained types of conflict resolution as showed in this section.

5   Conclusions and Directions for Further Research

We devised and discussed a logic programming based framework for agents on the Semantic Web, where agents are capable of expressing preferences on the rules or on the call literals in their knowledge. Those preferences enabled the resolution of conflicts with the most preferred solution. In case an agent has no preferences but is part of a web of trusted agents, we showed how the agent can replenish its own preferences based on the preferences of trusted agents.

The preferred answer set semantics from Section 2, i.e. without calls, was implemented by the OLPS solver [26], available at http://tinf2.vub.ac.be/olp/. For a given OLPC, i.e. a program with calls and an order on those rules, different plug-ins are envisaged to be written, depending on the type of desired calls. Such a plug-in's main task would be to execute the decision problem associated with a particular call, e.g. check the satisfiability of a concept with the FACT [21] DL reasoner, and subsequently calculate the call-free reduct and the reduced order on this reduct, which are then to be fed to OLPS.

References

1. K. Arisha, T. Eiter, S. Kraus, F. Ozcan, R. Ross, and V. S. Subrahmanian. IMPACT: Interactive Maryland Platform for Agents Collaborating Together. *IEEE Intelligent Systems*, 14(2):64–72, 1999.
2. F. Baader, D. Calvanese, D. McGuinness, D. Nardi, and P. Patel-Schneider. *The Description Logic Handbook*. Cambridge University Press, 2003.
3. C. Baral. *Knowledge Representation, Reasoning and Declarative Problem Solving*. Cambridge Press, 2003.
4. S. Bechhofer, F. van Harmelen, J. Hendler, I. Horrocks, D. L. McGuinness, P. F. Patel-Schneider, and L. A. Stein. OWL Web Ontology Language Reference, 2004.
5. K. Van Belleghem, M. Denecker, and D. De Schreye. A Strong Correspondence between DLs and Open Logic Programming. In *Proc. of ICLP'97*, pages 346–360, 1997.
6. E. Dantsin, T. Eiter, G. Gottlob, and A. Voronkov. Complexity and Expressive Power of Logic Programming. *ACM Comput. Surv.*, 33(3):374–425, 2001.
7. L. Ding, L. Zhou, and T. Finin. Trust Based Knowledge Outsourcing for Semantic Web Agents. In *Proc. of the 2003 IEEE/WIC International Conference on Web Intelligence*, 2003.
8. F. M. Donini, M. Lenzerini, D. Nardi, and A. Schaerf. AL-log: Integrating Datalog and Description Logics. *J. of Intell. and Cooperative Information Systems*, 10:227–252, 1998.
9. T. Eiter, W. Faber, N. Leone, G. Pfeifer, and A. Polleres. Planning under Incomplete Knowledge. In *Proc. of CL 2000*, volume 1861 of *LNCS*, pages 807–821. Springer, 2000.
10. T. Eiter, G. Gottlob, and H. Veith. Modular Logic Programming and Generalized Quantifiers. In *Proc. of LPNMR*, pages 290–309, 1997.
11. T. Eiter, T. Lukasiewicz, R. Schindlauer, and H. Tompits. Combining Answer Set Programming with DLs for the Semantic Web. In *Proc. of KR 2004*, pages 141–151, 2004.
12. T. Eiter, V. S. Subrahmanian, and G. Pick. Heterogeneous Active Agents, I: Semantics. *Artif. Intell.*, 108(1-2):179–255, 1999.

13. M. Gelfond and V. Lifschitz. The Stable Model Semantics for Logic Programming. In *Proc. of ICLP'88*, pages 1070–1080, Cambridge, Massachusetts, 1988. MIT Press.
14. Y. Gil and V. Ratnakar. Trusting Information Sources One Citizen at a Time. In *Proc. of International Semantic Web Conference (ISWC 2002)*, pages 162–176, 2002.
15. J. Golbeck and J. Hendler. Inferring Reputation on the Semantic Web. In *Proc. of WWW 2004*. ACM, 2004.
16. J. Golbeck, B. Parsia, and J. Hendler. Trust Networks on the Semantic Web. In *Proc. of Cooperative Intelligent Agents 2003*, 2003.
17. B. N. Grosof, I. Horrocks, R. Volz, and S. Decker. Description Logic Programs: Combining Logic Programs with Description Logic. In *Proc. of WWW 2003*, pages 48–57, 2003.
18. James Hendler. Agents and the Semantic Web. *IEEE Intelligent Systems Journal*, 16(2), 2001.
19. S. Heymans, D. Van Nieuwenborgh, and D. Vermeir. Nonmonotonic Ontological and Rule-based Reasoning with Extended Conceptual Logic Programs. In *Proc. of ESWC 2005*, number 3532 in LNCS, pages 392–407. Springer, 2005.
20. S. Heymans, D. Van Nieuwenborgh, and D. Vermeir. Preferential Reasoning on a Web of Trust. Technical report, Vrije Universiteit Brussel, Dept. of Computer Science, 2005. `http://tinf2.vub.ac.be/~{}sheymans/tech/aspc-tech.ps.gz`.
21. I. Horrocks. The FaCT system. In *Proc. of Tableaux'98*, number 1397, pages 307–312. Springer-Verlag, 1998.
22. I. Horrocks and P. Patel-Schneider. Reducing OWL Entailment to Description Logic Satisfiability. *J. of Web Semantics*, 1(4):345–357, 2004.
23. U. Hustadt, B. Motik, and U. Sattler. Reducing $\mathcal{SHIQ}^-$ Description Logic to Disjunctive Datalog Programs. FZI-Report 1-8-11/03, Forschungszentrum Informatik (FZI), 2003.
24. V. Lifschitz. Answer Set Programming and Plan Generation. *Journal of Artificial Intelligence*, 138(1-2):39–54, 2002.
25. B. Motik, R. Volz, and A. Maedche. Optimizing Query Answering in Description Logics using disjunctive deductive databases. In *Proc. of KRDB'03*, pages 39–50, 2003.
26. D. Van Nieuwenborgh, S. Heymans, and D. Vermeir. An Ordered Logic Program Solver. In *Proc. of PADL 2005*, number 3350 in LNCS, pages 128–142. Springer, 2005.
27. C. H. Papadimitriou. *Computational Complexity*. Addison Wesley, 1994.
28. M. Richardson, R. Agrawal, and P. Domingos. Trust Management for the Semantic Web. In *Proc. of ISWC 2003*, pages 351–368. Springer-Verlag, 2003.
29. R. Rosati. Towards Expressive KR Systems Integrating Datalog and Description Logics: Preliminary Report. In *Proc. of DL'99*, pages 160–164, 1999.
30. D. Van Nieuwenborgh and D. Vermeir. Preferred Answer Sets for Ordered Logic Programs. In *Proc. of JELIA 2002*, volume 2424 of *LNAI*, pages 432–443. Springer, 2002.
31. Matthias Wagner, Thorsten Liebig, Olaf Noppens, Steffen Balzer, and Wolfgang Kellerer. Towards Semantic-based Service Discovery on Tiny Mobile Devices.

Resolution-Based Approximate Reasoning for OWL DL[*]

Pascal Hitzler and Denny Vrandečić

AIFB, Universität Karlsruhe, Germany
{hitzler, vrandecic}@aifb.uni-karlsruhe.de

Abstract. We propose a new technique for approximate ABox reasoning with OWL DL ontologies. Essentially, we obtain substantially improved reasoning performance by disregarding non-Horn features of OWL DL. Our approach comes as a side-product of recent research results concerning a new transformation of OWL DL ontologies into negation-free disjunctive datalog [1, 2, 3, 4], and rests on the idea of performing standard resolution over disjunctive rules by treating them as if they were non-disjunctive ones. We analyse our reasoning approach by means of non-monotonic reasoning techniques, and present an implementation, called SCREECH.

1 Introduction

Knowledge representation and reasoning on the Semantic Web is done by means of ontologies. While the quest for suitable ontology languages is still ongoing, OWL [5] has been established as a core standard. It comes in three flavours, as OWL Full, OWL DL and OWL Lite, where OWL Full contains OWL DL, which in turn contains OWL Lite. The latter two coincide semantically with certain description logics [6] and can thus be considered fragments of first-order predicate logic.

OWL ontologies can be understood to consist of two parts, one intensional, the other extensional. In description logics terminology, the intensional part consists of a TBox and an RBox, and contains knowledge about concepts (called *classes*) and the complex relations between them (called *roles*). The extensional part consists of an ABox, and contains knowledge about entities and how they relate to the classes and roles from the intensional part. For the Semantic Web, TBox and RBox shall provide background vocabulary, while (annotated) web-pages etc. constitute ABoxes which are interlinked with intensional knowledge. The Semantic Web thus envisions a distributed knowledge source, built from OWL ontologies and intertwining the knowledge like the World Wide Web interconnects websites.

[*] The authors acknowledge support by the German Federal Ministry of Education and Research (BMBF) under the SmartWeb project, and by the European Commission under contract IST-2003-506826 SEKT and under the KnowledgeWeb Network of Excellence. The expressed content is the view of the authors but not necessarily the view of any of the projects as a whole.

Y. Gil et al. (Eds.): ISWC 2005, LNCS 3729, pp. 383–397, 2005.
© Springer-Verlag Berlin Heidelberg 2005

With an estimated 25 million active websites today and correspondingly more webpages, it is apparent that reasoning on the Semantic Web will have to deal with very large ABoxes. Complexity of ABox reasoning — also called *data complexity* — thus measures complexity in terms of ABox size only, while considering the intensional part of the ontology to be of constant size. For the different OWL variants, data complexity is at least NP-hard, which indicates that it will not scale well in general [7]. Methods are therefore being sought to cope with large ABoxes in an approximate manner.

The approach which we propose is based on the fact that data complexity is polynomial for non-disjunctive datalog. We utilise recent research results [1,2,3,4] which allow the transformation of OWL DL ontologies into disjunctive datalog. Rather than doing (expensive) exact reasoning over the resulting disjunctive datalog knowledge base, we do approximate reasoning by treating disjunctive rules as if they were non-disjunctive ones. The resulting reasoning procedure is complete, but may be unsound in cases. Its data complexity is polynomial. We are also able to give a characterization of the resulting approximate inference by means of standard methods from logic programming semantics.

This paper is structured as follows. In Section 2, we first discuss the general rationale behind approximate reasoning, and how it relates to other reasoning frameworks. We then recall formal terminology and notation for OWL DL, and shortly review datalog and SLD-resolution. Then, in Section 4, we explain how OWL DL ontologies can be transformed into disjunctive datalog. In Section 5 we introduce the new approximate SLD-resolution procedure which we propose. The presentation of our implementation SCREECH in Section 6 is followed by an Example in Section 7, and an experimental evaluation in Section 8. We conclude and discuss future work in Section 9.

2   Non-classical Reasoning — Common Grounds

The sophisticated reasoning tasks required when dealing with expressive knowledge representation languages like those based on description logics are known to be of high computational complexity. In the face of ever increasing data quantities to be processed, new methods are needed to obtain usable systems. As the high computational complexity of the reasoning tasks is unavoidable, the method of choice for obtaining scalable systems is to use *approximate reasoning* techniques. In a nutshell, approximate reasoning rests on the idea of decreasing the complexity of a problem by imposing controlled changes on either the language used or the inference operation used for the deduction. The resulting lower complexity and consequent speed-up thus comes at the price of unsoundness or incompleteness (or both), but in a controlled and well-understood manner which allows to assess the quality of the deduction made by the approximate reasoner. So-called *anytime algorithms* develop the idea a bit further and guarantee convergence to exact answers given enough time, while providing approximate results during the reasoning process.

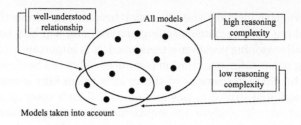

Fig. 1. Semantic view on approximate reasoning

A semantic perspective on approximate reasoning is depicted in Figure 1. When a theory is being considered, classical reasoning may be of high computational complexity and thus be unsuitable for time-critical tasks. By taking different models into account than the classical ones, the complexity of reasoning can be reduced. The resulting approximate inference may be incomplete or unsound with respect to classical inference, but in a controlled and well-understood manner, which makes the inferences suitable for further use.

Similar situations occur in the context of other sophisticated reasoning techniques. For non-monotonic reasoning, for example, a subset of the classical models is usually considered, which is selected by means of e.g. additional syntax constructs or by redefining the semantics of existing ones. Non-monotonic reasoning thus allows to arrive at conclusions which cannot be derived using classical reasoning: It is complete, but unsound, and can be described as *supraclassical* [8]. The rationale in this case is to model aspects of human commonsense reasoning like *jumping to conclusions*, again in a controlled and well-understood manner. Complexity considerations are often treated as secondary in this context.

Paraconsistent reasoning — or reasoning with inconsistency — can be approached from a similar perspective. While inconsistent knowledge bases have no classical models, paraconsistent reasoning strives to identify suitable models to be assigned to the knowledge base nevertheless, in order to allow the inference of meaningful consequences. As such, paraconsistent reasoning is sound, but incomplete with respect to classical logic, and can thus be termed *subclassical*.

Table 1 summarizes our discussion. While the table can certainly be extended further taking other forms of reasoning into account, we restrict ourselves to the mentioned examples, as the main goal of this paper is to present an approximate reasoning method for OWL DL, and not a comparative theory of reasoning

Table 1. Comparision of non-classical reasoning approaches

reasoning approach	focus	models taken into account	typical complexity
classical		all classical models	high
non-monotonic	commonsense	some classical models	very high
paraconsistent	inconsistency	more than the classical models	high
approximate	performance	variable	low

approaches. We have included this discussion because it explains the general rationale behind our approximate reasoning method, and will help us in analyzing it. Indeed, in all reasoning paradigms mentioned, it is important to obtain a clear understanding of the inference relation computed. This can be done by semantic analyses, i.e. by characterizations of the models taken into account. From the general perspective described in this section, it will later come as no surprise to the reader that we will analyze our approximate reasoning methods by means of standard techniques from non-monotonic reasoning. Indeed, in our particular case the models taken into account for approximate reasoning will turn out to be a subset of the classical models, as in non-monotonic reasoning.

3   Preliminaries

3.1   OWL DL Syntax and Semantics

OWL DL is a syntactic variant of the $\mathcal{SHOIN}(\mathbf{D})$ description logic [9]. Hence, although several XML and RDF syntaxes for OWL DL exist, it will be convenient to use the traditional description logic notation since it is more compact, and we recall the notation below. For the correspondence between this notation and various OWL DL syntaxes, see [9].

We indeed assume that the reader is familiar with OWL and thus with $\mathcal{SHOIN}(\mathbf{D})$, as space restrictions forbid to reintroduce them, but recall that $\mathcal{SHOIN}(\mathbf{D})$ supports reasoning with concrete datatypes, such as strings or integers [10]. Recall also that the description logic syntax for concepts in $\mathcal{SHOIN}(\mathbf{D})$ is defined as follows, where A is an atomic concept, R is an abstract role, S is an abstract simple role, $T_{(i)}$ are concrete roles, d is a concrete domain predicate, a_i and c_i are abstract and concrete individuals, respectively, and n is a non-negative integer:

$$C \rightarrow A \mid \neg C \mid C_1 \sqcap C_2 \mid C_1 \sqcup C_2 \mid \exists R.C \mid \forall R.C \mid \geq nS \mid \leq nS \mid \{a_1, \ldots, a_n\} \mid$$
$$\mid \geq nT \mid \leq nT \mid \exists T_1, \ldots, T_n.D \mid \forall T_1, \ldots, T_n.D$$
$$D \rightarrow d \mid \{c_1, \ldots, c_n\}$$

The $\mathcal{SHIQ}(\mathbf{D})$ description logic is obtained from $\mathcal{SHOIN}(\mathbf{D})$ by disallowing nominal concepts of the form $\{a_1, \ldots, a_n\}$ and $\{c_1, \ldots, c_n\}$, and by allowing qualified number restrictions of the form $\geq nS.C$ and $\leq nS.C$, for C a $\mathcal{SHIQ}(\mathbf{D})$ concept and S a simple role.

As description logics, $\mathcal{SHOIN}(\mathbf{D})$, i.e. OWL DL, and $\mathcal{SHIQ}(\mathbf{D})$ inherit their semantics from first-order logic by the standard translations known e.g. from [11], which we do not repeat here.

3.2   Datalog and SLD-Resolution

A (*definite* or *negation-free*) *disjunctive logic program* P consists of a finite set of *clauses* or *rules* of the form

$$\forall x_1 \ldots \forall x_n.(H_1 \vee \cdots \vee H_m \leftarrow A_1 \wedge \cdots \wedge A_k),$$

commonly written as

$$H_1 \vee \cdots \vee H_m \leftarrow A_1, \ldots, A_k,$$

where $x_1, \ldots, x_n$ are exactly all variables occuring in $H_1 \vee \cdots \vee H_m \leftarrow A_1 \wedge \cdots \wedge A_k$, and all H_i and A_j are atoms over some given first-order language Σ. The disjunction $H_1 \vee \cdots \vee H_m$ is called the *rule head*, and the conjunction $A_1 \wedge \cdots \wedge A_k$ is called the *rule body*. The set of all ground instances of atoms defined over Σ is called the *Herbrand base* of P and is denoted by B_P. The set of all ground instances of rules in P is denoted by ground(P). A rule is said to be *non-disjunctive* if $m = 1$. It is called a *fact* if $k = 0$. We abstract from the order of the atoms in the heads respectively bodies; it is not important for our results. A disjunctive logic program is called a *(disjunctive) datalog* program if it does not contain function symbols.

Note that we do not consider logic programs to come with one specific semantics. Some people for example associate datalog with the minimal model semantics only. For our treatment, datalog and logic programs are defined via syntax only. We do not specify a specific semantics because in the following we will discuss *different* semantics for logic programs in their relation to proof procedures. One of the semantics we will consider is the semantics coming from interpreting logic programs as a set of first order formulas, and in this case we use $\models$ to denote entailment in classical first-order predicate logic.

SLD-resolution (see e.g. [12]) is an efficient top-down query-answering technique for programs consisting of non-disjunctive rules, and has been implemented and successfully applied in standard Prolog systems.[1] In this framework, a ground atom can be derived from a program if and only if it is true in the least (and thus in all) Herbrand models of the program.

In the following, we mean by a *conjunctive query* simply a conjunction $B_1 \wedge \cdots \wedge B_n$ of atoms. The query is called *ground* if it does not contain any variables.

Given a conjunctive query $B_1 \wedge \cdots \wedge B_n$, an *SLD-resolution step* on the atom B_i with a non-disjunctive rule $H \leftarrow A_1, \ldots, A_k$ produces a conjunctive query

$$B_1\theta \wedge \cdots \wedge B_{i-1}\theta \wedge A_1\theta \wedge \cdots \wedge A_k\theta \wedge B_{i+1}\theta \wedge \cdots \wedge B_n\theta$$

where θ is the most general unifier of B_i and H. An *SLD-refutation* of a conjunctive query $B_1 \wedge \cdots \wedge B_n$ in a non-disjunctive program P is a finite sequence of conjunctive queries $Q_0, \ldots, Q_n$, where (*i*) $Q_0 = B_1 \wedge \cdots \wedge B_n$, (*ii*) each Q_i with $i > 0$ is obtained from Q_{i-1} by an SLD-resolution step with some rule from P on some literal B_i, and (*iii*) $Q_n = \square$, i.e. the conjunctive query Q_n does not contain any literals. If an SLD-refutation of $B_1 \wedge \cdots \wedge B_n$ in P exists, we write $P \vdash B_1 \wedge \cdots \wedge B_n$.

One of the fundamental results in logic programming states that $A \in B_P$ can be proven by SLD-resolution if and only if A is a logical consequence of P, i.e. if and only if A is true in the least Herbrand model of P:

---

[1] Like SWI or XSB Prolog, http://www.swi-prolog.org, http://xsb.sourceforge.net.

Theorem 1 ([12]). *For a ground conjunctive query $B_1 \wedge \cdots \wedge B_n$ and a non-disjunctive program P, $P \vdash B_1 \wedge \cdots \wedge B_n$ if and only if $P \models B_1 \wedge \cdots \wedge B_n$. In other words, entailment of ground conjunctive queries under SLD-resolution is entailment in predicate logic.*

SLD-resolution also allows to derive answers to non-ground queries: For a conjunctive (and not necessarily ground) query Q there exist an SLD-refutation if and only if $P \models \exists x_1 \ldots \exists x_n.Q$, where $x_1, \ldots, x_n$ are the variables occuring in Q. By keeping track of the most general unifiers used in the process, it is also possible to obtain bindings for (some of) the x_i in the form of (answer) substitutions θ, such that $P \models \exists y_1 \ldots \exists y_k(Q\theta)$, where the y_i are exactly those variables occurring in $Q\theta$. In order to keep our exhibition focused, we will only deal with ground queries.

4   Reducing OWL DL Knowledge Bases to Disjunctive Datalog Programs

We utilise recent research results about the transformation of OWL DL ontologies into disjunctive datalog, and perform approximate reasoning by transforming the disjunctive database into a non-disjunctive one. The transformation is based on the fact that OWL DL is a subset of first-order logic. OWL axioms can thus be translated directly into logical formulas and transformed into clausal form using any of the standard algorithms. The resulting clauses can be represented as disjunctive datalog rules which do not contain negation.

Note, however, that due to possible skolemization steps in the clausal form translation, the resulting datalog rules may contain function symbols. In general, datalog with function symbols is undecidable, but since we obtain the datalog program by a translation from OWL DL, which is decidable, inferencing over the resulting program must be decidable. Standard datalog engines, however, do in general not terminate in the presence of function symbols. To cope with this problem, a sophisticated method has been presented in [2, 3] which allows to get rid of the function symbols without loosing ABox consequences. As a result, we obtain a function- and negation-free disjunctive datalog program, which can be dealt with using standard techniques.

There is one other catch: The approach presented in [2, 3] does not yet allow to deal with nominals, i.e. it supports only $\mathcal{SHIQ}(\mathbf{D})$ instead of $\mathcal{SHOIN}(\mathbf{D})$ (the latter is the description logic coinciding with OWL DL). We remark that to date — and to the best of our knowledge — no reasoning algorithms for $\mathcal{SHOIN}(\mathbf{D})$ have been implemented. We will return to a possible treatment of nominals in our approach later.

The translation algorithm is schematically depicted in Figure 2. It transforms a $\mathcal{SHIQ}(\mathbf{D})$ knowledge base KB into a disjunctive datalog program $DD(KB)$. The steps of the algorithm are as follows. (1) Transitivity axioms are removed by adding axioms of a form similar to $\forall S.C \sqsubseteq \forall S.(\forall S.C)$ for transitive roles S. (2) The knowledge base is translated into clausal form by standard transformations based on first-order predicate logic. This introduces function symbols due

Fig. 2. Algorithm for Reducing $\mathcal{SHIQ}(\mathbf{D})$ to Datalog Programs

to necessary skolemization steps. (3) The TBox of the knowledge base is partially saturated by adding logical consequences. This is the crucial step of the algorithm. (4) The saturation from step (3) now allows to remove all function symbols which were introduced in step (2). Some additional axioms are added to ensure that the algorithm remains sound and complete. (5) The knowledge base is translated into disjunctive datalog clauses; this step is now straightforward.

It shall be noted that the details of the crucial step (3) are very sophisticated. They guarantee that the removal of function symbols in step (4) is at all possible. Step (3) is of exponential complexity, however for the ABox reasoning task which we focus on in this paper, Step (3) can in principle be performed offline, as this step is independent of the ABox – but note that this offline computation may still be difficult if the TBox is large, which is a seperate issue and deserves further in-depth studies which are outside the scope of this paper. A full presentation of the translation with correctness proofs is technically involved and lengthy, and space restrictions forbid to go into further detail; we refer the interested reader to [2, 3]. In [1] full proofs are given which show amongst other things that KB is unsatisfiable if and only if $DD(KB)$ is unsatisfiable. This suffices for reasoning over KB as reasoning tasks can be transformed into unsatisfiability checks.

5   Approximate Resolution

While approximate reasoning methods for propositional and first-order logic have been proposed (see e.g. [13, 14, 15, 16, 17, 18]), they have hardly been applied in the context of Semantic Web technologies. The few exceptions are reported e.g. in [19, 20, 21] — to the best of our knowledge, this list is exhaustive. The success of the approaches is mixed. [21] reports on an analysis indicating that straightforward adaptations of methods proposed by [14] do not suffice. [20] reports good results but is not an approximate reasoning method in the more narrow sense as the reasoning performed is exact, and thus does not address the complexity problems underlying OWL DL reasoning. [19] deals with approximating queries, while we focus on ABox reasoning. We will now present a novel approach based on the translation of OWL DL to disjunctive datalog, as presented earlier.

5.1   Approximate SLD-Resolution

Having obtained the translated knowledge base in the form of a disjunctive datalog program, ABox reasoning remains NP-hard, and thus untractable. If the datalog program is non-disjunctive, though, reasoning is polynomial in the size of the ABox. We therefore propose the following approximate reasoning technique in order to facilitate this insight. Given a conjunctive query $B_1 \wedge \cdots \wedge B_n$, an *approximate SLD-resolution step* on the atom B_i with a disjunctive rule $H_1 \vee \cdots \vee H_m \leftarrow A_1, \ldots, A_k$ is a conjunctive query

$$B_1 \theta \wedge \cdots \wedge B_{i-1} \theta \wedge A_1 \theta \wedge \cdots \wedge A_k \theta \wedge B_{i+1} \theta \wedge \cdots \wedge B_n \theta$$

such that θ is the most general unifier of B_i and some H_j. *Approximate SLD-refutation* is defined analogously to SLD-refutation, where approximate SLD-resolution steps are used instead of (usual) SLD-resolution steps.

It is necessary to pursue the question what notion of entailment underlies the approximate reasoning technique we propose. Following the spirit of the obervations from Section 2, we want to identify the set of models which underly the inference relation provided by approximate SLD-resolution. For this purpose, we need the following notion, which is derived from standard notions in non-monotonic reasoning over logic programs.

Definition 1 (cf. [22, 23, 24]). *A model M of a disjunctive program P is called* well-supported *if there exists a function $l : B_P \to \mathbb{N}$ such that for each $A \in M$ there exists a rule $A \vee H_1 \vee \cdots \vee H_m \leftarrow A_1, \ldots, A_k$ in* ground(P) *with $M \models A_i$ and $l(A) > l(A_i)$ for all i and k.*

Definition 1 is a straightforward adaptation of the notion of well-supported model for non-disjunctive programs, as given in [23]. For non-disjunctive (and negation-free) programs, the well-supported models are exactly the minimal ones, but this is not in general the case for disjunctive programs: Just consider the program consisting of the single rule $p \vee q \leftarrow$. Then $\{p, q\}$ is a well-supported model, but is not minimal.

Lifted appropriately to (non-disjunctive) programs with negation, the well-supported models coincide with the well-known stable models. This was shown in [23] and studied in-depth in [24, 25]. Stable models [26] provide the base for the most popular non-monotonic reasoning paradigm called *Answer Set Programming*, of which the two most prominent implementations are DLV and SMODELS [27, 28]. Our results thus stand within this well-established tradition.

It is apparent that $A \in B_P$ is entailed by a (disjunctive) program P by approximate SLD-resolution if and only if it is true in at least one well-supported model of P. This is called *brave reasoning with well-supported models*. A formal proof of the following proposition is omitted for space restrictions.

Proposition 1. *Entailment of ground conjunctive queries under approximate SLD-resolution is brave reasoning with well-supported models.*

As an example, consider the (propositional) program consisting of the two rules $p \vee q \leftarrow$ and $r \leftarrow p \wedge q$. Its minimal models are $\{q\}$ and $\{p\}$, so r is not bravely entailed by reasoning with minimal models. However all of $\{q\}$, $\{p\}$, $\{p, q\}$ and $\{p, q, r\}$ are well-supported models, so r is bravely entailed by reasoning with well-supported models.

There is an alternative way of formalizing approximate SLD-resolution using a modified notion of *split program* [29]. Given a rule

$$H_1 \vee \cdots \vee H_m \leftarrow A_1, \ldots, A_k,$$

the *derived split rules* are defined as:

$$H_1 \leftarrow A_1, \ldots, A_k \quad \ldots \quad H_m \leftarrow A_1, \ldots, A_k.$$

For a given disjunctive program P its *split program* P' is defined as the collection of all split rules derived from rules in P. Approximate SLD-resolution on P is obviously identical to SLD-resolution over P'.

Minimal models are well-supported, as can be seen from the following result which was obtained along the lines of research laid out in [24, 25].

Theorem 2 ([30]). *Let P be a disjunctive program. Then a model M of P is a minimal model of P if and only if there exists a function $l : B_P \to \mathbb{N}$ such that for each A which is true in M there exists a rule $A \vee H_1 \vee \cdots \vee H_m \leftarrow A_1, \ldots, A_k$ in $\mathsf{ground}(P)$ with $M \models A_i$, $M \not\models H_k$ and $l(A) > l(A_i)$ for all i and k.*

We hence have the following result, noting that $P \models Q$ for any ground conjunctive query Q and program P if and only if Q is true in all minimal models of P.

Proposition 2. *Let P be a (possibly disjunctive) program and Q be a ground conjunctive query with $P \models Q$. Then there exists an approximate SLD-refutation for Q.*

We remark that for negation-free disjunctive programs minimal models again coincide with *answer sets* [26], as in the currently evolving *Answer Set Programming Systems*, as already mentioned.

5.2   Approximate Resolution for OWL DL

Our proposal is based on the idea of converting a given OWL DL knowledge base into a function-free definite disjunctive logic program, and then to apply approximate resolution for ABox reasoning.

In order to be able to deal with all of OWL DL, we need to add a pre-processing step to get rid of nominals, i.e. we need to compile $\mathcal{SHOIN}(\mathbf{D})$ ontologies to $\mathcal{SHIQ}(\mathbf{D})$. We can do this by *Language Weakening* as follows: For every occurrence of $\{o_1, \ldots, o_n\}$, where $n \in \mathbb{N}$ and the o_i are abstract or concrete individuals, replace $\{o_1, \ldots, o_n\}$ by some new concept name D, and add ABox assertions $D(o_1), \ldots, D(o_n)$ to the knowledge base. Note that the transformation just given does in general not yield a logically equivalent knowledge base, so some information is lost in the process. Putting all the pieces together, we propose the following subsequent steps for approximate ABox reasoning for OWL DL.

1. Apply Language Weakening as just mentioned in order to obtain a $\mathcal{SHIQ}(\mathbf{D})$ knowledge base.
2. Apply transformations as in Section 4 in order to obtain a negation-free disjunctive datalog program.
3. Apply approximate SLD-resolution for query-answering.

The first two steps can be considered to be preprocessing steps for setting up the intensional part of the database. ABox reasoning is then done in the last step. From our discussions, we can conclude the following properties of approximate ABox reasoning for $\mathcal{SHIQ}(\mathbf{D})$.

- It is complete with respect to first-order predicate logic semantics.
- It is sound and complete wrt. brave reasoning with well-supported models.
- Data complexity of our approach is polynomial.

6   Screech OWL

A preliminary implementation of our approach is available as the SCREECH OWL approximate reasoner.[2] It is part of the KAON2 OWL tools.[3]

KAON2[4] is the KArlsruhe ONtology framework, which includes a fast OWL reasoner based on the transformation algorithms mentioned in Section 4, and also includes many other features helpful to work with ontologies. Among the KAON2 OWL tools, deo performs the language weakening step described in Section 5.2 in order to obtain a $\mathcal{SHIQ}(\mathbf{D})$ knowledge base. As KAON2 implements the sophisticated translation algorithms described in Section 4, we can convert an OWL ontology into a disjunctive datalog program, e.g. by using the dlpconvert KAON2 OWL tool with the -x switch.

SCREECH then accesses the results of the translation through the KAON2 API, creates the corresponding split programs and serialises them as Horn logic programs in Edinburgh Prolog syntax. The result can be fed to any Prolog interpreter — or other logic programming engine —, which in turn can be used to perform ABox reasoning and inferencing over the knowledge base.

For completeness, we need to mention that in general support for concrete domains and other features like integrity constraints is not necessarily implemented in off-the-shelf logic programming systems. In these cases, concrete domains etc. cannot be used. The KAON2 OWL tool ded,[3] for example, performs a language weakening step by removing all concrete domains, and may come in handy in such situations.

7   An Example

We demonstrate our approach by means of a simple OWL DL ontology. It contains only a class hierarchy and an ABox, and no roles, but this will suffice to display the main issues.

---

[2] http://logic.aifb.uni-karlsruhe.de/screech
[3] http://www.aifb.uni-karlsruhe.de/WBS/dvr/owltools
[4] http://kaon2.semanticweb.org

$$\text{serbian} \sqcup \text{croatian} \sqsubseteq \text{european}$$
$$\text{eucitizen} \sqsubseteq \text{european}$$
$$\text{german} \sqcup \text{french} \sqcup \text{beneluxian} \sqsubseteq \text{eucitizen}$$
$$\text{beneluxian} \equiv \text{luxembourgian} \sqcup \text{dutch} \sqcup \text{belgian}$$

serbian(ljiljana)   serbian(nenad)   german(pascal)   french(julien)
croatian(boris)   german(markus)   german(stephan)   croatian(denny)
indian(sudhir)   belgian(saartje)   german(rudi)   german(york)

Fig. 3. Example ontology

The ontology is shown in Figure 3, and its intended meaning is self-explanatory. Note that the fourth line,

$$\text{beneluxian} \equiv \text{luxembourgian} \sqcup \text{dutch} \sqcup \text{belgian},$$

translates into the four clauses

$$\text{luxembourgian}(x) \lor \text{dutch}(x) \lor \text{belgian}(x) \leftarrow \text{beneluxian}(x), \qquad (1)$$
$$\text{beneluxian}(x) \leftarrow \text{luxembourgian}(x),$$
$$\text{beneluxian}(x) \leftarrow \text{dutch},$$
$$\text{and} \qquad \text{beneluxian}(x) \leftarrow \text{belgian}(x).$$

Thus, our approach changes the ontology by treating the disjunctions in line (1) as conjunctions. This change affects the soundness of the reasoning procedure. However, most of the ABox consequences which can be derived by approximate SLD-resolution are still correct. Indeed, there are only two derivable facts which do not follow from the knowledge base by classical reasoning, namely

$$\text{dutch(saartje)} \qquad \text{and} \qquad \text{luxemburgian(saartje)}.$$

All other derivable facts are correct.

SCREECH translates the ontology from Figure 3 into the Prolog program listed in Figure 4. As standard implementations of SLD-resolution do not use fair selection functions and also use depth-first search for higher efficiency, they may sometimes fail to produce answers because they run into infinite branches of the search tree. This occurs, for example, when using SWI-Prolog[5]. A reordering of the clauses may improve the results, but does not solve the problem entirely. More satisfactory performance can be obtained by using SLD-resolution with tabling, as implemented e.g. in the XSB Prolog system[6]. In this case, all desired consequences can be derived.

[5] http://www.swi-prolog.org/
[6] http://xsb.sourceforge.net

```
serbian(ljiljana).    serbian(nenad).      german(pascal).    french(julien).
croatian(boris).      german(markus).      german(stephan).   croatian(denny).
indian(sudhir).       belgian(saartje).    german(rudi).      german(york).
european(X)           :- serbian(X).
european(X)           :- croatian(X).
european(X)           :- eucitizen(X).
eucitizen(X)          :- german(X).
eucitizen(X)          :- french(X).
eucitizen(X)          :- beneluxian(X).
beneluxian(X)         :- luxembourgian(X).
beneluxian(X)         :- dutch(X).
beneluxian(X)         :- belgian(X).
dutch(X)              :- beneluxian(X).
luxembourgian(X)      :- beneluxian(X).
belgian(X)            :- beneluxian(X).
```

Fig. 4. Example SCREECH output

8   Experiments and Evaluation

An approximate reasoning procedure needs to be evaluated on real data from practical applications. Handcrafted examples are of only limited use as the applicability of approximate methods depends on the structure inherent in the experimental data.

For our evaluation we have performed experiments with the OWL DL version of the GALEN Upper Ontology,[7] as it appears to be sufficiently natural and realistic. As it is a TBox ontology only, we populated GALEN's 175 classes randomly with 500 individuals.[8] GALEN does not contain nominals or concrete domains. GALEN has 673 axioms (the population added another 500). The TBox translation to disjunctive datalog took about 2300 ms, after which we obtained 2687 disjunctive datalog rules containing 267 disjunctions within 133 rules. Among these were 152 integrity constraints (i.e. rules with empty head), which we removed for our experiment as they led to inconsistency of the database.[9] After splitting disjunctive rules, we arrived at 2802 Horn rules.

We then randomly selected classes and queried for their extension using the KAON2 datalog engine, both for processing the disjunctive datalog program and for the split program. Some of the typical results are listed in Table 2, which indicates a significant speed-up of more than 40% on average, while the vast majority of the retrieved answers is correct. Note that we obtain significant speed-up although the KAON2 datalog engine is not optimized for Horn programs, but rather tuned to efficient performance on definite disjunctive datalog.

---

[7] http://www.cs.man.ac.uk/~rector/ontologies/simple-top-bio/
[8] Using the pop KAON2 OWL tool.
[9] This is an expected effect. Removal of the integrity constraints does not destroy completeness of the approximate reasoning procedure.

Table 2. Performance comparison for instance retrieval using disjunctive datalog (DD) vs. the corresponding split program (SPLIT), on the KAON2 datalog engine. *Instances* indicates the number of instances retrieved using DD versus SPLIT, e.g. class *Multiple* contained 9 individuals, while the split program allowed to retrieve 13 (i.e. the 9 correct individuals plus 4 incorrect ones). The full name of the class in the last row is Biological_object_that_has_left_right_symmetry.

Time (DD)	Time (SPLIT)	Instances	Class Name
11036 ms	6489 ms	154/154	Biological_object
11026 ms	5959 ms	9/9	Specified_set
11006 ms	6219 ms	9/13	Multiple
11015 ms	5898 ms	16/16	Probe_structural_part_of_heart
11036 ms	7711 ms	4/4	Human_red_blood_cell_mature
11055 ms	5949 ms	24/58	Biological_object_that...

The times were obtained with initial Java VM memory set to 256 MByte. Under memory restrictions, the speed-up is more significant, which is probably caused by the necessity to allocate additional memory for the DD reasoning task. Corresponding figures are given in Table 3. Our experiments also indicate that SCREECH may be useful when hardware is limited, for example in portable devices.

9   Conclusions and Further Work

In a nutshell, our proposed procedure approximates reasoning by disregarding non-Horn features of OWL DL ontologies. We argue that this is a reasonable approach to approximate reasoning with OWL DL in particular because many of the currently existing ontologies rarely use language constructs that do not fall into the Horn fragment of OWL DL [31]. So it can be projected that even in the future these constructs will play a minor role and thus should be the first to be tempered with in order to gain tractable reasoning.

Our approach provides ABox reasoning with polynomial time complexity. While it is complete, it is also unsound with respect to first-order logic. We have shown, however, that the inference underlying our approach can be characterized using standard methods from the area of non-monotonic reasoning. We have also presented our implementation SCREECH, and verified the usefulness of our approach by means of experiments.

Table 3. Performance comparison as in Table 2, but with 128 MByte intial memory

Time (DD)	Time (SPLIT)	Instances	Class Name
32997 ms	4817 ms	154/154	Biological_object
33028 ms	4947 ms	9/9	Specified_set
32927 ms	4987 ms	9/13	Multiple
32977 ms	4957 ms	16/16	Probe_structural_part_of_heart
32987 ms	7350 ms	4/4	Human_red_blood_cell_mature
32947 ms	4796 ms	24/58	Biological_object_that...

The checking whether a conjunctive query is a predicate logic consequence of a (negation-free) disjunctive logic program P amounts to checking whether the query is valid in *all* minimal models of P, i.e. corresponds to *cautious* reasoning with minimal models. Theorem 2 suggests how an anytime algorithm for this might be obtained: After performing approximate SLD-resolution, it remains to be checked whether there is any (ground instance of a) rule used in the refutation of the query, which has an atom A in its head besides the one used in the refutation and such that A is (cautiously) entailed by the program. Such an algorithm might then first find a brave proof of a query, and then substantiate this proof by subsequent calculations. Our approach may also be useful for the quick derivation of *possible* answers to a query, which may then be used for efficient guidance of the search within a sound and complete OWL reasoner. These and other issues are currently under investigation.

Acknowledgement. We are grateful for discussions with Boris Motik about his and our work.

References

1. Hustadt, U., Motik, B., Sattler, U.: Reasoning for Description Logics around $\mathcal{SHIQ}$ in a Resolution Framework. Technical Report 3-8-04/04, FZI, Karlsruhe, Germany (2004) http://www.fzi.de/wim/publikationen.php?id=1172.
2. Hustadt, U., Motik, B., Sattler, U.: Reducing $\mathcal{SHIQ}^-$ Description Logic to Disjunctive Datalog Programs. In: Proc. of the 9th Conference on Knowledge Representation and Reasoning (KR2004), AAAI Press (2004)
3. Hustadt, U., Motik, B., Sattler, U.: Reasoning in description logics with a concrete domain in the framework of resolution. In de Mántaras, R.L., Saitta, L., eds.: Proceedings of the 16th Eureopean Conference on Artificial Intelligence, ECAI'2004, including Prestigious Applicants of Intelligent Systems, PAIS 2004, Valencia, Spain, August 22-27, 2004, IOS Press (2004) 353–357
4. Motik, B., Sattler, U., Studer, R.: Query answering for OWL-DL with rules. In: Proceedings of the 3rd International Semantic Web Conference (ISWC2004), Hiroshima, Japan, November 2004. (2004) To appear.
5. W3C: Web ontology language (OWL). www.w3.org/2004/OWL/ (2004)
6. Baader, F., Calvanese, D., McGuinness, D., Nardi, D., Patel-Schneider, P., eds.: The Description Logic Handbook. Cambridge University Press (2003)
7. Hustadt, U., Motik, B., Sattler, U.: Data complexity of reasoning in very expressive description logics. In Kaelbling, L.P., Saffiotti, A., eds.: Proceedings of the Nineteenth International Joint Conference on Artificial Intelligence, Edinburgh, Scotland. (2005) 466–471
8. Makinson, D.: Bridges from Classical to Nonmonotonic Logic. Volume 5 of Texts in Computing. King's College Publications, London (2005)
9. Horrocks, I., Patel-Schneider, P.F.: A Proposal for an OWL Rules Language. In: Proc. of the Thirteenth Int'l World Wide Web Conf.(WWW 2004), ACM (2004)
10. Lutz, C.: Description Logics with Concrete Domains — A Survey. In: Advances in Modal Logics. Volume 4., King's College Publications (2003)
11. Horrocks, I., Sattler, U., Tobies, S.: Practical Reasoning for Very Expressive Description Logics. Logic Journal of the IGPL **8** (2000) 239–263
12. Lloyd, J.W.: Foundations of Logic Programming. Springer, Berlin (1988)

13. Selman, B., Kautz, H.A.: Knowledge compilation using Horn approximations. In: Proceedings of the Ninth National Conference on Artificial Intelligence (AAAI-91). (1991) 904–909
14. Schaerf, M., Cadoli, M.: Tractable reasoning via approximation. Artificial Intelligence **74** (1995) 249–310
15. Dalal, M.: Anytime clausal reasoning. Annals of Mathematics and Artificial Intelligence **22** (1998) 297–318
16. Cadoli, M., Scarcello, F.: Semantical and computational aspects of Horn approximations. Artificial Intelligence **119** (2000)
17. van Harmelen, F., ten Teije, A.: Describing problem solving methods using anytime performance profiles. In: Proceedings of ECAI'00, Berlin (2000) 181–186
18. Groot, P., ten Teije, A., van Harmelen, F.: Towards a structured analysis of approximate problem solving: a case study in classification. In: Proceedings of the Ninth International Conference on Principles of Knowledge Representation and Reasoning (KR'04), Whistler, Colorado (2004)
19. Stuckenschmidt, H., van Harmelen, F.: Approximating terminological queries. In Larsen, H., et al, eds.: Proc. of the 4th International Conference on Flexible Query Answering Systems (FQAS)'02). Advances in Soft Computing, Springer (2002)
20. Horrocks, I., Li, L., Turi, D., Bechhofer, S.: The Instance Store: DL reasoning with large numbers of individuals. In: Proceedings of the International Workshop on Description Logics, DL2004, Whistler, Canada. (2004) 31–40
21. Groot, P., Stuckenschmidt, H., Wache, H.: Approximating description logic classification for semantic web reasoning. In Gómez-Pérez, A., Euzenat, J., eds.: The Semantic Web: Research and Applications, Second European Semantic Web Conference, ESWC 2005, Heraklion, Crete, Greece, May 29 - June 1, 2005, Proceedings. Volume 3532 of Lecture Notes in Computer Science., Springer (2005) 318–332
22. Apt, K.R., Blair, H.A., Walker, A.: Towards a theory of declarative knowledge. In Minker, J., ed.: Foundations of Deductive Databases and Logic Programming. Morgan Kaufmann, Los Altos, CA (1988) 89–148
23. Fages, F.: Consistency of Clark's completion and existence of stable models. Journal of Methods of Logic in Computer Science **1** (1994) 51–60
24. Hitzler, P., Wendt, M.: A uniform approach to logic programming semantics. Theory and Practice of Logic Programming **5** (2005) 123–159
25. Hitzler, P.: Towards a systematic account of different semantics for logic programs. Journal of Logic and Computation **15** (2005) 391–404
26. Gelfond, M., Lifschitz, V.: Classical negation in logic programs and disjunctive databases. New Generation Computing **9** (1991) 365–385
27. Eiter, T., Leone, N., Mateis, C., Pfeifer, G., Scarcello, F.: A deductive system for nonmonotonic reasoning. In Dix, J., et al, eds.: Proceedings of the 4th International Conference on Logic Programming and Nonmonotonic Reasoning (LPNMR'97). Volume 1265 of Lecture Notes in Artificial Intelligence., Springer, Berlin (1997)
28. Simons, P., Niemelä, I., Soininen, T.: Extending and implementing the stable model semantics. Artificial Intelligence **138** (2002) 181–234
29. Sakama, C., Inoue, K.: An alternative approach to the semantics of disjunctive logic programs and deductive databases. Journal of Automated Reasoning **13** (1994) 145–172
30. Knorr, M.: Level mapping characterizations for quantitative and disjunctive logic programs. Bachelor's Thesis, Department of Computer Science, Technische Universität Dresden, Germany (2003)
31. Volz, R.: Web Ontology Reasoning with Logic Databases. PhD thesis, AIFB, University of Karlsruhe (2004)

Reasoning with Multi-version Ontologies: A Temporal Logic Approach

Zhisheng Huang and Heiner Stuckenschmidt

AI Department, Vrije Universiteit Amsterdam, The Netherlands
{huang, heiner}@cs.vu.nl

Abstract. In this paper we propose a framework for reasoning with multi-version ontology, in which a temporal logic is developed to serve as its semantic foundation. We show that the temporal logic approach can provide a solid semantic foundation which can support various requirements on multi-version ontology reasoning. We have implemented the prototype of MORE (Multi-version Ontology REasoner), which is based on the proposed framework. We have tested MORE with several realistic ontologies. In this paper, we also discuss the implementation issues and report the experiments with MORE.

1 Introduction

When an ontology is changed, the ontology developers may want to keep the older versions of the ontology. Although maintaining multi-version ontologies increases the resource cost, it is still very useful because of the following benefits:

- **Change Recovery.** For ontology developers, the latest version of an ontology is usually less stable than the previous ones, because the new changes have been introduced on it, and those changes and their consequences have not yet been fully recognized and evaluated. Maintaining the previous versions of the ontology would allow the possibilities for the developers to withdraw or adjust the changes to avoid unintended impacts.
- **Compatibility.** Ontology users may still want to use an earlier version of the ontology despite the new changes, because they may consider the functionalities of the earlier version of the ontology are sufficient for their needs. Furthermore, multi-version ontologies may have different resource requirement. Ontology users may prefer an earlier version with less resource requirement to a newer version with higher resource requirement.

The list above is not complete. We are going to discuss more benefits in the next section. Those benefits can justify to some extent that multi-version ontology management and reasoning systems are really useful. The change recovery requires that the system provides a facility to evaluate the consequences raising from ontology changes and a tool to compare multi-versions of the ontology. Selecting a compatible version needs a system that can support a query language for reasoning on a selected version of the ontology. This requires a query language which can express

Y. Gil et al. (Eds.): ISWC 2005, LNCS 3729, pp. 398–412, 2005.

the temporal aspects of the ontology changes. Intuitively multiple versions of an ontology can be considered as a temporal sequence of change actions on an ontology. That serves as our departure point in this paper. In this paper we will investigate how temporal logics serve as the semantic foundation of multi-version ontology reasoning. We propose a framework of reasoning with multi-version ontologies which is based on a temporal logic approach. We will show that the temporal logic can provide a solid semantic foundation which serve as an extended query language to detect the ontology changes and their consequences. We have implemented the prototype of MORE (Multi-version Ontology REasoner), which extends existing systems for querying Description Logic Ontologies with temporal operators that support the maintenance of multiple versions of the same ontology. We discuss the implementation of the MORE prototype and report the preliminary experiences with applying MORE to realistic ontologies.

This paper is organized as follows: Section 2 provides a brief survey on ontology evolution and versioning. Section 3 discusses the problem of multi-version ontology reasoning. Section 4 presents a temporal logic for reasoning with multi-version ontologies. Section 5 shows how the proposed temporal logic can serve as a query language for reasoning with multi-version ontologies. Section 6 discusses the implementation issues of MORE and reports the experiments with MORE. Section 7 discusses related work, further work, and concludes the paper.

2 Solved and Open Problems in Ontology Evolution

Database schema evolution is an important area related to the problem of ontology evolution. In the following, we summarize some of the basic requirements for schema evolution and versioning that have been stated in connection with the problem of schema evolution for object oriented databases that are most relevant for the problem of ontology evolution.

Evolvability. The basic requirement in connection with schema evolution is the availability of a suitable apparatus for evolving the schema in terms of *change operations* and a *structure for representing changes.*

Integrity. An important aspect of schema evolution is to preserve the integrity of the database during change. *Syntactic conflicts* may occur for example due to multiply defined attribute names in the same class . Further, *semantic conflicts* can appear if changes to the schema break up referential integrity or if the modification of an integrity constraints makes it in compatible with another one.

Compatibility. The literature mentions two aspects of compatibility: *downward compatibility* means that systems that were based on the old version of the schema can still use the database after the evolution. *Upward compatibility* means that system that are built on top of the new schema can still access the old data.

In principle, the issues discussed above are also relevant for the problem of ontology evolution. In the following, we summarize recent work that addressed the different aspects mentioned above for the special case of ontologies.

Evolvability. The evolvability of ontologies has been addressed by different researchers by defining change operations and change representations for ontology languages. Change operations have been proposed for specific ontology languages. In particular change operations have been defined for OKBC, OWL [12] and for the KAON ontology language [15]. All approaches distinguish between atom and complex changes. Different ways of representing ontological changes have been proposed: besides the obvious representation as a change log that contains a sequence of operations, authors have proposed to represent changes in terms of mappings between two versions of the same ontology [13].

Integrity. The problem of preserving integrity in the case of changes is also present for ontology evolution. On the one hand the problem is harder here as ontologies are often encoded using a logical language where changes can quickly lead to logical inconsistency that cannot directly be determined by looking at the change operation. On the other hand, there are logical reasoners that can be used to detect inconsistencies both within the ontology and with respect to instance data. As this kind of reasoning is often costly, heuristic approaches for determining inconsistencies have been proposed [16, 12]. While deciding whether an ontology is consistent or not can easily be done using existing technologies, repairing inconsistencies in ontologies is an open problem although there is some preliminary work on diagnosing the reasons for an inconsistency which is prerequisite for a successful repair [14].

Compatibility. The problem of compatibility with applications that use an ontology has received little attention so far. The problem is that the impact of a change in the ontology on the function of the system is hard to predict and strongly depends on the application that uses the ontology. Part of the problem is the fact that ontologies are often not just used as a fixed structure but as the basis for deductive reasoning. The functionality of the system often depends on the result of this deduction process and unwanted behavior can occur as a result of changes in the ontology. Some attempts have been made to characterize change and evolution multiple versions on a semantic level [10, 9]. This work provides the basis for analyzing compatibility which currently is an open problem.

We conclude that at the current state of research the problem of defining the basic apparatus for performing ontology evolution in terms of change operations and representation of changes is understood. Open questions with respect to ontology evolution mainly concern the problem of dealing with integrity problems and with ensuring compatibility of the ontology with existing applications. The basic problem that has to address in the context of both of these topic lies in the logical nature of many ontology specifications. We therefore need methods that work a the semantic level and are aware of logical implications caused by changes. The formal characterization of ontology evolution provided by Heflin is a step in the right direction, but it does not provide any concrete methods for supporting evolution that are necessary to resolve existing problems with respect to dealing with inconsistency or determining compatibility.

3   Multi-version Management: An Open Problem

The aim of this work is to provide basic support for solving the open problems in ontology evolution, in particular with respect to the problem of compatibility to existing applications. As argued above, in order to support compatibility an analysis of changes on a syntactic and structural level is not sufficient as the function of applications often depends on the result of reasoning processes.

Our goal is to provide ontology managers and users with a tool that helps to detect effects of changes in ontologies and select versions based on their propoerties. Another more ambitious goal for the future is to also provide support for predicting such effects before the ontology has actually been changed [7]. In this section, we introduce the general idea of providing tool support for this purpose and identify relevant use cases for the technology.

3.1   Application Scenarios

The development of our method is based on the assumption that different versions of an ontology are managed on a central server. In a commercial setting, ontologies are normally created and maintained on a development server. Stable versions of the ontology are moved to a production server which publishes the corresponding models and therefore plays the role of the central server. Further Compatangelo et al propose a blackboard architecture [5] that also allows the centralized management of different ontology versions in distributed environments and makes our approach applicable also in the distributed setting. Based on this general assumption, there are a number of quite relevant application scenarios for the version management technology sketched above. In the following, we provide a number of use cases for Multi-version Reasoning including typical relevant questions about the relation between statements in different versions of an ontology.

Semantic Change Log.   The ontology provider wants to inform the users of the ontology about changes in the new version. The idea is that the new version of the ontology is added to the system which automatically computes all changes with respect to a certain facts. A typical case would be that all subsumption relations are checked. The system outputs a list of obsolete subsumption relations and a list of new subsumption relations.

Version Selection.   The user needs an ontology with particular properties for his application. He wants to know which version of ontology fits his specific requirements best. For this purpose, the user defines a number of statements that he wants to hold. The systems identifies the latest version of the ontology in which the required statements hold.

Evolution Planning.   Based on customer feedback and requests, the ontology provider wants to determine useful and harmful changes to plan the future evolution of the ontology. In particular this includes determining necessary changes that will make it possible to derive certain wanted statements and the analysis of different development choices using defeasible reasoning techniques.

3.2   The General Approach

The different use cases described above have quite different requirements with respect to inferences that have to be supported. The common feature of all use cases, however, is that they require to reason in the individual ontologies and about the whole set of versions and their relations to each other. While there are existing tools for reasoning with ontologies (i.e. Description Logic Reasoners), being able to reason about different versions is an open issue. In our approach, we mainly address this issue of reasoning about the set of all versions. We do this based on the notion of a version space. A version space is a graph in which different versions of the same ontology form the nodes. Edges represent change operations that led to a new version. We use modal logic to make statements about version spaces, interpreting each version of the ontology as a possible world and change operations the accessibility relation. Queries about a concrete set of versions can now be formulated as a formula in modal logics and model checking techniques can be used to determine whether the version space at hand has the properties specified in the query. In order to determine the facts that hold in a particular world, we use an existing reasoner to derive statements implied by a certain version of the ontology.

The choice of the concrete approach and in particular, the concrete logic to be used to reason about the version space strongly depends on the requirements of the use case. When we look at the three use cases mentioned above, we can see that they have quite different requirements with respect to the expressive power of the query language. The semantic change log only need a very simple logic enabling us to compare different worlds and the statements that hold in each of them. As we will see below, this can be done using a simple temporal logic. Version selection requires explicit references to possible worlds that represent certain versions. This kind of expressiveness is provided by hybrid modal logics [2]. In contrast to the other use cases, evaluation planning requires explicit representations of change operations in the logical language. This requirement is met by dynamic logics [8] that would be appropriate for this use case.

In the remainder of this paper, we discuss a concrete implementation of the general approach outlined above. This concrete implementation addresses the first of the use cases, namely the semantic change log and makes a number of simplifying assumptions in terms of the structure of the version space and the types of statements about an ontology that can be used in queries about the version space. These simplifying assumptions are not general limitations of the approach but address the practical needs of our work in the context of the SEKT Project. In future work, we will extend the MORE system to also meet the requirements of the other use cases.

4   A Temporal Logic for Multi-version Ontology Reasoning

Temporal logics can be classified as two main classes with respect to two different time models: linear time model and branching time model. The linear time logics which express properties over a single sequence of states. This view is suitable for the retrospective approach to multi-ontology reasoning where we assume a sequence of versions. Branching time logics express properties across different sequences of states. This feature would be needed for the prospective approach where we consider different possible sequences of changes in the future. The linear temporal logic **LTL** is a typical temporal logic for modeling linear time, whereas the computation tree logic **CTL** is a typical one for modeling branching time [3, 4].

Temporal logics are often future-oriented, because their operators are designed to be ones which involve the future states. Typical operators are: the operator **Future** ϕ which states that 'ϕ holds sometimes in the future with respect to the current state', and the operator **Alwaysf** ϕ which states that 'ϕ always holds in the future with respect to the current state', and the operator ϕ **Until** ψ which states that 'ϕ always holds in the future until ψ holds'. For a discrete time model, the operator **Next** ϕ is introduced to state that ϕ holds at the next state with respect to the current state. For the retrospective reasoning, we only need a temporal logic that only talks about the past. Namely, it is one which can be used to compare the current state with some previous states in the past. It is natural to design the following past-oriented operators, which correspond with the counterparts of the future oriented temporal operators respectively:

- the previous operator states that a fact ϕ holds just one state before the current state the current state.
- the sometimes-in-the past operator states that a fact ϕ holds sometimes in the past with respect to the current state.
- the always-in-the-past operator states that ϕ holds always in the past with respect to the current state.

In this paper, we use a linear temporal logic, denoted as **LTLm**, which actually is a restricted linear temporal logic **LTL** to past-oriented temporal operators.

4.1 Version Spaces and Temporal Models

In the following, we will define the formal semantics for the temporal operators by introducing an entailment relation between a semantic model (i.e., multi-version ontologies) and a temporal formula. We consider a version of an ontology to be a state in the semantic model. We do not restrict ontology specifications to a particular language (although OWL and its description logics are the languages we have in mind). In general, an ontology language can be considered to be a set of formulas that is generated by a set of syntactic rules in a logical language $\mathcal{L}$.

We consider multi-versions of an ontology as a sequence of ontologies which are connected each other via change operations. Each of these ontologies has a unique name. This is different from the work in [10], in which an ontology is considered as one which contains the set of other ontologies which are backwards compatible with. We have the following definition.

Definition 1 (Version Space). *A version space S over an ontology set Os is a set of ontology pairs, namely, $S \subseteq Os \times Os$.*

We use version spaces as a semantic model for our temporal logic, restricting our investigation to version spaces that present a linear sequence of ontologies:

Definition 2 (Linear Version Space). *A linear version space S on an ontology set Os is a version space which is a finite sequence of ontologies*

$$S = \{\langle o_1, o_2\rangle, \langle o_2, o_3\rangle, \cdots, \langle o_{n-1}, o_n\rangle\}$$

such that $i \neq j \Rightarrow o_i \neq o_j$. Alternatively we write the sequence S as follows:

$$S = (o_1, o_2, \cdots, o_n)$$

We use $S(i)$ to refer the i_th ontology o_i in the space. For a version space $S = (o_1, o_2, \cdots, o_n)$, We call the first ontology $S(1)$ in the space the *initial version of the version space*, and the last ontology $S(n)$ the *latest version of the version space* respectively.

We introduce an ordering $\prec_S$ with respect to a version space S as follows:

Definition 3 (Ordering on Version Space). $o \prec_S o'$ *iff o occurs prior to o' in the sequence S, i.e., $S = (\cdots, o, \cdots, o', \cdots)$.*

It is easy to see that the prior version relation $\prec_S$ is a linear ordering.

4.2 Syntax and Semantics of LTLm

The Language $\mathcal{L}+$ for the temporal logic **LTLm** can be defined as an extension to the ontology language $\mathcal{L}$ with Boolean operators and the temporal operators as follows:

$q \in \mathcal{L} \Rightarrow q \in \mathcal{L}+$
$\phi \in \mathcal{L}+ \Rightarrow \neg\phi \in \mathcal{L}+$
$\phi, \psi \in \mathcal{L}+ \Rightarrow \phi \wedge \psi \in \mathcal{L}+$
$\phi \in \mathcal{L}+ \Rightarrow \mathbf{PreviousVersion}\,\phi \in \mathcal{L}+$
$\phi \in \mathcal{L}+ \Rightarrow \mathbf{AllPriorVersions}\,\phi \in \mathcal{L}+$
$\phi, \psi \in \mathcal{L}+ \Rightarrow \phi\,\mathbf{Since}\,\psi \in \mathcal{L}+$

Where the negation $\neg$ and the conjunction $\wedge$ must be new symbols that do not appear in the language $\mathcal{L}$ to avoid the ambiguities. Define the disjunction $\vee$, the implication $\rightarrow$, and the bi-conditional $\leftrightarrow$ in terms of the conjunction and the negation as usual. Define $\bot$ as a contradictory $\phi \wedge \neg\phi$ and $\top$ as a tautology $\phi \vee \neg\phi$ respectively.

Using these basic operators, we can define some addition operators useful for reasoning about multiple versions. We define the **SomePriorVersion** operator in terms of the **AllPriorVersions** operator as

$$\mathbf{SomePriorVersion}\phi =_{df} \neg\mathbf{AllPriorVersions}\,\neg\phi$$

The always-in-the-past **AllPriorVersions** operator is one which does not consider the current state. We can define a strong always-in-the-past **AllVersions** operator as

$$\mathbf{AllVersions}\phi =_{df} \phi \wedge \mathbf{AllPriorVersions}\,\phi,$$

which states that 'ϕ always holds in the past including the current state'.

Let S be a version space on an ontology set Os, and o be an ontology in the set Os, we extend the entailment relation for the extended language $\mathcal{L}+$ as follows:

$$
\begin{aligned}
&S, o \models q && \text{iff } o \models q, \text{ for } q \in \mathcal{L}. \\
&S, o \models \neg\phi && \text{iff } S, o \not\models \phi. \\
&S, o \models \phi \wedge \psi && \text{iff } S, o \models \phi, \psi. \\
&S, o \models \textbf{PreviousVersion}\,\phi && \text{iff } \langle o', o \rangle \in S \text{ such that } S, o' \models \phi. \\
&S, o \models \textbf{AllPriorVersions}\,\phi && \text{iff } \text{for any } o' \text{ such that } o' \prec_S o, S, o' \models \phi. \\
&S, o \models \phi\textbf{Since}\psi && \text{iff } \exists(o_1 \ldots o_i)(\langle o_1, o_2\rangle, \ldots, \langle o_{i-1}, o_i\rangle \in S \text{ and } o_i = o) \\
&&& \text{such that } S, o_j \models \phi \text{ for } 1 \le j \le i \text{ and } S, o_1 \models \psi.
\end{aligned}
$$

For a linear version space S, we are in particular interested in the entailment relation with respect to its latest version of the ontology $S(n)$ in the version space S. We use $S \models \phi$ to denote that $S, S(n) \models \phi$. Model checking has been proved to be an efficient approach for the evaluation of temporal logic formulas [4]. In the implementation of MORE, we are going to use the standard model checking algorithm for evaluating a query in the temporal logic **LTLm**. Therefore, we do not need a complete axiomatization for the logic **LTLm** in this paper.

5   LTLm as a Query Language

There are two types of queries: reasoning queries and retrieval queries. The former concerns with an answer either 'yes' or 'no', and the latter concerns an answer with a particular value, like a set of individuals which satisfy the query formula. Namely, the evaluation of a reasoning query is a decision problem, whereas the evaluation of a retrieval query is a search problem. In this section, we are going to discuss how we can use the proposed temporal logic to support both reasoning queries and retrieval queries.

5.1   Reasoning Queries

Using the **LTLm** logic we can formulate reasoning queries over a sequence of ontologies that correspond to the typical questions mentioned in Section 3.

Are all facts still derivable? This question can be answered for individual facts using reasoning queries. In particular, we can use the query $\phi \wedge \textbf{PreviousVersion}\,\phi$ to determine for facts ϕ derivable from the previous version whether they still hold in the current version. The same can be done for older versions by chaining the **PreviousVersion** operator or by using the operator **AllVersions** to ask whether formulas was always true in past versions and is still true in the current one ($\textbf{AllVersions}\,\phi$).

What facts are not derivable any more? In a similar way, we can ask whether certain facts are not true in the new version any more. This is of particular use for making sure that unwanted consequences have been excluded in the new version. The corresponding query is $\neg\phi \wedge$ **PreviousVersion**ϕ. Using the **AllPriorVersions** operator, we can also ask whether a fact that was always true in previous versions is not true anymore.

What facts are newly derivable from the new version? Reasoning queries can also be used to determine whether a fact is new in the current version. As this is true if it is not true in the previous version, we can use the following query for checking this $\phi \wedge \neg$**PreviousVersion** ϕ. We can also check whether a new fact never holded in previous versions using the following query $\phi \wedge \neg$**SomePriorVersion** ϕ.

What is the last version that can be used to derive certain facts? Using reasoning queries we can check whether a fact holds in a particular version. As versions are arranged in a linear order, we can move to a particular version using the **PreviousVersion** operator. The query **PreviousVersion PreviousVersion** ϕ for instance checks whether ϕ was true in the version before the previous one. The query ϕ**Since**ψ states that ϕ always holds since ψ holds in a prior version.

A drawback of reasoning queries lies in the fact, that they can only check a property for a certain specific fact. When managing a different versions of a large ontology, the user will often not be interested in a particular fact, but ask about changes in general. This specific functionality is provided by retrieval queries.

5.2   Retrieval Queries

Many Description Logic Reasoners support so-called retrieval queries that return a set of concept names that satisfy a certain condition. For example, a children concept c' of a concept c, written $child(c, c')$, is defined as one which is subsumed by the concept c, and there exists no other concepts between them. Namely,

$$child(c, c') =_{df} c' \sqsubseteq c \wedge \not\exists c''(c' \sqsubseteq c'' \wedge c'' \sqsubseteq c \wedge c'' \neq c \wedge c'' \neq c').$$

Thus, the set of new/obsolete/invariant children concepts of a concept on an ontology o in the version space S is defined as follows

$$newChildren(S, o, c) =_{df} \{c'|S, o \models child(c, c') \wedge \neg\textbf{PreviousVersion } child(c, c')\}.$$

$$obsoleteChildren(S, o, c) =_{df} \{c'|S, o \models \neg child(c, c') \wedge \textbf{PreviousVersion } child(c, c')\}.$$

$$invariantChildren(S, o, c) =_{df} \{c'|S, o \models child(c, c') \wedge \textbf{PreviousVersion } child(c, c')\}.$$

The same definitions can be extended into the cases like parent concepts, ancestor concepts, descendant concept and equivalent concepts. Those query supports are sufficient to evaluate the consequences of the ontology changes and the differences among multi-version ontologies. We will discuss more details in the section about the tests on MORE.

5.3   Making Version-Numbers Explicit

Temporal logics allow us to talk about temporal aspects without reference to a particular time point. For reasoning with multi-version ontologies, we can also talk about temporal aspects without mentioning a particular version name. We know that each state in the temporal logic actually corresponds with a version of the ontology. It is not difficult to translate temporal statements into a statement which refers to an explicit version number. Here are two approaches for it: relative version numbering and absolute version numbering.

Relative version numbering. The proposed temporal logic is designed to be one for past-oriented. Therefore, it is quite natural to design a version numbering which is relative to the current ontology in the version space. We use the formula $\textbf{Version}_0 \phi$ to denote that the property holds in the current version. Namely, we refer to the current version as the version 0 in the version space, and other states are used to refer to a version relative to the current version, written as $\textbf{Version}_{-i}$ as follows:

$$\textbf{Version}_0 \phi =_{df} \phi.$$

$$\textbf{Version}_{(-i)} \phi =_{df} \textbf{Previous Version}(\textbf{Version}_{(1-i)} \phi).$$

The formula $\textbf{Version}_{-i} \phi$ can be read as 'the property ϕ holds in the previous i-th version'.

Absolute version numbering. Given a version space S with n ontologies on it, i.e., $|S| = n - 1$. For the latest version $o = S(n)$, it is well reasonable to call the i-th ontology $S(i)$ in the version space the version i of S, denoted as $\textbf{Version}_{i,S}$. Namely, we can use the formula $\textbf{Version}_{i,S} \phi$ to denote that the property ϕ holds in the version i in the version space S. Thus, we can define the absolute version statement in terms of a relative version statement as follows:

$$\textbf{Version}_{(i,S)} \phi =_{df} \textbf{Version}_{(i-n)} \phi.$$

Explicit version numbering provides the basis for more concrete retrieval queries. In particular, we now have the opportunity to compare the children of a concept c in two specific ontologies i and j in the version space S. The corresponding definitions are the following:

$newChildren(S, c)_{i,j} =_{df} \{c' | S \models \textbf{Version}_{(i,S)} \, child(c, c') \wedge \neg \textbf{Version}_{(j,S)} \, child(c, c')\}.$

$obsoleteChildren(S, c)_{i,j} =_{df} \{c' | S \models \neg \textbf{Version}_{(i,S)} \, child(c, c') \wedge \textbf{Version}_{(j,S)} \, child(c, c')\}.$

$invariantChildren(S, c)_{i,j} =_{df} \{c' | S \models \textbf{Version}_{(i,S)} \, child(c, c') \wedge \textbf{Version}_{(j,S)} \, child(c, c')\}.$

Again, the same can be done for other predicates like parent-, ancestor or descendant concepts.

6   Implementation of MORE

We implemented a prototypical reasoner for multi-version ontologies called MORE based on the approach described above. The system is implemented as an intelligent interface between an application and state-of-the art description logic reasoners (compare Fig.1) and provides server-side functionality in terms of an XML-based interface for uploading different versions of an ontology and posing queries to these versions. Requests to the server are analyzed by the main control component that also transforms queries into the underlying temporal logic queries if necessary. The main control element also interacts with the ontology repository and ensures that the reasoning components are provided with the necessary information and coordinates the information flow between the reasoning components. The actual reasoning is done by model checking components for testing temporal logic formulas that uses the results of an external description logic reasoner for answering queries about derivable acts in a certain version.

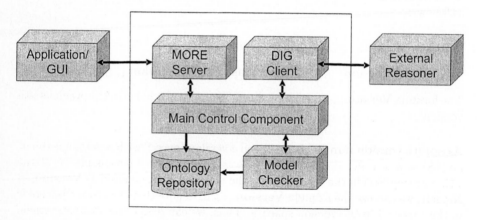

Fig. 1. Architecture of MORE

The MORE prototype is implemented in Prolog and uses the XDIG interface [11], an extended DIG description logic interface for Prolog[1]. MORE is designed to be a simple API for a general reasoner with multi-version ontologies. It supports extended DIG requests from other ontology applications or other ontology and metadata management systems and supports multiple ontology languages, including OWL and DIG [1][2]. This means that MORE can be used as an interface to any description logic reasoner as it supports the functionality of the underlying reasoner by just passing requests on and provides reasoning functionalities across versions if needed. Therefore, the implementation of MORE will be independent of those particular applications or systems. A prototype of MORE is available for download at the website: `http://wasp.cs.vu.nl/sekt/more`.

---

[1] http://wasp.cs.vu.nl/sekt/dig
[2] http://dl.kr.org/dig/

6.1   Experiments with MORE

We have tested the current implementation of the MORE system on different versions of real life ontologies from different domains. In the following, we briefly report experiments we performed on detecting changes in the concept hierarchy of the following two ontologies.

The OPJK Ontology.   The OPJK Ontology (Ontology of Professional Judicial Knowledge) is a legal Ontology that has been developed in the SEKT project[3] to support the content-based retrieval of legal documents[3]. We used five different versions of the ontology from different stages of the development process. Each of these version contains about 80 concepts and 60 relations.

The BiosSAIL Ontology.   The BioSAIL Ontology which was developed within the BioSTORM project[4]. It has been used in earlier experiments on change management reported in [12]. The complete data set consists of almost 20 different versions of the ontology. We take three versions of the BioSAIL ontology for the tests reported below. Each version of BioSAIL ontology has about 180 classes and around 70 properties.

Those two ontologies have been tested with different temporal reasoning queries. We concentrated on retrieval queries about the structure of the concept hierarchy. In particular, we used retrieval queries with explicit version numbering as introduced in section 5.3. In Fig.2 we show the results for the queries about the new and obsolete child, parent, ancestor, and descendant relations in the concept hierarchy.

It has to be noted that the result are not the result of a syntactic analysis of the concept hierarchy, but rely on description logic reasoning. This means that we also detect cases where changes in the definition of a concept lead to new concept relations that are only implicit in the Ontology. The results of these queries can be found at http://wasp.cs.vu.nl/sekt/more/test/. In a semantic change log, of course, the concrete changes between the versions will be represented. We aggregate the results due to space limitations. What we can immediately see from these numbers alone is that the versions become more stable over time. Especially in the case of the legal ontology, the number of changes from one version to the other becomes significantly lower over time. This can be seen as a sign of maturity.

Besides this change log functionality, arbitrary temporal queries using the operators introduced in this paper can be formulated and executed. The only limitation is the interface to the underlying DL reasoner, that currently is only implemented for queries about the concept hierarchy. This can easily be extended to any functionality provided by the RACER system [6]. A list of the template queries for temporal reasoning queries are available at the MORE testbed, which can be downloaded from the MORE website. The average time cost for each temporal reasoning query is about 7 seconds for the OPJK Ontology and 3 seconds for the BioSAIL ontology on a PC with 2Ghz CPU 512 MB memory under Windows 2000.

---

[3] http://www.sekt-project.com/
[4] http://smi-web.stanford.edu/projects/biostorm/

Results for the BioSAIL Ontology										
Version(from)	Version(to)	NC	OC	NP	OP	NA	OA	ND	OD	Total
BioSAILv16	BioSAILv20	136	10	123	49	228	104	227	32	909
BioSAILv20	BioSAILv21	54	1	42	21	193	32	192	1	536

Results for the OPJK Ontology										
Version(from)	Version(to)	NC	OC	NP	OP	NA	OA	ND	OD	Total
ontoRDF	ontoRDF2	82	25	53	10	141	16	141	74	542
ontoRDF2	ontoRDF3	82	17	49	13	144	17	144	21	487
ontoRDF3	oblk	49	43	36	20	70	20	54	85	377
oblk	opjk	4	7	2	1	8	6	8	18	54

NC = New Children concept relation, OC = Obsolete Children concept relation, NP = New Parent concept relation, OP = Obsolete Parent concept relation, NA = New Ancestor concept relation, OA = Obsolete Ancestor concept relation, ND = New Descendant concept relation, and OD = Obsolete Descendant concept relation.

Fig. 2. MORE Tests on Concept Relations

7   Discussion and Conclusions

In this paper, we discussed the integrated management of multiple versions of the same ontology as an open problem with respect to ontology change management. We proposed an approach for multi-version management that is based on the idea of using temporal logic for reasoning about commonalities and differences between different versions. For this purpose, we define the logic **LTLm** that consists of operators for reasoning about derivable statements in different versions. We show that the logic can be used to formulate typical reasoning and retrieval queries that occur in the context of managing multiple versions. We have implemented a prototypical implementation of the logic in terms of a reasoning infrastructure for ontology-based systems and successfully tested it on real ontologies.

Different from most previous work on ontology evolution and change management our approach is completely based on the formal semantics of the ontologies under consideration. This means that our approach is able to detect all implications of a syntactic change. In previous work, this could only be done partially in terms of ontologies if changes and heuristics that were able to predict some, but not all consequences of a change. Other than previous work on changes at the semantic level which were purely theoretical, we have shown that out approach can be implemented on top of existing reasoners and is able to provide answers in a reasonable amount of time. In order to be able to handle large ontologies with thousands of concepts, we have to think about optimization strategies. Existing work on model checking has shown that these methods scale up to very large problem sets if optimized in the right way. This makes us optimistic about the issue of scalability.

One of the reasons for the efficiency of the approach is the restriction to the retrospective approach, that only considers past versions. This restriction makes linear time logics sufficient for our purposes. A major challenge is the extension of our approach with the prospective approach that would allow us to reason about future versions of ontologies. This direction of work is challenging, because it requires a careful analysis of a minimal set of change operators and their consequences. There are proposals for sets of change operators, but these operators have never been analyzed form the perspective of dynamic temporal logic. The other problem is that taking the prospective approach means moving from linear to branching time logic which has a serious impact on complexity and scalability of the approach.

Acknowledgements. We want to thank Pompeu Casanovas and Nuria Casellas Caralt for providing the OPJK ontology, and thank Michel Klein for providing the BiosSAIL Ontology for the tests. The work reported in this paper was partially supported by the EU-funded SEKT project(IST-506826).

References

1. Sean Bechhofer, Ralf Möller, and Peter Crowther. The DIG description logic interface. In *International Workshop on Description Logics (DL2003)*. Rome, September 2003.
2. P. Blackburn and M. Tzakova. Hybrid languages and temporal logic. *Logic Journal of the IGPL*, 7(1):27–54, 1999.
3. V.R. Benjamins P. Casanovas, J. Contreras, J. M. López-Cobo, and L. Lemus. Iuris-ervice: An intelligent frequently asked questions system to assist newly appointed judges. In V.R. Benjamins et al, editor, *Law and the Semantic Web*, pages 205–522. Springer-Verlag, London, Berlin, 2005.
4. Edmund M. Clarke, Orna Grumberg, and Doron A. Peled. *Model Checking*. The MIT Press, Cambridge, Massachusetts, 1999.
5. E. Compatangelo, W. Vasconcelos, and B. Scharlau. Managing ontology versions with a distributed blackboard architecture. In *Proceedings of the 24th Int Conf. of the British Computer Societys Specialist Group on Artificial Intelligence (AI2004)*. Springer-Verlag, 2004.
6. Volker Haarslev and Ralf Möller. Description of the racer system and its applications. In *Proceedings of the International Workshop on Description Logics (DL-2001)*, pages 132–141. Stanford, USA, August 2001.
7. Peter Haase, Frank van Harmelen, Zhisheng Huang, Heiner Stuckenschmidt, and York Sure. A framework for handling inconsistency in changing ontologies. In *Proceedings of ISWC2005*, 2005.
8. D. Harel. Dynamic logic. In D. Gabbay and F. Guenther, editors, *Handbook of Philosophical Logic Volume II — Extensions of Classical Logic*, pages 497–604. D. Reidel Publishing Company: Dordrecht, The Netherlands, 1984.
9. J. Heflin and J. Hendler. Dynamic ontologies on the web. In *Proceedings of the Seventeenth National Conference on Artificial Intelligence (AAAI-2000)*, pages 443–449. AAAI/MIT Press, Menlo Park, CA., 2000.
10. J. Heflin and Z. Pan. A model theoretic semantics for ontology versioning. In *Proceedings of ISWC2004*, pages 62–76, Hiroshima, Japan, 2004. Springer.
11. Zhisheng Huang and Cees Visser. Extended DIG description logic interface support for PROLOG. Deliverable D3.4.1.2, SEKT, 2004.
12. M. Klein. *Change Management for Distributed Ontologies*. Phd thesis, Vrije Universiteit Amsterdam, 2004.
13. N.F. Noy and M.A. Musen. The prompt suite: Interactive tools for ontology merging and mapping. *International Journal of Human-Computer Studies*, 59(6):983–1024, 2003.

14. S. Schlobach and R. Cornet. Non-standard reasoning services for the debugging of description logic terminologies. In *Proceedings of IJCAI2003*, Acapulco, Mexico, 2003. Morgan Kaufmann.

15. L. Stojanovic. *Methods and Tools for Ontology Evolution.* Phd thesis, University of Karlsruhe, 2003.

16. H. Stuckenschmidt and M. Klein. Integrity and change in modular ontologies. In *Proceedings of IJCAI2003*, Acapulco, Mexico, 2003. Morgan Kaufmann.

Piggy Bank: Experience the Semantic Web Inside Your Web Browser

David Huynh[1], Stefano Mazzocchi[2], and David Karger[1]

[1] MIT Computer Science and Artificial Intelligence Laboratory,
The Stata Center, Building 32, 32 Vassar Street, Cambridge, MA 02139, USA
{dfhuynh, karger}@csail.mit.edu
[2] MIT Digital Libraries Research Group,
77 Massachusetts Ave., Cambridge, MA 02139, USA
stefanom@mit.edu

Abstract. The Semantic Web Initiative envisions a Web wherein information is offered free of presentation, allowing more effective exchange and mixing across web sites and across web pages. But without substantial Semantic Web content, few tools will be written to consume it; without many such tools, there is little appeal to publish Semantic Web content.

To break this chicken-and-egg problem, thus enabling more flexible informa-tion access, we have created a web browser extension called Piggy Bankthat lets users make use of Semantic Web content within Web content as users browse the Web. Wherever Semantic Web content is not available, Piggy Bank can invoke screenscrapers to re-structure information within web pages into Semantic Web format. Through the use of Semantic Web technologies, Piggy Bank provides direct, immediate benefits to users in their use of the existing Web. Thus, the ex-istence of even just a few Semantic Web-enabled sites or a few scrapers already benefits users. Piggy Bank thereby offers an easy, incremental upgrade path to users without requiring a wholesale adoption of the Semantic Web's vision.

To further improve this Semantic Web experience, we have created Semantic Bank, a web server application that lets Piggy Bank users share the Semantic Web information they have collected, enabling collaborative efforts to build so-phisticated Semantic Web information repositories through simple, everyday's use of Piggy Bank.

1 Introduction

The World Wide Web has liberated information from its physical containers—books, journals, magazines, newspapers, etc. No longer physically bound, information can flow faster and more independently, leading to tremendous progress in information usage.

But just as the earliest automobiles looked like horse carriages, reflecting outdated assump-tions about the way they would be used, information resources on the Web still resemble their physical predecessors. Although much information is already in structured form inside databases on the Web, such information is still flattened out for

Y. Gil et al. (Eds.): ISWC 2005, LNCS 3729, pp. 413–430, 2005.

presentation, segmented into "pages," and aggregated into separate "sites." Anyone wishing to retain a piece of that information (originally a structured database record) must instead bookmark the entire containing page and continuously repeat the effort of locating that piece within the page. To collect several items spread across multiple sites together, one must bookmark all of the corresponding containing pages. But such actions record only the pages'URLs, not the items'structures. Though bookmarked, these items cannot be viewed together or organized by whichever properties they might share.

Search engines were invented to break down web sites'barriers, letting users query the whole Web rather than multiple sites separately. However, as search engines cannot access to the struc-tured databases within web sites, they can only offer unstructured, text-based search. So while each site (e.g., epicurious.com) can offer sophisticated structured browsing and searching experi-ence, that experience ends at the boundary of the site, beyond which the structures of the data within that site is lost.

In parallel, screenscrapers were invented to extract fragments within web pages (e.g., weather forecasts, stockquotes, and news article summaries) and re-purpose them in personalized ways. However, until now, there is no system in which different screenscrapers can pool their efforts together to create a richer, multi-domained information environment for the user.

On the publishing front, individuals wishing to share structured information through the Web must think in terms of a substantial publication process in which their information must be care-fully organized and formatted for reading and browsing by others. While Web logs, or blogs, enable lightweight authoring and have become tremendously popular, they support only unstruc-tured content. As an example of their limitation, one cannot blog a list of recipes and support rich browsing experience based on the contained ingredients.

The Semantic Web [22] holds out a different vision, that of information laid bare so that it can be collected, manipulated, and annotated independent of its location or presentation format-ting. While the Semantic Web promises much more effective access to information, it has faced a chicken-and-egg problem getting off the ground. Without substantial quantities of data avail-able in Semantic Web form, users cannot benefit from tools that work directly with information rather than pages, and Semantic Web-based software agents have little data to show their useful-ness. Without such tools and agents, people continue to seek information using the existing web browsers. As such, content providers see no immediate benefit in offering information natively in Semantic Web form.

1.1 Approach

In this paper, we propose Piggy Bank, a toolintegrated into the contemporary web browser that lets Web users extract individual information items from within web pages and save them in Semantic Web format (RDF [20]), replete with metadata. Piggy Bank then lets users make use of these items right inside the same web browser. These items, collected from different sites, can now be browsed, searched, sorted, and organized together, regardless of their origins and types. Piggy Bank's use of Semantic Web technologies offers direct, immediate benefits to Web users in their everyday's use of the existing Web while incurring little cost on them.

By extending the current web browser rather than replacing it, we have taken an incremen-tal deployment path. Piggy Bank does not degrade the user's experience of the Web, but it can improve their experience on RDF-enabled web sites. As a consequence, we expect that more web sites will see value in publishing RDF as more users adopt Piggy Bank. On sites that do not publish RDF, Piggy Bank can invoke screenscrapers to re-structure information within their web pages into RDF. Our two-prong approach lets users enjoy however few or many RDF-enabled sites on the Web while still improving their experience on the scrapable sites. This solution is thus not subject to the chicken-and-egg problem that the Semantic Web has been facing.

To take our users'Semantic Web experience further, we have created Semantic Bank, a com-munal repository of RDF to which a community of Piggy Bank users can contribute to share the information they have collected. Through Semantic Bank, we introduce a mechanism for light-weight structured information publishing and envision collaborative scenarios made possible by this mechanism.

Together, Piggy Bank and Semantic Bank pave an easy, incremental path for ordinary Web users to migrate to the Semantic Web while still remaining in the comfort zone of their current Web browsing experience.

2   User Experience

First, we describe our system in terms of how a user, Alice, might experience it for the task of collecting information on a particular topic. Then we extend the experience further to include how she shares her collected information with her research group.

2.1 Collecting Information

Alice searches several web sites that archive scientific publications (Figure 1). The Piggy Bankextension in Alice's web browser shows a "data coin" icon in the status bar for each site, indicat-ing that it can retrieve the same information items in a "purer" form. Alice clicks on that icon to collect the "pure" information from each web site. In Figure 2, Piggy Bank shows the information items it has collected from one of the sites, right inside the same browser window. Using Piggy Bank's browsing facilities, Alice pinpoints a few items of interest and clicks the corresponding "Save" buttons to save them locally. She can also tag an item with one or more keywords, e.g., the topic of her search, to help her find it later. The "tag completion" dropdown suggests previously used tags that Alice can pick from. She can also tag or save several items together.

Alice then browses to several RSS-enabled sites from which she follows the same steps to collect the news articles relevant to her research. She also 'googles'to discover resources that those publication-specific sites do not offer. She browses to each promising search result and uses Piggy Bank to tag that web page with keywords (Figure 3).

After saving and tagging several publications, RSS news articles, and web pages, Alice browses to the local information repository called "My Piggy Bank" where her saved data resides (Figure 4). She clicks on a keyword she has used to tag the collected items (Figure 4) and views them together regardless of their types and origins (Figure 5). She can sort them all together by date to understand the overall progress made in her research topic over time, regardless of how the literature is spread across the Web.

Now that the information items Alice needs are all on her computer, rather than being spread across different web sites, it is easier for her to manage and organize them to suit her needs and preferences. Throughout this scenario, Alice does not need to perform any copy-and-paste opera-tion, or re-type any piece of data. All she has to do is click "Save" on the items she cared about and/or assign keywords to them. She does not have to switch to a different application—all inter-actions are carried out within her web browser which she is already familiar with. Furthermore, since the data she collected is saved in RDF, Alice accumulates Semantic Web information simply by using a tool that improves her use of Web information in her everyday's work.

2.2 Sharing Information

Alice does not work alone and her literature search is of value to her colleagues as well. Alice has registered for an account with the her research group's Semantic Bank, which hosts data published by her colleagues[1] With one click on the "Publish" button for each item, Alice publishes information to the Semantic Bank. She can also publish the several items she is currently seeing using the "Publish All" button. She simply publishes the information in pure form without having to author any presentation for it.

Alice then directs her web browser to the Semantic Bank and browses the information on it much like she browses her Piggy Bank, i.e., by tags, by types, by any other properties in the information, but also by the contributors of the information. She sifts through the information her colleagues have published, refining to only those items she finds relevant, and then clicks on the "data coin" icon to collect them back into her own Piggy Bank.

Bob, one of Alice's colleagues, later browses the Semantic Bank and finds the items Alice has published. Bob searches for the same topic on his own, tags his findings with the same tags Alice has used, and publishes them to the bank. When Alice returns to the bank, she finds items Bob has published together with her own items as they are tagged the same way. Thus, through Semantic Bank, Alice and Bob can collaborate asynchronously and work independently from each other.

3 Design

Having illustrated the user experience, we now describe the logical design of our system—Piggy Bank and Semantic Bank—as well as their dynamics.

---

[1] To see a live Semantic Bank, visit http://simile.mit.edu/bank/.

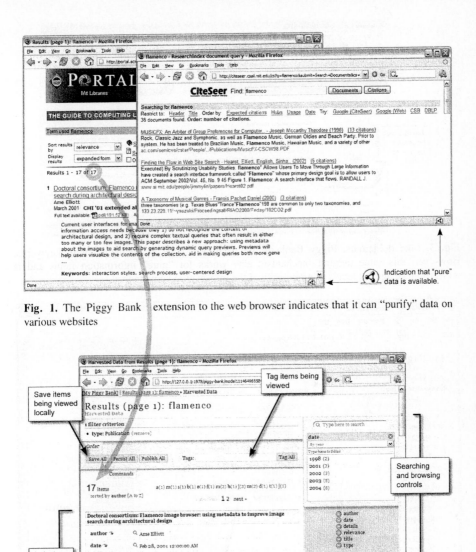

Fig. 1. The Piggy Bank extension to the web browser indicates that it can "purify" data on various websites

Fig. 2. Piggy Bank shows the "pure" information items retrieved from ACM.org. These itemscan be re.ned further to the desired ones, which can then be saved locally and tagged with keywords for more effective retrieval in the future.

Fig. 3. Like del.icio.us, Piggy Bank allows each web page to be tagged with keywords. How-ever, this same tagging mechanism also works for "pure" information items and is indiscriminate against levels of granularity of the information being tagged.

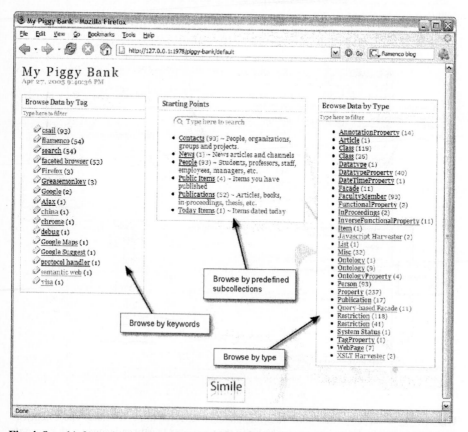

Fig. 4. Saved information items reside in "My Piggy Bank." The user can start browsing them in several ways, increasing the chances of re-finding information.

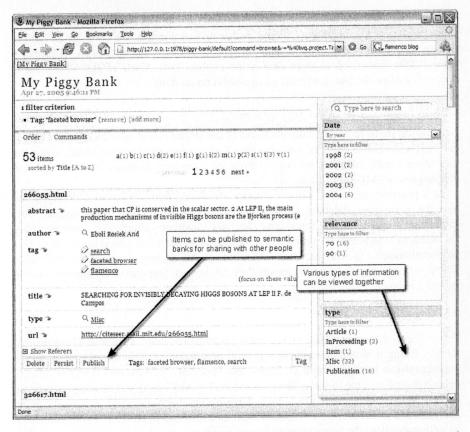

Fig. 5. All locally saved information can be browsed together regardless of each item's type and original source. Items can be published to Semantic Banks for sharing with other people.

3.1 Collect

Core in Piggy Bank is the idea of collecting structured information from various web pages and web sites, motivated by the need to re-purpose such information on the client side in order to cater to the individual user's needs and preferences. We consider two strategies for collecting structured information: with and without help from the Web content publishers. If the publisher of a web page or web site can be convinced to link the served HTML to the same information in RDF format, then Piggy Bank can just retrieve that RDF. If the publisher cannot be persuaded to serve RDF, then Piggy Bank can employ screenscrapers that attempt to extract and re-structure information encoded in the served HTML.

By addressing both cases, we give Web content publishers a chance to serve RDF data the way they want while still enabling Web content consumers to take matter into their own hands if the content they want is not served in RDF. This solution gives consumers benefits even when there are still few web sites that serve RDF. At the same time, we believe that it might give pro-ducers incentive to serve RDF in order to control how their data is received by Piggy Bank users, as well as to offer competitive advantage over other web sites.

In order to achieve a comprehensible presentation of the collected RDF data, we show the data as a collection of "items" rather than as a graph. We consider an item to be any RDF resource annotated with rdf:type statements, together with its property values. This notion of an item also helps explain how much of the RDF data is concerned when the user performs an operation on an item.

3.2 Save

Information items retrieved from each source are stored in a temporary database that is gar-bage-collected if not used for some time and reconstructed when needed. When the user saves a retrieved item, we copy it from the temporary database that contains it to the permanent "My Piggy Bank" database.

In a possible alternative implementation, retrieved items are automatically saved into the permanent database, but only those explicitly "saved" are flagged. This implementation is space-intensive. As yet another alternative, saving only "bookmarks" the retrieved items, and their data is re-retrieved whenever needed. This second alternative is time-intensive, and although this ap-proach means "saved" items will always be up to date, it also means they can be lost. Our choice of implementation strikes a balance.

3.3 Organize

Piggy Bank allows the user to tag each information item with several keywords, thereby fitting it simultaneously into several organizational schemes. For example, a photograph can be tagged both as "sepia" and "portrait", as it fits into both the "effect" organizational scheme (among "black & white," "vivid," etc.) and the "topic" scheme (among "landscape," "still life," etc.). Tagging has been explored previously as an alternative to folder hierarchies, which incur an over-head in creation and maintenance as well as disallow the co-existence of several organizational schemes on the same data ([37, 38, 42]).

We support tagging through typing with dropdown completion suggestions. We expect that such interaction is lightweight enough to induce the use of the feature. As we will discuss further in a later section, we model tags as RDF resources named by URIs with keyword labels. Our sup-port for tagging is the first step toward full-fledged user-friendly RDF editing.

3.3 View

Having extracted "pure" information from presentation, Piggy Bank must put presentation back on the information before presenting it to the user. As we aim to let users collect any kind of information they deem useful, we cannot know ahead of time which domains and ontologies the collected information will be in. In the absence of that knowledge, we render each informa-tion item generically as a table of property/values pairs. However, we envision improvements to Piggy Bank that let users incorporate on-demand templates for viewing the retrieved information items.

3.4 Browse/Search

In the absence of knowledge about the domains of the collected information, it is also hard to provide browsing support over that information, especially when it is heterogeneous, containing information in several ontologies. As these information items are faceted in nature—having sev-eral facets (properties) by which they can be perceived—we offer a faceted browsing interface (e.g., [41], [43]) by which the user can refine a collection items down to a desired subset. Figure 5 shows three facets—date, relevance, and type—by which the 53 items can be refined further.

Regardless of which conceptual model we offer users to browse and find the items they want, we still keep the Web's navigation paradigm, serving information in pages named by URLs. Us-ers can bookmark the pages served by Piggy Bank just like they can any web page. They can use the Back and Forward buttons of their web browsers to traverse their navigation histories, just like they can while browsing the Web.

Note that we have only criticized the packaging of information into web pages and web sites in the cases where the user does not have control over that packaging process. Using Piggy Bank, the user can save information locally in RDF, and in doing so, has gained much more say in how that information is packaged up for browsing. It is true that the user is possibly constrained by Piggy Bank's user interface, but Piggy Bank is one single piece of software on the user's local machine, which can be updated, improved, configured, and personalized. On the other hand, it is much harder to have any say on how information from several web sites is packaged up for browsing by each site.

3.5 Share

Having let users collect Web information in Semantic Web form and save it for themselves, we next consider how to enable them to share that information with one another. We again apply our philosophy of lightweight interactions in this matter. When the user explicitly publishes an item, its properties (the RDF subgraph starting at that item and stopping at non-bnodes) are sent to the Semantic Banks that the user has subscribed to. The user does not have fine-grained control over which RDF statements get sent (but the items being handled are already of possibly much finer granularity compared to full webpages). This design choice sacrifices fine-grained control in or-der to support publishing with only a single-click. Thus, we make our tools appealing to the "lazy altruists", those who are willing to help out others if it means little or no cost to themselves.

Items published by members of a Semantic Bank get mixed together, but each item is marked with those who have contributed it. This bit of provenance information allows information items to be faceted by their contributors. It also helps other members trace back to the contributor(s) of each item, perhaps to request for more information. In the future, it can be used to filter informa-tion for only items that come from trusted contributors.

3.6 Collaborate

When an item is published to a Semantic Bank, tags assigned to it are carried along. As a conse-quence, the bank's members pool together not only the information items they have collected but also their organization schemes applied on those items.

The technique of pooling together keywords has recently gained popularity through services such as del.icio.us [6], Flickr [25], and CiteULike [4] as a means for a community to collab-oratively build over time a taxonomy for the data they share. This strategy avoids the upfront cost for agreeing upon a taxonomy when, perhaps, the nature of the information to be collected and its use are not yet known. It allows the taxonomy to emerge and change dynamically as the information is accumulated. The products of this strategy have been termed folk taxonomies, or folksonomies.

Another beneficial feature of this strategy is that the collaborative effect may not be inten-tional, but rather accidental. A user might use keywords for his/her own organization purpose, or to help his/her friends find the information s/he shares. Nevertheless, his/her keywords automati-cally help bring out the patterns on the entire data pool. Our one-click support for publishing also enables this sort of folksonomy construction, intentional or accidental, through Piggy Bank users' wishes to share data.

While a taxonomy captures names of things, an ontology captures concepts and relation-ships. We would like to explore the use of RDF to grow not just folksonomies, but also folk-sologies (folk ontologies). For this purpose, we model tags not as text keywords, but as RDF re-sources named by URIs with keywords as their labels, so that it is possible to annotate them. For example, one might tag a number of dessert recipes with "durian"$_{tag}$ then tag the "durian"$_{tag}$ itself with "fruit"$_{tag}$. Likewise, the user might tag several vacation trip offers as "South-East Asia"$_{tag}$ and then tag "South-East Asia"$_{tag}$ with "location"$_{tag}$. It is now possible to create a relationship between "fruit"$_{tag}$ and "location"$_{tag}$ to say that things tagged as "fruit"$_{tag}$ "can be found at"$_{rel}$ things tagged with "location"$_{tag}$. (Arbitrary relationship authoring is not yet supported in Piggy Bank's user interface.)

By modelling tags not as text keywords but as RDF resources, we also improve on the ways folksonomiescan be grown. In existing implementations of text keyword-based tagging, if two users use the same keyword, the items they tag are "collapsed" under the same branch of the taxonomy. This behavior is undesirable when the two users actually meant different things by the same keyword (e.g., "apple" the fruit and "apple" the computer company). Conversely, if two us-ers use two different keywords to mean the same thing, the items they tag are not "collapsed" and hence fall under different branches of the taxonomy (e.g., "big apple" and "new york"). These two cases illustrate the limitation in the use of syntactic collision for grouping tagged items. By modeling tags as RDF resources with keyword labels, we add a layer of indirection that removes this limitation. It is now possible to separate two tags sharing the same keyword label by adding annotations between them, to say that one tag is OWL:differentFrom another tag. Similarly, an OWL:sameAs predicate can be added between two tags with different labels.

In Piggy Bank and Semantic Bank, when two different tags with the same label are encoun-tered, the user interface "collapse" their items together by default. Though the user interface cur-rently behaves just like a text keyword-based implementation, the data model allows for improve-ments to be made once we know how to offer these powerful capabilities in a user-friendly way.

3.7 Extend

We support easy and safe installation of scrapers through the use of RDF. A scraper can be described in RDF just like any other piece of information. To install a scraper in Piggy Bank, the user only needs to save its metadata into his/her Piggy Bank, just like she would any other information item, and then "activates" it (Figure 6). In activation,

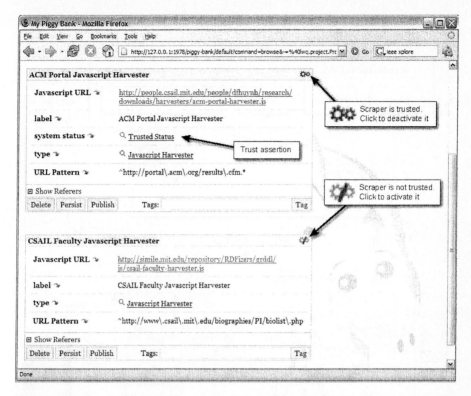

Fig. 6. Installation of a scraper involves saving its metadata and then activating it to indicate that it is trusted to be used within the system

Piggy Bank adds an assertion to the scraper's metadata, saying that it is "trusted" to be used by the system. (This kind of as-sertion is always removed from data collected from websites, so that saving a scraper does not inadvertently make it "trusted".)

4 Implementation

In this section, we discuss briefly the implementation of our software, keeping in mind the logical design we needed to support as discussed in the previous section.

4.1 Piggy Bank

First, since a core requirement for Piggy Bank is seamless integration with the web browser, we chose to implement Piggy Bank as an extension to the web browser rather than as a stand-alone application (cf. Haystack [39]). This choice trades rich user interface interactions available in desktop-based applications for lightweight interactions available within the web browser. This tradeoff lets users experience the benefits of Semantic Web technologies without much cost.

Second, to leverage the many Java-based RDF access and storage libraries in existence, we chose to implement Piggy Bank inside the Firefox browser [7], as we had

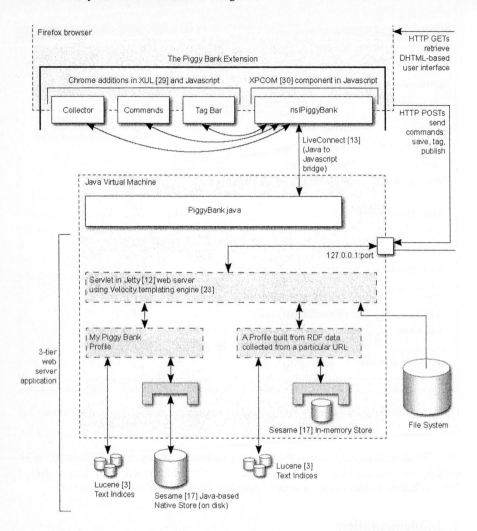

Fig. 7. Piggy Bank's architecture—a web server within the web browser. The embedded Java-based web server resolves queries, fetches data from several backend databases, and generates a DHTML [34]-based user interface on-the-fly using a templating engine. It also processes HTTP POSTs to respond to Save, Tag, and Publish commands. Chrome additions to the Firefox browser detect document loading events, invoke scrapers' Javascript code on document DOMs [24], and provide XUL [29]-based UIs for interacting with the extension. An XPCOM [30] component called nsIPiggyBank written in Javascript provides a bridge over to Piggy Bank's Java code.

found a way to integrate these Java-based RDF libraries into Firefox. By selecting Java as Piggy Bank's core implementation language, we also opened ourselves up to a plethora of other Java libraries for other functionalities, such as for parsing RSS feeds [21] (using Informa [11]) and for indexing the textual content of the information items (using Lucene [3]).

In order to make the act of collecting information items as lightweight as possible, first, we make use of a status-bar icon to indicate that a web page is scrapable, and second, we support collecting through a single-click on that same icon. Piggy Bank uses any combination of the fol-lowing three methods for collection:

- Links from the current web page to Web resources in RDF/XML [19], N3 [18], or RSS [21] formats are retrieved and their targets parsed into RDF.
- Available and applicable XSL transformations [31] are applied on the current web page's DOM [24].
- Available and applicable Javascript code is run on the current web page's DOM, retrieving other web pages to process if necessary.

Once the user clicks on the data coin icon, we need to present the collected information items to him/her. As mentioned above, we wanted to keep the Web's navigation paradigm by allow-ing the user to browse collected information as web pages named by URLs. This design choice required Piggy Bank to generate its user interface as DHTML [34]. Since Piggy Bank must gen-erate its DHTML-based user interface on-the-flybased on data dynamically collected and saved, we decided to make use of a servlet capable of generating DHTML ^{2}.

This design turns Piggy Bank into a 3-tier Java-based web server application, replete with (RDF) database backend, templating engine, and DHTML frontend, all embedded within the Firefox web browser (Figure 7).

In fact, Piggy Bank has several databases: a permanent "My Piggy Bank" database for stor-ing saved information and several temporary databases, each created to hold information col-lected from a different source. The Save command causes data to be copied from a temporary database to the permanent database. Commands such as Save, Tag, and Publish are implemented as HTTP POSTs, sent from the generated DHTML-based user interface back to the embedded web server. Tag completion suggestions are supported in the same manner.

4.2 Semantic Bank

Semantic Bank shares a very similar architecture to the Java part of Piggy Bank. They both make use of the same servlet that serves their DHTML-based faceted browsing user interface. They make use of several profiles for segregating data models. Semantic Bank gives each of its subscribed members a different profile for persisting data while it keeps another profile where "published" information from all members gets mixed together.

Semantic Bank listens to HTTP POSTs sent by a user's piggy bank to upload his/her data. All of the uploaded data goes into that user's profile on the Semantic Bank, and those items marked as public are copied to the common profile. Each published item is also linked to one or more members of the semantic bank who have contributed that item.

5   Related Work

We will now take a trip back in history to the birth of the World Wide Web, and witness that even at that time, adhoc solutions were already suggested to combat the highly flexible but still constraining information model of the Web.

---

^{2} The DHTML-based faceted browsing engine of Piggy Bank is Longwell version 2.0. Longwell 1.0 was written by Mark Butler and the Simile team.

5.1 Consumption

When the number of web sites started to accumulate, directories of web sites (e.g., Yahoo! [32]) were compiled to give an overview of the Web. When the number of sites continued to grow, search engines were invented to offer a way to query over all sites simultaneously, substantially reducing concerns about the physical location of information, thereby letting users experience the Web as a whole rather than as loosely connected parts. Capable of liberating web pages from within web sites, search engines still cannot liberate individual information items (e.g., a single phone number) from within their containing pages. Furthermore, because these third-party search engines do not have direct access into databases embedded within web sites, they cannot support structured queries based on the schemas in these databases but must resolve to index the data already rendered into HTML by the web sites.

Another invention in the early days of the Web was web portals which provided personaliz-able homepages (e.g., My Netscape [14]). A user of a portal would choose which kinds of infor-mation to go on his/her portal homepage, and in doing so, aggregate information in his/her own taste. Such an aggregation is a one-time costly effort that generates only one dynamic view of information, while aggregation through Piggy Bank happens by lightweight interactions, gener-ating many dynamic views of information through the act of browsing. During the evolution of the web portal, the need for keeping aggregated news articles up-to-date led to the invention of RSS (originally Rich Site Summary) [21] that could encode the content of a web site chronologi-cally, facilitating the aggregation of parts of different sites by date. RSS was the first effort to fur-ther reduce the granularity of the information consumption on the web that achieved widespread adoption. RSS feeds are now used by web sites to publish streams of chronologically ordered information for users do consume. RSS was also the first example of a pure-content format, firmly separating the concern of data production and data consumption and allowing innovative user interfaces to exist (e.g., [16]).

Also early in the history of the World Wide Web came screenscrapers—client-side programs that extract information from within web pages (e.g., stockquotes, weather forecasts) in order to re-render them in some manners customized to the needs of individual users. The news aggregators (e.g., [8]) juxtaposed fragments ripped out from various news web sites together to make up a customized "front page" for each user according to his/her news taste. More recently, client-side tools such as Greasemonkey [9] and Chickenfoot [33] let advanced users themselves prescribe manipulations on elements within web pages, so to automate tedious tasks or to customize their Web experience. Additions to web browsers such as Hunter-Gatherer [40] and Net Snippets [15] let users bookmark fragments within web pages, and Annotea [36] supports annotation on such fragments.

Piggy Bank adopts the scraping strategy but at a platform level and also introduces the use of RDF as a common data model wherein results from different scrapers can be mixed, thus allow-ing for a unified experience over data scraped from different sources by different scrapers. Piggy Bank is capable of storing more than just XPaths [28] pointing to information items as Hunter-Gatherer [40], and it allows users to extract data rather than annotate documents as Annotea [36] does. Piggy Bank does not rely on heuristics to re-structure information as Thresher [35] does, but rather requires people write easily distributable scraping code. It is possible to make use of Thresher [35] as a scraper writing tool.

5.2   Production

On the production side, HTTP [10] natively supports posting of data to a URL, though it leaves the syntax and semantic of that data as well as how the data is used to the web server at that URL. Web sites have been employing this mechanism to support lightweight authoring activities, such as providing registration information, rating a product, filling out an online purchase order, signing guestbooks, and posting short comments.

A more sophisticated form of publishing is Web logs, or blogs. Originally written by tech-savvy authors in text editors (e.g., [1]), blogs have morphed into automated personal content management systems used by tech-unsavvy people mostly as online journals or for organizing short articles chronologically. Using RSS technology, blog posts from several authors can be extracted and re-aggregated to form "planets".

Unlike blog planets, wikis [27] pool content from several authors together by making them collaborate on the editing of shared documents. This form of collaborative, incremental author-ing, while strongly criticized for its self-regulating nature and generally very low barrier to entry [5], has been proven incredibly prolific in the creation of content and at the same time very popu-lar. (Wikipedia [26] is visited more often than the New York Times. [2])

The effectiveness of socially scalable solutions is also evident in the more recent social book-marking services (e.g., del.icio.us [6]) where content authoring is extremely lightweight (assign-ing keywords) but the benefit of such authoring effort is amplified when the information is pooled together, giving rise to overall patterns that no one user's data can show.

6   Conclusion

In adopting Piggy Bank, users immediately gain flexibility in the ways they use existing Web information without ever leaving their familiar web browser. Through the use of Piggy Bank, as they consume Web information, they automatically produce Semantic Web information. Through Semantic Bank, as they publish, the information they have collected merges together smoothly, giving rise to higher-ordered patterns and structures. This, we believe, is how the Semantic Web might emerge from the Web. In this section, we discuss how the rest of the story might go.

6.1   Scraping the Web

Our story is about empowering Web users, giving them control over the information that they encounter. Even in the cases where the web sites do not publish Semantic Web information di-rectly, users can still extract the data using scrapers. By releasing a platform on which scrapers can be easily installed and used, and they can contribute their results to a common data model, we have introduced a means for users to integrate information from multiple sources on the Web at their own choosing.

In this new "scraping ecosystem," there are the end-users who want to extract Semantic Web information, scraper writers who know how to do so, and the publishers who want to remain in control of their information. We expect that many scraper writers will turn their creativity and expertise at scraping as many sites as they can so to liberate the information within.

The explosion of scrapers raises a few questions. Will there be a market where scrapers for the same site compete on the quality of data they produce? Will there be an explosion of several ontologies for describing the same domain? How can a user find the "best" scraper for a site? Which kinds of site will be more susceptible to scraping?

As a possible scenario, a centralized service could host the metadata of scrapers in order to support easy or automatic discovery of scrapers for end-users while allowing scraper writers to coordinate their work. Such a centralized service, however, is a single point of failure and a single target for attack. An alternative is some form of peer-to-peer scraper-sharing network.

6.2 Information Wants to Be Free

Our system goes beyond just collecting Semantic Web information but also enables users to publish the collected information back out to the Web. We expect that the ease with which publishing can be done will encourage people to publish more. This behavior raises a few questions. How can we build our system to encourage observance of copyright laws? How will publishers adapt to this new publishing mechanism? How will copyright laws adapt to the fine-grained nature of the information being redistributed? Is a Semantic Bank responsible for checking for copyright infringement of information published to it? Will scraper writers be held responsible for illegal use of the information their scrapers produce on a massive scale?

In order to remain in control of their information, one might expect publishers to publish Semantic Web information themselves so to eliminate the need for scraping their sites. They might include copyright information into every item they publish and hold Piggy Bank and Semantic Bank responsible for keeping that information intact as the items are moved about.

Perhaps it is in the interest of publishers to publish Semantic Web information not only to retain copyright over their information but also to offer advantages over their competitors. They can claim to publish richer, purer, more standard-compliant, more up-to-date, more coherent, more reliable data that is more usable, more mixable, more trustable. They can offer searching and browsing services directly on their web sites that are more sophisticated than what Piggy Bank can offer. They can even take advantage of this new publishing mechanism to spread their advertisements more easily.

Acknowledgements

This work is conducted by the Simile Project, a collaborative effort between the MIT Librar-ies, the Haystack group at MIT CSAIL, and the World Wide Web Consortium. We would like to thank Eric Miller, Rob Miller, MacKenzie Smith, Vineet Sinha, the Simile group, the User Interface Design group, and the Haystack group for trying out Piggy Bank and for their valuable feedbacks on this work. Last but not least, we are in debt to Ben Hyde for having infected us with the idea of a "scraping ecosystem."

References

[1] 9101 -- /News.
[2] http://www.w3.org/History/19921103-hypertext/hypertext/WWW/News/9201.html.
[3] Alexa Web Search - Top 500.
[4] http://www.alexa.com/site/ds/top_sites?ts_mode=lang&lang=en.
[5] Apache Lucene. http://lucene.apache.org/.
[6] CiteULike: A free online service to organise your academic papers
[7] http://www.citeulike.org/.
[8] Criticism of Wikipedia. http://en.wikipedia.org/wiki/Criticism_of_Wikipedia.
[9] del.icio.us. http://del.icio.us/.
[10] Firefox - Rediscover the web. http://www.mozilla.org/products/firefox/.
[11] Google News. http://news.google.com/.
[12] Greasemonkey. http://greasemonkey.mozdev.org/.
[13] HTTP - Hypertext Transfer Protocol Overview. http://www.w3.org/Protocols/.
[14] Informa: RSS Library for Java. http://informa.sourceforge.net/.
[15] Jetty Java HTTP Servlet Server. http://jetty.mortbay.org/jetty/.
[16] LiveConnect Index. http://www.mozilla.org/js/liveconnect/.
[17] My Netscape. http://my.netscape.com/.
[18] Net Snippets. http://www.netsnippets.com/.
[19] NewsMap. http://www.marumushi.com/apps/newsmap/newsmap.cfm.
[20] openRDF.org - home of Sesame. http://www.openrdf.org/.
[21] Primer - Getting into the semantic web and RDF using N3.
[22] http://www.w3.org/2000/10/swap/Primer.html.
[23] RDF/XML Syntax Specifications (Revised). http://www.w3.org/TR/rdf-syntax-grammar/.
[24] Resource Description Framework (RDF) / W3C Semantic Web Activity.
[25] http://www.w3.org/RDF/.
[26] RSS 2.0 Specifications. http://blogs.law.harvard.edu/tech/rss.
[27] Semantic Web project. http://www.w3.org/2001/sw/.
[28] Velocity. http://jakarta.apache.org/velocity/.
[29] W3C Document Object Model. http://www.w3.org/DOM/.
[30] Welcome to Flickr - Photo Sharing. http://flickr.com/.
[31] Wikipedia. http://www.wikipedia.org/.
[32] Wiki Wiki Web. http://c2.com/cgi/wiki?WikiWikiWeb.
[33] XML Path Language (XPath). http://www.w3.org/TR/xpath.
[34] XML User Interface Language (XUL) Project. http://www.mozilla.org/projects/xul/.
[35] XPCOM. http://www.mozilla.org/projects/xpcom/.
[36] XSL Transformations (XSLT). http://www.w3.org/TR/xslt.
[37] Yahoo!. http://www.yahoo.com/.
[38] Bolin, M., M. Webber, P. Rha, T. Wilson, and R. Miller. Automation and Customization of Rendered Web Pages. Submitted to UIST 2005.
[39] Goodman, D. Dynamic HTML: The Definitive Reference. 2nd. O'Reilly & Associates, Inc., 2002.
[40] Hogue, A. and D. Karger. Thresher: Automating the Unwrapping of Semantic Content from the World Wide Web. In Proc. WWW 2005.
[41] Kahan, J., Koivunen, M., E. Prud'Hommeaux and R. Swick. Annotea: An Open RDF Infrastructure for Shared Web Annotations. In Proc. WWW 2001.
[42] Lansdale, M. The Psychology of Personal Information Management. Applied Ergonomics 19(1), 55–66, 1988.

[43] Malone, T. How Do People Organize Their Desks? Implications for the Design of Office Information Systems. ACM Transactions on Office Information Systems 1(1), 99–112, 1983.

[44] Quan, D. and D. Karger. How to Make a Semantic Web Browser. In Proc. WWW 2004.

[45] schraefel, m.c., Y. Zhu, D. Modjeska, D. Wigdor, and S. Zhao. Hunter Gatherer: Interaction Support for the Creation and Management of Within-Web-Page Collections. In Proc. WWW 2002.

[46] Sinha, V. and D. Karger. Magnet: Supporting Navigation in Semistructured Data Environments. In Proc. SIGMOD 2005.

[47] Whittaker, S. and C. Sidner. Email Overload: Exploring Personal Information Management of Email. In Proc. SIGCHI 1996.

[48] Yee, P., K. Swearingen, K. Li, and M. Hearst. Faceted Metadata for Image Search and Browsing. In Proc. CHI 2003.

BRAHMS: A WorkBench RDF Store and High Performance Memory System for Semantic Association Discovery[*]

Maciej Janik and Krys Kochut

Large Scale Distributed Information Systems (LSDIS) Lab,
Department of Computer Science, University of Georgia,
415 Boyd Graduate Studies Research Center, Athens, GA 30602-7404
{janik, kochut}@cs.uga.edu

Abstract. Discovery of semantic associations in Semantic Web ontologies is an important task in various analytical activities. Several query languages and storage systems have been designed and implemented for storage and retrieval of information in RDF ontologies. However, they are inadequate for semantic association discovery. In this paper we present the design and implementation of BRAHMS, an efficient RDF storage system, specifically designed to support fast semantic association discovery in large RDF bases. We present memory usage and timing results of several tests performed with BRAHMS and compare them to similar tests performed using Jena, Sesame, and Redland, three of the well-known RDF storage systems. Our results show that BRAHMS handles basic association discovery well, while the RDF query languages and even the low-level APIs in the other three tested systems are not suitable for the implementation of semantic association discovery algorithms.

1 Introduction

Semantic Web ontologies are envisioned to represent knowledge bases containing millions of entities [26] interconnected with relationships. The relationships form the foundation of the Semantic Web [28] and enable the discovery and interpretation of semantic associations existing between entities in the ontology. Although, it is known that searching for simple paths in graphs is NP-complete [16], there is a great need for software tools that allow searching for relationship paths in a reasonable time, especially if the paths are of a limited length.

A semantic association path connecting two entities, as defined in [5], is a sequence of meaningful relationships connecting the two entities. The semantic association describes how the two entities relate to each other. We also say that two entities are semantically related to each other if a semantic association path exists

---

[*] This research has been supported by the National Science Foundation Grant No. IIS-0325464 entitled "SemDIS: Discovering Complex Relationships in the Semantic Web".

Y. Gil et al. (Eds.): ISWC 2005, LNCS 3729, pp. 431–445, 2005.

between them. Query languages that are available for RDF bases [20] allow the specification of certain patterns of semantic associations between entities as well as expressing various restrictions on the relationships participating in associations. However, they are not designed for the discovery of semantic associations [4]. The main problem is that in the semantic association discovery neither the length of the association path nor the relations included in it or their directionality are known a priori. These features of the semantic association discovery make the current high-level RDF query languages not suitable for this purpose, as the path expressions that they can create specify relationships of fixed length and directionality.

A possible solution to this problem is in the creation of graph-based algorithms that utilize API-level graph primitives, such as the fast computation of a node neighborhood. Several RDF storage base implementations have been described in the literature and a number of such implementations are available on the Web. All of them include high-level query languages such as RQL [13], RDQL [22], SquishQL [17], and SPARQL [29]. However, only a few of them have a lower-level API suitable to operate directly on the internal graph representation structures. Implementations providing such a low-level API include Jena [15], Sesame [8] and Redland [7]. Unfortunately, all of them have certain drawbacks and limitations when it comes to discovering longer semantic associations in large ontologies.

In order to overcome some of the limitations of the current RDF store implementations, we have created BRAHMS – a workBench Rdf store And High performance Memory System, which provides a suitable basis for the implementation and testing of semantic association discovery algorithms.

2 Motivation

Imagine an analyst investigating how a person X is may be related to a person Y, based on the facts that are stated in an RDF description base. Such requirement routinely occurs in examples such as Anti-money Laundering [23], Threat Assessment [27] and Risk Assessment. Such work requires discovering association paths existing between these two people, represented as resources in the RDF base. The semantic associations are usually of unknown and variable length, and the relations that connect the intermediate resources can be of any directionality. Non-directionality is a necessary requirement, as the two resources may not be linked by a directed path, but they may be connected by a path that includes inverse relations, representing potentially vital information about the semantic linkage existing between the resources in question. The discovered association paths should be built from instance resources, as they represent facts in knowledge base. Literal values and schema types represent important and valuable information for understanding the meaning of the path, but in this case they should not be included as the building blocks of the path itself.

The discovery of short (2-3 relations) association paths is quite fast even in larger RDF graphs, due to the limited search space. Obviously, it is not the case when it comes to finding longer paths in large graphs. The searches may take a much longer time, or be simply infeasible, as searching for simple paths in graphs is NP-Complete.

On the other hand, applications such as the anti-money laundering systems [14] search for and favor longer semantic associations while operating on large datasets. Our own experience shows that with a highly optimized implementation, searching for longer semantic associations, even in bigger graphs, may be done in almost real time.

One of the possible solutions is to use a system that keeps the whole graph structure in main memory, since accessing the disk-based or remote databases slows the search process to an unacceptable level. Therefore, an RDF store must have a memory efficient data representation that leaves enough space for the operation of search algorithms. Currently available RDF data stores are not suitable for association discovery due to their unacceptable performance and high memory requirements. During our own work on the semantic discovery project [24], we have created the following list of necessary features needed for the fast semantic association discovery in large graphs. These include the ability to:

- search for associations of variable length and unspecified directionality,
- work on large RDF graphs in main memory with leaving a sufficient amount of memory for the operation of the search algorithms,
- limit traversal paths to instance resources only (or only to schema level resources),
- produce the results within a reasonable time (on the order of a few minutes), and
- allow a fast start-up of the system by utilizing a pre-loaded RDF storage image.

The above set of requirements was the main motivating factor in creating our own RDF storage system, BRAHMS.

BRAHMS has been already used successfully in the Insider Threat project [2], which proved its value as an RDF storage system offering the necessary foundation for the implementation of fast semantic associations discovery algorithms. In this paper, we describe the design of BRAHMS and present its performance results in comparison to a few of the other available RDF store implementations.

3   RDF Storage Systems and Query Languages

3.1   RDF Query Languages in Association Discovery

Presently available RDF/OWL query languages do not directly support association discovery. Languages such as RQL, RDQL, and SquishQL offer support for path expressions but even though it is possible to specify a template search pattern of resources and relations connecting them, they are not suitable for semantic association discovery. The main problem is that the created path expressions can match only paths of a fixed length and of specified directionality of participating relations. Let us demonstrate it on the example of finding all paths of length up to two relations between two resources, startURI and endure, using the RDQL query language:

```
SELECT ?startURI, ?property_1, ?endURI
FROM (?startURI ?property_1 ?endURI)

SELECT ?startURI, ?property_1, ?endURI
FROM (?endURI ?property_1 ?start)
```

```
SELECT ?startURI, ?property_1, ?x, ?property_2, ?endURI
FROM (?startURI ?property_1 ?x)(?x ?property_2 ?endURI)
WHERE ?startURI ne ?x && ?endURI ne ?x

SELECT ?startURI, ?property_1, ?x, ?property_2, ?endURI
FROM (?startURI ?property_1 ?x)(?endURI ?property_2 ?x)
WHERE ?startURI ne ?x && ?endURI ne ?x

SELECT ?startURI, ?property_1, ?x, ?property_2, ?endURI
FROM (?x ?property_1 ?startURI)(?x ?property_2 ?endURI)
WHERE ?startURI ne ?x && ?endURI ne ?x

SELECT ?startURI, ?property_1, ?x, ?property_2, ?endURI
FROM (?x ?property_1 ?startURI)(?endURI ?property_2 ?x)
WHERE ?startURI ne ?x && ?endURI ne ?x
```

The above queries represent the following patterns to be matched:

```
[startURI  --property_1->  endURI]
[startURI  <-property_1--  endURI]
[startURI  --property_1->  x  --property_2->  endURI]
[startURI  --property_1->  x  <-property_2--  endURI]
[startURI  <-property_1--  x  --property_2->  endURI]
[startURI  <-property_1--  x  <-property_2--  endURI]
```

As shown above, six different queries are required to find all paths of length at most two that connect two selected resources. As the path length increases, the number of the required queries grows exponentially, due to non-directionality of relationships. Additionally, because we search for simple paths, each query must have conditions, which guarantee that each resource appears only once in a given path. As a result, even though it is possible to discover semantic associations using the current RDF query languages, it is prohibitively expensive.

3.2 Review of Existing RDF Storage Systems

There are already many existing and widely used RDF storage systems. In this paper, we evaluate Jena, Sesame, and Redland from the point of view of their suitability to the semantic association discovery. The three systems are arguably the most popular ones today. In addition, each one of them has an API for direct RDF querying on the storage or model. As discussed previously, such an API is necessary for implementing association discovery algorithms, because higher-level languages are unsuitable for expressing path queries of unknown length and directionality.

Jena (version 2.1) [12] is an RDF/OWL storage and querying engine (RDQL) implemented in Java. It can store graphs in main memory and in a database. The storage is organized in a triple-centric way. To get the neighborhood of a node, we have to use a general method for finding all triples that satisfy a given pattern. For neighborhood triples, the node plays the role of either a subject or an object. Due to the available indexing of triples, such searches are performed fast. Unfortunately, the in-memory implementation of the data graph requires large amounts of memory.

Redland (version 1.0.0) [21] is an RDF storage and querying engine implemented in C. It can store graphs in main memory, databases, and files. This RDF storage system is also triple-centered, but in the available 'hashes' memory-model, suitable indexes can be constructed to enable a fast computation of the node neighborhood. Surprisingly, the neighborhood search is slower than in the Java implementations of the two other storage systems and the memory consumption for the 'memory-hashes' is also very high. For our tests, we had to patch Redland to optimize its speed with two indexes in order to get a fast lookup of nodes pointing to and pointed by a specific resource. The patch was done according to the suggestions from the author of Redland [6]. In this way, we have avoided full table scans for each node neighborhood search, which was present in the original version of Redland.

Sesame (version 1.1) [25] is an RDF/OWL storage and querying engine (SeRQL) implemented in Java. It can store graphs in main memory, databases and in files. Only this RDF store has an available node-centric organization, where the neighborhood a given node can be directly extracted. The clear architecture of this system makes it easy to understand and use. Unfortunately, the in-memory implementation of the graph/model requires a large amount of memory, which in turn does not leave much space available for the search algorithms to operate on larger knowledge bases.

4 BRAHMS

BRAHMS has been designed to be a fast main memory-based storage system for RDF, capable of storing large description bases and serving as a base for efficient implementation of semantic association discovery algorithms. The first consequence of our design decisions was to make the description base read-only. BRAHMS has not been designed for modifications of RDF bases, but only for querying them. An updated BRAHMS storage image must be recreated from an updated RDF/RDFS description base. Such an approach allows us to optimize the memory usage, and to use specialized data structures and also to create all of the indexes only once.

The memory usage restriction required us to use a compact representation of the triples, nodes, their values, and storing only the most necessary structural data. On the other hand, the speed requirement demanded creating indexes for fast access and search. Taking into consideration the semantic association discovery algorithms that would be implemented using BRAHMS and the memory size limitations, we have created only the hash tables for matching string URIs with resource nodes as well as basic node-centric indexes that can be used to implement more complex queries and algorithms. The triples of instance resources are indexed as follows:

- subject → object, predicate
- object → subject, predicate
- predicate → subject, object.

These indexes are needed for a fast retrieval of node neighborhoods, as well as searching for and merging of neighborhoods during the semantic association discovery process.

Another design decision was to separate the instance resources, properties, literals and classes as they represent different pieces of information. Literals, properties and schema type resources are kept in separate memory structures with their own, similar indexes.

The final design decision addresses the optimization of the startup time. Some of the most time consuming operations while working on RDF data stored in main memory are the loading and parsing of the RDF file, together with the creation of suitable indexes. BRAHMS uses the Raptor RDF parser [19] for the initial load of the RDF file into the internal memory structures. The file load and the construction of indexes can be done only once and the created structures can be written to disk as a memory image of the internal representation for the future use. This requires that the internal memory structures do not use direct memory addresses, as those cannot be preserved in an image file. As an added bonus, this allows us to easily coalesce the memory image fragments into one compact memory block.

BRAHMS has been implemented in C++. All data is stored in a logically contiguous memory block and all internal references are made relative to the origin of the memory space. Each resource, class, property and literal is identified by a unique numeric identifier in its group. To minimize the memory usage, the internal data stores operate on these identifiers, keeping their string values in separate tables. BRAHMS uses the following types of internal data stores:

- the list of triples that contain only numerical identification of resources, properties, classes or literals together with indexes for fast access to them,
- the list of resources, properties, classes and literals that match ID with proper label/URI, and
- the list of resource values (URIs) and literal values.

5 Experiment Design

In our tests, we have compared our own system, BRAHMS, with the three RDF storage systems discussed previously: Jena 2.1 (Java), Sesame 1.1 (Java) and Redland 1.0.0 (C).

5.1 Tested Functions and Algorithms

We have selected the depth-first search and the bi-directional breadth-first exhaustive search algorithms for our tests, since many of the semantic association search methods are based on either of the two basic algorithms. As a result, the performance of these two algorithms offers a good insight into how a variety of other related semantic search algorithms would perform when implemented on the tested RDF storage systems.

We have performed the following three tests on each of the compared RDF stores:

- loading a dataset into memory, in order to estimate the memory consumption and the required load time,
- executing a basic depth-first search (DFS) algorithm in order to find semantic associations up to a given (fixed) length; DFS requires very little memory, as it is restricted by the maximum length of the association path,
- executing a bi-directional breadth-first search (bi-BFS) utilizing a trie representation of the search structures in order to find semantic associations up to given (fixed) length; this algorithm uses an exponential amount of memory as a function of the path length.

All of the above tests have been performed on the main memory storage implementations. The bi-directional breadth-first search is an algorithm that searches for the association paths by growing path frontiers from both endpoints of the search. A join of the two frontiers is performed at each step to find the complete paths.

5.2 Data Sets

In all of the tests, we have used both synthetic and real-life datasets. These included:

- SWETO (Semantic Web Testbed Ontology) [3] which is a dataset that contains real-world information about publications in computer science, including authors and co-authors, conferences, and journals. We have used two sets in our tests:
  - a small set of 14Mb, containing 187,507 statements, 55,876 unique resources with the average node degree of 2.16 in the biggest connected component; this dataset was used in our semantic association ranking experiments [11].
  - a big set of 255Mb, containing 3,196,692 statements, 813,479 unique resources and the average node degree of 3.90 in the biggest connected component.
- a small synthetic dataset, generated to include three ontologies (business, sports, and entertainment); 14Mb in size, containing 104,891 statements, 29,825 unique resources and the average node degree of 3.86 in the biggest component, and
- a big synthetic set, generated as Univ(50, 0) using the Lehigh University Benchmark [10], 556Mb in size, containing 6,888,642 statements, 1,082,818 unique resources and the average node degree of 6.09.

We did not use TAP [9] for testing purposes, because the number of entities in it is relatively low in comparison to SWETO and, what is more important, very few of the entities are linked by longer semantic association paths. Although this dataset represents an important knowledge base of facts and entities, its low connectivity makes it unsuitable for testing of discovering longer semantic associations.

5.3 Endpoint Resources

We have used the following resources as the endpoints in the depth-first search and bi-directional breadth-first search algorithm tests, as presented in Table 1.

When using the small SWETO knowledge base, we chose the same endpoints that were used for the on-line demo of association ranking. We have used the same endpoints when using the big version of SWETO in order to demonstrate the difference in the number of possible paths between the same resources as the size of the knowledge base increases.

For tests on the small synthetic graph, the sample endpoints were taken from [18].

The big synthetic graph was created as Univ(50,0) using the Lehigh University Benchmark, exactly as presented by the authors in their paper. Two professors from two distant universities were chosen as the endpoints. Our choice was random, but in most of the resources we have tested, we were able to find connections to all other resources in the graph using paths of length six or seven.

Table 1. Datasets and endpoint resources

Data set	Start resource	End resource
Small SWETO	http://lsdis.cs.uga.edu/proj/ semdis/testbed/#SWEET_215003 Chee-Keng Yap	http://lsdis.cs.uga.edu/proj/ semdis/testbed/ #SWEET_949653 Ravi Ramamoorthi
Big SWETO	http://lsdis.cs.uga.edu/proj/ semdis/testbed/#SWEET_215003 Chee-Keng Yap	http://lsdis.cs.uga.edu/proj/ semdis/testbed/ #SWEET_949653 Ravi Ramamoorthi
Small synthetic	http://lsdis.cs.uga.edu/semdis/ sports/Athlete_7271	http://lsdis.cs.uga.edu/semdis/ business/Spokesperson_7611
Big synthetic Univ(50, 0)	http://www.Department0. University0.edu/FullProfessor0	http://www.Department0. University49.edu/ FullProfessor0

5.4 Test System Environment

All of the tests were performed on a dual-processor computer system with the following configuration:

- 2 Intel(R) Xeon(TM) CPUs running at 3.06GHz; 4Gb memory (3Gb available for a single user process); 220GB of hard disk available
- Red Hat 9.0 Enterprise Linux operating system,
- Java SDK 1.4.1_02; 1800Mb of maximum heap size for loading the bigger data sets and 512Mb of maximum heap size for loading the smaller data sets,
- gcc (GCC) 3.2.2 20030222 (Red Hat Linux 3.2.2-5), C/C++ code compiled with the '–O6' optimization flag.

6 Experiment Results

In the performed tests, we have concentrated both on the speed and on the memory requirements. The memory requirements of the tested systems varied greatly, and the amount of the free memory available for the search algorithms after the data set has been loaded strongly influenced the choice of the search algorithm. The memory efficient but slow DFS, could be used with all storage implementations, as its memory requirements were very small. The bi-directional BFS was much faster, but it had high (exponential) memory requirements.

In the first experiment, we measured the time needed for each system to parse the RDF file and load its contents into memory. This value represents the time needed for a cold start. In addition, we measured the amount of memory needed to load each of the datasets. This showed how compact the memory representation was and which search algorithm was applicable for each of the test data sets.

6.1 RDF Data Load Tests

In this experiment, we measured the time needed to load an RDF file to memory and initialize the system. The time was measured using the time system call under Unix. The results are shown in Fig. 1.

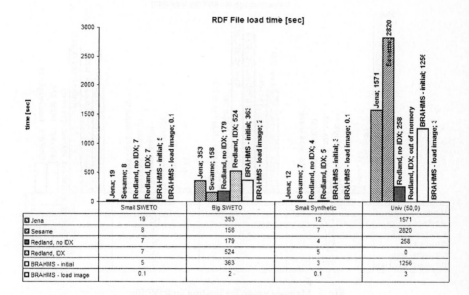

Fig. 1. RDF file initial load time

Two different loads were performed in Redland and in BRAHMS:

- "Redland no IDX" represents the unmodified Redland, without the additional indexes.
- "Redland IDX" stands for the patched Redland with two additional indexes: subject to predicate, object and object to predicate, subject.
- "BRAHMS initial" is the time needed by BRAHMS to parse and load the RDF file, create the indexes, and save the memory image file containing the internal data structures to disk.
- "BRAHMS load image" stands for BRAHMS utilizing a previously created memory image file.

Only one load operation was performed in Jena and Sesame.

As expected, for the smaller datasets the differences are not that significant, and the data load operation taking even twenty seconds is still acceptable. However, significant differences are evident for the bigger datasets, where the load times are on the order of magnitude longer.

This is the reason why we have decided for BRAHMS to be able to create and load a memory image of the internal data structures. Parsing the RDF file and creating the indexes is performed only once, and all of the subsequent experiments require only a very fast load of the previously prepared memory image file.

6.2 Memory Usage Tests

Along with measuring the time needed to load the datasets into memory, we also measured the memory usage of each tested system. The results are shown in Fig. 2.

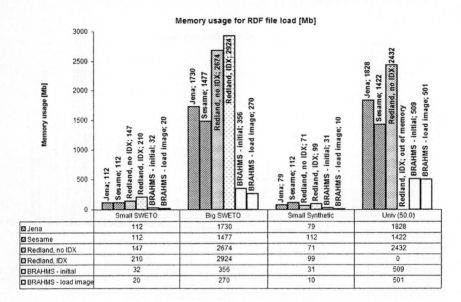

	Small SWETO	Big SWETO	Small Synthetic	Univ (50,0)
Jena	112	1730	79	1828
Sesame	112	1477	112	1422
Redland, no IDX	147	2674	71	2432
Redland, IDX	210	2924	99	0
BRAHMS - initial	32	356	31	509
BRAHMS - load image	20	270	10	501

Fig. 2. Memory usage for loading an RDF file

The memory requirements for the smaller datasets are insignificant for all the tested RDF stores, as they occupy only a small fraction of the available memory. For the big datasets, this becomes an important issue. The loaded datasets can occupy hundreds of megabytes or even gigabytes of memory. Some systems have almost reached the hard memory limits in the test computer system. Such high memory usage does not leave much runtime space for any faster algorithms relying on large workspaces.

The restrictions placed on the size of the used data structures allow BRAHMS to use much less memory than required by the other tested systems. This allows BRAHMS to load larger datasets for experiments and still have sufficient memory available for running search algorithms.

6.3 Semantic Association Search Tests

In this section, we present the timing results from running DFS and bi-BFS algorithms on different datasets using Jena, Sesame, Redland and BRAHMS.

For our tests, we have used Redland patched with the additional indexes in order to reach the speeds comparable to the other tested systems. BRAHMS tests used the memory image file that was created prior to the timing experiments.

Search on Small SWETO Dataset. Using the small SWETO, we tested both the classic DFS and the bi-BFS algorithms. Because it is a relatively small dataset, it is still feasible to perform the DFS and obtain the results within an acceptable time.

The results include the time used only for running the algorithms. The time needed to load the data file to memory (or the memory image in case of BRAHMS) has been excluded.

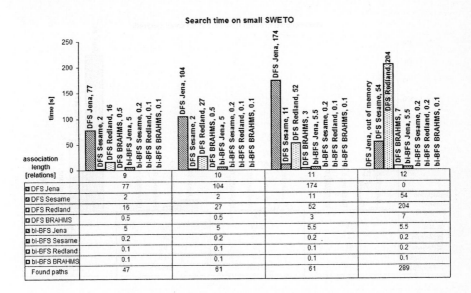

association length [relations]	9	10	11	12
◻ DFS Jena	77	104	174	0
◻ DFS Sesame	2	2	11	54
◻ DFS Redland	16	27	52	204
◻ DFS BRAHMS	0.5	0.5	3	7
◻ bi-BFS Jena	5	5	5.5	5.5
◻ bi-BFS Sesame	0.2	0.2	0.2	0.2
◻ bi-BFS Redland	0.1	0.1	0.1	0.2
◻ bi-BFS BRAHMS	0.1	0.1	0.1	0.1
Found paths	47	61	61	289

Fig. 3. Timing results from DFS and bi-BFS on small SWETO

As shown in Fig. 3, DFS is significantly slower than the bi-BFS. The differences were up to a few orders or magnitude, but this came with high memory requirements for bi-BFS. On the smaller or less connected datasets, the differences may be not as significant (seconds or a few minutes), which may be acceptable for the analyst. On the bigger or highly connected datasets, the DFS and related algorithms may be unacceptable.

Search on Small Synthetic Dataset. This synthetically generated dataset has a normal distribution of node degrees, which differs from the real-life SWETO. Although the average node degree is similar and the size of the dataset resembles the size of the small SWETO dataset, the number of located paths is much higher.

In this and further experiments, we have used only the bi-BFS, as it is a much faster algorithm. The timing results produced by DFS would be unacceptable and take in excess of several hours. The results are shown in Fig. 4.

Opposite to the small SWETO, the number of discovered paths grows into millions as the path length exceeds 10. Still, all of the tested RDF stores can compute the paths in a reasonably short time without facing the memory limitation problems. This situation changes drastically for the bigger datasets.

Search on Big Datasets. The path search algorithms tests using the big datasets were limited to paths of length up to 10. Even with this maximum length, the number of all located simple paths between the two selected entities has grown above tens of millions. The search for longer paths caused the expansion of the search space beyond the available memory, in most cases.

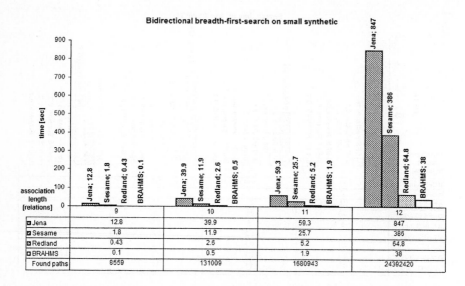

Fig. 4. Timing results from bidirectional BFS on small synthetic dataset

Using the big SWETO dataset, we were able to perform the search only using BRAHMS. The other systems have run out of memory during the search, and were even not able to discover paths of length six or seven. The results are presented in Table 2.

The synthetic dataset Univ(50, 0) required a smaller memory for the search than the big SWETO for association paths up to length 10. Sesame was able to successfully run the bi-BFS search and produce results, but the computation time was much longer than that of BRAHMS. The results are shown in Fig. 5.

The modified Redland could not load this dataset into memory and consequently no associations could be discovered in the Univ(50, 0) dataset. These could be still computed using the database storage model, but that resulted in much higher run times (not reported here).

Jena was able to load this dataset to memory, but due to the high memory usage, no associations could be discovered using bi-BFS. The system did not allow allocating enough of the additional memory.

Table 2. bi-BFS results using BRAHMS on the big SWETO dataset

Association length [relations]	6	7	8	9	10
BRAHMS execution [sec]	0.1	0.1	0.8	1.1	66.4
Number of found paths	202	202	214,778	214,778	46,641,867

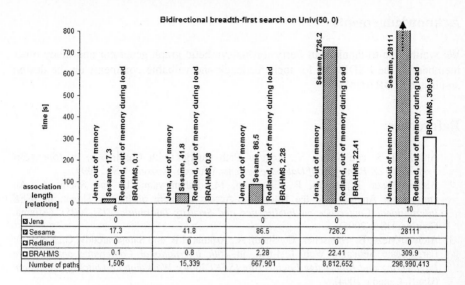

Fig. 5. Timing results from bi-BFS on Univ(50, 0) dataset

7   Conclusions and Future Work

In this paper we presented BRAHMS, the storage system for RDF, and its applicability for fast discovery of semantic associations in relatively large description bases. We compared its capabilities with three other, publicly available RDF/OWL storage systems, both in terms of speed and memory requirements. Even for smaller data sets, BRAHMS was able to compute semantic associations faster than the other RDF stores, using the same search algorithms. Longer semantic associations in bigger graphs could not be computed in a reasonable amount of time by the other systems due to their high memory requirements, while BRAHMS has been able to produce results and in within an acceptable time. This shows that semantic association discovery can become a reality, even on relatively large RDF data sets.

The discovery of semantic associations is still difficult for the presently available RDF query languages. Some of them support path expressions, but they are limited to paths of known length and defined relationship directionality.

In the near future, we plan to experiment with a variety of semantic association discovery algorithms, utilizing a language for defining regular paths, similar to [1]. The regular expressions defined over the RDF resources and types (including subsumption and class hierarchy) will enable us to define the association paths of interesting patterns and significantly restrict the search space of the semantic association discovery. Further development of semantic association search algorithms and their improvements may lead to a new perspective for knowledge discovery and searching in the Semantic Web.

Acknowledgements

We would like to thank Matt Perry for his synthetic graph generator and many other members of the LSDIS lab for their feedback and valuable comments on the design and usage of BRAHMS.

References

1. Abiteboul, S. and Vianu, V., Regular Path Queries with Constraints. in *16th ACM Symposium on Principles of Database Systems*, (Tuscon, Arizona, USA, 1997).
2. Aleman-Meza, B., Burns, P., Eavenson, M., Palaniswami, D. and Sheth, A., An Ontological Approach to the Document Access Problem of Insider Threat. in *IEEE International Conference on Intelligence and Security Informatics (ISI-2005)*, (Atlanta, Georgia, USA, 2005).
3. Aleman-Meza, B., Halaschek, C., Sheth, A., Arpinar, I.B. and Sannapareddy, G., SWETO: Large-Scale Semantic Web Test-bed. in *16th International Conference on Software Engineering and Knowledge Engineering (SEKE2004): Workshop on Ontology in Action*, (Banff, Canada, 2004).
4. Angles, R. and Gutierrez, C., Querying RDF Data from a Graph Database Perspective. in *2nd. European Semantic Web Conference (ESWC2005)*, (Heraklion, Greece, 2005).
5. Anyanwu, K. and Sheth, A., r-Queries: Enabling Querying for Semantic Associations on the Semantic Web. in *The Twelfth International World Wide Web Conference*, (Budapest, Hungary, 2003).
6. Beckett, D. Creating additional storage hashes, 2003, redland-dev - Redland development mailing list.
7. Beckett, D., The Design and Implementation of the Redland RDF Application Framework. in *Tenth International World Wide Web Conference*, (Hong Kong, 2001), ACM.
8. Broekstra, J., Kampman, A. and Harmelen, F.v., Sesame: A Generic Architecture for Storing and Querying RDF and RDF Schema. in *International Semantic Web Conference 2002*, (Sardinia, Italy, 2002).
9. Guha, R.V. and McCool, R. The tap knowledge base.
10. Guo, Y., Pan, Z. and Heflin, J., An Evaluation of Knowledge Base Systems for Large OWL Datasets. in *Third International Semantic Web Conference*, (Hiroshima, Japan, 2004), Spinger, 274-288.
11. Halaschek, C., Aleman-Meza, B., Arpinar, I.B. and Sheth, A.P., Discovering and Ranking Semantic Associations over a Large RDF Metabase. in *30th International Conference on Very Large Data Bases*, (Toronto, Canada, 2004).
12. Jena. http://www.hpl.hp.com/semweb/jena.htm.
13. Karvounarakis, G., Alexaki, S., Christophides, V., Plexousakis, D. and Scholl, M., RQL: A Declarative Query Language for RDF. in *The Eleventh International World Wide Web Conference*, (Honolulu, Hawaii, USA, 2002), ACM.
14. Krebs, V. Mapping Networks of Terrorist Cells. *Connections*, 24 (3). 43-52.
15. McBride, B., Jena: Implementing the RDF Model and Syntax Specification. in *Tenth International World Wide Web Conference: Semantic Web Workshop*, (Hong Kong, 2001).
16. Mendelzon, A.O. and Wood, P.T., Finding Regular Simple Paths In Graph Databases. in *15th Conference on Very Large Databases*, (Amsterdam, The Netherlands, 1989), Morgan Kaufman pubs. (Los Altos CA).
17. Miller, L., Seaborne, A. and Reggiori, A., Three Implementations of SquishQL, a Simple RDF Query Language. in *First International Semantic Web Conference on The Semantic Web*, (Sardinia, Italy, 2002), Springer-Verlag, 423 - 435.

18. Milnor, W.H., Ramakrishnan, C., Perry, M., Sheth, A.P., Miller, J.A. and Kochut, K.J., Discovering Informative Subgraphs in RDF Graphs - Preliminary Results (submitted to). in 4th International Semantic Web Conference (ISWC 2005), (Galway, Ireland, 2005).
19. Raptor. http://librdf.org/raptor/.
20. RDF. http://www.w3.org/RDF/.
21. Redland. http://librdf.org/.
22. Seaborne, A. RDQL - A Query Language for RDF, 2004.
23. Semagix. Anti-Money Laundering - CIRAS. http://www.semagix.com/solutions_ciras.html.
24. Semantic Discovery: Discovering Complex Relationships in Semantic Web. http://lsdis.cs.uga.edu/Projects/SemDis/.
25. Sesame. http://www.openrdf.org/.
26. Sheth, A., From Semantic Search & Integration to Analytics. in Dagstuhl Seminar Proceedings 04391, (Dagstuhl, Germany, 2005).
27. Sheth, A., Aleman-Meza, B., Arpinar, I.B., Halaschek, C., Ramakrishnan, C., Bertram, C., Warke, Y., Avant, D., Arpinar, F.S., Anyanwu, K. and Kochut, K. Semantic Association Identification and Knowledge Discovery for National Security Applications. Journal of Database Management.
28. Sheth, A., Arpinar, B. and Kashyap, V. Relationships at the Heart of Semantic Web: Modeling, Discovering and Exploiting Complex Semantic Relationships. in Nikravesh, M., Azvin, B., Yager, R. and Zadeh, L.A. eds. *Enhancing the Power of the Internet Studies in Fuzziness and Soft Computing*, Springer-Verlag, 2003.
29. SPARQL. Query Language for RDF. Prud'hommeaux, E. and Seaborne, A. eds., 2005.

A Template-Based Markup Tool for Semantic Web Content

Brian Kettler, James Starz, William Miller, and Peter Haglich

ISX Corporation, 4301 N. Fairfax Drive, Suite 370, Arlington VA 22203 USA
{bkettler, jstarz, wmiller, phaglich}@isx.com

Abstract. The Intelligence Community, among others, is increasingly using document metadata to improve document search and discovery on intranets and extranets. Document markup is still often incomplete, inconsistent, incorrect, and limited to keywords via HTML and XML tags. OWL promises to bring semantics to this markup to improve its machine understandability. A usable markup tool is becoming a barrier to the more widespread use of OWL markup in operational settings. This paper describes some of our attempts at building markup tools, lessons learned, and our latest markup tool, the Semantic Markup Tool (SMT). SMT uses automatic text extractors and templates to hide ontological complexity from end users and helps them quickly specify events and relationships of interest in the document. SMT automatically generates correct and consistent OWL markup. This comes at a cost to expressivity. We are evaluating SMT on several pilot semantic web efforts.

1 Introduction

The Intelligence Community (IC), among others, is increasingly using document metadata to improve document search and discovery on intranets and extranets.[1] Document markup is still often incomplete, inconsistent, incorrect, and limited to keywords via HTML and XML tags. This can lead to poor search performance, even if the search tool has the ability to search structured metadata.[2] Tools to date have focused on metadata annotation by authors at document production time. Some (e.g., In.vision's Xpress Author [6]) integrate with MS Word and other popular document editing tools to create metadata during the document creation, review, and dissemination process. More recent IC efforts have focused on post-production markup in which a user other than the author creates markup, perhaps leveraging the output of an automated document classification tool. These tools tend to focus on pulling out known keywords (e.g., the names of countries), mapping them to terms in a controlled vocabulary (e.g., the ISO 3166 country codes), and then outputting matched terms as tags (e.g., in XML or HTML) in (or associated with) the original document. This is a ripe application area for markup in the Web Ontology Language

---

[1] This paper uses the terms "web" to refer to unclassified and classified intranets and extranets (as well as the World Wide Web).

[2] Google and similar search engines are still the predominant tools in operational use although extensions to these are the subject of advanced technology pilot projects.

Y. Gil et al. (Eds.): ISWC 2005, LNCS 3729, pp. 446–460, 2005.

(OWL) [11], which can capture the semantics of terms used in markup – including markup of content and the relationships within – and bridge diverse metadata vocabularies across the production community.

This paper describes our latest markup tool, the Semantic Markup Tool (SMT), which was developed for use on an IC pilot effort and applied on several other projects employing semantic web technology. The SMT has benefited from lessons learned in developing and using previous versions, some of which are also described in this paper. The SMT employs an innovative combination of automated text extraction technology (using a variety of commercial products), manual markup through a form-based interface, and the use of markup templates which hide ontological complexity from end users. The SMT outputs correct and consistent OWL markup that feeds other semantic web tools for content exploitation by machines and humans

A usable markup tool is becoming a barrier to the more widespread use of OWL markup in operational settings. The SMT explores a particular point in the tradeoff space between usability and expressivity. We are evaluating SMT on several pilot semantic web efforts. This paper also describes related and future work.

2   Motivation and Requirements

Metadata markup can improve information retrieval and discovery. Metadata needs to be done consistently: e.g., by using controlled vocabularies that are machine-interpretable. Metadata using HTML or XML tag sets can often be ambiguous, as the meaning of the tag is often built into the software that creates or exploits the tags. Although they can require significant effort to configure and maintain, automatic text extraction tools, such as Lockheed's AeroSwarm/AeroText [10], can pull out entities from the text and classify them according to a vocabulary. Some can also extract simple relationships (values for entity attributes, etc.). These tools are still limited by the state of the art in natural language processing in their understanding of the text and are thus unable to capture more complex relationships. The output of these tools can be automatically converted markup in HTML, XML, or even OWL.

In a previous IC project we were involved with, we helped build a manual tool for the capturing of more complex relationships in a document and representing them in automatically generated OWL markup.[3] This tool allowed a user (a subject matter expert) to add facts, represented in OWL, to a document using a form-based interface. This tool automatically generated OWL (in the RDF serialization) that was then combined with OWL-encoded assertions (statements) from multiple documents (and databases translated automatically into OWL) into a logically centralized Knowledge Base, which could then be queried and browsed by users through web-based tools.

A user could say almost anything about a document that the ontologies supported. Users could pick classes and properties of interest from one or more OWL ontologies presented in tree. The number of "root" classes and properties was in the hundreds. This made it hard for a user unfamiliar with the ontology to determine which classes and properties might be appropriate. Even a user familiar with the ontology would have to find those few classes and properties pertinent to the current document. A text

---

[3] The original version of this was based on the pioneering work resulting in U. Maryland's SHOE Knowledge Annotator [3].

search capability[4] would have been helpful in finding classes and properties in the ontology, but that would have been highly sensitive to how those were named by the original ontology author(s).

Often a user would desire to represent a fact involving multiple classes and properties: e.g., Bob Smith and Fred Jones attended a meeting in San Francisco, CA. The user would need to determine the following:

- Bob Smith and Fred Jones should be instances of class *Person* (or a subclass of *Person*).
- Their names should be represented as values for attributes (datatype properties) *firstName* and *lastName* of these instances.
- A meeting is represented as an instance of class *MeetingEvent* (or one of its subclasses).
- Attendance is represented by the property *hasParticipant* (defined for class *Event* and its subclasses).
- A meeting's location is represented as an instance, linked to an *Event* via property *hasLocation.*

The class instances (which we term "Knowledge Objects" after they are stored in our persistent repository) and properties involved are shown in Figure 1.

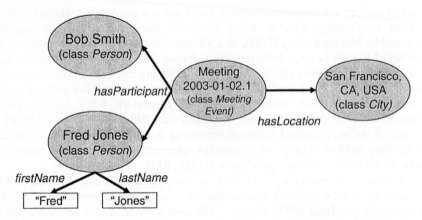

Fig. 1. An "Idiom" for Representing Knowledge Objects (Class Instances) for a Meeting

This is only one of the ways in which the above fact could be represented. Other ontologies would have different representations. Using the previous markup tool, this fact could take quite a while to enter, despite having pick lists, etc. for selecting classes and properties. Representing multiple facts in a document could take hours. The point is that having a user learn these ontology-specific "idioms" or patterns for representing facts burdens the markup process (even when the markup tool is handling the encoding into OWL/RDF/XML). Furthermore, the user is not insulated from the "raw" ontologies and thus potentially has to relearn these idioms when ontologies change.

---

[4] Such as Stanford's Protégé tool provides [11].

Thus while the previous markup tool provided great flexibility, we could not find many users willing to pay the price in effort to use it. This was especially true in IC organizations dealing with large volumes of highly varied, unstructured content (e.g., web and text documents) to process. The SMT's design, described in the following section, is an attempt to explore another point in the flexibility-usability tradeoff space.

Another lesson learned from our prior experience is the need to provide immediate added value to the user doing the markup, who may or may not be the document author. Although many of the users doing markup will also benefit from the markup later on (e.g., via using newly enabled search capabilities), there must also be some more immediate benefit. One technique investigated for SMT is the automated production of a document summary, which is often required for intelligence product publication, from the user's input. This is described in more detail in Section 3.3.

A major shift in our philosophy of markup has been to view markup as not replacing a document's content (even just its textual – versus multimedia – content), but rather providing a semantically grounded "index" entry for the document (in addition to any text indices for the document). The markup in a document will provide additional information – represented using one or more OWL ontologies – through which to find that document through higher precision, semantically grounded search. A user can then drilldown to the document's text to see its content that has not been modeled. An "index" here is stored in a knowledge base and contains multiple such entries. This index is unlike a book's index in that the former can itself be used to answer some queries, as well as located information. Thus the SMT is focused on support the manual markup of just a few key facts per document.

To summarize the motivation for SMT, our previous work has led us to a point where we are focused on automated markup for the generation of high volume, low "fidelity" assertions; more usable but less flexible tools for manual markup of key facts; and support for document search with some inferencing and question-answering potential via a "meaningful" index aggregated from these assertions. How the SMT does this is the subject of the next section.

3 The Semantic Markup Tool

This section presents additional details on the Semantic Markup Tool (SMT), the IC application in which it is embedded, and some initial results.

3.1 The Application Context

The IC application has the wider goal of providing web users (analysts and warfighters) with improved search and discovery capabilities by integrating techniques for keyword search (a la Google), metadata search, and retrieval of knowledge objects, assertions collected from facts in OWL markup of documents and data sources. The application collects and processes web documents (in HTML) to (1) extract and normalize (administrative) metadata (e.g., author, producing organization, date published, etc.), (2) convert the HTML to text, and (3) index the document's content by its keywords and ontologically described entities and relationships. Figure 2 shows this process and the components involved.

The entities and relationships will be described in OWL markup that references OWL ontologies. Because of the projected volume of web documents to process, a major requirement for a markup tool was the minimization of human effort required. The initial concept of operations was that most documents would be processed through an automatic extractor to capture entities and simple relationships from the text. Only a fraction of documents would be augmented with manual markup to describe more complex relationships beyond the capabilities of text extractors to find. The application uses a web service wrapping one or more commercial text extractors.

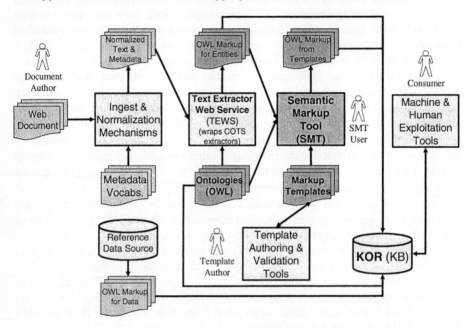

Fig. 2. Functional application architecture in which SMT is embedded

The Semantic Markup Tool (SMT) supports the markup of OWL documents by subject matter experts (SME's). It uses a hybrid manual-automatic approach to markup of document content in OWL. Steps include:

1. A document is ingested from the web. This document can be in HTML and several other types. The document is converted to text. Metadata in the document (e.g., in HTML tags) extracted and normalized (e.g., dates, country codes, etc are converted to a canonical format). Statistical categorizers assign topic codes) to the document if necessary. The document is indexed by its keywords using a commercial text indexer.

2. A document is then processed by the commercial text extractors, wrapped by the Text Extractor Web Service (TEWS).[5] The TEWS returns a list of entities (e.g., "Prime Minister Berlusconi", "Italy"), entity types (classes in an OWL ontology: e.g., Person, Country), and entity offsets with the

---

[5] This service was developed by another IC organization, which hosts it for multiple clients (including our application).

document. The TEWS also extracts some relationships (e.g., for an event) and returns entity offsets within the original document text. The TEWS outputs OWL markup describing the entities and relationships extracted.

3. The SMT receives a queue of ingested and normalized along with the OWL markup of any entities and relationships automatically extracted. The OWL markup produced automatically by the TEWS is automatically saved for storage in a knowledge base, the KOR (Knowledge Object Repository). This markup is higher volume (i.e., more assertions) than that produced through manual markup via the SMT, but is generally of lower quality and accuracy. The latter is due to errors made in the extraction of entities and their classification by type (ontology class).

4. An SMT user can then select a document and one or more markup templates (Section 3.2). Markup templates are used to describe events and other complex entities of interest mentioned in the document. The SMT can recommend markup templates to the user based on the entities extracted from the document. The types (ontology classes) for these entities are matched to the types of classes specified as legal values for template slots in a template's definition.

5. A user fills out ("instantiates") a markup template using entities from the TEWS, values he supplies, etc. The SMT's graphical user interface provides several ways to fill in templates (see Section 3.3). Uses may also choose to augment or change the type classification of one or more entities made by the TEWS.

6. Once a template is filled in, a user can save it. This causes OWL markup to be automatically generated. Currently this markup is not stored within the original web document but rather logically linked to the original web document through metadata (including the source document's URL) a we save on a per-assertion basis (via RDF's reification mechanism).[6]

A number of OWL-aware semantic web applications can process the OWL markup generated by the SMT. In our application, this markup is stored in the Knowledge Object Repository (KOR) for later exploitation by humans (via visualization, navigation, and query tools) and machine agents. The KOR is built on top of the Sesame triple store [2] and is one of the tools in ISX's Semantic Object Web framework [8].

Additional tools (such as Stanford's Protégé tool [12]) are used to author and validate the ontologies used. This markup can then be loaded into a knowledge base, such as our Knowledge Object Repository (KOR). Facts from the markup will be integrated with existing knowledge loaded from reference data sources (whose data has been converted to OWL). The KOR can be exploited by visualization, browsing, and navigation tools for human use and by software agents for knowledge discovery and other applications.

3.2 Markup Templates

As mentioned previously, the SMT's predecessors presented users with the complexity of all the classes and properties in a set of ontologies to use. Providing a

---

[6] In our IC environment, we are not allow to modify the source web documents.

usable interface for quickly visualizing, navigating, and selecting classes and properties from large, graph-structured ontologies proved difficult.

An innovation in the SMT was the use of markup templates to hide ontological complexity from users. For example, a user describes a meeting event by picking the class Meeting and selecting and filling out (allowable) properties. The values of properties could be literals (e.g., numbers and strings) or entities that in turn could have their own properties. This also makes document markup easier and faster. Markup templates can be viewed as somewhat analogous to database forms and database views, which serve to hide the complexity of multiple underlying database tables from a user entering data or performing queries. A database view can span multiple tables, much as a template can span multiple classes in one or more ontologies.

The use of templates comes at a cost of limiting the kinds of facts that can be expressed about the document. For example, to describe reports of meetings, a Meeting template might be defined with slots for participant, location, topic, start date, end date, etc. An SMT user fills out a slot by supplying a value, ideally by selecting one or more entities automatically extracted from the document by the TEWS. These slots are the *only* things a user can say about the meeting, for example. This is the expressivity limitation that is due to our approach of shielding a user from the full complexity of the OWL ontologies. If the user wishes to specify the weather during the meeting, he can either bring up a weather template (if available) or utilized a "power user" features that lets him add a single assertion (specified using terms from one or more ontologies) about one or more entities.

The SMT generates OWL markup from the filled in template, which, when loaded in the KOR, will result in a knowledge object (KO) of type (ontology class) Meeting. Other KO's may also be created. From a meeting template, for example, KO's and the links between them – including those shown in Figure 1 – are created.[7]

Template definitions thus contain the mappings from instances (KOs) and slots to classes and properties in one or more OWL ontologies. Thus if an SMT user supplies a value for participant (e.g., "Fred Jones"), a KO for that participant will be specified in the markup sent to the KOR. The KO will have properties that correspond to the slot values: e.g., filling slot Location with entity "San Francisco" will result in the KO for the meeting being linked to the KO for *SanFrancisco* (an instance of class *City*) via the property *hasLocation*.

Templates can also contain metadata (template author, version, etc.) and constraints. The latter can be used to populate and validate a template. Implicit constraints come from the ontologies referenced. For example, the ontology might specify that the property *hasLocation* (corresponding to slot *Location*) can only have a single value of type Location. Explicit constraints can state a relationship that must hold between the user-supplied values for slots: e.g., value for slot *Start Date* must be less than value for slot *End Date*.

---

[7] KO's for cities and countries, for example, will likely already exist in the KOR. In this case, a collection of heuristic matching techniques are used to match KO's asserted in the newly created markup with those already in the KOR. We term this process "co-reference resolution" between KO's. This involves comparing KO's potentially populated from multiple documents (and reference data sources). Entities within a *single* document are co-referenced using by the TEWS using synonym lists, anaphoric binding techniques from linguistics, etc.

Template definitions are stored as XML files and validated using an XML schema. These can be created and edited by trained subject matter experts using XML authoring tools or ISX's DTV tool.[8] We envision templates being created for individual production organizations, communities of interest, and community-wide use. Such templates can be used to enforce markup standards such as required document metadata, etc.

3.3 Semantic Markup Tool User Interface

Figure 3 shows the SMT's graphical user interface (GUI) in the midst of markup by a user for a test document (and test markup template) about a meeting between Italian PM Silvio Berlusconi and U.S. envoy James Baker on January 19, 2004. The upper right-hand (Document) pane shows the document with the entities extracted by the TEWS underlined (entities applicable to the selected slot are shown in red). A user can quickly check the output of the TEWS. The user can mouse-over an entity is to view its type (ontology class), shown as a tool tip. He can change its type or even designate a selection of text as an entity in the event the TEWS missed it. Thus, the user can optionally correct the output of the TEWS.

After reading the document, the user next selects a markup template. The SMT can recommend templates to the user based on the entities the TEWS found. These recommendations are presented in relevance-ranked order. The user can also choose a template that is not recommended. We anticipate that there will be about a dozen templates a user might use on a regular basis. Each template would have about 5-10 slots. This is in contrast to the direct use of the ontologies in which the user might have to select from among hundreds of classes and properties.

The template is displayed in the left-hand (Template) pane: e.g., a template for a Meeting. When a template comes up, the SMT tries to fill in as many of the template's slots as it can to reduce the burden on the user. For a given slot, the SMT matches its value type – an ontology class specified in the template definition – to the types (ontology classes) of entities from the TEWS. For example, for the slot *Participant* (of the Meeting template) can be filled by entities of type (class) *Person* or *Organization* extracted from the document such as "James Baker", "President Bush", "Prime Minister Berlusconi". If only one entity and appropriate type for a slot is found, the SMT fills it in as the default value for slot *Participant* (a lightning bolt icon is displayed next to the slot to indicate this). In the example, multiple entities could fill the *Participant* slot, so the SMT lists those (and only those) entities in a pull-down menu for value for slot *Participant* and the user can select from among these (or supply an alternative value by designating another entity in the document as a location).

For some slots (e.g., *Event Title*), the user can type in values directly. The SMT can validate these values generally: e.g., flag a non-date value entered for one of the *Date* slots. Some slots are required (designated by a "*"). Users can select "Unknown" for a value. Some slots can have multiple values (as specified in the template definition). In the example shown, slot *Participant* can have multiple instantiations (the user clicks on the + to add additional ones), each with a different value (i.e., a facility).

---

[8] The DIONE Template Versioning Tool (DTV) supports the authoring and automatic validation of templates against changing ontologies. ISX developed DTV as part of the ontology versioning work with Lehigh University for DARPA's DAML Program.

454   B. Kettler et al.

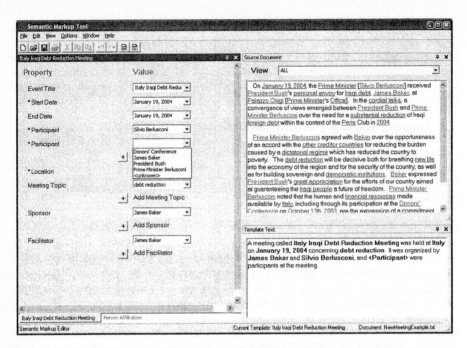

Fig. 3. Semantic Markup Tool's Main Graphical User Interface

The SMT tries to apply additional rules to fill in slots automatically. These include constraints specified in templates. For example, the Meeting template has the constraint mentioned above that the value for slot *Start Date* must be earlier than the value for slot *End Date*. Assume there are 3 date entities extracted from the document: "1/17/2004", "1/18/2004", and "1/19/2004". If the user selects 1/19/2004 from the pull-down menu for the value of slot Start Date, then the pull-down menu for the value of slot End Date will default to "1/19/2004" (since "1/17/2004" and "1/18/2004" are earlier than "1/19/2004" and hence invalid for *End Date* given the constraint). By managing the contents of pull-down menus and populating default values, the SMT tries to minimize user effort required to populate the template. More sophisticated business rules for computing default values and validating values filled in could be implemented. We are investigating the use of SWRL [5] for representing such rules, perhaps using the Jess [15] engine to execute them.

A user can fill in slots directly from the document view by right clicking on an entity. The SMT displays a list of slots that that entity could fill. For example, right clicking on the entity "James Baker" would list slots *Sponsor* and *Facilitator* as alternatives that could be filled by that entity. The SMT has no special domain (or linguistic) knowledge built in to allow it to determine that this entity might be more likely the value of slot *Facilitator* rather than slot *Sponsor* or vice versa. In some cases, the TEWS can apply linguistic rules to determine from the text describing an event (e.g., a Bombing) who the victim, perpetrator, etc. are. When such knowledge is available, the SMT can leverage it to automatically fill in one or more slots. Thus as text extractors improve, the SMT can leverage the improvements to populate more of the template automatically.

As a template is populated, the lower right-hand (Template Text summary) pane shows a stylized English text with placeholders corresponding to some of the template's slots. As slots are filled in, the text is fleshed out. A user can edit the sentences directly by typing into the sentence pane. A user can also fill in slots from this pane by right clicking on a slot name and selecting a value.

This provides a third alternative way (counting the template and document panes) by which a user can populate a template. We believe giving users these choices will allow them to use whichever method proves the easiest or fastest for them. The user can hide an unused pane, for example, if he finds it distracting. The sentences generated are stored with the document metadata as a summary to be used later (e.g., displayed in list of documents, etc.).

The user can instantiate multiple templates for a document. For example, the document might describe a meeting and a bombing, requiring two kinds of templates to mark up both events. Each template is shown on a separate tab panel. The user can easily switch between these tabs to go back and forth between filling out templates.

Some templates may be linked: i.e., the value of one template may determine the values in another template. For example, a Meeting template has slot Location. A user can link a Location Detail template to that slot to describe additional properties about the location besides just its name (e.g., perhaps its address, lat/lon, etc.). These additional properties are slots in the Location Detail template.

Once the user fills in the template(s), the SMT generates OWL markup using information from the template definition(s), which links slots to ontology properties, etc. The OWL markup generated can be quite sophisticated. This operation is hidden from the user. OWL markup from the TEWS (or another extractor) for entities is also saved. This is tagged as non-user-validated (versus markup specified through an SMT template).

For most uses, we anticipate the user will open a document, choose a template from a small set of frequently used templates, fill in a few slots (in addition to those the SMT auto-populates from the TEWS), and save the result.

The SMT is implemented in C# in Microsoft's .NET environment using Infragistics' GUI components.

3.4 Applications and Results

On several projects, we have demonstrated that the SMT can produce markup quickly that is more consistent, correct, and complete than our previous methods. Templates can enforce slot entry, helping to ensure the markup generated will be complete. The SMT can validate slots against constraints and business rules, helping to improve correctness. The entities a user puts in a slot must match the slot definition in type. The output of OWL is handled automatically, reducing the potential for syntactic errors, etc. Organizational and community standards can be embodied in markup templates to improve consistency of markup across users and organizations, respectively.

A trained SMT user can mark up most documents in well under a minute by filling in a template. In fact, in many cases the limiting factor on using the SMT tends to be the time for the user to read the actual document. The SMT has been vetted with several intelligence analysts, and their feedback incorporated into its design.

4 Related Work

Markup tools differ in the information they aim to capture (administrative and/or content metadata), their output language (e.g., HTML, XML, OWL, etc), and the level of automation provided. Several tools are embedded with common user applications to create markup as a by-product of authoring. These include Teknowledge's prototype MS PowerPoint-based tool (Briefing Associate) and MS Word-based tool (Semantic Word) from DARPA's DAML program that produce OWL markup [16]. Adobe's XMP uses RDF and metadata templates for metadata markup [1]. In.vision's Xpress Author for Word product integrates with MS Word to generate (XML) markup automatically [6]. XML publishing tools such as Arbortext's products also support metadata capture.

Table 1 compares several tools that use ontologies to generate markup.[9] The table was populated primarily based on documentation found at the various web sites. In some cases (e.g., OntoMat, Protégé, and SMORE) the tools were installed and run. Thus we apologize in advance for any inadvertent misrepresentation of the tools. The reader should refer to the web sites for the latest features. The tools include: (ISX), KIM (OntoText) [9], Melita (U. Sheffield) [3], MnM (Open Univ.) [13], OntoMat-Annotizer (U. Karlsruhe) [17], Protégé (Stanford)) [12], Semantic Word (Teknowledge) [16], SMORE (U.Maryland) [20], and SMT (ISX).

The table shows 3 sets of features including Input Parameters (unshaded rows at top), User Interface (shaded rows in middle), and Output (unshaded rows at bottom).

Most of these tools mark up web pages using OWL or RDF Schema ontologies. About half are Java-based. Some support the creation of ontologies on the fly during markup, including the finding and reuse of existing web ontologies. Some pull instances from a knowledge base (KB). Most allow either form-based specification of assertions (triples) and many support drag-and-drop from the document's text (and/or selecting text then selecting a class or property). Most support domain and range validation on assertions. About half interface with a text extractor to automatically find named entities in the text that can be used in assertions. Several tools (e.g., MnM and Melita) use learning techniques to improve automatic extraction/annotation. The tools differ in how OWL markup (typically containing individuals and their relationships) is output or stored.

Only 3 tools support templates, which facilitate the entry of assertions and can hide ontological complexity from end users. Protégé's templates are really custom forms that support the easy entry of property values for single (versus multiple) individuals. Templates can, as previously discussed, limit what can be expressed in the markup generated. To our knowledge, the SMT provides a unique combination of features including template-based markup leveraging the output of an automatic entity extractor, several GUI markup "modes", and maturity beyond "research-ware".

See, for example, [14] for another comparison of semantic annotation tools.

---

[9] Most of these were listed on http://annotation.semanticweb.org/tools/.

Table 1. Comparison of Related Markup Tools

Tool \ Feature	KIM	Melita	MnM	OntoMat Annotizer (V0.8)	Protégé (w/ Custom Forms)	Semantic Word	SMORE	SMT
Version / Status / Availability	Plug-in (Free for Research)	Limited Distrib.	2.1 Open Source	V0.8 (Free)	3.1 Open Source	1.0 Alpha (free)	V5.0 (free)	V1.0 Prototype (GOTS)
Platform	MS IE Plug-in & Server	Java Client & Server	Java	Java	Java	Visual Basic plug-in to Word, Java	Java	MS .NET (C#) Application
Object of Markup	web page	web page	web page	web page	any (doc not visible)	MS word doc	web page	web page
Kind of Ontologies Supported?	KIM Ont. (RDFS)	yes but kind??	RDF, DAML+OIL	OWL	OWL	OWL	OWL	OWL
Ontology Creation Supported?	no	no	no	yes	yes	no	yes	no
Ontology Web Search Capability?	no	no	no	no	no	no	yes	no
Templates Supported?	no	no	no	yes (forms)	yes	no	no	yes
Instance KB Access?	yes	no	yes	no	yes	no	no	no
Pre-population of Assertions or Slots?	entities from Text Extractor (GATE)	entities from Text Extractor (Amil-care)	entities from Text Extractor (various)	no	no	entities from Text Extractor	no	entities & relationships from Text Extractor (various)
Entry/Editing modes	only auto-generated (named) entity annotations supported	text entity select;	select/click text	form, doc text drag/drop, OWL editing	form, copy/paste, wizards	doc text select/click	doc text drag/drop or select/click; triple formats	form, doc text drag/drop, text entity
Constraint Checking of Assertions or Slots?	N/A	N/A	yes (domain & range)	yes (domain & range)	yes (domain & range)	yes (domain & range)	yes (domain & range)	yes
Content of Markup Generated	individuals & doc metadata	individuals	individuals, & relationships	classes, individuals, relationships	classes, individuals, relationships	individuals & relationships	classes, individuals, relationships	individuals, relationships
Expressivity of Markup	all classes in the ontology	all classes in the ontology	all classes & props in the ontology	all classes & props in the ontology	all classes & props in the ontology (without forms)	all classes & props in the ontology	all classes & props. in the ontology	limited to classes & props in templates
Format of Markup	output stored in KB	OWL	XML, RFD, DAML+OIL	OWL (embedded in HTML)	OWL	MS Word file or XML	OWL	OWL (in separate doc)
Other Features		system learns annotation rules	KB population; learning to extract		many plug-ins provide additional functionality	markup within MS Word	supports HTML editing	generates doc summary text

5 Future Work

We are investigating the SMT in a number of other semantic web applications. For our primary IC application, SMT has not yet entered operational use, however. This is primarily due to a recent change of program direction to explore how far fully automated (yet "lower grade") markup can take us, given the high volume of documents that must be processed. Another issue to be resolved is organizational and concerns who in the current production workflow will be responsible for doing any manual markup (presumably on a high-value subset of those documents).

Other applications being investigated for SMT include the CAST project for an IC organization to provide tools for analysts that allow them to capture complex relationships in documents (via OWL) and use those relationships to organize the documents around their task context: e.g., current set of analysis tasks and hypotheses. The AFRL Effects-Based Operations-Center of Gravity Analysis (EBO/COG-A) project is planning to use the SMT to extract from documents information about the interrelationships of complex target systems to aid military planners. We have proposed using the SMT markup templates for querying a knowledge base of markup as well.

Proposed enhancements to the SMT include more sophisticated automation to select template and populate slots; integration of the SMT with a knowledge base to assist in template population and reasoning; a richer language (e.g., SWRL (Horrocks *et al.* 2004)) to express constraints; and numerous usability enhancements. We are working to handle additional document types without having to convert them to text first (e.g., HTML documents).

We have begun to extend the SMT to handle the markup of images. In this version of the SMT, the TEWS-extracted text entities are instead image "primitives" extracted by feature extractors (perhaps with assistance from human photo/imagery analysts): e.g., Image X contains a truck, road, security fence, and 4 persons. The SMT could then be used to instantiate a template by filling in slots with these extracted features: e.g., a template for an arms delivery event. The template would assign roles (via slots) to the components of the image: e.g., arms dealer, truck driver, security goon, and arms recipient. A template could markup several related images to show different temporal slices of an event. The OWL generated from the template would support image retrieval, real-time monitoring, and other applications.[10]

6 Conclusions

This paper has presented the SMT, a template-based tool for the markup of SMT documents. The SMT provides a hybrid manual-automatic markup tool for the rapid use specification of relationships in the document content in addition to the entities extracted automatically. Via templates, the SMT generates OWL markup that is more complete and consistent than previous methods. The SMT has been vetted with several intelligence analysts and is being used on a several pilot applications.

The XML-based representation of templates is general purpose. Template hide ontological complexity from end users, enable automation (using constraints and rules), and generate correct and complete OWL markup. End users, leveraging the output of an automated text extractor such as the TEWS, can fill in templates quickly. In addition to OWL markup (using the RDF/XML serialization), the SMT could be easily modified to generate XML markup. Additional tools to support the easy authoring and validation of templates (against evolving ontologies) have been developed.

The machine-understandable OWL markup generated by the SMT can be exploited by a growing set of semantic web tools and applications to provide improved search, discovery, and knowledge management capabilities. Providing users with usable tools

---

[10] There are several other tools that image markup: e.g., PhotoStuff [12].

for human augmentation of semantic markup and with incentives to use them – both in direct value-added functionality from the markup tools themselves and from exploitation tools to be used later – will be essential for the semantic web to move towards widespread adoption.

Acknowledgments

The authors wish to thank the IC sponsors of this work. Much of this work was done under a subcontract to ISX Corporation from Computer Sciences Corporation (CSC). Dr. Joseph Rockmore of Cyladian Technology Consulting provided valuable inputs into the design, as did Gary Edwards, Mark Hoffman, and Joe Roberts of ISX Corporation. Previous versions of the SMT were funded by DARPA under the DARPA Agent Markup Language (DAML) and benefited from the insights of Dr. James Hendler, Mr. Murray Burke, and Dr. Mark Greaves. Dr. Greaves has sponsored the work on the DIONE project which has supported the SMT work through the development of template authoring and validation/versioning tools (among others). Several of those versions were developed by NGIT. Dr. Jeff Heflin (now at Lehigh University) developed the SHOE Knowledge Annotator which was one of the first ontology markup-based tools for the Web, as part of the pre-DAML work done by the University of Maryland under the direction of Dr. James Hendler.

References

1. Abobe, Inc. Extensible Metadata Platform (XMP).
   http://www.adobe.com/products/xmp/main.html.
2. Broekstra, J. et al., 2002. Sesame: A generic architecture for storing and querying RDF and RDF schema. In *The Semantic Web - ISWC 2002*, volume 2342 of *Lecture Notes in Computer Science*, Springer Verlag.
3. Dingli, A. (University of Sheffield). Melita.
   http://www.dcs.shef.ac.uk/~alexiei/WebSite/University/Melita/index.htm
4. Heflin, J., and Hendler, J., 2000. Dynamic Ontologies on the Web. In *Proceedings of American Association for Artificial Intelligence Conference (AAAI-2000)*. Menlo Park, Calif.: AAAI Press.
5. Horrocks, I. *et al.*, 2003. SWRL: A Semantic Web Rule Language Combining OWL and RuleML. World Wide Web Consortium Submission, 19 November 2003. http://www.daml.org/2003/11/swrl/
6. In.vision Research. Xpres Author for Word. http://www.invisionresearch.com/xpress.htm
7. Kalyanpur, A. et al., 2004. Hypermedia Inspired Ontology Engineering Environment: SWOOP. In *Proceedings of the International Semantic Web Conference (ISWC)*.
8. Kettler, B. *et al.*, 2003. The Semantic Object Web: An Object-Centric Approach to Knowledge Management and Exploitation on the Semantic Web. ISX Corporation Whitepaper. Presented as a poster at the 2nd International Semantic Web Conference. http://www.semanticobjectweb.isx.com
9. Kiryakov, A. et al. (Ontotext). KIM Semantic Annotation Platform,
   http://www.ontotext.com/kim
10. Lockheed Martin, AeroSWARM
    http://ubot.lockheedmartin.com/ubot/hotdaml/aeroswarm.html

11. McGuinness, D. and van Harmelen, F. 2004. Web Ontology Language (OWL) Overview. World Wide Web Consortium Recommendation, 10 February 2004. http://www.w3.org/TR/owl-features/

12. Noy, N.F., M. Sintek, S. Decker, M. Crubezy, R. W. Fergerson, and M. A. Musen, 2001. Creating Semantic Web Contents with Protege-2000. *IEEE Intelligent Systems* 16(2):60-71. http://protege.stanford.edu

13. Open University. MnM. http://kmi.open.ac.uk/projects/akt/MnM/

14. Reeve, L. and H. Han, 2005. Survey of Semantic Annotation Platforms. In *2005 ACM Symposium on Applied Computing.*

15. Sandia National Labs. Java Expert Systems Shell (JESS). http://herzberg.ca.sandia.gov/jess/

16. Tallis, M. et al., 2001. The briefing associate: A role for cots applications in the semantic web. In *Semantic Web Working Symposium (SWWS)*, Stanford, California, USA. http://mr.teknowledge.com/daml/software.htm

17. Univ. of Karlsruhe. OntoMat-Annotizer. http://annotation.semanticweb.org/ontomat.html

18. Univ. of Maryland at Baltimore County. Swangler. http://swangle.projects.semwebcentral.org/

19. Univ. of Maryland at College Park (MINDSWAP Lab). PhotoStuff. http://www.mindswap.org/2003/PhotoStuff/

20. Univ. of Maryland at College Park (MINDSWAP Lab). SMORE. http://www.mindswap.org/2005/SMORE/

Representing Web Service Policies in OWL-DL

Vladimir Kolovski[1], Bijan Parsia[2], Yarden Katz[2], and James Hendler[2]

[1] Maryland Information and Network Dynamics Laboratory Lab,
University of Maryland , College Park , MD 20740
[2] Dept. of Computer Science, University of Maryland, College Park, MD 20742
{kolovski, hendler}@cs.umd.edu, bparsia@isr.umd.edu, yarden@umd.edu

Abstract. Recently, there have been a number of proposals for languages for expressing web service constraints and capabilities, with WS-Policy and WSPL leading the way. The proposed languages, although relatively inexpressive, suffer from a lack of formal semantics. In this paper, we provide a mapping of WS-Policy to the description logic fragment species of the Web Ontology Language (OWL-DL), and describe how standard OWL-DL reasoners can be used to check policy conformance and perform an array of policy analysis tasks. OWL-DL is much more expressive than WS-Policy and thus provides a framework for exploring richer policy languages.

1 Introduction

To provide for a robust development and operational environment, web services are described using machine-readable metadata. This metadata serves several purposes, one of them being describing the capabilities and requirements of a service – often called the service policy. Recently, there have been many different web service policy language proposals, all of them describing languages with varying degrees of expressivity and complexity [17, 4, 1]. However, with most current proposals it is difficult to determine their expressivity and computational properties as most lack formal semantics. One characteristic of the proposed languages is that they involve policy assertions and combinations of assertions. For example, a policy might assert that a particular service requires some form of reliable messaging or security, or it may require both reliable messaging and security. Several industrial proposals (e.g., WS-Policy [17] and Features and Properties [4]) appear to restrict them to a kind of propositional logic with policy assertions being atomic propositions and the combinations being conjunction and disjunction. By mapping the policy language constructs into a logic (e.g., some variant of first order logic) we can acquire a clear semantics for the languages, as well as a good sense of the computational aspects.

Additionally, if we can map the policy languages into a standardized logic, we can benefit from the tools and general expertise one expects to come with a reasonably popular standard. By mapping two policy languages into the same background formalism, we will be able to provide some measure of interoperability between policies written in distinct languages. If we are smart in our mapping, we should also be able use pre-existing reasoners for the standardized logic to do policy processing.

Y. Gil et al. (Eds.): ISWC 2005, LNCS 3729, pp. 461–475, 2005.

Our language of choice is the Web Ontology Language, OWL [2], and the Resource Description Framework, RDF [11]. Both RDF and OWL are strict subsets of first order logic, with the subspecies OWL-DL being a very expressive yet decidable subset. OWL-DL builds on the rich tradition of description logics where the tradeoff between computational complexity and logical expressivity has been precisely and extensively mapped out and practical, reasonably scalable reasoning algorithms and systems have been developed.

In this paper, we have translated one of the policy languages, WS-Policy, to OWL-DL. WS-Policy is being developed by IBM, Microsoft, BEA, and other major web services vendors and is generally considered to be the policy language with the most momentum. Our approach maps policies to OWL-DL classes. With this, we are able to use our OWL-DL reasoner, Pellet [15] as a policy processor with analysis services that go far beyond what is usually offered. We also tackle another policy-related proposal, Features and Properties, and describe how its boolean predicates can also be translated to OWL-DL. In our evaluation section, we demonstrate how generic OWL-DL reasoners can easily handle processing moderately sized policies.

2   WS-Policy Overview

WS-Policy provides a general purpose model and syntax to describe the policies of a Web service. It specifies a base set of constructs that can be used and extended by other Web service specifications to describe a broad range of service requirements and capabilities. WS-Policy's scope is limited to allowing endpoints to specify requirements and capabilities needed for establishing a connection. Its goal is not be used as a language for expressing more complex, application-specific policies that take effect after the connection is established.

For this purpose, WS-Policy introduces a simple and extensible grammar for expressing policies and a processing model to interpret them. A policy, as defined in the specification is composed from a combination of assertions and alternatives.

An assertion is the basic, atomic unit of a policy. For example, an assertion could declare that the message should be encrypted. The actual definitions and meaning of the assertions are domain-dependent and not defined in WS-Policy. An assertion is defined by a unique Qualified Name, and can be a simple string or a complex object with many sub elements and attributes. A set of assertions can be termed an alternative.

A policy is built up using assertions and nested combinations of the operators `wsp:All`, `wsp:ExactlyOne`, and the attribute `wsp:Optional`. This policy syntax is used to describe acceptable combinations of assertions for a given Web service invocation.

2.1   Mapping WS-Policy Operators to OWL

In this section, we describe our mapping of the WS-Policy constructs from a normal form policy expression into OWL expressions. A policy in a normal form is a straightforward XML Infoset representation, enumerating each of its alternatives that in turn enumerate each of its assertions. Following is a schema outline for the normal form of a policy expression:

```
<wsp: Policy>
   <wsp:ExactlyOne>
      [ <wsp:All> [<Assertion>  </Assertion>]* </wsp:All> ]*
   </wsp:ExactlyOne>
</wsp:Policy>
```

Listing 1. Normal form of a policy expression

Policy expressions can also be represented in more compact forms, using additional operators such as `wsp:Optional`, however as shown in [17] the policy expressions can all be expanded to normal form. Therefore we only provide a mapping of the constructs used in a normal form policy expression: `wsp:ExactlyOne` and `wsp:All`.

First, we map policy assertions directly into OWL-DL classes (which correspond to atomic propositions). Though WS-Policy assertions often have some discernible substructure, it is not key to their logical status in WS-Policy. Or rather, that substructure is idiosyncratic to the assertion set, rather than being a feature of the background formalism. So a general WS-Policy engine must be adapted to deal with their structure, if it is to do so. The WS-Policy specification asserts: "Assertions indicate domain-specific (e.g., security, transactions) semantics and are expected to be defined in separate, domain-specific specifications."

It seems unfortunate that each domain-specific specification comes with its own domain specific syntax. If we are to capture the semantics of each assertion language, we must separately map each assertion language into OWL. We do provide a general strategy for mapping WS-Policy assertions in the next section.

Mapping `wsp:All` to an OWL construct is straightforward because `wsp:All` means that all of the policy assertions enclosed by this operator have to be satisfied in order for communication to be initiated between the endpoints. Thus, it is a logical conjunction and can be represented as an OWL intersection. Each of the members of the intersection is a policy assertion, and the resulting class expression is a custom-made policy class that expresses the same semantics as the WS-Policy one.

Handling `wsp:ExactlyOne` might be trickier, depending on the interpretation of the operator. There are two possible interpretations:

- `wsp:ExactlyOne` means that a policy is supported by a requester if and only if the requester supports at least one of the alternatives in the policy. In the previous version of WS-Policy there was a `wsp:OneOrMore` construct capturing this meaning. In such case, the `wsp:ExactlyOne` is an inclusive OR , and can be mapped using `owl:unionOf`.
- `wsp:ExactlyOne` means that only one, not more, of the alternatives should be supported in order for the requester to support the policy. This is supported

by [17], where it is stated that although policy alternatives are meant to be mutually exclusive, it cannot be decided in general whether or not more than one alternative can be supported at the same time. Our translation covers this more complicated case.

Wsp:ExactlyOne can be translated to OWL in the following way: for n different policy assertions, expressed as OWL classes themselves, wsp:ExactlyOne is the class expression consisting of the members of each separate policy class that do **not** also belong to another policy class. In OWL terms, it is the union of all of the classes with the complement of their pair-wise intersections. Because of the pair-wise intersections there is a quadratic increase in the size of the OWL construct that is used as a mapping for wsp:ExactlyOne.

Table 1. Mapping of WS-Policy Constructs to OWL

WS-Policy Construct	OWL Expression
Wsp:All (policies A and B)	owl:intersectionOf(A B)
Wsp:ExactlyOne (policies A and B)	intersectionOf(complementOf(intersectionOf(A B)) unionOf(A B))

To more compactly express complex policies, WS-Policy allows nesting of operators. To convert a policy from a compact to a normal form, the properties of wsp:ExactlyOne and wsp:All can be used. If we are to show that our translation correctly captures the meaning of wsp:ExactlyOne and wsp:All, we need to prove that the mappings from Table 1. have the same properties as the WS-Policy operators. wsp:ExactlyOne and wsp:All have the following properties: *commutativity, associativity, idempotency* and *distributivity*. It can be easily shown that our mappings, which are essentially a logical conjunction and explicit disjunction, also satisfy these properties.

2.2 Mapping Policy Assertions to OWL

In this section we provide a mapping for the building blocks of a policy expression, the policy assertions. Our proposal for mapping assertions is first to create a base class for every general policy assertion, e.g., *wsp:Language, wsp:TextEncoding,wsse:BinarySecurityToken* would be mapped to OWL classes BaseLanguage, BaseTextEncoding, BaseBinarySecurityToken. A WS-Policy assertion in normal form consists of attributes and elements. We describe how these are handled separately:

– for attributes, we create a datatype property representing that attribute and use the owl:hasValue restriction on that property to create a new class corresponding to the assertion.

- for elements, we create separate classes for all of the elements contained in the policy assertion. Then, the specific assertion class is created by placing `owl:allValuesFrom` restrictions on properties that relate the base assertion class with the generated classes for the elements.

In order to illustrate the approach, consider the following assertion:

```
<wsse:Integrity wsp:Preference="100">
      <wsse:Algorithm  Type="wsse:AlgCanonicalization"
                URI="http://www.w3.org/Signature/xml-exc-c14n"/>
</wsse:Integrity>
```

The translation of this assertion would produce two classes, $Integrity_1$ and $Algorithm_1$, shown below:

Table 2. Translation of Example Policy Assertion

$Integrity_1 \equiv ((\forall \text{ hasAlgorithm. } Algorithm_1) \cap (=1 \text{ hasAlgorithm.} Algorithm_1) \cap (\exists \text{hasPreference.100}) \cap \text{BaseIntegrity})$
$Algorithm_1 \equiv ((=1 \text{ hasType.}\{"wsse:AlgCanonicalization"\}) \cap (=1 \text{ hasURI.}\{"http://www.w3.org/Signature/xml-exc-c14n"\}) \cap \text{BaseAlgorithm})$

Having this information in hand, we developed an XSL script[1] that takes a WS-Policy expression in normal form and produces valid OWL-DL. For demonstrative purposes, we translated a subset of WS-PolicyAssertions using the approach specified above.

2.3   WS-Policy Merge and Intersection

In this section, we discuss the possibility of expressing `Merge` and `Intersection`.

`Merge` is the process of combining sub-policies together to form a single policy. This operation is needed because a policy might be specified in a distributed way, having its fragments defined in separate files. It is necessary to combine all these policy fragments together to form a single merged policy which could be processed further.

`Merge` works on policies already converted to normal form. The merged policy is a Cartesian product of the alternatives in the first policy and the alternatives in the second policy. There is a straightforward way of doing the `Merge` operation in OWL-DL. First, we translate each of the input policies into OWL-DL as described above. Then, the merged policy is simply the *intersection* of the input policies. Thus, `Merge` also maps cleanly onto OWL-DL. An outline of the proof is shown in Appendix 1.

---

[1] http://www.mindswap.org/2005/services-policies/wsp2owl.xsl

The goal of WS-Policy is to allow endpoints to specify requirements for starting a web service interaction. To achieve this goal, the `Intersection` operation compares two Web services policies for common alternatives. Interaction is possible only when both of the endpoints agree on at least one policy alternative.

Like in `Merge`, the process of coming up with an intersection is carried out in a cross product fashion, comparing each alternative from the first policy with every alterantive from the other one. However, in the case of `Intersection`, if the two alternatives that are being combined do not agree on the same vocabulary, then they combined alternative is not added to the new policy. A vocabulary of an alternative is simply defined as the set of QNames of the assertions in that alternative.

`Intersection` cannot be mapped into a single OWL construct, however using our OWL mappings of the policy assertions it is not difficult to rule out the incompatible alternatives. If the policy assertions are mapped to classes, then to check whether two alternatives are equal, we need to see whether the assertions in the two alternatives are derived from the same base clases. Specifically, evey assertion in the first alternative needs to be derived from the same base class with some assertions from the second alternative, and vice-versa, for the alternatives to be compatible.

3   Policy Processing

One of our arguments for expressing policies using OWL was the ability to reason about policy containment - whether the requirements for supporting one policy are a subset of the requirements for another. That would allow us to be more flexible in determining whether a particular requestor supports a policy, in the cases where the requestor supports a superset of the requirements established by the policy.

In general, we get the following inferences out of the box:

1. policy inclusion (if x meets policy A then it also meets policy B; a.k.a., A rdfs:subClassOf B);
2. policy equivalence (A owl:equivalentTo B);
3. policy incompatibility (if x meets policy A then it cannot meet policy B; a.k.a, A owl:disjointWith B);
4. policy incoherence (nothing can meet policy A; a.k.a., A is unsatisfiable)
5. policy conformance (x meets policy A; a.k.a, x rdf:type A)

One futher reasoning service supported by Pellet, and integrated with Swoop [10], is explanations for inconsistencies [14], which can be used to help debug policy incompatibility, incoherence, and the like. As we add further explanation capability to our systems, this debugging power will grow.

Thus we see that with a fairly simple mapping, we can use an off the shelf OWL reasoner as a policy engine and analysis tool, and an off-the-shelf OWL editor as a policy development and integration environment. OWL editors can also be used to develop domain specific assertion languages (essentially, domain

Ontologies) with a uniform syntax and well specified semantics. We can also experiment with extensions to WS-Policy, by using more expressive constructs from OWL at the policy language, as well as the assertion language, level. We can experiment with extensions before having to write a yet another processor for them. Of course, if it turns out that we really want to restrict ourselves to a very inexpressive subset, then we may still want to build specific reasoners and processors that are tuned for that sublanguage. But there again, our tools can help us. Pellet does expressivity analysis of ontologies, so can help determine what logic we are really using and the price of extensions.

Furthermore, ontology development techniques can be useful for policy development as well. Most human generate ontology develop iteratively, with specializations added to the class tree over time. Similarly, we can build up our policies from more general ones. A general policy could be very restrictive, setting tough guidelines for all of a companies policies.

If we have a similar style mapping for another policy language, we will be able to do policy analysis and integration across policy languages. We have taken the first steps in this direction with providing a translation of the Features and Properties compositors.

However, some care must be taken given the open world semantics of OWL. For example, an OWL reasoner does not assume that because it cannot prove that x conforms to policy A, that x does not conform to policy A. It is unclear what the WS-Policy authors intend, though a closed world assumption is not unlikely. However, even if there is a closed world assumption on WS-Policies, we can handle at least some of those cases by adding explicit disjoint statements at translation time. In the following section, we delve into the issue of open vs. closed world semantics.

4   The Semantics of Policies

Many of the current web policy languages do not have a formal semantics, leaving the meaning of certain language constructs unclear. The WS-Policy language provides for a good example. In our translation of WS-Policy documents into OWL, we assume, of course, OWL's *open world* semantics. Under this assumption, the failure to *prove* an assertion leaves us with no conclusion about the assertion's truth or falsity. That is, in light of incomplete knowledge, some statements about policies simply remain *unknown*. By contrast, in the *closed world* assumption the failure to prove an assertion ϕ leads to the conclusion that $\neg\phi$ is the case.

While the open world assumption was made for OWL ontologies, and the choice can certainly be justified[2], it seems that WS-Policy operates under closed world assumption. The Intersection operation in WS-Policy, which is used to

---

[2] The idea behind the open world assumption is that if an assertion is not made in your knowledge base, you should not infer that it is false, because the assertion might still be made in some other ontology on the Web. Thus, the open world assumption is more "web like."

determine the policy on which both endpoints agree, does not include those alternatives that have no matching assertions. In other words, if the provider has an assertions indicating support of a specific functionality, and the requester is missing that assertions in his policy, then they are not compatible with each other.

Let us contrast open and closed world assumptions. Suppose that a policy is devised to express the constraints for gaining web access. A person fulfills the requirement for web access if he or she are either a registered user or a guest user. The policy can be expressed in OWL as follows:

Table 3. Web Access Policy class definition

```
WebAccessPolicy ⊑ Policy
WebAccessPolicy ≡ (RegisteredUser ⊔ GuestUser)
                  ⊓ ¬(RegisteredUser ⊓ GuestUser)
```

It is easy to see what kind of individual will fail to belong to `WebAccessPolicy`. Since our definition of this class corresponds to the WS-Policy `ExactlyOne` operator, its members must be instances of either `GuestUser` or `RegisteredUser`, but *not both*. However, as a consequence of OWL's open world semantics, it is not enough for an individual i to simply belong to `GuestUser` or `RegisteredUser` (and not to both) for i to satisfy the second conjunct of the `WebAccessPolicy` class definition. Rather, in the case that i : `RegisteredUser`, it must *also* be provable that i : ¬`GuestUser`, and vice versa.

Contrast this with a translation of the above policy into a closed world language, such as Prolog, given below.[3]

```
not(X, Y) :- \+ X ; \+ Y.
policy(X) :- webAccessPolicy(X).
webAccessPolicy(X) :- (guestUser(X) ; registeredUser(X)),
                      not(guestUser(X), registeredUser(X)).
```

Unlike in the OWL case, the knowledge base consisting of the assertions {`guestUser(bob)`, `regularUser(john)`} will be sufficient to conclude that both `webPolicyAccess(bob)` and `webPolicyAccess(john)`. Since it is not provable that `guestUser(john)` and `regularUser(bob)` (which would disqualify both from our policy), we simply assume that they are *not* such. This constitutes the closed world assumption. The behavior of this example might be more reasonable than its OWL counterpart, depending on the specific policy and associated knowledge base.

4.1   Bridging Open and Closed Assumptions

It would be desirable to have a way to 'turn on' the closed world effect as needed in our own policies, depending on the specific application, without committing to

---

[3] Note that in Prolog, ; stands for disjunction, \+ for negation, and , for conjunction.

it across the board (which Prolog does.) Furthermore, there are cases where the open world effect can force us to model our policies unnaturally. These counter intuitive results of open world semantics for policy developers can be handled with a closed world mechanism. Consider the following example:

A research lab in College Park uses OWL to specify its policies. In the research lab, there are two types of employees: senior employees and non-senior (regular) employees, both subclassed from the Employee class. A senior employee is modelled as a kind of regular employee. Every employee has been specified a set of rights for use of devices in the lab. While senior employees are able to delegate rights to use certain devices, regular employees cannot. For example, a senior employee might delegate the right to use the conference room printer to a regular employee. Now consider two individuals, Evren who is a regular employee, and Ryu who is a senior one. If we specify that Ryu delegates the right to Evren to use the conference room printer, there is no harm done since Ryu is a Senior Employee. However, if we specify that Evren delegates the right to use the, say, conference printer to Ryu, we would expect a contradiction since regular employees are not able to delegate rights. However, because of the open world assumption, the fact that Evren is delegating rights, and isn't defined to be a *non-senior* employee, allows the OWL reasoner to *infer* that Evren is a *senior* employee. This is the opposite of what the policy writer had in mind. The undesirable consequence is illustrated below.

Table 4. Undesirable consequence of OWA for policy modelling

Policy definition
DelegationConfPrinter $\sqsubseteq$ Delegation
DelegationConfPrinter $\equiv$ $\exists$delegationGiver.SeniorEmployee
$\qquad$ $\sqcap$ $\exists$delegationType.RightToUseDevices
RightToUseConfPrinter $\sqsubseteq$ RightToUseDevices

Knowledge base
evren : RegularEmployee
ryu : SeniorEmployee
badOWA : DelegationConfPrinter
delegationGiver(badOWA, evren)
delegationReceiver(badOWA, ryu)

The above policy, paired with the shown knowledge base, will yield the inference that Evren is of type SeniorEmployee. A possible fix for the problem would be to make SeniorEmployee and RegularEmployee disjoint, though this would break the perfectly correct modeller's intuition that: (1) the two kinds of employees should share the superclass Employee, and (2) a senior employee is a regular employee *plus some privileges*, captured by making the former of a subclass of the latter.

A better solution that would allow us to keep the current class hierarchy intact is to use a *default rule*. Essentially, we'd like to enforce that any individual who is not *already known* to be a senior employee does not have delegation rights. The individual `ryu` in the above knowledge base clearly does not fall in this category, being asserted to be a senior employee. The modal operators **K** and **A**, discussed as an extension for the description logic $\mathcal{ALC}$ in [3], allow us to express this constraint as a sentence in the knowledge base.[4] The **K** operator can be read as what is "known" to be the case, while the **A** operator can be read as a "default assumption":

$$\text{KEmployee} \sqcap \neg\text{ASeniorEmployee} \sqsubseteq \neg\text{Delegation}$$

Which can be read as "If one is known to be an employee, but is not already a senior employee, then one does not have the ability to delegate rights." Note that the use of **K** and **A** here introduces a closed world assumption with respect to the rule. If it is only asserted that `evren` is an `Employee` for example, then by default he is *not* a `SeniorEmployee`, preventing us from erroneously inferring that he is one.

5   WSDL

In addition to WS-Policy, we explored another proposal, Features and Properties [4] that has also been put forth as a candidate for describing web service policies. Integrating WSDL 2.0 with Features and Properties produced a framework that allows users to specify web service capabilities and requirements in the service description, with expressiveness similar to WS-Policy. The framework in question is based on three concepts, `Features`, `Properties` and `Compositors`. Simply put, a `Feature` represents a piece of functionality, identified by a URI. An example of a `Feature` would be encryption. `Properties` are the parameters of a `Feature`, also identifiable by a URI. For an encryption `Feature`, `Property` might be the algorithm used, part of message encrypted, etc. `Compositors` are used for combining multiple `Features` and `Properties`. There are four `Compositors` defined in the proposal:

1. *all*: this compositor specifies that a service invocation MUST comply with all the children elements
2. *choice*: specifies that a service invocation MUST comply with exactly one of the possibly many children elements
3. *one-or-more*: specifies that a service invocation MUST comply with at least one of the possibly many children elements
4. *zero-or-more*: specifies that a service invocation MAY comply with one or more of the children elements

The compositors in WSDL do provide more options than WS-Policy, however they too can be mapped to OWL, as shown in the following table:

---

[4] Two similar solutions are possible using these operators. The **K** operator can also be used to formulate an equivalent constraint in the form of a query. Another alternative is to use a *default rule*; we refer the reader to [3] for the details of both alternatives.

Table 5. Mapping of Features and Properties Compositors to OWL

WSDL Compositor	OWL Expression
all (policies A and B)	owl:intersectionOf(A B)

choice
(policies A and B)
	intersectionOf(
	    complementOf(intersectionOf(A B))
	    unionOf(A B))

one-or-more	owl:unionOf
zero-or-more	means *optional*, not mapped to any OWL expressions

6   Evaluation

One of the benefits of expressing policies in OWL is the possibility of using an off-the-shelf OWL reasoner as a policy engine and analysis tool. In this section, we show that currently available DL reasoners can easily process moderately-sized policies. For the purpose of our evaluation, we have selected three reasoners, Pellet [15], FaCT [8] and Racer [6]. We also created a random policy generator, a script that creates policy assertions and specific policy classes and individuals that have the structure of a WS-Policy in OWL form. The translation of the synthetic WS-Policies to OWL-DL took neglibile time (<0.3 sec) using the XSLT mentioned above.

Table 6 summarizes the results of classifying these policy ontologies with the reasoners.

Table 6. Classifying Policy ontologies using off-the-shelf DL reasoners

Policy Size (assertions, policies)	Pellet (sec.)	Racer (sec.)	FaCT (sec.)
(100,10)	0.81	0.91	1.03
(100,20)	1.00	1.32	1.20
(200,20)	1.53	1.45	1.55
(200,40)	2.17	1.75	2.30
(1000,100)	15.54	22.32	16.22

Every policy in the test samples contains multiple (at most 8) alternatives, and each alternative has multiple assertions, thus the samples represent reasonably complex policies. Even in a case with 200 assertions and 40 policies, all of the reasoners performed well (around 2 sec.) The evaluation supports our claim that OWL Reasoners are more than ready to be used as policy processing tools.

7   Related Work

To the best of our knowledge, there have been no previous attempts of expressing WS-Policy in OWL. There have been, however, numerous proposals for web service policy languages based on XML or OWL. The main difference between our work and related policy languages is the level of expressivity - WS-Policy is focused on those aspects of a service required to establish a connection between endpoints and it does not require a great deal of expresivitiy. Most of the languages discussed in this section on the other hand, have a bigger scope of being able to specify high-level, application-specific, heterogeneous policies.

First, we look at XML-based policy languages. The Web Services Policy Language [1], developed at Sun Microsystems, is suitable for specifying a wide range of policies, including authorization, quality-of-service, quality-of protection, reliable messaging, privacy, and application-specific service options. WSPL is of particular interest in several respects. It supports merging two policies, resulting in a single policy that satisfies the requirements of both, assuming such a policy exists. Policies can be based on comparisons other than equality, allowing policies to depend on fine-grained attributes such as time of day, cost, or network subnet address. By using standard data types and functions for expressing policy parameters, a standard policy engine can support any policy. The syntax is a strict subset of the OASIS eXtensible Access Control Markup Language (XACML [5]) Standard.

In essence, a WSPL policy is a sequence of one or more rules, where each rule represents an acceptable alternative. A rule contains a number of predicates, which correspond to policy assertions in WS-Policy. All of the predicates need to be satisfied for the rule to be satisfied. However, only one of the rules can be satisfied for the policy to be satisfied. A WSPL Policy on an operator level is in Disjunctive Normal Form, thus expressible in OWL-DL.

WSPL defines a standard language for use in specifying predicates that constrain domain-specified vocabulary items. Each predicate places a constraint on the value of an Attribute. Possible constraints are: equals, greater than, greater than or equal to, less than, less than or equal to, setequals and subset. Unfortunately , the OWL datatyping formalism is not expressive enough to generally represent datatype predicates such as the ones mentioned. There has been a recent proposal of an extension to OWL-DL, caled OWL-E [13] which adds datatype group-based class constructors to allow the use of datatype expressions in class restrictions. OWL-E is interesting because it adds much more datatype expressiveness and it is still decidable.

The Platform for Privacy Preferences Project (P3P [12]) enables Web sites to express their privacy practices in a standard XML-based format that can be retrieved automatically and interpreted easily by user agents. Similar to what we hav edone with WS-Policy, there has been a number of attempts to use an RDF or OWL schema to describe the semantics of P3P. According to [18], there exists a data-centric relational semantics for P3P in which a P3P policy is modeled as a relational database, that further allows to express P3P using RDF. However, it is important to take note that modal logical statements can be made about data types in the P3P schema. This issue is investigated in detail by Hogben [7], which provides a complete OWL schema that captures the semantics of P3P. Having P3P modelled in OWL allows the authors to perform syntactic and semantic validation on the policies.

Moving to OWL-based systems, Rei [9] is a policy specification language based on a combination of OWL-Lite, logic-like variables and rules. It allows users to develop declarative policies over domain specific ontologies in RDF, DAML+OIL and OWL. Rei allows policies to be specified as constraints over allowable and obligated actions on resources in the environment. A distinguishing feature of Rei is that it includes specifications for speech acts for remote policy management and policy analysis specifications like what-if analysis and use-case management.

KaOS Policy and Domain Services [16] use ontology concepts encoded in OWL to build policies. These policies constrain allowable actions performed by actors which might be clients or agents. The KAoS Policy Service distinguishes between authorizations and obligations. The applicability of the policy is defined by a class of situations which definition can contain components specifying required history, state and currently undertaken action.

8   Conclusion and Future Work

In this section we provide a summary of our contributions and possible future directions:

1. By providing a mapping for the formalism of WS-Policy we have shown that it is an expressive subset of OWL-DL
2. Currently available OWL reasoners perform reasonably well as policy processors, without any modification, and we have preliminary empirical results to show for it.
3. OWL-DL provides an interesting framework for exploring richer policy languages with minimal implementation cost. An interesting direction would be integration of our policy mapping with OWL-S profiles, which seems like a natural next step.
4. In the cases when OWL is not suitable, we have clear extensions we can add to address these issues. We covered the K operator and OWL with datatype predicates in this paper.
5. Finally, since other policy languages (WSDL, WSPL) also seem to be subsets of (a slightly extended) OWL, OWL-DL seems to be the right language for specifying policies in general.

Acknowledgements

This work was completed with funding from Fujitsu Laboratories of America-College Park, Lockheed Martin Advanced Technology Laboratory, NTT Corp., Kevric Corp., SAIC, National Science Foundation, National Geospatial-Intelligence Agency, DARPA, US Army Research Laboratory, NIST, and other DoD sources.

474   V. Kolovski et al.

References

1. A. H. Anderson. An introduction to the web services policy language. In *Fifth IEEE International Workshop on Policies for Distributed Systems and Networks (POLICY'04)*, 2004.
2. M. Dean and G. Schreiber. Owl web ontology language reference w3c recommendation., feb 2004.
3. F. M. Donini, D. Nardi, and R. Rosati. Description logics of minimal knowledge and negation as failure. *ACM Transactions on Computational Logic*, pages 1529–3785, 2001.
4. J. D. et al. Wsdl annotation proposal.
   http://lists.oasis-open.org/archives/wsrm/200403/msg00082.html.
5. S. Godik and T. Moses. Oasis extensible access control markup language (xacml) version 1.1. oasis committee specification, July 2003.
6. V. Haarslev and R. Mller. Racer: A core inference engine for the semantic web. *Proceedings of the 2nd International Workshop on Evaluation of Ontology-based Tools*, 2003.
7. G. Hogben. Describing the p3p base data schema using owl. In *A WWW2005 Workshop on Policy Management for the Web*, 2005.
8. I. Horrocks. The fact system. http://www.cs.man.ac.uk/ horrocks/FaCT/.
9. L. e. a. Kagal. A policy language for a pervasive computing environment. In *IEEE 4th International Workshop on Policies for Distributed Systems and Networks*, June 2003.
10. A. Kalyanpur, B. Parsia, and J. Hendler. A tool for working with web ontologies. In *In Proceedings of the International Journal on Semantic Web and Information Systems, Vol. 1, No. 1, Jan - March*, 2005.
11. O. Lassila and R. Swick. Resource description framework (rdf) model and syntax specification, February 1999.
12. P3P. Platform for Privacy Preferences Project. http://www.w3.org/P3P/.
13. J. Z. Pan and I. Horrocks. Owl-e: Extending owl with expressive datatype expressions. Technical report, Victoria University of Manchester, 2004.
14. B. Parsia, E. Sirin, and A. Kalyanpur. Debugging owl ontologies. In *The 14th International World Wide Web Conference (WWW2005)*, Chiba, Japan, May 2005.
15. Pellet. Pellet - owl dl reasoner, 2003. http://www.mindswap.org/2003/pellet.
16. A. Uszokand and J. Bradshaw. Kaos policies for web services. In *W3C Workshop on Constraints and Capabilities for Web Servies*, October 2004.
17. WS-Policy. Web services policy framework (ws-policy).
   http://www-106.ibm.com/developerworks/library/specification/ws-polfram/.
18. T. Yu, N. Li, and A. Anton. A formal semantics for p3p. In *ACM Workshop on Secure Web Services*, October 2004.

9   Appendix

Theorem 1. *Merge between two policies, as defined in WS-Policy, is equivalent to the conjunction of the OWL translations of the two policies.*

Proof: Consider two policies, P1 and P2 in normal form:
$P_1 = \text{ExactlyOne}(A_1, A_2, A_3, ... A_n)$
$P_2 = \text{ExactlyOne}(B_1, B_2, B_3, ... B_n)$

Then, their translations to OWL would have the following form:
$$O_1 = (A_1 \cup A_2 \cup A_3 \cup ... \cup A_n) \bigcap \neg((A_1 \cap A_2) \cup (A_1 \cap A_3) \cup ... \cup (A_{n-1} \cap A_n))$$
$$O_2 = (B_1 \cup B_2 \cup B_3 \cup ... \cup B_n) \bigcap \neg((B_1 \cap B_2) \cup (B_1 \cap B_3) \cup ... \cup (B_{n-1} \cap B_n))$$

A merged policy can be mapped to the following OWL expression,
$P1$ merge $P_2 = ((A_1 \cap B_1) \cup (A_1 \cap B_2) \cup ... \cup (A_n \cap B_m)) \bigcap$
$\neg((A_1 \cap B_1 \cap A_1 \cap B_2) \cup (A_1 \cap B_1 \cap A_1 \cap B_3) \cup ... \cup (A_n \cap B_{m-1} \cap A_n \cap B_m))$.

We are going to show that $(O_1 \cap O_2) \Leftrightarrow (P_1$ merge $P_2)$. The proof follows the divide and conquer approach - we first split up both of the expressions in two disjoint parts, then show that the subexpressions are equivalent.

For the first part,
$$((A_1 \cap B_1) \cup (A_1 \cap B_2) \cup ... \cup (A_n \cap B_m)) \Leftrightarrow$$
$$(A_1 \cup A_2 \cup A_3 \cup ... \cup A_n) \cap (B_1 \cup B_2 \cup B_3 \cup ... \cup B_n)$$
holds because $\cap$ distributes over $\cup$.

After eliminating $\neg$, the second part is to prove that

$$((A_1 \cap B_1 \cap A_1 \cap B_2) \cup (A_1 \cap B_1 \cap A_1 \cap B_3) \cup ... \cup (A_n \cap B_{m-1} \cap A_n \cap B_m)) \quad (1)$$

is equivalent to:

$$((A_1 \cap A_2) \cup (A_1 \cap A_3) \cup ... \cup (A_{n-1} \cap A_n)) \cap ((B_1 \cap B_2) \cup ... \cup (B_{n-1} \cap B_n)) \quad (2)$$

After applying distributive law, (2) can be written in DNF as well:

$$((A_1 \cap A_2 \cap B_1 \cap B_2) \cup (A_1 \cap A_2 \cap B_1 \cap B_3) \cup ... \cup (A_n - 1 \cap A_n \cap B_{(m-1)} \cap B_m)) \quad (3)$$

Having both of the expressions in DNF, we can easily show that each disjunct from (1) can be expressed using a combination of disjuncts in (3), and vice-versa. Having (1) $\subseteq$ (3) and (3) $\subseteq$ (1) means that (1) = (3), thus these subexpressions are equivalent,too. Having proven that the corresponding subexpressions are equivalent, we conclude that $(O_1 \cap O_2) \Leftrightarrow (P_1$ merge $P_2)$.**Q.E.D**

Information Modeling for End to End Composition of Semantic Web Services

Arun Kumar, Biplav Srivastava, and Sumit Mittal

IBM India Research Laboratory,
Block 1, IIT Campus, Hauz Khas, New Delhi 110016, India
{kkarun, sbiplav, sumittal}@in.ibm.com

Abstract. One of the main goals of the semantic web services effort is
to enable automated composition of web services. An end-to-end view
of the service composition process involves automation of composite service creation, development of executable workflows and deployment on
an execution environment. However, the main focus in literature has
been on the initial part of formally representing web service capabilities
and reasoning about their composition using AI techniques. Based upon
our experience in building an end-to-end composition tool for application integration, we bring out issues that have an impact on information
modeling aspects of the composition process. In this paper, we present
approaches for solving problems relating to scalability and manageabil-
ity of service descriptions and data flow construction for operationalizing
the composed services.

1 Introduction

In many industrial applications such as mobile telephony, service providers face
intense competition. In response, they need to continually develop compelling
applications (e.g., movie recommendation system) to attract and retain end-
users, with quick time-to-market. Much of this service/application development
is currently done manually in an ad hoc manner, without standard frameworks
or libraries, thus resulting in poor reuse of software assets. When a new service
is needed, the desired capability is informally specified and then, an application
developer must create this capability using component services available in-house
or from known vendors. A component-oriented software development approach to
application integration where each software is wrapped as a web service would
offer substantial benefits in creating new services by leveraging web services
composition.

Web services composition involves concepts from the AI domain as well as
software engineering/programming domain. When viewed as a *program*, input
and output parameters become important whereas when viewed as an *action*,
the preconditions and effects become dominant [19]. However, most of the work
in semantic web services community has focused on the AI approach of formally
representing web service capabilities in ontologies like OWL-S [15], and reasoning about their composition using goal-oriented inferencing techniques from

Y. Gil et al. (Eds.): ISWC 2005, LNCS 3729, pp. 476–490, 2005.

planning[11]. An end-to-end view of web service composition starting from new service specification to an executing instance of the composed service is missing. To address this view, we have developed a prototype of a tool for facilitating new service creation and application integration for telecom service providers [1].

Our solution takes an end to end view and synergistically combines the AI approach of reasoning about web services functionality based on their preconditions and effects, and the distributed programming approach of selecting instances to optimize end-to-end runtime metrics, currently adopted by semantic web community and the industry, respectively. The solution drives the composition process right from specification of the business process in OWL-S, through creation of desired functionality using planning techniques into an abstract plan (workflow), through generation of a deployable workflow by selection and binding of appropriate service instances (specified using WSDL[1]), to finally deploying and running the composite service (specified using BPEL [5]).

The web service modeling efforts in the semantic web community, however, fall short of expectations of real world applications. During the course of our prototype development, we ran into several important modeling issues. We find that existing OWL-S service support is insufficient for the end-to-end composition vision because (a) the modeling does not allow for best knowledge engineering practices of modularity, conciseness and generality and (b) composed web services cannot be automatically operationalized due to lack of contextual information associated with input and output parameters.

A few alternative formalisms have been proposed to address OWL-S deficiencies but they focus more on foundational frameworks to overcome representational weaknesses [14, 21] rather than address ways for efficient, automatic, end-to-end composition. In this paper, we investigate information modeling issues for end-to-end composition of web services and propose related pragmatic extensions to OWL-S. Most specifically, our contributions through this work are:

- We differentiate web service types from service instances. This helps in organizing the expected thousands of web services into categories, allows the scaling of OWL-S ontology for inferencing and permits systematic treatment of non-functional requirements.
- We define support for context to disambiguate intended meanings of input and output (i/o) parameters. In other words, we introduce semantics for i/o parameters to construct the data flow after the control flow has been worked out by planning.

Representation and reasoning go hand-in-hand in any application. While we mainly focus on information modeling when using contingent planning for web service composition, we clarify at the outset that the proposed solution is also applicable if a different planner or a more complex planning formalism were to be used. More details of planning is given in the related works.

The rest of the paper is organized as follows. Section 2 describes a motivating scenario, highlighting the problems that surface while using OWL-S for end-to-

---

[1] http://www.w3.org/TR/wsdl

end composition. Section 3 discusses the issue of scaling of services ontology. Section 4 deals with generation of data flow to operationalize the composite service. Section 5 briefly describes our implementation. Section 6 gives some related work and Section 7 concludes the paper.

2 A Motivating Scenario

Suppose a telco wishes to offer its telecom and IT infrastructure to enterprise clients, by creating and deploying services that would enable automation of the client's business processes. An example of such a business process is a simple Customer Order Management System for a *FlowerDelivery* service. Assume that the registry of available services in the telco's infrastructure consists of a *Directory service*, one or more flower selling services - *FreshFlowerShop service, Fragrant-FlowerShop service*, etc., multiple credit card services such as *VisaCard service, MasterCard service* etc. and a *Dispatch service*. Figure 1 shows the ≺Inputs, Outputs, Preconditions, Effects≻ (IOPEs) of these services.

The figure also shows a feasible plan for the new service obtainable with an AI planner. The plan consists of invocations to directory service for obtaining

```
New Service Requirement
Name: FlowerDeliveryService
Input: PersonName, PersonName, FlowerName, NumOfFlowers, CreditCard
Output: OrderReceipt, DeliveryReceipt
Precon: PersonName notNullᵃ, PersonName notNull, NumOfFlowers <= 1000,
        FlowerName oneOf FLOWERLIST, CreditCard hasBalance
Effect: Packet deliveredTo PersonName, OrderReceipt sentTo PersonName,
        DeliveryReceipt sentTo PersonName, CreditCard debited

Services in Registry
Name: FreshFlowerShop Service              Name: Directory Service
Input: Address, Address, FlowerName, NumOfFlowers    Input: Name
Output:OrderReceipt, Packet, Amount        Output: Address
Precon:Address available, Address available,    Precon: Name notNull
       FlowerName oneOf FLOWERLIST,
       NumOfFlowers <= 1500
Effect: OrderReceipt sentTo Address,       Effect: Address available
        Amount available, Packet available

Name: FragrantFlowerShop Service           Name: VisaCard Service
Input: Address, Address, FlowerName, NumOfFlowers    Input: Amount, CreditCard
Output:OrderReceipt, Packet, Amount        Output: Authorization
Precon:Address available, Address available,    Precon: Amount available,
       FlowerName oneOf FLOWERLIST,             CreditCard hasBalance
       NumOfFlowers <= 1200
Effect: OrderReceipt sentTo Address,       Effect: CreditCard debited,
        Amount available, Packet available          Authorization available

Name: CheapFlowerShop Service              Name: Dispatch Service
Input: Address, Address, ItemCode, NumOfItems    Input: Authorization, Address, Address, Packet
Output:Acknowledgment, Packet, Charges     Output: DeliveryReceipt
Precon:Address available, ItemCode oneOf ITEMLIST, Precon: Authorization available, Address available,
       Address available, NumOfItems <= 100        Address available, Packet available
Effect: Acknowledgment sentTo Address,     Effect: DeliveryReceipt sentTo Address,
        Amount available, Packet available          Packet deliveredTo Address

A plan for FlowerDelivery Service
// I is for input and O is for output
Step 1: Directory Service1(I:N1, O:A1)
        Directory Service2(I:N2, O:A2)
Step 2: FreshFlowerShop Service(I:A3, I:A4, I:FN, I:NUM, O:ORCPT, O:PKT, O:AMT)
Step 3: VisaCard Service(I:AMT, I:CC, O:AUTH)
Step 4: Dispatch Service(I:AUTH, I:A5, I:A6, I:PKT, O:DRCPT)
```

ᵃ The string in **boldface** is the predicate and the associated strings are its parameters

Fig. 1. The FlowerDelivery Service composition scenario

addresses of the sender and the recipient. This is followed by invocation to one of the flower shop services for obtaining desired flowers. An order receipt is sent to the sender. Pricing details are passed on to the credit card payment gateway and on successful authorization, shipping details and the flower packet are handed over to the dispatch service for delivery. A delivery receipt is now sent to the sender. In generating an end-to-end deployable plan for this scenario, we faced the modeling problems listed below.

Service Types Vs Instances: The scenario described above has multiple flower shop services. These services can offer different kinds of flower packages (e.g. bouquets, decoration styles etc.), but essentially they are all flower shops. This fact can be very useful for efficient representation of such services. Unfortunately, OWL-S does not capture the notion of service *types*. Each OWL-S description currently pertains to a single instance of a service.

There are several drawbacks with this approach. First, given the requirements of the new *FlowerDelivery service* as shown in Figure 1, the composition tool needs to consider and evaluate each and every instance of such FlowerShop kind of service available. This seriously affects the performance and scalability of the composer (planner) since there may be hundreds of such FlowerShop service instances available whereas for obtaining a feasible functional composition, different instances of similar kinds of services need not be considered.

The second drawback of the current approach is related to standardization. Since there is nothing common defined for similar services, a composition tool cannot infer anything about the degree of similarity or dissimilarity of these services. In our scenario, each of the FlowerShop services have different profiles even though their underlying process model may be the same. In Figure 1 the FreshFlowershop Service has a different profile than that of CheapFlowerShop Service. We can try to rectify this by adding some relations in the ontology such as *OrderReceipt* **isEquivalentTo** *Acknowledgment*, but it does not always work as in the case of FlowerName and ItemCode. Since the profile model is used to advertise a service, these two would appear as different kinds of services.

The third drawback relates to the service grounding part. Since grounding is specific to each service instance, a composition taking that into account is less likely to be stable - changes at the level of individual service instance operation take place much more frequently than those at the level of service functionality. The composition becomes prone to small implementation changes made to the service instance. For example, if the VisaCard Service originally supported 64-bit encryption protocol (specified in its grounding, not shown in figure) then the plan in Figure 1 may break if VisaCard service upgrades to 128-bit encryption.

Support for Data Flow Construction: When we seek to operationalize composed plans, we are in fact generating programs. A program contains the specification of both its control flow (the dependence among activities) and the data flow (the dependence among data manipulations). Planning techniques can be used to easily generate the control flow for the composite service given the precondition and effect information for available service types, but generating the complete data flow needs reasoning with contexts of inputs and outputs.

For the full composition, data flow has to be produced between dependent services to make the plan executable. In Figure 1, the FreshFlowerShop Service accepts two addresses - one of these addresses is that of the sender and the other is that of the recipient. Even if this distinction of their semantics is not necessary for generating the control flow, it could be important for the data flow. Specifically, the two addresses can have different meanings and different data (message) types. In the FlowerDelivery scenario, to determine the relation between input/output of component services, we must (automatically) figure out things such as the following:

DF1: CreditCard information from the user goes directly to the VisaCard Service.

DF2: distinguish the semantics of the two Address inputs each to the Fresh-FlowerShop Service and the DispatchService.

DF3: map the Address outputs from invocation of the two DirectoryService instances to the Address inputs of both the FreshFlowerShop Service as well as the DispatchService.

DF4: DeliveryReceipt from DispatchService and OrderReceipt from Fresh-FlowerShop Service together constitute the output for the user.

In programming languages this issue is resolved by specifying an ordering among the parameters of a function or procedure. A human developer could then look at the language specification and specify the parameters accordingly. However, in the web service composition scenario, software programs cannot automatically derive and interpret semantics of all parameters just from the available ordering. The context for the inputs and outputs need to be made explicit. One provision to model the semantics associated with the input/output parameters is by creating new concepts in the domain ontology. But this will make the ontology large and brittle. The latter consequence is well understood in knowledge engineering[18] and that is the reason very specific terms are not recommended in an ontology.

In the following two sections, we will look into these modeling issues more closely and propose approaches for resolving them.

3   Scaling Services Ontology

In order to work with large collections of web services – categorizing them, supporting multiple views [10], standardization and for stable functional compositions – we need to support web service *types* that are described independent of individual web service *instances*. The approach of separating type definitions from instance definitions has been used successfully in data models for distributed systems management [13] and has various modeling benefits. In this section, we first delve into the classification of services into types and instances, then look at the support for this classification in OWL-S and finally discuss the issue of modeling non functional service capabilities.

3.1   Classifying Services into Types and Instances

Our proposal raises the question of what kind of relationship a web service type has with its various instances. A web service type captures the core functionality of a class of web services. Individual instances belonging to that class of services must adhere to the basic type definition but may be allowed to offer minor variations under some constraints. An important desiderata is that any composition which is produced with the web service type should be still valid when any of its web service instance is selected. This is ensured if the precondition of a web service type is more specific than precondition of its instances and its effect is more general than effect of any of its instances. We can summarize the relationship as:

If $S^{instance}$ is of S^{type},

1. $S^{type}_{precondition} \vdash S^{instance}_{precondition}$ and

2. $S^{type}_{effect} \dashv S^{instance}_{effect}$

The above relationship states that the precondition of the service type entails the precondition of the service instance so that the latter is satisfied whenever the former is. For effects, the reverse is true. With this, given a web service request R, when the request matches a service type ($R \bowtie S^{type}$), the relationship between R and the web service instances would be:

1. $R_{precondition} \bowtie S^{type}_{precondition} \Rightarrow (\forall S^{instance}: S^{type}) R_{precondition} \bowtie S^{instance}_{precondition}$ and

2. $R_{effect} \bowtie S^{type}_{effect} \Rightarrow (\forall S^{instance}: S^{type}) R_{effect} \bowtie S^{instance}_{effect}$

According to it, if a request R matches a web service type, where matching can be exact or defined over a range as in [16], all the instances of the web service type will also match. While this relationship would guarantee that compositions are valid when the abstract plan is concretized, it can be overly restrictive because the precondition of the web service type is required to be more specific than all its instances. We will call this as the *strict* relation. To relax the restriction, we use the insight that eventually each web service type referred in the abstract plan will be instantiated by only one web service instance. Therefore, as long as we could guarantee that if a request R matches a web service type, some but at least one instance of the web service type will also match, the abstract will be successfully concretized and the composition will succeed. That is,

1. $R_{precondition} \bowtie S^{type}_{precondition} \Rightarrow (\exists S^{instance-i}: S^{type}) R_{precondition} \bowtie S^{instance-i}_{precondition}$ and

2. $R_{effect} \bowtie S^{type}_{effect} \Rightarrow (\exists S^{instance-j}: S^{type}) R_{effect} \bowtie S^{instance-j}_{effect}$ and

3. instance-i = instance-j

The decision of whether to follow the *strict* or *relaxed* relationship during domain modeling is one of balancing tradeoffs. With the former, the abstract plans can be automatically concretized because all its service instances are guaranteed to preserve composition. With the latter, a service type has to be more specific than at least one of its instance and this would simplify building of the services ontology (e.g., more instances for a type). During the concretization of abstract plan, all instances might need to be explored for say, optimality. In that case, additional constraints will have to be checked for instances whose preconditions are more specific than that of their type. Checking these additional constraints may require the intervention of a developer.

We adopt the *relaxed* relation above as the guideline for our domain modeling. In Figure 2, FlowerShopService type captures the category of flower shop services whose instances are Fresh, Fragrant and Cheap Flower shop services. The preconditions of FlowerShopService type is the same as Fresh and Fragrant service instances (disregarding the non-functional requirement of *NumOfFlowers*, see below) but different from precondition of Cheap Flower service which has a restriction on *ItemCode*.

Fig. 2. Proposed modeling for FlowerDelivery scenario with svc. types, roles & NFCs

3.2   Support for Service Types

As previously noted, currently OWL-S is designed to model a single web service instance [15]. It consists of a *ServiceProfile* that describes the interface of the service, a *ServiceModel* that describes the details of its operation and a *ServiceGrounding* that provides information about interoperation with that service using messages.

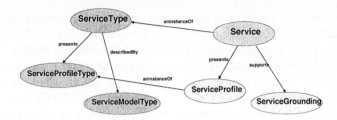

Fig. 3. *Modified OWL-S* upper ontology

We propose to separate the representation of web service type definitions from instance definitions. This means that the OWL-S upper ontology needs enhancements to have a *ServiceType* class hierarchy in addition to the *Service* hierarchy (see Fig. 3). The *ServiceProfile* model of the current OWL-S *Service* hierarchy is essentially a type definition and can be moved to the *ServiceType* hierarchy. The *ServiceProfile* of an instance will now point to the corresponding *ServiceProfileType* for structure, and contain the actual values of the Inputs, Outputs, Preconditions and Effects (IOPE) parameters applicable for that service instance.

ServiceGrounding is a concept that applies to instances rather than types and can stay as it is. *ServiceModel* should ideally be encapsulated inside the service interface and not exposed to the external world. Making the model visible outside the service is useful only if it describes the conversational aspect of the web service that would be needed to interoperate with it. In such a case, it should be included in the *ServiceType* hierarchy since a common conversation model should be applicable to all instances of a service type. In other words, we propose to have an ontology for service types that consists of *ServiceProfileType* and *ServiceModelType* model. This would be in addition to an ontology for service instances that consists of a *ServiceProfile* and a *ServiceGrounding*.

With this representation, a new kind of service can be specified in the ontology by adding an object of type *serviceType*, without having to create an actual running instance first. This is not possible in the current OWL-S ontology. Creating an object of ServiceType would include defining the parameters in its profile by populating the *ServiceProfileType* model, and describing the conversation model by populating the *ServiceModelType* model. Each actual running instance of this web service would be represented by an object of type *Service* and include a reference to its *ServiceType* object. Its *ServiceProfile* model would contain the actual values of the parameters listed in the corresponding *ServiceProfileType*.

3.3   Modeling Non Functional Service Capabilities

The functional capability (FC) of a web service describes its core functionality. It is expressed through IOPEs that capture the transformation performed by this service. The non-functional capabilities (NFCs), on the other hand, help in characterizing the service further by capturing its optional features, such as cost, QoS etc. OWL-S has provision to represent NFCs through profile attributes which may contain parameters other than the functional IOPEs.

Since NFCs inherently capture properties of service instances (and not of types), they are not needed during functional composition. In contrast, FCs form the core of the functional composition process. NFCs play an important role during selection of appropriate service instances in order to meet the end-user requirements. The current OWL-S only deals with service instances and therefore all the functional as well as non-functional attributes are in the ServiceProfile. In our modified OWL-S upper ontology (presented in Figure 3), the FCs get represented in ServiceProfileType. The ServiceProfile of an instance inherits these FCs from the ServiceProfileType and adds the NFCs to it.

In some domains it may be desirable to model certain service features as mandatory for all instances of a service type. In military applications, for example, it may be necessary to make all service instances secure. For such domains, it seems logical to model NFCs such as security in the service type itself. These non-functional capabilities now form a part of the core functionality. They are included in ServiceProfileTypes and are utilized in selecting service types during the logical composition phase.

Table 1 shows the NFCs for the FlowerShop service instances. Note that NumOfFlowers is not modeled in FlowerShopService type in Figure 2, as opposed to Figure 1 where it is included as a part of precondition of the services. The NumOfFlowers requirement in the desired composite service was for $\prec 1000$ and this would be ensured while picking instances.

Table 1. Representing Instances for FlowerShop Services

Instance Name	Security Level	Response Time	Max #Flowers
FreshFlowerShopService	Restricted	70 sec	1500
FragrantFlowerShopService	Confidential	240 sec	1200
CheapFlowerShopService	Public	30 sec	100

4   Generation of Data Flow

One of the main differences between knowledge engineering and programming, as described in [18][2], is that while logic sentences in the former tend to be self-contained, the statements in a program depend heavily on surrounding context. To operationalize the workflow of the composite service, we need support for incorporating context with IO parameters of component web services. One option is to introduce specific terms in the domain ontology, one for each possible concept and each valid context. However, this makes the ontology large and brittle. The consequence of this is well understood in knowledge engineering [18] and that is the reason very specific terms are not recommended in an ontology.

---

[2] Chapter 8, Page 222.

The semantics of each input/output parameter can be expressed along two dimensions. The first one specifies the meaning of the parameter as intended by the service designer. For instance, the designer of FreshFlowerShop Service could designate one Address parameter as the *From* address and the other one as the *To* address. The second dimension is dictated by the composition of which this service becomes a component. If in a composition, the input parameter Name to the Directory Service is assigned the label *From*, the output Address should be assigned the same label.

4.1 Context Resolution Using Roles

We seek to solve the problem of context resolution by explicitly encoding the context for inputs and outputs using the notion of *roles*. A role is a term that *qualifies* a concept. That is, for any concept φ, (ψ φ) specifies that the role played by φ is ψ. Roles are optionally specified on the inputs and outputs by the service developer. They come from a separate ontology, and are structured and standardized in a domain similar to concepts. Figure 4 shows a sample role ontology for roles that could be played during categorizing offerings, item transfer and expertise lookup. Depending on need, a parameter can have either one, multiple or no specific roles. In Figure 2, the user assigns the roles of *From* and *To* to the two input addresses in the input specification.

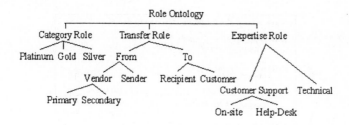

Fig. 4. Sample Role Ontology

In [8], the authors give an extensive coverage of how context is handled in knowledge representation in AI. Their solution is to explicitly model context as a resource and they introduce terms to specify *lifting rules* so that propositions could be generalized across contexts to serve their data aggregation application. In comparison to the roles, the context of [8] means that if *ist(c_i, φ)*, the proposition φ is true in context c_i. The two usages can be combined - for example, *ist(c_i, ψ φ)* means that the proposition φ has the role ψ in the context c_i. Currently OWL-S does not support the notion of roles for service representation.

A key motivation for defining roles is that they should be generic in nature. If a role can be attached with multiple concepts, it reduces brittleness in the ontology by eliminating the need for specific terms. Introduction of roles, however, requires the developer to define the roles played by the input and output parameters in her specification of the service.

4.2 Role Propagation

Roles can be propagated so that input or output or both can be associated with new roles in the presence of roles coming from requirement specification and/or those of other services. New roles can be acquired while matching a specification with a service instance or from the input to the output of a service and vice-versa. When a role can or cannot be propagated will be specified by the service modeler for a service using some rule language like SWRL. Some rules are given in Figure 5. Rule 1 says that a role from the specification can be propagated to input of an instance. In Figure 2, using this rule, the roles *From* and *To* from the requirements specification are transferred to the corresponding inputs of the Directory service instances. Rule 2 says that roles can be propagated from the input to the output of a service. In our scenario, using this rule, the role of input *From* or *To* to the Directory service is carried to its output. Rule 3 says that role can be propagated from the output of one service instance to input of a successor, if the successor does not have roles assigned for its inputs. Rule 4 says that if the inputs (or outputs) of a service has parameters of the same type (with no roles assigned), no role is propagated. This is because having the same parameter type introduces ambiguity for propagation. For example, if roles were not assigned to the two Address inputs of the FlowerShop Service by the service developer, no role for them can be inferred automatically from the composition.

Given service S with inputs I and outputs O

1. IF $\psi_I^{instance} = \{\}$ and $\psi_I^{spec} \neq \{\}$
   THEN $\psi_I^{instance} = \psi_I^{spec}$

2. IF $\psi_O = \{\}$ and $\psi_I \neq \{\}$
   THEN $\psi_O = \psi_I$

3. IF $\psi_I^{next-instance} = \{\}$ and $\psi_O^{prev-instance} \neq \{\}$
   THEN $\psi_I^{next-instance} = \psi_O^{prev-instance}$

4. IF $((\exists I_i, I_j, i \neq j \text{ s.t. } I_i^{type} = I_j^{type}) \vee$
   $(\exists O_i, O_j, i \neq j \text{ s.t. } O_i^{type} = O_j^{type})$
   THEN do not propagate

Fig. 5. Some rules for role propagation

The rules cannot be generic because role propagation should depend on the way the service processes its inputs to generate outputs, something best known to the service developer. Therefore, we advocate that rules be provided on a per service basis, taking into account the way service has been implemented.

4.3 Data Flow Construction Using Roles

Going back to the data flow problems raised in Section 2, credit card and receipts can be deduced from the IO data types of the services in the composition. For address, the role propagation rules can be used with Directory Service to automatically deduce the data flow as follows. Rule 1 will associate different roles

From and *To* to the two directory Service instances and Rule 2 will propagate them to the outputs. Now, using the roles on outputs of Directory Services, the data flow with the next services - FlowerShop Service and Dispatch Service - is found by simple role alignment.

Assigning roles has two benefits - on the one hand, role disambiguates between multiple instances of the same concept in a service profile thus clarifying the intended usage of the concept in the service. On the other hand, it enables the creation of a context using which the data flow from other service to this service. Association of roles with parameters of a web service also provides an extra dimension for matching requirements. A match-making tool would try to search services for which the input parameters have roles that fit the description of the requirement.

4.4 Discussion

In [8], the authors point out that while the aim of a context mechanism is to qualify information, in the semantic web, the mechanism should additionally be able to handle its large scale and distributedness, i.e., the mechanism should yet be easy to inference with and easy to use. They argue that the best way to approach a context mechanism is by focusing on the needs of a specific application, and they focus on data integration. In this section, we presented roles as a pragmatic approach for resolving ambiguities during service composition.

However, there are other kinds of situations where roles are not sufficient. To illustrate, in situation DF3 mentioned in Section 2, the data flow could be constructed using roles under the assumption that an output from a service is unconstrained. For example, the solution assumed that an output can serve as input for more than one service later in the plan. Modeling of such assumptions is not handled. Full automation of data flow construction needs full support for contextual reasoning.

5   Implementation

We have implemented a prototype tool that allows end to end composition of web services [1]. The composition is basically done in two stages:

1. **Logical Composition:** This phase provides functional composition of *service types* to create new functionality that is currently not available.
2. **Physical Composition:** This phase enables the selection of component *service instances* based on non-functional (e.g. QoS) requirements, that would then be bound together for deploying the newly created composite service.

In the absence of tools to support our modified OWL-S ontology (introduced in Section 3), we used the current OWL-S Profile model to represent the service types. The combination of SNOBASE[3] and PSME [6] was used as registry for service type definitions. The logical phase uses service types for creation of

---

[3] http://www.alphaworks.ibm.com/tech/snobase

abstract composition(s) delivering the desired functionality. Once an abstract composition is obtained then the physical phase uses a registry of web service instances to select appropriate instances satisfying the user's non-functional requirements. We used Web Service Matchmaking Engine (WSME) [7] as a service instances registry to contain Web Service Description Language (WSDL) specifications for each advertised service along with its non-functional capabilities. The tool produces deployable and executable composite service represented in BPEL language.

We have implemented a Role Ontology for the flower shop scenario and modified our OWL-S service descriptions to incorporate role information along with each input/output parameter. The roles help in guiding the data flow construction as discussed.

6   Related Work

Information modeling for end-to-end web services composition is challenging. The composition problem poses challenge to existing planning methods in representation of complex actions, handling of richly typed messages, dynamic object creation and specification of multi-partner interactions [20]. We are using *limited* contingent planning for generating the control flow during web service composition [12, 1]. Contingent planning (CP) deals with planning for domain with incomplete knowledge and sensing. In the case of web services, the value of all logical terms may not be known in the initial state but they can be found at the runtime using sensing actions. Our planner can also take input about selective conditions from the user and then uses it to efficiently focus search. But the modeling solutions are applicable independent of the form of planning used.

Many authors have raised issues about OWL-S. For example, [14] gives a list of problems with OWL-S: conceptual ambiguity (e.g., what is a service?), poor axiomatization (there is no firm concept or relation hierarchy and several relations take placeholders in the domain or range), loose design (support for multiple views is needed at different levels of granularity), and narrow scope on information systems which does not make distinction with real world objects and events. However, it does not deal with scalability, service quality and assessment which is essential for end to end composition.

The end-user requirements for the composite service, like that of any software program, can consist of functional as well as non-functional requirements. The non-functional attributes relate to performance, reliability and other user-acceptance issues. [4] describes how such requirements can be qualitatively arranged as goal structures and used to design systems. Their framework allows treating requirements as potentially conflicting or synergistic goals to achieve during the software development process. A middleware for composing web services with QoS in mind is presented in [22]. We characterize how to model non-functional capabilities for the composition process.

Our solution regarding generation of data-flow is related to [9] which describes an environment for building reusable ontologies based on the concept of roles. This work informally defines role as a characteristic that a basic domain concept exhibits in a context. We can use their tool to build role ontology in parallel with the domain ontology. Our solution is in the spirit of [3] where a formal framework was proposed for data integration based on dynamic logic. An alternative proposal to OWL-S is the SESMA [17] model which directly handles inputs and outputs. Here, a notion of conversation data set is introduced to hold the input and output variables with values, and these could be evaluated as part of reasoning with the service's preconditions and effects.

Problem of data flow analysis in programs has been studied extensively in the compiler domain. Gathering knowledge of how data flows in a program is conceptualized using the life-cycle and scope of variables [2]. Analyzing the data flow should be differentiated from generation of the flow itself. The former arises when component modules have already been integrated and bounded using variables. The latter presents itself while the developer is trying to integrate the modules, and is therefore the harder issue to resolve.

7   Conclusion

Current efforts in the world of semantic web services focus on formally representing service capabilities and on reasoning about composition of services using AI techniques. We presented several issues that arise when we view the composition of web services from an end-to-end perspective. Concretely, we delved into the aspects related to scaling of service ontologies and support for generation of data flow information to operationalize a composite workflow. We discussed the need for separating service type from service instances and introduced the notion of roles to help disambiguate the semantics of IO parameters. We showed that the proposed guidelines are helpful in an end-to-end composition scenario.

References

1. V. Agarwal, K. Dasgupta, N. Karnik, A. Kumar, A. Kundu, S. Mittal, and B. Srivastava. A Service Creation Environment based on End to End Composition of Web Services. In *Proceedings of the 14th International World Wide Conference*, May 2005.
2. A. V. Aho, R. Sethi, and J. Ullman. *Compilers: Principles, Techniques and Tools*. Addison-Wesley, 1986.
3. Diego Calvanese, Giuseppe De Giacomo, Maurizio Lenzerini, Daniele Nardi, and Riccardo Rosati. Description logic framework for information integration. In *Principles of Knowledge Representation and Reasoning*, pages 2–13, 1998.
4. L. Chung and B. A. Nixon. Dealing with Non-Functional Requirements: Three Experimental Studies of a Process-Oriented Approach. In *International Conference on Software Engineering*, pages 25–37, 1995.
5. F. Curbera et al. Business Process Execution Language for Web Services. http://www-106.ibm.com/developerworks/webservices/library/ws-bpel/, 2002.
6. P. Doshi, R. Goodwin, R. Akkiraju, and S. Roeder. Parameterized Semantic Matchmaking for Workflow Composition. Technical Report RC23133, March 2004.

7. C. Facciorusso, S. Field, R. Hauser, Y. Hoffner, R. Humbel, R. Pawlitzek, W. Rjaibi, and C. Siminitz. A Web Services Matchmaking Engine for Web Services. In *Proc. 4th Intl. Conf. on e-Commerce and Web technologies*, Sep. 2003.

8. R. Guha, R. McCool, and R. Fikes. Contexts for the Semantic Web. In *Proceedings of the International Semantic Web Conference*, 2004.

9. K. Kozaki, Y. Kitamura, M. Ikeda, and R. Mizoguchi. Hozo: An Environment for Building/Using Ontologies Based on a Fundamental Consideration of "Role" and "Relationship". In *13th Int. Conf. on Knowledge Engg. and Knowledge Management*, 2002.

10. R. Lara, H. Lausen, S. Arroyo, J. de Bruijn, and D. Fensel. Semantic Web Services: Description Requirements and Current Technologies. In *International Workshop on Electronic Commerce, Agents, and Semantic Web Services*, September 2003.

11. S. McIlraith, T. C. Son, and H. Zeng. Semantic Web Services. *IEEE Intelligent Systems, Special Issue on the Semantic Web.*, 16(2):46–53, March/April 2001.

12. A. Mediratta and B. Srivastava. User-driven search control in contingent planning and an application. In *IBM Research Report*, 2005.

13. Common Information Model (CIM) Metrics Model, Version 2.7. Distributed Management Task Force, http://www.dmtf.org/standards/documents/CIM/DSP0141.pdf, June 2003.

14. P. Mika, D. Oberle, A. Gangemi, and M. Sabou. Foundations for Service Ontologies: Aligning OWL-S to DOLCE. In *Proceedings of the 13th International World Wide Web Conference*, 2004.

15. OWL Services Coalition. OWL-S: Semantic Markup for Web Services. http://www.daml.org/services/ owl-s/1.0/owl-s.html, Nov. 2003.

16. M. Paolucci, T. Kawamura, T. R. Payne, and K. Sycara. Semantic matching of web services capabilities. In *Proceedings of the First International Semantic Web Conference, LNCS 2342*, pages 333–347. Springer-Verlag, 2002.

17. J. Peer. Semantic service markup with SESMA - language specification, version 0.7. In *http://elektra.mcm.unisg.ch/pbwsc/docs/sesma_0.7.pdf*, 2004.

18. S. Russell and P. Norvig. Artificial Intelligence: A Modern Approach (First Ed.). Prentice Hall Publication, ISBN: 0131038052., 1995.

19. Marta Sabou, Debbie Richards, and Sander van Splunter. An Experience Report on using DAML-S. In *Proceedings of 12th International World Wide Web Conference, (WWW)*, May 2003.

20. B. Srivastava and J. Koehler. Web Service Composition - Current Solutions and Open Problems. ICAPS 2003 Workshop on Planning for Web Services, 2003.

21. WSMO. Web Services Modeling Ontology. http://www.wsmo.org, 2004.

22. L. Zeng, B. Benatallah, A. Ngu, M. Dumas, J. Kalagnanam, and H. Chang. QoS-Aware Middleware for Web Services Composition. In *IEEE Transactions on Software Engineering*, pages 311–327, 2004.

Searching Dynamic Communities with Personal Indexes

Alexander Löser[1], Christoph Tempich[3], Bastian Quilitz[1], Wolf-Tilo Balke[2],
Steffen Staab[4], and Wolfgang Nejdl[2]

[1] CIS,University of Technology Berlin, Einsteinufer 17, 10587 Berlin, Germany
{aloeser, baqui}@cs.tu-berlin.de
[2] L3S, University of Hannover, 30167 Hannover, Germany
balke, nejdl@l3s.de
[3] AIFB, University of Karlsruhe 76128 Karlsruhe, Germany
tempich@aifb.uni-karlsruhe.de
[4] ISWeb, University of Koblenz Landau 56016 Koblenz, Germany
staab@uni-koblenz.de

Abstract. Often the challenge of finding relevant information is reduced to find the 'right' people who will answer our question. In this paper we present innovative algorithms called INGA (Interest-based Node Grouping Algorithms) which integrate personal routing indices into semantic query processing to boost performance. Similar to social networks peers in INGA cooperate to efficiently route queries for documents along adaptive shortcut-based overlays using only local, but semantically well chosen information. We propose active and passive shortcut creation strategies for index building and a novel algorithm to select the most promising content providers depending on each peer index with respect to the individual query. We quantify the benefit of our indexing strategy by extensive performance experiments in the SWAP simulation infrastructure. While obtaining high recall values compared to other state-of-the-art algorithms, we show that INGA improves recall and reduces the number of messages significantly.

1 Introduction

Finding relevant information from a heterogeneous set of information resources is a longstanding problem in computing. In everyday life we observe that there are successful strategies for finding relevant information in a social network of people. Studies of social networks show that the challenge of finding relevant information may be reduced to find the 'right' people. 'The right people' generally are the ones who either have the desired piece of information and can directly provide the relevant content or the ones who can recommend 'the right people'. Milgram's [15] and Kleinberg's [12] experiments illustrated that people with only local knowledge of the network (i.e. their immediate acquaintances) were quite successful at constructing acquaintance chains of short length, leading to 'small world' networks. In such a network, a query is forwarded along that outgoing link which takes it 'closest' to the destination. We observe that such mechanisms in social networks work although

Y. Gil et al. (Eds.): ISWC 2005, LNCS 3729, pp. 491–505, 2005.

- people may not always be available to respond to requests,
- people may shift their interests and attention,
- people may not have exactly the 'right' knowledge, but only knowledge which is *semantically close*.

I.e., the real-world social network is *highly dynamic* with regard to availability of peers and with regard to expertise about topics and it needs *semantic similarity* in order to determine 'the right person'.

Inspired by these observations and focussed by the requirements of semantic search in the setting of distributed autonomous information sources, we have conceived INGA a novel peer-to-peer algorithm where each peer plays the role of a person in a social network. In INGA , facts are stored and managed locally on each peer constituting the 'topical knowledge' of the peer. A peer responds to a query be providing an answer matching the query or by forwarding the query to what he deems to be the most appropriate peers. For the purpose of determining the most appropriate peers, each peer maintains a *personal semantic shortcut index*. The index is created and maintained in our highly dynamic setting in a lazy manner, i.e. by analyzing the queries that are initiated by users of the peer-to-peer network and that happen to pass through the peer.

The personal semantic shortcut index maintained at each peer reflects that a peer may play the following four different roles for the other peers in the network (in decreasing order of utility):

- The best peers to query are always those that already have answered the query or a semantically similar query in the past successfully. We call such peers *content providers*.
- If no content providers are known, peers are queried that have *issued semantically similar queries* in the past. The assumption is that this peer has been successful in getting matching answers and now we can directly learn from him about suitable content providers. We call such peers *recommenders*.
- If we do not know either of the above we query peers that have established a good social network to other persons over a variety of general domains. Such peers form a *bootstrapping network*.
- If we fail to discover any of the above we fall back to the default layer of neighboring peers. To avoid overfitting to peers already known we occasionally select random peers for a query. We call this the *default network*.

Seen from a local perspective, each peer maintains in its index information about some peers, about what roles these peers play for which topic and how useful they were in the past. Seen from a global perspective, each of the four roles results in a network layer of peers that is independent from the other layers.

1.1 Related Work

The first approaches for efficient indexing in P2P architectures were central indices, that have to transmit either meta data about the available content to central indexing peers, like e.g. GlOSS [9] or *Napster*. One of today's main technique for indexing P2P systems are so-called distributed hash tables (DHTs),(e.g. [1] or see [4] for a survey) that without need of a central index allows to route queries with certain keys to particular peers containing the desired data. But to provide this functionality all new content in the network has to be published at the node for the respective key, if new data on a peer arrives or a new peer joins the network. And in case that a peer leaves the network the information about its content has to be unpublished. Recent research in [14] shows that due to the publishing/unpublishing overhead, DHTs lack efficiency when highly replicated items are requested and in practical settings perform even worse than flooding approaches degrading further if network churn is introduced.

While the visualization of keys and objects in the same name space used in structured overlays provides an elegant clean solution to routing within logarithmical bounds it comes at the significant cost of destroying the locality of the content: Content at a user's desktop is co-located with other relevant items, structured overlays destroy this locality meaning that enhanced opportunities for browsing and pre-fetching are lost [11]. Unstructured networks, such as Gnutella, keep this locality, since a query is forwarded to randomly picked neighbors. To bound the number of hops it can travel, each query is tagged with a maximum number of hops (TTL). In addition Gnutella employs a duplicate detection mechanism, so that peers do not forward queries that they have already previously forwarded. To improve the efficiency of Gnutella routing indices local index information are first introduced by [8]. This indexing strategy locally stores information about specific queries and what peers were successfully queried in the past. Edutella [16] combines a super-peer network with routing indices and an efficient broadcast. While its routing approach is efficient, especially when churn is high its performance suffers from (de-)registering complex semantics in the distributed indices. [18] first considers the semantics of the query to exploit interest-based locality in a static network. They use shortcuts that are generated after each successful query and are used to further requests, hence they are comparable to content provider shortcuts. However their search strategy differs from ours, since they only follow a shortcut if it matches exact with a query, else they use a flooding approach. To update the index they use a LRU strategy. Similar, [5] uses a local routing index for content provider shortcuts for the specific scenario of top k retrieval in P2P networks. Local indices are maintained in a static super-peer network. Their index policy considers temporal locality, each index entry has a certain time to live after which the shortcut has to be reestablished for the next query on that topic. REMINDIN [19] used a routing table storing content provider shortcuts and a relaxation based routing strategy. The approach was only designed for a static setting without any index size limitation, an assumption that is not realistic.

1.2 Contributions and Paper Organisation

In this paper, we propose an improved shortcut selection strategy able to identify and group peers with similar interests efficiently in a dynamic setting. To our best knowledge, this is the first approach simulating volatile shortcut networks without any static peers. To adapt to the dynamics of the networks and to bound the local index we present an index update policy combining temporal, semantic and community locality. We show, that by indexing shortcuts linking only to a small fraction of peers we perform like an 'unlimited' index. To further boost performance and enhance recall in a dynamic setting we introduce in INGA two additional types of overlays, namely recommender and bootstrapping overlays. We have built a network simulator and conducted extensive experiments under realistic conditions. Results show that INGA outperforms other state-of-the-art approaches significantly.

We describe the infrastructure to maintain the index and the semantic similarity function to select peers in section 2. Section 3 shows the index structure and update strategy for each type of shortcut. Section 4 presents our dynamic routing model. Section 5 describes our simulation methodology and the results of our simulations.

2   Basic Building Blocks of an INGA Peer

Our peer selection strategies described in section 3 are implementation independent. For evaluation purposes, though we use the SWAP infrastructure [10]. We recall that it provides all standard peer-to-peer functionality such as information sharing, searching and publishing of resources. Specifically it comprises the following main building blocks:

- The *network component's* task is to provide core network functionality, such as maintaining network connections to other peers and to provide a unique peer identifer (PID).
- Similar to file sharing networks each peer may publish all resources from its *local content database*, so other peers can discover them by its requests (this also applies to resources downloaded from other peers). All information is wrapped as RDF statements and stored in an RDF repository [1]. Additionally to local meta data (*MMusen isOrganizerOf ISWC2005*) each resource is assigned a topic (*ISWC2005 isTypeOf SemanticWebConference*) and hierarchical information about the topics is stored (*SemanticWebConference subTopicOf Conference*). The topics a peer stores resources for are subsequently referred to as the peers own topics. Note, that our algorithm does not require a shared topic hierarchy, although it is advantageous for it (*cf.* 2).
- For successful queries (own queries or those of other peers), which returned at least one match, the *shortcut management component* extracts information about answering and forwarding peers to create, update or remove shortcuts in the *local shortcut index*. Contrary to related approaches, such as DHTs, INGA peers only index 'egoistically', i.e. shortcuts on topics they requested themselves.
- The *routing logic* selects 'most suitable' peers to forward a query to, for all own queries or queries forwarded from remote peers. The selection depends on the knowledge a peer has already acquired for the specific query and the similarity between the query and locally stored shortcuts.

For simplicity throughout this paper we will assume peers not to be malicious (i.e. they do not intentionally return false shortcuts); strategies for identifying malicious peers in overlay networks are e.g. given in [6].

---

[1] http://www.openrdf.org/

Query and Result Messages. We use a simple query message model which is similar to the structure of a Gnutella query message. Each query message is a quadruple: $QM(q, b, mp, qid)$ where q is a SERQL query (*cf.* footnote 1). We support any SERQL queries, however for routing purposes only the topic information is used. From a query for all *SemanticWebConferences* organized by *MMusen*, only *SemanticWebConference* is utilized for routing. b is the bootstrapping capability of the querying peer to allow the creation of bootstrapping shortcuts, mp the message path for each query message containing the unique PIDs of all peers, which have already received the query, to avoid duplicated query messages, and qid a unique query ID to ensure that a peer does not respond to a query it has already answered. Unique query IDs in INGA are computed by using a random number generator that has sufficiently high probability of generating unique numbers. A result message is a tuple: $RM(r, mp, qid)$ where r represents the answer to the query. We just consider results which exactly match the query. Besides the message path mp is copied to the answer message to allow the creation of recommender and content provider shortcuts.

Semantic Similarity Function. In case the peers in the network share a common topic hierarchy our routing algorithm uses not only exact index hits, but also exploits the semantic similarity between a query and an indexed shortcut. We define the similarity function between a query q and a shortcut sc, which are both given by query terms in the same topic hierarchy as $sim : q \times sc \rightarrow [0; 1]$. Such similarity metrics are often domain specific and depend on the query semantics. In our implementation we use a similarity metric for topic hierarchies proposed by [13] (but of course any other suitable similarity can be used):

$$sim_{Topic}(q, sc) = \begin{cases} e^{-\alpha l} \cdot \frac{e^{\beta h} - e^{-\beta h}}{e^{\beta h} + e^{-\beta h}} & \text{if } q \neq sc \\ 1 & \text{otherwise} \end{cases} \quad (1)$$

where l is the length of the shortest path between q and sc in the graph spanned by the sub topic relation and h is the minimal level in the topic hierarchy of either q or sc. α and β are parameters scaling the contribution of shortest path length l and depth h, respectively. Based on the benchmark data set given in [13], we chose $\alpha = 0.2$ and $\beta = 0.6$ as optimal values.

3   Building and Maintaining of the Index

Each peer is connected to a set of other peers in the network via uni-directional shortcuts. Hence, each peer can locally select all other peers it wants to be linked to. However, due to limited local resources and each peer's specific interests, peers only maintain a bounded index of shortcuts . The decision of replacing a shortcut from the index, i.e. promoting new peers as shortcut acquaintances, depends on the history of the responses to previous requests issued by each peer. We now will propose index building and update strategies for each shortcut type that efficiently limit the index size to only the most useful shortcuts for each local peer. Following the social metaphors in section 1, we generally distinguish between four types of shortcuts.

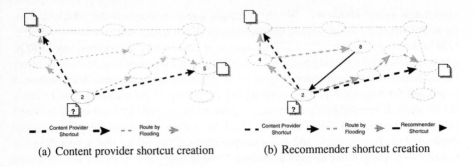

(a) Content provider shortcut creation   (b) Recommender shortcut creation

Fig. 1. Topic specific shortcut creation

3.1   Content Provider Layer

The design of the content provider shortcut overlay departs from existing work as published by [18], [19], or [7] and exploits the simple, yet powerful principle of interest-based locality. That means if a content provider peer has a particular piece of content that a peer is interested in, it can be considered very likely that the content provider will also have other interesting items for that peer.

Discovery and Creation. When a peer joins the system, it may not have any information about the interest of other peers. It first attempts to receive answers for its queries by exploiting lower layers of the INGA peer network, e.g. by flooding. The lookup returns a set of peers that store documents for the topic of the query. These peers are potential candidates to be added to the content provider shortcut list. Each time the querying peer receives an answer from a remote peer, content provider shortcuts sc to new remote peers are added to the list in the form: *sc(topic, pid, query hits,'c', update)*, where *topic* is the query terms taken from the query message, *pid* is the unique identifier of the answering peer, *query hits* is the number of returned statements, *'c'* is the type of content provider shortcuts and *update* is the time, when the shortcut was created or the last time, when the shortcut was used successful. The content provider shortcut list will grow with each submitted query until the maximum number of content provider peers is reached. Subsequent queries of the local peer or of a remote peer are matched against the topic column of the content provider shortcut list. If a peer cannot find suitable shortcuts in the list, it issues a lookup through lower layers, and repeats the process for adding new shortcuts. Consider figure 1(a). Peer 2 discovers shortcuts for the topic */Education/UML* by flooding the default network with a maximum number of hops (TTL) of three hops and creates two content provider shortcuts to peer 3 and peer 5.

3.2   Recommender Layer

Very active peers issue many successful queries and produce many shortcuts. If a remote peer issues many queries that are similar to one's own interests, it will be beneficial to establish links to this peer. The reason is that, if a remote peer has established a shortcut to an interesting content provider, it is likely that this peer will issue other queries on related topics that one will be interested in, too. Such recommender shortcuts thus represent a new kind of links in the semantic overlay structure. If a peer can not directly determine a content provider peer for a given query, it can always forward the query to the best matching recommender.

Creation by controlled listening. To foster the learning process of recommender short-cuts, especially for new peers in the network, we consider the incoming queries that are routed through ones peer. A recommender shortcut *sc(topic,pid,query hits maxsim,r, update)* is created, where *topic* is the set of query terms from the query message. The *pid* for a respective shortcut is extracted from the query message as the ID of the query-ing peer. Since we will get no information about the number of results retrieved for the query, we set the number of *queryhits* to 1. Finally *r* indicates the type of the shortcut for passive recommender shortcut and *update* is the time, when the shortcut was created or the last time, when the shortcut was used successfully. Consider again Figure 1(b). Peer 2 issues the query /Top/Education/UML. Peer 8 creates a shortcut to peer 2 since this query was routed through peer 8.

3.3   Content Provider and Recommender Index

We assume that each peer may only store a limited amount of shortcuts, hence only knows a limited set of topic specific neighbors it can route a query to. If the local index size is reached a peer has to decide, which shortcut should be deleted from the index. For each shortcut in the index we compute a rank based on the following types of localities:

Semantic locality. We measure the maximum semantic similarity $maxsim$ between the topic of a shortcut and the topics represented by the local content of a peer according to equation 1. Hence, we retain a shortcut about topic t to a remote peer, if t is close to our own interests.

LRU locality. To adapt to changes in the content and interests we use a LRU replace-ment policy [2]. Shortcuts that have been used recently receive a higher rank. Each local shortcut is marked with a time stamp when it was created. The time stamp will be updated, if the shortcut will be used successful by the local peer. There is thus an 'oldest' and 'latest' shortcut. The value $update \in [0..1]$ is calculated as difference between the shortcuts time stamp and the 'oldest' time stamp divided by the difference between the 'latest' and the 'oldest'.

Community locality. We measure how close a shortcut leads us to a document. Con-tent provider shortcuts, marked with a c, provide a one hop distance, we set $type = 1$. Recommender shortcuts, marked with a r require at least two hops to reach a peer with relevant documents, we set $type = 0.5$.

We weight the localities and compute the index relevance according to equation 2.

$$relevance = \frac{a * maxsim + b * type + c * update}{a + b + c} \qquad (2)$$

Shortcuts with the highest relevance are ranked at the top of the index, while peers with a lower relevance are deleted from the index.

3.4   Bootstrapping Layer

Bootstrapping shortcuts link to peers that have established many shortcuts for different query topics to a lot of remote peers. We determine the bootstrapping capability by analyzing the in-degree and out-degree of a peer. We use the out-degree as a measure of how successful a peer discovers other peers by querying. To weight the out-degree, we measure the amount of distinct sources a peer receives queries from. We use the in-degree as a measure, that such a peer may share prestigious shortcuts with a high availability. By routing a query along bootstrapping shortcuts, we foster the probability to find a matching shortcut for a query and avoid the drawbacks of having to select peers randomly, e.g. by flooding.

Discovery and Update. Each incoming query that is stored in our index includes the bootstrapping information of the querying peer. While a peer is online it continually updates its bootstrapping index based on incoming queries and stores bootstrapping shortcuts in the form *sc(pid, bo)*, where *pid* is the PID of the querying peer and *bo* its bootstrapping capability. Once an initial set of bootstrapping nodes is found, a peer may route its queries to the nodes with the highest *bo* value. One calculates its *bo* value using equation 3

$$Bo = (1 + |outdegree|) \times (1 + |indegree|) \tag{3}$$

where *out-degree* is the number of distinct remote peers one's knows. To compute an approximation of the *in-degree* without any central server we count the number of distinct peers that send a query via one's peer. To do this from the message path of indexed recommender shortcuts we scrutinize the pen-ultimate peers. The number of distinct pen-ultimate peers denotes one's in degree. To avoid zero values we limited the minimum for both values to one.

3.5   Default Network Layer

When a new peer enters the network, it has not yet stored any specific shortcuts in its index. Default network shortcuts connect each peer p to a set of other peers (p's neighbors) chosen at random, as in typical Gnutella-like networks (e.g. using rendezvous techniques).

4   Dynamic Shortcut Selection

The basic principle of shortcuts consists of dynamically adapting the topology of the P2P network so that the peers that share common interests spontaneously form well-connected semantic communities. It has been shown that users are generally interested in only some specific types of content. Therefore being part of a community that shares common interests is likely to increase search efficiency and success rate. To optimize the overall message traffic we will now propose a dynamic shortcut selection strategy, where each peer selects only a certain number k of most promising shortcuts for query forwarding. Then we will evaluate our approach against related approaches.

4.1 Overview

INGA consists of several steps executed locally and across the network when recommending peers for a query and retrieving or returning results. Consider a query posed to the P2P network. Necessary steps are:

Across the network:Recommending. Whenever a peer receives a query message, it first extracts meta-information about the querying peer and updates its bootstrapping and recommender index if needed. Then our forwarding strategy is invoked to select a set of k peers which appear most promising to answer the query successfully. Finally the original query message is forwarded to these k peers.

Across the network: Answering Queries. When a peer receives a query, it will try to answer the query with local content. We only return non-empty, exact results and route them directly to the querying peer. If the maximum number of hops is not yet reached, the query is forwarded to a set of peers selected as above.

Locally: Receiving Results. On the arrival of result items a querying peer analyzes the message path and the respective number of results to create or update local content provider and recommender shortcuts.

4.2 Selecting Best Matching Shortcuts

The task of the INGA shortcut selection algorithm is to determine best matching candidates to which a query should be forwarded. We rely on forwarding strategies, depending on the local knowledge for the topic of the query a peer has acquired yet in its index:

- We only forward a query via its k *best matching* shortcuts.
- We try to select content and recommender shortcuts before selecting bootstrapping and default network shortcuts.
- To avoid overfitting and accommodate a little volatility (especially in the form of new joining peers), queries are also randomly forwarded to some peers.

The following algorithm shows the basic peer selection procedure:The algorithm works as follows: in step 1 we select k peers from content or recommender shortcuts that match the topic of the query with the highest similarity. To avoid forwarding queries along shortcuts with only low similarity we introduce a minimum similarity threshold t_{greedy}.

Algorithm 1. Dynamic

Require: Query q, **int** k, **int** t_{Greedy}
Ensure: $TTL_q < maxTTL$
 1: $s \leftarrow$ *TopGreedy(q, Content/RecommenderShortcuts,(k,t_{Greedy}))*
 2: **if** $(|s| < k)$ **then**
 3:     $s \leftarrow s +$ *TopBoot(BootstrappingShortcuts,($k - |s|$))*
 4: **end if**
 5: $s \leftarrow$ *RandomFill(s,defaultNetworkShortcuts,f,k)*
 6: **Return** s.

Algorithm 2. TopGreedy

Require: Query q, **Set** $QueryDependentShortcuts$, **int** k, **int** t_{greedy}
1: $topShortcuts \leftarrow \{\}$
2: $s\_tmp \leftarrow QueryDependentShortcuts$
3: **while** (s_tmp *is* not empty) $\wedge$ ($k > 0$) **do**
4:    $Next \leftarrow maxSim_{Topic}(q, s\_tmp)$
5:    **if** sim_{Topic} $(q,Next) > t_{greedy}$ **then**
6:       $s\_tmp \leftarrow s\_tmp - (Next)$
7:       **if** (*Next* routes not to a peer in *topShortcuts*) **then**
8:          $topShortcuts \leftarrow topShortcuts + Next$
9:          $k \leftarrow k - 1$
10:      **end if**
11:   **else**
12:      break
13:   **end if**
14: **end while**
15: **Return** *topShortcuts*

If found less then k shortcuts we select the top bootstrapping shortcuts (step 3). Finally we fill the up remaining shortcuts randomly from the default network and return the set of selected shortcuts. The algorithm terminates if the query has reached its maximum number of hops. We will now show all subroutines for shortcut selection in more details. Algorithm *TopGreedy* allows for selecting the top peers above a similarity threshold. The algorithm browses trough the index of all topic dependent shortcuts (step 3) and identifies the most similar matching shortcuts for a query (step 4) above t_{greedy} (step 5). If two shortcuts have the same similarity, we choose the shortcut with the higher query hits value. The algorithm carefully selects the top-k peers for a query by avoiding different shortcuts with overlapping peers step (7-8).[2] The *TopBoot* Algorithm (omitted here due to space restrictions) works similar to the *TopGreedy* Algorithm, but selects the best peers with highest known bootstrapping capability. It also avoids overlapping peers within the set of selected shortcuts. The task of algorithm *RandomFill* is twofold: if the other subroutines fail to discover k peers for a query, it fills up remaining peers until k is reached (step 12-14). The second task of the algorithm is to contribute some randomly chosen peers to the selected set of k peers to avoid overfitting of the selection process as known from simulated annealing techniques. In step 2 the algorithm determines if new peers should be added to the already selected set, or if peers have to be exchanged. Depending on the probability f in step 6-7 the algorithm exchanges already selected peers with randomly chosen ones.

5   Experimental Evaluation

Open Directory (DMOZ) as real world data set. We simulated our approach with three different data sets [3] with similar results. Trough space limitations we only show the

---

[2] Due to limited space details have been omitted.
[3] The data sets are available at $http : //ontoware.org/projects/swapsim/$.

Algorithm 3. RandomFill

Require: Set *preSelected*, **Set** *defaultNetWorkShortcuts*, **int** f, **int** k
1: **Set** *postSelected* $\leftarrow \{\}$
2: **if** ($\frac{k-|preSelected|}{k} < f$) **then**
3:    **while** (*preSelected is* not empty) **do**
4:       *Next* $\leftarrow$ *next(preSelected)*
5:       *preSelected* $\leftarrow$ *preSelected* $-$ (*Next*)
6:       **if** (*rand*(0,1) $> f$) **then**
7:         *postSelected* $\leftarrow$ *postSelected* $+$ *Next*
8:       **end if**
9:    **end while**
10: **end if**
11: $k \leftarrow k - |postselected|$
12: **while** $k > 0$ **do**
13:    *postSelected* $\leftarrow$ *postSelected* $+$ *next(defaultNetworkShortcuts)*
14:    $k \leftarrow k - 1$
15: **end while**
16: **Return** *postSelected*

results of the open directory *DMOZ.org* data set. It consists of realistic data about the content distribution among persons within a large community. For the topic distribution we select the 1657 topics in the first three levels of the DMOZ hierarchy that have one or more editors assigned to them . We represent one editor by one peer and assume that peers that are interested in a topic also store resources for this topic. We observed that editors are distributed with a heavily tailored Zipf popularity over the topics: 755 topics have 1 editor; 333 topics have 2 editors; 204 topics have 3 editors; . . . ; 44 topics have 6 editors; . . . ;14 topics have 10 editors ;1 topic has 32 editors. Furthermore some editors are interested in more than one topic. Again we observed a heavily tailored Zipf distribution: 991 editors only have one topic; 295 two topics; 128 three topics; ... one editor has 18 topics; one editor 20 topics and one editor has 22 topics.

Query Distribution. Queries are generated in the experiments by instantiating the blueprint $(*; isTypeOf; topic)$, with topics arbitrarily chosen from the set of topics that had at least one document. We generated 30000 queries, uniformly distributed over the 1657 different topics. We distribute the queries uniformly over the peers, hence each peer may issue a query to any topic and each topic is requested with the same probability. We choose a uniform query distribution instead of a ZIPF-distribution, which is typically observed in file sharing networks [17]. This simulates the worst case scenario, where we do not take advantage of often repeated queries for popular topics.

Gnutella style network. The simulation is initialized with a network topology which resembles the small world properties of file sharing networks[4]. We simulated 1024 peers. In the simulation, peers were chosen randomly and they were given a randomly selected query to question the remote peers in the network. The peers decide on the basis of their local short cut which remote peers to send the query to. Each peer uses INGA to

---
[4] We used the Colt library http://nicewww.cern.ch/~hoschek/colt/

select up to $pmax = 2$ peers to send the query to. Each query was forwarded until the maximal number of hops $hmax = 6$ was reached.

Volatile network and interest shifts. We implemented the dynamic network model observed for Gnutella networks of [17] in our simulation: 60% of the peers have a availability of less than 20%, while 20% of the peers are available between 20 and 60% and 20 % are available more than 60%. Hence only a small fraction of peers is available more than half of the simulation time, while the majority of the peers is only online a fraction of the simulation time. Users' interest may change over time, e.g. to account for different search goals [3]. To simulate the effect of changing interests in the network, after 15 queries, equal to ca. 15.000 queries over all peers, each peer will ask for a completely different set of topics.

Evaluation Measures. We measure the search efficiency using the following metrics:

- **Recall** is a standard measure in information retrieval. In our setting, it describes the proportion between all relevant documents in peer network and the retrieved ones.
- **Messages** represent the required search costs per query that can be used to indirectly justify the system scalability.
- **Message Gain** compares the recall per message, hence the proportion of messages with respect to to the achieved recall.

5.1   Comparing INGA with State-of-the-Art Approaches

As a baseline we compare INGA with an index size of 40 entries against the interest based locality strategy (IBL) of [18] with an LRU strategy and an index size of 40 entries, the naive algorithm of Gnutella (Naive) and REMINDIN [19].

INGA outperforms in terms of messages and message gain. Figure 2(a) shows the recall in contrast of the maximum possible recall in a dynamic network. After only 15 queries INGA nearly doubles the recall of the naive approach and drastically outperforms *IBL*. Since INGA and REMINDIN use similar strategies for creating shortcuts both archive a similar recall. However, after introducing new topics in the network, INGA 's outperforms REMINDIN due to its optimized index for a dynamic network. Figure 3(b) shows the number of messages. Due to bootstrapping peers, that focus queries to a fraction of peers in the network, INGA outperforms and halves the messages in contrast to a naive approach. In contrast to REMINDIN INGA reduces the number of messages from about 85 to 58 messages. Figure 3(b) shows, that in terms of message gain INGA outperforms all approaches dramatically. Due to its improved indexing and shortcut selection strategy INGA nearly doubles the message gain of REMINDIN.

Each layer contributes. Figure 3(a) shows the message gain of the different layers. Only using content provider shortcuts (Content-40) performs poorly, a combination of content and recommender shortcuts raise the message gain (Content Recommender-40) and finally the introduction of bootstrapping peers (INGA-40) additionally boosts INGA performance.

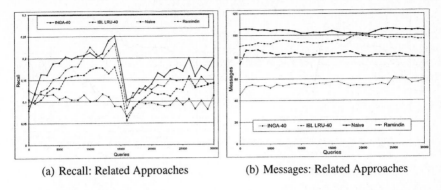

(a) Recall: Related Approaches   (b) Messages: Related Approaches

Fig. 2. Comparison Recall and Message: Dynamic Network 1024 Peers, 6 Hops, k=2

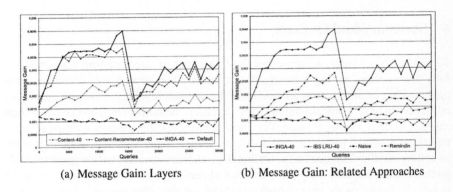

(a) Message Gain: Layers   (b) Message Gain: Related Approaches

Fig. 3. Message Gain: Dynamic Network 1024 Peers, 6 Hops, k=2

5.2   Setting Optimal Index Size and Weights

Limiting index size performs similar to an unlimited index. We conducted experiments
with an unlimited index size and a maximum size of 100, 40, 20 shortcut entries. Figure
4(a) shows that an index size of 100 entries performs as good as an unlimited index while
an index of 40 entries still is a reasonable tradeoff between size and routing efficiency.

Combined weighting is ideal, community weight outperforms. To determine an optimal weighting of the parameter (a, b, c) of the index policy, we conducted experiments
where we only consider the similarity locality ($a = 10, b = 0, c = 0$) , where we
only consider the community locality (with $a = 0, b = 10, c = 0$), where we only
consider the LRU-Locality ($a = 0, b = 0, c = 10$) and an 'optimal' combination
($a = 3, b = 6, c = 1$). [18] proposes a LRU strategy to update the index. We found
out that there are better strategies. Figure 4(b) shows a similarity and LRU strategy,
both perform worse and are alone not capable to adopt to the dynamics of the network and the changing interests of each peer. The community locality raises the message gain, even after changing the interests of each peer, while the combined strategy
performs best.

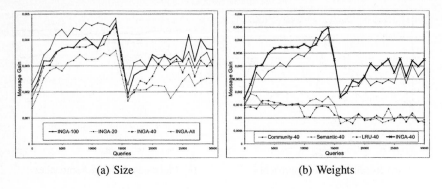

(a) Size   (b) Weights

Fig. 4. Index Behavior: Dynamic Network 1024 Peers, 6 Hops, k=2

6   Summary and Outlook

To our best knowledge we presented the first semantic query routing algorithm in a fully decentralized setting without any super peers. The novel design principle of our approach lies in the dynamic adaptation of the network topology, driven by the history of successful or semantically similar queries. This is memorized by using bounded local shortcut indexes storing semantically labelled shortcuts and a dynamic shortcut selection strategy, which forwards queries to a community of peers that are likely to best answer queries. Shortcuts connect peers that share similar interests and thus spontaneously form semantic communities. The clustering of peers within semantically communities drastically improves the overall performance of our algorithm even in a highly volatile setting, while our index policy keeps the shortcuts to the 'right' peers, that provide facts to the core interests of a requesting peer.

An interesting additional problem is the generalization of our approach for a network with individual semantics on each peer. Peers within the same community may share its facts and possibly agree on a common set of semantics. Such a community search engine would enable flexible and efficient wide area knowledge sharing applications without the maintenance of central indexing servers or a static semantic structure.

Acknowledgement. Research reported in this paper has been partially financed by EU in the IST project SEKT (IST-2003-506826) and EU IST ASG. Alexander Löser was generously funded by the German Research Society, Berlin-Brandenburg School in Distributed Information Systems (DFG grant GRK 316/3).

References

1. K. Aberer, P. Cudre-Mauroux, M. Hauswirth, and T. van Pelt. GridVine: Building Internet-Scale Semantic Overlay Networks. In 3rd. International Semantic Web Conference (ISWC), Hiroshima, Japan, 2004.
2. A. V. Aho, P. J. Denning, and J. D. Ullman. Principles of optimal page replacement. J. ACM, 18(1):80-93, 1971.

3. J. Allan. Incremental relevance feedback for information filtering. In SIGIR '96: Proceedings of the 19th annual international ACM SIGIR conference on Research and development in information retrieval, pages 270-278, New York, NY, USA, 1996. ACM Press.

4. S. Androutsellis-Theotokis and D. Spinellis. A survey of peer-to-peer content distribution technologies. ACM Comput. Surv., 36(4):335-371, 2004.

5. W.-T. Balke, W. Nejdl, W. Siberski, and U. Thaden. Progressive distributed top-k retrieval in peer-to-peer networks. In 21st International Conference on Data Engineering (ICDE), Tokyo, Japan, 2005.

6. T. Condie, S. Kamvar, and H. Garcia-Molina. Adaptive Peer-to-Peer Topologies. In Int. Conf. on Peer-to-Peer Computing (P2P), Zurich, Switzerland, 2004.

7. B. Cooper. Guiding queries to information sources with InfoBeacons. In ACM/IFIP/USENIX 5th International Middleware Conference, Toronto, 2004.

8. A. Crespo and H. Garcia-Molina. Routing indices for peer-to-peer systems. In International Conference on Distributed Computing Systems, july 2002.

9. L. Gravano and H. Garc´ýa-Molina. Generalizing GlOSS to vector-space databases and broker hierarchies. In International Conference on Very Large Databases, VLDB, pages 78-89, 1995.

10. P. Haase et al. Bibster - a semantics-based bibliographic peer-to-peer system. In Proc. of the 3rd International Semantic Web Conference, Japan. Springer, 2004.

11. P. J. Keleher, B. Bhattacharjee, and B. D. Silaghi. Are virtualized overlay networks too much of a good thing? In IPTPS '01: Revised Papers from the First International Workshop on Peer-to-Peer Systems, pages 225-231. Springer-Verlag, 2002.

12. J. Kleinberg. Navigation in a small world. Nature, 406, 2000.

13. Y. Li, Z. Bandar, and D. McLean. An Approach for messuring semantic similarity between words using semantic multiple information sources. In IEEE Transactions on Knowledge and Data Engineering, volume 15, 2003.

14. B. Loo, J. Hellerstein, R. Huebsch, S. Shenker, and I. Stoica. Enhancing p2p file-sharing with an internet-scale query processor. In In Proc. of Int. Conf. on Very Large Databases (VLDB), Toronto, 2004.

15. 15. S. Milgram. The small world problem. Psychology Today, 67(1), 1967.

16. W. Nejdl, M. Wolpers, W. Siberski, A. L¨oser, I. Bruckhorst, M. Schlosser, and C. Schmitz. Super-Peer-Based Routing and Clustering Strategies for RDF-Based Peer-To-Peer Networks. In 12th International World Wide Web Conference, Budapest, Hungary, May 2003.

17. S. Saroiu, P. K. Gummadi, and S. D. Gribble. A measurement study of peer-to-peer file sharing systems. Multimedia Systems, 9(2), 2003.

18. K. Sripanidkulchai, B. Maggs, and H. Zhang. Efficient Content Location Using Interest Based Locality in Peer-to-Peer System. In Infocom. IEEE, 2003.

19. C. Tempich, S. Staab, and A. Wranik. REMINDIN:Semantic Query Routing in Peer-to-Peer Networks based on Social Metaphors. In Proceedings of the 13th WWW Conference New York. ACM, 2004.

RUL: A Declarative Update Language for RDF*

M. Magiridou[1], S. Sahtouris[2], V. Christophides[2], and M. Koubarakis[1]

[1] Dept. of Electronic and Computer Engineering,
Technical University of Crete GR73100 Chania, Greece
{magiridou, manolis}@intelligence.tuc.gr
[2] Institute of Computer Science FORTH,
Vassilika Vouton P.O. 1385 Heraclion, Greece
{saxtouri, christop}@ics.forth.gr

Abstract. We propose a declarative update language for RDF graphs
which is based on the paradigms of query and view languages RQL and
RVL. Our language, called RUL, ensures that the execution of the update
primitives on nodes and arcs neither violates the semantics of the RDF
model nor the semantics of the given RDFS schema. In addition, RUL
supports fine-grained updates at the class and property instance level,
set-oriented updates with a deterministic semantics and takes benefit of
the full expressive power of RQL for restricting the range of variables to
nodes and arcs of RDF graphs.

1 Introduction

Semantic Web applications are striving nowdays for managing changes of persistent resource descriptions created according to RDFS schemata [1, 2]. The
majority of ontology-based authoring and annotation tools [3] requires first to
manually edit the resource descriptions and thereafter reloading them into an
RDF Store from scratch. This approach offers rather limited functionality especially in the case of deletions and modifications. To overcome these limitations, some RDF Stores [4] have implemented suitable update APIs [5, 6, 7, 8].
However, forcing developers to code in advance all possible updates of resource
descriptions (using these APIs) is not a viable solution for dynamic Semantic
Web applications employing non trivial RDFS schemata. In this context, designing a declarative update language offering complete (i.e., all valid RDF changes
should be specifiable by one or by a sequence of update primitives from a minimal set) and sound (i.e., every primitive is guaranteed to maintain consistency
of resource descriptions w.r.t. the employed RDFS schemata) primitives is a
challenging issue.

In this paper, we propose a declarative update language for RDF graphs
which is based on the paradigms of query and view languages RQL [9] and
RVL [10]. Our language, called RUL, ensures that the execution of the update
primitives on nodes and arcs neither violates the semantics of the RDF model
(e.g., insert a property as an instance of a class) nor the semantics of a specific

---

* Supported in part by European project OntoGrid - http://www.ontogrid.net.

Y. Gil et al. (Eds.): ISWC 2005, LNCS 3729, pp. 506–521, 2005.

RDFS schema (e.g., modify the subject of a property with a resource not classified under its domain class). This main design choice has been made in order to take into account the fact that updates are fairly destructive operations and change the state of an RDF graph. Thus, type safety for updates is even more important than type safety for queries. The more errors we can catch at compile time the less costly runtime checks (and possibly expensive rollbacks) we need. The rest of RULs design choices concern (a) the *granularity* of the supported update primitives; (b) the *deterministic or not* behavior of the executed sequences of update statements; and (c) the *smooth integration* with an underlying RDF/S query language. To the best of our knowledge, RUL is the first declarative language supporting fine-grained updates at the class and property instance level, has a deterministic semantics for set-oriented updates and takes benefit of the full expressive power of RQL for restricting the range of variables to nodes and arcs of RDF data graphs. However, our design can be also immediately transferred to other RDF query languages (e.g., RDQL [11], or SPARQL [12]) offering less expressive pattern matching capabilities [13].

None of the RDF update languages proposed so far [14, 15] supports the aforementioned functionality. The most interesting proposal is MEL that has been developed in the framework of QEL and it is based on Datalog [14]. MEL primitive commands consist of a statement specification and an optional query constraint, declared as a QEL query. The granularity of the operations follows a subgraph-centered approach but consistency of updates w.r.t the employed RDFS schemata is not respected. Furthermore, no formal semantics or detailed behavior description have been given for MEL. The rdfDB Query Language [15] supports SQL-like updates (insert and delete) by following a statement-centered approach and does not integrate smoothly with the query language. In fact, the update operations can affect only specific statements without variables and thus their execution semantics is trivial.

From knowledge representation languages in the semantic data modelling tradition, Telos [16] is probably the closest to RDF. Telos has inspired the RDF data model behind the query language RQL and the hybrid framework of [17]. Work on update languages for Telos is reported in [16, 18, 19] However, the statements UNTELL and RETELL discussed in these papers concentrate on the temporal features of Telos and pay no attention to the many issues regarding update side-effects as discussed in this paper.

The rest of the paper is organized as follows. Section 2 introduces the syntax of RUL in an incremental, informal way by giving examples and intuitive explanations while Section 3 clarifies RULs formal semantics and in particular its deterministic behavior for set-oriented updates. Our conclusions as well as some challenges for future work are given in Section 4.

2   The Syntax of RUL

RUL can be used to express updates to RDF graphs i.e., insertions, deletions and modifications of nodes and arcs. We consider an RDF graph to follow the

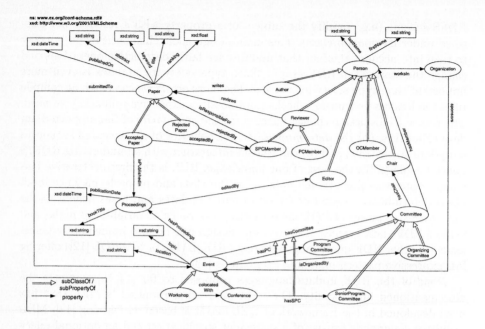

Fig. 1. RDF Schema in graphical form for the conference organization example

formal model for RDF proposed in [20]. The main constraints this model imposes to RDF Semantics [21] can be summarized as follows: *the domain and range of properties should always be defined, both of these declarations have to be unique* and *class and property definitions have to be complete.*

In this section, we present the syntax of RUL in an incremental, informal way by giving examples and intuitive explanations based on the RDF schema of Figure 1 dealing with the organization of scientific conferences, and Figure 2 where the effects and side-effects of each operation are analyzed in detail. Section 3 presents the formal semantics of RUL.

We assume that the vocabularies used in the RDF graphs have been defined using RDF Schema. RUL does not deal with schema updates. We also do not deal with blank nodes, containers, collections or reification in this paper.

2.1   Updating Class Instances

Instances of classes can be updated using the INSERT, DELETE or MODIFY statements. The syntax of the INSERT statement is as follows:

```
INSERT QualClassName(ResourceExp)
[FROM VariableBinding]   [WHERE Filtering] [USING NAMESPACE NamespaceDefs]
```

The INSERT operation introduces new nodes in an RDF graph and classifies them, or inserts new classification links for existing nodes. The expression

`ResourceExp` denotes a node and can be a constant URI or a variable. In the former case, `ResourceExp` determines a unique graph node, while in the latter, the clause `FROM` determines the bindings of this variable (i.e., a set of nodes) as in RQL. The expression `QualClassName` denotes the class to which the new nodes will become instances or to which the new classification links from existing nodes will be created.

The clause `WHERE` gives as usual the filtering conditions for the variables bindings introduced in the clause `FROM`. The clause `USING NAMESPACE` gives a list of namespaces that disambiguate the use of names in the other clauses. The clauses `FROM, WHERE` and `USING NAMESPACE` are optional. In the rest of this paper, we show the `USING NAMESPACE` clause when we are presenting the syntax of RUL but avoid any namespace information in the examples for reasons of brevity (i.e., all the names employed in the examples are unique and they are defined in the schema namespace `ns` of Figure 1).

As in RQL, RUL distinguish between direct and indirect instances of a class `C` or property `P` (equivalently, between direct and indirect instantiation links). A resource node `r` is a *direct* instance of class `C` if it has been introduced in the graph by an appropriate update statement. A resource node `r` is an *indirect* instance of class `C` if r is a direct instance of a subclass of `C`. The definition is similar for properties. An RDF graph *has no redundancies* with respect to instantiation if there is no instance of a class or a property that is both a direct and an indirect instance. All the update operations defined below result in RDF graphs with no redundancies with respect to instantiation.

The *effects* and *side-effects* of an `INSERT` operation with the above syntax are presented graphically in Figure 2(I). If node `ResourceExp` exists in the graph and it is classified under a superclass of `QualClassName` (Case (I.1) in Figure 2), the effect of `INSERT` is that a new classification link is inserted between `ResourceExp` and `QualClassName`. In this case, the operation has the side-effect that the prior classification link is deleted (since it is implied by the new classification link). On the other hand, if `ResourceExp` exists in the graph and it is classified under a subclass of `QualClassName` (Case (I.3) where D is a subclass of C), the `INSERT` operation has no effects. Obviously, if the node exists as a direct instance of `QualClassName`, the operation has no effects too. Finally, if node `ResourceExp` exists in the graph and it is classified under a class which is not related through a subclass relation to `QualClassName` (Case (I.2)), the result is a multi-classified node (&d1 is classified both under B and D classes) without any side-effects.

Example 1. Make the resource with URI `http://www.ex.org/paper1.pdf` an instance of the class `AcceptedPaper`:

`INSERT AcceptedPaper(&http://www.ex.org/paper1.pdf)`

`paper1.pdf` is not already an instance of class `AcceptedPaper` or one of its subclasses (if it had any). In other words, the execution of an `INSERT` operation leaves us with an RDF graph with no redundancies with respect to instantiation.

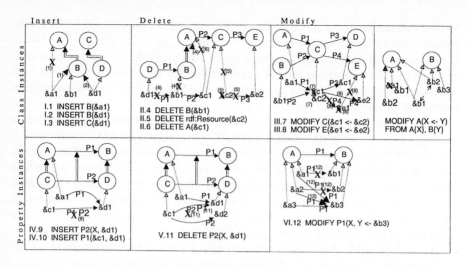

Fig. 2. RUL operations effects and side-effects

Example 2. Classify as reviewers all members of the OC of ISWC05:

```
INSERT Reviewer(X)
FROM {Y}isOrganizedBy.hasMember{X;OCMember}
WHERE Y = &http://www.iswc05.org
```

The above example demonstrates the use of variables in the INSERT clause and the use of RQL *path expressions* for navigating RDF graphs in the FROM clause. More precisely, variable X will be range restricted to instances of class OCMember involved in the OrganizingCommittee of the ISWC05 Event. This update operation will multiply classify OCMember instances under the class Reviewer.

The syntax of the DELETE operation is as follows:

```
DELETE QualClassName(ResourceExp)
[FROM VariableBinding] [WHERE Filtering] [USING NAMESPACE NamespaceDefs]
```

The DELETE operation deletes classification links and possibly nodes from an RDF graph (Figure 2 (II)). The expression ResourceExp, which denotes the node from which the classification link to be deleted originates, can be a URI or a variable. The effect of the DELETE operation is to remove the direct or indirect classification link of ResourceExp to class QualClassName and replace it by the link of ResourceExp to all the immediate super-classes of QualClassName if any (e.g., in Figure 2(II.4), &b1 is now classified under class A). If ResourceExp is multi-classified (e.g., &c1 in Figure 2(II.6)), then the classification link of ResourceExp to QualClassName is deleted without being replaced by another. Finally, if QualClassName is the top of the class hierarchy rdf:Resource, the effect is the deletion of ResourceExp node along with all its classification links (Figure 2(II.5)).

It should be stressed that, all classification links that are added by a DELETE operation must take the semantics of INSERT into account, so that the resulting RDF graph remains without redundancies.

The side effects of DELETE in any of the above cases are caused by the changes in the classification of a node. To be more specific, all property arcs emanating from the note denoted by ResourceExp that have as domain (or range) a class, to which ResourceExp is no longer an instance, are also deleted. These side-effects are necessary to keep the graph consistent, since ResourceExp does no longer belong to the declared classification. To illustrate these, consider the properties P1 and P3 in Figure 2(II), which are deleted when the respective classification links are removed (statements (II.4) and (II.6)).

Example 3. Delete all papers submitted by the PC chair(s) of ISWC05:

```
DELETE Paper(X)
FROM {Y}writes{X}, {Z;Conference}hasPC.hasChair{Y}
WHERE Z=&http://www.iswc05.org
```

The above DELETE operation will be effective only if the node bindings of variable X are classified under the class ns:Paper or one of its subclasses (e.g., AcceptedPaper). It is worth noticing that these nodes will still be present in the output RDF graph of the previous update operation, but only as instances of the top class rdf:Resource (since ns:Paper has no other superclasses).

Finally, the syntax of the MODIFY operation is:

```
MODIFY QualClassName(OldResourceExp <- NewResourceExp)
[FROM VariableBinding] [WHERE Filtering] [USING NAMESPACE NamespaceDefs]
```

The expressions OldResourceExp and NewResourceExp can be constants or variables as in other statements. The arrow <- has the meaning of an *assignment* operation. The MODIFY operation is not a sequence of DELETE and INSERT. The effect of the MODIFY operation (Figure 2(III)) is to completely remove the node(s) denoted by OldResourceExp and then insert the node(s) denoted by NewResourceExp as an instance of QualClassName. The insertion of NewResourceExp has the same semantics as the INSERT operation presented earlier (see cases III.7 and III.8). The first side effect of MODIFY is that all properties emanating from (or ending at) the resource denoted by OldResourceExp are completely removed. The other side effect is that the previously removed properties became now properties emanating from (or ending at) the resource denoted by NewResourceExp (e.g., in Case III.8, property arc P4 which ends at &e1, is removed, while another property arc P4 which ends at &e2, is inserted).

Example 4. The information that paper1.pdf is an accepted paper is incorrect. The correct information is that paper101.pdf has been accepted.

```
MODIFY AcceptedPaper(&http://www.ex.org/paper1.pdf <- &http://www.ex.org/
paper101.pdf)
```

If paper1.pdf had title "The language SQL", we could equivalently write:

```
MODIFY AcceptedPaper(X <- &http://www.ex.org/paper101.pdf)
FROM {X}title{Y}
WHERE Y="The language SQL"
```

2.2   Updating Property Instances

The `INSERT`, `DELETE` and `MODIFY` statements can also be used to update the properties of resources i.e., arcs in an RDF graph. The syntax of the `INSERT` statement in this case is as follows:

```
INSERT QualPropertyName(SubjectExp, ObjectExp)
[FROM VariableBinding] [WHERE Filtering] [USING NAMESPACE NamespaceDefs]
```

The above `INSERT` operation adds to resource node `SubjectExp` a new property arc that is an instance of property `QualPropertyName` and has value `ObjectExp`. `SubjectExp` and `ObjectExp` can be constants or variables with bindings determined in the FROM clause. In both cases RQL typing rules for triples must be respected: `SubjectExp` must evaluate to a URI, instance of the domain of property `QualPropertyName`, and `ObjectExp` must evaluate to a URI or literal value instance of the range of property `QualPropertyName`.

    We now detail the semantics of this operation by referring to Figure 2(IV). The variable X, that has not been given a range, should be assumed to range over all nodes shown in the figure. As in the case of resources, if a property arc from `SubjectExp` to `ObjectExp` exists and it is an instance of a super-property of `QualPropertyName` (Figure 2(IV.9)), then the operation's effect is the deletion of the instantiation link of the arc and the introduction of a new link to `QualPropertyName` (e.g., the arc from `&c1` to `&d1` becomes an instance of property P2). However, when `SubjectExp` and `ObjectExp` are not instances of the domain and range of `QualPropertyName` this operation has no effect (e.g., P1 between `&a1` and `&d1` is not affected by the insertion IV.9). If the property arc exists as an instance of a subproperty of `QualPropertyName` (Figure 2 (IV.10)), then the operation has also no effect. It is obvious that there are no side-effects in this operation.

Example 5. Make "IR" a keyword of paper `http://www.ex.org/paper1.pdf`.

```
INSERT keyword(&http://www.ex.org/paper1.pdf, "IR")
```

Example 6. Make Oracle a sponsor of every database conference.

```
INSERT sponsors(&http://www.oracle.com, X)
FROM {X;Conference}topic{Y}
WHERE Y like "*database*"
```

Example 7. Make editors of the proceedings of ISWC05 the chair(s) of the PC and the chair(s) of the OC.

```
INSERT editedBy(X,Y)
FROM {Q}hasProceedings{X}, {Q}@P.hasChair{Y},
WHERE Q = &http://www.iswc05.org and (@P=isOrganizedBy or @P=hasPC)
```

This example demonstrates the use of *schema querying* in the FROM clause of RUL. Variables prefixed by @ are RQL *property variables* implicitly restricted to range over the set of all data properties.

The syntax of the DELETE operation is as follows:

```
DELETE QualPropertyName(SubjectExp, ObjectExp)
[FROM VariableBinding] [WHERE Filtering] [USING NAMESPACE NamespaceDefs]
```

As in the case of resources, the DELETE operation (Figure 2(V)) removes essentially the instantiation link between QualPropertyName and the property arc from SubjectExp to ObjectExp (e.g., the arc from &c1 to &d1 is not anymore an instance of P2) and inserts a link from the arc to the super-property of QualPropertyName (e.g., the arc from &c1 to &c2 becomes an instance of P1), as we discussed in the property INSERT operation. If the arc is not an instance of QualPropertyName (e.g. the arc from &a1 to &d1 not classified under P2), then the operation has no effect. This update operation has also no side-effects.

Example 8. Delete keyword "IR" from paper http://www.ex.org/paper2.pdf:

```
DELETE keyword(&http://www.ex.org/paper2.pdf, "IR")
```

Example 9. Remove assigned papers on web services from reviewer Smith:

```
DELETE reviews(&http://www.uni-ex.edu/~smith, X)
FROM {X}paperKeyword{Y}
WHERE Y like "*web services*"
```

Example 10. Delete all sponsors of ISWC05:

```
DELETE sponsors(X, &http://www.iswc05.org)
FROM Organization{X}
```

The syntax of the MODIFY operation is:

```
MODIFY QualPropertyName([OldSubjectExp <-] NewSubjectExp,
                        [OldObjectExp  <-] NewObjectExp)
[FROM VariableBinding] [WHERE Filtering] [USING NAMESPACE NamespaceDefs]
```

As we can see in Figure 2(VI), the effect of the operation is to delete the arc between the resources denoted by the OldSubjectExp and OldObjectExp and insert a new arc from NewSubjectExp to NewObjectExp (e.g., the arc between &a1 and &b1 is removed and a new arc between &a1 and &b3 is inserted). If OldSubjectExp (resp. OldObjectExp) or NewSubjectExp (resp. NewObjectExp) is not an instance of a class in the domain (resp. range) of QualPropertyName, the operation has no effect. If the arc from NewSubjectExp to NewLObjectExp already exists and it is an instance of QualPropertyName, it is not inserted (e.g., the arc between &a2 and &b3), so that redundancies are avoided, as we discussed in the property INSERT operation. No other arcs are affected as a side-effect of the above operation.

Example 11. Change the keyword "IR" to "Information Retrieval" in the papers where this keyword appears:

```
MODIFY keyword(X, "IR" <- "Information Retrieval")
FROM Paper{X}
```

Example 12. Make the publication date of every accepted paper to be the same as the publication date of the proceedings where it is published:

```
MODIFY publishedOn(Y, Z <- X)
FROM {Y;AcceptedPaper}isPublishedIn.publicationDate{X},{Y}publishedOn{Z}
```

The above examples demonstrate the modification of a property's object. The following example illustrates a case where the subject of a property is updated.

Example 13. Pass all the reviews to be done by Prof. Smith to his Ph.D. student Jones:

```
MODIFY reviews(&http://www.ex.org/~smith <- &http://www.ex.org/~jones, Y)
FROM Paper{Y}
```

Example 14. The information "Oracle sponsors WWW 2005" in our graph is incorrect. The correct information is "Google sponsors ISWC 2005".

```
MODIFY sponsors(&http://www.oracle.com <- &http://www.google.com,
               &http://www.www05.org <- &http://www.iswc05.org)
```

This example demonstrates the change of both subject and object of a property.

We close this section by pointing out that it is a design choice of RUL to have one syntax for updates of instantiation links (unary predicates) and a *different syntax* for updates of property arcs (binary predicates) to remind the user of the *different semantics* of these operations (i.e., we do not believe that a uniform syntax based on triples and `rdf:type` would be appropriate for RUL).

2.3   More Expressive Updates

The syntax of RUL presented above allows us to express two kinds of updates: *primitive* ones where a node or arc of an RDF graph is inserted or deleted (with appropriate side-effects), and *set-oriented* ones where an atomic update of the same kind (e.g., an insertion) is performed repeatedly for all resource tuples calculated by evaluating the FROM and WHERE clauses of an INSERT, DELETE or MODIFY statement. Of course, by writing multiple RUL statements, we can also express *sequences* of such updates. In this section, we extend the above syntax to be able to express sequences of primitive updates inside a *single* RUL statement, and show with examples why such an extension is a useful feature of RUL. A discussion of the problems involved and how they can be addressed effectively is postponed until Section 3.3.

The first extension that we propose is to allow multiple atomic formulas, in an INSERT, DELETE or MODIFY clause. In this way, we can express sequences of primitive updates of the *same* kind.

Example 15. Make resource &http://www.ex.org/paper3.pdf authored by Smith an instance of class Paper.

```
INSERT Paper(&http://www.ex.org/paper3.pdf),
    writes(&http://www.uni-ex.edu/~smith, &http://www.ex.org/paper3.pdf)
```

Note that even in sequences of primitive insertions as in the above example, the order of execution of each individual update *does* matter (we cannot insert a property `writes` for resource `paper3.pdf` before we make it an instance of the range of `writes`). This is in direct contrast with updates in relational languages [22, 23] where order does not matter in sequences of updates of the same kind. Thus, the order of execution for update statements with multiple predicates is from left to right and the comma operator signifies sequence.

Example 16. Reject all papers with ranking less than 4, and add the SPC member responsible for the paper as the person who made the final recommendation.

```
INSERT RejectedPaper(X), rejectedBy(X,Y)
FROM {X;Paper}ranking{Z},
     {X}submittedTo.hasSPC.hasMember{Y;SPCMember}, {Y}isResponsibleFor{X}
WHERE Z < 4
```

This example shows clearly why the proposed enhancement of the RUL syntax is useful. In this case additions to the graph come "in pairs"; thus, the example is impossible to express without variables and sequencing.

Apart from sequences of updates of the same kind, RUL can also express sequences of updates of *different* kinds. This is done by allowing multiple INSERT, DELETE or MODIFY clauses before the FROM clause of an update statement.

Example 17. Form the Program Committee of ISWC06 by taking the set of all PC members of ISWC05 except those that reviewed less than 5 papers for ISWC05, and adding to this set the members of the OC of ISWC05.

```
INSERT hasPCMember(&http://www.iswc06.org#pc, X)
DELETE hasPCMember(&http://www.iswc06.org#pc, Y)
INSERT hasPCMember(&http://www.iswc06.org#pc, Z)
FROM   {W}hasPCMember{X}, {W}hasPCMember{Y},
       {W}hasOCMember{Z}
WHERE  W = &http://www.iswc05.org#pc
       and count(SELECT Q FROM {Y}reviews{Q}, {Q}submittedTo{W}) <5
```

This last extension to the syntax of RUL also allow us to express updates with effects that depend on the order of execution of the primitive updates captured by the clauses INSERT, DELETE or MODIFY (e.g., in Example 17, all the Program Committee members of ISWC05 have to be made Program Committee members for ISWC06 *before* those of them that reviewed less than 5 papers for ISWC05 are deleted). The order of execution for multiple update clauses in an RUL update statement is from top to bottom. Thus, update clauses with multiple predicates can be trivially translated into sequences of update statements with a single predicate. We will discuss these issues in detail in Section 3.3 where the semantics of set-oriented updates are discussed in every detail.

2.4   Safety

The presence of variables in RUL statements forces us to impose an easily verifiable syntactic notion of safety as in relational updates [22]. An RUL statement is *safe* if all the variables appearing in INSERT, DELETE or MODIFY clauses also appear in the FROM clause of the statement. Thus, if an RUL statement is safe, no new values can be inserted in the graph except the ones present in the update statement itself.

Example 18. Let us revisit Example 11. If the user writes the unsafe statement

MODIFY keyword(X, "IR" <- "Information Retrieval")

an RUL compiler can easily translate this into the safe statement of Example 11 since domain(keyword)=Paper. This is one of the benefits of adopting the RQL typing framework [9].

3   The Semantics of RUL

In this section we give a formal semantics to RUL. We start by defining the concepts of RDF that we need using the formal model introduced in [9]. The important contribution of [9] is the introduction of a rich type system for RDF and RDFS that has been proved valuable in the implementation of RQL. Because RUL updates are destructive operations that change the state of an RDF graph, type safety for RUL updates is even more important than type safety for RQL queries. The more errors we can catch at compile time, the less costly runtime checks (and possibly expensive rollbacks) we will need.

We start by defining the concepts of RDF graph and RDFS graph. We slightly modify the definitions of [9] to cover only the concepts of RDF used in this paper (we do not deal with blank nodes, containers, collections or reification).

Let LT be the set of XML Schema data types that can be used in RDF. Let T be the set of types in the RDF/S type system defined in [9]. Let $Values(T)$ be the set that includes all typed literals with types from T and all URIs.

Definition 1. *An* RDFS graph *is a 6-tuple* $S = (VS, ES, C, P, \prec, \Theta, \Lambda)$ *where* VS *is a set of nodes,* $ES \subseteq V \times V$ *is a set of edges,* C *is a set of class names,* P *is a set of property names,* $\prec$ *is a partial order on* $C \cup P$, $\Theta : VS \cup ES \to C \cup P$ *is a function mapping nodes to classes and edges to properties, and* $\Lambda : VS \cup ES \to T$ *is a typing function that returns the type of each node or edge.*

Definition 2. *An* RDF graph *over the RDFS graph* $(VS, ES, C, P, \prec, \Theta, \Lambda)$ *is a quadruple* $G = (V, E, \nu, \lambda)$ *where* V *is a set of nodes,* $E \subseteq V \times V$ *is a set of edges,* $\nu : V \to Values(T)$ *is a value function that assigns a value from* $Values(T)$ *to each node in* V *and* $\lambda : V \cup E \to 2^{C \cup P} \cup LT$ *is a typing function which satisfies the following: (i) For each node a in V, λ returns a set of class or data type names $c \in C \cup LT$ such that $\nu(a)$ belongs to the interpretation of each c. (ii) For each edge $(a, b) \in E$, λ returns a property name $p \in P$ such that $(\nu(a), \nu(b))$ belongs to the interpretation of p.*

Note that λ contains all classes (resp. properties) that a node (resp. property arc) is an instance of directly or indirectly.

Let *Query* be the set of queries that can be expressed in RQL and *Tuple* the set of tuples of arbitrary arity formed by elements of $Values(T)$. We assume that the function $\mathcal{E} : Query \times Graph \rightarrow Tuple$ gives the semantics of RQL query evaluation as defined in [9]. If q is an RQL query and G is an input RDF graph then the answer to query q is the set of tuples $\mathcal{E}(q, G)$.

Let $Graph$ be the set of all possible RDF graphs and $Update$ be the set of all possible updates that can be expressed in RUL. The semantics of RUL statements are captured by the semantic function $\mathcal{A} : Update \times Graph \rightarrow Graph$. When an update u is applied to a graph $G \in Graph$ and appropriate preconditions are satisfied, u affects a set of nodes and arcs of G and produces a new graph given by $\mathcal{A}(u, G)$.

An RUL update is called *primitive* if it is of the form INSERT $c(i)$, DELETE $c(i)$, INSERT $p(i, i)$, DELETE $p(i, j)$ where c is a class, p is a property and i, j are URIs. If τ and τ' are two updates then their *composition* is a *complex* update denoted by $\tau; \tau'$. The semantics of composition are given by the equation $\mathcal{A}(\tau; \tau', G) = \mathcal{A}(\tau', \mathcal{A}(\tau, G))$. Composition is an associative operation thus $\mathcal{A}(\tau_1; \cdots; \tau_n, G) = \mathcal{A}(\tau_n, \mathcal{A}(\ldots, \mathcal{A}(\tau_1, G)))$.

3.1   The Semantics of INSERT

Let $G = (V, E, \nu, \lambda)$ be an RDF graph over the RDFS graph $(VS, ES, C, P, \prec, \Theta, \Lambda)$. The effect of update INSERT $c(i)$ in G is captured by $\mathcal{A}(\text{INSERT } c(i), G) = (V', E, \nu', \lambda')$ where V', ν', λ' are defined as follows. If there is no node $a \in V$ with $\nu(a) = i$ then $V' = V \cup \{a_0\}$ where a_0 is a brand new node symbol. Additionally, ν' extends ν such that $\nu'(a_0) = i$ and λ' extends λ such that $\lambda'(a_0) = \{c\}$. On the other hand, if there is a node $a \in V$ with $\nu(a) = i$ then $V' = V$ and ν' is the same as ν. In this case, if $c \in \lambda(a)$ then $\lambda' = \lambda$. If $c \notin \lambda(a)$ but there exist classes $c_1, \ldots, c_k \in \lambda(a)$ such that $c \prec c_1, \ldots, c \prec c_k$ then λ' is the same as λ with the exception that $\lambda'(a) = (\lambda(a) \setminus \{c_1, \ldots, c_k\}) \cup \{c\}$. Otherwise, λ' is the same as λ with the exception that $\lambda'(a) = \lambda(a) \cup \{c\}$.

The preconditions for the execution of the primitive update INSERT $p(i_1, i_2)$ in G is that i_1 is a URI and instance of $domain(p)$, and i_2 is a URI or literal and instance of $range(p)$. The effect of this update is captured by $\mathcal{A}(\text{INSERT } p(i_1, i_2), G) = (V', E', \nu', \lambda')$ where V', E', ν' and λ' are defined as follows. If i_2 is a literal of type t and there is no $a \in V$ such that $\nu(a) = i_2$ then $V' = V \cup \{a_0\}$ where a_0 is a brand new node symbol such that $\nu'(a_0) = i_2$ and $\lambda'(a_0) = t$ (function ν' is identical to ν for all other values in its domain). Otherwise, $V' = V$ and $\nu' = \nu$. Now let $a_1, a_2 \in V'$ be nodes such that $\nu(a_1) = i_1$ and $\nu(a_2) = i_2$. If $p \in \lambda((a_1, a_2))$ then $E' = E$ and $\lambda' = \lambda$. If $p \notin \lambda((a_1, a_2))$ but there are properties $p_1, \ldots, p_k \in \lambda((a_1, a_2))$ such that $p \prec p_1, \ldots, p \prec p_k$ then $E' = E$ and λ' is the same as λ with the exception that $\lambda'((a_1, a_2)) = (\lambda((a_1, a_2)) \setminus \{p_1, \ldots, p_k\}) \cup \{p\}$. Otherwise, $E' = E \cup \{(a_1, a_2)\}$ and λ' is the same as λ with the exception that $\lambda'((a_1, a_2)) = \lambda((a_1, a_2)) \cup \{p\}$.

The semantics of INSERT statements with multiple predicates in the INSERT clause can now be defined using composition as follows:

$$\mathcal{A}(\text{INSERT } c_1(i_1), \ldots, c_n(i_n), p_1(j_1, j_1'), \ldots, p_m(j_m, j_m'), \ D) =$$
$$\mathcal{A}(\text{INSERT } c_1(i_1); \cdots; \text{INSERT } c_1(i_k); \text{INSERT} p_1(j_1, j_1'); \cdots; \text{INSERT} p_m(j_m, j_m'), \ D).$$

3.2   The Semantics of DELETE

Let $G = (V, E, \nu, \lambda)$ be an RDF graph over the RDFS graph $(VS, ES, C, P, \prec$
$, \Theta, \Lambda)$. The precondition for the execution of the primitive update DELETE $c(i)$
in G is that i is an instance of class c. The effect of this update is captured by
$\mathcal{A}(\text{DELETE } c(i), G) = (V', E', \nu, \lambda')$ where V', E', λ' are defined as follows. Let
$a \in V$ be the node with $\nu(a) = i$. If $c = \text{rdf:Resource}$ then $V' = V \setminus \{a\}$
otherwise $V' = V$.

   If $c \in \lambda(a)$ then let C_1 be the set $\{c_1 : c_1 \preceq c \wedge c_1 \in \lambda(a)\}$. Then λ' is the same
as λ with the exception that $\lambda'(a) = \lambda(a) \setminus C_1$. In addition, $E' = E \setminus (\{(a, b) :$
$\lambda((a, b)) = p \wedge (\exists c_1 \in C_1) domain(p) = c_1\} \cup \{(b, a) : \lambda((b, a)) = p \wedge (\exists c_1 \in$
$C_1) range(p) = c_1\})$.

   If $c \notin \lambda(a)$ but there is a class c' such that $c' \prec c$ and $c' \in \lambda(a)$ then λ' is the
same as λ with the exception that $\lambda'(a) = (\lambda(a) \setminus C_1) \cup C_2$ where $C_1 = \{c_1 \in$
$\lambda(a) : c' \preceq c_1 \preceq c\}$ and $C_2 = \{c_2 \in \lambda(a) : c \prec c_2 \wedge \neg(\exists c_3)(c \prec c_3 \prec c_2)\}$. In
addition, $E' = E \setminus (\{(a, b) : \lambda((a, b)) = p \wedge (\exists c_1 \in C_1) domain(p) = c_1\} \cup \{(b, a) :$
$\lambda((b, a)) = p \wedge (\exists c_1 \in C_1) range(p) = c_1\})$.

   In a similar way, one can define the semantics of DELETE for the case of
properties. The semantics of DELETE statements with multiple predicates can
then be easily defined as in the case of INSERT using composition. Finally, the
semantics of MODIFY can also be defined similarly and are omitted.

3.3   Set-Oriented Updates

The syntax of RUL allows us to express set-oriented updates using variables in
the INSERT, DELETE or MODIFY clause as we showed with examples in Section 2.

   The semantics of update statements with a single INSERT, DELETE or MODIFY
clause with variables can easily be defined using the operation of composition
and function $\mathcal{E}$ that formalizes the evaluation of RQL queries. For example,

$$\mathcal{A}(\text{INSERT } c(x) \text{ FROM } b(x) \text{ WHERE } f(x), D) = \mathcal{A}(\text{INSERT } c(i_1); \cdots ; \text{INSERT } c(i_k), D)$$

where $i_1, \ldots, i_k$ are URIs such that $\mathcal{E}(\text{SELECT } x \text{ FROM } b(x) \text{ WHERE } f(x), D) =$
$\{(i_1), \ldots, (i_k)\}$. The semantics can be given similarly if we have a predicate
$p(x, y)$ in the INSERT clause. The same holds for statements with a single DELETE
clause with variables. The case of MODIFY is slightly more involved: the order of
execution of the actions involved is as it was explained in Section 2.

   The situation becomes more complex when we consider multiple predicates
in an INSERT, DELETE or MODIFY clause, or multiple INSERT, DELETE or MODIFY
clauses in a single update statement. Obviously, clause order matters in this
case as we have already demonstrated in Example 15 where we consider multiple
updates of the same kind without variables. The following examples illustrate
the issues involved when multiple updates of different kinds are allowed.

Example 19. Let us assume an RDFS schema with two classes A and B and an
RDF graph with a single node with URI i1 that is an instance of class A (so
class B has no instances). Let us now consider the following statements:

(1)   DELETE B(X) INSERT B(X)   (2)   INSERT B(X) DELETE B(X)
       FROM A{X}   FROM A{X}

The effect of Statement (2) is to leave class B in the same state (i.e., with no instances) while Statement (1) forces i1 to become an instance of B as well.

There is also a deeper issue regarding the order of execution for the different tuples of values of the variables that satisfy the FROM and WHERE clauses.

Example 20. Let us revisit the above example and introduce a new class C in the schema, and a second resource node with URI i2 that is an instance of class C. Let us now consider the following statement:

DELETE B(X) INSERT B(Y)
FROM A{X}, C{Y}
WHERE X != Y

The set of tuples satisfying the FROM and WHERE clause are (i1,i2),(i2,i1). The following orders of execution are possible for the DELETE-INSERT block:

DELETE B(i1); DELETE B(i2); INSERT B(i2); INSERT B(i1)
DELETE B(i1); INSERT B(i2); DELETE B(i2); INSERT B(i1)
DELETE B(i2); INSERT B(i1); DELETE B(i1); INSERT B(i2)

These different orders result in different states of the graph. In the first case class B ends up with instances i1, i2, in the second case it has instance i1, and in the third case it has instance i2.

It is possible to give *non-deterministic* semantics to RUL that allow all of the above executions. In this case $\mathcal{A}$ must be allowed to be a *relation* i.e., a subset of $Update \times Graph \times Graph$. Non-deterministic update languages have been considered in the past for other data models e.g., by Abiteboul and Vianu for the relational model [22, 23]. For practical reasons we have chosen to avoid non-determinism in RUL.

We solve the dilemma of examples such as the above by adopting a semantics similar to the one proposed in [24] where a procedural language with a for each iterator for deductive database updates is proposed. Let $U_1, \ldots, U_n$ be INSERT or DELETE. The semantics of updates with multiple INSERT or DELETE clauses with variables is captured by the following:

$$\mathcal{A}(U_1\ c_1(x_1) \cdots U_n\ c_n(x_n)\ \text{FROM}\ b(x_1, \ldots, x_n)\ \text{WHERE}\ f(x_1, \ldots, x_n), D) =$$
$$\mathcal{A}(U_1\ c_1(i_1^1); \cdots; U_1\ c_1(i_1^k); \cdots; U_n\ c_n(i_n^1); \cdots; U_n\ c_n(i_n^k), D)$$

where $i_1^1, \ldots, i_n^1, \ldots, i_1^k, \ldots, i_n^k$ are URIs such that

$$\mathcal{E}(\text{SELECT}\ x_1, \ldots, x_n\ \text{FROM}\ b(x_1, \ldots, x_n)\ \text{WHERE}\ f(x_1, \ldots, x_n), D) =$$
$$\{(i_1^1, \ldots, i_n^1), \ldots, (i_1^k, \ldots, i_n^k)\}.$$

In other words, the FROM and WHERE clauses are evaluated first to compute a set of valid bindings. Then, each one of the INSERT or DELETE statements is executed in turn for *all* elements of the set of bindings. The semantics can be given similarly if multiple class or property predicates are allowed in the INSERT or DELETE clauses. Since update clauses with multiple predicates are trivially translated into sequences of update statements with a single predicate then our semantics cover this case as well.

4   Conclusions

We have presented an expressive declarative language for updating RDF graphs while ensuring that insertion/deletion/modification of nodes and arcs violates the semantics neither of the RDF model nor of the specific RDFS schema. More precisely, we have carefully designed the effects and side-effects of each RUL operation to always result in a consistent state of the updated graph. There is an ongoing implementation of RUL using the existing ICS-FORTH RQL code base. In future work, we plan to precisely characterize the expressive power of the language we have developed (in the spirit of [22, 23]) and consider schema updates and schema evolution. Our work on RUL should be considered as a first necessary step towards this direction.

References

1. Das, A., Wu, W., McGuinness, D.: Industrial Strength Ontology Management. In: The Emerging Semantic Web. (IOS Press)
2. May, W., J. Alferes, F.B.: Towards Generic Query, Update, and Event Languages for the Semantic Web. In: Proc. 2nd PPSWR. (2004)
3. Perez, A.G.: A Survey on Ontology Tools. Deliverable 1.3 IST Project OntoWeb (2002)
4. Magkanaraki, A., Karvounarakis, G., Christophides, V., Plexousakis, D., Anh, T.: Ontology Storage and Querying. ICS-FORTH Technical Report No 308 (2002)
5. Seaborne, A.: An RDF NetAPI. In: Proc. 1st ISWC. (2002) 399–403
6. Broekstra, J., Kampman, A., van Harmelen, F.: Sesame: A Generic Architecture for Storing and Querying RDF and RDF Schema. In: Proc. 1st ISWC. (2002)
7. Oberle, D., Volz, R., Motik, B., Staab, S.: KAON Server Prototype. Deliverable 6, IST Project WonderWeb (2002)
8. Sarkar, S., Ellis, H.: Five Update Operations for RDF. Rensselaer at Hartford Technical Report, RH-DOES-TR 03-04 (2003)
9. Karvounarakis, G., Alexaki, S., Christophides, V., Plexousakis, D., Scholl, M.: RQL: A declarative query language for RDF. In: Proc. 11th WWW. (2002)
10. Magkanaraki, A., Tannen, V., Christophides, V., Plexousakis, D.: Viewing the Semantic Web Through RVL Lenses. In: Proc. 2nd ISWC. (2003)
11. Seaborn, A.:   RDQL - A   Query   Language   for   RDF. (http://www.w3.org/Submission/RDQL)
12. Clark, K.: SPARQL Protocol for RDF. http://monkeyfist.com/kendall/sparql-protocol/ (2004)
13. Haase, P., Broekstra, J., Eberhart, A., Volz, R.: A Comparison of RDF Query Languages. In: Proc. 3rd ISWC. (2004) 502–517
14. Nejdl, W., Siberski, W., Simon, B., Tane, J.: Towards a Modification Exchange Language for Distributed RDF Repositories. In: Proc. 1st ISWC. (2002) 236–249
15. Guha, R.V.: Rdfdb ql. (http://www.guha.com/rdfdb/query.html)
16. Mylopoulos, J., Borgida, A., Jarke, M., Koubarakis, M.: Telos: Representing Knowledge about Information Systems. ACM Transactions on Information Systems **8** (1990) 325–362
17. Nejdl, W., Dhraief, H., Wolpers, M.: O-Telos-RDF: a Resource Description Format with Enhanced Meta-Modeling Functionalities Based on O-telos. (In: Workshop on Knowledge Markup and Semantic Annotation at the 1st K-CAP)

18. Koubarakis, M., Mylopoulos, J., Stanley, M., Jarke, M.: Telos: Features and Formalization. Technical Report KRR-TR-89-4, Dept. of Computer Science, University of Toronto (1989)
19. Plexousakis, D.: Semantical and Ontological Considerations in Telos: a Language for Knowledge Representation. Computational Intelligence 9 (1993) 41–72
20. Alexaki, S., Christophides, V., Karvounarakis, G., Plexousakis, D., Tolle, K.: The ICS-FORTH RDFSuite: Managing Voluminous RDF Description Bases. In: Proc. 2nd SemWeb. (2001)
21. Hayes, P.: RDF Semantics. http://www.w3.org/TR/rdf-mt/ (2004)
22. Abiteboul, S., Vianu, V.: A Transcation Language Complete for Database Update and Specification. In: Proc. 6th PODS. (1987) 260–268
23. Abiteboul, S., Vianu, V.: Procedural and Declarative Database Update Languages. In: Proc. 7th PODS. (1988) 240–250
24. Wallace, M.: Compiling Integrity Checking Into Update Procedures. In: Proc. 12th IJCAI. (1991) 903–908

Ontologies Are Us: A Unified Model of Social Networks and Semantics

Peter Mika

Vrije Universiteit, Amsterdam,
1081HV Amsterdam, The Netherlands
pmika@cs.vu.nl

Abstract. In our work we extend the traditional bipartite model of ontologies with the social dimension, leading to a tripartite model of actors, concepts and instances. We demonstrate the application of this representation by showing how community-based semantics emerges from this model through a process of graph transformation. We illustrate ontology emergence by two case studies, an analysis of a large scale folksonomy system and a novel method for the extraction of community-based ontologies from Web pages.

1 Introduction

According to the most cited definition of the Semantic Web literature, an ontology is an explicit specification of the conceptualization of a domain [1]. Guarino clarifies Gruber's definition by adding that the AI usage of the term refers to "an engineering artifact, constituted by a specific vocabulary used to describe a certain reality, plus a set of explicit assumptions regarding the intended meaning of the vocabulary words" [2]. An ontology is thus engineered by -but often for- members of a domain by explicating a reality as a set of agreed upon terms and logically-founded constraints on their use.

Conceiving ontologies as engineering artifacts allows us to objectify them, separate them from their original social context of creation and transfer them across the domain. Problems arise with this simplistic view, however, if we consider the temporal extent of knowledge. As the original community evolves through members leaving and entering or their commitments changing, a new consensus may shape up invalidating the knowledge codified in the ontology.

To address the problem of ontology drift, several authors have suggested *emergent semantics* as a solution [3]. The expectation is that the individual interactions of a large number of rational agents would lead to global effects that could be observed as semantics. Ontologies would thus become an emergent effect of the system as opposed to a fixed, limited contract of the majority. While the idea quickly caught on due to the promise of a more scalable and easily maintainable Semantic Web, the agreement so far only extends to the basic conditions under which emergence would take place. The vision is a community of self-organizing, autonomous, networked and localized agents co-operating in dynamic, open environments, each organizing knowledge (e.g. document instances) according to a

Y. Gil et al. (Eds.): ISWC 2005, LNCS 3729, pp. 522–536, 2005.

self-established ontology, establishing connections and negotiating meaning only when it becomes necessary for co-operation. Beyond the reasonable belief that individual actions in such a semantic-social network would lead to ontology emergence, there is a lack of an abstract model of such a system that could also explain the process of emergence. Thus there appears to be a large conceptual gap in the literature between the vision and the details of implementations of various semantic architectures based on P2P, Grid, MAS and web technology.

In this paper, we take a step back and formulate a generic, abstract model of semantic-social networks (Section 2), which we will call the Actor-Concept-Instance model of ontologies. This model is built on an implicit (albeit crucial) realization of emergent semantics, namely that meaning is necessarily dependent on a community of agents. Inspired by social tagging mechanisms, we represent semantic-social networks in the form of a tripartite graph of person, concept and instance associations, extending the traditional concept of ontologies (concepts and instances) with the social dimension. We will show how lightweight ontologies of concepts and social networks of persons emerge from this model through simple graph transformations. In Section 3 we will demonstrate these effects based on two independent, large scale datasets. In Section 4, we evaluate one of our emergent ontologies (the result of a social-network based ontology extraction process) against the results of the traditional method of ontology extraction based on co-occurrence. Lastly, we conclude by a summary and a discussion of future work in Section 5.

2   A Tripartite Model of Ontologies

While expert systems designed for centralized, controlled environments benefit greatly from the increasing expressivity of ontology languages such as OWL, especially in domains that lend naturally to formalization such as engineering and medicine, lightweight ontologies expressed in RDF(S) have spread and caught on in the loosely controlled, distributed environment of the Web [4].

The tendency towards lightweight, easily accessible mechanism for ontology and metadata creation is best evidenced by the recent appearance of folksonomies. Folksonomy (from folk and taxonomy) is a neologism for a practice of collaborative categorization using freely chosen keywords. Folksonomies (also called social tagging mechanisms) have been implemented in a number of online knowledge sharing environments since the idea was first adopted by social bookmarking site del.icio.us in 2004.

The idea of a folksonomy is to allow the users to describe a set of shared objects with a set of keywords of their own choice. What the objects are depends on the goal of the site: while bookmarks are the object of classification in del.icio.us, photos are shared in Flickr, scientific publications are tagged in CiteULike, while 43Things allows users to share their goals and plans (e.g. to travel or loose weight) by annotating their descriptions with keywords and connecting users with similar pursuits[1].

---

[1] del.icio.us, www.flickr.com, www.citeulike.org, www.43things.com

It is important to note that in terms of knowledge representation, the set of these keywords cannot even be considered as vocabularies, the simplest possible form of an ontology on the continuous scale of Smith and Welty [6]. First, the set of words is not fixed. In fact, the users form no explicit agreement at all about the use of words, not even in the form of incremental, need-based, local and temporary agreements suggested by the research on emergent semantics [3]. Yet, the basic conditions of emergent semantics are given and as we will show there is semantics emerging at the scale of these systems. Second, although we use the term concept in the following, it is clear that there is no one-to-one correspondence between concepts and keywords. It is not always possible for the users to express a complex concept with a single keyword and thus they may use more than one tag to express the concept association that the item brings up in them. Lastly, the instances of folksonomies are instances only in the sense of classification.

In order to model networks of folksonomies at an abstract level, we will represent such a system as a tripartite graph with hyperedges. The set of vertices is partitioned into the three (possibly empty) disjoint sets $A = \{a_1, \ldots, a_k\}$, $C = \{c_1, \ldots, c_l\}$, $I = \{i_1, \ldots, i_m\}$ corresponding the set of actors (users), the set of concepts (tags, keywords) and the set of objects annotated (bookmarks, photos etc.) In effect, we extend the traditional bipartite model of ontologies (concepts and instances) by incorporating actors in the model.

In a social tagging system, users tag objects with concepts, creating ternary associations between the user, the concept and the object. Thus the folksonomy is defined by a set of annotations $T \subseteq A \times C \times I$. Such a network is most naturally represented as hypergraph with ternary edges, where each edge represents the fact that a given actor associated a certain instance with a certain concept. In particular, we define the representing hypergraph of a folksonomy T as a (simple) tripartite hypergraph $H(T) = \langle V, E \rangle$ where $V = A \cup C \cup I$, $E = \{\{a, c, i\} \mid (a, c, i) \in T\}$.

Tripartite graphs and hyperedges are rather cumbersome to work with. However, we can reduce such a hypergraph into three bipartite graphs (also called two-mode graphs) with regular edges. These three graphs model the associations between actors and concepts (graph AC), concepts and objects (graph CO) and actors and instances (graph AI). For example, the AC valued bipartite graph is defined as follows:

$$AC = \langle A \times C, E_{ac} \rangle, \ E_{ac} = \{(a, c) \mid \exists i \in I : (a, c, i) \in E\}, \ w : E \to \mathbb{N}, \ \forall e = (a, c) \in E_{ac}, \ w(e) := |\{i : (a, c, i) \in E)\}|$$

In words, the bipartite graph AC links the persons to the concepts that they have used for tagging at least one object. Each link is weighted by the number of times the person has used that concept as a tag. This kind of graph is known in the social network analysis literature as an affiliation network [7], linking people to affiliations with weights corresponding to the strength of the affiliation. An affiliation network can be used to generate two simple, weighted graphs (one-mode networks) showing the similarities between actors and events, respectively. (At this point it is recommended to dichotomize the graph by applying some threshold.)

The process of folding a bipartite graph (the extraction of a one-mode network) can be most easily understood by looking at the matrix form of the graph. Let's denote this matrix as $\mathbf{B} = \{b_{ij}\}$. As discussed before, $b_{ij} = 1$ if actor a_i is affiliated with concept c_j. We define a new matrix $\mathbf{S} = \{s_{ij}\}$, where $s_{ij} = \sum_{x=1}^{k} b_{ix}b_{xj}$. In matrix notation $\mathbf{S} = \mathbf{BB}'$. This matrix, known as the co-affiliation matrix, defines a social network that connects people based on shared affiliations. In our case the links are between people who have used the same concepts with weights showing the number of concepts they have used in common. The dual matrix, $\mathbf{O} = \mathbf{B}'\mathbf{B}$ is a similar graph showing the association of concepts, weighted by the number of people who have used both concepts as tags. Note that in both graphs the diagonal of the corresponding matrices contains the counts of how many concepts or persons a given person or concept was affiliated with in the bipartite graph. We can use these values to normalize the association weights (e.g. by calculating the Jaccard-coefficient) and then filtering again based on the relative weights. In case of the $\mathbf{S}$ social network, for example, this means that we have taken into account the relative importance of the link between persons.

In summary, the AC graph, the affiliation network of people and concepts can be folded into two graphs: a social network of users based on overlapping sets of objects and a lightweight ontology of concepts based on overlapping sets of communities. Thus in this simple model, social networks and semantics are just flip-sides of the same coin: the original bipartite graph contains all the information to generate these networks, while it is not possible to re-generate the original graph from them.

The other two bipartite graphs that we derived from the original tripartite model can also be folded into one-mode networks in a similar fashion. In particular, the CI graph leads to another semantic network, where the links between terms are weighted by the number of instances that are tagged with both terms. This type of semantic network is a much more familiar kind: it mimics the basic method applied in text mining, where terms are commonly associated by their co-occurrence in documents. The AI graph results in another social network of persons, where the weight of a pair is given by the number of items they have both tagged. We also get a network of instances, with associations showing the number of people who have tagged a given pair of instances.

In the following we focus our attention to the two lightweight ontologies based on overlapping communities (O_{ac}) and overlapping sets of instances (O_{ci}).[2] The analysis of the emergent social networks is outside the scope of the current paper.

---

[2] Recall that $O_{ac} = \mathbf{B}'\mathbf{B}$, where $\mathbf{B} = \{b_{ij}\}$ with $b_{ij} = 1$ if actor a_i is affiliated with concept c_j; and $O_{ci} = \mathbf{D}'\mathbf{D}$, where $\mathbf{D} = \{d_{pq}\}$ with $d_{pq} = 1$ if concept c_p is used to tag the instance i_q.

2.1   Ontology Enrichment

The community-based lightweight ontology O_{ac} that we extract from the affiliation network is rather peculiar from a knowledge representation perspective. Unlike the manually constructed thesauri known in the Semantic Web literature (such as Wordnet [8]), it more closely resembles the association thesauri studied in linguistics. An example is the Edinburgh Associative Thesaurus (EAT)[3], which was collected in 1973 via an experiment using a group of university students as subjects [9]. The experiment consisted of handing a list of words to students who were instructed to write down against each stimulus word the first word it made them think of, working as quickly as possible. The obtained words were used in a next round of the experiment. (The cycle was repeated three times, by then the number of different responses was so large that they could not all be re-used as stimuli.)

Our associative ontology is similar to the EAT in that the weights of the links between terms are expressed as the number of people who make that association. The difference is that in the EAT collection, people are prompted explicitly to create links between concepts, while we deduce such links by observing tagging behavior. More importantly, however, both methods have the crucial property that the result clearly depends on the community of people who take part in experiment. The method of ontology engineering is particularly revealing, because once the initial set of words is selected there is only one parameter to the process: the population chosen. (In particular, the knowledge engineer has no other role than handing out questionnaires and collecting the responses.) Some of the results are likely to hold for other communities (like the overwhelming reaction of saying *Noah* when hearing the word *ark*), but many of the aggregated associations are driven by the collective mind set of the subjects of the experiment. A collective mindset that is likely shaped by the well-known law of community formation: interaction creates similarity, while similarity creates interaction.

We can not only repeat the experiments with different communities, but given some information about the social structure of the community, we could also extract local ontologies by limiting our tripartite ontology to the associations of a certain sub-community of actors. Note that this is the principle of locality in action, one of the expected hallmarks of emergent semantics [3]. We will demonstrate this effect in Section 3.2 where we extract an ontology of research topics in the Semantic Web domain.

In modern terms, the EAT is an emergent ontology based on empirical data. Unlike ontologies that are meant to codify fixed agreements, all graphs that we derive are also emergent in the sense of evolving dynamically with the Actor-Concept-Instance network. Changes in the original network can occur in a number of ways. Users may join or leave the community, changing the set of actors. The focus of the community may shift, affecting the set of items tagged and the concepts used. Last, the understanding and use of terms may change, reflecting in the set of associations between concepts and instances created by the users.

---

[3] Consult the EAT online at http://www.eat.rl.ac.uk/

Although our association networks are very simple ontological structures, there are several opportunities of enriching them with additional semantics. We start by observing that a significant drawback of the EAT is the heterogeneity of terms. Our emergent ontologies will also likely to contain a diverse mixture of specific and generic terms, i.e. terms that we can unambiguously place in a clearly defined context (e.g. instances such as *Peter*) and terms that can occur in multiple contexts of use (e.g. *war*). From a network view, general words are therefore more likely to bridge different clusters of words, while specific terms are expected to exhibit a dense clustering in their neighborhood. This suggest an opportunity to distinguish between these two categories by computing the *clustering coefficient*, the *(local) betweenness centrality* or the *network constraint* on our terms[7,10]. These well-known ego-network measures of Social Network Analysis are readily available in popular network analysis packages such as Pajek[11] and UCINET[12]. Based on the same observation, we also expect that clustering algorithms can help us in finding synonym sets of the more specific terms. There is a wide range of clustering algorithms available in the above mentioned network analysis packages, based on different definitions of cohesiveness.

We may also extract broader/narrower term relations typical of thesauri using set theory. In an ideal situation, we would say that Concept A is a super-concept of Concept B if the set of entities (persons or items) classified under B is a subset of the entities under A ($B \subseteq A \leftrightharpoons A \cap B = B$). We might also add the criterium that the set of A should be significantly larger then the set of B, i.e. $|B|/|A| < k$ for some value of k. In principle, such an ordering allows us to define a Galois lattice using the subset relation. In practice, such a lattice would be very sparse (considering the number of entities and the number of possible subsets over them), so we will approximate this method by looking for near-perfect overlaps, i.e. $|A \cap B|/|B| < n$ for some value of n. Finding appropriate values for the k, n parameters of the model is the task of the researcher.

The reader should note that the meaning of these broader/narrower relations are very different, depending on whether we analyze the O_{ci} or the O_{ac} ontology. In the first case, the interpretation is that all (or most) of the items classified under the narrower term also appear under the broader term. In other words, what we extract is a classification hierarchy. In the second case, the meaning is that all the persons associated with the narrower term are also associated with the broader term. In other words, we extract a hierarchy based on sub-community relationships.

3   Case Studies

In the following, we demonstrate the broad applicability of the Actor-Concept-Instance model of ontologies by looking at two different semantic social networks. Our first data set comes from an existing web-based social bookmarking tool called del.icio.us (Section 3.1), while the second case is built on synthetic data obtained by using web mining techniques (Section 3.2). We will show how the abstract model applies to the particular cases and demonstrate our method of ontology emergence based on the graph transformation described above.

3.1   Ontology Emergence in del.icio.us

According to the definition of author Joshua Schachter, del.icio.us is a social bookmarking tool. Much like the similar functions of browsers, del.icio.us allows users to manage a personal collection of links to web sites and describe those links with one or more keywords. Unlike stand-alone tools, del.icio.us is a web-based system that allows users to share bookmarks with each other. Bookmarks can be browsed by user, by keywords (tags) or by a combination of both criteria. Further, the user interface encourages exchange by showing how bookmarks are linked together via users and tags. In terms of the Actor-Concept-Instance model, registered users of del.icio.us are the actors who create or remove associations between terms and webpages (instances) by adding or deleting bookmarks.

From the perspective of studying emergence, del.icio.us is remarkable for the dynamics of its user base. The young, technologically aware community gathering around the site closely follows the latest news and trends in web technology as well as the evolving vocabulary of the field. Beyond technology, del.icio.us users also post bookmarks related to current topics in politics, media, business and entertainment. The emphasis on timeliness is reinforced by listing bookmarks in a backward-chronological order as it is typical for blogs.

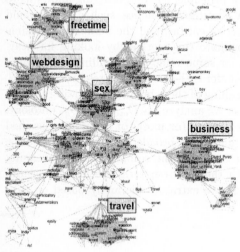

Fig. 1. The del.icio.us tags associated through co-occurrence on items and the clusters emerging

Table 1. The five main clusters of interest based on the Concept-Object network

travel	cote, provence, villa, azur, mas, holiday, vacation, tourism, france, heritage
business	venture_capital, enterprise, up, start, venture, newspaper, capital, Segev, pitango, vc
free time	procrastination, info, advice, gtd, life, notes, planning, daily, reading, forums
sex	hot, to, street, pictures, on, photos, free, celeb, adult, lesbian
web design	design, designer, webdesign, premium, logo, logos, dreamweaver, templates, best, good

The process of annotation is made as easy as possible. A single textbox allows users to enter a set of words without any recommendations made by the system. On the downside, this means that synonyms are common in the folksonomy, e.g. "semanticweb", "semweb" are different keywords. Ambiguity is also present, since users often pick overly general terms to describe items (such as "web", "tool" and other popular terms). Further, users often make the mistake to enter key phrases instead of keywords (e.g. "Bill Clinton"), where the words are subsequently parsed as separate tags ("Bill" and "Clinton"); or they escape the one-word-only limitation by concatenating words. Case sensitivity and the use of punctuation marks further pollute the del.icio.us namespace. However, at the scale of system (over 30 thousand registered users in December, 2004) the imperfections of tagging are reduced to an acceptable level. On the plus side, users benefit from instant gratification in the form of linkage to other relevant, timely, socially-ranked posts.

del.icio.us exposes tagging data in the form of RSS feeds, which we have collected using a focused RDF crawler. The crawler was initialized with the single most popular tag ("web") and have traversed the RSS network in a breadth-first-search manner, following links to tags mentioned in the descriptions of items. The sample data that we collected - over a million triples of RDF - was stored using the Sesame storage and query facility [13]. The sample represents 51852 unique annotations of 30790 URLs, by 10198 persons using 29476 unique tags. [4]

Next, we have generated both the Actor-Concept and Concept-Instance graphs. In order to scale down the dataset (without loosing much information) and to avoid strong associations with a low support we have filtered out those entities that had only a minimal number of connections, i.e. those tags that had less than ten items classified under them and those persons who have used less than five concepts.

Subsequently, we have extracted the above mentioned two kinds of ontologies by folding these graphs using the network analysis package Pajek. As a reminder, the first ontology (O_{ac}) is based on actors sharing concepts as interests, i.e. the associations reflect overlapping communities of interests, while the second network (O_{ci}) reflects the co-occurrence of tags on items. We have filtered the networks based on the absolute strength of associations. Next, we applied geometric normalization to the resulting graphs and filtered edges again based on the relative strength of the associations. We have chosen the thresholds in such a way to obtain networks of equal size (438 concepts). Figure 1 shows a high level view of the O_{ci} graph, Figure 2 shows a detailed view of the O_{ac} graph.

The results show clear evidence of emerging semantics in both cases, but the networks we obtain still show very different pictures. With an equal number of vertices, the densities of the two networks are quite different (0.01 for the O_{ci} network, 0.006 for the O_{ac} network), and so is the amount of clustering present (the average clustering coefficients are 0.2 and 0.03, respectively).

The selection of concepts in the two networks is also very different: only 64 concepts are present in both networks of the total of 438 nodes in each graph.

---

[4] This is a sample of the complete data set because the RSS feeds expose only the latest thirty items for each tag. Futher, we stopped crawling after reaching this size. To our knowledge this is still the largest ontology annotation data set ever studied.

(A sample is included in Table 2.) A closer look reveals that the concepts within the clusters of the first network are often very specialized terms, while those in between the clusters are overly general terms. A look at the terms with the lowest clustering and highest betweenness centrality confirms this hypothesis. The top five terms with highest betweenness are *up, cool, hot, in, to.* Noticeable also is that the terms with the highest clustering and lowest network constraint are those related to sex. As mentioned before, the second network shows much less clustering: overly general and overly specific terms are both missing.

Table 2. Terms starting with "A" or "a" in the two lightweight ontologies generated from the del.icio.us network

O_{ci}	*/GoogleHacks, _0, 04, 1, 2, 2005, 3g, a, A, a9, Aaron_Mankovski, actona, actors, adult, aduva, advice, ajax, all, Allegrini, america, an, and, angeles, apparel, Apple, as, assembly, attempt, attention, attention.xml, aviv, axml, azur
O_{ac}	.net, 3d, 43folders, academic, accessibility, acronym, actionscript, activism, ad, ads, adsense, advertising, advice, advisories, adwords, agile, ajax, amazon, amer-ica, analysis, and, Apache, apache, api, app, apple, application, architecture, archive, Art, art, articles, asia, astronomy, atlas, Audio

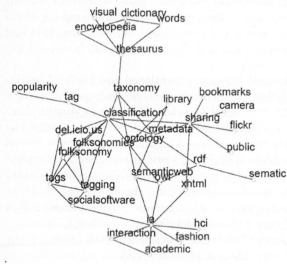

Fig. 2. Detail view of the del.icio.us tags associated through users: a 3-neighborhood of the term ontology. Note that the term *sematic* is correctly associated, despite the obvious typo.

Table 3. Broader/narrower term relations in the technology domain, based on sub-communities in del.icio.us

Broader	Narrower
rss	atom
cmyk	rgb
cell	umts, wcdma, ev-do
phone	cell
ajax	json
xml	xslt
rdf	owl
flickr	gmail, picasa
ruby	rails
mac	iphoto
java	j2ee
google	gds
search	a9, engine
linux	ubuntu, gnome
flash	actionscript
flickr	lickr, photoset
javascript	xmlhttprequest, dom, sarissa

The clue to the different qualities of these networks lies in the difference in the way associations are created between the concepts. In the first case, there exist a strong association between concepts if they share a large percentage of items, *independent of the number of users interested in them and regardless if these associations were added by the same users or not.* The resulting distribution of association weights shows a very slow decline, the average weight is fairly high. In the second case, there is a strong association in the network if two concepts share a large fraction of the users among them, *independent of the number of instances associated with them and regardless whether these terms were added to the same instances or not.* The resulting weight distribution shows a very steep decline, the average weight is fairly low.

This suggest that the first network (O_{ci}) is more appropriate for concept mining. In fact, a λ-set analysis performed with UCINET on a slightly larger network of 751 concepts resulted in meaningful clusters of specific terms, representing various domains of interests in the del.icio.us community. At a level of $\lambda = 20$, we found 5 cohesive groups of concepts that we identified as interests related to travel, business, free time, porn and web design (see Figure 1 and Table 1).

However, the O_{ci} semantic network ignores the relevance of the individual concepts from the user perspective and as such it gives an inaccurate picture of the community. Concepts related to sex, for example, get a misleadingly high centrality in the network due to the specificity and extent of the vocabulary used to describe sex-related sites. On the other hand, the more evenly distributed community-based network (O_{ac}) contains concepts that are actually important to del.icio.us users. These concepts almost all come from the computer domain, the apparent core interest of users. The strength of links between the concepts are also a more accurate representation of reality as they are not biased by the actual number of items that have been tagged with them.

The ignorance of the item-based extraction method towards the number of users also makes it problematic to extract taxonomic relations. Namely, many of the relations we extracted are based on the word usage of a small number of users, and in the worst case a single user. The Concept-Actor ontology yields much more easily interpretable results, shown in Figure 3. As discussed before, these are sub-community relations: the community associated with a narrower term is a sub-community of the community associated with the broader term. Nevertheless, even here we find an association created by a single story marked by a large number of users. This suggests an improvement to our original method, namely filtering out concepts that have only a limited number of items or persons associated to them. We take this into account as we move on to generalize our method to community-based ontology extraction from Web pages.

We conclude by noting the potential application of the results to improving del.icio.us itself, e.g. by offering search and navigation based on broader/narrower terms. Considering the dynamics of the community and the extent of neologism, the ontologies emerging from folksonomies such as del.icio.us also have a large potential for enriching established, but slowly evolving linguistic ontologies such as Wordnet [8].

3.2 Community-Based Ontology Extraction from Web Pages

Folksonomies such as del.icio.us are effective, because they attract sizeable sub-communities of users pursuing similar interests. Nevertheless, the community of del.icio.us is still a niche compared to the general web population, just as the number of web sites tagged is only a fraction of the number of pages on the Web.

We would like to show in the following that even without explicitly assigned tags, it is possible to extend the idea of community-based ontology extraction to the Web. Let's suppose that we have a selected a community, whose members will play the role of Actors in our model, and we have prepared a list of terms whose associations we are interested in. The instances of our model are the pages of the Web. Further, we assume that a web page is tagged by a concept if the concept occurs on the page.

Based on these assumptions, the Concept-Instance ontology is straightforward to create: we can use a search engine to obtain page counts for all pairs of concepts and then normalize by their separate page counts. This is the basic co-occurrence analysis method of text mining.

Generating the Actor-Concept ontology requires another broad assumption. We will say that there is an association between a concept, a person and a web page if the name of the person and the label of the concept co-occur on the page. This association represents a weaker commitment than in the case of folksonomies, because it is not guaranteed that the association is made *by* the person. Nonetheless, we can now generate the bipartite graph of persons and concepts by measuring the association using page counts from the search engine.

First, we measure the association between a person (e.g. *"Peter Mika"*) and a concept (e.g. *"Semantic Web"*) by submitting a boolean query combining the two terms (e.g. *"Peter Mika" AND "Semantic Web"*). We normalize the result with the number of pages where the concept occurs. We then repeat this with the same concept and the names of all other members of the target community. We calculate the mean strength of association with the concept of *"Semantic Web"*. Lastly, we associate those members of the community with this concept whose association strength is at least one standard deviation higher than the mean. (Note that this is a slightly more sophisticated method of filtering than a general threshold.) We can now fold the bipartite graph of actors and concepts to obtain the O_{ac} ontology.

Our method of community-based ontology extraction have been implemented as part of the Flink system. The system is a web-based presentation of the social networks and research interests of Semantic Web researchers[5]. The community of researchers represented in Flink includes all authors, program committee members and organizers of all past international Semantic Web events from 2001, altogether 607 persons. The system extracts the social network of researchers as described in [14] and associates them with research topics using the search engine Google.

Flink can also be used to perform co-occurrence analysis and generate the O_{ci} ontology. We improve the basic method by adding the disambiguation term

---

[5] Flink itself uses Semantic Web technology and is the winner of the Semantic Web Challenge of 2004. See http://flink.semanticweb.org and http://challenge.semanticweb.org

"Semantic Web" OR ontology to the queries sent to the search engine, limiting the items returned to those relating to the Semantic Web.

The resulting ontological structures are not included here due to limitations of space, but we strongly encourage the reader to consult them online[6]. To make the networks comparable, we have included only the 100 strongest associations in each network. Again, we see a significant difference in the set of concepts remaining in the networks. Namely, from the original 60 terms (selected manually from the proceedings of the ISWC events), the method of text mining found the strongest associations between more general terms. Specific concepts related to the Semantic Web seem to float to the periphery and are misplaced in general. For example, the term *FOAF* is related to *XML* and *OWL-S*, technologies not directly related to FOAF. *Annotation* is related to *alignment* and *databases*. The term *ontology* is associated, among others, with *HTML*, *XML* and *databases*, concepts not directly related to the understanding of ontologies in the Semantic Web community.

The O_{ac} association network represents a clear improvement in these respects. The method found correct associations between domain specific concepts. For example, the term *FOAF* is linked here to *Redland* and *Sesame*, the triple stores preferred by FOAF developers for their scalability. Terms related to ontology languages (*OWL*, *RDF*, *OIL*, *DAML+OIL*, *ontology languages* etc.) are correctly clustered together, just as the technologies related to ontology storage (query languages, triple stores), with terms related to ontology development (*OilEd*, *OntoEdit*, *ontology development*) connecting the two clusters. More general technologies are also placed correctly in context, i.e. corresponding to the way they are used in the Semantic Web. For example, *NLP* is tied to the notions of *annotation* and *ontology learning*.

The difference in the node sets can be explained in a similar way as in the case of del.icio.us: the O_{ci} network ignores the overall relevance of these concepts to the Semantic Web community. Considering the associations, we believe that there is another effect in play. By querying the associations of persons first and then linking concepts through overlapping communities, we simulate the effect of first asking the members of the community to associate themselves with certain research interests and then relating these interests through overlapping communities. Overlapping communities turn out to be a stronger link than overlapping sets of web pages. A possible explanation is that even after including the disambiguating term in the query, the search engine still suffers from *knowing too much*, blurring away community-specific interpretations.

4   Evaluation

In absence of a golden standard, evaluating the results of ontology learning or ontology mapping is a difficult task: inevitably, it requires consulting the community or communities whose conceptualizations are being learned or mapped. In order to evaluate our results, we have thus approached in email 61 researchers active in the Semantic Web domain, most of whom are members of the ISWC community and

---

[6] http://www.cs.vu.nl/~pmika/research/iswc2005/

many of them are in the graph-theoretical core of the community[7]. The single question we asked was *In terms of the associations between the concepts, which ontology of Semantic Web related concepts do you consider more accurate?* Lacking a yardstick, there is no principled correct answer to this question that we expected to receive. Instead, we were interested to find out if there is a majority opinion emerging as an answer and if yes, which of the two ontologies (produced by the two different methods) would that majority accept as more accurate.

Many respondents expressed difficulty in answering the question due to the (intentional) lack of further explanations or instructions, e.g. what the associations mean, but also due to the very different node sets of the two semantic networks. Nonetheless, out of the 33 respondents only three persons were not willing to express any preference (even if a slight one) for one network or the other. 23 respondents were members of the ISWC community and 15 of them belong to the core of the community.

The distribution of the answers for the various subgroups are summarized in Table 4. First, taking all responses into account, we can conclude that the participants consider the O_{ac} network as a more accurate representation of associations between the concepts than the O_{ci} network (the result is significant at a level of $p = 0.01$). The majority vote becomes

Table 4. Results for the comparison of the community-based (O_{ac}) and item-based (O_{ci}) ontology extraction methods

	N	O_{ac}	O_{ci}	Ratio	Sign.
All	30	22	8	73.3%	0.0055
ISWC	23	18	5	78.3%	0.0040
ISWC-core	15	13	2	86.7%	0.0032

even stronger if we consider only the members of the ISWC community, i.e. the persons whose name has been used to extract the semantic network. Thus as a second finding we can also conclude that the O_{ac} network is considered more accurate particularly by those whose names were used in the extraction process. The results become even more conclusive if we only consider the votes from the core members of the community. Based on this finding and assuming a continuum, we can state that the O_{ac} network better reflects the conceptualizations of those closer to the core of the community. Combined together, our findings confirm that the O_{ac} network better reflects the conceptualizations of those involved in Semantic Web research, and this holds especially for those most actively involved in Semantic Web research.

5   Conclusions and Future Work

The Semantic Web is a web for machines, but the process of creating and maintaining it is a social one. Although machines are helpful in manipulating symbols according to pre-defined rules, only the users of the Semantic Web have the necessary interpretive and associative capability for creating and maintaining ontologies. Ontology creation necessitates a social presence as it requires an actor to

---

[7] We performed a categorical core/periphery analysis with correlation optimization using UCINET 6 based on the connected part of the Flink social network data (N=528), available at http://prauw.cs.vu.nl:8080/flink/graph. The results show a clear C/P structure with 63 persons in the core and 465 persons on the periphery.

reliably predict how other members of the community would interpret the symbols of an ontology based on their limited description. With incorporating the notion of semantics into the web architecture, we have thus made the users of the system a critical part of the design.

We have argued elsewhere for a three layered view of the Semantic Web, namely the layer of communities and their relations, the layer of semantics (ontologies and their relations) and the layer of content items and their relations (the hypertext Web) [15]. In this paper we have formalized this view as a tripartite model of ontologies with three different classes of nodes (actors, concepts, and instances) and hyperedges representing the commitment of a user in terms of classifying an instance as belonging to a certain concept. We have shown the usefulness of this model by generating two kinds of association networks: the well-known co-occurrence network of ontology learning and a novel semantic network based on community relationships. Among the future work is the study of the two emerging social networks, based on object and concept overlaps.

The general advantage of the incorporation of the social context into the representation of ontologies is the possibility of studying emergence from user actions. Emergent semantics is likely to best complement well-established, but slowly evolving ontologies such as WordNet [8], which lack the associative component.[8] We have also compared the two networks based on object and person overlap and noted the advantage of the second network: the possibility to extract semantics pertinent to a sub-community of the user network. In some sense, this is the opposite of mining general knowledge from search engines as in the work of Cimiano et al. or Etzioni et al. [16,17]. In comparison to these systems, our community-based ontology extraction has a great potential in extracting ontologies that more closely match the conceptualization of a particular community. For example, when trying to find associations between concepts used by the Web Services community, it is natural to consider only the associations created (explicitly or implicitly) by those involved in developing Web Services. As we have shown, using this method the resulting ontology is more likely to be accepted as accurate by the community itself.

It seems that ontologies are us: inseparable from the context of the community in which they are created and used. A greater acknowledgement of this state -by incorporating the link between actors and concepts into the model of ontologies-have only benefits to bring in terms of more meaningful and easily maintainable conceptual structures. While we are only at the beginning of realizing these benefits, there is a clear magic as we see semantics emerge from the individual actions of a community at work.

---

[8] For example, according to WordNet the distance of the terms *Noah* and *ark* is quite large: their closest common ancestor in the hypernym tree is *object, physical object*. Yet, the Edinburgh master's students overwhelmingly associate the term *Noah* with *ark* and vice versa. The association is so strong in fact (78 and 79 percent of all terms mentioned in response, respectively) that it is safe to say that in the mind of the students these terms are solely defined by each other, in the context of the biblical story of Noah's ark.

References

1. Gruber, T.R.: Towards Principles for the Design of Ontologies Used for Knowledge Sharing. In Guarino, N., Poli, R., eds.: Formal Ontology in Conceptual Analysis and Knowledge Representation, Deventer, The Netherlands, Kluwer Academic Publishers (1993)
2. Guarino, N.: Formal Ontology in Information Systems. IOS Press (1998)
3. Aberer, K., Cudré-Mauroux, P., Ouksel, A.M., Catarci, T., Hacid, M.S., Illarramendi, A., Kashyap, V., Mecella, M., Mena, E., Neuhold, E.J., Troyer, O.D., Risse, T., Scannapieco, M., Saltor, F., de Santis, L., Spaccapietra, S., Staab, S., Studer, R.: Emergent Semantics Principles and Issues. In: Database Systems for Advanced Applications 9th International Conference, DASFAA 2004. Volume 2973 of LNCS. (2004) 25–38
4. Mika, P., Akkermans, H.: Towards a New Synthesis of Ontology Technology and Knowledge Management. Knowledge Engineering Review (To appear.)
5. van Elst, L., Abecker, A.: Ontologies for information management: balancing formality, stability, and sharing scope. Expert Systems with Applications **23** (2002) 357–366
6. Smith, B., Welty, C.: Ontology: Towards a new synthesis. In: Formal Ontology in Information Systems, Ongunquit, Maine, ACM Press (2001) iii–x
7. Wasserman, S., Faust, K., Iacobucci, D., Granovetter, M.: Social Network Analysis: Methods and Applications. Cambridge University Press (1994)
8. Fellbaum, C., ed.: WordNet - An electronic lexical database. MIT Press (1998)
9. Kiss, G., Armstrong, C., Milroy, R., Piper, J.: An associative thesaurus of English and its computer analysis. Edinburgh University Press (1973)
10. Burt, R.S.: Structural Holes: The Social Structure of Competition. Harvard University Press (1995)
11. Batagelj, V., Mrvar, A.: Pajek - Program for Large Network Analysis. Connections **21** (1998) 47–57
12. Borgatti, S., Everett, M., Freeman, L.: Ucinet for Windows: Software for Social Network Analysis. (Harvard: Analytic Technologies)
13. Broekstra, J., Kampman, A., van Harmelen, F.: Sesame: An Architecture for Storing and Querying RDF and RDF Schema. In: Proceedings of the First International Semantic Web Conference (ISWC 2002). Number 2342 in Lecture Notes in Computer Science (LNCS), Springer-Verlag (2002) 54–68
14. Mika, P.: Social Networks and the Semantic Web: An Experiment in Online Social Network Analysis. In: Proceedings of the IEEE/WIC/ACM International Conference on Web Intelligence, Beijing, China (2004)
15. Mika, P.: Social Networks and the Semantic Web: The Next Challenge. IEEE Intelligent Systems **20** (2005)
16. Cimiano, P., Handschuh, S., Staab, S.: Towards the Self-Annotating Web. In: Proceedings of the 13th International World Wide Web Conference, New York, USA (2004) 462–471
17. Etzioni, O., Cafarella, M., Downey, D., Kok, S., Popescu, A.M., Shaked, T., Soderland, S., Weld, D.S., Yates, A.: Web Scale Information Extraction in KnowItAll (Preliminary Results). In: Proceedings of the 13th International World Wide Web Conference, New York, USA (2004) 100–111

OMEN: A Probabilistic Ontology Mapping Tool

Prasenjit Mitra[1], Natasha F. Noy[2], and Anuj Rattan Jaiswal[1]

[1] The Pennsylvania State University, University Park, PA 16802, U.S.A.
{pmitra, ajaiswal}@ist.psu.edu
http://www.psu.edu/
[2] Stanford University, Stanford, CA 94305, U.S.A.
noy@smi.stanford.edu
http://smi.stanford.edu/

Abstract. Most existing ontology mapping tools are inexact. Inexact ontology mapping rules, if not rectified, result in imprecision in the applications that use them. We describe a framework to probabilistically improve existing ontology mappings using a Bayesian Network. OMEN, an Ontology Mapping ENhancer, is based on a set of meta-rules that captures the influence of the ontology structure and the existing matches to match nodes that are neighbours to matched nodes in the two ontologies. We have implemented a protype ontology matcher that can either map concepts across two input ontologies or enhance existing matches between ontology concepts. Preliminary experiments demonstrate that OMEN enhances existing ontology mappings in our test cases.

1 Introduction

Information sources, even those from the same domain, are heterogenous in nature. The semantics of the information in one source differs from that of the other. In order to enable interoperation among heterogenous information sources or to compose information from multiple sources, we often need to establish mappings among database schemas and among ontologies. These mappings capture the semantic correspondence between the schemas or the concepts in the ontologies.

Several problems arise when an expert entrusted with matching two ontologies constructs the semantic mappings between them. First, the expert needs automatic or semi-automatic means for establishing the mappings. Often, the schemas or ontologies are quite large. Manually establishing the mappings among large ontologies is prohibitively expensive or downright impossible due to the sheer number of entities that the expert needs to match. Thus, an expert needs an automated ontology matching tool. However, automatic tools often use heuristics and may be imprecise. The expert would like to specify, along with each mapping, the amount of uncertainty associated with it. Second, precise mappings may not even exist. Even a human expert may be able to come up only with approximate mappings. In particular, the expert may not be able to come up with precise mappings if the expert has incomplete information about class definitions. Therefore, we introduce **probabilistic mappings** that map each pair

Y. Gil et al. (Eds.): ISWC 2005, LNCS 3729, pp. 537–547, 2005.

of concepts from two sources and the mapping between them has an associated probability.

Our main premise in this work is the following: if we know a mapping between two concepts from the sources, we can use the mapping to infer mappings between related concepts. For example, if two properties are equivalent, and so are their domains, we can infer (with some certainty) that their ranges are equivalent as well. Therefore, we can build a Bayes Net with the concept mappings. The Bayes Net uses a set of *meta-rules* that expresses how each mapping affects other related mappings. We can use existing automatic and semi-automatic tools to come up with initial probability distributions for mappings. Next, we use this probability distribution to infer probability distributions for other mappings.

We have implemented a tool, OMEN, an Ontology Mapping Enhancer. OMEN uses a Bayes Net to provide probabilistic inference and aids in enhancing existing ontology mappings by deriving missed matches and invalidating existing false matches. Preliminary results show that using OMEN an expert can enhance the quality of existing mappings between concepts across ontologies.

The primary contributions of this paper are as follows:

1. We introduce a probabilistic method of enhancing existing ontology mappings by using a Bayes Net to represent the influences between potential concept mappings across ontologies.
2. In OMEN, we provide an implemented framework where domain knowledge of mapping influences can be input easily using simple meta-rules. We demonstrate the effectiveness of OMEN in our preliminary experiments.

To the best of our knowledge, no existing work has extensively used a probabilistic representation of ontology mapping rules and probabilistic inference to improve the quality of existing ontology mappings.

The rest of the paper is organized as follows. Section 2 contains a description of the knowledge model used to represent the ontologies and the mapping expressions, In Section 3, we discuss the use of meta-rules to generate new probability distributions based on existing ones. Section 4 contains a description of how the Bayes Net that OMEN uses is constructed. In Section 5, we briefly outline our prototype implementation and provide the results of our experiments. Section 6 describes some open issues and scope for future work. In Section 7, we discuss the related work and conclude the paper in Section 8.

2   Knowledge Model and Mapping Expressions

We assume a simple ontology model (that is more or less similar to RDF Schema or a subset of OKBC with more commonly used facets). We use the following components to express ontologies:

Classes. Classes are concepts in a domain, organized in a subclass–superclass hierarchy with multiple inheritance.

Properties. Properties describe attributes of classes (which are primitive values, such as numbers, strings, etc., and we omit these from mapping consideration) and relationships between classes. Properties have one or more **domains**, which are classes to which the property can be attached; and one or more **ranges**, which restrict the classes for the values of property.

Given two ontologies, O and O', a **mapping** between two concepts, $C \in O$ and $C' \in O'$, $m(C, C')$ (C and C' can be either classes or properties), is one of the following values:

- $=$ if the concepts are equivalent;
- $\subset$ if C is a specialization of C';
- $\supset$ if C' is a generalization of C;
- $\cap$ if there is an overlap between C and C';
- $\times$ if C and C' are not related.

Note, that we may not know the value of the mapping at all. In other words, if $(m(C, C')) = \times$, then we *know* that they are not related, which is different from not knowing what their relationship is.

Therefore, for each mapping $m(C, C')$, we can talk about a **probability distribution** over the mapping values $\{=, \subset, \supset, \cap, \times\}$. For each mapping $m(C, C')$, the sum of the values in the distribution must be less than or equal to 1. It is less than one if we do not have complete information about the distribution.

3   Meta-rules for Generating New Probability Distributions

In this section, we show examples of meta-rules that are used to match the ontologies and discuss how the algorithm generates new probability distributions depending upon the existing ones. The algorithm starts the process by initializing probability distributions for some of the mappings, using the output of various automatic mapping tools. It then uses a set of meta-rules to derive new mappings based on existing ones.

3.1   Examples of Meta-rules

Before giving an example of a meta-rule, we describe the notations and shorthands that we use for brevity. In all the rules for mapping between two ontologies, O and O', we use the following:

- all concepts from O have no prime ('); all concepts from O' have a prime (');
- upper-case C with or without a subscript is a class;
- lower-case q with or without a subscript is a property;
- $P(C_1 \theta C_2, x)$ indicates that the probability of the match $(C_1 \theta C_2)$ is x.

The following is an example of a meta-rule to generate a mapping between classes in the range of a property based on the mapping of the properties themselves and their domains. Not included explicitly in the rule (for brevity) is an assumption that both properties, q and q', have a single domain and range.

$$P(C_d = C'_d, x) \wedge P(q = q', 1) \wedge$$
$$domainOf(q, C_d) \wedge domainOf(q', C'_d) \wedge$$
$$rangeOf(q, C_r) \wedge rangeOf(q', C'_r)$$
$$\Rightarrow P(C_r = C'_r, x)$$

Below are some (informal) examples of other metarules:

Mappings between superclasses and all but several siblings: Here we can probably still say something about the probabilities that the rest of the siblings match in a pairwise fashion. (If these are later combined with rules producing other evidence, such an observation will be helpful).

Mappings between a property and domain of a property: **Natasha, can you please fill in what you meant by this**

Mapping between properties: If two classes are ranges for matching properties, then they may match (but probabilities are reduced somewhat compared to the case when the domains match as well).

Mappings between superclasses and all but one sibling: In this case, we say that the existing matches between the superclasses and the matched siblings result in the remaining siblings matching with high probability.

3.2 Combining the Results from Several Rules for the Same Mapping

Consider a pair of classes, C and C' (Figure 1). Let us assume that initially we do not have any probability distribution for $m(C, C')$. Then a number of meta-rules affect the probability distribution for $m(C, C')$. In the example in the figure, the following rules and mappings affect the result:

– A mapping between superclasses of C and C'; mappings between the siblings of C and C'. Let's say we know that $P(C_0 = C'_0, x)$, for some $x < 1$, and $P(C_0 \subset C'_0, y)$, for some $y < 1$, $(x + y \leq 1)$, and $P(C_1 = C'_1, 1)$. We then use the following rule (we omit the relationships that are obvious from the figure, such as $subclassOf(C, C_0)$ from the rule):

$$p(C_0 =/ \subset C'_0, x) \wedge p(C_1 = C'_1, 1) \Rightarrow$$
$$p(C =/ \subset C', x)$$

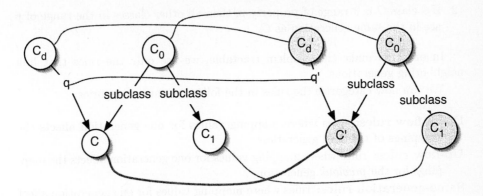

Fig. 1. The probability distribution for the mapping between C and C' is affected by the mappings between their superclasses, siblings, and domains of the properties q and q' for which C and C' are ranges

- A mapping between properties q and q' ($P(q = q', 1)$) for which C and C' are ranges respectively, and mappings between domains of q and q' ($P(C_d = C'_d, z)$). We are assuming that both q and q' have a single domain and range each.

$$P(C_d = C'_d, z) \land P(q = q', 1) \Rightarrow$$
$$P(C = C', z)$$

For the moment, let us assume that there are no more influences on the mapping $m(C, C')$.

We now need to combine the following three results of the rules above:

1. $P(C = C, x)$
2. $P(C \subset C, y)$
3. $P(C = C', z)$

We also know that $x + y \leq 1$. The algorithm must combine probabilitic influences of different rules and determine the probability distribution of the matching nodes.

In theory, we could introduce some certainty factor into the rules. However, an easier solution would be to use probabilities to reflect that. For example, if the rule is fairly certain, then we simply propagate the initial probability x (as in the rules above). If the rule is more speculative, we can reduce the probability in the result of the rule by some factor.

3.3 Eliminating Circular Dependencies

We define a **generation** of classes in the following way:

1. All subclasses of the same superclass (siblings) belong to the same generation.

2. If a class C is a range of property p, then all other classes in the range of p are in the same generation as C.

In order to make the problem tractable, we use only the rules that link neighboring generations.

We can now categorize the rules in the following three categories:

Down-flow rules: rules where mapping values for one generation affects the mappings of the *next* generation

Up-flow rules: rules where mapping values for one generation affects the mappings for the *previous* generation

Same-generation rules: rules where mapping values for one generation affect mapping values for the same generation.

Combination rules: any combination of the above.

In order to avoid circular dependencies, we use the following restrictions:

1. In same-generation rules, only the values that were available prior to the current iteration, can be used in the antecedent of rules. Same-generation rules that introduce cycles are broken arbitrarily by dropping some edges.
2. Each iteration is either a down-flow iteration or an up-flow iteration. The only rules that are allowed in a down-flow (up-flow) iteration are down-flow (up-flow) rules, same-generation rules, and combination rules with only down-flow (up-flow) rules.

For the rest of this note, we only consider a down-flow iteration.

During a down-flow iteration, a mapping between two classes, $m(C, C')$ is affected by the mappings between:

– their superclasses;
– their siblings;
– the properties for which C and C' are ranges, the domains of these properties, and other ranges of these properties.

Note that all the examples of the rules in section 3are down-flow, same-generation, or combination rules (where combination is same-generation and down-flow). In other words, all these rules can be used in a down-flow iteration.

4   Construction of the Bayesian Network

We construct a Bayes Net to represent the influences and inter-relationships between ontology matches as described below. We describe the construction of a down-flow graph, that is a graph constructed using only the down-flow rules, or same-generation rules. An up-flow graph can be constructed correspondingly.

4.1   The BN-Graph

Initially, we construct all possible nodes representing all possible matches across the two ontologies. That is, if ontology $O1$ contains n nodes, and ontology $O2$ contains m nodes, we construct $m \times n$ nodes in the Bayes Net graph representing all possible matches. Each node in the Bayes Net graph represents a unique match between two concepts in the source ontologies. That is, each node represents a match from a pair of concepts such that no two concepts in a pair come from the same ontology and no two nodes represent the same set of concepts. As is evident, we create a large number of matches that are very unliquely to exist in practice. We discuss later how we can reduce the number of nodes in the Bayes Net for large ontologies.

Down-flow edges: The down-flow edges in the graph are constructed as follows. Let there be parent concepts P_1 and P_1' such that concepts C_1 and C_2 are the children of the parent concepts respectively in the source ontologies. For all possible quadruple (P_1, P_2, C_1, C_2), a directed edge between nodes $n1$ and $n2$ is added to the graph, where node $n1$ represents the match between P_1 and P_2 and node $n2$ represents the match between C_1 and C_2.

In the current implementation, we do not add any same-generation edges to avoid creating cycles. Recall, the graph in a Bayes Net must not contain cycles and is a DAG. How same-generation information can be introduced in a Bayes Net is left for future work.

4.2   Apriori Probabilities and Evidence

The "root" nodes in the BN-Graph, that is nodes that have no parents, must be provided with a set of apriori probabilities. This set of apriori probabilities is obtained from the previous matching – the output of a matcher that is input to OMEN. [1] We assume that the previous matching matched the source ontologies and generated probabilities that model the certainty of all possible candidate matches (or at least the matches represented by the root nodes in the BN-Graph). OMEN also obtains the evidence to the Bayes Net from the final result of the previous matcher.

4.3   Meta-rules and Conditional Probability Tables

The meta-rules form the basis for constructing the conditional-probability tables(CPTs) for each node. The construction of appropriate conditional probability tables is the hardest and most subjective task in the design of our Bayes Net . Yet, the accuracy of the CPTs deeply influence the veracity of the results obtained from any Bayes Net .

The interface to OMEN allows external functions to generate and provide the tool with appropriate CPTs. These functions are called on a per node basis and

---

[1] Recall, that OMEN enhances existing ontology matches.

passed a neighbourhoods (in the source ontologies) of the two concepts that the node represents as arguments.

OMEN also provides internal functions that generate the CPTs based on meta-rules and the apriori probabilities. Ideally, the CPTS should not depend upon the apriori probabilities of the nodes and an expert will indicate how one match in the Bayes Net influences other matches and also provide the probability tables expressing such an influence. However, when such an expert is absent, we have empirically observed that using the apriori probabilities in conjunction with the meta-rules to generate the CPTs provides better matches than those obtained by just using the meta-rules.

4.4   Reducing the Number of Nodes

If the source ontologies are very large, the number of nodes in the Bayes Net being quadratic in the number of nodes in the source ontologies, are extremely large too. We reduce this number by removing nodes in the Bayes Net that do not have any parents or children. We observed empirically that there are a significant number of such nodes.

The Bayes Net that is constructed is a collection of DAGs. Consider a node present in a DAG none of whose nodes are supplied as evidence. This situation happens because all the nodes in the DAG represent matches that are deemed unrealistic by the previous matcher. In absence of a single evidence in the entire DAG, the Bayes Net cannot perform any inference in that DAG. Therefore, we can reduce the Bayes Net by removing that DAG from the collection of DAGs altogether.

If we want to reduce the number of nodes even further, we can adopt the following policy. Before the Bayes Net is constructed, identify the evidence nodes — those that are classfied as matches by the previous matcher. Now create a node in the Bayes Net only for those pairs of nodes such that their distance from the evidence node is at most k, where k is a small integer $(1, 2, 3, ...)$. This restriction implies that any node in the Bayes Net represents nodes in the ontology whose distance from a node (in the ontology) that has been matched by the previous matcher is at most k.

5   Implementation and Experimentation

OMEN uses BNJ, Version 2.0 [1] as its probabilistic inference engine. In the current implementation, only down-flow meta-rules were used. The experiments were run on ...

6   Future Work

Up-flow rules: The current implementation takes into account only down-flow rules. In the future, we intend to perform experiments to determine whether the system based on up-flow rules outperform one based on down-flow rules and to identify the scenarios when one outperforms the other.

Multiple iterations: We start with some initial set of probability distributions and use a down-flow iteration to create new probability distributions for mappings. A case could be made to combine successive passes of down-flow and up-flow iterations using the down-flow and up-flow meta-rules alternately. Ideally, the system will perform multiple iterations until it meet some convergence criteria (or have done some "sufficient" number of iterations). The usefulness of performing multiple iterations needs to be empirically verified in the future. We also need to characterize whether the system automatically converges or whether there needs to be an arbitrary cut-off on the number of passes done. Another issue is whether the same meta-rules and CPTs be used during mutliple iterations or should different CPTs be generated for different passes?

Using inferred mappings in rules: We start with a set of mappings that we get "from the outside" as an initial sample of values. These mappings are set and we do not alter them. We generate new mappings and posterior probabilities in the first pass. Should the second pass, the first up-flow pass be performed using the output of the first pass? Or should it be performed on the original results and the results of the two independent passes combined to get better results. Should the evidence provided by the previous matcher be constantly treated as evidence, or should it be changed depending upon the posterior probabilities generated by the several iterations of OMEN?

Other mappings to consider: For now, all the rules are "symmetric" in the way we treat generations. For example, the mappings between superclasses and some of their siblings affect the mapping between the remaining siblings. What if we have a mapping between two classes, C and C', some of their subclasses, but then a subclass of C is mapped to a class in O' that is not closely related to C' (definitely not its subclass)?

7   Related Work

Two research directions are related to our work: automatic or semi-automatic discovery of ontology mappings and the use of uncertainty in knowledge-based systems.

7.1   Automatic Ontology Mapping

Over the past decade, researchers have actively worked on developing methods for discovering mappings between ontologies or database schemas. These method employ a slew of different techniques. For example, Similarity Flooding [8] and AnchorPrompt [10] algorithms *compare graphs* representing the ontologies or schemas, looking for similarities in the graph structure. GLUE [3] is an example of a system that employs *machine-learning techniques* to find mappings. GLUE uses multiple learners exploiting information in concept instances and taxonomic structure of ontologies. GLUE uses a probabilistic model to combine results of different learners. Hovy [5] describes a set of heuristics that researcher-sat ISI/USC used for semi-automatic alignment of domain ontologiesto a large central ontology. Their techniques are based mainly on*linguistic analysis* of concept names and natural-languagedefinitions of concepts. A number of researchers propose *similarity metrics* between concepts in different ontologies based on their relations to other concepts. For example, a similarity metric between concepts in OWL ontologies developed by Euzenat and Volchev [4] is a weighted combination of similarities of various features in OWL concept definitions: their labels, domains and ranges of properties, restrictions on properties (such as cardinality restrictions), types of concepts, subclasses and superclasses, and so on. Finally, approaches such as ONION [9] and Prompt [11] use a combination of *interactive specifications* of mappings and *heuristics* to propose potential mappings.

The approach that we describe in this paper is complementary to the techniques for automatic or semi-automatic ontology mapping. Many of the methods above produced pairs of matching terms with some degree of certainty. We can use these results as input to our network and run our algorithm to improve the matches produced by others or to suggest additional matches. In other words, our work complements and extends the work by other researchers in this area.

7.2 Probabilistic Knowledge-Based Systems

Several researchers have explored the benefits of bringing together Nayes Nets an knowledge-based systems and ontologies. For instance, Koller and Pfeffer [7] developed a "probabilistic frame-based system," which allows annotation of frames in a knowledge base with a probability model. This probability model is a Bayes Net representing a distribution over the possible values of slots in a frame. In another example, Koller and colleagues [6] have proposed probabilistic extensions to description logics based on Bayesean Networks.

In the context of the Semantic Web, Ding and Peng [2] have proposed probabilistic extensions for OWL. In this model, the OWL language is extended to allow probabilistic specification of class descriptions. The authors then build a Bayesean Network based on this specification, which models whether or not an individual matches a class description and hence belongs to a particular class in the ontology.

Researchers in machine learning have employed probabilistic techniques to find ontology mappings. For example, the GLUE system mentioned earlier [3], uses a Bayes classifier as part of its integrated approach. Similarly, Prasad and colleagues [12] use a Bayesean approach to find mappings between classes based on text documents classified as exemplars of these classes. These approaches, however, consider instances of classes in their analysis and not relations between classes, as we do. As with other approaches to ontology mapping, our work can be viewed as complementary to the work done by others.

8 Conclusion

We have outlined the design and implementation of OMEN, an ontology match enhancer tool, that improves existing ontology matches based on a probabilistic inference. This tool is dependent upon a set of meta-rules which express the influences of matching nodes on the existence of other matches across concepts in source ontologies that are located in the proximity of the matching nodes. We described how we implemented a simple first version of the matching tool and discussed our preliminary results. We have also outlined several improvements that can be made to the tool and identified several open questions that if resolved can make the performance of the tool even better.

References

1. Bayesian network tools in java(bnj), version 2.0, July 2004.
2. Z. Ding and Y. Peng. A probabilistic extension to ontology language owl. In *37th Hawaii International Conference On System Sciences (HICSS-37)*, Big Island, Hawai, 2004.
3. A. Doan, J. Madhavan, P. Domingos, and A. Halevy. Learning to map between ontologies on the semantic web. In *The Eleventh International WWW Conference*, Hawaii, US, 2002.
4. J. Euzenat and P. Valtchev. Similarity-based ontology alignment in OWL-Lite. In *The 16th European Conference on Artificial Intelligence (ECAI-04)*, Valencia, Spain, 2004.
5. E. Hovy. Combining and standardizing largescale, practical ontologies for machine translation and other uses. In *The First International Conference on Language Resources and Evaluation (LREC)*, pages 535–542, Granada, Spain, 1998.
6. D. Koller, A. Levy, and A. Pfeffer. P-Classic: a tractable probabilistic description logic. In *14th National Conference on Artificial Intelligence (AAAI-97)*, 1997.
7. D. Koller and A. Pfeffer. Probabilistic frame-based systems. In *Fifteenth National Conference on Artificial Intelligence (AAAI-98)*, Madison, Wisconsin, 1998. AAAI Press.
8. S. Melnik, H. Garcia-Molina, and E. Rahm. Similarity flooding: A versatile graph matching algorithm and its application to schema matching. In *18th International Conference on Data Engineering (ICDE-2002)*, San Jose, California, 2002. IEEE Computing Society.
9. P. Mitra, G. Wiederhold, and S. Decker. A scalable framework for interoperation of information sources. In *The 1st International Semantic Web Working Symposium (SWWS'01)*, Stanford University, Stanford, CA, 2001.
10. N. F. Noy and M. A. Musen. Anchor-PROMPT: Using non-local context for semantic matching. In *Workshop on Ontologies and Information Sharing at the Seventeenth International Joint Conference on Artificial Intelligence (IJCAI-2001)*, Seattle, WA, 2001.
11. N. F. Noy and M. A. Musen. The PROMPT suite: Interactive tools for ontology merging and mapping. *International Journal of Human-Computer Studies*, 59(6):983–1024, 2003.
12. S. Prasad, Y. Peng, and T. Finin. A tool for mapping between two ontologies using explicit information. In *AAMAS 2002 Workshop on Ontologies and Agent Systems*, Bologna, Italy, 2002.

On the Properties of Metamodeling in OWL

Boris Motik

FZI Research Center for Information Technologies at the University of Karlsruhe,
Karlsruhe, Germany
motik@fzi.de

Abstract. A common practice in conceptual modeling is to separate
the intensional from the extensional model. Although very intuitive, this
approach is inadequate for many complex domains, where the borderline
between the two models is not clear-cut. Therefore, OWL-Full, the most
expressive of the Semantic Web ontology languages, allows combining
the intensional and the extensional model by a feature we refer to as
metamodeling. In this paper, we show that the semantics of metamodeling adopted in OWL-Full leads to undecidability of basic inference problems, due to free mixing of logical and metalogical symbols. Based on this
result, we propose two alternative semantics for metamodeling: the *contextual* and the *HiLog* semantics. We show that $\mathcal{SHOIQ}$— a description
logic underlying OWL-DL— extended with metamodeling under either
semantics is decidable. Finally, we show how the latter semantics can be
used in practice to axiomatize the logical interaction between concepts
and metaconcepts.

1 Introduction

A common practice in conceptual modeling is to separate the *intensional* from
the *extensional* model of a domain. The intensional model is analogous to a
database schema and it describes the general structure and the regularities of
the world. The extensional model is analogous to a database instance and it
describes a particular state of the world. Such a modeling style has also influenced
the design of the Ontology Web Language (OWL) [14], the W3C standard for
building ontologies in the Semantic Web. Namely, OWL provides concepts and
properties for building the intensional model, and individuals and relationships
among them for building the extensional model.

To better understand this duality, consider the following example, originally
presented in [16]; a similar example may be found in [15]. A natural way to
represent kinship between animal species is to organize them in a hierarchy of
concepts. For example, the concept *Bird* represents the set of all birds, and the
concept *Eagle* is a subconcept of *Bird*, stating that all eagles are birds. This is
an example of intensional knowledge, as it is concerned with defining the general
notions of birds and eagles. Knowledge about concrete animals is represented by
extensional knowledge, e.g. by stating that the individual *Harry* is an instance
of *Eagle*. Now the intensional knowledge implies that *Harry* is an *Bird* as well.

Y. Gil et al. (Eds.): ISWC 2005, LNCS 3729, pp. 548–562, 2005.

However, one might also make statements about individual species, such as "eagles are listed in the IUCN Red List[1] of endangered species." Notice an important distinction: we do not say that each individual eagle is listed in the Red List, but that the eagle species as a whole is. Hence, we introduce a concept *RedListSpecies*, and consider the relationship between *RedListSpecies* and *Eagle*. Making the former a superconcept of the latter is incorrect, as it would imply that *Harry* is a *RedListSpecies* — clearly an undesirable conclusion. It is better to say that *Eagle* is a *type of RedListSpecies*. Thus, *RedListSpecies* acts as a *metaconcept* for *Eagle*. The style of modeling which provides for metaconcepts is called *metamodeling*, and it can be used to build concise models if we precisely axiomatize the properties of metaconcepts. For example, by stating that "it is not allowed to hunt the individuals of species listed in the Red List", we formalize the logical properties of the metaconcept *RedListSpecies*, allowing us to deduce that "it is not allowed to hunt *Harry*."

The examples such as the one given above are often dismissed with an argument that "eagle as a species" and "eagle as a set of all individual eagles" are not the one and the same thing, and should not be referred to using the same symbol. Whereas an in-depth philosophical investigation might provide a more definitive answer, we simply observe that the word "eagle" in most people's minds invokes a notion of a "mighty bird of prey." The interpretation of this notion as a concept or as an individual is secondary and is often context-dependent, so using different symbols for the same intuitive notion makes the model unnecessarily complex.

Metamodeling is provided in OWL-Full, the most expressive language of the OWL family. However, its semantics is controversial, mainly because it is non-standard, and therefore makes realizing practical reasoning systems difficult [5]. Therefore, OWL-DL was conceived as a "well-behaved" subset of OWL-Full by imposing the following restrictions: (i) the sets of logical and metalogical symbols are strictly separated, (ii) the sets of symbols used as concepts, roles and individuals are strictly separated, and (iii) restrictions required to yield a decidable logic, such as the one on simple roles in number restrictions [7], are enforced. These restrictions make OWL-DL a syntactical variant of the $\mathcal{SHOIN}(\mathbf{D})$ description logic, which is known to be decidable. This is desirable since, to practically implement reasoners for expressive logics, advanced optimization techniques are essential, and these are much easier to develop if the logic is decidable [1–ch. 9].

Since it does not enforce (iii), OWL-Full is trivially undecidable. To obtain a decidable logic supporting metamodeling, it is natural to ask whether OWL-DL, extended with metamodeling in the style of OWL-Full, remains decidable. However, in Section 2 we show that even the basic description logic $\mathcal{ALC}$ becomes undecidable if restrictions (i) and (ii) are not enforced.

We analyze this undecidability result, and show that it is actually due to (i), that is, to free mixing of logical and metalogical symbols. In a way, metamodeling in OWL-Full goes beyond its original purpose, and allows the user to tamper with

---

[1] http://www.redlist.org/

the semantics of the modeling primitives themselves. Therefore, in Section 3 we present two alternative semantics for metamodeling: a *contextual* or π-semantics, which is essentially first-order, and a *HiLog* or ν-semantics, which is based on HiLog [4] — a logic providing a second-order syntax for first-order logic. We show that, under some technical assumptions, both semantics can be combined with $\mathcal{SHOIQ}$, a description logic underlying OWL-DL, yielding a decidable fragment of OWL-Full without increasing the complexity of reasoning. Furthermore, we present a resolution-based decision procedure for the $\mathcal{SHIQ}$ fragment which, we believe, provides a basis for a practical implementation. Finally, in Section 4 we discuss the added expressivity of metamodeling on a concrete example. Technical details from this paper are presented in the technical report [9].

2   Undecidability of Metamodeling in OWL-Full

The semantics of OWL-Full [14] is quite technical, so we introduce $\mathcal{ALC}$-Full— an extension the basic description logic $\mathcal{ALC}$ with metamodeling in the style of OWL-Full. We use *rdf:*, *rdfs:* and *owl:* for the standard namespace prefixes.

Definition 1. *Let V be the* vocabulary *set consisting of these symbols:*

> *owl:Thing, owl:Nothing, rdf:type, rdfs:subClassOf, owl:sameAs,*
> *owl:differentFrom, owl:complementOf, owl:unionOf$_1$, owl:unionOf$_2$,*
> *owl:intersectionOf$_1$, owl:intersectionOf$_2$, owl:someValuesFrom,*
> *owl:allValuesFrom, owl:onProperty*

Let N be the set of names such that $V \subseteq N$. An $\mathcal{ALC}$-Full knowledge base KB is a finite set of triples of the form $\langle s, p, o \rangle$, where $s, p, o \in N$.

An interpretation I is a triple $(\triangle^I, \cdot^I, EXT^I)$, where $\triangle^I$ is a non-empty set, $\cdot^I : N \rightarrow \triangle^I$ is a name interpretation function and $EXT^I : \triangle^I \rightarrow 2^{\triangle^I \times \triangle^I}$ is an extension function. Let $CEXT^I : \triangle^I \rightarrow 2^{\triangle^I}$ be the concept extension function defined as $CEXT^I(x) = \{y \mid (y, x) \in EXT^I(rdf{:}type^I)\}$. An interpretation I is a model of KB if it satisfies all conditions from Table 1. KB is satisfiable if and only if a model of KB exists.

$\mathcal{ALC}$-Full differs from OWL-Full in that: (*i*) it does not provide concrete predicates, (*ii*) it does not include the meta-level resources such as *owl:Class*, and (*iii*) it allows only binary union and intersection. These distinctions are not relevant for our undecidability proof. We use $\langle a \sqcup b, p, o \rangle$ as a syntactic shortcut for $\langle x, p, o \rangle$, $\langle x, owl{:}unionOf_1, a \rangle$ and $\langle x, owl{:}unionOf_2, b \rangle$, where x is a fresh name. We use similar shortcuts for $\langle s, p, a \sqcup b \rangle$ and for $\sqcap$.

We show the undecidability of $\mathcal{ALC}$-Full by a reduction from the well-known *domino tiling* problem [3]. A *domino system* is a triple $\mathcal{D} = (D, H, V)$, where $D = \{D_1, \ldots, D_n\}$ is a finite set of *domino types*, and $H \subseteq D \times D$ and $V \subseteq D \times D$ are *horizontal* and *vertical compatibility relations*, respectively. A $\mathcal{D}$-*tiling* of an infinite grid is a function $t : \mathbb{N} \times \mathbb{N} \rightarrow D$ such that $t(0,0) = D_0$ and, for all $i, j \in \mathbb{N}$, $(t(i,j), t(i, j+1)) \in H$ and $(t(i,j), t(i+1, j)) \in V$. For an arbitrary domino system $\mathcal{D}$, determining whether a $\mathcal{D}$-tiling exists is undecidable [3].

Table 1. Semantics of $\mathcal{ALC}$-Full

---

1. $\langle s, p, o \rangle \in KB$ implies $(s^I, o^I) \in \mathrm{EXT}^I(p^I)$
2. $\mathrm{CEXT}^I(owl\text{:}Thing^I) = \triangle^I$
3. $\mathrm{CEXT}^I(owl\text{:}Nothing^I) = \emptyset$
4. $(x, y) \in \mathrm{EXT}^I(rdfs\text{:}subClassOf^I)$ implies $\mathrm{CEXT}^I(x) \subseteq \mathrm{CEXT}^I(y)$
5. $(x, y) \in \mathrm{EXT}^I(owl\text{:}sameAs^I)$ implies $x = y$
6. $(x, y) \in \mathrm{EXT}^I(owl\text{:}differentFrom^I)$ implies $x \neq y$
7. $(x, y) \in \mathrm{EXT}^I(owl\text{:}complementOf^I)$ implies $\mathrm{CEXT}^I(x) = \triangle^I \setminus \mathrm{CEXT}^I(y)$
8. $(x, y) \in \mathrm{EXT}^I(owl\text{:}unionOf_1^I)$ and $(x, z) \in \mathrm{EXT}^I(owl\text{:}unionOf_2^I)$ imply
   $\mathrm{CEXT}^I(x) = \mathrm{CEXT}^I(y) \cup \mathrm{CEXT}^I(z)$
9. $(x, y) \in \mathrm{EXT}^I(owl\text{:}intersectionOf_1^I)$ and $(x, z) \in \mathrm{EXT}^I(owl\text{:}intersectionOf_2^I)$ imply
   $\mathrm{CEXT}^I(x) = \mathrm{CEXT}^I(y) \cap \mathrm{CEXT}^I(z)$
10. $(x, y) \in \mathrm{EXT}^I(owl\text{:}someValuesFrom^I)$ and $(x, p) \in \mathrm{EXT}^I(owl\text{:}onProperty^I)$ imply
    $\mathrm{CEXT}^I(x) = \{w \mid (w, z) \in \mathrm{EXT}^I(p) \wedge z \in \mathrm{CEXT}^I(y)\}$
11. $(x, y) \in \mathrm{EXT}^I(owl\text{:}allValuesFrom^I)$ and $(x, p) \in \mathrm{EXT}^I(owl\text{:}onProperty^I)$ imply
    $\mathrm{CEXT}^I(x) = \{w \mid (w, z) \in \mathrm{EXT}^I(p) \rightarrow z \in \mathrm{CEXT}^I(y)\}$

For a domino system $\mathcal{D}$, let $KB_\mathcal{D}$ be the $\mathcal{ALC}$-Full knowledge base consisting of triples (1) – (9). Lemma 1 shows that satisfiability of $KB_\mathcal{D}$ exactly encodes the problem of deciding whether a $\mathcal{D}$-tiling exists.

$$\langle D_i \sqcap D_j, rdfs\text{:}subClassOf, owl\text{:}Nothing \rangle \text{ for } 1 \leq i < j \leq n \tag{1}$$

$$\langle GRID, rdfs\text{:}subClassOf, D_1 \sqcup \ldots \sqcup D_n \rangle \tag{2}$$

$$\langle NotGRID, owl\text{:}complementOf, GRID \rangle \tag{3}$$

$$\langle D_i, rdfs\text{:}subClassOf, \alpha_i \rangle, \langle \alpha_i, owl\text{:}onProperty, owl\text{:}allValuesFrom \rangle, \tag{4}$$
$$\langle \alpha_i, owl\text{:}allValuesFrom, NotGRID \sqcup \bigsqcup_{(D_i, d) \in H} d \rangle \text{ for } 1 \leq i \leq n$$

$$\langle D_i, rdfs\text{:}subClassOf, \beta_i \rangle, \langle \beta_i, owl\text{:}onProperty, rdf\text{:}type \rangle, \tag{5}$$
$$\langle \beta_i, owl\text{:}allValuesFrom, NotGRID \sqcup \bigsqcup_{(D_i, d) \in V} d \rangle \text{ for } 1 \leq i \leq n$$

$$\langle GRID, owl\text{:}someValuesFrom, GRID \rangle \tag{6}$$

$$\langle GRID, owl\text{:}onProperty, owl\text{:}allValuesFrom \rangle \tag{7}$$

$$\langle GRID, owl\text{:}onProperty, rdf\text{:}type \rangle \tag{8}$$

$$\langle GRID, rdfs\text{:}subClassOf, owl\text{:}allValuesFrom \rangle \tag{9}$$

$$\langle rdf\text{:}type, owl\text{:}sameAs, owl\text{:}onProperty \rangle \tag{10}$$

$$\langle a_{0,0}, rdf\text{:}type, GRID \sqcap D_0 \rangle \tag{11}$$

Lemma 1. *A $\mathcal{D}$-tiling exists if and only if $KB_\mathcal{D}$ is satisfiable.*

Proof. ($\Rightarrow$) For a $\mathcal{D}$-tiling t, let I be an interpretation depicted in Figure 1, with $\mathrm{CEXT}^I(GRID^I) = \{a_{i,j}\}$ and $\mathrm{CEXT}^I(D_k^I) = \{a_{i,j} \mid t(i, j) = D_k\}$, for $i, j \geq 0$ and $1 \leq k \leq n$. The triples (3) – (5) encode the compatibility relations of $\mathcal{D}$ (including $NotGRID$ into (3) and (4) ensures that compatibility is enforced only among instances of $GRID$). Hence, it is easy to see that I is a model of $KB_\mathcal{D}$.

($\Leftarrow$) Let I be a model of $KB_\mathcal{D}$. An excerpt of I is shown in Figure 1, in which a triple $\langle s, p, o \rangle$ is represented as an arc pointing from the node s to the

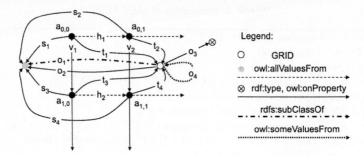

Fig. 1. Grid Structure in a Model of $KB_\mathcal{D}$

node o, whereas p is encoded by the line type according to the legend. To refer easily to arcs, we assign them labels t_i, h_i and v_i (these do not correspond to p). For example, the arc s_1 represents the triple $\langle a_{0,0}, rdf{:}type, owl{:}allValuesFrom \rangle$. Due to (10), $rdf{:}type$ and $owl{:}onProperty$ are synonyms, so s_1 also represents the triple $\langle a_{0,0}, owl{:}onProperty, owl{:}allValuesFrom \rangle$. By an abuse of notation, we do not distinguish between the symbols and their interpretations.

Due to (11), $a_{0,0}$ is linked by t_1 to $GRID$. Due to (6), (7) and (8), $a_{0,0}$ is linked to $a_{0,1}$ and $a_{1,0}$ through h_1 and v_1, respectively, and $a_{0,1}$ and $a_{1,0}$ are in the concept extension of $GRID$ by t_2 and t_3, respectively. Due to (6) and (7), $a_{1,0}$ is linked by h_2 to $a_{1,1}$, and by t_4 to $GRID$. Finally, by (9), all $a_{i,j}$ are in the concept extension of $owl{:}allValuesFrom$, that is, all $a_{i,j}$ have an s_l arc to it.

Consider now the arcs at the node $a_{1,0}$. The arc s_3 can, due to (10), be read as $\langle a_{1,0}, owl{:}onProperty, owl{:}allValuesFrom \rangle$. By applying Item 11 of Table 1 for $x = a_{1,0}$ and $y = a_{1,1}$, we conclude that, if w is in the concept extension of $a_{1,0}$ and it is connected via $p = owl{:}allValuesFrom$ to some z, then z must be in the concept extension of $a_{1,1}$. However, we may now set $w = a_{0,0}$ due to v_1, and $z = a_{0,1}$ due to h_1; this implies that $a_{0,1}$ is in the concept extension of $a_{1,1}$, that is, that $a_{0,1}$ is connected to $a_{1,1}$ by v_2. Hence, $a_{0,0}$, $a_{0,1}$, $a_{1,0}$ and $a_{1,1}$ are arranged in a two-dimensional grid, which continues indefinitely due to (6) – (8).

A node $a_{i,j}$ in I is allowed to have multiple $owl{:}allValuesFrom$ and $rdf{:}type$ successors, and all $a_{i,j}$ need not be distinct, so I need not be a two-dimensional grid. However, a two-dimensional grid can easily be extracted from I: one can choose any $owl{:}allValuesFrom$ successor $a_{i,j+1}$ and any $rdf{:}type$ successor $a_{i+1,j}$ of $a_{i,j}$, as well as any $owl{:}allValuesFrom$ successor $a_{i+1,j+1}$ of $a_{i+1,j}$. Regardless of the choices, $a_{i,j+1}$ is always connected to $a_{i+1,j+1}$ by $rdf{:}type$, so $a_{i,j}$, $a_{i,j+1}$, $a_{i+1,j}$ and $a_{i+1,j+1}$ are connected in a grid-like manner.

Hence, I contains a two-dimensional infinite grid in which $owl{:}allValuesFrom$ are horizontal, and $rdf{:}type$ are vertical arcs. The triples (1) – (5) ensure that each grid node is assigned a single domino type corresponding to the compatibility relations H and V of $\mathcal{D}$, so a $\mathcal{D}$-tiling can easily be constructed from I.   □

Together with [3], Lemma 1 immediately implies the following result:

Theorem 1. *Checking satisfiability of an $\mathcal{ALC}$-Full knowledge base KB is undecidable.*

3   Two Decidable Approaches to Metamodeling

The proof of Lemma 1 reveals the causes for the undecidability of metamodeling in OWL-Full. Namely, this logic not only allows treating concepts as individuals, but it also allows mixing logical and metalogical symbols, and exposes its modeling primitives as individuals. We exploited this in axioms (5) and (6) of $KB_{\mathcal{D}}$, by stating an existential restriction on *owl:allValuesFrom* and *rdf:type* symbols and thus affecting their semantics. One would easily agree that tampering with the semantics of the ontology language is hardly desirable in practice, so in this section we present two alternative semantics for metamodeling.

In the following, we consider the description logic $\mathcal{SHOIQ}$, since it acts as the logical underpinning of the OWL family of languages. We do not consider datatypes here for the sake of simplicity. However, in [9] we show that, as long as datatypes are not subjected to metamodeling, they do not affect our results. We believe that this is not a practically relevant restriction: treating datatype individuals as concepts and vice versa will just unnecessarily confuse the users.

3.1   The Syntax and Semantics of $\mathcal{SHOIQ}$ with Metamodeling

Definition 2 (Syntax). *For N_a a set of atomic names, the set of names is defined as $N = N_a \cup \{n^- \mid n \in N\}$. For each $n \in N$, let $\mathsf{Inv}(n) = n^-$ and $\mathsf{Inv}(n^-) = n$. A $\mathcal{SHOIQ}$ RBox $KB_{\mathcal{R}}$ is a finite set of transitivity axioms $\mathsf{Trans}(R)$ and role inclusion axioms $R \sqsubseteq S$, where $R, S \in N$. As usual, we assume that $R \sqsubseteq S \in KB_{\mathcal{R}}$ implies $\mathsf{Inv}(R) \sqsubseteq \mathsf{Inv}(S) \in KB_{\mathcal{R}}$, and that $\mathsf{Trans}(R) \in KB_{\mathcal{R}}$ implies $\mathsf{Trans}(\mathsf{Inv}(R)) \in KB_{\mathcal{R}}$. Let $\sqsubseteq^*$ be the reflexive-transitive closure of $\sqsubseteq$. A name R is simple if for each name $S \sqsubseteq^* R$, $\mathsf{Trans}(S) \notin KB_{\mathcal{R}}$. A set of $\mathcal{SHOIQ}$ concepts over $KB_{\mathcal{R}}$ is inductively defined as follows: each $A \in N$ is a concept and, for R and i names, S a simple name, C and D $\mathcal{SHOIQ}$ concepts and n a non-negative integer, $\{i\}$, $\neg C$, $C \sqcap D$, $C \sqcup D$, $\exists R.C$, $\forall R.C$, $\geq n\,R.C$ and $\leq n\,R.C$ are also $\mathcal{SHOIQ}$ concepts. A $\mathcal{SHOIQ}$ TBox $KB_{\mathcal{T}}$ is a finite set of concept inclusion axioms of the form $C \sqsubseteq D$, where C and D are $\mathcal{SHOIQ}$ concepts. A $\mathcal{SHOIQ}$ ABox $KB_{\mathcal{A}}$ is a finite set of assertions of the form $C(a)$, $R(a,b)$ or (in)equality axioms of the form $a \circ b$, where $\circ \in \{\approx, \not\approx\}$, C is a $\mathcal{SHOIQ}$ concept, and R, a and b are names. A $\mathcal{SHOIQ}$ knowledge base KB is a triple $(KB_{\mathcal{R}}, KB_{\mathcal{T}}, KB_{\mathcal{A}})$. The logic $\mathcal{ALCHOIQ}$ is a fragment of $\mathcal{SHOIQ}$ without the transitivity axioms. The logics $\mathcal{ALCHIQ}$ and $\mathcal{SHIQ}$ are the fragments of $\mathcal{ALCHOIQ}$ and $\mathcal{SHOIQ}$, respectively, without the nominal concepts $\{i\}$.*

The major difference of Definition 2 to the usual definitions is that the sets of concept, role and individual names are not disjoint, but are merged into one set of names. We denote with N_{KB} the subset of those names that occur in KB, and with $|KB|$ the *size* of KB with the numbers coded in unary. We now define the so-called *contextual* semantics for $\mathcal{SHOIQ}$.

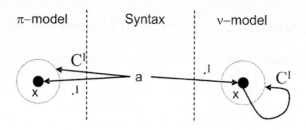

Fig. 2. π- and ν-models of the Axiom $a(a)$

Definition 3 (Contextual Semantics). *For a $\mathcal{SHOIQ}$ knowledge base KB, a π-interpretation I is a 4-tuple $(\triangle^I, \cdot^I, C^I, R^I)$ where $\triangle^I$ is a non-empty domain set, $\cdot^I : N \to \triangle^I$ is a name interpretation function, $C^I : N \to 2^{\triangle^I}$ is an atomic concept extension function and $R^I : N \to 2^{\triangle^I \times \triangle^I}$ is a role extension function. The function C^I is extended to concepts as specified in Table 2, upper left section, where symbols are interpreted* contextually, *that is, depending on their syntactic position. A π-interpretation I is a π-model of KB if it satisfies all conditions from Table 2, lower left section. The notions of π-satisfiability, π-unsatisfiability and π-entailment (written $\models_\pi$) are defined as usual.*

The contextual semantics is essentially equivalent to the one from [4] and to standard first-order semantics. Namely, in a first-order formula, the role of a symbol can be inferred from the place at which the symbol occurs in a formula, so the set of constant, function and predicate symbols need not be disjoint. We use π-semantics mainly as a baseline for a comparison with the HiLog semantics, defined below. This semantics is more in the spirit of OWL-Full, and is based on HiLog [4].

Definition 4 (HiLog Semantics). *For a $\mathcal{SHOIQ}$ knowledge base KB, a ν-interpretation I is a 4-tuple $(\triangle^I, \cdot^I, C^I, R^I)$ where $\triangle^I$ is a non-empty domain set, $\cdot^I : N \to \triangle^I$ is a name interpretation function, $C^I : \triangle^I \to 2^{\triangle^I}$ is an atomic concept extension function, and $R^I : \triangle^I \to 2^{\triangle^I \times \triangle^I}$ is a role extension function. The extension of the function C^I to concepts and the interpretation of axioms are specified in Table 2, right section. The notions of ν-satisfiability, ν-unsatisfiability and ν-entailment (written $\models_\nu$) are defined as usual.*

To understand the essential difference between these two semantics, consider the knowledge base *KB* containing only the axiom $a(a)$, where the symbol a is used both as an individual and as a concept. A π-model of *KB* is depicted on the left-hand side of Figure 2: both the individual interpretation $\cdot^I$ and the concept interpretation C^I are assigned directly to the symbol a. A ν-model of *KB* is depicted on the right-hand side of Figure 2: the individual interpretation $\cdot^I$ assigns the domain individual x to the symbol a; however, the concept interpretation is not assigned to a, but to x. We discuss the consequences that such a definition of semantics has on entailment in Section 4.

Table 2. Two Semantics for $\mathcal{SHOIQ}$ with Metamodeling

	π-semantics	ν-semantics
	Extending C^I to concepts	
A	$C^I(A) \subseteq \Delta^I$	
$\{i\}$	$\{i^I\}$	
$\neg D$	$\Delta^I \setminus C^I(D)$	
$D_1 \sqcap D_2$	$C^I(D_1) \cap C^I(D_2)$	C^I and the interpretation of
$D_1 \sqcup D_2$	$C^I(D_1) \cup C^I(D_2)$	axioms are obtained from the
$\exists S.D$	$\{x \mid (x,y) \in R^I(S) \land y \in C^I(D)$	ones for π-semantics by apply-
$\forall S.D$	$\{x \mid (x,y) \in R^I(S) \to y \in C^I(D)$	ing the following changes:
$\leq n\,S.D$	$\{x \mid \sharp\{y \mid (x,y) \in R^I(S) \land y \in C^I(D)\} \leq n\}$	
$\geq n\,S.D$	$\{x \mid \sharp\{y \mid (x,y) \in R^I(S) \land y \in C^I(D)\} \geq n\}$	$C^I(A) \rightsquigarrow C^I(A^I)$
	Interpretation of axioms	
	$R^I(S) = R^I(\mathsf{Inv}(S))^-$	$R^I(S) \rightsquigarrow R^I(S^I)$
$S \sqsubseteq T$	$R^I(S) \subseteq R^I(T)$	$R^I(T) \rightsquigarrow R^I(T^I)$
$D_1 \sqsubseteq D_2$	$C^I(D_1) \subseteq C^I(D_2)$	
$\mathsf{Trans}(S)$	$R^I(S)^+ \subseteq R^I(S)$	$R^I(\mathsf{Inv}(S)) \rightsquigarrow R^I(\mathsf{Inv}(S)^I)$
$D(a)$	$a^I \in C^I(D)$	
$S(a,b)$	$(a^I, b^I) \in R^I(S)$	
$a \approx b$	$a^I = b^I$	
$a \not\approx b$	$a^I \neq b^I$	

Note: $\sharp S$ is the number of elements in S, S^+ is the transitive closure of S, and S^- is the inverse relation of S.

Neither semantics requires different names to be interpreted as different domain objects. If this is required, the *unique name assumption* should be axiomatized explicitly, by introducing an axiom $n_i \not\approx n_j$ for each $n_i, n_j \in N$, $n_i \neq n_j$.

Since the contextual semantics is essentially first-order, it can be decided using known algorithms, such as [8]. Therefore, we focus on deciding ν-satisfiability. In Subsection 3.2 we consider $\mathcal{ALCHOIQ}$ knowledge bases, in Subsection 3.3 we discuss the problems introduced by transitivity axioms, and in Subsection 3.4 we present a resolution-based practical decision procedure for the $\mathcal{ALCHIQ}$ fragment.

3.2 Deciding ν-Satisfiability of $\mathcal{ALCHOIQ}$

An equivalence relation $\mathcal{E}$ over a set of names N induces a set or equivalence classes, so for each equivalence class we may arbitrarily select one *representative name* from it. For a name n, let n/ε denote the representative name chosen for the equivalence class of n, and for α an $\mathcal{ALCHOIQ}$ concept (axiom), let α/ε denote the concept (axiom) obtained from α by replacing each name n with n/ε. Finally, let KB be an $\mathcal{ALCHOIQ}$ knowledge base and $\mathcal{E}$ an equivalence relation over N_{KB}; then KB/ε is the knowledge base obtained from KB by (i) replacing each axiom α with α/ε, and by (ii) appending an axiom $n_i/\varepsilon \not\approx n_j/\varepsilon$ for each pair of names $n_i, n_j \in N_{KB}$ such that $n_i/\varepsilon \neq n_j/\varepsilon$.

An algorithm for checking ν-satisfiability of KB can be easily obtained by non-deterministically guessing an equivalence relation $\mathcal{E}$ over N_{KB}, and then by checking π-satisfiability of KB/ε. The correctness of the algorithm is demonstrated by the following lemma:

Lemma 2. *An $\mathcal{ALCHOIQ}$ knowledge base KB is ν-satisfiable if and only if an equivalence relation $\mathcal{E}$ over N_{KB} exists, such that KB/ε is π-satisfiable.*

Proof. ($\Leftarrow$) Let $\mathcal{E}$ be an equivalence relation over N_{KB} and I^{π} a π-model of KB/ε. We construct a ν-interpretation I_{ν} by setting $\triangle^{I_{\nu}} = \triangle^{I_{\pi}}$, $n^{I_{\nu}} = (n/\varepsilon)^{I_{\pi}}$, $C^{I_{\nu}}(n^{I_{\nu}}) = C^{I_{\pi}}(n/\varepsilon)$, $R^{I_{\nu}}(n^{I_{\nu}}) = R^{I_{\pi}}(n/\varepsilon)$, for each $n \in N_{KB}$ and, finally, $C^{I_{\nu}}(x) = C^{I_{\pi}}(x)$ and $R^{I_{\nu}}(x) = R^{I_{\pi}}(x)$ for each $x \in \triangle^{I_{\nu}}$ such that there is no $n \in N_{KB}$ with $n^{I_{\nu}} = x$. Due to inequality axioms $n_i/\varepsilon \not\approx n_j/\varepsilon$, we have $I_{\pi}(n_i/\varepsilon) \neq I_{\pi}(n_j/\varepsilon)$, so the construction assigns a unique value to $C^{I_{\nu}}(x)$ and $R^{I_{\nu}}(x)$ for each $x \in \triangle^{I_{\nu}}$, and I_{ν} is correctly defined. Furthermore, for each concept X, $C^{I_{\nu}}(X) = C^{I_{\pi}}(X/\varepsilon)$, so I_{ν} is obviously a ν-model of KB.

($\Rightarrow$) Let I_{ν} be a ν-model of KB. We define $\mathcal{E} = \{(n_i, n_j) \mid n_i{}^{I_{\nu}} = n_j{}^{I_{\nu}}\}$ and construct a π-interpretation I_{π} by setting $\triangle^{I_{\pi}} = \triangle^{I_{\nu}}$, $(n/\varepsilon)^{I_{\pi}} = n^{I_{\nu}}$, $C^{I_{\pi}}(n/\varepsilon) = C^{I_{\nu}}(n^{I_{\nu}})$ and $R^{I_{\pi}}(n/\varepsilon) = R^{I_{\nu}}(n^{I_{\nu}})$, for each $n \in N_{KB}$. Again, for each concept X, $C^{I_{\pi}}(X/\varepsilon) = C^{I_{\nu}}(X)$, so I_{π} is a π-model of KB/ε. $\square$

Now Lemma 2 immediately implies the following result:

Theorem 2. *Checking ν-satisfiability of an $\mathcal{ALCHOIQ}$ knowledge base KB can be performed in non-deterministic exponential time, assuming numbers are coded in unary.*

Proof. Observe that $|N_{KB}|$ is linear in $|KB|$, and that each equivalence relation $\mathcal{E}$ is a subset of $N_{KB} \times N_{KB}$. Hence, the number of possible equivalence relations is exponential in $|KB|$. A decision procedure for checking ν-satisfiability of KB can systematically examine all equivalence relations $\mathcal{E}$ and for each one perform a π-satisfiability check of KB/ε. The last step can be performed in non-deterministic exponential time, since $\mathcal{ALCHOIQ}$ is a fragment of $\mathcal{C}^2$ — the two-variable first-order logic with counting, which is decidable in NExpTime assuming numbers are coded in unary [12]. Hence, the overall algorithm runs in non-deterministic exponential time as well. $\square$

We briefly compare the results of Theorems 1 and 2. The main feature of ν-semantics is the reification of concept and role names. However, it is more like π-semantics and less like OWL-Full semantics in the way it handles the modeling primitives. In particular, in ν- and π-semantics, these are expressed as formulae and are not accessible as individuals in the knowledge base. On the contrary, OWL-Full reifies the modeling primitives as well, and thus allows their semantics to be altered by the statements in the knowledge base.

3.3   HiLog Semantics and Transitivity

The differences between the algorithms for checking ν- and π-satisfiability are minor. Since the latter algorithm can easily handle transitive roles, one might expect the former one to be easily extended to handle transitivity as well. However, consider the following knowledge base KB:

$$\top \sqsubseteq \geq 3\, S \qquad (12)$$

$$S \approx T \qquad (13)$$

$$\mathsf{Trans}(T) \qquad (14)$$

Notice that KB is a $\mathcal{SHOIQ}$ knowledge base: the role S is simple, since it passes the syntactic criterion specified in Definition 2 (i.e., it is neither transitive nor it has transitive subroles). However, in any ν-interpretation I, (13) ensures that $S^I = T^I = \alpha$. Furthermore, due to (14), $R^I(\alpha)$ is transitive. Effectively, in (12) a transitive role is used in a number restriction, even though S is syntactically a simple role.

Since equality of role names might be non-trivially entailed by KB, identifying this requires theorem proving itself. This makes a check for simple roles under ν-semantics difficult, if not impossible. Because allowing transitive roles in number restrictions leads to undecidability [7], we get the following result:

Proposition 1. *Checking ν-satisfiability of a $\mathcal{SHOIQ}$ knowledge base KB is undecidable.*

Decidability can be regained by using *unique role assumption*, requiring symbols used as roles in KB to be interpreted as distinct domain individuals.

Definition 5 (Unique Role Assumption). *A $\mathcal{SHOIQ}$ knowledge base KB employs* unique role assumption *(URA) if it contains an axiom $S \not\approx T$ for each two distinct names S and T occurring as roles in KB.*

If KB employs URA or if it contains neither explicit equality statements nor number restrictions, role interpretations of different symbols can be assumed to be independent. Then, simple roles can be checked as usual, and transitivity axioms of KB can be eliminated by transforming KB into an equisatisfiable $\mathcal{ALCHOIQ}$ knowledge base $\Omega(KB)$, as done in [10]. Roughly speaking, a transitivity axiom $\mathsf{Trans}(S)$ is replaced with axioms of the form $\forall R.C \sqsubseteq \forall S.(\forall S.C)$, for each R with $S \sqsubseteq^* R$ and C a concept occurring in KB. This transformation is polynomial, so it does not increase the complexity of reasoning. Hence, ν-satisfiability of a $\mathcal{SHOIQ}$ knowledge base KB employing URA can be deiced by checking ν-satisfiability of the $\mathcal{ALCHOIQ}$ knowledge base $\Omega(KB)$.

3.4   A Practical Reasoning Procedure for $\mathcal{ALCHIQ}$

The reasoning procedure from Section 3.2 is worst-case optimal, but is unlikely to be effective in practice, since it systematically examines exponentially many equivalence relations. Therefore, we now present a practical, resolution-based algorithm for $\mathcal{ALCHIQ}$. It is an extension of our algorithm for deciding π-satisfiability from [10], and extending it to handle nomials is part of our ongoing work. Using the transformation of transitivity axioms from the previous subsection, this algorithm can also decide ν-satisfiability of $\mathcal{SHIQ}$ knowledge bases. Due to space constraints, we omit many technical details, which are given in [9]. We assume familiarity with first-order logic and resolution theorem proving.

Table 3. ν-semantics by Mapping into First-order Logic

Mapping Concepts to FOL

$$\nu_y(A, X) = \mathsf{isa}(A, X)$$
$$\nu_y(\neg D, X) = \neg\nu_y(D, X)$$
$$\nu_y(D_1 \sqcap D_2, X) = \nu_y(D_1, X) \wedge \nu_y(D_2, X)$$
$$\nu_y(D_1 \sqcup D_2, X) = \nu_y(D_1, X) \vee \nu_y(D_2, X)$$
$$\nu_y(\forall S.D, X) = \forall y : \mathsf{arole}(S, X, y) \rightarrow \nu_x(D, y)$$
$$\nu_y(\exists S.D, X) = \exists y : \mathsf{arole}(S, X, y) \wedge \nu_x(D, y)$$
$$\nu_y(\leq n\, S.D, X) = \forall y_1, \ldots, y_{n+1} : \bigwedge \mathsf{arole}(S, X, y_i) \wedge \bigwedge \nu_x(D, y_i) \rightarrow \bigvee y_i \approx y_j$$
$$\nu_y(\geq n\, S.D, X) = \exists y_1, \ldots, y_n : \bigwedge \mathsf{arole}(S, X, y_i) \wedge \bigwedge \nu_x(D, y_i) \wedge \bigwedge y_i \not\approx y_j$$

Mapping Axioms to FOL

$$\nu(D_1 \sqsubseteq D_2) = \forall x : \nu_y(D_1, x) \rightarrow \nu_y(D_2, x)$$
$$\nu(S \sqsubseteq T) = \forall x, y : \mathsf{arole}(S, x, y) \rightarrow \mathsf{arole}(T, x, y)$$
$$\nu(D(a)) = \nu_y(D, a)$$
$$\nu(S(a, b)) = \mathsf{arole}(S, a, b)$$
$$\nu(a \circ b) = a \circ b \text{ for } \circ \in \{\approx, \not\approx\}$$

Mapping KB to FOL

$$\nu(S) = \forall x, y : \mathsf{arole}(S, x, y) \leftrightarrow \mathsf{arole}(S^-, y, x)$$
$$\nu(KB) = \bigwedge_{\alpha \in KB_\mathcal{R} \cup KB_\mathcal{T} \cup KB_\mathcal{A}} \nu(\alpha) \wedge \bigwedge_{S \in N_{KB}} \nu(S)$$

Notes:

   (i): X is a meta variable and is substituted by the actual variable,

   (ii): ν_x is defined as ν_y by substituting x, x_i and ν_x for y, y_i and ν_y, respectively.

Translation into First-order Logic. Our algorithm is based on resolution, so in Table 3 we define an operator ν which translates KB into a formula $\nu(KB)$ of first-order logic with equality. As shown by the following lemma, $\nu(KB)$ is first-order satisfiable if and only if KB is ν-satisfiable. Intuitively, for a name n, $\mathsf{isa}(n, x)$ encodes the concept extension of n and $\mathsf{arole}(n, x, y)$ encodes the role extension of n. Therefore, a ν-interpretation I_ν of KB can be easily converted into a first-order interpretation I of $\nu(KB)$ and vice versa.

Lemma 3. *For an $\mathcal{ALCHIQ}$ knowledge base KB, KB is ν-satisfiable if and only if a first-order model of $\nu(KB)$ exists.*

Basic Superposition Calculus. We decide first-order satisfiability of $\nu(KB)$ by *basic superposition* [2] ($\mathcal{BS}$), a clausal calculus optimized for theorem proving with equality. The calculus is parameterized by a certain term ordering and a selection function. It consists of resolution and superposition rules, which are applied only to literals in clauses designated by the chosen parameters. A set of clauses N is *saturated* by $\mathcal{BS}$ if applying a rule of $\mathcal{BS}$ to premises from N produces an already derived clause. $\mathcal{BS}$ is sound and complete: a saturated set of clauses N is unsatisfiable if and only if it contains the empty clause.

Decision Procedure by $\mathcal{BS}$. In order to apply $\mathcal{BS}$, we transform $\nu(KB)$ into the set of clauses $\Xi_\nu(KB)$ using the so-called *structural transformation* [11], which ensures that this step is polynomial.

We now saturate $\Xi_\nu(KB)$ by $\mathcal{BS}_{DL}$, where $\mathcal{BS}_{DL}$ denotes the $\mathcal{BS}$ calculus parameterized as discussed in [9]. It is possible to show that during such a saturation, only clauses of a certain syntactic form are derivable, and that the number of possible derived clauses is exponential in $|KB|$. Therefore, saturation by $\mathcal{BS}_{DL}$ will terminate after an exponential number of steps. Since $\mathcal{BS}_{DL}$ is sound and complete, it decides satisfiability of $\Xi_\nu(KB)$ and, by Lemma 3, ν-satisfiability of KB. The actual algorithm has to deal with several techical issues, for which we direct the reader to [9]. Hece we just state our main result:

Theorem 3. *For an $\mathcal{ALCHIQ}$ knowledge base KB, saturation of $\Xi_\nu(KB)$ by $\mathcal{BS}_{DL}$ decides ν-satisfiability of KB and runs in time exponential in $|KB|$, assuming numbers are coded in unary.*

4 Expressivity of Metamodeling

We now discuss the benefits of metamodeling in terms of additional consequences that can be drawn. These results are similar to the ones for HiLog from [4].

It is easy to see that ν-satisfiability is a strictly stronger notion than π-satisfiability. Consider the following knowledge base[2] KB:

$$Eagle(Harry) \tag{15}$$

$$\neg Aquila(Harry) \tag{16}$$

$$Eagle \approx Aquila \tag{17}$$

Under the contextual semantics, the interpretations of the symbols *Eagle* and *Aquila* as concepts and as individuals are independent, so KB is π-satisfiable. However, KB is ν-unsatisfiable: in each ν-interpretation $Eagle^I = Aquila^I = \alpha$, so it cannot be that $Harry^I \in C^I(Eagle^I)$ and $Harry^I \notin C^I(Aquila^I)$. For the other direction, we have the following lemma:

Lemma 4. *A ν-satisfiable $\mathcal{SHOIQ}$ knowledge base KB is also π-satisfiable.*

Proof. Let I_ν be a ν-model of an $\mathcal{SHOIQ}$ knowledge base KB. We construct a π-interpretation I_π as follows: $\triangle^{I_\pi} = \triangle^{I_\nu}$, $n^{I_\pi} = n^{I_\nu}$, $C^{I_\pi}(n) = C^{I_\nu}(n^{I_\nu})$ and $R^{I_\pi}(n) = R^{I_\nu}(n^{I_\nu})$, for each $n \in N_{KB}$. By a straightforward induction on the concept structure it can be shown that, for each concept X, $C^{I_\pi}(X) = C^{I_\nu}(X)$, so I_π is a π-model of KB.   □

Furthermore, for a knowledge base with unique name assumption or without equality (either explicit or implicit, introduced through number restrictions), π-satisfiability and ν-satisfiability coincide:

Lemma 5. *Let KB be an $\mathcal{SHOIQ}$ knowledge base such that it employs unique name assumption, or it contains neither explicit equality statements nor number restrictions. Then KB is π-satisfiable if and only if it is ν-satisfiable.*

---

[2] "Aquila" is the Latin name for "eagle."

Proof. The ($\Leftarrow$) direction follows from Lemma 4. For the ($\Rightarrow$) direction, let KB be π-satisfiable in some model I_π. Since KB either employs unique name assumption or it does not employ equality, without loss of generality, we may assume that for each $n_i, n_j \in N$, $n_i \neq n_j$ implies $n_i^{I_\pi} \neq n_j^{I_\pi}$.

We now construct a ν-interpretation I_ν as follows: $\triangle^{I_\nu} = \triangle^{I_\pi}$, $n^{I_\nu} = n^{I_\pi}$, $C^{I_\nu}(n^{I_\nu}) = C^{I_\pi}(n)$ and $R^{I_\nu}(n^{I_\nu}) = R^{I_\pi}(n)$, for $n \in N_{KB}$. Furthermore, for all $x \in \triangle^{I_\nu}$ such that there is no $n \in N_{KB}$ with $x = n^{I_\nu}$, let $C^{I_\nu}(x) = R^{I_\nu}(x) = \emptyset$. Since we can assume that different names of N_{KB} are interpreted as different elements of $\triangle^{I_\nu}$, the construction assigns a unique value to $C^{I_\nu}(x)$ and $R^{I_\nu}(x)$ for each $x \in \triangle^{I_\nu}$, so I_ν is correctly defined. By a straightforward induction on the concept structure it can be shown that, for each concept X, $C^{I_\nu}(X) = C^{I_\pi}(X)$. Therefore, I_ν is a ν-model of KB.   □

To summarize, ν-semantics allows deriving new consequences only if it is possible to derive that two symbols are equal; for example, from (15) and (17) it is possible to derive $Aquila(Harry)$. Furthermore, if the unique name assumption is employed, as it is often the case in practice, ν-semantics does not yield any additional consequences. This seems to suggest that the benefits of ν-semantics do not outweigh its drawbacks, namely, the fact that it is non-standard and that it introduces problems for transitive roles. Moreover, π-semantics might be sufficient for many practical applications.

However, ν-semantics unlocks its full potential when combined with a language more expressive than OWL. For example, by combining ν-semantics with the Semantic Web Rule Language (SWRL) [6], one can explicitly axiomatize the semantics of metaconcepts. Consider the example from Section 1. By (18) we state that *Eagle* is an *RedListSpecies*, and by a SWRL rule (19) we state that instances of species listed in the Red List are not allowed to be hunted. Notice that in atom $S(I)$ we use the variable S at the position of a predicate. Under ν-semantics this is equivalent to $isa(S, I)$, but under π-semantics this would not be possible without leaving the confines of first-order logic. Now from (15), (18) and (19), we may infer $CannotHunt(Harry)$, so *RedListSpecies* semantically acts as a metaconcept of the *Eagle* concept.

$$RedListSpecies(Eagle) \tag{18}$$

$$RedListSpecies(S) \wedge S(I) \rightarrow CannotHunt(I) \tag{19}$$

To summarize, from the logical perspective, ν-semantics alone does not bring much, and π-semantics may be sufficient for numerous applications. However, ν-semantics provides a sound foundation for metamodeling, which, when combined with expressive logical formalisms such as SWRL, allows precisely axiomatizing the interaction between concepts and metaconcepts. Thus, we believe ν-semantics to be very relevant for the future extensions of OWL.

5   Related Work

The definition of ν-satisfiability given in Section 3 is inspired by HiLog [4], a logic in which general terms are allowed to occur in place of function and predicate symbols in formulae. The semantics is defined by interpreting each individual as a member of the interpretation domain, and by assigning a functional and a relational interpretation to domain objects. The authors show that HiLog can be considered "syntactic sugar", since each HiLog formula can be encoded into an equisatisfiable first-order formula. The definition of the ν operator in Table 2 closely resembles this encoding. Finally, the authors show that a satisfiable first-order formula without equality is also satisfiable under HiLog semantics.

In [13], the RDFS Model Theory was criticized for allowing infinite number of meta-layers. The authors argue that such semantics is inadequate for the Semantic Web because (i) it does not provide adequate support for inferencing, (ii) it allows defining classes containing themselves, which may lead to paradoxes, and (iii) by adding classes, one necessarily introduces objects in the interpretation universe. The authors propose RDFS-FA, a stratified four-level approach, consisting of the meta-language layer, the language layer, the ontology layer and the instance layer. In [5] similar arguments were used to criticize the semantics of OWL-Full. We follow the principles of RDFS-FA by strictly separating the modeling primitives from the ontology and the instance layers. However, to allow metamodeling, our definition of ν-semantics merges the ontology and the instance layers into one. Furthermore, we show that (iii) affects the logical consequences only if equality reasoning is required, which matches well with the intuition behind metamodeling.

In [16] the authors point out the usefulness of metamodeling in many application domains. They propose separation of modeling layers, which are connected using so-called *spanning instances*. However, the authors do not consider the logical consequences of their approach.

6   Conclusion

In this paper we have analyzed the metamodeling features of OWL-Full, the most expressive of the Semantic Web ontology languages. We have shown that the style of metamodeling adopted in OWL-Full leads to undecidability of basic reasoning problems, due to mixing logical and metalogical primitives. In order to obtain a decidable and expressive language supporting metamodeling, we have proposed two alternative semantics: the contextual one, which is essentially first-order, and the HiLog one, which is more in the spirit of OWL-Full. Under certain technical assumptions, both semantics are decidable when combined with the description logic $\mathcal{SHOIQ}$. Furthermore, we have presented a practical resolution-based decision procedure for reasoning with $\mathcal{SHIQ}$ knowledge bases under HiLog semantics, thus obtaining practical support for a logic with metamodeling whose expressivity is between OWL-Lite and OWL-DL.

We have analyzed the added expressivity of metamodeling and have shown that the HiLog semantics allows deriving new conclusions only by equality reasoning. However, this approach unlocks its full potential if combined with expressive extensions, such as SWRL, since it allows axiomatizing the logical interaction between concepts and their metaconcepts.

In future, we shall attempt to extending the practical decision procedure from Subsection 3.4 to handle nominals as well, and thus to cover all of OWL-DL.

Acknowledgements

This work was partially funded by the EU IST project DIP 507483. We thank the anonymous reviewer for valuable comments regarding Subsection 3.2.

References

1. F. Baader, D. Calvanese, D. McGuinness, D. Nardi, and P. Patel-Schneider, editors. *The Description Logic Handbook*. Cambridge University Press, January 2003.
2. L. Bachmair, H. Ganzinger, C. Lynch, and W. Snyder. Basic Paramodulation. *Information and Computation*, 121(2):172–192, 1995.
3. R. Berger. The undecidability of the dominoe problem. *Memoirs of the American Mathematical Society*, 66, 1966.
4. W. Chen, M. Kifer, and D. S. Warren. HILOG: a foundation for higher-order logic programming. *Journal of Logic Programming*, 15(3):187–230, 1993.
5. I. Horrocks and P. F. Patel-Schneider. Three Theses of Representation in the Semantic Web. In *Proc. WWW 2003*, pages 39–47. ACM, 2003.
6. I. Horrocks and P. F. Patel-Schneider. A Proposal for an OWL Rules Language. In *Proc. WWW 2004*. ACM, 2004.
7. I. Horrocks, U. Sattler, and S. Tobies. Practical Reasoning for Very Expressive Description Logics. *Logic Journal of the IGPL*, 8(3):239–263, 2000.
8. I. Horrocks, U. Sattler, and S. Tobies. Reasoning with Individuals for the Description Logic $\mathcal{SHIQ}$. In *Proc. CADE 2000*, number 1831 in LNAI, pages 482–496. Springer, 2000.
9. U. Hustadt, B. Motik, and U. Sattler. Reasoning for Description Logics around $\mathcal{SHIQ}$ in a Resolution Framework. Technical Report 3-8-04/04, FZI, Karlsruhe, Germany, April 2004. http://www.fzi.de/ipe/publikationen.php?id=1172.
10. U. Hustadt, B. Motik, and U. Sattler. Reducing $\mathcal{SHIQ}^-$ Description Logic to Disjunctive Datalog Programs. In *Proc. KR 2004*, pages 152–162, Menlo Park, California, USA, June 2004. AAAI Press.
11. A. Nonnengart and C. Weidenbach. Computing Small Clause Normal Forms. In A. Robinson and A. Voronkov, editors, *Handbook of Automated Reasoning*, volume I, chapter 6, pages 335–367. Elsevier Science, 2001.
12. L. Pacholski, W. Szwast, and L. Tendera. Complexity Results for First-Order Two-Variable Logic with Counting. *SIAM Journal on Computing*, 29(4):1083–1117, 2000.
13. J. Pan and I. Horrocks. RDFS(FA) and RDF MT: Two Semantics for RDFS. In *Proc. ISWC 2003*, number 2870 in LNCS, pages 30–46. Springer, 2003.
14. P. F. Patel-Schneider, P. Hayes, and I. Horrocks. OWL Web Ontology Language; Semantics and Abstract Syntax. http://www.w3.org/TR/owl-semantics/, 2002.
15. G. Schreiber. The Web is not well-formed. *IEEE Intelligent Systems*, 17(2):79–80, March/April 2002. Contribution to the section "Trends & Controversies: Ontologies KISSES in Standardization", edited by S. Staab.
16. C. Welty and D. Ferrucci. What's in an instance? Technical Report 94-18, Max-Planck-Institut, 1994. RPI Computer Science.

A Bayesian Network Approach to Ontology Mapping

Rong Pan, Zhongli Ding, Yang Yu, and Yun Peng

Department of Computer Science and Electrical Engineering,
University of Maryland, Baltimore County,
Baltimore, Maryland, USA
{pan.rong, zding1, yangyu1, ypeng}@umbc.edu

Abstract. This paper presents our ongoing effort on developing a principled methodology for automatic ontology mapping based on *BayesOWL*, a probabilistic framework we developed for modeling uncertainty in semantic web. In this approach, the source and target ontologies are first translated into Bayesian networks (BN); the concept mapping between the two ontologies are treated as evidential reasoning between the two translated BNs. Probabilities needed for constructing conditional probability tables (CPT) during translation and for measuring semantic similarity during mapping are learned using text classification techniques where each concept in an ontology is associated with a set of semantically relevant text documents, which are obtained by ontology guided web mining. The basic ideas of this approach are validated by positive results from computer experiments on two small real-world ontologies.

1 Introduction

Uncertainty concerns every aspect of semantic web ontologies. In many applications, overlapping between concepts/classes cannot be represented logically by OWL constructs. Even if they can, the degree of overlapping is not represented (e.g., how close a class A is to its super class B?). A description about an unknown concept or object input to an OWL reasoner may be uncertain (e.g., x is an instance of class A and is moderately likely to have property p related with class B). In a previous work, we have developed a Bayesian network based framework *BayesOWL*, to address representation and reasoning with uncertainty within a single ontology ([5], [6]).

Uncertainty becomes more prevalent in concept mapping between two ontologies where it is often the case that a concept defined in one ontology can only find partial matches to one or more concepts in another ontology. Semantic similarities between concepts are difficult, if not impossible to be represented logically, but can easily be represented probabilistically. This has motivated recent development of ontology mapping taking probabilistic approaches (GLUE [7], CAIMAN [11], OntoMapper [19], and OMEN [13]) (See [14] for a survey of existing approaches to ontology mapping, including those based on logical translation, syntactical and linguistic analysis). However, these existing approaches fail to completely address uncertainty in mapping. For example, GLUE captures similarity between two concepts onto1:A and onto2:B by joint probability distribution $P(A, B)$ obtained by text classification of exemplars (semantically relevant text documents) to each concept. Then onto1:A is mapped to onto2:C whose similarity to onto1:A, measured by, say their Jaccard coef-

Y. Gil et al. (Eds.): ISWC 2005, LNCS 3729, pp. 563–577, 2005.
© Springer-Verlag Berlin Heidelberg 2005

ficients [21] (computed from the joint distribution), passes a threshold and is highest among all concepts in onto2. Here, onto1:A is taken as (semantically) equivalent to onto2:C, the degree of similarity between them will not be considered in future reasoning (e.g., subsumption within onto2). Also ignored are the other concepts that are also similar to onto1:A (albeit at smaller degree).

The work reported in this paper extends *BayesOWL* in a number of significant ways so that uncertainty in ontology mapping can be dealt with properly. As depicted in Figure 1 below, this new framework consists of three components: 1) a text classification based *learner* to learn from web data the probabilistic ontological information within individual ontologies and between concepts in two different ontologies; 2) a *BayesOWL* module to translate given ontologies (together with the learned uncertain information) into BNs; and 3) a concept *mapping module* which takes a set of learned raw similarities as input and finds mappings between concepts from two different ontologies based on evidential reasoning across two BNs.

Before describing the BN Mapping module and the learner in detail (Sections 3 and 4), we first provide some background information in Section 2. This includes a brief summary of *BayesOWL*, and introductions to Jeffrey's rule and iterative proportional fitting procedure (IPFP), two techniques used in this work. Methods and results of computer experiments with two small ontologies are given in Section 5. The paper concludes with discussions and directions of future research in Section 6.

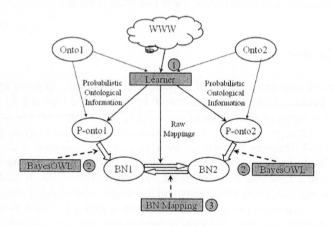

Fig. 1. The framework

2   Background

As background, we briefly introduce Jeffrey's rule, IPFP, and *BayesOWL* here.

2.1   Techniques for Updating Probability Distributions

Two techniques for updating a probability distribution by another distribution used in this work are briefly described below.

Jeffrey's rule, also known as rule of *probability kinematics* or *J-conditioning*, was proposed by Richard Jeffrey [9] to revise a probability measure (e.g., a joint distribution $P(x)$) by another probability function (e.g., a prior $Q(x_i)$ in another distribution). The rule can be written as follows in this context: if $P(x_i)$, our belief on $X_i \in X$, is changed to $Q(x_i)$, then the beliefs of other variables $X_{j \neq i} \in X$ shall be changed to

$$Q(x_j) = \sum_{x_i} P(x_j \mid X_i = x_i) Q(X_i = x_i) \tag{2.1}$$

if $P(x_j \mid x_i)$ is invariant with respect to $Q(x_i)$.

Jeffrey's rule can be used as a mechanism to update a distribution by soft evidence, represented as a distribution such as $Q(x_i)$. The rule then can be written as

$$P(x_i \mid se) = Q(x_i), \text{ and} \tag{2.2}$$

$$
\begin{aligned}
Q(x_{j \neq i}) &= P(x_j \mid se) \\
&= \sum_{x_i} P(x_j \mid X_i = x_i) P(X_i = x_i \mid se) \\
&= \sum_{x_i} P(x_j \mid X_i = x_i) Q(X_i = x_i)
\end{aligned} \tag{2.3}
$$

Pearl ([16], [17]) has shown that the virtual evidence, a method widely adopted in Bayesian network (BN) inference, can be viewed as formally equivalent to the likelihood ratio version of Jeffrey's rule. This is done by adding a virtual node ve_i which has X_i as its only parent in the BN, related by likelihood ratio:

$$L(X_i) = \frac{P(ve_i \mid X_i)}{P(ve_i \mid \overline{X_i})} = \frac{P(X_i)Q(\overline{X_i})}{Q(X_i)P(\overline{X_i})} \tag{2.4}$$

when X_i is binary. Soft evidence update (eqs. 2.2 and 2.3) can be realized by BN belief update with ve_i instantiated to true. It can be shown that $L(X_i)$ for multivalued variables can also be calculated from $P(x_i)$ and $Q(x_i)$ [17].

As will be seen shortly, we use Jeffrey's rule to propagate probabilistically beliefs on variables between two BNs that are translated from two ontologies during mapping.

IPFP. (Iterative Proportional Fitting Procedure) is a computational procedure that updates a given distribution $Q_0(x)$ to satisfy a set of probability constraints $R = \{R_i(y^i)\}$ where each $R_i(y^i)$ is a distribution over $Y^i \subseteq X$ [10]. Roughly speaking, IPFP iterates over constraints in $\{R_i(y^i)\}$ in cycle, at each iteration, the current distribution is updated by one constraint according to

$$Q_k(x) = Q_{k-1}(x) \cdot \frac{R_i(y^i)}{Q_{k-1}(y^i)} \tag{2.5}$$

It has been proved based on *I-divergence* geometry ([4], [22]) that IPFP converges to an unique distribution $Q^*(x)$, which 1) satisfies all $R_i(y^i)$ in R, i.e., $Q^*(y^i) = R_i(y^i)$ for $R_i \in R$, and 2) has the smallest Kullback-Leibler distance (or I-divergence) to $Q_0(x)$ among all distributions $Q(x)$ that satisfy all constraints in R, i.e.,

$$I(Q^* \parallel Q_{(0)}) = \sum_x Q^*(x) \log \frac{Q^*(x)}{Q_{(0)}(x)} \tag{2.6}$$

is minimized. $Q^*(x)$ is called I_1-projection of $Q_0(x)$ on R. Bock [1] and Cramer [2] extended IPFP to conditional IPFP (CIPFP) to allow constraints with the form of conditional probability distributions and proved its convergence.

If we consider $Q(y^i)$ as soft evidence on a collection of variables Y^i, then IPFP can be considered as another mechanism of processing soft evidence [20]. The difference between Jeffrey's rule and IPFP in this regard is that the former requires the invariance of domain knowledge (i.e., $P(x_j | x_i)$ remains unchanged in $Q(x)$) while the latter requires minimizing I-divergence which in general destroys the invariance in the updated $Q^*(x)$. How to combine these two techniques together when used in ontology to BN translation and in concept mapping will be given in Subsection 2.2 and Section 3.

2.2 BayesOWL

BayesOWL ([5], [6]) is a framework which augments and supplements OWL for representing and reasoning with uncertainty based on Bayesian networks. This framework provides a set of rules and procedures for direct translation of an OWL ontology into a BN structure (a directed acyclic graph or DAG) and a method based on IPFP that utilizes available probability constraints about classes and interclass relations in constructing the conditional probability tables (CPTs) of the BN. The translated BN, which preserves the semantics of the original ontology and is consistent with the probabilistic constraints, can support ontology reasoning, both within and across ontologies, as Bayesian inferences.

Structural translation. The general principle underlying the structural translation rules is that all classes (specified as "subjects" and "objects" in RDF triples of the OWL file) are translated into nodes in BN, and an arc is drawn between two nodes in BN if the corresponding two classes are related by a "predicate" in the OWL file, with the direction from the superclass to the subclass.

The model-theoretic semantics of OWL treats the domain as a non-empty collection of individuals. If class A represents a concept, the node it is translated to is treated as a binary random variable of two states a and $\bar{a}$, and we interpret $P(A = a)$ as the prior probability or one's belief that an arbitrary individual belongs to class A, and $P(a | b)$ as the conditional probability that an individual of class B also belongs to class A. Similarly, for $P(\bar{a})$, $P(\bar{a} | b)$, $P(a | \bar{b})$, and $P(\bar{a} | \bar{b})$, we interpret the negation as "not belonging to".

Control nodes are created during the translation to facilitate modeling relations among class nodes that are specified by OWL *logical* operators, and there is a converging connection from each of the concept nodes involved in this logical relation to its specific control node. There are five types of control nodes in total corresponding to the five types of logical relations: "and" (owl:intersectionOf), "or" (owl:unionOf), "not" (owl:complementOf), "disjoint" (owl:disjointWith), and "same as" (owl:equivalentClass).

Constructing CPTs. The nodes in the DAG obtained from the structural translation step can be divided into two disjoint groups: X_R, regular nodes representing concepts in ontology, and X_C, control nodes for bridging logical relations. The CPT for a control node in X_C can be determined by the logical relation it represents so that when its state is "True", the corresponding logical relation holds among its parent nodes. When all the control nodes' states are set to "True" (denote this situation as CT), all the logical relations defined in the original ontology are held in the translated BN. The remaining issue is then to construct the CPTs for node in X_R so that $P(X_R|CT)$, the joint distribution of all regular nodes in the subspace of CT, is consistent with all the given probabilistic constraints about classes and relations between classes. These constraints include, most likely, priors for classes $P(C)$, conditionals $P(C|D)$ for relations between classes C and D. Several suggestions have been made to encode probability constraints in semantic web languages (e.g., [6] with OWL, and [8] with RDF). These constraints can be obtained from the ontology designers or learned from data (an approach that learns these constraints from web is described in Section 4).

In principle, IPFP can be applied to construct CPTs to satisfy all the given probabilistic constraints. Two difficulties exist. First, as we mentioned earlier, direct application of IPFP may destroy the existing interdependencies between variables (i.e., the given DAG becomes invalid). Secondly, IPFP is computationally very expensive since every entry in the joint distribution of the BN must be updated at each iteration. To overcome these difficulties, we developed an algorithm named D-IPFP that decomposes IPFP so that each iteration only updates a small portion of the BN that are directly involved with the chosen constraint, and the update is done only to CPTs while keeping the DAG of the network intact [18]. In particular, when each of the given constraints involves only one variable C_i and a set of zero or more of its parents L_i, (2.5) of IPFP becomes [5]

$$\begin{cases} Q_k(c_i \mid \pi_i) = Q_{k-1}(c_i \mid \pi_i) \cdot \dfrac{Q(c_i \mid L_i)}{Q_{k-1}(c_i \mid L_i)} \\ Q_k(c_j \mid \pi_j) = Q_{k-1}(c_j \mid \pi_j) \qquad \forall j \neq i \end{cases} \tag{2.7}$$

The *BayesOWL* framework can support common ontology reasoning tasks as probabilistic inferences in the translated BN. For example, given a concept description e, it can answer queries about concept satisfiability (whether $P(e|CT) = 0$), about concept overlapping (how close e is to a concept C as $P(e|C,CT)$), and about concept subsumption (find the concept which is most similar to e) by defining some similarity measures such as Jaccard coefficient [21].

3 Concept Mapping Between Ontologies Using BN Mapping

It is often the case when attempting to map concept A defined in Ontology 1 to Ontology 2, there is no concept in Ontology 2 that is semantically identical to A. Instead, A is similar to several concepts in Ontology 2 with different degree of similarity. A solution to this so-called one-to-many problem, as suggested by [19] and [7], is to map A to the target concept B which is most similar to A by some measure. This simple approach would not work well because 1) the degree of similarity between A and B is not reflected in B and thus will not be considered in reasoning after the mapping;

2) potential information loss because other similar concepts are ignored in the mapping; 3) it cannot handle the situation where A itself is uncertain; and 4) it does not work well when more than one concepts need to be mapped. To see the last point, consider a situation where concept x defined as intersection of A and B in onto1 is to be mapped to onto2. Suppose the most similar concepts to A in onto2 are C and D, and those to are B are E and D, it would be difficult to determine which of the three $(C, D, \text{and } E)$ x should be mapped to.

These difficulties in ontology mapping can be dealt with properly in our framework. We assume that pair-wise similarity measures are available between any concepts in two ontologies onto1 and onto2 (or between variables in BN1 and BN2, respectively). We take mapping as update on probability distribution of variables in BN2 by distributions of variables in BN1 in accordance to the similarity measures between these variables. Further inferences (e.g., finding the most probable subsumer in onto2 for a concept defined in onto1) can be drawn by Bayesian inference with the updated distribution of BN2. We present our approach starting with the basis: 1) a notion of *probabilistic semantic linkage* between a pair of concepts/variables; 2) the "1 to n" mapping (one variable in BN1 mapped to multiple similar ones in BN2); and 3) the "m to n" mappings where multiple variables in BN1 need to be mapped.

3.1 Pair-Wise Probabilistic Semantic Linkage

We assume the similarity information between variable A in BN1 and B in BN2 is captured by the joint distribution $P(A, B)$. This distribution is in a probability space, denoted as $PS^{1,2}$, which is related but different from the spaces for A and B, denoted as PS^1 and PS^2, respectively. Moreover, since this measure is based on the semantic similarity intrinsic to the meanings of these two variables, $P(A, B)$ is assumed invariant with respect to changes in PS^1 and PS^2. That is, beliefs on variables in A and B may change when evidence is presented but not that of $P(A, B)$ in $PS^{1,2}$.

Probabilistic semantic linkage between A and B, which serves as a basis mapping mechanism between similar variables, is defined as

$$SL_{A,B}^{1,2} = <PS^1, PS^2, A, B, P(A, B)>,$$

where $A \in PS^1$, and $B \in PS^2$, and $P(A, B)$ measures the semantic similarity between A and B. Then the influence to B by A via the single linkage $SL_{A,B}^{1,2}$ changes $P(B)$ to $Q(B)$ by $P(A)$. This update can be viewed as twice applications of Jeffrey's rule across these three spaces, first from PS^1 to $PS^{1,2}$, then $PS^{1,2}$ to PS^2, as depicted in Figure 2 below. Since A in PS^1 is identical to A in $PS^{1,2}$, $P(A)$ in PS^1 becomes soft evidence $Q(A)$ to $PS^{1,2}$ by (2.2), the distribution of B in $PS^{1,2}$ is updated by (2.3) to

$$Q(B) = \sum_A P(B \mid A)Q(A), \tag{3.1}$$

$Q(B)$ is then applied as soft evidence from $PS^{1,2}$ to node B in PS^2, updating distribution of other variables C in PS^2 by (2.3) as

$$Q(C) = \sum_B P(C \mid B)Q(B) = \sum_B P(C \mid B)\sum_A P(B \mid A)P(A). \tag{3.2}$$

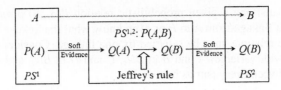

Fig. 2. Mapping concept A to B via semantic linkage $SL_{A,B}^{1,2}$

3.2 Multiple Semantic Linkages

Usually, A in onto1 may be semantically similar to more than one concept in onto2. For, example, if A is fairly similar to B in onto2, it would also be similar to all super concepts and also some sub-concepts of B, possibly with different similarity measures. In other words, mapping A to BN2 amounts mapping it through all semantic linkages that initiate from A and end at each similar concept B^J in BN2. Probabilistically, BN2 can be seen as receiving n soft evidences, one for a linkage from A to B^J for each concept B^J in BN2. This requires 1) all similarity measures $P(A, B^J)$ remain invariant, and 2) conditional dependencies among variables in BN2 also remain invariant. This "1 to n" mapping can be carried out by a process that combines both Jeffrey's rule and IPFP. Like IPFP, this process is iterative over these linkages in a cycle until convergence.

This process can be realized by generalizing Pearl's virtual evidence approach for soft evidence update [15]. In this method of ours, each node B^J is attached a virtual evidence node. At iteration step k, if linkage from A to B^J is chosen, then we first calculate likelihood $L_K(B^J)$ for virtual evidence node ve^J that will be used to simulate soft evidence $Q(B^J)$ by

$$L_K(B^J) = \frac{Q_{K-1}(B^J)Q(\overline{B^J})}{Q(B^J)Q_{K-1}(\overline{B^J})}, \qquad (3.3)$$

and then apply Jeffrey's rule of (3.1) and (3.2) with the modified likelihood to update variable beliefs in BN2. Note that (3.3) is the same as (2.4) except for $Q_{k-1}(B^J)$, the new distribution obtained at step k-1 is used rather than the initial $P(B^J)$. Also note that this process does not explicitly modify the joint distribution of BN2 as the standard IPFP would do, instead, it modifies the likelihood associated with each virtual evidence node ve^J while keep the joint distributions $P(A, B^J)$ and CPT's in BN2 unchanged. It can be shown that when the process converges, beliefs on variables in BN2 are consistent with all similarity measures $P(A, B^J)$ and $P(A)$, the belief of A in BN1.

Mapping Reduction. Using all n linkages in "1 to n" type of mapping, as described above, is computationally very expensive because the IPFP process takes a number of iterations to converge, and each iteration involves belief update of BN2, which itself is exponential to the size of BN2. The problem gets worse for "m to n" type of mapping where what needs to be mapped is a composite concept that is defined as a conjunction (intersection) of several variables or their negations in BN1.

Fortunately, satisfying a given probabilistic relation $P(A, B)$ does not always require the use of a linkage from A to B or even know what the linkage looks like. Several probabilistic relations may be satisfied by one linkage. Consider a simple example in Figure 3 with variables A and B in BN_1, C and D in BN_2, and similarity (joint probabilities) between every pair as below:

$$P(C, A) = \begin{pmatrix} 0.3 & 0 \\ 0.1 & 0.6 \end{pmatrix}, \quad P(D, A) = \begin{pmatrix} 0.33 & 0.18 \\ 0.07 & 0.42 \end{pmatrix},$$

$$P(C, B) = \begin{pmatrix} 0.3 & 0 \\ 0.16 & 0.54 \end{pmatrix}, \quad P(D, B) = \begin{pmatrix} 0.348 & 0.162 \\ 0.112 & 0.378 \end{pmatrix}$$

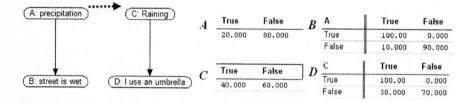

Fig. 3. Mapping Reduction Example

However, we do not need to set up linkages for all these relations. As Figure 3 depicts, when we have a linkage from A to C, all these relations are satisfied (the other three linkages are thus redundant). This is because not only beliefs on C, but also beliefs on D are properly updated by the mapping A to C.

Several experiments with large BNs have shown that only a very small portion of all $n_1 \cdot n_2$ linkages are needed in satisfying all probability constraints. This, we suspect, is due to the fact that some of these constraints can be derived from others based on the probabilistic interdependencies among variables in the two BNs. We are currently actively working on developing a set of rules that examine the BN structures and CPTs so that redundant linkages can be identified and removed.

4   Learning Probabilities from Web Data

In this work, we use prior probability distributions $P(C)$ to capture the uncertainty about concepts (i.e., how likely an arbitrary individual belongs to class C), conditional distributions $P(C|D)$ for relations between C and D in the same ontology (e.g., how likely an arbitrary individual in class D is also in D's subclass C), and joint probability distributions $P(A,B)$ for semantic similarity between concepts C and D from different ontologies. Often these kinds of probabilistic information are not available and are difficult to obtain from domain experts. Our solution is to learn these probabilities using text classification technique ([3], [12]) by associating a concept with a group of sample text documents called *exemplars*. The idea is inspired by those machine learning based semantic integration approaches such as [7], [11], and [19], where the meaning of a concept is implicitly represented by a set of exemplars that are relevant to it.

Learning the probabilities for semantic similarity between concepts in two ontologies is straightforward, assuming we have sufficient exemplars of good quality associated with each concept. First, we can build a model (classifier) for each concept in Ontology 1 according to the statistical information in that concept's exemplars using a text classifier such as Rainbow[1] or Bayesian text classifier dbacl[2]. Then concepts in Ontology 2 are classified into classes of Ontology 1 by feeding their respective exemplars into the models of Ontology 1 to obtain a set of probabilistic scores. These scores showing the inter-concept similarity in a probability form. Concepts in Ontology 1 can be classified in the same way into classes of Ontology 2. This cross-classification process (Figure 4) helps find a set of raw mappings between Ontology 1 and Ontology 2. Similarly, we can obtain prior or conditional probabilities related to concepts in a single ontology through self-classification with the models learned for that ontology.

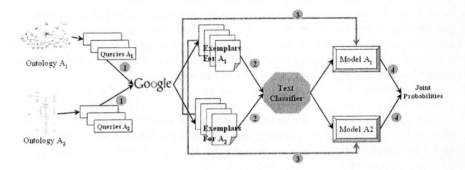

Fig. 4. Cross-classification using Text Classifiers on Web Data

The quality of these text classification based methods is highly dependent on the quality of text exemplars to each concept, which together should well capture the meaning of the concept. Two criteria are seen to be crucial in assessing the quality of exemplars: each exemplar (at least most of them) should be *relevant* to the meaning of the concept, and that these exemplars together should well *cover* all aspects of that concept. For example, articles on computer games are very relevant to the concept of "computer applications", but they alone hardly cover all computer applications.

The need to find sufficiently many relevant exemplars for a large number of concepts greatly reduces the attractiveness and applicability of these machine learning based approaches. It would be a very time-consuming task for knowledge workers to find high quality text exemplars manually, as apparently the case for GLUE [7]. Our approach is to use search engines such as Google[3] to retrieve text exemplars for each concept node automatically from WWW, the richest information resource available nowadays. The goal is to search for documents in which the concept is used in its

---

[1] http://www-2.cs.cmu.edu/~mccallum/bow/rainbow
[2] http://www.lbreyer.com/
[3] http://www.google.com

intended semantics. The rationale is that the meaning of a concept can be described or understood by the way it is used.

To find out what documents are relevant to a term, one cannot simply use the words in the name of the term as keywords to query the search engine. This because a word may have multiple meanings (word senses) and a query using only the name of the term in attention may return documents related to a meaning different from the intended semantics of the term. For example, in an ontology for "food", a concept named "apple" is a subconcept of "fruit". If one only uses "apple" as the keyword for query, documents showing how to make an apple pie and how to use an iPod may both be returned. Clearly, the documents using "apple" for its meaning in computer field is irrelevant to "apple" as a fruit. Fortunately, since we are dealing with concepts in well defined ontologies, the semantics of a term is to a great extent specified by the other terms used in defining this concept in the ontology, including names of its super and subconcept classes and the properties of this concept and its super classes. This semantic information can thus be used to guide the web search with increased relevancy. There are a number of ways the semantic information can be used to help search. The simplest one, and the one we have experimented so far is to form search query for one concept by combining all the terms on the path from root to that concept node in the taxonomy. In the "apple" example, the query would then become "food fruit apple", and documents about iPod and Apple computers would not be returned.

In the experiments, for each concept A, we search the web to obtain two sets of exemplars: U^{A+} containing exemplars that support (or positively related to) A; and U^{A-}, containing exemplars that support the negation of (or negatively related to) A. Exemplars in U^{A+} are obtained by searching the web for pages that contain A and all names of A's ancestors on the taxonomy, while that for U^{A-} are obtained by search pages that contain all names of A's ancestors but not A.

With all these documents, we can obtain joint probabilities of A and B by text classification, similar to what is done in GLUE [7]: applying the classifiers of concepts A and B to all text documents in U, and classify them into four categories: U^{A+B+}, U^{A+B-}, U^{A-B+}, and U^{A-B-}. Then the joint probabilities can be obtained by counting the items in each category, e.g., $P(A, B)= |U^{A+B+}| / |U|$. If we only search for positive exemplars U^{A+} and U^{B+}, then only conditional probability $P(B|A)$ can be obtained (by applying B's classifier to A's supportive exemplars to obtain U^{A+B+} and compute $P(B|A) = |U^{A+B+}| / |U^{A+}|$). The first approach is the one that works for our purpose.

5 Experiments

We have performed computer experiments on two small-scale real-world ontologies. Our goals are to find how good the learning can be with the exemplars mined from the web, and how the uncertainty inference across multiple Bayesian networks could help ontology mapping.

Translating Taxonomies to BNs. We took the Artificial Intelligence sub-domain from ACM Topic Taxonomy[4] and DMOZ[5] (Open Directory) hierarchies and pruned

---

[4] http://www.acm.org/class/1998/
[5] http://dmoz.org/

some concepts to form two ontologies, both of which have a single root node *Artificial Intelligence*. All other concepts in the hierarchies are sub categories of AI. These two hierarchies differ in both terminologies and modeling methods. DMOZ categorizes concepts by popularities of web pages to facilitate people's easy access to these pages, while ACM topic hierarchy categorizes concepts from super to sub to structure a classification primarily for academics.

Table 1. Statistics of the expirements

Taxono-mies	# Nodes	Depth	Total Exemplar size	Avg. Exemplar Size	# Exemplar	Avg. # Exp./node
ACM AI	15	3	19.7 MB	698 KB	24533	1636
DMOZ AI	25	3	29.2 MB	612 KB	35148	1406

For every concept, except the root, we obtained exemplars by querying Google as described in the previous section. The statistics of these web pages is listed in Table 1. We used Bayesian text classifier dbacl to create a model for each non-root concept X and obtained the pair-wise conditional probability $P(X \mid Parent(X))$. The root nodes were assigned a prior probability as (0.5, 0.5).

Then, using *BayesOWL*'s translation rules, the two ontologies were translated into two BNs as shown in Figure 5.

Learning uncertainty mappings. Raw mappings $P(A, B)$ were computed for each pair of concepts of the two BNs. The similarity between A and B were measured by their Jaccard coefficient, computed from the joint probability. Table 2 lists the five most similar concepts and five most different concepts in the learning result. The top three most similar concepts are actually identical concepts. However, besides these three, another pair of identical concepts is not measured as highly related. They are */Learning/Connectionism & Neural Net* in ACM topic and */Machine Learning/Neural Network* in DMOZ. Their similarity is only 0.61. We speculate this is because the term "connectionism" is not as popular as when ACM topic hierarchy was constructed, and thus is not used along with "*Neural Network*" in most web pages.

Inference with BN Mappings. Treating ontology mapping as Bayesian network mapping as described here allows us to conduct probabilistic reasoning far beyond finding the best concept match. We are currently actively investigating this issue and developing related algorithms. To illustrate our point, consider the example of finding a description of DMOZ's */Knowledge Representation/Semantic Web* (*dmoz.sw*) in ACM topic. There is no ACM concept that is identical to *dmoz.sw*, it must be described by a composite expression involving multiple ACM concepts. The two most semantically similar concepts to *dmoz.sw* in ACM are */Knowledge Representation and Formalism Method/Relation System* (*acm.rs*) and */Knowledge Representation and Formalism Method/Semantic Network* (*acm.sn*) with the joint distributions

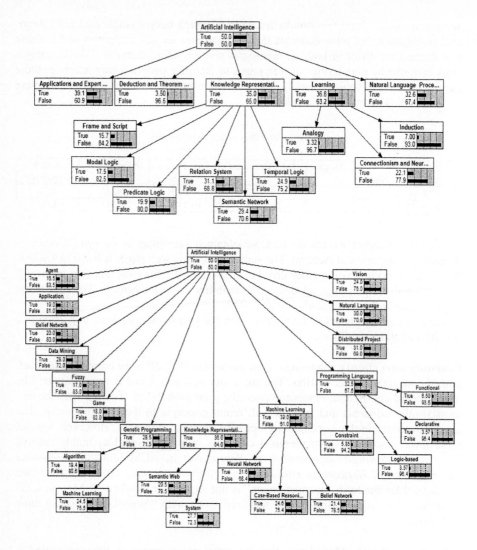

Fig. 5. Bayesian network for ACM topics' AI sub-domain and DMOZ's AI sub-domain

$$P(dmoz.sw, acm.rs) = \begin{pmatrix} 0.60 & 0.12 \\ 0.21 & 0.07 \end{pmatrix} \text{ and } P(dmoz.sw, acm.sn) = \begin{pmatrix} 0.58 & 0.13 \\ 0.25 & 0.04 \end{pmatrix},$$

and respective Jaccard coefficients $J(dmoz.sw, acm.rs) = 0.64$, and $J(dmoz.sw, acm.sn) = 0.61$.

From the two joint probabilities, we can see that *dmoz.sw* is not a subconcept of either *acm.rs* or *acm.sn*, but had a sizable overlap with each of them. From the following joint probabilities

$$P(acm.rs, acm.sn) = \begin{pmatrix} 0.2612 & 0.0498 \\ 0.0323 & 0.6557 \end{pmatrix},$$

we can see that *acm.rs* and *acm.sn* also overlap with each other. Figure 6 illustrates the overlap of these three concepts.

Table 2. Five most similar concepts and most different concepts in the learning result. The root concept's name is omitted.

ACM topic	DMOZ	Similarity
/Knowledge Representation & Formalism Method	/Knowledge Representation	0.96
/Natural Language Processing	/Natural Language	0.90
/Learning	/Machine Learning	0.88
/Learning	/Knowledge Representation	0.81
/Applications & Expert System	/Knowledge Representation	0.79
......		
/Fuzzy	/Learning/Analog	0.03
/Learning/Induction	/Learning/Game	0.02
/Deduction & Theorem Proving	/Programming Language/Declarative	0.02
/Learning/Induction	/Application	0.01
/Learning/Analogy	Agent	0.01

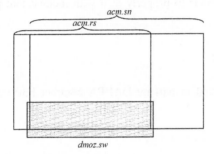

Fig. 6. The Venn diagram for *dmoz.sw*, *acm.rs*, and *acm.sn*

This leads to a conjecture that *dmoz.sw* may be described in terms of *acm.rs* and *acm.sn*. To validate this conjecture, we need to have the conditional probability $P(acm.rs= true, acm.sn = true| dmoz.sw = true)$. This can be obtained as follows.

1. Using learned probabilities $P(dmoz.sw, acm.rs)$ and $P(dmoz.sw, acm.sn)$, two semantic linkage were created, from *dmoz.sw* to *acm.rs* and to *acm.sn*, respectively.
2. Instantiate *dmoz.sw* as *true*, and compute the likelihoods for the two virtual evidence nodes associated with *acm.rs* and *acm.sn*.
3. Compute $P(acm.rs= true, acm.sn = true| dmoz.sw = true)$ by any Bayesian network inference algorithm with the two virtual evidence nodes set to true.

In our experiment, this probability was computed to be 0.851. From this we could conclude that intersection of *acm.rs* and *acm.sn* is the highly probable subsumer of *dmoz.sw*. More detailed analysis may require having the joint distribution of the three concept nodes (in two ontologies/BNs) or distribution involving additional relevant ACM concepts (with similarity measure lower than those of *acm.rs* and *acm.sn*). These distributions can be computed in the similar fashion.

6 Discussion and Future Work

This paper describes our ongoing research on developing a probabilistic framework for automatic ontology mapping. In this framework, ontologies (or parts of them) are first translated into Bayesian networks, and then the concept mapping is realized as evidential reasoning between the two BNs by Jeffrey's rule. The probabilities needed in both translation and mapping can be obtained by using text classification programs, supported by associating to individual concepts relevant text exemplars retrieved from the web.

We are currently actively working on each of these components. In searching for relevant exemplars, we are attempting to develop a measure of relevancy so that less relevant documents can be removed. We are also investigating how semantic information can be utilized to post-process text documents mined from the web so that less relevant ones can be identified and excluded. We are expanding the ontology to BN translation from taxonomies to include properties, and develop algorithms to support common ontology-related reasoning tasks. As for a general BN mapping framework, our current focus is on linkage reduction. We are also working on the semantics of BN mapping and examining its scalability and applicability. Future work also includes developing methods to properly deal with inconsistent probability constraints in IPFP process.

Acknowledgement

This work was supported in part by DARPA contract F30602-97-1-0215 and NSF award IIS-0326460.

References

1. Bock, H. H. 1989. A Conditional Iterative Proportional Fitting (CIPF) Algorithm with Applications in the Statistical Analysis of Discrete Spatial Data. *Bull. ISI, Contributed Papers of 47th Session in Paris*, 1: 141-142.
2. Cramer, E. 2000. Probability Measures with Given Marginals and Conditionals: *I*-projections and Conditional Iterative Proportional Fitting. *Statistics and Decisions*, 18: 311-329.
3. Craven, M.; DiPasquo, D.; Freitag, D.; McCallum, A.; Mitchell, T.; Nigam, K.; and Slattery, S. 2000. Learning to Construct Knowledge Bases from the World Wide Web. *Artificial Intelligence*, 118(1-2): 69-114.
4. Csiszar, I. February 1975. *I*-divergence Geometry of Probability Distributions and Minimization Problems. *The Annuals of Probability*, 3(1): 146-158.
5. Ding, Z.; Peng, Y.; and Pan, R. November 2004. A Bayesian Approach to Uncertainty Modeling in OWL Ontology. In *Proceedings of 2004 International Conference on Advances in Intelligent Systems - Theory and Applications (AISTA2004)*. Luxembourg-Kirchberg, Luxembourg.
6. Ding, Z.; and Peng, Y. January 2004. A Probabilistic Extension to Ontology Language OWL. In *Proceedings of the 37th Hawaii International Conference on System Sciences (HICSS-37)*. Big Island, Hawaii.

7. Doan, A.; Madhavan, J.; Domingos, P.; and Halevy, A. 2004. Ontology Matching: A Machine Learning Approach. *Handbook on Ontologies in Information Systems*, S. Staab and R. Studer (eds.), Springer-Velag, 2004. Invited paper. P397-416.
8. Fukushige, Y. October 2004. Representing Probabilistic Knowledge in the Semantic Web. Position paper for *the W3C Workshop on Semantic Web for Life Sciences*. Cambridge, MA, USA.
9. Jeffery, R. 1983. *The logic of Decisions 2nd Edition*, University of Chicago Press.
10. Kruithof, R. Telefoonverkeersrekening, *De Ingenieur* 52, E15-E25, 1937.
11. Lacher, M.; and Groh, G. May 2001. Facilitating the Exchange of Explicit Knowledge through Ontology Mappings. In *Proceedings of the 14th International FLAIRS Conference*. Key West, FL, USA.
12. McCallum, A.; and Nigam, K. 1998. A Comparison of Event Models for Naive Bayes Text Classification. *AAAI-98 Workshop on "Learning for Text Categorization"*.
13. Mitra, P.; Noy, N. F.; and Jaiswal, A. R. 2004. OMEN: A Probabilistic Ontology Mapping Tool. In *Workshop on Meaning Coordination and Negotiation at the Third International Conference on the Semantic Web (ISWC-2004)*. Hisroshima, Japan.
14. Noy, N. 2004. Semantic integration: A survey of ontology-based approaches. *SIGMOD Record*.
15. Pan, R.; and Peng, Y.;. 2005. A Framework for Bayesian Network Mapping. (Extend Abstract). Accepted by *AAAI-05*.
16. Pearl, J. 1988. Probabilistic Reasoning in Intelligent Systems: Networks of Plausible Inference. Morgan Kaufman, San Mateo, CA.
17. Pearl, J. 1990. Jeffery's rule, passage of experience, and neo-Bayesianism. In H.E. et al. Kyburg, Jr., editor, *Knowledge Representation and Defeasible Reasoning*, pages 245-265.
18. Peng, Y.; and Ding, Z. July 2005. Modifying Bayesian Networks by Probability Constraints. *Proceedings of the 24th Conference on Uncertainty in AI (UAI 2005)*. Edinburgh, Scotland.
19. Prasad, S.; Peng, Y.; and Finin, T. 2002. A Tool For Mapping Between Two Ontologies (Poster), *International Semantic Web Conference (ISWC02)*.
20. Valtorta, M.; Kim, Y.; and Vomlel, J. 2002. Soft Evidential Update for Probabilistic Multiagent Systems. *International Journal of Approximate Reasoning*, 29(1): 71-106.
21. van Rijsbergen, C. J. 1979. *Information Retrieval*. London: Butterworths. Second Edition.
22. Vomlel J. 1999. Methods of Probabilistic Knowledge Integration. *PhD thesis*, Department of Cybernetics, Faculty of Electrical Engineering, Czech Technical University.

Ontology Change Detection Using a Version Log

Peter Plessers[*] and Olga De Troyer

Vrije Universiteit Brussel, Pleinlaan 2, 1050 Brussel, Belgium
{Peter.Plessers, Olga.DeTroyer}@vub.ac.be

Abstract. In this article, we propose a new ontology evolution approach that combines a top-down and a bottom-up approach. This means that the manual request for changes (top-down) by the ontology engineer is complemented with an automatic change detection mechanism (bottom-up). The approach is based on keeping track of the different versions of ontology concepts throughout their lifetime (called virtual versions). In this way, changes can be defined in terms of these virtual versions.

1 Introduction

With the emergence of the Semantic Web [1], a new dimension has been added to the World Wide Web (WWW). Before, the information and functionality provided on the WWW was primarily tailored towards human interpretation, limiting the possibilities for machine processing. The Semantic Web has been proposed as an answer to these shortcomings by making the semantics of the web content explicit. Two major building blocks are used to realize this vision: ontologies as a formal, explicit specification of a conceptualization [2], and semantic annotations connecting web content and ontologies to enrich the web content with semantic information. Besides containing semantically annotated web pages, the Semantic Web is also a true 'web of ontologies' meaning that ontologies are interconnected, as they are reused and linked to each other.

The subject of this paper concerns ontology evolution. Evolution is an intrinsic part of the Semantic Web: alterations in a particular domain, changes of user requirements or corrections of design flaws, they all may induce changes to the corresponding ontologies and to semantic annotations. Moreover, changes to one ontology may have implications on many depending artifacts (other ontologies, annotations, applications, etc. based on the changed ontology) [3]. The manual handling of this evolution process of ontologies in a distributed, decentralized environment as the Semantic Web is not feasible as it is a too laborious, time intensive and complex process [12]. Therefore, it is vital that an approach is provided guiding the ontology engineer in this complex ontology evolution process.

To be able to understand the modifications applied to an ontology, the changes should be formally represented and captured. This is usually done through an evolu-

[*] This research is partially performed in the context of the e-VRT Advanced Media project (funded by the Flemish government) which consists of a joint collaboration between VRT, VUB, UG, and IMEC.

tion log listing all applied changes. Furthermore, the change representation used should be sufficient expressive (i.e. able to specify all possible changes to an ontology), and should support different levels of granularity (i.e. fine-grained changes (e.g. the creation of a single class) opposed to coarse-grained changes (e.g. the movement of sibling classes to a different parent)). In current approaches, the evolution log is a direct result of the changes requested by the ontology engineer. In this paper, we argue that such an approach may lead to a limited evolution log, missing valuable information. This makes it harder for (other) users and machines to understand and interpret the ontology modifications. Therefore, we propose an ontology evolution approach combining a top-down and a bottom-up approach. This means that the manual request for changes by ontology engineers (top-down) is complemented with an approach of automatic change detection (bottom-up).

The paper is structured as follows. Section 2 presents an overview of current practices in the domain of ontology evolution. Section 3 gives a general outline of the ontology evolution approach focusing on the different phases of the approach. Section 4 introduces the *version log*, which forms the basis of our approach. In the subsequent sections, the relevant phases of our approach are elaborated in more detail: section 5 discusses the Change Request phase, section 6 presents the Change Implementation phase, the Change Detection mechanism is given in section 7, while section 8 presents the Change Recovery phase. Finally, section 9 discusses the advantages of our approach and provides conclusions.

2   Ontology Evolution

In this section, we give an overview of current practices in the domain of ontology evolution. Stojanovic [11] has defined ontology evolution as the timely adaptation of an ontology to the arisen changes and the consistent propagation of these changes to depending artifacts. In [10] the authors identified a possible evolution process. The core phases of this process can be summarized as follows:

- *Change representation*: in the context of a change request, the necessary changes have to be identified and represented in a suitable format.
- *Semantics of change*: changes to an ontology can induce inconsistencies in other parts of the ontology or to other depending artifacts. The task of this phase is to solve these inconsistencies by requesting new deduced changes.
- *Change propagation*: the task of this phase is to bring all dependent artifacts in a consistent state by propagating changes to these depending artifacts.
- *Change implementation*: this phase is used to inform an ontology engineer about all the consequences of a change request, to apply all requested and deduced changes and to keep track of all these applied changes in an evolution log.

To represent changes, they introduced in [6] three levels of abstractions of ontology changes for the KAON language. They distinguished: elementary changes (modifications to one single ontology entity), composite changes (modifications to the direct neighborhood of an ontology entity) and complex changes (modifications to an arbitrary set of ontology entities). Also Klein [5] makes a similar taxonomy for the OWL language for which he defines both basic and complex change operations. Basic change operations are changes to one single ontology entity whereas complex change operations are a mechanism for grouping basic change operations together to form a logical unit. The set of elementary changes and basic change operations (further called *basic changes*) is exhaustive as it is derived from the underlying ontology language; the set of composite changes, complex changes and complex change operations (further called *composite changes*) is infinite as new composite changes can always be defined [5]. The benefit of composite changes is that ontology engineers can formulate their change requests at a higher-level of abstraction, corresponding to their mental model of the change, instead of forcing them to think in terms of individual basic changes.

In [4] the usefulness of a composite change detection approach was already indicated. They introduced a detection mechanism based on rules and heuristics to detect composite changes between two ontology versions (V_{old} and V_{new}). While their approach is applicable in specific cases, in general, the approach has serious limitations:

- The approach requires that V_{old} is still available, because detection rules rely on both V_{old} and V_{new}. Unfortunately, when an ontology is modified, the original version is often no longer available.

- Multiple changes to V_{old} may interfere possibly invalidating defined change detection rules. Take for example the composite change 'moveSiblings' (representing the movement of all siblings to a different parent). A detection rule can be formulated checking if all siblings of a parent A in V_{old} have a new parent B in V_{new}. Assume that after the move of the siblings, one of the siblings was removed. This would mean that the rule, as formulated, no longer applies. Nevertheless, the 'moveSiblings' change did occur.

The authors of [4] try to overcome these problems by introducing heuristics to change the precise criteria of the rules to approximations. While heuristics may provide the ontology engineer with some flexibility in the rule definitions, it is clear that it doesn't offer a bullet-proof solution as it makes the detection process imprecise and unpredictable.

We argue that, when the ontology engineer solely specifies changes manually, the log of changes may be missing valuable information. This is because of the following reasons:

- It is not always trivial for ontology engineers to select the intended composite change they want to apply due to the complexity involved. Instead they rely on basic changes to achieve step by step the desired result, evaluating the progress after each step. As a consequence, the intended composite change will not be listed in the evolution log.

- A same ontology modification can be achieved in different ways, using composite changes that may differ in level of granularity (and therefore also have different semantics) (e.g. 'moveClasses' and 'moveSiblings'). The ontology engineer will only select one change, meaning that the others will not be listed in the evolution log.

- Meta-changes (information about changes) are valuable to understand occurred ontology modifications as they define the implication of a change. They are, unfortunately, not useful for ontology engineers, as they don't specify 'what' has to change. Therefore, they don't get listed in the log of changes.

- The number of possible composite changes is infinite. Nevertheless, ontology engineers only use a finite number of these composite changes. If a fixed set of composite changes is defined, this means that users are restricted to this set to understand the occurred modifications, although other composite changes may be more appropriate for them.

3   Overview of the Approach

In this section, we will give an overview of the different phases of our ontology evolution approach. Some of the phases resemble phases from the evolution process proposed in [10], but the incorporation of a change detection mechanism has influenced these phases. The five phases of our approach are: (1) Change Request, (2) Change Implementation, (3) Change Detection, (4) Change Recovery and (5) Change Propagation. An overview of the phases is shown in Figure 1.

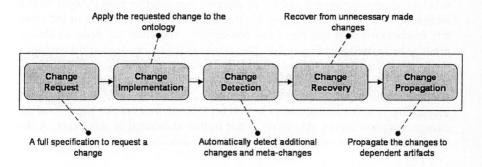

Fig. 1. Five phases of the ontology evolution approach

The purpose of the different phases is summarized as follows:

1. *Change Request:* In this phase, it is specified which changes need to be applied to the ontology. The phase is divided into two steps. In the first step, the ontology engineer specifies the request for change in terms of basic and composite changes. In the second step, it is checked whether the ontology remains consistent if the requested change would be applied. If this is not the case, new changes (called deduced changes) are added to the change request to solve the inconsistencies. Note that this is an iterative process: new deduced changes may result in additional deduced changes. The result of this phase is a *complete change request specification* composed of requested and deduced changes that transform an ontology from one consistent version into another consistent version. In our example (see Figure 2), two change requests are specified: (1) 'removeSubtype(B, A)' with deduced change 'removePropertyInstantiation($p, I, "abc"$)', and (2) 'addSubtype(B, C)'. This phase is further elaborated in Section 5.

2. *Change Implementation:* This phase takes as input the complete change request specification of the previous phase, and executes the specified changes on the ontology (see Figure 2b+c). We keep track of all changes applied through an *evolution log,* i.e. a log that stores all changes applied. A detailed overview of this phase is presented in Section 6.

3. *Change Detection:* In this phase, it is checked whether other (composite) changes (besides the one specified in the change request) or meta-changes occur as a consequence of the ontology modification. This is done by comparing *change definitions* to the modifications kept in *a version log* (see section 4). The change is added to the *evolution log,* when a combination of modifications of the version log meets the definition of that particular change. E.g. for Figure 2c, a composite change 'changeSubclassRelation' can be detected. We discuss this phase in detail in Section 7.

4. *Change Recovery:* In this phase, the deduced changes from the Change Request phase are checked and possibly need to be revised. We clarify this with the example. When we specified during change request to remove the subclass relation between *B* and *A*, a deduced change was added to remove the property instantiations of *p* for *I* to maintain consistency (Figure 2b). When we later on created a new subclass relation between *B* and *C*, we detected that together both changes form a composite change (e.g. changeSubclassRelation) and that the remove of the property instantiation *p* of instance *i* was unnecessary. Therefore this deduced change needs to be revised (see Figure 2d). This results in a new iteration of the evolution process. A detailed description of this phase is given in Section 8.

5. *Change Propagation:* In this phase, depending artifacts are brought into a consistent state by propagating changes listed in the evolution log to these depending artifacts. Due to space limitations as well as because the focus of this paper is on the change detection aspect, this phase is not further elaborated in this paper. A detailed approach concerning change propagation is described in [7, 8].

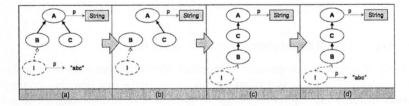

Fig. 2. An example illustrating an evolution process

For this paper, we assume that an ontology is defined in terms of classes, properties and individuals. The definition of classes, properties and individuals is specified by instantiating either built-in or user-defined properties. We therefore define an ontology as a five-tuple $O = (C, P, I, PI, D)$ where:

C is the set of Classes
P is the set of Properties

I	is the set of Individuals
PI	is the set of Property Instantiations
D	is the set of all data values

A property instantiation pi $\in$ PI is a three-tuple $pi = (p, s, t)$ where:

$p \in P$	is a property
$s \in C \vee s \in P \vee s \in I$	is the source of the property instantiation
$t \in C \vee s \in P \vee s \in I \vee t \in D$	is the target of the property instantiation

4 Version Log

Before discussing the different phases of our approach, we first present one of the key elements in our ontology evolution approach i.e. the *version log*. This log keeps track of the different versions, called *virtual versions*, an ontology concept passes during its lifetime: starting from the creation of the concept, over its modifications until its retirement. Note the difference between the version log and the evolution log: the former lists the different versions of the ontology concepts, the latter lists the interpretations of these versions in terms of changes. We use the version log to keep ontologies consistent; to serve as the basis for the definition of changes; and as source for change detection. We will first explain the structure and the concepts used in this log. The concepts used in this log are defined by means of an ontology, called the *version ontology*, and discussed in detail in subsection 4.1. In subsection 4.2, we introduce the *change definition language*. The changes, used by ontology engineers to specify their change requests, are defined in terms of this language. Change definitions are treated in subsection 4.3.

4.1 Version Ontology

The version log captures, for each concept of the ontology, its different versions. Each version represents the definition of the concept at a moment in time. For each class, property and individual that is created in the ontology, we create an associated instance in the version log. This instance is an instance of the *EvolutionConcept* class. Such an EvolutionConcept instance keeps, besides a reference to the concept in the ontology (for which it was created – called the referred concept), a list of past and current versions of the referred concept.

Whenever a change request for a concept in the ontology is executed, a new *Version instance* is added to the associated EvolutionConcept instance, representing the new version of the referred concept. Such a Version instance has (1) a transaction time property i.e. the moment in time the modification was applied to the ontology *(hasTransactionTime)*, (2) a *causes* (and inverse *causedBy*) property to express which version causes which other versions, reflecting the relation between requested changes and deduced changes in the change request, (3) a state property *(hasState)* to reflect the state of the version (pending or confirmed) and (4) optionally (if it exists) the ID of the referred concept *(hasID)*. Figure 3 gives an overview.

To capture a version of a concept, we have to file all its property instantiations that together form its definition. To do this independently of the ontology language used, we have defined a number of classes and properties to capture the most common ontology language constructs (e.g. complement, union and intersection of classes; symmetric and transitive characteristics of properties; etc.). We have defined the classes *IndividualVersion*, *PropertyVersion* and *ClassVersion* to capture the version of respectively individuals, properties and classes. Because space is limited, we cannot describe the complete version ontology, therefore we only discuss some parts. The interested reader is referred to the full specification of the version ontology[1].

For an IndividualVersion we specify that the referred individual is an instance of a certain EvolutionConcept instance *(instanceOf)* and capture the user-defined PropertyInstantiations that form the definition of the individual *(hasPI)*. For a PropertyVersion we can specify for the referred property (among other properties) the domain and range *(hasDomain, hasRange)*. Also cardinality and value constraints may be specified *(hasConstraint)*. For a ClassVersion we can specify for the referred class (among other properties) a subtype relation *(subTypeOf)*, possible cardinality and value constraints *(hasConstraint)*, and an enumeration of individuals *(enumerates)* that together form the definition of the class.

Note that for the cardinality and value constraints mentioned above, we make a distinction between global and local constraints, referring to the scope of the constraint. Global constraints apply to every instantiation of a given property. Local constraints only hold for those instantiations of a given property when used in a particular class.

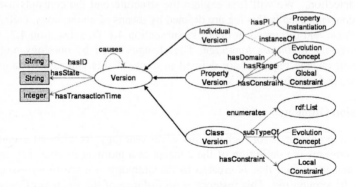

Fig. 3. The Version concepts of the version ontology

An extract of an example version log is given below. The extract shows an EvolutionConcept representing the different versions a class 'Student'. The first version represents the initial version of the class. In the second version, we see that the class includes a subtype relation. Note that the version log doesn't specify 'what' has changed; it only lists the successive versions.

```
<EvolutionConcept rdf:ID="fd42cc20">
   <refersTo rdf:resource=".../university#Student"/>
   <hasVersion>
      <ClassVersion rdf:ID="389a99b0">
         <hasTransactionTime>624</hasTransactionTime>
```

[1] See http://wise.vub.ac.be/ontologies/versionontology.owl.

```
      <hasState>confirmed</hasState>
      <hasID>Student</hasID>
    </ClassVersion>
  </hasVersion>
  <hasVersion>
    <ClassVersion rdf:ID="389a99b1">
      <hasTransactionTime>628</hasTransactionTime>
      <hasState>confirmed</hasState>
      <hasID>Student</hasID>
      <subtypeOf rdf:resource="#fd42cc22" />
    </ClassVersion>
  </hasVersion>
</EvolutionConcept>
```

4.2 Change Definition Language (CDL)

The version log uses an explicit timeline for the different versions. The 'hasTransactionTime' sequentially orders all versions across all EvolutionConcepts. Note that versions originating from the same change request (i.e. user-specified and deduced changes) will have the same transaction time. The order between such versions is defined by the 'causes' and 'causedBy' properties. As previously mentioned, these properties define which version causes which other versions, reflecting the relation between requested changes and deduced changes. This information is required to be able to undo changes (see Section 8). Figure 4 shows the timeline (T_A and T_B) for two EvolutionConcept instances A and B. The transaction times of the different versions refer to the timeline T. A variable cv refers to the current version of a concept. If $n \in$ $\mathbb{N}$ specifies the total amount of versions of one EvolutionConcept, than we can use cv - a (where $a \in N$, $a \leq n$) to refer to the $(n - a)^{\text{th}}$ version of that concept. We also define a variable cv_p (where $p \in P$). This variable takes only those versions into account where the instantiation of the given property p was changed; cv_p refers to the last one of these versions, cv_p-1 to the previous one, etc.

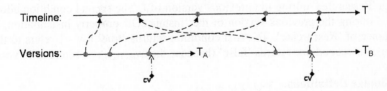

Fig. 4. Timeline introduced by the version log

This time aspect allows us to check properties of past versions of ontology concepts [9]. This is done by means of *conditions*. These conditions are used to formulate change definitions (see section 4.3). The conditions are resolved using pattern matching. We use the following syntax to define conditions on versions (Note that V defines a set of variables):

```
<property>(<source>, <target>, [<version>])
```

where

- <property> is the property we want to retrieve;
- <source> is the source of the queried property or a variable that substitutes the source. <source> ∈ C or <source> ∈ P or <source> ∈ I or <source> ∈ V;
- <target> is the target of the queried property or a variable that substitutes the target. <target> ∈ C or <target> ∈ P or <target> ∈ I or <target> ∈ D or <target> ∈ V;
- <version> is a reference to a version using the cv or cv_p variable or a variable that substitutes the version. Omitting a version reference means we refer to the current version of the <target> (cv). <version> ::= $cv_{[<property>]}$[- <a>] (where <a> ∈ ℕ) or <version> ∈ V.

We illustrate this with an example. Table 1 shows three versions of an individual i. In the first version, i is an instance of 'Student'. In a second version, i becomes an instance of 'Researcher', and in version three i "publishes a first article".

Table 1. Different versions of an example individual i

Versions	Statements
1st version	instanceOf(i, 'Student')
2nd version	instanceOf(i, 'Researcher')
3rd version	instanceOf(i, 'Researcher')
	publishes(i, 'article_001')

The following are two conditions:

```
Condition 1: instanceOf(i, 'Researcher', cv - 1)
Condition 2: instanceOf(i, 'Researcher', cv_instanceOf - 1)
```

The first condition allows to check if the individual $i \in$ I was an instance of the concept 'Researcher' during the previous version of i. The second condition allows to check if during the previous version of the 'instanceOf' property instantiation, i was an instance of 'Researcher'. The first condition returns 'true' (cv - 1 refers to the 2nd version), the second one returns 'false' (because the $cv_{instanceOf}$ - 1 refers to 1st version).

4.3 Change Definitions

The Change Definition Language introduced in the previous subsection is used to specify *change definitions*. A *change* is an interpretation of an ontology modification i.e. the definition of a change formally specifies the modifications that correspond with this change. These change definitions are used in two ways in our approach. Firstly, ontology engineers specify their change requests in terms of change definitions. The definition of the change specifies how the ontology has to change (see section 5). Secondly, these same change definitions allow detecting other changes (not specified during change request). This is possible because we are able to verify whether some change definitions are satisfied by the modifications that occurred (see section 7).

Both [5] and [6] distinguish basic and composite changes where composite changes are defined in terms of basic and other composite changes (i.e. a functional definition). In our approach, we define changes declaratively in terms of changing versions. It is exactly this declarative definition of changes that will allow us to detect changes based on the versions kept in the version log.

We make a distinction between *changes* (i.e. define 'what' has changed) and *meta-changes* (i.e. define the implications of a change). Changes are further classified into *basic* and *composite* changes. Basic changes can be expressed as a modification of exactly one element of the version log by only imposing conditions on the changing element (e.g. createSubtypeOf, deleteHasDomain, etc.). These basic changes are sufficient to express any desirable change. A Composite change is either a modification of exactly one element but also imposes conditions on other elements, or a modification of more than one element.

As examples, we define the basic change 'addDomain', the composite change 'moveUpDomain' and the meta-change 'restrictProperty'.

The basic change 'addDomain' adds A as domain of property p. Note that the definition only expresses a condition on the element that changes (hasDomain of a property p). The definition specifies that A is the domain of p in the current version, but wasn't in a previous version.

$$\forall \ p \in P, \ A \in C: \ \text{addDomain}(p, \ A) \ \leftarrow$$
$$\neg\text{hasDomain}(p, \ A, \ cv-1) \ \wedge$$
$$\text{hasDomain}(p, \ A, \ cv)$$

The composite change 'moveUpDomain' moves the domain of a property p up in the hierarchy of classes. So if p has as domain the class A, the domain will be changed to a superclass of A. Note that this change expresses an additional condition on the subtype relation between A and B.

$$\forall \ p \in P, \ A, \ B \in C: \ \text{moveUpDomain}(p, \ A, \ B) \ \leftarrow$$
$$\text{hasDomain}(p, \ A, \ cv_{\text{hasDomain}}-1) \ \wedge$$
$$\neg\text{hasDomain}(p, \ A, \ cv_{\text{hasDomain}}) \ \wedge$$
$$\neg\text{hasDomain}(p, \ B, \ cv_{\text{hasDomain}}-1) \ \wedge$$
$$\text{hasDomain}(p, \ B, \ cv_{\text{hasDomain}}) \ \wedge$$
$$\text{subtypeOf}(A, \ B, \ cv)$$

As an example of a meta-change, we define the 'constraintWeakening' meta-change indicating a weakening of constraints as a consequence of the change. Different modifications to an ontology can lead to a weakening of constraints, e.g. the raise of a cardinality constraint or the extension of a value constraint, a change to a subtype relation, etc. This means that multiple definitions exist for the 'constraintWeakening' each reflecting different causes. For this example, we define the 'constraintWeakening' meta-change in the case of a replacement of class B as the domain of property p by class A, where A is a superclass of B. This is a weakening of constrains as first only instances of class B could instantiate property p, now also individuals of class A can. Note that the definition uses the 'moveUpDomain' change definition.

$$\forall \ p \in P: \ \text{constraintWeakening}(p) \ \leftarrow$$
$$\exists \ A, \ B \in C: \ \text{moveUpDomain}(p, \ B, \ A)$$

5 Change Request

Ontology engineers express their change requests (i.e. 'what' has to change) in terms of the change definitions (as defined in section 4.3). Applying these changes directly to the ontology may cause inconsistencies, meaning that the ontology would no longer conform to the constraints imposed by the ontology language used. To avoid this, we first process the requested change in the version log. To check if a requested change can be applied, the conditions in the change definitions are tested. The conditions in the change definition that refer to past versions form a pre-condition that needs to be satisfied. If this pre-condition is not satisfied, the requested change cannot be applied and the change request will be rejected. Otherwise, the changes are recorded in the version log by adding new versions to the EvolutionConcepts referring to the ontology concept to be changed so that the new current version satisfies the post-conditions in the change definition. The conditions in the change definition that refer to current versions form a post-condition. Note that these new versions are marked in the version log with the value 'pending' for the property 'hasState' indicating that they are not yet applied to the ontology itself.

Next, we have to check whether the ontology would remain consistent if we would apply these new versions to the ontology itself. The consistency check is based on a consistency model i.e. a model that restricts the version ontology so that it conforms to the constraints imposed by the ontology language used (explained in section 5.1). If it turns out that the requested change would cause inconsistencies, additional changes should be added to the change request to solve these inconsistencies. Note that in our approach, it is currently still the responsibility of the ontology engineer to specify the additional changes. Keep in mind that the deduction of additional changes is an iterative process. Every new deduced change creates a new version in the version log, and the consistency check is reapplied. The 'cause' and 'causedBy' properties are used to express the causal relation between versions to reflect the causal relation that exists between requested and deduced changes.

The result of this phase is a *complete change request* (consisting of requested and deduced changes) that transforms an ontology from a consistent version to another consistent version. The actual implementation of the complete change request to the ontology is done in the next phase (Change Implementation).

5.1 Consistency Model

To check for consistency, we make use of a *consistency model*. Such a consistency model is a formal meta-model that restricts the version ontology so that it is conforms to the constraints imposed by the ontology language used. This means that whenever the latest version stored in the version log conforms to the consistency model, the requested changes can be applied. Note that different consistency models may exist for different ontology languages or different variants of an ontology language (e.g. OWL Lite and OWL DL).

To clarify the consistency model, we give a number of example constraints that represent constraints from OWL.

- In OWL, a subtype relation can only be defined between either two classes (sub-ClassOf) or two between two properties (subPropertyOf):

$$\forall\ a,\ b:\ \texttt{subTypeOf}(a,\ b)\ \Rightarrow\ (a \in C \land b \in C)\ \lor$$
$$(a \in P \land b \in P)$$

- In OWL, a property may have a domain and the domain of a property is a class:

$$\forall\ a,\ b:\ \texttt{hasDomain}(a,\ b)\ \Rightarrow\ a \in P \land b \in C$$

- In OWL DL and Full, the value of a cardinality constraint is a non-negative integer:

$$\forall\ C,\ v:\ \texttt{hasCardinality}(C,\ v)\ \Rightarrow\ v \in \mathbb{IN} \land v \geq 0$$

- In OWL Lite however, the previous constraint would not hold as the value of a cardinality constraint is in this case restricted to 0 or 1. The previous constraint is replaced by the following:

$$\forall\ C,\ v:\ \texttt{hasCardinality}(C,\ v)\ \Rightarrow\ v \in \{0,\ 1\}$$

6 Change Implementation

The objective of this phase is twofold. The first objective of the change implementation phase is to synchronize the ontology with the latest version of EvolutionConcept(s) in the version log, i.e. the requested changes need to be applied to the ontology. The second objective is to add the changes listed in the change request to the *evolution log*. This log keeps track of all applied changes and gives an overview of the complete evolution history of the ontology in terms of changes.

The process of applying changes to the actual ontology is quite simple. The concepts that need to modify (obtained using the *refersTo* property in the version log) just have to be replaced by the current version specified in the version log. To perform the synchronization, a mapping between the concepts of the version ontology and the elements of the chosen ontology language needs to be provided. Figure 5 shows an example.

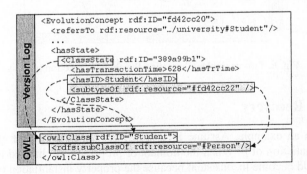

Fig. 5. Example mapping between Version log and an OWL ontology

7 Change Detection

After the execution of the previous phases, the version log has been modified, the ontology has been synchronized with the version log and the requested changes have been added to the evolution log. The changes specified in the change request are only one way to see (interpret) the modification made to the ontology. From all the changes defined (by means of change definitions), other definitions may also be satisfied by the ontology modification and therefore these changes have also occurred. To detect these additional changes, we use the following procedure. For each change definition specified, we check if its definition is satisfied. As change definitions are given in terms of conditions on the version log, a change definition is satisfied if all conditions of its definition are satisfied. The changes, whose definitions are met, are subsequently added to the evolution log. Note that this change detection process isn't limited to the ontology owner, but can be performed for all maintainers of artifacts depending on the ontology. This makes it possible for maintainers of depending artifacts to specify their own set of change definitions, independently of the set of change definitions of the ontology owner or other maintainers.

Notice that this change detection process is particularly flexible i.e. the detection process is not dependent on the steps taken to achieve a particular change neither on the order of these steps. Figure 6 illustrates this with two situations where both the 'moveUpDomain' change will be detected. In the first situation (1), the domain of property p is changed from class B to class A being a superclass of B. This change confirms to the definition of 'moveUpDomain' (see Section 4.3). In the second situation (2), the domain of property p is changed from class B to class A. This change doesn't conform to the definition of 'moveUpDomain' as the subtype condition is not met. However, when in a next step, the subclass relation between B and A is added, this modification will result in the detection of the 'moveUpDomain' change as all conditions are now met.

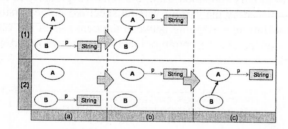

Fig. 6. Two examples illustrating the change detection process

8 Change Recovery

We start with an example. Assume for Figure 6(2) an instance i of class B with a property instantiation of p. When the domain of property p is changed to class A, the ontology would become inconsistent because the property instantiation of p for i is no longer valid. To overcome this inconsistency, the change request will be extended with an additional change to remove the property instantiation from i. When in the next step, the subtype relation is added between B and A, we will detect the 'move-

UpDomain' change (see previous section). It becomes now clear that the removing of the property instantiation of p from i was not necessary. This example illustrates the necessity to be able to recover from deduced changes when detecting changes.

When a composite change is detected, the change recovery process is as follows:

1. As presented in section 4.3, the definition of a change is specified in terms of conditions. For each property, possible pre-conditions and post-condition are specified in terms of past and current versions. In this first step, from the versions of the version log that satisfy the definition of the detected change (in this example 'move-UpDomain'), we select those versions that satisfy the conditions in the change definition that form the post-condition (Figure 6(2b + c)).
2. In a second step, all versions that are caused by one of the selected versions are undone. In our example, this means undoing the remove of property instantiation p for i. This is possible by following the 'causes' property from the selected versions in the version log. In this way, we undo all deduced changes. Undoing changes is trivial as we can easily return to the previous version (found in the version log).
3. The version log is checked for inconsistencies. If it appears to be consistent, the changes will be applied to the ontology. If not, additional changes need to be formulated by the ontology engineer to solve any inconsistency. This step is repeated until consistency is reached. Note that this step is similar to the process described in section 5. In our example, the ontology is consistent as the property instantiation p of individual i became valid by adding the subtype.

9   Discussion and Conclusions

The change detection mechanism as presented here has a number of advantages:

1. *Implicitly detection of changes.* It is not always easy for ontology engineers to select the correct, intended composite change that reflects the modifications they have in mind. Therefore, they will opt for basic changes to achieve step by step the desired result. In the end, they might have applied a composite change, not realizing they did. The detection mechanism proposed is able to automatically detect these implicitly executed composite changes.
2. *Allowing different levels of granularity.* Several composite changes, with different levels of granularity (and also different semantics), may result in the same ontology modification. Consider for example the composite changes 'moveClasses' and 'moveSiblings'. 'moveSiblings' provides more semantics than 'moveClasses' (difference in granularity). The same modification can be achieved using either of these changes. When an ontology engineer opts for the 'moveClasses' change to actually execute a 'moveSiblings' change, valuable information is lost because the most accurate change is not registered. The change detection mechanism overcomes this problem, as the more accurate change will be detected.
3. *Meta-changes are automatically detected.* Meta-changes are not useful for ontology engineers to specify change requests as they don't define 'what' has to change. Furthermore, ontology engineers don't want to be burden with the task of manually specifying them. However, these meta-changes are definitely valuable for understanding occurred ontology changes. The change detection mechanism is able to detect such meta-changes.

4. *Different sets of change definitions.* Ontology engineers may use a fix set of composite change definitions to specify their change requests, although an infinite number of composite changes may exist. Our approach makes it possible for maintainers of depending artifacts to define additional composite change definitions, which are more appropriate for their purpose. The occurrence of these additional changes can be detected using our change detection mechanism.

As a conclusion, we summarize the contributions of this paper. We have presented a new ontology evolution approach that includes an automatic change detection mechanism. The key element of our approach is the version log, which maintains the different versions of the ontology concepts. Change definitions as well as the consistency model are defined in terms of this version log. Because the version log is independent of the ontology language used, also change definitions are defined independently of the used ontology language. Different ontology languages are supported by defining a proper consistency model and specifying a mapping between the version ontology and the ontology language used.

References

1. Berners Lee, T., Hendler, J., Lassila, O.: The semantic web: A new form of web content that is meaningful to computers will unleash a revolution of new possibilities. Scientific American (2001) 5(1)
2. Gruber, T.: A Translation Approach to Portable Ontology Specifications. Knowledge Acquisition 5(2) (1993) 199-220
3. Klein, M., Fensel, D.: Ontology versioning for the Semantic Web. In Proceedings of the First International Semantic Web Working Symposium (SWWS), Stanford University, California, USA (2001) 75-91
4. Klein, M., Fensel, D., Kiryakov, A., Ognyanov, D.: Ontology versioning and change detection on the web. In 13th International Conference on Knowledge Engineering and Knowledge Management (EKAW02), Sigüenza, Spain (2002)
5. Klein, M.: Change Management for Distributed Ontologies. PhD Thesis (2004)
6. Maedche, A., Stojanovic, L., Studer, R., Volz, R.: Managing multiple ontologies and ontology evolution in OntoLogging. In Proceedings of the Conference on Intelligent Information Processing (IIP-2002), Montreal, Canada (2002) 51-63
7. Maedche, A., Motik, B., Stojanovic, L., Managing multiple and distributed ontologies on the Semantic Web. TheVLDB Journal - Special Issue on Semantic Web 12 (2003) 286-302
8. Maedche, A., Motik, B., Stojanovic, L., Studer, R., Volz, R.: An Infrastructure for Searching, Reusing and Evolving Distributed Ontologies, In Proceedings of the Twelfth International World Wide Web Conference (WWW 2003), Budapest, Hungary, ACM (2003) 439-448
9. Plessers, P., De Troyer, O., Casteleyn, S.: Event-based Modeling of Evolution for Semantic-driven Systems. In Proceedings of the 17th Conference on Advanced Information Systems Engineering (CAiSE'05), Publ. Springer-Verlag, Porto, Portugal (2005)
10. Stojanovic, L., Maedche, A., Motik, B., Stojanovic, N.: Userdriven Ontology Evolution Management. In Proceeding of the 13th European Conference on Knowledge Engineering and Knowledge Management EKAW, Madrid, Spain (2002)
11. Stojanovic, L.: Methods and Tools for Ontology Evolution. Phd Thesis (2004)
12. Tallis, M., Gil, Y.: Designing scripts to guide users in modifying knowledge-based systems. In Proceedings of the 14th National Conference on Artificial Intelligence (AAAI/IAAI 1999), Orlando, Florida, USA (1999) 242-249

RelExt: A Tool for Relation Extraction from Text in Ontology Extension

Alexander Schutz and Paul Buitelaar

German Research Center for Artificial Intelligence (DFKI GmbH),
Language Technology Lab,
Stuhlsatzenhausweg 3,
Saarbrücken, Germany
{aschutz, paulb}@dfki.de

Abstract. Domain ontologies very rarely model verbs as relations holding between concepts. However, the role of the verb as a central connecting element between concepts is undeniable. Verbs specify the interaction between the participants of some action or event by expressing relations between them. In parallel, it can be argued from an ontology engineering point of view that verbs express a relation between two classes that specify domain and range. The work described here is concerned with relation extraction for ontology extension along these lines. We describe a system (RelExt) that is capable of automatically identifying highly relevant triples (pairs of concepts connected by a relation) over concepts from an existing ontology. RelExt works by extracting relevant verbs and their grammatical arguments (i.e. terms) from a domain-specific text collection and computing corresponding relations through a combination of linguistic and statistical processing. The paper includes a detailed description of the system architecture and evaluation results on a constructed benchmark. RelExt has been developed in the context of the SmartWeb project, which aims at providing intelligent information services via mobile broadband devices on the FIFA World Cup that will be hosted in Germany in 2006. Such services include location based navigational information as well as question answering in the football domain.

1   Introduction

An investigation of the structure of existing ontologies via the Swoogle ontology search engine [1] [1] has shown that domain ontologies very occasionally model verbs as relations holding between their concepts. However, the role of the verb as a central connecting element between concepts is undeniable. Verbs specify the interaction between the participants of some action or event by expressing relations between them.

In parallel, it can be argued from an ontology engineering point of view, that verbs express a relation between two classes that specify the domain and range of some action or event. For instance,consider the following German sentence from the football domain:

Ballack schiesst das Leder ins Netz.

---

[1] http://swoogle.umbc.edu/

Y. Gil et al. (Eds.): ISWC 2005, LNCS 3729, pp. 593–606, 2005.

(Ballack shoots the ball into the net.)

A valuable contribution for an ontology in the football domain would be that the verb "schiessen" (to shoot) as a relation holds between the concept FOOTBALLPLAYER, instantiated as "Ballack", as domain and the concept BALLOBJECT, instantiated as "Leder" ("leather, ball") as range, that is:

Rel:SHOOT (Dom:FOOTBALLPLAYER, Range:BALLOBJECT)

The work described here is concerned with the extension of a football ontology along these lines, in the context of the SmartWeb [2] project. SmartWeb aims at providing services accessible via mobile broadband devices in the context of the FIFA World Cup, which is hosted in Germany in 2006. Such services include location based infrastructural information (i.e. "Show me the fastest route to the stadium.") as well as question answering in the football domain (i.e. "Who caused the penalty that Ballack converted?").

The ontology that was constructed for this purpose consists of the following components: the upper model DOLCE [2] as foundational ontology, SUMO [3] for describing cross-domain concepts, the domain-specific SportEventOntology, which was modelled by domain experts and is focused mainly on football, and other components such as the navigation and discourse ontology. As of now [3], the ontology contains 1570 direct classes (concepts) and 487 direct relations. Relations relevant for the football domain are mostly properties of some class such as "hasAge", "hasName", "atMinute". SUMO does model verbal relations between classes, for instance "causes", "connects", "knows" or "shows", but these are still rather abstract. However, in domain ontologies relations need to be specified more precisely.

Therefore, in the approach we present here we implemented a system (RelExt) that is capable of automatically identifying highly relevant *triples* (pairs of *concepts* connected by a *relation*) that can be integrated in an (already existing) ontology. RelExt works by extracting relevant terms and verbs from a given text collection and computing relations between them through a combination of linguistic and statistical processing.

The remainder of this document is structured as follows. Section 2 compares our approach to other ongoing relevant research in relation extraction and ontology learning in general. In Sect. 3, we give a detailed overview of the components used in the system, as well as the processing steps undertaken. Section 4 describes the evaluation strategy and the methods we used for evaluation, and goes on with interpreting our results. Finally, Sect. 5 points out ideas for further work to be carried out in this direction and closes with concluding remarks.

2   Related Work

A large collection of methods for ontology learning from text have developed over recent years as witnessed by the proceedings of various workshops in this area, e.g.

---

[2] http://www.smartweb-projekt.de/
[3] July 2005.

at ECAI 2002[4], ECAI 2004[5]. Unfortunately, there is not much consensus within the ontology learning community on the exact task they are concerned with, which makes a comparison of approaches difficult[6].

In order to estimate the state-of-the-art in ontology learning, we first need to establish the subtasks that together constitute the complex task of ontology development (either manual or with any level of automatic support). Ontology development is primarily concerned with the definition of concepts and relations between them. In our case this implies the acquisition of linguistic knowledge about the terms that are used to refer to a specific concept in text and possible synonyms of these terms. An ontology further consists of a taxonomy backbone (is-a relation) and other, non-hierarchical relations.

Recent work on relation extraction from text, other than the is-a relation, has been addressed primarily within the biomedical field as there are very large text collections readily available (e.g. PubMed[7]) for this area of research. The goal of this work is to discover new relationships between known concepts (i.e. symptoms, drugs, diseases) by analyzing large quantities of biomedical scientific articles (see e.g. [5] [6] [7]).

Most of the work on text mining combines statistical analysis with more or less complex levels of linguistic analysis, e.g. by exploiting syntactic structure and dependencies for relation extraction as reported for instance by [8], [9] and [10]. Relation extraction is therefore also very much related to the problem of acquiring selection restrictions for verb arguments in NLP (compare [11]), as witnessed for instance by the ASIUM system that enables an integrated acquisition of relations between concepts identified in text and so-called sub-categorization frames for the verbs that underlie these relations [12].

Relation extraction through text mining for ontology development was introduced in work on association rules in [13]. Of specific interest to the work described here is also recent research by Reinberger and Spyns [14], and by Sabou [15], both of which employ dependency structure for ontology learning.

While Reinberger and Spyns employ mainly statistical methods based on frequency information over linguistic dependencies (predicate-object, preposition-headnoun) in order to establish relations between entities from a corpus of the biomedical domain, they are not concerned with labelling the discovered relations, which moves their research more towards the work proposed by Maedche and Staab [13].

Sabou conducts her research on a corpus of controlled language from Web Service descriptions, that consists of simple sentence constructions from which ontology fragments can be extracted easily. Unfortunately, the proposed evaluation of Sabou's system cannot be performed automatically and needs a lot of manual interference.

3 Approach

Here we describe an approach to relation extraction for ontology extension based on linguistic analysis and a predefined ontology that we intend to extend with relations derived from predicate argument structure.

---

[4] http://www-sop.inria.fr/acacia/WORKSHOPS/ECAI2002-OLT/
[5] http://olp.dfki.de/ecai04/cfp.htm
[6] A start towards surveying research in this area has been made by OntoWeb deliverable 1.5 [4].
[7] http://www.pubmedcentral.nih.gov/

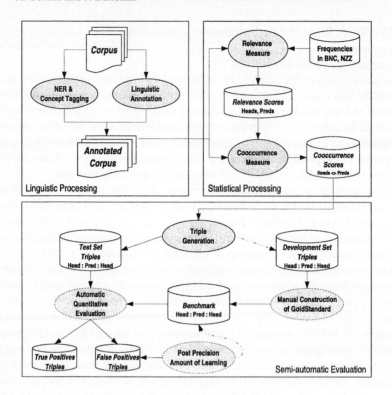

Fig. 1. System processing architecture

What follows is the description of the corpus we used (3.1) and the system architecture, including linguistic annotation (3.2), the various stages of statistical processing and filtering (3.3), and finally, after the identification of relevant terms and relations, the construction of triples. The processing pipeline is sketched in Fig. 1.

3.1 Corpus Description

We worked on a document collection compiled from the football domain, consisting of 0.5 mio tokens in 1219 documents. [8] The documents comprise minute-by-minute (live-ticker) reports on football matches from the first and second German division. Figure 2 shows an example document of the corpus.

The benefits of this kind of text compared to the much more detailed match reports are twofold: Firstly, the sentences are rather concise, which significantly reduces the error rate of grammatical function assignment of our parser. Secondly, the language used in the minute-by-minute texts is not as prosaic as the language used in the detailed match reports, which reduces the amount of (sometimes newly invented) synonyms for domain specific terms. The average sentence length of the corpus is approximately 13 words.

---

[8] The corpus was compiled from http://www.kicker.de

```
Anpfiff
16: Überraschende Führung für Energie Cottbus: Miriuta zirkelt einen Freistoß
    über die Bremer Mauer ins rechte obere Toreck.
34: Nach einem öffnenden Zuspiel von Skripnik kommt auf der rechten Seite Stalteri
    an den Ball, dringt in den Strafraum ein und überwindet mit einem Rechtsschuss
    den herauseilenden Gäste-Keeper Piplica.
...
Schlusspfiff
```

```
Kickoff
16: Energie Cottbus surprisingly take the lead: Miriuta curls a freekick over the
    Bremen wall into the top corner.
34: From a penetrating pass by Skripnik, Stalteri takes possession on the right
    wing, moves into the penalty area and beats the on rushing visitor's keeper
    Piplica with a right footer.
...
Final whistle
```

Fig. 2. Example document from the corpus

3.2 Linguistic Analysis

For the linguistic annotation, we used the SCHUG-system [16] [17] , which provides a multi-layered XML-format for a given text, specifying *dependency structure* along with *grammatical function assignment*, *phrase structure*, *part-of-speech* and *lemmatization* (including *decomposition*, which is useful in particular for German where compound nouns are often used). Figure 3 provides an example.

Dependency Structure. As mentioned before in Sect. 1, verbs specify an action or event, whereas the semantic classes of their syntactic arguments account for the class of participants in that event. Exploiting this information could be very useful when it comes to restricting a relation to hold only between a small set of semantic classes.

On the phrase level, SCHUG is able to provide a detailed analysis of syntactic arguments, which involves decomposition of complex NPs into nominal head, pre- and post modifier. Considering the whole NP as a candidate term for relation extraction would introduce data sparseness, and therefore, it is important to normalise a complex NP to its headnoun. Using only headnouns can be seen as a step towards normalisation, which eases concept tagging and therefore, broadening coverage.

Named Entity Recognition / Concept Tagging. In order to map instances of football players in the corpus to existing ontology class labels, we performed Named Entity Recognition (NER), based on gazetteer lists. The gazetteers were automatically generated from semi-structured documents about football matches in the first and second German division, containing formal data, such as team lineup, referee names and further information about a given match. For instance, if we encountered the string "Oliver Kahn" [9] (or "Kahn", or "O. Kahn"), we tagged the tokens with the correct named entity type, in this case GOALKEEPER. For NER, we distinguished only between 4 different ontology classes: GOALKEEPER, FOOTBALLPLAYER, TEAM and COACH.

---

[9] A German goalkeeper.

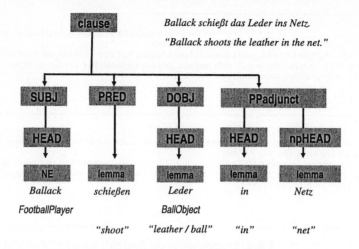

Fig. 3. Analyzed dependency structure for "Ballack schießt das Leder ins Netz."

Furthermore, a concept tagging step was undertaken, in order to map synonyms for given terms to the corresponding ontology concepts. For this purpose we used synonyms that the SportEventOntology specifies for a given *concept label* in German and English. For instance, the concept DEFENDER has a synonym list with the following elements: [DE: *Abwehrspieler, Abwehr, Verteidiger*] [EN: *Defender, Defense, Back, Fullback, Defenceman*]. We exploited this information also for mapping terms from more specific subclasses to more general superclasses, i.e. if we encountered the token "Manndecker" (stopper / DEFENDER), we tagged the token with the more general term/label FOOT-BALLPLAYER instead, in order to reduce the sparse data problem. Ambiguity in concept tagging is not really an issue here as we are working with a domain specific corpus and ontology in which there is mostly a one-to-one mapping between terms and concepts.

3.3   Statistical Processing

In order to identify the most relevant terms and relations for the football domain, it is necessary to filter out more general terms. As our goal was not only to find single relevant terms, but highly relevant triples, a single statistical ranking step was not sufficient in order to produce satisfactory results. In fact, we had to perform several computations on the extracted data, starting from *relevance ranking*, and *cross-referencing* relevant nouns and verbs with the predicate-argument-pairs, to computing *co-occurrence*-scores in order to construct triples that are specifically used in the football domain.

Relevance Measure. In the context of *ontology learning*, a promising approach is to select the *nominal heads* of noun phrases as candidates to be modelled as classes in an ontology, while verbs (or rather the *predicates* they express) bear information about the relationship between two classes. We therefore exploit the rich linguistic information provided by SCHUG and extracted two lists from the processed corpus. The first list contains lemmatized headnouns, while the second list consists of lemmatized predicates.

Adopting the methods of [18](chapter 5.3), a χ^2 test was used to compute a relevance ranking, comparing the observed frequencies of headnouns in the domain specific corpus with the frequencies of the same headnouns in a larger and more general corpus. As a general corpus, we relied on the British National Corpus (90 mio tokens) for English texts, and a corpus compiled from Swiss newspapers (9 mio tokens) for German texts. The same procedure was used to rank the predicates. The formula for χ^2 is given below.

$$\chi^2 = \sum_{i,j} \frac{(O_{i,j} - E_{i,j})^2}{E_{i,j}} \cdot \tag{1}$$

However, since we are dealing with 2x2 contingency tables only, it simplifies to

$$\chi^2 = \frac{N(O_{11}O_{22} - O_{12}O_{21})^2}{(O_{11} + O_{12})(O_{11} + O_{21})(O_{12} + O_{22})(O_{21} + O_{22})} \cdot \tag{2}$$

where the indices refer to the column and row of the table, O is the observed frequency and N the sample size.

For instance, the noun "Ball" *(ball)* occurred 6849 times in our corpus of approx 0.5 mio tokens and only 511 times in the approx 9 mio tokens general corpus, obtaining a higher χ^2-score than "Tor" *(goal)*, which occurred more frequently than "Ball" in our corpus, due to the squared sums of the mean error.

According to this ranking, we obtained three lists ordered by relevance, one for headnouns, a second list for headnouns mapped to ontology class labels, and a third list for predicates. To illustrate highly relevant terms for the football-domain, Table 1 lists the top 10 for headnouns and Table 2 gives the top 10 class labels after mapping headnouns to the ontology. Table 3 displays highly relevant lemmatized verbs used in the football-domain.

Table 1. χ^2-top lemmatized headnouns

Rank	χ^2-score	Headnoun	Frequency
1	125245.24	Ball *(ball)*	6849
2	121888.52	Tor *(goal)*	7767
3	95003.21	Meter *(meters)*	5967
4	64157.18	Schuss *(shot / drive)*	3575
5	57185.76	Eck *(corner)*	3132
6	45474.96	Strafraum *(penalty area)*	2298
7	34668.11	Freistoss *(freekick)*	1752
8	30017.75	Leder *(leather / ball)*	1561
9	27989.09	Flanke *(cross)*	1479
10	27414.66	Pfosten *(post)*	1457

Co-occurrence Measure. After filtering out those elements from the χ^2-sorted lists where the score did not indicate strong relevance for the football-domain, we examined the dependency structure of the remaining predicates. We considered only those predicate-argument-pairs for further investigation, where a highly ranked predicate co-occurred with a highly ranked headnoun. We then ranked the resulting list of predicate-argument-pairs again by further statistical processing. Assuming a headnoun together with its grammatical function as one unit, *co-occurrence*-scores were computed again with χ^2, as described below.

Table 2. Top ontology class labels after NER and concept tagging

Rank	Class Label	Frequency
1	FOOTBALLPLAYER	28494
2	GOALOBJECT	8188
3	BALLOBJECT	7249
4	GOALKEEPER	6887
5	SHOOT	3578
6	TEAM	2477
7	PENALTYAREA	2298
8	FREEKICK	1752
9	WING	1482
10	POST	1457

Table 3. χ^2-top lemmatized predicates

Rank	χ^2-score	Predicate	Frequency
1	27167.41	flanken *(to cross / to centre)*	1373
2	22045.39	klaeren *(to clear)*	1435
3	21908.37	schiessen *(to shot)*	1503
4	20439.09	koepfen *(to head)*	1033
5	16342.99	lassen *(to let / to leave)*	826
6	9563.41	ziehen *(to pull / to drag)*	1548
7	9468.57	passen *(to pass / to play)*	814
8	7752.84	spielen *(to play / to pass)*	1559
9	7653.68	lenken *(to divert)*	537
10	7637.45	parieren *(to parry / to save)*	405

We obtained a ranked (by χ^2-score) list, consisting of predicates paired up with one of their arguments in a specific grammatical function. A higher score for a predicate-headnoun-pair with a particular grammatical function means that this headnoun occurring with this particular grammatical function is statistically more likely to appear for that predicate than the same headnoun in any other grammatical function.

By this computation, we determined the *selectional preferences* of each predicate, which are semantic restrictions on syntactic arguments of the grammatical function for a given predicate and headnoun, and which in turn were used for the construction of triples. Selectional preferences have been used also in previous research on ontology learning [19].

Table 4 illustrates some of the selectional preferences for the verb "flanken" *(to cross)* and the verb "pruefen" *(to try / to test)*, computed by the χ^2-algorithm. We exploited the computed selectional preferences in order to find the most preferred *subjects* for a given verb as well as the most preferably selected *direct* and *indirect objects*.

Relation Extraction. The triples were constructed from the selected headnoun-predicate pairs, where the subject was chosen as the domain of the relation, while the (direct and indirect) objects as well as the adjuncts defined the range, as shown in Table 5. The steps undertaken for each verb (in order to combine it with appropriate terms for domain and range) were as follows:

1. compose a sub-unit consisting of a predicate and a highly ranked OBJ or NP-Head of PP_ADJUNCT
2. glue a highly ranked SUBJ to the lefthand side of the sub-unit
3. SUBJ + sub-unit constitutes a triple

Table 4. Selectional preferences for "flanken" *(to cross)* vs. "pruefen" *(to try / to test)*

Predicate	ARG-CLASS	GF	χ^2
flanken *(to cross)*	FOOTBALLPLAYER	SUBJ	25.03
flanken	REFEREE	SUBJ	0.05
flanken	FOOTBALLPLAYER	DOBJ	34.77
flanken	REFEREE	DOBJ	0.01
flanken	FOOTBALLPLAYER	IOBJ	10.63
flanken	REFEREE	IOBJ	0.01
pruefen *(to try / to test)*	FOOTBALLPLAYER	SUBJ	3.09
pruefen	GOALKEEPER	SUBJ	0.63
pruefen	FOOTBALLPLAYER	DOBJ	0.20
pruefen	GOALKEEPER	DOBJ	20.60
pruefen	FOOTBALLPLAYER	IOBJ	0.96
pruefen	GOALKEEPER	IOBJ	7.69

Table 5. Examples of constructed triples

Domain	Relation	Range
FOOTBALLPLAYER	flanken *(to cross)*	FOOTBALLPLAYER
FOOTBALLPLAYER	flanken_auf *(to cross to)*	FOOTBALLPLAYER
FOOTBALLPLAYER	flanken_zu *(to cross to)*	FOOTBALLPLAYER
FOOTBALLPLAYER	pruefen *(to test)*	GOALKEEPER

Our inspections however showed that the huge amount of single occuring predicate-headnoun-pairs (which unfortunately obtained a high χ^2 value) biased the construction of accurate, relevant triples to a large extent. We therefore introduced a threshold, considering only those elements for triple construction that co-occured more than once.

4 Evaluation

A big problem for ontology learning efforts is performance evaluation, as performance in an open set is to be measured. How would one want to measure something that has been learned, but which is not yet known? Because, if it had been known in the first place, there would not have been the need for a learning effort.

As of now, various promising proposals have been made for comparing ontologies on the lexical as well as on the taxonomic level [20], which could be used in order to evaluate against a *gold standard*. Still, what happens when something learned shows up that is not covered by the gold standard? Certainly, these are problems that have to be addressed as well.

4.1 Benchmark Construction

Nevertheless, we did measure the performance of our system against a gold standard that we constructed to benchmark different parameters. For this purpose, we split up the corpus into 4 equally sized sub-corpora of 300 documents, from which we used one sample for benchmark construction.

From this sample (consisting of 101536 tokens) we generated 192 triples and presented these to 3 domain experts. It was their task to determine whether a given triple was an appropriate one for the football domain, or not. We also allowed an "in-between" rating, to be used if the annotator could not make up his mind. The annotation process was

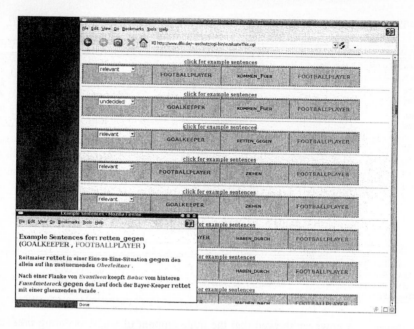

Fig. 4. WWW evaluation interface

performed via a web-based interface, as shown in Fig. 4. The Kappa-statistic [21], which was computed in order to determine agreement among the 3 annotators, was found to be at roughly 27%. As this value was rather low, we additionally considered the per-class agreement [22] of the annotators, as presented in Table 6. Given reasonable agreement among the annotators' judgement on appropriate and not appropriate generated relations, we constructed two benchmarks. The strict benchmark GS_{strict} consists of 26 elements, containing only those triples which all annotators agreed upon to be appropriate. The relaxed benchmark $GS_{relaxed}$ excluded all those triples, which were rated as not appropriate by at least one of the domain experts, leading to a set of 38 triples.

Table 6. Per-class agreement among the 3 annotators for evaluation of 192 triples

Judgement	Assigned	Agreed	Disagreed	Agr. Ratio
appropriate	202	264	140	65%
undecided	112	50	174	22%
not appropriate	262	300	224	57%

4.2 Experiment

As it was our aim to find relations for the extension of the SmartWeb SportEventOntology, we put the following restrictions on generated triples: Firstly, we considered only those triples, where the terms for domain and range could already be mapped to ontology classes. Secondly, we further reduced the sets of triples to be evaluated by removing items containing auxiliary and modal verbs.

Setup. Introducing a parametrizable setup option for triple construction, we distinguished between two setups which controlled the amount of triples to be generated. Setup I generated only one triple per verb (namely the best, according to the selectional preferences for SUBJs, OBJs and NP-heads of PP_ADJUNCTs), while setup II generated all possible triples (by considering less preferred SUBJs and OBJs for triple composition), resulting in a set of triples with larger size.

We therefore generated 6 sets of triples, 2 for each of the 3 test corpora. Furthermore, we introduced a linear order based on the sum of the selectional preferences that were used in order to compose a given triple.[10] This enabled us to rank the triples within a set.

According to the ranking, we constructed 2 samples of different size. The first sample (A) was scaled exactly to the size of the Gold Standard by considering only the first best triples, and the second sample (B) simply contained all triples of the set.

As a result, we now obtained highly relevant relations connecting two highly relevant terms. Some examples are given in Table 5.

Metrics and Results. Various contributions in recent and ongoing work (i.e. [23], [24] or [25]) are concerned with establishing metrics for quantitative evaluation for ontology learning. However, as pointed out briefly in the introduction of this section, this effort is rather difficult. Sabou [23] proposes an evaluation strategy to be carried out over different stages, addressing issues like *extraction performance*, *ontology building support*, *domain coverage* and *fitness for the task at hand*. Therefore, the well-established metrics *recall* and *precision* are employed, and from them, new derived metrics like *Lexical Overlap* or *Ontological Improvement* are proposed to operate on the ontological level. Still, many of the evaluation stages rely on a manual inspection or consultation of domain experts.

As we are evaluating triples against a gold standard, we decided to use only the classic metrics *recall* and *precision* which are given below, measuring the system's performance on the 3 test corpora which were not used for benchmark creation.

$\mathbf{T}_s$ reflects the set of triples for a given sample, while $\mathbf{GS}$ denotes the set of triples contained in the benchmark.

$$recall = \frac{|\mathbf{T}_s \cap \mathbf{GS}|}{|\mathbf{GS}|} \tag{3}$$

$$precision = \frac{|\mathbf{T}_s \cap \mathbf{GS}|}{|\mathbf{T}_s \cup \mathbf{GS}|} \tag{4}$$

Table 7 and Table 8 display the evaluation results for the 3 test corpora with different samples, as described in Sect. 4.2.

With respect to the benchmark, recall improves with a larger sample, but precision remains low around 10%. However, an inspection of the false positives showed that some triples were in fact appropriate [11], although they were not contained in the gold standard. Clearly, those cases affect particularly the precision score of the evaluation in a negative manner. In order to account for this situation, Kavalec and Svátek [25] have proposed an additional notion of *posterior precision*, to be assessed after inspection and

---

[10] The selectional preferences for verb-OBJ (range) and verb-SUBJ (domain), intuitively.

[11] After re-consultation of the annotators.

Table 7. Performance for samples generated with setup I from 3 different test-corpora

Corpus		# of Evaluated Triples	Recall	Precision				
				a priori		a posteriori		
				percentage	true positives	percentage	true positives	
# of	1	38	15.8%	8.6%	6	20.0%	14	
Triples	2	38	23.7%	13.4%	9	23.9%	16	
= |GS|	3	38	15.8%	8.6%	6	20.0%	14	
	Average over Samples		18.4%	10.2%		21.3%		
# of	1	95	39.5%	12.7%	15	24.6%	29	
Triples	2	84	34.2%	11.9%	13	23.9%	26	
= ALL	3	92	34.2%	11.1%	13	23.1%	27	
	Average over Samples		36.0%	11.9%		23.9%		

Table 8. Performance for samples generated with setup II from 3 different test-corpora

Corpus		# of Evaluated Triples	Recall	Precision				
				a priori		a posteriori		
				percentage	true positives	percentage	true positives	
# of	1	38	13.2%	7.0%	5	18.3%	13	
Triples	2	38	21.1%	11.8%	8	19.1%	13	
= |GS|	3	38	15.8%	8.6%	6	15.7%	11	
	Average over Samples		16.7%	9.1%		17.7%		
# of	1	148	44.7%	10.1%	17	20.7%	35	
Triples	2	136	42.1%	10.1%	16	20.3%	32	
= ALL	3	146	42.1%	9.5%	16	19.6%	33	
	Average over Samples		43.0%	9.9%		20.2%		

re-consultation of a domain expert or ontology engineer. Following their line of research, triples from the set of false positives which were found to be relevant, were treated as such, and a recomputation of precision (*a posteriori*) was performed, leading to a significant improvement of the value reported as *a priori* precision. The difference between *prior precision* and *posterior precision* would be a possible way of measuring the amount of learning.

5   Conclusions and Future Work

In this paper we described an approach for extracting and evaluating highly relevant relations holding between ontology classes in the football domain. In contrast to the majority of the work carried out in ontology learning, we are concerned with the extraction of domain specific verbal relations other than *is-a*. As our approach is directed towards ontology extension, we rely on an already existing ontology for some domain, in order to map highly relevant headnouns to concept labels. Given that, we claim our approach to be robust and easily adjustable to different domains, as the main steps rely on statistical processing of formerly extracted linguistic information.

We are not (yet) concerned with clustering of extracted relations, which would bring together different predicates as synonyms for a single more abstract relation label. In this way, the relation will be defined as an abstraction over individual English or German verb forms (i.e. predicates).

The *RelExt*-system is implemented as a modular system, which contributes methods for the extraction procedure, the various statistical filtering steps and the triple generation.

Its modular structure allows for easy integration of new methods and composition of processing steps at will, which we think is very beneficial for tuning efforts.

The evaluation procedure we pursued supplies us with insights into overall system performance, while the different setups allow conclusions to be drawn about the performance of subcomponents of the system. As one further step, we propose the incremental extension of the gold standard.

An aspect that certainly has to be focussed on is the generation of higher quality triples, in order to improve precision without lowering recall. This can be done by taking external linguistic resources into account, i.e. interfacing with WordNet [26] or accessing information from subcategorization frame lexica for a given verb.

As SCHUG (the linguistic analysis) introduces a lot of ambiguity in grammatical function assginment (i.e. specifying multiple subjects and/or direct objects per clause), the work carried out here has a very nice side effect. The computed *selectional preferences* can be used in order to support SCHUG when it cannot decide wich grammatical function to assign to a given phrase, which will in turn produce linguistic annotations of higher quality.

Acknowledgements

This research has been supported by BMB+F (German Ministry of Education and Research) grant 01 IMD01 A for the SmartWeb project.

References

1. Ding, L., Finin, T., Joshi, A., Pan, R., Cost, R.S., Peng, Y., Reddivari, P., Doshi, V.C., Sachs, J.: Swoogle: A Search and Metadata Engine for the Semantic Web. In: Proceedings of the Thirteenth ACM Conference on Information and Knowledge Management, ACM Press (2004)
2. Gangemi, A., Guarino, N., Oltramari, A., Schneider, L.: Sweetening ontologies with dolce. In: Proceedings of EKAW 2002, Siguenza, Spain (2002)
3. Niles, I., Pease, A.: Towards a standard upper ontology. In: FOIS '01: Proceedings of the international conference on Formal Ontology in Information Systems, ACM Press (2001) 2–9
4. Gomez-Perez, A., Manzano-Macho, D.: A survey of ontology learning methods and techniques. deliverable 1.5, ontoweb project (2003)
5. Rindflesch, T., Tanabe, L., Weinstein, J., Hunter, L.: Edgar: Extraction of drugs, genes, and relations from biomedical literature. In: Pacific Symposium on Biocomputing. (2000)
6. Pustejovsky, J., Castano, J., Zhang, J., Cochran, B., Kotecki, M.: Robust relational parsing over biomedical literature: Extracting inhibit relations. In: Pacific Symposium on Biocomputing. (2002)
7. Vintar, S., Todorovski, L., Sonntag, D., Buitelaar, P.: Evaluating context features for medical relation mining. In: ECML/PKDD Workshop on Data Mining and Text Mining for Bioinformatics. (2003)
8. Buitelaar, P., Olejnik, D., Sintek, M.: A protégé plug-in for ontology extraction from text based on linguistic analysis. In: Proceedings of the 1st European Semantic Web Symposium (ESWS). (2004)

9. Ciramita, M., Gangemi, A., Ratsch, E., Saric, J., Rojas, I.: Unsupervised learning of semantic relations between concepts of a molecular biology ontology. In: Proceedings of the 19th International Joint Conference on Artificial Intelligence. (2005) accepted for publication.
10. Gamallo, P., Gonzalez, M., Agustini, A., Lopes, G., de Lima, V.S.: Mapping syntactic dependencies onto semantic relations. In: Proceedings of the ECAI Workshop on Machine Learning and Natural Language Processing for Ontology Engineering. (2002)
11. Resnik, P.: Selection and information: A class-based approach to lexical relationships (1993)
12. Faure, D., Nedellec, C.: A corpus-based conceptual clustering method for verb frames and ontology. In Velardi, P., ed.: Proceedings of the LREC Workshop on Adapting lexical and corpus resources to sublanguages and applications. (1998) 5–12
13. Maedche, A., Staab, S.: Discovering conceptual relations from text. In Horn, W., ed.: Proceedings of the 14th European Conference on Artificial Intellignece (ECAI'2000). (2000)
14. Reinberger, M.L., Spyns, P.: Discovering knowledge in texts for the learning of DOGMA-inspired ontologies. In: Proceedings of the ECAI 2004 Workshop on Ontology Learning and Population. (2004) 19–24
15. Sabou, M.: Extracting ontologies from software documentation: a semi-automatic method and its evaluation. In: Proceedings of the ECAI-2004 Workshop on Ontology Learning and Population (ECAI-OLP). (2004)
16. Declerck, T.: A set of tools for integrating linguistic and non-linguistic information. In: Proceedings of SAAKM (ECAI Workshop). (2002)
17. Buitelaar, P., Declerck, T., Sacaleanu, B., Vintar, S., Raileanu, D., Crispi, C.: A multi-layered, xml-based approach to the integration of linguistic and semantic annotations. In: Proceedings of EACL 2003 Workshop on Language Technology and the Semantic Web, Budapest, Hungary (2003)
18. Manning, C.D., Schütze, H.: Foundations of statistical natural language processing. MIT Press (1999)
19. Faure, D., N'edellec, C.: Asium: Learning subcategorization frames and restrictions of selection. In Kodratoff, Y., ed.: 10th Conference on Machine Learning (ECML 98) – Workshop on Text Mining. (1998)
20. Maedche, A., Staab, S.: Measuring similarity between ontologies. In: EKAW '02: Proceedings of the 13th International Conference on Knowledge Engineering and Knowledge Management. Ontologies and the Semantic Web, Springer-Verlag (2002) 251–263
21. Carletta, J.: Assessing agreement on classification tasks: the kappa statistic. Comput. Linguist. **22** (1996) 249–254
22. Poesio, M., Vieira, R.: A corpus-based investigation of definite description use. Comput. Linguist. **24** (1998) 183–216
23. Sabou M., Wroe C., G.C., G., M.: Learning domain ontologies for web service descriptions: an experiment in bioinformatics. In: Proceeedings of the 14th International World Wide Web Conference WWW2005. (2005)
24. Spyns, P., Reinberger, M.L.: Evaluating ontology triples generated automatically from texts. In: Proceedings of the second European Conference on the Semantic Web, LNCS, Springer Verlag (2005)
25. Kavalec, M., Svaték, V.: A study on automated relation labelling in ontology learning. In Buitelaar, P., Cimiano, P., Magnini, B., eds.: Ontology Learning from Text: Methods, Evaluation and Applications. IOS Press (2005) 44–58
26. Fellbaum, C.: WordNet: An Electronic Lexical Database. MIT Press (1998)

Containment and Minimization of RDF/S Query Patterns

Giorgos Serfiotis[1,2], Ioanna Koffina[1,2], Vassilis Christophides[1,2], and Val Tannen[3]

[1] Institute of Computer Science, Foundation for Research and Technology – Hellas,
P.O. Box 1385, 71110 Heraklio, Greece
{koffina, christop}@ics.forth.gr
[2] Department of Computer Science, University of Crete,
P.O. Box 2208, 71110 Heraklio, Greece
serfioti@csd.uoc.gr
[3] Department of Computer and Information Science, University of Pennsylvania,
200 South 33rd Street, Philadelphia, Pennsylvania
val@cis.upenn.edu

Abstract. Semantic query optimization (SQO) has been proved to be quite useful in various applications (e.g., data integration, graphical query generators, caching, etc.) and has been extensively studied for relational, deductive, object, and XML databases. However, less attention to SQO has been devoted in the context of the Semantic Web. In this paper, we present sound and complete algorithms for the containment and minimization of RDF/S query patterns. More precisely, we consider two widely used RDF/S query fragments supporting pattern matching at the data, but also, at the schema level. To this end, we advocate a logic framework for capturing the RDF/S data model and semantics and we employ well-established techniques proposed in the relational context, in particular, the Chase and Backchase algorithms.

1 Introduction

Semantic query optimization (SQO) is the process of increasing the potential for an efficient evaluation of queries by using intentional information about the contents of a database. The essential idea is to use knowledge (e.g., under the form of integrity constraints) about the data to reformulate a query into a more efficient but semantically equivalent one. SQO has been proved to be quite useful in various applications. For example, when integrating information sources, the composition of user queries with publishing views that establish mappings between data sources, often results in redundant queries. Moreover, when queries are produced automatically – e.g., from graphical query generators in portals – and not from humans, they are very likely to be redundant. Redundancy can be eliminated using query minimization techniques. Finally, in order to exploit cached query results we need to be able to identify query containment. In this way queries can be (partially or completely) answered, thus, avoiding costly access to remote data sources.

SQO has been extensively studied in the context of relational [19], deductive [4][6][16], object [11] [8] and, recently, XML databases [9][10][18][24]. However, less attention to SQO has been devoted in the context of the Semantic Web. In [1] the authors propose a graphical interface that produces on-the-fly minimal RQL queries while the user navigates through an RDF/S schema. The key idea to query

Y. Gil et al. (Eds.): ISWC 2005, LNCS 3729, pp. 607 – 623, 2005.
© Springer-Verlag Berlin Heidelberg 2005

minimization is that when navigating through hierarchies of classes (properties), the path expressions get refined by taking into account the subclasses (subproperties) currently visited. In [23] the author proposes a graph-based approach for identifying RDF/S queries that are subsumed by (i.e., contained in) queries whose results are already cached. If a query A, issued on an RDF/S description base DB, subsumes a query B, then query B needs not be executed on DB; it can be instead evaluated on the cached results of query A. However, both approaches consider only a limited fragment of RDF/S queries featuring pattern matching against data graphs (i.e., similar to relational queries).

In this paper, we study SQO for more expressive fragments of patterns supported by declarative RDF/S query languages. More precisely, we consider two fragments of increasing expressiveness allowing complex pattern matching at the data, but also, at the schema level. The main contribution of this work is to present sound and complete algorithms for both checking the containment of RDF/S query fragments and minimizing them, which generalize previous results [9] for unions of conjunctive queries under disjunctive embedded dependencies. The rest of the paper is organized as follows: Section 2 introduces the logic framework that allows us to reduce the containment and minimization problems to the relational equivalent. Section 3 presents the two expressive RDF/S query fragments for which our algorithms apply. Section 4 and 5 describe the proposed containment and minimization algorithms, which are based on the Chase and Backchase (C&B) algorithms as were introduced in [8] and extended in [9]. Our conclusions, as well as some challenges for future work, are given in Section 6.

2   From RDF/S to SWLF

In this section we will present our logic framework, termed *Semantic Web Logic Framework* (SWLF), consisting of six first-order logic (FOL) predicates for capturing RDF/S schemas and description bases, as well, as a set of appropriate FOL constraints under the form of *disjunctive embedded dependencies* (DEDs).

Table 1. FOL predicates for RDF/S

Predicate	Type
CLASS	Set <name: Class>
PROP	Set <domain: Class, name: Property, range: Class>
C_SUB	Set <subC: Class, class: Class>
P_SUB	Set <subP: Property, prop: Property>
C_EXT	Set <class: Class, inst: Resource>
P_EXT	Set <subject: Resource, prop: Property, object: Resource>

Definition 1. RDF/S schemas and description bases are represented by a set of FOL predicates (relations), namely $R=\{CLASS, PROP, C\_SUB, P\_SUB, C\_EXT, P\_EXT\}$. Each predicate R_i has a set of attributes A_i, as shown in **Table 1**, whose domains have one of the following types T_i in T, $T=\{Class, Property, Resource\}$.

The meaning of these predicates is given below:

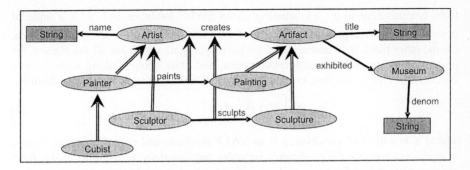

Fig. 1. An RDF/S schema

- CLASS(c) iff *c* is a class.
- PROP(a, p, b) iff *p* is a property having class *a* as domain and class *b* as range.
- C_SUB(c, a) iff class *c* is a (direct or not) subclass of class *a*.
- P_SUB(q, p) iff property *q* is a (direct or not) subproperty of property *p*.
- C_EXT(c, x) iff resource *x* is in the proper extent – is a direct instance – of class *c*.
- P_EXT(x, p, y) iff the ordered pair (*x*, *y*) (formed from resources *x*, *y*) is in the proper extent – is a direct instance – of property *p*.

The translation of a specific RDF/S schema in SWLF is straightforward: the predicates CLASS, PROP, C_SUB and P_SUB get instantiated for every class, property and direct subclass/subproperty relationship. For example, some of the facts we generate for the RDF/S schema of **Fig. 1** are:

```
CLASS(Artist), PROP(Artist,creates,Artifact), C_SUB(Painter,Artist),
P_SUB(paints,creates), P_SUB(sculpts,creates)
```

Definition 2. Disjunctive embedded dependencies (DEDs) are FOL formulas of the following general form:

$$\forall \overline{x} \left[\varphi(\overline{x}) \rightarrow \bigvee_{i=1}^{l} \exists \overline{y_i} \overline{\varphi_i'}(\overline{x}, \overline{y_i}) \right]$$

where $\overline{x}$, $\overline{y_i}$ are tuples of variables and φ, φ_i' are conjunctions of relational atoms of the form $R(\omega_1, ..., \omega_l)$ and equality atoms of the form $\omega = \omega'$, where $\omega_1, ..., \omega_l, \omega, \omega'$ are variables or constants; φ may be the empty conjunction.

In particular, in order to capture the intended meaning of an RDF/S schema two types of constraints are considered in SWLF; for each predicate, many constraints existentially quantifying its variables and one constraint universally quantifying them. The constraints of the former type provide partial (incomplete) knowledge of the RDF/S schema and have the general form:

$$\exists \overline{y} \overline{\varphi'}(\overline{y}) \tag{1}$$

where $\overline{y}$ is a tuple of variables and φ' is a conjunction of one SWLF predicate and equalities between the variables of one of the SWLF predicates and constants. This form is equivalent to $\varphi'(\bar{y})$, where φ' is an SWLF predicate and $\bar{y}$ is a tuple of constants, and corresponds to the form of the facts generated for an RDF/S schema. On the other hand, the constraints of the latter type state which are all the classes, the properties and the subsumption relationships, and, thus, provide along with those of the previous type a complete knowledge of the RDF/S schema. Their general form is:

$$\forall \bar{x} \left[\varphi(\bar{x}) \rightarrow \bigvee_{i=1}^{l} \varphi_i'(\bar{x}) \right] \tag{2}$$

where $\bar{x}$ is a tuple of variables, φ is an SWLF predicate and each φ_i' is a conjunction of equalities between the predicate's variables and constants. Constraints of this form capture also the reflexivity and transitivity of class and property subsumption relationships. **Table 2** shows the constraints of form (2) introduced for the P_SUB predicate given the RDF/S schema of **Fig. 1**.

Table 2. Example of constraints introduced for P_SUB given the RDF/S schema of **Fig. 1**

Constraint universally quantifying P_SUB's variables
$\forall$subP $\forall$prop (P_SUB(subP, prop) $\rightarrow$ (subP="creates" $\wedge$ prop="creates") $\vee$ (subP="paints" $\wedge$ prop="creates") $\vee$ (subP="paints" $\wedge$ prop="paints") $\vee$ (subP="sculpts" $\wedge$ prop="creates") $\vee$ (subP="sculpts" $\wedge$ prop="sculpts"))

In order to capture the semantics of the RDF/S data model, i.e., of every RDF/S schema and description base, we consider a set of constraints, called δ_{Mod}.

Definition 3. δ_{Mod} is the set of the following disjunction-free DEDs:

- Every resource in the extent of a class implies the existence of the corresponding class: $\forall c,x$ C_EXT(c,x) $\rightarrow$ CLASS(c)
- The subclass relationship relates classes: $\forall c,d$ C_SUB(c,d) $\rightarrow$ CLASS(c) $\wedge$ CLASS(d)
- The domain and range of every property is a class: $\forall a,p,b$ PROP(a,p,b) $\rightarrow$ CLASS(a) $\wedge$ CLASS(b)
- The domain and range of every property is unique: $\forall a,p,b,c,q$ d PROP(a,p,b) $\wedge$ PROP(c,q,d) $\wedge$ p=q $\rightarrow$ a=c $\wedge$ b=d
- Every statement in the extent of a property implies the existence of the corresponding property: $\forall x,p,y$ P_EXT(x,p,y) $\rightarrow$ $\exists c,d$ PROP(c,p,d)
- The subproperty relationship relates properties: $\forall p,q$ P_SUB(p,q) $\rightarrow$ $\exists a,b,c,d$ PROP(a,p,b) $\wedge$ PROP(c,q,d)
- Every class is a subclass of itself: $\forall c$ CLASS(c) $\rightarrow$ C_SUB(c,c)
- The subclass relationship is transitive: $\forall a,c,e$ C_SUB(e,c) $\wedge$ C_SUB(c,a) $\rightarrow$ C_SUB(e,a)
- Every property is a subproperty of itself: $\forall c,p,d$ PROP(c,p,d) $\rightarrow$ P_SUB(p,p)
- The subproperty relationship is transitive: $\forall p,q,r$ P_SUB(p,q) $\wedge$ P_SUB(q,r) $\rightarrow$ P_SUB(p,r)
- A class is both subclass and superclass of itself: $\forall a,c$ C_SUB(a,c) $\wedge$ C_SUB(c,a) $\rightarrow$ a=c

- A property is both subproperty and superproperty of itself : $\forall p,q \; P\_SUB(p,q) \wedge P\_SUB(q,p) \rightarrow p=q$
- In a valid RDF description schema the domain (range) of every subproperty is subsumed by the domain (range) of its superproperty: $\forall a,p,b,c,q,d \; P\_SUB(q,p) \wedge PROP(a,p,b) \wedge PROP(c,q,d) \rightarrow C\_SUB(c,a) \wedge C\_SUB(d,b)$
- In a valid RDF description base the subject/object resources in every statement are (direct or indirect) instances of the property's domain/range classes: $\forall a,p,b,x,y \; PROP(a,p,b) \wedge P\_EXT(x,p,y) \rightarrow \exists c,d \; C\_SUB(c,a) \wedge C\_SUB(d,b) \wedge C\_EXT(c,x) \wedge C\_EXT(d,y)$

It should be stressed that, compared to the RDF/S Semantics given in [14], SWLF *(i)* distinguishes between the different RDF/S abstraction layers (data, schema and metaschema), *(ii)* enforces that a property's domain and range are always defined and unique, *(iii)* does not allow the existence of cycles in the class and property hierarchies, *(iv)* states that the set inclusion of the domain and range are preserved for specialized properties and *(v)* demands that in each statement the subject and object resources are (direct or not) instances of the domain and range classes of the property, respectively. These additional constraints are employed to reason over queries (and not on data as in [14]), clarify the semantics of classes and properties and decrease the complexity of RDF/S query containment and minimization.

In this context, we consider the following two additional sets of constraints capturing (partially or completely) the semantics of a particular RDF/S schema:

Definition 4. δ_{RDF} is the set of disjunction-free DEDs consisting of δ_{Mod} and the constraints of form (1).

Definition 5. Δ_{RDF} is the set of DEDs consisting of δ_{Mod} and the constraints of forms (1) and (2).

Having in mind the FOL predicates R and the aforementioned sets of constraints, the formal definitions of an RDF/S *description base* and a *description schema* are:

Definition 6. An RDF/S (description) schema DS in SWLF is an instantiation of the relational schema $R_S=\{CLASS, PROP, C\_SUB, P\_SUB\}$ satisfying δ_{Mod}.

Definition 7. An RDF/S description base DB in SWLF given a DS is an instantiation of the relational schema $R_B=\{C\_EXT, P\_EXT\}$ satisfying δ_{Mod}.

3   RDF/S Query Languages' Fragments

All RDF/S query languages provide pattern matching facilities against schema and/or data graphs. The main difference in their expressiveness is related to their ability to support either exact or extended pattern matching by taking into account the subsumption relationship of classes and properties defined in an RDF/S schema. When only exact matching is supported, patterns of schema-agnostic RDF/S query languages (e.g., SPARQL [21]) can be divided into two main fragments: The first includes patterns for pure data matching given as input the schema classes and properties (i.e., as in relational queries), while the latter includes patterns that

Table 3. RDF/S query patterns categorization

		Property Patterns	Class Patterns
RQL_{UCQ}		{X; $C}@P{Y; $D}	$C{X; $D}
		{$C}@P{$D}	$C{$D}
		{X}@P{Y}	$C{X}
		{X}^p{Y}	^c{X}
	RQL_{CORE}	{X}p{Y}	c{X}
		{X; c}p{Y; d}	c{X; d}

arbitrary mix schema and data querying. When both exact and extended matching is supported, patterns of schema-aware RDF/S query languages (e.g., RQL [15]) can be similarly divided into the previous two fragments while the latter also includes patterns for exact matching of schema and data graphs.

Table 3 presents the basic RDF/S class and property patterns of RQL (capital letters denote variables, and small letters denote constants), as well as introduces the fragments that these patterns belong to. With the exception of the RQL distinction between exact (denoted with '^') and extended pattern matching for class (^c{X} and c{X}) and property ({X}^p{Y} and {X}p{Y}) instances, all the other patterns are encountered in the majority of the RDF/S query languages. In this context, the SQO algorithms presented in this paper for the two most expressive previous RQL fragments [12] can be naturally applied to other RDF/S query languages as long as the appropriate translations of their patterns to SWLF are provided.

In particular, in this paper we focus on unions of RQL conjunctive queries, called RQL_{UCQ}, that are defined analogously to unions of relational conjunctive queries; the only difference lies to the fact that RQL class/property patterns are used instead of simple relational predicates. Indeed, according to the declarative semantics given in [15], RQL patterns have the same meaning as conjunctions of relational atoms.

Definition 8. An RQL conjunctive query is a FOL formula of the following form:

$$ans(\overline{u}) : - ..., E_i(\overline{u_i}),...,u_m = u_n$$

where $\overline{u}$ is a tuple of variables or constants, $E_i(\overline{u_i}$)'s are class/property patterns (see **Table 3**) and $u_m=u_n$'s are equalities between variables and/or constants. Each $\overline{u_i}$ involves the variables X_i, C_i, @P_i, Y_i, D_i – where @P_i is a property variable, C_i and D_i are class variables, X_i and Y_i are resource variables – or a subset of them.

Note that RQL conjunctive queries must be *safe*, i.e., their variables must be range restricted as for relational queries [2]. By extending the above formalism, we get the following definition.

Definition 9. RQL_{UCQ} queries have the form: $\bigcup_k Q_k$

where Q_k's are RQL conjunctive queries whose heads have the same type.

Definition 10. RQL_{CORE} is a subset of RQL_{UCQ} including patterns for pure data matching (see **Table 3**).

The complete list of the property patterns for both RQL_{UCQ} and RQL_{CORE} fragments is given in the Appendix (class patterns are defined in a similar way). As we will see in the sequel, the gain from limiting the expressiveness of RQL_{UCQ} queries to RQL_{CORE} is double. First of all, the partial knowledge of the RDF/S schema offered from δ_{RDF} suffices to solve the containment and minimization problems for the RQL_{CORE} (i.e., we do not need complete schema information). Additionally, considering only the information provided from δ_{RDF} leads to lower execution costs of the containment, equivalence and minimization algorithms, which stems from the fact that the involved *chase* algorithm considers only disjunction-free constraints (see Section 4).

RQL_{UCQ} (RQL_{CORE}) queries can be translated into unions of relational conjunctive queries expressed in terms of SWLF (see Appendix for the complete list of property pattern translation). The translation is straightforward: given an RQL_{UCQ} (RQL_{CORE}) query, class/property patterns get substituted by the corresponding SWLF predicates.

Example 1. Take a look at the translation of the RQL_{UCQ} query[1] retrieving cubists who have painted artefacts that are exhibited.

```
SELECT      X
FROM        {X; Cubist}paints{Y}, {Y}exhibited
```

By replacing the constants found in the patterns with variables and adding the corresponding equalities we get:

```
SELECT      X
FROM        {X; $C}@P₁{Y}, {Y}@P₂
WHERE       $C=Cubist and @P₁=paints and @P₂=exhibited
```

Now, the query can be rewritten in SWLF as follows:

```
ans(X):- {X; $C}@P₁{Y}, {Y}@P₂, $C=Cubist, @P₁=paints,
@P₂=exhibited
```

The corresponding SWLF query is produced by employing P_SUB to navigate through the subproperties of *paints* and *exhibited*, P_EXT to retrieve the direct instances of these subproperties, C_SUB to retrieve *Cubist*'s subclasses and C_EXT to retrieve the direct instances of these subclasses. Finally, C_SUB and PROP are used to ensure that *Cubist* is a subclass of *paint*'s domain.

```
ans(x):- PROP(a,p₁,b), P_SUB(q₁,p₁), P_EXT(x,q₁,y), C_SUB(c,a),
C_SUB(e,c), C_EXT(e,x), P_SUB(q₂,p₂), P_EXT(y,q₂,z),
c="Cubist", p₁="paints", p₂="exhibited"
```

4   RQL Query Containment and Equivalence

For the RQL_{UCQ} and RQL_{CORE} fragments we define containment and equivalence as follows:

Definition 11. An RQL_{UCQ} (RQL_{CORE}) query Q_1 is contained in an RQL_{UCQ} (RQL_{CORE}) query Q_2 ($Q_1 \subseteq Q_2$) given an RDF description schema *DS* iff for every RDF

---

[1] For simplicity, in all RQL queries presented in this paper namespaces are disregarded.

description base *DB* conforming to *DS*, the result of Q_1 is contained in that of Q_2 ($\forall$DB Q₁(DB)⊆Q₂(DB)).

Definition 12. An RQL$_{UCQ}$ (RQL$_{CORE}$) query Q_1 is equivalent to an RQL$_{UCQ}$ (RQL$_{CORE}$) query Q_2 ($Q_1 \equiv Q_2$) given an RDF description schema *DS* iff for every RDF description base *DB* conforming to *DS*, the result of Q_1 is equivalent to that of Q_2 ($\forall$DB Q₁(DB)≡Q₂(DB)).

As stated previously, we reduce the RQL query containment and equivalence problems to the relational ones under constraints. In this section we introduce the *chase* algorithm and present how it can be employed in our RQL$_{UCQ}$ (RQL$_{CORE}$) containment and equivalence checking.

4.1 Chase Algorithm

The core chase consists of a sequential execution of a number of chase steps. For example, given the constraint $\forall x \forall y\ A(x, y) \rightarrow B(x)$ and the query Q(x) :- A(x, y), the chase step leads to query Q(x) :- A(x, y), B(x). When no more chase steps can apply the chase ends and the query outputted is called the *universal plan*.

Unfortunately, the chase with an arbitrary set of DEDs is not guaranteed to terminate. However, in [9] the authors introduced a syntactic restriction, namely *stratified-witness*, which ensures termination of the chase under a set of disjunction-free DEDs. When a set of DEDs respects stratified-witness, no sequence of chase steps can force the chase to diverge. Stratified-witness can be extended in order to handle constraints that use disjunction, too (see [22] for further details). The key idea lies on the splitting of disjunctive constraints into disjunction-free ones and checking whether one of the possible combinations of disjunction-free constraints leads to an endless execution of chase steps by checking them for stratified-witness.

In [7] the author proves soundness of the chase-based containment algorithm for conjunctive queries under a set of DEDs. In the sequel, we extend this algorithm to unions of conjunctive queries:

Theorem 1. Given two unions of conjunctive queries Q_1, Q_2 and a set D of DEDs, assume that the chase of Q_1 with D terminates rendering the universal plan U_1. Then, Q_1 is contained in Q_2 under D (Q₁⊆$_D$Q₂) iff[2] for every i there is a j such that U_{1i} is contained in Q_{2j}, i.e., there is a containment mapping from Q_{2j} into U_{1i}.

Moreover, it is obvious that two queries Q_1, Q_2 are equivalent under a set D of constraints iff Q₁⊆$_D$Q₂ and Q₂⊆$_D$Q₁. Therefore, at least one and at most two containment checks are needed in order to decide the equivalence of queries under constraints.

4.2 Checking Containment and Equivalence of RQL$_{CORE}$ Queries

The algorithm for checking whether an RQL$_{CORE}$ query is contained in another is based on Theorem 1. It takes as input the two SWLF queries and δ$_{RDF}$, which is a set

---

[2] In contrast to [7] and without loss of generality, after each chase step we check the query for inconsistencies, i.e. equalities between distinct constants.

of DEDs that behaves as if stratified-witness[3] was present and, therefore, ensures the termination of chase and, thus, soundness of the containment check.

Example 2. Assume that we want to check the containment of the query retrieving people having painted

```
SELECT      X
FROM        {X}paints
```

in the query returning all artists

```
SELECT      X
FROM        Artist{X}
```

The queries are translated, respectively, into SWLF as follows:

```
ans(x):-P_SUB(q,p),  P_EXT(x,q,y),  p="paints"
ans(x):-C_SUB(c,a),  C_EXT(c,x),  a="Artist"
```

By chasing the first query with the basic constraint $\forall p \forall q \; P\_SUB(q, p) \rightarrow \exists a_1 \exists a_2 \exists b_1 \exists b_2 \; PROP(a_2, q, b_2) \land PROP(a_1, p, b_1)$ we get the query[4]:

```
ans(x):-P_SUB(q,p), P_EXT(x,q,y), PROP(a₁,p,b₁), PROP(a₂,q,b₂),
p="paints"
```

The next chase step involves the first domain/range constraint:

```
ans(x):-P_SUB(q,p), P_EXT(x,q,y), PROP(a₁,p,b₁), PROP(a₂,q,b₂),
C_SUB(a₂,a₁), C_SUB(b₂,b₁),  p="paints"
```

The following one involves the second domain/range constraint:

```
ans(x):-P_SUB(q,p), P_EXT(x,q,y), PROP(a₁,p,b₁), PROP(a₂,q,b₂),
C_SUB(a₂,a₁),  C_SUB(b₂,b₁),  C_SUB(c,a₂),  C_SUB(d,b₂),
C_EXT(c,x),  C_EXT(d,y),  p="paints"
```

After a number of chase steps we reach the following (incomplete) universal plan:

```
ans(x):-P_SUB(q,p),  P_EXT(x,q,y),  PROP(a₁,p,b₁),  PROP(a₂,q,b₂),
C_SUB(a₂,a₁),  C_SUB(b₂,b₁),  C_SUB(c,a₂),  C_SUB(d,b₂),
C_EXT(c,x),  C_EXT(d,y),  C_SUB(c,a₁),  C_SUB(h,g),  C_SUB(c,g),
p="paints", a₁=h="Painter", b₁="Painting", g="Artist"
```

Since there is a containment mapping from the second input query to the chased query ($\{c \rightarrow c, a \rightarrow g, x \rightarrow x\}$), the first query is contained in the second one.

Using the same algorithm we can prove that the query of Example 1 is contained in the first query of Example 2. Having reduced the RQL_{CORE} containment problem to a relational one, the equivalence problem gets reduced to the relational one as well.

4.3 Checking Containment of RQL_{UCQ} Queries

The same algorithm can be used for checking containment between RQL_{UCQ} queries. It takes as input the two SWLF queries and the set of constraints Δ_{RDF}, which ensures the termination of chase and, thus, soundness of the containment check.

---

[3] δ_{RDF} (and Δ_{RDF}) is a set of DEDs not satisfying stratified-witness. However, it does not allow the introduction of an infinite number of fresh variables [22].

[4] The predicates triggering the chase step are underlined while the introduced ones are given in bold.

Example 3. Assume that we want to check the containment of the following query retrieving people who have painted artefacts that are exhibited somewhere

```
SELECT     X
FROM       {X}paints{Y}, {Y}exhibited
```

in the query returning people having exclusively painted (i.e., in the proper interpretation of *paints*) something

```
SELECT     X
FROM       {X}^paints
```

The input queries are translated respectively into SWLF as follows:

```
ans(x):-P_SUB(q₁,p₁), P_EXT(x,q₁,y), P_SUB(q₂,p₂),
P_EXT(y,q₂,z), p₁="paints", p₂="exhibited"
```

and

```
ans(x):-P_EXT(x,p,y), p="paints"
```

After a number of chase steps the first query reaches the (incomplete) universal plan[5]:

```
ans(x):- P_SUB(q₁,p₁), P_EXT(x,q₁,y), P_SUB(q₂,p₂),
P_EXT(y,q₂,z), p₁=q₁="paints", p₂=q₂="exhibited"
```

There is a containment mapping from the second input query to the chased query ($\{p \rightarrow q_1, x \rightarrow x, y \rightarrow y\}$). Therefore, the first query is contained in the second one.

As with RQL_{CORE}, the RQL_{UCQ} equivalence problem is also reduced to the relational one.

In the beginning of this section we have claimed that containment of RQL_{UCQ} queries can be checked in presence of Δ_{RDF}. It should be stressed that any restriction of Δ_{RDF}, either by employing δ_{RDF} or by considering the set of constraints that excludes from Δ_{RDF} the constraints of form (1), affects the soundness of the containment (see [22] for further details). The same stands for the minimization algorithm presented in the next section.

The complexities of both containment (equivalence) algorithms depend on the cost of the chase algorithm to reach the universal plan and the cost of the simple containment check at the end. In this context, the chase depends on the set of constraints considered (δ_{RDF} for RQL_{CORE} and Δ_{RDF} for RQL_{UCQ}) and on the size of the input queries (in presence or not of union). Note that the chase with disjunction-free constraints satisfying stratified-witness (or behaving as if satisfying it, like δ_{RDF}) is NP-complete [20].

5 RQL Query Minimization

In this section, we detail how we can minimize RQL_{UCQ} (RQL_{CORE}) queries using the *backchase* algorithm. Furthermore, we highlight how the produced minimal SWLF queries can be translated both to schema-aware RDF/S query languages, like RQL, and to schema-agnostic languages, like SPARQL.

Definition 13. Given an RDF description schema *DS* an RQL_{UCQ} (RQL_{CORE}) query *Q* gets minimized when replaced with a minimal equivalent query *SQ* ($\forall$DB $Q(DB) \equiv SQ(DB)$).

---

[5] If we applied all possible chase steps, the constraints would introduce union in the universal plan.

A *minimal* RQL$_{UCQ}$ (RQL$_{CORE}$) query uses fewer and/or simpler RQL patterns than the original query. The intuition is that a class pattern is simpler than a property one; a pattern involving proper interpretations (for RQL$_{UCQ}$) and/or fewer variables is simpler than one involving extended interpretations and/or more variables. The above hypotheses are made by taking into account that the evaluation of a simpler pattern is more efficient that the original one.

5.1 Backchase Algorithm

The core algorithm is the backchase, which, given a query's universal plan, checks all its subqueries for minimality and equivalence to the original query using chase. According to the following theorem introduced in [9] the backchase is guaranteed to find all minimal equivalent subqueries when the chase terminates and, thus, ensures completeness of the minimization algorithm.

Theorem 2 [9]. Given a union of conjunctive queries Q and a set C of DEDs, if the chase of Q with C terminates yielding the universal plan of U, all C-minimal reformulations of Q are subqueries of U.

5.2 Minimization of RQL$_{CORE}$ Queries Using Schema Knowledge

In order to minimize an RQL$_{CORE}$ query the universal plan of the original SWLF query and δ_{RDF} are given as input. Since the chase with δ_{RDF} terminates, the backchase always finds all minimal equivalents of an RQL$_{CORE}$ query.

Example 4. Assume the following query

```
SELECT      X
FROM        Cubist{X}, Painter{X}
```

which was introduced in Example 3. Its SWLF translation will chase to:

```
ans(x):-C_SUB(c₁,a₁), C_EXT(c₁,x), C_SUB(c₂,a₂), C_EXT(c₂,x),
C_SUB(e,d), a₁=d="Painter", a₂=e="Cubist"
```

If we examine its subquery retrieving the extended interpretation of *Cubist*

```
ans(x):-C_SUB(c,a), C_EXT(c,x), a="Cubist"
```

we will conclude that it is δ_{RDF}-minimal and δ_{RDF}-equivalent to the query given as input. Thus, this query will be produced by our minimization algorithm.

It is worth noticing that RQL$_{CORE}$ queries demonstrate a very interesting and useful feature: they have only one minimal equivalent! As we will explain in the next subsection, more than one minimal query can occur only by replacing extended interpretations with proper ones, which are not supported by RQL$_{CORE}$.

5.3 Minimization of RQL$_{UCQ}$ Queries Using Schema Knowledge

Similarly, minimization of RQL$_{UCQ}$ is always successful since the set of constraints employed in this case – Δ_{RDF} – guarantees termination.

Example 5. Assume the query of Example 4. If considered as an RQL$_{UCQ}$ query, it will minimize to the query retrieving the proper interpretation of *Cubist*

```
ans(x):-C_EXT(c,x), c="Cubist"
```

The difference in the minimal query is due to the fact that the backchase has the additional knowledge that *Cubist* has no subclass than itself. As we will see in the sequel, unlike RQL_{CORE}, RQL_{UCQ} queries may have more than one minimal equivalent.

Example 6. Assume the query

```
SELECT     $A, X
FROM       $A{X; Artist}
```

and its SWLF translation

```
ans(a,x):-C_SUB(c,a), C_SUB(e,c), C_EXT(e,x), c="Artist"
```

If we execute the C&B algorithms, we will find three (!) minimal equivalent queries:

(1st) `ans(a,x):-C_SUB(e,a), C_EXT(e,x), a="Artist"`
(2nd) `ans(a,x):-C_EXT(a,x), a="Artist"`
  ∪ `ans(a,x):-C_EXT(e,x), a="Artist", e="Sculptor"`
  ∪ `ans(a,x):-C_SUB(e,c), C_EXT(e,x), a="Artist", c="Painter"`
(3rd) `ans(a, x):- C_EXT(a, x), a="Artist"`
  ∪ `ans(a, x):-C_EXT(e, x), a="Artist", e="Sculptor"`
  ∪ `ans(a, x):-C_EXT(e, x), a="Artist", e="Painter"`
  ∪ `ans(a, x):-C_EXT(e, x), a="Artist", e="Cubist"`

The most interesting minimal queries are the first and third ones. In the first one redundancy has been removed without resolving the navigational part occurring from traversing the subclass hierarchy of *Artist*; this is why the extended interpretation of *Artist* is used. On the contrary, in the third minimal query schema information has been completely unfolded, introducing a union involving only the proper interpretations of *Artist*'s subclasses. When the former will be executed against an RDF/S store, it will still require schema navigation, while the latter contains all necessary schema information to retrieve the resources and, thus, it can be used by schema-agnostic languages. The second query lies somewhere in the middle; since both proper and extended interpretations are used, a part of the schema information has been unfolded, while some other has not. This form seems useful when the results of some of the constituent conjunctive queries are already cached.

In general, the number of minimal queries depends on the constraints considered, i.e., the size of the RDF/S schema, and the query given as input. As they grow, the number of minimal equivalents considerably increases. Every RQL_{UCQ} query has one minimal equivalent query where schema information is completely unfolded. This means that if the original query does not involve pattern matching at the data level, minimization practically answers the original query; the result is a constant query, i.e., a query were only equalities appear in the body. Apart from it, there usually exists one minimal query where the unfolding has not introduced union and several ones where partial unfolding has taken place.

5.4 Minimization of RQL_{UCQ} Queries by Ignoring Schema Knowledge

Our minimization technique can, also, be used for minimizing RQL patterns in their general form without taking into consideration specific RDF/S schemas [22]; therefore the chase in this case considers only δ_{Mod}.

Example 7. Assume the RQL$_{UCQ}$ query

```
ans(X, @P, Y):-{X; $C}@P{Y; $D}, cond(X, @P, Y)
```

involving the pattern we want to simplify and a dummy predicate *cond* stating the conditioned variables. The equivalent SWLF query is:

```
ans(x,p,y):-PROP(a,p,b), P_SUB(q,p), P_EXT(x,q,y),
C_SUB(c,a), C_SUB(d,b), C_EXT(c,x), C_EXT(d,y), cond(x,p,y)
```

If we inspect the universal plan of the query above during backchase, we will reach the subquery

```
ans(x,p,y):- P_SUB(q,p), P_EXT(x,q,y), cond(x,p,y)
```

which is both δ_{Mod}-minimal and δ_{Mod}-equivalent. Interestingly, it corresponds to the RQL$_{UCQ}$ query

```
ans(X, @P, Y):-{X}@P{Y}, cond(X, @P, Y)
```

Thus, the pattern *{X; $C}@P{Y; $D}* gets simplified to pattern *{X}@P{Y}* when only variables *X*, *@P*, *Y* are either conditioned or projected.

5.5 Backward Translation

As a matter of fact, in some cases we would like to restore the initial form (i.e., RQL$_{UCQ}$ or RQL$_{CORE}$) of a minimal query expressed in terms of SWLF. In the case of RQL$_{CORE}$ the backward translation is simple since only two RQL patterns, in particular *$C{X}* and *{X}@P{Y}*, may appear in the body of an RQL$_{CORE}$ minimal query. On the contrary, the translation becomes somehow more complicated for RQL$_{UCQ}$. Initially, we need to identify simple patterns in the SWLF query and combine them in order to form more complex ones. For example, the patterns *{X}@P*, *{$C}@P*, *$C{X}* correspond to the RQL pattern *{X; $C}@P*. For both RQL$_{UCQ}$ and RQL$_{CORE}$ minimal queries we have to reduce the number of employed variables and replace with constants as many variables as possible by using the equalities between the variables and constants. The following example illustrates the backward translation of an SWLF query into RQL$_{UCQ}$.

Example 8. In the first phase, the first minimal query of Example 6 translates into:

```
SELECT      $A, X
FROM        $A{X}
WHERE       $A=Artist
```

The second phase does not affect the query. Finally, by incorporating the only available equality in the FROM and SELECT clauses we get the RQL$_{UCQ}$ query

```
SELECT      Artist, X
FROM        Artist{X}
```

There are two tricky issues regarding the backward translation. Firstly, δ_{Mod} implies the equivalence of the predicates CLASS(c), C_SUB(c, c) and PROP(a, p, b), P_SUB(p, p). However, C_SUB(c, c) and P_SUB(p, p) result in redundant processing from an RDF/S query engine. Additionally, there is no RQL pattern corresponding to P_SUB(p, p). Thus, for these predicates we employ the translations of CLASS(c) – i.e., *$C* – and PROP(a, p, b) – i.e., *@P* -, respectively. Secondly, although they do not belong to the RQL$_{UCQ}$ fragment, the functions *domain(@P)* and *range(@P)* should be used for some SWLF queries due to the lack of an RQL pattern that would explicitly impose a restriction on a property's domain/range.

Example 9. Assume the RQL$_{UCQ}$ query of Example 6. The translation of the third minimal query into RQL and SPARQL[6] is given below.

SPARQL	RQL

SELECT ?C ?X
WHERE {{?X rdf:type :Artist . ?C rdf:type rdfs:Class .
    FILTER ?C = :Artist}
UNION
WHERE {{?X rdf:type :Sculptor . ?C rdf:type rdfs:Class .
    FILTER ?C = :Artist}
UNION
WHERE {{?X rdf:type :Painter . ?C rdf:type rdfs:Class .
    FILTER ?C = :Artist}
UNION
WHERE {{?X rdf:type :Cubist . ?C rdf:type rdfs:Class .
    FILTER ?C = :Artist}
	SELECT Artist, X
	FROM ^Artist{X}
	UNION
	SELECT Artist, X
	FROM ^Sculptor{X}
	UNION
	SELECT Artist, X
	FROM ^Painter{X}
	UNION
	SELECT Artist, X
	FROM ^Cubist{X}

The complexities of all the previous minimization algorithms depend on the backchase which, in turn, depends on the chase and the simple containment check – employed in order to reach the universal plan and check all its subqueries for minimality. The full optimization corresponds to an exponential number of NP-complete problems [20].

6 Summary and Future Work

In this paper we studied SQO of patterns supported by expressive RDF/S query languages, like RQL. Nevertheless, our results are valid for less expressive query languages, too. In order to deal with the SQO problem, we advocate a logic framework that enables to reduce the containment and minimization problems for unions of RDF/S conjunctive queries into relational equivalents.

In particular, the C&B algorithms, which we employed for RDF/S SQO, were initially developed in the context of conjunctive queries issued against relational schemas and matched (exclusively) against data by taking into account embedded dependencies [2] (for capturing key and foreign key constraints, as well as views). In our context, we consider unions of conjunctive queries for checking containment and minimization of queries built on expressive RDF/S query patterns asking for both schema and data matching over class (or property) subsumption hierarchies, and constraints under the form of disjunctive embedded dependencies. In contrast to relational queries, RDF/S queries usually contain a schema navigational part (e.g., in order to obtain the extended instances of a class, we need to consider the instances of all its direct and transitive subclasses). Therefore, the goal of RDF/S SQO is twofold: (a) the schema navigational part must be pruned as much as possible and (b) redundant data access should be eliminated as in the case of traditional SQO in relational databases. In conjunction with the aforementioned variation of SQO for the Semantic Web (SW) is the fact that the RQL$_{UCQ}$ minimization algorithm always generates a minimal query where no further schema querying is needed in order to answer it.

---

[6] For simplicity reasons namespaces' definitions are disregarded.

As a future work we are planning to study SQO of ontology constructs originating from more expressive SW languages, such as OWL's inverse properties as well as disjointness of class and property interpretations. Moreover, we plan to study SQO of richer RDF/S query fragments involving functions – like domain, range, subclassof, subpropertyof and aggregate ones – as well as nested queries.

Acknowledgements

We would like to thank Alin Deutsch and Nicola Onose for fruitful discussions on relational and XML SQO.

References

[1] Nikos Athanasis, Vassilis Christophides, and Dimitris Kotzinos. *Generating on the Fly Queries for the Semantic Web: The ICS-FORTH Graphical RQL Interface (GRQL)*. In Proceedings of the 3rd International Semantic Web Conference, Japan, 2004.

[2] Serge Abiteboul, Richard Hull, and Victor Vianu. *Foundations of Databases*. Addison-Wesley, 1995.

[3] Tim Bray, Eve Maler, Jean Paoli, and C. M. Sperberg-McQueen. *Extensible Markup Language (XML) 1.0*. W3C Recommendation, 6 October 2000.

[4] Francois Bry. *Query Answering in Information Systems with Integrity Constraints*. In Proceedings of the 1st Working Conference on Integrity and Internal Control in Information Systems: Increasing the confidence in Information Systems, Zurich, 1997.

[5] Tim Berners-Lee, James Hendler, and Ora Lassila. *The Semantic Web: A new form of Web content that is meaningful to computers will unleash a revolution of new possibilities*. Scientific American, 17 May 2001. Available at http://www.scientificamerican.com/print_version.cfm?articleID=00048144-10D2-1C70-84A9809EC588EF21

[6] Upen S. Chakravarthy, John Grant, Jack Minker. *Logic-Based Approach to Semantic Query Optimization*. ACM Transactions on Database Systems 15(2): 162-207 (1990)

[7] Alin Deutsch. *XML Query Reformulation over Mixed and Redundant Storage*. PhD Thesis, University of Pennsylvania, 2002.

[8] Alin Deutsch, Lucian Popa, and Val Tannen. *Physical Data Independence, Constraints and Optimization with Universal Plans*. In Proceedings of the 25th International Conference on Very Large Databases (VLDB), Edinburgh, 1999.

[9] Alin Deutcsh and Val Tannen. *Reformulation of XML Queries and Constraints*. In Proceedings of the 9th International Conference on Database Theory (ICDT), Italy, 2003.

[10] Xin Dong, Alon Y. Halevy, and Igor Tatarinov. *Containment of Nested XML Queries*. In Proceedings of 30th International Conference on Very Large Databases (VLDB), Toronto, Canada, 2004.

[11] John Grant, Jarek Gryz, Jack Minker, and Louiqa Raschid. *Semantic Query Optimization for Object-Databases*. In Proceedings of the 13th International Conference on Data Engineering, Birmingham U.K, 1997.

[12] Peter Haase, Jeen Broekstra, Andreas Eberhart, and Raphael Volz. *A Comparison of RDF Query Languages*. In Proceedings of the 3rd International Semantic Web Conference, Japan, 2004.

[13] Frank Van Harmelen and Deborah L. McGuinness. *OWL Web Ontology Language Overview*. W3C Recommendation, 10 February 2004.

[14] Patrick Hayes. *RDF Semantics*. W3C Recommendation, 10 February 2004.

[15] Gregory Karvounarakis, Aimilia Magkanaraki, Sofia Alexaki, Vassilis Christophides, Dimitris Plexousakis, Michel Scholl, and Karsten Tolle. *Querying the Semantic Web with RQL*. Computer Networks 42(5): 617-640, 2003.

[16] Alon Levy and Yehoshua Sagiv. Semantic Query Optimization in Datalog Programs. In Proceedings of the 8th International Conference on Data Engineering, Tempe, Arizona 1992.

[17] Frank Manola and Eric Miller. *RDF Primer*. W3C Recommendation, 10 February 2004.

[18] Gerome Miklau and Dan Suciu. *Containment and equivalence for an XPath fragment*. In Proceedings of the 21st ACM SIGMOD-SIGACT-SIGART symposium on Principles of database systems. Madison, Wisconsin, 2002.

[19] Hwee Hwa Pang, HongJun Lu, and Beng Chin Ooi. An Efficient Semantic Query Optimization Algorithm. In Proceedings of the 7th International Conference on Data Engineering, Japan, 1991.

[20] Nicola Onose. *Extensions of the Relational Chase*. Project Report of End of Studies, 2005.

[21] Eric Prud'hommeaux, and Andy Seaborne. *SPARQL Query Language for RDF*. W3C Working Draft, 19 April 2005.

[22] Giorgos Serfiotis. Optimizing and Reformulating RQL Queries on the Semantic Web. Master's Thesis, University of Crete, 2005.

[23] Heiner Stuckenschmidt. *Similarity-Based Query Caching*. In Proceedings of the 6th International Conference on Flexible Query Answering Systems, Lyon, 2004.

[24] Cong Yu and Lucian Popa. *Constraint-Based XML Query Rewriting For Data Integration*. In Proceedings of the ACM SIGMOD International Conference on Management of Data, Paris, 2004.

Appendix: Translations of $RQL_{UCQ}(RQL_{CORE})$ Patterns into SWLF

Property Pattern	Translation	Fragment
@P ^@P	PROP(a,p,b)	
{X; $C}@P{Y; $D} {$C}@P{Y; $D} {X; $C}@P{$D}	PROP(a,p,b), P_SUB(q,p), P_EXT(x,q,y), C_SUB(c,a), C_SUB(d,b), C_SUB(e,c), C_SUB(f,d), C_EXT(e,x), C_EXT(f,y)	RQL_{CORE} when $C=c$, $D=d$, @P=p
{X; $C}@P{Y} {$C}@P{Y} {X; $C}@P	PROP(a,p,b), P_SUB(q,p), P_EXT(x,q,y), C_SUB(c,a), C_SUB(e,c), C_EXT(e,x)	
{X}@P{Y; $D} {X}@P{$D} @P{Y; $D}	PROP(a,p,b), P_SUB(q,p), P_EXT(x,q,y), C_SUB(d,b), C_SUB(f,d), C_EXT(f,y)	RQL_{UCQ}
{X}@P{Y} {X}@P @P{Y}	P_SUB(q,p), P_EXT(x,q,y)	
{$C}@P{$D} {$C}^@P{$D}	PROP(a,p,b), C_SUB(c,a), C_SUB(d,b)	
{$C}@P {$C}^@P	PROP(a,p,b), C_SUB(c,a)	
@P{$D} ^@P{$D}	PROP(a,p,b), C_SUB(d,b)	
{X; ^$C}@P{Y; ^$D}	PROP(a,p,b), P_SUB(q,p), P_EXT(x,q,y), C_SUB(c,a), C_SUB(d,b), C_EXT(c,x), C_EXT(d,y)	
{X; ^$C}@P{Y} {X; ^$C}@P	PROP(a,p,b), P_SUB(q,p), P_EXT(x,q,y), C_SUB(c,a), C_EXT(c,x)	
{X}@P{Y; ^$D} @P{Y; ^$D}	PROP(a,p,b), P_SUB(q,p), P_EXT(x,q,y), C_SUB(d,b), C_EXT(d,y)	RQL_{UCQ}
{X; $C}@P{Y; ^$D} {$C}@P{Y; ^$D}	PROP(a,p,b), P_SUB(q,p), P_EXT(x,q,y), C_SUB(c,a), C_SUB(d,b), C_SUB(e,c), C_EXT(e,x), C_EXT(d,y)	
{X; ^$C}@P{Y; $D} {X; ^$C}@P{$D}	PROP(a,p,b), P_SUB(q,p), P_EXT(x,q,y), C_SUB(c,a), C_SUB(d,b), C_SUB(f,d), C_EXT(c,x), C_EXT(f,y)	

{X; ^$C}^@P{Y; ^$D}	PROP(a,p,b), P_EXT(x,p,y), C_SUB(c,a), C_SUB(d,b), C_EXT(c,x), C_EXT(d,y)	
{X; ^$C}^@P{Y} {X; ^$C}^@P	PROP(a,p,b), P_EXT(x,p,y), C_SUB(c,a), C_EXT(c,x)	
{X}^@P{Y; ^$D} ^@P{Y; ^$D}	PROP(a,p,b), P_EXT(x,p,y), C_SUB(d,b), C_EXT(d,y)	
{X; $C}^@P{Y; ^$D} {$C}^@P{Y; ^$D}	PROP(a,p,b), P_EXT(x,p,y), C_SUB(c,a), C_SUB(d,b), C_SUB(e,c), C_EXT(e,x), C_EXT(d,y)	
{X; ^$C}^@P{Y; $D} {X; ^$C}^@P{$D}	PROP(a,p,b), P_EXT(x,p,y), C_SUB(c,a), C_SUB(d,b), C_SUB(f,d), C_EXT(c,x), C_EXT(f,y)	
{X; $C}^@P{Y; $D} {$C}^@P{Y; $D} {X; $C}^@P{$D}	PROP(a,p,b), P_EXT(x,p,y), C_SUB(c,a), C_SUB(d,b), C_SUB(e,c), C_SUB(f,d), C_EXT(e,x), C_EXT(f,y)	
{X; $C}^@P{Y} {$C}^@P{Y} {X; $C}^@P	PROP(a,p,b), P_EXT(x,p,y), C_SUB(c,a), C_SUB(e,c), C_EXT(e,x)	
{X}^@P{Y; $D} {X}^@P{$D} ^@P{Y; $D}	PROP(a,p,b), P_EXT(x,p,y), C_SUB(d,b), C_SUB(f,d), C_EXT(f,y)	
{X}^@P{Y} {X}^@P ^@P{Y}	P_EXT(x,p,y)	

Class Pattern	SWLF Translation	Fragment
$C ^$C	CLASS(c)	RQL$_{CORE}$ when $C=c, $D=d RQL$_{UCQ}$
$C{$D} ^$C{$D}	C_SUB(d,c)	
$C{X}	C_SUB(d,c), C_EXT(d,x)	
$C{X; $D}	C_SUB(d,c), C_SUB(e,d), C_EXT(e,x)	
^$C{X}	C_EXT(d,x)	RQL$_{UCQ}$
^$C{X; $D}	C_SUB(d,c), C_SUB(e,d), C_EXT(e,x), C_EXT(c,x)	
$C{X; ^$D}	C_SUB(d,c), C_EXT(d,x)	
^$C{X; ^$D}	C_SUB(d,c), C_EXT(c,x), C_EXT(d,x)	

A String Metric for Ontology Alignment

Giorgos Stoilos, Giorgos Stamou, and Stefanos Kollias

Department of Electrical and Computer Engineering,
National Technical University of Athens,
Zographou 15780, Greece

Abstract. Ontologies are today a key part of every knowledge based system. They provide a source of shared and precisely defined terms, resulting in system interoperability by knowledge sharing and reuse. Unfortunately, the variety of ways that a domain can be conceptualized results in the creation of different ontologies with contradicting or overlapping parts. For this reason ontologies need to be brought into mutual agreement (aligned). One important method for ontology alignment is the comparison of class and property names of ontologies using string-distance metrics. Today quite a lot of such metrics exist in literature. But all of them have been initially developed for different applications and fields, resulting in poor performance when applied in this new domain. In the current paper we present a new string metric for the comparison of names which performs better on the process of ontology alignment as well as to many other field matching problems.

1 Introduction

It is widely recognized today that ontologies are going to play a key role in the realization of almost all modern knowledge based application. They have already been successfully applied in fields like the World Wide Web [1], intelligent multimedia systems [2] and many more. Ontologies are used in order that distributed and disparate applications and systems overcome semantic heterogeneity and enable them interchange knowledge for the completion of more complex tasks. But, the various ways that different organizations conceptualize a domain or the fact that they purpose ontologies for different applications, thus modelling a different perspective of the world or the same but with different constraints and properties, results in heterogeneous ontologies which still have to be brought into mutual agreement.

To overcome this heterogeneity, scientist have developed methodologies and tools for assisting the (still) semi-automatic process of ontology alignment. This process provides us with semantic correspondences among the entities that exist within two heterogeneous ontologies. Nowadays, many techniques have been developed, or borrowed from other fields, in order to discover the semantic correspondences among entities. Among these methods a very popular one is the comparison of the class and property names of the ontologies using a string distance metric so as to produce a degree of similarity. Such a technique is referred

Y. Gil et al. (Eds.): ISWC 2005, LNCS 3729, pp. 624–637, 2005.

to as *terminological matching*. Even if the core methodology of a platform is not based on this technique an initial similarity extraction step is usually performed using this method. This technique is based on the fact that the same concepts are likely to be modelled using quite similar names. Many platforms that use such a methodology to compute similarities between ontologies exist in literature; some examples are, Anchor-PROMPT [3], QOM [4], Cupid [5] and many more.

Though powerful string metrics exist in literature, and have been used successfully in the past, from our experience with the development of a new ontology alignment platform, they don't perform well when used in this new demanding and complex domain. In this paper we present a new string metric which is created by paying special care to each different characteristic of the process of ontology alignment, thus leading to a metric with very good performance.

The rest of the paper is organized as follows. In section 2 we review the most frequently used string metrics found in literature. In section 3 we present the requirements that the field of ontology alignment introduces and explain why the usual string metrics fail to satisfy these requirements by giving small examples. These specifications will guide us during the definition of the new string metric which is introduced in section 4. In section 5, we present two evaluation experiments and strength our points about the bad behavior of the classical metrics. In section 6 we integrate our new metric in a new ontology alignment platform to see its behavior when it is used in a more complete ontology platform and at last section 7 concludes the paper.

2   Related Work

Today quite a lot of string metrics exist in literature. These string metrics have been developed and applied in different scientific fields like statistics, for probabilistic record linkage [6], database, for record matching [7], Artificial Intelligence, for supervised learning [8], and Biology, for identifying common molecular subsequences [9]. In the current paper we have considered the *Levenstein* [10] distance, which counts the insertions and deletions needed to match two strings, the *Needleman-Wunsch* [11] distance, which assigns a different cost on the edit operations, the *Smith-Waterman* [9], which additionally uses an alphabet mapping to costs and the *Monge-Elkan* [7], which uses variable costs depending on the substring gaps between the words. Moreover we used the *Jaro-Winkler* [12,6] similarity, which counts the common characters between two strings even if they are misplaced by a "short" distance, the *Q-Gram* [13], which counts the number of tri-grams shared between the two strings and the *sub-string* distance [14] which searches for the largest common substring.

3   Desired Properties

Ontology alignment is a relatively new field in computer science. Thus, none of the classical string metrics has been created having the properties and characteristics of this field in mind. Algorithms that are used in ontology alignment are very complex and contain many features and parameters that can affect the performance even of commonly accepted and "good" string metrics, when they are used in this new context. Features like the threshold (the value above which two pairs are considered identical), or the cardinality of mappings ("one-to-one, one-to-many" etc.) play a key role in ontology alignment and as we will see the metrics found in literature sometimes fail to give satisfactory results cause of the existence of these parameters. Thus, before we define our string metric we think that it is crucial to state the specifications that we want such a string metric to fulfill. More precisely we want the new metric to be:

1. **Fast:** Since ontologies are used in applications that demand processing in real-time, like the semantic web or intelligent retrieval tasks, the complexity of the string metric should be very low, leading to a fast matching procedure.
2. **Stable:** As we aforementioned, one very crucial parameter of ontology alignment algorithms is their threshold. When we will demand from alignment platform to automatically operate on the semantic web their threshold would probably be fixed at a value considered optimal by their authors. Though some methods that automatically adjust the threshold during runtime exist in literature [15] it cannot be proved that they select the optimum value for threshold each time an alignment is performed. Thus, we demand by the string metrics to be as "stable" as possible. By "stability" we define the ability of a string metric to perform almost optimal even if small diverges from the optimal threshold take place. As we will see all metrics fail to satisfy this crucial property. Even worst, classical metrics are really sensitive in small changes of the threshold, and while they can provide good results if the threshold is optimized, this performance can rapidly decrease if we slightly disturb the value of the threshold.
3. **Intelligent:** When operating for example in the semantic web context, it is likely that an ontology be compared to an irrelevant one, but with which string resemblances occur. In this case we want our metric to identify all the differences and provide us with correct results. But it is not uncommon the situation where usual string metrics fail to identify cases where two strings represent completely different concepts but resemble a lot. Consider for example the words "score" and "store". They represent two completely different concepts. Though this is true the Monge-Elkan, Levenstein, SubString, Needleman-Wunsch, Q-Gram and Jaro-Winkler metrics rate the pair with a similarity degree of 0.68, 0.8, 0.6, 0.9, 0.57 and 0.88 which are relatively hight values. In contrast our string metric assigns a value of 0.45.
4. **Discriminating:** One of the most usual cardinalities requested for alignment mappings is the "one-to-one" cardinality. As it is obvious in an "one-to-one" mapping if a string in a reference ontology is mapped with the same similarity degree to more than one in the second ontology it is very probable that the algorithm fails to pick the correct pair from the set of pairs. Hence, we would like from our similarity metric to rarely assign the same similarity degree when we compare one particular string to several others.

Many times during the experiments we faced situations where several runs of an alignment between two ontologies using the same configuration produced different precision and recall [16] values cause of this phenomenon.

From the above analysis it is obvious that ontology alignment is indeed a demanding and delicate process that adds many constraints to the string metrics used in it.

4 Definition of the String Metric

In the current section we sill introduce the new string metric, using as our guide the properties and features introduced in the previous section.

The new metric is based on the intuitions presented in [17] about the similarity between two entities. We argue that the similarity among two entities is related to their commonalities as well as to their differences. Thus, the similarity should be a function of both these features. This feature also appears, sometimes implicitly, in other measures as well. For example, in those measures that perform string editing, such operation can be considered as a form of difference counting, while non-editing can be considered as similarity counting. Thus, our metric is defined by the following equation:

$$Sim(s_1, s_2) = Comm(s_1, s_2) - Diff(s_1, s_2) + winkler(s_1, s_2) \qquad (1)$$

where $comm(s_1, s_2)$ stands for the commonality between s_1 and s_2, $diff(s_1, s_2)$ for the difference and $winklerImpr(s_1, s_2)$ for the improvement of the result using the method introduced by Winkler in [6]. We now have to define the functions of commonality and difference.

The function of commonality is motivated by the substring string metric. In the substring metric the biggest common substring between two strings is computed. This process is further extended by removing the common substring and by searching again for the next biggest substring until no one can be identified. The sum of the lengths of these substrings is then scaled with the length of the strings. The intuition behind this extension of the substring metric is the following. In the field of Computer Science researchers tend to use descriptive names for their variables or the units that represent real world entities. In other cases they tend to concatenate words and create new ones. For example in order to represent the concept of the number of pages of a book it is likely that someone uses the word "numberOfPages" or someone else might use the word "numPages". As one can see these two strings share not one but two common substrings which is very crucial to identify in order to approximate their real similarity as much as possible. Moreover, we can now distinguish cases like the above with cases where the substring "Pages" is shared but the rest of the strings are quite different, thus satisfying the specification for an intelligent metric. Hence, the function of commonality is given by the following equation:

$$Comm(s_1, s_2) = \frac{2 * \sum_i length(maxComSubString_i)}{length(s_1) + length(s_2)} \qquad (2)$$

As for the difference function, this is based on the length of the unmatched strings that have resulted from the initial matching step. Moreover, we believe that difference should play a less important role on the computation of the overall similarity. Our choice was the Hamacher product [18], which is a parametric triangular norm. This leads us to the following equation:

$$Diff(s_1, s_2) = \frac{uLen_{s_1} * uLen_{s_2}}{p + (1-p) * (uLen_{s_1} + uLen_{s_2} - uLen_{s_1} * uLen_{s_2})} \quad (3)$$

where $p \in [0, \infty)$, and $uLen_{s_1}$, $uLen_{s_2}$ represent the length of the unmatched substring from the initial strings s_1 and s_2 scaled with the string length, respectively. Observer that the parameter p can be adjusted at will giving a different importance on the difference factor. From experiments we performed we concluded that a value of 0.6 gives very good results. In Fig. 1 a three dimensional plot of the Hamacher function is illustrated.

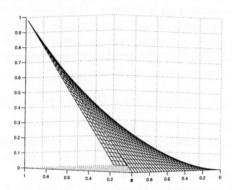

Fig. 1. Hamacher t-norm curve

As it is obvious from (1), our similarity measure takes values from the interval $[-1, 1]$. The majority of string metrics found in literature range over $[0, 1]$, but other metrics that extend this interval can be found, like the Resnik similarity [19] for taxonomies.

The incorporation of a difference factor to the overall similarity is the key feature for the satisfiability of the rest of specifications introduced in section 3. The dissimilarity stretches the range of our similarity metric over the interval $[-1, 1]$ performing a somewhat "clean-up" of the crucial space between 0.4 to 0.7, where a threshold can range, by discarding highly dissimilar pairs close to -1. In other string metrics this interval is cramped with false and true positive values. This fact makes these metrics very sensitive on the choice of the threshold. Moreover, this stretching makes it less probable to get same values for a string when it is compared to a large set of other strings, and thus satisfying the property of discrimination. At last the complexity of our string is polynomial to the size of the input strings, satisfying the property of a fast metric.

5   Evaluation

We have conducted two kinds of experiments. The first one is about ontology alignment, where we used a terminological matcher in order to compare the various string metrics. The second one is performed with classical benchmarks found in literature for data integration and retrieval [20].

5.1   Ontology Alignment

The ontology test set used to perform the experiments was that of the EON ontology alignment contest [21,22]. This test set consists of one reference ontology (33 classes, 59 properties, 56 individuals and 20 anonymous individuals), for a bibliographic domain, to be compared with other ontologies. Most of these ontologies originate from the reference ontology by making some hand made changes. These changes were for example the extension, or shrinkage of the ontology hierarchy, the use of synonyms, foreign names, removal of class properties and many more. Most of these modifications are devised in order to evaluate ontology alignment platforms and algorithms, as a whole, that might use other ontology features, or external sources like multilingual dictionaries or lexicons as well and not just terminological matching. Thus from the initial test set we only used those that involved alternations of the strings of classes and properties, excluding synonyms, foreign languages and randomly generated strings. Clearly, such occasions cannot be handled by terminological matching and including them would not provide us with valuable results. The evaluation sets we used are the following:

1. **101:** In this test set the reference ontology is compared with itself.
2. **204:** In this test the reference ontology is compared with a modified one. These modifications involved naming conventions like the insertion of underscores, abbreviations, upper-cased and lower-cased strings.
3. **301,302,303,304:** The reference ontology is compared with four real-life ontologies for bibliographic references found on the web and left unchanged.

Table 1. Precision and Recall of string metrics for various ontology alignment tests

Test	String Metrics															
	Levenstein		Sub-String		Jaro-Winkler		Monge-Elkan		Q-Gram		Smith-Waterman		Needleman-Wunsch		Sim	
	Pre.	Rec.	Pre.	Rec.	Pre.	Rec.	Pre.	Rec.	Pre.	Rec.	Pre.	Rec.	Pre.	Rec.	Pre.	Rec.
101	1.0	1.0	1.0	1.0	1.0	1.0	.88	.88	1.0	1.0	.88	.88	1.0	1.0	1.0	1.0
204	.967	.967	.822	.804	.965	.923	.695	.695	.857	.847	.793	.75	.926	.829	.978	.978
301	.8	.786	.872	.786	.81	.557	.833	.737	.872	.786	.511	.754	.857	.786	.9	.786
302	.6	.645	.367	.666	.363	.666	.34	.625	.666	.666	.375	.625	.35	.687	.72	.645
303	.764	.812	.622	.791	.754	.833	.571	.66	.677	.833	.581	.666	.904	.791	.754	.833
304	.972	.947	.8	.96	.923	.947	.776	.776	.972	.947	.789	.789	.972	.947	.972	.947
312	.794	.968	.911	.968	.862	.781	.823	.875	.939	.968	.794	.843	.76	1.0	.911	.968
Pre.=Pecision, Rec.=Recall																

Furthermore, we performed an additional experiment, named **312**, aligning the two ontologies of experiments 301 and 302.

In order to perform the alignment and evaluation experiments we used the API for ontology alignment introduced by Euzenat [23]. We used the sample implementations found in the API after performing some slight modifications on them, in order to include all the metrics and exclude from the alignment references to external entities. In order to evaluate each metric we have used the classical measures from the field of information retrieval of precision and recall [16]. Algorithms to compute precision and recall, given a proposed and a correct reference alignment, can also be found in the API.

For each metric and for each experiment we were changing the threshold of the algorithm (the value below which a mapping between strings is discarded) in order to achieve the highest precision for the highest recall that is possible by a metric. The reason for giving maximum importance to the recall measure is the following. Since ontology alignment is likely to stay a semi-automatic process, human intervention will eventually be needed to complete an alignment. Since the burden of deleting false identified pairs by a platform is minimal compared to the burden of traversing two heterogeneous ontologies that might include thousands of concepts and attributes and identify similar entities, recall is a much more important measure. Furthermore, the choice of not keeping the threshold constant is that different metrics have different mathematical properties thus one optimal threshold for one metric could be a worst for all the others, and vice versa. The complete set of experiments and the values of precision and recall using several string metrics is depicted in Table 1, where our metric appears in the last column.

From Table 1 we can immediately see that the Monge-Elkan and Smith-Waterman metrics perform worst than any other metric. In experiment 101 we can see the point made in section 3 about the use of an "one-to-one" mapping and the optimistic behavior of some metrics. In all other experiments their performance is kept in low levels. On the other hand our metric, on average, performs better compared to the other metrics. It manages to achieve high precision while retaining recall at high levels. Even in cases where a slightly better recall was achieved by other measures, the price to pay was a dramatically low precision, such that in some cases even up to 50 or 40 false positive pairs were retrieved. For example, Needleman-Wunsch metric achieves a better recall in experiments 302 and 312 but the precision is so poor that up to 56 and 10 false negative pairs, respectively, have to be removed later, possibly by human intervention. The same thing happens with Sub-String (Jaro-Winkler) distance, in experiments 302 and 304 (302), where the price for the slightly better recall are 55 and 18 (56) false positive pairs, respectively.

As we mentioned before, achieving a very high recall is crucial for the process of creating mappings between ontologies. But at the same time precision must be kept at high levels since having to discard up to 50 pairs, as it happened in the experiments when a good recall was achieved for such small ontologies, is not desired at all. It would be interesting to see in the cases where other metrics achieve better recall but substantially lower precision what happens if we drop recall at the same level as the one achieved by our metric. Even if this happens most metrics still achieve substantially low precision. More precisely in 302, for the same recall, Needleman-Wunsch achieves 0.57 precision, Jaro-Winkler 0.607 and Sub-String 0.62. Only Q-Gram achieves 0.775. At last Sub-String, in 304, achieves the same precision (0.972), and Needleman-Wunsch in experiment 312, 0.861.

In order to give a more intuitive view of the strength of the new metric, we have computed the precision and recall for each experiment and for each experiment for nine different threshold values, ranging from 0.1 to 0.9. Then we computed the average precision and recall of all experiments for all these different thresholds and we have created an average precision vs. average recall chart. This can be depicted in Fig. 2. We have excluded from these charts Monge-Elkan and Smith-Waterman metrics since their performance is very poor when applied to our field of interest.

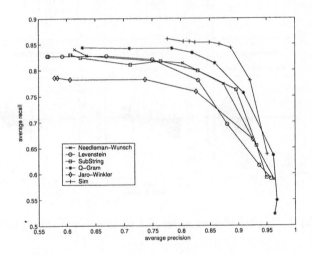

Fig. 2. Average Precision vs. Average Recall values

In Fig. 2 we can immediately see that our metric achieves at the same time a substantially better precision and recall. While other metrics have scored their best recall when precision is at a very low levels (and subsequently decrease recall to increase precision), our metric can simultaneously achieve high values on both these measures.

Additionally, since curves in Fig. 2 are interpolated, we have put "marks" on each one of these to denote the points where average precision and average recall is computed for different threshold values. Concerning our string metric we can identify an area of seven different threshold values where average precision is increasing while at the same time average recall still stays at high levels. This is the area where recall ranges from 0.86 to 0.85 while precision ranges from 0.77

to 0.88. In all the other curves, after the third or forth threshold value (where average precision vs. recall is at acceptable levels), we can observe a very high decrease of recall when a higher threshold is set. In other words the area that our metric achieves a high recall combined with a very high precision is a highly unstable area for all the other metrics. If not a highly optimal threshold is set in an ontology platform that uses such a metric, there is a high risk that low results are obtained.

In order to give a more clear picture on the stability of our metric, in Fig. 3 we present the number of pairs assigned a particular similarity degree in all six experiments.

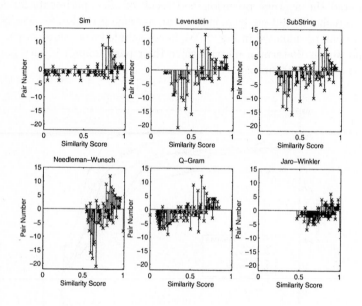

Fig. 3. Number of pairs assigned a particular similarity values

From Fig. 3 we can immediately deduce that the Needleman-Wunsch and Jaro-Winkler metrics are highly instable. Notice how many pairs have been accumulated within a small interval of the similarity degree axis. Clearly a small variation in the threshold of an alignment platform that uses one of these metrics could wreck the performance. Moreover, all the other metrics suffer too by a bad stability. Observe for example the diagram for the Levenstein distance. Within the interval of [0.4, 0.6] where, according to Fig. 2, average precision vs. average recall is at its best levels, the metric retrieves 16 true positives and 79 false negatives. As it is obvious a slight disturbance of the threshold might fetch many of the false pairs or loose many of the correct ones. Sub-String and Q-Gram metrics are a bit more stable. Sub-String has the interval of (0.4, 0.6] where 8 true and 46 false positives exist (without including 0.4 where 16 more false positives appear). Q-Gram, on the other hand, ranks 9 true positives and 44 false negatives within the interval [0.3, 0.5], where obviously the same problem as before exists.

When it comes to our metric its stability is obvious. The highly dissimilar pairs have too early been discarded close to -1 and the danger of fetching too many of them if an optimal threshold is not chosen is very small. Into the interval $[0.5, 0.7]$, only 4 true positives and 17 false positives appear. Thus, with this property satisfied we can more easily choose a threshold where the maximum recall strength of the metric is being used and at the same time not worry if we are at a point where low precision is encountered. At last observe that in our case, under the interval where the majority of true positives is present, a very low number of false positives exist, which justifies the results of the high precision.

5.2   Census and Field Matching

Even though our metric was originally designed for the domain of ontology alignment it still is a string metric in the classical sense. Thus we could not resist but to evaluate it with classical benchmarks found in literature like the ones in [7,8,24,20]. The list of the datasets used can be found in Table 2 as well as the number of strings that each dataset includes.

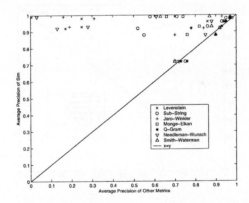

Fig. 4. Average Precision of string metrics vs. our metric

Each dataset contains two relations. Each relation contains a number of strings where each string is compared with all the strings of the other relation. Each comparison of two strings is assigned a similarity degree. Every entry for a string contains a key which is purposed for the identification of the correctness of a pair. In order to evaluate our metric against these datasets we used the SecondString open-source library [20]. This library contains all these datasets as well as algorithms to compute the average precision and maximum F1 measure for each test. The F1 measure is an aggregation of the precision and recall measures.

In Figs. 4 and 5 we can see two scatter plots. The former is about the average precision achieved in all experiments by all classical metrics, relative to our

Table 2. Datasets used in experiments

Name	Strings
bird1	377
bird2	982
bird3	98
bird4	719
park	654
restaurant	863
peopleMatch	90
census	841

metric, while the latter one is about the maximum F-measure. As we can see from these plots our metric performs better in the majority of experiments performed with the data sets presented in Table 2. Only in five cases in average precision and equal times in maximum F1 looses with a small difference.

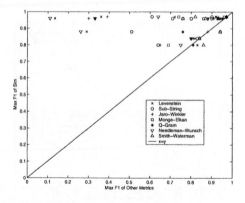

Fig. 5. Maximum F1 of string metrics vs. our metric

At last these experiments also gave us results about the complexity of the metrics. Our metric comes second, very close to the substring metric, with which has a large resemblance. Both these metrics are far from competition, relative to time execution, from the other metrics from which perform about 5 to 20 times faster when it comes to experiments with big strings to be compared.

6   A Sample Implementation

At last, we have started the integration of the similarity metric in an ontology alignment platform. This way we can test the behavior of our metric when the aggregation of more than one methods for computing similarity is involved. The platform features three kinds of matching methods, as described in [14]. These are the following:

- **Terminological Matching:** This method is the standard terminological method, which computes similarities based on the strings of class and property names.
- **Structural Internal Matching:** In this method we refine the similarity computed by terminological matching, for two classes, by a portion of the similarities between the names of their properties.
- **Structural External Matching:** In this method we again refine the similarity between two classes by a portion of the similarity computed for the superclasses of the two classes.

The similarities computed by the above methods are aggregated to produce an overall similarity. In this aggregation we give more importance to similarities computed for class and property names, by the terminological method, and less importance to the other methods.

Table 3. Precision, Recall and fallout for the experiments

	Precision	Recall	F-Measure
101	1.0	1.0	1.0
201	0.926	0.692	0.792
204	0.989	0.978	0.983
222	0.966	0.945	0.955
223	0.956	0.956	0.956
230	0.962	1.0	0.98
301	0.98	0.79	0.874
302	0.857	0.625	0.722
303	0.816	0.83	0.824
304	0.92	0.90	0.915
312	0.967	0.937	0.95

In order to evaluate the sample implementation we have again used the evaluation experiments from [21,22]. Additionally to the experiments used for the evaluation of the string matching method we have included experiments, 201, 222, 223 and 230. The reader is referred to [22] for a detailed description of the experiments.

In the following table we can see the precision, recall and f-measure achieved by the sample ontology alignment platform. In all experiments we have used a fixed threshold, set at value 0.65.

7   Conclusions

Ontology alignment platforms have been benefited a lot by the use of string distance metrics in order to discover semantic mappings between ontologies. Though powerful metrics exist in literature they have been developed and purposed for different domains and applications. The delicate and demanding features of the process of ontology alignment, such as speed, threshold, cardinality, or the potentially short size of ontologies can badly affect the performance of classical metrics which usually are "optimistic", to the degrees they assign, or accumulate values close to one another.

These demanding features has led us to the creation of a new string metric taking extra care to satisfy each one of them. Experiments has shown that the new metric performs better on average by the classical ones, when optimal configurations are used, and can greatly outperform them when no a priory knowledge for the alignment task is known. Furthermore, experiments with classical benchmarks for field and census matching has show that our metric is still very powerful to be used in such domains and for such tasks, too. At last, all this interestingly good performance comes with a low complexity.

Acknowledgements

This work is supported by the FP6 Network of Excellence EU project Knowledge Web (IST-2004-507482).

References

1. Berners-Lee, T., Hendler, J., Lassila, O.: The semantic web. Scientific American **279** (2001)
2. Benitez, A., Smith, J., Chang, S.F.: Medianet: A multimedia information network for knowledge representation. Volume 4210., IS&T/SPIE-2000 (2001)
3. Noy, N., Musen, M.: Anchor-prompt: Using non-local context for semantic matching. In: Proc. IJCAI 2001 workshop on ontology and information sharing, Seattle (WA US). (2001) 63–70
4. Ehrig, M., Staab, S.: Qom - quick ontology mapping. In: Proc. of the 3rd International Semantic Web Conference, Hiroshima (JP). Volume volume 3298 of LNCS. (2004) 683–697
5. Madhavan, J., Berstein, P., Rahm, E.: Generic schema matching using cupid. In: Proc. of the 27th VLDB, Roma (IT). (2001) 48–58
6. Winkler, W.: The state record linkage and current research problems. Technical report, Statistics of Income Division, Internal Revenue Service Publication (1999)
7. Monge, A., Elkan, C.: The field-matching problem: algorithm and applications. In: Proceedings of the second international Conference on Knowledge Discovery and Data Mining. (1996)
8. Tejada, S., Knoblock, C.A., Minton, S.: Learning object identification rules for information integration. Information Systems **26** (2001) 607–633
9. Smith, T.F., Waterman, M.S.: Identification of common molecular subsequences. Journal of Molecular Biology **147** (1981) 195–197
10. Levenstein, I.: Binary codes capable of correcting deletions, insertions and reversals. Cybernetics and Control Theory (1966)
11. Needleman, S.B., Wunsch, C.D.: A general method applicable to the search for similarities in the amino acid sequence of two proteins. Molecular Biology **48** (1970) 444–453

12. Jaro, M.: Probabilistic linkage of large public health data files (disc. p687-689). Statistics in Medicine **14** (1995) 491–498
13. Sutinen, E., Tarhio, J.: On using q-gram locations in approximate string matching. In: ESA '95: Proceedings of the Third Annual European Symposium on Algorithms, Springer-Verlag (1995) 327–340
14. Euzenat, J., Le Bach, T., Barrasa, J., Bouquet, P., De Bo, J., Dieng-Kuntz, R., Ehrig, M., Hauswirth, M., Jarrar, M., Lara, R., Maynard, D., Napoli, A., Stamou, G., Stuckenschmidt, H., Shvaiko, P., Tessaris, S., Van Acker, S., Zaihrayeu, I.: State of the art on ontology alignment. deliverable 2.2.3 (2004)
15. Ehrig, M., Sure, Y.: Ontology mapping - an integrated approach. In: Proceedings of the First European Semantic Web Symposium. Volume 3053. (2004) 76–91
16. Do, H., Melnik, S., Rahm, E.: Comparison of schema matching evaluations. In: Proceedings of the 2nd International Workshop on Web Databases. (2002)
17. Lin, D.: An information-theoretic definition of similarity. In: Proc. 15th International Conf. on Machine Learning, Morgan Kaufmann, San Francisco, CA (1998) 296–304
18. Hamacher, H., Leberling, H., Zimmermann, H.J.: Sensitivity analysis in fuzzy linear programming. Fuzzy Sets and Systems **1** (1978) 269–281
19. Resnik, P.: Using information content to evaluate semantic similarity in a taxonomy. In: Proceedings of the IJCAI-95. (1995) 448–453
20. Cohen, W., Ravikumar, P., Fienberg, S.: A comparison of string metrics for matching names and records. In: Proc. KDD-2003 Workshop on Data Cleaning and Object Consolidation. (2003)
21. Euzenat, J.: Evaluating ontology alignment methods. In: Proc. Dagstuhl seminar on Semantic interoperability and integration, Wadern (DE). (2004) 47–50
22. Sure, Y., Corcho, O., Euzenat, J., Hughes, T., eds.: Proceedings of the 3rd Evaluation of Ontology-based tools (EON). (2004)
23. Euzenat, J.: An api for ontology alignment. In: Proc. 3rd conference on international semantic web conference (ISWC), Hiroshima (JP). (2004) 698–712
24. Cohen, W.: Data integration using similarity joins and a word-based information representation language. ACM Transactions on Information Systems **18** (2000) 288–321

An Ontological Framework for Dynamic Coordination

Valentina Tamma[1], Chris van Aart[2], Thierry Moyaux[1],
Shamimabi Paurobally[1], Ben Lithgow-Smith[1], and Michael Wooldridge[1]

[1] Dept of Computer Science, University of Liverpool,
Liverpool L69 7ZF, UK
[2] Acklin BV,
Taxandriaweg 12b,
5142 PA Waalwijk, The Netherlands

Abstract. Coordination is the process of managing the possible interactions between activities and processes; a mechanism to handle such interactions is known as a coordination regime. A successful coordination regime will prevent negative interactions occurring (e.g., by preventing two processes from simultaneously accessing a non-shareable resource), and wherever possible will facilitate positive interactions (e.g., by ensuring that activities are not needlessly duplicated). We start from the premise that effective coordination mechanisms require the sharing of knowledge about activities, resources and their properties, and hence, that in a heterogeneous environment, an ontological approach to coordination is appropriate. After surveying recent work on dynamic coordination, we describe an ontology for coordination that we have developed with the goal of coordinating semantic web processes. We then present a implementation of our ideas, which serves as a proof of concept for how this ontology can be used for dynamic coordination. We conclude with a summary of the presented work, illustrate its relation to the Semantic Web, and provide insights into future extensions.

1 Introduction

Coordination is one of the fundamental problems in systems composed of multiple interacting processes. Such processes will need to coordinate their activities if ever there is a possibility that these activities may interact with one-another. As an example, imagine two processes making use of a non-shareable resource. If both processes attempt to use the resource simultaneously, we will naturally have problems - a lost update at best, perhaps damage to the resource at worst. The processes thus need to *coordinate* their activities, to make use of the non-shareable resource. Although such a scenario represents the best-known type of possible coordination interaction, there are many other less obvious ways in which coordination may be mutually beneficial. For example, imagine two e-science processes carrying out some computational task, where both processes require the results of some intermediate computation; then, it makes sense for them to adopt a policy of pro-actively exchanging information that may be of use to other processes. Here, coordination is not *required* for the agents to be successful in their tasks, but there is a global benefit to be gained by adopting this rule.

Coordination in the limited sense of synchronisation (preventing scenarios such as simultaneous access to a non-shareable resource) has long been a central topic of

Y. Gil et al. (Eds.): ISWC 2005, LNCS 3729, pp. 638–652, 2005.

research in the concurrency community [1]. However, the pre-dominant approach to handling coordination has been to *hard-wire* the coordination mechanism into the system structure (for example by means of semaphores, monitors, or locks). In more open systems, where the processes and resources of which the system is comprised are not known at design time, such an approach is often impossible. In such systems, it may be desirable to allow the relevant processes to communicate their intentions with respect to future activities and resource utilisation, and get them to *reason* about coordination at run time, with the goal of preventing negative interactions, and facilitating positive interactions. This is a *dynamic* approach to coordination, since the coordination requirement is handled at *run-time*, rather than design time. Note that the communication implied by this approach requires an agreed common vocabulary for coordination, with a precise semantics, and hence we have an ontological approach to dynamic coordination, in short.

Our goal in this paper is to describe such an ontological approach to coordination, and present our results with respect to a proof-of-concept implementation of the approach. We begin in the following section with a brief survey of previous work on coordination, which has been carried out largely within the multi-agent systems community. In section 3, we give an informal overview of our coordination ontology; the key concepts, their attributes, and their relationships. In section 4, we present a proof-of-concept implementation of the ontological approach to coordination, in which multiple processes detect coordination relationships using a Jess/Protégé implementation of the ontology. We conclude with some conclusions and pointers to further work.

2   Background

Coordination is perhaps the defining problem in cooperative working. Since much work on coordination (and in particular, the precursors to our own work) arises from the multi-agent systems community [2], we will adopt the convention of referring to the processes which need to coordinate as "agents". The coordination problem is that of *managing relationships between the activities of agents* [3]. Coordination is essential if the activities that agents engage in can *interact* in any way. Consider the following examples.

- *You and I both want to leave the room, and so we independently walk towards the door, which can only fit one of us. I graciously permit you to leave first.* In this example, our activities need to be coordinated because there is a resource (the door) which we both wish to use, but which can only be used by one person at a time.
- *I intend to submit a grant proposal, but in order to do this, I need your signature.* In this case, my activity of sending a grant proposal depends upon your activity of signing it off – I cannot carry out my activity until yours is completed. In other words, my activity *depends* upon yours.
- *I obtain a soft copy of a paper from a Web page. I know that this report will be of interest to you as well. Knowing this, I pro-actively photocopy the report, and give you a copy.* In this case, our activities do not strictly need to be coordinated – since the report is freely available on a Web page, you could download and print your own copy. But, by pro-actively printing a copy, I save you time.

Notice that coordination, defined in this way, subsumes the well-known (and widely studied) concept of *synchronisation* [1]. Synchronisation is generally concerned with the rather restricted case of ensuring that processes do not destructively interact with one another. While solving this problem certainly requires coordination, the concept of coordination is actually much broader than this. Standard solutions to synchronisation problems involve *hard-wiring* coordination regimes into program code. Thus, for example, a JAVA method may be flagged as `synchronized` by a programmer, indicating that a certain access regime is enforced whenever this method is invoked. However, in large-scale, dynamic, open systems, of the kind we are concerned within this project, such hard-wired regimes are too limiting. We ideally want computational processes to be able to *reason about* the coordination issues in their system, and resolve these issues *autonomously*.

In order to build agents for semantic web applications that can reason about coordination issues dynamically, we must first identify the possible interaction relationships that may exist in these applications. Hence, the goal, here, is to derive and formally define the possible interaction relationships that may exist between activities. There is some prior work on this topic — von Martial [4] puts forward a high-level typology for coordination relationships. He suggested that, broadly, relationships between activities could be either *positive* or *negative*. Positive relationships "are all those relationships between two plans from which some benefit can be derived, for one or both of the agents plans, by combining them" [5, p. 111]. Such relationships may be *requested* (I *explicitly* ask you for help with my activities) or *non-requested* (it so happens that by working together we can achieve a solution that is better for at least one of us, without making the other any worse off). Von Martial distinguishes three types of non-requested relationships:

The action equality relationship: We both plan to perform an identical action, and by recognizing this, one of us can perform the action alone, and so, save the other effort.

The consequence relationship: The actions in my plan have the side-effect of achieving one of your goals, relieving thus you of the need to explicitly achieve it.

The favour relationship: Some part of my plan has the side effect of contributing to the achievement of one of your goals, perhaps by making it easier (e.g., by achieving a precondition of one of the actions in it).

Another major body of work on this issue is that on *Partial Global Planning* [6]. The basic idea of partial global planning is that agents develop and exchange plans of local activity in order to identify possible interactions (positive or negative). The ideas were refined in Decker's subsequent work on *Generalised Partial Global Planning* (GPGP) in the TÆMS testbed [7]. GPGP makes use of five techniques for coordinating activities:

- *Updating non-local viewpoints*: Agents have only local views of activities, and so, sharing information can help them achieve broader views. In his TÆMS system, Decker uses three variations of this policy: communicate no local information, communicate all information, or an intermediate level.

- *Communicate results*: Agents may communicate results in three different ways. A minimal approach is where agents only communicate results that are essential to satisfy obligations. Another approach involves sending all results. A third is to send results to those with an interest in them.
- *Handling simple redundancy*: Redundancy occurs when efforts are duplicated. This may be deliberate – an agent may get more than one agent to work on a task because it wants to ensure the task gets done. However, in general, redundancies indicate wasted resources, and are therefore to be avoided. The solution adopted in GPGP is as follows. When redundancy is detected, in the form of multiple agents working on identical tasks, one agent is selected at random to carry out the task. The results are then broadcast to other interested agents.
- *Handling hard coordination relationships*: "Hard" coordination relationships are essentially the "negative" relationships of von Martial. Hard coordination relationships are thus those that threaten to prevent activities being successfully completed. Thus a hard relationship occurs when there is a danger of the agents' actions destructively interfering with one another, or preventing each others actions being carried out. When such relationships are encountered, the activities of agents are rescheduled to resolve the problem.
- *Handling soft coordination relationships*: "Soft" coordination relationships include the "positive" relationships of von Martial. Thus, these relationships include those that are not "mission critical", but which may improve overall performance. When these are encountered, then rescheduling takes place, but with a high degree of "negotiability": if rescheduling is not found possible, then the system does not worry about it too much.

Based on all this body of work, we have designed an ontology for coordination, which is presented in the next section. Although ontologies for service based computing have been developed, such as OWL-S [8] and WSMO [9], they mainly focus on describing the services and their orchestration/composition. We argue that our ontology is complementary to existing efforts. Coordination is indeed an important aspect of service based computing, however it addresses the way in which *independent*, and possibly conflicting agents choreograph with others. While in efforts like OWL-S and WSMO the interaction and composition of processes are modelled as a workflow that is determined *a priory* and that is executed by a workflow execution component, in agent-based coordination, the choreography is determined by the exchange of messages among the agents that need to interact (*protocol*). However, OWL-S first order logic representation of process theory based on PSL [18] could be integrated in our ontology, in a future implementation.

3 An Ontology for Coordination

As described above, we define an ontology for coordination. The basic idea is to enable agents to reason about the relationships of their activities to the activities of other agents. So, the fundamental purpose of the ontology is to answer the following questions:

- what is a *coordinable activity*?
- what *coordination relationships* such activities have to one another?

In the sub-sections that follow, we give an overview of the ontology: the key concepts, the slots associated with these concepts, the relationships between these concepts, and axioms. In the interests of comprehensibility, we do not present all the components of the ontology. Also note that our presentation is informal: we aim to give an overview of the ontology, rather than present all the low-level technical details. The "definitive" version of the ontology is maintained using Protégé [10] and is illustrated in in Figure 1.

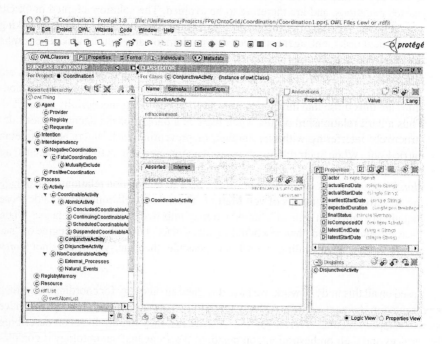

Fig. 1. The Protégé version of the coordination ontology

3.1 Agents

Our starting concept is *Agent*. The idea is, obviously enough, that this concept relates to the agents in the system, i.e., the things that do the actions in the system needing to be coordinated. For the purposes of the coordination ontology, agents have just one slot: *id*, which is a string representation of the unique identifier for the agent (e.g., a URI).

3.2 Processes and Activities

Our next concept is *Process*. A process is an activity that changes the state of the environment in some way. It may be terminating or non-terminating, and be carried out by a human or other agent, or be a natural (physical) process.

The process concept has two sub-classes: the most important of which is that of a *CoordinableActivity*. A coordinable activity is a process that can be managed in such a way as to be coordinated with other coordinable activities. For example, executing the process of invoking a web service would be a coordinable activity, in the sense that the invocation of such a service can be managed so as to coordinate with other invocations. For example, suppose we have two agents, both of which want to invoke the same web service, with different parameters. Then, in general, the agents could manage their invocations so as not to interfere with one another.

Not all processes of interest to a system are coordinable – hence we have the *NonCoordinableActivity* concept. We intend this concept to capture all those processes whose coordination is not possible by the agents within the system to which a particular knowledge base refers. This will include at least the following two types of process (although we do not represent these as concepts):

- *Natural events*: These are physical processes that will take place irrespective of what any agent in the system does. An extreme example would be the decay of an atom, caused by essentially random quantum events. Clearly, such processes cannot be coordinated with other processes: they will take place (or not take place) irrespective of what the agents in the system do.
- *External processes*: These are processes – either physical world processes or natural processes – which are simply outside the control of the system, in that they cannot be managed by the agents in the system. Notice that such processes may be coordinated by entities *outside* the system: the point is, that for the purposes of the system to which the knowledge base refers, they cannot be coordinated.

Another way of thinking about the distinction between a coordinable and a non-coordinable activity is that there is always an agent (i.e., a software agent within the system) associated with a coordinable activity, whereas there is no such agent associated with a non-coordinable activity.

We think of particular *CoordinableActivity* as being arranged into an and/or tree hierarchy of activities, with *AtomicActivity*s as leaves of the tree. Thus a *CoordinableActivity* is *composedOf* possibly many other *Activity*s, and may be:

- a *ConjunctiveActivity*: in this case, it is composed of a number of other activities, which must *all* be successfully completed in order for the overall activity to be completed;
- *DisjunctiveActivity*: it is composed of a number of other activities, of which *at least one* must be successfully completed in order for the overall activity to be completed; or
- *AtomicActivity* – in which case the activity is composed of *no* further activities. (The set of *CoordinableActivity*s of which this activity is composed is empty.)

In future work, it may be interesting to compare these notions with those of the OWL-S model of processes, and one possibility is to attempt to align them in some way [8][1]. We can further identify the following sub-classes of *AtomicActivity*:

---

[1] The point is that there may be some relation at this point to the process model in OWL-S, so perhaps an *AtomicActivity* is a sub-class of an OWL-S process, and similarly for OWL-S composite processes.

- *ConcludedCoordinableActivity*: an activity that has taken place in the past, and is now fully concluded;
- *ContinuingCoordinableActivity*: this is an activity that is currently in progress;
- *ScheduledCoordinableActivity*: this is an activity that it is expected *will* take place, in the sense that it is scheduled for execution by some agent[2];
- *SuspendedCoordinableActivity*: this is an activity that whose status is undetermined.

Let us briefly consider slots and properties of our concepts. A *CoordinableActivity* will have the following slots:

- *actor*: an *Agent*, i.e., the agent that intends to carry out, or has carried out this activity;
- *earliest start date*: either a date or `null`, with a date indicating the earliest date at which the activity may begin; `null` indicates that this information is not known;
- *latest start date*: either a date or `null`, with a date indicating the latest date at which the activity may begin; `null` indicates that this information is not known;
- *expected duration*: either a natural number, indicating the number of milliseconds the activity is expected to take, or `null` indicates an unknown duration;
- *latest end date*: either a date or `null`, with a date indicating the latest date at which the activity may end; `null` indicates that this information is not known;
- *actual start date*: either a date or `null`, with a date indicating the date at which the activity actually began; `null` indicates that this information is not known;
- *actual end date*: either a date or `null`, with a date indicating the date at which the activity actually ended; `null` indicates that this information is not known;
- *final status*: an enumeration type, either `succeeded`, `failed`, or `null`.

There are a number of axioms that may be introduced at this point. With respect to *Conjunctive* and *DisjunctiveActivity*s, we have the following:

- a *ConjunctiveActivity* has successfully terminated if all its components have successfully terminated;
- a *DisjunctiveActvity* has successfully terminated if at least one of its components has successfully terminated.

With respect to the relationship between scheduled activities and their successful completion, we have the following:

- if an activity is scheduled, then it should have a `null` actual start date and actual end date.
- if an activity is concluded, then the final status must be non-`null`;
- if an activity started before its earliest start date, then it has `failed`;
- if an activity started after its latest start date, then it has `failed`.

---

[2] We do not worry about exactly what "scheduled for execution" means: we simply assume that some agent is expected to carry out the activity, or that the activity appears in some agent's plan.

3.3   Resources

Next, we have the *Resource* concept. The idea of this concept, as we discussed in the introduction, is that a resource is something that may be required to expedite an activity. Thus, we have a one-to-many relationship between *AtomicActivity*s and *Resource*s. Note that we regard this set as being fixed, for any given activity. The *Resource* concept has the following slots:

- *viable*: a Boolean value, indicating whether the resource is still in a state to be used; a value of `false` here would indicate that the resource could not be used by any activity (even if these activities *Require* it). Another simple way to think about *viable* is that it indicates whether a resource is "broken" or "working" or not.
- *consumable*: a Boolean value, which indicates whether the use of the resource will reduce subsequent availability of the resource in some way; more precisely, whether the repeated use of the resource in activities would make the resource non-viable.
- *shareable*: a Boolean value, indicating whether a resource may be used by more than one agent at any given time.
- *cloneable*: a Boolean value, indicating whether or not the resource is cloneable (= `true`), or unique and not-cloneable (= `false`). An example of a cloneable resource would be a dataset or a digital document. An example of a unique resource would be a physical artefact produced as the output of a particular experiment, or a human being.
- *owner*: either an *Agent* (in which case this is the agent that owns the resource), or `null` (in which case the semantics are that the resource may be used by any agent at no cost). If a resource is owned by an agent, and another agent wishes to use this resource, then it may be necessary to enter into negotiation over the exploitation of the resource.

3.4   Interdependencies Between Activities

We now turn to the interrelationships that exist between activities. Our first concept is that of an *Interdependency*. The interdependency concept has the following slots:

- *source* and *target*: both slots are *Activities*, the idea being that these are the two activities which are interdependent.
- *isHard*: a Boolean value, which indicates whether the relation is "soft" (= `false`) or "hard" (= `true`), with the following semantics:
  - a *hard* relation is one which will materially affect the success or otherwise of the activities;
  - a *soft* relation is one which *may* affect the activities, positively or negatively, but will not affect whether they are successful or not.

Sub-classes of *CoordinationRelation* are:

- *NegativeCoordination*: an interaction which, if it occurs, will lead to a reduction in the quality of the solution or the utility of the participants;

- *PositiveCoordination*: an interaction which, if it occurs, will lead to an increase in the utility of the participants or the quality of the solution.

We have a further sub-class of *NegativeCoordination*: *FatalCoordination* is a hard coordination relationship which, if it occurs, will inevitably lead to the failure of one or more of the component activities. Note that instances of $FatalCoordination$ relationships are always $hard$. As sub-classes of *FatalCoordination*, we have:

- $MutuallyExclude$: an instance of this relationship will exist between two *AtomicActivity*s iff:
    1. they both $Require$ some resource r,
    2. the actual or scheduled usage of r by both activities overlaps;
    3. r is non-shareable.

  The idea is thus that these two activities will be mutually exclusive, in the sense that they cannot possibly both succeed, as they require access to a resource that cannot be shared.
- $ResourceContention$: an instance of this relationship will exist between two *AtomicActivity*s iff:
    1. they both $Require$ some resource r;
    2. resource r is consumable.

  The idea here is thus that one of the activities (the earlier one) could prevent the successful completion of the other activity, by depleting it or rendering it unviable. We do not require that $ResourceContention$ relationships are $hard$, although, of course, they could be.
- $Disables$: one activity will disable another if the occurrence of it will definitively prevent the occurrence of the other.

Sub-classes of *PositiveCoordination* are:

- *ConditionallyFeeds*: in such a coordination, the occurrence of activity A_1 will subsequently make possible the occurrence of activity A_2, but it is nevertheless possible that A_2 could occur (i.e., the occurrence of A_1 is a sufficient but not necessary event for the occurrence of A_2);
- *Enables*: the occurrence of activity A_1 is both necessary and sufficient for the occurrence of A_2;
- *IsSubsumedBy*: activity A_1 is subsumed by activity A_2 if A_2 contains all the activities of A_1.;
- *Subsumes*: the inverse of $IsSubsumedBy$;
- *Favors*: an activity A_1 favors another activity A_2 if its prior occurrence will subsequently improve the overall quality of A_2. We include this as a "catch all". This is a $soft$ relationship.

3.5   Operational Relationships

In order to *resolve* a coordination relationship between two activities, we may have to appeal to the *operational relationships* that exist between the agents that will carry them out. Intuitively, operational relationships exist between agents that carry out activities, and by understanding these relationships, it can help to resolve the coordination relationships. The main concept here is *OperationalRelationship*. This concept has two slots, both of which are *Agents*: *source* and *target*. Sub-classes of *OperationalRelationship* include:

- *LegalAuthority*: this sub-class indicates that *source* has legal authority over *target* (of course, this begs the question of what "legal authority" means in the context of semantic web services and processes, but this is outside the scope of our current work, and is left as a placeholder for the future);
- *ContractualAuthority*: this indicates that *source* has contractual authority over *target* (i.e., that both agents "belong" to the same organisation, and that in the context of this organisation, *source* should take precedence over *target*);
- *ProducerConsumer*: this indicates that *source* is the *owner* of a *Resource* that is to be used by *target*;
- *ConsumerProducer*: the inverse of *ProducerConsumer*;
- *Peer*: two agents that work as peers, i.e., that neither has any authority over the other.

We have developed a prototype as a proof-of-concept for our ontology. The current state of its development is now presented.

4   Implementation

We have implemented our prototype with the plug-in JessTab 1.1 [11] in Protégé 3.0. JessTab is a plug-in integrating the inference engine Jess (in its version 6.1p7 [12] in our case) with Protégé, so that Jess can carry out inferences on the knowledge base in Protégé. More precisely, JessTab enables Jess to work with a Protégé knowledge base, i.e., Jess can (i) access the ontology and the instances represented in Protégé, (ii) directly manipulate these ontology and instances, (iii) infer new facts deduced from these ontology and instances, and (iv) perform all the other programming tasks permitted by Jess, such as calculating or launching Java operations.

In our prototype, we use these capabilities of JessTab in the following way. We first design an ontology for our agents in OWL [13] using Protégé. For this proof of concept we restrict our attention to few concepts and types of coordination and we do not implement the whole ontology described in Section 3. In our implementation, concepts in the ontology are translated into Jess facts, whilst the coordination strategy is translated into a set of Jess rules. In our ontology , we create the class *Agent*, with subclasses *Provider*, *Requester* and *Registry*, as well as the classes required by these three types of *Agent*s, i.e., *RegistryMemory*, *Intention* and *Resource*, which are now outlined.

A *RegistryMemory* is related to an instance of *Registry* by the property "hasMemory". Every instance of *RegistryMemory* represents either a *Requester* and one of its *Intention*s, or a *Provider* and one of its capabilities and associated *Resource*s.

The second element, *Intention*, is related to instances of *Agent* to describe one of the activities planned by a particular *Agent*. Besides an *Agent*, an *Intention* may also be linked to a *RegistryMemory* to enable a *Registry* to memorize an *Agent*'s *Intention*.

The third class is *Resource*, which contains the name of a resource (we assume this name is a unique identifier for this resource) and the flag "isShareable".

After the creation of the classes of this ontology, we populate the ontology with instances. In our example, we instantiate one resource *Provider*, two resource *Requesters* and one *Registry*. These first two steps related to ontology building do not require JessTab, but only Protégé. Finally, we add Jess rules to "animate" our instances. These rules implement the choreography between the instanciated *Agent*s. These three stages are detailed in the following subsections.

4.1   Classes in the Ontology

As noted, we basically deal with three different classes, namely *Provider, Requester* and *Registry*. Each time a *Provider* or a *Requester* registers to a *Registry*, this *Registry* records the information sent by this *Provider/Requester* by creating a *RegistryMemory*, which means that a *RegistryMemory* is very similar to a *Provider/Requester* and thus to an *Agent* (of course, only from an ontological viewpoint, like everything in this subsection!). To record a *RegistryMemory*, *Registry* has an object property called "hasMemory" listing instances of *RegistryMemory* used by this *Registry*. "hasMemory" is the only property of interest in a semantic *Registry*, even if a *Registry* inherits all the properties of an *Agent*, namely "hasName", "hasCapabilities", "hasGoals", "hasIntention" and "hasResource".

It is worth noting the difference we make between "hasGoals" and "hasIntention": in a similar way to the BDI (Belief, Desire and Intention) architecture [14], an agent desires to achieve its multiple goals, and as a result, this agent selects and adopts the appropriate intention (which is a plan of actions in the BDI architecture). In our ontology, we translate this in the following way: an *Agent* has a property "hasGoals" pointing to several instances of *Intention*, and one property "hasIntention" pointing to one of these instances of *Intention*. This latter *Intention* represents what current action this *Agent* currently tries to achieve. Indeed, this is the main difference between a *RegistryMemory* and an *Agent*: only an *Agent* has a property "hasIntention", while both *RegistryMemory* and *Agent* have a property "hasGoals". A semantic *Registry* uses the property "hasGoals" to register in one of its *RegistryMemory*s what it knows about an *Agent*'s planned activities. In other words, there is one *RegistryMemory* per *Agent* (normally, this *Agent* should be a *Requester*), and as many properties "hasGoals" per *RegistryMemory* as the *Agent* communicates to the *Registry*.

Finally, all *Agent*s may have object properties "hasResource" of type *Resource*, and "hasCapabilities" of type *string*. As previously stated, there is one *RegistryMemory* per *Agent* (this *Agent* should now be a *Provider*), and as many properties "hasResource" and "hasCapabilities" per *RegistryMemory* as the *Agent* communicates to the *Registry*.

A *Resource* describes a resource, such as a CPU, a hard drive, a printer, ... and datatype properties "hasCapabilities" of type string, e.g., saving-information, calculating, printing, etc. In addition, *RegistryMemory* has two datatype properties "agentName" and "agentRef" to respectively record the name (which is the string an *Agent* records in its datatype property "hasName") and the address of the agent.

4.2   An Example of Instances for Our Ontology

As a case study, we have implemented a system with four agents, in which "Requester 1" and "Requester 2" look for the non-shareable resource called "Printer", while "Provider

Printer" manages this resource. Requester 1 has "intention1", which describes the fact that this agent has scheduled to use Printer from the date 5 and for a duration of 10 time units. Figure 2 displays this Requester 1's intention to use Printer, as well as Requester 2's.

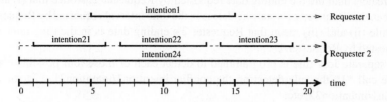

Fig. 2. Gantt chart of Requester 1 and Requester 2's schedules for Printer

In this figure, we can also see that the property "hasGoals" of Requester 2 points to four intentions, namely intention21, 22, 23 and 24, and that intention24 is at the same time as intention21, 22 and 23. We assume that Agent2 has not seen this overlapping in its own schedule, and the registry should thus detect this clash among Agent2's goals. The registry should also detect the clashes between Agent2's goals and Agent1's.

4.3   Orchestration Implemented in the Prototype

The Jess program roughly adopts the following four steps. By "roughly", we mean that these steps are interlaced in practice, while we are now presenting them sequentially:

- *Step 1*: The Protégé classes, instances and templates are translated into Jess. This is performed by the JessTab command (mapclass :THING) that translates the root node of the Jess ontology, as well as all its children up to the instances, into Jess. Note that this command is an addition of JessTab to Jess.
- *Step 2*: Every agent sends (i.e., asserts) a registration message to every registry. This message contains the description of this agent, one of its capabilities, one of its goals and one of its resources. The agent sends several messages to register all its capabilities, goals and resources, and can write "none" if it does not have one of these features.
- *Step 3*: Every registry receives these messages and saves their content by creating *RegistryMemorys*. One *RegistryMemory* is created for each registering *Agent*, and this *RegistryMemory* is almost a copy of *Agent* reconstructed from the registration messages.
  In practice, the JessTab commands make-instance and slot-set add instances and slots in the Protégé base, and then mapinstance converts this information into Jess, so as the consistency is maintained between Jess and Protégé knowledge bases.
- *Step 4*: Every semantic *Registry* detects clashes between non-shareable resources. Intention21, 22, 23 and 24 in Figure 2 represent the four possible types of clash with intention1. For example, intention1/intention21 is a conflict in which the beginning of the time interval represented in intention1 overlaps the end of intention21. This

conflict is characterized by the following conjunction: (i) the starting date requested by Requester 1 is later (greater) than the starting date requested by Requester 2, (ii) the starting date requested by Requester 1 is earlier (lower) than the ending date requested by Requester 2, (iii) the ending date requested by Requester 1 is later (greater) than the the ending date requested by Requester 2. Notice that (i) and (ii) mean that Requester 1's starting date is in the time interval requested by Requester 2, while (ii) and (iii) mean that Requester 2's ending date is in the time interval requested by Requester 1.

A separate Jess rule is programmed to detect each of these four possible clashes. We call *1* the rule detecting the conflict intention1/intention21, *2* for intention1/intention22, etc.

4.4 Results

The execution trace in JessTab is displayed in Figure 3, in which we can see seven conflicts, each one beginning with the name of the rule that detected it followed by some explanations. For example, the first conflict was detected by the rule *2*, and is thus of

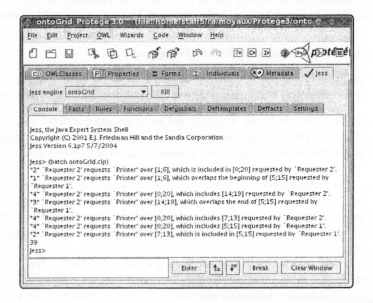

Fig. 3. JessTab detects the conflicts in the schedule of the non-shareable resource

the type intention1/intention22, but this first conflict is not between Requester 1's intention1 and Requester 2's intention22. In fact, this conflict is due to the fact that Requester 2 wants to use Printer both over [1;6] and [0;20], and thus, the former time interval is included in the latter while Printer is non-shareable.

Conversely to this, the second clash is between two different requesters. In other words, inter-agent as well as intra-agent conflicts are detected. We have checked that it is possible to add more instances of resources, providers, requesters and registries and JessTab still detects the conflicts.

5 Conclusions

The effectiveness of the Semantic Web relies on enabling technologies that permit the various components – ontologies, reasoning engines, and agents – to work harmoniously together. The interactions need to be managed according to a theory that is understood and agreed upon by all the components (in the paper we loosely referred to these components as *agents*). Coordination is the process of managing the possible interactions between activities and processes. The premise of the work presented in this paper is that effective coordination requires the sharing of knowledge about activities, resources and their properties. Typically, this sharing is achieved statically, by hard-coding at design time the coordination mechanism in the agents. However, in more open systems, where the processes and resources of which the system is comprised are not known at design time, such an approach is often impossible. A viable alternative in this type of systems would be a *dynamic* approach, in which the coordination requirement is handled at *run-time*, rather than design time. Such approach allows the relevant processes to communicate their intentions with respect to future activities and resource utilisation, and gets them to "reason" about coordination at run time, with the goal of preventing negative interactions, and facilitating positive interactions. The communication implied by this solution requires an agreed common vocabulary for coordination, with a precise semantics, that is, an ontological approach to dynamic coordination.

This paper describes such an ontological approach to coordination, and presents our results with respect to a proof-of-concept implementation of the approach, in which multiple processes detect coordination relationships using a Jess/Protégé implementation of the ontology. This prototype is only intended to show how an inference engine may be used to perform coordination tasks in Semantic Web Services. In fact, inference engines have already been being used to check semantic consistency, e.g., Racer [15] both checks semantic consistency and improves the organization of Protégé knowledge bases.

This work is still at an embryonic stage, the results obtained by the proof-of-concept implementation are very promising and encourage us to proceed towards the development of a representation of coordination mechanisms using Semantic Web rule languages. One possible implementation strategy consists of representing the rules in SWRL [16] and using a reasoner such as Vampire [17], to reason about the coordination rules. This strategy raises a number of research issues, such as whether the choice of rules will fail to provide a definitive answer due to the undecidability of SWRL. As an improvement on our prototype, we could:

- *Make every agent register to only one registry* instead of every possible registry;
- *Add other protocols*: e.g, some methods of clash resolution, and the update of *Registrys* by *Agents*;
- *Add message format*: at the moment, we only handle a basic registration message;
- *Looking for the maximum size of a semantic registry*: how many resources, providers, and requesters make the semantic registry too slow (in a dynamic environment, unlike our prototype).

Acknowledgements

The work presented in this paper is partially funded by the FP6 EU project Ontogrid (FP6-511513). The authors would like to thank Sean Bechofer and Terry Payne for their insightful comments on this work.

References

1. Ben-Ari, M.: Principles of Concurrent and Distributed Programming. Prentice Hall (1990)
2. Wooldridge, M.: An Introduction to Multiagent Systems. John Wiley & Sons (2002)
3. Malone, T.W., Crowston, K.: The interdisciplinary study of coordination. ACM Computing surveys **26** (1994) 87–119
4. von Martial, F.: Coordinating Plans of Autonomous Agents (LNAI Volume 610). Springer-Verlag: Berlin, Germany (1992)
5. von Martial, F.: Interactions among autonomous planning agents. In Demazeau, Y., Müller, J.P., eds.: Decentralized AI — Proceedings of the First European Workshop on Modelling Autonomous Agents in a Multi-Agent World (MAAMAW-89), Elsevier Science Publishers B.V.: Amsterdam, The Netherlands (1990) 105–120
6. Durfee, E.H.: Coordination of Distributed Problem Solvers. Kluwer Academic Publishers: Dordrecht, The Netherlands (1988)
7. Decker, K., Lesser, V.: Designing a family of coordination algorithms. In: Proceedings of the First International Conference on Multi-Agent Systems (ICMAS-95), San Francisco, CA (1995) 73–80
8. OWL-S: OWL Semantic Web Services (2004): http://www.daml.org/services/.
9. WSMO: Web Service Modelling Ontology (2004): http://www.wsmo.org.
10. Stanford Medical Informatics: Protégé (2005) http://protege.stanford.edu/ (accessed 31 March 2005).
11. Eriksson, H.: JessTab (2005) http://www.ida.liu.se/~her/JessTab/ (accessed 31 March 2005).
12. Friedman-Hill, E.: Jess (2005) http://herzberg.ca.sandia.gov/jess/
13. W.W.W. Consortium: Web site for the specification of OWL (2004) http://www.w3.org/2004/OWL/.
14. Agent Oriented Software Group: Company web site (2004).
15. Haarslev, V., Möller, R.: Web site for the software Racer (2005) http://www.cs.concordia.ca/Ehaarslev/racer/download.html
16. SWRL. (http://www.w3.org/Submission/2004/SUBM-SWRL-20040521/)
17. Tsarkov, D., Riazanov, A., Bechofer, S., Horrocks, I.: Using Vampire to reason with OWL. In McIlraith, S.A., Plexousakis, D., van Harmelen, F., eds.: Proc. of the 2004 International Semantic Web Conference (ISWC 2004). Number 3298 in Lecture Notes in Computer Science, Springer (2004) 471–485
18. PSL, process specification language. (http://www.mel.nist.gov/psl/)

Introducing Autonomic Behaviour
in Semantic Web Agents

Valentina Tamma, Ian Blacoe, Ben Lithgow-Smith, and Michael Wooldridge

Department of Computer Science, University of Liverpool,
Liverpool L69 3BX, United Kingdom

Abstract. This paper presents SERSE – SEmantic Routing SystEm– a distributed multi-agent system composed of specialised agents that provides robust and efficient gathering and aggregation of digital content from diverse resources. The agents composing SERSE use ontological descriptions to search and retrieve semantically annotated knowledge sources, by maintaining a *semantic index* of the instances of the annotation ontology. The efficient retrieval is made it possible through the semantic routing mechanism, that permits to identify the agent indexing the resources requested by a user query without having to maintain a central index, and by reducing the number of messages broadcasted to the system. The system is also capable of exhibiting autonomic behaviour. Autonomic behaviour is characterised by self configuration and self healing capabilities, aimed at permitting the system to manage the failure of one of its agents and ensure continuous functioning.

1 Introduction

The Semantic Web primarily aims to share knowledge from distributed, dynamic, and heterogeneous sources, whose content is expressed in a machine-readable format by means of languages such as RDF [1] and OWL, in a similar way to that in which information is shared on the World Wide Web. Agents play an integral role in this vision; they use these machine-readable representations to gather and aggregate knowledge, as well as to reason in order to manage inconsistencies, and to infer new facts. Together with their ability to process Semantic Web content, agents contribute features, such as distribution, autonomy, and social ability, that make them particularly suited to manage large, heterogenous, and distributed knowledge bases. In recent years, many tools have been developed for managing traditional knowledge sources, but such approaches usually imply a centralised, and static environment where the ultimate control is centralised. This type of approach does not promise to scale well to the Semantic Web, which is an open, dynamic, and often chaotic environment.

Distributed, decentralised systems are thought to be a better alternative for scalability [2]; their architecture is characterised by system components each with equal roles and the capability to exchange knowledge and services directly with each other. Peer-to-peer technology (P2P) such as Edutella [2] or Morpheus [3] is a possible answer to this quest for decentralisation. P2P systems are networks of peers with equal roles and capabilities, and recently peer-based management systems have been proposed, which exploit P2P technology for sharing and retrieving huge amounts of data [4]. However,

Y. Gil et al. (Eds.): ISWC 2005, LNCS 3729, pp. 653–667, 2005.

most approaches are oriented at file sharing, rather than at the management of semantically enriched content as provided by the Semantic Web. The agent paradigm seems to offer equally good prospects for the management of semantically annotated content: on the one hand, agents are intrinsically distributed, and platforms for agent oriented programming offer standardised communication protocols and management mechanisms (for instance, Jade [5]). On the other hand agents can provide "smart", service-based support for autonomous semantic web tools, and well-automated discovery mechanisms for advertising and locating resources within an open framework, established trust and reputation frameworks, and proactive support for fact maintenance [6]. One way in which the adoption of the agent-oriented paradigm can be beneficial to semantic web applications is by making them exhibit *autonomic behaviour*. Autonomic computing is an emerging branch of software engineering promoting the design and implementation of self-managing systems, many of which consist of several interacting, autonomous components that in turn comprise large numbers of interacting, autonomous, self-governing components at the next level down [7]. This type of behaviour is intended to make it easier to manage the complexity and scalability of complex distributed systems, such as those to manage Semantic Web content.

In this work we concentrate on the *robust* and *efficient* gathering and aggregation of digital content from diverse resources. We developed a multi-agent system composed of specialised agents that is able to search and retrieve semantically annotated knowledge sources. In addition to searching for digital content, the semantic information used to annotate resources is used to explore the addition of autonomic features to the system, in order to equip it with self-management and self-healing capabilities, aimed at permitting the system to manage the failure of one of its agents and ensure continuous functioning. In this paper we introduce the system SERSE (SEmantic Routing SystEm) and its main functionalities. This paper extends our previous work in this area [8,9] by introducing the autonomic behaviour features exhibited by SERSE and by presenting details of its multi-platform implementation. In the remainder of this paper we describe the system's conceptual architecture and the information flow between the system components. We examine the two main functionalities offered by the system, namely query management and autonomic behaviour, and we present a set of experiments aimed at evaluating the performance for each of these functionalities.[1]

2   SERSE

SERSE's primary goal is to enable the semantic retrieval and aggregation of the digital content of web resources. SERSE is designed as a multi-agent system composed of specialised agents capable of functioning in a scalable, self-managing, open, and dynamic fashion. The system requires resources to be semantically annotated according to one or more ontologies expressed in OWL, and at present is not capable of discovering annotated resources autonomously. For this purpose SERSE relies on the Annotation System component of Esperonto, that informs it of newly acquired content providing references

---

[1] SERSE was developed as part of the now concluded Esperonto projectIST-2001-34373 whose aim was to provide a set of tools for performing the transition from the traditional web to the semantic web [8].

to both the resources and their RDF annotations. The description of the Annotation System is outside the scope of this paper. However, for the purpose of describing SERSE, it is sufficient to say that annotations are semi-structured representations of information referencing instances (of one or more concepts in the annotation ontology) that appear in the content of web resources. [2]

The core of the system is represented by a network of specialised agents providing *indexing* and *routing* functionalites, that permit them to efficiently retrieve resources based on the semantics of their content. Each agent is *specialised* with respect to a concept, meaning that it can access the resources whose annotations contain instances of that concept, and it is only aware of those agents specialised with concepts that are *similar* or *related* to its own. Therefore, the agent network is organised into *semantic neighbourhoods* that mirror the structure of the ontology (in terms of the hierarchical and specific relationships defined in the ontology).

Neighbourhoods are partially overlapping, and this permits the routing mechanism to find the answer to a query in a limited number of hops, without having to browse the whole ontology and without having to flood the network with a large number of messages. Semantic neighbourhoods are automatically determined when the system receives a notification of new ontological content – received as new concepts are used to annotate resources. The neighbourhoods are not static but they dynamically change as the system is required to handle further notification of new ontological content, or if the ontology is modified (and a new version of the ontology is used in the annotation). In this way, we have multiple overlapping neighbourhoods, each centred on one concept, and agents have knowledge only of the agents composing their neighbourhood.

Indexing ontological content consists of creating structures that link resources, identified through their URLs, to RDF statements describing instances of the concepts in the ontologies. The routing functionality permits SERSE to route queries to the agents that are capable of retrieving the resources annotated with the concepts they are specialised on. SERSE handles queries expressed in RDQL [10] (an RDF query language developed by HP as part of the Jena toolkit) [11] on any combination of concepts and concepts properties (including object properties). Complex queries are decomposed into simple ones, each regarding a single concept. Each simple query is sent to one of the agents in the network of routers, and the agent consults its index to determine whether it can answer the query. If the agent cannot answer the query, then it routes the request to the agent in its neighbourhood that handles the concept *closest* to the one in the query. We evaluate similarity between concepts according to the approach proposed by [12]. However, we modified the algorithm so that it exhibits a greedy but less precise behaviour, implemented through heuristics, and that provides a higher number of potential matches. Ehrig and Staab's approach is aimed at ontology mapping, a process that can be taken off line and requires high precision in order to establish the correct mappings. Semantic routing is different in nature: the evaluation of similarity should be sufficiently precise to determine a new agent to whom the query can be routed, not necessarily the *best* agent. In addition, semantic routing is a dynamic process executed on line, and therefore it requires fast computation in order to minimise the time spent by the user waiting for an answer. We discuss in more detail the indexing and routing in Section 4,

---

[2] We are currently working at making SERSE a standalone system.

where these functionalities are related to the component of SERSE's architecture that provides them.

In addition to the main indexing and routing facilities, the system is also intended to be self-governing; it uses autonomic computing techniques to preserve index knowledge and to adjust the index connections when one or more indices within the system are unavailable. Autonomic behaviour is also used to maintain the system operative in case of failure of one agent or one platform. Section 5 describes the mechanisms used to implement autonomic behaviour in SERSE.

3   Conceptual Architecture

SERSE's conceptual architecture is composed of six types of specialised agents providing different functionalities. The heart of the architecture is composed by the network of Router agents, providing indexing and routing capabilities. These agents are complemented by a number of other specialised agents providing ancillary services, that implement system management functions. Figure 1 shows the different roles played by agents in SERSE and the message flow in the system.

SERSE is built within JADE – a FIPA compliant agent deployment environment [5]. The system is designed to be distributed over a number of JADE platforms, on different host machines, with each platform containing a part of the indexing system and its own interface agent set. This enables the system to operate even when reduced to one platform, and to dynamically reconfigure the index network in response to temporary or permanent outages of agents and platforms in the system. It also uses the JENA semantic web toolkit to handle RDFS, OWL, and RDQL. SERSE is able to use ontological

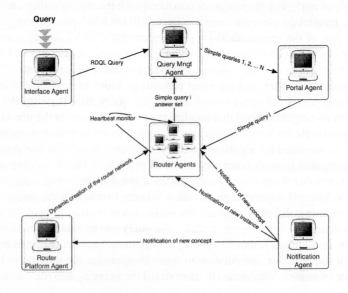

Fig. 1. SERSE conceptual architecture

definitions expressed in either RDFS or OWL (Lite and DL), using the full range of expressions available. The different roles that agents play in SERSE are described below, and Figure 2 shows the interactions between the different types of agents on a single platform and on multiple platforms.

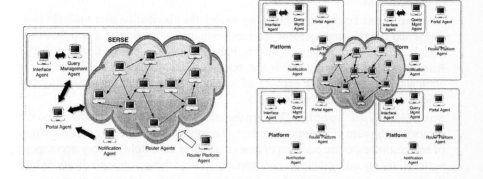

Fig. 2. SERSE architecture on a single platform and distributed over multiple platforms

- **Router Agents:** Router agents provide the core functionalities of the system: indexing, routing and self-management. In order to provide these functionalities agents maintain two types of indices, a *content index* and a *routing index*. The content index stores the URI identifying the RDF statements referring to instances of some resources, together with the URLs used to identify them. The routing index stores the communications address and concept handled by each of the router agents that are semantic neighbours. Routing indexes contain entries for three types of neighbour links:
    - *actual*: neighbour concepts which are handled by existing agents;
    - *ontology*: neighbouring concepts (according to the ontology) for which no agent yet exists; and
    - *implied*: concepts outside the neighbourhood that are presumed to exist, and to be linked to existing concepts. These links can be implied from the absence of one or more ontology neighbours.

Implied and ontology neighbours are used to provide some of the self management functionalities described in Section 5 and are used to query the routers even if the generation of the network is not complete, and, more in general, in all cases when a path between two agents should have been established, because they concern concepts in the ontology that are related, but the link has not been created, yet. By means of this mechanism, each agent is responsible for a sub-set of the total system knowledge and has only localised knowledge of its semantic neighbours.

Router agents are also equipped with self management capabilities that allow them to actively respond to changes in the state of their neighbourhood. In order to ascertain the actual status of their neighbourhood, Router agents employ two types of messages: they both monitor the result of their outgoing routing messages (to verify that they do not return an error), and they periodically send *heartbeat messages* [7] that "ping" their neighbour. In addition, Router agents periodically save the state of their content and routing indexes enabling the knowledge to be recovered following any failure of the agent. Router agents are distributed over multiple platforms, while the other agents described below are replicated for each of the platforms.

- `Router Platform Agents`: They enable the distribution over multiple platforms and provide management services, such as the creation of a new `Router agent`, for each agent platform on which the network of routers is distributed. The `Router Platform Agent` is also responsible for triggering the dynamic creation and adjustment of the network of routers upon receipt of the notifications of new content, as described in Section 5

- `Notification Agents`: They are the interface between each platform and the Annotation System of Esperonto, and receive notifications regarding the annotation of new resources, or the addition of new concepts in the ontology. They decompose notifications regarding multiple concepts and re-send these atomic notifications into the `Router Agents` network as Agent Communication Language messages.

- `Interface Agents`: They provide a connection between each agent platform and the software components operating outside the platform, such as the web-based query interface, by creating a socket interface and passing query and response objects across it.

- `Query Management Agents (QMA)`: They decompose complex queries, that involve multiple concepts linked by logical connectives, into atomic queries. The atomic queries are then sent into the `Router Agent` network; when the QMA receives the responses to each query, these are aggregated by re-applying the logical connectives, thus producing a set of web resources that match the constraints expressed in the complex query. During the process duplicate instances are identified and removed.

- `Portal Agents`: They act as a gateway into the `Router Agent` network, through which all atomic notifications and queries are passed. Each platform in the system has a `Portal Agent`, that maintains a list of *significant points* within the router system, and send messages into the network by initially routing them to the most appropriate of these points.

Finally, the other main component of SERSE is the web-based query interface. This enables the construction of queries using concepts from multiple ontologies, logical connectives between the concepts, and specification of the values of concept properties. Responses to queries are displayed as lists of web resources, identified by URLs, that match query constraints together with the URIs of the instances that annotate them. In addition, query replies also contain a list of the concepts that are neighbours of each the responding agents. This enables follow-up queries in which the original query is modified by changing property values of concepts, exchanging one concept for a similar one, broadening or narrowing a query by substituting ontological ancestors or descendents of a concept, etc.

4   Query Management

As mentioned in Section 2, SERSE handles queries specified in RDQL on any combination of concepts and concept properties (including object properties). Queries are sent from the local Interface Agent to the local QMA, where they are decomposed into atomic queries. Query decomposition is achieved by syntactically parsing the query and identifying blocks that form atomic queries, but preserve the semantics of the original query.

The QMA sends each atomic query to the local Portal Agent, which forwards each of them to the most competent Router Agent known to the local Portal Agent. In the current implementation of SERSE, these agents are those which have knowledge of the root nodes of each of the ontologies that have been notified to the system. The purpose of this initial semantic routing is to enter the router network in the general semantic area of the queried concept improving the efficiency of the routing process. Although routing first to the root node agents might potentially be perceived as a bottleneck, these agents are effectively those that are likely to have the smallest workload from handling queries. In fact, in the domain ontologies used by SERSE, as well as in most domain ontologies, the majority of the instances are direct instances of very specific concepts (leaf nodes), whilst root nodes have few (if any) instances. Therefore, the additional routing effort of these agents is compensated by answering fewer queries. In addition, any set of significant entry points could become a bottleneck, and alternatives are constrained by the processing necessary to identify the best entry point, and message workloads.

Once an atomic query is received by the appropriate Router Agent, it extracts the query constraints expressed in RDQL, then it consults its content index to check if it stores the URI of instances of the query concept. Any instances that match the query contribute to the answer set, which consists of a list of resources that are described by matching instances, and is returned directly to the QMA that sent out the query. Included in the query reply is information about the concepts handled by the replying Router Agent and the agents address which is then used in follow-up queries. This then enables users to semantically browse from one concept to other closely related concepts, using knowledge about these relationships held by the Router Agent and revealed by the original query.

If no instance is referenced in the content index, the query is routed to the semantic neighbour with the most similar expertise This semantic routing mechanism is designed to move messages in a series of hops across the network of Router Agents, until the message is addressed to the Router Agent indexing instances of the concept in the message.

5   Autonomic Behaviour

SERSE has been designed to autonomously react to a number of events that can affect its processing. These include the notification of new ontology, but also exceptional events such as the controlled shut down of an agent. The aim is to have a system that can work in an open environment, such as the Semantic Web, and that is scalable, robust, and requires limited human intervention for its functioning. For this reason, SERSE has been designed as a multi-agent system in which agents can join and leave the system without having to take (part of) the system off-line, or without degrading the performance of the system.

Autonomic behaviour in SERSE supervises two main functionalities: dynamic management of the network of router agents, and failure management.

The management of the router agents consists mainly of the of the operations to create the network of routers from scratch once the system is notified by the Notification Agent that a new ontology is available. Failure management consist of the functionalities that enable the system to continue to operate despite the temporary or permanent loss of agents or whole platforms from an existing index network. Autonomic behaviour is achieved by a number of different mechanisms:

- *Creation requests messages*: When the Notification Agent in one of the platforms receives a notification of new annotation ontology, it determines autonomously the root concept(s) and generates a creation request message for each of these concepts, to be sent to the Router Platform Agent, that in turns, creates a router agent for each root concept.
- *Router network population*: The population of the network of routers is triggered by the notification of new content messages received by SERSE. If the message notifies instances of a concept for which a router agent has not yet been created, the Router Platform Agent creates a new Router agent, and each of the neighbouring router agents affected by this event update their neighbourhood indices, with the pointers to the new actual neighbours. In this situation, ontology and implied links are created, in order to fill gaps between the existing routers and the newly created one.
- *Heartbeat monitor*: Router Agents monitor the success of messages sent to neighbours, and record this in their routing index. When messages are unsuccessful the neighbour is first set to a warning level, and if failure continues for a short time the entry is marked as unavailable. The neighbour will be considered available again if a message is received from it within a time period, but otherwise will eventually be removed from the neighbourhood.
- *Index backup and backup recovery*: Router Agents periodically save their knowledge to an XML backup file, which enables the recovery of knowledge following the failure of the Router Agent or platform. The knowledge stored in the file consists of the contents of both the content index and routing index. Recovery from failure of a platform is addressed by having the Router Platform Agent on start-up (following a manual platform re-start) check for saved state files, and, if any are found, re-creating Router Agents using the stored knowledge. Recovery from the failure of individual Router Agents is addressed by them contacting the local Router Platform Agent when they shut-down, and the Router Platform Agent will then use the saved state to re-create the Router Agent.
- *Router Agent shutdown procedure*: When Router Agents are subject to a controlled shut-down of their platform, they immediately save their knowledge to file, and then contact each of their neighbours to inform them of the shut-down.

This enables the neighbours to reactively adapt their neighbourhood connections to reflect the loss of neighbour. Recovery from shut-down, like that for failure, is initially a manual process but once started the `Router Platform Agent` will detect the saved-states and restore the `Router Agents`.

6   Experimental Evaluation

We conducted a number of experiments aimed to analyse the performance of the two main functionalities provided by the system: query management, and autonomic behaviour. In our experiments, we used two ontologies developed as part of the use-cases of Esperonto, the Fund Finder and the Cultural Tour ontologies for which we had also the annotated documents storing the instances of the concepts. The Fund Finder is expressed in OWL-Lite, and it is composed of around 50 concepts (12 of which are root concepts), and of 118 instances. The Cultural Tour ontology is an RDFS ontology composed of 60 concepts, and has more that 61000 instances.

In order to test the performance of the query management process we measured, for each ontology, the round-trip reply time for a set of twenty fixed queries, listed in increasing order of complexity. Figure 5 and Figure 6 illustrate the last query we posed for each of the ontologies, in order to show the level of complexity of the queries used in the experiments. The queries were posed to SERSE in sequence, and for each query we performed 1000 repetitions, in order to guarantee the reliability of the results. Figure 3 shows the response time, averaged over the repetitions, for each of the ontologies. We have compared these results with those obtained by qurying the static RDF model in Jena, the response times averaged over 100 repetitions for each query are depicted in Figure 4.

With respect to the autonomic behaviour exhibited by SERSE, we measured, for each of the two ontologies, the query response time in two different scenarios. Scenario 1 aims to test how well SERSE copes with the notifications of new content. This was achieved by creating new `Router agents` along the route of a query, by means of in-

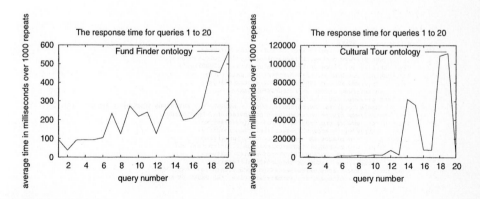

Fig. 3. SERSE response times in relation to queries about the Fund Finder and Cultural Tour ontology

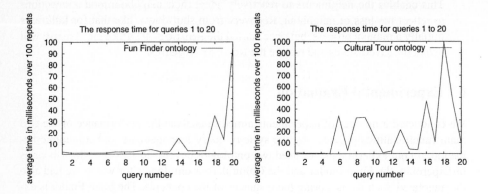

Fig. 4. Jena response times in relation to the same queries for each of the two ontologies

```
SELECT ?x, ?z WHERE
(?x, <http://www.w3.org/1999/02/22-rdf-syntax-ns#type>,
        <http://www.blacoe.uk/Fund_Finder.owl#Discount>)
(?x, <http://www.blacoe.uk/Fund_Finder.owl#Aims>, ?y)
(?y, <http://www.w3.org/1999/02/22-rdf-syntax-ns#type>,
        <http://www.blacoe.uk/Fund_Finder.owl#Objective>)
(?y, <http://www.blacoe.uk/Fund_Finder.owl#objectiveName>, "Company_Creation")
(?x, <http://www.blacoe.uk/Fund_Finder.owl#negotiated_by>, ?u)
(?u, <http://www.w3.org/1999/02/22-rdf-syntax-ns#type>,
        <http://www.blacoe.uk/Fund_Finder.owl#Negotiator_Body>)
(?u, <http://www.blacoe.uk/Fund_Finder.owl#actsForBody>, ?t)
(?t, <http://www.w3.org/1999/02/22-rdf-syntax-ns#type>,
        <http://www.blacoe.uk/Fund_Finder.owl#State_Funding_Body>)
(?z, <http://www.w3.org/1999/02/22-rdf-syntax-ns#type>,
        <http://www.blacoe.uk/Fund_Finder.owl#subvention>)
(?z, <http://www.blacoe.uk/Fund_Finder.owl#Deadline>, "30-juny-2005")
(?z, <http://www.blacoe.uk/Fund_Finder.owl#Aims>, ?w)
(?w, <http://www.w3.org/1999/02/22-rdf-syntax-ns#type>,
        <http://www.blacoe.uk/Fund_Finder.owl#Objective>)
(?w, <http://www.blacoe.uk/Fund_Finder.owl#objectiveName>, "Quality")
(?z, <http://www.blacoe.uk/Fund_Finder.owl#hasRelatedRegulation>, ?v)
(?v, <http://www.w3.org/1999/02/22-rdf-syntax-ns#type>,
        <http://www.blacoe.uk/Fund_Finder.owl#Diari_Oficial_de_la_Generalitat_de_Catalunya>)
(?v, <http://www.blacoe.uk/Fund_Finder.owl#date>, "26/04/1996")
```

Fig. 5. Query number 20 for the Fund Finder ontology

```
SELECT ?x, ?z WHERE
(?x, <http://www.w3.org/1999/02/22-rdf-syntax-ns#type>,
        <http://www.blacoe.uk/tesauro#RelacionExistenciaPersona>)
(?x, <http://www.blacoe.uk/tesauro#referencia>, "500001146")
(?x, <http://www.blacoe.uk/tesauro#entidad_existente>, ?y)
(?y, <http://www.w3.org/1999/02/22-rdf-syntax-ns#type>,
        <http://www.blacoe.uk/tesauro#Persona>)
(?y, <http://www.blacoe.uk/tesauro#fuente>,
        "Nadia Sokolova [Barcelona (CapCom) : Espaa?, ? - Barcelona (CapCom) : Espaa?, ?]")
(?y, <http://www.blacoe.uk/tesauro#autor_anotacion>, "prototipo")
(?z, <http://www.w3.org/1999/02/22-rdf-syntax-ns#type>,
        <http://www.blacoe.uk/tesauro#RelacionCreacion>)
(?z, <http://www.blacoe.uk/tesauro#estado>, "provisional")
(?z, <http://www.blacoe.uk/tesauro#creacion_relacionada>, ?w)
(?w, <http://www.w3.org/1999/02/22-rdf-syntax-ns#type>,
        <http://www.blacoe.uk/tesauro#ObraLiteraria>)
(?w, <http://www.blacoe.uk/tesauro#tipo_obra_literaria>, "articulo")
(?w, <http://www.blacoe.uk/tesauro#referencia>, "EL PASEO DE ROSALES ")
```

Fig. 6. Query number 20 for the Cultural Tour ontology

troducing messages notifying the acquisition of new content – that is, of new resources containing instances of some concept that was not instantiated before. The experiment was designed to implement the following procedure:

1. Remove all notifications concerning resources containing instances of a concept, for instance Organisation Applicant in the Fund Finder ontology;
2. Add a new notification for the concept SME, subsumed by Organisation Applicant;
3. Build SERSE: this consists of starting the Router Platform agent for the platforms, loading the ontology model and the notifications, and the dynamic generation of the network of routers from the notifications;
4. Run query no. 1, an atomic query with subject SME;
5. Notify one resource with instances of Organisation Application;
6. Run query no. 2, an atomic query with subject SME;
7. Notify one resource with instances of Company;
8. Run query no. 3, an atomic query with subject SME;

Figure 7 illustrates the relations existing between the concepts in the ontology that are used in the notifications and queries of Scenario 1. Scenario 2 aims to test how the system responds to an increase in the workload due to introducing agents in the semantic neighbourhood, and hence to the increase in the number of semantic similarity (and relatedness) calculations that needs to be performed during the semantic routing process. The process followed to set up the experiment mirrors the process followed in Scenario 1, but it uses different parts of the ontologies, and receives notifications related to five concepts.

Figure 8 shows the response times for the queries posed to the system in both scenarios. The experimental data concerning the round trip response time to different queries shows that the query management process implemented in SERSE takes a longer time to answer the queries when compared with Jena. This result is quite predictable because SERSE adds the overhead of the messages exchanged in order to enable the semantic routing and the system's self management. However, SERSE is still quite efficient, keeping the response time generally under the second. In that respect the results obtained are very promising. However, there some anomalies with queries number 14, 15, 18, and 19 in the Cultural Tour ontology. We have identified a number of reasons that contribute to these anomalies:

Fig. 7. The Fund Finder concepts used in the experiments of Scenario 1

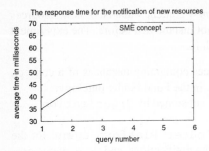
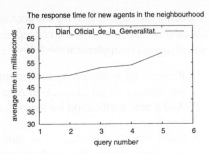

Fig. 8. Response times in relation to the queries in Scenario 1 and Scenario 2

1. Number of instances returned by each atomic query: For each query we match large sets of instances by URI, and then we match them with the corresponding resources by URL.
2. The time that RDQL takes to process the RDF model: This time varies considerably, as it can be seen by the values in Figure 3, and it is proportional to the number of statements in the RDF model.
3. Large sets of instances and resources returned: the resulting query result messages are quite large and the transmission time increases.
4. Time necessary to check for duplicates when large number of resources are returned as results of complex queries.
5. Number of semantic calculations performed: that is the length of the routing path and the number of neighbours for each of the agents in the path. The effect of the increase in the number of calculations is, however, negligible, as confirmed by the experiments for Scenario 1 and Scenario 2.

With respect to the results obtained when testing the autonomic behaviour, we can see that SERSE is able to dynamically adjust its network of routers in order to cope with the notification of new content and with the addition of new agents to the neighbourhood, without degrading the performance in terms of response time. Figure 8 shows how the increase in response time remains controlled despite the introduction of new content and new agents in the neighbourhood.

7   Related Work

Autonomic computing is a new engineering paradigm that aims at building computing systems that are *self managing* [7]. Usually, self managing systems are expected to exhibit four main properties:

1. *self configuration*: the ability to configure itself according to high level goals;
2. *self optimisation*: the ability to optimise the use of resources;
3. *self healing*: the ability to *react* to the signs of a possible problem, by detecting it, and, if possible, fixing it;
4. *self protection*: the ability to defend itself from malicious attacks as well as from human error.

These characteristics remind of those defining the notion of *agency* and in [7] the authors claim that "autonomy, proactivity, and goal-directed interactivity with their environment are distinguishing characteristics of software agents [13]. Viewing autonomic elements as agents and autonomic systems as multiagent systems makes it clear that agent-oriented architectural concepts will be critically important". Hence, it is not surprising that many notions of autonomic computing are found in multi-agent systems (MAS) literature. An example is the use of an *hearbeat* message broadcasted regularly in a MAS, organised as in peers or as a network, in order to monitor the status of the other agents [14].

Self healing has been analysed in [15], where the authors present a team of broker agents, which share global knowledge about the system. This global knowledge is used to discover that a broker has been disconnected from the rest of the system and to inform the other brokers of the event. IBM has developed theABLE agent platform [16] that reduces the workload of the system administrator by supporting autonomic agents. Finally, in [17] provide a review of the various architectural issues in autonomic computing.

From the multi-agent literature perspecitve, SERSE can be classified among the cooperative information agents, such as RETSINA [18], and InfoSleuth [19]. RETSINA is a matchmaker based information system where collaborative task execution is achieved through matching service providers and requesters over the web (and more recently, over the Semantic Web). InfoSleuth explicitly deals and reconciles multiple ontologies by means of specialised ontology agents that collectively maintain a knowledge base of the different ontologies used to specify requests, and return ontology information as requested.

As mentioned in Section 1, P2P systems have been recently used to reduce the complexity of distributed knowledge management applications. A typical example of such an application is EDUTELLA [2], a hybrid P2P architecture for sharing metadata, that implements an RDF-based metadata infrastructure for JXTA [22]. However, the emphasis is more on RDF repositories of metadata rather than on the representation of semantic information in possibly heavy-weight ontologies. Some other projects use "super-peers", which start the semantic routing process in the right direction.

An aspect of peer-to-peer networks that needs to be especially analysed is *scalability*. The way in which queries are propagated in the network determines how the network itself will scale. Networks where queries are broadcasted to all peers will hardly scale, unlike those networks implementing intelligent mechanisms for broadcasting the queries only to those few selected peers that are able to answer the queries. At this end have been developed several routing protocols that manage distributed indices used to handle complex queries. Examples of such protocols are CAN [23] and Chord [24].

Other approaches emphasise the use of semantics represented in ontologies. Among these there is the SWAP project [25]. In SWAP, each node is responsible for a single ontology: ontologies might represent different views of a same domain, multiple domains with overlapping concepts, or might be obtained by partitioning an upper level ontology. Knowledge sharing is obtained through ontology mapping and alignment, however mappings are not dynamically obtained.

More recently, GridVine [28] support complex queries in RDQL, that consist of triple patterns with more than one bound variable, thus providing the possibility of asking sophisticated queries, and thus implementing scalable semantic overlay networks. However, GridVine does not deal with ontology management operations in each of its peers.

8 Conclusion

In this paper we presented SERSE – SEmantic Routing SystEm– a distributed multi-agent system composed of specialised agents that provides robust and efficient gathering and aggregation of digital content from diverse resources. The agents composing SERSE use ontological descriptions to search and retrieve semantically annotated knowledge sources, by maintaining a *semantic index* of the instances of the annotation ontology. The efficient retrieval is made it possible through the semantic routing mechanism, that permits to identify the agent indexing the resources requested by a user query without having to maintain a central index, and by reducing the number of messages broadcasted to the system. The system is also capable of exhibiting autonomic behaviour. Autonomic behaviour is characterised by self-management and self-healing capabilities, aimed at permitting the system to manage the failure of one of its agents and ensure continuous functioning.

We tested the performance search and retrieval capabilities of the system, and the experimental data shows that SERSE generates generally maintains the response times under the second, showing that the overhead produced by the indexing and routing mechanisms does not impact the system performance. We also tested the autonomic behaviour, and the experimental results show how the system is able to efficiently self configure.

Acknowledgements

The authors would like to thank Terry Payne for his comments on this paper.

References

1. Decker, S., *et al.*: The semantic web: The roles of XML and RDF. IEEE Internet Computing **4** (2000) 63–74
2. Nejdl, W., *et al.*: EDUTELLA: A p2p networking infrastructure based on rdf. In: Proceedings of the WWW2002, Honolulu, Hawaii, USA (2002) 604–615
3. The Morpheus website. (http://musiccity.com)
4. Halevy, A., *et al.*: Schema mediation in peer data management systems. In: Proceedings of the International Conference on Data Engineering (ICDE03), Bangalore, India (2003)
5. Bellifemine, F., *et al.*: JADE a white paper. EXP In search of innovation **3** (2003)
6. Tamma, V., Payne, T.: Toward semantic web agents: Agentlink and knowledge web. AgentLink newsletter **19** (2005)
7. Kephart, J., Chess, D.: The vision of autonomic computing. Computer magazine **36** (2003) 41–51

8. Tamma, V., *et al.*: SERSE: searching for semantic web content. In: Proceedings of ECAI 2004. (2004)
9. Tamma, V., *et al.*: SERSE: searching for digital content in esperonto. In: Proceedings of EKAW 2004. (2004)
10. RDQL (http://www.w3.org/Submission/2004/SUBM-RDQL-20040109/)
11. The Jena website. (http://www.hpl.hp.com/semweb/jena2.htm)
12. Ehrig, M., Staab, S.: QOM quick ontology mapping. Number 3298 in LNCS (2004) 683–697
13. Wooldridge, M., Jennings, N.: Intelligent agents: Theory and practice. Knowledge engineering review **10** (1995) 115–152
14. Sterritt, R., Bustard, D.: Towards an autonomic computing environment. Proceedings of 14th International Workshop on Database and Expert Systems Applications, 2003
15. Kumar, S., Cohen, P.: Towards a fault-tolerant multi-agent system architecture. In: Proceedings of Agents 2000.
16. Bigus, J.P., *et al.*: ABLE: A toolkit for building multiagent autonomic systems. IBM Systems Journal **41** (2002)
17. McCann, J., Huebscher, M.: Evaluation issues in autonomic computing. International Workshop on Agents and Autonomic Computing and Grid Enabled Virtual Organizations (AAC-GEVO04), Wuhan, China (2004)
18. Sycara, K., *et al.*.: Dynamic service matchmaking among agents in open information systems. ACM SIGMOD Record. Special Issue on semantic interoperability in global information systems (1998)
19. Bayardo, Jr., R., *et al.*: InfoSleuth: Agent-based semantic integration of information in open and dynamic environments. In: Proceedings of the ACM SIGMOD International Conference on Management of Data. Volume 26,2., New York, ACM Press (1997) 195–206
20. Ehrig, M., *et al.*: The SWAP data and metadata model for semantics-based peer-to-peer systems. In: Proceedings of MATES-2003. Number 2831 in LNAI, Springer (2003)
21. Castano, S., *et al.*: Ontology-addressable contents in p2p networks. In: Proc. of WWW'03 1st SemPGRID Workshop. (2003)
22. Project JXTA. (http://www.jxta.org)
23. Ratnasamy, *et al.*: A scalable, content addressable network. In: Proceedings of ACM SIGCOMM. (2001)
24. Stoica, I., *et al.*: Chord: a scalable peer-to-peer lookup service for internet applications. In: Proceedings of ACM SIGCOMM. (2001)
25. SWAP: Semantic web and peer-to-peer. (http://swap.semanticweb.org)
26. Arumugam, M., *et al.*: Towards peer-to-peer semantic web: A distributed environment for sharing semantic knowledge on the web. In: Proceedings of WWW2002, Honolulu, Hawaii, USA (2002)
27. Lima, T., *et al.*: Digital library services supporting information integration over the web. In: Proceedings of WIIW 2001. (2001)
28. Aberer, K., *et al.*: Gridvine: Building internet-scale semantic overlay networks. Number 3298 in LNCS (2004) 107–121

Combining RDF and Part of OWL with Rules: Semantics, Decidability, Complexity

Herman J. ter Horst

Philips Research, Eindhoven, The Netherlands
herman.ter.horst@philips.com

Abstract. This paper extends the model theory of RDF with rules, placing an emphasis on integration with OWL and decidability of entailment. We start from an abstract syntax that views a rule as a pair of rule graphs which generalize RDF graphs by also allowing rule variables in subject, predicate and object positions. We include RDFS as well as a decidable part of OWL that weakens D-entailment and OWL Full. Classes can be used as instances. Almost all examples in the DAML set of test rules are covered by our approach.

For a set of rules R, we define a general notion of R-entailment. Extending earlier results on RDFS and OWL, we prove a general completeness result for R-entailment. This result shows that a restricted form of application of rules that introduce blank nodes is sufficient to determine R-entailment. For rules that do not introduce blank nodes, we prove that R-entailment and R-consistency are decidable and in PSPACE. For rules that do not introduce blank nodes and that satisfy a bound on the size of rule bodies, we prove that R-consistency is in P, that R-entailment is in NP, and that R-entailment is in P if the target RDF graph is ground.

1 Introduction

There is much interest in combining the standard Semantic Web languages RDF and OWL with facilities for expressing and reasoning with rules. There is not yet a standard Semantic Web language for rules. The purpose of this paper is to extend the model theory of RDF [8] with rules, while integrating OWL. We focus specifically on decidability of entailment and on exploring the computational complexity of entailment.

It is well known that OWL Full entailment is undecidable and that OWL DL entailment is decidable and NEXPTIME-complete [9]. OWL DL is integrated with rules in SWRL [10]. Consistency and entailment for SWRL are undecidable [10]. OWL DL's direct model-theoretic semantics [16] has been extended for SWRL [10]. OWL DL's RDF-compatible semantics and correspondence theorem [16] have not been extended to SWRL.

In this paper we present basic definitions of an RDF-compatible semantics of rules. We combine this semantics with a non-standard semantics involving the OWL vocabulary, with lower computational complexity than OWL DL, so

Y. Gil et al. (Eds.): ISWC 2005, LNCS 3729, pp. 668–684, 2005.

that there is greater scope for arriving at a decidable combination of ontologies and rules. In [11] the pD^* semantics was defined as a weakened variant of OWL Full. In [12] the pD^* semantics was extended to apply to a larger subset of the OWL vocabulary, which includes FunctionalProperty, Inverse-FunctionalProperty, sameAs, SymmetricProperty, TransitiveProperty, inverseOf, equivalentClass, equivalentProperty, hasValue, someValues-From, allValuesFrom, differentFrom and disjointWith. The pD^* semantics is in line with and extends the 'if-semantics' of RDFS [8], and is weaker than the 'iff-semantics' of D-entailment and OWL Full. As an example, the pD^* semantics assumes, like RDFS, that if c is a subclass of d, then each instance of c is an instance of d, but does not assume, like OWL does, that the converse condition also holds. While classes can be used as instances, fewer entailments are supported that relate to datatypes or entire classes or properties. The pD^* semantics seems to be sufficient for many applications where an ontology is used in combination with data relating to instances. There is a complete set of simple entailment rules for pD^* entailment which extend the standard entailment rules for RDFS; pD^* consistency is in P, while pD^* entailment is NP-complete, and in P if the target RDF graph has no blank nodes [12].

The model-theoretic semantics for RDF integrated with rules described in this paper includes the pD^* semantics. We show that the decidability and complexity results for the pD^* semantics can be extended to include a large class of rules. The resulting combination includes meta-modeling expressivity and uses a simple, uniform framework involving (entailment) rules also for RDFS and part of OWL. This leads to a relatively low threshold for implementation.

In this paper we describe some of the background to pD^* entailment, but refer to [12] for the underlying model theory. See [12], Sections 1.8 and 5.1, for an extensive discussion and comparison of the pD^* semantics and the semantics of OWL DL and Full. This paper does not contain complete proofs.[1]

2   Abstract Syntax, Examples, Overview, Discussion

2.1   Abstract Syntax for Rules

A rule is viewed as a pair of rule graphs; a rule graph is a set of *triple patterns*[2] which generalize RDF triples [13] by also allowing rule variables in subject, predicate and object positions. If $\rho = (\rho_l, \rho_r)$ is a rule, then ρ_l is called the body or left-hand side of the rule, and ρ_r is called the head or right-hand side of the rule. We impose the common condition that each rule variable in the head of a rule also appears in the body of the rule. We also require that the body of a rule cannot contain blank nodes. It should be noted, however, that in an application of a rule, a rule variable in the body of the rule can be matched with a blank node in an RDF graph.

---

[1] A version of this paper with complete proofs is available on request.

[2] This term is used in the same way by [18].

If the body and the head of a rule ρ are both nonempty, then ρ will be called a *proper rule* and will be written informally as: IF ρ_l THEN ρ_r.

If the body of a rule ρ is empty, then the rule is viewed as specifying certain axioms. In this case ρ is called an *axiom rule*, written as: AXIOMS ρ_r.

If the head of a rule ρ is empty, then the rule is interpreted as specifying that a certain pattern of RDF statements should be viewed as inconsistent. In this case, ρ is called an *inconsistency rule*, written informally as: NOT ρ_l. Compare the standard equivalence of the formulas $P \Rightarrow Q$ and $\neg P \vee Q$.

In the following examples we use the N-Triples syntax for RDF [6] for bodies and heads of rules, writing rule variables for example as ?x.

2.2   Example: Uncle

The well-known uncle example displays a widely-used kind of rule that cannot be expressed in OWL:

```
IF    ?a ex:hasParent ?b .
      ?b ex:hasBrother ?c .
THEN ?a ex:hasUncle ?c .
```

2.3   Example: Entailment for RDFS and OWL

RDFS-entailment [8] is characterized by entailment rules (see Table 1 below), which can be viewed as being defined by proper rules. Along the same lines, the pD^* semantics [12] involving the OWL vocabulary is characterized by entailment rules, which can also be viewed as being defined by proper rules. The pD^* semantics can be realized by 1 axiom rule, 23 proper rules (none of which introduces blank nodes; cf. Table 2) and 2 inconsistency rules. We give two examples, the inconsistency rule for differentFrom and the proper rule for FunctionalProperty (cf. entailment rule rdfp1, see Table 2):

```
NOT ?v owl:differentFrom ?w .
    ?v owl:sameAs ?w .

IF    ?p rdf:type owl:FunctionalProperty .
      ?u ?p ?v .
      ?u ?p ?w .
THEN ?v owl:sameAs ?w .
```

2.4   Example: intersectionOf

Although the pD^* semantics does not explicitly include unionOf and intersectionOf, half of OWL's iff conditions for these constructs are available in an alternative way, by means of rdfs:subClassOf [12]. For example, the fact that a class c is contained in the intersection of the classes $c_1, \ldots, c_n$ can be expressed by saying that c is a subclass of each class c_j. The converse condition, and thereby OWL's complete semantic condition for intersectionOf, can be realized by adding a proper rule:

```
IF     ?x rdf:type c₁ .
       . . .
       ?x rdf:type cₙ .
THEN ?x rdf:type c .
```

2.5   Example: disjointProperties

Rules can be used for meta-modeling, for example to extend OWL. OWL's `disjointWith` primitive applies to classes: OWL does not have a similar notion for properties. Such a primitive can be added with an inconsistency rule and an axiom rule:

```
NOT ?p ex:disjointProperties ?q .
    ?a ?p ?b .
    ?a ?q ?b .
```

```
AXIOMS ex:disjointProperties rdfs:domain rdf:Property .
       ex:disjointProperties rdfs:range rdf:Property .
```

2.6   Example: someValuesFrom

The $pD*$ semantics [12] includes the complete iff condition for `hasValue` from the OWL semantics [16] (cf. entailment rules rdfp14a and rdfp14bx in Table 2 below), while including an if condition for `someValuesFrom` and `allValuesFrom` (cf. entailment rules rdfp15 and rdfp16 in Table 2). An additional proper rule can be used to obtain OWL's complete iff condition for `someValuesFrom`:[3]

```
IF     ?v owl:someValuesFrom ?w .
       ?v owl:onProperty ?p .
       ?u rdf:type ?v .
THEN ?u ?p  b  .
       b  rdf:type ?w .
```

This rule introduces a new blank node, which is denoted by b.

2.7   Example: Rules for Role-Value-Maps

A role-value-map [1] is a definition of a class in terms of the composite of certain properties p_i and q_j:

$$C = \{x : \forall y \ (x,y) \in p_1 \circ \ldots \circ p_m \Rightarrow (x,y) \in q_1 \circ \ldots \circ q_n\}$$

Role-value-maps arise in a number of applications and are difficult to combine with description logics. The inclusion $\subseteq$ can be written as: if $x \in C$ and $(x,y) \in p_1 \circ \ldots \circ p_m$, then $(x,y) \in q_1 \circ \ldots \circ q_n$. It is not difficult to see that this if condition can be expressed by a proper rule that introduces $n-1$ new blank nodes.

---

[3] This proper rule induces entailment rule rdf-svx: see [12], Section 6.

2.8   Example: Airports and Map Points

For the final example we switch to the N3 syntax [2], which can be used to give a succinct representation of rules that introduce blank nodes. The following rule (by Mike Dean) from the DAML set of test rules[4] states that for each airport there is a map point with the same location, which is the underlying object of the airport, and has the appropriate label:

```
{ ?airport              a airport-ont:Airport;
                        airport-ont:latitude ?lat;
                        airport-ont:longitude ?lon;
                        airport-ont:name ?name }
=> { :layer map:object  [a map:Point;
                        map:Location [a map:Location;
                           map:latitude ?lat; map:longitude ?lon];
                        map:underlyingObject ?airport;
                        map:label ?name].}.
```

This is the original version of the rule, which introduces two blank nodes. See [10] for an alternative representation of this rule in SWRL, which uses two someValuesFrom statements.

2.9   Overview and Discussion

In this paper we present basic definitions of an RDF-compatible semantics of rules and give a model-theoretic definition of R-*entailment*, which describes in a mathematical way what it means if a (source) RDF graph S entails a (target) RDF graph G with respect to a set of rules R. R-entailment is taken to be an extension of RDFS entailment, extending the meta-modeling capabilities of RDFS. R-entailment also incorporates pD^* entailment [12] and thereby part of OWL. Most examples in the DAML set of test rules (cf. Example 2.8) are covered by our approach; in this paper we do not consider the use of arithmetic, e.g. for conversion of different units. We prove a general completeness result for R-entailment, which shows that a restricted form of application of rules that introduce blank nodes is in general sufficient to determine R-entailment. For rules that do not introduce blank nodes, we prove that R-entailment and R-consistency are decidable and in PSPACE. For rules that do not introduce blank nodes and that satisfy a bound on the size of rule bodies, we prove that R-consistency is in P, that R-entailment is in NP, and that R-entailment is in P if target RDF graphs do not have blank nodes. These results are proved, as in [12], by showing that entailment rules can be used to form a partial closure graph H of the source graph S that is sufficient to decide consistency and entailment, that is polynomially bounded in size, and that can be computed in polynomial time if there is a bound on the size of rule bodies. S R-entails a target graph G if replacements can be made of the blank nodes in G that turn G into a subset of H; this can be checked with a non-deterministic guess, which is not needed if

---

[4] http://www.daml.org/2003/06/ruletests/translation-1.n3

G does not have blank nodes. S is R-inconsistent if H contains a set of triples that matches with an inconsistency rule.

The rules considered here are analogous to and simpler than datalog rules; triple patterns take the place of first-order atoms. Datalog and description logics do not use blank nodes. The PSPACE complexity of R-entailment for rules that do not introduce blank nodes compares favorably with the complexity of OWL DL (NEXPTIME-complete [9]) and datalog (EXPTIME-complete [4]); the latter results form points of comparison for combination formalisms (cf. Section 5). The data complexity of pure datalog is P (in fact P-complete [4]). If rules do not introduce blank nodes, then R-entailment (and R-consistency) with respect to a fixed set of rules is also in P. This compares favorably with the coNP-hard data complexity reported for systems that extend a description logic with datalog rules (see Section 5). The gain in complexity can be 'understood' in part by noting that part of OWL is captured as part of R-entailment with (pD^* entailment) rules by the results of [12].

3   Background

This section summarizes part of the material used from [13] [8] [12].

3.1   URI References, Blank Nodes, Literals

The symbol U denotes the set of *URI references*, B denotes the set of *blank nodes*, i.e. (existentially quantified) variables, and L denotes the set of *literals*, i.e. data values such as strings and integers. L is the union of the set L_p of *plain literals* and the set L_t of *typed literals*. A typed literal l consists of a lexical form s and a datatype URI t: we write l as a pair, $l = (s,t)$. The sets U, B, L_p and L_t are pairwise disjoint. A *vocabulary* is a subset of $U \cup L$. The symbol T denotes the set of all *RDF terms*, i.e. $T = U \cup B \cup L$. The notion 'RDF term' is used in the same way by [18].

3.2   Generalized RDF Graphs

A *generalized RDF graph* G [12] is defined to be a subset of the set

$$U \cup B \ \times \ U \cup B \ \times \ U \cup B \cup L. \tag{1}$$

The elements (s, p, o) of a generalized RDF graph are called *generalized RDF statements* or *generalized RDF triples*, which consist of a *subject*, a *predicate* (or *property*) and an *object*, respectively. We write triples as $s\,p\,o$. RDF graphs [13] [8] require properties to be URI references; generalized RDF graphs, which also allow properties to be blank nodes, were introduced in [12] to solve the problem that the standard set of entailment rules for RDFS [8] is incomplete.

If the projection mappings on the three factor sets of the product set given in (1) are denoted by π_i, the *set of RDF terms* of a generalized RDF graph G is

$$T(G) = \pi_1(G) \cup \pi_2(G) \cup \pi_3(G).$$

The set of *blank nodes* of a generalized RDF graph G is denoted by $bl(G) = T(G) \cap B$. The *vocabulary* of a generalized RDF graph G is the set $V(G) = T(G) \cap (U \cup L)$. Two generalized RDF graphs G and G' are *equivalent* if there is a bijection $f : T(G) \to T(G')$ such that $f(bl(G)) \subseteq bl(G')$, such that $f(v) = v$ for each $v \in V(G)$, and such that $s\,p\,o \in G$ if and only if $f(s)\,f(p)\,f(o) \in G'$.

A generalized RDF graph is *ground* if it has no blank nodes.

Given a partial function $h : B \rightharpoonup T$, an *instance* of a generalized RDF graph G is the generalized RDF graph G_h obtained from G by replacing the blank nodes v in G and the domain of h by $h(v)$.

Given a set S of generalized RDF graphs, a *merge* of S is a generalized RDF graph that is obtained by replacing the generalized graphs G in S with equivalent generalized graphs G' that do not share blank nodes and by taking the union of these generalized graphs G'. The merge of a set of generalized RDF graphs S is uniquely defined up to equivalence. A merge of S will be denoted by $M(S)$.

3.3   Simple Interpretations

A *simple interpretation* [8] I of a vocabulary V is a 6-tuple $I = (R_I, P_I, E_I, S_I, L_I, \mathrm{LV}_I)$, where R_I is a nonempty set, called the set of *resources*, P_I is the set of *properties*, LV_I is the set of *literal values*, which is a subset of R_I that contains at least all plain literals in V, and where E_I, S_I and L_I are functions: $E_I : P_I \to \mathcal{P}(R_I \times R_I)$, $S_I : V \cap U \to R_I \cup P_I$, $L_I : V \cap L_t \to R_I$. Here $\mathcal{P}(X)$ denotes the power set of the set X, i.e. the set of all subsets of X. If I is a simple interpretation of a vocabulary V, then I also denotes a function with domain V, in the following way. For $l \in L_p \cap V$, we have $I(l) = l \in \mathrm{LV}_I$. For $l \in L_t \cap V$, $I(l) = L_I(l)$. For $a \in U \cap V$, $I(a) = S_I(a)$.

If $E = s\,p\,o$ is a ground triple, then a simple interpretation I of a vocabulary V is said to *satisfy* E if $s, p, o \in V, I(p) \in P_I$ and $(I(s), I(o)) \in E_I(I(p))$. If G is a ground RDF graph, then I satisfies G if I satisfies each triple $E \in G$.

Given a simple interpretation I and a partial function $A : B \rightharpoonup R_I$, a function I_A is defined that extends I by using A to give an interpretation of blank nodes in the domain of A. If $A(v)$ is defined for $v \in B$, then $I_A(v) = A(v)$. If G is any generalized RDF graph, then I *satisfies* G if I_A satisfies G for some function $A : bl(G) \to R_I$, i.e. if, for each triple $s\,p\,o \in G$, we have $I_A(p) \in P_I$ and $(I_A(s), I_A(o)) \in E_I(I_A(p))$. If I is a simple interpretation and S a set of generalized RDF graphs, then I satisfies S if I satisfies G for each G in S; it is not difficult to see that I satisfies S if and only if I satisfies $M(S)$.

3.4   RDFS Entailment and D^* Entailment

The notion of D^* entailment [11] [12] generalizes RDFS entailment [8] to include reasoning with datatypes from a given datatype map D [8]. If D contains only the standard datatype rdf:XMLLiteral, then D^* entailment coincides exactly with RDFS entailment. Table 1 lists a complete set of entailment rules for D^* entailment. In this table, prefixes such as rdf: are omitted from e.g. the URI rdf:type. These rules consist of the 18 rules defined in [8] for RDFS, with two differences that affect rules rdf2 and rdfs7. Rule rdfs7x corrects an error overlooked in [8] and [11] (see [12], Section 1.5): it differs from rule rdfs7 in that it can produce generalized RDF triples with blank nodes in predicate position when applied to ordinary RDF triples. To handle datatypes, rule rdf2 is replaced by the more general rule rdf2-D. Use is made of new blank nodes b_l, called *surrogate blank nodes*, allocated by rule lg ('literal generalization') to literals l. In rule rdfs1, b_l is a blank node allocated by rule lg to a plain literal $l \in L_\mathrm{p}$. In rule rdf2-D, b_l is a blank node allocated by rule lg to a well-typed D-literal l: $l \in L_D^+$. The only inconsistencies that can arise for the $D*$ semantics are D-clashes, which generalize XML-clashes [8]: given a datatype map D, a D-*clash* is a triple b type Literal, where b is a blank node allocated by rule lg to an ill-typed D-literal l: $l \in L_D - L_D^+$.

Table 1. $D*$ entailment rules [12]

	If G contains	where	then add to G
lg	$v \, p \, l$	$l \in L$	$v \, p \, b_l$
gl	$v \, p \, b_l$	$l \in L$	$v \, p \, l$
rdf1	$v \, p \, w$		p type Property
rdf2-D	$v \, p \, l$	$l = (s, a) \in L_D^+$	b_l type a
rdfs1	$v \, p \, l$	$l \in L_\mathrm{p}$	b_l type Literal
rdfs2	p domain u		
	$v \, p \, w$		v type u
rdfs3	p range u		
	$v \, p \, w$	$w \in U \cup B$	w type u
rdfs4a	$v \, p \, w$		v type Resource
rdfs4b	$v \, p \, w$	$w \in U \cup B$	w type Resource
rdfs5	v subPropertyOf w		
	w subPropertyOf u		v subPropertyOf u
rdfs6	v type Property		v subPropertyOf v
rdfs7x	p subPropertyOf q		
	$v \, p \, w$	$q \in U \cup B$	$v \, q \, w$
rdfs8	v type Class		v subClassOf Resource
rdfs9	v subClassOf w		
	u type v		u type w
rdfs10	v type Class		v subClassOf v
rdfs11	v subClassOf w		
	w subClassOf u		v subClassOf u
rdfs12	v type Container-MembershipProperty		v subPropertyOf member
rdfs13	v type Datatype		v subClassOf Literal

$D*$ entailment is weaker than D-entailment [8]. For example, with regard to the XML Schema datatype xsd:boolean, the three triples $a \, p$ true, $a \, p$ false, b type boolean D-entail the triple $a \, p \, b$, but this is not a $D*$ entailment. It is possible to 'recover' certain missing D-entailments by using meta-modeling statements. See [12], Section 1.7, for an example that uses the $pD*$ semantics. It is also possible to use rules and R-entailment for this purpose.

3.5 pD^* Entailment

The notion of pD^* entailment was introduced in [11] [12] as a variant of OWL
entailment, weakening OWL Full (see Section 1). The 18 D^* entailment rules
of Table 1 become complete for pD^* entailment by adding the 23 P-entailment
rules of Table 2 [12]. In addition to rule rdfp15, there is a second entailment rule
for someValuesFrom, called rdf-svx (see 2.6 and [12], Section 6) and analogous to
rule rdfp16 for allValuesFrom. This rule introduces a new blank node and can
be added for R-entailment; it is not supported by the pD^* semantics because
the proof of decidability given in [12] does not extend to the use of this rule.
For the pD^* semantics, in addition to D-clashes, another type of inconsistency
is formed by P-clashes: a *P-clash* is either a combination of two triples of the
form v differentFrom w, v sameAs w, or a combination of three triples of the
form v disjointWith w, u type v, u type w.

4 Rules and R-Entailment

In this section we define a model-theoretic semantics integrating RDF with rules
and extend the completeness, decidability and complexity results obtained in
[12]. Starting in 4.4, we make the combination with the pD^* semantics for OWL
[12]. It is also possible to start from simple entailment or RDFS entailment,
which would simplify some results; for example, P-entailment rules could be
subsumed under R-entailment rules. However, an advantage of the chosen setup
is that a closer connection is obtained to the semantic conditions of OWL.

4.1 Definition (Rule Graph)

In our definition of rules we use a set of *rule variables* X which is assumed to be
disjoint from the set T of RDF terms: $X \cap T = \emptyset$. Rule variables will also briefly
be called *variables*. A *rule graph* G is defined to be a set of *triple patterns*, i.e. a
subset of the product set

$$U \cup B \cup X \times U \cup B \cup X \times U \cup B \cup L \cup X. \qquad (2)$$

Given a rule graph G, we denote the union of the projection mappings π_i on the
three factor sets of the product set given in (2), applied to G, by

$$\pi(G) = \pi_1(G) \cup \pi_2(G) \cup \pi_3(G).$$

The set of variables of a rule graph G is denoted by $\text{var}(G) = \pi(G) \cap X$, the
set of blank nodes of G by $bl(G) = \pi(G) \cap B$, and the vocabulary of G by
$V(G) = \pi(G) \cap (U \cup L)$.
    Two kinds of *instances* of rule graphs are defined, with respect to variables
and with respect to blank nodes. Given a rule graph G and a function $\varphi :$
$\text{var}(G) \to T$, the instance of G with respect to φ is the generalized RDF graph
G_φ obtained from G by replacing the variables $v \in \text{var}(G)$ by $\varphi(v)$. Similarly,

Table 2. P-entailment rules [12]

	If G contains	where	then add to G
rdfp1	p type FunctionalProperty		
	$u\,p\,v$		
	$u\,p\,w$	$v \in U \cup B$	v sameAs w
rdfp2	p type Inverse-FunctionalProperty		
	$u\,p\,w$		
	$v\,p\,w$		u sameAs v
rdfp3	p type SymmetricProperty		
	$v\,p\,w$	$w \in U \cup B$	$w\,p\,v$
rdfp4	p type TransitiveProperty		
	$u\,p\,v$		
	$v\,p\,w$		$u\,p\,w$
rdfp5a	$v\,p\,w$		v sameAs v
rdfp5b	$v\,p\,w$	$w \in U \cup B$	w sameAs w
rdfp6	v sameAs w	$w \in U \cup B$	w sameAs v
rdfp7	u sameAs v		
	v sameAs w		u sameAs w
rdfp8ax	p inverseOf q		
	$v\,p\,w$	$w, q \in U \cup B$	$w\,q\,v$
rdfp8bx	p inverseOf q		
	$v\,q\,w$	$w \in U \cup B$	$w\,p\,v$
rdfp9	v type Class		
	v sameAs w		v subClassOf w
rdfp10	p type Property		
	p sameAs q		p subPropertyOf q
rdfp11	$u\,p\,v$		
	u sameAs u'		
	v sameAs v'	$u' \in U \cup B$	$u'\,p\,v'$
rdfp12a	v equivalentClass w		v subClassOf w
rdfp12b	v equivalentClass w	$w \in U \cup B$	w subClassOf v
rdfp12c	v subClassOf w		
	w subClassOf v		v equivalentClass w
rdfp13a	v equivalentProperty w		v subPropertyOf w
rdfp13b	v equivalentProperty w	$w \in U \cup B$	w subPropertyOf v
rdfp13c	v subPropertyOf w		
	w subPropertyOf v		v equivalentProperty w
rdfp14a	v hasValue w		
	v onProperty p		
	$u\,p\,w$		u type v
rdfp14bx	v hasValue w		
	v onProperty p		
	u type v	$p \in U \cup B$	$u\,p\,w$
rdfp15	v someValuesFrom w		
	v onProperty p		
	$u\,p\,x$		
	x type w		u type v
rdfp16	v allValuesFrom w		
	v onProperty p		
	u type v		
	$u\,p\,x$	$x \in U \cup B$	x type w

given a rule graph G and a partial function $h : B \rightharpoonup T$, the instance of G with respect to h is the rule graph G_h obtained from G by replacing the blank nodes v in G and the domain of h by $h(v)$. Given a rule graph G combined with $h : B \rightharpoonup T$ and $\varphi : \mathrm{var}(X) \to T$, $G_{h\varphi}$ is the instance of G_h with respect to φ.

4.2   Definition (Rule)

A *rule* is defined as a pair of rule graphs $\rho = (\rho_1, \rho_r)$ that are not both empty and that satisfy the conditions $\mathrm{var}(\rho_r) \subseteq \mathrm{var}(\rho_1)$ and $bl(\rho_1) = \emptyset$. If $\rho = (\rho_1, \rho_r)$ is a rule, then ρ_1 is called its left-hand side or body, and ρ_r is called its right-hand side or head. Given a rule ρ, the set of variables of ρ is denoted by $\mathrm{var}(\rho) = \mathrm{var}(\rho_1)$, the set of blank nodes of ρ by $bl(\rho) = bl(\rho_r)$, and the vocabulary of ρ by $V(\rho) = V(\rho_1) \cup V(\rho_r)$. If R is a set of rules, then $V(R) = \bigcup_{\rho \in R} V(\rho)$. A rule ρ is said to *introduce blank nodes* if $bl(\rho) \neq \emptyset$. A rule ρ is called *finite* if both ρ_1 and ρ_r are finite. As was already mentioned in 2.1, a rule ρ is called a *proper rule* if ρ_1 and ρ_r are both nonempty, an *axiom rule* if $\rho_1 = \emptyset$ and an *inconsistency rule* if $\rho_r = \emptyset$.

4.3   Definition (Satisfaction)

Given a simple interpretation I (see 3.3) and a partial function $Z : X \rightharpoonup R_I$, a function I_Z is defined that extends I by setting $I_Z(v) = Z(v)$ if $Z(v)$ is defined for $v \in X$. If, in addition, a partial function $A : B \rightharpoonup R_I$ is given, a function I_{ZA} is defined that extends I_Z further by setting $I_{ZA}(v) = A(v)$ if $A(v)$ is defined for $v \in B$. If G is any rule graph, I a simple interpretation and $Z : \mathrm{var}(G) \to R_I$ a function, then I_Z is said to *satisfy* G if there is a function $A : bl(G) \to R_I$ such that for each triple pattern $s\,p\,o \in G$ we have $I_{ZA}(p) \in P_I$ and $(I_{ZA}(s), I_{ZA}(o)) \in E_I(I_{ZA}(p))$.

A simple interpretation I *satisfies* a rule ρ if $I(p) \in P_I$ for each $p \in U$ that appears in predicate position in a triple pattern in ρ_1 or ρ_r, and if I also satisfies the following conditions:

- If ρ is an axiom rule, then I satisfies ρ_r.
- If ρ is a proper rule and $Z : \mathrm{var}(\rho) \to R_I$ a function such that I_Z satisfies ρ_1, then I_Z also satisfies ρ_r.
- If ρ is an inconsistency rule, then there is no function $Z : \mathrm{var}(\rho) \to R_I$ such that I_Z satisfies ρ_1.

4.4   Definition (R-Interpretations, R-Entailment)

If R is a set of rules and D a datatype map, an R-*interpretation* of a vocabulary V is a pD^* interpretation [12] of $V \cup V(R)$ that satisfies each rule $\rho \in R$.

Given a set of rules R, a set S of generalized RDF graphs is called R-*consistent* if there is an R-interpretation that satisfies S.

Given a set of rules R, the set of R-*axiomatic triples* is the generalized RDF graph obtained by taking the merge of the generalized RDF graphs ρ_r where ρ

ranges over the axiom rules in R, by adding the triples p type Property for each $p \in U$ appearing in predicate position in a triple pattern in a body or head of a rule $\rho \in R$, and by adding the triples v type Resource for each $v \in U \cap V(R)$.

Given a set of rules R, an R-*clash* is a generalized RDF graph that forms an instance $\rho_{l\varphi}$ of the body ρ_l of an inconsistency rule $\rho \in R$ for a function $\varphi : \mathrm{var}(\rho) \to T$.

Table 3. Three R-entailment rules (see 4.5 for the R-entailment rules rdfρ)

	If R contains	where	then add to G
lg-R	$v\,p\,l$	$l \in L$	b_l type Resource
rdf2-DR	$v\,p\,l$	$l = (s,a) \in L_D^+$	b_l type a
rdfs1-R	$v\,p\,l$	$l \in L_\mathrm{p}$	b_l type Literal

Given a datatype map D and a set of rules R, a set S of generalized RDF graphs R-*entails* a generalized RDF graph G if each R-interpretation I that satisfies S also satisfies G. In this case, we write $S \models_R G$.

4.5   Definition (R-Entailment Rules)

See Table 3 for the definition of the R-entailment rules lg-R, rdf2-DR and rdfs1-R, given a set of rules R and a datatype map D. In this table the phrase "If R contains $v\,p\,l$" stands for "If R contains a rule ρ such that ρ_l or ρ_r contains the triple pattern $v\,p\,l$". These rules are similar to rules lg, rdf2-D, rdfs1: see 3.4. For each proper rule $\rho \in R$, the R-entailment rules also include an entailment rule **rdfρ**, defined in the following way. If a given generalized RDF graph G contains the triples in the instance $\rho_{l\varphi}$ of ρ_l for a function $\varphi : \mathrm{var}(\rho) \to T(G)$, where $\varphi(x) \in U \cup B$ for each $x \in (\pi_1(\rho_r) \cup \pi_2(\rho_r)) \cap X$, then rdf$\rho$ prescribes the following two steps:

- Replace the rule graph ρ_r with the instance ρ_{rh} of ρ_r by replacing the blank nodes b in ρ_r with blank nodes $h(b)$ that do not appear in G; here $h : bl(\rho_r) \to B$ is assumed to be an injective function.
- Add the triples in the instance $\rho_{rh\varphi}$ of ρ_{rh} to G.[5]

4.6   Definition (Partial and Full R-Closures)

The rule system described in this paper is declarative; the entailment rules of Tables 1 and 2 and the preceding definition can be applied in any order (cf. Theorem 4.10). However, in order to prove decidability, we consider a special

---

[5] Note, as an example, that the syntactic conditions imposed in Table 2 on the pD^* entailment rules (e.g. the condition $v \in U \cup B$ of rule rdfp1) are realized exactly by the general syntactic condition of the entailment rules rdfρ that arise from the corresponding proper rules.

way of applying the entailment rules. Suppose that D is a datatype map, R a set of rules and G a generalized RDF graph. Suppose that K is a nonempty subset of the positive integers $\{1, 2, ...\}$ chosen in such a way that for each container membership property [8] $\mathtt{rdf:\_i} \in V(G) \cup V(R)$ we have $i \in K$. The *partial R-closure* G_{RK} of G is defined in the following way, refining the definitions of partial D^* and pD^* closure [12]. In the first step, all RDF, RDFS, D-axiomatic triples and P-axiomatic triples [12] are added to G, except for the axiomatic triples that include $\mathtt{rdf:\_i}$ such that $i \notin K$. Moreover, the R-axiomatic triples are added in such a way that G does not contain any blank node that appears in the merge of the generalized RDF graphs ρ_r, where ρ ranges over the axiom rules in R. In the next step, rules lg and lg-R are applied to each triple in G that contains a literal and to each triple pattern (in a rule in R) that contains a literal that does not appear in G, in such a way that distinct well-typed D-literals with the same value are associated with the same surrogate blank node b_l. Then, rules rdf2-D and rdfs1 are applied to each triple in G containing a well-typed D-literal or a plain literal, respectively. Next, rules rdf2-DR and rdfs1-R are applied to each triple pattern that appears in a rule in R and that contains a well-typed D-literal or plain literal that has not yet been handled by rules rdf2-D and rdfs1, respectively. The generalized RDF graph that has now been obtained is denoted by G_0. The partial R-closure G_{RK} is defined in a recursive way: $G_{RK} = \bigcup_{n=0}^{\infty} G_n$. Suppose that G_n has been defined. Then, G_{n+1} is the generalized RDF graph that extends G_n by making all possible applications to triples in G_n for each of the remaining D^* entailment rules, P-entailment rules and rule lg; moreover, for each entailment rule rdfρ arising from a proper rule $\rho \in R$, one application is made for each instance $\rho_{l\varphi}$ of ρ_l for a function $\varphi : \mathrm{var}(\rho) \to T(G_n)$, where $\varphi(x) \in U \cup B$ for each $x \in (\pi_1(\rho_r) \cup \pi_2(\rho_r)) \cap X$, such that $\rho_{l\varphi} \subseteq G_n$, and, if ρ introduces blank nodes, such that there is no function $h : bl(\rho_r) \to T(G_n)$ such that $\rho_{rh\varphi} \subseteq G_n$.[6] This completes the definition of the partial closure G_{RK}. Theorem 4.11 shows that this restricted use of proper rules that introduce blank nodes is in general sufficient to determine R-entailment. It should be noted that applications of rule lg in the last, recursive step do not lead to new blank nodes b_l. The *full R-closure* G_R of G is defined by taking $G_R = G_{R\{1,2,...\}}$.

4.7   Lemma

Let D be a finite datatype map. If R is a finite set of finite rules that do not introduce blank nodes and G a finite generalized RDF graph, then each partial R-closure G_{RK} of G is finite for K finite, and of size bounded by a polynomial in $|G|$, $|K|$ and $\sum_{\rho \in R}(|\rho_l| + |\rho_r|)$. If there is a bound on the size of rule bodies (e.g. if R is fixed), then a partial R-closure of a finite generalized RDF graph G can be computed in polynomial time, and it is possible to determine in polynomial time if a finite generalized RDF graph contains an R-clash.

---

[6] For example: for the proper rule for $\mathtt{someValuesFrom}$ (see 2.6) no application needs to be made if (the term matched by) $?u$ is already $?p$-related to a term of type $?w$.

Proof. This can be proved by refining the proof of Lemma 4.8 in [12].   □

In the remainder of this section D is a given datatype map.

4.8   Definition (R-Herbrand Interpretation)

Given a set of rules R and a generalized RDF graph G, an R-*Herbrand interpretation* $R_K(G)$ is defined in a similar way to a D^* Herbrand interpretation $S_K(G)$ (see [12], Definition 4.9). The only difference is that, throughout the definition, $V(G_s)$ is replaced by $V(G_R) \cup V(R)$, $bl(G_s)$ by $bl(G_R)$ and $G_{s,K}$ by G_{RK}.

4.9 R-Satisfaction Lemma

Let R be a set of rules and G a generalized RDF graph. If the partial R-closure G_{RK} of G does not contain an R-clash, P-clash or D-clash, then $R_K(G)$ is an R-interpretation that satisfies G_{RK}.

Proof. This can be proved by extending the proofs of the D^* and pD^* satisfaction lemmas (Lemmas 4.10 and 5.10 in [12]).   □

4.10   Theorem (R-Entailment Lemma)

Let R be a set of rules, S a set of generalized RDF graphs and G a generalized RDF graph. Then, $S \models_R G$ if and only if there is a generalized RDF graph H that can be derived from $M(S)$ merged with RDF, RDFS, D-axiomatic triples, P-axiomatic triples and R-axiomatic triples, by application of D^* entailment rules, P-entailment rules and R-entailment rules, and that either contains an instance of G as a subset or contains an R-clash, P-clash or D-clash.

4.11   Theorem (R-Entailment Lemma: Alternative Statement)

Let R be a set of rules, S a set of generalized RDF graphs and G a generalized RDF graph. Let H be a partial R-closure $M(S)_{RK}$ of $M(S)$ and suppose that $i \in K$ for each $\mathtt{rdf}\!:\!\_i \in V(G)$. Then, $S \models_R G$ if and only if either H contains an instance of G as a subset or H contains an R-clash, P-clash or D-clash.

4.12   Corollary

If D is finite, then the R-entailment relation $S \models_R G$ between finite sets S of finite generalized RDF graphs, finite sets R of finite rules that do not introduce blank nodes, and finite generalized RDF graphs G is decidable and in PSPACE. If there is a bound on the size of rule bodies, then this problem is in NP, and in P if G is ground.

4.13   Theorem (R-Consistency Lemma)

Let R be a set of rules, S a set of generalized RDF graphs and H a partial R-closure of $M(S)$. Then, S is R-consistent if and only if H does not contain an R-clash, P-clash or D-clash.

4.14   Corollary

If D is finite, then the problem to determine if a finite set of finite generalized RDF graphs is R-consistent with respect to a finite set R of finite rules that do not introduce blank nodes is decidable and in PSPACE, and in P if there is a bound on the size of rule bodies.

Proof. The proof of Theorems 4.10, 4.11 and 4.13 builds further on the proof of Theorems 5.11, 5.12 and 5.15 of [12]. The proof of the corollaries is based on the computation of a partial R-closure $H = M(S)_{RK}$, following the steps described in Definition 4.6. Lemma 4.7 and its proof show that this computation can be done in polynomial space and that it can be done in polynomial time if there is a bound on the size of rule bodies. For Corollary 4.12, a non-deterministic guess is used of an instance function h such that $G_h \subseteq H$ (by Savitch's theorem, NPSPACE=PSPACE); this is not needed if G is ground.   □

If R is allowed to vary without restrictions, then R-consistency is NP-hard, even if only inconsistency rules are used. This can be shown with a transformation from the standard NP-complete problem conjunctive boolean query.

5   Related Work

SWRL combines ontologies with rules by extending OWL DL with datalog rules, i.e. function-free Horn rules [10]. Rules may include DL atoms and `sameAs` and `differentFrom` statements; unlike the approaches that will be mentioned next, in SWRL rules cannot include non-DL atoms. Consistency and entailment for SWRL are undecidable, by a reduction from the domino problem [10]. For SWRL a prototype implementation has been described which makes use of first-order reasoning, necessarily without guarantee of completeness [10].

Several formalisms have been investigated which impose restrictions on the extension of a description logic with datalog rules in order to obtain decidable inference problems (cf. 2.9). $\mathcal{AL}$-log [5] allows the addition to rule bodies of atoms that specify that a constant or variable belongs to a class defined in the DL $\mathcal{ALC}$. The resulting combination is shown to be decidable and in NEXPTIME by using a tableau algorithm in combination with constrained SLD-derivation. As an example, the standard NP-complete problem graph 3-colorability is encoded with a knowledge base [5], which shows that data complexity of $\mathcal{AL}$-log is coNP-hard [3]. A similar encoding cannot be used with the approach described in this paper because it uses the union construct to express that each node in the input graph belongs to one of three colors (cf. 2.4).

The CARIN approach [14] includes a more powerful description logic ($\mathcal{ALCNR}$) and has more possibilities allowing concepts and roles in datalog rules. Much attention is devoted to the "existential entailment problem": for two or more Horn rules, it may occur that either the antecedents of one rule are satisfied or the antecedents of another rule are satisfied, while it is not known which of these possibilities occurs, so that all possibilities need to be considered, thus increasing the computational complexity. This contrasts with traditional Horn systems and the approach described in this paper, where the application of rules can be considered in isolation. In [14], several restrictions are discussed which guarantee decidability, leading to coNP-complete data complexity, i.e. complexity of inference in the number of ground facts.

One of these restrictions requires that each variable in a Horn rule appears in a non-DL-atom in the body of the rule. This "DL-safety" condition is also used to achieve decidability in [15] and [17], with formalisms that include increasingly expressive DLs. According to [15], DL-safety amounts to the condition that "the identity of all objects is known". R-entailment, on the other hand, allows variables in bodies of rules to be matched with blank nodes.

DLP captures part of OWL DL with datalog rules [7]. Datalog is EXPTIME-complete [4]. DLP does not include the same expressivity as R-entailment. For example, sameAs and FunctionalProperty are not supported by DLP. Unlike the R-semantics, the formalisms mentioned in this section do not include the full semantics of RDF and meta-modeling capabilities as provided by RDFS. For example, DLP is restricted to the "DAML+OIL subset of RDFS" [7].

This paper uses a simple, uniform approach which, unlike in e.g. [5], does not involve a hybrid system that incorporates two distinct reasoning paradigms. Just like RDF and OWL and unlike [5] [14] [17], this paper does not make a unique names assumption. To recapitulate, DLP seems to be the approach that is most similar to R-entailment; compared with other formalisms that combine ontologies and rules, R-entailment does not include the same expressivity but leads to improved complexity and adds meta-modeling expressivity.

6   Conclusion

In this paper we have defined a semantic extension of RDF that incorporates rules. We started from an abstract syntax that considers a rule as a pair of rule graphs which extend RDF graphs with the possibility to include rule variables. For a set of rules R, we defined a general notion of R-entailment, which extends RDFS and its meta-modeling capabilities. R-entailment also extends a decidable part of OWL that weakens D-entailment and OWL Full. We proved a general completeness result for R-entailment, which shows that a restricted form of application of rules that introduce blank nodes is in general sufficient to determine R-entailment. For rules that do not introduce blank nodes, we proved that R-entailment and R-consistency are decidable and in PSPACE. For rules that do not introduce blank nodes and that satisfy a bound on the size of rule bodies, we proved that R-consistency is in P, that R-entailment is in NP, and that R-entailment is in P if the target RDF graph is ground.

Acknowledgment. Many thanks to Warner ten Kate, Jan Korst and the anonymous reviewers for their useful comments about the manuscript.

References

1. F. Baader et al. (Eds.), *The Description Logic Handbook*, Cambridge, 2003.
2. T. Berners-Lee, S. Hawke, D. Connolly, Semantic Web Tutorial Using N3, May 2004, http://www.w3.org/2000/10/swap/doc/
3. M. Cadoli, L. Palopoli, M. Lenzerini, Datalog and Description Logics: Expressive Power, Proceedings of the 6th International Workshop on Database Programming Languages (DBPL1997), pp. 281-298, 1997.
4. E. Dantsin, T. Eiter, G. Gottlob, A. Voronkov, Complexity and Expressive Power of Logic Programming, ACM Computing Surveys, 33 (2001) 374-425.
5. F.M. Donini, M. Lenzerini, D. Nardi, A. Schaerf, $\mathcal{AL}$-log: Integrating Datalog and Description Logics, Journal of Intelligent Information Systems, 10 (1998) 227-252.
6. J. Grant, D. Beckett (Eds.), RDF Test Cases, W3C Recommendation, 10 February 2004, http://www.w3.org/TR/2004/REC-rdf-testcases-20040210/
7. B. Grosof, I. Horrocks, R. Volz, S. Decker, Description Logic Programs: Combining Logic Programs with Description Logic, Proceedings of the 12th International Conference on the World Wide Web (WWW2003), pp. 48-57, 2003.
8. P. Hayes (Ed.), RDF Semantics, W3C Recommendation, 10 February 2004, http://www.w3.org/TR/2004/REC-rdf-mt-20040210/
9. I. Horrocks, P.F. Patel-Schneider, Reducing OWL Entailment to Description Logic Satisfiability, Journal of Web Semantics 1 (2004) 345-357.
10. I. Horrocks, P.F. Patel-Schneider, S. Bechhofer, D. Tsarkov, OWL Rules: A Proposal and Prototype Implementation, J. Web Semantics 3 (2005) 23-40.
11. H.J. ter Horst, Extending the RDFS Entailment Lemma, Proceedings 3rd Int. Semantic Web Conference (ISWC2004), Springer LNCS 3298, pp. 77-91, 2004.
12. H.J. ter Horst, Completeness, Decidability and Complexity of Entailment for RDF Schema and a Semantic Extension Involving the OWL Vocabulary, Revised and extended version of [11], Journal of Web Semantics 3 (2005) 79-115.
13. G. Klyne, J. Carroll (Eds.), Resource Description Framework (RDF): Concepts and Abstract Syntax, W3C Recommendation, 10 February 2004, http://www.w3.org/TR/2004/REC-rdf-concepts-20040210/
14. A.Y. Levy, M.-C. Rousset, Combining Horn Rules and Description Logics in CARIN, Artificial Intelligence 104 (1998) 165-209.
15. B. Motik, U. Sattler, R. Studer, Query Answering for OWL-DL with Rules, Journal of Web Semantics 3 (2005) 41-60.
16. P.F. Patel-Schneider, P. Hayes, I. Horrocks (Eds.), OWL Web Ontology Language Semantics and Abstract Syntax, W3C Recommendation, 10 February 2004, http://www.w3.org/TR/2004/REC-owl-semantics-20040210/
17. R. Rosati, On the Decidability and Complexity of Integrating Ontologies and Rules, Journal of Web Semantics 3 (2005) 61-73.
18. RDF Data Access Working Group, W3C, http://www.w3.org/2001/sw/DataAccess/

Benchmarking Database Representations of RDF/S Stores

Yannis Theoharis[1,2], Vassilis Christophides[1,2], and Grigoris Karvounarakis[3]

[1] Institute of Computer Science, FORTH, Vassilika Vouton,
P.O.Box 1385, GR 71110
[2] Department of Computer Science, University of Crete, P.O.Box 2208, GR 71409,
Heraklion, Greece
{theohari, christop}@ics.forth.gr
[3] Department of Computer and Information Science, University of Pennsylvania,
3330 Walnut St., Philadelphia, PA 19104, USA
gkarvoun@cis.upenn.edu

Abstract. In this paper we benchmark three popular database representations of RDF/S schemata and data: (a) a schema-aware (i.e., one table per RDF/S class or property) with explicit (ISA) or implicit (NOISA) storage of subsumption relationships, (b) a schema-oblivious (i.e., a single table with triples of the form ⟨subject-predicate-object⟩), using (ID) or not (URI) identifiers to represent resources and (c) a hybrid of the schema-aware and schema-oblivious representations (i.e., one table per RDF/S meta-class by distinguishing also the range type of properties). Furthermore, we benchmark two common approaches for evaluating taxonomic queries either on-the-fly (ISA, NOISA, Hybrid), or by precomputing the transitive closure of subsumption relationships (MatView, URI, ID). The main conclusion drawn from our experiments is that the evaluation of taxonomic queries is most efficient over RDF/S stores utilizing the Hybrid and MatView representations. Of the rest, schema-aware representations (ISA, NOISA) exhibit overall better performance than URI, which is superior to that of ID, which exhibits the overall worst performance.

1 Introduction

Several RDF stores have been developed during the last five years for supporting real-scale Semantic Web applications. They usually rely on (main-memory) virtual machine implementations or on (object-) relational database technology, while employing a variety of storage schemes. The most popular database representations for shredding RDF/S resource descriptions into relational tables are: the *schema-oblivious* (also called *generic* or *vertical*), the *schema-aware* (also called *specific* or *binary*) and a *hybrid* representation, combining features of the previous two. In *schema-oblivious*, a single table is used for storing both RDF/S schemata and resource descriptions under the form of triples (⟨subject-predicate-object⟩). In *schema-aware*, each property (or class) defined in an RDF/S schema is represented by a separate table. In hybrid one table per RDF/S meta-class is

Y. Gil et al. (Eds.): ISWC 2005, LNCS 3729, pp. 685–701, 2005.
© Springer-Verlag Berlin Heidelberg 2005

created, namely, for class and property instances with different range values (i.e., resource, string, integer, etc.). Several variations (e.g., with explicit or implicit database representation of subsumption relationships, use of resource URIs vs IDs, etc.) of these three core storage schemes have also been implemented in existing RDF stores [2,15,24,4,16,19,22,13] (see [20] for an extensive survey). In terms of inferring triples from schema information there exist two approaches: either to precompute them (at compile-time) or to compute them on demand (at run-time). The *schema-oblivious* (URI and ID), as well as, approaches using materialized views (MatView) adopt the former approach, while *schema-aware* (ISA and NOISA) and Hybrid adopt the latter. On demand computations can be performed either in main memory (as in ISA) or in secondary memory (as in NOISA and Hybrid). All these representations have pros and cons for different Semantic Web application scenarios, and, thus, benchmarking their performance is an important, but also a challenging task.

In this paper, we focus on the efficient evaluation of *taxonomic* RDF/S queries, retrieving the proper or transitive instances of a particular class or property. A key point affecting the performance of such queries is the representation of subsumption relationships and thus, the cost of traversing persistent class (or property) hierarchies. For this reason, we have developed a synthetic RDF/S generator, which takes as input the size of the subsumption hierarchies, the number of classified resources, as well as their distribution under classes or properties at various levels in the hierarchy and produces RDF/S schemas and resource descriptions that match these specifications. Then, we have conducted extensive experiments on the aforementioned RDF/S storage schemes on top of the object-relational DBMS PostgreSQL. The main conclusion drawn from these experiments is that the evaluation of taxonomic queries is most efficient over RDF/S stores utilizing the Hybrid and MatView representations. This result is especially interesting in the case of Hybrid which is also optimal in terms of storage space requirements, in contrast with MatView which relies on Transitive Closure (TC) precomputation over the database instances, that incurs a huge storage overhead. Of the rest, *schema-aware* representations (ISA, NOISA) exhibit as expected overall better performance than URI, which is superior to that of ID, that exhibits the worst performance.

Experimental results reported in [1] and [2] also highlight the performance gains of the *schema-aware* representation compared to the *schema-oblivious* one. The main reason is that in the former, tuples contain only the property values involved in a given query, while in the latter, tuples contain both property names and values and, thus, imply an additional filtering phase on the property name on a significantly larger table (i.e., extra overhead for schema filtering in all queries) to locate the tuples actually involved in a query. However, a comparative evaluation of taxonomic queries against different database representations of subsumption relationships is not provided in any of these studies. Furthermore, the statistical analysis presented in [14], [21] highlights the structural characteristics of RDF schemata employed by popular or emerging SW applications. However, these studies do not benchmark intensional (i.e., schema) or extensional (i.e., data) queries formulated against secondary memory-based RDF/S stores. Moreover, in [5] an extensive benchmarking of intensional taxonomic queries has been presented for various families of encodings, using real data from the Open Directory Portal as a testbed. In this paper, we take one step further, by evaluating both intensional and extensional taxonomic queries against various synthetic RDF/S schemata and resources descriptions, corresponding to different Semantic Web application needs. The goal of the experiments reported in [8] was to evaluate the trade-off between the materialization of the TC, including triples that are inferred by the schema, and its run-time computation using a DL (Description Logic) reasoner. Their main conclusion was that the use of materialized views in a database managed by a DL reasoner leads to increasing result completeness, while the query response time is considerably low. Furthermore, authors in [23] worked on the problem of incremental maintenance of materialized ontologies using logic reasoners by taking into account the RDF/S model semantics [11]. They also noted the trade-off between inferencing time, storage space and access time. Compared to these studies we provide precise formulas to estimate the storage overhead of the materialized approach.

The remainder of this paper is organized as follows: Section 2 surveys the main storage schemes adopted by existing RDF/S stores. Moreover, we illustrate the translation of taxonomic queries against each of the three possible RDF/S relational representations. Section 3 introduces our synthetic RDF/S generator based on different distribution modes of resources under the classes of a schema. Section 4 presents the results of our experimental evaluation using the qualitative and quantitative parameters considered by our RDF/S generator. Finally, Section 5 concludes our paper and discusses possible future directions in RDF/S benchmarking.

2   RDF/S Storage Schemes

The three widely used storage schemes for shredding RDF/S resource descriptions into relational tables are:

Schema-oblivious (also called *generic* or *vertical*): One ternary relation is used to store any RDF/S schema or resource description graph. This table contains triples of the form ⟨subject-predicate-object⟩ where attribute subject represents a resource that is the source of a property, whose name is given in attribute predicate, while attribute object represents a destination resource or a literal value for this property (see Figure 1). Different properties of a specific resource are tied together using the same subject URI.

Schema-aware (also called *specific* or *binary*): Unlike the previous representation one table per RDF/S schema property or class is used (see Figure 2).

Hybrid: In this representation (see Figure 3), there is a ternary relation for every different property range type and a binary relation for all class instances (as in *schema-aware*). On the other hand, property (class) instances with range values of the same type are stored in the same relation, distinguished by the property (class) id (as in *schema-oblivious*).

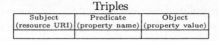

Fig. 1. Schema-oblivious representation

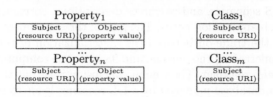

Fig. 2. Schema-aware representation

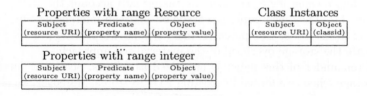

Fig. 3. Hybrid representation

Schema evolution is straightforward in the *schema-oblivious* approach, whereas the addition (deletion) of a new property requires the addition (deletion) of a table in the *schema-aware* approach. On the other hand, the former approach disregards type information, since all property values are usually stored as VARCHARs (i.e., strings) in the object attribute, whereas the latter entails a significant overhead when managing a potentially large number of tables (for voluminous RDF/S schemata). In Hybrid, schema evolution can be easily supported (as in *schema-oblivious*), while preserving type information (as in *schema-aware*).

The main variations of the *schema-aware* scheme concern the representation of subsumption relationships of classes and properties, defined in one or more RDF/S schemata. The first, called ISA, exploits the object-relational features of SQL99 [18] for representing subsumption relationships using sub-table definitions (see subsection 2.1). The second, called NOISA, ignores this feature and stores RDF/S data using a standard relational representation as depicted in Figure 2. Furthermore, two variations of the *schema-oblivious* scheme have been proposed, which differ in the way they store resources' URIs. The former, called URI, stores the URIs in the table holding the triples (usually repeating the same URI, e.g., in multiple triples that refer to properties of the same resource), while the latter, called ID, relies on integer identifiers to represent resources and properties in the triple table and stores them only once in a separate table (called "instance"). It should be stressed that the redundancy in the URI representation incurs a significant storage overhead. On the other hand, the ID representation suffers

Table 1. RDF/S storage schemes and systems

RDF/S Stores	Schema-aware			Hybrid	Schema-oblivious	
	ISA	NOISA	MatView	Hybrid	URI	ID
RDFSuite[2]	X	X		X		
Jena[15,24]	X				X[24]	X[15]
Sesame[4]	X					X
DLDB[16]			X			
RStar[13]						X
KAON[22]						X
PARKA[19]		X				
3Store[9]						X

from the need of an additional join operation at the end of every query, in order to retrieve the actual resource URIs.

Except from the triples which are explicitly defined in an RDF graph, many other can be inferred by the semantics of the schema (see RDF/S model semantics [11]). Two main approaches have been proposed to address this issue: the *a priori* (at compile-time) materialization in the persistent store or the *a posteriori* (at run-time) computation of the inferred triples. The former approach avoids to recomputing TCs for every query, but incurs a storage overhead and makes data updates harder, while the latter has less storage requirements, although its scalability is limited by the main memory space that is required for the run-time TC computations.

Existing RDF/S stores employing either URI or ID, the two *schema-oblivious* variations, usually adopt the former (materialized) approach,[1] while [16] proposes to store the precomputed triples as materialized views: for each class or property, a table holds its proper instances while a materialized view holds both proper and transitive instances. In order to create this view, the table with the proper instances is "unioned" with the views of its direct subclasses. Henceforth, we call this storage scheme MatView. On the other hand, RDF/S stores employing one of the two variations of the *schema-aware*, ISA and NOISA, as well as the Hybrid usually adopt the former (virtual) approach. It is worth noticing that both Hybrid and NOISA employ an internal encoding of subsumption relationships using interval-based labels of persistent classes and properties [5]. This encoding ensures an efficient evaluation of taxonomic queries in secondary storage, by transforming costly TC computations into appropriate range queries and reduces main memory requirements of the TC computation.

Table 1 summarizes the storage schemes implemented by existing RDF/S stores. Other approaches exist, but they are beyond the scope of our paper. For example, [6] focuses on how to derive an efficient *schema-aware* representation without any a priori knowledge of the employed RDF/S schemata. Although quite interesting, this work leads to more complex implementations of declarative query language interpreters running on the top of application-specific RDF/S

---

[1] Although SQL99 [18] defines a syntax for expressing transitive joins the existing implementations are not efficient [17].

stores. Furthermore, in [7], the authors employ the *schema-oblivious* approach for building persistent Semantic Web applications on top of existing RDF/S stores. Finally, native stores like Redland [3] or YARS [10] employ lower level database techniques to manage RDF/S data such as Hash Tables and B⁺-trees, but do not provide full-fledged database functionality.

2.1   Translation of Taxonomic RDF/S Queries

In this subsection, we present the translation of the core RDF/S taxonomic queries into SQL over the relational schemas considered by the *schema-aware* (ISA and NOISA), the Hybrid and the *schema-oblivious* (URI and ID) representations illustrated in Figures 1, 2 and 3.

Consider, for instance, the (binary) tree-shaped class hierarchy of Figure 4. The label of each class is composed of two integers: the *end* number denotes the unique classid obtained when traversing the hierarchy in post-order, while the *start* is the *end* number of the leftmost descendant of the class. Then, to find all subclasses of the Root we sim-

ply need to issue a query with the filtering condition $1 \leq start, end \leq 7$ (i.e., returning the classes whose label is included in the interval of the Root). The labels of classes and properties, as well as their subsumption relationships are stored into two auxiliary tables called SubClass and SubProperty. In this context,

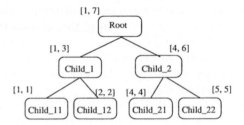

Fig. 4. Example of a labeled RDF/S schema

each extensional taxonomic query issued against the NOISA and Hybrid representations (i.e., find all transitive instances of the Root) also implies an intensional query involving a range condition on class or property labels.

In the following we show the SQL translation of taxonomic queries at Root level (given its label) over our testbed representations:

– **Schema-aware** NOISA: the SQL translation of our example taxonomic query in this representation is performed in two phases. First we need to find all the subclasses of the Root class:

```
select  S.end
from    SubClass S
where   S.start >= RootStart and S.end <= RootEnd
```

Next, we need to scan sequentially all the tables holding the instances of the previously retrieved subclasses, in the order determined by the query plan:

```
(select URI from Child_11) UNION ALL (select URI from Child_12) UNION ALL
(select URI from Child_1)  UNION ALL (select URI from Child_21) UNION ALL
(select URI from Child_22) UNION ALL (select URI from Child_2)  UNION ALL
(select URI from Root)
```

Note that, internally, the unique classid (i.e., the post order number) is used as table name (rather than a string as depicted in Figure 2) and no elimination of duplicates is required (UNION ALL) to assemble resource URIs.

- **Schema-aware ISA**: the SQL translation of our example taxonomic query in this representation is left entirely to the internal implementation of the PostgreSQL table inheritance feature:

```
select URI from Root;
```

where all the tables of the involved subclasses are sequentially scanned. As a matter of fact, PostgreSQL relies on a special catalog table, called *pg_inherits*, to store the subsumption relationships of tables defined in an object-relational schema. This table holds a unique id for each sub-table, along with the id of its parent table and the number of table occurrences in the hierarchy (in case of multiple inheritance). Then, a C program uses this information to compute the sub-tables involved in an SQL query: first, the tableID is inserted into an empty list; then, the direct children of this table are found, by performing a selection on *pg_inherits*, and their tableIDs are appended to the list. This process is repeated recursively for each new tableID that is appended to the list, until a fixpoint is reached. After that, PostgreSQL scans all tables in the order in which they appear in the list.

- **Hybrid**: the SQL translation of our example taxonomic query in this representation is simpler, since it requires only one phase for both schema filtering and instance scanning:

```
select  I.URI
from    ClassInstances I
where   I.classid >= RootStart and I.classid <= RootEnd;
```

- **Schema-oblivious URI**: the SQL translation of our example taxonomic query in this representation is:

```
select  T.SubjectURI
from    Triples T
where   T.predicate = 'typeof' and T.object = 'Root';
```

- **Schema-oblivious ID**: the SQL translation of our example taxonomic query includes a join operation between the table holding triples and the one holding resources' URIs. Below, *typeofID* stands for the identifier of the property *typeOf*:

```
select  I.URI
from    Triples T, Instance I
where   T.predicate = typeofID and T.ObjectID = RootID and I.ID = T.SubjectID;
```

- **MatView:** the SQL translation of our example taxonomic query involves a simple scan on the materialized view which stores the proper and transitive instances of the Root class.

```
select  MV.URI
from    Mat_View_Root MV;
```

3   Synthetic RDF Data Generation

As we will explain in the sequel, for relatively small schema sizes, *the hierarchy structure (i.e., shape and arity) does not affect the performance of (intensional or extensional) taxonomic queries*; as a matter of fact, *their performance only depends on the number of nodes in the hierarchy*. For this reason, our RDF/S generator produces only binary-tree-shaped subsumption hierarchies rather than more exotic structures of class or property lattices.

More precisely, the three critical parameters of our generator are (a) the depth of the tree; (b) the total number of classified resources; and (c) their distribution mode under nodes at various hierarchy levels. It should be stressed that the tree depth determines the size of an RDFS schema and therefore the number of tables we have to create in the two *schema-aware* representations (i.e., for complete binary trees $2^{depth+1} - 1$ tables). In our benchmark we consider three categories of schemata, namely, *small* (up to 4 levels, i.e., 31 nodes), *medium* (up to 6 levels, i.e., 127 nodes), and *large* (more than 7 levels). In addition, the number of resources that we consider in our experiments is 10,000, 100,000 and 1,000,000.

3.1   Distribution of Resources

In average case analysis, we can consider a uniform distribution of resources under the nodes of the tree-shaped subsumption hierarchy. However, this is not a realistic assumption for real-life Semantic Web applications. For instance, in some SW applications, such as Semantic Web Portals [5], leaf classes are highly populated compared to the intermediate ones while in other applications such as Knowledge Bases (e.g., the IMDB[2] wrapped in RDF/S) some class subtrees are heavier than others in terms of classified resources. Our RDF/S generator relies on the zipfian distribution [25] to simulate the classification of resources in Semantic Web applications.

Definition 1. *The distribution of occurrence probabilities of resources under the schema classes follows the zipfian law:*

$$Zipf(A, i) = A/(i^z * h)$$

where A is the total number of resources to be distributed, i is the rank value given to each class, N is the total number of classes, z is a skew parameter and $h = \sum_{j=1}^{N} 1/j^z$.

After assigning an increasing rank to each class, the probability that a resource is classified under a class according to the zipfian distribution essentially follows a power-law: the number of resources classified under the class with the 1st rank is i^z times larger than the class with the ith rank. When $z = 0$, resources are uniformly classified, while when $z > 0$ some classes are more frequently populated than others. In this work we consider that $z = 1$ and thus, a class with i-th rank, can be populated with $A/(i * h)$ resources. In a nutshell, our generator considers the following resource distribution modes:

---
[2] Url: www.imdb.com

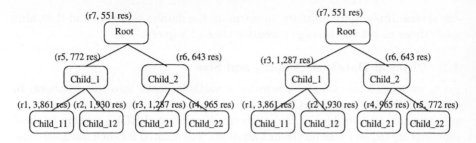

Fig. 5. Zipfian Distribution favouring leaves vs favouring subtrees

- *Uniform distribution of resources to tree classes ($z = 0$)*: in this case, resource distribution is determined only by the total number of schema classes (i.e., the tree depth). For instance, with a uniform classification of 10,000 resources under the seven nodes of our example schema depicted in Figure 4, in the case of ISA and NOISA we need to insert $10,000/7 = 1428$ tuples in each class instance table, while in Hybrid 10,000 tuples will be inserted into the single class instance table (Hybrid), 1/7 of which will have the classid of the Root class as the value of the attribute object, 1/7 of which will have the classid of the Child_1, etc.
- *Zipfian distribution of resources favouring tree leaves ($z = 1$)*: in this case, lower rank values are given to leaf classes while the Root class has the highest rank. Using this class ranking, the classification of 10,000 resources under our example schema is illustrated in the left part of Figure 5 (for each class its rank value and number of classified resources is shown).
- *Zipfian distribution of resources favouring sub-trees ($z = 1$)*: in this case, lower rank values are given to the classes of a sub-tree. The generator is parameterized to take into account the depth of the root class of a sub-tree. For instance, the lower rank values are given to the classes of the first (leftmost) sub-tree whose root (Child_1) is located at depth 1 of our example schema. Using this class ranking, the classification of 10,000 resources under our example schema is illustrated in the right part of Figure 5 (for each class its rank value and number of classified resources is shown).

4   Experimental Evaluation

In this section, we present a performance evaluation of taxonomic queries issued against six relational representations (ISA, NOISA, MatView, Hybrid, URI and ID), using the synthetic RDF/S schemata and data created by our generator. The objective of our study is to measure the effect of the schema size in intensional taxonomic queries, as well as, the effect of resource number and distribution modes in extensional taxonomic queries. Experiments were carried out on a pc with a Pentium III 1 GHz processor and 256MB of main memory, over Suse Linux (v9.2) using PostgreSQL (v7.4.6) with Unicode configuration and 10,000 buffers (8KB each), used for data loading, index creation and querying. Each query was run several times: once, initially, to warm up the database buffers and then nine more times to get the average execution time of a query.

4.1 Physical Database Schema and Size

First, we loaded tree-shaped schemata of variable depth into the database. In ISA and NOISA, tables **SubClass** (or **SubProperty**) were populated with the subsumption relationships of the synthetically generated RDFS schema In these representations, an index on the uri attribute was created for each instance table of a specific schema class. To speed-up sequential access, each instance table was clustered according to this index. In Hybrid, a B^{+}-tree index was created on the classid attribute of the single table that holds the instances of all classes. This table was clustered according to classid, in order to minimize the I/Os required when fetching the resources that are classified under a specific class.

Then, we generated various datasets according to the distribution modes presented in the previous section and load them into the instance tables of each representation. To compute the physical database size for each representation we consider that the attribute uri has the type VARCHAR(1000), while classid in Hybrid has the type int4. Moreover, we took into account the extra storage cost per tuple due to an internal id of 40 bytes generated by PostgreSQL to identify the physical location of a tuple within its table (block number, tuple index within block). PostgreSQL also incurs an overhead of 4 bytes for the storage of strings. In *schema-oblivious*, the attribute predicate has the type VARCHAR(20). Table 2 summarizes the size of the database for the three different numbers of resources, distributed uniformly among the schema classes.

- ISA and NOISA: For each tuple $((1000*1+4)+40)$ Bytes $= 1$KB are needed.
- Hybrid: For each tuple $((1000*1+4)+4+40)$ Bytes $= 1$KB are needed. Also for each entry of the index constructed on classid, PostgresSQL holds 8 bytes for the 'row pointer' and 4 bytes for the int4 type of the search key. Since 12 Bytes are needed per index entry, the expected index size for 10,000 resources is around 12KB. However, PostgreSQL fills, as expected, each index page until the fill-factor of 70%. As a result, for 10,000 resources the index size is approximately $1.3 * 12$KB $= 15.6$KB.
- Schema-oblivious: For each tuple $(2 * (1000 * 1 + 4) + (20 * 1 + 4))$ Bytes $= 2$KB are needed.

The following lemma gives a precise measure of the storage overhead of TC precomputations, in *schema-oblivious* and MatView.

Lemma 1. *Consider a complete-binary tree shaped RDFS schema and uniform resource distribution. Let d be the depth of the tree and A be the number of triples explicitly given. Then the number of total triples (those explicitly given and those inferred due to class or property subsumption) is: $totalTriples(A,d) \simeq d * A$*

Proof. Let A be the total number of triples. Then, each class has $y = A/2^{d+1} - 1$ triples. Computing inferred triples for each class in a bottom-up fashion results in the following total number of triples:

Table 2. Database size

# of Resources	ISA,NOISA,Hybrid	URI	ID	MatView
10,000	10 MB	$depth * 20$ MB	$\simeq$ 10-14 MB	$depth * 10$ MB
100,000	100 MB	$depth * 200$ MB	$\simeq$ 100-140 MB	$depth * 100$ MB
1,000,000	1 GB	$depth * 2$ GB	$\simeq$ 1-1.4 GB	$depth * 1$ GB

$$TA = \sum_{i=0}^{d} 2^i * (2^{d+1-i} - 1) * y = y * (\sum_{i=0}^{d} 2^{d+1} - 2^i) = y * ((d+1) * 2^{d+1} - \sum_{i=0}^{d} 2^i) = y * ((d+1) * 2^{d+1} - (2^{d+1} - 1)) = A * ((d+1) * 2^{d+1} / (2^{d+1} - 1) - 1) \simeq d * A$$
$\square$

Lemma 1 presumes a complete, binary-tree-shaped schema. It should be also stressed that, a zipfian distribution of resources favouring leaves or subtrees implies that a larger number of resources will be located deeper in the tree. Since MatView, URI and ID duplicate the resources classified under a class in the instance tables of all of its superclasses, the storage overhead in these representations is more significant in the case of the zipfian than in the case of the uniform distribution.

Increasing the number of triples during TC precomputation implies a direct increase of the database size. URI's storage requirements are obviously d times larger than without precomputed TCs. On the other hand, ID hold triples of the type $\langle$int4, int4, int4$\rangle$ and resource URIs are only stored once. Hence, the storage overhead in ID is significantly smaller than in URI. More precisely, each triple needs $3 * 4 + 40 = 52$ Bytes (vs 2KB in URI).

Finally, in MatView, each view is of type $\langle$resourceURI, id$\rangle$. The aforementioned storage overhead of this representation can be computed in a similar way by changing the meaning of A, from "total number of triples" to "total number of resources".

4.2   The Effect of Schema Size

As we have already explained in Section 2.1, taxonomic queries involve two filtering phases, an intensional (i.e., at the schema) and an extensional (i.e., at the data). During the former, we need to compute all the subclasses of the root class whose transitive instances need to be retrieved. Recall that, in NOISA and Hybrid, this computation is performed by a range query on the classes' interval-based labels, while in ISA a TC is performed internally on the structural information of the inheritance table catalog (*pg_inherits*) maintained by PostgreSQL. During the extensional filtering phase of a taxonomic query, *schema-aware* (both ISA and NOISA) needs to scan a number of (possibly empty) tables, containing the instances of the schema classes, while all the other representations need to scan only one (possibly empty) table, regardless of the number of the schema classes under which resources are classified.

In order to measure the cost of the schema filtering in taxonomic queries, we have executed the same query (i.e., transitive instances of the Root class) against an empty database created according to the six possible representations. As we can see from Figure 6, in *schema-aware* the execution *time of taxonomic queries depends on the size of the schema in terms of number of classes or properties* (and thus on the depth of our complete binary tree)

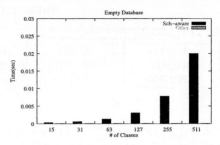

Fig. 6. Querying an empty database

while the execution *time in the other storage schemes is independent from the schema size* (almost 0 seconds). The extra cost of the *schema-aware* is due to the I/O seek time of empty tables.

Moreover, since the physical size of a resource's URI in ISA and NOISA is 1KB and each PostgreSQL buffer requires 8 KB (out of which only 8,152 Bytes of them are used - the other 40 Bytes hold block information), only 7 tuples (i.e., 7 resources) can be stored in one block. Thus, the last block of each table may contain from 1 up to 7 resources. This factor incurs an extra storage overhead, which in the worst case (i.e., 511 classes for $depth = 8$) can be up to 4MB.

4.3   The Effect of Resource Distribution Mode

Recall that, taxonomic queries in Hybrid are evaluated in one phase, where both schema and data filtering are performed against the single table used to store all class instances. Then, to find the transitive instances of a specific class (e.g., Root) we only need to perform an index scan on the `classid` (filtering condition on the labels of the descendant classes) and table clustering on this attribute is high beneficial for query performance. Hence, as we can see in Figure 7, the execution *time in* Hybrid *scales linearly with respect to the size of the database (i.e., the number of classified resources)*. Similar behaviour is exhibited by *schema-oblivious* and MatView, also evaluating taxonomic queries in one phase due to the TCs precomputation.

Before further detailing our experimental results, we would like to point out that ISA and NOISA exhibit the same behavior in terms of all the aforementioned factors affecting the evaluation of taxonomic queries. They only differ in the fact that schema filtering (as the first evaluation phase of taxonomic queries in *schema-aware*) in ISA is performed in main-memory by PostgreSQL, while in NOISA it is handled by a separate query. However, for small schema sizes the main-memory and the persistent processing of the schema filtering phase comes with almost the same execution cost. For this reason, both representations gave the same measurements in all experiments and thus we are going to refer to both of them in the figures below as *schema-aware*.

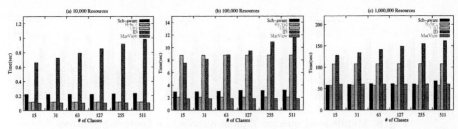

Fig. 7. Root Queries: variable depth and number of uniformly distributed resources

Querying the Root Class: Figure 7 depicts the execution times for a query requesting the transitive instances of the **root** class, in the case of the uniform distribution, over each representation. The performance figures for the two zipfian distributions were very similar to Figure 7, thus we conclude that *the distribution mode doesn't affect execution time of taxonomic queries at the root class.*

It is worth noticing that the schema size affects query evaluation time only in the case of *schema-aware*, due to the storage overhead explained previously. As we can see in Figure 7(a), this overhead, which varies between 0 and 4MB, has a significant effect for 10,000 resources (i.e., of size 10 MB), while Figures 7(b),(c) depict that it is not as important for larger numbers of resources, where the *schema-aware* representations achieve similar performance to that of Hybrid and MatView. Furthermore, comparing Hybrid and URI, we can easily observe that URI exhibits very similar performance to Hybrid in the case of 10,000 resources (Figure 7(a)), while Hybrid clearly outperforms URI in the other two cases (Figures 7(b),(c)). The reason for the latter is that the physical size of triples involved in the query in URI is twice as large as the size of the tuples involved in the **ClassInstances** table of Hybrid, thus additional I/O activity is required for this representation. Regarding ID, in all figures it exhibits the worst performance, because it requires an extra join to retrieve the actual resource URI. This join is very costly, given that the number of triples involved is, on average, *depth* times larger than the actual triples existing in the RDF graph (Lemma 1). Finally, MatView is the only representation, between those who precompute TCs, which achieves good performance, since taxonomic query evaluation only involves a sequential scan over the corresponding view. However, precomputing the TCs (also for URI and ID) both incurs a huge storage overhead and also creates the need for a view-update strategy.

Querying a Middle Level Class: Figure 8 depicts the execution times over each representation, for a query requesting the transitive instances of a **middle** level class, in the case of a zipfian distribution favouring subtrees (note that the y axis is drawn in logarithmic scale). Clearly, for a *small* and *medium* number of resources, Hybrid and MatView exhibit the overall best performance, while for a *large* number of resources *schema-aware* and MatView outperform all other representations. Of the rest ID performs better than URI, but they are both far worse than the previous three representations.

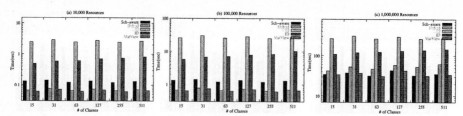

Fig. 8. Middle level queries: Zipfian distribution favouring subtrees

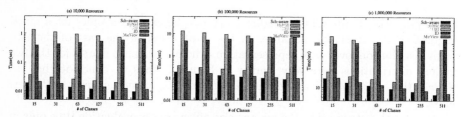

Fig. 9. Leaf level queries: Zipfian distribution favouring leaves

In the case of middle level queries we have to access a smaller number of subclasses, as well as of classified resources, than in the case of querying the root class. In order to measure the effect of distribution modes in query evaluation we need to compute the selectivity of the filtering conditions on the instance tables of each representation. A zipfian distribution favouring subtrees leads to query selectivity of 35% and 45%, while favouring leaves leads to selectivity between 45% and 55%[3]. We should point out that, since in the two zipfians distributions (favouring subtrees or leaves) the subtrees rooted at a **middle** level have different weights (i.e., number of classified resources) we choose in our experiments to query the heaviest subtrees.

The varying selectivity rapidly affects query evaluation time in Hybrid and URI. In the case of Hybrid, an index scan is performed on the **ClassesInstances** table, using the B^+-tree index on the attribute `classid` where the selectivity is fairly high, as opposed to the sequential scan required to retrieve the instances of the root class. As one would expect, the higher the selectivity, the higher is the benefit of choosing an index scan. On the other hand, when the selectivity is low, the I/O cost of accessing and using the index may be greater than the benefit; hence, index scan is efficient in the case of a uniform distribution, while it incurs an execution overhead in the case of the two zipfian distributions. This behaviour is reflected in Figure 8(c), where Hybrid exhibits worse performance than *schema-aware* and MatView for a *large* number of resources. Also the index scan on table **Triples** in URI uses a B^+-tree index on the `object` attribute. The overhead of accessing the index in this case is even bigger than in Hybrid, since the index size in URI (index on a `VARCHAR(1000)` attribute) is much bigger than

---

[3] On the other hand, a uniform distribution leads to increased selectivity, starting from 80% for *depth* = 3 and increasing up to 94% for *depth* = 8.

in Hybrid (index on an `int4` attribute). As a result, URI exhibits the overall worst performance. Finally, in the case of ID the query plan produced by PostgreSQL do not use the index on `object`, but a sequential scan on table **Triples**. Hence, what really affects the evaluation of taxonomic queries in ID is not the distribution mode, but the depth of the subsumption hierarchy, since the total number of triples is depth times larger (Lemma 1) than the original one.

Querying Leaves. In this case we have to access only a single class and a smaller number of classified resources. The former implies no additional I/Os for the *schema-aware* representations due to space left at the end of blocks. Hence, *schema-aware* exhibits the same (overall best) behaviour as MatView (Figure 9, note that the y axis is drawn in logarithmic scale). Furthermore, the selectivity is higher than in the case of queries at **middle** level, and ranges between 70% and 85% in the two zipfian distributions.[4] (we queried the **leaf** class with the largest weight). As a result, the perfomance figures of Hybrid converge with those of *schema-aware* and MatView, while URI and ID follow by far.

Due to space limitations, we are not showing the experimental results for the cases of querying middle level and leaf classes, when resources are distributed uniformly. However, the results in those cases illustrate the same trends, with the exception that URI performs better than ID.

5   Summary and Future Work

The main conclusion that can be drawn from our experiments is that Hybrid and MatView achieve the best performance in terms of query execution times of taxonomic queries. Both exhibit very similar performance in the cases of *small*, *medium* and *large* numbers of resources (namely 10,000, 100,000 and 1,000,000, respectively) and queries on the **root** or **leaf** classes, while MatView outperforms Hybrid in the case of queries on **middle** level classes.

However, the performance of MatView relies on the duplication of resources in the instance tables of all superclasses of the class under which they are classified, which incurs a huge storage overhead. Moreover, MatView comes with the additional cost of data updates in materialized views, which can be a decisive factor in applications involving frequent updates (URI and ID also suffer from the same drawbacks). Unlike MatView, Hybrid achieves competitive performance without having to precompute TCs, by taking advantage of the encoding of subsumption hierarchies (the attribute `classid`) that is stored with the data (resource `uri`), enabling to evaluate taxonomic queries in a single phase.

Of the rest, *schema-aware* representations achieve similar performance to Hybrid and MatView for *medium* and *large* number of resources and queries on **root** class. Additionally, *schema-aware* exhibit the overall best performance in the case of taxonomic queries at **leaf** level classes. Furthermore, *schema-aware* is better than URI for *medium* and *large* number of resources and queries on root,

---

[4] Compared to selectivity ranging between 94% and 99.8% in a uniform distribution.

and clearly for queries at **middle** or **leaf** level classes. Note that, URI is sensitive to the size of the main-memory used for caching: as this size increases, URI's performance improves for larger number of resources. It is worth noticing that queries in our benchmark were executed against databases that only contained resources classified under classes. The addition of property-related triples in a single **Triples** table, in the case of *schema-oblivious* representations (URI, ID) would further degrade the performance of the two *schema-oblivious* representations.

Finally, apart from the case of taxonomic queries at **middle** or **leaf** level classes and zipfian resource distribution where ID outperforms URI, ID exhibits the worst performance, mainly because of the costly join operation it has to perform, and also suffers from the same drawbacks as MatView and URI (although the storage overhead is much smaller than in the case of URI).

It should be stressed that the conclusions drawn from our experiments are also confirmed by the independently conducted benchmarking of XML database implementations [12], where the combination of *document-dependent* partitioning (as in schema-aware) with the use of interval-based encoding for containment joins (similar to taxonomic queries) yields superior performance, compared to document-indepedent (similar to schema-oblivious) approaches. As a next step, we plan to extend our testbed to other categories of queries involving schema and data path expressions, that are translated to SQL queries with joins over the underlying RDBMS. To that end, we need to extend our generator with appropriate distribution modes of properties over (domain or range) classes. Conclusions of [21] could offer a basis for our attempt to model more sophisticated schema structures.

References

1. R. Agrawal, A. Somani, and Y. Xu: Storage and Querying of E-Commerce Data. In Proc. of VLDB 2001.
2. S. Alexaki, V. Christophides, G. Karvounarakis, D. Plexousakis: On Storing Voluminous RDF Descriptions: The case of Web Portal Catalogs. In Proc. of WebDB'01 (co-located with ACM SIGMOD'01).
3. D. Beckett: Redland RDF Application Framework, 2003.
4. J. Broekstra, A. Kampman and F. van Harmelen: Sesame: A generic Architecture for Storing and Querying RDF and RDF Schema. In Proc. of the ISWC'02.
5. V. Christophides, M. Scholl, D. Plexousakis., S. Tourtounis: On Labelling Schemes for the Semantic Web. In Proc. of the 12th Intern. World Wide Web Conference (WWW'03), 2003.
6. L. Ding, K. Wilkinson, C. Sayers, H. Kuno: Application-Specific Schema Design for Storing Large RDF Datasets. In Proc. of the PSSS'03, collocated with ISWC'03.
7. M. Gertz, K.-U. Sattler: A Model and Architecture for Conceptualized Data Annotations. Technical Report CSE-2001-11, Dept. of Computer Science, University of California, Davis, 2001.
8. Y. Guo, J. Heflin, Z. Pan: Benchmarking DAML+OIL Repositories. In Proc. of ISWC'03.

9. S. Harris, and N. Gibbins: 3Store: Efficient Bulk RDF Storage. In Proc. of 1st International Workshop on Practical and Scalable Semantic Web Systems 2003.
10. A. Harth, S. Decker: Yet Another RDF Store: Perfect Index Structures for Storing Semantic Web Data With Contexts. DERI Technical Report, 2004.
11. P. Hayes: RDF Semantics. W3C Working Draft, World-Wide Web Consortium (W3C), 2003.
12. H. Lu, J. X. Yu, G. Wang, S. Zheng, H. Jiang, G. Yu, A. Zhou: "What Makes the Differences: Benchmarking XML Database Implementations", ACM TOIT, Vol.5, No.1, Feb'05, p 154–194.
13. L. Ma, Z. Su, Y. Pan, L. Zhang, T. Liu: RStar: An RDF Storage and Query System for Enterprise Resource Management. In Proc. of the ACM CIKM 2004.
14. A. Magkanaraki et al: Benchmarking RDF schemata for the Semantic Web. In Proc. of the 1st International Semantic Web Conference (ISWC'02), 2002.
15. B. McBride. Jena: Implementing the RDF Model and Syntax Specification. 2001, Technical report Hewlett Packard Laboratories.
16. Z. Pan, J. Heflin: DLDB: Extending Relational Databases to Support Semantic Web Queries. In Proc. of PSSS'03, collocated with ISWC'03.
17. G. Schadow, M. Barnes, and C. McDonald, Representing and querying conceptual graphs with relational database management systems is possible, In Proc. of AMIA Symposium 2001:598-602
18. SQL99 Standard, NCITS/ISO/IEC 9075-1 01-Jan-1999 Information Technology - Database Languages - SQL - Part 1: Framework.
19. K. Stoffel, M. Taylor, J. Hendler: Efficient Management of Very Large Ontologies. In Proc. of American Association for Artificial Intelligence Conference (AAAI'97), 1997.
20. SWAD-Europe Deliverable 10.2: Mapping Semantic Web Data with RDBMSs.
21. C. Tempich, R. Volz: Towards a benchmark for Semantic Web reasoners - an analysis of the DAML ontology library. In Proc. of The 2nd Int. Workshop on Evaluation of Ontology-based Tools, EON2003.
22. R. Volz, D. Oberle, B. Motik, S. Staab: KAON SERVER - A Semantic Web Management System. In Proc. of the Atlantic Web Intelligence Conference (AWIC'03), 2003.
23. R. Volz, S. Staab, B. Motik: Incremental Maintenance of Materialized Ontologies. Proc. of ODBase'03, 2003.
24. K. Wilkinson, C. Sayers, H. A. Kuno, D. Raynolds: Efficient RDF Storage and Retrieval in Jena2. In Proc. of SWDB'03 (co-located with VLDB'03).
25. G. K. Zipf: Human Behaviour and the Principle of Least Effort. Addison-Wesley, Reading, Massachusetts, 1949.

Towards Imaging Large-Scale Ontologies for Quick Understanding and Analysis[*]

KeWei Tu, Miao Xiong, Lei Zhang, HaiPing Zhu, Jie Zhang, and Yong Yu

Department of Computer Science and Engineering,
Shanghai JiaoTong University, Shanghai, 200030, P.R. China
{tkw, xiongmiao, zhanglei, zhu, zhangjie, yyu}@apex.sjtu.edu.cn

Abstract. In many practical applications, ontologies tend to be very large and complicated. In order for users to quickly understand and analyze large-scale ontologies, in this paper we propose a novel ontology visualization approach, which aims to complement existing approaches like the hierarchy graph. Specifically, our approach produces a holistic "imaging" of the ontology which contains a semantic layout of the ontology classes. In addition, the distributions of the ontology instances and instance relations are also depicted in the "imaging". We introduce at length the key techniques and algorithms used in our approach. Then we examine the resulting user interface and find it facilitates tasks like ontology navigation, ontology retrieval and ontology instance analysis.

1   Introduction

Ontologies play a key role in the Semantic Web. More and more ontologies have been developed to formalize the conceptualization of a domain. In some applications, such conceptualization is so large and complicated that the resulting ontology will contain hundreds to tens of thousands of concepts and relations. For instance, the OWL version of the National Cancer Institute Ontology [1] contains more than twenty-seven thousand classes and seventy properties.

In order for users to understand and hence make use of such large-scale ontologies, there must be effective ways to present ontologies and facilitate user browsing and searching. Presenting a large ontology in plain text (e.g. XML files) is obviously unacceptable, as in this way users can learn nothing more than some individual statements. Almost all ontology engineering tools provide form-like UI to present interrelated statements together. For example, a typical "class view" gives an orderly list of the name, description, sub-classes, super-classes and properties of a certain class. However, such a view only presents to users a local view of the ontology, leaving users unaware of the ontology's holistic content and structure. A widely used ontology visualization approach is to draw an ontology as a graph (as in [2,3]), with nodes representing classes and edges representing relations in most cases. In this way, users gain a much larger view of the ontology and could more conveniently navigate between different ontological

---

[*] This work was supported by IBM China Research Lab.

Y. Gil et al. (Eds.): ISWC 2005, LNCS 3729, pp. 702–715, 2005.

elements. In spite of these advantages, however, for large ontologies users' visual field in such an approach is often rather local. This is because when scaling the whole ontology graph to the screen size, one can often see nothing but a mess of lines.

An advisable visualization principle is to organize an ontology by its class hierarchy. Most ontology tools use trees to present the ontology hierarchy, although it is actually a directed acyclic graph (DAG). A hierarchy structure is a semantic organization of an ontology, so users can gain a holistic sense of an ontology when looking at the top levels of the hierarchy. In addition, seeking a certain concept in a hierarchy is much easier, as one can gradually narrow his searching scope when going deeper in the hierarchy. Apart from these merits, however, our practical experience shows that there are several shortcomings of hierarchical visualization.

- Hierarchy can not visualize some important information of an ontology such as the relations between classes.
- When users go deeper into a hierarchy, it is very easy for them to get lost and be unable to find the way home to the root.
- There is no semantic organization for sibling classes (i.e. the direct subclasses of a certain class). Typically they are listed alphabetically, and when the list is very long it becomes somewhat unreadable.
- Browsing a hierarchy is kind of inconvenient as it requires sometimes too many mouse-clicks to expand the nodes.

In this paper we propose a novel visualization approach to attack the deficiencies of current approaches. The main feature of our approach is that it presents a large-scale ontology by a holistic "imaging" which is semantically organized for quick understanding of the subject and content of the ontology. The semantic organization takes into account not only the class hierarchy information, but also other information such as relations and class similarities. Easy and friendly browsing and searching functions are provided on top of our visualization approach.

Another concern for ontology visualization is upon instances. In practice the number of instances populated in an ontology is often orders of magnitude larger than the class/relation number. A good visualization approach should also facilitate the analysis of ontology instances and instance relations. While most existing approaches do little on this aspect, our approach aims to meet this request.

It should be noticed that our approach is to complement existing approaches, instead of replacing them. In other words, our approach aims to facilitate the quick understanding and analysis of large-scale ontologies, while functions such as the details display of ontological elements are not provided. So one should use our approach together with existing approaches to achieve the best efficiency.

The rest of this paper is organized as follows. Section 2 presents the main techniques and algorithms used in our approach. Section 3 demonstrates the resulting visualization system by a few user scenarios. Finally we discuss the related work in section 4 and conclude the paper in section 5.

2   Techniques and Algorithms

In this section we present our approach of generating from an ontology its imaging. We use a simple RDF ontology (Figure 1) as the sample ontology throughout the procedure. Notice that, however, (i) our approach could be applied to other kinds of ontology as well, such as OWL ontology, and (ii) our approach is specially designed for large-scale ontology.

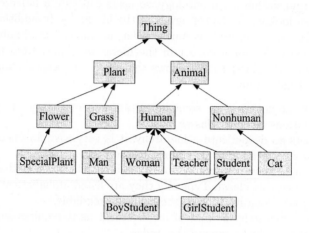

Fig. 1. The sample ontology (only the class hierarchy is shown, while the properties are omitted)

2.1   Semantic Connection Calculation

While an ontology is mainly composed of a set of classes, we need to lay them out in an Euclidean space to facilitate visualization. In order for such layout to be semantically meaningful, we first need to calculate the semantic connections between the classes.

As we know, a higher semantic similarity implies a stronger semantic connection, so we first calculate the semantic similarities between classes. The most classic semantic similarity calculation is based on the class hierarchy. For example, [4] proposed a formula as follows.

$$Sim_1(c_1, c_2) = \frac{2 \times N_3}{N_1 + N_2 + 2 \times N_3}$$

where N_1 and N_2 are the numbers of sub-class relations from c_1 and c_2 to their most specific common superclass C, and N_3 is the number of sub-class relations from C to the root of the class hierarchy.

Another kind of similarity calculation is based on the feature of the classes, such as the parts and attributes. For our sample RDF ontology, the only feature is the properties of a class. The following formula is proposed by [5].

$$Sim_2(c_1, c_2) = \frac{\|C_1 \cap C_2\|}{\|C_1 \cap C_2\| + \alpha \|C_1 - C_2\| + (1 - \alpha)\|C_2 - C_1\|}$$

where C_1 and C_2 are the feature sets of c_1 and c_2, and for our sample ontology they are the sets of properties of c_1 and c_2. α is defined as $\min(N_1, N_2)/(N_1 + N_2)$.

Besides class similarity, one may agree that the number of relations defined between two classes also contributes to the semantic connection, because more relations between two classes implies that they are more relative, and hence have a stronger semantic connection. This is depicted by the following formula.

$$Rel(c_1, c_2) = \frac{1 - e^{-n}}{1 + e^{-n}}$$

where n is the number of relations between c_1 and c_2.

In our approach, we take the weighted average of the three above-calculated values as the final evaluation of the semantic connection. The weights are customized by users, so that they can control what information would be presented in the visualization result. In order to speed up the subsequent processing, we set a connection threshold and discard those connections that are too weak. This threshold is also customizable, specifying the compromise between running speed and result quality.

For our sample ontology, the following table shows a part of the resulting semantic connections, i.e. those between the **Student** class and the other classes, with the threshold set to 0.6.

$$
\begin{array}{lll}
\text{Student} - \text{Teacher} & : & 0.7257 \\
\text{Student} - \text{Animal} & : & 0.6333 \\
\text{Student} - \text{Human} & : & 0.8214 \\
\text{Student} - \text{Man} & : & 0.7175 \\
\text{Student} - \text{Woman} & : & 0.7175 \\
\text{Student} - \text{BoyStudent} : & & 0.8497 \\
\text{Student} - \text{GirlStudent} : & & 0.8497 \\
\end{array}
$$

2.2 Layout

After semantic connections are calculated, we can now lay classes out in a 2D plane, with strong connections implying small distances and vice versa. There are several algorithms that can be used to lay out a set of elements based on their preferred distances, such as Multidimensional Scaling (MDS) [6] and Force Directed Placement (FDP, also called Spring Embedder) [7]. In our approach we choose the FDP algorithm, because although it only achieves local optimality of the layout, it has some fast variations and could be used incrementally.

In standard FDP, elements are first randomly placed. With the forces between elements defined by their preferred and actual distances, they are moved according to the combined forces on them, until convergence. To speed up this procedure, we adopt a preprocessing method proposed in [8] before the standard FDP.

Figure 2 shows the result of running FDP on our sample ontology. As we see, classes with strong semantic connections, such as those human classes, are

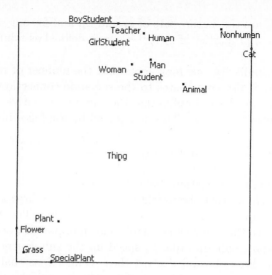

Fig. 2. Sample ontology: the result of FDP

clustered together, while classes with weak connections, such as the plant classes and the animal classes, are far away from each other.

2.3   SOM

The layout produced by FDP reflects fairly well the semantic organization of the ontology. However, similar classes are often placed together in a small area, while there are often large areas with few classes in it. In most cases the class clusters are more important to users' understanding of the ontology, but the small space those clusters occupy make class labelling/annotation very inefficient, or even impossible. So we try to alleviate this problem by distorting the layout using Self-Organizing Maps (SOM) [9].

A SOM network is composed of $n \times n$ neurons, where n is determined by the number of classes, so that on average each class will own tens of SOM neurons. The neurons are first randomly placed in the 2D plane where the FDP layout is. In training, they will first be gradually organized to form a smooth network (the self-organizing phase), and then be converged to the positions where the classes are (the convergence phase).

Figure 3(a) shows the resulting SOM network in the original 2D plane. By spreading the $n \times n$ network to form a grid, we get Figure 3(b), the resulting layout, where a class is represented by its nearest neuron. We can see in the resulting layout that classes in clusters tend to occupy much larger space than before, thus could be labelled clearly.

Notice that for each neuron, we can assign it to its nearest class. In this way each class would own a set of neurons. In other words, in the resulting layout each class would occupy an area, in addition to a point, as shown in Figure 3(b). The

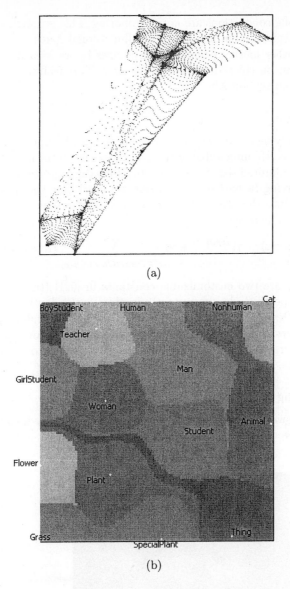

(a)

(b)

Fig. 3. Sample ontology: the result of SOM

semantic organization of the ontology is now exactly visualized by *the neighborhood of these areas*: two neighboring areas implies a strong semantic connection between the two corresponding classes. For example, in Figure 3(b), Woman and Man are neighboring because they have a strong semantic connection, while Woman and Plant are separated by two other classes, which indicates that their semantic connection is not so strong. One may also find out from the figure that sometimes this layout can not perfectly visualize the semantic connections: some classes with strong connections are not neighboring. This is inevitable, however, as we have to display an ontology in a two-dimensional space.

There is another merit of representing a class by an area in addition to a point: classes can be colored much more clearly. This facilitates our instance visualization, as in section 2.5.

2.4 Labelling

Although by applying SOM classes tend to occupy much larger space, for large-scale ontolgies it is still impossible to label all classes when the layout is displayed in a screen with a limited size. So we have to assess the importance of each class, and when displaying (a part of) the layout, we label only the most important classes that fall into the screen. Currently we simply compute the importance based on the class hierarchy.

$$Importance(c) = \gamma_1{}^{depth(c)} + \gamma_2 \sum_{c_i \in DirectChildren(c)} Importance(c_i)$$

where γ_1 and γ_2 are two customizable constants in $[0,1]$ (their default values are 0.5 and 1 respectively in our system), $depth(c)$ is the depth of c in the class hierarchy, and $DirectChildren(c)$ is the set of the direct children of c in the hierarchy. The first part of the formula gives more importance to the classes higher in the hierarchy, while the second part gives more to the classes with more descendants.

2.5 Visualizing Instance

In our approach we visualize the distribution of the ontology instances and instance relations.

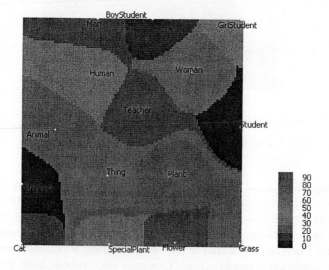

Fig. 4. Sample ontology: the instance distribution

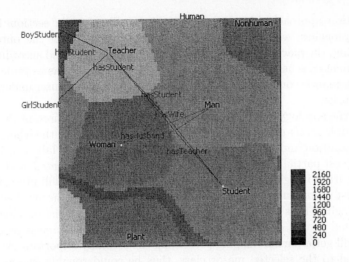

Fig. 5. Sample ontology: the instance relations (zoomed-in vision)

For ontology instances, we use different colors to represent different instance numbers of classes. Since a class could be represented by an area, we just fill the area with the corresponding color. Two modes are provided to count the instance number of a class. The first mode only takes into account those instances whose types are explicitly declared as the class, while the second also includes those that are declared as the instances of the sub-classes of that class. Figure 4 is the resulting imaging.

For instance relations, we draw a line between two classes to represent a relation between the instances of the two classes. Like in visualizing the instance distribution, we use the line color to indicate the number of instance pairs that have the relation. Notice that here we use the point representation of classes. Also there are two modes to count the number, based on whether the instances of a class's sub-classes should be included into the instances of that class. To prevent showing too many lines simultaneously, we select only those with the largest numbers of instance pairs. Figure 5 shows the sample visualization of the instance relations.

3   User Interface

Now we will review the user interface of our visualization approach under different tasks, i.e. ontology navigation, ontology retrieval and ontology instance analysis.

3.1   Ontology Navigation

Ontology navigation, i.e. navigating the content of an ontology, is the most basic task for an ontology visualization tool. For large-scale ontologies, traditional visualization approaches become inefficient, as discussed in section 1. Unlike those approaches, we present to users a holistic imaging of the ontology. In the imaging, the placement of classes are semantically arranged according to the measurements discussed in section 2.1, so that neighboring classes typically have stronger semantic connections. Such placement may facilitate user understanding of the ontology.

Since the ontology being visualized may be very large, we present the imaging with multiple *levels-of-detail*. In other words, we first present the whole imaging at low resolution and with only limited information directly labelled, but upon users' request partial imagings with more details can be presented, and the more local an partial imaging is, the more detailed information it will present. In this way, at first users could see several most important classes of the ontology marked in the imaging, thus roughly understanding the subject of the ontology. If one is interested in one of these major classes, by clicking that class or a nearby area he will get a partial imaging presenting the secondly important classes that are related to the selected major class, thus he could roughly understand the related part of the ontology. This procedure could go on until the most detailed information is presented.

Figure 6 gives an example of this procedure. The ontology visualized is the Semantic Web Technology Evaluation Ontology (SWETO)[1], which contains more than one hundred classes.

When a user is viewing a partial imaging, he could choose to switch to another partial imaging near the current one. This is useful because that, as the imaging is semantically organized, based on the current partial imaging the user may guess the position of a class and wish to seek it in a nearby area. Besides, the user could also choose to go back to a higher level-of-detail (i.e. with lower resolution).

We also provide a thumbnail of the imaging to facilitate the navigation. The area that is currently displayed is highlighted in the thumbnail, so as to help the user locate himself. Another function of thumbnail is that, by clicking on the thumbnail the user could switch between different areas conveniently.

Notice that our visualization approach is designed to complement other approaches instead of replacing them, so we integrate our visualization tool into an ontology engineering environment, i.e. ORIENT [10], which provides most kinds of traditional visualization tools like the form view, tree view and graph view (Figure 7). Such integration doubtless maximizes the overall navigation utility. For example, one could first get an overall understanding of the ontology from our visualization approach, and then scrutinize the formal details of several interesting classes using the traditional views.

3.2   Ontology Retrieval

In some applications, such as semantic annotation, users need to find from an ontology a class or classes that meet certain conditions. For large-scale ontologies,

---

[1] Available at http://lsdis.cs.uga.edu/Projects/SemDis/sweto/

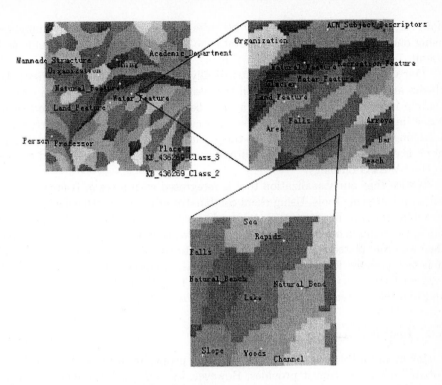

Fig. 6. Multiple levels of detail

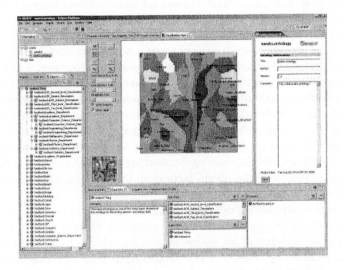

Fig. 7. Integrated into an ontology engineering environment

however, the searching process may be quite laborious and time-consuming. So using ontology visualization to facilitate the searching process is advisable and useful.

Our visualization approach is intrinsically applicable to searching. First, the classes are semantically organized in the resulting imaging, so finding a certain class in it would be easier than in a mere list. Second, the *level-of-detail* technique introduced in the previous section enables users to gradually narrow the searching scope and finally find the target class in the finest level-of-detail. Figure 6 is exactly an example procedure of searching for the water-related classes in the SWETO ontology.

Notice that our visualization tool is integrated with a set of traditional ontology engineering tools. Using them combinatorially could further facilitate the searching process. For example, one may have already found a class by the traditional tools and hence have gotten the class's position in our imaging, so he could then find the related classes just by looking into the nearby area of the position. It is also possible for users to get a set of class candidates by traditional tools (e.g. an RDF query answerer), then he could map these classes to the imaging and find the desired one based on their positions.

3.3   Instance Analysis

Facing an ontology with large-scale instances, people are usually at a loss in the "ocean" of information it provides. However, by "imaging" the distribution of the ontology instances and instance relations using our visualization approach, we are able to make quick analysis, at the instance level, about which topics in the ontology are "hot", and which classes are more actively inter-connected and thus strongly associated.

Take for example the imaging of a university ontology shown in Figure 8. In the areas depicting professors (the upper part), Naval_Architecture_and_Ocean_En-gineering_Professor, Mechanical_and_Power_Engineering_Professor, Electronics_and_Electric_Engineering_Professor, and Material_Science_and_Engineering_Professor are assigned hotter colors than other professor classes, which means they own more instances. Analogous situation happens to the student classes (the lower part), as the classes such as Naval_Architecture_and_Ocean_Engineering_Student, Mechanical_and_Power_Engineering_Student, Electronics_and_Electric_Engineering_Student, and Material_Science_and_Engineering_Student are hotter than the others. So users could quickly infer from the above facts that these engineering-related schools are of more importance in that university.

Inter-relationship among different classes is another important and interesting factor that can be easily investigated using our visualization approach. For instance, in the imaging of an online store's knowledge base of its customers' purchasing records, by observing the Middle-Aged class one can find that, the two lines representing the Purchased property connecting the class respectively to the Classical_Literature class and to the Traditional_Opera class are more prominent (which means more property instances within) than those Purchased lines connecting Middle-Aged to Pop_Music and to Animation. For the Youth class,

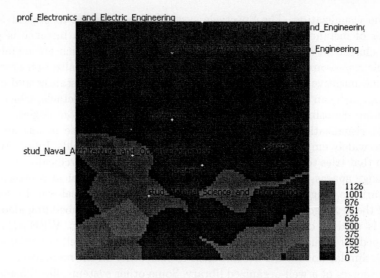

Fig. 8. Instance analysis for a university ontology

the situation is just the opposite. Therefore the store holder can learn from the imaging how to associate and recommend proper categories of commodities to the customers of different age. Similarly, other shopping habits among buyers of different gender, occupation, region, etc., can also be analyzed in our ontology visualization.

The level-of-detail, searching and overview functions provided by our visualization approach can be used to further enhance the instance analysis process.

4   Related Work

A number of previous work have contributed to the ontology visualization field. OntoViz[2] targets at the precise visualization of the ontology structure, using rectangles for classes/instances and lines for relations, while exploring ontology in OntoViz is somewhat inconvenient. TGVizTab[3] also tries to draw a precise graph of the ontology with concepts as nodes and relations as edges, and it employs a spring-embedding algorithm to implement a customizable layout. Jambalaya[11] displays information in a similar way, but adds in a level-of-detail feature, allowing users to browse the ontology detail at several levels. In a word, all these methods try to draw a precise graph of the ontology, so they have a common drawback that if the ontology is very large, the visualization result will become unreadable. In contrast, our approach presents a holistic view which is applicable to large ontologies.

Currently most ontology visualization methods do not well support the analysis of large-scale instances. Our approach, however, manages to visualize the distribution of ontology instances and instance relations. There are also some other ontology visualization methods that aim to integrate instance information into the visualization. The Spectacle system[12] is designed to present a large number of instances with a simple ontology to users. Each instance is placed into a cluster based on its class membership. Instances which are members of multiple classes are placed in overlapping clusters. This visualization provides a clear and intuitive depiction of the relationships between instances and classes. Our approach can not visualize the instance overlap like Spectacle, which is the cost of our choosing to present a holistic view of large-scale ontologies.

The visualization techniques and algorithms that we use in our approach are also widely employed in other knowledge visualization fields. Infosky[13] is a system that tries to enable the exploration of large and hierarchically structured knowledge spaces, and it presents a two-dimensional graphical representation with variable magnification, much like providing users a real-world telescope. One of the key algorithms employed in InfoSky is a spring-embedding algorithm, which is used to cluster documents or document collections. WEBSOM[14] is developed for visualizing document clusters based on the Self-Organizing Map (SOM). Similar documents become close to each other on the map, like the books on the shelves of a well-organized library. Some other systems, like Themescape by Cartia Inc. and ET-Map[15], also visualize large numbers of documents or websites using the SOM algorithm.

5   Conclusion and Future Work

In this paper we present a novel ontology visualization approach that aims to facilitate user understanding and analysis of large-scale ontologies. Specifically, our approach produces a holistic imaging of the ontology that contains a semantic layout of the ontology classes, with the distribution of instances and instance relations also visualized. We scrutinize the resulting user interface and find it facilitates tasks like ontology navigation, ontology retrieval and ontology instance analysis.

As the next step, we are planning to conduct a comprehensive user-based study, so as to better evaluate our approach. In addition, while currently our system can visualize an ontology with hundreds of classes in minutes, we will try to further speed up our approach by using more optimization techniques, especially for the FDP and SOM algorithms, which are the main source of the time complexity of our approach. We also plan to extend our approach to visualize ontology evolution. Since both the FDP and the SOM algorithm could be adapted to run incrementally, it is possible to produce two comparable imagings of the ontology before and after changing, thus highlighting the ontology changes.

References

1. Available at http://www.mindswap.org/2003/CancerOntology/.
2. Sintek, E.: OntoViz Tab: Visualizing protege ontologies. Available at http://protege.stanford.edu/plugins/ontoviz/ontoviz.html (2003)

3. Alani, H.: TGVizTab: An ontology visualization extension for protege. In: in Knowledge Capture 03 - Workshop on Visualizing Information in Knowledge Engineering, Sanibel Island, FL (2003)

4. Wu, Z., Palmer, M.: Verbs semantics and lexical selection. In: Proceedings of the 32nd conference on Association for Computational Linguistics, Morristown, NJ, USA, Association for Computational Linguistics (1994) 133–138

5. Rodríguez, M.A., Egenhofer, M.J., Rugg, R.D.: Assessing semantic similarities among geospatial feature class definitions. In: Interoperating Geographic Information Systems (Interop'99). LNCS 1580, Springer-Verlag (1999) 189–202

6. Kruskal, J.B., Wish, M.: Multidimensional Scaling. Beverly Hills and London: Sage Publications (1984)

7. Fruchterman, T.M.J., Reingold, E.M.: Graph drawing by force-directed placement. Software - Practice and Experience 21 (1991) 1129–1164

8. Mutton, P., Rodgers, P.: Spring embedder preprocessing for www visualization. In: Proceedings of Information Visualisation 2002 (IV02). (2002)

9. Kohonen, T.: Self-Organizing Maps. Springer (1995)

10. Zhang, L., Yu, Y., Lu, J., Lin, C., Tu, K., Guo, M., Zhang, Z., Xie, G., Su, Z., Pan, Y.: ORIENT: Integrate ontology engineering into industry tooling environment. In: Proceedings of the 3rd International Semantic Web Conference (ISWC2004). (2004)

11. Storey, M.A.D., Noy, N.F., Musen, M.A., Best, C., Fergerson, R.W., Ernst, N.: Jambalaya: an interactive environment for exploring ontologies. In: International Conference on Intelligent User Interfaces (IUI). (2002) 239–239

12. Fluit, C., Sabou, M., van Harmelen, F.: Ontology-based information visualization. In: Proceedings of Information Visualization '02. (2002)

13. Andrews, K., Kienreich, W., Sabol, V., Becker, J., Droschl, G., Kappe, F., Granitzer, M., Auer, P., Tochtermann, K.: The infosky visual explorer: exploiting hierarchical structure and document similarities. Information Visualization 1 (2002) 166–181

14. Kaski, S., Honkela, T., Lagus, K., Kohonen, T.: Websom - self-organizing maps of document collections. Neurocomputing 21 (1998) 101–117

15. Chen, H.C., Schuffels, C., Orwig, R.: Internet categorization and search: A self-organizing approach. Journal of Visual Communication and Image Representation 7 (1996) 88–102

Automatic Evaluation of Ontologies (AEON)

Johanna Völker, Denny Vrandečić, and York Sure

Institute AIFB, University of Karlsruhe
{voelker, vrandecic, sure}@aifb.uni-karlsruhe.de

Abstract. OntoClean is a unique approach towards the formal evaluation of ontologies, as it analyses the intensional content of concepts. Although it is well documented in numerous publications, and its importance is widely acknowledged, it is still used rather infrequently due to the high costs for applying OntoClean, especially on tagging concepts with the correct meta-properties. In order to facilitate the use of Onto-Clean and to enable proper evaluation of it in real-world cases, we provide AEON, a tool which automatically tags concepts with appropriate OntoClean meta-properties. The implementation can be easily expanded to check the concepts for other abstract meta-properties, thus providing for the first time tool support in order to enable intensional ontology evaluation for concepts. Our main idea is using the web as an embodiment of objective world knowledge, where we search for patterns indicating concepts meta-properties. We get an automatic tagging of the ontology, thus reducing costs tremendously. Moreover, AEON lowers the risk of having subjective taggings. As part of the evaluation we report our experiences from creating a middle-sized OntoClean-tagged reference ontology.

1 Introduction

Providing a shared conceptualization of a domain of interest, ontologies have become an important means for knowledge interchange and integration. The raise of the Semantic Web leads to distributed nets of knowledge, and plenty of reasoning will take place on heterogeneously created ontologies. For reasoning algorithms to yield useful results the underlying ontologies need to offer a high quality. Their wide-spread use leads to an increasing need for domain-independent methodologies and guidelines for ontology engineering and evaluation.

OntoClean [10] is a well-known methodology for the formal analysis of taxonomic relationships based on philosophical notions such as *essence*, *unity* or *identity*. Several tools supporting the OntoClean methodology have been developed and integrated into ontology editors such as ODEClean for WebODE [7], OntoEdit [17] or Protégé [15]. Given a taxonomy of concepts annotated with respect to a set of meta-properties, all these tools are able to perform an automatic analysis of the taxonomic relationships in order to detect cases of invalid generalization. Nevertheless, since this annotation has to be done manually, the evaluation of ontologies according to the OntoClean methodology remains a difficult and time consuming, thus very expensive task.

Y. Gil et al. (Eds.): ISWC 2005, LNCS 3729, pp. 716–731, 2005.

In order to solve this problem, we have developed an approach for the automatic tagging of concepts with respect to the meta-properties which constitute the basis for the OntoClean methodology. We provide an implementation of our approach, AEON[1], which makes use of the World Wide Web as the currently biggest existing source of common sense knowledge. In line with several approaches such as [4] and [5] we defined a set of domain independent patterns which can be considered as indicators for or against Rigidity, Identity, Unity and Dependence of given concepts in an ontology.

In the next section we give a brief introduction to the OntoClean methodology, in particular to the core notions of Rigidity, Unity, Dependence and Identity. Thereafter, we describe our approach to an automatic annotation of concepts with respect to these meta-properties (section 3). For the evaluation we needed a tagged ontology. In Section 4 we describe its creation and the problems we faced. Section 5 presents the evaluation setting and the results of the evaluation. In section 6 we discuss some related work, before we finally conclude with a short summary and an outlook to future work (section 7).

2   OntoClean in Theory

We provide a brief introduction to OntoClean, for a more thorough description refer to [10], for example. In the OntoClean vocabulary, *properties* are what is commonly called *concepts* or *classes*. *Meta-properties* are therefore properties of properties. Within this paper we will use the term *meta-property* in the usual OntoClean way, whereas we will refrain from using the term *property* but rather stick to the more common term *concept*. OntoClean consists of two steps: first every single concept needs to be tagged with occurrences of the core meta-properties, which are described below. Thus, every concept will have a certain tagging like $+R+U-D+I$. We call an ontology with tagged concepts a tagged ontology (wrt. OntoClean, to be precise). After the tagging, the second step of OntoClean is to check all subsumption relations of the ontology (also called Subclass-relations). OntoClean constraints the possible taxonomic relations by disallowing subsumption relations between specific combinations of tagged concepts. This way, OntoClean provides a unique approach by formally analyzing the concepts intensional content and their subsumption relationships.

We now briefly present the four main meta-properties and rules which belong to OntoClean. The four meta-properties are: *Rigidity (R)*, *Unity (U)*, *Dependence (D)* and *Identity (I)*. They base on philosophical notions dating back to Aristotle. Here we will offer a short description of these meta-properties.

Rigidity. Rigidity is based on the notion of *essence*. A concept is essential for an instance *iff* it is necessarily an instance of this concept, in all worlds and at all times. *Iff* a concept is essential to all of its instances, the concept is called rigid and is tagged with $+R$. *Iff* it is not essential to some instances, it is called non-rigid, tagged with $-R$. An anti-rigid concept is one that is not essential to

---

[1] http://ontoware.org/projects/aeon/

all of its instances. It is tagged $\sim R$. An example of an anti-rigid concept would be *teacher*, as no teacher has always been, nor is necessarily, a teacher, whereas *human* is a rigid concept because all humans are necessarily humans and neither became nor can stop being a human at some time.

Unity. Unity is about "What is part of something and what is not?" This answer is given by an **Unity Criterion** (UC), which is true for all parts of an instance of this concept, and for nothing else. For example, there is an unitiy criterion for the parts of a human body, as we can say for every human body which parts belong to it. Concepts carrying an UC have Unity and are tagged $+U$ else $-U$.

Dependence. A concept C_1 is dependent on a concept C_2 (and thus tagged $+D$), *iff* for every instance of C_1 an instance of C_2 must exist. An example for a dependent concept would be *food*, as instances of food can only exist if there is something for which these instances are food. Another way to regard dependency is to distinguish between intrinsic and extrinsic concepts. Intrinsic concepts are independent, whereas extrinsic concepts need to be given to an instance by circumstances or definitions.

Identity. A concept with Identity is one, where the instances can be identified as being the same at any time and in any world, by virtue of this concept. This means that the concept carries an **Identity Criterion** (IC). It is tagged with $+I$, and with $-I$ otherwise. It is not important to answer the question of what this IC is (this may be hard to answer), it is sufficient to know that the concept carries an IC. For example, the concept *human* carries an IC, as we are able to identify someone as being the same or not, even though we may not be able to say what IC we actually used for that. On the other hand, a concept like *red* would be tagged $-I$, as we cannot tell instances of red apart because of its color.

On a tagged ontology, we can use the existing OntoClean rules to check the ontology for consistency. Here, we will give only one illustrative example for these rules. For a full list refer to [11]. As shown in [17] such rules can be formalized as logical axioms and validated by an inference engine.

$\sim R$ can't subsume $+R$. Having a concept C subsuming the concept D, with C tagged $\sim R$ and D tagged $+R$, would lead to the following inconsistency: D must always hold true for all of its instances. D, as a subsumed concept, would always imply C for all of its instances. Therefore there are at least some instances of C that are necessarily C as they are D. Thus C can not be anti-rigid, as the tagging says, because this would mean that it is not necessarily true for any of its instances – which would be a contradiction. The classic example is *student*, an anti-rigid concept, subsuming *human*, a rigid concept, which is obviously wrong: whereas every student is free to leave the university and stop being a student, humans cannot stop being humans. As every human would be a student, according to the example, they never could stop being a student, which contradicts the previous sentence.

3   Approach

Our approach for the automatic assignment of meta-properties according to the OntoClean methodology is based on three fundamental assumptions. First, we believe that the nature of concepts is to some degree reflected by human language and what is said about instances of these concepts in the language corpus. Because of this, we consider statistics about the occurrences of lexico-syntactic patterns (see section 3.2) as a feasible means to capture the meta-properties of ontological concepts. Second, in line with similar approaches by [9], [14], [16], [3] and [4] we think that using the Web as a corpus is an effective way of addressing the typical data sparseness problem one encounters when working with natural language corpora. Finally, from our point of view, the Web being the biggest source of common-sense knowledge available constitutes a perfect basis for computational comprehension of human intuition as to the philosophical notions of essence, unity and identity.

3.1   Architecture and Implementation

In order to evaluate our approach we developed AEON, a tool which matches lexico-syntactic patterns on the Web to obtain positive and negative evidence for rigidity, unity, dependence and identity of concepts in an RDFS or OWL ontology. The architecture of AEON is roughly depicted by figure 1. It consists of an *evaluation component*, which is responsible for training and evaluation, a *classifier* for mapping given sets of evidence to meta-properties such as +R or -U, a *pattern library* and a *search engine wrapper*.

The **pattern library** is initialized by means of an XML file containing a set of abstract patterns for each meta-property (see listing 1.1). Each of these patterns include a specification of the type of evidence it produces, e.g. negative evidence for rigidity. Moreover, it contains a declaration of one or more variables and a set of Web queries which can be instantiated by replacing the regarding

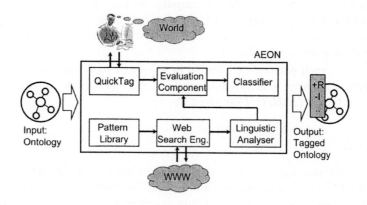

Fig. 1. Architecture of AEON

variables by the labels of the concepts to be analysed. Finally, a linguistic filter, i.e. a regular expression over tokens and part-of-speech tags, is defined for filtering the results obtained by the above mentioned queries (see section 3.3).

Listing 1.1. Negative Evidence for Rigidity (R)

```
<pattern>
  <variable name="x" />
  <evidence type="false" for="R" />
  <google regex="is\t\w+ no\t\w+ longer\t(DT\w+\t)?(NN|NP
      |NNS|NPS) x\t[^(NN|NP|NNS|NPS)]">
    <query string="is no longer a x" />
    <query string="is no longer an x" />
    <query string="is no longer x" />
  </google>
</pattern> %
```

Given a set of instantiated patterns (e.g. *"is no longer a student"*) the **search engine wrapper** uses the Google™ API in order to retrieve web pages or snippets, i.e. parts of web pages containing the regarding search string, from the Web. For normalization purposes (see below) it also queries the web for all occurrences of the regarding concept, such as *"student"* for example.

The **linguistic analyser** provides methods for tokenization, lemmatizing and part-of-speech (POS) tagging, which are required for some fundamental preprocessing of the snippets and HTML pages obtained from the Web and for an appropriate matching of the linguistic patterns described above. By what we call *Linguistic Filtering* we analyse, for example, all those snippets returned by Google™, which satisfy the query "is no longer a computer" (cf. listing 1.1). If the regular expression associated with the query does not match, the particular snippet is not counted as a hit and thus does not provide any evidence with respect to the rigidity of `computer`. This way, we avoid false matches in case of statements such as "He is no longer a computer hacker." or (this would yield false evidence for the unity of `employee`) when we find a phrase like "the computer of an employee consists of". Of course, linguistic filtering is also applied in the normalization process (see above).

Finally, for each pattern i contained in the above mentioned pattern library the positive or negative evidence $evidence(p, i, c)$ for a concept c having a certain meta-property $p \in \{R, U, D, I\}$ is given by:

$$evidence(p, i, c) = \frac{\sum_{q \in Q_i} lf(hits(q_c))}{lf(hits(c))},$$

where Q_i is the set of queries associated with pattern i, q_c is the instantiation of query q for concept c, and $hits(q_c)$ and $hits(c)$ are the number of hits obtained for q_c or c respectively. lf is a function implementing the linguistic filtering described above.

Given a concept c and the evidence values obtained for all patterns the decision whether or not a meta-property p applies to c is made by a classifier. A set of classifiers – one for each meta-property – has been trained on a small number of examples provided by human annotators (cf. section 5). The manual effort rests with the creating of a gold standard ontology and classifiers to be trained on this ontology.

3.2 Patterns

During the last decades, lexico-syntactic patterns have become generally accepted as an effective means for extracting various types of lexical and ontological relationships such as hyponymy and meronymy (cf. [13], [2], [12]). Nevertheless, there has been little if any work on the use of pattern-based approaches towards the extraction of meta-properties, i.e. properties of concepts or relations. So, we performed an extensive evaluation of many different pattern candidates before finally choosing a small subset of particularly promising patterns for the evaluation of our approach. All of these patterns are domain-independent, thus being well suited for the WWW as a very heterogeneous corpus.

Rigidity. The intuition behind the patterns we defined for Rigidity is the following: If any individual can become or stop being a member of a certain class, then it holds that the membership of this class, e.g. the property *being a student*, is not essential for all its individuals. Therefore, we can obtain **negative** evidence with respect to Rigidity from the following patterns:

```
is no longer (a|an)? CONCEPT
became (a|an)? CONCEPT
while being (a|an)? CONCEPT
```

Unity. As explained in section 2 a concept is tagged with $+U$ if for each of its instances all parts can be identified and if they share a common Unity Criterion which holds true for exactly these parts. Because of this, in order to determine whether a given concept has unity or not we have to find answers to questions such as *"what is part of an object? and what is not?"* or *"under which conditions is the object a whole?"*. If we can answer these questions for at least most of the instances of the concept, we can take this as **positive** evidence for Unity.

```
part of (a|an)? CONCEPT
```

Moreover, since instances of concepts which are not countable usually do not carry a unity criterion, we can get **positive** evidence for Unity by searching for the following patterns:

```
(one|two) CONCEPT
```

Of course, one and two seem to be somewhat arbitrary, but since Google™is not yet able to process queries containing regular expressions we had to confine ourselves to what we considered as the most frequent of all possible variations of this pattern.

Similarly, **negative** evidence can be obtained by a pattern which indicates non-countability of a concept.

```
amount of CONCEPT
```

Identity. According to [11] identity is given by the fact that two instances of a concept are the same *iff* they have the same parts. This is known as *mereological extensionality* and can be expressed by the following patterns providing **positive** evidence for Identity:

```
CONCEPT consists of (two|three) parts
CONCEPT is composed of (two|three) parts
```

Additional **positive** evidence for identity can be obtained by the rather straight-forward pattern:

```
CONCEPT is identified by
```

Negative and **positive** evidence respectively can be obtained by these merely linguistic patterns checking whether the name of the concept is an adjective or a noun.

Both patterns are matched on the results of Google™queried for nothing but the concept name. Please note that linguistic preprocessing as described in section 3.1 is required to allow this kind of lexico-syntactic pattern matching, since these patterns assume the text to be an alternate sequence of words and POS tags. The tags *JJ, JJR* and *JJS* indicate an adjective, whereas *NN, NP, NNS* and *NPS* are indicators for a common or proper noun.

```
(JJ|JJR|JJS) CONCEPT
(NN|NP|NNS|NPS) CONCEPT
```

Also, countability means that the instances of a concept are obviously identifiable (or else they would not be countable). Therefore we reuse the same patterns that we have already used as positive or negative evidence for Unity.

```
(one|two) CONCEPT
amount of CONCEPT
```

Dependence. Among the meta-properties Rigidity, Unity, Identity and Dependence we consider Dependence as the most difficult one to learn automatically. Maybe, this is because of the fact that relational knowledge, i.e. knowledge involving more than one concept, is required in order to detect Dependence. Nevertheless, we tried to capture Dependence of concepts by the following pattern:

```
cannot be (a|an)? CONCEPT without
```

Additional Patterns. Due to the flexible architecture of AEON, adding further patterns is a very easy task. It simply requires the addition of the pattern in described format to the XML file.

We had some more patterns in mind, but preliminary testing in Google™ revealed often only a small number of hits, which would only lower the efficiency of the system and not improve the output of the system adequately.

3.3   Discussion

The described approach is original, and quite a number of problems were raised. We solved many of them, but some remain for further research. Both kinds are described in this section.

Certain patterns could return a lot of inappropriate evidence. Searching for the fragment *"is no longer a computer"* would also return *"is no longer a computer hacker"*, which is false evidence about the Rigidity of computers. To solve this problem we introduced linguistic preprocessing and patterns that recognize *computer* not being the subject of the given example. Thus we can get rid of a lot of false evidence.

The other problem occurs with high level, abstract or seldom used concepts: they just do not return hits, or return only a small, and thus usually unreliable number of evidence. However, we do not consider this as a big problem in general, since this kind of very abstract concepts mostly appear in upper-level ontologies which are typically smaller and less dynamic than domain ontologies. If we do not get any hits, the concept will not be part of possible constraint errors. So it does not really bother the user with wrong warnings but rather simply ignores this concept.

A much bigger problem is given by the highly ambiguous nature of human language. So far, our approach does not distinguish between different concepts which could be meant by the word "glass", for example. Whereas the "glass" which can be used to drink water certainly has Unity, the "glass" windows are made of does not have Unity. Linguistic patterns do not help in this case. We will try to solve this problem by comparing the context of the word – given by a Google™snippet or a Web page – with the semantic neighborhood of the regarding concept.

Natural language is not as strict and formal as the OntoClean meta-properties. The best known example is the English verb *to be*, which can have various meanings based heavily on context, like subsumption, definition or constitution. But exactly these different meanings play a crucial role within the OntoClean methodology. Thus, the translation of the OntoClean definitions of meta-properties to commonly used language patterns was quite challenging. With the patterns given in this section we hope to have achieved a good balance between language ambiguity, pragmatic indication of meta-properties and number of occurrences for a wide range of concepts.

The combination of negative and positive evidence right now just happens by simple subtraction. Maybe more complex combinations will yield even better results. This is an open issue. So is the difference between Non-, Anti- and Semi-Rigidity. Right now we just consider Rigidity and Non-Rigidity, but the more detailed division may lead to an even better evaluation of the ontology.

4   OntoClean in Practice

For the evaluation and training of our automatic methods, we needed a gold standard tagging of an ontology with the OntoClean meta-properties. Although

OntoClean is already some years old and appeared in a number of publications, actual tagged ontologies were found only extremely scarcely. Our best resource was the example ontology in [11] and some examples in the other publications. This amounted to about 30-40 tagged concepts. [20] describes the creation of another ontology evaluated with OntoClean, but this is not publicly available. To the best of our knowledge there are no further available tagged ontologies.

So we decided to tag an ontology on our own. We wanted a generic, domain-independent ontology with a not too small number of concepts. This is to ensure that the experience we gain and the classifiers trained will be most reusable for further ontologies evaluated with AEON in the future. We chose Proton[2], a freely available upper level ontology developed by OntoText within the European IST project SEKT[3]. We merged the System, Top and Upper modules of Proton, and the merged ontology contained 266 concepts, as diverse as *Accident*, *Alias*, *Happening* or *Woman*.

We asked methodology and ontology engineering experts to tag Proton according to the OntoClean methodology, because we wanted to base the evaluation of our own techniques on this human tagging. Most of them told us that based on their experience with OntoClean the manual tagging of an ontology such as Proton would take more than one week. Some even considered this as an effort of one month – which would of course render any evaluation of the ontology far too expensive to be efficient. Finally, we were able to convince two of them to create a manual tagging of Proton. The third tagging we used for our evaluation was done by one of the authors of this paper.

The tagging itself was very strenuous, and often uncertainty arose. Decisions were debatable and the documentation of OntoClean was open to interpretation. The experts tagged the ontology in the given time of four to six hours, but they achieved an agreement far lower than expected (refer to table 2). Concepts similar to those in the example ontology in [11] were often tagged consistently, but the agreement on the other concepts was low (close to the baseline given by random tagging). This suggests that the experts rather worked by analogies (not surprisingly, given the time constraints) to the examples (an approach that is very common for humans) than by applying the definitions of the meta-properties.

Taking into account that OntoClean is only a method to evaluate the taxonomic relationships of an ontology, these findings point to doubts concerning the efficiency of manual tagging. Although there are some implementations that support the tagging with OntoClean meta-properties in existing ontology engineering environments (refer to section 6), the number of actually tagged ontologies is obviously far too low. This again points to a discrepancy between the expected work and the expected benefit of using OntoClean. To turn OntoClean into a feasible and more often used ontology evaluation method, a far more precise and yet broader understandable description of OntoClean must become available, or else an approach for the automatic tagging of concepts must lower the time to

---

[2] http://proton.semanticweb.org
[3] http://www.sekt-project.com

tag ontologies dramatically. The latter approach requires far less training to the individual ontology engineer and evaluator.

The upper level ontology DOLCE was created with the principles of Onto-Clean in mind. WordNet on the other hand was not created with ontological categories in mind, but rather adhering to linguistic structures. Aligning those two should reveal numerous errors in WordNet, by OntoClean standards, due to the different nature of the two. In [8], where this task is described, the authors say that the alignment of DOLCE and WordNet yielded almost only constraint violations regarding rigidity and much less on all other meta-properties. Thus it was essential to get reliable results for rigidity, more than for the other meta-properties.

Another problem is that tagging an ontology implies further ontological decisions possibly unintended by the ontology creators. Subjective point of views going further than the ontology is already committed to can be introduced through the tagging. For example, regarding the concept *Dalai Lama* we could state this concept is not rigid: a person is chosen to become the *Dalai Lama*. Thus a question of believe becomes relevant: buddhist religion claims that one does not become the *Dalai Lama*, but rather that one is the *Dalai Lama* since birth - or not. It is not a role a person plays, but rather it is the identity moving from body to body through the centuries. Simply tagging an ontology therefore reduces its possible audience by further ontological commitments.

We see that this contradicts to the definition of Rigidity, as there seem to be possible worlds where the concept is rigid and possible worlds in which it is not. Our approach dodges this problem by basing the taggings on statistics over a large corpus instead of an individual or small group's subjective point of view.

5   Evaluation

As described in section 4 we decided to use the System, Top and Upper module of the Proton ontology for the evaluation of our approach. The merged ontology consists of 266 concepts, most of them annotated with a short natural language description. The list of all concepts together with their descriptions was given to three human annotators in the following called A_1, A_2 and A_3. All of them were considered to be experts in using the OntoClean methodology. Nevertheless, whereas Rigidity, Identity and Dependence were considered by all annotators, only two of them also assigned Unity labels to some of the concepts. Table 1 shows the number of concepts and their corresponding taggings created by each of the human annotators. The data sets labelled A_1/A_2, A_1/A_3, A_2/A_3 were obtained by building the intersection of two of the single data sets. Obviously, $A_1/A_2/A_3$, which is the intersection of all three data sets – the set of concepts which are tagged identically by all human annotators – is extremely sparse.

In order to illustrate how difficult it was for the human annotators to tag the ontology according to the OntoClean methodology we measured the human agreement between the data sets. *strict* means that two taggings were considered equal only if they were totally identical. *relaxed* means that − and ~ were

Table 1. Tagged Concepts

	R			U			I			D		
	+	-	~	+	-	~	+	-	~	+	-	~
A_1	147	69	50	156	81	29	194	61	11	151	110	3
A_2	208	39	0	103	138	3	189	58	0	31	203	13
A_3	201	64	0	0	0	0	223	42	0	63	1	0
avg	**185.3**	**57.3**	**16.7**	**86.3**	**73.0**	**10.7**	**202.0**	**53.7**	**3.7**	**81.7**	**104.7**	**5.3**
A_1 / A_2	122	3	20	77	61	11	134	17	4	23	94	3
A_1 / A_3	125	27	15	0	0	0	171	18	1	47	1	0
A_2 / A_3	161	14	0	0	0	0	163	12	0	9	0	0
avg	**136.0**	**14.7**	**11.7**	**25.7**	**20.3**	**3.7**	**156.0**	**15.7**	**1.7**	**26.3**	**31.7**	**1.0**
A_1 / A_2 / A_3	106	2	6	0	0	0	126	8	0	9	0	0

Table 2. Human Agreement

	A_1 / A_2		A_1 / A_3		A_2 / A_3		A_1 / A_2 / A_3	
	relaxed	strict	relaxed	strict	relaxed	strict	relaxed	strict
R	58.7%	50.6%	63.0%	57.4%	71.1%	71.1%	46.3%	43.9%
U	61.1%	56.6%	N/A	N/A	N/A	N/A	N/A	N/A
I	66.4%	64.8%	71.7%	71.3%	71.1%	71.1%	54.5%	54.5%
D	48.9%	45.7%	75.0%	75.0%	15.0%	15.0%	15.0%	15.0%
avg	**58.8%**	**54.2%**	**69.9%**	**67.9%**	**52.4%**	**52.4%**	**38.6%**	**37.8%**

considered the same. Since our approach so far does not distinguish between Semi- and Anti-Rigidity, for example, the strict agreement can be neglected for the following evaluation. As shown by table 2 the average human agreement is extremely low, which means close to the random baseline and sometimes much lower than the results we obtained by automatic tagging. Given these figures indicating the difficulty of this task, we believe any kind of automatic support could be of great use for formal ontology evaluation.

Baseline. In order to obtain an objective baseline for the evaluation of AEON which is statistically more meaningful than the human agreement (see table 2) we computed a random baseline for the F-Measure as follows: Let x be the overall number of concepts to be tagged, p the number of positive and $n = x - p$ the number of negative examples. Given a random tagging for all n concepts we can assume that half of them are tagged as $+$ and how many are tagged as $-$. Of course, the fraction of positives within the whole data set tends to be the same as in each of the randomly chosen subsets S_+ and S_- of size $\frac{n}{2}$. Therefore, the number of true positives (TP) and true negatives (TN) is given by $TP = \frac{p}{x} * \frac{x}{2} = \frac{p}{2}$ and $FP = (1 - \frac{p}{x}) * \frac{x}{2} = \frac{x}{2} - \frac{p}{2} = \frac{x-p}{2} = \frac{n}{2}$ whereas the false positives (FP) and false negatives (FN) can be computed by $TN = \frac{n}{x} * \frac{x}{2} = \frac{n}{2}$ and $FN = (1 - \frac{n}{x}) * \frac{x}{2} = \frac{x}{2} - \frac{n}{2} = \frac{x-n}{2} = \frac{p}{2}$.

Obviously, the Precision P_+ for the positive examples (for example, all concepts tagged as $+R$) is given by $P_+ = TP/(TP + FP)$, whereas the Precision

Table 3. Random Baseline (F-Measure)

	R			U			I			D		
	+	-	M-avg	+	-	M-avg	+	-	M-avg	+	-	M-avg
A_1	52.5	47.2	49.9	54.0	45.3	49.6	59.3	35.1	47.2	53.5	45.9	49.7
A_2	62.7	24.0	43.4	45.8	53.6	49.7	60.5	32.0	46.2	20.1	63.6	41.8
A_3	60.1	32.6	46.4	N/A	N/A	N/A	62.7	24.1	43.4	66.3	3.0	34.7
avg	58.4	34.6	46.6	49.9	49.5	49.7	60.8	30.4	45.6	46.6	37.5	42.1
A_1 / A_2	62.7	24.1	43.4	50.8	49.1	50.0	63.6	20.4	42.0	27.7	61.8	44.7
A_1 / A_3	60.0	33.5	46.7	N/A	N/A	N/A	64.3	16.7	40.5	66.2	4.0	35.1
A_2 / A_3	64.8	13.8	39.3	N/A	N/A	N/A	65.1	12.1	38.6	66.7	N/A	N/A
avg	62.5	23.8	43.1	50.8	49.1	50.0	64.3	16.4	40.4	53.5	32.9	39.9
A_1 / A_2 / A_3	65.0	12.3	38.7	N/A	N/A	N/A	65.3	10.7	38.0	66.7	N/A	N/A

Table 4. Rigidity (Best Results with Linguistic Filtering)

	P		R		F					Classifier
	+	-	+	-	+	-	M-avg	baseline	no LF	
A_1	59.0	51.4	69.5	40.0	63.8	45.0	54.4	49.9	61.6	RandomForest
A_2	86.9	31.8	91.0	23.3	88.9	26.9	57.9	43.4	47.8	ADTree
A_3	76.5	23.5	76.1	24.0	76.3	23.8	50.1	46.4	44.8	RandomTree
avg	74.1	35.6	78.9	29.1	76.3	31.9	54.1	46.6	51.4	
A_1 / A_2	91.3	64.3	94.9	50.0	93.1	56.3	74.7	43.4	69.4	ADTree
A_1 / A_3	78.2	66.7	98.0	12.9	87.0	21.6	54.3	46.7	62.6	DecisionStump
A_2 / A_3	93.8	11.1	93.8	11.1	93.8	11.1	52.5	39.3	48.2	RandomTree
avg	87.8	47.4	95.6	24.7	91.3	29.7	60.5	43.1	60.1	
A_1 / A_2 / A_3	95.5	0.0	100.0	0.0	97.7	0.0	48.9	38.7	48.4	NBTree

for the negative examples can be obtained by $P_- = TN/(TN + FN)$. Recall can be computed by $R_+ = TP/(TP + FN)$ and $R_- = TN/(TN + FP)$ respectively.

Given Recall and Precision we can obtain the F-Measure for positive and negative examples by $F_+ = \frac{2*P_+*R_+}{P_++R_+}$ and $F_- = \frac{2*P_-*R_-}{P_-+R_-}$. This leads to an *macro-average F-Measure* of $F = \frac{1}{2} * (F_+ + F_-)$, which we consider as a reasonable baseline for the evaluation of our approach. A detailed overview of the concrete baselines we determined for all data sets is given by table 3.

Setting. Since we decided to evaluate our system separately for R, U, I and D, we made 2*7*4=56 experiments (one for each human annotator, each meta-property, with and without linguistic filtering) using a number of Weka[4] classifiers. In order to detect the limitations of our approach and to see what we can potentially get out of the data we are able to provide, we first tried many different types of classifiers, such as Support Vector Machines, Bayesian classifiers and Decision Trees. Since the latter turned out to perform best we finally decided to focus on the class of Decision Trees – among them ADTree, RandomForest and

---

[4] http://www.cs.waikato.ac.nz/ml/weka/

Table 5. Identity (Best Results with Linguistic Filtering)

	P		R		F					Classifier
	+	-	+	-	+	-	M-avg	baseline	no LF	
A_1	75.0	34.8	84.1	23.2	79.3	27.8	53.6	47.2	49.5	ADTree
A_2	79.4	37.5	86.3	26.8	82.7	31.3	57.0	**46.2**	45.0	ADTree
A_3	87.3	55.0	95.8	26.8	91.4	36.1	63.8	43.4	47.9	RandomForest
avg	**80.6**	**42.4**	**88.7**	**25.6**	**84.5**	**31.7**	**58.1**	**45.6**	**47.5**	
A_1 / A_2	87.0	13.3	90.7	10.0	88.8	11.1	50.0	42.0	54.1	RandomTree
A_1 / A_3	93.0	46.7	95.2	36.8	94.1	41.2	67.7	40.5	50.8	NBTree
A_2 / A_3	95.7	57.1	98.1	36.4	96.9	44.4	70.7	38.6	48.2	ADTree
avg	**91.9**	**39.0**	**94.7**	**27.7**	**93.3**	**32.2**	**62.8**	**40.4**	**51.0**	
A_1 / A_2 / A_3	95.3	66.7	99.2	25.0	97.2	36.4	66.8	38.0	48.5	RandomForest

Table 6. Unity (Best Results with Linguistic Filtering)

	P		R		F					Classifier
	+	-	+	-	+	-	M-avg	baseline	no LF	
A_1	69.5	49.5	63.6	56.2	66.4	52.6	59.5	49.6	58.8	DecisionStump
A_2	43.0	61.2	46.0	58.3	44.4	59.7	52.1	47.7	57.8	ADTree
A_3	N/A	N/A	N/A	N/A	N/A	N/A	N/A	N/A	N/A	N/A
avg	**56.3**	**55.4**	**54.8**	**57.3**	**55.4**	**56.2**	**55.8**	**48.7**	**58.3**	
A_1 / A_2	57.6	53.6	51.5	59.7	54.4	56.5	55.5	50.0	60.2	ADTree
A_1 / A_3	N/A	N/A	N/A	N/A	N/A	N/A	N/A	N/A	N/A	N/A
A_2 / A_3	N/A	N/A	N/A	N/A	N/A	N/A	N/A	N/A	N/A	N/A
avg	**57.6**	**53.6**	**51.5**	**59.7**	**54.4**	**56.5**	**55.5**	**50.0**	**60.2**	
A_1 / A_2 / A_3	N/A	N/A	N/A	N/A	N/A	N/A	N/A	N/A	N/A	N/A

J48, for example. The features given to these classifiers were sets of evidences obtained by all patterns for the regarding meta-property (see section 3.1). Precision, Recall and F-Measure for both positive and negative examples as well as the macro-average F-Measure were determined by a 10-fold cross-validation. Please note that for training and evaluation we only used those concepts which were annotated in the regarding data set and for which we obtained at least some evidence. The percentage of tests which failed, because we did not get any Google™hits for the instantiated patterns was about 20% for rigidity, 5% for identity and around 10% for unity. Because of this, in many cases the number of examples we gave to the classifiers was extremely low - especially for the agreement data sets A_1/A_2, A_1/A_3, A_2/A_3 and $A_1/A_2/A_3$. The reason why the results are nevertheless very promising, certainly is the good quality of the classification features we get by using a pattern-based approach.

Results. One of the main findings of our experiments was that linguistic filtering really helps in the task of pattern-based ontology evaluation. As shown by tables 4, 5 and 7 without linguistic filtering the baseline for macro-average F-Measure was missed several times. And especially for *Identity* we noticed that the results could be improved by around 30% with the help of linguistic filtering. Another interesting result of the evaluation was that on average our system performed significantly better on the agreement, i.e. the intersection of two or three data sets, than on the single data sets. This is probably due to the fact that those concepts which were tagged identically by at least two of the human annotators are easier to tag – maybe, because they are less ambiguous.

Table 7. Dependence (Best Results with Linguistic Filtering)

	P		R		F					Classifier
	+	-	+	-	+	-	M-avg	baseline	no LF	
A_1	68.2	40.9	69.8	39.1	69.0	40.0	54.5	**49.7**	**39.1**	RandomTree
A_2	30.0	81.5	23.1	86.3	26.1	83.8	55.0	41.8	56.7	RandomForest
A_3	100.0	0.0	100.0	0.0	100.0	0.0	50.0	34.7	50.0	ADTree
avg	**66.1**	**40.8**	**64.3**	**41.8**	**65.0**	**41.3**	**53.2**	**42.1**	**48.6**	
A_1 / A_2	45.5	70.0	45.5	70.0	45.5	70.0	57.8	**44.7**	**35.3**	ADTree
A_1 / A_3	100.0	0.0	100.0	0.0	100.0	0.0	50.0	35.1	40.0	ADTree
A_2 / A_3	100.0	0.0	100.0	0.0	100.0	0.0	50.0	N/A	50.0	ADTree
avg	**81.8**	**23.3**	**81.8**	**23.3**	**81.8**	**23.3**	**52.6**	**39.9**	**41.8**	
A_1 / A_2 / A_3	N/A	N/A	N/A	N/A	N/A	N/A	N/A	N/A	N/A	N/A

The overall conclusion we draw from the evaluation of AEON was that despite the weaknesses of our pattern-based approach (see section 3.3) the first results are already very promising. Given the small amount of training data we had and the fact that we used standard Weka classifiers without much parameter tuning we hope to get even better results in future experiments.

6   Related Work

Applying OntoClean for ontology evaluation has been proposed e.g. for traditional ontology engineering methodologies such as [6,18]. Checking for the described constraint violations after tagging reveals any design errors during the cyclic engineering of ontologies. There are several OntoClean plug-ins created for ontology engineering suites to support this, in particular for Protégé [15], WebODE [1] and OntoEdit [17]. They allow the manual tagging of ontologies, integrated within the ontology engineering task, and also partially check the consistencies according to the OntoClean rules described in section 2. As we have seen in section 4, the biggest problem when applying OntoClean is not the proper user interface for a manual tagging nor the possibility to check the ontology for formal taxonomic constraints, but rather the high cost of tagging itself. This is where the work presented here comes into play. To the best of our knowledge no other approach is known which automatizes the OntoClean tagging task as we do. DILIGENT [19] is the only known ontology engineering methodology right now, that explicitly integrates computational agents to be actors participating in ontology engineering tasks just like human users. The integration of our approach into DILIGENT is on our agenda.

7   Conclusion and Outlook

Despite the fact that ontology evaluation is a critical task for ontology engineering there currently exist only few approaches. OntoClean is the only known approach, where the intension of the concepts are taken into account when checking the taxonomic structure of the ontology. Tagging ontological concepts according to OntoClean is very expensive as it requires a lot of experts time and knowledge. The approach provided in this paper is giving a helpful hand by enabling an automatic tagging. Instead of claiming full automatic tagging and evaluation against OntoClean's meta-properties, we only take into account the concepts we are pretty sure of in our tagging and point to potential formal errors in the taxonomy at hand. But, such a tagging is only the beginning and a small building block for a next generation integrated ontology engineering environment. While the user is creating or evolving an ontology, the system checks the taxonomical relationships in the background, pointing to possible inconsistencies and likely errors. For those taggings where the system's confidence is not that high, suggestions will be given. These suggestions can be substantiated with an explanation based on the patterns found on the Web, which is much more intuitive than the formal definition of a meta-property.

The flexible architecture described in section 3 can easily be extended to check for further constraints, not represented by OntoClean's rules. For example, if we find evidence that *human being* consists of *amount of matter* then we could conclude that there is probably no taxonomic relationship between both concepts. Mereological relationships may be regarded as well. Due to the strong usage of Google™and its snippets, we are even able to pinpoint to the very evidence of why two relationships should or should not exist. This way the automatic tagger can act as a full agent, who does not just point to errors, but also explains why a certain change is needed.

With the availability of the software presented in this paper we hope to turn the usage of OntoClean from a few experts method to a widespread and standard technique for the intensional ontological analysis for every ontology, raising the quality of ontologies in common use.

Acknowledgements. Research reported in this paper has been partially financed by the EU in the IST-2003-506826 project SEKT (http://www.sekt-project.com). Special thanks go to Aldo Gangemi and Daniel Oberle for their time spent on tagging our reference ontology and thus making the evaluation possible. We thank Andreas Hotho, Philipp Cimiano, Peter Haase, Stephan Bloehdorn and Christoph Tempich for helpful comments and interesting discussions.

References

1. J. C. Arpírez et al. WebODE: a scalable workbench for ontological engineering. In *Proc. of Int. Conf. on Knowledge Capture (K-CAP), Victoria, Canada*, 2001.
2. E. Charniak and M. Berland. Finding parts in very large corpora. In *Proc. of the 37th Annual Meeting of the ACL*, pages 57–64, 1999.

3. P. Cimiano, S. Handschuh, and S. Staab. Towards the self-annotating web. In *Proceedings of the 13th World Wide Web Conference*, pages 462–471, 2004.
4. P. Cimiano, G. Ladwig, and S. Staab. Gimme' the context: Context-driven automatic semantic annotation with c-pankow. In *Proc. 14th WWW*. ACM, 2005.
5. O. Etzioni et al. Web-scale information extraction in KnowItAll (preliminary results). In *Proc. 13th WWW Conf.*, pages 100–109, 2004.
6. M. Fernández-López et al. Building a chemical ontology using Methontology and the Ontology Design Environment. *IEEE Int. Systems*, 14(1), Jan/Feb 1999.
7. M. Fernández-López and A. Gómez-Pérez. The integration of ontoclean in webode. In *Proc. of the EON2002 Workshop at 13th EKAW*, 2002.
8. A. Gangemi et al. Sweetening WordNet with Dolce. *AI Magazine*, Fall 2003.
9. G. Grefenstette. The WWW as a resource for example-based MT tasks. In *Proc. of ASLIB'99 Translating and the Computer 21*, 1999.
10. N. Guarino and C. A. Welty. A formal ontology of properties. In *Knowledge Acquisition, Modeling and Management*, pages 97–112, 2000.
11. N. Guarino and C. A. Welty. An overview of OntoClean. In S. Staab and R. Studer, editors, *Handbook on Ontologies in Inf. Sys.*, pages 151–172. Springer, 2004.
12. U. Hahn and K. Schnattinger. Towards text knowledge engineering. In *Proc. of AAAI'98/IAAI'98*, 1998.
13. M. Hearst. Automatic acquisition of hyponyms from large text corpora. In *Proc. 14th Int. Conf. on Computational Linguistics*, pages 539–545, 1992.
14. F. Keller, M. Lapata, and O. Ourioupina. Using the web to overcome data sparseness. In *Proc. of EMNLP-02*, pages 230–237, 2002.
15. N. Noy, R. Fergerson, and M. Musen. The knowledge model of Protégé-2000: Combining interoperability and flexibility. In R. Dieng and O. Corby, editors, *Proc. of the 12th EKAW*, LNAI, pages 17–32, Juan-les-Pins, France, 2000. Springer.
16. P. Resnik and N. A. Smith. The Web as a parallel corpus. *Computational Linguistics*, 29(3):349–380, 2003.
17. Y. Sure, J. Angele, and S. Staab. OntoEdit: Multifaceted inferencing for ontology engineering. *Journal on Data Semantics*, LNCS(2800):128–152, 2003.
18. Y. Sure, S. Staab, and R. Studer. Methodology for development and employment of ontology based knowledge management applications. *SIGMOD Rec.*, 31(4), 2002.
19. C. Tempich et al. An argumentation ontology for distributed, loosely-controlled and evolving engineering processes of ontologies (DILIGENT). In C. Bussler et al., editors, *ESWC 2005*, LNCS, Heraklion, Crete, Greece, 2005. Springer.
20. C. Welty, R. Mahindru, and J. Chu-Carroll. Evaluating ontology cleaning. In D. McGuinness and G. Ferguson, editors, *AAAI2004*. AAAI / MIT Press, 2004.

A Method to Combine Linguistic Ontology-Mapping Techniques

Willem Robert van Hage[1], Sophia Katrenko[2], and Guus Schreiber[3]

[1] TNO, Science and Industry,
wrvhage@few.vu.nl
[2] Free University Amsterdam, Computer Science
schreiber@cs.vu.nl
[3] University of Amsterdam, Informatics Institute
katrenko@science.uva.nl

Abstract. We discuss four linguistic ontology-mapping techniques and evaluate them on real-life ontologies in the domain of food. Furthermore we propose a method to combine ontology-mapping techniques with high Precision and Recall to reduce the necessary amount of manual labor and computation.

1 Introduction

Ontologies are widely used to provide access to the semantics of data. To provide integrated access to data annotated with different, yet related, ontologies, one has to relate these ontologies in some way. This is commonly done by cross-referencing concepts from these ontologies. In different contexts this practice is called ontology mapping, schema matching, or meaning negotiation. In the literature one can find surveys of the widely varying methods of automated ontology mapping. For instance, in the surveys done by Kalfoglou and Schorlemmer [5]; and Rahm and Bernstein [8]. The latter organized the methods hierarchically. The ontology-mapping methods we develop in this paper fall in the categories *schema-only based*, which means they work on the conceptual part of the ontology and not on the annotated individuals and *linguistic*, since we use the labels of the concepts. The techniques we use come from the field of *information retrieval* (IR).

The work in this paper is done within the scope of the Adaptive Information Disclosure (AID) project, which is part of the greater effort of the Dutch "Virtual Labs for e-Science" project (VL-e) [1]. The AID project focusses on facilitating access to domain-specific text corpora, in particular articles about food. When the semantics of data sources or the information needs are of increasing complexity old-fashioned information-retrieval systems can fail to deliver due to the following reasons:

---

[1] http://www.vl-e.nl

Y. Gil et al. (Eds.): ISWC 2005, LNCS 3729, pp. 732–744, 2005.

- Domain-specific terms can have homonyms in a different domain. For instance, "PGA" stands for "Polyglandular Autoimmune Syndrome" and the "Professional Golfers' Association".
- Synonyms used by different communities can be difficult to relate to each other. For instance, some refer to "stomach acid" with "Betaine HCl", others use "Hydrochloric Acid".
- Skewed term-frequency distributions can lead to failing weighting schemes. For instance, the term "cancer" occurs as frequently as some stop words in the medical MedLine corpus, but it is an important term.

Ontologies pave the way for new techniques to facilitate access to domain-specific data. Semantic annotation of text resources can help to subdue jargon. [6,10] Obviously accessing annotated data sources is not without problems of its own. In practice different data sources are often annotated with different ontologies.[2] In order to provide integrated access using multiple ontologies, some form of ontology mapping needs to be done.

Within AID we focus on food information corpora. This domain–like the medical domain–struggles with an information overload and jargon issues. For instance, everyday household terms are intermingled with names of proteins and other chemical compounds. This complicates the formulation of good search queries. In this paper we test the applicability of four automated ontology-mapping techniques on real-life ontologies in the domain of food and assess their practical use. Specifically we try to map the USDA Nutrient Database for Standard Reference, release 16 (SR-16) [3] onto the UN FAO AGROVOC thesaurus (AGROVOC) [4] using that yield RDFS [1] subClassOf relations. The four techniques we discuss are listed below.

1. Learn subclass relations between concepts from AGROVOC and SR-16 by querying Google for Hearst patterns. [4]
2. Learn subclass relations by extracting them from Google snippets returned by the same queries with the help of shallow parsing using the TreeTagger part-of-speech tagger. [9]
3. Learn subclass relations by extracting them from a semi-structured data source, the CooksRecipes.com Cooking Dictionary, with MINIPAR [7].
4. Use the Google hits method as a sanity check to filter the dictionary mining results.

In Section 2 we discuss some related work to give an impression of current practice in relation extraction. In Section 3 we describe the experimental set-up we used in which we tested the four mapping techniques. In Section 4 we describe the four techniques in great detail and discuss the acquired results. In Section 5 we propose a method for applying the techniques in practice and we show how much manual labor can be saved.

---

[2] We use the term ontologies to include light-weight ontologies such as vocabularies and thesauri.
[3] http://www.nal.usda.gov/fnic/foodcomp/Data/SR16/sr16.html
[4] http://www.fao.org/agrovoc

2   Related Work

Brin proposed a method called Dual Iterative Pattern Relation Extraction (DIPRE) in his paper from 1998 [2]. He tested the method on part of his Google corpus–which at the time consisted of about 24 million web pages–to learn patterns that link authors to titles of their books. These patterns were then used to retrieve author-title relation instances from the same corpus. An example of such a pattern is the HTML bit: "<li>*title* by *author*".

In 1992 Hearst devised a set of lexico-syntactic patterns for domain aspecific hyponym extraction [4]. His patterns found entrance in many applications such as Cimiano and Staab's PANKOW system. [3] The first method we discuss in this paper is similar to their work.

In their 2004 paper Cimiano and Staab try to accomplish two things. The first is a instance classification task: to classify geographical entities such as Amsterdam (City), Atlantic (Ocean), etc. The second is a subclass learning task: to reconstruct a subclass hierarchy of travel destinations mentioned in the LonelyPlanet website[5]. The method they use is the same for both tasks. They send Hearst patterns describing the relation they want to test to the Google API and depending on the number of hits Google returns they accept of reject the relation. For instance, the query "cities such as Amsterdam" yields 992 hits. Depending on which threshold they put on the number of hits they achieved Precision between .20 and .35 and Recall somewhere between .15 and .08. The higher the threshold, the higher the Precision and the lower Recall.

What we want to accomplish is a bit more complicated than either of Cimiano and Staab's tasks for two reasons. The food domain is less well-defined than the geographical domain, in which there are exhaustive thesauri such as TGN. The relations between the concepts are clearly defined. Countries have exactly one capital. Countries can border each other, etc. In the food domain such consensus does not exist. This means the evidence for relations that can be found in Google can be expected to be more ambiguous in the food domain than in the geographical domain.

3   Experimental Set-Up

Our set-up consists of the two thesauri we want to connect, the auxiliary sources of knowledge we use to learn the mappings from, and a gold-standard mapping to assess the quality of the learnt relations. In Section 3.3 we discuss the gold standard and the evaluation measures we use.

3.1   Thesauri

AGROVOC. This is a multi-lingual thesaurus made by the Food and Agriculture Organization of the United Nations (FAO). It consists of roughly 17,000

---

[5] http://lonelyplanet.com/destinations

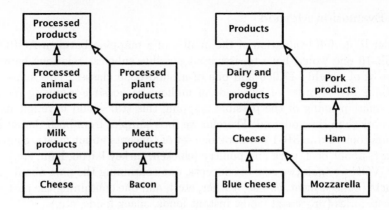

Fig. 1. excerpts from AGROVOC (left) and SR-16 (right)

concepts and three types of relations derived from the ISO thesaurus standard: use (preferred term), rt (related term) and bt (broader term). We use a RDFS version of this thesaurus where the broader term relation is represented with the RDFS subClassOf relation. The maximum depth of AGROVOC's subclass hierarchy is eight. Figure 1 shows an excerpt from AGROVOC. The text boxes are classes with their names and the arrows stand for subclass relations.

SR-16. This is the Nutrient Database for Standard Reference version 16 (SR-16) made by the United States Department of Agriculture (USDA), converted to RDFS and OWL by the AID group. It consists of roughly 6500 concepts and one relation, RDFS subClassOf. The maximum depth of the subclass hierarchy of SR-16 is four. Figure 1 shows an excerpt from SR-16.

3.2   Auxiliary Knowledge Sources

We used one general and one domain-specific source. The general source is Google and the domain-specific source is the CooksRecipes.com's Cooking Dictionary.

Google. Google [6] is an open domain search engine. At the moment (mid 2005) Google indexes more than 8 billion pages. The large size of Google allows makes it possible to use it for statistical comparison of words. Google has a programming interface called the Google API, that at the moment allows researchers to pose 1000 queries per day.

CooksRecipes.com's Cooking Dictionary. The CooksRecipes.com Cooking Dictionary provides definitions for ingredients, culinary terms and cooking techniques. It contains 1076 definitions. An example entry is: "**Basmati** an aged, aromatic long-grain rice grown in the Himalayan foothills; has a creamy yellow color, distinctive sweet, nutty aroma and delicate flavor..."

---

[6] http://www.google.com

3.3   Evaluation Method

In order to do full evaluation of the quality of a mapping between AGROVOC and SR-16 one would have to assess all possible subclass relations between a thesaurus of roughly 17,000 and one of around 6500 classes. This sums up to something of the order of hundreds of millions of possible mapping relations. With smart pruning of the possible mapping this still would have left us with more work than time allowed. Therefor we took samples from both thesauri on a common topic. From SR-16 we took one set of concepts about meats, containing the parts about beef, pork and poultry (chicken, turkey bacon, ham, etc.). From AGROVOC we took two sets of concepts, one containing the part about animal products (minced meat, cheese, leather, etc.), and one containing the part about food categories (processed foods, instant foods, snack foods, etc.).

For the experiments with Google we created a gold standard mapping by hand from the set of SR-16 concepts to both sets of AGROVOC concepts. The size of the mapping from meats to animal products is 31 relations out of 3696 possible relations. The size of the mapping from meats to food categories is 32 relations out of 792 possible relations.

The experiments with the CooksRecipes.com Dictionary yielded few results, distributed evenly over the thesauri, which made it hard to choose a subset of the thesaurus that contained a reasonable number of mapping relations. Therefor, we evaluated only the returned results. This means we are unable to say anything about Recall of the techniques using the CooksRecipes.com Dictionary.

The measures we used are Precision, Recall and F-Measure as used throughout the literature.[7] The F-Measure we use gives Precision and Recall an equal weight.

Protocol. The protocol we used can be summarized as follows: All concepts are to be interpreted in their original context. For instance, in AGROVOC chicken is a subclass of product, which means none of the individuals of the chicken class are live chickens. Taking this into account chicken is not a subclass of frozen foods, because some chicken products are never frozen, but chicken is a subclass of poultry, because all chicken products qualify as poulty.

4   Experiments

4.1   Hearst Patterns and Google Hits

The mapping technique described in this section is approximately the same as Cimiano and Staab's "Learning by Googling" method. It derives relations from Google hit counts on certain queries.

Method

1. **Create hypothetical relations between pairs of concepts from both thesauri.** For this experiment we chose to investigate all possible relations

---

[7] http://en.wikipedia.org/wiki/Information_Retrieval

Table 1. Hearst patterns used in this paper

	concept₁ such as	*concept₂*
such *concept₁* as		*concept₂*
	concept₁ including	*concept₂*
	concept₁ especially	*concept₂*
	concept₁ and other	*concept₂*
	concept₁ or other	*concept₂*

from any of the concepts in the predefined set of SR-16 concepts to any of the concepts in both of the predefined sets of AGROVOC concepts (see Section 3.3).

2. **Construct Google queries containing Hearst patterns for each pair of concepts.** We chose to use the same Hearst patterns as Cimiano and Staab [3] except the apposition and copula patters, to reduce the number of Google queries, because these patterns did not yield enough results to be useful. The patterns are listed in the Table 1. Since we are only interested in the combined result of all the patterns we can further reduce the number of queries by putting the patterns in a disjunction. We chose the disjunction to be as long as possible given the limit Google imposes on the number of terms in a query (which was 32 at the time).

3. **Send the queries to the Google API.**

4. **Collect the hit counts for all Heart patterns that give evidence for the existence of a relation.** For instance, add the hits on the queries "milk products such as cheese", "milk products including cheese", etc. Since all these hits give a bit of evidence that cheese is a subclass of milk products.

5. **Accept all hypothetical relations that get more hits than a certain threshold value.** Reject all others.

Results. The average number of hits for the mapping to food categories is about 2.5 and to animal products it is about 1.3. Only about 2.5% of the patterns had one or more hits. The maximum number of hits we found was in the order of 1000, while Cimiano and Staab find hit counts in the order of 100,000. We suspect that this is the case because people rarely discuss the ontological aspects of food, because it is assumed to be common knowledge–everybody knows beef is a kind of meat–and hence can be left out. Since the total number of hits is so low we chose not to use a threshold, but to accept all relations that had one or more hits instead. Precision and Recall are shown in Table 2.

Table 2. Results of the Google hits experiment

	Precision	Recall	F-Measure
to animal products	.17 (10/58)	.32 (10/31)	.22
to food categories	.30 (17/56)	.53 (17/32)	.38

Discussion. The performance of the PANKOW system of Cimiano and Staab on geographical data is a Precision of .40 with a Recall of around .20 for instance classification and a Precision of .22 and a Recall of .16 for subclass extraction.

Overall Recall seems to be less of a problem in the food domain than in the geographical domain. The decent Recall values can be explained by the large size of the current Google corpus. On simple matters it is quite exhaustive. Even though the total hit counts in the food domain are lower than in the geographical domain it seems that a greater percentage of the relations is mentioned in Google. Apparently not all LonelyPlanet destinations have been discovered by the general web public. If you are interested in really high Recall in the field of geography you can simply look up your relations in the Getty Thesaurus of Geographic Names (TGN) [8].

Precision of the mapping to animal products seems to be comparable to the subclass learning task Cimiano and Staab set for themselves. The overall low Precision can be explained by the fact that when you use Google as a source of mappings between two thesauri you turn it from one into two mapping problems: from the thesaurus to Google; and then from Google to the other thesaurus. That means you have to bridge a vocabulary gap twice and hence introduce errors twice.

Precision of mapping to food categories using Google hits seems to be comparable to that of instance classification. Mapping to animal products, i.e. mapping between concepts of similar specificity, appears to be more difficult.

4.2   Hearst Patterns and Google Snippets

The second mapping technique is a modification of the previous technique. Instead of deriving relations from Google hit counts we analyze the snippets presented by Google that summarize the returned documents. We try to improve performance by shallow parsing the context of the occurrence of the Hearst pattern and remove false hits.

Method

1. **Follow step 1 through 3 from the "Hearst patterns and Google hits" method.**
2. **Collect all the snippets Google returns.** Snippets are the short exerpts from the web pages that show a bit of the context of the query terms.
3. **Extract the patterns.** To accomplish this we part-of-speech tag the snippets with TreeTagger and recognize sequences of adjectives and nouns as concept names. Then we try find all Hearst patterns over the concept names in the snippets.
4. **Discard all patterns that contain concept names that do not exactly match the original concept names.** For instance, if the original pattern looked like "soup such as chicken", discard the matches on "soup such as chicken soup", because these give false evidence for the relation

---

[8] http://www.getty.edu/research/conducting_research/vocabularies/tgn

chicken subClassOf soup. We ignore prefixes to the concept names from the following list: "other", "various", "varied", "quality", "high quality", "fine", "some", and "many". This unifies concept names such as "meat products" and "high quality meat products".

5. **Count every remaining occurrence of the pattern as evidence that the relation holds.**

6. **Follow step 4 and 5 from the "Hearst patterns and Google hits" method.**

Results. Analysis of the snippets improves Precision while sacrificing Recall. Overall performance indicated by the F-Measure does not chance much. Shallow parsing the snippets removed many false hits. For instance, "salads such as chicken salad" does not lead to chicken subClassOf salad anymore. The exact Precision and Recall are shown in Table 3.

Table 3. Results of the Google snippets experiment

	Precision	Recall	F-Measure
to animal products	.38 (7/18)	.22 (7/31)	.27
to food categories	.50 (12/24)	.37 (12/32)	.42

Discussion. Even the Precision achieved with mapping to concepts of similar specificity (to animal products) is comparable to the level PANKOW achieves for instance classification. The mapping to food categories, which is closer to the instance classification task, now achieves a higher Precision and Recall than PANKOW.

As Cimiano and Staab noted downloading the whole documents for analysis could further improve the results. This might even improve Recall a bit if these documents contain more good Hearst patterns than those that caused them to appear in Google's result set.

4.3   Extraction from a Dictionary

With the third mapping technique we try to exploit the implicit editor's guidelines of a dictionary to achieve an even higher grade of Precision than the Google Snippets technique described in the previous section. As an example we took a dictionary that includes terms from both thesauri, the CooksRecipes.com Cooking Dictionary. This dictionary is relatively small compared to the thesauri, but it covers about the same field as SR-16.

Method

Find regularities in the dictionary that highly correlate with subclass relations. We found that the editor of the dictionary often starts a definition with the superclass of the described concept. The following steps are tailored to exploit this regularity.

1. **Select all entries describing a concept that literally matches a concept from AGROVOC or SR-16.**
2. **Parse the entry with MINIPAR.**
3. **Extract the first head from the parse tree.** For instance, the entry of the concept basmati starts with "an aged, aromatic long-grain rice grown in ..." The first head in this sentence is "rice".
4. **Check if the first head corresponds to a concept in the other thesaurus** If basmati is a concept from AGROVOC, try to find the concept rice in SR-16 and vice versa.
5. **Construct a subclass relation between the concept matching the entry name and the one matching the first head.**

Results. More than half of all the returned relations, even those failing the check in step 4, are correct subclass relations according to our strict evaluation protocol. As expected, given the relatively wide scope of the dictionary, step 4 eliminates most of the results. However the mapping relations that are left are of high quality. The exact results are shown in Table 4.

Table 4. Results of the dictionary extraction experiment

	Precision
relations not forming a mapping	.53 (477/905)
mapping entire AGROVOC–SR-16	.75 (16/21)

Discussion. We exploited a regularity in the syntax of the data. This yields high Precision results. Clearly, Recall of this method is dependent on the size of the dictionary and the overlap between the dictionary and the thesauri.

We noticed that most of the errors could have been filtered out by looking for evidence on Google. For instance, the entry: "**leek** a member of the lily family *(Allium porrum)*; ..." would cause our technique to suggest the relation leek subClassOf member. One query could have removed this false relation from the result list, because "member such as leek" gives no hits on Google.

4.4   Combination of Google Hits and Dictionary Extraction

The fourth technique is an improvement to the dictionary extraction technique. We use the Google hits technique to filter false relations out of the list of results provided by extraction.

Method

1. **Follow all the steps of the Dictionary Extraction method.** This yields a list of relations.
2. **For each extracted relation follow step 2–5 from the Google hits method.** This filters out all relations for which no evidence can be found on Google using Hearst patterns.

Results. Applying the Google hits technique as a sanity check on the extraction results greatly reduces the number of relations. Precision of this smaller result set is higher than with both the Google hits and dictionary extraction technique. Around 63% of the correct results were removed versus 92% of the incorrect results. The results are shown in Table 5.

Table 5. Results of combining dictionary extraction and Google hits

	Precision
relations not forming a mapping	.53 (477/905)
after Google hits sanity check	.84 (178/210)
mapping entire AGROVOC to SR-16	.75 (16/21)
after Google hits sanity check	.94 (15/16)

Discussion. The combination of Google hits and a dictionary gave the best Precision of the four techniques. Most of the mismatches caused by definitions that did not exactly fit the regularity that we exploited with the dictionary extraction technique were removed by applying the Google hits technique. On the other hand, a substantial portion of the correct results was also removed.

We noticed that most of the incorrect relations that were not removed are easily recognizable by hand. If the superclass is not directly food related the relation is usually false. For instance, mayonnaise subClassOf cold. Most relations to latin names of plants were inverted. For instance, rosmarinus officinalis subClassOf rosemary. There is another member of the rosemary family, "Rosmarinus eriocalix", so rosmarinus officinalis should be a subclass.

5   Method Proposal

As we discussed in Section 3.3 simply checking all possible relations between two ontologies is task of quadratic complexity. In theoretical computer science this might qualify as a polynomial with a low degree, but for a mapping technique that uses the Google API (which only allows 1000 queries per account per day) this means it does not scale well. Furthermore, assessing a quadratic number of relations by hand is often not feasible. Therefor we propose to combine high Precision techniques and techniques that achieve a high Recall per human assessment. The method we propose is as follows:

1. **Find a small set of high Precision mapping relation as starting points, preferably distributed evenly over the ontologies.** This could be done with the last two techniques we described or with tools such as PROMPT [9]. Which technique works best depends largely on the naming conventions used in the ontologies.
2. **Manually remove all the incorrect relations.** Assessing the results of the dictionary extraction technique took about one man hour.

---

[9] http://protege.stanford.edu/plugins/prompt/prompt.html

3. **For each correct relation select the concepts surrounding the subject and object concepts.** For instance, if the SR-16 concept cheese (see Figure 1) was correctly mapped as a subclass of the AGROVOC concept Milk products, one would select a subclass tree from SR-16 that contains cheese and a subclass tree from AGROVOC that contains Milk products. This can be accomplished in the following two steps:

   (a) **Travel up the subclass hierarchy from the starting point.** Go as far as possible as long as it is still clear what is subsumed by the examined concept, without having to examine the subtrees of the sibling concepts. A suitable top concept from SR-16 could be Dairy and egg products because it is immediate clear to us what is subsumed by this concept without having to look at the Pork products concepts. A suitable top concept from AGROVOC could be Processed animal products.

   (b) **Select all subclasses of the two top concepts.** Collect the concepts as two sets.

   This could be done using tools such as Triple20 [10] or Sesame [11].

4. **Find relations between the two sets of concepts returned in the previous step.** This could be done with the Google snippets technique.

5. **Manually remove all incorrect relations.** The evaluation of the mapping between the AGROVOC animal product concepts and the SR-16 meat concepts took us four man hours. Assessing all the mappings returned by the previous steps could take days. The higher the applied mapping techniques' Precision, the less time this step takes.

6. **Manually add all omissions.** Creating a list of omissions during the assessments of the previous step reduces the amount of work in this step. The higher the applied mapping techniques' Recall, the less time this step takes.

This method reduces the search space by eliminating cross-references between concepts in unrelated parts of the ontologies. For instance, possible relations between concepts in the part of AGROVOC about legumes and in the part of SR-16 about poultry would be ignored if step 1 did not yield any relations between those parts. Hence the number of queries we have to send to Google is reduced along with the number of necessary manual assessments low.

6 Discussion

We discussed four ontology mapping techniques and evaluated their performance. There is a clear trade-off between Precision and Recall. The more assumptions we make the higher Precision gets and the lower Recall. We showed that exploiting syntactic information by using a part-of-speech tagger can improve Precision of ontology-mapping methods based on Google hits such as our Google hits method and possibly PANKOW.

---

[10] http://www.swi-prolog.org/packages/Triple20
[11] http://www.openrdf.org

We showed that in our experiments finding subclass relations to generic concepts such as food categories is easier than mapping concepts that are roughly equal in specificity. We hypothesize that this is because the former discriminate more clearly between different interpretations of concepts and are therefor used more often. For instance, the phrase "chickens such as roosters" is less discriminating about the meaning of the word "rooster" than "poultry such as roosters" or "birds such as roosters".

Furthermore, we introduced a method that extends the PANKOW two-step method by Cimiano and Staab to decrease the number of necessary Google queries and the amount of manual work.

Acknowledgements

This paper has benefitted from input from the AID group's participants: Pieter Adriaans, Jan van Eijck, Leonie IJzereef, Machiel Jansen, Hap Kolb, Maarten de Rijke and the authors of this paper. Sophia Katrenko provided the RDFS and OWL version of SR-16. We want to thank Marco Roos and Scott Marshall from the Micro Array Department of the University of Amsterdam, Michel Klein at the Computer Science department of the Free University Amsterdam for valuable discussions, Victor de Boer who organized the Ontology Learning and Population Workshop at the Human-Computer Studies Laboratory of the University of Amsterdam and and everybody who attended. Furthermore we want to thank Thijs de Graaf, Wessel Kraaij and Dolf Trieschnigg at the Signal Processing group at TNO Science and Industry.

References

1. Dan Brickley and Ramanathan Guha. *Resource description framework (RDF) schema specification 1.0.* W3C, March 2000.
2. Sergey Brin. Extracting patterns and relations from the world wide web. In *WebDB Workshop at 6th International Conference on Extending Database Technology, EDBT'98*, 1998.
3. Philipp Cimiano and Steffen Staab. Learning by googling. *SIGKDD Explor. Newsl.*, 6(2):24–33, 2004.
4. Marti Hearst. Automatic acquisition of hyponyms from large text corpora. In *Proceedings of the 14th International Conference on Computational Linguistics*, 1992.
5. Yannis Kalfoglou and Marco Schorlemmer. Ontology mapping: the state of the art. *The knowledge engineering review*, 18(1):1–31, march 2003.
6. Jaap Kamps. Improving retrieval effectiveness by reranking documents based on controlled vocabulary. In *Advances in Information Retrieval: 26th European Conference on IR Research (ECIR)*, 2004.
7. Dekang Lin. Dependency-based evaluation of minipar. In *Proceedings of the Workshop on the Evaluation of Parsing Systems, First International Conference on Language Resources and Evaluation*, Granada, Spain, May 1998.
8. Erhard Rahm and Philip A. Bernstein. A survey of approaches to automatic schema matching. *VLDB Journal*, 10(4), 2001.

9. Helmut Schmid. Probabilistic part-of-speech tagging using decision trees. In *Proc. of International Conference on New Methods in Language Processing*, 1994.
10. H. Stuckenschmidt, F. van Harmelen, A. de Waard, T. Scerri, R. Bhogal, J. van Buel, I. Crowlesmith, Ch. Fluit, A. Kampman, J. Broekstra, and E. van Mulligen. Exploring large document repositories with rdf technology: The dope project. *IEEE Intelligent Systems*, 19(3):34–40, 2004.

Debugging OWL-DL Ontologies: A Heuristic Approach

Hai Wang, Matthew Horridge, Alan Rector,
Nick Drummond, and Julian Seidenberg

Department of Computer Science,
The University of Manchester,
Manchester M13 9PL, UK
{hwang, mhorridge, rector, ndrummond, jms}@cs.man.ac.uk

Abstract. After becoming a W3C Recommendation, OWL is becoming increasingly widely accepted and used. However most people still find it difficult to create and use OWL ontologies. On major difficulty is "debugging" the ontologies - discovering why a reasoners has inferred that a class is "unsatisfiable" (inconsistent). Even for people who do understand OWL and the logical meaning of the underlining description logic, discovering why concepts are unsatisfiable can be difficult. Most modern tableaux reasoners do not provide any explanation as to why the classes are unsatisfiable. This paper presents a 'black boxed' heuristic approach based on identifying common errors and inferences.

1 Introduction

One of the advantages of logic based ontology languages, such as OWL, in particular OWL-DL or OWL-Lite, is that reasoners can be used to compute subsumption relationships between classes and to identify unsatisfiable (inconsistent) classes. With the maturation of tableaux algorithm based DL reasoners, such as **Racer** [11], **FaCT** [8], **FaCT++** [7] and **PELLET** [4], it is possible to to perform efficient reasoning on large ontologies formulated in expressive description logics.

However, when checking satisfiability (consistency) most modern description logic reasoners can only provide lists of unsatisfiable classes. They offer no further explanation for their unsatisfiability. The process of "debugging" an ontology - i.e. determining why classes are unsatisfiable - is left for the user. When faced with several unsatisfiable classes in a moderately large ontology, even expert ontology engineers can find it difficult to work out the underlying error. This is a general problem which gets worse rather than better with improvements in DL reasoners; the more powerful the reasoner the greater its capacity to make non-obvious inferences.

Debugging an ontology is a non-trivial task because:

- *Inferences can be indirect and non-local.* Axioms can have wide-ranging effects which are hard to predict.
- *Unsatisfiability propagates.* Therefore, a single root error can cause many classes to be marked as unsatisfiable. Identifying the root error from amongst the mass of unsatisfiable classes is difficult.

Y. Gil et al. (Eds.): ISWC 2005, LNCS 3729, pp. 745–757, 2005.

2 A Heuristic Approach to Ontology Debugging

In short, the current state of ontology development environments and reasoning services within these environments is akin to having a programming language compiler detect an error in a program, without explaining the location of the error in the source code.

Over the past five years we have presented a series of tutorials, workshops and post-graduate modules on OWL-DL and its predecessors. Based on our experience, a list of frequently made errors have been identified as reported in [10]. This catalogue of common errors has been used in turn to develop a set of heuristics that have been incorporated into debugging tool for Protégé-OWL [5]. The examples in this paper are all taken from these tutorials and use the domain of Pizzas used in the introductory tutorial.

The heuristic debugger treats the tableaux reasoner as a 'black box'or 'oracle'. This 'black box' approach has the advantage that it is independent of the particular reasoner used. It works with any DIG [1]compliant reasoner, even ones which have been specially augmented or adapted. [1]

Being independent of the reasoner has advantages even if only as single reasoner is to be used. Many modern reasoners transform the input ontology in order to optimise the reasoning process. Although logically equivalent, the internal representation may bear little resemblance to the ontology as it was constructed by the user. Given such transformations, even it were possible for the reasoner to 'explain' its actions, the explanation in terms of the transformed ontology would be unlikely to be of direct use to the user. An additional advantage of the 'black box' approach is that it is independent of such transformations.

3 Background

3.1 OWL Overview

OWL [2] is the latest standard in ontology languages, which was developed by members of the World Wide Web Consortium[2] and Description Logic community.

An OWL ontology consists of classes, properties and individuals. Classes are interpreted as sets of objects that represent the individuals in the domain of discourse. Properties are binary relations that link individuals and are represented as sets of ordered pairs that are subsets the cross product of the set of objects.

OWL classes fall into two main categories – named classes and anonymous (unnamed) classes. Anonymous (unnamed) classes are formed from logical descriptions. They contain the individuals that satisfy the logical description. Anonymous classes may be sub-divided into restrictions and 'logical class expressions'. Restrictions act along properties, describing sets of individuals in terms of the types of relationships that the individuals participate in.

---

[1] The DIG Interface is a standard DL reasoner communication protocol that sits between DL based applications and DL reasoners, thereby allowing these applications to communicate with different third party DL reasoners.

[2] http://www.w3.org

Logical classes are constructed from other classes using the boolean operators AND (⊓), OR (⊔) and NOT (¬).

An important point to note from the point of view of debugging is that OWL allows the nesting of anonymous class expressions to arbitrary levels. For example, the expression:

Pizza ⊓ ∃ hasTopping (PizzaTopping ⊓ ∃ hasIngredient (SpicyIngredient ⊓ ∃ hasColour RedColour)) describes the individuals that are pizzas that have pizza toppings that have ingredients which are spicy ingredients that are coloured red.

Disjoint Axioms. All OWL classes are assumed to overlap unless it is otherwise stated that they do not. To specify that two classes do not overlap they must be stated to be *disjoint* with each other using a *disjoint axiom*. The use (and misuse) of disjoint axioms is one of the primary causes of unexpected classification results and inconsistencies [10]. Disjoint axioms are 'inherited' by their subclasses. For example if Pizza is disjoint from PizzaTopping then all subclasses of Pizza will be disjoint from all subclasses of PizzaTopping. This can make debugging difficult for ontologies that have deep taxonomical hierarchies.

Describing Classes. Named OWL classes are described in terms of their named and anonymous super classes, equivalent classes and disjoint classes. When a restriction is added to a named class, it manifests itself as an anonymous superclass of the named class.

For example the named class SpicyPizzaTopping might have a named superclass called PizzaTopping and also the anonymous super class ∃ hasSpicyIngredient SpicyIngredient. That is, things that are SpicyPizzaToppings are also PizzaToppings and things that have at least one SpicyIngredient. We refer to these super classes as *conditions*, as they specify the conditions for membership of a given class.

In summary, OWL has three types of class axioms:

– **Subclass axioms** – These axioms represent *necessary* conditions.
– **Equivalent class axioms** – These axioms represent *necessary & sufficient* conditions.
– **Disjoint axioms** – These axioms represent additional *necessary* conditions.

Domain and Range Axioms. OWL also allows 'global' axioms to be put on properties. In particular, the *domain* and *range* can be specified for properties. In many other languages, domain and range are commonly used as constraints that are checked and generate warnings or errors if violated. Hence domain and range constraints can be used in inference and are a potential cause of unsatisfiability.

3.2 Unsatisfiable OWL Classes

An OWL class is deemed to be unsatisfiable (inconsistent) if, because of its description, it cannot possibly have any instances. While there are many different ways in which the axioms in an ontology can cause a class to be unsatisfiable, the key observation in heuristic debugging is that there are limited number of root causes for the unsatisfiability.

In general, there are three categories of causes.

Local unsatisfiability. The combination of directly asserted restrictions and named superclasses are unsatisfiable.

Propagated unsatisfiability. The combination of directly asserted restrictions and named superclasses would be satisfiable except that some class used in them is unsatisfiable.

Global unsatisfiability. There is some global constraint, usually a domain or range constraint, from which along with other information in the ontology it can be inferred that the class is unsatisfiable.

Local unsatisfiability is usually easy to spot. Section 4.5 describes the various reasons that may lead to a class being locally unsatisfiable. Propagated unsatisfiabiity is more difficult. There are two primary mechanisms for propagation:

Unsatisfiable ancestor classes. All descendant classes of an unsatisfiable class are unsatisfiable. Therefore unsatisfiability propagates down the subclass hierarchy.

Unsatisfiable fillers of existential restrictions. Any existential (or minimum cardinality) restriction with an unsatisfiable filler is itself unsatisfiable.

A single error can cause large swathes of the ontology to be unsatisfiable. The key strategy of the heuristic debugger is to collect all global conditions so that they can be treated as local.

4   Heuristic Debugging Process

Figure 1 gives a principled view of the heuristic debugging process; in practice this is optimised.

- Check that the selected class is indeed unsatisfiable
- Determine the *basic debugging necessary conditions*

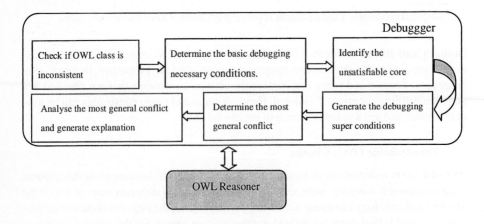

Fig. 1. The debugging process

- Identify the *unsatisfiable core*, or smallest set of unsatisfiable subset of the *basic debugging necessary conditions*
- Generate the the *debugging super conditions*, which are the conditions that are implied by the conditions in the *unsatisfiable core*.
- Determine the *most general conflicting* class set based on the *unsatisfiable core*.
- Analyse the most general conflict in order to produce an explanation of why the class is unsatisfiable.

Each step is examined in detail below.

4.1 Determining the *Basic Debugging Necessary Conditions (BDNC)*

As discussed in section 3.1 OWL uses three kinds of class axioms:

- **Subclass axioms** – *necessary* conditions.
- **Equivalent class axioms** – *necessary & sufficient* conditions.
- **Disjoint axioms** – *necessary* conditions.

An OWL class is unsatisfiable if and only if a subset of the above conditions, which we refer to as the *basic debugging necessary conditions* is unsatisfiable. The first step of the debugging process is the generation the *'basic debugging necessary conditions'*. This is achieved by collecting together the *necessary*, and *necessary & sufficient* conditions of the class that is being debugged, and then adding a condition for each class that the given class is disjoint with, which represents the complement class of each disjoint class. For example, suppose the class in question was disjoint with class D. The condition $\neg D$ would be added to the set of basic debugging necessary conditions.

4.2 Identifying the Unsatisfiable Core

After obtaining the set of basic debugging necessary conditions, they are refined and reduced to obtain the *unsatisfiable core*. The *unsatisfiable core* is the smallest unsatisfiable subset of the basic debugging necessary conditions. The *unsatisfiable core* is defined as follows:

Definition 1. *Let $BDNC(C)$ be the 'basic debugging necessary conditions' of a unsatisfiable Class C. An **unsatisfiable core** $(UC(C))$ of the class C is a set of OWL class descriptions, such that:*

1. *$UC(C) \subseteq BDNC(C)$*
2. *Intersection of all the concepts belonging to $UC(C)$ is unsatisfiable.*
3. *For every set of class descriptions CD:*
   $CD \subset UC(C) \Rightarrow$ *Intersection of all the concepts belonging to CD is satisfiable $\vee CD = \emptyset$*

Condition 3 ensures that an *unsatisfiable core* is the most minimal possible set of conditions. An unsatisfiable class could have more than one *unsatisfiable core*, in which case the first is analysed.

Rule 1: Named class rule
    (a) **IF** $C_1 \in DSC(C) \wedge C_1 \sqsubseteq C_2$, where C_1 is a named OWL class
        THEN $C_2 \in DSC(C)$
    (b) **IF** $C_1 \in DSC(C)$ and $Disj(C_1, C_2)$, where C_1 and C_2 are named
        OWL classes
        THEN $\neg C_2 \in DSC(C)$

Rule 2: Complement class rule
    (a) **IF** $\neg C_1 \in DSC(C)$, where C_1 is a named OWL class
        THEN IF $C_2 \sqsubseteq C_1$, **THEN** $\neg C_2 \in DSC(C)$
              IF $C_1 \equiv C_2$, **THEN** $\neg C_2 \in DSC(C)$
    (b) **IF** $\neg C_1 \in DSC(C)$, where C_1 is an anonymous OWL class
        THEN $NORM(C_1) \in DSC(C)$

Rule 3: Domain/Range rule
    (a) **IF** $\exists S.C_1 \in DSC(C) \vee \geq n\,S \in DSC(C) \vee = n\,S \in DSC(C)$,
        where $n > 0$, and $DOM(S) = C_2$
        THEN $C_2 \in DSC(C)$
    (b) **IF** $\exists S.C_1 \in DSC(C) \vee \geq n\,S \in DSC(C) \vee = n\,S \in DSC(C)$,
        and where $n > 0$, $INV(S) = S_1$ and $RAN(S_1) = C_2$
        THEN $C_2 \in DSC(C)$
    (c) **IF** $\exists S.C_1 \in DSC(C) \vee \geq n\,S \in DSC(C) \vee = n\,S \in DSC(C)$,
        where $n > 0$, and $RAN(S) = C_2$
        THEN $\forall S.C_2 \in DSC(C)$

Rule 4: Functional/Inverse functional property
    (a) **IF** $\exists S.C_1 \in DSC(C)$ or $\geq n\,S \in DSC(C)$ or $= n\,S \in DSC(C)$,
        where $n > 0$ and S *is functional*
        THEN $\leq 1\,S \in DSC(C)$
    (b) **IF** $\exists S.C_1 \in DSC(C)$ or $\geq n\,S \in DSC(C)$ or $= n\,S \in DSC(C)$,
        where $n > 0$ and $INV(S) = S_1$, S_1 *is inverse functional*
        THEN $\leq 1\,S \in DSC(C)$

Rule 5: Inverse Rule
        IF $\exists S.C_1 \in DSC(C)$ and $INV(S) = S_1$,
        and $C_2 \sqsupseteq C_1$ and $C_2 \sqsubseteq \forall S_1 C_3$
        THEN $C_3 \in DSC(C)$

Rule 6: Symmetric Rule
        IF $\exists S.C_1 \in DSC(C)$ and S is a symmetric property,
        and $C_2 \sqsupseteq C_1$ and $C_2 \sqsubseteq \forall S C_3$
        THEN $C_3 \in DSC(C)$

Rule 7: Transitive Rule
        IF $\forall S.C_1 \in DSC(C)$ and S is a transitive property,
        THEN $\forall S\,\forall S.C_1 \in DSC(C)$

Rule 8: Intersection Rule
        IF $C \wedge C_1 \in DSC(C)$,
        THEN $C \in DSC(C)$ and $C_1 \in DSC(C)$

Rule 9: Subproperty Rule
    (a) **IF** $\forall S.C_1 \in DSC(C)$ and $S_1 \sqsubset S$, **THEN** $\forall S_1.C_1 \in DSC(C)$
    (b) **IF** $\leq nS \in DSC(C)$ and $S_1 \sqsubset S$, **THEN** $\leq nS_1.C_1 \in DSC(C)$
    (c) **IF** $\exists S.C_1 \in DSC(C)$ and $S_1 \sqsupset S$, **THEN** $\exists S_1.C_1 \in DSC(C)$
    (d) **IF** $\geq nS \in DSC(C)$ and $S_1 \sqsupset S$, **THEN** $\geq nS \in DSC(C)$

Rule 10: Other inference Rule
        IF C_1 can be inferred by any subset of $UC(C)$, where C is a named class
        THEN $C_1 \in DSC(C)$

Fig. 2. Rules for the membership of Debugging Super Conditions (DSC)

4.3   Generating the Debugging Super Conditions

The *unsatisfiable core* merely identifies the set of axioms which have resulted in the inconsistency. However, as described above, the inconsistency may have been caused by global conditions (section 3.1). The debugging process, therefore, 'collects' global axioms – primarily domain/range and disjoint axioms – and maps them into local axioms – i.e. sets of necessary conditions. These are the *debugging super conditions*. The set of *debugging super conditions* is expanded by recursive application of the rules in Figure 2, the most important of which are explained below.

Debugging Super Condition Generation Rules

Named class rule (Rule 1): If an OWL named class C_1 is added to the debugging super conditions, all its direct super classes are also added to the debugging super conditions. For each OWL class C_2 which is asserted to be disjoint with C_1, $\neg C_2$ will be added to the debugging super conditions.

Complement class rule (Rule 2): If an OWL complement class $\neg C_1$ is added to the debugging super conditions, it will be converted to negation normal formal (NNF) so that negations only appear directly before named classes. For example $\neg(\forall\ eats\ Plant) \equiv \exists\ eats\ \neg Plant$. Futhermore, if C_1 is a named class, the complement of all the subclasses of C_1 will be added. The complement of each necessary & sufficient conditions of C_1 will also be added.

Domain/Range axioms (Rule 3): As explained in section 3.1, in OWL, domain restrictions act as universal restrictions such that the all individuals to the property is applied can be inferred to be of the type indicatged by the domain. Therefore, if an existential (someValuesFrom) restriction acting along the property P is added to the debugging super conditions, and P has a domain of C_d, then C_d is also added to the debugging super conditions. (Note that the domain of P might have been declared as the range of its inverse.)

Functional /Inverse functional property (Rule 4): If an existential restriction (someValuesFrom) or a hasValue restriction is added to the debugging super conditions, and the property that the restriction acts along is a functional property P^3, then a $\leq$ 1 P restriction (max cardinality restriction) is added to the debugging super conditions.

Intersection Rule (Rule 8): If an OWL class $C_1\ \sqcap\ C_2$ is added to, then both C_1 and C_2 are added to the debugging super conditions.

4.4   Determining the Most General Conflict

Determining the most general conflict is based on a simple observation: If an OWL class C conflicts with another class D, then then it conflicts with any subclass of D). Therefore we can can eliminate any classes that are subclasses of other classes already in the *Debugging super conditions*.

The most general conflict – *MGC(C)* – is therefore defined as follows.

---

[3] A functional property implies that an individual may only be related to at most one other individual via that property.

Definition 2. *Let* $DSC(C)$ *to debugging super conditions of the unsatisfiable Class* C. *The **most general conflict** ($MGC(C)$) of C is a set of OWL class descriptions, such that:*

1. $MGC(C) \subseteq DSC(C)$
2. *Intersection of $MGC(C)$ of all the concepts belonging to is unsatisfiable.*
3. $\forall C_1 : MGC(C), C_2 : MGC(C)$, *such that* $C_1 \sqsubseteq C_2 \Rightarrow C_1 = C_2$
4. $\nexists C_1 : DSC(C)$, *such that*
   $C_2 \ni MGC(C)$ *and* $\exists C_2 : MGC(C)$ *such that* $C_2 \sqsubseteq C_1$ *and*
   Intersection of all the concepts belonging to $MGC(C) \cup \{C_1\} - \{C_2\}$ is unsatisfiable

Condition 3 ensures that no class in $MGC(C)$ is subclass of another class in $MGC(C)$. Condition 4 ensures that if we replace any class in $MGC(C)$ with one of its superclass in $DSC(C)$, the intersection of $MGC(C)$ will become satisfiable.

4.5   Analysing the Most General Conflict

Having determined the most general conflict set, the final step is to analyse it to find the route use of the conflict and provide the explanation to users about the reason these set of axioms are conflicted. Although there theoretically indefinitely many ways in which inconsistencies may arise, we have found empirically that most can be boiled down to a small number of 'error patterns' to be checked by the heuristic debugger.

There are two broad classes of reasons that the *Most general conflict set* can be unsatisfiable.

- It can contain one or more classes – including restrictions – that are themselves unsatisfiable
- The intersection of two or more classes could be unsatisfiable.

Each of these cases will be dealt with in turn; the debugger generates suitable error messages for each case.

Unsatisfiable Superclasses

Existential (someValuesFrom) restriction. There are three common reasons for an existential restriction to be unsatisfiable:

- Its filler may be unsatisfiable, in which case the filler must be analysed to find the root cause from which the unsatisfiability propagated. In this case the debugger will suggest that the filler should be the next class to be debugged.
- The filler may be disjoint from the range of the property. In this case the debugger will suggest that the filler and property range should be examined to determine why they are disjoint.
- The property may have an unsatisfiable domain. In this case the domain class will have already been added to the debugging super conditions and will therefore be found to be the cause of unsatisfiability.

Universal (allValuesFrom) restriction. A universal restriction alone will never be unsatisfiable. Since a universal restriction does not imply that anything actually exists, it can be trivially satisfied. A universal restriction only leads to an inconsistency when there is a corresponding existential restriction along the same property that has a filler which is disjoint from the filler of the universal restriction. However, universal restrictions that are only trivially satisfiable are usually errors. Later addition of existential restrictions are likely to cause classes to become unsatisfiable. Therefore, the debugger generates warnings for trivially satisfied restrictions.

Maximum/Minimum/Equality cardinality restriction. In OWL, cardinality restrictions do not specify a filler [4]. Therefore, the only common situation in which they themselves can be unsatisfiable is if the restricted property has an unsatisfiable domain and the restriction is a minimum cardinality greater than zero restriction. In this case the domain class will have been added to the debugging super conditions and will therefore be found to be the cause of unsatisfiability.

Intersection condition. An intersection condition will be unsatisfiable if at least one of the operand classes is unsatisfiable. All of conditions that represent the operand classes will have been added to the debugging super conditions and therefore the cause of unsatisfiability will be found by examining these operand conditions.

Union condition. A union conditions will only be unsatisfiable if *all* of its operand classes are unsatisfiable. In this case the debugger will suggest that all of the operand conditions should be debugged by individually checking them.

Complement condition. If a complement condition is unsatisfiable the operand class must be equal or be inferred equal to owl:Thing.

hasValue restriction. If a hasValue restriction is unsatisfiable, the filler individual is a member of an unsatisfiable class or a class disjoint with the range of the property in question. In this case the debugger will suggest that the class which the filler is a member of should be debugged.

Contradictory Super Conditions. The second common cause of a class being unsatisfiable is that two or more *debugging super conditions* contradict each other, i.e. their conjunction is unsatisfiable. This situation can arise for a variety of reasons as described below. Unless otherwise stated, the debugger generates an explanation for the user.

- The class in question has been asserted to be disjoint with one of its super conditions.
- A universal (allValuesFrom) and an existential (someValuesFrom) that act along the same property have disjoint fillers. In this case the debugger will suggest that the intersection of the two fillers should be debugged in order to determine why the fillers are disjoint from each other.
- A universal (allValuesFrom) has an unsatisfiable filler (owl:Nothing) which conflicts with any existential or minimum cardinality restriction on the same property.
- The super conditions contain a maximum (or equality) cardinality restriction, limiting the number of relationships along property P to n, but there are more than n disjoint filler classes implied by existential and/or minimum cardinality constraints.
- The super conditions contain two or more cardinality restrictions that act along the same property but contradict each other. For example, $\leq 2P$ and $\geq 3P$.

---

[4] i.e. there are no "qualified cardinality restrictions".

5 Case Study

This section illustrates the use of the debugger with an example taken from an ontology about pizzas [5]. The pizza ontology contains the class hierarchy shown in Figure 3. The ontology also contains the property hasTopping, which has a domain of Pizza. The ontology contains the following class axioms:

IceCreamWithChocolateSauce ⊑ ∃ hasTopping ChocolateSauce

Pizza ⊑ ¬ (∃ hasTopping ¬ PizzaTopping)

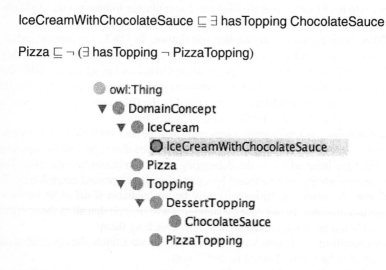

Fig. 3. ExampleHierarchy

When the ontology is classified, it is found that the class IceCreamWithChoco-lateSauce is unsatisfiable. In order to debug this class, the debugger is started and the class is selected. With the debugger running, the user is lead through the steps shown in Figure 4. At the end of each debugging step, the debugger presents a tree of conditions, which represent the conditions that instances of the class being debugged must fulfil – the parent child relationships in the tree are *is-generated-from*. For example, at the end of the first debugging step depicted in Figure 4, all instances of Ice-CreamWithChocolateSauce must also be instances of Pizza, which was generated from ∃ hasTopping ChocolateSauce due to the fact that Pizza is in the domain of the hasTopping property. Conditions that cause an unsatisfiability are boxed in red, and an explanation is generated. In this case the conditions ∃ hasTopping ChocolateSauce and ∀ hasTopping PizzaTopping contradict each other – the explanation being "The universal restriction means that all relationships along hasTopping must be to individuals that are members of PizzaTopping. However, the existential restriction means that there must be at least one relationship to an individual from ChocolateSauce, which is disjoint from PizzaTopping." After the user has has pressed the Continue button, the debugger suggests that the next step is to determine why PizzaTopping and Chocolate-Sauce are disjoint from each other. At the end of this final step the debugger explains

---

[5] We typically use the domain of pizzas as it is easily understood but rich enough to illustrate key principles and common errors [6].

Explanation of the cause of unsatisfiability   Conditions that cause the unsatisfiability are highlighted

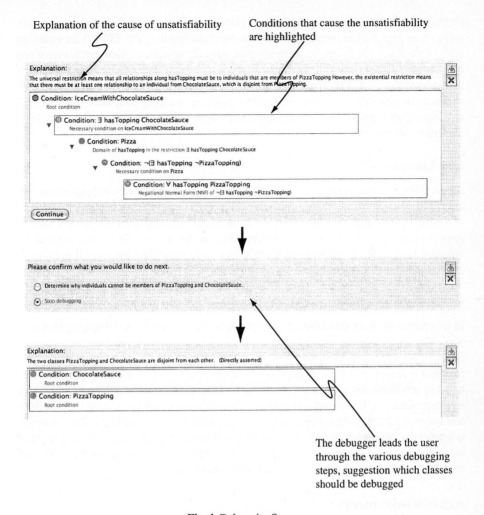

Fig. 4. DebuggingSteps

that the classes PizzaTopping and ChocolateSauce are disjoint from each other because PizzaTopping is disjoint with DessertTopping which is an ancestor class of ChocolateSauce – the explaination being "The two classes ChocolateSauce and PizzaTopping are disjoint from each other. DessertTopping, which is an ancestor class of ChocolateSauce, has been asserted to be disjoint with PizzaTopping."

6   Related Work and Conclusions

6.1   Related Work

Work in the area of reasoner explanation is still in its infancy. Other approaches were discussed at the 3rd International Semantic Web Symposium (ISWC 2004) held in Hiroshima, Japan, where the Pellet reasoner [4] team's future work includes the development of an explanation mechanism for concept satisfiability. The OWL-Lite ontology editor OntoTrack [9], is able to generate explanations for subsumption, equivalence and concept satisfiability using algorithms based on the work of Borgida et. al. in explaining subsumption in $\mathcal{ALC}$ [3]. The OntoTrack team implemented their own tableaux based explanation generator, which is currently limited to working with unfoldable ALEN ontologies, and generates an explanation corresponding to the stages of the tableaux algorithm expansion.

6.2   Limitations

As the title of this paper suggests, the debugger is based on heuristics and pattern matching. The debugger cannot determine the root cause of unsatisfiability in every case, and is therefore not complete. However, we have found that this does not have a serious impact on the usefulness of the debugger, since in most cases the mistakes made by ontologists, ranging from students to experts, can be described by a small number of error patterns that the debugger is adept at spotting.

6.3   Conclusions and Future Work

In this paper we have described a heuristic approach to ontology debugging that uses a DL Reasoner, treating the reasoner as a 'black box'. This means that the debugger is totally reasoner independent, thereby affording the user the benefits of being able to select a reasoner that is appropriate for their needs. The black box approach also helps to minimise any potential versioning problems between the debugger and future advancements in DL reasoners, since the debugger does not need to know the details of any internal tableaux algorithms, reasoner optimisations or capabilities. The debugger is useful for beginners constructing small ontologies, through to domain experts and ontology engineers working with large complex ontologies, as it reduces the amount of time and frustration involved in tracking down ontological inconsistencies.

Acknowledgements

This work was supported in part by the CO-ODE project funded by the UK Joint Information Services Committee and the HyOntUse Project (GR/S44686) funded by the UK Engineering and Physical Science Research Council and by 21XS067A from the National Cancer Institute. Special thanks to all at Stanford Medical Informatics, in particular Holger Knublauch, for their continued collaboration and to the other members of the ontologies and metadata group at Manchester for their contributions and critiques.

References

1. Sean Bechhoffer. The dig description logic interface: Dig/1.1. Technical report, The University Of Manchester, The University Of Manchester, Oxford Road, Manchester M13 9PL, 2003.
2. Sean Bechoffer, Frank van Harmlen, Jim Hendler, Ian Horrocks, Deborah McGuinnes, Peter Patel-Schneider, and Lynn Andrea Stein. Owl web ontology langauge reference, February 2004.

3. A Borgida, E Franconi, I Horrocks, D McGuinness, and P Patel-Schneider. Explaining alc subsumption. In *Description Logics*, 1999.

4. Bijan Parsia Evren Sirin. Pellet: An owl dl reasoner. In Ralf Moller Volker Haaslev, editor, *Proceedings of the International Workshop on Description Logics (DL2004)*, June 2004.

5. Alan Rector Holger Knublauch, Mark Musen. Editing description logic ontologies with the protege-owl plugin. In *International Workshop on Description Logics - DL2004*, 2004.

6. Matthew Horridge, Holger Knublauch, Alan Rector, Robert Stevens, and Chris Wroe. A practical guide to building owl ontologies using protégé-owl and the co-ode tools. Available from http://www.co-ode.org/resources, 2004.

7. Ian Horrocks. Fact++ web site. http://owl.man.ac.uk/factplusplus/.

8. Ian Horrocks. The fact system. In *Automated Reasoning with Analytic Tableaux and Related Methods: International Conference Tableaux'98*, pages 307 – 312. Springer-Verlag, May 1998.

9. Thorsten Liebig and Olaf Noppens. Ontotrack: Combining browsing and editing with reasoning and explaining for owl lite ontologies. In S.A. McIlraith et al., editor, *Proceedings of the 3rd International Semantic Web Conference (ISWC2004)*. Springer-Verlag, 2004.

10. Alan L. Rector, Nick Drummond, Matthew Horridge, Jeremy Rogers, Holger Knublauch, Robert Stevens, Hai Wang, and Chris Wroe. Owl pizzas: Practical experience of teaching owl-dl: Common errors and common patterns. In *Proceedings of Engineering Knowledge in the Age of the Semantic Web*, 2004 2004.

11. Ralf Moller Volker Haarslev. Racer system description. In *International Joint Conference on Automated Reasoning, IJCAR 2001*, 2001.

Rapid Benchmarking for Semantic Web Knowledge Base Systems

Sui-Yu Wang, Yuanbo Guo, Abir Qasem, and Jeff Heflin

Computer Science and Engineering Department, Lehigh University, Bethlehem,
PA 18015, USA
{syw2, yug2, abq2, heflin}@cse.lehigh.edu

Abstract. We present a method for rapid development of benchmarks for Semantic Web knowledge base systems. At the core, we have a synthetic data
generation approach for OWL that is scalable and models the real world data.
The data-generation algorithm learns from real domain documents and generates benchmark data based on the extracted properties relevant for benchmarking. We believe that this is important because relative performance of systems
will vary depending on the structure of the ontology and data used. However,
due to the novelty of the Semantic Web, we rarely have sufficient data for
benchmarking. Our approach helps overcome the problem of having insufficient real world data for benchmarking and allows us to develop benchmarks
for a variety of domains and applications in a very time efficient manner. Based
on our method, we have created a new Lehigh BibTeX Benchmark and conducted an experiment on four Semantic Web knowledge base systems. We have
verified our hypothesis about the need for representative data by comparing the
experimental result to that of our previous Lehigh University Benchmark. The
difference in both experiments has demonstrated the influence of ontology and
data on the capability and performance of the systems and thus the need of using a representative benchmark for the intended application of the systems.

1 Introduction

As the Semantic Web catches on we should expect to see a large growth of Web data
that has formal semantics and an increasing number of systems that process them.
Now that OWL is a W3C recommendation it is quite foreseeable that a fair share of
those data will be marked up in OWL and we will have a variety of tools that will
process these knowledge bases (KB). We should also see a lot of companies attempting to adapt the technology but finding it very difficult to choose the right tool.
Historically this has been the case for various "killer" technologies like databases and
object oriented systems. Companies have invested millions of dollar in technologies
that eventually had to be discarded [3]. It would be prudent for us in the Semantic
Web community to have tools and techniques ready for evaluating these emergent
systems, so we are not caught off guard and benefit from a proactive strategy. It is
therefore critical that we explore various approaches for evaluating these KB processing tools in an objective and practical manner.

Benchmarking has been a powerful tool for evaluation and comparison of computer systems. However, benchmarking of Semantic Web KB systems is challenging

Y. Gil et al. (Eds.): ISWC 2005, LNCS 3729, pp. 758–772, 2005.
© Springer-Verlag Berlin Heidelberg 2005

due to a) the wide variety of types and sizes of KBs b) the difference in reasoning tasks involved and c) the breadth of the application domains. First, if the data is large, scalability and efficiency become crucial issues. Second, the system must provide sufficient reasoning capabilities to support the semantic requirements of the application. However, increased reasoning capability usually means an increase in query response time as well. An important question is how well existing systems support these conflicting requirements. Finally, different domains and their associated applications may place emphasis on different requirements. As such, any data that is used in the benchmark has to be a good representative of the domain.

In our previous work [12, 13] we have considered the first two issues. This resulted in the Lehigh University Benchmark (LUBM). LUBM is intended to evaluate the performance of OWL repositories with respect to extensional queries over a large dataset that commits to a single realistic ontology. It consists of the ontology, customizable synthetic data, a set of test queries, and several performance metrics. The main features of the benchmark include simulated data for the university domain, and a repeatable data set that can be scaled to an arbitrary size.

In this paper we address the third issue of benchmarking Semantic Web KB systems with respect to a given domain. The synthetic data generator for LUBM was bound to a particular ontology and the data was generated by rules specified a priori based on subject matter expert's knowledge of the domain. To extend the benchmark over different domains, we have to be capable of generating synthetic data of different ontologies due to insufficient quantities of real data at the current stage of the Semantic Web development. We present a probabilistic model that, given representative data of some domain, can capture the properties of the data and generate synthetic data that has similar properties. To the best of our knowledge, this is the first work to model Semantic Web knowledge bases.

In our previous LUBM experiment [13] we have evaluated four KB systems for the Semantic Web from several different aspects. We evaluated two memory-based systems (memory-based Sesame and OWLJessKB) and two systems with persistent storage (database-based Sesame and DLDB-OWL).

To evaluate our new approach, we have created the Lehigh BibTeX Benchmark (LBBM) and used this benchmark to evaluate the same systems. We are interested not only in testing the systems against the new benchmark but also in seeing the potential difference in the performances of the systems between the two benchmarks.

Finally, to evaluate the performance of the LBBM, we collected a fair amount of OWL data, randomly selected a subset from the data, and used the subset as the training file for the data-generator. The synthetic data, the original data, and two other sets of data (one generated completely randomly by only looking into the ontology and one generated based on the authors' knowledge about what the data is like) are compared by using them to benchmark the memory-based Sesame system. The results showed that although the synthetic data still performs differently from the original data in some queries, the synthetic data always outperforms the completely random dataset.

We believe our approach to data generation for OWL KB system benchmarks has three distinct advantages over a more static data generation approach. First, it reduces the benchmark development time drastically. Second, it allows the same systems to be tested against KBs that commit to different ontologies, because data sets for new ontologies can be quickly generated. A third advantage is more representative benchmark data, because it is statistically based on actual data, as opposed to the developer's knowledge of the domain. We presented a comparison between benchmarks of synthetic data and the real data and showed that the performances are very similar.

In Section 2 of the paper we describe the new data generation approach in detail and discuss its validity. In Section 3 we describe the LBBM experiment and compare it to the LUBM. In Section 4 we present the experiment that evaluates our new data generation technique. In Section 5 we talk about related work and in Section 6 we conclude.

2   Using a Learned Probabilistic Model to Generate Data

The main idea behind our approach is to extract properties relevant for benchmarking from real world data, and then use them to guide the generation of the synthetic data. In this section we first define terminologies and notations that are used in formalizing the problem, then describe the property-learning algorithm. Following that we describe a Monte Carlo algorithm that utilizes the discovered properties to generate synthetic data.

2.1   Pattern-Extraction Problem

The property-discovering process is motivated by the desire to solve the problem of not having enough real-world data for benchmarking a semantic web KB system. In a real-world OWL dataset, there are governing rules behind the generation of the data that are not observable from the ontology itself. Some parts of the ontology may be used more frequently than others. Take the BibTeX data for example, while assertions like each journal paper must have at least one author can be defined in the ontology, the probability that a paper has three authors cannot be obtained by simply looking at the ontology. We wanted to discover these properties, and use them to synthetically generate data that is a legitimate substitute for the real data. This is especially critical since we still do not have enough real OWL data on the Web, but at the same time we need sufficient and credible data to develop effective benchmarks.

Given representative actual data of some domain, the probabilistic modeling of the data can capture the features important for benchmarking in the data. We tried only to capture the statistical features of the data concerning the classes and properties. The actual content, or values, of the triples are filled with strings with similar length to that of the original file. Such simplification largely reduces the complexity of the tool, while preserving the performance of the benchmark using the synthetic data.

We assume that each individual only belongs to one most specific class. Although this is not always true, this assumption is valid for a reasonably large portion of existing Semantic Web data. In our model, an individual has a probability of being a member of a particular class, while a member of a particular class has a probability of a particular cardinality for each property. This model differs from the LUBM in that the LUBM assumes a minimum/maximum cardinality and an uniform distribution of cardinalities, while this new model can be used to simulate more complex real world distributions, thus giving the benchmark more power in dealing with different forms of ontologies/data. We will first introduce the terminology used in the model, then present an algorithm that can extract features from the data.

We first define the predicate type(x,y) to indicate if an individual x is an instance of the class y. Let an RDF triple Tp be represented as $Tp=(s,p,o)$, where s, p, o are the subject, predicate, and object, respectively. An individual $Ind(S_{ID})$ is then the set of RDF triples $Ind(S_{ID}) = \{Tp_1, Tp_2, ..., Tp_n\}$ such that for each triple Tp_i of the form $Tp_i =(s_i,p_i,o_i)$, $s_i=S_{ID}$.

We next define the *property pattern*, which plays a key role in mining patterns in the training data. Let C be the set of classes, P be the set of properties that are defined in the ontology and G be [RDF literals $\cup$ XML Schema datatypes$\cup$ C]. A *property pattern Prop* is a 4-tuple $Prop =(c, p, g, \delta_{Prop})$ where: 1) $c \in C$, 2) $p \in P$, 3) $g \in G$, and 4)δ_{Prop}: a probability distribution function. Also, an RDF triple Tp is said to *match* some property pattern $Prop$, $match(Tp, Prop)$, iff type$(s_i,c)\wedge(p_i = p)\wedge$type$(o_i,g)$. The probability δ_{Prop} distribution is then defined as

$$\delta_{Prop}(n) = P(\sum_{Tp\in Ind(s_{ID})} I(match(Tp,Prop)) =n \mid type(s_{ID},c), Ind(s_{ID})\in KB) \tag{1}$$

where I is an indicator function[1], and KB denotes the pool of individuals in the training file. $\delta_{Prop}(n)$ is then the probability that there are n triples in some individual $Ind(S_{ID})$ in the training file KB that matches $Prop$. $\delta_{Prop}(n)$ is then describing how likely for an individual $Ind(S_{ID})$ to have n triples that matches the property pattern $Prop$.

A *property pattern set* for a class c, $ppSet(c)$, is the set of property patterns $ppSet(c) = \{Prop_1, Prop_2, ..., Prop_m\}$, such that $c_i = c, \forall i, i = 1,...,m$. The property pattern set denotes all the property patterns we discovered for the individuals of the class c, thus is the basis for generating data about class c. When generating an individual, the property pattern set determines the kind of contents/triples the individual should have.

The synthetic data generation is divided into two phases, the property-discovering phase, and the data generation phase. We now describe the procedure of discovering properties in the training data. The knowledge of the algorithm about the training file is denoted as Γ, a collection of property pattern sets. The algorithm goes through the training data only once. Initially the algorithm has no knowledge about the training file, $\Gamma = \varnothing$. As it goes through the data on the basis of individuals, it will either 1) create new property pattern set of the class c based on the information/individuals encountered so far, if there is no property pattern set of the class c in its knowledge, or 2) update its current knowledge. Then the collected information determines the following parameters: 1) h, the number of property pattern sets, 2) $\Gamma = \{ppSet(c_1), ppSet(c_2), ..., ppSet(c_h)\}$ such that $c_i \neq c_j, i \neq j$, 3) a set of values $\{\tau_1,\tau_2,...,\tau_h\}$, where. $\sum_{k=1}^{j} \tau_k = 1$. τ_k is defined to be the proportion of individuals of the class c_k. The algorithm is shown in Fig 1.

As the algorithm goes through the data, it will continuously update its *knowledge* about the data, where the knowledge in the form of property pattern sets for different

---

[1] The indicator function has value 1 if the event is true, and zero otherwise.

classes, Γ, and the corresponding *Count_$\tau(k)$*, the number of individuals of class c_k in KB. τ_k is then obtained by normalizing *Count_$\tau(k)$* at the end of the algorithm. In practice, we define an additional function, *Count_$\delta Prop(n)$*, which can be viewed as a histogram, with x-axis being n, and y axis being the number of individuals of the class c that matches *Prop*. $\delta Prop(n)$ is obtained by performing normalization on *Count_$\delta Prop(n)$* after all data has been processed.

Initial Condition: $\Gamma = \varnothing$ (h=0)
For all individuals *Ind(SIDi)*, $i = 1, 2, \ldots,$ u, with triples $Tp_j = (s_{ij}, p_{ij}, o_{ij}) \in Ind(S_{IDi})$

   If there are triples in the individual that match property patterns in current knowledge,
   if $\exists Prop = (c_k, p, g, \delta Prop)$ s.t. *match(Tpj, Prop)*:
      Update Prop: check n, the number of triples in current individual *Ind(SIDi)*
        that matches *Prop*, then increase the value of *Count_$\delta Prop$ (n)* by one.
   Else
      Initialize Prop: generate a new instance of property pattern *Prop=(c_k, p, g, $\delta Prop$)*
        s.t. $\text{type}(s_{ij}, c_k) \wedge \text{type}(o_{ij}, g)$, with *Count_$\delta Prop$ (n)* =1 where n is the number of triples
        in current individual *Ind(SIDi)* that matches *Prop*, zero elsewhere.
      If there is property pattern set of the class c_k in current knowledge, $\exists ppSet(c_k)$ s.t.
      $\text{type}(s_{ij}, c_k)$:
          $ppSet(c_k) \leftarrow ppSet(c_k) \cup Prop$
      Else
          $h \leftarrow h+1$, $\Gamma \leftarrow \Gamma \cup \{ppSet(c_k)\}$ where $ppSet(c_k) = \{prop\}$
   Count_$\tau(k)$ $\leftarrow$ *Count_$\tau(k)$+1*

Normalize:
   For all property patterns: $\delta_{\text{Pr}op}(i) = Count\_\delta_{\text{Pr}op}(i) \Big/ \sum_{j=0}^{\infty} Count\_\delta_{\text{Pr}op}(j), i = 1, \ldots, \infty$
   For all $i=1,\ldots,h$: $\tau_i = Count\_\tau(i) \Big/ \sum_{j=1}^{h} Count\_\tau(j)$

Fig. 1. Algorithm *Extract* for extracting property patterns from training file

2.2   The Monte Carlo Data Generation Algorithm

The algorithm presented in this section is capable of generating synthetic data that has a structure similar to that of the training data. Inherited from the nature of Monte Carlo methods [20], this is a scalable algorithm that can generate files of arbitrary sizes that have similar properties to that of the training data. The algorithm will initialize the "framework" of the synthetic data first, that is, it first generates a set of individuals and assigns a class to each, then the algorithm goes on to generate the properties and corresponding vales to each individual. Define Rand(χ) to be a random number generator with seed χ that generates random number between [0, 1]. Let the function F(x) be the *cumulative distribution function* of δ:

$$F(x) = \sum_{i=0}^{x} \delta(i) \tag{2}$$

Note that in practice, the range of i such that $\delta(i) > 0$ is finite, that is, $\delta(i) = 0$ $\forall i > \varepsilon$, where ε is some threshold. Let $\Pi = \{ \pi_1, \pi_2, ..., \pi_h \}$ be the set of generated individuals, where π_i is the set of individuals generated according to the distribution of the property pattern set $ppSet(c_i)$.

Initial conditions: $\Pi = \varnothing$, $i = 1, ..., h$.

Given the total number of desired individuals λ in the document to be generated, initialize the set of individuals according to the desired number of individuals. These individuals only have id and classes assigned, without detail of properties and values assigned yet.

For all individuals
  For all the property patterns $Prop_{ij}(c_i, p_{ij}, g_{ij})$ of the class c_i
    Find y such that $Rand(\chi_{ij}) = F_{ij}(y)$

      Generate y RDF triples according to $Prop_{ij}$, if $g_{ij} \in$ C, then randomly select y members from π_k, type(π_k, g_{ij}), as the objects. Otherwise generate the objects such that they are random values of type g_{ij}.

Fig. 2. Algorithm *Generate* for generating synthetic data

Note that we skip the details of generating the values of the properties. For benchmarking purposes, the content itself is less important as long as the generated content has similar "features" to the training data. The feature can refer to the length of the string, the range of the integer value, etc.

2.3 Probabilistic Model Versus the Power Law

Since we are trying to generate data that resembles the real world data, a key question is how representative our synthesized data is. The first claim of our tool is its scalability. One may argue that real-world data should be self-similar, that is, some complex patterns emerge when the size of the data increases. We argue the legitimacy of the scalability in the fundamental inapplicability of the power law on our approach.

The power-law specifies a relationship between two variables such that one is proportion to the power of the other [11]. This law has been shown to hold in many different kinds of network. Take the World-Wide-Web for example, the number of links to a certain node can be predicted by the rank[2] of the node. However, in a structural dataset like OWL, the distribution of the links is often constrained by the type of link it is. Take the Bibtex domain for example, although the out- link of the ObjectProperty "editor" of a certain publication may vary over a wide range, most of them have 1-3 editors. If the power-law applies, then as the size of the file increases, the maximum number of editors will also increase, without limit, which is clearly not true. No matter how big the file size is, the maximum number of authors is unlikely to exceed 5 people. Still, there could be links where the power law is valid. In the FOAF

---

[2] The index in the order of decreasing measurements (in-degree, out-degree, etc.).

domain, the number of acquaintances one has, as the community of FOAF increases, could also increase without boundary. In such cases, the data generation is scalable to the size of the real world data as long as the training file is a representative subset of the real world data. When we say representative subset, we mean when the sample is being drawn, we collect all the information about the sample, that is, when an individual is being collected to the subset, all the links it has are also taken into the subset.

3 LBBM: A New Benchmark

The data generation method described in previous section allows us to rapidly develop a benchmark that is specific to a domain and then conduct experiments based on it. We highlight the workflow in the following. First we choose an ontology that represents the domain in question. Then we collect sample data and create synthetic test data that commits to that ontology by utilizing the new data generation approach. We use this approach to generate a new benchmark for the Bibtex domain. At the end we compare the LBBM to our previous approach, the LUBM.

3.1 Lehigh Bibtex Benchmark (LBBM)

To test drive our approach, we have used it to create a new benchmark named Lehigh BibTeX Benchmark (LBBM). We have used the Lehigh University BibTeX ontology as our domain definition [18]. This ontology is a modified version of the Bibtex ontology 0.1 by MIT [4]. It is important to note our rationale behind choosing this particular ontology. Tempich and Volz [23] have done some preliminary work towards a benchmark for Semantic Web reasoners. Though their benchmark is still under construction, they analyze the publicly available ontologies and report them to be clustered into three categories: description logic-style, database schema-like, and terminological ontologies.

The BibTeX ontology is expressed in OWL Lite and consists of 28 classes and 80 properties, half of which are datatype properties. According to the classification of [23], the ontology is more of a database schema-like ontology. The classes and properties in the BibTeX ontology used by LBBM correspond to entries and fields in Bib-TeX respectively.

We designed test queries as realistic as possible against the benchmark data. Moreover, we choose the queries that cover a range of types in terms of input size, selectivity, complexity, required hierarchy information, and required OWL inference. We designed twelve test queries in LBBM. A complete list of the queries can be found in [24]. Because of the nature of the ontology and the data, most of queries are RDF style queries and only one of them assumes OWL inference.

In order to acquire a suitable set of training data, we take advantage of the fact that there are plenty of BibTeX files on the Web, and convert them into OWL format by the Java BibTeX to RDF Converter 1.0 developed by the University of Karlsruhe [15] and the perl DAML+OIL conversion script by BBN. This resulted in a 2.4 MB OWL file which was used as our training data. We then used our tool to identify patterns from the training data and generate synthetic benchmark data based on those patterns.

In order to test a system in the benchmark framework, we wrap the system with an instantiation of the predefined interface between the benchmark test module and the target system. This involves the implementation of Java APIs for operations such as loading and query execution.

Query response time is collected in the way based on the process used in database benchmarks [5, 6, 9, 22]. To account for caching, each query is executed for ten times consecutively and the average time is computed. The elapsed time is counted from when the query is issued till the result set is returned and traversed from the beginning to the end. We also measure query completeness and soundness. We do not measure them with a coarse distinction of yes or no. Instead, we measure the degree of completeness as the percentage of the entailed answers that are returned by the system, and the degree of soundness as the percentage of the answers returned by the system that are actually entailed [13].

3.2 An Experiment Using LBBM

We have conducted an experiment based on LBBM. Although newer systems with improved performance had been introduced, for the sake of comparison, we have evaluated the same systems as in our previous LUBM experiment, including DLDB-OWL (04-03-29 release), Sesame (both main memory-based and database-based, v1.0), and OWLJessKB (04-02-23 release). First we briefly introduce the reasoning features of these systems.

DLDB-OWL [21] loosely couples a relational database system (MS Access) with a description logic reasoning reasoner (FaCT). Sesame [7] is a storing and querying facility for RDF and RDF Schema (RDFS). Sesame is an incomplete reasoner for OWL Lite. We evaluate two implementations of Sesame, i.e., main memory-based and database-based. For brevity, we hereinafter refer to them as Sesame-DB and Sesame-Memory respectively. OWLJessKB [17] is a memory-based reasoning tool for OWL implemented as a set of JESS production rules.

We have tested the above systems against four datasets, the largest one consisting of 320 OWL files totaling 189MB and containing over 2,600,000 triples. The test queries are expressed in RQL [16], a KIF-like language and JESS and issued to Sesame, DLDB-OWL and OWLJessKB respectively. The experiment is conducted on a PC with following environment 1) 1.80GHz Pentium 4 CPU, 2) 256MB of RAM, 3) 80GB of hard disk, 4) Windows XP Professional OS, and 5) Java SDK 1.4.1, 512MB of max heap size.

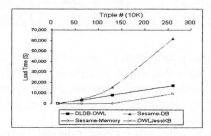

Fig. 3. Load Time

Table 1 shows the load time of each system and the consequent repository sizes of DLDB-OWL and Sesame-DB. Fig. 3 depicts how the load time grows as the data size increases. It needs to be mentioned that OWLJessKB has failed to load the smallest dataset even after we increased the max heap size to 1GB. Consequently we will not include OWLJessKB in the subsequent discussion except for query completeness and soundness.

Impressively, Sesame-Memory could load all of the datasets, despite that it nearly reached the memory limitations when loading the largest dataset. Furthermore, it is the fastest system to load every dataset. As for the two systems with secondary storage, DLDB-OWL could obviously scale better than Sesame-DB. We will return to this in next section.

Fig. 4 compares the selected query response time between DLDB-OWL and Sesame systems. A complete set of results can be found at [24]. Sesame-Memory performed the best in querying too. It was the fastest system in answering the queries upon the four of the datasets, with a few exceptions at the largest dataset when its performance went down drastically (e.g. Queries 4, 10, and 12). We believe this was caused by frequent page swapping due to main memory limitations. For the other two systems, Sesame-DB was faster than DLDB-OWL to answer almost all the queries. Furthermore, for most of the queries, Sesame-DB has showed no proportional increase in the response time as the data size grows.

Table 1. Load time and repository sizes

	Data Set	Data Size (MB)	Triple #	Load Time	Repository Size (KB)
DLDB-OWL	LBBM(1)	9.46	130,138	00:07:44	19,005
Sesame-DB				00:07:14	54,788
Sesame-Memory				00:00:12	-
OWLJessKB				failed	-
DLDB-OWL	LBBM(2)	47.3	651,392	01:00:03	86,606
Sesame-DB				01:13:18	261,390
Sesame-Memory				00:01:09	-
DLDB-OWL	LBBM(3)	94.8	1,302,952	02:14:56	172,130
Sesame-DB				04:17:57	521,110
Sesame-Memory				00:02:54	-
DLDB-OWL	LBBM(4)	189	2,606,739	4:43:18	342,458
Sesame-DB				17:09:55	1,039,991
Sesame-Memory				02:37:26	-

Next we look at the query completeness and soundness of each system. In order to get a flavor of its capability in this aspect, we have tested OWLJessKB on a single file extracted from the test dataset. It turned out that all the systems were sound in answering the twelve queries. However, they differed from each other in query completeness.

Specifically, all of them could answer Query 1 through Query 9 as well as Query 12 completely. However, while Sesame and OWLJessKB were complete, DLDB-OWL could only find partial answers (about 98%) for Query11 since it does not make inferences about the domain of properties. Moreover, as expected, OWLJessKB was the only system that could answer Query10, which requires *owl:inverseOf* inference.

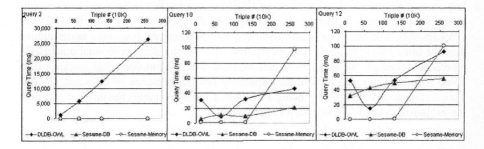

Fig. 4. Comparison between different systems for selected queries

3.3 Comparison to the LUBM Experiment

As noted, the same systems have previously been evaluated with our other benchmark: LUBM. The scales of the datasets used herein are also close to the first four datasets in the LUBM experiment respectively. The major difference between the two benchmarks lies in the ontology, the data model, and the test queries. We are interested to see how these have influenced the performance of each system.

In terms of loading, DLDB-OWL was the system showing the best scalability in both experiments. Large scales of data remain a big challenge for OWLJessKB. It could load only the smallest dataset in the LUBM experiment after spending much longer time than the others. In this experiment, it was still slow in loading and could not even handle the smallest dataset.

In contrast, Sesame systems have performed quite better in this experiment. Sesame-Memory succeeded to load a considerably larger size of data. Sesame-DB still faces the scalability problem, but it is much less prominent than in the LUBM experiment. We have considered Sesame's inability to scale in loading to relate to two reasons. One is its use of forward-chaining inference and the overhead of recording the dependency among statements. The other reason is the time cost of ID management for resources and literals during loading. (Readers are referred to [13] for a detailed discussion.). Compared to LUBM, LBBM's ontology and data are more simplistic and as a result, there are less inferred statements by Sesame during loading. In addition, there are fewer unique literals in the data. We think these could account for the significant scalability improvement of Sesame.

It turned out that the difference between both benchmarks have also influenced the query performance, especially for Sesame. In the LUBM experiment, Sesame-DB was very slow in answering some of the queries (particularily those do not contain a specific URI as the subject or object in the statements and have a complex pattern of relationships among the individuals concerned). Given the simplicity of the BibTeX ontology and the model of the test data, we have not found any appropriate queries representing complex connections between individuals. For the present queries in LBBM, Sesame was able to answer them rather quickly.

The ontology and test data used in our LBBM, although described in OWL language, is essentially an RDFS ontology. The case is similar for the test queries. It is known that Sesame is developed as an RDF repository. We believe it is more optimized for processing RDF-style data and queries than systems like DLDB-OWL and OWLJessKB. The result has clearly showed that Sesame has become a better choice than the other two systems for the applications in a similar domain to what our LBBM represents. Overall, the experiment has verified that the ontology and instance data could make a difference in both the capability and performance of the same system. This demonstrates the need for using a benchmark that resembles the domain in which the evaluated systems are intended to be applied.

4   Evaluation of the Data Generation Technique

We claimed our tool is capable of generating a legitimate substitute to the real data. To examine this assumption, we take subsets of the original file, generate synthetic data using the subset as the training file, and compare the benchmark result of the synthetic file to that of the original file. A subset was derived by randomly selecting an individual and taking it along with all neighboring individuals two hops away from it into the subset. The definition of neighboring individuals, however, is a tricky question. Consider the data as a huge directed graph. The resulting sets of neighbors are different when considering neighbors via link direction or just via links. We take both subset selection schemes into consideration.

In additional to the synthetic data and the original data, we also generated two other sets of data for comparison. They both use a tool that can parse a given ontology, let user specify the kind of triples and the min/max cardinality of that kind of triple, let user specify min/max number of individuals of a certain class, and generate data according to the given parameters in a uniform distribution. The first set of data has parameters assigned by a domain expert (based on knowledge about the kinds of triples and approximate ratio between different classes of individuals). The second set is generated by assigning the parameters according to a series of random numbers.

The size of the original file is one million. We have subsets of sizes 125, 250, 500, 1000, 5000, 10000, 20000, and 50000 triples. For each size, we have a subset that includes directional neighbors and one that includes neighbors regardless of directions. These subsets are used as training files to generate a set of synthetic data consisting of one million triples. The two data sets generated according to domain knowledge and completely randomly also consist of one million triples.

The system for evaluation is the memory-based Sesame-DB. Eleven queries were designed so that the first half of the queries are bound to have results in almost any kind of data, while the second part is more likely to have answers for more realistic data. The set of queries can be found at [24]. The experiment is conducted on a PowerBook G4 with environment as follows: 1) 1.0GHz PowerPC G4 CPU; 2) 512MB of RAM; 60GB of hard disk; 3) Mac OS X 10.3.9; 4)Java SDK 1.4.2.

Fig 5. shows the result of the query time verses the size of the training files for selected queries. In the legends, "orig" refers to the result from the original Bibtex data, "man" refers to the data generated with domain knowledge, "rand" refers to the set of data generated completely randomly, "dir" refers to the set of results with training files subsetted with direction of the links considered, while "non-dir" refers to those that does not. Other queries have either close-to-zero query time or zero results thus are less valuable to present here. In Fig 5. Q5, the performance from the completely random dataset is omitted, because it performs so bad that it will flatten out other information in the graph. The query time for query 5 in the completely random dataset is 330493ms.

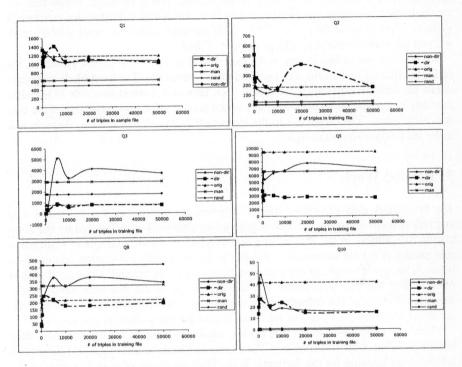

Fig. 5. Query Time verse different sizes of training file in selected queries

For Fig 5 Q3, the data from non-directional scheme returns far more results than the original file, while the data from directional scheme performs reasonably well. This query asks for all InProceedings that have at least one author and one editor. One possible explanation is that while almost all InProceedings have at least one author, the number of InProceedings having editors are relatively fewer. At the same time, the probability that someone is an editor isn't uniform either: some people are more likely to be editors for several publications. In the non-directional selection scheme, as long as we selected a publication with editors, or selected someone being editor, the probability of the data two hops away having the property editor is higher than normal.

In Fig 5 Q5, the non-directional selection scheme outperforms the directional one. The query is asking for people with more than two publications. This might be explained by that when an individual is selected, it is less likely for the directional scheme to get all the publication from someone because the link's direction is from publication to author/person. Fig 5 Q8 might be explained similar to that in Q3. This query asks for publication with publisher specified. For the non-directional scheme, it is likely to select a bunch of individuals from the same source Bibtex file, thus more likely than normal to have the attribute publisher.

From the figures we can see that the benchmark result of the synthetic data given representative training data, can be almost identical to the original file at best, and still better than completely random data at worst. Furthermore, these results can be achieved with a training set of only 10000 triples. The experiment shows that the synthetic data generator presented here can be a reasonable substitute for benchmark systems if insufficient data is available, or if the user wishes to create a benchmark without the pain of collecting a large amount of data.

Ideally, we would like to repeat the experiment on other ontologies. However, the lack of sufficient real-world data had made this impossible. The most likely next candidate for such experiments is the FOAF data. However, current available FOAF data can only contribute about 60000 triples, which is only a fraction to the size of the current experiment. The difference in the magnitude in the size of the two datasets will make the comparison meaningless.

5   Related Work

The benchmark data generation tries to discover the patterns in the real world data and reflect them in the synthetic data generation. Our work is influenced by the association rule mining in the data-mining research [1]. A classic example of association rule mining is for the supermarket retailers to try to identify association relationships between the items bought in one customer transaction. For example discover if milk is often bought together with bread. We take advantage of the structural nature of the Semantic Web data. The definition of a transaction is analogous to that of the individual in our approach, and patterns are found within the transaction/individual.

There are some other works that exploit similar techniques for the Semantic Web but for different purposes from ours. For example, Maedche and Staab [19] have studied ontology learning for the Semantic Web. They make use of a modification of the generalized association rule learning algorithm for discovering properties between classes.

Our work on benchmarking Semantic Web KB systems has emphasized on the support of evaluating the systems with respect to large amount of data and extensional queries upon the data. This makes our work different from others. For instance, Alexaki et al. [2] have developed some benchmark queries for RDF, however, these are mostly intensional queries. Some attempts have been done by Elhaik et al [10] and Horrocks and Patel-Schneider [14] to benchmark description logic systems. The emphasis of this work is to evaluate the reasoning algorithms in terms of the tradeoff between expressiveness and tractability in description logic. Our work is not a description logic benchmark. Moreover, unlike our approach, such benchmark data generation as used in [10] does not take account of simulating the real world data. Lastly, the Web Ontology Working Group provides a set of OWL test cases [8]. They are intended to provide examples for, and clarification of, the normative definition of OWL and focus on the completeness and soundness with respect to individual features. Different from our benchmarks, they are not suitable for the evaluation of scalability.

6 Conclusion

In this paper, we have considered the issue of rapid development of benchmarks for Semantic Web knowledge base systems. In our previous work, we have used the Lehigh University Benchmark (LUBM) to evaluate several contemporary systems. LUBM is bound to a specific ontology and its data generation is based on statically encoded rules. The university ontology that we used in LUBM is categorized as a description logic-style ontology. The benchmark represents certain classes of Semantic Web applications but not all. It is difficult and inefficient if not completely impossible to generate benchmarks that will cover the wide variety of Semantic Web applications that are possible. In light of this, in this work, we have moved forward by introducing a method for generating benchmark data of any chosen domain in a very time efficient manner. We have achieved this by developing a data generation approach that does not depend on statically encoded rules. This method constructs a probabilistic model that can extract statistical features from real world data that are important for benchmarking. A Monte Carlo algorithm is used to generate synthetic data that have similar features to that of the real world data based on the model constructed. Experiments have been conducted to show that the benchmark using the synthetic data has a performance very similar to the one that uses real world data at best, and still outperforms the data generated without knowledge of the real-world data at worst. We have shown that our data generation provides a reasonable substitute for large quantity of real world data.

We have used this new approach to create another benchmark called Lehigh BibTeX Benchmark (LBBM) within a considerably short period. LBBM is different from LUBM in the sense that it represents the use of a database schema-like ontology and more RDF-style data and queries. We have used this new benchmark to evaluate two main memory-based systems (memory-based Sesame and OWLJessKB) and two systems with persistent storage (database-based Sesame and DLDB-OWL). They are the same systems in our previous LUBM experiment. We compared both experiments and pointed out the difference between their results. The experiment has verified that the characteristics of ontology and data used in the benchmark can make a difference in the evaluation of the systems. We argue this demonstrates the necessity of choosing a representative benchmark for the intended application of the systems and thus the need for a variety of Semantic Web knowledge base benchmarks. We intend for our approach presented herein to play a promotional role in this regard.

Acknowledgements

This material is based on work supported by the National Science Foundation under account No. IIS-0346963. We thank Paul Koget for suggestions that synthetic data generators could be learned from existing data.

References

[1] Agrawal, R. Imielinski, T., and Swamy, A. Mining association rules between sets of items in large databases. In Proc, of ACM SIGMOD Intl. Conf. on Management of Data, May 1993.

[2] Alexaki, S. et al. On Storing Voluminous RDF Description: The case of Web Portal Catalogs. In Proc. of the 4th International Workshop on the Web and Databases, 2001.

[3] Beall, S and Hodges, R. Application & Systems Program Development: Software Directory Columns. Gartner Corporation Technical Report, 1997.

[4] Bibtex Definition in OWL Version 0.1. http://www.visus.mit.edu/bibtex/0.1/

[5] Bitton, D., DeWitt, D., and Turbyfill, C. Benchmarking Database Systems, a Systematic Approach. In Proc. of the 9th International Conference on Very Large Data Bases, 1983.

[6] Bitton, D. and Turbyfill, C. A Retrospective on the Wisconsin Benchmark. In Readings in Database Systems, Second Edition, 1994.

[7] Broekstra, J. and Kampman, A. Sesame: A Generic Architecture for Storing and Querying RDF and RDF Schema. In Proc. of ISWC2002.

[8] Carroll, J.J. and Roo, J.D. ed. OWL Web Ontology Test Cases. http://www.w3.org/TR/2004/REC-owl-test-20040210/

[9] Cattell, R.G.G. An Engineering Database Benchmark. In Readings in Database Systems, Second Edition, 1994.

[10] Elhaik, Q, Rousset, M.C., and Ycart, B. Generating Random Benchmarks for Description Logics. In Proc. of DL' 98.

[11] Faloutsos M. and Faloutsos, P. and Faloutsos, C.. On Power-law Relationships of the Internet Topology. Pages 251-262, SIGCOMM '99

[12] Guo, Y., Heflin, J., and Pan, Z. Benchmarking DAML+OIL Repositories. In Proc. of ISWC2003.

[13] Guo, Y., Pan, Z. and Heflin, J. LUBM: A Benchmark for OWL Knowledge Base Systems. In Journal of Web Semantics, Vol 3, Issue 2, 2005

[14] Horrocks, I. and Patel-Schneider, P. DL Systems Comparison. In Proc. of DL' 98.

[15] Java BibTeX-To-RDF Converter. http://www.aifb.uni-karlsruhe.de/WBS/pha/bib/

[16] Karvounarakis, G. et al. Querying Community Web Portals. http://www.ics.forth.gr/proj/isst/RDF/RQL/rql.pdf

[17] Kopena, J.B. and Regli, W.C. DAMLJessKB: A Tool for Reasoning with the Semantic Web. In Proc. of ISWC2003.

[18] Lehigh University Bibtex Ontology. http://www.cse.lehigh.edu/~syw/bib-bench.owl

[19] Maedche, A and Staab, S. Ontology learning for the semantic web. IEEE Intelligent Systems, 16(2): 72-79. 2001.

[20] Manno, I. Introduction to the Monte Carlo Method. Budapest, Hungary: Akadémiai Kiadó, 1999.

[21] Pan, Z. and Heflin, J. DLDB: Extending Relational Databases to Support Semantic Web Queries. In Workshop on Practical and Scalable Semantic Systems, ISWC2003.

[22] Stonebraker, M. et al. The SEQUIOA 2000 Storage Benchmark. In Readings in Database Systems, Second Edition. 1994.

[23] Tempich, C. and Volz, R. Towards a benchmark for Semantic Web reasoners–an analysis of the DAML ontology library. In Workshop on Evaluation on Ontology-based Tools, ISWC2003.

[24] Wang, Sui-Yu, Guo, Yuanbo, Qasem, Abir, and Heflin, J. Rapid Benchmaring for Semantic Web Knowledge Base Systems, Technical Report LU-CSE-05-026, Dept. of Computer Science and Engineering, Lehigh University, 2005.

Using Triples for Implementation: The Triple20 Ontology-Manipulation Tool

Jan Wielemaker[1], Guus Schreiber[2], and Bob Wielinga[1]

[1] University of Amsterdam, Human Computer Studies (HCS),
Kruislaan 419, NL-1098 VA Amsterdam, The Netherlands
{wielemak, wielinga}@science.uva.nl
[2] Free University Amsterdam, Computer Science,
De Boelelaan 1081a, NL-1081 HV Amsterdam, The Netherlands
schreiber@cs.vu.nl

Abstract. Triple20 is a ontology manipulation and visualization tool for languages built on top of the Semantic-Web RDF triple model. In this article we explain how a triple-centered design compares to the use of a separate proprietary internal data model. We show how to deal with the problems of such a low-level data model and show that it offers advantages when dealing with inconsistent or incomplete data as well as for integrating tools.

1 Introduction

Triples are at the very heart of the Semantic Web [1]. RDF, and languages built on top of it such as OWL [2] are considered *exchange* languages: they allow exchanging knowledge between agents (and humans) on the Semantic Web through their *atomic* data model and well-defined semantics. The agents themselves often employ a data model that follows the design, task and history of the software. The advantages of a proprietary internal data model are explained in detail by Noy *et al.* [3] in the context of the Protégé design.

The main advantage of a proprietary internal data model is that it is neutral to external developments. Noy *et al.* [3] state that this enabled their team to quickly adopt Protégé to the Semantic Web as RDF became a standard. However, this assumes that all tool components commit to the internal data model and that this model is sufficiently flexible to accommodate new external developments. The RDF triple model and the higher level Semantic Web languages have two attractive properties. Firstly, the triple model is generic enough to represent *anything*. Secondly, the languages on top of it gradually increase the semantic commitment and are extensible to accommodate to almost any domain. Our hypothesis is that a tool infrastructure using the triple data model at its core can profit from the shared understanding when using the triple model for *exchange*. We also claim that, where the layering of Semantic Web languages provide different levels of understanding of the same document, the same will apply for tools operating on the triple model.

Y. Gil et al. (Eds.): ISWC 2005, LNCS 3729, pp. 773–785, 2005.

In this article we describe the design of Triple20, an ontology editor that runs directly on a triple representation. First we introduce our triple store, followed by a description on how the model-view-controller design can be extended to deal with the low level data model. In Sect. 4.1 to Sect. 6.2 we illustrate some of the Triple20 design decisions and functions, followed by some metrics, related work and discussion.

2   Core Technology: Triples in Prolog

The core of our technology is Prolog-based. The triple-store is a memory-based extension to Prolog realising a compact and highly efficient implementation of **rdf/3** [4]. Higher level primitives are defined on top of this using Prolog *backward chaining* rather than *transformation* of data structures. A simple example:

```
class(Sub, Super) :-
    rdf(Sub, rdfs:subClassOf, Super),
    rdf(Sub, rdf:type, rdfs:'Class'),
    rdf(Super, rdf:type, rdfs:'Class').
```

The RDF infrastructure is part of the Open Source SWI-Prolog system[1] and used by many internal and external projects. Higher-order properties can be expressed easily and efficiently in terms of triples. Object manipulations, such as defining a class are also easily expressed in terms of adding and/or deleting triples. Operating on the same triple store, triples not only form a mechanism for *exchange* of data, but also for cooperation between *tools*. Semantic Web standards ensure consistent interpretation of the triples by independent tools.

3   Design Principles

Most tool infrastructures define a data model that is inspired by the tasks that have to be performed by the tool. For example, Protégé, defines a flexible meta-data format for expressing the basic entities managed by Protégé: classes, slots, etc. The GUI often follows the model-view-controller (MVC) architecture [5]. This design is illustrated in Fig. 1. There are some issues with this design we would like to highlight.

- All components in the tool set must conform to the same proprietary data model. This may harm maintainability and complicates integrating tools designed in another environment.
- Data is translated from/to external (file-)formats while loading/saving project data. This poses problems if the external format contains information that cannot be represented by the tool's data model.

The MVC design pattern is commonly used and successful. In the context of the Semantic Web, there is an alternative to the proprietary tool data model provided by the stable RDF triple model. This model was designed as an *exchange*

---

[1] http://www.swi-prolog.org

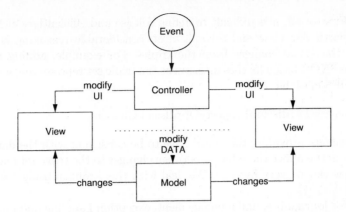

Fig. 1. Model-View-Controller (MVC) design pattern. Controllers modify UI aspects of a *view* such as zooming, selection, etc. directly. During editing the *controller* modifies the *model* that in turn informs the views. Typically, the data structures of the *Model* are designed with the task of the application in mind.

model, but the very same features that make it good for exchange also make it a good candidate for the internal tool data model. In particular, the *atomic* nature of the model with its standardised semantics ensure the cooperating tools have a sound basis.

In addition to providing a sound basis, the triple approach deals with some serious consistency problems related to more high-level data models. All Semantic Web data can be expressed precisely and without loss of information by the toolset, while each individual tool can deal with the data using its own way to view the world. For example, it allows an RDFS tool to work flawlessly with an OWL tool, although with limited understanding of the OWL semantics. Different tools can use different subsets of the triple set, possibly doing different types of reasoning. The overall semantics of the triple set however is dictated by stable standards and the atomic nature should minimise interoperability problems. Considering editing and browsing tools, different tools use different levels of abstractions, viewing the plain triples, viewing an RDF graph, viewing an RDFS frame-like representation or an OWL/DL view (Fig. 4, Fig. 5).

Finally, the minimalist data model simplifies general tool operations such as *undo*, save/load, client/server interaction protocols, etc.

In the following architecture section, we show how we deal with the low-level data model in the MVC architecture.

4   Architecture

Using a high-level data model that is inspired by the tasks performed by the tools, mapping actions to changes in the data model and mapping these changes back to the UI is relatively straightforward. Using the primitive RDF triple model, mapping changes to the triple store to the views becomes much harder for two reasons. First of all, it is difficult to define concise and efficiently which changes affect a particular view and second, often considerable reasoning is involved deducing the visual changes from the triples. For example, adding the triple below to a SKOS-based [6] thesaurus turns the triple set representing a thesaurus into a RDFS class hierarchy:[2]

skos:narrower rdfs:subPropertyOf rdfs:subClassOf .

The widgets providing the 'view' have to be consistent with the data. As we can see from the above the relation between changes to the triple set and changes to the view can be very indirect. We deal with this problem using *transactions* and *mediators* [7].

Both for journalling, undo management, exception handling and maintaining the consistency of views, we introduced transactions. A transaction is a sequence of elementary changes to the triple-base: *add, delete* and *update*,[3] labeled with an identifier and optional comments. The comments are used as a human-readable description of the operation (e.g. "Created class Wine"). Transactions can be nested. User interaction with a controller causes a transaction to be started, operations to be performed in the triple-store and finally the transaction to be committed. If anything unexpected happens during the transaction, the changes are discarded, providing protection against partial and inconsistent changes by malfunctioning controllers. A successful transaction results in an *event*.

Simple widgets whose representation depends on one or more direct properties of a resource (e.g., a label showing an icon and label-text for a resource) register themselves as simple representation of this resource. They will be informed if the resource appears in the *subject* or *object* of an affected triple or the `rdfs:subPropertyOf` hierarchy is modified in the committed transaction. In most cases this will cause the widget to do a simple refresh.

Complex widgets, such as a hierarchical view, cannot use this schema as they cannot easily define the changes in the database that will affect them and re-computing and refreshing the widget is too expensive for interactive use. It is here that we introduce *mediators*. A *mediator* is an arbitrary (Prolog Herbrandt-)term that is derived from the triple set through a defined function. For example, the term can be an ordered list of resources that appear as children of a particular node in the hierarchy which is computed using an OWL reasoner. Widgets register a mediator whenever real-time update is considered too expensive. The function and its parameters are registered with the *updater*. The *updater* is running in a separate thread of execution, updating all mediators after each successfully committed transaction. If a mediator is different from the previous result, the controllers that registered the mediator are notified and will update using the high-level representation provided by the model term. This approach has several advantages.

---

[2] Whether this interpretation is correct is not the issue here.

[3] The *update* change can of course be represented as a delete-and-add, but a separate primitive is more natural, requires less space in the journal and is easier to interpret while maintaining the view consistency.

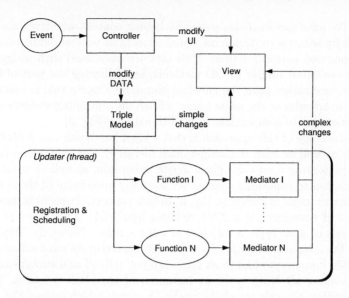

Fig. 2. Introducing *mediators* to bridge the level of abstraction between triples and view. Update is performed in a different thread to avoid locking the UI.

- The UI remains responsive while updating the mediators.
- Updates can be aborted as soon as a new transaction is committed.
- Multiple widgets depending on the same mediator require only one computation.
- The updater can schedule on the basis of execution time measured last time, frequency of different results and relation of dependent widgets to the 'current' widget.[4]
- One or multiple update threads can exploit multi-cpu (SMP) hardware as well as schedule updates over multiple threads to ensure likely and cheap updates are not blocked for a long time by unlikely expensive updates.

4.1   Rules to Define the GUI

The interface is composed of a hierarchy of widgets, most of them representing one or more resources. We have *compound* and *primitive* widgets. Each widget is responsible for maintaining a consistent view of the triple set as outlined in the previous section. Triple20 widgets have small granularity. For example, most resources are represented by an icon and a textual label. This is represented as a compound widget which controls the icons and displays a primitive widget for the textual label.

In the conventional OO interface each compound widgets decides which member widgets it creates and what their their configuration should be, thus generating the widget hierarchy starting at the outermost widget, i.e. the toplevel

---

[4] This has not yet been implemented in the current version.

window. We have modified this model by having context-sensitive rule sets that are called by widgets to decide on visual aspects as well as define context sensitive menus and perform actions. Rule sets are associated with widget classes. Rules are evaluated similar to OO methods, but following the part-of hierarchy of the interface rather than the subclass hierarchy. Once a rule is found, it may decide to wrap rules of the same name defined on containing widgets similar to sending messages to a superclass in traditional OO (Fig. 3).

The advantage of this approach is that widget behaviour can inherit from its containers as well as from the widget class hierarchy. For example, a compound widget representing a set can offer a *delete* menu-item as well as the method to handle deletion to contained widgets without any knowledge of these widgets.

Another example is shown in Fig. 3. In this context, Triple20 is used to view the results of transforming a XML Schema into RDF. XSD types are created as subclasses of `xsd:Type`, a subclass of `rdfs:Class`.[5] Normally, Triple20 does not show the instances of *meta-classes* in the hierarchy. As most schemas do not contain that many types and most types are not defined as a subtype of another type, expanding all XSD types as instances of the class is useful. The code fragment refines the rule for **child_cache/3**, a rule which defines the *mediator* for generating the children of a node in the hierarchy window (Fig. 5). The `display` argument says the rule is defined at the level of display, the outermost object in the widget part-of hierarchy and therefore acts as a default for the entire interface. The `part` argument simply identifies the new rule set. The first rule says the mediator for expanding a `xsd:Type` node is the set of resources linked to it using V `rdf:type` R, sorted by label name (**lsorted**(V)). The second rule simply calls the default behaviour.

```
:- begin_rules(display, part).

child_cache(R, Cache, rdf_node) :-
        rdfs_subclass_of(R, xsd:'Type'),
        rdf_cache(lsorted(V), rdf_has(V, rdf:type, R), Cache).
child_cache(R, Cache, Class) :-
        super::child_cache(R, Cache, Class).

:- end_rules.
```

Fig. 3. Redefining the hierarchy expansion for `xsd:Type`. This rule set can be loaded without changing anything to the tool.

Rule sets are translated into ordinary Prolog modules using the Prolog pre-processor.[6] They can specify behaviour that is context sensitive. Simple refinement can be achieved loading rules without defining new widgets. More complicated customization is achieved by defining new widgets, often as a refinement

---

[5] That is, schema types are considered classes in a hierarchy of types.
[6] Realised using **term_expansion/2**.

of existing ones, and modify the rules used by a particular compound widget to create its parts.

5   User-Interface Principles

RDF documents can be viewed at different levels. Our tool is not a tool to support a particular language such as OWL, but to examine and edit arbitrary RDF documents. It provides several views, each highlighting a particular aspect:

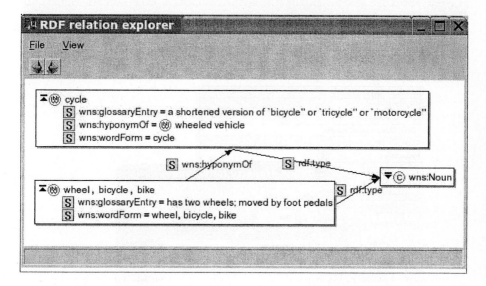

Fig. 4. Triple20 graph diagram. Resources are shown using just their label or as a frame. Values or properties can be dragged from a frame to the window to expand them.

- The *diagram* view (Fig. 4) provides a graph of resources. Resources can be shown as a label (*Noun*) or expanded to a frame (*cycle*). Elements from the frame can be dragged to the diagram as natural user-controlled mechanism to expand the graph. This tool simply navigates the RDF graph and works on any RDF document.
- The *hierarchy* view (Fig. 5, left window) shows different hierarchies (class, property, individuals) in a single view. The type of expansion is indicated using icons. Expansion can be controlled using *rules* as explained in Sect. 4.1.
- A tabular window (Fig. 5, right window) allows for multiple resource specific representations. The base system provides an *instance* view and a *class* view on resources.

  Editing and browsing are as much as possible integrated in the same interface. This implies that most widgets building the graphical representation of the data

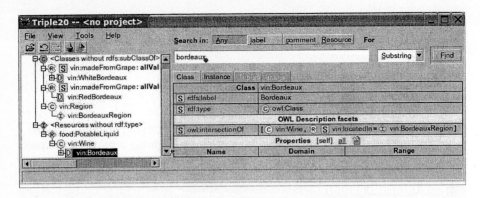

Fig. 5. Triple20 main window after a search and select

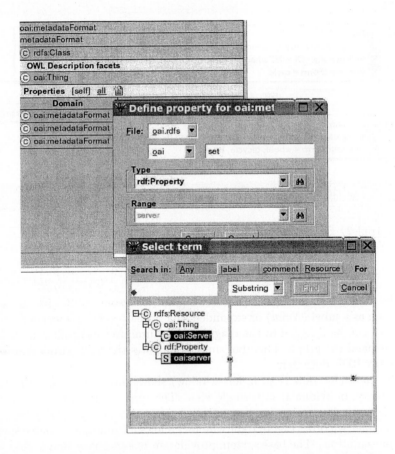

Fig. 6. Select a resource by typing, in this example *server*. The style indicates the status and is updated after each keystroke. Green (here) means there are multiple resources with this name. Hitting the *binocular* icon shows all matches in the hierarchy, allowing the user to select.

are sensitive. Visual feedback of activation and details of the activated resource are provided. In general both menus and drag-and-drop are provided. Context-specific rules define the possible operations dropping one resource on another. Left-drop executes the default operation indicated in the status bar, while right-drop opens a menu for selecting the operation after the drop. For example, the default for dropping a resource from one place in a hierarchy on another node is to *move* the resource. A right-drop will also offer the option to associate an additional parent. Rules also provide context-sensitive menus on resources.

Drag-and-drop can generally be used to add or modify properties. Before one can drop an object it is required to be available on the screen. This is often impractical and therefore many widgets provide menus to modify or add a value. This interface allows for typing the value using completion, selecting from a hierarchy as well as search followed by selection. An example is shown in Fig. 6.

6   Implementation

6.1   The Source of Triples

Our RDF store is actually a quadruple store. The first three fields represent the RDF triple, while the last identifies the source or sub-graph it is related too. The source is maintained to be able to handle triples from multiple sources in one application, modify them and save the correct triples to the correct destination.

Triple20 includes a library of background ontologies, such as RDFS and OWL as well as some well-known public toplevel ontologies. When a document is loaded which references to one of these ontologies, the corresponding ontology is loaded and flagged 'read-only', meaning no new triples will be assigned to this source and it is not allowed to delete triples that are associated to it. This implies that

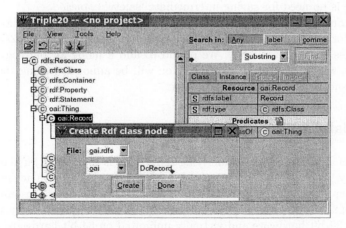

Fig. 7. Create a new class. The system proposes the file the class will be saved to as well as the namespace based on the properties of the super class. Both can be changed.

trying to delete such a triple inside a transaction causes the operation to be aborted and the other operations inside the transaction to be discarded.

Other documents are initially flagged 'read-write' and new triples are associated to sources based on rules. Actions involving a dialog window normally allow the user to examine and override the system's choice, as illustrated in Fig. 7.

Although *referring* to other documents should be the dominant technique for reusing material on the Semantic Web, Triple20 allows for moving triples from one source to another realising reuse through copy, possibly followed by adjustment to the new context.

6.2   Projects

As an ontology editor, Triple20 is designed to operate in two modes. For simple browsing and minor editing of relatively small projects it can simply open (load) a RDF document. It will automatically load referenced documents from its library, providing access to the document in its context. The ontology can be edited and saved similar to editing text documents with a word processor.

The above does not scale very well. It requires the relatively slow load and save from RDF/XML serialization and does not preserve specific settings of the editor related to the document, such as namespace abbreviations (e.g., rdfs for `http://www.w3.org/2000/01/rdf-schema#`), loading of related documents from locations outside the library, etc. For this reason, Triple20 provides *projects*. A project is simply a journal of all actions that can be reloaded by *replaying* it. Operations of committed transactions are simply appended to the project file. For documents that are loaded we save a snapshot with MD5 signature in the internal quick-load format, providing reliable and fast loading of the same triple set. The project approach has several advantages for dealing with the development of large documents.

- There is no need for saving intermediate 'safety' copies.
- The commented sequence of transactions allow for reviewing the changes, both for the author as a *change log* and for a reviewer that has to authorize changes for a central copy. We intend to add a mode for ontology maintenance, where each finished transaction will be annotated using the author, data and a motivation by the author.

7   Scalability

The aim of Triple20 and the underlying RDF store is to support large ontologies in memory. In-memory storage is much faster than what can be achieved using a persistent store [4], a requirement to deal with the low-level reasoning at the triple level. The maximum capacity of the triple store is approximately 40 million triples on 32-bit hardware and virtually unlimited on 64-bit hardware.

We summarise some figures handling WordNet [8] in RDF. The measurements are taken on a dual AMD 1600+ machine with 2GB memory running SuSE Linux.

The 5 WordNet files contain a total of 473,626 triples. The results are shown in Tab. 8. For the last test, a small file is added that defines the `wns:hyponymOf` property as a sub property of `rdfs:subClassOf` and defines `wns:LexicalConcept` as a subclass of `rdfs:Class`. This reinterprets the WordNet hierarchy as an RDFS class hierarchy. Note that this work is done by the separate update thread recomputing the mediators and thus does not block the UI.

8   Related Work

Protégé [9] is a landmark in the world of ontology editors. We have described how our design differs in Sect. 3. Where Protégé is primarily designed as an *editor*, Triple20 is primarily a *browser*. To avoid cluttering the view with controls, Triple20's widgets concentrate on popup menus, drag-and-drop and direct manipulation techniques. Protégé has dedicated support for ontology engineering, which Triple20 lacks.

Table 1. Some figures handling WordNet on a dual AMD 1600+ machine. Loading time is proportional to the size of the data.

Operation	Time (sec)
Load from RDF/XML	65.4
Load from cache	8.4
Re-interpret as class hierarchy	16.3

OntoPlugin [10] is the plugin system of OntoEdit. The integration is not targeted at the data level, but at the tool level, dealing with integration of init, exit, menu options, etc. They aim at integrating larger components, making no commitment on a common data model.

JENA [11] is a Java-based environment for handling RDF data. The emphasis in this software lies on the RDF API and on the querying functionality, and not so much on ontology ontology editing, browsing and manipulation.

Similarly, the Sesame software [12] can be seen as complementary to Triple20, providing client/server-based access to RDF data repositories. Software for using our infrastructure and Sesame together is available from the SWI-Prolog web-site.

KAON [13] is an extensible ontology software environment. The main difference with Triple20 is that the KAON software is mainly aimed to provide middleware; the environment focuses on integrating distributed applications.

In [14], Miklós et al. describe how they reuse large ontologies by defining *views* using an F-logic based mapping. In a way our *mediators*, mapping the complex large triple store in a manageable structure using Prolog can be compared to this, although their purpose is to map one ontology into another, while our purpose is to create a manageable structure suitable for driving the visualisation.

9   Discussion

We believe the main weakness in our infrastructure is Prolog's poor support for
declarative inferencing. We identify the following problems. Firstly, bad ordering
in conjunctions may lead to poor performance. In another project[7] we have found
that dynamic reordering is feasible and efficient. Secondly, frequent recomputation
as well as commonly occurring loops in RDF graphs result in poor performance
and complicated code to avoid loops. We plan to add tabling to SWI-Prolog to
improve on this, in a similar way as tabling is realised in XSB Prolog [15].

We plan to study the possibility of adding external (DL) reasoners to the
infrastructure. The can be handled elegantly as another type of *mediator*, connected through the SWI-Prolog XDIG [16] interface. We are afraid though that
the communication overhead will be unacceptable for large triple stores.

We have realised a tool architecture that is based directly on the RDF triple
model. The advantage of this approach over the use of a tool oriented intermediate model is that any Semantic Web document can be represented precisely
and tools operating on the data can profit from established RDF-based standards on the same grounds as RDF supports exchange between applications.
With Triple20, we have demonstrated that this design can realise good scalability, providing multiple consistent views (triples, graph, OWL) on the same triple
store. Triple20 has been used successfully as a stand-alone ontology editor, as a
component in other applications and as a debugging tool for other applications
running on top of the Prolog triple store.

Software Availability

Triple20 is available under Open Source (LGPL) license from the SWI-Prolog
website.[8] SWI-Prolog with graphics runs on MS-Windows, MacOS X and almost
all Unix/Linux versions, supporting both 32- and 64-bit hardware.

Acknowledgements

The Triple20 type-icons are partly taken from and partly inspired by the Protégé
project. This work is partly supported by the Dutch BSIK project MultiMedian.

References

1. Brickley, D., Guha (Eds), R.V.: Resource description framework (RDF) schema
specification 1.0. W3C Recommendation (2000) http://www.w3.org/TR/2000/CR-
rdf-schema-20000327/.
2. Dean, M., Schreiber, A.T., Bechofer, S., van Harmelen, F., Hendler, J., Horrocks, I.,
MacGuinness, D., Patel-Schneider, P., Stein, L.A.: OWL Web Ontology Language
Reference. W3C Recommendation, World Wide Web Consortium (2004) Latest
version: http://www.w3.org/TR/owl-ref/.

---

[7] http://www.swi-prolog.org/packages/SeRQL/
[8] http://www.swi-prolog.org/packages/Triple20

3. Noy, N.F., Sintek, M., Decker, S., Crubezy, M., Fergerson, R.W., Musen, M.A.: Creating Semantic Web contents with protege-2000. IEEE Intelligent Systems **16** (2001) 60–71
4. Wielemaker, J., Schreiber, G., Wielinga, B.: Prolog-based infrastructure for RDF: performance and scalability. In Fensel, D., Sycara, K., Mylopoulos, J., eds.: The Semantic Web - Proceedings ISWC'03, Sanibel Island, Florida, Berlin, Germany, Springer Verlag (2003) 644–658 LNCS 2870.
5. Krasner, G.E., Pope, S.T.: A cookbook for using the model-view-controller user interface paradigm in smalltalk-80. Technical report, Palo Alto (1988)
6. Miles, A.J.: Owl ontology for thesaurus data. Deliverable, SWAD-Europe (2001)
7. Wiederhold, G.: Mediators in the architecture of future information systems. IEEE Computer **25** (1992) 38–49
8. Miller, G.: WordNet: A lexical database for english. Comm. ACM **38** (1995)
9. Musen, M.A., Fergerson, R.W., Grosso, W.E., Noy, N.F., Crubézy, M., Gennari, J.H.: Componentbased support for building knowledge-acquisition systems. In: Conference on Intelligent Information Processing (IIP 2000), Beijing, China (2000) http://smi-web.stanford.edu/pubs/SMI_Abstracts/SMI-2000-0838.html.
10. Handschuh, S.: OntoPlugins a flexible component framework. Technical report, University of Karlsruhe (2001)
11. McBride, B.: Jena: Implementing the rdf model and syntax specification. In: Semantic Web Workshop, WWW 2001. (2001)
12. Broekstra, J., Kampman, A., van Harmelen, F.: Sesame: An architecture for storing and querying rdf and rdf schema. In: Proc. First International Semantic Web Conference ISWC 2002, Sardinia, Italy. Volume 2342 of LNCS., Springer-Verlag (2002) 54–68
13. Oberle, D., Volz, R., Motik, B., Staab, S.: An extensible ontology software environment. In Staab, S., Studer, R., eds.: Handbook on Ontologies. International Handbooks on Information Systems. Springer (2004) 311–333
14. Miklos, Z., Neumann, G., Zdun, U., Sintek, M.:   Querying semantic web resources using triple views.   In Kalfoglou, Y., Schorlemmer, M., Sheth, A., Staab, S., Uschold, M., eds.: Semantic Interoperability and Integration. Number 04391 in Dagstuhl Seminar Proceedings, Internationales Begegnungs- und Forschungszentrum (IBFI), Schloss Dagstuhl, Germany (2005) <http://drops.dagstuhl.de/opus/volltexte/2005/47> [date of citation: 2005-01-01].
15. Freire, J., Warren, D.S., Sagonas, K., Rao, P., Swift, T.: XSB: A system for efficiently computing well-founded semantics. In: Proceedings of LPNMR 97, Berlin, Germany, Springer Verlag (1997) 430–440 LNCS 1265.
16. Huang, Z., Visser, C.: An extended dig description logic interface for prolog. Deliverable, SEKT (2003) http://wasp.cs.vu.nl/sekt/dig/.

A Little Semantic Web Goes a Long Way in Biology

K. Wolstencroft, A. Brass, I. Horrocks, P. Lord, U. Sattler,
D. Turi, and R. Stevens

School of Computer Science, University of Manchester, UK

Abstract. We show how state-of-the-art Semantic Web technology can be used in e-Science, in particular, to automate the classification of proteins in biology. We show that the resulting classification was of comparable quality to that performed by a human expert, and how investigations using the classified data even resulted in the discovery of significant information that had previously been overlooked, leading to the identification of a possible drug-target.

1 Introduction

Semantic Web research has seen impressive strides in the development of languages, tools, and other infrastructure. In particular, the OWL ontology language, the Protégé ontology editor, and OWL reasoning tools such as FaCT++ and Racer are now in widespread use.

In this paper, we report on an application of Semantic Web technology in the domain of biology, where an OWL ontology and an OWL classification tool called the *Instance Store* were used to automate the classification of protein data. We show that the resulting classification was of comparable quality to one performed by a human expert, and how investigations using the classified data even resulted in either the discovery of new information or that which had been overlooked.

While this example focuses on a particular protein family and a particular set of model organisms, the technique should be applicable to other protein families, and to data from any sequenced genome—in fact we believe that similar techniques should be applicable to a wide range of investigations in biology, and in e-Science more generally. If this proves to be the case, then Semantic Web technology is set to have a major impact on e-Science.

Background and Motivation. The volume of genomic data is increasing at a seemingly exponential rate. In particular, *high throughput* technology has enabled the generation of large quantities of DNA sequence information. This sequence data, however, needs further analysis before it is useful to most biologists. This process, called *annotation*, augments the raw DNA sequence, and its derived protein sequence, with significant quantities of additional information describing its biological context.

Y. Gil et al. (Eds.): ISWC 2005, LNCS 3729, pp. 786–800, 2005.

One important process during annotation is the classification of proteins into different families. This is an important step in understanding the molecular biology of an organism. Attempts to automate this procedure have, however, not generally matched the gold-standard set by human experts. Human expert classification has been more accurate because their expertise allows them to recognise the properties that are sufficient, for example, to place an individual protein into a specific subfamily class. Automated methods have, in contrast, often failed to achieve the same level of specificity. Our goal, therefore, was to improve the precision of automatic protein classification, and bring it up to the same level as that achieved by human experts.

Overview of Our Technique. Given a set of proteins, each with a (partial) description of its properties, the objective is to find, for each of these proteins, the most specific protein family classes of which it is an instance. To describe protein family classes, we use an OWL-DL ontology; this enables us to specify necessary and sufficient conditions for a protein to be an instance of a given protein class. The ontology models the biology community's view of the current knowledge of protein classification. We then take protein data derived using standard bioinformatics analysis tools, translate these data into OWL-DL instance descriptions that use terms from the ontology, and use the Instance Store to classify these instances.

Empirical Evaluation. We have tested our system using data sets from both the human and *Aspergillus fumigatus* (a pathogenic fungus) genomes. We found that our automatic classification process performed at least as well as a human expert: it allows a fast and repeatable classification process, and the explicit representation of human expert knowledge means that there is a clear and explicit evidence base for the classification. Moreover, the precise and methodical classification of the data led to the discovery of new information about these proteins, including a protein subclass that seems to be specific to pathogenic fungi, and could thus be an important drug-target for pharmaceutical investigations.

2   Science and Technology

In this section, we describe the biology problem we have tackled and the Semantic Web technology that we used to achieve an appropriate solution.

2.1   Classifying Proteins

The process of annotation follows the "central dogma" of molecular biology. In broad outline, this process consists of the following steps: firstly DNA is sequenced; then genes are identified in this DNA; the DNA is then translated into a protein sequence; the proteins are then analysed and annotated with information useful for further biological investigation. As the majority of the functions of a cell are carried out by proteins, it is those proteins in which most biologists are interested. Proteins are classified into families that both reflect the functions they carry out in the cell, as well as often giving clear indications as to the biological processes in which they are involved. It is this classification, along with other and diverse kinds of information, which makes up the annotation of a protein and makes the large data sets manageable, enabling biologists to perform more thorough investigations.

In the last decade, various steps of this process have been automated, and thus their speed has increased enormously. Sequencing of whole genomes[1] is now routine. Gene discovery is technically challenging, but responds well to the increasing availability of CPU cycles. However, this still leaves a large number of protein sequences—approximately 30 000 in the human genome, a quantity that is more or less in other species. This quantity is far more than that with which the individual biologist can cope.

The automation of the annotation process has, however, lagged behind advances in other parts of this process. To date, automated approaches have proven to be quicker than human expert annotation, but the level of detail is often reduced [26,6]. As a consequence, many protein sequences are not annotated with the accurate, specific information necessary for bioinformatics analyses. Thus useful resources for further biological discovery remain untapped.

In this investigation, we have used one protein family, the *protein phosphatase* family, as a case study to demonstrate a new, ontology-based method for automated annotation. This method was designed to combine the speed of automated annotation with some of the detailed knowledge that experts use in annotation.

Protein phosphatases are a large and varied protein family. Together with another family, the protein kinases, they are critically involve in controlling the activity of many other proteins, thereby forming an essential part of the feedback control mechanism within the cell.

Given this pivotal role, it is perhaps unsurprising that many protein phosphatases have been implicated in various diseases of great medical importance, including diabetes, cancer, and neurodegenerative conditions. Phosphatases are therefore a major subject of medical and pharmaceutical research.

In general, proteins are relatively modular and comprise of a number of different *protein domains*. Using a protein sequence, it is often possible to computationally determine the protein domains of which it is composed. For many protein families, including the protein phosphatases, it is possible to classify their members based on the protein domains of which they are composed. To avoid confusion with interpretation domains or the domain of a property, for the remainder of this paper, we use "p-domain" for protein domain.

The different p-domain composition of proteins suggests the specific function of a protein. , Individual p-domains, however, often have specific and separate functions from the protein as a whole. For example, an enzyme will have a catalytic p-domain that performs the catalysis on the substrate molecule, but it will also contain structural p-domains and binding p-domains that ensure that the substrate can interact with the catalytic p-domain. Therefore, a specific

---

[1] A genome is the entirety of DNA in a cell.

combination of p-domains is required for a protein to function correctly. In some cases, the presence of a certain p-domain is *diagnostic* for membership in a particular protein family, i.e., some p-domains only occur in a single protein family. If a protein contains one of these diagnostic p-domains, it must belong to that particular family. For example, the protein tyrosine kinase catalytic p-domain is diagnostic for the tyrosine kinases.

Most protein families are, however, defined by a non-trivial combination of p-domains. For example, as you descend the hierarchical structure, extra p-domains (and therefore more specific functional properties) are observed in the protein class definitions. For example, an R5 phosphatase is a type of classical receptor tyrosine phosphatase. As a tyrosine phosphatase, it contains at least one phosphatase catalytic p-domain and, as a receptor tyrosine phosphatase, it contains a transmembrane region. The R5 type actually contains two catalytic p-domains and a fibronectin p-domain, identifying it as an instance of even more specific subclasses.

Identifying the p-domain composition of a protein is, therefore, a first step towards its classification. There are databases describing functional p-domains, for example, PROSITE [17], SMART [20] and INTERPRO [23], and these databases come with specific tools, such as INTERPROSCAN, which can report the presence of these p-domains in a novel protein sequence. Bioinformaticians are, however, usually required to perform the analysis that places a protein (with its set of p-domains) into a particular protein family. The whole process of classifying proteins from a genome can be accomplished with the following steps:

1. Given a genome, we extract DNA gene sequences, which we then translate into the set of protein sequences. If we are interested in a particular protein family, we can sub-select sequences containing p-domains diagnostic of that family.
2. On each of the extracted proteins, we use INTERPROSCAN to determine its p-domain composition.
3. For each of these compositions, we identify the protein family or subfamily to which it belongs by comparing them to the available biological knowledge.

The final step currently requires the most human analysis and expert knowledge. Manual classification methods are carried out by protein family experts to interpret these data and use their expert knowledge to classify proteins to a fine-grained level. To the best of our knowledge, no automated method has yet been able to replicate this expert level of detail and precision.

2.2   Ontologies and the Instance Store

Ontologies, with their intuitive taxonomic structure and class based semantics, are widely used in domains like bio- and medical-informatics, where there is a tradition of establishing taxonomies of terms. The recent W3C recommendation of OWL[2] as the language of choice for web ontologies also underlines the long

---

[2] See http://www.w3.org/2004/OWL/ or [11].

term vision that ontologies will play a central role in the Semantic Web. Most importantly, as shown in [4], most of the available OWL ontologies can be captured in OWL-DL—a subset of OWL for which highly optimised Description Logic [2] reasoners can be used to support ontology design and deployment.

Unfortunately, existing reasoners (and tools), while successful in dealing with the (relatively small and static) class level information in ontologies, fail when presented with the large volumes of instance level data often required by realistic applications, hampering the use of reasoning over ontologies beyond the class level. The system we have used—the instance Store (IS) [14]—addresses this problem using a hybrid database/reasoner architecture: a relational database is used to make instances persistent, while a class level ("TBox" in Description Logic terms) reasoner is used to infer ontological information about the classes to which they belong. Moreover, part of this ontological information is also made persistent in the database. The IS currently only supports a rather limited form of reasoning about individuals: it takes an ontology (without instances), a set of axioms asserting class-instance relationships, and answers queries asking for all the instances of a class description. The classes in both axioms and queries can be arbitrarily complex OWL-DL descriptions, and a DL reasoner is used to ensure that *all* instances (explicit and implicit) of the query concept are returned. In the remainder of this paper, we use "class-level ontology" for an ontology in which no instances occur. From a theoretical perspective, this might seem un-interesting; the IS is, however, able to deal with much larger numbers of individuals than would be possible using a standard DL reasoner. More importantly, this kind of reasoning turns out to be useful in a range of applications, in particular those such as the one presented here where a domain model is used to structure and classify large data sets.[3]

There is a long tradition of coupling databases to knowledge representation systems in order to perform reasoning, most notably the work in [5]. However, in the IS, we do not use the standard approach of associating a table (or view) with each class and property. Instead, we have a fixed and relatively simple schema that is independent of the structure of the ontology and of the instance data. The IS is, therefore, agnostic about the provenance of data, and uses a new, dedicated database for each ontology (although the schema is always the same).

The basic functionality of the IS system are illustrated in Figure 1. At startup, the `initialise` method is called with a relational database, an OWL-DL class reasoner such as Racer [9] or Fact++ [30], and a class-level OWL-DL ontology. The method creates the schema for the database if needed (i.e., if the IS is new), parses the ontology, and loads it into the reasoner. To populate the IS, the `addAssertion` method is called repeatedly. Each assertion states that an instance (identified by a URI) belongs to class (which is an arbitrary OWL-DL description). Once the IS has been populated with some—possibly millions of—instances, it can be queried using the `retrieve` method. A query again consists of an arbitrary (possibly complex) OWL-DL class description; the result is the set of all instances belonging to the

---

[3] The IS was initially developed for use in a Web Service registry application, where it was used to classify and retrieve (large numbers of) descriptions of web services.

```
initialise(database: Database, reasoner: OWLReasoner, ontology: OWLOntology)
addAssertion(instance: URI, class: OWLDescription)
retrieve(query: OWLDescription): Set ⟨URI⟩
```

Fig. 1. The IS API

query class, and is returned by `retrieve` as a set of URIs. The IS uses database queries to return individuals that are "obviously" instances of the query class, and to identify those instances where the DL reasoner is needed in order to determine if they form part of the answer set.

3   Description of the Experiments Undertaken

The method we present could be applicable in general to many protein families, but to demonstrate the technique and the fine-grained classification possible, we present the analysis of one family, the protein phosphatases, in the human and *Aspergillus fumigatus* genomes.

We have combined automated reasoning techniques [9,14] with elements of a service-oriented architecture [27,19] to produce a system to automatically extract

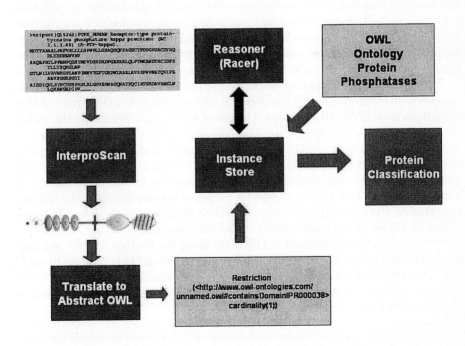

Fig. 2. The Ontology Classification System Architecture

and classify the set of protein phosphatase from an organism.[4] Figure 2 shows the components in our protein classification experiment. An OWL class-level ontology describes the protein phosphatase family, and this ontology is pre-loaded into the Instance Store. Protein instance data is extracted from the protein set of a genome, and the p-domain composition is determined using INTERPROSCAN. These p-domain compositions are then translated into OWL descriptions and compared to the OWL definitions for protein family classes using the Instance Store which, in turn, uses a DL reasoner (Racer in this case), to classify each such instance. For each protein class from our ontology, it returns those proteins that can be inferred to be an instance of this class.

In the remainder of this section, we will describe the relevant components of this architecture in more detail, and explain the outcomes of this experiment from a biology perspective. In the next section, we describe the experience gained and lessons learnt from a computer science perspective.

3.1   The Ontology

In this section, we describe how we capture the expert knowledge for phosphatase classification in an OWL-DL ontology. All the information used for developing our ontology comes from peer-reviewed literature from protein phosphatase experts. The family of human protein phosphatases has been well characterised experimentally, and detailed reviews of the classification and family composition are available [1,7,18]. These reviews represent the current community knowledge of the relevant biology. If, in the future, new subfamilies are discovered, the ontology can easily be changed to reflect these changes in knowledge; we will comment on this in Section 4.

Fortunately for this application, there are precise rules,[5] based on p-domain composition, for protein family membership, and we can express these rules as class definitions in an OWL-DL ontology. The use of an ontology to capture the understanding of p-domain composition enables the automation of the final analysis step which had previously required human intervention, thus allowing for full automation of the complete process. In biology, the use of ontologies to capture human knowledge of a particular domain and to answer complex queries is becoming well established [8,28]. Less well established is the use of reasoning systems for data interpretation. In this study, we present a method which makes use of ontology reasoning and illustrates the advantages of such an approach.

The ontology was developed in OWL-DL using the Protégé editor,[6] and currently contains 80 classes and 39 properties; it is available at (http://www.bioinf.man.ac.uk/phosphabase/download). Part of the subsumption hierarchy inferred from these descriptions can be seen in the left-hand panel of Figure 3, which shows the OWL ontology in the Protégé editor.

---

[4] Due to the relatively small test-set used, the case study reported here could have been carried out using Racer [9] only, i.e., without the IS. However, larger sets of protein data will necessitate the use of IS or a similar tool.

[5] We use "rules" here in a completely informal way.

[6] We used Protégé 3.0 with OWL plugin 1.3, build 225.1.

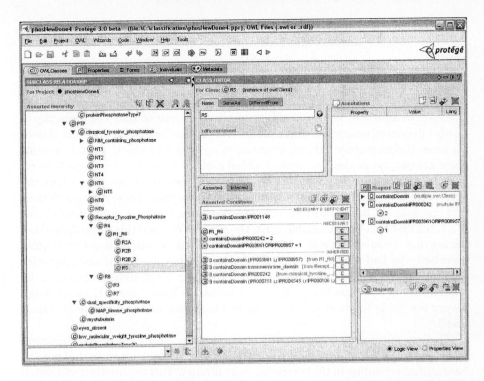

Fig. 3. A screenshot of the phosphatase ontology in the OWL ontology editor Protégé

More precisely, for each class of phosphatase, this ontology contains a (necessary and sufficient) definition. For this family of proteins, this definition is, in most cases, a conjunction of p-domain compositions, i.e., a typical case of a phosphatase class definition looks as follows, where X_i are p-domains:

If a Y protein contains at least n_1 p-domains of type X_1 and ... and at least n_m p-domains of type X_m, then this protein also belongs to class Z.

For example, receptor tyrosine phosphatases contain one or two phosphatase catalytic p-domains, and receptor tyrosine R2B phosphatases contain exactly 2 tyrosine phosphatase catalytic p-domains, one transmembrane p-domain, at least one fibronectin p-domain, and at least one immunoglobulin p-domain. In some cases, X_i is a disjunction of p-domains. P-domains come with a rather "flat" structure, i.e., only few p-domains are specialisations of others. Clearly, "counting" statements such as the one above go beyond the expressive power of OWL since they would require (the OWL equivalent of) *qualified* cardinality restrictions [10], whereas OWL only provides unqualified cardinality restrictions through its `restriction(U minCardinality(n))` and `restriction(U maxCardinality(n))` constructs. In contrast, this kind of expressive means was provided by DAML+OIL [15], i.e., we could have defined the above mentioned receptor tyrosine phosphatases using the expression

IntersectionOf (Restriction(contains minCardinality(1) PhCatalDoms)
                 Restriction(contains maxCardinality(2) PhCatalDoms)

To overcome this problem, we used a well-known work-around.[7] For each X_i that we would have liked to use in a qualified number restriction, we introduced a subproperty containsX_i of contains, and set the range of containsX_i to the class X_i. In addition, we added sub-property assertions so that the hierarchy of newly introduced properties containsX_i reflects the class hierarchy of the classes X_i used. Unfortunately, this work-around is not always correct. That is, assume there are two ontologies, one with qualified number restrictions and one that resulted from the application of this work-around. Then there are cases where the first one implies a subsumption relationship between two classes, whereas the second one does not imply this subsumption. Similarly, a class may be unsatisfiable w.r.t. the first one, but satisfiable w.r.t. the second. We used this work-around believing that it was correct and, when we learned that it sometimes is not, were quite surprised—we had "cluttered" our ontology with a large number of new properties without this guaranteeing the desired effect. However, we then checked that, in the special case of our experiment, this work-around is indeed correct, even though we are not going to prove this here. We will comment more on this in Section 4 and 5.

Having captured the expert knowledge in this way, we are left with the problem of dealing with the potentially very large numbers of protein instances that need to be classified according to the corresponding ontology. This requirement motivated our use of the IS.

3.2   The Data Sets

This study focuses on the previously identified and described human phosphatases [1,24], and the less well characterised A. fumigatus protein phosphatases. The human phosphatases, having been carefully hand-classified, form a control group for our automated protein phosphatase classification. Previous classification of human phosphatases by biological experts provides a substantial test-set for our approach. If the IS can classify the characterised proteins (at least) as well as human experts, then this would increase our confidence when using our method on unknown genomes. The A. fumigatus genome falls between these extremes, and thus offers a unique insight into the comparison between the automated method and the manual. The A. fumigatus genome has been sequenced, and annotation is currently underway by a team of human experts [22]. We have considered 118 human phosphatases and 45 from A. fumigatus.

Pre-Screening. Isolation of the protein phosphatase sequences from the protein set of the genome was achieved by screening for diagnostic phosphatase motifs, i.e. for specific patterns. These are

1. the protein tyrosine phosphatase active site motif H-C-X(5)-R
2. the protein serine/threonine phosphatase motif [LIVMN]-[KR]-G-N-H-E

---

[7] See, e.g., http://www.cs.vu.nl/~guus/public/qcr.html

3. the protein phosphatase C signature motif [LIVMFY]-[LIVMFYA]-[GSAC]-[LIVM]-[FYC]-D-G-H-[GAV].

The EMBOSS program, PATMATDB [25] was used to perform the pre-screening process. Performing an INTERPROSCAN on every protein sequence from the genome would also have isolated the protein phosphatase sequences, but each INTERPROSCAN can take several minutes. PATMATDB can screen the whole genome in the time taken to run one INTERPROSCAN, so we decided to use IN-TERPROSCAN only for the detailed analysis of each sequence identified as being a protein phosphatase.

3.3 Queries Asked and Results

The purposes of the human and *A.fumigatus* studies were different. The human study was a proof of concept to demonstrate the effectiveness of the automated method. The *A.fumigatus* study was more focused towards biological discovery.

For the human phosphatases, we were interested in comparing the automated classification with the thorough, human expert classification. Therefore, we browsed the class hierarchy of our phosphatase ontology and, for each class, we retrieved those proteins for which the IS inferred that this class was the most specific one. We were also interested in identifying instances that did not fit any of the ontology class definitions (i.e., whose most specific class was the top class).

For the *A.fumigatus* phosphatases, we browsed the class hierarchy in a similar way but, as the phosphatases from this organism were less well characterised, we were particularly interested in the differences between the human and *A.fumigatus* set, i.e., we were interested in finding classes that had instances of the human proteins, but not of the *A.fumigatus* proteins, and vice versa. All these queries could be answered easily and quickly using the IS.

The results of this experiment were three-fold. Firstly, we found that the automated classification of the human protein phosphatases performed as well as the manual classification by phosphatase experts. Since the same protein instances were used in the automated and manual studies, we could compare these two classifications, and it turned out that both classifications put almost all phosphatases into the same place in the class hierarchy. This evidence shows proof of concept, and suggests that the automated approach could be used to solve the current annotation bottleneck. Secondly, in the few cases where the automatic and the manual classification differed, detailed investigations by a domain expert revealed that the automatic one was actually "more correct": we discovered two proteins for which no appropriate class was available, i.e. they were classified by the automatic classification as instances of the top phosphatases class.

This discovery lead to a modification of the ontology, and thus of the expert knowledge on proteins. One of these phosphatases was DUSP10 (Dual specificity phosphatase 10). It was found to contain an extra p-domain, a *disintegrin*. This particular p-domain is not found in any other protein phosphatase and poses interesting questions about possible protein functions to the biologists. Our automated classification method was able to find these mis-classifications because the IS applied the expert knowledge systematically and consistently.

The automated classification of the *A.fumigatus* phosphatases revealed large differences from the human phosphatases. Not only were there fewer individual proteins, but whole subfamilies were missing. Some of these differences can be attributed to the differences in the two organisms. Many phosphatases in the human classification were tissue-specific variations of tissue-types that do not occur in *A.fumigatus*. Since *A.fumigatus* is pathogenic to humans, these differences are important avenues of investigation for potential drug targets. The most interesting discovery in the *A.fumigatus* data set was the identification of a novel type of calcineurin phosphatase, i.e., again, a phosphatase that was classified automatically only as an instance of the top class. Calcineurin is well conserved throughout evolution and performs the same function in all organisms. However, in *A.fumigatus*, it contains an extra functional p-domain. Further bioinformatics analyses revealed that this extra p-domain also occurs in other pathogenic fungus species, but in no other organisms, suggesting a specific functional role for this extra p-domain. Previous studies have identified divergences in the mechanism of action of calcineurin in pathogenic fungi as being linked to virulence, so this protein is an interesting drug-target for future study.

4   Lessons Learnt

As we have seen, we have successfully used Semantic Web technology in a bioinformatics application. Besides finding new protein families that are of interest to biologists, we have shown that automated classification can indeed compete with manual classification, and is sometimes even superior. Our approach to automated classification combines the advantages of speed of the automated methods and accuracy of human expert classification, the latter being due to the fact that we captured the expert knowledge in an OWL ontology. The combination of the two, namely speed and expert knowledge, provides a quick and efficient method for classifying proteins on a genomic scale, and offers a solution to the current annotation bottleneck.

Our approach was made possible by the development of state-of-the-art Semantic Web technology, such as the OWL ontology language, the Protégé OWL ontology editor, the OWL Instance Store, and the Racer OWL reasoner; this technology did not emerge overnight, but is based on decades of research in logic-based knowledge representation and reasoning. Although neither Racer nor the IS support all of OWL-DL,[8] these tools proved more than adequate for our experiment.

In contrast, a limitation in the expressive power of OWL-DL *did* cause considerable problems: the lack of qualified number restrictions (also called qualified cardinality restrictions). In order to overcome this limitation, we had to employ a work around and verify that this work around, even though not correct in general, was correct for our ontology and instance data. This work around introduced a significant overhead, and was only possible through a close co-operation between the

---

[8] Racer does not support individual names in complex class descriptions (so-called nominals—see [16]), and the current version of IS does not support role assertions between individuals.

biologists and computer scientists. We, therefor, cannot recommend such an approach in general. Additionally, we observe that, from a theoretical and practical perspective, this work around should not be necessary since (a) reasoners such as Racer and Fact [9,13] support qualified number restrictions, (b) for all Description Logics we are aware of that support (unqualified) number restrictions, the worst-case complexity of reasoning remains the same when they are extended with qualified number restrictions (see, e.g., [29]), and (c) the latest version of Protégé-OWL now supports qualified number restrictions. Hence we can, in the future, run similar experiments without having to resort to this work around, provided that we are willing to diverge from the current OWL standard.

The ability to run such experiments is of considerable importance since there is a wealth of unannotated and partially annotated data in the public domain, to which we plan to apply our approach. New genomes are being sequenced continually, and some existing genomes have not been annotated to any degree of detail. Now that the ontology system architecture is in place, new proteins can be quickly and successfully classified as members of protein phosphatase subfamilies. Development of other ontologies, would enable the application of this technique to some of the 1,000's of other protein families.

This paper demonstrates a proof of concept for the automated classification of proteins using automated reasoning technologies. From a study involving a single protein family and two species, we were able to identify a new protein subclass. As this class of protein appears to be specific to pathogenic fungi, it is potentially useful for further pharmaceutical investigations. Automated reasoning over instance data has therefore enabled us to generate new hypotheses which will require significiant further laboratory experimentation, which, in turn, will potentially improve our understanding of protein phosphorylation.

Finally, we would like to point out that the ontology definitions are produced from expert protein family knowledge. Therefore, they reflect what is currently known in the research community, and are made explicit in a machine-understandable format, namely OWL-DL. This has several important consequences. Firstly, the construction of such an ontology can help in the development of a consensus from within the community [3], and even if the community fails to agree on a single ontology, automated classification could be used to enable "parallel" alternative annotations. Secondly, if the community knowledge of the protein family changes, the ontology can easily be altered, and the protein instances can be re-classified accordingly. Lastly, if the definitions are based on what is known, proteins that do not fit into any of the defined classes are easily identified, making the discovery of new protein subfamilies possible.

5   Outlook and Future Work

Our plans for future work are manifold. Basically, we want to do more "automated" biology, but we are thereby pushing the current state-of-art in logic-based knowledge representation, automated reasoning, and Semantic Web technology. Within this section, we only discuss three of the related issues.

Firstly, we observe that a protein is a sequence of amino acids, and thus sequences can be seen as strings over a twenty letter alphabet since there are only twenty amino acids. In our current ontology, we do not capture this sequence information, and thus cannot answer queries related to these sequences. From a biology perspective, however, queries such as "give me all proteins whose amino acid sequence contains an M followed by some arbitrary sub string, which is then followd by a NEN" would be really valuable. From a computer science perspective, we could easily express (and query over) these strings using a simple form of concrete domains, so-called datatypes [21,12]. However, the datatypes currently available in OWL do not provide predicates that compare a given string with a regular expression, a comparison that would reflect the above example query.

Secondly, we are currently concerned with a single class of components of an organism, namely the proteins. In the future, we want to use the available technology to automate investigations into their interaction, and also represent and reason about larger structures such as genomes and cells. We could easily model interactions between proteins using a property `interact` to make statements such as "proteins of class X only interact with proteins of class Y". However, we would also need to make statements on an instance level such as "this protein instance interacts with that protein instance", which is possible in OWL-DL, but goes beyond the capabilities of the current IS. We are currently extending the IS to handle statements of this kind, and we will see if this extension is able to cope with the large volumes of data that will be needed in biology applications.[9]

Thirdly, we will "roll back" the work-around we used to cope with the absence of qualified number restrictions, both in our ontology and in the instance data, instead using the form of qualified number restrictions provided by Protégé, Racer, and the IS. This will greatly enhance the interpretability of the current ontology and also make its extension to other families of proteins more straight-forward.

Acknowledgements. This work was funded by an MRC PhD studentship, the myGrid e-science project, University of Manchester with the UK e-science programme EPSRC grant GR/R67743 and the ComparaGRID project, BBSRC grant BBS/B/17131. Preliminary sequence data was obtained from *The Institute for Genomic Research* website at http://www.tigr.org from Dr Jane Mabey-Gilsenan. Sequencing of *A.fumigatus* was funded by the National Institute of Allergy and Infectious Disease U01 AI 48830 to David Denning and William Nierman, the Wellcome Trust, and Fondo de Investicagiones Sanitarias.

References

1. A. Alonso, J. Sasin, N. Bottini, I. Friedberg, I. Friedberg, A. Osterman, A. Godzik, T. Hunter, J. Dixon, and T. Mustelin. Protein tyrosine phosphatases in the human genome. *Cell*, 117(6):699–711, 2004.

---

[9] Racer can already handle such statements, but can only deal with a relatively small number of individuals.

2. F. Baader, D. Calvanese, D. McGuinness, D. Nardi, and P. Patel-Schneider, editors. *The Description Logic Handbook: Theory, Implementation and Applications.* Cambridge University Press, 2003.
3. M. Bada, D. Turi, R. McEntire, and R. Stevens. Using Reasoning to Guide Annotation with Gene Ontology Terms in GOAT. *SIGMOD Record (special issue on data engineering for the life sciences)*, 2004.
4. S. Bechhofer and R. Volz. Patching syntax in OWL ontologies. In *Proc. of the 3rd International Semantic Web Conference (ISWC)*, 2004.
5. A. Borgida and R. J. Brachman. Loading data into description reasoners. In *Proceedings of the ACM SIGMOD International Conference on Management of Data*, pages 217–226, 1993.
6. K. Carter, A. Oka, G. Tamiya, and M. I. Bellgard. Bioinformatics issues for automating the annotation of genomic sequences. *Genome Inform Ser Workshop Genome Inform*, 12:204–11, 2001.
7. P. T. Cohen. Novel protein serine/threonine phosphatases: variety is the spice of life. *Trends Biochem Sci*, 22(7):245–51, July 1997.
8. Gene Ontology Consortium. Gene ontology: Tool for the unification of biology. *Nature Genetics*, 25(1):25–29, 2000.
9. V. Haarslev and R. Möller. RACER system description. In *Proceedings of the International Joint Conference on Automated Reasoning (IJCAR-01)*, volume 2083 of *Lecture Notes in Artificial Intelligence*, pages 701–705. Springer-Verlag, 2001.
10. B. Hollunder and F. Baader. Qualifying number restrictions in concept languages. In *Proceedings of the Second International Conference on the Principles of Knowledge Representation and Reasoning (KR-91)*, pages 335–346, 1991.
11. I. Horrocks, P. F. Patel-Schneider, and F. van Harmelen. From SHIQ and RDF to OWL: The making of a web ontology language. *Journal of Web Semantics*, 1(1), 2003.
12. I. Horrocks and U. Sattler. Ontology reasoning in the SHOQ(D) description logic. In *Proceedings of the Seventeenth International Joint Conference on Artificial Intelligence*, 2001.
13. I. Horrocks. Using an expressive description logic: FaCT or fiction? In *Proceedings of the Sixth International Conference on the Principles of Knowledge Representation and Reasoning (KR-98)*, pages 636–647, 1998.
14. I. Horrocks, L. Li, D. Turi, and S. Bechhofer. The instance store: DL reasoning with large numbers of individuals. In *Proc. of the 2004 Description Logic Workshop (DL 2004)*, 2004. available at CEUR, www.ceur.org, see also instancestore.man.ac.uk.
15. I. Horrocks, P. Patel-Schneider, and F. van Harmelen. Reviewing the design of DAML+OIL: An ontology language for the semantic web. In *Proc. of the 18th Nat. Conf. on Artificial Intelligence (AAAI 2002)*, pages 792–797. AAAI Press, 2002.
16. I. Horrocks and U. Sattler. A tableaux decision procedure for SHOIQ. In *Proc. of the 19th Int. Joint Conf. on Artificial Intelligence (IJCAI 2005)*, 2005.
17. N. Hulo, C. J. Sigrist, V. Le Saux, P. S. Langendijk-Genevaux, L. Bordoli, A. Gattiker, E. De Castro, P. Bucher, and A. Bairoch. Recent improvements to the prosite database. *Nucleic Acids Res*, 32:134–7, 2004.
18. P. J. Kennelly. Protein phosphatases–a phylogenetic perspective. *Chem Rev*, 101(8):2291–312, 2001.
19. K. Wolstencroft, P. Lord, L. Tabernero, A. Brass, and R. Stevens. Intelligent classification of proteins using an ontology. Submitted, 2005.

20. I. Letunic, R. R. Copley, S. Schmidt, F. D. Ciccarelli, T. Doerks, J. Schultz, C. P. Ponting, and P. Bork. Smart 4.0: towards genomic data integration. *Nucleic Acids Res*, 32:142–4, 2004.

21. C. Lutz. Description logics with concrete domains—a survey. In *Advances in Modal Logics Volume 4*. World Scientific Publishing Co. Pte. Ltd., 2003.

22. J. E. Mabey, M. J. Anderson, P. F. Giles, C. J. Miller, T. K. Attwood, N. W. Paton, E. Bornberg-Bauer, G. D. Robson, S. G. Oliver, and D. W. Denning. Cadre: the central *aspergillus* data repository. *Nucleic Acids Res*, 32:401–5, 2004.

23. N. J. Mulder, R. Apweiler, T. K. Attwood, et al. Interpro, progress and status in 2005. *Nucleic Acids Res*, 33:201–5, 2005.

24. T. Mustelin, T. Vang, and N. Bottini. Protein tyrosine phosphatases and the immune response. *Nat Rev Immunol*, 5(1):43–57, January 2005.

25. P. Rice, I. Longden, and A. Bleasby. EMBOSS: the European molecular biology open software suite. *Trends Genet*, 16(6):276–7, June 2000.

26. T. F. Smith and X. Zhang. The challenges of genome sequence annotation or "the devil is in the details". *Nat Biotechnol*, 15(12):1222–3, 1997.

27. R. Stevens, H. Tipney, C. Wroe, T. Oinn, M. Senger, P. Lord, C. Goble, A. Brass, and M. Tassabehji. Exploring Williams Beuren Syndrome Using MyGrid. In *Bioinformatics*, volume 20, pages 303–310, 2004. Intelligent Systems for Molecular Biology (ISMB) 2004.

28. R. Stevens, C. Wroe, P. Lord, and C. Goble. Ontologies in bioinformatics. In S. Staab and R. Studer, editors, *Handbook on Ontologies*, pages 635–657. Springer, 2003.

29. S. Tobies. *Complexity Results and Practical Algorithms for Logics in Knowledge Representation*. PhD thesis, RWTH Aachen, 2001. electronically available at http://www.bth.rwth-aachen.de/ediss/ediss.html.

30. D. Tsarkov and I. Horrocks. Efficient reasoning with range and domain constraints. In *Proceedings of the 2004 Description Logic Workshop (DL 2004)*. CEUR, 2004. Available from ceur-ws.org.

Provenance-Based Validation of E-Science Experiments

Sylvia C. Wong, Simon Miles, Weijian Fang, Paul Groth, and Luc Moreau

School of Electronics and Computer Science,
University of Southampton, UK
{sw2, sm, wf, pg03r, l.moreau}@ecs.soton.ac.uk

Abstract. E-Science experiments typically involve many distributed services maintained by different organisations. After an experiment has been executed, it is useful for a scientist to verify that the execution was performed correctly or is compatible with some existing experimental criteria or standards. Scientists may also want to review and verify experiments performed by their colleagues. There are no exsiting frameworks for validating such experiments in today's e-Science systems. Users therefore have to rely on error checking performed by the services, or adopt other ad hoc methods. This paper introduces a platform-independent framework for validating workflow executions. The validation relies on reasoning over the documented *provenance* of experiment results and *semantic descriptions* of services advertised in a registry. This validation process ensures experiments are performed correctly, and thus results generated are meaningful. The framework is tested in a bioinformatics application that performs protein compressibility analysis.

1 Introduction

Very large scale computations are now becoming routinely used as a methodology to undertake scientific research: success stories abound in many domains, including physics (griphyn.org), bioinformatics (mygrid.org.uk), engineering (geodise.org) and geographical sciences (earthsystemgrid.org). These large scale computations, which underpin a scientific process usually referred to as *e-Science*, are ideal candidates for use of Grid technology [1].

E-Science experiments are typically formed by invoking multiple services, whose compositions are modelled as workflows [2]. Thus, experimental results are obtained by executing workflows. As part of the scientific process, it is important for scientists to be able to verify the correctness of their own experiments, or to review the correctness of their peers' work. Validation ensures results generated from experiments are meaningful.

Traditionally, program validation has been carried out in two complementary manners. On the one hand, *static verification* analyses program code before it is executed and establishes that the program satisfies some properties. These verifications are extensively researched by the programming language community. Examples include type inference, escape analysis and model checking. They typically depend on the semantics of the programming language being analysed. On the other hand, static verification is complemented by *run-time* checking, which is carried out when the program executes, and verifies that data values satisfy constraints, expressed by either types or assertions.

Y. Gil et al. (Eds.): ISWC 2005, LNCS 3729, pp. 801–815, 2005.

Such validation methods suffer from limitations in the context of large e-Science experiments, potentially carried out in open environments. First, programs (or workflows) may not be expressed in languages that analysis tools operate on, or may not be directly available because they are exposed as services, hereby preventing static analysis. Second, in general, in open environments, we cannot make the assumption that services always check that their inputs or outputs match their interface specifications (if available at all); furthermore, such interfaces may be under-specified (for instance, many bioinformatics services tend to process and return strings encoding specific biological sequence data); as a result, no guarantee exists that types will be checked dynamically. Third, studies of user practice have shown that rapid development cycles are being adopted by e-Scientists, in which workflows are frequently modified and tuned and scientific models are evolved accordingly. As a result, it is important for scientists to be able to verify that previous experimental results are compatible with recent criteria and requirements. Since these models did not necessarily exist at experiment design or execution time, it is a necessity to perform such validation *after* the experiment has been completed.

The *provenance* of a piece of data denotes the process by which it is produced. Provenance-aware applications are applications that record documentation of their execution so that the provenance of the data they produce can be obtained and reasoned over. In this paper, our thesis is that provenance-based validation of experiments allows us to verify the validity after experiments have been conducted. Specifically, our contributions are: (a) a provenance-based architecture to undertake validation of experiments; (b) the use of semantic reasoning in undertaking validation of experiments; (c) an implementation of the architecture and its deployment in a bioinformatics application in order to support a set of use cases. Our experimentation with the system shows that our approach is tractable and performs efficiently.

The structure of the paper is as follows. Section 2 describes some use cases we have identified that require experiment validation. Section 3 briefly discusses current approaches to e-Science experiment validation and explains why it is necessary to perform validation after an experiment was executed. Section 4 introduces the proposed framework for validation of workflow execution. Section 5 then describes how the architecture can be applied to the use cases introduced in Section 2. In Section 6, we discuss how semantic reasoning is essential in properly establishing the validity of experiments. Section 7 then presents results from an implementation of the validation framework with an e-science application (specifically, the protein compressibility analysis experiment). The paper finishes with discussion in Section 8 and conclusions in Section 9.

2   Use Cases

The motivation for this work comes from real problems found by scientists in their day to day work. Therefore, in this section, we introduce a number of use cases in the bioinformatics domain where it is necessary to perform some form of validation of experiments after they have been completed.

Use Case 1 (Interaction validity, interface level). *A biologist, B, performs an experiment on a protein sequence. One stage of this experiment involves generating a pre-specified number of permutations of that sequence. Later, another biologist, R, judges the experiment results and considers them to be suspicious. R determines that the number of permutations specified was an invalid value, e.g. it was negative.* □

In this example, we consider that the service provider could have specified a restriction for the number of permutations to non-negative integers in the service schema, since the parameter only makes sense for non-negative integers. However, this does not guarantee that the service will validate the data against the schema at run-time. In general, whether validation is carried out at run-time is service specific.

In Use Case 1, B could have entered a negative value for the number of permutations. In this case, the value is incorrect because it does not conform to the restrictions and requirements as specified by the interface document of the service. By validating the experiment using its provenance, R can determine that B entered an invalid value for the number of permutations, and thus the results generated by the experiment were not meaningful.

Use Case 2 (Interaction validity, domain level). *A bioinformatician, B, downloads a file containing sequence data from a remote database. B then processes the sequence using an analysis service. Later, a reviewer, R, suspects that the sequence may have been a nucleotide sequence but processed by a service that can only analyse meaningfully amino acid sequences. R determines whether this was the case.* □

Nucleotides and amino acids are two separate classes of biological sequences, but the symbols used in the syntax of nucleotides are a subset of those used for amino acids. Therefore, it is not always possible to detect which type of sequence is used by superficially examining the data. The service used in Use Case 2 could require an amino acid sequence as its input. If a nucleotide sequence was accidentally used rather than an amino acid sequence, the problem would not be detected at run-time, and the experiment results would not be meaningful.

Given that many bioinformatics services operate on strings, the biological interpretation of a piece of data is information not directly available from interface specification, and cannot be easily derived from the data itself. Typically, such additional description that is useful or of interest to the user has to be made explicit elsewhere. Thus, the interaction in an experiment can be correct according to service interface specifications, but incorrect according to the domain level understanding of the problem.

Use Case 3 (Ontology revision). *A bioinformatician, B, performs an experiment on a sequence downloaded from a remote database. Later, another bioinformatician, D, updates the ontology that classifies sequences stored in the database to correct an error in the previous version. B checks if the experiment is compatible with the new version of the ontology.* □

Ontologies are invaluable in describing domain specific knowledge such as DNA and RNA sequences are subtypes of nucleotide sequences, as illustrated by the Gene Ontology [3]. If a service advertises that it accepts nucleotide sequences, we can infer that the service can also meaningfully process DNA and RNA sequences.

Similar to Use Case 2, the bioinformatician B in Use Case 3 wants to validate the interactions in the experiment according to their domain-level characterisation (specifically, biological sequence types). However, in this use case, the ontology describing the gene sequences is revised after the experiment has been conducted. Therefore, to ensure results of the experiment are not affected by this error in the ontology, B validates the execution against the revised ontology.

Use Case 4 (Conformance to plan). *A biologist, B, creates a plan for an experiment by defining the type of analysis to perform at each stage of the experiment. B then performs an experiment that is intended to follow the plan. Later another biologist, R, determines whether each operation performed in the experiment fulfilled an intended operation in the plan.* □

In Use Case 4, the plan defined by B is abstract in nature. To verify whether the experiment conformed to the original plan, R examines the *tasks* the services perform. In other words, R is interested in verifying the properties of the services, not the interactions between the services. This is in contrast to the previous use cases, where the validation is performed on the types of the data provided and accepted by the services.

Use Case 5 (Patentability of results). *A biologist, B, performs an experiment. Later, B wishes to patent the results. A reviewer, R, checks that no service used in the experiment has legal restrictions such that the results could not be patented.* □

In Use Case 5, R is interested in attributes such as condition of use, legal constraints and patents. These conditions are (probably) unforeseen by biologist B when he designed and performed the experiment.

3   Current Validation Approaches

Web Services are described by a WSDL interface [4] that specifies the operations they support, the inputs they expect, and the outputs they produce. The inputs and outputs of an operation are part of a message and their structure, referred to as interface type, is commonly specified using XML Schema [5]. In other words, it is the type expected by the transport layer (i.e., SOAP [6]). It is generally (but not always) the role of the service provider to publish interface type definitions.

We augment interface types with further descriptions that characterise additional invariants of interest to the user. For instance, in the previous section, we discussed a characterisation of data in domain-level terms. OWL-S [7] allows for semantic types expressed using the OWL ontology to be added to the service profile. Given that the world is evolving, we consider that several views about an object may co-exist. Hence, it is permitted to associate several semantic types to a given entity: this is the approach adopted by myGrid [8], which also relies on the OWL ontology language to give a classification of biological data. Such descriptions are not restricted to inputs and outputs, but can be annotations to service interfaces that identify the functions they perform or the resources they rely upon. Such information may be provided by the service provider, or by a third party, and published in a registry such as the myGrid/Grimoires registry [9].

In the introduction, we discussed two commonly used forms of validation: static and dynamic. *Static validation* operates on workflow source code. The vast array of static analyses devised by the programming language community is also applicable to workflows, such as type inference, escape analysis, etc. Some analysis were conceived to address problems that are specific to workflows. Examples of these include workflow concurrency analysis [10], graph-based partitioning of workflows [11], and model checking of activity graphs [12]. Yang et al. [13] devise a static analysis to infer workflow quality of service. However, the workflow script may not always be available, or it may be expressed in a language for which we do not have access to a static analyser.

Hence, validation may be performed at run-time. In its simplest form, validation is *service-based*. In Web Services, a validating XML parser verifies all XML documents sent to a service conform to its specified schema. Thus, if all the services used in a workflow employ validating parsers, the workflow execution is guaranteed to satisfy syntactic types required by services. We note however that many XML parsers are non-validating by default, such as Apache Axis (ws.apache.org/axis) and JAXB (java.sun.com/xml/jaxb), because validation is an expensive operation that affects the performance of web services. Therefore, most XML parsers used by web services simply check if XML documents are well-formed, and if they can be unmarshalled into compiled classes.

Other forms of validation and analysis can take place at run-time. The Pegasus planner is capable of analysing a workflow and re-planning its execution at run-time so as to make use of existing available resources [14]. Policy languages such as KAoS are used to perform semantic reasoning and decide if access can be granted to services as they are being invoked [15].

Service-based validation can only be performed at run-time. However, it is sometimes necessary to validate an experiment after it has been executed. This has been identified in Use Cases 3 and 5. Third parties, such as reviewers and other scientists, may want to verify that the results obtained were computed correctly according to some criteria. These criteria may not be known when the experiment was designed. This is because as science progresses, criteria evolve. Thus, it is important that previously computed results can be verified according to revised sets of criteria.

4   Provenance-Based Validation Architecture

We propose a provenance-based approach to workflow validation. The provenance of an experiment contains a record of all service invocations such that the information is sufficient to reproduce the exact experiment. A provenance-based approach lends itself easily to third party validation as scientists can share provenance data with other scientists. Also, as validation criteria evolve, the validation process can be repeated without re-executing the experiment.

Figure 1 explains our proposed provenance-based semantic validation framework. Service providers host services on the Grid and advertise them in a registry. Since we wish to support multi-level descriptions beyond interface types, possibly provided by third parties, the registry provides support for semantic annotations [9]. An interface for metadata publication allows for metadata annotations to services, individual opera-

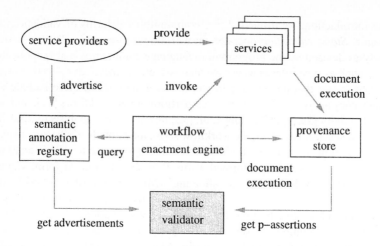

Fig. 1. Provenance-based validation architecture

tions (within a service), their inputs and outputs; likewise, a query interface caters for metadata-based discovery.

Users construct workflows for their experiments. The workflow enactment engine queries the registry for services that provide the tasks requested in the workflow and calls the appropriate services in the correct order. The services and the workflow enactment engine document the execution of the experiment using a provenance store. We refer to the provenance of some experimental result as the documentation of the process that led to that result. Each client and service (collectively, *actors*) in an experiment can assert facts about that experiment, called *p-assertions* (assertions, by an actor, pertaining to provenance). A p-assertion may state either the content of a message sent by one actor to another, an *interaction p-assertion*, or the state of an actor when an interaction took place, an *actor state p-assertion*. Examples of actor state p-assertions range from the workflow that is being executed, to the amount of disk and CPU a service used in a computation [16].

After the experiment is carried out, validation is performed using the algorithm outlined in Figure 2. Validation is done on a per activity basis. In this context, activities are service invocations in the experiment. The list of activities in an experiment is provided by the provenance store. For each activity, a, the validator computes two values for comparison — a requirement on the value of some property, R, and the actual value of that property used in the activity A. The validator then performs semantic reasoning over A and R to see if A fulfils all the requirements specified in R. If A satisfies R, then a is deemed to be valid. An experiment is valid when all activities are proved to be valid.

Figure 3 explains how requirement R and actual value A are calculated for a given activity a. First, the validator obtains provenance p-assertions for a from the provenance store. Using this provenance information, the validator fetches services' advertisements and semantic annotations from the registry. The user supplies extra information needed for validation, such as the bioinformatics ontology in Use Case 3 and the legal descriptions in Use Case 5.

```
isValid ← true
for all activities a do
    (R, A) ← Compute(a)
    isValid ← isValid ∧ (A satisfies R)
end for
```

Fig. 2. Algorithm for provenance-based validation. Requirement R and actual value A are calculated using the *Compute* function shown in Figure 3.

```
Function:  Compute requirement R and actual value A
Require:  activity a
    Retrieve p-assertions from provenance store
    Get advertisements from registry
    Get user supplied information
    R ← Compute requirements
    A ← Compute trace
```

Fig. 3. Algorithm to compute requirement R and actual value A

The type of information to obtain from the provenance store, the registry and the user depends on the actual validation to be performed. Similarly, the semantic reasoning needed to compare requirement R and actual value A also depends on the type of validation. The next section explains how the semantic validator implements the various types of validations identified by the use cases using the algorithms introduced in this section. Section 6 then discusses the semantic reasoning performed.

5   Validation Algorithms for the Use Cases

Figure 3 presented a generic algorithm for computing requirement R and actual value A of an activity by querying the provenance store and the registry. In this section, we apply the algorithm in Figure 3 to the use cases in Section 2.

5.1   Interface Level Interaction Validity

Use Case 1 requires the validation of workflow interactions at the interface level. A workflow is valid if data passed to all activities in the workflow conform to specifications in their WSDL interface documents, defined in XML schema. Specifically, the validator validates input XML documents (actual value A) against the schemas (requirement R). For each activity a, R and A are computed according to Figure 4. The validator queries the provenance store for the service and operation names of activity a. These names are used to obtain the WSDL document for the activity from the registry. The provenance store also provides the validator with a copy of the data passed to the activity in the experiment.

> Retrieve service/operation names of a from provenance store
> $R \leftarrow$ Get WSDL document for a from registry
> $A \leftarrow$ Retrieve input to a from provenance store

Fig. 4. Interface-level interaction validation: computing requirement R and actual value A for activity a

5.2 Domain Level Interaction Validity

To support Use Cases 2 and 3, we validate all interactions in a workflow execution using domain-level knowledge. For each activity a, we wish to compare the domain-level types of the data expected by the activity (R) with the actual data used (A). The domain-level type of the actual data passed to activity a is derived from the output of preceding operation p. (By preceding, we refer to the service that precedes activity a in terms of data flow, not time). In the simplest case, an interaction is considered domain-level valid if A is either the same type or a subtype of R. Figure 5 summarises how the two values R and A are computed. First, the validator queries the provenance store to obtain the service and operation names of activity a and preceding activity p. With the service and operation names, the validator retrieves the metadata attached to the WSDL message parts from the registry. Specifically, the validator is interested in the metadata for the output message part of operation p, and the metadata for the input message parts of the current operation a. The last piece of information the validator requires is the ontology. This is supplied by the user.

> Retrieve service/operation names of a from p-assertions
> Retrieve service/operation names of preceding activity p from p-assertions
> $R \leftarrow$ Get input domain-level type of a from registry
> $A \leftarrow$ Get output domain-level type of p from registry
> Get ontology from user

Fig. 5. Domain-level interaction validation: computing requirement R and actual value A for activity a

5.3 Activity Validity

To support Use Cases 4 and 5, we verify that the metadata associated with services conforms to certain criteria. We use the myGrid profile [17] to identify the tasks services perform. (The myGrid profile is an extension of the OWL-S profile [7]). Likewise, the profile also specifies databases usage restrictions. Thus, the process of verifying the activity validity of an experiment involves checking that each activity's profile satisfies the requirements specified for it. The requirement can be different for each activity, as in Use Case 4. In other situations, the requirement can be the same for every activity in the workflow, such as in Use Case 5.

An activity is considered to fulfil requirement R if the metadata annotation for the operation (A) is of the same class or is a subclass of R. Figure 6 shows the algorithm used for computing the values R and A for activity a. The validator first obtains the names of the service and operation for activity a from the provenance store. It then retrieves the semantic annotations of operation a from the registry. The user supplies the requirement R for the activity. In Use Case 4, R is the original plan of the experiment. In Use Case 5, R is the set of legal requirements devised according to patenting needs. Any required ontology is also supplied by the user.

Retrieve service and operation names of a from p-assertions
$A \leftarrow$ Get semantic annotation of a from registry
$R \leftarrow$ Get requirements from user
Get ontology from user

Fig. 6. Activity validation: computing requirement R and actual value A for activity a

After the validator computed the values R and A, it can verify whether A satisfies R, as shown in Figure 2. For Use Case 1, verification of satisfaction is performed using a validating XML parser. For the other use cases, semantic reasoning is required. This will be explained in the next section.

6   Semantic Reasoning for Validation

All of the algorithms presented in the previous section require some properties (type, legal restrictions etc.) of multiple entities to be compared. An exact match of types is inadequate for validation of an experiment, as illustrated in the examples below, and so semantic reasoning allows our architecture to take full advantage of the relationship between types encoded in ontologies. In this section, we illustrate some of the reasoning that can be employed by our validation architecture, with examples taken from a bioinformatics application in which we have tested a implementation of our architecture (see Section 7).

6.1   Validation by Generalisation

The simplest and most commonly required form of reasoning is to compare two types where one is a super-class of the other.

For example, database D may advertise its download operation as returning *RNA sequences*. Analysis service A advertises its analysis operation taking as input *nucleotide sequences*. The ontology specifies that both *DNA* and *RNA sequences* are subclasses of *Nucleotide sequences*. Therefore, the interaction between the download operation D and analysis service A is valid as the input type of A is a superclass of the output type of D.

Similarly, in Use Case 4, a plan is defined using high-level concepts to describe the operations to be performed at each stage of the experiment. For example, in the experiment plan for our sample bioinformatics application, one of the steps requires a *Compression* algorithm. The provenance records that a *PPMZ* algorithm was used in the experiment and, in the ontology, *PPMZ* algorithm is defined as a sub-class of *Compression* algorithm. Therefore, the semantic validator can verify that this operation conforms to the one in the original plan.

6.2 Validation of Inter-parameter Constraints

The same experiment provides cases for more novel forms of semantic description and reasoning in validation. One service, *gcode*, in our bioinformatics workflow takes two parameters: a sequence and a grouping alphabet. The sequence, which may represent either an amino acid sequence or a nucleotide sequence, is encoded as a sequence of symbols. The grouping alphabet specifies a set of non-overlapping groups of symbols, each group having a symbolic name. Service *gcode* replaces each symbol in the input sequence with the name of the group to which it belongs, so that the output of the service is a sequence of group names of the same length as the original sequence.

In order for the workflow to be semantically valid, the symbols used in the input sequence of *gcode* must have the same meaning as those making up groups in the grouping alphabet. That is, if the grouping alphabet specifies groups of nucleotides (A, G, C and T/U) then the input sequence should be a nucleotide sequence, and if the alphabet specifies groups of amino acids (A, B, C, D, E...) then the input sequence should be an amino acid sequence.

The ontology contains the concepts *Sequence* and *GroupingAlphabet* both of which are parameterised on the types of their elements, which can be either *Nucleotides* and *Amino Acids*. In the registry, the *gcode* service is annotated with metadata defining the semantic types of its input parameters. We wish to advertise the fact that the arguments used as input parameters to this service must have corresponding BaseTypes: if the sequence is made up of amino acids, the alphabet should also be. That is, one is a *Sequence* with property *hasElementType* with target X, the other is is a *GroupingAlphabet* with property *hasLetterType* with target Y and X is equal to Y. Because X and Y effectively denote variables to be instantiated in different ways in different experiments, it is impossible to express this constraint with OWL alone. Instead we can use technologies such as the Semantic Web Rule Language [18] or *role-value maps* [19], with which we can express that the value of one concept's property (X) must be equal to the value of another concept's property (Y) without giving the type of those values. This mechanism has also been used to specify configuration policies of registries [20].

The input sequence and the grouping alphabet are provided to *gcode* by two other actors, and these interactions are recorded in a provenance store. From the provenance data, the element type of the input sequence and the letter type of the grouping alphabet in a particular experiment can be determined.

7   Evaluation

In this section, we present our evaluation of validation framework in satisfying two of the use cases (Use Case 2 and Use Case 4) in a sample bioinformatics experiment.

For completeness, we briefly explain the intent of the experiment used in evaluating our architecture. A more detailed description of this experiment and its workflow can be found in [21]. The experiment, developed by Klaus-Peter Zauner and Stefan Artmann, studies the structure of protein sequences by analysing their compressibility. Proteins are amino acid chains that fold into unique 3D structures. This 3D shape of the protein determines its function. The structure of protein sequences is of considerable interest for predicting which sections of the DNA encode for proteins and for predicting and designing the 3D-shape of proteins. For comparative studies of the structure present in an amino acid, it is useful to determine their compressibility. This is because compression exploits context-dependent correlations within a sequence. The fraction of its original length to which a sequence can be losslessly compressed is an indication of the structure present in the sequence.

For the evaluation, we ran the workflow multiple times and recorded the executions in the provenance store. Both the provenance store and the registry were implemented as Web Services (available for download at pasoa.org and grimoires.org respectively). The semantic validation component was implemented in Java and used Jena 2.1 for reasoning over the ontology. The ontology itself was specified in OWL and based on the ontology developed by the bioinformatics Grid project, myGrid. After a set of workflow runs, each analysing one sample, the provenance store contains records of interactions between services. Each interaction record contains the invocation message that occurred in the workflow, which specifies the operation invoked and data exchanged as arguments. In addition to the message itself, the services record data links that specify when the output of one service has been used as the input of another service. Collectively, the data links describe the data flow throughout the experiment. The full provenance data for one workflow run was approximately 1 MB in size. For the

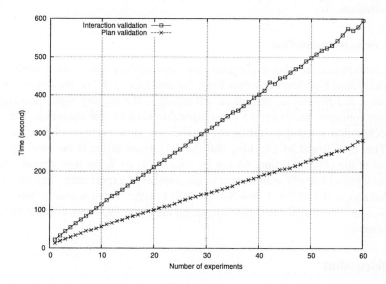

Fig. 7. Evaluation of interaction validity and conformance to plan for an increasing number of experiments

evaluation, we deployed the registry on a Windows XP PC with Pentium 4 CPU, 3 GHz, 2 GB RAM, and the provenance store and semantic validator on another Windows XP PC with Pentium 4 CPU, 1.5 GHz, 2 GB RAM. The PCs were connected by a 100Mb local ethernet. The results of each experiment is described in further detail below.

Two forms of validation were implemented, corresponding to Use Cases 2 and 4, implementing the algorithms in Figures 5 and 6 respectively. Given that we intend large numbers of experiments to be performed, it is critical to that our approach scales well as the amount of data in the provenance store expands. Therefore, we performed the validation process on all experiments in the provenance store as we increase the number of experiments. Figure 7 shows the performance of the semantic validation architecture as the number of experiments for which provenance documentation is recorded and are to be validated increases.

7.1   Interaction Validity, Domain Level

In the interaction validity experiment, the type of each output message part in the experiment was compared with the type of the input message part of the succeeding invocations in which it was used. We obtained the names of the input and output message parts from the provenance store. We then use these names to obtain their domain level types from the registry. The domain level types are ontology terms. The comparison is done by checking if the output type is the same class or a subclass of the input type. Specifically, we use the member functions hasSuperClass and equals of the OntClass interface in Jena. As can be seen in Figure 7, the time required for validation increases linearly with respect to the number of experiments. In total, one test included a total of $452N + 1$ Web Service calls to either the provenance store and registry plus $48N$ occurrences of reasoning using the ontology, where N is the number of experiments.

7.2   Conformance to Plan

In the conformance to plan experiment, the planned data flow of each experiment is expressed using high-level concepts from the ontology to define the operations to be performed, and the service operations advertised in the registry were annotated with low-level concepts specifying the exact algorithm used by that operation. The validator checked that every data link in the provenance store corresponded to one in the plan. This is achieved by checking that the performed action is the same class or a subclass of the planned action. As can be seen in Figure 7, the time required for validation increases linearly with respect to the number of experiments. In total, one test included a total of $260N + 1$ Web Service calls to either the provenance store and registry plus $48N$ occurrences of reasoning using the ontology, where N is the number of experiments.

8   Discussion

The myGrid and CombeChem (combechem.org) projects have also worked on the problems of provenance recording and service description, and adopted RDF-based approaches, making ontology-based reasoning a possibility. However, neither identify the architectural elements required for validation nor provide a generic, domain-independent way to satisfy use cases such as those presented in this paper.

As our design is dictated by pragmatic considerations, we have adopted a hybrid approach to information representation. Provenance information is made available by the provenance store as XML documents. Inside the data structure representing provenance, we may find assertions, made by some actors. These assertions may be expressed using semantic web technologies. For instance, the function performed by a service or a description of its internal state expressed using OWL. In the registry, annotations provided by third parties may be encoded in the formalism of their choice. We have explicitly experimented with OWL and RDFS. Therefore, semantic reasoning (based either on OWL or RDFS technology) only operates on a subset of the provenance representation and some descriptions published in the registry.

This hybrid approach to representation suits the intensive data processing requirements of Grid applications. For roughly 10 days of computation over 100 nodes, we expect our provenance store to accumulate approximately $10 \times 100 \times 24 \times 60 \times 60 \times 20 = 1,728,000,000$ invocations to be described for the provenance of a data set. Selectively identifying the elements to reason over is therefore essential. All our use cases operate using the same reasoning pattern, which consists of identifying the provenance of some data and iterating on all its records. More advanced use cases will result in new patterns of processing. As all possible patterns cannot be anticipated, we allow users to use declarative specifications of what they expect from computations. Policy languages such as KAoS [20] are strong contenders for this problem. KAoS positive and negative obligations allow us to encode what has to occur, or what should not occur. For example, we can introduce a policy for a transactional system that requires every action to be committed or rolled back by the end of an experiment. The challenge will be to integrate the KAoS reasoner (also OWL based) with the potentially large size of the provenance store.

9 Conclusions

Grid based e-Science experiments typically involve multiple heterogeneous computing resources across a large, open and distributed network. As the complexity of experiments grows, determining whether results produced are meaningful becomes an increasingly difficult task. In this paper, we studied the problem of validation on such experiments. Traditionally, program validation is carried out either statically or at run-time. However, the usefulness of either approach is limited for large scale e-Science experiments. Static analyses rely on the availability of workflow scripts. These scripts may not be expressed in languages that analysis tools operate on, or may not be available because they are exposed as web services. Run-time service-based error checking is service dependent and users may not have control over its configuration.

We propose an alternative, provenance-based approach to experiment validation. The provenance of an experiment documents the complete process that led to the results. As a result, validation is not reliant on the availability of workflow scripts or service configurations. Moreover, as science progresses, criteria for validation evolve. Using a provenance-based approach, the validation process can be repeated without re-running the experiment. By employing technologies for provenance recording, annotation of service descriptions and semantic reasoning, we have produced an effective solution to the validation problem. Algorithms working over the automatically recorded documentation of experiments and utilising the semantic descriptions of experimental services in registries can test the validity of results to satisfy various domain-independent and domain-specific use cases.

To demonstrate the viability of our semantic validation architecture, we have discussed how it can be used with various algorithms and forms of semantic reasoning to satisfy five use cases. We have also implemented two of the use cases. Performance tests show our algorithms scale linearly as the amount of provenance documentation recorded increases.

Acknowledgements

This research is funded in part by the Grimoires (EPSRC Grant GR/S90843/01), my-Grid (EPSRC Grant GR/R67743/01) and PASOA (EPSRC Grant GR/S67623/01) projects. The authors would also like to thank Klaus-Peter Zauner and Stefan Artmann for providing us with the bioinformatics experiment.

References

1. Foster, I., Kesselman, C., Tuecke, S.: The anatomy of the grid: Enabling scalable virtual organizations. International Journal of High Performance Computing Applications **15** (2001) 200–222
2. Gil, Y., Deelman, E., Blythe, J., Kesselman, Tangmunarunkit, H.: Artificial intelligence and grids: workflow planning and beyond. IEEE Intelligent Systems **19** (2004) 26–33
3. Consortium, T.G.O.: The Gene Ontology (GO) database and informatics resource. Nucleic Acids Research **32** (2004) 258–261
4. Christensen, E., Curbera, F., Meredith, G., Weerawarana, S.: Web services description language (WSDL) 1.1. Technical report, W3C Note, http://www.w3.org/TR/wsdl (2001)
5. Fallside, D.C., Walmsley, P.: XML schema part 0: Primer second edition. Technical report, W3C Recommendation, http://www.w3.org/TR/xmlschema-0 (2004)
6. Mitra, N.: SOAP version 1.2 part 0: Primer. Technical report, W3C Recommendation, http://www.w3.org/TR/soap12-part0 (2004)
7. Martin, D., Burstein, M., Hobbs, J., Lassila, O., McDermott, D., McIlraith, S., Narayanan, S., Paolucci, M., Parsia, B., Payne, T., Sirin, E., Srinivasan, N., Sycara, K.: OWL-S: Semantic markup for web services. Technical report, W3C Member Submission, http://www.w3.org/Submission/OWL-S (2004)
8. Wroe, C., Goble, C., Greenwood, M., Lord, P., Miles, S., Papay, J., Payne, T., Moreau, L.: Automating experiments using semantic data on a bioinformatics grid. IEEE Intelligent Systems **19** (2004) 48–55
9. Miles, S., Papay, J., Luck, M., Moreau, L.: Towards a protocol for the attachment of metadata to grid service descriptions and its use in semantic discovery. Scientific Programming **12** (2004) 201–211

10. Lee, M., Han, D., Shim, J.: Set-based access conflicts analysis of concurrent workflow definition. In: Proceedings of Third International Symposium on Cooperative Database Systems and Applications, Beijing, China (2001) 189–196
11. Baresi, L., Maurino, A., Modafferi, S.: Workflow partitioning in mobile information systems. In: Proceedings of IFIP TC8 Working Conference on Mobile Information Systems (MOBIS 2004), Oslo, Norway, Springer (2004) 93–106
12. Eshuis, R., Wieringa, R.: Verification support for workflow design with uml activity graphs. In: Proceedings of the 24th International Conference on Software Engineering. (2002) 166–176
13. Yang, L., Bundy, A., Berry, D., Huczynska, S.: Inferring quality of service properties for grid applications. In: CS poster, EPSRC e-Science Meeting, Edinburgh, UK, NeSC (2004) static analysis of workflows.
14. Blythe, J., Deelman, E., Gil, Y.: Planning for workflow construction and maintenance on the grid. In: ICAPS 2003 workshop on planning for web services. (2003)
15. Uszok, A., Bradshaw, J.M., Jeffers, R.: KAOS: A policy and domain services framework for grid computing and semantic web services. In Jensen, C., Poslad, S., Dimitrakos, T., eds.: Trust Management: Second International Conference (iTrust 2004) Proceedings. Volume 2995 of Lecture Notes in Computer Science., Oxford, UK, Springer (2004) 16–26
16. Miles, S., Groth, P., Branco, M., , Moreau, L.: The requirements of recording and using provenance in e-science experiments. Technical report, Electronics and Computer Science, University of Southampton (2005)
17. Wroe, C., Stevens, R., Goble, C., Roberts, A., Greenwood, M.: A suite of DAML+OIL ontologies to describe bioinformatics web services and data. nternational Journal of Cooperative Information Systems 12 (2003) 197–224
18. Horrocks, I., Patel-Schneider, P.F., Boley, H., Tabet, S., Grosof, B., Dean, M.: SWRL: A semantic web rule language combining OWL and RULEML. Technical report, DARPA Agent Markup Language (DAML) Program, http://www.daml.org/2003/11/swrl/ (2003)
19. Schmidt-Schauss, M.: Subsumption in KL-ONE is undecidable. In Brachman, R.J., Levesque, H.J., Reiter, R., eds.: Proceedings of the 1st International Conference on the Principles of Knowledge Representation and Reasoning (KR89), Morgan Kaufmann (1989) 421–431
20. Moreau, L., Bradshaw, J., Breedy, M., Bunch, L., Johnson, M., Kulkarni, S., Lott, J., Suri, N., Uszok, A.: Behavioural specification of grid services with the KAOS policy language. In: Proceedings of Cluster Computing and Grid (CCGrid), Cardiff, UK (2005)
21. Groth, P., Miles, S., Fang, W., Wong, S.C., Zauner, K.P., Moreau, L.: Recording and using provenance in a protein compressibility experiment. In: Proceedings of the 14th IEEE International Symposium on High Performance Distributed Computing (HPDC-14), NC, USA (2005)

Semantic Service Integration for Water Resource Management

Ross Ackland[1], Kerry Taylor[1], Laurent Lefort[1], Mark Cameron[1],
and Joel Rahman[2]

[1] CSIRO, ICT Centre, GPO Box 664, Canberra, ACT 2601, Australia
{ross.ackland, kerry.taylor, laurent.lefort,
mark.cameron}@csiro.au
http://www.ict.csiro.au/
[2] eWater Cooperative Research Centre, CSIRO Land and Water,
GPO Box 1666, Canberra ACT, 2601, Australia
joel.rahman@csiro.au
http://www.catchment.crc.org.au

Abstract. Water resource management is becoming increasingly difficult due to the interaction of conflicting factors such as environmental sustainability and economic constraints. In Australia, the introduction of a water rights management framework is an administrative attempt to facilitate the resolution of this complex and multi-faceted problem. Policies relating to water allocation and trading have already advanced beyond our abilities to monitor, measure, report and enforce these policies. Mismanagement of this valued resource can have severe damaging long term environmental and economic effects. We believe that Semantic Web Services technologies will help decision makers minimise the risk of mismanagement. In this paper, we discuss the potential application of our dynamic service composition approach and its compatibility with other solutions. We identify the benefits for the different categories of users and discuss how ontologies can help to bridge the gap between specialists and non-specialists, or specialists focusing on separate aspects of the overall problem.

1 Introduction

Water is becoming a highly valued resource not only in Australia but in many countries around the world. This value is driving the need for improving the efficiency of water management practices. In the Australian context, water management is a complex relationship between demand and supply, moderated by water rights trading. Intelligent water allocation, extraction and trading are essentially a process of economic optimization integrated with hydrologic network modelling. Decisions need to be made at both the micro (irrigator on farm) and macro (government policy making) levels. Water resource allocation is driven by a variety of environmental, economic and social factors, as well as physical constraints of the distribution systems. Decisions on water usage are based on data from information sources that include historical datasets, policy information, real time data and predictive simulation models that need to be executed at the time of decision making and evaluated on an ongoing basis.

Decisions are made by a variety of stakeholders, each operating on a different time horizon (from days to years) at different geographic extents, with different decision

Y. Gil et al. (Eds.): ISWC 2005, LNCS 3729, pp. 816–828, 2005.

making goals and from very different contexts. For example, an individual farmer makes decisions about ordering water from a reservoir for extraction from the river in a matter of days. A regional water management agency may allocate water to consumptive users within a large catchment on an annual or seasonal timescale.

In this paper, we examine issues associated with water resource management in Australia in the context of allocation and trading. We then look at current information systems used by decision makers and the need for improved model data fusion. We introduce the need for a framework in which a new class of applications can exist and show how semantic technologies are a critical component to this framework in order to improve present approaches for linking data and models together. We characterise the data management and model integration problem to be addressed within the Australian context. We discuss how our approach to service composition can complement the existing approaches and identify the potential benefits.

2 Water Resource Management in Australia

The Australian climate is dry and highly erratic with long droughts alternating with periods of intensive and localized flooding. Additionally, water use has increased dramatically over the last two decades due mainly to the increase in irrigated agriculture. Producers are continually planning to avoid losses by protecting themselves against drought, as well as capitalising on high rainfall years. Water management is defined and regulated by each of the State and Territory Government authorities and in most states a licencing system regulates water access and distribution [3]. In most cases, a water licence is no absolute, but gives a right to use a specified amount of the available resource for a given time and within a given region. Water rights can also be withdrawn or altered at any time without any statutory guarantee of compensation. Water rights are defined in volumetric terms with several classes of rights. The two broad categories of water rights are surface water rights (access to streams and rivers) and groundwater rights (access to artesian aquifers). Within these categories water rights are classified into several priority classes that entitle the holder access to a share of the water available to each class.

2.1 Water Allocation

Allocation is the process of establishing and enforcing water demand. Planning for both environmental allocation and irrigation demand is undertaken by the relevant agencies within each state or territory. Unfortunately there have been a number of instances of over allocated systems, where too many licences have been issued for consumptive use such that the extraction of the total licenced volume would threaten the minimum reserve required for environmental sustainability. These situations are not necessarily the result of poor planning but more an indication of the complexity of the interaction between economic, social and environmental benefits and costs at different levels of geographic scale.

In an attempt to alleviate the situation of allocation errors, agencies are adopting adaptive management practices where they can respond more rapidly to changing circumstances such as unpredicted climatic change, new scientific evidence, changing community values and so on. The downside of this approach is that increased government intervention can have an adverse affect on financial investments that rely on water allocation. We are currently faced with the difficulty in determining whether the environmental allocations are actually achieved, due to the limited measuring and reporting that takes place, especially where a distributor provides water to users on a commercial basis.

2.2 Water Trading

Now that availability of water is becoming increasingly scarce, water trading is emerging as a means of efficiently allocating rights. In moving toward free trading of water rights, market based solutions for water management will be difficult to implement. Long term commitment is needed by governments and the private sector and the dynamics of a market system for a natural resource such as water include some unique difficulties, such as:

- Long distance trading – losses that occur between original and new locations;
- Exchange rate is difficult to calculate due to hydrological differences when trading occurs across catchments;
- Wide variety of transaction costs;
- The drivers for permanent and temporary water entitlements are different.

Water trading has been in existence in Australia for some time and tentative steps have already been taken with trial systems for interstate water trading [4], [16]. The success of these trials has resulted in the creation of water markets now covering larger geographic areas and involving a greater number of traders and brokers.

Water management, in particular allocation and trading, is essentially a process of optimization that involves the integration of water balance models, climatic models and economic models. Traditionally, the process has comprised the selection and development of appropriate modelling tools to support policy development and decision making processes by water authorities. While the tools themselves may originate from different domains (hydrologic and economic) there also exists a broader community of potential users that could benefit from access to these tools.

Irrigators and allocators (authorities responsible for establishing and regulating water allocation limits) require access to the same information and services although they are engaged in addressing problems at differing geographic and temporal scales. Allocators need to consider the conflicting interests of the different stakeholders which include environmental interests as well as economic [13].

Water trading has been available to land holders with water entitlements in the Southern NSW and Victorian regions of Australia since the completion of the Murray-Darling pilot project[1]. Watermove[2] is one example of an online web based water exchange facility operated by Goulburn-Murray Water Authority. An irrigator's decision to trade water will be sensitive to water prices as well as current and future farm product prices [18] and seasonal conditions [1]. As the Watermove web site

---

[1] http://www.mdbc.gov.au/naturalresources/watertrade/pilot_watertrade.htm
[2] http://www.watermove.com.au

suggests, there are a number of factors a trader should take into account when considering an offer. These include: seasonal allocation compared with previous seasons, water use in current season compared with previous seasons, cost of alternatives. (e.g. dairy farmers buying feed), prices paid for temporary water in the region, price trends, price volatility, water volumes available, tariff structures and whether any delivery charge will apply to water purchased and used. Although the establishment of zones, trading rules and exchange rates are fairly static compared with other trading systems such as energy and finance, it becomes increasingly difficult to predict outcomes as the geographic scale increases. For example, the trading variations occur across zones which contain separate tributaries that may impact down stream water balances. Add to this unpredictable climatic conditions and the dynamics of the system become much more interesting to all parties. To define long term policies for catchment or basin level regions, we need appropriate data and predictive models for all types of water use that allow analysis at a whole of system level in order to support the next round of water reforms.

It is clear that an environment that can provide requirements based problem expression, resource discovery, service composition and iterative problem execution, will potentially benefit a broad community of users.

3 Current Approaches in Model and Data Integration

There has been an increasing emphasis in recent years on providing more integrated information services to Australian natural resource managers. However these initiatives have typically focused either on data delivery or on simulation modelling and rarely on both. These new services have introduced considerable flexibility to their consumers, but are still based on relatively rigid models of interaction, and each are configured to answer a limited set of questions at very specific spatial and temporal scales.

3.1 Data Services

Natural resource managers regularly require access to spatial and temporal data, which in Australia is held by a variety of organizations in each jurisdiction. This data is gradually being made available through online data portals, such as the Victoria Water Resource Data Warehouse[3]. The range of natural resource data available online in Australia includes hydrologic data[4], climate data[5], soils information[6] and various derivative products, such as Sentinel Hotspots[7] used for bushfire detection. CANRI[8] and the NSW Natural Resource Atlas[9] are good examples of web based access to natural resource datasets available to a broad user community.

---

[3] http://www.vicwaterdata.net
[4] Ibid
[5] http://www.nrm.qld.gov.au/silo/, http://www.bom.gov.au
[6] http://www.asris.csiro.au
[7] http://www.sentinel.csiro.au
[8] http://www.canri.nsw.gov.au
[9] http://www.nratlas.nsw.gov.au

While these and other services represent an improvement over previous, more manual forms of data provision and exchange, they still suffer from a number of problems, particularly a lack of integration with models. Many users of data services expect to use the data as input to models, although often significant and time consuming pre-processing must occur before the data can be used.

Additionally there is increasing need to use real-time data sourced from sensor networks that allow monitoring and control of water use. To meet this need, such data must be provided dynamically and in a form to support its ready integration with a wide variety of other information resources.

3.2 Model Services

Predictive modelling is becoming central to natural resource management for purposes such as considering the impacts of a new policy, or performing a priority allocation of restoration funding in order to achieve a desired outcome. There is a need for models to become more accessible, for use by a wide range of stakeholders, and more integrative, by including a range of biophysical considerations. Several large modelling initiatives have, in recent years, addressed these issues of accessibility and integration of models developed to match the requirements of different categories of users [6], [12].

3.3 Model Integration Services

Model integration frameworks have been designed to facilitate the integration from broad scale water quality models[10] to complex models examining water allocation scenarios in circumstances ranging from 'what-if' analyses in public stakeholder workshops to seasonal water allocations by legislative authorities. The Catchment Modelling Toolkit[11] is a suite of environmental modelling products, engineered with high level user interfaces delivered through an online community and supported through regular training workshops. The toolkit has made its suite of catchment models available to a wide range of industry stakeholders and consultants. Central to the Toolkit is a framework, TIME [14], that supports toolkit model development and integration. TIME is based on the Microsoft .NET[12] platform and supports the development of spatial and temporal models in standard programming languages.

The Harmon-IT[13] project focuses on integrating existing catchment models by defining a standard protocol for communications between models called openMI[14]. Using this approach, wrappers can be created for legacy models, while models under active development can have the protocol embedded directly.

The Dynamic Information Architecture System DIAS[15], is designed for the simulation of complex dynamic systems and supports both the development of new models and the integration, through wrappers of legacy models.

---

[10] For example, CMSS: http://www.clw.csiro.au/products/cmss
[11] http://www.toolkit.net.au
[12] http://www.microsoft.com/net
[13] www.harmonit.org
[14] http://www.openmi.org
[15] http://www.dis.anl.gov/DIAS

RIMIS [7] is a Web Services based system designed to support regional landscape managers in posing 'what if' questions for catchment-scale salinity and water quality problems. RIMIS integrates hydrological, economic and social simulation models and is built on an infrastructure that enables distributed data and service coordination across organizations. This allows catchment managers to describe their problems and scenarios using data and modelling services from participating state government and local council organizations. RIMIS uses workflow technologies to provide a solution to the problem of obtaining data and coordinating model execution. However, the construction of workflows is not based on semantic descriptions of data and services, making it a difficult task for domain experts.

Hydra3 [15] is an older model integration technology which lacked the modern advantages offered by Web Services for interoperability but attempted to drive model-data and model-model integration through the use of declarative specifications of mapping relationships. This approach to interoperability is now driving much of the semantic web services research agenda.

3.4 Limitations of Current Systems

Water resources management is dependent on information about water distribution, utilization and knowledge of water quality and availability. Improvements in water resource management will be driven by our ability to improve access to environmental data integrated with predictive models. Data and models currently exist in abundance as isolated self contained systems that make integration across these systems problematic. Recent advances in environmental sensing technologies provide an opportunity to collect information about our environment at much higher spatial and temporal resolutions. However, without an underlying framework to facilitate intelligent integration of models and data there will be little benefit gained in generating orders of magnitude more data from real time sensor networks.

Environmental Modelling Frameworks like TIME and OpenMI are an improvement over product-centered integration approaches such as Arc Hydro[16], and HEC[17], but they do not solve all the issues linked to model complexity [11] and component interoperability over multiple frameworks [2] for which Web Services with richer semantics are seen as a viable option. Semantic technologies will mean that integrated, problem based software applications will no longer need to "hardcode what to do with each data item" [17], so that the task of investigating problems and making decisions can be placed in the hands of key information users, without the mediation of software technologists.

4   A Framework for Water Resources Monitoring and Management

The Water Resources Observation Network (WRON) is a concept envisioned by CSIRO as a distributed network integrating a range of technologies for acquiring,

---

[16] http://www.crwr.utexas.edu/giswr/hydro
[17] http://www.hec.usace.army.mil

storing, analyzing, visualizing and interpreting environmental and economic data relating to water resource management at a national scale. WRON will require collaboration and participation by many agencies and stakeholders within Australia. The goal for WRON is to facilitate the development of next generation modelling and decision support tools and be able to deliver those tools to a much wider range of water resource users utilizing dynamic model-data fusion techniques. Essential to WRON will be the efficient and seamless linkage of the following elements:

- Legacy databases held by various custodians. These are typically spatial databases such as terrain, soil and land cover datasets, also time series hydrometric data (eg: climate, water levels and physio-chemical parameters);
- Field based sensor networks that measure climatic, in stream, groundwater, landscape and ecosystem parameters in real time at much higher resolutions (both spatially and temporally) than currently available;
- Remotely sensed data sources such as soil moisture, soil temperature, evapotranspiration, vegetation indexes and land use activities, reported in near real time;
- Predictive models and decision support tools for uncertainty estimation, optimization and multi-criterion analysis available as re-useable building blocks rather than self contained systems;
- Computational resources that automatically enable the execution of compute intensive applications deployed across the network.

We identify three categories of users for the WRON. These are: users with an administrative role in charge of reporting water usage on the basis of the presently available data and knowledge; users with an operational role, in charge of day-to-day management of some parts of the system; and users with a planning role, preparing decisions affecting the future on the basis of 'what if' models.

The common theme among these users is that they are all working within a scenario driven environment where problem expression capabilities would range from specification (*how much water should I buy/sell today?*) through simulation (*what is the effect on diversion limits if demand increases by 20%*), analysis (*given current climatic conditions, and my usage profile, actions recommended include …*), monitoring (*I need to know when consumption is exceeding diversion limits*) and evolution to reiterate the problem definition. Enabling flexible and efficient problem management is a key component in translating WRON's technological underpinnings into domain specific problem focused tools that have meaning and impact for users.

5   Semantic Web Services Composition

There are many desirable features of current and emerging semantic web tools that can provide solutions to the WRON needs, especially those tools developing around Semantic Web Services. It is particularly attractive to leverage the high-impact Web Services standards together with the emerging descriptive and inferencing capability of the Semantic Web. Our work is adopting these tools for resource description, workflow enactment, and service interoperability, together with declarative data integration technology, to address the WRON needs. In this section we emphasise the need for machine interpretable resource description, and outline how this can be used, together with other intelligent technologies, to realise the WRON.

5.1 Why We Need Formal Resource Descriptions

In order to support the wide diversity of rich data and processing resources required for water resources management, as well as the wide diversity of expected users, it is important to have declarative, computationally-interpretable resource descriptions.

A traditional approach to resource descriptions would have a body of like-minded people recognising a common information need to meet and establish a data format standard for information exchange. Nowadays, such a format would certainly rely on XML. Once a resource can be encoded in a standard format it can also be described with external metadata in a fairly simple way following another standard such as ANZLIC[18] or Dublin Core[19]. Inevitably, any previous standard for data format encoding or metadata will be either too broad (requiring coverage of areas that are of no interest to the current problem) or too narrow (not supporting sufficiently specific description for the current problem). Large scale attempts to standardise a common information model for frameworks such as the WRON, either in terms of data formats or metadata formats, are doomed to fail [17]. They will be expensive and slow and will surely hinder development in a multi-party environment that requires infrastructure development to proceed within widely varying time, budget and goal constraints of participating organisations and application needs.

A computationally interpretable resource description has many advantages in making software components more generally applicable over a range of evolving, different, flexible resource types. This capability is a much more natural fit with the nature of feasible WRON development. For example, the use of hierarchical classifications to support discovery of modelling components has been established in the natural resources domain [10] and using the added value of OWL[20] to support contextually-based discovery of resources of software modules, has been demonstrated in [9].

An important feature of formal resource descriptions is that there is no reason for any particular classification to be authoritative: multiple independent or co-dependent ontologies may be created to meet community needs as they arise. Software tools to navigate, select, and manipulate data may be entirely independent of any particular ontology because the ontology itself is manipulated as a data object with well defined semantics, amenable to semantic inferencing.

What can this semantic inferencing offer? Firstly, it offers an advantage for rapid ontology design through acquisition and merging of multiple pre-existing ontology resources. Information sources containing the standard knowledge shared by specialists in their domain of expertise are readily found and can be converted into formal domain ontologies. Semantic inferencing assists in the construction of sound and non-trivial ontologies.

Secondly, it offers a degree of automation in classification of resources, described using ontological terminology. This classification is valuable for software components, data types, data models, and structured data sets, including databases. It can

---

[18] http://www.anzlic.org.au
[19] http://dublincore.org
[20] http://www.w3.org/TR/owl-features

assist in both resource discovery (through support for classification, browsing and querying ontological structures), and resource assembly (through machine assisted goal seeking and data type inference). For example, it will be possible for a WRON user to describe their problem domain in terms of an ontology, rather than in terms of WRON resources. Good resource descriptions will enable the expertise embedded in models to be exposed: constraints relating to time, location, and physical parameters can be interpreted by software to validate their use in a user problem context. Data format translation services will be invoked automatically as necessary.

Thirdly, it offers some resilience to change in domain applications assembled from underlying resources. If the assembly of resources to meet application goals is specified at a conceptual, abstract level, and machine processable inference can be employed to ground the specification to concrete resources, then the abstract specification will be isolated from many of the changes at the resource level. This is analogous to the value gained from interpreters and compilers for high level programming languages—they enable a machine recompilation step to translate a high level specification to work for different platform architectures.

Fourthly, and perhaps most importantly, semantic inferencing is crucial to avoiding death by standardisation. Where community standards can be developed or pre exist for data formats and terminology, they are very valuable community assets. But where they don't exist, semantic descriptions, coupled with machine interpretable mapping rules and semantic inferencing can be used to relate pre existing WRON resources to an application domain model of choice at run time. For example, provided that a water quality time series dataset description formally identifies that the "BOD" element corresponds to "bio chemical oxygen demand" and that it is measured in "milligrams per litre", on a "daily timestep", at a fixed geo-location, the integration of this information with another biological oxygen demand measurement data set, recorded and labelled in a different format, but described in a consistent terminology, is straightforward machine processing. Furthermore, appropriate machine generated metadata (itself amenable to semantic inferencing) should be attached to generated information products by this method, so that there is also the potential to explain any deficiencies or assumptions made in creating the new information for scientific scrutiny.

The need for the WRON computational infrastructure to support heterogeneity in data resources is only exacerbated by the desire to provide data access for real time sensor networks. Autonomous water quality sensors are themselves an emerging technology: their capabilities for measurement parameters vary widely already and divergence will continue over time as legacy sensors will co-exist with modern types. This makes it very important to capture descriptions of sensor capability and limitation within the computational infrastructure, so that machine reasoning, as before, can be used to match sensor data to the requirements of an application problem.

5.2   How the WRON Might Work

Our vision for the WRON comprises basic resources, reference ontologies and mappings, a problem definition tool, and a sophisticated Web Services based run time environment. Basic resources are published to the WRON with Web Service interfaces. These resources comprise data as files, databases, sensors, and complex software components embedding expert knowledge such as model algorithms. These resources are enriched with extra information as resource descriptions in terms of a reference ontology and mappings that permit computational interpretations. For data resources such as databases, this description is centred on the data model itself. For services exposing software components such as hydrological models, it also provides an understanding of the functional meaning to assist the selection of the right model and capture knowledge on how to link models from various origins together. This approach is workable if and only if resource specific concepts are managed independently of each other.

Reference ontologies, like "neutral ontologies" [17], capture domain knowledge in a resource independent manner. Basic resources are related to one or more reference ontologies through machine interpretable, declarative mappings. Logical languages provide a very good basis for this purpose [5], [8] but closer integration with ontology languages is still needed. While there may be considerable effort in establishing the semantic content, especially to generate large reference ontologies, this activity is useful in more than one way. The information collected can also be used to generate metadata to document and complete the translation done at the various stages of the service composition. That is, much of the metadata for problem specific composed services may be produced for free.

Specification of application problems proceeds through user interaction with the resources and ontologies in an "ontology based specification" approach as described in the following section. This interaction produces an artefact which we call a problem definition. Queries expressed in terms of the problem definition are answered in a run time environment that dynamically interprets the definition and coordinates services to respond with an integrated result.

5.3 How a User Works with the WRON

At one level, a user may interact with the WRON in a very traditional way - to use the rich resource descriptions to locate web services and data resources to meet their needs. A simple application would provide a search based interface for a web user to discover datasets based on metadata keywords for example. However, much of the perceived benefit for WRON relies on providing the capability to create new resources or services out of the basic resources. These new resources would be available for reuse just as basic resources are. To describe how this works, we focus on a scientific expert WRON user – someone aiming to offer their expertise into the community through development of a specialist application, perhaps to assist irrigators in water allocation decisions.

We envisage the development of a new application to proceed as follows. A domain expert works with a specialist tool (we call it the "Composers Workbench") to browse reference ontologies as sources of knowledge about the target application domain concepts. In doing so, the expert selects domain concepts and defines a problem specification for the application in mind. By virtue of the fact that network resources have been previously linked to reference ontologies, the domain expert is also simultaneously selecting an assembly of resources to satisfy the specification. By employing rich semantic descriptions to the full, the expert is free to be only as specific about the exact resource selection as desirable for the problem at hand. The expert may supplement the definition with specific calibration or parameter data appropriate to the problem. The problem itself will certainly evolve as the expert redefines and tests the automatically generated service implementation. When complete, the expert may deploy the service composition as a first class resource, the interface of which is exposed as yet another web service. The service conceptual description (as OWL) and interface (as WSDL), together with a computational implementation of the service may be automatically derived from the specification. That is, the service now becomes a WRON accessible Web Service resource available to the wider community of users. Depending on the application needs, the Web Service may need to be supplemented with a specialist GUI for presentation and user interaction, such as that offered by the Catchment Modelling Toolkit for example.

When using the service, a specific run time query is combined with the abstract specification of the service and transformed at run time to an executable workflow. We use an automated planner to derive an optimal, executable process specification with temporal relationships between component execution derived automatically. Declarative constraints on component applicability are interpreted in the context of the run time data. The workflow may be generated in a choice of languages, including the Web standard BPEL4WS[21]. A workflow engine is used to orchestrate the calls to each individual resource in an asynchronous manner. These workflows may coordinate tens or hundreds of activities, including activities for authorisation, multi database semi joins, translations of data types and units of measurement, data chunking to match service capability, computational and data intensive models, and managing temporary storage of intermediate results.

6 Conclusions

To improve our understanding of the impact of Water Reforms and monitoring the state of catchments with a range of multi disciplinary focuses, we need to keep pace with the rapidly increasing volume and availability of data and the increasing richness and sophistication of models available. Environmental Modelling frameworks are now adopting appropriate standards and common software engineering practices which will facilitate the move to Web Services. It is for this reason we believe the timing is ideal to consider the adoption of Semantic Web technologies. We believe the semantic richness required to work on hydrological problems is already expressed in "de facto standards" from collaborative projects (Arc Hydro, HydroML[22], HarmonIT, Harmoniqua[23], CUAHSI[24]) and further refined in the work to develop the Upper Ontology for Hydrology[25] developed at Drexel University and other projects such as SWEET[26].

A large part of our work to date has been in building domain-independent infrastructure tools for ontology engineering, problem definition, query planning, work-

---

[21] Developed by Microsoft, IBM, and BEA http://www.oasis-open.org

[22] http://water.usgs.gov/nwis_activities/XML/nwis_hml.htm

[23] http://harmoniqua.wau.nl

[24] http://www.cuahsi.org

[25] http://loki.cae.drexel.edu/~how/upper/2003/12/upper.html

[26] http://sweet.jpl.nasa.gov/ontology

flow generation and workflow execution. Prototype versions of our tools now exist and the next stage will be the deployment and evaluation of these tools in variety of application domains. Our work permits a fine grained approach to service interaction whereby process-oriented workflows are automatically generated from declarative specifications. This means the resulting workflows may be more complex and better optimised than those created from flow-based specification tools. For example, Oracle's BPEL Designer[27], which provides a neat graphical user interface to describe a workflow, is inappropriate for editing and maintaining workflows that invoke hundreds of services. We are also developing tools that can assist domain specialists in the creation of ontologies from content available in a range of existing formats. Many sources of knowledge rich content are presently under exploited and we hope to improve what is often seen as a tedious and timely process. We believe the increased level of automation these semantic tools can provide has the potential to significantly reduce the effort required in building applications and to enable knowledge specialists to effectively build their own applications without the need for the software specialist.

References

1. Appels, D., Douglas, R., Dwyer, G.: Responsiveness of Demand for Irrigation. Water: A Focus on the Southern Murray-Darling Basin August 2004. http://www.pc.gov.au/research/swp/rdia/rdia.pdf
2. Argent, Y. R. and Rizzoli, A. E.: Development of Multi-Framework Model Components Proceedings of iEMSs 2004, Osnabrück, Germany, 14-17 June 2004. http://www.iemss.org/iemss2004/pdf/integratedmodelling/argedeve.pdf
3. Banks, G.: Water Rights Arrangements in Australia and Overseas. Australian Government Productivity Commission Research Paper. ISBN 1-74037-131-3. October 2003.
4. Bjornlund, H.: Efficient Water Market Mechanisms to Cope with Water Scarcity. Water Resources Development, Vol. 19, No. 4, 553–567, December 2003. http://www.utsc.utoronto.ca/~02wongwb/Bjornlund%202003.pdf
5. de Bruijn, Jos., Polleres, Axel.: Towards an Ontology Mapping Specification Language for the Semantic Web. DERI Technical Report 2004-06-30 June 2004. http://www.deri.at/publications/techpapers/documents/DERI-TR-2004-06-30.pdf
6. Bury, H., Durakova, D., Dysarz, T., Eleftheriadou, E., Kochanek, K., Owsinski, J. W., Rapantova, N., Unucka, J.: Transcat. The State-of-art in European Water Resource Related DSS Systems and Methodologies. http://www.transcat-project.net/Deliverables/WP5/DL-51-02.doc
7. Cameron, M.A., Corke, B., Taylor, K.L., Walker, G., Watson, B.: Regional Integrated Management Information System Proceedings of iEMSs 2002, Lugano, Switzerland, 24–27 June, 2002. http://www.iemss.org/iemss2002/proceedings/pdf/volume%20uno/304_cameron.pdf
8. Cameron, M.A., Taylor, K.L.: First-Order Patterns for Information Integration, 5th International Conference on Web Engineering (ICWE 2005), Sydney, Australia, July 27-29, 2005, Lecture Notes in Computer Science, Volume 3579, Jul 2005, Pages 173 – 184
9. Caprotti, O., Dewar, M., Turi, D.: Mathematical Service Matching Using Description Logic and OWL. Proceedings 3rd Int'l Conference on Mathematical Knowledge Management (MKM'04). Volume 3119 of Lecture Notes in Computer Science, Springer-Verlag (2004).

---

[27] http://otn.oracle.com/bpel

10. Guariso, G., Tracanella, E., Piroddi, L., Rizzoli, A.: A Web Accessible Environmental Model Base: a Tool for Natural Resources Management. Proc MODSIM 97, International Congress on Modelling and Simulation, Hobart, Australia, pp 657-662, December 1997.

11. Harvey, H. Feedback on the OpenMI Architecture reports A & B version 0.6. Water and Environmental Management Research Centre. http://www.cen.bris.ac.uk/pgra/dph/publications/2003-05-28-openmi1.pdf

12. Marston, F., Argent, R., Vertessy, R., Cuddy, S., Rahman, . J. The Status of Catchment Modelling in Australia. CSIRO Land and Water Technical Report 02/4 March 2002 http://www.toolkit.net.au/pdfs/technical200204.pdf

13. Prasad, A., Khan, S. Synthesis Report Murray-Darling Basin Dialogue on Water and Climate - River Symposium Brisbane 6 September 2002. http://www.wac.ihe.nl/dialogue/Basin/Murray-Darling/documents/Murray-Darling%20Report.pdf

14. Rahman, J.M., Seaton, S., Cuddy, S.M.: Making Frameworks More Useable: Using Model Introspection and Metadata to Develop Model Processing Tools. Proceedings of iEMSs 2002, Lugano, Switzerland, 24–27 June, 2002. http://www.iemss.org/iemss2002/proceedings/pdf/volume%20tre/382_rahman.pdf

15. Taylor, K., Walker, G., Abel D.: A Framework for Model Integration for Spatial Decision Support Systems. International Journal of Geographic Information Science, 13(6), pp 533-555, 1999.

16. Tisdell, J., Ward, J., Grudzinski, T.: 2002, The development of Water reform in Australia. CSIRO Land and Water Technical Report 02/5, May 2002, pp45-47. http://www.catchment.crc.org.au/pdfs/technical200205.pdf

17. Uschold, M., Gruninger, M.: Ontologies and Semantics for Seamless Connectivity. SIGMOD Record, 33 (4), pp 58-64 December 2004.

18. Wijedasa, H. A., Malano, H. M., McMahon, T. A., Turral, H. N., Smith, G. S.: Water Trading in the Goulburn-Murray Irrigation Scheme. Technical Report 02/9 December 2002. http://www.gu.edu.au/school/eve/research/watertrading/download/Trading_GM.pdf

Towards a Killer App for the Semantic Web

Harith Alani, Yannis Kalfoglou, Kieron O'Hara, and Nigel Shadbolt

Intelligence, Agents, Multimedia,
School of Electronics and Computer Science,
University of Southampton, UK
{ha, y.kalfoglou, kmo, nrs}@ecs.soton.ac.uk

Abstract. Killer apps are highly transformative technologies that create new markets and widespread patterns of behaviour. IT generally, and the Web in particular, has benefited from killer apps to create new networks of users and increase its value. The Semantic Web community on the other hand is still awaiting a killer app that proves the superiority of its technologies. There are certain features that distinguish killer apps from other ordinary applications. This paper examines those features in the context of the Semantic Web, in the hope that a better understanding of the characteristics of killer apps might encourage their consideration when developing Semantic Web applications.

1 Introduction

The Semantic Web (SW) is gaining momentum, as more researchers gravitate towards it, more of its technologies are being used, and as more standards emerge and are accepted. There are various visions of where the technology might go, what tasks it might help with, and how information should be structured and stored for maximum applicability [4][21][30]. What is certainly clear is that no-one who wishes seriously to address the problems of knowledge management in the twenty-first century can ignore the SW.

In many respects, the growth of the SW mirrors the growth of the World Wide Web (WWW) in its early stages, as the manifest advantages of its expressivity became clear to academic users. However, once the original phase of academically-led growth of the WWW was over, to the surprise of many commentators, the web began its exponential growth, and its integration with many aspects of ordinary life. Technologies emerged to enable users to, for example, transfer funds securely from a credit card to a vendor's account, download large files with real time video or audio, or find arbitrary websites on the basis of their content.

Most realistic visions of the SW include a version of this exponential growth. The SW infrastructure should be put in place to enable such growth. With a clean, scalable and unconstraining infrastructure, it should be possible for users to undertake all those tasks that seem to be required for the SW to follow the WWW into the stratosphere, such as publishing their RDF, converting legacy content, annotating, writing ontologies, etc.

However, that something is possible does not entail that it is inevitable. So the question arises of how developers and users might be persuaded to come to the SW. This type of growth of a network has often been observed in the business literature. Many technologies depend for their usability on a large number of fellow users; in this context

Y. Gil et al. (Eds.): ISWC 2005, LNCS 3729, pp. 829–843, 2005.

Metcalfe's Law [15] states that the utility of a network is proportional to the square of the number of users.

Technologies which have this effect are called *killer apps*. Exactly what is a killer app is to a large extent in the eye of the beholder; in the WWW context, killer apps might include the Mosaic browser, Amazon, Google, eBay or Hotmail. Hotmail attracted over 30 million members in less than three years after its 1996 launch; eBay went from nothing to generating 20% of all person-person package deliveries in the US in less than 2 years. Of course, the WWW was a useful enough technology to make its own way in the world, but without the killer apps it might not have broken out of the academic/nerdy ghetto. By extension, it is a hope of the SW community that the SW might take off on the back of a killer app of its own.

The dramatic development of the WWW brought with it a lot of interest from the business community, and the phenomenon of killer apps has come under much scrutiny [10][19]. Attempts have been made to observe the spread of killer apps, and to generalise from such observations; the tight development cycles of WWW technology have helped such observations.

In this paper, our aim is to consider the potential for development of the SW in the light of the killer app literature from the business community. Of course, it is impossible to forecast where the killer app for the SW will come from. But examination of the literature might provide some pointers as to what properties such an application might have, and what types of behaviour it might need to encourage.

2   Killer Apps and the Semantic Web

Killer apps emerge in the intersection between technology, society and business. They are technological in the broad sense of being artificial solutions to perceived problems, or artificial methods to exploit perceived opportunities (which is not to say that they need to have been developed specifically with such problems or opportunities in mind). Mere innovation is not enough. Indeed, a killer app need not be at the cutting edge of technological development at all. The killer app must meet a need, and be usable in some context, such as work or leisure or commerce. It must open up some kind of opportunity to bring together a critical mass of users.

To do this, killer apps have a number of features which have been catalogued by commentators. In this section, we will examine and reinterpret such features in the context of the SW. We reiterate that these features may not all be necessary, and they certainly are not sufficient; however they can act as an interesting framework to our thought on this topic.

The main point, of course, about a killer app is that it enables a superior level of service to be provided. And equally clearly, the SW provides an important opportunity to do this, as has been argued from the beginning [4]. There are obvious opportunities for any knowledge-based task or enterprise to improve its performance once knowledge sources are integrated and more intelligent information processing is automated.

2.1   The Bottom Line: Cost vs Benefit

However, merely providing the opportunity is not enough. Cost-benefit analysis is essential [10]. There are several aspects to costs. Obviously, there are financial costs; will people have to pay for the killer apps on the SW? Maybe not; there are many examples of totally free Internet applications, such as Web browsers, search engines, and chat messengers. Such applications often generate large revenues through online advertising. According to the Interactive Advertising Bureau UK[1] and PriceWaterhouseCoopers[2], the market size of online advertising in the UK for 2004 was £653.3m, growing more than 60% in one year. Free products may be very important in this context [19], and indeed killer apps are often cheaper than comparable alternative products [7].

But such costs are not the only ones incurred. There are also important resource issues raised by any plan to embrace the SW.

Conversion Cost: As well as investing in technologies of certain kinds, organisations and people will have to convert much of their legacy data, and structure newly-acquired data, in particular ways. This immediately requires resources to support the development of ontologies, the formatting of data in RDF, the annotation of legacy data, etc., not to mention potential costs of exposing data in RDF to the wider world (particularly where market structures reward secrecy). Furthermore, the costs of developing smart formalisms that are representationally adequate (the fun bit) are dwarfed by the population of informational structures with sufficient knowledge of enough depth to provide utility in a real-world application [12]. Note also that such a process will require ascent of some very steep learning curves.

Maintenance Cost: In a very dynamic domain, it may be that ontologies have to be updated rapidly [20][5]. The properties of ontologies are not as well-understood as they might be; areas such as mapping ontologies onto others, merging ontologies and updating ontologies are the focus of major research efforts. It is currently unknown as to how much such maintenance effort would cost over time.

Organisational Restructuring Costs: Information processing is integrated into an organisation in subtle ways, and organisations often subconsciously structure themselves around their information processing models [11], a fact implicitly accepted by the knowledge engineering community [27]. Surveys of organisations, for example, reveal that ontologies are used in relatively primitive ways; indeed, in the corporate context, the term 'ontology' is a generic, rarely defined catch-all term. Some are no more than strict hierarchies, some are more complex structures allowing loops and multiple instantiations, still others are in effect (sometimes multilingual) corporate vocabularies, while others are complex structures holding metadata [22]. Whatever their level of sophistication, corporate ontologies support the systematisation of large quantities of knowledge, far from the traditional AI view of their being highly detailed specifications of well-ordered domains. Ontologies may refer to an internal view of the organisation (marketing, R&D, human resources, etc) or an external one (types of supplier and supplies,

---

[1] www.iabuk.net
[2] http://www.pwc.com/

product types, etc). A recent survey showed that only a relatively small number (under a quarter) of corporate ontologies were derived from industry standards. The big issue for many firms is not representational adequacy but rather the mechanics of integration with existing systems [12].

Transaction Costs: On the other hand, it is also true that if the SW does alter information gathering and processing costs, then the result will inevitably be some alteration of firms' management structures. The result will be leaner firms with fewer management layers, and possibly different ways of processing, storing and maintaining information. Such firms may provide opportunities for new SW technologies to explore, and a gap in the market from which a killer app may emerge.

It has long been argued that the size and structure of firms cannot be explained simply by the price mechanism in open competitive markets [8]. The allocation of resources is made using two mechanisms - first (between firms and consumers) by distributed markets and coordinated by price, but also (within firms) by the use of authority within a hierarchy (i.e. people get ordered to do things). The question then is how this relates to a firm's structure - when a firm needs some service, does it procure it from outside and pay a market price, or does it get it done in-house, using workers under some contractual obligation, and why?

It is generally thought that such organisational questions are determined by the *transaction costs* within a firm [33][34]. The promise of the SW is that many of the information gathering costs will be ameliorated. The general result of this is likely to be a continuation of trends that we have seen in economies since the widespread introduction of IT, which is the removal of middle management ("downsizing"), and the outsourcing of many functions to independent suppliers. In the SW context, of course, many of those independent suppliers could well be automatic agents, or providers of web services. If the SW contains enough information about a market, then we might well expect to see quite transformative conditions, and several market opportunities. The killer app for the business aspects of the SW may well be something that replaces the coordinative function of middle management.

But we should add a caveat here: the marginal costs of information gathering will be ameliorated, but equally there will, as noted above, be possibly hefty sunk costs up front, as firms buy or develop ontologies, convert legacy data to RDF, lose trade secrets as they publish material, etc. These initial costs may prove an extensive barrier to change.

Reducing Costs: Here we see the importance of the increase in size of the user base. For example, the costs of developing and maintaining ontologies are high, but can be shared. Lightweight ontologies are likely to become more important [31]; not only are they cheaper to build and maintain, but they are more likely to be available off the shelf [22]. Furthermore, they are more likely to be easily understandable, mappable, maintainable, etc. The development of such lightweight multi-purpose ontologies will be promoted as the market for them gets bigger.

Similar points can be made about ontology development tools. Better tools to search for, build or adapt ontologies will spur their use or reuse, and again such tools will appear with the demand for them. And in such an environment, once an ontology has been developed the sunk costs can be offset by licensing the use of that ontology by other organisations working in that domain. The costs, in such a networked environment, will come down over the period of use; if a single firm took on the costs of developing and licensing an ontology for a domain, that firm could also take on the maintenance costs. Organisations that specialised in ontology maintenance and training for users could spring up, given sufficient demand for their services.

Increasing Benefit: Similarly to data restructuring; there has to be some discernible benefit for organisations putting their data in RDF, and these benefits will become more apparent the more published data in RDF there is. So the issue here, which a killer app might help with, is that there seems to be little or no advantage for an individual firm in moving first. A firm that publishes its data in RDF early incurs costs early and takes a risk, but gets little benefit; and vice versa. Nevertheless, being first in a new market is a distinct advantage [10][7], but late entrants can also succeed if they outperform existing services [13] (e.g. Google). So there is a Prisoner's Dilemma to be sorted out.

Berners-Lee argues that the killer app for the SW is the *integration* [2]. Once distributed data sources are integrated, the sky becomes the limit. This of course could be true, but it will be hard to convince data providers to publish in RDF and join the SW movement without concrete examples of benefit. This is probably supported by Berners-Lee suggestion that we need to "Justify on short/medium term gain, not network effect" [3]. Integration alone might not be seen as a gain on its own, especially when considering costs and privacy issues.

In a survey for business use cases for the SW, researchers of the EU *Knowledge Web*[3] emphasised the importance of proper targeting for SW tasks [24] to avoid applying SW technologies to where they do not offer any clear benefit, which may discourage industry-wide adoption. The survey concluded that the areas which seem to benefit more from this sort of technology are *data integration* and *semantic search*. It was argued that these areas could be accommodated with technologies for *knowledge extraction*, *ontology mapping* and *ontology development*. Similarly, Uschold and Gruninger [31] argue that ontologies are useful for better *information access*, *knowledge reuse*, *semantic-search*, and *inter-operability*. They also list a number of assumptions to be made to progress towards a fully automated semantic integration of independent data sources. Fensel et al [14] describe the beneficial role of ontologies in general *knowledge management* and *eCommerce* applications. They also list a number of obstacles that need to be overcome to achieve those benefits, such as *scalable ontology mapping*, *instantiation*, and *version control*. Other obstacles, such as *trust*, *agent co-ordination*, *referential integrity*, and *robust reasoning* have also been discussed [18].

2.2   Leveraging Metcalfe's Law

The relevance of Metcalfe's Law, that the utility of a network is proportional to the square of the number of its members [15], is clear in the context of this examination of the nature of the costs It is often cited in other contexts as an explanatory variable for killer apps [10][19][13]. There are two stages to the process of growing a network;

---
[3] http://knowledgeweb.semanticweb.org/

first get the network's growth accelerating, and second preserve the network once it is in place, in order to create a *community of practice (CoP)*.

Communities of Practice: A CoP [32] is an informal, self selecting, group of people sharing some work- or leisure-related practice. The CoP that springs up around such a practice acts as a kind of support network for practitioners. It provides a language (or informal ontology) for people to communicate with, a corporate memory, and a means of spreading best practice.

This self-selection, and informality of CoPs, makes a community very hard to develop, because the community is a second-order development. So, we might take the example of Friend of a Friend *(FOAF)*[4]. FOAF is a basic ontology that allows a user to express simple personal information (email, address, name, etc) as well as information about people they know. Many SW enthusiasts considered FOAF to be *cool* and *fun* and started publishing their FOAF ontologies. Currently there are millions of FOAF RDF triples scattered over the Web, perhaps far more than any other type of SW annotations.

Social Network Applications: Surprisingly, there exist many Web applications that allow users to represent networks of friendships, such as Friendster[5], Okrut[6], LinkedIn[7], TheFacebook[8], SongBuddy[9], to name just a few. However, FOAF has simply become a more convenient form for representing, publishing, and sharing information. Even though none of the applications above are entirely based on FOAF, some have already begun reading and exporting FOAF files. FOAF is certainly helping spread RDF, albeit in a way limited to part of the SW community, and could therefore be regarded as a facilitator or a medium for possible killer apps that could make use of available FOAF files and provide some useful service.

Sustaining Network Growth: However, one interesting obstacle in the way of FOAF creating the nexus of users that will launch the SW is that a network is generally self-selecting and second order. One obvious benefit of FOAF is that, as a pretty simple ontology, it provides a relatively painless way of ascending the learning curve for non-users of SW technology. However, to sustain the network growth, there is still need to something underlying such networks, some practice, shared goal, or other practical purpose.

It may well be that a potentially more fruitful approach would be to support existing communities and try to expand SW use within them, so that little Semantic Webs emerge from them, as SW technologies and techniques reach saturation point within them [18]. And because CoP overlap, and converge on various boundary objects and other linking practices and artefacts [32]. There are many obvious aids to such a development strategy; for instance, good-quality ontologies could be hand-crafted for particular domains. But also, it turns out that a number of the best SW tools at the moment

---

[4] http://www.foaf-project.org/
[5] http://www.friendster.com/
[6] http://www.orkut.com/
[7] https://www.linkedin.com/
[8] http://www.thefacebook.com/
[9] http://www.songbuddy.com/

also support this "filling out" technique. For instance CS AKTive Space [28] specifically enables people to find out about the state of the discipline of computer science in the UK context; a limited but useful domain. Flink [23] generates FOAF networks for SW researchers. CS AKTive Space and Flink are winners of the 2003 and 2004 Semantic Web Challenges respectively.

Open Systems and Social Aspects: One other useful aspect of Flink is that it integrates FOAF profiles with ordinary HTML pages, and therefore sets up an explicit link between the SW and the WWW. Direct interaction with other existing systems increases the value of a system by acquiring additional value from those systems [19]. One good example is Protégé, an ontology editor from Stanford [25]. By being open source and extendable, Protégé allowed many existing systems and tools to be linked or integrated with it, thus increasing its use and value. For this reason, and for being free, Protégé has quickly become one of the most popular ontology editing tools available today.

This openness is of course built into the very conception of the SW; the integration of large quantities of data, and the possibility of inference across them, is where much of the power stems from. As with the WWW, this does require a major programme of voluntary publication (e.g. to simply and conveniently compare prices across retailers over the WWW). The SW would add value (or reduce information processing costs) still more by allowing agents to do the same thing and more [17].

And as with the WWW, if this process takes off, then more and more vendors would have to publish their data in RDF, even if they are initially reluctant. The argument in favour of such coercion is that everyone benefits eventually, and that early movers not only gain, but force laggards to follow suit.

Privacy and Trust: Transparency and the removal of restrictions to publication are not undiluted goods. It may be that certain pieces of information benefit some organisations only as long as they withhold them from public view (trade secrets). Or that issues such as privacy and anonymity will rear their heads here. Or even that differing intellectual property regimes and practices will lead to competitive advantage being lost in some economies.

In particular, integrating large quantities of information across the Internet and reasoning across them raises potential problems. Firstly, it is the integration of information that threatens to allow harmful inference; information is quite often only harmful when seen in the right (or wrong) context. But the SW is the tool *par excellence* for doing that. And secondly, publication of information (e.g. FOAF) in a friendly and local context can quickly get out of one's control.

It is often argued that standard data protection legislation is adequate for the new online contexts, but that policing is the problem. As it stands, traditional restrictions on the gathering of information are becoming decreasingly relevant as information crosses borders so easily. More plausible is policing restrictions on how information can be used once collected.

Furthermore, formalising or externalising knowledge, for example in the creation of ontologies, can have a number of effects. First of all, knowledge that is codified can become more 'leaky', i.e. it is more likely to leave an organisation. Secondly, it will tend to reduce the competitive advantage, and therefore income, of certain experts. Thirdly, much depends on whether a consensus exists about the knowledge in the first place.

2.3   Creativity and Risk

Killer app development cannot follow from careful planning alone. As we have noted already, there is no algorithm for creating a killer app. They tend to emerge from simple and inventive ideas; they get much of their transformative power by destroying hitherto reliable income streams for established firms. Christensen [7] points out that most killer apps are developed by small teams and start-ups. Examples include Google, eBay, and Amazon, which were all created by a few dedicated individuals. Giant industrial firms are normally reluctant to support risky projects, because they are generally the ones profiting from the very income streams that are at risk [10].

However, even though most semantic web applications have so far been built in research labs and small groups and companies, there is clear interest expressed by the big players as well. So, for example, Hewlett Packard has produced Jena [6], a Java library for building SW applications, and IBM has developed WebFountain [16], a heavy platform for large scale analysis of textual web documents using natural language analysis and taxonomies for annotations. Adobe has perhaps gone further than many; Acrobat v5 now allows users to embed RDF metadata within their PDF documents and to add annotations from within Web browsers which can be stored and shared via document servers.

The SW provides a context for killer app development, a context based on the ability to integrate information from a wide variety of sources and interrogate it. This creates a number of aspects for the potential for killer apps. First of all, SW technologies might essentially be expected to enable the retrieval of data in a more efficient way that possible with the current WWW which is often seen as a large chaotic library.

On the other hand, it may be that the SW might take off in an original and unpredictable direction. The clean infrastructure that the W3C ensures is in place could act as a platform for imaginative methods of collating and sifting through the giant quantities of information that is becoming available. This might result in a move away from the webpage paradigm, away from the distinction between content providers and consumers, as for example with efforts like CS AKTive Space [28], or a move towards a giant, relatively uniform knowledge base (of the CYC variety) that could cope with all those complexities of context that foiled traditional AI approaches [1]. The ultimate vision of the SW that prevails should affect not only the standards developed for it [21], but also where we might look for killer apps.

2.4   Personalisation

Personalisation has been a common thread in the development of killer apps. Customers tend to become more loyal to services they can customise to their liking [10]. Many of today's killer apps have some level of personalisation; Amazon for example makes recommendations based on what the customer buys or looks at; Auto Trader[10] and

---

[10] http://www.autotrader.co.uk

Rightmove[11] save customers' searches and notify them via emails when a new result to their query is available; personalised web services attract more customers (if done properly!) and provide better tailored services [13].

Personalisation is often the key to providing the higher service quality than the opposition. The service itself need not be provided in any better ways, but the personalised aspect gives it the extra that is needed to defeat the alternatives. Such a connection could be indirect; for example, an Amazon-style recommender system, linked with an advertising platform, could help find alternative revenue streams and therefore drive down the cost to the consumer.

It goes without saying that personalisation is a hot topic on the SW, as well-annotated knowledge sources can be matched against RDF statements about individual consumers, to create recommendations or targeted products. There may well be major advantages to be had in systems that can feed information discreetly into recommender systems [26][9].

Nevertheless, it is the personalisation aspect that has much potential for the SW, as long as the provision of enough information for the system to work interestingly is not too painful.

2.5   Semantic Web Applications

There have been few sustained attempts to try to promote SW applications. For instance, the important work of the W3C naturally is focused on the standards that will create the clean platform that is a necessary but sadly not sufficient condition for the SW to take off. But one of the most interesting and inspired is the series of Semantic Web challenges, which we will discuss briefly in the next section.

3   The Semantic Web Challenge

The annual International Semantic Web Challenge[12] (SWC), has been a deserved success, sparking interest and not a little excitement. It has also served to focus the community. Applications should "illustrate the possibilities of the Semantic Web. The applications should integrate, combine, and deduce information from various sources to assist users in performing specific tasks." Of course, to the extent that it does focus the community, the SWC will naturally influence the development of the SW.

Submissions to the SWC have to meet a number of minimum requirements, viz:

- First, the information sources used
  - should be geographically distributed,
  - should have diverse ownerships (i.e. there is no control of evolution),
  - should be heterogeneous (syntactically, structurally, and semantically), and
  - should contain real world data, i.e. are more than toy examples.
- Second, it is required that all applications assume an open world, i.e. assume that the information is never complete.

---

[11] http://www.rightmove.co.uk
[12] http://challenge.semanticweb.org/, where the criteria quoted below are to be found.

- Finally, the applications should use some formal description of the meaning of the data.

Secondly, there are desiderata that act as tiebreakers.

- The application uses data sources for other purposes or in another way than originally intended
- Using the contents of multi-media documents
- Accessibility in multiple languages
- Accessibility via devices other than the PC
- Other applications than pure information retrieval
- Combination of static and dynamic knowledge (e.g. combination of static ontologies and dynamic work-flows)
- The results should be as accurate as possible (e.g. use a ranking of results according to validity)
- The application should be scalable (in terms of the amount of data used and in terms of distributed components working together)

In the light of our discussion above, these are interesting criteria. Many of them are straightforwardly aimed at ensuring that the characteristic possibilities of the SW are realised in the applications. For instance, the SW would have little point indeed if it only worked on toy examples, did not scale, could not work with distributed information sources, or if it required some kind of closed world to work.

However that may be, what is of interest here is the relation to the SWC criteria and the literature on killer apps. What the SWC is intended to uncover are new ways of exploiting information, particularly distributed information, and demonstrating the power of interrogation. In this respect, the challenge can only raise the profile of the SW, and help extend its community to more people and organisations. The SWC is an excellent vehicle for demonstrating where added value may come from. And as we have seen, increasing the size of the network will bring with it exponentially-increasing benefits.

But the SWC looks unlikely to furnish us with a (prototype of a) killer app, because the criteria focus on interesting results, rather than on usability, superiority or the alteration of old habits. Some of the criteria are slightly double-edged. For example, it is essential that an application uses a formal description of the meaning of the data. This, of course, is a deliberate attempt to ensure that one of the most contentious aspects of the SW (one of the most commonly-cited causes of scepticism about the SW's prospects) is incorporated. That is, the use of ontologies to provide understanding of terms in knowledge from heterogeneous sources. However, the way the challenge is constructed means that what is bound to happen in many if not most applications is that the developers will create their system with a possibly very painstakingly constructed ontology in mind, rather than taking the more difficult option of employing a very lightweight system that could work with arbitrary ontologies. The situation is somewhat similar to the knowledge engineering Sisyphus challenges, where KE methodologies were tested and compared by being applied to the same problem. However, as the methodologies were applied by their developers, the results were less than enlightening; a later attempt to try to measure how difficult methodologies were to use by non-specialists suffered from an unwillingness of most developers to discover this key fact about their methods [29].

There is little here to create the genuine community (as opposed to a large network); to promote the idea that users have something of a responsibility not to free ride, and to publish RDF data. Neither is there much to promote personalisation within that community. There is little to protect privacy, little to reduce the pain of annotating legacy data or building ontologies, and, although the focus of the SWC is the results of information-processing, little to ensure that such processing can integrate into the organisational workflow. Surprisingly few of the traditional requirements, from a business perspective, appear in the SWC criteria.

None of this, let us hastily add, is intended as a criticism of the SWC, which has publicised the SW and drawn a lot of attention to the extra power that it can provide. Our point is merely that there is a lot more to finding a killer app than producing an application that does brilliant things.

4   Discussion

Killer apps must provide a higher service quality, and evolve (pretty quickly) into something perceived as indispensable, conferring benefits on their users without extra costs or steep learning curves. Individual users should coalesce into a community of practice, and their old habits should change in accordance with the new possibilities provided by the app. This is particularly important as the SW is likely to impose new costs on users in the short term, for example through having to annotate legacy content, develop ontologies, etc.

As the SW is in a relatively early stage of development, it is not currently clear exactly what threats and opportunities it provides (and, of course, the future form of the SW will conversely depend on what applications for it are successful). There has been some speculation about how the SW will develop, and what extensions of the WWW will be appropriate or desirable. For instance, consider a recent attempt by Marshall and Shipman to understand potential development routes for the SW [21], which sets out three distinct but related visions of the SW.

I *SW technology could bring an order and consistent structure to the chaotic Web. So information access would be assisted by semantic metadata.* This vision envisages that humans will continue to be the chief agents on the SW, but that information could now be represented and stored in ways to allow its use in situations far beyond those foreseen by its original authors. In other words, the SW will extend the existing Web, but exactly how is hard to predict. In order for potential SW Killer Apps to respond to this vision should, ideally, have the following properties in particular:

- They should help foster communities of users (that is, at some level, users should want to interact, and share experiences, with others). SW technology is expected to facilitate knowledge sharing and bringing more people together.
- Users should not feel submerged in a mass, but should retain their individuality with personalised products. With more machine readable information becoming available (eg FOAF), better personalisation should be feasible.
- Users should be able to bring as much of their legacy content up to date with relatively painless maintenance techniques. So, for example, applications

should be able to leverage comparatively simple ontologies; ontology construction, merging and selection should be made easier, and we should be able to move away from handcrafting; annotation methods and interfaces have to be easy. In all these cases, the existence of a community of interested users will provide the initial impetus for the user to ascend the learning curve.

II *The Web will be turned, in effect, into a globally distributed knowledge base, allowing software agents to collect and reason with information and assist people with common tasks, such as planning holidays or organising diaries.* This vision seems close to Berners-Lee et al's SW grand vision [4]. In many ways it is the composition of the other visions, assuming machine processing and global representation of knowledge. It is also a vision that will require more from a potential Killer App:

- They should exploit integrated information systems to make inferences that could not be made before. Showing added value is key to encourage businesses and content providers to participate in the SW.
- They should help remove the rather painful need to annotate, build ontologies, etc.
- The new application should fit relatively smoothly into current work or leisure experiences. Little change in habits is acceptable, assuming some returned benefit, but too much change is a problem!

III *The SW will be an infrastructure, made up of representation languages, communication protocols, access controls and authentication services, for coordinated sharing of knowledge across particular domain-oriented applications.* Information is used largely for the original purposes of its author, but that much more machine processing will take place. If this vision prevails, then a prospective SW Killer app should pay special attention to the following:

- It should not compromise other important aspects of users' lives, for instance by threatening privacy to a dangerous degree, either by making inappropriate surveillance possible, or by facilitating torts such as identity theft.
- Furthermore, if such a vision comes to pass, then the opportunities for killers apps are all the greater, in that any such standards-driven platform approach should make it possible for as many applications to flourish on top of it as possible. Whether such applications will ever be acknowledged as SW apps rather than general WWW applications is open to debate!

These conditions for each vision of the SW are, of course, necessary yet not sufficient! Furthermore, all of the conditions apply, to some degree, to each of the three visions.

We have seen that killer apps appear when there are opportunities to make progress on costs, communities, creativity and personalisation. All new technologies begin with a handicap in these areas. They impose costs, of retooling, of learning curves and of business process rescheduling. There is always a chicken and egg problem with the development of a community of users – the technology of necessity precedes the community. The risks of creative thought become clearer at the outset; the benefits only appear later. And the dialectic between personalisation and creating economies of scale often means that the latter are pursued long before the former. As an added handicap, it is often the case that the costs are borne disproportionately by early adopters.

The opportunities of the SW are also therefore counterbalanced by the risks. We note that we cannot predict where new killers will come from. The transformations that such applications wreak make the future very different from the present. Hence we can't be concretely prescriptive. But the general requirements for killer apps that emerge from our review of the business/management literature suggest certain routes for development, in addition to sensible lists of characteristics such as the criteria for the SW challenges, or the conditions listed at the beginning of this section.

So it is probably uncontroversial to assume that any SW killers will have to provide (1) a service that is not possible or practical under more traditional technologies, (2) some clear benefit to developers, data providers, and end users with minimum extra costs, and (3) an application that becomes indispensable to a user-base much wider than the SW researchers community. But additionally, research should be focusing on four important areas. First of all, perhaps most important, the cost issue should be addressed. Either the potentially large costs of annotating, ontology development, etc, should be mitigated, or side-stepped by thinking of types of application that can work with minimal non-automatic annotation, low cognitive overhead, or ontologies that sacrifice expressivity for simplicity. Secondly, another way of improving the cost/benefit ratio is to increase benefits, in which case the fostering of user communities looks like a sensible way forward. This means that applications in real-world domains (preferably in areas where the Internet was already important, such as media/leisure or e-science) look more beneficial than generic approaches. Thirdly, creativity is important, so radical business models are more interesting than simply redoing what the WWW already does. And fourthly, personalisation needs to be addressed, which means that extended user models are required.

When we look at the three visions outlined by Marshall and Shipman, vision III appears to be the one most amenable to the development of killer apps, in that it envisages a platform upon which applications sit – the form of such applications is left relatively open. In contrast, vision I, for example, doesn't see too much of a change for the WWW and the way it is used, and so there are fewer opportunities opening up as a result. Indeed, when we look at vision I, assuming that the SW does improve the navigation of the chaotic web, it might even be appropriate to say, not that there is a killer app for the SW, but rather that the SW is the killer app for the WWW. Whereas, with Marshall and Shipman's vision III, the vision is of a garden in which a thousand flowers bloom. On this vision, it is the painstaking, pioneering and often tedious negotiations of standards that will be key; such standards need to support the right kind of research.

5 Conclusions

Killer apps are very difficult things to monitor. They are hard to describe, yet you know one when you see one. If you are finding difficulty persuading someone that something is a killer app, it probably is not! A lot depends on the bootstrapping problem for the SW – if the SW community is small then the chances of someone coming up with a use of SW technology that creates a genuinely new use for or way of producing information are correspondingly small. For it is finding the novelty that is half the battle. There is unlikely to be much mileage in simply reproducing the ability to do something that is already possible without the SW. Furthermore, it is likely that a killer app for the SW will exploit SW technology integrally; merely using RDF will not quite do the trick [30]. The willingness of the producers of already-existing killers to use SW technology, like Adobe, is encouraging, but again will not necessarily provide the killer app for the SW. The checklist of criteria for the SWC gives a good list of the essentials for a genuinely SW application.

This is not simply a matter of terminology. The SW is more than likely to thrive in certain restricted domains where information processing is important and expensive. But the ambitions of its pioneers, rightly, go beyond that. For that to happen, killer apps need to happen. We hope we have given some indication, via our examination of the business literature, of where we should be looking.

Acknowledgments

This work is supported under the Advanced Knowledge Technologies (AKT) Interdisciplinary Research Collaboration (IRC), which is sponsored by the UK Engineering and Physical Sciences Research Council under grant number GR/N15764/01. The AKT IRC comprises the Universities of Aberdeen, Edinburgh, Sheffield, Southampton and the Open University. The views and conclusions contained herein are those of the authors and should not be interpreted as necessarily representing official policies or endorsements, either express or implied, of the EPSRC or any other member of the AKT IRC.

References

1. T. Berners-Lee. The semantic web road map. *http://www.w3.org/DesignIssues/Semantic. html*, 1998.
2. T. Berners-Lee. Iswc2003 keynote. http://www.w3.org/2003/Talks/1023-iswc-tbl/, 2003. 2nd International Semantic Web Conference (ISWC2003), Florida, USA.
3. T. Berners-Lee. Www2004 keynote. http://www.w3.org/2004/Talks/0519-tbl-keynote/, 2004. 13th Int. World Wide Web Conf., New York.
4. T. Berners-Lee, J. Hendler, and O. Lassila. The semantic web. *Scientific American*, May 2001.
5. S. Buckingham-Shum. Contentious, dynamic, information-sparse domains. and ontologies? *IEEE Intelligent Systems*, pages 80–81, Jan/Feb 2004.
6. J. J. Carroll, I. Dickinson, C. Dollin, D. Reynolds, A. Seaborne, and K. Wilkinson. Jena: Implementing the semantic web recommendations. Technical report, HP Laboratories Bristol, HPL-2003-146, Dec. 24, 2003.
7. C. M. Christensen. *The Innovator's Dilemma*. Harvard Business School Press, 1997.
8. R. Coase. *The Nature of the Firm, Economica 1937, reprinted in Oliver E. Williamson & Sidney G. Winter (eds.) The Nature of the Firm: Origins, Evolution and Development.* Oxford: Oxford University Press, 1991.
9. S. Cox, H. Alani, H. Glaser, and S. Harris. The semantic web as a semantic soup. In *Proc. 1st Workshop on Friend of a Friend*, Galway, Ireland, 2004.
10. L. Downes and C. Mui. *Unleashing the Killer App*. MIT Press, Harvard Business School Press, 2000.
11. K. Eischen. The social impact of informational production: Software development as an informational practice. Cgirs working paper 2002-1, Center for Global International and Regional Studies, University of California, Santa Cruz, 2002.

12. J. Ellman. Corporate ontologies as information interfaces. *IEEE Intelligent Systems*, pages 79–80, Jan/Feb 2004.

13. P. Evans and T. Wurster. *Blown to Bits*. Harvard Business School Press, 2000.

14. D. Fensel, C. Bussler, Y. Ding, V. Kartseva, M. Klein, M. Korotkiy, B. Omelayenko, and R. Siebes. Semantic web application areas. In *Proc. 7th Int. Workshop on Applications of Natural Language to Information Systems (NLDB 2002)*, Stockholm, Sweden, 2002.

15. G. Gilder. Metcalfe's law and legacy. *Forbes ASAP*, 13 September 1993.

16. D. Gruhl, L. Chavet, D. Gibson, J. Meyer, P. Pattanayak, A. Tomkins, and J. Zien. How to build a webfountain: An architecture for very large-scale text analytics. *IBM Systems Journal*, 43(1):64–76, 2004.

17. J. Hendler. Agents and the semantic web. *IEEE Intelligent Systems*, pages 30–37, March/April 2001.

18. Y. Kalfoglou, H. Alani, M. Schorlemmeret, and C. Walton. On the emergent semantic web and overlooked issues. In *Proc. 3rd Int. Semantic Web Conf. (ISWC)*, Japan, 2004.

19. K. Kelly. *New Rules for the New Economy: 10 Radical Strategies for a Connected World*. Penguin Books, 1998.

20. M. Klein and D. Fensel. Ontology versioning on the semantic web. In *Proc. 1st Int. Semantic Web Working Symp.*, pages 75–91, Stanford University, CA, USA, 2001.

21. C. Marshall and F. M. Shipman. Which semantic web? In *Proc. 14th HyperText Conf. (HT'03)*, pages 57–66, Nottingham,UK, 2003. ACM.

22. D. L. McGuinness. *Ontologies Come of Age*. in D. Fensel, J. Hendler, H. Lieberman, and W. Wahlster editors. Spinning the Semantic Web: Bringing the World Wide Web to Its Full Potential, MIT Press, 2002.

23. P. Mika. Social networks and the semantic web: The next challenge. *IEEE Intelligent Systems*, 19:82–82, 2005.

24. L. Nixon. Prototypical business use cases. FP6 IST NoE Deliverable D1.1.2, KnowledgeWeb EU NoE - FP6 507482, Dec. 2004.

25. N. F. Noy, M. Sintek, S. Decker, M. Crubezy, R. W. Fergerson, and M. A. Musen. Creating semantic web contents with protege-2000. *IEEE Intelligent Systems*, pages 60–71, March/April 2001.

26. M. C. schraefel, A. Preece, N. Gibbins, S. Harris, and I. Millard. Ghosts in the semantic web machine? In *Proc. 1st Workshop on Friend of a Friend, Social Networking and the Semantic Web*, Galway, Ireland, 2004.

27. G. Schreiber, H. Akkermans, A. Anjewierden, R. de Hoog, N. Shadbolt, W. V. de Velde, and B. Wielinga. *Knowledge Engineering and Management: The CommonKADS Approach*. MIT Press, 1999.

28. N. Shadbolt, m. schraefel, N. Gibbins, and S. Harris. Cs aktive space: or how we stopped worrying and learned to love the semantic web. In *Proc. 2nd Int. SW Conf*, Florida, 2003.

29. N. Shadbolt, K. O'Hara, and L. Crow. The experimental evaluation of knowledge acquisition techniques and methods: history, problems and new directions. *International Journal of Human-Computer Studies*, 51:729–755, 1999.

30. M. Uschold. Where are the semantics in the semantic web? *AI Magazine*, 24(3), 2003.

31. M. Uschold and M. Gruninger. Ontologies and semantics for seamless connectivity. *SIGMOD Record*, 33(4), 2004.

32. E. Wenger. *Communities of Practice: Learning, Meaning and Identity*. Cambridge University Press, 1998.

33. O. E. Williamson. *Markets and Hierarchies*. New York: Free Press, 1975.

34. O. E. Williamson. *The Nature of the Firm: Origins, Evolution and Development*. Oxford: Oxford University Press, 1991.

Enterprise Architecture Reference Modeling in OWL/RDF

Dean Allemang, Irene Polikoff, and Ralph Hodgson

TopQuadrant Inc,
141 Howard Drive, Beaver Falls, PA
{dallemang, irene, ralph}@topquadrant.com

Abstract. This paper describes the design of and the deployment options for the Federal Enterprise Architecture Reference Model Ontology (FEA-RMO). The goal of any reference model is to provide a basis or starting point for some design process. While this is a laudable goal, it poses an immediate problem for representation; how can a model be represented in such a way that it can be extended in certain ways (for application to a particular problem), but not without regard to the advice that it gives? Reference models are usually expressed in natural language. At their best, such models provide a starting point for designers, and a checklist for their designs, to see that they conform to industry best practices. At worst, reference models expressed in natural language become a source of busy work; designers do not use the models during the design process, instead they spend time after the fact writing up an explanation of how and why they are compliant with the reference framework they've never seriously considered. In this paper, we have used Semantic Web technologies (in particular, RDF and OWL) to represent a reference mode for enterprise architecture in the US government. The content of the model comes from the recent Federal Enterprise Architecture Reference Model effort. We use the capability of RDF to distribute structured information to allow the reference model to be extended (as intended in its design). We use OWL to maintain the consistency of those extensions. The model has been used as the basis for an implementation of an FEA registry, a web-based system for managing enterprise architectures based on the FEA. The work of representing the FEA as formal ontologies was funded in part by GSA.[1]

Keywords: Government Sector, Portals, Knowledge Management.

1 Introduction

Reference models have been developed for a number of areas, ranging from highly technical areas like networking and distributed processing ([10], [11]), social areas like library and archiving ([9]) and even culturally focused areas like Cultural Heri-

[1] We would like to thank Rick Murphy, Enterprise Architect and George Thomas, Chief Enterprise Architect of the Office of CIO of GSA for their vision, support and contribution to the use cases described in this paper.

Y. Gil et al. (Eds.): ISWC 2005, LNCS 3729, pp. 844 – 857, 2005.

tage and Museum management ([12]). In all these cases, the reference model represents some agreement on good practices which, if followed, will provide some specific value to designers of systems in each of these areas.

The reference models themselves are not system models; they are blueprints, templates, or starting points for system design. The intended use of a reference model is as an aid for a designer. It gets past the "blank slate" problem of a design from scratch, by providing a starting point. It also provides guidance to the design, so that the designer can reuse known and proven solution patterns. . The reference model also encourages independent design teams to conform to core principles that will facilitate future integration.

This role of a Reference Model in the design process poses very particular challenges: a reference model must be represented as a reusable asset, which is not a system design in its own right. The engineering of a reference model is therefore a problem of "design for reuse". In short, how can a reference model be represented in such a way that it simultaneously makes enough design commitments to advise a system designer (involved with a system that was not even conceived at the time of reference model development), while leaving that same designer enough latitude to customize a design to the particular needs of the problem at hand. This kind of engineering problem is called by the name "domain modeling for asset reuse" [13].

In this paper, we will use a particular reference model as a case study. In response to a presidential initiative for e-government, the US federal government has developed the Federal Enterprise Architecture (FEA, [1]) a reference model for enterprise architecture. The basic idea of the FEA is that each government agency supports services, functions, operations and technologies that are not unique to their agency. The government as a whole would run more smoothly if all the agencies were to "align" their operations. In 2004, the first full version of the FEA Reference Model (FEA RM) was released. Like other reference models, this is not an enterprise architecture in itself, but a model to guide enterprise architects in government agencies as they create their own, agency-specific, enterprise architectures. Like other reference models, it provides design guidance, while allowing for a certain latitude for the specific agencies.

Reference models are typically written in natural language, and are presented as some form of human-readable document. The reference models of the FEA are no exception.[2] This form of presentation has the advantage that the reference models can be read by anyone who can read PDF files; but it has the disadvantage that the process of reusing the reference model ("alignment") can only be verified by an interpretation process whereby an enterprise architect (or whoever has the job of making the alignment) determines what the reference architecture means, and argues for the particular alignment of their architecture to the model. This is a highly ambiguous and subjective task, and is prone to errors and even misuse.

A formal representation of a reference model addresses this problem by providing an unambiguous (or at least, less ambiguous) representation of the reference model,

---

[2] Some of the FEA models are available in XML as well as in natural language. However, XML alone (not being a graph representation) can not describe all the relationships within and between the models. RDFS and OWL layered on top of XML provide us with all the language constructs needed to represent FEA.

and allows for the definition of objective criteria for whether an architecture is actually conformant.

But a formal representation brings up a new issue: while some value can be gained from simple formal representations (e.g., the list of business areas, lines of business, and subfunctions found in the Business Reference Model), most reference models have more complex structure than simple lists, or even hierarchies. Furthermore, description of how an enterprise architecture aligns with such a reference model architecture requires more complex consistency checking than is usual even for a taxonomy.

Fortunately, 2004 also saw the adoption by the W3C of the OWL standard for representing *ontologies*, which are formal models that allow the sort of complexity required by enterprise architecture reference models. Furthermore, the OWL standard provides a formal semantic for the meaning of these models, which addresses the issues of fragility and ambiguity of informal models. Finally, OWL provides a framework for combining ontologies and checking their consistency, thereby providing the framework for a systematic discipline for determining how well proposed architectures match the reference model.

1.1 Federal Enterprise Architecture

The FEA has five models: the Performance Reference Model (PRM), the Business Reference Model (BRM), the Service Component Reference Model (SRM), and the Technology Reference Model (TRM) and the Data Reference Model (DRM) Each of these is, at its core, a taxonomic structure of enterprise architecture entities.

The idea of providing a reference model for enterprise architecture is that each agency should be able to use the reference model as a starting point for documenting its own enterprise architecture. The current draft of the FEA RM contains some ambiguity about just how the FEA RM can/may be adapted to apply to a particular agency's enterprise architecture. By examining the example of the DOD [14] and other vanguard agencies who are already applying the FEA RM, we have determined that the following types of adaptations to the FEA RM are being done:

- Some agencies are making extensions to the reference model (describing entities in more detail than given in the FEA RM)
- Additions to the model (adding more siblings to an entity in the FEA RM) are also being done
- Finally, some agencies are making deletions (leaving out entities from the model) and replacements (leaving an entity out while noting that it is being replaced by one or more new entities)

While each agency has considerable autonomy, there are many benefits to having a central reference model to which each agency refers.

1.2 The FEA RM Ontology

We have constructed a number of ontologies using the W3C standard Web Ontology Language OWL that reflects the structure of the published FEA RM. Collectively, these models make up the FEA RM Ontology, or FEA-RMO for short.

The FEA Reference Model Ontology architecture mirrors that of the FEA RM itself [1], that is, the Performance Reference Model (PRM) organizes the overall architecture, making reference to the other models as needed. The Business Reference Model (BRM) draws upon the Service Reference Model (SRM), the Data Reference Model (DRM) and the Technical Reference Model (TRM). In section 0, we describe how OWL was used to represent the various dependencies of these models upon one another, in particular, a recurring design pattern we call the "*Class-instance Mirror Pattern*" that is essential for representing the reference models.

Performance Reference Model

The PRM is organized into layers called Measurement Areas, Measurement Categories and Generic Indicators.

Business Reference Model

The BRM is organized into Business Areas, Lines of Business and Subfunctions.

Service Component Reference Model

The SRM is organized into Service Domains, Service Types and Components.

Technology Reference Model

The TRM is organized into core Service Areas, Service Categories, Service Standards and Service Specifications.

FEA Core Ontology

The FEA-RMO includes a model that is not explicitly called out in the FEA RM, where concepts and properties that are common to all the reference models are defined. This provides modularity to the ontology design that allows for simplified maintenance and integration of the models.

2   Use Cases for FEA-RMO

We have identified several use cases for FEA-RMO [2], but in this paper we will report on those that are supported by the current models and the semantic applications we have built around them. Many of the other use cases rely on modifications to government workflow beyond the technical scope of the FEA-RMO pilot.

2.1   Use Case: FEA Browser

Actor: Enterprise Architect, system developer, project manager. Anyone who needs to consult the FEA for any purposes.

Stakeholders: FEA Program Management Office (PMO), Agency that Enterprise Architect works for, Agency employees and administrators.

Goal: Gain better understanding of the FEA, understand how enterprise entities are aligned with the FEA RM.

Precondition:

A browsing system for the FEA RM. General purpose modeling tools like SWOOP [7] and Protégé [4] can provide some assistance for this purpose.

Steps:

1. User selects an entity from one of the reference models (e.g., a Line of Business from the BRM)
2. System displays information about that entity (e.g., quotes from the RM documents), and the entities adjacent to it (e.g., the Business Area that is comprised of it, the subfunctions that it is comprised of).
3. System displays a legend to orient the user in the appropriate RM document.
4. In the case of agency extensions (see next use case), system displays FEA core and agency extension entities separately.
5. User selects another related entity to browse, or uses a search function to search the FEA for a concept of interest.

Postcondition: none

Outcome:

User viewed and inspected any supported perspectives on the FEA.

2.2 Use Case: Agency Extension

Actor: Agency Enterprise Architect designing agency-specific modifications to the core FEA RM.

Stakeholders: FEA PMO, Agency that the Enterprise Architect works for

Goal: Maintain agency extensions separately from core model, while aligning the modifications with the appropriate parts of the model. Make these extensions available for the Browse use case.

Precondition:

Agency has accepted the FEA RM as a starting point for enterprise architecture modeling, and has access to the FEA.

Steps:

1. User identifies agency to which extensions belong, and validates identity credentials.
2. User selects an element in one of the reference models where a modification is to be made.
3. System provides guidance (based on the current reference model) for extensions, and records the extensions made by the user.

Postcondition:

Model and extensions are in a satisfactory state. The Browse use case is applicable in determining this postcondition.

Outcome:

Agency-specific modifications are stored independently (with appropriate access protections) of the reference model, but are available for browsing.

3 Application of Semantic Web Technology

There are two features of the FEA RM requirements that made RDF(S) and OWL Semantic Web technologies particularly appropriate. In fact, these requirements were so well suited to these technologies, that had we not used RDF and OWL, we would have needed to have invented similar knowledge representation technologies to have completed the project.

There are two other issues for which the current RDF and OWL standards posed some problems.

In this section we outline these features, the ways in which Semantic Web technologies were particularly well suited as solutions, and the ways in which we were able to work around the shortcomings.

3.1 Issue: Remote Composability

A major feature of a reference model is that it has been designed as a re-usable object. It is useful only inasmuch as it can be added to, changed, or otherwise edited. This makes the design of a reference model different from most engineering design.

In order to make use of a reference model, its users have to be able to reference any part of the model, and relate new items to those parts. This requires a robust system for extending and connecting to reference-able entities.

The match of this requirement to RDF is almost definitional. RDF is a graph-based modeling language, in which the identity of nodes and links (the modeling constructs) are done using URIs (making them web-worthy). The primitive operation in RDF is the graph merge; two graphs are made into one by unifying any references in one graph to nodes that are mentioned in the other.

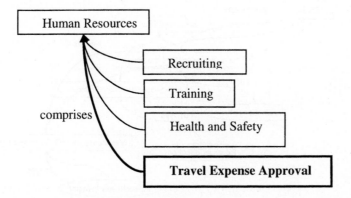

Fig. 1. Human Resources is comprised of several service types

The application of this to a reference model is perfectly straightforward. The reference model is expressed as an RDF graph, in which the parts of the model to be extended are published (as URIs). Then anyone in the world can express an extension to the model, simply by referring to it (importing it), and asserting new triples that refer to the nodes in the reference model.

As an example, the SRM identifies a Service Type for Human Resources, which is comprised of several Service Components, like Health and Safety, Recruiting, Training, etc. Suppose that the Federal Junket Agency (FJA) wants to add more service types here, having to do with how they manage travel. In terms of RDF triples, this is simply a matter of storing new triples, shown in **bold** in the Figure 1.

RDF allows the FJA to store the triple (<Travel Expense Approval> <comprises> <Human Resources>) in a separate web page from the FEA RM triples, but have any RDF application treat it as appearing at the appropriate part of the SRM.

3.2 Issue: Inter-model Consistency

The FEA expresses certain constraints between the various models. For example, the PRM makes use of BRM constructs in a number of ways. We will take a fairly simple one as an example.

The PRM specifies that "[T]he PRM's Measurement Categories are the same as the BRM's Lines of Business." This poses a problem for our second use case. If we simply construct our PRM model according to this rule, then when an agency adds new Lines of Business to the BRM, they will not be considered as Measurement Categories, and this rule will not be maintained. We could write a complex procedure to maintain the consistency between the models, but this adds a level of maintenance complexity that could severely restrict the applicability of the project.

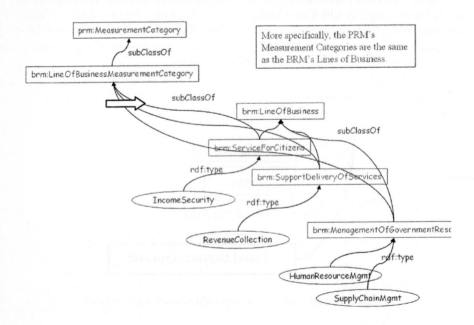

Our solution was to allow the OWL[3] reasoner to maintain this kind of connection between the models. We modeled the connection using OWL [4, 5], and allowed the reasoner to maintain consistency. In this case, the connection between the models was simply a few well-placed subClassOf triples between PRM and BRM entities, as shown by the arrow in the diagram above:

In particular, these subClassOf relations (between the appropriate subclasses of Lines of Business and the PRM Measurement Category) imply (according to the formal semantics of OWL) that any Line of Business will also be considered as a Measurement Category. This greatly simplifies maintenance of the models as agencies make changes; no special-purpose code is required, simply an OWL-compliant reasoner.

3.3 Issue: Removal of Triples

RDF's data model has been described by the slogan, "anyone can say anything about any topic." This feature was very well suited for our first issue, but it brings in a problem as well; it does not provide a direct way for anyone to *gainsay* what another has said. In the FEA case, it does not allow an agency to remove or replace triples from the core FEA-RMO.

One solution to this issue would be to simply insist that no agency be permitted to remove triples from the FEA-RMO; after all, the FEA RM can't provide much guidance, if agencies are permitted unrestricted deletions and additions to it. Nevertheless, it seems that the agencies are already reserving the right to remove triples as well as add them, so we need to support this capability in our modeling system.

Our solution to this problem is to introduce a new owl:ObjectProperty of our own called "replaces", that an agency can use to state explicitly that they are not using some element from the FEA-RMO. Returning to the Federal Junket Agency, the SRM actually already includes a consideration for Travel; but the FJA wants to replace this with a number of travel-related services, as shown below:

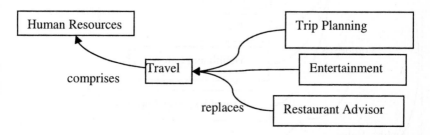

Fig. 2. Replacements for the Travel service

This solution can be made to work, but requires special-purpose code to interpret when displaying the agency modified model. On the other hand, this method does

---

[3] For this simple example, only RDFS reasoning was required; for more involved constraints, we required some reasoning from OWL, in particular, the use of inverses, transitive properties, and elementary reasoning about the owl:hasValue restriction.

have the advantage that it forces the agency to be specific about the parts of the FEA-RMO that it has chosen to ignore.

3.4 Issue: Individuals as Classes in OWL-DL

So far, we have only discussed the taxonomic portions of the FEA. There are more parts to the FEA, however, which involve referencing the taxonomies in various ways. For the most part, this does not raise any special issues. However, there is one issue that is relevant to modeling in OWL, and in particular, to modeling in OWL-DL. This is the issue that some entities in the taxonomy are occasionally referred to as individuals, and occasionally as classes. This double-usage is not allowed in OWL-DL.

Fortunately, the W3C is aware of this issue, and the Best Practices Working Group has published a Working Draft [3] to address exactly this point. We have used Pattern 2 from this draft (which we prefer to call the "*Class-Instance Mirror pattern*") over 200 times in the construction of the FEA-RMO.

As a simple example, consider once again the Human Resources aspects of the FJA. In the original diagram Human Resources is an instance, and it is related to several other instances with the '*comprises*' property, as already shown in Fig. 1. Now suppose that we want to refer to the *Class* of all service types that comprise Human Resources (say, to be used as described in section 0 or 0). We can't use the Human Resources instance; that isn't the Class of all things that comprise Human Resources.

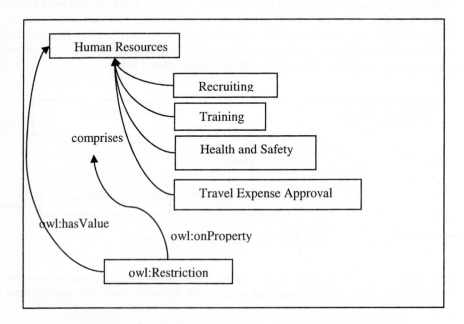

Fig. 3. Restriction onProperty comprises hasValue Human Resources

Fortunately, there is a simple OWL construct that does just this; the (**Restriction onProperty** *comprises* **hasValue** *Human Resources*). This is shown in Fig. 3. The OWL inference engine will maintain the instances of this class, to be exactly those instances which comprise Human Resources. Since this is maintained by the inference engine, it will remain consistent even when new service types are added.

We call this the "Class-Instance Mirror pattern" to highlight the relationship between the instance ("Human Resources") and the Class (an anonymous Restriction).This class exists only to provide a handle on the instances related to the instance, figuratively providing a "mirror image" of the instance in the Class world.

The pattern relies on very simple OWL reasoning (the ability to assign values according to the owl:hasValue restriction, and the ability to classify instances according to the same restriction), so this reasoning can be done quite reliably and efficiently.

4 Implementation: A Portal for the FEA Registry

We used these models to produce a web portal that displays the parts of the FEA, and allows agencies to make extensions to the FEA-RMO. The portal is a pilot project; that is, while it is fully functional and available on the web [6], it has not been deployed for use by enterprise architects in the agencies. In this section, we will highlight some of its functionality as it pertains to the use cases given here and the issues discussed above. The system was implemented using the RDF Gateway product from Intellidimension.

The basic portal is a model-driven web application; every page is generated from information in the FEA RM (with agency additions, when appropriate). A sample page from the application is shown, along with a fragment of the model that generated it.

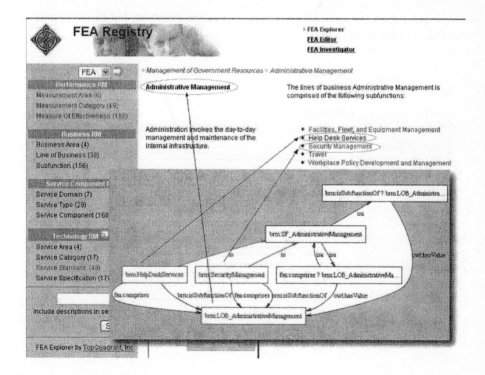

The registry portal allows users to browse all parts of the four models, either in the core FEA-RMO itself, or with agency extensions. Each entity in the portal links to another place in the model.

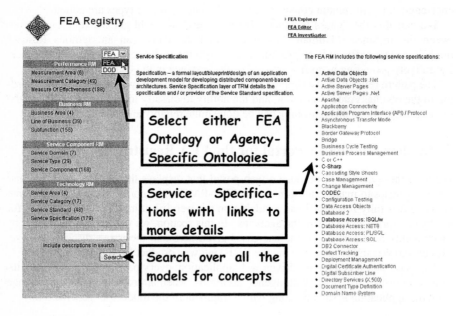

A search capability uses simple regular expression matching, but shows results in the context of the model itself.

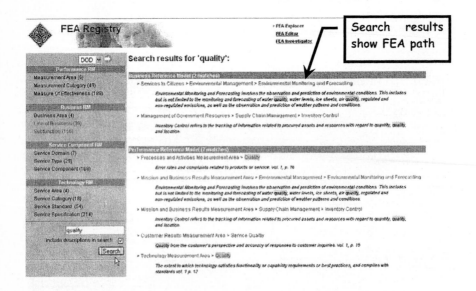

Finally, an agency can make additions or changes to some part of the model and review the changes using a number of reports.

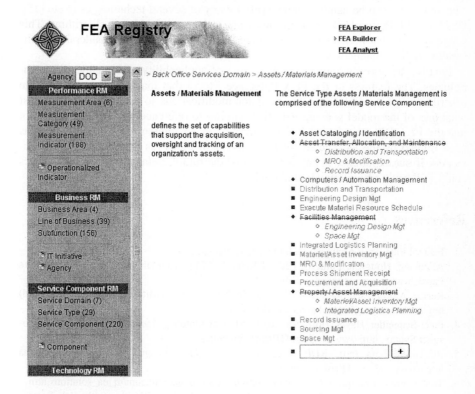

5   Conclusions and Lessons Learned

The entire development process for the FEA-RMO took just about three months, from project inception to delivery. This suggests to us that it is possible to deliver semantic technology solutions in short time frames. A key to this speedy development was a good starting point; the published FEA RM, though it was developed and delivered as a natural language publication, was highly structured and quite consistent. This allowed the modeling process to proceed smoothly and with minimal ambiguity.

Another key to the project's success was the availability of design patterns to help guide model development. We had to document some patterns ourselves [2], but others were available from the W3C [3]. As the craft of ontology engineering develops, more such patterns will be available, making this process simpler.

The role of RDF and OWL cannot be overstated here. RDF as a foundation technology provided a great deal of the functionality needed to support distribution of the models in a coherent and semantically consistent way.

The role of OWL was a bit more subtle. While the reasoning capabilities of OWL were essential in allowing the models to express the appropriate constraints between the elements, the actual reasoning capabilities required were considerably less than those specified in the OWL standard [4]. In fact, the only reasoning that was needed could be achieved with a very simple reasoner that can do RDFS reasoning, combined with a-box reasoning on inverses, transitive properties, and owl:hasValue restrictions. This reasoning can be handled quite easily by any of several technologies (Rete [15], Datalog [16], Prolog [17], etc.), and need not make use of tableaux algorithms. This suggests to us that perhaps other reasoning strategies could have considerable applicability in the semantic web.

Finally, this project suggests a whole area of applicability of semantic web technologies. The features of the FEA Reference Model that made RDF so appropriate (distribution of modifications, the need for modifications to be able to specify just what part of the model is being modified) applies to reference models in general, not just the FEA RM. We feel that the success of many reference model activities has been limited by the weaknesses of the delivery methods (as natural language documents). If our experience is any indication of the future, Semantic Web technologies could well bring a revolution to this field.

References

1. Federal Enterprise Architecture, http://www.feapmo.gov/
2. Allemang, Hodgson, Polikoff, Federal Reference Model Ontologies (FEA-RMO), White Paper, www.topquadrant.com. Feb. 2005.
3. Rector, A. Representing Specified Values in OWL: "value partitions" and "value sets" (ed) http://www.w3.org/TR/swbp-specified-values/
4. Patel-Schneider, Hayes, Horrocks (ed). OWL Web Ontology Language Semantics and Abstract Syntax, http://www.w3.org/TR/owl-semantics/
5. Brickley, Guha (ed). RDF Vocabulary Description Language 1.0: RDF Schema http://www.w3.org/TR/rdf-schema/
6. TopQuadrant, Enterprise Architecture, http://www.topquadrant.com/tq_ea_solutions.htm
7. Aditya Kalyanpur, Bijan Parsia, James Hendler "A Tool for Working with Web Ontologies," *In Proceedings of the International Journal on Semantic Web and Information Systems, Vol. 1, No. 1, Jan-Mar 2005*
8. J. Gennari, M. A. Musen, R. W. Fergerson, W. E. Grosso, M. Crubézy, H. Eriksson, N. F. Noy, S. W. Tu The Evolution of Protégé: An Environment for Knowledge-Based Systems Development. 2002.
9. Consultative Committee for Space Data Systems. Reference Model for an Open Archival Information System (OAIS). (CCSDS 650.0-R-1, Red Book, 1999) (http://ssdoo.gsfc.nasa.gov/nost/isoas/ref_model.html).
10. Zimmerman, H. "OSI reference model - the ISO model of architecture for open systems intercommunications, IEEE Transactions on Communications vol. COM-28 pp. 425-432 April 1980
11. Reference Model of Open Distributed Processing (RM-ODP). ISO/IEC 10746.
12. ICOM/CIDOC Documentation Standards Group, CIDOC Conceptual Reference Model, http://www.ville-ge.ch/musinfo/cidoc/oomodel/.
13. Simos, M. "Juggling in Free Fall: Uncertainty Management Aspects of Domain Analysis Methods," 512-521. Fifth International Conference on Information Processing and Management of Uncertainty in Knowledge-Based Systems. Paris, France, July 4-8, 1994. Berlin, Germany: Springer-Verlag, 1995.
14. Army Enterprise Transformation Guide, http://www.army.mil/aeioo/aetg/activities.htm

15. Charles Forgy, "Rete: A Fast Algorithm for the Many Pattern/Many Object Pattern Match Problem", Artificial Intelligence, 19, pp 17-37, 1982
16. Ceri, S., Gottlob, G., Tanca, L.: What you always wanted to know about Datalog (and never dared to ask). IEEE Transactions on Knowledge and Data Engineering 1(1) (1989) 146-166
17. K. L. Clark and F. G. McCabe. PROLOG: A Language for Implementing Expert Systems. In J. E. Hayes, D. Michie, and Y.-H. Pao, editors, Machine Intelligence, volume 10, pages 455--470. Ellis Horwood, Chichester, 1982.

MediaCaddy - Semantic Web Based On-Demand Content Navigation System for Entertainment

Shishir Garg, Amit Goswami, Jérémy Huylebroeck,
Senthil Jaganathan, and Pramila Mullan

France Telecom R&D, 801 Gateway Boulevard, Suite 500, South San Francisco, CA, USA
{shishir.garg, amit.goswami, jeremy.huylebroeck,
senthil.jagnathan, pramila.mullan}@rd.francetelecom.com

Abstract. This paper is aimed at documenting the role of Web services and specifically Semantic Web Services in serving the needs of the entertainment industry by enabling the users to easily research and explore the large volume meta-content (content about content e.g. entertainment news, articles, reviews, interviews, trailers etc) and eventually leading them to FIND right content (Music, Movies TV program etc). In this scenario, semantic web techniques are used to not only develop and populate the ontology from different meta-content sources, but also to annotate them semantically to provide personalize meta content based Search-Find experience for main content. The paper outlines an application scenario where this is applied in a demonstrated proof of concept and articulates the next steps in the evolution of this architecture.

1 Overview of the Entertainment Industry

For the entertainment industry, traditional approaches to delivering meta-content about movies, music, TV shows, etc. were through reviews, articles etc that were done and published in traditional media such as newspapers, magazines, TV shows, etc. These entertainment magazine/new papers have provided extensive Subjective analysis of Movies, TV shows, Events and music, hence played a very critical role in influencing consumer's opinion about different types of contents. In other words, Consumer has used these sources to search and find right content for him/her.

With the introduction of the internet, non-traditional forms of delivering entertainment started surfacing. The third quarter of 2003 in the U.S was the best ever for broadband penetration bringing such services as content on-demand and mobile multimedia, back from hibernation. 2003 also witnessed the beginning of the on-line content explosion and a flood of new, more capable terminals. Users are accessing content via their television set top boxes, ISP portals, and smart phones, interactively. As of today more than 5000 movies and 2,500,000 songs are available online. In the next couple of years this figure is expected to grow in leaps and bounds. With such a phenomenal rise in content over IP, a new need for secondary meta-content related to the movies/music emerged. Initially this was through movie reviews or music reviews, etc. published on web portals such as Yahoo, MSN, etc and online magazine portals as well as entertainment sales sites such as Netflix.com. Amazon.com etc... Most Consumers today get information about media content

Y. Gil et al. (Eds.): ISWC 2005, LNCS 3729, pp. 858–871, 2005.

primarily from reviews/articles in entertainment/news magazines, their social network of friends (one user recommends a song or movie to a friend) and acquaintances, and advertisements. In most of the cases, one or all of the above influence user's opinion about any content she chooses to consume. In addition, a new breed of customizable meta-content portals has emerged, which specifically targets for the entertainment industry. Examples of such portals include, Rotten Tomatoes, IMDB, etc. However, these services today are typically accessed via portals thereby limiting the interactions and access to the information to exchanges between a user and the source for non-PC environment.

Today, Content on demand is finally taking off due to boost in digital TV infrastructure and added intelligence in Set Top Boxes—by 2008 more than 40 million set top boxes will have advanced OS and hardware. Interactive Program Guides (IPGs) are becoming the entertainment portal for TV viewers, and In-Stat/MDR expects the worldwide IPG market value to grow to nearly $1 Billion (US) by 2008. IPGs will help end-users to find a TV program, movie or sporting event from among listings of thousands of available options, and then make it easy for them to select the program for viewing, tag it with a reminder for later, or even set up a recording to capture the show for time-shifting on a Personal Video Recorder.

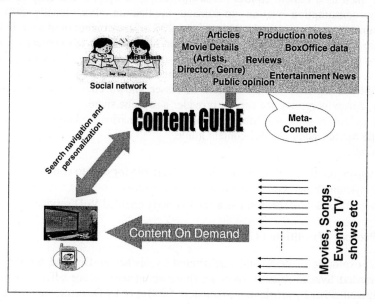

Fig. 1. Conceptual Model of Content Navigation System

This paper discusses a service concept for a recommendation engine called MediaCaddy which leverages semantic web technology to build intelligence in IP based content portals for any connected device. It is a recommendation and aggregation service built around a self-learning engine, which analyzes a click stream generated by user's interaction and actions with meta-content displayed on UI. This meta-content (Music /Movies/ TV reviews/ article/ synopsis/ production notes) is accessed from multiple Internet sources and structured as an Ontology using a semantic inferencing platform. This provides multiple benefits, both allowing for a uniform mechanism for aggregating disparate sources of content, and on the other hand, also allowing for complex queries to be executed in a timely and accurate manner. The platform allows this information to be accessed via Web Services APIs, making integration simpler with multiple devices and UI formats. Another feature that sets MediaCaddy apart is its ability to achieve a high level of personalization by analyzing content consumption behavior in user's personal Movie/Music Domain and his social network and using this information to generate music and movie recommendations. Fig 1 explains conceptual model of MediaCaddy.

2 Service Opportunities

It has been proven from business cases of Internet e-commerce vendor Amazon and DVD rental portal Netflix [1] as well as TV Guide/PVR service Tivo [2] that simple user assistance/ recommendation engines can drive revenues up by 30% and 60% respectively. With the explosion of on-demand content, more intelligent methods can be developed to help a user navigate through a content reservoir using a limited device such as a remote control. Such an intelligent system will help in increasing content consumption via an on-demand application. Traditionally 80% of the entertainment industry revenues come from 20% of the content produced. In a typical revenue share model, users pay $2 to $4 per film, wherein the content owner takes 30% to 60% of it and the rest goes to a service provider. The more popular the content, the larger the content owner's revenue share. MediaCaddy thus can be used to enable an increase in consumption of lesser known content, where margins are higher, hence increasing the service provider's revenue share.

Let us look at some real life scenarios. These scenarios explain a user's interaction with the MediaCaddy enabled content guide.

Assumptions:

- At least three thousand content titles are available for user to consume.
- The system knows a user's content purchase history
- Every IM buddy of the user has a MediaCaddy enabled VoD service.

2.1 Pretext: (Traditional Content Guide)

User is exploring content catalogue offered by his/her on-Demand service provider. On Demand System doesn't know anything about user, hence offers list of content categorized either by artists (approximately 5000+) or by Directors (approx 2000+) or by Genres (100+).

2.2 Scenario #1: (Content navigation Guide powered by MediaCaddy)

Along with traditional categories (Sort by name or Sort by Genre) offered by service providers, MediaCaddy offers three more categories. Each of these categories is explained in more detail.

The first category is a single comprehensive listing of recommended content. These movies/music tracks are suggested based on past purchase history of user. This personalized list of is generated based on Components (Artists, directors, Genre, basic keyword based content description, MPAA rating, reviewers which had facilitated past purchases etc) of movies/music tracks purchased by the user in the past.

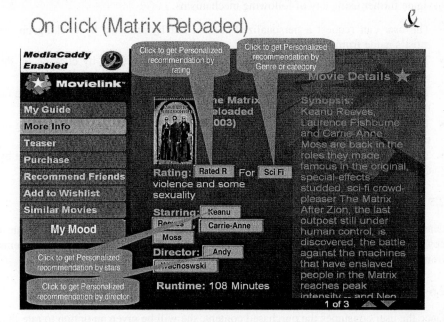

Fig. 2. Sample User Interface of Content Navigation System

The second category is a listing of content from a user's friend circle. This category will offer content recommended by the user's active friends (compiled from messenger buddy list) and movies liked by passive buddies (people of similar interests, compiled from comprehensive listing of "friends of friends")

The third category is a listing of content based on the user's current mood, generated based on interest shown by the user in the current session. The user's interest is captured by analyzing the clicks she made on any of the ontological entities displayed in the UI e.g. artist, genre, movie/music, producer, etc. (see Fig. 2). For example, a user comes home and is interested in watching an action movie by either Tom Cruise or by Tom Hanks. The movie should also be either a spy thriller or a super natural thriller. She starts browsing the catalogue, and based on her interests captured by following and analyzing clicks made in the current session, a list of movies is offered that fits her interest.

2.3 Scenario #2: (Content navigation Guide powered by MediaCaddy)

Once the user selects a movie from one of these four sources (system recommendations, social network, mood based or from catalogue), she can get more detailed information such as artists, director, category, synopsis, personalized reviews by her preferred reviewers (generated based on past performance of reviewers in influencing user's past purchases), recent news items from preferred news sources, productions notes, box office results, public consensus etc.

2.4 Scenario #3: (Content navigation Guide powered by MediaCaddy)

Upon viewing the details of a selected movie, if the user is not interested in it, she can navigate further using any of following mechanisms:

- The user can request a personalized content list by an artist by clicking on the artist's name from the current screen.
- The user can request a personalized content list by a director by clicking on the director's name from the current screen.
- The user can request a personalized content list by a genre/category by clicking on the genre/category's from current screen.
- The user can request a personalized list of movies by MPAA rating by clicking on the MPAA rating from current screen.
- The user can request a personalized list of movies similar to a particular movie by clicking on it. This holds true for other content types as well.

2.5 Scenario #4: (Content navigation Guide powered by MediaCaddy)

Once a personalized list of movies is displayed, the user can also request the latest news either for the selected artist or director. The user will be offered news items from her preferred news sources.

2.6 Scenario #5: (Content navigation Guide powered by MediaCaddy)

Once the user consumes the purchased content, she will be given an option to rate that content on a scale of one to five. She can also recommend content to her active buddies. User participation into the system is encouraged in this manner.

3 Implementation Architecture

The following figure provides an overview of the implementation architecture used for MediaCaddy development. The development was done completely in a Java and J2EE environment, using an open source application server called JOnAS from ObjectWeb.org. The components include:

- Automated meta-content gathering engine: The meta-content gathering engine is a series of extraction agents, built as a Classifier Committee, using a combination of statistical, probabilistic and knowledge based data to populate the ontology from semi-structured and non-structured data sources. Trusted partner data, available in structured form is populated into the ontology server directly.
- Meta-content repository: basically refers to the ontology server (containing an ontology representation as well as instance data), which is based on off the shelf technology from a third party, and is a core asset used in producing recommendations. A REST based Web service API is available to browse the ontology and run inference queries on it. The technology is described here [3]
- Social Network components: These are built using EJBs for the core server with business logic built in plain java objects, and is based on a Cosine similarity algorithm. The cosine algorithm simply computes the cosine value between two

vectors of any dimension. The space considered is orthogonal in this implementation. These components are not detailed in this paper.

- MediaCaddy Server: This is the heart of the system. The MediaCaddy server performs data transformations across various data types and formats, by defining a system wide standard XML format that all components should adhere to. The MediaCaddy server is also interfaces with other components of the system including user profiling, session management and impulse generation, social network, etc. Naturally, the MediaCaddy server also interfaces with the Ontology server via the query interfaces provided by the ontology server. For this, the MediaCaddy server also defines a Query Management API to standardize the interactions with the ontology server.

Scalability issues discussed in previous projects such as [4] are not addressed.

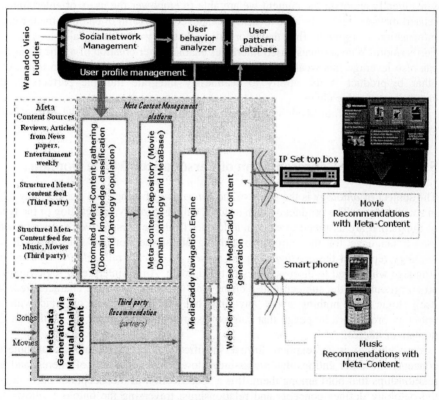

Fig. 3. MediaCaddy component level view

4   How Semantic Web Technologies Address the Needs of the Entertainment Domain?

A Semantic web approach to this problem is interesting as the entertainment domain offers a vast set of resources that are available, often for free, to be leveraged in developing a complex system such as MediaCaddy. In working with commercial third-party sources, we are able to use structured data to populate the ontology, while the ontology has been completely pre-designed by hand.

Using a non-semantic, simple XML and XML-Schema based system would limit the levels of flexibility we are able to achieve. While XML provides for well formed messaging, the more sophisticated Semantic web technologies provide support for complex querying and inferencing. Machine readability and automated processing, key tenets of the Semantic web world, are key requirements for the MediaCaddy platform. Every query made by the user is translated into several system level queries. It is not possible to cover the details of the syntax used within the system to describe the ontology in this paper.

By leveraging Web services for their ability to easily integrate multiple heterogeneous sources of meta-content and leveraging semantic web technologies to semantically annotate the content we are able to empower the users of entertainment related meta-content to be able to easily maneuver the wealth of entertainment-related information in order to find the information that they are specifically looking for. Furthermore, Web services based interfaces enable easier creation of applications that can also leverage this wealth of information in unique ways to present to users. One other by-product is the ability to seamlessly integrate multiple partners in the entertainment value chain.

The following four sections represent the main components of the MediaCaddy system.

5 Ontological Representation of Personalized Movie Domain

The subject of *ontology* is the study of the *categories* of things that exist or may exist in some domain. The product of such a study, called *ontology*, is a catalog of the types of things that are assumed to exist in a domain from the perspective of a person who uses a language for the purpose of talking about the domain. The types in the ontology represent the *predicates*, *word senses*, or *concept and relation types* of the language when used to discuss topics in the domain. An un-interpreted logic imposes no constraints on the subject matter or the way the subject may be characterized. By itself, logic says nothing about anything, but the combination of logic with an ontology provides a language that can express relationships about the entities in the domain of interest.

An ontology is an explicit formal specification for representation of objects, concepts and other entities that are assumed to exist in some area of interest and the relationships that hold among them. It is a specification of a conceptualization. Since the ontology defines concepts and relationships, traversing the ontology allows for discovery of relationships that exist between entities, thus enabling an ontology inference layer to return deterministic responses to queries.

In order to ensure success in this experiment, it was important to select a domain where the number of entities is stable and relatively small. Also, it is desirable to have sufficient existing information about the domain that needs to be modeled using the ontology. The entertainment domain fits these requirements well, and the movie domain specifically is extremely well suited with a lot of disparate yet structured sources available that can be used not only as knowledge sources to model the ontology but also as sources to populate the entity instances.

The MediaCaddy ontology defines several entities as discussed in Figure 4. The main entities, the movie entity and the user entity, define the relationships that exist between these entities and several other entities. The relationships can be categorized into the following types:

- Direct entity-entity relationships: These are the various relationships such as movie-review, movie-director, movie-artist, etc. They are defined as explicit relationships that help ascertain the unique relationship between these entities. For example, the movie-director relationship is defined as "is directed by", etc. There are several user related relationships as well, such as user-artist and user-reviewer, that are used extensively within MediaCaddy to personalize the system for the user's needs
- There are a few entity-same entity relationships as well, that are meant to define relationships between similar instances. In the case of users, it is used to define affinity between individuals.
- Multi-hop relationships: These are used to traverse relationships between multiple entities and to infer details not obvious without traversing the defined links. For example, by traversing the user -> reviewer -> movie graph, additional movie instances are revealed than originally anticipated. Such traversals are key to the MediaCaddy system.

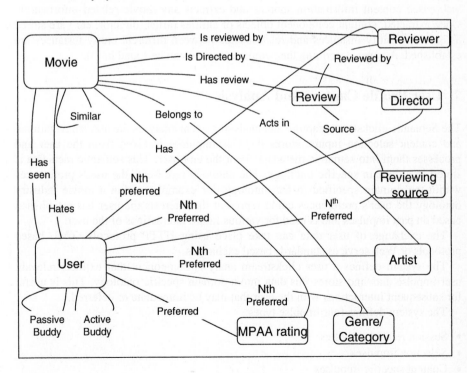

Fig. 4. Movie Ontology

Ontological relationships between entities are used to infer more information about a user profile than is seen explicitly from a user's behavior. Furthermore the system constantly captures user activity (Clicks made on UI e.g. Fig 2) which in turn updates the user profile. This approach distinguishes MediaCaddy's semantic ontology approach from traditional recommendation systems.

For a novice user the recommendation made by the system is of generic nature (default settings) but as the usage increases the recommendations are more accurate and ontological relationships helps in building a better user profile by inferring different types of possible relationships between entity instances. User preferences are updated on a timely basis based on usage patterns and the user profile is then built by correlating previous patterns with the current pattern. The profile is then reflected back in the ontology.

There are several additional pieces of information stored in the ontology, such as content related metadata (e.g. year of release, length, etc.) and other details that are not clearly exposed in the metadata described as they are stored as attributes of the entities defined.

6 Content Knowledge Capture (Ontology Building)

MediaCaddy utilizes a third party component to perform crawling, indexing and population of Ontological entities. The third party component crawls through different web based content information sources and extracts any movie related information. Once extracted, content component objects or entities (artist, director, etc.) are stored as ontology entity instances and relationships between different entity instances are established. A paper describing the components used can be found in [3].

7 User Profile Capture and Analysis

The Semantic clickstream capture and analysis system analyses the user's navigational and content selection inputs, stores them as impulses received from the user and processes them into semantic metadata about the end-user. This semantic metadata is stored in a domain specific ontology. The ontology represents the user's preferences within the domain specified in the ontology, for example, within a movie industry ontology the user's preferences could represent the interests the user has established based on past impulses and is used for various future interactions of the user.

The exchange of user data can take place using HTTP protocols, XML based protocols or Web services standards based exchanges.

The system defines a user clickstream analysis component that extracts relevant user impulse data and stores this data into a domain specific ontology. This is useful for subsequent interactions with the user that may be immediate or deferred.

The system defines four impulse types:

- Session related activities
- Selection impulses
- Content specific impulses
- Meta-data related impulses

These user impulses are then analyzed and aggregated and the user information is extracted into the ontology of the user.

8 Content Navigation Via Semantic Queries

8.1 Personalized Content Navigation in Movie Domain

MediaCaddy offers three different types of content navigation methods.

8.1.1 User Profile Based Navigation

The user profile section explains how a detailed analysis of the user's behavior and interaction with content ontology, generates user profile, which is nothing but couple of lists of preferred directors, artists, news sources, review sources, reviewers, genre/category/keywords, active buddy and passive buddy. These lists will be used for personalization of navigation output. To understand personalized content navigation, we need to understand entry points in the Content Ontology domain. Please see Fig. 5 and Fig. 6 to understand flow of content navigation.

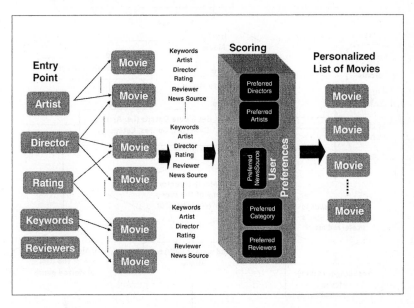

Fig. 5. Content navigation based on different entry points of Movie Domain

The following is a representation of personalized weight for every movie while performing navigation by artist, director or genre.

- (AW)= Weight of artist as a movie component in User's Movie Ontology
- (DW) = Weight of Director as a movie component in User's Movie Ontology
- (GW) = Weight of Genre as a movie component in User's Movie Ontology
- (RW) = Weight of Reviewer as a movie component in User's Movie Ontology

- (Ng) = Number of genres of movie
- (Na) = Number of Artists of movie
- (Nd) = Number of Directors of movie
- (Nr) = Number of Reviewers of movie
- (MW) = Personalized weight of a movie.
- N = Index of preferred artist, director, genre, reviewer, review sources and news source tables of user's profile. If entry is not found in table value of N will be zero.

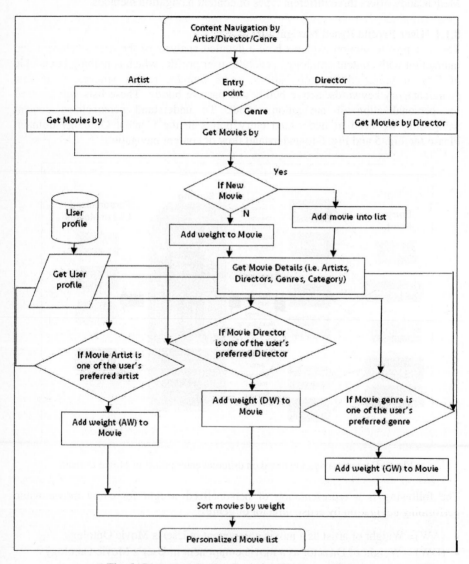

Fig. 6. Content navigation by Artist, Director or Genre

$$\text{Personalized Movie Weight (MW)} = \sum_{i=0}^{i=Na}(AWi \,/\, Ni) + \tag{1}$$

$$\sum_{i=0}^{i=Nd}(DWi \,/\, Ni) + \sum_{i=0}^{i=Ng}(GWi \,/\, Ni) + \sum_{i=0}^{i=Nr}(RWi \,/\, Ni)$$

There are multiple Entry points in Movie knowledge domain graph. Typically one of the following will be used to request personalized movie listing.

1. Artists: User can request a personalized list of movies, jut by clicking name of any of the artist from any of the guide's screen. Please refer 0 and 0.
2. Director: User can also request a personalized list of movies, just by clicking name of any of the director from any of the guide's screen. Please refer 0 and 0.
3. Genre/Keyword/Category: Third entry point in Movie knowledge domain can be genre/category/Keyword. User can request a personalized list of movies, just by clicking names of any of the category/keyword/Genre. Please refer 0 and 0.
4. User: user can also request a simple personalized list of movies based on his user profile.

8.1.2 Mood Based Content Navigation

Both of the above discussed content navigation methods heavily depend on user's profile, but its very difficult to profile human behavior, hence this one is totally independent of user profile. Mood based content navigation method, analyzed user's intentions by monitoring his/her activities in current navigation session and generates list of movies based on user's intentions. Mood based content navigation system has following three stages.

1. **Impulse capture:** In MediaCaddy, mood is defined as user's intentions in current session. MediaCaddy logs user's every interaction with system, between login and logout (or timeout)
2. **Intelligent knowledge extraction or mood analysis:** During this stage, user's interaction with content guide is analyzed and knowledge is extracted. During this knowledge extraction process, any of the user's clicks which were directly or indirectly related to any movie domain, are filtered. Once filtered, these clicks represent entity instances (name or artist, genre, director or movies) in Movie Domain.
3. **Content navigation:** All the entity instances filtered during knowledge extraction stage become entry points for content navigation in Movie domain ontology. Please refer to Fig. 4.In previous example Tom Cruise and Tom Hanks represents instances of artist entity, Action and Thriller are instances of genre entity, and Top Gun and Forest Gump represents Movie entity instances, these entity instances become entry point for Content navigation process.

9 Findings

One of the goals of our study was to give some elements in order to compare our approach in a future paper with the collaborative filtering based recommendation engine, especially since the main goal was to develop a content navigation system. We believed that bringing more information to the recommendation engine about all the entities would provide more relevant recommendation results. The actual system is based on a more semantically rich analysis than just the objects themselves and their consumption statistics. Those multiple ontological relationships between entities allowed more complex inferring bringing therefore more details about the actual user profile, and then the recommendation made to him, than what the user behavior tracking component only could capture. The relevance of the recommendation allowed to put them at the core of the navigation system instead of using a simple catalog browsing.

The system is designed to leverage the openness of services, thanks to a standards based way to describe them, in addition to techniques to map different contextual information such as content information or user profiles.

Nevertheless, a lack of XML usage within the entertainment industry has been observed, requiring multiple ways to aggregates the information within the ontology, making the architecture and mostly the maintenance of the system more complex. Promote the usage of semantic technologies and XML representation in general would definitely ease the creation of such a system.

Secondly, the lack of a common identification of content and related entities such as actors, directors, with one or a few generic IDs, makes the mapping of the information tricky, sometimes with a high degree of uncertainty. It basically creates incorrect recommendations. To minimize this effect, more complexity in the ontology creation and traversing had to be used.

Finally, the implementation of our system didn't take into consideration at every step the need of efficiency and speed. Most of the computation is done every time, after a very fast information retrieval from the ontology. We found that caching or storing the intermediate computation is possible and would bring more responsiveness. For example, intermediate results could be put back into the ontology to create more weighted relationships between entities that would be used in the traversing, which is in this case optimized. In our case, it is particularly true concerning the user related information and relationships.

10 Next Steps

A first version of this prototype is completed. For next steps, the entertainment industry is vast and consists of many facets that are not represented in this solution yet. A next step will be to incorporate additional entity classes to expand the size of the ontology. (e.g. different kind of content) and more relationships (e.g. more granular information about the content).

The current system doesn't use OWL [5]. Enhancing, importing and exporting the ontology using the OWL format is a one of the necessary next step to make the system more open and easier to maintain in the long run.

In this goal of making the system more open, use of standards to represent the user profile information (in a general meaning) will be studied. Schematic representations such as FOAF, OPML or attention.xml [6] are tracks that will be followed to understand how to import and also export user related information.

From a long term perspective, context extraction of a particular piece of information is helps indexing this information. Examples of such techniques exist to auto categorize web pages for instance, based on the content of the page itself. Similar approach would be explored for the entities categorization within the ontology.

Additionally, the definition of categories needs more analysis. A bottom up community approach will definitely be considered. This approach would require more analysis and processing of the information. The goal would be to develop automatic, and dynamic if possible, system for a particular context. Folksonomy in a specific community is an interested manual process to do such a thing as a first step, especially for its contextual and distributed effort aspects that reduces the resources needed and creates quickly large corpus of valuable information.

References

1. Netflix: http://www.netflix.com
2. Tivo: http://www.tivo.com
3. A. Sheth and C. Ramakrishnan, "Semantic (Web) Technology in Action": Ontology Driven Information Systems for Search, Integration and Analysis, In IEEE Data Engineering Bulletin, Special issue on Making the Semantic Web Real, Decmber 2003.
4. International Multimedia Conference: Multimedia information services enabling: an architectural approach: Proceedings of 2001 ACM workshops on Multimedia Pages 18-23
5. Web Ontology Language (OWL):: http://www.w3.org/2004/OWL/
6. attention.xml: http://developers.technorati.com/wiki/attentionxml

LKMS – A Legal Knowledge Management System Exploiting Semantic Web Technologies

Luca Gilardoni, Chistian Biasuzzi, Massimo Ferraro, Roberto Fonti,
and Piercarlo Slavazza

Quinary - Via Pietrasanta 14 – 20141 Milan – Italy
{gil,bic,fem,for,slp}@quinary.com

Abstract. Semantic Web, using formal languages to represent document content and providing facilities for aggregating information spread around, can improve the functionalities provided nowadays by KM tools. This paper describes a Knowledge Management system, targeted at lawyers, which has been enhanced using Semantic Web technologies. The system assists lawyers during their everyday work, and allows them to manage their information and knowledge. A semantic layer has been added to the system, providing capabilities that make system usage easier and much more powerful, adding new and advanced means for create, share and access knowledge.

1 Introduction

After years of hype, there is clear evidence of an up-take of knowledge management in corporations. Today, knowledge is recognized as a strategic resource, with major key drivers being the need to cut time to market and the fear of missing business opportunities in a global market where companies have to cope with new products and services. At the same time, there is a general acknowledgement that existing technology behind most knowledge management products has somehow reached its limits. Current knowledge management systems are indeed still mostly built on top of conventional document management systems, without real 'understanding' layers. Tools are mostly designed as aids to human centered activities with a set of low level tools needing human guidance to deliver results [1]. Albeit relying on web technologies, built as intranet portal tools, current state of the art does not really leverage the expected potential of the semantic web. To go to the next step, we should move towards a architecture and an infrastructure providing a foundation for new generation services, semantically aware tools and proactive agents, able to better support human actors.

Technology born to support the development of the Semantic Web may be used to build such foundation. Moreover, the 'inside web', that is the web constituted by intranets, KM environments, portals, is worth to users as much – and often more – than the 'web out there'. If we consider the whole world of professional users within corporation – and to some extent even some virtual community build within closed spaces – we find out a huge amount of information available. The fact that such information is not available to the general public is scarcely relevant, as whenever we consider ourselves, we find that, in our space of accessible information, the outer web

Y. Gil et al. (Eds.): ISWC 2005, LNCS 3729, pp. 872 – 886, 2005.

and inside web often play an equally relevant role. What's even more notable is that the relevance is often in our capacity to connect internal information and external one. A collaborative environment, such as those currently found behind most intranets, could provide a natural place to add semantic capabilities, while the organization work which is behind most intranet initiatives provides the economic support and impulse to add what's needed – organized information and knowledge – to implement the semantic layer.

The system described in this paper is centered around this assumption. Based on a long experience in building advanced knowledge management systems, and derived from research made in the framework of the Dot.Kom project ([2]), we built an enhanced solution integrating such a semantic layer into an existent KM environment.

The semantic layer is founded over an ontology repository supporting knowledge integration and fusion and acting as the common glue for share and reuse services for knowledge management. Ontologies indeed play a key role in the context of the Semantic Web: they formalize the knowledge about the concepts related to the "world" of interest. Once the proper knowledge framework is defined through ontologies, one can identify in documents instances of the concepts described, and relations between them. Accordingly, they also play a key role in supporting knowledge management tools, making them a bit more 'knowledge aware'. Semantic annotations, whether manually generated, or derived by information extraction techniques or other automatic processes, can provide a major framework for generating, preserving and sharing knowledge. Annotations provide the basis for advanced information retrieval, and for providing proactive services.

We will describe here a specific vertical solution targeting law firms. The described system has already been deployed in a major Italian law firm, and is currently a key component of our company offering for the legal market.

2 Knowledge in the Legal World

Law is a knowledge-based profession. Since law firms and law departments are knowledge-based organisations, knowledge management becomes critical to their continuing success. A knowledge management system enables lawyers to work more efficiently and to provide legal services quicker than ever before. By creating processes to support and facilitate the identification, capture and dissemination of a firm's knowledge, knowledge management systems leverage a law firm collective wisdom.

The legal industry has faced significant pressures in recent years, making knowledge management a business imperative. In the age of instant communication, lawyers have been forced to find quicker ways to deliver traditional legal services. Law firm clients have become very sophisticated buyers of legal services and therefore they expect a faster turnaround time.

Several components of knowledge management, such as precedent libraries or work product repositories, already exist in law firms. Innovative law firms however are already working to find a more efficient way to work, leveraging the knowledge of their experts by delegating work to more junior staff and hence looking for better ways to improve knowledge sharing and exploitation processes.

Work of professionals within a law firm – or a legal department in a corporation - ultimately leads to production of documents: acts, contractsor opinions. In this sense work processes are document centric. This is one of the reasons why most KM solutions targeting law professionals focuses on document management issues. However, from the point of view of knowledge building and sharing, what is really relevant is the intellectual process carried on to delivery the document.

The outcome of this process is constrained on one side by the task and the specific matter, from the other by contextual knowledge.

The context should be maintained, because it is this contextual knowledge that enables, for example, to maintain and revise documents (.. this clause was made this way because of that law ...; if the law is later amended, or a different interpretation given by the supreme court, that clause has to be revised in future contracts and effects on old contracts has to be evaluated). Legal documents, moreover, are inherently interrelated; and so may be the

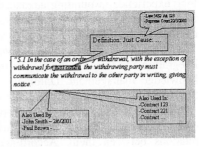

process that leads to them. A contract – legal act binding two or more parties - may be designed taking legal opinions into account, and it may be in turn the source of a case which leads to production of legal acts discussing it, these in turns taking other opinions into account. Legal opinions - written by lawyers on request of customers who need advise on some topic - are also based in turn on decisions taken in courts on specific cases. Being able to keep track of context hence results to be of paramount importance.

The context is given as well by the work process. Lawyers, as many other professionals, are compelled by the need to share knowledge and competencies. Findings derived by analysis of a court sentence have to be somehow saved for usage by other members of the firm. Too many times people end up redoing the same work as the guy next door in the office. Even a search made against a database looking for specific cases may be reused in similar cases.

The more a law firm tends to specialize in specific sector, which is often the case, the more sharing this kind of knowledge gives the competitive advantage. Specific law firm knowledge is so relevant that the area of practice a law firm is specialized in highly qualifies the firm. A primary concern and a major activity directly functional to the primary process is therefore to keep this background knowledge up to date through knowledge maintenance processes.

One way to share this knowledge is by similarity, which is often the approach taken by case based reasoning systems, which sometimes work rather reasonably. Point is that current tools reason by similarity at the textual level, which may work reasonably to find out similarity in matter (e.g. two employment contracts for managers with similar bonus plans) but can hardly support in linking at the clause level (to stay within contracts) or to maintain connections to supporting cases. Similarity is not taken to the conceptual level, and hidden links and background knowledge are ... just treated as hidden.

Hence knowledge management system to prove effective must support, other than 'conventional' search, a way to annotate and hyperlink elements to the surrounding context, and be able to navigate and search hyperlinks. To be usable, however, the system must be able to support automatic (at least partially) hyper-linking, and make easy to manage annotations.

A rich knowledge layer and semantic web technologies provide the foundation to enhance existing knowledge sharing environments supporting these functionalities. In a sense, this is not surprising, as the same rationale (adding a semantic layer to enhance sharing providing a better user experience) is also behind the Semantic Web. Moreover, in a world where more and more information is going online, and where a number of public initiatives (e.g. NormeInRete, see [3]) are strongly driving to make available public legal information on the web, the more the technology supports integration of internal law firm material (the 'inside web') with external material, the more users are likely to take advantage of it.

3 System Description

LKMS (Legal Knowledge Management System) is a collaborative web-based platform for knowledge management, supporting law firms in managing a document base and the processes around it. LKMS is a vertical solution for the legal market built on top of "K@", a generic KM system developed by Quinary since 2002.

With LKMS users can access and share a common repository of documents while the system keeps track of people interaction. Documents, including both physical documents residing inside the law firm, external URLs, notes and Wiki pages, may be organized according to one or more taxonomies, supporting multiple inheritance (DAGs): the environment provides a basic framework for sharing information by matching the way an organization is structuring its processes.

The core system supports browsing and searching using free text queries and provides a number of tools to track user behavior (who added a document or a node in a taxonomy, who added classification links between nodes and taxonomies, who visited nodes or read documents) to facilitate sharing and keeping track of workgroup activities.

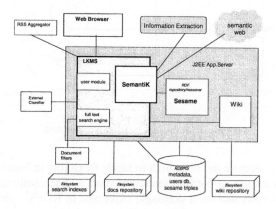

Fig. 1. LKMS Architecture

The system also includes a document drafting component, based on XML technology, enabling to build template documents as aggregate of clauses and composition logic. Drafts can then be built from templates by specifying constraints through a user friendly query answer interface.

The core version of LKMS has been enhanced in 2004, now it is able to maintain the association between documents and semantic annotations with respect to a formal ontology according to Semantic Web standards. Figure below outlines the overall system architecture.

Semantic Layer Overview. The core KM framework has been enriched with the SemantiK plugin to provide a semantic layer over documents repository. SemantiK is a platform featuring presentation, editing, integration, and searching of knowledge expressed through the RDF language. SemantiK has been integrated with LKMS as a plugin, allowing for connecting annotations to documents on evidence that, in most cases, annotations are motivated by or related to document content.

Storage and inferencing over annotations is given by an underlying RDF repository (Sesame, see [4]). The main purpose of SemantiK is to provide a middleware for high-level access to an RDF knowledge base, supported by a knowledge integration layer, and a web GUI for maintenance of RDF annotations tailored to end users habits. Main functionalities include:

- ontology supported GUI for viewing, browsing and editing annotations through web forms;
- support for semantic search;
- support for knowledge integration and resources disambiguation;
- interface and support for automatic annotation extraction from documents.

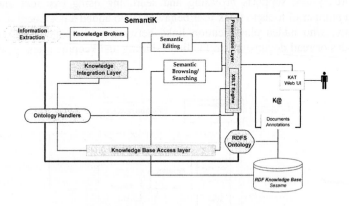

Fig. 2. SemantiK Internal Architecture

The whole architecture has been built to tackle flexibility in handling of specialized ontologies, with respect to both presentation issues and semantic integration. LKMS comes with a precompiled legal ontology, expressed in RDFS[1], which may however

---

[1] Enhanced with few custom meta-properties – porting to OWL is being considered.

be extended. The ontology is complemented by Ontology Handlers, a set of Java classes supporting specializations dependent on specific entities.

Moreover, Information Extraction services enable to extract annotations from documents or, more in general, fetch them from external data sources. Plugins has been developed for a number of information extraction systems.

The Ontology. The general legal ontology shipping with LKMS was created in cooperation with our first customer and has been only slightly modified since then (only manual adaptation is handled so far).

The ontology covers three main areas.

Laws. This area includes most of the subdivision of the Italian legislation. It also copes with law's articles and articles' subparts. Each concept is characterized by a minimal set of properties aiming at uniquely identifying each concept, such as law date and number. Given this information it is then also possible to compute URNs, that is a standard unique identifier used, in this case, in order to build links to the public site NormeInRete ([3]). Besides, name, description, source and references to other laws can be defined.

Legal Documents. This part of the ontology describes different kind of legal documents: contracts, legal Opinions, Sentences from the different kind of Italian or European Courts, Regulations, Decisions, legal doctrine, etc. Aside, we also include entities describing actors – i.e. organizations such as Tribunals and Judges, and other supporting entities (e.g. grades of legal cases, possible outcomes of "Supreme Court Decisions" etc).

Juridical Concepts. These kinds of concepts are expected to take over the glossary keywords normally used by lawyers, enabling annotating content on the basis of relevant matters. They have been derived transforming a digital glossary from a book about labor law into a structured and organized ontology. It resulted in a complex hierarchy of 1442 Legal Keywords, with references to each other and to more than 3500 laws or regulations automatically extracted from the same book too. An RDF representation of all instances was created and uploaded in the system, and at the same time patterns (a JAPE grammar) were automatically generated to support a Legal NEA IE tool – described later.

Knowledge Handlers. SemantiK has been tailored to the legal domain by providing a set of Ontology Handlers matching the legal concept classes described in the previous paragraph.

An Ontology Handler is a Java class that is bound to some RDFS class and that is in charge of handling a number of actions regarding instances of that RDFS class – such as rendering, searching, knowledge integration. The Java hierarchy must of course respect the RDFS hierarchy: this way, specialization of actions can be achieved straightforwardly. The root of the hierarchy is a Java class that by default is responsible for the instances of the RDFS class Resource – that is, of all resources in the KB.

Ontology Handlers may provide customization such as to find and match legal documents by number and date (as opposed for example to judges, matched primarily by name and surname), to render links to external resources for laws, and to generate automatic label for structured legal documents.

The Presentation Layer. Given a set of triples all having as subject a certain resource (in particular an annotation associated to a document in LKMS), the SemantiK presentation layer is able to render it (for viewing or editing) in a domain dependent way by means of XSL transformations, applied to XML-ization of the triples.

Using custom CSS we have been able to harmonize the output with web-application environment that constitutes the user interface of LKMS.

SemantiK uses custom meta-properties associated to RDF Resources and Properties for defining a number of presentation details like properties order, visibility and cardinality.

Moreover SemantiK can highlight annotated text in documents, given that the RDF resources annotated have an offset –automatic Information Extraction tools described later on provide such offsets. Annotations are given different colors to distinguish RDF Classes and are hyperlinked for fast querying.

Annotation Production and Knowledge Integration. Data can be inserted in SemantiK by manual editing or by means of external IE engines. In both cases, before instances are added to the Knowledge Base, they are passed through the SemantiK integration layer, which is in charge of detecting whether the intended resources exist already in the KB.

Manual editing is supported by the ontology management module: when creating new instances, the user is asked to choose the *type* of the new resource if more than one is possible: the RDFS classes are displayed in a tree-like manner in a listbox, and possibly some branches of the tree are collapsed (the behavior can be set using meta-properties). The wizard-like UI allows the user for expanding the class tree until the right type is found.

When the user is editing an annotation, given a certain property, he is asked to formulate a query in order to find in the Knowledge Base the intended instances. The query is dispatched to the proper Ontology Handler depending on the range of the property. In general, each Ontology Handler is responsible for parsing the query (for it could have a peculiar syntax) and then trying to use some specific method or heuristic in order to find some results, as already mentioned above.

In general, a fuzzy measure of closeness is computed between the candidate resource and the existing ones; then, the user is presented with the closest resources (if any) and is asked for disambiguate his intent. Note that the usage of a fuzzy match allows coping with misspelled words.

In the case of automatic annotation using a Knowledge Broker, the Ontology Handlers try to automatically defuzzify the closeness measures using a proper threshold.

Anyway, given some existing resource, at any moment the user is able to merge it with other existing resources, which can be selected from a list automatically generated of possibly similar resources, or manually searched.

Semantic Annotation Extraction. The Legal IE Application is the module in charge of automatically extracts annotations from documents. It is targeted at the legal domain and its task is to get as input a document, extract references to legal documents and juridical concepts, and get them back in RDF format (referring to the legal ontology).

SemantiK is responsible for calling the Legal IE Application passing a plain text version of the document (conversion from PDF, MS Word and RTF is supported by the base system) and for integrating the resulting RDF in the semantic repository. The Legal IE Application, wrapped in a web service based on AXIS [9], performs analysis and, using the legal ontology as reference ontology, returns RDF annotations. The analysis may be based on different engines. We integrated and tested a GATE [5] based NEA, Amilcare [6] and TIES [7].

The Legal IE Application uses GATE as processing framework and each external processing component is connected using a GATE component. There are four GATE components: Linguistic component, which uses Italian Linguistic tools to perform the basic linguistic analysis (tokenization, POS tagging, lemmatization); Legal NEA component, which uses JAPE grammar [8] and performs a NE analysis focused on legal entities; Amilcare component and TIES component, which use respectively Amilcare and TIES to perform IE processing.

The application is configurable to possibly use only some of the components (e.g. there can be different legal IE applications working concurrently, using different components).

Document Similarity Measures. An algorithm for computing documents similarity basing on RDF annotation has been developed in SemantiK. Roughly speaking, comparing annotations is accomplished by recursively following resources properties and values and counting matching values. The obtained measure is used to suggest similar documents motivated by semantic similarity. Experiments are ongoing to exploit the similarity measure for automatic document classification.

4   LKMS in Use

LKMS environment was designed in order to support a lawyer in his everyday work within a law firm. Accordingly, the system is used to maintain, in a centralised repository, and share between lawyers a number of documents, both coming from outside the law firm and produced inside.

By supporting indexing by semantic content, LKMS enables to perform better searches, based not simply on full text but on semantic content – or, better, on both. Moreover, it becomes possible to support better automatic classification, and to develop triggers based on content; hence people working on specific cases can be signaled about changes in relevant regulations or news about the specific matter.

Next picture shows the situation where a lawyer, browsing LKMS within a specific legal case, comes across a significant document. Starting from the SemantiK document info panel on top, the user can examine the annotations (in this example a number of references to laws). Then the lawyer can follow the hyperlinks leading to more specific information about a particular annotation (an article of law) and, possibly, to other useful information (juridical concepts) or related documents. Please note that in the example the relation between the source document and the one 'discovered' by following the semantic links is derived through the semantic layer through common references, while in a traditional KM system or DMS, such link should have been explicitly stated.

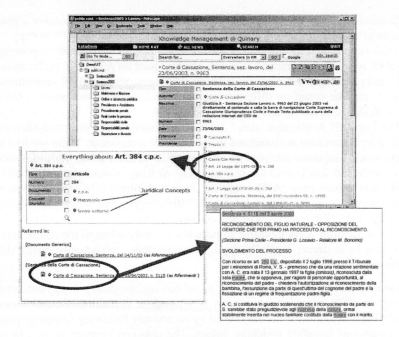

Fig. 3. SemantiK Browsing

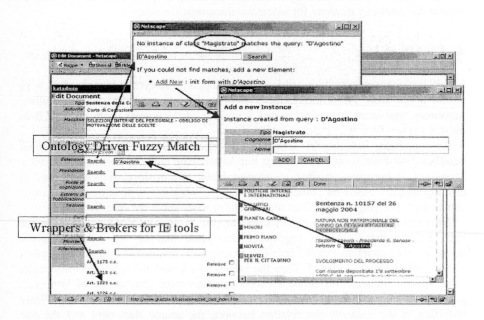

Fig. 4. Sentence Annotation

Annotation such as the ones just shown can derive from both manual annotation and semi-automatic information extraction processes. In this scenario a lawyer imports the sentence in the system, and gets a partial annotation of the new content, making use of some of the available IE modules. The lawyer may then further edit the annotation in SemantiK, removing mistakes and adding missed references.

An essential requirement to reach the LKMS goals introduced above is the development of tools supporting annotation of new documents inserted in the repository, keeping the complexity of the semantic representation behind the scenes.

Our feeling is that with SemantiK we are going in the right direction. The tool supports a lawyer with a point and click, workflow-based user interface, driving the user to a progressive refinement of the annotation with respect to our legal ontology.

In figure 4, editing of annotations is done within the browser having side by side the form based annotation panel on the left and the text with annotations highlighted in the context of the document on the right, rendered as hyperlink to the system knowledge base. Defining new annotations (e.g. adding a legal concept reference, or one of the expected attributes of the sentence) may be done very simply by dragging text elements from right to left. SemantiK features for fuzzy matching and the possibility to exploit ontological information to drive the GUI properly constraining input values, enable to minimize user burden in obtaining a rich and precise annotation.

Founding on a semantic layer also paves the way to development of new drafting tools, able to associate pertinent matter while editing legal documents. We are currently experimenting with tools enabling in-place annotation of text, such as AktiveDoc [26], developed during the course of Dot.Kom project by the University of Sheffield.

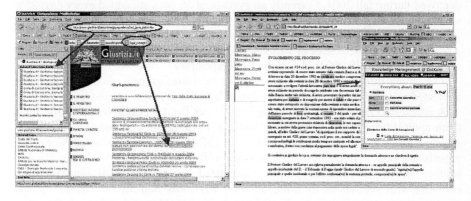

Fig. 5. Enhanced Semantic Web Surfing – Kzilla on the left, Magpie on the right

LKMS's semantic knowledge base can be exploited proactively when the lawyer is browsing the web, either following links from online journals or institution web sites (e.g. during normal monitoring activities of selected sources) or actively searching for something relevant for a case he is working on. Tools like Magpie [24], a browser add-on that uses an ontology infrastructure to semantically markup web documents on-the-fly - which we tested integrated in SemantiK deriving automatically references for Juridical Concepts from our ontology - may support the user in making sense of browsed pages on the web against internal knowledge, highlighting references to annotated material of LKMS stored documents (see **Fig. 5**). By clicking on the highlighted concept the user can follow the contextual link and browse the concept ontology in LKMS, reaching documents already in the system related to that specific concept and helping him to quickly make sense of new material. For the same purpose, we also developed Kzilla, a web browser plugin enabling to match browsed material against content of the LKMS internal repository, much alike what services like Alexa do for generic browsing.

LKMS Evaluation. Currently LKMS has been deployed in an Italian legal firm grouping about 50 lawyers. LKMS hosts now more than 30000 documents. Most material is in PDF - a large number however constituted by scanned images - and Word format, plus a number of XML documents generated by an automated drafting systems, a number of simple textual notes and a number of html documents or URLS (specialized publishers, newspapers, Italian and European public institutions).

Material includes legal documents produced within the firm or by other parts in cases, significant legal documents (cases, opinions etc) gathered from different sources, plus a number of general documents from newspapers. Material partly comes in from batch imports from older repositories, partly from daily work, with a minor part gathered by a specialized spider. Some types of documents (e.g. news from press and some legal related publication) is added by clerks and later on classified/annotated by lawyers, other are added by lawyers directly into the system or indirectly coming from the case management system (e.g. docs from corresponding parties).

The first LKMS version enhanced by the semantic layer SemantiK has been deployed during fall 2004. Currently an average of 50 docs are added every day, 25% of which are manually annotated. Most of them only hold generic metadata such as authors or sources, but there are also more than 400 references through laws or articles, about 150 sentences of various kinds and about 100 acts, laws, circulars etc, for a total of about 30.000 triples in the RDF repository.

The strong directives issued from the law firm management about having richly annotated material are by itself a clear sign of usefulness judged by end users eyes.

A recent experiment has been made in the legal firm: focusing on a specific topic ('non-competition pact'), 8 younger lawyers have been 'commanded' to collect selected material on the subject, add it to LKMS and properly annotate it. The experiment took 96 hours of work - including collecting and analyzing material – and resulted in 117 documents, properly annotated against the legal ontology, and enriched with references to laws, authors, keywords and so on. While manual annotation proved a daunting task, such work was judged useful and worth the effort from the senior partner's side.

Automatic Annotations. It is well evident that automatic IE support is what's needed to step up, as manual annotation may be accepted (and has been accepted - once suitable support for minimizing the burden has been put in place!) for documents where IE is not feasible (e.g. scanned documents), in case of major features (e.g. main metadata for a Supreme Court Sentence), full annotation on all material is out of question.

Usage of tools and IE techniques has however been explored and developed by the authors in the framework of the Dot.Kom project. An automatic information extraction application has been derived and already tested, and it is likely to be setup in production in short time. During the test, made on real data from the law firm, the system produced a number of automatically extracted annotations on a selected corpus of 1200 documents. 5800 references where extracted to a total number of about 250 laws, opinions or articles. 1150 articles to laws were identified. The repository was filled with 70000 triples.

The automatically extracted annotations have been evaluated qualitatively on random elements and judged of relevant quality.

A formal test has been done in parallel – in the framework of the Dot.Kom project - using a legal corpus composed of 197 Sentences from Corte Cassazione (the Italian High Court) in HTML format (2500 - 3000 words each). This corpus was fully annotated according to our legal ontology, starting from an automatic pass made using a NEA based IE module and further manually edited in order to remove mistakes and adding missing elements. While being very specific in coverage (i.e. it is based only on Supreme Courts Sentences) the corpora has the advantage of being based on public material, unlike most other legal documents, and sufficiently generic in both domain (the sentences are not only related to labor law but cover different topics) and in linguistic aspects. The structure of the documents is rather standardized, but the content vary; for example, considering legal references, a wide variety of forms is used, reasonably reflecting a much wider set of documents.

Results of the formal evaluation are listed in a forthcoming Dot.Kom deliverable, but results for all the system tested show average precision over .85 for recalls ranging between .70 and .80 depending on IE subsystem used, with better values for most frequent and useful entities.

Overall results from both tests has been judged more than adequate, and the manual work eventually needed to amend annotations has been judged feasible, given that the error rate is sufficiently low, and anyway worth while pursuing in the light of advantages in using annotated material.

5 Related Work

The idea of using Semantic Web technologies to enhance and facilitate the use of a Knowledge Management System is shared by several others systems such as, for example, KIM and Haystack. KIM [16] is a platform for semantic annotations of texts, supporting semantic indexing and retrieval, which also shares with our system the use of some underlying technologies (GATE, Sesame and Lucene). Haystack [17] as well aims at giving users a unified access to their own corpora of knowledge for organization, navigation, and search, enabling users to import a variety of information types (documents, email, calendar, web pages) into a single unified RDF repository. In either case the two platforms however focuses on general functionalities, while the system described here is strongly focused on the legal domain, making possible to tackle a number of specificities and to take into account peculiarities of legal processes. Another example of vertical solution – for the Environmental domain - is the Semantic Web Environmental Directory (SWED) [18].

Other systems, whose goal is to support the creation of semantic portals, have some similarities with our system. We can cite ODESeW [19], OntoWebber [20], SEAL [21], OntoWeb [22] and OntoView [23]. Other tools share with LKMS the semantic browsing approach, such as already mentioned Magpie [24], or Topicalla [25], a client application for the Semantic Web which allows one to view information using a UI that is generated based on the kind of data available. However these tools and platforms aim mainly to support accessing and retrieval of information, while the purpose of our system is to support the whole knowledge creation process.

The legal area is subject of a growing interest, and there is a lot of work ongoing - see e.g. the recent book on Law and the Semantic Web [10]. Moreover a number of EU funded projects, including e-Court [11], e-Power [12], CLIME [13], FF Poirot [14], and SEKT [15], coped to different extent with exploitation of Semantic Web technologies in the legal domain. To our knowledge however no system aims at supporting the whole knowledge lifecycle and none has yet reached the stage of deployment in a production environment.

6 Conclusions and Future Work

In this paper we have presented a knowledge management solution for lawyer enhanced by a number of semantic web technologies. The system has already reached the commercial stage, where most features has already been incorporated in a commercial solution, deployed in a main Italian law firm and likely to be deployed at other sites on finalization of ongoing deals.

A number of other features are currently in the research and development pipeline. We are currently doing preliminary experimentations on classifiers working on RDF expressions attached to documents – derived automatically from texts and enhanced by additional information derived from public web services based on partial data extracted. We also are experimenting Collaborative Filtering techniques to generate suggestion of interest, mixing data from user tracking – who read what where – with documents semantic features.

Work done, and feedback got, clearly showed usefulness of rich representation framework in knowledge intensive environments, and capacity of semantic web derived technologies and tools to effectively support end users in everyday work. It also showed feasibility of a number of features still too often confined to experimental labs. Work done also enabled to better assess and investigate a number of issues related to matching organizations knowledge resources against public web material, including expected role of end user's as active annotators vs. automatic information extraction, and influences of the new features on ways of working within legal organizations. Attention paid to GUI issues, to flexibility in handling different ontology entities, to tools supporting 'making sense' of raw material has been functional to take end users within the loop. Several issues have still to be solved, and most relate to exploitation of machine learning techniques [27] to ease building of the semantic web. However we feel that as semantic web technology is a key element to step up knowledge management systems, we also believe that knowledge sharing environments like the one described, able to really exploit users knowledge through the organization, will be strong drivers to support building of the Semantic Web itself.

Acknowledgements

Part of the R&D activities behind the work reported has been carried out within the IST-Dot.Kom project (http://www.dot-kom.org), sponsored by the European Commission as part of the framework V, (grant IST-2001-34038). Dot.Kom involves the University of Sheffield (UK), ITC-Irst (I), Ontoprise (D), the Open University (UK), Quinary (I) and the University of Karlsruhe (D). Its objectives are to develop Knowledge Management and Semantic Web methodologies based on Adaptive Information Extraction from Text.

References

1. Salzburg Research and EC IST DG Unit E2, "The Future of electronic publishing towards 2010", http://ep2010.salzburgresearch.at, 2003
2. J. Iria, F. Ciravegna, P. Cimiano, A. Lavelli, E. Motta, L. Gilardoni and E. Mönch: "Integrating Information Extraction, Ontology Learning and Semantic Browsing into Organizational Knowledge Processes", Workshop on the application of Language and Semantic Technologies to support Knowledge Management Processes at the 14th International Conference on Knowledge Engineering and Knowledge Management EKAW 2004, 5-8th October 2004 - Whittlebury Hall, Northamptonshire, UK
3. NormeInRete project. http://www.normeinrete.it
4. J. Broekstra, A. Kampman, F. van Harmelen, "Sesame: A Generic Architecture for Storing and Querying RDF and RDF Schema", Lecture Notes in Computer Science, Volume 2342, Jan 2002
5. H. Cunningham, D. Maynard, K. Bontcheva, V. Tablan, "GATE: A Framework and Graphical Development Environment for Robust NLP Tools and Applications", Proceedings of the 40th Anniversary Meeting of the Association for Computational Linguistics (ACL'02), Philadelphia, July 2002.
6. F. Ciravegna, "Adaptive information extraction from text by rule induction and generalisation", Proceedings of 17th International Joint Conference on Artificial Intelligence (IJCAI), Seattle, 2001.
7. ITC-IRST "TIES. Trainable Information Extraction System". http://tcc.itc.it/research/textec/projects/dotkom/ties.html
8. H. Cunningham, D. Maynard, V. Tablan. "JAPE: a Java Annotation Patterns Engine (Second Edition)", Technical report CS--00--10, University of Sheffield, Department of Computer Science, 2000.
9. "Apache Axis, an implementation of the SOAP " http://ws.apache.org/axis/
10. V.R. Benjamins, P. Casanovas, J. Breuker, A. Gangemi"Law and the Semantic Web: Legal Ontologies, Methodologies, Legal Information Retrieval, and Applications", Vol. 3369, Springer, 2005.9.
11. "Electronic Court: Judicial IT-based management". http://laplace.intrasoft-intl.com/e-court/
12. "European Programme for an Ontology based Working Environment for Regulations and legislation", http://www.belastingdienst.nl/epower/
13. "Computerised Legal Information Management and Explanation", http://www.bmtech.co.uk/clime/
14. IST 2001-38248. "Financial Fraud Prevention-Oriented Information Resources using Ontology Technology", http://www.starlab.vub.ac.be/research/projects/poirot/
15. "Semantically-Enabled Knowledge Technologies", http://sekt.ijs.si/.

16. B. Popov, A. Kiryakov, D. Ognyanoff, D. Manov, A. Kirilov, "KIM - a semantic platform for information extraction and retrieval", Journal of Natural Language Engineering, Vol. 10, Issue 3-4, Sep 2004, pp. 375-392, Cambridge University Press.

17. D. Quan, D. Huynh, and D. R. Karger, "Haystack: A Platform for Authoring End User Semantic Web Applications", Proceeding of the 2nd International Semantic Web Conference, Florida, October 2003.

18. "The Semantic Web Environmental Directory" http://www.swed.org.uk/swed/index.html.

19. O. Corcho, A. Gomez-Perez, A. Lopez-Cima, V. Lopez-Garcia, and M. Suarez-Figueroa, "ODESeW. Automatic generation of knowledge portals for Intranets and Extranets", The Semantic Web - ISWC 2003, vol. LNCS 2870, pp. 802-817, 2003.

20. Y. Jin, S. Xu, S. Decker, and G. Wiederhold, "OntoWebber: a novel approach for managing data on the Web", International Conference on Data Engineering, 2002.

21. N. Stojanovic, A. Maedche, S. Staab, R. Studer, and Y. Sure, "SEAL - a framework for developing semantic portals", Proceedings of the International Conference on Knowledge capture, pp. 155-162, 2001.

22. P. Spyns, D. Oberle, R. Volz, J. Zheng, M. Jarrar, Y. Sure, R. Studer, and R. Meersman, "OntoWeb - a semantic Web community portal", Fourth International Conference on Practical Aspects of Knowledge Management, 2002.

23. E. Mäkelä, E. Hyvönen, S. Saarela, K. Viljanen, "OntoView - A Tool for Creating Semantic Web Portals", Proceeding of the 3rd International Semantic Web Conference, Hiroshima, November 2004.

24. M. Dzbor, J.B. Domingue, E. Motta, "Magpie - towards a semantic web browser", Proceeding of the 2nd Intl. Semantic Web Conf., October 2003, Florida US.

25. "Topicalla", http://topicalla.mozdev.org/index.hml.

26. V. Lanfranchi, F. Ciravegna, D. Petrelli: "Semantic Web-based Document: Editing and Browsing in AktiveDoc", Proceedings of the 2nd European Semantic Web Conference , Heraklion, Greece, May 29-June 1, 2005

27. F. Ciravegna, N. Kusmerick, S Staab, C Knoblock. "Machine learning for the Semantic Web" Dagstuhl workshop 13-18 February 2005, Dagstuhl, Germany. http://www.smi.ucd.ie/Dagstuhl-MLSW/

Definitions Management: A Semantics-Based Approach for Clinical Documentation in Healthcare Delivery

Vipul Kashyap[1], Alfredo Morales[2], Tonya Hongsermeier[1], and Qi Li[1]

[1] Clinical Informatics R&D, Partners Healthcare System, 93 Worcester St, Suite 201, Wellesley, MA 02481, USA
{vkashyap1, thongsermeier, qli5}@partners.org
[2] Cerebra, 5963 La Place Court, Suite 200, Carlsbad, CA 92008, USA
Alfredo.Morales@cerebra.com

Abstract. Structured Clinical Documentation is a fundamental component of the healthcare enterprise, linking both clinical (e.g., electronic health record, clinical decision support) and administrative functions (e.g., evaluation and management coding, billing). Documentation templates have proven to be an effective mechanism for implementing structured clinical documentation. The ability to create and manage definitions, i.e., *definitions management,* for various concepts such as diseases, drugs, contraindications, complications, etc. is crucial for creating and maintaining documentation templates in a consistent and cohesive manner across the organization. Definitions management involves the creation and management of concepts that may be a part of controlled vocabularies, domain models and ontologies. In this paper, we present a real-world implementation of a semantics-based approach to automate structured clinical documentation based on a description logics (DL) system for ontology management. In this context we will introduce the ontological underpinnings on which clinical documents are based, namely the domain, document and presentation ontologies. We will present techniques that leverage these ontologies to render static and dynamic templates that contain branching logic. We will also evaluate the role of these ontologies in the context of managing the impact of definition changes on the creation and rendering of these documentation templates, and the ability to retrieve documentation templates and their instances precisely in a given clinical context.

1 Introduction

Structured Clinical Documentation is a fundamental component of the healthcare enterprise linking both clinical (e.g., electronic health record, clinical decision support) and administrative functions (e.g., evaluation and management coding, billing). At its core, Structured Clinical Documentation consists of template-based, logically driven instruments designed to facilitate and minimize the guesswork of coding and documenting information regarding a patient throughout the continuum of care. When well implemented in the context of the clinical workflow, these instruments can save clinicians' time as well as well as assure clinical thoroughness, thus reducing the chance of medical errors.

Stakeholders in basic sciences, health services and medical informatics research recognize the importance of information captured directly from episodes of clinical

Y. Gil et al. (Eds.): ISWC 2005, LNCS 3729, pp. 887–901, 2005.
© Springer-Verlag Berlin Heidelberg 2005

care for research, real-time decision support and patient screening for clinical trials or clinical syndromes [1,2]. Structured entry and reporting systems promise to meet this need by enabling health care providers to document clinical encounters through selection from pre-defined categories [3-6].

Structured entry and reporting systems are designed to enhance the process of clinical documentation by both presenting useful categorical concepts in a user interface and capturing input from the end user though the interface as machine-readable data. Structured entry is achieved as the end user navigates through lists of relevant concepts and sets status (e.g. present/absent, etc.) or strongly typed values. The main objectives of these systems are:

- Capture of raw data in a consistent and cohesive manner enabling generation and delivery of reminders and alerts to the point of care while providing an infrastructure for clinical research. This leads to enhancement of patient care.
- Reduce variability in the quality and quantity of concepts recorded as part of the medical record. This enables research investigators to seamlessly integrate research questions without impacting the clinical workflow.

Although the benefits of structured entry and reporting systems have been well documented, their widespread implementation and consequent adoption has been limited due to the following reasons [8-11]:

- Inefficiency, complexity and slow pace of navigating through user interfaces to find relevant content
- Inflexibility for documenting unforeseen findings
- Lack of integration with clinical applications
- Deficiencies in both coverage by and goals of the underlying domain and document models.
- Lack of consistency and maintenance of documentation templates in the context of evolving domain and document models.
- Decreased overall efficiency for generating complex documents.

We present a semantics-based infrastructure that seeks to address some of the abovementioned issues. The ability to create and manage definitions, i.e., *definitions management,* for various concepts such as diseases, drugs, complications, etc. is crucial for consistent maintenance and creation of documentation templates across the organization. Definitions management involves the creation and management of concepts and other knowledge objects that could be components of controlled vocabularies, domain models and ontologies. In this paper, we present a real world implementation of a semantics-based approach, with ontological underpinnings to automate execution and maintenance of documentation templates based on description logics (DL) system for ontology management.

The ontological underpinnings of the proposed infrastructure help address issues related to the evolution of the underlying document and domain models. We leverage ontologies and semantic inferences to automate the process of generating and rendering complex documents and enable precise location of relevant clinical content referenced in these documents. These techniques enable rendering static and dynamic templates that contain branching logic and manage the impact of definition changes on the creation and rendering of these documentation templates.

The organization of the paper is as follows. In Section 2, we present a real-world scenario and use case that describes an actual documentation template implemented at Partners HealthCare. Section 3 discusses the document and domain ontologies used in the system. We present and discuss the architecture of the system in Section 4. In Sections 5 and 6, we present the functionality of the clinical documentation system in the clinical and maintenance contexts. The role of semantic inference is explored in Section 7. Section 8 presents conclusions and future work.

2 Use Case and Scenario

A sample clinical documentation template being implemented at Partners HealthCare System is presented. It consists of a set of questions that elicit information related to patient state, including diseases, active medications and other important clinical information such as lab results and conditions or situations that makes a given therapy, treatment or procedure inadvisable (this is known as contraindications.)

```
PATIENT QUESTIONNAIRE

1.  Do you know if there any contraindications to fibric
    acid for this patient?
    __ Yes
    __ No
2.  Does this patient suffer from gallstones?
    __ Yes
    __ No
3.  What is the AST Value for this patient?
    _____ mg/ml?
4.  Which of the following range of values does the AST
    values for this patient apply to?
    _ < X
    _ [X,Y]
    _ [Y,Z]
    _ > Z
5.  Are the liver panel values more than the normal value
    for this patient?
    __ Yes
    __ No
6.  If the answer to Question 5 is Yes, then the liver
    panel values are:
    __ 2 x Normal
```

The above instrument contains a set of *data collection items*, each of which attempts to elicit some information about the patient. It may be noted that some of the information might either be elicited directly from the physician and some of it may be populated from the Electronic Medical Record (EMR).

The conventional approach to automate this template involves the design of tightly coupled structures incorporating information to be collected embedded within the business logic and presentation logic required to present them to the end user. Variations of this approach attempt to separate presentation logic from business logic and the data structures where the captured information is stored.

Adopting either approach poses significant challenges. The maintainability and extensibility of the resulting documentation template may require significant additional investment as changes in the information requirements occur along with changes in presentation and business logic requirements. A different approach, based on the composition of the underlying information and domain knowledge models based on their underlying semantics, is needed to facilitate the development and delivery of documentation templates as adaptive knowledge assets. If we adopt the above approach to defining and creating a template, the following observations can be made:

- A distinction needs to be made between the questions being asked and the information about which the enquiry is being made. For instance, in Question 1, there is a distinction between *contraindication to fibric acid* as opposed to *does this patient have contraindication to fibric acid?*
- The values displayed as potential answers to a question may not cover all the possible values associated with an information item. For instance, in Question 4, the values displayed as potential responses for *AST* may not cover all potential values of *AST* observed in practice. This template may be intended for a specialized subset of patients, which could be reflected in the potential choices available.
- Most questions on the template are related to some attributes of the patient state. For instance, various questions in the questionnaire refer to *contraindications*, clinical conditions (*suffer*), clinical laboratory tests (*AST, Liver Panel*)
- There is branching logic embedded in this questionnaire. For instance, Question 6 becomes relevant only when the answer to Question 5 is *Yes*. This is just a simple example. In general there might be complicated patterns for *branching logic* that might be represented as a graph or a tree structure.
- Some of the information being discussed in the question might be *composite* in structure. For instance, the information item, *Liver Panel* in Question 5 consists of a set of laboratory tests that are used to determine the liver condition of a patient
- Some of the values displayed as potential answers to the questions may be *derived* from the actual values. For instance in Question 6, the answers are based on the *normal AST* (e.g., *2 x Normal*), where *normal* describes the range of values for that given laboratory test that are considered within the norm. These values may either be derived via statistical processes or stored as default values associated with the information item. The latter is typically the case in biomedical information systems such as an EMR
- Some of the answers to a question might be intervals of values. This is illustrated in Question 4

The observations above suggest a need to delineate between information related to the document template (questions, attributes, values) and information related to the biomedical concepts referred to in the documentation template. This helps us identify the two types of ontologies, viz. document and domain ontologies that underpin the system. Functionality needed to enable presentation and rendering of templates can now be specified in terms of operations on the underlying ontologies. In the next section, we illustrate these two types of ontologies represented using OWL-DL expressions that were constructed using the Cerebra Construct workbench.

3 Ontological Underpinnings

The content and structure of a documentation template can be decomposed and modeled using three types of ontologies:

Document Ontologies: Documentation aspects of the template, such as the data collection item, the questions being asked, the properties about the patient state about which the question is being asked, the set of proposed responses are modeled using document ontologies. These ontologies conform to a document template meta-model that determines the composition and the logical organization of a document template, and may be viewed as a container framework where biomedical knowledge is referred to and accessed while presenting the template to a physician in the context of a clinical encounter. **Fig. 1.** illustrates the representation of the documentation template presented in the previous section as a document ontology. This representation was made using Cerebra Construct, a MS Vision add-on that allows modeling of ontologies following a visual paradigm producing OWL-DL as output. In the example, the document template ontology consists of a concept *Document* corresponding to the template. The *Document* concept contains concepts such as "Section" which contains concepts related to each of the questions such as *Known Contraindications to Fibric Acid?*, *Known Gallstones History?*, etc. Each of these questions contains references to biomedical concepts such as *FibricAcidContraindication*, *Patient*, etc.

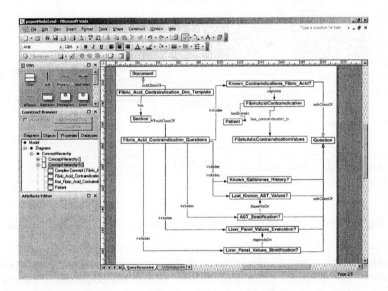

Fig. 1. Sample Documentation Template Ontology as Represented in Cerebra Construct

Domain Ontologies: Biomedical knowledge referenced in the documentation template is modeled using domain specific ontologies. This description will include concepts that may have their origin in controlled vocabularies, e.g., SNOMED CT [16], LOINC [17], ICD-9-CM[18], complex concepts that may arise from their combination following a logical prescription, relationships among those concepts as well as restrictions over the concepts imposed by characterizations of their attributes and the values that they may assume. The concepts, restrictions and attributes modeled in the use case are represented in **Fig. 2.**

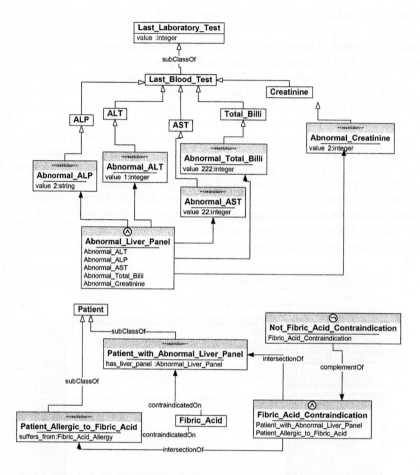

Fig. 2. Representation of Domain Ontology for Sample Documentation Template

- **Patient:** This refers to the subject of the documentation template which is a patient. The questions in the questionnaire refer to the properties of patient state, such as **has_contraindication,** which specifies a patient's contraindications to drugs and therapies; **suffers_from,** which specifies a patient's conditions or problems; **has_AST_value,** a data type property that specifies the results of an AST test on the patient; **has_liver_panel,** which specifies liver panel values of a patient.
- **Contraindications:** This refers to a set of contraindications
- **Fibric_Acid:** This refers to the compound Fibric Acid

Information Ontology

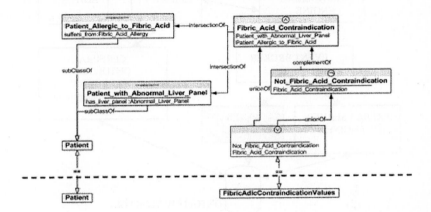

Document Ontology

Fig. 3. Composition Ontology

- **Fibric_Acid_Contraindication:** This refers to a subclass of contraindications that deal with Contraindication to Fibric Acid and can be defined as:

```
Fibric_Acid_Contraindication ⊆
                  ∀has_liver_panel.AbnormalLiverPanel ∩
                                  ∀suffers_from. Fibric_Acid_Allergy
```

- **Gallstones:** This refers to the concept Gallstones
- **AST_Value:** This is a datatype which refers to a range of valid AST values. Cerebra Server provides a mechanism to define ranges as restrictions based on values of the datatype.
- **Liver_Panel:** This is a composite concept that is a cross product (intersection) of the concepts, ASTValue, ALTValue, AlkalinePhosphateValue, TotalBilirubin-Value. The DL expression for LiverPanel can be given as:

```
LiverPanel ⊆ ∀has_AST_value.ASTValue ∩ ∀has_ALT_value.ALTValue ∩
             ∀has_AP_value.AlkalinePhosphateValue ∩
             ∀has_TB_value.TotalBilirubinValue
```

Composition Ontologies: Constitute a set of **inter-ontology articulations** between elements in the document ontology and domain ontologies. These articulations capture the association between a documentation template and the domain knowledge it contains. **Fig. 3.** presents the inter-ontology articulations between the document ontology and the domain ontology for the sample documentation template.

4 Architecture

The architectural components of the clinical documentation engine being implemented at Partners HealthCare are presented in **Fig. 4.**

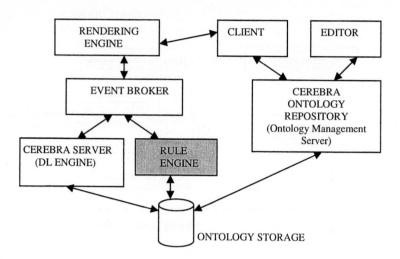

Fig. 4. Clinical Documentation System Architecture

- **Client/Editor:** User interfaces are needed in tow contexts. In the transactional or execution context, the *clinician* will enter data into the documentation template. In the maintenance context, the *knowledge engineer* will make editorial changes to the underlying ontologies and templates.
- **Rendering Engine:** The rendering engine acts as a presentation logic layer. It consumes the data collection items presented to it by the **event broker** component, applies style sheet templates and presents them to the user interface.
- **Event Broker:** The event broker implements a blackboard architecture where it receives a stream of data collection items and decides based on appropriate criteria whether the data collection item needs to be processed by the **DL Engine** or the **Rules Engine**. When the event broker receives a patient id it is forwarded to appropriately components to retrieve an initial set of data collection items.
- **DL Engine:** This component processes OWL-DL based ontologies and provides inferencing capabilities in the execution and maintenance contexts. The DL engine computes potential responses for questions associated with data collection items and identifies redundant questions in the context of interactions between the clinician and the documentation system. In the maintenance context, the DL engine interacts with the **Ontology Management Server** when the domain and/or document ontologies change, and checks for contradictions and equivalences. The DL engine is implemented by the Cerebra Server.
- **Rules Engine: DL engines** cannot reason with spatio-temporal information required by some documentation templates. In these cases, the **event broker** invokes the rules engine to perform the appropriate computations. In the maintenance context, DL engines and Rule engines interact with each other to address changes in ontology and the resulting changes in rule bases (and vice versa).

- **Ontology Management Server:** The ontology management server manages changes in the domain and document ontologies in the maintenance context. It propagates the impact of changes in the domain ontology to the document ontology. It invokes the **DL engine** to check whether the changes introduced are consistent, and to identify new contradictions and equivalences that might surface.
- **Ontology Storage:** This is the repository which stores the ontologies and instances and might be implemented in a relational database management system.

5   The Execution Context: Rendering and Instantiation of Documentation Templates

Documentation templates become alive or are "played" in the execution context, i.e. when a clinician enters data in a documentation template in the context of a clinical encounter with a patient. We assume that the clinician enters the patient id and the documentation system retrieves the appropriate template(s). The DL engine may be invoked to determine the relevant template(s) to be displayed to the clinician. Each new data collection item in the documentation template is viewed as an *event*, which triggers various computational processes.

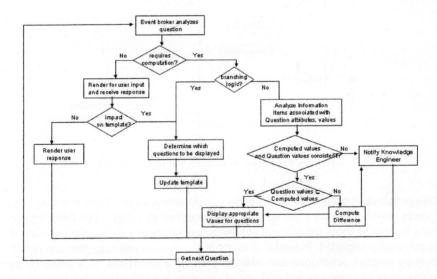

Fig. 5. The Event processing framework

The event processing framework is illustrated in **Fig. 5**. The workflow provides a mechanism to define how a documentation template will be presented to a clinician at the point of care. It will also evaluate at execution time whether inconsistencies have arisen. These would be communicated to the knowledge engineer, who would address them in maintenance mode.

6 The Maintenance Context: Tracking and Maintenance of Domain and Document Ontologies

In this section, we discuss scenarios related to changes in the definition of domain ontology concept by a knowledge engineer. The **ontology management server** enables propagation of changes in the domain ontology elements to the relevant document ontology elements as illustrated in the taxonomy in **Fig. 6**. The possible scenarios in which a knowledge engineer may be notified are:

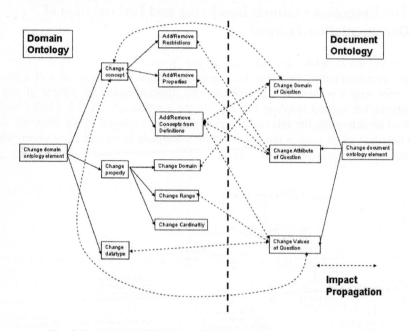

Fig. 6. Taxonomy of Changes in Domain and Document Ontologies

Change in concept definitions: A concept could appear as the domain or range of an attribute (associated with a question) in the document ontology. The knowledge engineer is notified about the relevant attributes and values of a data collection item that are potentially impacted. Potential changes in the domain ontology that can result in changing concept definitions are: adding/removing a restriction on a property, adding/removing of properties and addition of concepts to a definition. For example, one may redefine the concept Patient as SeverelyIllPatient by adding a property severity-level with the restriction that it has a value "high".

Patient changes to Patient ∩ ∀severity-level.{"high"}

Consider another example, where one may redefine the concept Contraindication-ToFibricAcid as a disjunction of AbnormalAST and AbnormalALT. i.e.,

ContraindicationToFibricAcid ≡ AbnormalAST
changes to ContraindicationToFibricAcid ≡ AbnormalAST ∪ AbnormalALT

Change in property definitions: A property typically appears as an attribute of a data collection item on which a question is posed. The knowledge engineer is notified of the questions impacted by this change. A definition can be changed by changing either its domain, range or cardinality. In each case the knowledge engineer should check that the domain and range associated with the relevant data collection items are consistent with the change. For example if the definition of the concept Patient is changed to FemalePatient, i.e., Patient <u>changes to</u> Patient ∩ Female, all the properties of FemalePatient, that appear in a data collection item are flagged and the knowledge engineer is notified. If the cardinality of a property changes from ≤ 1 to ≥ 1, then the user interface for a data collection item may need to be changed from a single select to multi-select.

Change in datatype definitions: Datatype definitions are represented using XML schema types and can be changed by changing the range of values associated with it. For example the value of normal LDL may be changed from < 100 to < 70. The data collection items where these datatypes appear as values are flagged and the knowledge engineer is notified.

7 The Role of Semantic Inferences

We now illustrate with examples, the role of semantic inferences in the execution and maintenance contexts.

Semantic Inferences in the Execution Context: The ability to retrieve relevant documentation templates based on properties of the patient state. Templates for patients suffering from Diabetes can be retrieved by performing the following inference:

$$\text{TBox} \models \text{Patient} \cap \exists\text{suffers-from.Diabetes} \equiv \mathbf{D} ?$$

where $\mathbf{D}$ is the information domain associated with a documentation template.

The ability to determine redundant questions based on a user response. For instance, if a patient has a contraindication to fibric acid, the question that seeks information on whether a patient suffers from gallstones becomes redundant. This redundancy can be identified by performing the following inference.

$$\text{TBox} \models \forall\text{suffers-from.Gallstones} \subseteq \\ \forall\text{has-contraindication.FibricAcidContraindication} ?$$

The ability to determine whether a question needs to be displayed based on the responses to earlier questions. Consider a patient P_1 for which some state properties are known. For question 6 (from the instrument) to be rendered, the answer to question 5 should be yes, i.e., the following statement should be satisfiable:

$$\text{ABox} \models P_1 \in \text{Patient} \cap \forall\text{has-liver-panel.AbnormalLiverPanel} ?$$

Semantic Inferences in the Maintenance Context: Whenever concept definitions in the domain ontology change, semantic inferences can be performed to enable:

Checking for consistency and contradictions: The DL engine checks whether the changes are consistent or whether they give rise to contradictions. For instance, clinical evidence may suggest that abnormal AST values are not possible in the presence of abnormal ATL values. This may result in the following constraint being added to the TBox with the following inference:

ASTValue ∩ ATLValue ≡ φ,TBox ⊨ AbnormalLiverPanel ≡ φ

This will have an impact on question 5 in the questionnaire as this will never have a valid response. The Knowledge Engineer will be notified of this possibility

Checking for equivalences: In this scenario, the DL engine checks whether the changes introduce new equivalences. For example, consider the following definition of FibricAcidContraindication:

FibricAcidContraindication ≡
∃has_liver_panel.AbnormalLiverPanel ∩ ∃suffers_from.Fibric_Acid_Allergy

Suppose the definition of FibricAcidContraindication changes to:

FibricAcidContraindication' ≡ ∃has_liver_panel.AbnormalLiverPanel

This creates a new equivalence which can be used by the DL engine to infer the-equivalence of questions 1 and 5, thus making one of them **redundant**, as follows:

TBox ⊨ Patient ∩ ∃has-contraindication.FibricAcidContraindication
       ≡ Patient ∩ ∃has_liver_panel.AbnormalLiverPanel

Identifying concept differences: Whenever a concept definition changes, the DL engine can identify the conceptual difference between the two versions of the concept and present the changes to the knowledge engineer. In the example given above, the knowledge engineer will be notified of the following conceptual difference:

TBox ⊨ FibricAcidContraindication' ∩ ∃suffers_from.Fibric_Acid_Allergy
                  ≡ FibricAcidContraindication

Datatype reasoning: Whenever the definition of a data type, e.g., AbnormalASTvalues changes, the DL engine can identify potential impacts, including contradictions this can introduce. For instance changing of normal ASTValues from [5,25] to [10, 30] would change the definition of normal LiverPanelValues which will affect the responses to Questions 5 and 6. These changes will be propagated and the Knowledge Engineer notified.

8   Conclusions and Future Work

Clinical documentation templates are an intrinsic part of the process of care in modern medicine and constitute one of the most valuable tools for providing both episodic and preventive care. Mainstream implementations of an electronic documentation template system normally involve representing and storing these ontological concepts and their relationships as fix structures in relational databases or XML stores, exposing them through a middleware layer of enterprise objects (.Net components or EJBs) which functionality would be presented to the end user via a framework of dynamically generated user interfaces.

The approach afore mentioned is intractable over time, as it will require continuous refactoring of enterprise objects and support for specialized data structures to handle dynamic knowledge evolution. This will translate to a high cost of ownership and jeopardize their long term viability. In order to cope with the rapid change of knowledge in medicine and its effect on biomedical concepts as illustrated in Sections 6 and 7, technology and techniques are needed that enable model-based dependency propagation and semantic inferences which are not currently supported by various middleware platforms and relational databases.

We have presented a model-based composition method for representing and delivering documentation templates to the point of care. This provides the foundation to define an infrastructure for creation and maintenance of documentation templates, clinical rules and other knowledge assets. Separation of the document model and the domain knowledge is the key architectural design, the adoption of which is expected to enable operational efficiencies at Partners HealthCare System. It is also anticipated that the cost of maintaining clinical documentation templates will be reduced over time generating more return on investment. This is expected to have a positive impact on the ability of the clinician to identify and complete patient relevant documentation in a streamlined manner.

We also introduce a reference semantics-based architecture with ontological underpinnings. The associated ontology management and inferencing capabilities are mechanisms that will enable Partners Healthcare to deliver adaptable documentation templates. These templates will be instantiated based on patient-state based classification. Semantics also provides a mechanism to manage the implications of knowledge change over time, including identification of inconsistencies, equivalences and redundancies that may arise as domain and document ontologies evolve.

It is expected that the modeling approach and implemented architecture, will enable adoption of a scalable, long term solution that integrates seamlessly with the overall knowledge management efforts in progress. This will enable enhancement of documentation templates beyond information gathering nature into a knowledge exploration and delivery mechanism.

A critical requirement for semantics and model based approaches is the availability of semantically rich knowledge that is loaded into the DL engine. Requirements related to clinical documentation will be analyzed and the set of biomedical terminologies and information models that will be identified. The following have been earmarked [14] as a starting set of standards that would constitute the foundational vocabularies and models. These will be represented in the OWL-DL format and preloaded into the DL engine for their use as descriptions of domain knowledge concepts. These standards are:

1. Health Level 7 (HL7) reference framework [15] for structuring and representing clinical information such as demographic information, clinical encounters, observations, diagnosis

2. The College of American Pathologists Systematized Nomenclature of Medicine Clinical Terms (SNOMED CT) [16] for anatomical descriptions, diagnosis documentation, descriptions of interventions and procedures.

3. Laboratory Logical Observation Identifier Name Codes (LOINC) [17] to standardize the electronic exchange of laboratory test orders and drug label section headers.

4. A set of federal terminologies related to medications, including the Food and Drug Administration's names and codes for ingredients, manufactured dosage

forms, drug products and medication packages, the National Library of Medicine's RxNORM [19] for describing clinical drugs, and the Veterans Administration's National Drug File Reference Terminology (NDF-RT) for specific drug classifications.
5. The Human Gene Nomenclature (HUGN) [20] for exchanging information regarding the role of genes in biomedical research in the federal health sector.
6. The Environmental Protection Agency's Substance Registry System [21] for non-medicinal chemicals of importance to health care.

The work described in the paper is an ongoing implementation of a definitions management infrastructure for clinical decision support at Partners HealthCare System. Some future initiatives we are looking at are:

*   The use of rule-based approaches to capture knowledge not expressible within current DL-based systems
*   The integration of the ontology management server with a content management server for a managing the lifecycle of models and ontologies.
*   The integration of the rules engine with a content management server for managing the lifecycles of rules in conjunction with their associated models and ontologies.
*   Explore the use of description logics that support inferences on spatial and temporal relationships.

References

1. Committee on Quality of Health Care in America: Using Information Technology. Crossing the Quality Chasm: A New Health System for the 21st Century. Washington, D.C.: IOM; 2001
2. Committee on Improving the Patient Record. The Computer-Based Patient Record: An Essential Technology for Health Care, 2 ed. Washington, DC: ION; 1991
3. Yoder JW, Schultz DF, Williams BT. The MEDIGATE graphical user interface for entry of physical findings: Design principles and implementation. Medical Examination Direct Iconic and Graphic Augmented Text Entry System. *J Med Syst* 1998;22(5):325-37.
4. Stead WW, Brame RG, Hammond WE, Jelovsek FR, Estes EH, Parker RT. A computerized obstetric medical record. *Obstet Gynecol* 1977;49(4):502-9.
5. Slack WV, Hicks GP, Reed CE, Van Cura LJ. A computer based medical-history system. *N Engl J Med* 1966;274(4):194-8.
6. Johnson KB, Cowan J. Clictate: a computer-based documentation tool for guideline-based care. *J Med Syst* 2002;26(1):47-60.
7. Kahn CE, Jr. Self-documenting structured reports using open information standards. *Medinfo 1998*;9(Pt 1):403-7.
8. McDonald CJ. The barriers to electronic medical record systems and how to overcome them. *J Am Med Inform Assoc* 1997;4(3):213-21.
9. Lum F, Schein O, Schachat AP, Abbott RL, Hoskins HD, Jr., Steinberg EP. Initial two years of experience with the AAO National Eyecare Outcomes Network (NEON) cataract surgery database. *Ophthalmology 2000*;107(4):691-7.
10. Poon AD, Fagan LM, Shortliffe EH. The PEN-Ivory project: exploring user-interface design for the selection of items from large controlled vocabularies of medicine. *J AmMed Inform Assoc* 1996;3(2):168-83.

11. Rosenbloom ST, Kiepek W, Belletti J, Adams P, Shuxteau K, Johnson KB, Elkin PL, Shultz EK. Generating Complex Clinical Documents using Structured Entry and Reporting. Medinfo 2004.
12. Goldberg H, Morales A, McMillan D, Quinlan M. An Ontology-Driven Application to Improve the Prescription of Educational Resources to Parents of Premature Infants. EON 2003
13. Goldberg H, Morales A. Improving information prescription to parents of premature infants through an OWL-based knowledge mediator. *Medinfo 2004*;11(Pt 1):361-5.
14. Presidential Initiative on Consolidated Health Informatics, http://www.whitehouse.gov/omb/egov/c-3-6-chi.html
15. Health Level 7, http://www.hl7.org
16. Snomed International, http://www.snomed.org
17. LOINC, http://www.regenstrief.org/loinc
18. International Classification of Diseases, Nine Revision, Clinical Modification – ICD-9-CM, http://www.cdc.gov/nchs/about/otheract/icd9/abticd9.htm
19. RxNORM, http://www.nlm.nih.gov/research/umls/rxnorm_main.html
20. HUGO Gene Nomenclature Committee, http://www.gene.ucl.ac.uk/nomenclature
21. EPA Substance Registry System, http://www.epa.gov/srs

Ubiquitous Service Finder
Discovery of Services Semantically Derived from Metadata in Ubiquitous Computing

Takahiro Kawamura[1], Kouji Ueno[1], Shinichi Nagano[1],
Tetsuo Hasegawa[1], and Akihiko Ohsuga[1]

Research and Development Center, Toshiba Corp.

Abstract. Metadata have been already given to most of the data and objects in the real world, such as books, foods, digital contents like movie, electric devices, and so forth. Further, they can be accumulated electronically by barcodes and RFIDs, which is expected to spread explosively in 2005. On the other hand, web services are getting popular in the internet, and UPnP services and ECHONET are penetrating into the home network. In our project, we propose a new handheld application called Ubiquitous Service Finder, in which user can intuitively browse as icons the metadata around him/her in a cellular phone, then invoke the services semantically related to the metadata by simple drag and drop operation.

1   Introduction

Objects and data are everywhere in the world, then most of them have their own descriptions, metadata. For example, industrial products have names and dates of manufacture and model numbers, and foods have production places and producers. As the already disseminated standards, there are EAN and UPC for barcodes, EPG for movie data, and ID3 for music data. Further, in near future RFIDs will lead to add PML and/or ucode to the products. Since food safety and recalls are common concerns these days, situations that people would need refer to such information will increase. On the other hand, there are lots of services and information in the internet, which can be related and used with such information. For example, manufacturers are providing their product catalog search service, and some public agencies are putting food safety information on the web. Further, map services, news search, and banking services, etc. became already quite popular. As their standards, there are RSS, FOAF, PICS, P3P for some kinds of web pages, and WSDL, OWL-S and WSMO for web services and their annotations. Services are not only in the internet, but also in the home network according to dissemination of home information appliances. For example, play and record functions of latest HDD recorders, temperature control functions of air conditioners, and surveillance cameras can be accessible via LAN. As their common standards, there are CC/PP for device profiles, UPnP and DLNA mainly for digital audiovisual players, and ECHONET for white

Y. Gil et al. (Eds.): ISWC 2005, LNCS 3729, pp. 902–915, 2005.

goods. Furthermore, the standards like RTMiddleware and RSi is now under consideration for coordination among home robots via the network near future.

That is, metadata and services are flooding around us, nevertheless, there is no simple and direct access method to them. You may have the following experiments: at inventory clearance users always need turn their PCs upside down to take a memo of small but long catalog numbers, and at stores need check tiny and illegible information on some food packages. Besides, you have no way to search the related information on the web at that moment. You first have to go home, and have a chair in front of your PC, then type that information by hand. In addition, we believe ubiquitous computing which is a product space of pervasive and mobile has two essentials: people can use the same services everywhere, and people can use the pinpoint services depending on that time and location.

Therefore, we have developed Ubiquitous Service Finder (USF) to provide the simple and direct access to ubiquitous metadata and services in a way of combining both essentials. Here, we took a cellular phone as a target device because of its ownership rate and adherence of younger people to bring it into their beds. Then, as the most intuitive and friendly interface for the people, we took an interface to represent metadata and services as icons. USF allows the user to browse a large variety of metadata and services surrounding him/her, and to invoke the services by icon-click and drag&drop operation. So that in cases that what specification does this PC have?, what songs are inside of this CD?, and when is the expiration date of this meat?, etc., you can just hold up your phone to them, and get displayed the objects as icons. Then, by simply clicking it you can see the content of their metadata, and store them locally. The user has no need to turn over something and take a memo by a pen. In addition to that, services in the internet and provided by the home information appliances are also displayed as icons in the phone, Then, by drag&dropping an object icon to a service icon you can just assign the metadata to the service inputs, and invoke it. The user has no need to start up your PC and type the keyboard.

In the rest of this paper, section 2 shows USF architecture and technical points inside, and section 3 illustrates three of typical usecases for USF. Then, we locate USF in the current ubiquitous computing research in section 4, and discuss the related activities in section 5. Finally, our status and future plan are summarized in section 6.

2   Proposal of Ubiquitous Service Finder

2.1   Architecture

In this paper, we have assumptions that metadata for the industrial products and foods can be looked up electronically, and web services in the internet and UPnP services in the office and home network can be accessed.

USF shown in fig. 1 is an application to coordinate those metadata with any of services. In this figure, you can see several kinds of icons which are corresponding

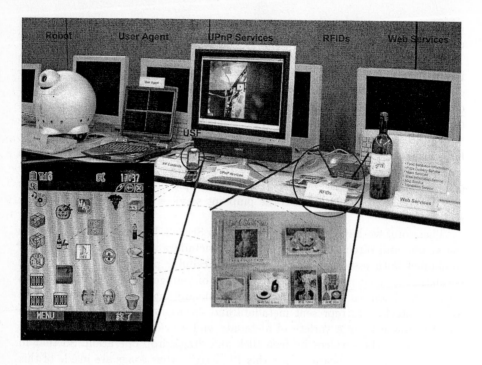

Fig. 1. Snapshot

to the real objects, data, and services. Note that the cellular phone is equipped with a touch panel as the screen.

Further, fig. 2 shows the internal architecture. Here we took SOA (Service Oriented Architecture) as our fundamental design, then services mean not only web and UPnP services, but also object and data (movie, music, photos, etc.) which only have outputs such as metadata and data themselves. In the following, we describe some of components in USF architecture.

WA2WS Getaway transforms web applications likes cgis to web services, which have WSDL interfaces to be published and are accessible via SOAP. The detailed description can be found in [1]. Also, Annotator which is under development suggests the related ontology classes to the service. The user can just select some of them to make it semantic web service.

UPnP2WS Getaway is another gateway to transform UPnP services to web services, which is combined with UPnP Control Point (hub to manage UPnP devices), and automatically finds UPnP services within a sub-domain, then publishes them as web services accessible via SOAP to User Agent below.

User Agent is assumed to be in a home server (or its corresponding PC) in the home, and/or in a PC for personal use in the office. It gets metadata corresponding to tag ids detected by RFID readers from Metadata DB, and shows them as icons on the following USF device, as well as the available services in the internet and the home network. Then, according to the user's

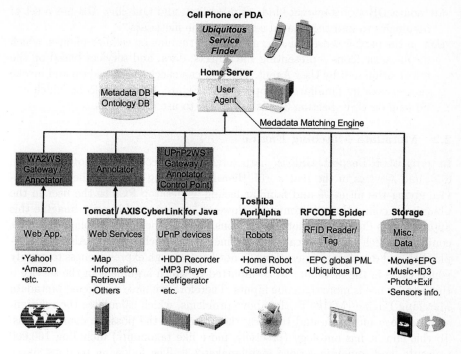

Fig. 2. USF Architecture

operation on USF device, it returns the content of metadata to USF device, and/or invokes web/UPnP services. User Agent includes a scripting system for sophisticated service flows, then if the user has some experiment on programming it is possible to add the user's own customization and batch processes. Further, Metadata Matching Engine described in the next section is included in User Agent.

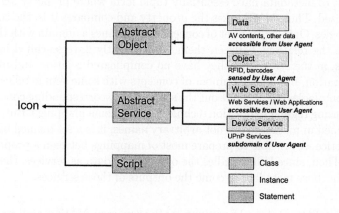

Fig. 3. Icons in USF

Metadata DB stores several kinds of metadata, and Ontology DB has a set of
ontologies to find the related services to the metadata.

USF in the narrow sense is a Java application running on cellular phones, which
displays the icons representing the objects, data, and services based on the
information sent by User Agent. The user can check the metadata and invoke
the services by familiar icon operations. Figure 3 lists the icons which can
be seen on USF. Section 3 illustrates how to use those icons.

2.2   Metadata Matching Engine

In terms of HCI aspect, USF is characterized by its icon abstraction of objects,
data and services in the real world, then by reflecting them on the mobile device giving the intuitive and familiar feeling as desktop PCs to the user in the
ubiquitous computing environment. However, as you would easily imagine this
approach has drawbacks that lots of icons flood in the small display, then it is
confusing which metadata can be combined with which services. Also, the simple click and drag&drop operations do not have enough expressiveness to specify
which value in the metadata to be inputted to which argument in the service if
that service needs more than one inputs. Therefore, we have developed Metadata
Matching Engine (MME) to the above problems, which calculates the relationship between metadata and services, then proposes the possible combinations.
To this end, it has ontology (precisely, more like taxonomy) including 160,000
concepts, and semantic service matchmaker[2,3]. The following sections shows
the feature of metadata matching.

Mapping from Metadata to Ontology. First of all, MME parses the target
metadata, and by comparison with ontologies stored in DB retrieves a meaning
(concept in DL sense) corresponding to each property in the metadata, such as
producer, production place, expiration date, and so forth. For now metadata have
several formats, and are under standardization by each industrial segment or organization. So that metadata parsers must be developed for each format, however, most of metadata have essentially tuple form where property and value(s)
are pairwised. Thus, MME takes the property and compares it to the concepts in
the ontologies. Ontology is a set of concepts that defines a domain with their properties and the relations between them. We currently have so-called lightweight
ontologies, in the sense that they have no complicated relation and philosophical deliberation, but a huge number of concepts with some simple relations. Base
on those ontologies, MME finds out the semantically corresponding concept to the
property using regular expression technique and schema mappings. But, the properties defined in metadata are not arbitrary names, it is a set defined in advance.
So in practice we are able to prepare most of mappings between a property and a
concept. Then, since USF handles the objects and data as services, the concepts
included in those metadata become the outputs of those services.

Discovery of the Related Services. As the next step, MME searches on services
which can be used with the metadata. The services must be annotated as semantic

web services[4] in advance. Semantic web services is an attempt of putting meta-data referring ontology to web services and their exploitation for service discovery and composition. Currently, we transformed 50 kinds of web applications to web services by WA2WS Gateway, and annotated them as semantic web services for this project. We hope to have publicly accessible semantic web services in the internet near future. In the above semantic web services, service description language OWL-S[5] assigns any of concepts to a category and each input/output, etc. Thus, MME calculates the relationship between the concepts returned from metadata in the previous section and the concepts assigned to the services. Since the ontology is defined based on Description Logic, MME checks to see if there is a relation like subsumption, union between those concepts. We developed a web services matchmaker to find the similar services based on ontology[2,3], so here extended it to metadata for objects, data and UPnP services. In practice, MME firstly determines whether there is a certain degree of similarity between the most representative concept of the metadata and the concept for the service category. Secondly, it checks if all of the concepts for the service inputs can be supplied by any of the output concepts in the metadata. That is, the service discovery has two-step approach with a class hierarchy of service categories and IO Type matching. Then, if a service which can take the outputs of the metadata as inputs is found, the next service which can take the outputs of the service as inputs will be searched. After repeating this process a certain times, a sequence of possible combinations of services can be found. USF will show this sequence as a directed link of icons highlighted with red arrows to the user. This behavior means a kind of simple reactive planning where the services descriptions are operators. If there are more than one operator to be connected, MME sorts the possible candidates according to distance of the concepts and certainty calculated from user contexts below. If the user does not like the proposed combination, he/she can get the next combination displayed. Note that MME is just suggesting the possible combinations by planning once or several times, and the service invocation is not automatic. It will be done by the user's drag&drop operation of the first icon to one of the icons on the directed link. After that, User Agent will pass the values corresponding to the properties (concepts) in the metadata to the service, and the output values of the service to the next service for the sequential service invocation. We will show some examples in section 3.

Further, USF also allows the user to make service flows in advance as script programs. In our first observation we thought it had a limit to define in advance the service flows with specific service bindings, because there would be tons of services in the internet and the information appliances vary in each home. Therefore, we have developed MME to automatically suggest the combinations of services based on semantics. However, as an intermediate way we are now providing so-called latebinding scripts, where abstract services can be defined in the flow without specific bindings, and at the runtime the services to be invoked will be searched. The abstract services have OWL-S, and the above matchmaker searches for the possible services to invoke. The user can describe his/her own script, and User Agent will execute it.

3   Usecases

As described in section 1, USF has been developed for the purpose of providing
an intuitive accessesor to metadata of objects and data around us and services
in the inter/home network. In this section, we introduce 3 useful cases: firstly
the user browses metadata bound to the physical objects, secondly the user
simply invokes a service with the data, lastly the user gets MME suggested a
service sequence from metadata and executes the service sequence. Further, we
summarize other features in USF.

3.1   Usecase 1: Metadata Scouter

Firstly, we show the simplest example that the user browses metadata surrounding him/her via USF (fig. 4(a)). In this example, we use RFIDs to find the
objects near the user carrying USF. There are already some mobile devices
attached with RFID readers, such as Ubiquitous Communicator[6], a cellular
phone[7]. Although we expect USF will be ported to those devices near future,
the current implementation is a simple but versatile one where a Java-enabled
cellular phone has a RFID in the back. RFID readers are connected to a PC

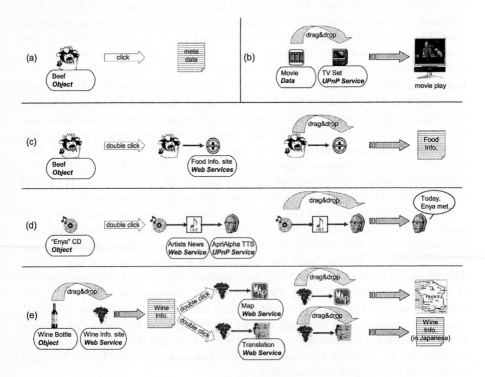

Fig. 4. Usecases

running User Agent, and controlled by the Agent. If User Agent detects the tag id assigned to the cellular phone, it determines other ids detected by the same reader as the user's neighborhood, and get icons corresponding the ids displayed on USF application in the phone.

For instance, when the user goes into the kitchen with USF, a tag attached to a beef pack bought at a store is detected, and a beef icon will appear on USF. Then, if the user clicks on the icon, User Agent accesses the metadata DB with the tag id to get the description about the cow's birth place and the expiration date, etc. and get that text information displayed on the user's USF. For the other use, it is useful for checking the specification of PCs and electronic equipment purchased some time ago, or for copying metadata of books and DVDs in the real shops into USF, then comparing their prices with the net shops in the home [1].

3.2   Usecase 2: Ubiquitous Remote

As the next step to just browsing metadata, the user will want to pour the information into any service, and invoke it. In this section, we show an example that the user operates home appliances with USF (fig. 4(b)). It is possible for USF to handle not only metadata for the real object, but also ones for electric data [2]. For example, if movie or music data are stored at a file server and they are accessible from User Agent, those icons will appear on USF. Also, if web and UPnP services are accessible from User Agent, those will appear as icons on USF. In practice, since UPnP services are available within a sub-domain, the accessible services are UPnP services detected by an UPnP Control Point in that sub-domain and web services in the internet. UPnP2WS Gateway also has the Control Point function as mentioned before. So if User Agent determines from the information of the RFID reader that the user who has USF is approaching a sub-domain, UPnP services detected by UPnP2WS Gateway will appear on USF.

For instance, when the user goes into the living room, movie data stored at a file server in the home network and a replay service provided by an UPnP-compliant HDD recorder will appear on USF. Then, if the user drag&drops a movie icon to the replay service icon, the actual movie is played by the HDD recorder. Further, if the user retires to his/her room, USF will show another playable service like a PC in the room, and the icon for the HDD recorder in the living room will disappear. Then, if the user drag&drops the movie icon to the new playable service, this time the movie is played by his/her PC [3].

---

[1] Note that there is an assumption here that the RFID tags are still active after purchases, and the tag information mainly annotated for SCM (Supply Chain Management) by manufacturers or distributors can be accessible from consumers. However, barcode DBs like UPC or EAN are accessible in fact.

[2] Needless to say, they are the metadata in its literal meaning. In this paper, we call explanatory data for the real object also as metadata.

[3] In the current implementation, the actual movie data is copied by User Agent and directly sent to the playable service which is published as an UPnP service. If DLNA[8] will disseminate in the digital audiovisual appliances near future, streaming would also be possible.

3.3   Usecase 3: Service Finder

The above two cases illustrated introduction of USF as a browser and a remote. However, as the number of icons increase, the icons flood in the display of USF and the user will be confused the possible combination of the icons. Further, in the previous example data themselves were inputted into a service, but metadata can also be inputted to a service. In that case, the user needs to indicate which property of the metadata is inputted to which argument for service inputs. Therefore, the above mentioned Metadata Matching Engine will become necessary. In the followings, we illustrate: discovery and invocation of web services, coordination of web services and services provided by home appliances, and interactive combination of data and services.

In the previous example, the user intuitively found the combination of the movie data and the playable service, but it would not be so easy to find which service is combined with the beef icon. In such a case, if the user double-clicks the beef icon, USF will pick, for example, a food safety service from the crowd of services, and link the beef icon to it with a red arrow. To this end, firstly MME gets a pair of the property and the value like *name: US beef* in the beef metadata, then according to the mapping from metadata to ontology described in section 2.2 specifies a concept representing Meat in a food ontology stored in the ontology DB. In the same manner, metadata like *production region: Pennsylvania* and *process day: 29/12/2004* are used to specify Location and Time concept. Secondly, according to the discovery of the related services in section 2.2, MME determines that the semantical distance between the Meat and the Food which is a category concept given to the food safety service are close enough. Then, the beef icon and the food service are linked after checking if the inputs of the food service are filled by the beef metadata. That is, USF are digging and proposing the possible services combined with the beef on behalf of the user. Finally, when the user drag&drops the beef icon to the food service icon, the information of the beef will be given to a search form for the food service, and the detailed safety information will be displayed. In fact, MME determines the information about Location, Time corresponds to inputs concepts for the food search service. Then, each value (Pennsylvania, 29/12/2004, etc.) are given to the search form, and the result is shown in a text dialog on USF. Figure 4(c) shows the above flow, and fig. 5(1)-(4) shows the actual screen shots, although a beef is replaced with a pumpkin.

For the other example, when the user double-clicks a CD icon, USF finds the search service on Yahoo! Music via Music concept, then further the Text-to-Speech service provided by a home robot via Text Information concept (see fig. 5(5)). This is an example of the services sequence composed by repeating the discovery of the services possibly combined twice. The length of the sequence can be set at User Agent, normally it should be 2 or 3 due to computational time. Figure 4(d) shows this flow.

On the contrary, it is possible to combine the services step by step. For example, after the user gets the information about a wine by drag&dropping a wine icon to a wine information service, then the user can search for the

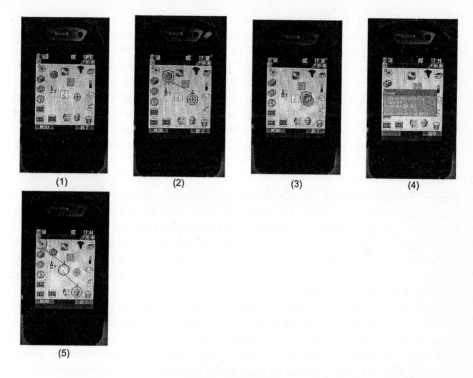

Fig. 5. Screenshots

next service combined with the wine information by double-clicking on the wine service. Further, if the user gets a map service from the wine service via Location concept and does not like it, double-clicking on the wine service again shows the next service such as a translation service and the previous TTS service. Figure. 4(e) explains this sequence.

Although all the above examples are for generic metadata for the object and the data, USF can handle metadata changing over time like MPEG-7, and find the different service depending on timing (scene) of the double-click during the play.

3.4   Additional Use

In this section, we show some of USF functions not mentioned before.

Metadata Search. In the previous section, we showed the examples that the services possibly combined with the object and the data are semantically searched. However, in the first place there is a case that the user wants to find icons for some specific objects, data, or services. For example, in a case of finding a particular author's book at a big bookstore or a library, it is impractical to check all the icons one by one. For such a case, we have provided the abstract icon. The abstract icon is a kind of folder predefined with search conditions.

By double-clicking it, the user can search metadata which satisfy the conditions from all the metadata currently detected. Setting of the conditions to the abstract icon is written in User Agent. In the above case, the user can prepare the abstract icon with the condition for the author and genre, and easily check existence and location of desired books by double-clicking it at the library.

In addition to this, it is possible to automatically add the user's context to the condition. The current implementation is only providing macros to get the user's current location and time as the context information, but using this information would be useful for finding the nearest shop to the current location, and so forth.

Script Definition. As already described, we also provides the script icon to execute the predefined flow. In a case that the user repeatedly uses the same services on a daily basis, the sequence of the services should be described in a script program at User Agent. In the script, a service definition can be written with a specific URL (binding), but it is also possible to define it with necessary metadata and get discovered the actual service at the invocation as described in section 2.2. In the internet, there are lots of web services which require the number of credit cards at the purchase. So that it would be useful for the user who occasionally buys something at a particular site to prepare a script which executes the necessary sequence by just drag&dropping the product metadata. Although the user can define my profile icon including name, address, phone numbers, etc. in USF, it would be safer to fill the important information like the card number into the script, and make it not readable.

Agent Mobility. In USF, User Agent is managing the user's conditions, scripts, and other preferences like history. So we have a plan to make User Agent mobile and follow the user to run on a home server when the user is in home, and migrate to the office when the user is at work. We have already developed lightweight mobile script system[9], and now merging it to MME.

4   Discussion

First of all, we locate USF in the ubiquitous computing research. We believe the user's icon choice in USF device represents the user's current interest, and it is like a snapshot of the user context. Then, USF is providing a mechanism to recommend the services according to the context. So that USF is regarded as so-called high-level service discovery, one of typical problems in this research area. Methodologies for service discovery in the ubiquitous computing have already been classified, however, at the same time it is well known that service discovery based on the context, that is, the high-level service discovery is still unsolved[10]. As a distinct feature of USF, it is exploiting ontologies rather than rules in lots of other systems to link the context to any service. Consequently, USF has some advantages like that reasoning process gets visible and it is easier to keep knowledge consistency, and recommendation gets faster, although the rules are still necessary to make eccentric combination. As the other feature, USF is adopting a forward chaining style in the sense that the proposed service is what the user is inspired by something just attracted at that moment. We believe it is more casual case for people than purposive behavior (backward chaining style) like service composition by planning techniques. Also, this mechanism can be seen as tracking associative relations with ontology. So the user might be able to find surprising combinations of metadata and services, and use it not for pragmatic use.

Also, USF has adopted Service Oriented Architecture as its basic design. In contrast that CS system assumes the other party to connect from the design phase, SOA system in its principle is that service providers provide services to a public space, then service requesters search for and try to connect the services if necessary. In USF, when the user enters a particular area, he/she tries to utilize the objects and data available in that area combining the accessible services. Therefore, it would be sort of a right design decision to take SOA as its base. Then, web services has been taken as the richest and semantic web friendly framework.

On the other hand, some people might wonder from practical standpoint due to its semantic approach. However, we are not aiming at the very intelligent task, but rather simple task where hard-coding is impractical. The recent web browsers have a function to automatically fill the user's name and address in the corresponding part of html form. In fact, USF is extending it with ontology for more general service invocation. Further, semantic web is now actively investigated in the world, and application of metadata and ontology on the web is growing faster. Semantic web services is one of such activities, and WSDL 2.0 which is a de-fact standard for web services has already included mapping to RDF[11]. Also, the next version of UDDI is considering to adopt OWL[12] for category description. These movement will support the semantic use of USF.

Finally, we mentioned why we took a cellular phone as the device in section 1, but we do not adhere to it in the implementation, because the technical strengths in our system are converged at User Agent. So we have some plan to port the front-end application to other devices like TV, PC, car navigation system, and so forth.

5   Related Works

Sakamura et al.[6] and KDDI[7] have already developed mobile devices with RFID readers. However, either one is only for tag detection, and has no mean to connect web/UPnP services on the network. We will consider to port USF to those devices.

Aura (Advanced User Resource Annotation System)[13] project in MS Research is providing an application for a mobile device with a barcode reader, by which the user can scan the barcode on products, and search the related data in UPC database or Google and eBay. Besides, the individual user can annotate it on the web, and share with other users. However, there is no semantic aspect, and service discovery and combination are not considered.

Another similar approach to USF is Task Computing of Fujitsu[14]. This allows the user to selectively combine and invoke a sequence of web and UPnP

ize to make the user build a sequence from a list of services on PCs in
the office environment.

Further, CALI[15] of Nokia is a reasoning engine to semantically combine the
user context written in DL with any services. They are using SIP for exchange
of the context, and have a plan to implement on a cellular phone near future.

Finally, especially in Japan there are some internet services, which makes the
user read QR code or barcode with cellular phones or Pocket PCs, and searches
for its price in Amazon, or public reviews with RSS over the internet. However,
those are also not considering semantics and web services invocation.

6 Conclusion and Future Works

In an industry segment it is expected that coordination among networked appliances in the home will become a big movement near future. Also, web services
in the internet was hype, but is growing constantly. On the other hand, SCM by
RFID is considered to be popular triggered by the admission of UHF tag. Also,
as HDD recorders and digital music players like iPod get popular, annotation to
digital data would make rapid progress.

In this circumstance, we developed USF aiming at simple coordination of
objects, data, and services, and took up two drawbacks of our approach: discovery of services and inputs to the services. Then, we proposed metadata mapping
and service combination using Metadata Matching Engine. Our current status is
that we have just developed the prototype, and now have evaluation on precision
ratio on the proposed services based on our ontologies and matching strategy
response time at multiple accesses. As future works, we have a plan of public
experiment with some target products within this year. We hope we will provide
a value-added ubiquitous solution with semantics based on the result.

References

1. H. P. Huy, T. Kawamura, T. Hasegawa, How to make Web sites talk together -
   Web Service Gateway Solution, Proceedings of 14th International World Wide Web
   Conference (WWW 2005), 2005.
2. M. Paolucci, T. Kawamura, T. R. Payne, K. Sycara, Semantic Matching of Web
   Services Capabilities, Proceedings of First International Semantic Web Conference
   (ISWC 2002), LNCS No. 2342, pp. 333-347, 2002.
3. T. Kawamura, J. D. Blasio, T. Hasegawa, M. Paolucci, K. Sycara, Public Deployment of Semantic Service Matchmaker with UDDI Business Registry, Proceedings
   of 3rd International Semantic Web Conference (ISWC 2004), LNCS 3298, pp. 752-
   766, 2004.

4. D. Martin, M. Paolucci, S. McIlraith, M. Burstein, D. McDermott, D. McGuinness, B. Parsia, T. Payne, M. Sabou, M. Solanki, N. Srinivasan, K. Sycara, Bringing Semantics to Web Services: The OWL-S Approach, Proceedings of International Workshop on Semantic Web Services and Web Process Composition (SWSWPC 2004), 2004.
5. OWL Services, http://www.daml.org/services/owl-s/.
6. Ubiquitous Communicator, http://www.ubin.jp/press/pdf/TEP040915-u01e.pdf
7. http://www.kddi.com/corporate/r_and_d/kaihatsu/ (in Japanese)
8. Digital Living Network Alliance, http://www.dlna.org
9. K. Ueno, T. Kawamura, T. Hasegawa, A. Ohsuga, M. Doi, Cooperation between Robots and Ubiquitous Devices with Network Script "Flipcast", Proceedings of Network Robot System: Toward intelligent robotic systems integrated with environments (IROS 2004 Workshop), 2004.
10. Hetal S., Standards for service discovery and delivery, IEEE Pervasive Computing vol. 1, no. 3, 2002.
11. Resource Description Framework, http://www.w3.org/RDF/.
12. Web-Ontology Working Group, http://www.w3.org/2001/sw/WebOnt/.
13. Annotate the Planet, http://aura.research.microsoft.com
14. R. Masuoka, B. Parsia, Y. Labrou, E. Sirin, Ontology-Enabled Pervasive Computing Applications, IEEE Intelligent Systems, vol. 18, no. 5, pp. 68-72, 2003.
15. D. Khushraj, O. Lassila, CALI: Context-Awareness via Logical Inference, Proceedings of Workshop on Semantic Web Technology for Mobile and Ubiquitous Applications, 2004.

Ontological Approach to Generating Personalized User Interfaces for Web Services

Deepali Khushraj and Ora Lassila

Nokia Research Center,
5 Wayside Road,
Burlington MA, USA

Abstract. Web services can be presented to end-users via user interfaces (UIs) that facilitate the invocation of these services. Standardized, interoperable mechanisms for describing Web service interfaces enable the generation of UIs automatically and dynamically, at least in principle; the emergence of *Semantic Web services* opens the possibility of improving the generation process. In this paper, we propose a scheme that extends the OWL-S ontology, an emerging standard for Semantic Web services, to better enable the creation of such dynamic interfaces.

Semantic Web services go beyond "classical" Web services in enabling enhanced *discovery, invocation* and *composition*. In our scheme, the integration of semantic descriptions of Web services with semantic models of the user's locally available data enables context-based personalization of dynamically created user interfaces, allowing us to minimize the number of necessary inputs. The need for this is compelling on mobile devices with limitations on input methods and screen size and where context data is readily available. The use of an underlying semantic model enables better accuracy than traditional form-filling techniques.

We propose an architecture for the creation and personalization of dynamic UIs from Web service descriptions. The key idea is to exploit the semantic relationships between type information of Web service input fields, and their association with information the system has about the user (such as the user's current context, PIM data, context history, usage history, corporate data etc.), in order to personalize and simplify the invocation of Web services.

1 Introduction

We observe that *Web service interfaces* [1] and *Web forms* [2, Chapter 17] bear a conceptual resemblance to one another: both specify a set of inputs and a method whose invocation yields some results. It is therefore possible to transform descriptions of Web services to form-based UIs (for invoking these services). Current formalisms for interface description, however, are not strong enough to communicate the *semantics* of services, a prerequisite for generating personalized UIs.

The *Semantic Web* is a vision of the next generation of the World Wide Web, characterized by the association of formally described semantics with content and services [3]. Work on realizing the Semantic Web is motivated by promises of greater

Y. Gil et al. (Eds.): ISWC 2005, LNCS 3729, pp. 916–927, 2005.

ease – and degree – of automation, as well as improved interoperability between information systems [4]. On the Semantic Web content and services are described using representation languages such as RDF [5] and OWL [6]. Representations refer to *ontologies*, specifications of conceptualizations [7], which, in turn, enable *reasoning* via the use of logic rules.

The application of Semantic Web technologies to Web services is referred to as *Semantic Web services* [8]: Descriptions of service interfaces are associated with formal semantics, allowing *agents* to describe their functionality, discover and "understand" other agents' functionality and invoke services provided by other agents; furthermore, it is possible to combine multiple services into new services. Work on Semantic Web services is – again – driven by the possibility to automate things that formerly have required human involvement, consequently leading to improved interoperability.

OWL-S [9,10] is one of the recently emerged ontologies for semantic annotation of Web service descriptions. The OWL-S ontology is written in the ontology language OWL. Web services annotated using OWL-S can be automatically discovered, composed into new services, invoked, and their execution automatically monitored. The process model of OWL-S is used to specify how a service works by providing a semantic description of its inputs, outputs, preconditions, post conditions and process flow. The OWL-S description can be grounded to a WSDL [1] description (and possibly other standards). The grounding part of the ontology enables mapping of OWL-S inputs and outputs to the corresponding inputs and outputs in the WSDL description of the service. Hence OWL-S can be used with SOAP based Web services, which provide a WSDL description, to create Semantic Web services.

In the next section we present an approach to generating user interfaces automatically from OWL-S profiles. These interfaces can be optimized and *personalized* using semantic information about the user, collected in a *semantic cache* (as presented in section 3). Section 4 then outlines the overall architecture of our system. Finally, we present a concrete example in the form of a simple usage scenario (section 5).

2   Generating User Interfaces

Our approach is to use the OWL-S *profile* and *process model* of a service as the basic representation from which to generate a form-based UI. OWL-S provides a rich vocabulary that can be used for describing not only the (call-)interface of a service, but also other aspects that may be helpful in UI generation. There are, however, aspects of UIs that are not "derivable" from OWL-S descriptions; for this purpose, we have extended the ontology with *user interface annotations*. The extensions provide cues about:

- *display labels* used for fields,
- preferred *widget types* for implementing fields (e.g. free-text input, checkbox),
- how to render *fields with pre-determined value ranges* (e.g., a selection list) as well as the *ordering of available values* in such fields,

- *grouping* of fields and subfields, and
- how to *generate the serialized RDF data* from inputs specified by the user (the generation of serialized RDF is a requirement for invoking Semantic Web services).

(The details of the extensions are presented below; an understanding of the OWL Web ontology language as well as the OWL-S ontology is required to grasp the details.)

Every *UIModel* is associated with an OWL-S service and has associated process UIs. Multiple UIs can be attached to a single process; hence each *ProcessUI* is linked to a specific OWL-S process and a *UIFieldMap* that provides cues pertaining to the input and output fields involved in the process interaction. UI-related cues for fields are specified by creating an instance of the *UIFieldMap* class (note that a set of related fields can then be grouped together by creating an instance of the *FieldMapList*, which has individual *UIFieldMap* instances as members). Every instance of the field map can specify the following properties:

- The *parameterName* property points to the input parameter resource used in the OWL-S profile or process model. Since every input and output parameter in OWL-S has an associated parameter type, it becomes easy to identify the semantic type associated with the field using this property.
- The *parameterTypePath* property specifies a path that is used to create an OWL instance from the specified user inputs in the generated UI.
- The *fieldType* property provides cues about the type of UI widget that should be used for the given field. For example, it could specify *single select, multiple select, check box*, etc. Or, it could specify the widget type at a higher level, such as "select one" or "select many" and a widget could then be chosen at runtime based on available data about the field. Or, it could be of *FieldSet* type to specify multiple subfields. For example, a currency converter service uses inputs "price" and "currency" as input fields. Input price could further have "amount" and "currency" as subfields. The subfields are specified using the *hasSubfieldMap* property that has *FieldMapList* as range.
- The *instanceDataLocation* property along with *instanceSelectionPath* and *displayLabelPath* are used for fields that have a pre-determined value range. The *instanceDataLocation* property specifies the URL from where the value range can be found. For example, a language translator service could specify possible values for input language and output language by pointing to an ontology about languages supported by the service. Multiple locations for loading instance data can be specified using this property. The *instanceSelectionPath* property is then used to specify the path query required to select instance data from the specified data locations. Finally, the path specified by the *displayLabelPath* property is used to find the label to be used to display the instance on the UI widget.

In addition to the above properties, the UI Model fields could specify information about how conservative the UI generation scheme must be. For example, using the

UI Model, strict ordering of input fields can be imposed, or strict ordering for elements in certain selection style widgets can be imposed.

When a Semantic Web service is accessed, the associated OWL-S description along with the *UIModel* gets loaded. The rendering algorithm[1] makes use of the extended OWL-S description associated with the service to generate the UI. Once the UI is generated and inputs are received from the user, an OWL instance is created for every input parameter specified in the OWL-S description, by using the *parameterTypePath* property. The data for creating an OWL instance could be received from a single widget or from multiple widgets. The algorithm uses grouping knowledge about fields along with the *parameterTypePath* to create a single OWL instance from multiple widgets.[2] Once the OWL instances are created, the OWL-S grounding is used to invoke the service with the specified inputs. Finally, outputs of the service invocation are presented to the user. A sample *UIModel* graph associated with AltaVista's "Babel Fish" language translator Web service along with the generated UI is presented in Appendix A.

3   "Semantic Caching"

As illustrated in section 2, it is possible to generate form-based UIs from "plain" OWL-S descriptions, and potentially better ones from OWL-S profiles augmented with UI cues. Using additional information about the user – such as the current context, history of actions, etc. – allows us to further improve the generated result. The repository that stores information about the user is called the *semantic cache*. The key idea is to exploit semantic relationships between type information of Web service input (and output) fields and their association with data in the semantic cache.

The semantic cache gets data from:

- User's personal profile,
- PIM information such as address book entries, calendar entries, etc.,
- user's current context and his context history, and
- the history of inputs/outputs in recently invoked services.
- corporate data, such as company phone book, organization hierarchies etc.

The data sources for the semantic cache could go beyond the ones above. The basic requirement for any data source is that it uses a semantic model to represent data objects. In our case, we make use of semantic models that are created using the OWL Web ontology language. Making use of all the available data would significantly increase the response time for generating UIs, therefore a subset of data objects from the sources are cached.

The semantic cache stores both semantic models and data annotated with these models. A cache management algorithm constantly adds objects to and evicts them

---

[1] Our rendering algorithm currently generates HTML forms based on UIModels, but the renderer can easily be extended to create either XHTML or XForms based UIs.

[2] A detailed discussion of this is beyond the scope of this paper.

from the cache based on the usage patterns of the data objects in the cache. A caching scheme that implements standard caching algorithms such as MRU or LRU cannot be used directly. The scheme should also take into account the semantic relationships between objects in the cache, since the addition or deletion of a set of semantically similar objects could be done together. Additionally, the scheme should take into account the nature of data sources involved. For example, the user's current context is transient, whereas his profile information mostly remains static.

While rendering a Semantic Web service, the *type* information associated with the involved input fields is used to retrieve objects from the cache (in our case, the *parameterType* property of OWL-S provides this information). The retrieved objects are essentially instances of the class specified as the *type* of the field. By making use of a reasoner, both explicit and implicit objects of a given *type* can be queried for. The retrieved objects are given weights based on the nature of the data sources involved and their frequency of occurrence. The semantic distance between prespecified objects used by fields of the service and data in the cache can also be used to determine the relevance of a given instance. In the case of composite Web services, the relevance of a semantic instance in the cache, can further be inferred based on the atomic services that constitute the service and based on the control constructs (such as Sequence, Split etc.) specified in the service's process model. Weights are additionally adjusted based on the current context. The cumulative weight of a given object helps in determining the relevance of its use. Finally, *customizations* are made using the objects retrieved:

- *Eliminating user input widgets* for fields where the answer is already known with sufficient certainty,
- *changing UI widgets* where the input values can be predetermined (e.g. change a free-text input widget to an editable selection list),
- providing *intelligent default values* for certain fields, and
- *reordering or narrowing down* element lists in widgets such as selection lists, checkboxes, etc.

Semantic Web techniques (ontologies, reasoning, rich semantic models, etc.) can also be used in determining the user's current *usage context* and managing definitions of contexts [11]. Making the context definitions derived via semantic reasoning available to the semantic cache, and consequently to the UI generation process, can improve the system's ability to discover implicit relationships between objects in the cache. The user's context can further be applied to limit the amount of data to be considered when rendering a UI. For example, in case of *location-based services*, only data relevant to the user's current location may be considered (or at least given priority). Additionally, considering context in UI generation will improve the user's perception that the system is behaving in a *context-aware* manner.

4   Component Architecture

Figure 1 shows the component architecture of our prototype implementation. The Semantic Web services expose their service description using OWL-S and the ex-

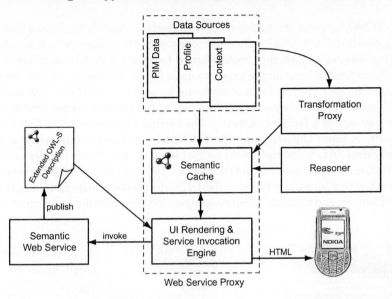

Fig. 1. System Components

tended UIModel ontology (as presented in section 2). The UIModel for a Web service could be provided by the Web service provider or by an intermediary such as an enterprise that is making services available to employees within an organization. The enterprise could thus make decisions about the allowed level of personalization, by appropriately configuring the UIModel.

When a service is to be invoked, the UI rendering engine uses the extended OWL-S description to render a dynamic web-based UI (possibly using HTML, XHTML or XForms). Additionally, it uses both explicit and implicit relationships in the semantic cache to render a personalized UI appropriate to the current context. Implicit relationships in the semantic cache are inferred using a reasoner. All data sources that feed data into the semantic cache have type information associated with them. Commonly occurring types in the semantic cache include: profile information, context history, PIM data, common sense information etc. The type information is used by the rendering algorithm to determine how relevant data from a given source is. The system can also support data originating from legacy applications using a transformational framework. In our system, the semantic cache along with the rendering engine are implemented as part of a Web service proxy. After the UI is rendered, user inputs are received to invoke the service. These inputs are used to further change the contents of the semantic cache. Finally the service is invoked and the outputs are presented as a UI.

5 Simple Usage Scenario

Our implementation was tested on a Nokia Series 60 phone with several atomic and composite real-world Web services. Example test services include, AltaVista's

"Babel Fish" language translator service, Barnes and Noble's book price finder service, zip code finder service etc. In order to test our system, the OWL-S descriptions from the *Mindswap* Web site[3] were adapted to have *UI Model* extensions. In this section, we present an example usage scenario based on some of our test services.

A mobile user visiting India is shopping for a souvenir to take back home. He makes use of the currency converter service on the phone to determine the price of the souvenir in a familiar currency. The currency converter takes three inputs: Input Price, Input Currency and Output Currency. The corresponding semantic types in the OWL-S description for each of these fields are: *XML Schema integer*, *Currency type* (represented as an OWL Class URI) and *Currency type*, respectively. The corresponding widget types in the *UI Model* are: free-text input, single select drop-down list and multiple select drop-down list, respectively (see Figure 2).

Fig. 2. Currency Converter   **Fig. 3.** Pages 1 & 2 of the currency list

Since the *Input Price* field uses a free-text input widget and has type XML Schema, only values entered by the user to invoke the same service in the recent past are used from the semantic cache. If the service was accessed recently, then the field is displayed as an editable select list, with cached values, else a free-text input widget is presented.

Since the *Input Currency* and *Output Currency* fields have the type Currency and use drop-down list widgets (with pre-determined value ranges), the currencies are ordered in the list so that relevant currencies appear on the top of the list. If any instances of Currency are found in the cache then they are likely to occur higher up on the list.

Additionally, the ordering of currencies is determined by using the semantic relationship of the Currency type class with other classes in its ontology. From the currency ontology, the rendering engine determines that every Currency object is associated with one or more countries. Hence it determines all relevant countries in the semantic cache to ascertain the ordering of currencies. In the rendered UI, USD appears high on the list because the user's profile indicates that he has an US residential address. The user's calendar information shows that he recently attended a meeting in Helsinki, his context history indicates that he recently traveled via

---

[3] www.mindswap.org

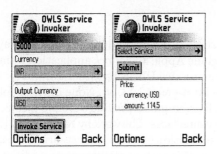

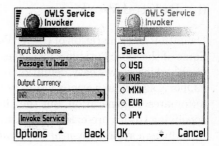

Fig. 4. Selected inputs & invocation results   **Fig. 5.** Book Price Finder

Tokyo and the use of GPS coordinates suggest that the user's current location is Bombay. By using simple geo-spatial reasoning, the cache determines that the user recently attended a meeting in Finland, that he recently traveled via Japan and that he is currently located in India; hence the currencies used in these countries (i.e. EUR, JPY and INR) appear high on the list. Similarly several other countries appear high on the list based on data in the semantic cache (See Figure 3). In the current context, the relevant inputs are INR as input currency and USD as output currency (See Figure 4). Due to the reordering of currencies in the drop-down list, based on data in the semantic cache, the hassle of browsing through a long list (of 98 currencies) is avoided in this case. Once the service is invoked, the results are displayed to the user, as shown in Figure 5.

Now let us assume that the user wants to buy a book, from a local store, and check its price in local currency before he gets to the store to pick it up. The user makes use of the store's book price finder service, which takes book name and output currency as inputs. The corresponding types for these fields are: *XML Schema string* and *Currency*. Since the INR object has semantic type Currency and was recently used as an input for service invocation, it appears higher on the list, making it easier to select (see Figure 5). Note that this service was never invoked in the past, yet personalization is done based on the semantic types of fields.

Personalization of the rendered UI can further be done based on knowledge about the atomic services involved. For example, the book price finder service, presented earlier, is a composite service based on three atomic services. It first makes use of a book details grabber service, which takes a book name as input and provides the ISBN number along with other details as output. It then makes use of a book price finder service, which takes the ISBN number and provides the price in USD as output. And finally, it makes use of a currency converter service to translate the price from USD to the desired currency. In the current scenario, knowledge about the currency converter atomic service helps in further deciding the weights given to individual currencies in the drop-down list.

We observe that the use of a semantic cache for rendering personalized UIs makes form-filling easier on devices with limited text-input methods, specially for the reduction in number of keystrokes used. Furthermore, it makes it easier to personalize the UI of services that were never invoked before or that are composed of atomic services that were invoked in the past.

6   Related Work

Definition and generation of UIs for Web services has been addressed in many ways. Some of the more notable approaches include Apple's *Sherlock* application framework[4] which allows easy definition of Web service UIs using either JavaScript or XQuery, as well as various industry specifications [12,13,14]. None of these fully automates UI generation, but they are all attempts to provide a simple means of specifying UIs for pre-existing Web service interfaces. The work by Kassoff et al [15] introduces a system for *near-automatic* generation of user interfaces from WSDL profiles; in addition to a WSDL document, this system requires some additional information to generate the UI. Furthermore, the approach to providing default values requires authoring new "virtual" WSDL profiles which specify these values explicitly.

Automated form-filling techniques are often used in the context of Web-based forms. Published work in this area often addresses issues of building automated Web robots (or "bots") that need to access pages that are only reachable via various (form-based) query interfaces [16,17, for example]. Furthermore, most modern Web browsers offer some means of automatic filling or "completing" of Web forms. Although these techniques make use of personal profile information and usage history, they cannot be used for rendering personalized Semantic Web service interfaces because they will not be able to exploit the associated semantic model. Due to the lack of semantic processing capabilities, personalization based on the current context, PIM information etc. will be limited.

In database research, semantic caching techniques are frequently used to cache database queries and associated results [18, for example]. Subsequent queries are then answered by determining their semantic locality with cached queries to improve response time. As described earlier, the term "semantic caching" is used in an entirely different manner in this paper; hence semantic caching techniques for databases cannot be applied to render personalized UIs for Web services.

7   Conclusions

There is a striking resemblance between Web service descriptions and Web forms. This strongly motivates the generation of dynamic UIs for Web service access. Our work clearly establishes the need for a UI layer extension to Semantic Web service descriptions and demonstrates the benefits of semantic caching techniques for personalization of Web service UIs. The fundamental idea is to enable personalization by exploiting the relationship of semantic objects in the user's cache with type information associated with Web service inputs. Additionally, the process model associated with composite services can also be used. The use of caching is emphasized because all data about the user cannot be used while rendering personalized UIs as this would considerably increase the time required for UI generation. Semantic caching based personalization enables automatic form-filling and other customizations to UIs for services that have never been accessed before. The proposed

---

[4] http://developer.apple.com/macosx/sherlock/

approach has great potential for access to services from mobile devices that have limited text-input capabilities but have context information, such as current location, social context etc., readily available. Our prototype implementation uses a Web service proxy based architecture, which enables semantic processing to occur either remotely or locally on the user's mobile device. The prototype implementation was tested using several real-world Web services and an evidence to the practical benefits of the proposed approach was established. Several optimizations can be performed on the algorithm used to query for semantic objects and manage semantic objects in the cache; we would like to address this in the future.

References

1. Christensen, E., Curbera, F., Meredith, G., Weerawarana, S.: Web Services Description Language (WSDL) 1.1. W3C Note, World Wide Web Consortium (2001)
2. Raggett, D., Hors, A.L., Jacobs, I.: HTML 4.01 Specification. W3C Recommendation, World Wide Web Consortium (1999)
3. Berners-Lee, T., Hendler, J., Lassila, O.: The Semantic Web. Scientific American **284** (2001) 34–43
4. Lassila, O.: Serendipitous Interoperability. In Eero Hyvönen, ed.: The Semantic Web Kick-off in Finland – Vision, Technologies, Research, and Applications. HIIT Publications 2002-001. University of Helsinki (2002)
5. Lassila, O., Swick, R.R.: Resource Description Framework (RDF) Model and Syntax Specification. W3C Recommendation, World Wide Web Consortium (1999)
6. McGuinness, D.L., van Harmelen, F.: OWL Web Ontology Language Overview. W3C Recommendation, World Wide Web Consortium (February 2004)
7. Gruber, T.R.: A Translation Approach to Portable Ontology Specifications. Knowledge Acquisition **5** (1993) 199–220
8. Payne, T., Lassila, O.: Semantic Web Services (guest editors' introduction). IEEE Intelligent Systems **19** (2004) 14–15
9. Ankolekar, A., Burstein, M., Hobbs, J.R., Lassila, O., McDermott, D., Martin, D., McIlraith, S.A., Narayanan, S., Paolucci, M., Payne, T., Sycara, K.: DAML-S: Web Service Description for the Semantic Web. In Horrocks, I., Hendler, J., eds.: The Semantic Web - ISWC 2002. Volume 2342 of Lecture Notes in Computer Science., Springer Verlag (2002) 348–363
10. Martin, D., Burstein, M., Hobbs, J., Lassila, O., McDermott, D., McIlraith, S., Narayanan, S., Paolucci, M., Parsia, B., Payne, T., Sirin, E., Srinivasan, N., Sycara, K.: OWL-S: Semantic Markup for Web Services. W3C Member Submission, World Wide Web Consortium (2004)
11. Khushraj, D., Lassila, O.: CALI: Context-Awareness via Logical Inference. In: ISWC 2004 workshop on Semantic Web Technology for Mobile and Ubiquitous Applications. (2004)
12. Anuff, E., Chaston, M., Moses, D., Kropp, A.: Web Service User Interface (WSUI) 1.0. Working Draft, Epicentric, Inc. (2001)
13. Kropp, A., Leue, C., Thompson, R.: Web Services for Remote Portlets Specification. OASIS Standard, Organization for the Advancement of Structured Information Standards (OASIS) (2003)

14. Arsanjani, A., Chamberlain, D., Gisolfi, D., Konuru, R., Macnaught, J., Maes, S., Merrick, R., Mundel, D., Raman, T., Ramaswamy, S., Schaeck, T., Thompson, R., Diaz, A., Lucassen, J., Wiecha, C.F.: (WSXL) Web Service Experience Language Version 2. IBM Note, IBM Corporation (2002)
15. Kassoff, M., Kato, D., Mohsin, W.: Creating GUIs for Web Services. IEEE Internet Computing **7** (2003) 66–73
16. Doorenbos, R.B., Etzioni, O., Weld, D.S.: A Scalable Comparison-Shopping Agent for the World-Wide Web. In Johnson, W.L., Hayes-Roth, B., eds.: Proceedings of the First International Conference on Autonomous Agents (Agents'97), Marina del Rey, CA, USA, ACM Press (1997) 39–48
17. Liddle, S.W., Yau, S.H., Embley, D.W.: On the Automatic Extraction of Data from the Hidden Web. In: Proceedings of the International Workshop on Data Semantics in Web Information Systems (DASWIS-2001). (2001)
18. Dar, S., Franklin, M.J., Jónsson, B.T., Srivastava, D., Tan, M.: Semantic Data Caching and Replacement. In Vijayaraman, T.M., Buchmann, A.P., Mohan, C., Sarda, N.L., eds.: VLDB'96, Proceedings of 22th International Conference on Very Large Data Bases, September 3-6, 1996, Mumbai (Bombay), India, Morgan Kaufmann (1996) 330–341

A   Example UI Model

AltaVista's Babel Fish translator Web service is used to translate text between a variety of languages. Figure 6 represents the RDF graph for the UI model of the

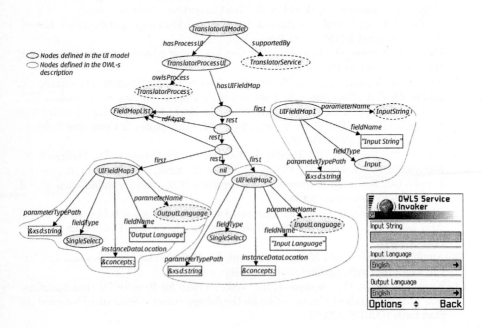

Fig. 6. Babel Fish Service & User Interface Model

service and the corresponding dynamic user interface generated by the rendering engine. The model extends from concepts defined in the OWL-S description of the service[5]. The UI model is supported by the *TranslatorService* and has an associated process UI. The specified process UI is created for the *TranslatorProcess* and has several UI fields. Each UI field is specified as a mapping between the associated parameter in the OWL-S description and other properties for rendering (and invoking) the UI. In the figure, we see three UI field map nodes, one for each of the OWL-S input parameters, namely Input String, Input Language and Output Language. A detailed explanation of all the properties emerging out of these nodes is provided in section 2.

---

[5] http://www.mindswap.org/2004/owl-s/1.0/BabelFishTranslator.owl

On Identifying Knowledge Processing Requirements[*]

Alain Léger[1], Lyndon J.B. Nixon[2], and Pavel Shvaiko[3]

[1] France Telecom R&D, Rennes, France
alain.leger@francetelecom.com
[2] Free University of Berlin, Berlin, Germany
nixon@inf.fu-berlin.de
[3] University of Trento, Povo, Trento, Italy
pavel@dit.unitn.it

Abstract. The uptake of Semantic Web technology by industry is progressing slowly. One of the problems is that academia is not always aware of the concrete problems that arise in industry. Conversely, industry is not often well informed about the academic developments that can potentially meet its needs. In this paper we present a first step towards a successful transfer of knowledge-based technology from academia to industry. In particular, we present a collection of use cases from enterprises which are interested in Semantic Web technology. We provide a detailed analysis of the use cases, identify their technology locks, discuss the appropriateness of knowledge-based technology and possible solutions. We summarize industrial knowledge processing requirements in the form of a typology of knowledge processing tasks and a library of high level components for realizing those tasks. Eventually these results are intended to focus academia on the development of plausible knowledge-based solutions for concrete industrial problems, and therefore, facilitate the uptake of Semantic Web technology within industry.

1 Introduction

The industrial uptake of Semantic Web technology is still slow. On the one hand, industry is not often well informed about the academic developments that can potentially meet its needs. On the other hand, academia is not always aware of the concrete problems that arise in industry, and therefore, the research agenda and the achievements thereof are not tailored for an easy migration to industrial applications. Thus, in order to increase the industrial uptake of Semantic Web technology, there is a clear need for researchers to have access to a study of industrial requirements, thereby focusing their activities on research challenges arising exactly from those requirements. Simultaneously, industry needs to have access to studies identifying plausible knowledge-based solutions to technological problems in their business scenarios, as well as to success stories which demonstrate the value of adopting knowledge-based technology.

On a large scale, industry awareness of the knowledge-based technology has started only recently, e.g., at the EC level with the IST-FP5 thematic network Ontoweb[1] which

---

[*] The work described in this paper is supported by the EU Network of Excellence Knowledge Web (FP6-507482).

[1] http://www.ontoweb.org/

Y. Gil et al. (Eds.): ISWC 2005, LNCS 3729, pp. 928–943, 2005.

had brought together around 50 companies worldwide which are interested in Semantic Web technology. These companies influenced significantly a global vision of Semantic Web technology developments, provided success stories and guidelines for best practices. Based on this experience, within the IST-FP6 network of excellence Knowledge Web[2], an in-depth analysis of the concrete industry needs in the key economic sectors has been identified as one of the next steps towards stimulating the industrial uptake of Semantic Web technology. To this end, this paper aims at identifying technology locks within the concrete business scenarios, and at discussing plausible knowledge-based solutions to those locks.

The contributions of the paper are:

- a collection of the use cases and their detailed technical analysis used to determine European industry needs with respect to knowledge-based technology;
- a typology of knowledge processing tasks and a library of high level components for realizing those tasks used to focus academia on the current industry requirements.

The rest of the paper is organized as follows. A set of use cases collected from industry and their preliminary analysis are presented in Section 2 and Section 3 respectively. Section 4 describes, via an example, a methodology for identifying technology locks occurring in the use cases and discusses the appropriateness of knowledge-based approaches for resolving those locks. Section 5 summarizes industrial knowledge processing requirements as a typology of knowledge processing tasks and a library of high level components. Section 6 considers the related efforts and industrial experiences with some components of the library proposed. Finally, Section 7 reports some conclusions and discusses the future work.

2   Use Case Collection

A major barrier between industry and research is that the former thinks in terms of problems and solutions and the latter thinks in terms of technologies and research issues. A business use case provides a brief description of a concrete business problem. A technical use case relates a business problem to a solution, and a solution to a technology, which, in turn, may lead to a research issue. Therefore, business use cases and their technical analysis provide an effective means for enterprises to argue and communicate their needs to academia.

In order to enable the collection of use cases we invited companies interested in Semantic Web technology to form an Industry Board (IB). Around 50 companies[3] from 12

---

[2] http://knowledgeweb.semanticweb.org/

[3] Some examples are Acklin; Amper; Berlecon Research GmbH; Biovista; Bitext; British Telecom, BT; Computas Technology; Daimler Chrysler; Deimos Space; Distributed Thinking; EADS Airbus Industry; France Télécom Division R&D; Green Cacti; HR-XML Consortium Europe; IFP Institut Français du Pétrole; IKV++ Technologies AG; Illycaffè S.p.A.; Labein; Merrall-Ross International Ltd; Neofonie Technology Development and Information Management GmbH; NIWA; Office Line Engineering; QUARTO Software; RIS-ARIS; Robotiker Tecnalia; Semtation GmbH; SNCF; Synergetics; Tecnologia, Información y Finanzas; TSF S.p.A.; Telefonica; Thalés; TXT e-solutions; WTCM, see for details http://knowledgeweb.semanticweb.org/o2i/

Table 1. The use cases collected in 2004

#	Use case name	IB member	Web page
1	Recruitment	WWJ GmbH	http://www.wwj.de
2	Multimedia content analysis	Motorola	http://www.motorola.com
3	eScience portal	Neofonie	http://www.neofonie.de
4	News aggregation service	Neofonie	http://www.neofonie.de
5	Product lifecycle management	Semtation	http://www.semtation.de
6	Data warehousing in healthcare	Semtation	http://www.semtation.de
7	B2C marketplace for tourism	France Telecom	http://www.francetelecom.com
8	Digital photo album	France Telecom	http://www.francetelecom.com
9	Geosciences project memory	IFP	http://www.ifp.fr
10	R&D support for coffee	Illy Cafe	http://www.illy.com
11	Real estate management	TrenItalia	http://www.trenitalia.com
12	Hospital information system	L&C	http://www.landcglobal.com
13	Agent-based system for insurance	Acklin	http://www.acklin.nl
14	DCVD Semantic Web portal	DaimlerChrysler	http://www.daimlerchrysler.com
15	Specialized web portals	Robotiker	http://www.robotiker.es
16	Integrated access to biology	Robotiker	http://www.robotiker.es

industry sectors[4] have joined the initiative so far. We asked the IB members to describe the actual or hypothetical deployment of Semantic Web technology in their business environments. Thus, in 2004, 16 use cases were provided by 12 companies, see Table 1. The breakdown of the use cases with respect to industrial sectors is shown in Figure 1. For example, the most active sectors (in providing use cases) were *service industry* and *media & communications*. A detailed description of all the use cases can be found in [19].

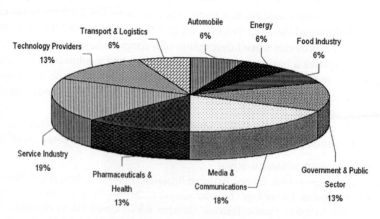

Fig. 1. Breakdown of the use cases by industry sectors

---

[4] These are: Health, Telecom, Automotive, Energy, Food, Media, Transport, Space, Publishing, Banking, Manufacturing, Technology sectors.

3   Preliminary Analysis of Use Cases

We have performed an initial analysis of the use cases of Table 1 aiming at an overview of the current industrial needs. The IB members were requested to point out technological problems they have encountered in their businesses as well as the knowledge-based approaches they view as plausible solutions to those problems. As a result, we obtained:

- a set of typical business problems for which an industry expert has determined that a plausible solution can come from the knowledge-based technology;
- a set of typical technological issues/locks (and corresponding research challenges) which knowledge-based technology is expected to overcome.

Figure 2 and Figure 3 illustrate the results of this preliminary analysis. The former shows the type of business/market needs for which Semantic Web was considered by the industry as a relevant technological approach. The latter shows the type of technological issues which industry considers that Semantic Web must be able to overcome. Let us discuss them in turn.

Figure 2 shows that in nearly half of the collected use cases industry has identified *data integration* and *semantic search* as typical business problems for which they expect Semantic Web to provide solutions. Below, we illustrate, with the help of two use cases, how a concrete business problem can indicate the need for a knowledge-based solution.

The first use case is taken from the Human Resources field. In this use case, the expert saw a solution needed for the problem of *matching between job offers and job seekers*. The key reason given by the expert for such a need was that "employee recruitment is increasingly being carried out online. Finding the best suited candidate in a short time should lead to cost cutting and resource sparing". The second use case is focused on the problem of data warehousing for a healthcare scenario. The solution is seen as being to *introduce a common terminology for healthcare data and wrap all legacy data in this terminology*. The key reason given by the expert for such a need was that "it reduces the time and cost involved in *data integration* and *consistency checking* of the data coming from different healthcare providers".

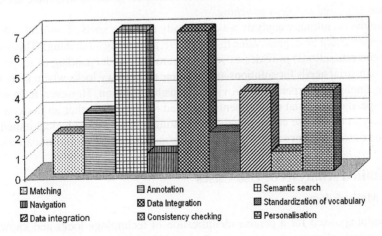

Fig. 2. Preliminary vision for solutions sought in the use cases

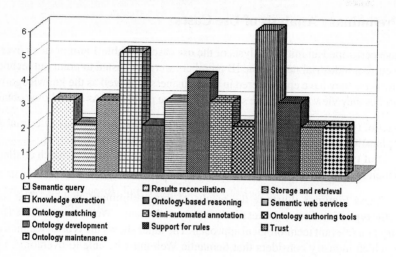

Fig. 3. Preliminary vision of technological issues in the use cases

Figure 3 shows the technological issues/locks which industry consider that Semantic Web approaches might overcome. Here, the key issues are: *ontology matching*, i.e., resolving semantic heterogeneity between heterogeneous ontologies; *knowledge extraction*, i.e., populating ontologies by extracting data from legacy systems; *ontology development*, i.e., modeling a business domain, authoring tools, re-using existing ontologies.

Let us now illustrate, with the help of yet another use case from our collection, how a concrete business problem can be used to identify such technology locks. The use case deals with the problem of providing unified access to biological repositories on the Internet. The problem is attacked by modeling those repositories (notice they may store their data according to various data/conceptual models) as ontologies. This, in turn, is performed by analyzing the underlying data instances. Finally, since those newly created ontologies will likely use different terminologies, mappings between them must also be established. Hence, in this case the technological issues to overcome are *knowledge extraction* and *ontology matching*.

From the preliminary analysis we can already draw the areas of Semantic Web research which could be of great value to industry (e.g., ontology matching). This analysis (by experts estimations) provides us with a preliminary understanding of scope of the current industrial needs for solutions and concrete technology locks where knowledge-based technology is expected to provide a plausible solution. However, to be able to answer specific industrial requirements, we need to conduct further an in-depth technical analysis of the use cases, thereby associating to each technological issue/lock a concrete knowledge processing task and a component realizing its functionalities.

4   Detailed Analysis of Use Cases

4.1   A Methodology

A methodology used for a precise identification of technology locks and knowledge processing tasks they require is based on Rational Unified Process (RUP) [1, 15] which, in turn, extensively exploits Unified Modeling Language (UML) [6]. Out of six standard steps of the RUP approach (i.e., *business modeling, service requirements, analysis, design, implementation,* and *validation*) we focus only on three of them, namely, *service requirements, analysis,* and *design*:

- *Service Requirements.* These are a set of services available from a system in order to implement a business case. They are determined through analysis of functional needs, which in turn imply some technical constraints (e.g., time response, number of connected customers) of a system to be developed. Service requirements are expressed via UML technical use cases.
- *Analysis.* This step performs initial system partitioning with respect to its main processing tasks and analyses the use cases in detail. In particular, use cases are refined with the help of UML sequence diagrams, which incorporate the modules for the architecture proposal and the information flow between these modules to fulfill the use case functionality. Notice that during this step we identify the use case's technology locks.
- *Design.* This step refines and homogenizes classes, and drafts the architecture design. It is partially specified in the context of our analysis, namely, it aims only at identifying knowledge processing tasks which resolve technology locks determined in the previous step. We structure knowledge processing tasks as primary and secondary tasks according to their influence on the architecture of a system to be developed. Primary tasks are the common parts for most of actions or parts of actions of the system. Secondary tasks are additional requirements, i.e., extensions of the common parts.

4.2   The Methodology by an Example

Let us discuss with the help of the B2C marketplace for tourism use case how the above introduced methodology is used for the identification of technology locks and possible knowledge processing tasks resolving them. We first provide a summary of the use case, then we discuss the service requirements, analysis, and design steps.

Use Case Summary. The B2C marketplace for tourism use case considers a scenario where users are offered an one-stop browsing and purchasing of personalized tourism packages by a dynamic combination of various tourism offers (e.g., travel, accommodation, meals) from different providers. A detailed description of this business scenario can be found in [19]. Figure 4 illustrates two primary use cases of the B2C marketplace system.

The first use case, which is called *to plan a nice weekend*, constitutes the entry point inside the marketplace allowing customers to define their personal needs. The platform takes care of identifying potentially useful contents and services, accessing multiple providers and selecting only the relevant ones.

The second use case, which is called *to package and purchase a nice weekend*, requires (i) a dynamic aggregation of relevant contents and services (e.g., transport, accommodation, leisure activities), (ii) an automated packaging of week-end proposals, and (iii) facilities for purchasing them on-line.

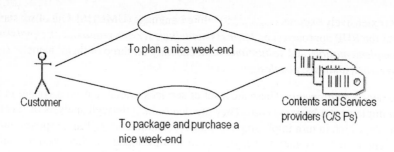

Fig. 4. UML use case diagram for B2C marketplace for tourism

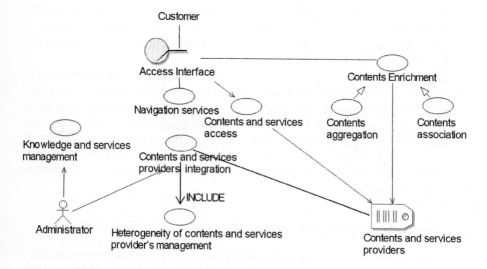

Fig. 5. UML technical use case diagram for B2C marketplace for tourism

Service Requirements. The technical use case diagram is presented in Figure 5. Let us discuss its actors.

Customer and Access Interface. A customer with the help of its access interface (e.g., mobile phone) accesses services available within the system through the authentication mechanism, personalization, and session management.

Contents and Services providers (C/S Ps). Contents and services providers manage their offers autonomously, i.e., the system does not impose any constraints. Each C/S P has its own rules for structuring information at the protocol, syntactical, and semantic levels. The system adapts itself via an Administrator or automatically.

Administrator performs (i) referencing of new contents and services providers, and (ii) internal knowledge representation and management.

Analysis. During this step, we analyze each technical use case of Figure 5 in detail. In particular, we consider *navigation services, contents and services access, contents en-*

richment, contents aggregation, contents association, contents and services provider's integration, heterogeneity of contents and services provider's management, and *knowledge and services management* technical use cases.

For lack of space we discuss here only the *contents aggregation* technical use case. First, we report the actors it involves, then we provide its summary, inputs and outputs, and finally we analyze with the help of sequence diagrams the flow of its events, possible technology locks and potential knowledge-based solutions.

Actors: Customer and Access Interface, C/S Ps.

Summary: The use case *contents aggregation* is inherited from the use case *contents enrichment*. A global schema, which is a model for the data of all the C/S Ps, captures the knowledge of the domain. The use case performs a fusion of the information issued by different C/S Ps. It aims at providing a user with the result which has the following characteristics:

– No duplication and redundant information;
– Avoid the user having to aggregate the contents issued from different C/S Ps.

Preconditions and inputs:

– The use case *contents and services access* has been executed;

Post-conditions and outputs:

– The aggregated contents are transferred to the access interface.

The flow of events for the *contents aggregation* technical use case is presented in Figure 6. Let us discuss it in detail. The system (ManageContentAggregation component) starts from mapping the data (potentially expressed using different data models) among C/S Ps involved in the processing of the request of a user. This step is essential in order to evaluate the contents of each C/S P, and hence, detect redundancies, complementary information, etc. The flow of events is as follows:

– Identification of the mappings between different data models (requestSchemas);
– Contents aggregation (manageContent): check for duplicated information, fusion of complementary information are operated by the ControlContent component;
– Transformation of the result of contents aggregation into XML formalism;
– The results encoded in XML are transferred to the access interface (loadXmlStream).

Technology locks identification: Technology locks are highlighted in Figure 6. These are the MappingContent and ControlContent components. Let us discuss them in turn.

It is crucial to be able to dynamically discover semantic mappings between the contents of different C/S Ps. The current solution follows the data integration approach which is to create static correspondences between data models [16]. In this case, mappings can be specified in a declarative manner (e.g., manually). However, this solution does not satisfy requirements of the business case. In fact, C/S Ps may appear and disappear over the network, change their contents, schemas, and so on. Thus, the problem is to determine those semantic correspondences dynamically. For example, given two XML schemas, suppose in the first schema the *address* element consists of the attributes

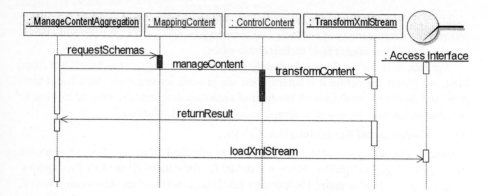

Fig. 6. Flow of events: Contents aggregation technical use case

name, *town*, and *postcode* and in the second schema the *address* element is split down into three sub elements *street_name*, *post_code*, and *town*. Then, a solution should be developed in order to determine correspondences between the semantically related entities, e.g., the *address* element in the first schema should be mapped to the *address* element in the second schema. A more complex solution is required to determine which attributes of the first schema are to be mapped to the elements of the second schema.

The second technology lock is to execute the correspondences (mappings) produced as output of the MappingContent component. As the use case requires, mapping's execution should not only translate the source data instances under the expected common schema, but also check for duplications, and, if any detected, discard them. This lock can be decomposed into two sub-locks. The first sub-lock is to generate query expressions (out of the correspondences determined in the previous step) that automatically translate data instances of the C/S P's schemas under an integrated schema. For example, [29] provides a standard data translation solution. Such a solution is based on the assumption that correspondences between schema elements are only identified (using a binary choice: a mapping exists or does not exist). However, if the correspondences between schema elements can be determined by providing a more informative specification, e.g., a particular type of the correspondence, namely a logical relation (equivalence, subsumption), then data translation operation could also be performed more accurately. The second sub-lock is to reconcile the data instances. Let us consider one example which deals with duplicates. The current solution interprets data instances as strings and checks if two strings are identical. However, in general, one C/S P may adopt the use of a standard while another C/S P adopts the use of fully expanded descriptions, and so on. For example, ⟨Oro Stube, Restaurant, Trento, TN, NULL⟩; ⟨Oro Stube, ristorante-pizzeria, Povo Trento, TN, I-38050⟩; ⟨Oro Stube, Trento, NULL, 38100⟩ all refer to the same place Oro Stube. Thus, a solution should be developed in order to detect (meaningfully) identical instances and discard the less informative ones.

Design. Having identified technology locks of the B2C tourism marketplace system, we are able to propose knowledge processing tasks required in order to develop plausible solutions to those technology locks. In particular, our technical use case requires the *matching*, *data translation*, and *results reconciliation* knowledge processing tasks:

- *Matching*. This task aims at (on-the-fly and automatic) determining semantic correspondences between the contents of C/S Ps and the global schema. It takes two data/conceptual models (e.g., XML schemas, OWL ontologies) and returns a set of mappings between the entities of those models that correspond semantically to each other. This task is necessary to ensure semantic homogeneity at schema level among C/S Ps, and therefore, it is classified as a primary task in the context of the B2C marketplace system.
- *Data translation*. This task aims at generating query expressions (out of mappings determined as a result of *matching*) that automatically translate data instances between heterogeneous information sources. This task is necessary to ensure semantic homogeneity at the level of data instances, and therefore, it is classified as a primary task in the context of the B2C marketplace system.
- *Results reconciliation*. This task aims at detecting redundancies, duplications, and complements among the data coming from different C/S Ps which are involved in the processing of the request of a user. It takes as input responses of each C/S P involved in the processing of the request, performs all the necessary operations (e.g., cleaning, fusion) and produces a reconciled result. This task is necessary to provide a user with an accurate way of accessing the requested data, and therefore, it is classified as a primary task.

In the above described manner we determine technology locks, discuss appropriateness of the knowledge-based technology, and required knowledge processing tasks for all the technical use cases of the B2C marketplace scenario. Also, we have considered some other business cases (e.g., recruitment of human resources (HR), multimedia content analysis and annotation (MCAA)) and we have analyzed them in detail as demonstrated above, see [26].

5   Knowledge Processing Tasks and Components

Based on the primary and secondary knowledge processing tasks determined during the technical use case analysis (conducted for four business cases, see [26]), we construct a typology of knowledge processing tasks and a library of components for realizing those tasks, see Table 2 and Table 3.

Our typology includes 9 primary tasks and 3 secondary tasks. Some tasks are required to be implemented within a single component. For example, (schema/ontology) matching, matching results analysis, and producing explanations of mappings are the functionalities of the match manager component. Thus, the library of high level components contains less components than the number of knowledge processing tasks identified. In particular, it consists of 9 components. Let us discuss knowledge processing tasks and components of Table 2 and Table 3 in more detail.

Ontology Management, Schema/Ontology Merging and Ontology Manager. These aim at (i) ontology maintenance, e.g., editing concepts, resolving name conflicts, browsing ontologies, and (ii) merging (multiple) ontologies, e.g., by taking the union of the

Table 2. Typology of knowledge processing tasks & components. Part 1 - Primary tasks.

#	Knowledge processing tasks	Components
1	Ontology Management	Ontology Manager
2	Matching	Match Manager
3	Matching Results Analysis	Match Manager
4	Data Translation	Wrapper
5	Results Reconciliation	Results Reconciler
6	Composition of Web Services	Planner
7	Content Annotation	Annotation Manager
8	Reasoning	Reasoner
9	Semantic Query Processing	Query Processor

Table 3. Typology of knowledge processing tasks & components. Part 2 - Secondary tasks.

#	Knowledge processing tasks	Components
1	Schema/Ontology Merging	Ontology Manager
2	Producing Explanations	Match Manager
3	Personalization	Profiler

axioms, according to evolving business requirements, see [9, 14, 17]. For example, let us consider the HR scenario. It requires exploiting a common HR ontology. Since the job market or some aspects of the recruitment domain such as qualifications may alter, the HR ontology has to be updated. In fact, with a globalization of the job market, recruitment applications might be submitted from new countries which have different educational systems. Therefore, higher level qualifications must be identified within the system and related to existing qualifications. Moreover, in a decentralized distributed environment such as the Web, it is reasonable to expect existence of multiple ontologies, even on the same topic. Thus, some of the relevant ontologies might be useful for extending the HR ontology, and, hence, are need to be merged into it.

Matching, Matching Results Analysis, Producing Explanations and Match Manager. These aim at discovering mappings between the entities of schemas/ontologies which correspond semantically to each other, see [23,24]. Mappings are typically specified (i) by using coefficients rating match quality in the [0,1] range, see [5, 10, 20, 30], or (ii) by using logical relations (e.g., equivalence, subsumption), see [11, 12]. For example, in the HR scenario, a requirement for Java programming skills may be matched against C++ programming skills as similar with a coefficient of 0.8 or as Java $\sqsubseteq$ C++.

Depending on the application requirements, some further manipulations with mappings (e.g., ordering, pruning) can be performed, see [8]. For example, in the HR scenario, the complexity of qualifications and work experience suggest that exact matches between job requirements and applicants are unlikely to happen; rather a ranking mechanism is required to express the extent to which, for example, the equivalence might be assumed. In fact, when an applicant states that (s)he has a proficiency in C++, how would this rank differently against vacancies requiring persons with skills in Java, Microsoft .NET, or object oriented programming?

State of the art matching systems may produce effective mappings. However, these mappings may not be intuitively obvious to human users, and therefore, they need to be explained, see [7, 25]. In fact, if Semantic Web users are going to trust the fact that two terms may have the same meaning, then they need to understand the reasons leading a matching system to produce such a result. Explanations are also useful when matching (large) applications with thousands of entities (e.g., business catalogs, such as UNSPSC and eCl@ss). In these cases automatic matching solutions will find a number of plausible mappings, hence, some human effort for performing the rationalization of the mapping suggestions is inevitable. Generally, the key issue here is to represent explanations in a simple and clear way to the user. For example, in the HR scenario, explanations should help users of the HR system to make informed decisions on why a job vacancy requirements meet a job applicant request.

Data Translation and Wrapper. These aim at an automatic manipulation (e.g., translation, exchange) of instances between information sources storing their data in different formats (e.g., OWL, XML), see [21, 28]. Usually, for the task under consideration, correspondences between semantically related entities among schemas/ontologies are assumed to be given. They are taken in input, processed according to an application requirements, and are returned in output as *executable* mappings. For example, in the HR scenario, a wrapper acts as an interface to the input data such that both requests from and responses to the system may be expressed in RDF while the underlying data continues to be stored in its original format.

Results Reconciliation and Results Reconciler. These aim at determining an optimal solution for returning results from the queried information sources. The problem should be considered at least at two levels: (i) contents, e.g., for discarding redundant information, and (ii) routing performance, e.g., for choosing the best (under the given conditions) plan for delivering results to the user, see [22]. In the B2C tourism marketplace scenario, this task prevents customers, for example, from encountering several (identical) responses about the same restaurants or different opening times for the same museum.

Composition of Web Services and Planner. These aim at an automated composition of the pre-existing web services into new (composed) web services, thereby enabling the latter with new functionalities, see [4]. Technically, composition is typically performed by using automated reasoning approaches (e.g., planning, see [27]). In the B2C tourism marketplace scenario, composition of web services is needed when organizing a travel journey. In particular, for the combination of transport and hotel reservation services.

Content Annotation and Annotation Manager. These aim at an automated generation of metadata for different types of contents, such as text, images, audio tracks, etc., see, for example [2]. Usually, an annotation manager has in input the (pre-processed) contents and some sources of explicitly specified domain knowledge and outputs content annotations. For example, in the MCAA scenario, knowledge-based analysis of the audiovisual content should automatically generate semantic metadata, for instance, by extracting the audiovisual features (e.g., color, shape) from visual objects, and by linking them to the semantically equivalent concepts defined in the MCAA ontologies.

Reasoning and Reasoner. These aim at providing a set of logical reasoning services (e.g., subsumption, instance checking tests, see [13]), which are (heavily) tuned to particular application needs. For example, when dealing with multimedia annotations, logical reasoning can be exploited in order to check consistency of the annotations against the set of spatial (e.g., left, right, adjacent, near) and modal (possibility, necessity) constraints. Thus, ensuring that the objects detected in the multimedia content correspond semantically to the concepts defined in domain ontologies. For example, in the football domain, it should be checked whether a goalkeeper is located *near* the goal and potentially holds a ball in his/her hands. The key issue here is in the development of optimizations over the standard reasoning techniques tailored to specific application tasks, because, in general, modal/temporal logic reasoning procedures do not scale well.

Semantic Query Processing and Query Processor. These aim at rewriting queries by exploiting terms from the pre-existing ontologies, thus, enabling a semantics-preserving query answering, see [2,18]. For example, in the MCAA scenario, query processor should be able to interpret queries by exploiting a set of domain ontologies in order to return relevant multimedia content (e.g., images, videos). Notice that the user should be able to specify queries in different ways, for example, as (i) high level concepts, e.g., *holiday*, *beach*; (ii) natural language expressions, e.g., *give me all the photos of Trento*; (iii) sample images.

Personalization and Profiler. These aim at an adaptation of functionalities available from a system to the needs of groups of users, see [3]. Typical tasks of a profiler include automatic generation and maintenance of user profiles, personalized content management and mining, etc. For example, in the MCAA scenario, users might want to participate in different social networks and to share some annotations over them. Thus, they need a support for new contact's recommendation, adaptive navigation through these new contacts, and so on. In turn, adaptation might be performed along different dimensions, where the use of Semantic Web technology is promising, namely: user' terminal (e.g., PDA, cell phone), external environment (e.g., language, location).

6   Discussion

The IST-FP5 project Ontoweb (2001-2004) has brought (EC) industry awareness of Semantic Web technology on a large scale. In particular, a special interest group on Industrial Applications[5] was formed. It collected over 50 use cases (notice, their majority dealt only with technology producers), which, in turn, provided a good overview of the expectations from Semantic Web technology. Based on those foundations, the subsequent IST-FP6 Network of Excellence Knowledge Web (2004-2007) has deliberately focused on the potential adopters of the technology and an in-depth analysis of the use cases.

In this paper, we report our first results of the business use cases collection and analysis as targeted by Knowledge Web. By a preliminary analysis of the collected use cases we categorized the types of solutions being sought for, and the types of technological locks which arise when realizing those solutions. By a detailed technical analysis of the

---

[5] http://sig4.ago.fr

selected use cases we identified precisely where in the business processes the technology locks occur, described the requirements for technological solutions that overcome those locks, and argued for the appropriateness of knowledge-based solutions. Moreover, a quick analysis of the other business cases of [19] have shown that most of the knowledge processing tasks of Table 2 and Table 3 repeat with some variations/specificity from use case to use case. This observation suggests that the constructed typology is stable, i.e., it contains (most of) the core knowledge processing tasks stipulated by the current industry needs. By drawing from concrete industrial use cases the knowledge processing tasks and components that can provide expected solutions, we link business problems to specific research challenges. We expect the Semantic Web research community to address those challenges. Once knowledge processing components are provided by research, their practical usefulness and contribution to technology transfer from academia to industry can be assessed through an extensive evaluation within different industrial contexts.

Thus, for example in the HR scenario, the sought-for solution is the *semantic* matching between job offers and job applications. By a technical use case analysis we located where in the business process the lock occurs and defined the requirements with respect to the *matching* task and the *match manager* component. Hence, we have already provided (i) a client industry with a clear identification of the place where the system requires knowledge-based solutions and (ii) researchers with a clear definition of the requirements that must be met by their prototypical implementations of knowledge processing components. In particular, in the HR scenario, some existing implementations of a match manager (e.g., [5,30]) have been plugged into the business process at the identified location. A prototype has been tested by the client industrial partner, and it had demonstrated a better characteristics (e.g., precision, recall) with respect to the legacy solution. Thus, experience of this use case and some other use cases (e.g., MCAA scenario) gives us a preliminary vision that the proposed approach is able to facilitate the industrial uptake of Semantic Web technology.

7   Conclusions and Future Work

We have presented a set of business cases collected from enterprises which are interested in Semantic Web technology. We discussed via examples a methodology for the identification of technology locks in business cases, appropriateness of the knowledge-based technology, and possible approaches resolving those locks. We summarized industry requirements with respect to the knowledge-based technology as a typology of knowledge processing tasks and a library of high level components for realizing those tasks. We intend our typology as a guide for academic activities, thereby connecting concrete industrial problems with research efforts. Thus, by facilitating the communication of industry requirements to academia and directing research results back to industry, where those results are relevant, we contribute to the process of increasing the industrial uptake of Semantic Web technology.

This work represents only an initial step. In fact, to build the typology presented in this paper we have conducted an in-depth analysis of 4 (out of 16) use cases. Thus, we still have to scrutinize the rest of the use cases and update our typology, although we have a preliminary vision that in those use cases, most of the knowledge processing tasks repeat

942 A. Léger, L.J.B. Nixon, and P. Shvaiko

the current typology. Emerging business cases will also be tracked, as they will likely generate new requirements. For example, future trends such as semantic web services, grid computing, social networking will give rise to knowledge processing components for web service discovery, orchestration; distributed reasoning; and so on.

References

1. Rational software corporation. http://www-306.ibm.com/software/rational/.
2. aceMedia project. Integrating knowledge, semantics and content for user centred intelligent media services. http://www.acemedia.org.
3. G. Antoniou, M. Baldoni, C. Baroglio, R. Baumgartner, F. Bry, T. Eiter, N. Henze, M. Herzog, W. May, V. Patti, R. Schindlauer, H. Tompits, and S. Schaffert. Reasoning methods for personalization on the Semantic Web. *Annals of Mathematics, Computing & Teleinformatics*, 2(1):1–24, 2004.
4. B. Benatallah, M.-S. Hacid, A. Léger, C. Rey, and F. Toumani. On automating web services discovery. *VLDB Journal*, (14(1)):84–96, 2005.
5. A. Billig and K. Sandkuhl. Match-making based on Semantic Nets: The XML-based approach of BaSeWeb. In *Proceedings of the workshop on XML-Technologien für das Semantic Web*, pages 39–51, 2002.
6. G. Booch, J. Rumbaugh, and I. Jacobson. *The Unified Modeling Language User Guide*. Addison-Wesley, 1997.
7. R. Dhamankar, Y. Lee, A. Doan, A. Halevy, and P. Domingos. iMAP: Discovering complex semantic matches between database schemas. In *Proceedings of SIGMOD*, 2004.
8. T. Di Noia, E. Di Sciascio, F. M. Donini, and M. Mongiello. A system for principled matchmaking in an electronic marketplace. In *Proceedings of WWW*, pages 321–330, 2003.
9. D. Dou, D. McDermott, and P. Qi. Ontology translation on the Semantic Web. *Journal on Data Semantics*, II:35–57, 2005.
10. J. Euzenat and P. Valtchev. Similarity-based ontology alignment in OWL-lite. In *Proceedings of ECAI*, pages 333–337, 2004.
11. F. Giunchiglia and P. Shvaiko. Semantic matching. *The Knowledge Engineering Review Journal*, (18(3)):265–280, 2003.
12. F. Giunchiglia, P. Shvaiko, and M. Yatskevich. Semantic schema matching. In *Proceedings of CoopIS*, 2005.
13. V. Haarslev, R. Moller, and M. Wessel. RACER: Semantic middleware for industrial projects based on RDF/OWL, a W3C Standard. `http://www.sts.tu-harburg.de/~r.f.moeller/racer/`.
14. Stanford Medical Informatics. Protégé ontology editor and knowldege aquisition system. http://protege.stanford.edu/index.html.
15. I. Jacobson, G. Booch, and J. Rumbaugh, editors. *The unified software development process*. Addisson-Wesley, 1999.
16. M. Lenzerini. Data integration: A theoretical perspective. In *Proceeding of PODS*, pages 233–246, 2002.
17. D. L. McGuinness, R. Fikes, J. Rice, and S. Wilder. An environment for merging and testing large ontologies. In *Proceedings of KR*, pages 483–493, 2000.
18. E. Mena, V. Kashyap, A. Sheth, and A. Illarramendi. OBSERVER: An approach for query processing in global information systems based on interoperability between pre-existing ontologies. In *Proceedings of CoopIS*, pages 14–25, 1996.
19. L. Nixon, M. Mochol, A. Léger, F. Paulus, L. Rocuet, M. Bonifacio, R. Cuel, M. Jarrar, P. Verheyden, Y. Kompatsiaris, V. Papastathis, S. Dasiopoulou, and A. Gómez Pérez. D1.1.2 Prototypical Business Use Cases. Technical report, Knowledge Web NoE, 2004.

20. N. Noy and M. Musen. PROMPT: Algorithm and tool for automated ontology merging and alignment. In *Proceedings of AAAI*, pages 450–455, 2000.
21. J. Petrini and T. Risch. Processing queries over RDF views of wrapped relational databases. In *Proceedings of the workshop on Wrapper Techniques for Legacy Systems*, 2004.
22. N. Preguica, M. Shapiro, and C. Matheson. Semantics-based reconciliation for collaborative and mobile environments. In *Proccedings of CoopIS*, pages 38–55, 2003.
23. E. Rahm and P. Bernstein. A survey of approaches to automatic schema matching. *VLDB Journal*, (10(4)):334–350, 2001.
24. P. Shvaiko and J. Euzenat. A survey of schema-based matching approaches. *Journal on Data Semantics*, IV, 2005.
25. P. Shvaiko, F. Giunchiglia, P. Pinheiro da Silva, and D. L. McGuinness. Web explanations for semantic heterogeneity discovery. In *Proceedings of ESWC*, pages 303–317, 2005.
26. P. Shvaiko, A. Léger, F. Paulus, L. Rocuet, L. Nixon, M. Mochol, Y. Kompatsiaris, V. Papastathis, and S. Dasiopoulou. D1.1.3 Knowledge Processing Requirements Analysis. Technical report, Knowledge Web NoE, 2004.
27. P. Traverso and M. Pistore. Automated composition of semantic web services into executable processes. In *Proceedings of ISWC*, pages 380–394, 2004.
28. Y. Velegrakis, R. J. Miller, and J. Mylopoulos. Representing and querying data transformations. In *Proceedings of ICDE*, pages 81–92, 2005.
29. L. Yan, R. Miller, L. Haas, and R. Fagin. Data driven understanding and refinement of schema mappings. *SIGMOD Record*, 30(2):485–496, 2001.
30. J. Zhong, H. Zhu, J. Li, and Y. Yu. Conceptual graph matching for semantic search. In *Proceedings of the ICCS*, pages 92–106, 2002.

An Application of Semantic Web Technologies to Situation Awareness

Christopher J. Matheus[1], Mieczyslaw M. Kokar[2],
Kenneth Baclawski[2], and Jerzy J. Letkowski[3]

[1] Versatile Information Systems, Inc. Framingham, Massachusetts USA
cmatheus@vistology.com
http://www.vistology.com
[2] Northeastern University Boston, Massachusetts USA
ken@baclawski.com mkokar@ece.neu.edu
[3] Western New England College, Springfield, MA, USA
jletkows@wnec.edu

Abstract. Situation awareness involves the identification of relationships among objects participating in an evolving situation. This problem in general is intractable and thus requires additional constraints and guidance defined by the user if there is to be any hope of creating practical situation awareness systems. This paper describes a Situation Awareness Assistant (SAWA) based on Semantic Web technologies that facilitates the development of user-defined domain knowledge in the form of formal ontologies and rule sets and then permits the application of the domain knowledge to the monitoring of relevant relations as they occur in a situations. SAWA includes tools for developing ontologies in OWL and rules in SWRL and provides runtime components for collecting event data, storing and querying the data, monitoring relevant relations and viewing the results through a graphical user interface. An application of SAWA to a scenario from the domain of supply logistics is presented along with a discussion of the challenges encountered in using SWRL for this task.

1 Introduction

The essence of situation awareness lies in the monitoring of various entities and the relations that occur among them. Since the properties of relations, unlike the properties of objects, are not directly measurable, one needs to have some background knowledge (such as ontologies and rules) to specify how to derive the existence and meaning of particular relations. For instance, in the domain of supply logistics, relations like "suppliable" or "projected undersupply within 2 days" need to be systematically specified. The number of potentially relevant relation types is practically unlimited. This presents a great challenge to developers of general-purpose situation awareness systems since it essentially means that such systems must have the potential to track any possible relation. In other words, the relation determination algorithms must be generic, rather than handcrafted for each special kind of relation. Furthermore, in order to derive a specific relation one often needs to access a number of data sources and then combine (i.e., fuse) their inputs. One way to address these challenges is to use generic reasoning tools, such as those based on the principles

Y. Gil et al. (Eds.): ISWC 2005, LNCS 3729, pp. 944–958, 2005.
© Springer-Verlag Berlin Heidelberg 2005

being employed by the Semantic Web. To take advantage of this approach, however, all information must be available in a formally defined knowledge base.

At Versatile Information Systems, Inc., we are developing a collection of flexible ontology-based information fusion tools needed for identifying and tracking user-defined relations. These tools collectively make up our **Situation Awareness Assistant (SAWA)**. The purpose of SAWA is to permit the offline development of problem specific domain knowledge and then apply it at runtime to the fusion and analysis of object-level data. Domain knowledge is captured in SAWA using OWL ontologies for describing the classes and properties of the domain and SWRL rules for defining the conditions of higher-order relations. The user controls the system situation monitoring requirements by specifying "standing relations", i.e., high-level relations or queries that the system is to monitor. SAWA provides a flexible query and monitoring language based on OWL-QL that can be used to request information about the current situation or to conduct what-if queries about possible future situations. In this paper we describe the structure and capabilities of SAWA and show its use on examples from the supply logistics domain. In particular, we show how to develop an appropriate ontology and associated rules, how SAWA collects and processes incoming events and how it communicates with the user. We also discuss the advantages and limitations of applying Semantic Web technologies to the problem of situation awareness.

2 General Approach

We view situation awareness as a fusion problem involving the identification and monitoring of higher-order relations among object-level objects. As mentioned in the introduction, practical solutions to this problem require user-defined constraints, which we usually identified with a corpus of knowledge specific to a domain of interest, otherwise known as *domain knowledge*. The use of domain knowledge requires a form of representation and a means for processing or reasoning about the knowledge representations. Rather than developing ad hoc representations we advocate the leveraging of existing standards. We also believe strongly in the value of formal representations that can be used in conjunction with generic yet formal reasoning systems. Our approach to domain knowledge representation, which we will describe shortly, is thus premised on use of standards-based formal representations.

Even with appropriate domain knowledge the number of possible relations definable within the domain knowledge constraints can remain intractable. To further constrain a situation we believe it is necessary to know something about the user's specific *goals*. By knowing more specifically what the user is looking for, automated systems can focus attention on just those events and candidate relations that are relevant. Our process for *relevance reasoning* has been reported elsewhere [1] and will not be explained in detail in this paper. We will summarize, however, by saying that relevance reasoning takes a *standing relation* (i.e. a goal) from the user, identifies the portion of the domain knowledge that is relevant to the standing relation, finds the attributes in the domain knowledge that must be grounded in input events and uses these attributes to identify what types of objects and which of their attributes need to be monitored in the event stream. With this mechanism, the large number of objects and attributes in a situation can be pared down to a more manageable stream of data in which only a comparatively small number of relevant relations must be monitored.

2.1 Ontology Representation in OWL

In our current efforts we have been exploring the use of recent developments for the Semantic Web [2]. In particular we have chosen to use the OWL Web Ontology Language [3] for defining ontologies that serve as the basis for data and knowledge representation within our situation awareness systems. The advantages of using OWL includes the fact that it is defined by a formal set of semantics and that there are a growing number of automated systems to formally process OWL documents, including editors, consistency checkers and reasoning engines [4].

OWL was designed to capture the classes, properties and restrictions pertinent to a specific domain. As such, OWL can capture basic class hierarchies, properties among classes and data and simple constraints on those properties and classes. OWL, however, cannot capture all types of knowledge relevant to a given domain. In particular, it does not provide a way to represent arbitrarily complex implications, in which knowledge of the existence of a collection of facts $(X_1, X_2...X_n)$ implies the truth of some other information (i.e., $X_1 \wedge X_2 \wedge ...X_n \rightarrow Y$). For example, there is no way in OWL to define the relationship of "uncle(X,Y)" which requires knowing that X is male, X has a sibling Z, and Z has a child Y. The joining of collections of interrelated facts into implication rules as illustrated in this example is very common when defining relationships important to domains involving situation awareness. We therefore need the ability to define portions of our domain knowledge using a rule language, and for this purpose we have selected the Semantic Web Rule Language, SWRL [5].

2.2 Rule Representation in SWRL

SWRL is built on top of OWL and, like OWL, has a formally defined semantics, making it a natural choice for use in our situation awareness applications. SWRL does, however, have some shortcomings that make it less than ideal. Because it was officially introduced as a draft recommendation in just the spring of 2004, it is relatively new and is still evolving; this means there are few tools and applications for use with SWRL and it remains a moving target which may undergo radical changes that will introduce inconsistencies for early adopters. Furthermore, SWRL requires the use of binary predicates. While it is possible to represent concepts dependent on higher-arity relations using SWRL, the process of doing so significantly complicates the resulting rules, making them difficult to read and maintain. As an example consider the concept of a "part" at a "facility" being in "critical supply" at a particular "time", meaning there is a greater need for the part than the number of units available. What we would like to do is create a rule with a predicate of the form criticalPartAtFacility(?Part,?Facility,?Time,?DeficitAmount)[1] as its head and additional predicates in the body that define the conditions under which this predicate should be deemed to be true. To do this in SWRL we need to convert this four-term predicate into an instance of a class (fabricated solely for this rule) that is the domain of four properties, one for each of the four terms.

In the nine rules for our Repairable Assets scenario in which we monitor for critical and marginal parts at a number of airbases this technique was employed nine

---

[1] Variables in the examples of SWRL code presented in this paper are indicated by being prefaced with a question mark, such as in ?Facility.

times and was usually repeated in the head and bodies of multiple rules. The need for this technique contributed greatly to the more than 1000 lines of SWRL code required to implement these nine relatively simple rules; this in turn made the debugging of the code very tedeous. Still, the advantages of SWRL – primary its formal semantics and its close association with OWL – were enough to encourage us to continue with our exploration of its use for situation awareness.

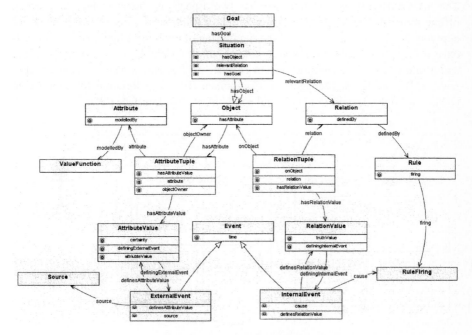

Fig. 1. SAW Core Ontology. This ontology serves as the basis for all domain specific ontologies and rule sets. According to the ontology a Situation consists of Objects and Relations and a Goal (standing relation). Objects have AttributeTuples that are associated with specific Attributes and a collection of AttributeValues defined according to ExternalEvents. Relations are realized through RelationTuples that connect pairs of Objects with RelationValues defining by the firing of Rules.

2.3   SAW Core Ontology

We are interested in building systems for situation awareness that are generic in nature. That is to say that the systems should be applicable to a wide variety of problem domains simply through the redefinition of the domain knowledge that they use. For this approach to work, some core concepts need to be established that will be used as the basis for the development of specific domain knowledge ontologies and rule sets. For this reason we have developed a SAW Core Ontology that serves as the representational foundation of all domain knowledge that is built on top of it. We have reported on this core ontology in earlier papers [6] and will not describe it in detail here. A simplified version of the ontology is shown in Fig. 1 with the key concepts being use of objects that have attributes with specific values being defined by external events that occur over time; in addition, relations combine pairs of objects with truth values defined over time by the firing of rules that define the relations.

3   SAWA High-Level Architecture

The SAWA High-Level Architecture has two aspects as shown in Fig. 2: a set of offline tools for Knowledge Management and a Runtime System of components for applying the domain knowledge to the monitoring of evolving situations. The knowledge management tools include an ontology editor, an ontology consistency checker and a rule editor. The runtime system consists of a Situation Management Component (SMC), an Event Management Component (EMC), a Relation Monitor Agent (RMA), a Triples DataBase (TDB) and a Graphical User Interface (GUI).

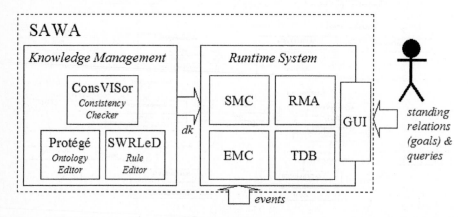

Fig. 2. SAWA High-Level Architecture. On the left side of the diagram is the Knowledge Management suite of tools used to develop the domain knowledge that serves as input to the Runtime System, shown on the right hand side. The user interacts with the system through the GUI by issuing standing relations (goals) and queries. Events from the outside world come into the runtime system and are processed for redistribution to other components by the Event Management Component (EMC).

4   SAWA Knowledge Management

Knowledge Management in SAWA is handled by a loosely coupled suite of tools for developing and maintaining OWL ontologies and SWRL rule sets.

4.1   Ontology Editor

The OWL language is based in RDF [7], which has an XML-based representation. As such, any text or XML editor could be used to develop OWL ontologies. The manual coding of OWL is, however, tedious and prone to error, making specialized editors highly desirable. There are a number of editors available for OWL [8] but the most widely used is Protégé [9]. Protégé is a general-purpose ontology management system developed long before OWL but for which OWL plug-ins have been developed. Using Protégé with the basic OWL plug-in permits the use of Protégé's frame-based editor to construct OWL classes, properties and restrictions among them as well as to develop annotations for OWL ontologies. This approach is adequate but not as convenient as a graphical editor that allows the visual display and manipulation of the relations between objects and properties. Fortunately there is a plug-in for Protégé called ezOWL that provides a graphical editor on top of the basic OWL-plugin. All of the ontologies depicted in this paper are screenshots taken from ezOWL. EzOWL has its limitations (for example it does not cleanly display more than two properties between two classes) and does not always produce correct OWL code, but it is currently the best available visual editor for OWL and does a satisfactory job, provided the resulting code is checked for consistency.

4.2 Consistency Checker

Developing an accurate and consistent ontology is not easy, particularly as the complexity of the domain increases. For all but the most trivial problems it is imperative that newly constructed ontologies be automatically validated for logical consistency; this is also invaluable when combining multiple ontologies that may individually be consistent but are collectively incompatible. It has been the authors' experience that seldom is the first design of an ontology complete and consistent, and the use of consistency checking tools has saved tremendous amounts of development time. SAWA includes ConsVISor [10], an OWL/RDF consistency checker, in its suite of knowledge management tools. ConsVISor is both a standalone Java application and a free Web Service available. at http://www.vistology.com/consvisor.

ConsVISor's purpose is to analyze OWL and RDF documents looking for symptoms of semantic inconsistencies. Not only does it detect outright semantic violations, it also identifies situations where logical implications have not been fully specified in a document. For example, if an ontology places a minimum cardinality constraint on a property for a specific class and an instance of that class is created without having the minimum number of property values, an informative message is provided as shown. Emphasis is placed on providing highly informative feedback about detected symptoms so as to aid the correction of underlying errors by the human user. ConsVISor's output however is based on an OWL-based Symptom Ontology [11] and as such can produce symptom reports in OWL that can be automatically processed by other OWL-cognizant programs.

4.3 Rule Editor

SWRL rules in their XML representation are syntactically and (frequently) semantically difficult to read and write. It was therefore decided that SAWA needed an easy to use editor to assist in the construction and maintenance of SWRL rules. With SWRL being so new, there were no SWRL editors available and so we decided to

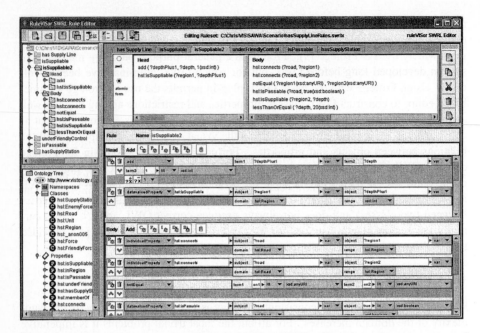

Fig. 3. RuleVISor. This screenshot of the RuleVISor SWRL editor shows its use on a set of rules used by the Supply Logistics scenario described in Section 6.

implement one, which we are calling RuleVISor. A screenshot of RuleVISor being used on a rule set for the Supply Logistics scenario described in Section 6 is shown in Fig. 3. The rules are displayed along the top left hand side of the editor in a directory style layout for easy selection and high-level scanning. The rule that is currently being edited appears in two forms in the right-hand section of the editor. At the top of this section is the display of the contents of the rule head and body in either an easy to read atomic form, which is shown in the screenshot, or as raw SWRL code (not shown). Below this display is the section where editing of the rule takes place, including the optional naming of each rule. This section is split into a portion at the top for editing the head followed by a portion for editing the body. Within either of these the user has the option of adding or deleting binary atoms, atomic atoms, instances, data value ranges and built-in functions simply by clicking on the appropriate icons. Each clause in a rule head or body appears in a three row region that provides the name of the atom, the terms it operates over and possibly other constraints such as term type restrictions. The values of the terms can either be typed in by the user or dragged from other areas of the editor. The primary source for dragged items is the Ontology Tree that appears in the lower left hand corner.

The Ontology Tree displays the contents of the ontologies upon which a rule set is to be built. Of most interest here are the Classes and Properties of the ontology, which are used to populate the term slots of atoms used in the rule heads and bodies. Class and Property names may be dragged to any text entry box in the editor but they will only be accepted by the box if the value being dragged matches the type that the box expects. This form of primitive type checking represents the beginning of a much more sophisticated policy for consistency checking based on ConsVISor that is planned for a future version of RuleVISor.

5 SAWA Runtime System

The SAWA Runtime System, also called the SAWA Engine, is depicted in Fig. 4 along with the communication channels between its sub-components. SAWA is implemented in Java, includes Jess as the basis for its reasoning functions and uses our proprietary RDF/OWL/XSD parser. The SAWA Engine consists of the following sub-components: the Situation Management Component (SMC) which is the system's central controller, the Event Management Component (EMC) which processes all incoming events, the Relation Monitoring Agent (RMA) which monitors relevant events for the status of relations occurring in the evolving situation, the Triples Data-Base (TDB) which maintains a historical record of all situation events and permits the processing of queries, and the Graphical User Interface (GUI) which handles all user interaction with the system. The function of each of these components is described further in the subsections that follow.

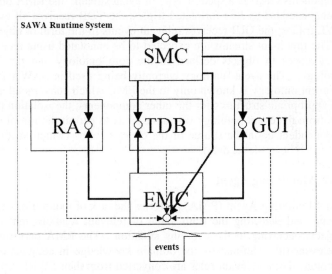

Fig. 4. SAWA Runtime System

5.1 Situation Management Component

The Situation Management Component (SMC) is the central controller for SAWA. It interacts with the GUI to provide options to the user and to accept the user's commands to start, stop and query situations. In addition, it serves as the communication channel between the GUI and the TDB and RMA. The SMC initializes the monitoring of situations by instructing the EMC to start listening to specific event streams and informs the RMA, TDB and GUI how to connect to the EMC to receive their appropriate streams of processed events. The SMC is also responsible for performing relevance reasoning, which is achieved through the application of XSLT scripts, and for passing the appropriate set of relevant rules to the RMA and the set of relevant objects and attributes to the EMC.

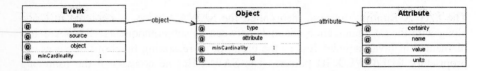

Fig. 5. Event Ontology. Simple ontology used to represent incoming events for processing by the EMC. Each Event describes one or more Objects each having one or more Attributes for which a value and certainty measure are defined.

5.2 Event Management Component

The Event Management Component (EMC) receives streams of raw event data and converts them into appropriate streams of events for the GUI, RMA and TDB. Each of these components receives a specific type of event stream: the RMA only receives relevant events encoded as Jess-formatted triples; the TDB receives all events in the form of OWL triples; the GUI receives relevant events in the form of object-attribute instances. The raw input streams are expected to be annotated using an event ontology with references to objects defined in the core ontology and the appropriate domain ontology. The event ontology currently being used in SAWA is shown in Fig. 5. This event ontology is known only to the EMC which converts all event information into appropriate structures for the other components; the isolation of the other components from the event ontology was done so as to permit the use of other event ontologies dependent upon the source of the event streams (which at this time is a simulator of fused object-level data).

5.3 Relation Monitoring Agent

The Relation Monitoring Agent (RMA) performs the task of monitoring the stream of relevant events and detecting the truth value of relevant relations that might exist between objects occurring in the evolving situation. The RMA performs this task using the relevant rules defined by the domain knowledge in conjunction with the standing relation. These relevant rules are converted from their SWRL representation into Jess rules using an XSLT script. The Jess rules are then processed in the forward-chaining Rete network of our enhanced Jess inference engine; some of the enhancements we have made to Jess include the support for over thirty of the SWRL built-ins which are implemented as procedural attachments in the form of Java method calls. As events come in, they are processed through the Rete network and as a result may end up firing one or more rules. The firing of a rule results in the instantiation of a relation that is then reported to the GUI via the SMC. At the moment all rule firings result in relations that have an associated certainty rating of 1.0 (i.e., 100%). We are working on a new implementation of the reasoning engine that will incorporate uncertainty reasoning and will thus afford the detection of relations having incomplete certainties.

5.4 Triples Database

In RDF and OWL all information is represented in the form of triples. Each triple represents a predicate that relates a subject to an object. For example, to state that S2 is a SupplyStation requires a triple of the form: S2 rdf:type SupplyStation. More complex knowledge structure can be represented using collections of interrelated triples [12]. The triples representing the domain knowledge, user input and the incoming events all need to be maintained in a way that they can be readily processed. In SAWA this is accomplished through the Triples DataBase (TDB).

The TDB's primary purpose is to maintain an accurate history of all events so that they can be queried by the user at any time. It is currently developed on top of Jess and makes use of Jess' built-in query capabilities to implement an engine for OQL: OWL Query language [13]. The TDB also supports "what-if" queries in which a set of hypothetical facts are asserted, a query is run to produce what-if results, and the hypothetical facts are retracted along with all facts deduced from them. The TDB accomplishes this what-if capability using the "logical" retraction feature of Jess. While both the general query mechanism and the what-if query mechanism work as designed, they are quite inefficient and not particularly suited for new real-time operations. Consequently we are in the process of developing our own inferencing and query engine optimized for the processing of triples.

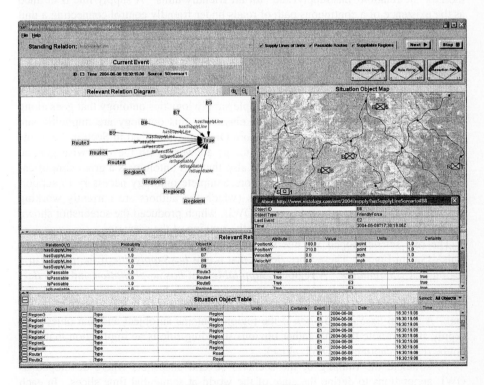

Fig. 6. The SAWA GUI

5.5 Graphical User Interface

The Graphical User Interface permits the user to define standing relations, execute queries and monitor the current state of events, objects, attributes and relations. Its use on a Supply Logistics scenario (described in the next section) is illustrated in Fig. 6. The GUI provides the means for specifying the standing relation (i.e., goal), executing queries, and monitoring the evolution of events, objects, attributes and relations. Objects and attributes are displayed in the Situation Object Table and also on the Situation Object Map. Relevant relations appear in the Relevant Relations table as well as in the Relevant Relation Diagram. Clicking on objects on the map or events, objects or relations in the tables brings up a sub window of supplemental information as shown in the figure for Unit B8. The dials in the upper right hand corner are used for monitoring the performance of the inferencing engine.

6 A Supply Logistics Scenario

SAWA is currently being applied to the domain of supply logistics for which we have developed two scenarios, supply line and repairable assets. In this section we focus on the first scenario that was constructed for the purposes of demonstrating the basic system functions. The goal or "standing relation" for this scenario is to constantly monitor the relation "hasSupplyLine" for all friendly units. A supply line is defined as the existence of a continuous path of roads under friendly control connecting a unit (e.g., B5, B6, etc.) to a supply station (e.g., S1). The specific layout for this scenario can be seen in the map display in the GUI screenshot in Fig. 6. Roads connect pairs of regions (their centroids indicated by solid dots). There are six friendly blue units (i.e., B5, B6, B7, B9 and S1), including one supply station (S1), and one unfriendly red unit (R1).

The screenshot in Fig. 7 shows the simple supply logistics ontology that goes along with this scenario. Note that all of the classes in this ontology are implicitly sub classes of the Object class in the SAW Core Ontology described in Section 2.2 – this is necessary for the domain specific ontology to work with the otherwise generic mechanisms of the SAWA Engine. Note also that this ontology is a gross simplification of what would be expected for a more complete ontology necessary to support more practical supply logistics scenarios (which the authors are currently working on). This ontology was created using ezOWL, which produced the screenshot shown in Fig. 7 as well as the OWL code used in the running of the scenario.

The rule set developed for this scenario is partially shown in the screenshot of RuleVISor in Fig. 3. These rules define that a unit *hasSupplyLine* if the unit is in a region that *isSuppliable*. A region *isSuppliable* if it *hasSupplyStation* and is *underFriendlyControl* or if it is connected to another region by a *Passable* road and that other region *isSuppliable*. A region is *underFriendlyControl* if it contains a friendly unit. A region *hasSupplyStation* if the region contains an object and that object is a supply station (note that this rather obvious sounding rule is an implication that cannot be readily captured in OWL alone).

To simulate the running of the scenario several snapshots where developed as OWL annotations to define the state of the world at sequential time slices. In each time slice one of the units was moved around in such a manner as to create changes in the set of relations that would hold true. These snapshots where then presented to a running SAWA application in which the user specified the standing relation to be *hasSupplyLine* as applied to all friendly units. The system correctly detected the standing relations that held true at each time slice and reported these back to the GUI which displayed them for the user; the GUI screenshot in Fig. 6 shows the display after a couple of time steps.

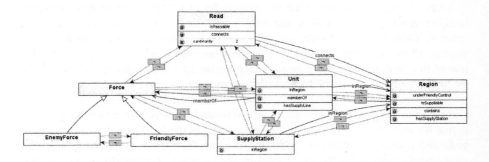

Fig. 7. Simple Supply Logistics Ontology. This ontology captures just enough information needed for reasoning about supply lines, which serves as the standing relation in our supply logistics scenario. Each of the classes represented in the ontology is a subclass of the Object class defined in the SAW Core Ontology shown in Fig. 1.

7 Semantic Web Technologies for Situation Awareness

The representational and reasoning requirements for Situation Awareness share much in common with those of the Semantic Web, with an added emphasis on the handling of time and uncertainty. Both need to be able to represent object-level information concerning classes and properties as well as higher-order relations that can occur among specific instances (e.g., a web site and its content, a web service and the set of users permitted to access it, etc.). Given our experience with using Semantic Web technologies it is natural to ask how well they fared when applied to Situation Awareness.

We have found the use of OWL to be generally quite suitable for representing taxonomies of classes and for capturing most of the properties of interest. There have been cases where we would have liked to have been able from within OWL to further constrain certain properties based on the values of other properties but instead were forced to use a rule. This is a well-known limitation of OWL [14] and is something that we have no problem with resorting to SWRL to resolve.

With regards to the use of SWRL there are a number of issues that we encountered (for more details see [15]). The lack of higher-order predicates is the most severe and was already illustrated in Section 2.2. Another issue we had to deal with was the declarative definitions of the SWRL built-ins. SWRL built-ins are defined without specification of the input/output nature of their terms. For example, swrlb:add(100,?X,?Y) is a perfectly valid use of the SWRL add built-in even though it defines an infinite set. It is also possible to use it in the following manner to implement subtraction, swrlb:add(100,50,?X), even though swrlb:subtract is also defined by the language. In practice "add" is generally needed as a function that binds to the variable in the first term position the summation of the remaining bound terms. In our implementation of the built-ins for Jess we require that there only be a single unbound variable and then use its occurrence in the list of terms to determine which function is to be used to calculate its value (this means you can, if you wish, use swrlb:add to perform subtraction); if more than one term is unbound an exception is thrown. This approach is not strictly conformant with the definition of SWRL but it represents a pragmatic approach that satisfies the requirements of a large number of problems.

Most rule languages have some mechanism for explicitly asserting new facts into working memory; in Jess this is achieved using (assert ...). There is no such construct in SWRL. Rather, SWRL only states that when the statements in the body of a true are all true then the statements in the head are also true. The natural interpretation of this from the context of an inference engine like Jess is that the statements in the head should be asserted into working memory, for otherwise these true statements would be inaccessible by any of the other rules. For this reason we translate the statements in the heads of rules into assert commands in Jess. We go one step further in that we also look for the occurrence of variables in the head that are unbound in he body and produce a "gensym" command to generate a new symbol to produce an anonymous object to fill the role played by the variable. Technically the occurrence of a variable in the head that is not bound in the body is prohibited in SWRL (these are referred to as *unsafe* rules owing to the existentially quantified variables in their heads). In practice it is very frequently necessary to construct anonymous objects of this sort and yet SWRL has no construct for doing so (i.e., it has no gensym operator).

SWRL also lacks user-defined procedural attachments, which greatly reduces it general usefulness in practical applications. There are many calculations that are simply more appropriately handled by writing a method in Java (or any other procedural language) than to force its computation using rules alone. In situation awareness applications this comes up in such tasks as calculating the aggregation of a set of objects into a group, finding the centroid of a set of objects, dynamically modeling the position of a moving object over time, etc.

Perhaps the most restrictive aspect of SWRL is its lack of negation and in particular negation as failure. In all of our rule-based applications we have encountered the need to use a closed world assumption when reasoning about the information at hand. Seldom in the real world is it the case that we will have all of the timely information needed to make a conclusion; we must therefore be able to write rules that can detect the absence of specific forms of information and make decisions accordingly. In SWRL there is no way to look for the absence of information owing to its strict adherence to the monotonic assumption inherited from OWL. In our SWRL applications we have been forced to violate this assumption and move outside of the language in order to fully represent the knowledge needed to define some of our rules.

8 Conclusion

This paper described the Situation Awareness Assistant, SAWA. SAWA is designed to monitor the evolution of higher-order relations within a situation using formal and generic reasoning techniques for level-two fusion. The system was developed to make use of the formal languages of OWL and SWRL, which permit the representation of ontologies and rules. For a specific application of SAWA, a domain theory consisting of a domain specific OWL ontology and a corresponding set of SWRL rules are first constructed or reused from a previous application. A standing relation, or goal, is then defined by the user, which is used to determine the relevant portion of the domain knowledge for the current objectives as well as to identify the relevant object and object-attributes that the system needs to monitor in the event stream. As relevant events are detected they are passed on to the relation-monitoring agent, which analyzes them for the possible occurrence of higher-order relations. As higher-order relations are detected they are passed onto the GUI, which displays them in both tabular and graphical forms for the user along with other data pertaining to the events, objects and their attributes. The GUI also provides the capability for querying the system's triple database using basic OQL queries or with "what-if" queries that can produce hypothetical situations against which a query is run. A scenario from the domain of supply logistics was briefly described and we high-lighted some of the issues we encountered in our effort to apply Semantic Web technologies to the problem of Situation Awareness.

References

1. C. Matheus, K. Baclawski and M. Kokar, Derivation of ontological relations using formal methods in a situation awareness scenario. In Proc of SPIE Conference on Multisensor, Multisource Information Fusion, pages 298-309, April 2003.
2. T. Berners-Lee, J. Hendler and O. Lassila, The Semantic Web: A new form of Web content that is meaningful to computers will unleash a revolution of new possibilities. Scientific American, May 2001.
3. M. Dean, G. Schreiber, S. Bechhofer, F. van Harmelen, J. Hendler, I. Horrocks, D. L. McGuinness, P. F. Patel-Schneider, and L. A. Stein. OWL Web Ontology Language Reference. W3C Recommendation 10 February 2004. http://www.w3.org/TR/owl-ref/
4. http://www.w3.org/2004/OWL/.
5. I. Horrocks, P. F. Patel-Schneider, H. Boley, S. Tabet, B. Grosof and M. Dean. SWRL: A Semantic Web Rule Language Combining OWL and RuleML. W3C Member Submission, 2004. http://www.w3.org/Submission/SWRL/.
6. C. Matheus, M. Kokar and K. Baclawski, A Core Ontology for Situation Awareness. In Proceedings of FUSION'03, Cairns, Queensland, Australia, pages 545-552, July 2003.
7. G. Klyne, J. J. Carroll, and B. McBride, Resource Description Framework (RDF) Concepts and Abstract Syntax.. W3C Recommendation 10 February 2004. Latest version is available at http://www.w3.org/TR/rdf-concepts/
8. European OntoWeb Consortium, A Survey of Ontology Tools, May 2002. http://ontoweb.aifb.uni-karlsruhe.de/About/Deliverables/D13_v1-0.zip.
9. J. Gennari, M. A. Musen, R. W. Fergerson, W. E. Grosso, M. Crubézy, H. Eriksson, N. F. Noy, S. W. Tu The Evolution of Protégé: An Environment for Knowledge-Based Systems Development. 2002.
10. ConsVISor, 2003. http://www.vistology.com/consvisor. See also K. Baclawski, M. Kokar, R. Waldinger and P. Kogut, Consistency Checking of Semantic Web Ontologies. 1st International Semantic Web Conference (ISWC)}, Lecture Notes in Computer Science, LNCS 2342, Springer, pp. 454--459, 2002.

11. K. Baclawski, C. Matheus, M. Kokar, J. Letkowski and P. Kogut, Towards a Symptom Ontology for Semantic Web Applications. In Proceedings of Third International Semantic Web Conference, Hiroshima, Japan, pages 650-667, November, 2004.
12. RDF Primer. W3C Working Draft. Edited by F. Manola and E. Miller, 2002. http://www.w3.org/TR/rdf-primer/
13. OQL: OWL Query Language, 2003.
14. M. K. Smith, Web Ontology Issue Status, 2003. http://www.w3.org/2001/sw/WebOnt/webont-issues.html#I3.2-Qualified-Restrictions
15. C. Matheus, Position Paper: Using Ontology-based Rules for Situation Awareness and Information Fusion. W3C Workshop on Rule Languages for Interoperability, Washington, D.C., April 2005. http://www.w3.org/2004/12/rules-ws/paper/74

Task Knowledge Based Retrieval for Service Relevant to Mobile User's Activity

Takefumi Naganuma and Shoji Kurakake

Network Laboratories, NTT DoCoMo Inc. 3-5 Hikari-no-oka,
Yokosuka-shi, Kanagawa, 239-8536 Japan
{naganuma, kurakake}@netlab.nttdocomo.co.jp

Abstract. Since mobile Internet services are rapidly proliferating, finding the most appropriate service or services from among the many offered requires profound knowledge about the services which is becoming virtually impossible for ordinary mobile users. We propose a system that assists non-expert mobile users in finding the appropriate services that solve the real-world problems encountered by the user. Key components are a task knowledge base of tasks that a mobile user performs in daily life and a service knowledge base of services that can be used to accomplish user tasks. We present the architecture of the proposed system including a knowledge modeling framework, and a detailed description of a prototype system. We also show preliminary user test results; they indicate that the system allows a user to find appropriate services quicker with fewer loads than conventional commercial methods.

1 Introduction

NTT DoCoMo is the premier mobile communications company in Japan and is providing mobile Internet services to over 44 million subscribers. Currently, widely diverse contents such as entertainment services (Ring-tone download, Games, etc), transaction services (Money transfer, Airline reservation, etc) and information services (Weather forecast, Maps and local information, etc) are being offered through more than 89,000 mobile Internet sites [1]. The market volume of mobile Internet content exceeded one hundred thousand million yen in 2003, which is more than the market volume of Internet content accessed through PCs, 760 hundred million yen. Moreover, 36.2% of people accessing the Internet via mobile phones used for-fee Internet contents, a larger proportion than personal computer users for which it is only 9.5% [2]. 3rd Generation mobile network service (3G), which continues to spread, enables the transmission of more voluminous and richer content by extension of the communication bands, so the market is expected to increase greatly. However, those rich network environments will increase the service provider's cost for developing and maintaining content. Furthermore, the market has, up to now, been dominated by a few popular entertainment services such as character download and ring-tone download, but these markets have already become saturated. If we are to expand overall market volume, it is necessary to expand the market volume of non entertainment services by increasing the frequency with which users can benefit from the rich contents possible in the 3G mobile network.

Y. Gil et al. (Eds.): ISWC 2005, LNCS 3729, pp. 959–973, 2005.
© Springer-Verlag Berlin Heidelberg 2005

We believe that the key to the next step in mobile Internet market growth is realizing the intelligent service platform, which will mediate between services and users by interpreting the user's activity in the real world. Because mobile handsets are the most appropriate devices for problem solving in daily life as users always carry them, there will be many more occasions for providing services compared to Internet services accessed by the PC. By realizing the intelligent service platform, users will be able to access the most appropriate services to help their activities in the real world anytime, anywhere, and service providers will gain more chances for providing new services.

Current methods for accessing Internet services, such as directory-type search methods and keyword-type full-text search methods, do not suit mobile computing environments. This is because mobile handsets have strong resource limitations such as relatively weak input methods and small displays, and most users are non-experts in that they have no computer literacy, i.e. the young generation or the aged. Furthermore, most mobile Internet services are accessed for just a few minutes in daily life such as when waiting for a train. Novice users obviously cannot perform service retrieval efficiently because they do not understand the overall directory structure and can not come up with the keywords that will exactly identify the service needed.

Many research activities are targeting the realization of efficient service retrieval in the mobile Internet environment such as a service retrieval system based on user's location [3]. However, this system simply provides a mechanism for associating Internet content with the user's location according to the address information written in the target document, its does not take into account the meaning of the user's activity. The contents supported by the above approach are very limited, and content that has no address information can not be retrieved even if it is very useful to the user.

We treat user activity in the real world as the semantics of services by using Semantic Web technology. To realize this, we propose a knowledge modeling framework that makes it easy to describe various user tasks in the real world as the semantics of services. We define "task" as what the user wants to do in the real world. And we also propose the task knowledge based service retrieval system based on the task knowledge base developed by using the knowledge modeling framework. The task knowledge base contains a variety of structured tasks in the real world and their relations with the information services available. Our system makes it easy for non-expert users of mobile services to retrieve the service appropriate to solve the user's problem by just inputting her currently desired task as a problem-solving request to the system.

We will present our approach and the high-level architecture of the proposed system. We then discuss the knowledge modeling framework including our strategy for realizing network-wide knowledge sharing, semantic description of task knowledge with OWL-S [10], and a task knowledge modeling environment and service retrieval system. Details are provided of the design of the system sequence, server component and client interface, all of which are intended to be implemented on actual mobile handsets. We also describe a prototype system for each part. The paper finishes with an evaluation by user testing and our conclusions.

2 Overview of Proposed System

A general approach to problem-solving is to divide the large or abstract original problem into several small or concrete sub-problems. Paper [8] shows that human daily life is driven by "proximal goals" (short-term goals), which are derived from "distal goals" (long-term goals). In the area of problem-solving by using information services, a problem that corresponds to a "distal goal" is divided into sub-problems that correspond to "proximal goals" where each of the sub-problems can be solved directly by using one information service. Our idea is to divide the user's "distal goal" into a couple of "proximal goals" and lead the user to appropriate services that can solve the "proximal goals".

To elucidate the above discussion we provide an example. Consider the real world problem: "I want to spend this weekend at amusement park XYZ, but I do not know how to get there". The information-seeking actions associated with this problem are represented by the following structure.

> Decide how to get to amusement park XYZ
> → Check route
> → Check distance and time required
> → Check for transfer instructions

In the above example, the problem of "Decide how to get to amusement park XYZ" corresponds to the "distal goal", and the sub-problems to realize it, "Check route", " Check distance and time required" and "Check for transfer instructions", correspond to "proximal goals". The user is assisted in solving the original problem by invoking a sequence of services, each of which handles a corresponding sub-problem.

To realize the above approach, we treat "what a user wants to do" as the user's task and structure knowledge that can be used to divide the task into sub-tasks as task knowledge. We have built a knowledge base that stores such structured task knowledge. Furthermore, we have developed knowledge of service usage (for example, "This service provides functions for reserving movie tickets") as service knowledge, and have built a knowledge base that stores service knowledge. We developed a task oriented service retrieval system that uses these two knowledge bases. Each task is represented as an individual node that we call task node, and task and sub-task structures in task knowledge are represented as a graph structure among task nodes yielding parent tasks and their sub-tasks; service knowledge is expressed by associating each task node with the URI (Uniform Resource Identifier) of the appropriate concrete information service.

2.1 High-Level Architecture

Fig. 1 shows the high-level architecture of the proposed system. The system is composed of two parts; the Knowledge Modeling Framework (KMF), which provides a task knowledge modeling environment to support task knowledge modeling and stores the described model in the Task Knowledge Base (Task KB), and the Service Retrieval Framework (SRF), which provides a task knowledge based service retrieval system for actual mobile handsets through the use of the Task KB and the Service Knowledge Base (Service KB). KMF provides an environment that makes it easy to describe and acquire task knowledge and that also supports interoperability within task knowledge because it is to be shared by many network service providers and content service providers. SRF provides the server module needed to retrieve appropriate knowledge from the Task KB and the Service KB according to the user's request, and the client module, which actually runs on a mobile handset to provide an easy-to-use user interface.

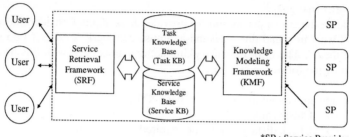

*SP : Service Provider

Fig. 1. High-level architecture of proposed system. The system is composed of two parts; 1)KMF, which provides a task knowledge modeling environment, and 2)SRF, which provides a task knowledge based service retrieval system that can be used from a mobile handset.

2.2 Research Challenges

1. The *Knowledge Modeling Framework (KMF)* must be capable of describing all tasks likely to be performed by mobile users in a structured way as task knowledge. The framework must make it easy to describe knowledge and to extend existing knowledge. We note that task knowledge will be created by multiple entities.
2. The *Service Retrieval Framework (SRF)* must enable a mobile user to retrieve appropriate services by entering a simple problem-solving request. The environment must provide components that run on commercial mobile handsets and provide a user interface that is easy to use and to understand. The environment also must handle a wide range of user requests such as abstract or concrete requests.

3   Designing Knowledge Modeling Framework

The Knowledge Modeling Framework (KMF) is designed to provide the ability to describe many kinds of task knowledge, and to extend existing knowledge or add external knowledge from a third party. We show details of this framework below.

3.1   Basic Approach for Task Knowledge Modeling in the Real World

It's important to manage and reuse already described knowledge because there are so many tasks in the real world. Much research has been conducted on the ontology for knowledge sharing in the engineering domain [12] [13], business domain [14] or problem-solving research area [15] [16]. The final goal of our research is to create large scale task ontology for modeling real world user activities. Towards this goal, first of all, we considered the strategy for extracting task knowledge that can be reused. Our approach is to extract task knowledge that depends on some specific place such as an amusement park or a department store at first, and next we extract the generic task knowledge from the place-dependent task knowledge. The advantage of this approach is that the extraction of the place-dependent task knowledge is easer to carry out by collecting and analyzing cases of service usage in the real world place. The category of the real-world place can be borrowed from commercial services such as a map service or car navigation service. In this research, we treat this category of place as a domain for classifying the task knowledge. Fig. 2 shows basic approach for task knowledge modeling in the real world.

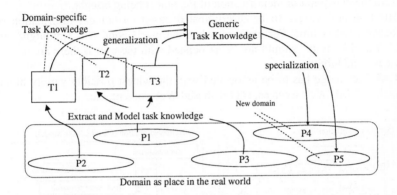

Fig. 2. Basic approach for task knowledge modeling in the real world

The generic task knowledge facilitates the reuse of knowledge. For instance, generic task knowledge such as "go to somewhere", which corresponds to the general process model to perform the activity of moving from a starting point to a destination, is common knowledge among specific task knowledge regarding going to specific places from specific places. The knowledge engineer can use such generic task knowledge to describe more specific task knowledge in a new domain which decreases the cost for expanding the coverage of task knowledge. We have constructed domain specific task knowledge for 12 domains so far.

3.2   Requirements for Semantic Description of Task Knowledge

Task knowledge consists of various kinds of task nodes and their relations. A good description of task knowledge is quite important for the management and reuse of knowledge. In addition, an interoperable standard format for knowledge representation is essential for network-wide knowledge sharing. By sharing the same description, we can combine different task knowledge such as knowledge created by a service provider and independent user groups of the service. We extracted the task knowledge description requirements which were based from the analysis of structured task knowledge developed in [4]. Fig. 3 shows an example of a generic task model and a specific task model and their relation based on the requirements.

1. The relations between task nodes must allow the discrimination of two relation types: "specialized" relation, which indicates that an *object* task node is more specific than a *subject* task node, and "achieved" relation, which indicates that an *object* task node is one of the divided task nodes that achieve a *subject* task node.
2. The achieved relation must be represented as a sequence of tasks by using some kind of control construct, such as Sequence, Exclusiveness, etc.
3. The achieved relation involves the role of each sub-task to achieve the task with which the sub-task is associated.
4. The specialized relation involves the viewpoint of the policy for categorization. For instance, "Buy products" and "Buy foods" are associated by a specialized relation from the viewpoint of identification of the object being bought.
5. The task nodes have to be discriminated based on context information such as location and/or time. For instance, when the user's context is "midnight", the task of "travel by train" should not be associated with the user if there are no train services in midnight.
6. Task knowledge has to be associated with the widest possible variety of services, such as XML Web services, HTML-based Web content, etc.

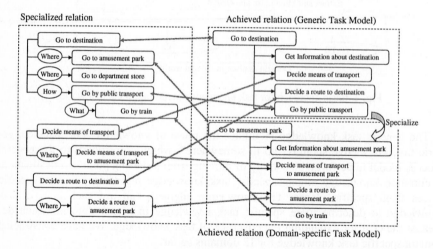

Fig. 3. An Example of structured task knowledge described with achieved relation and specialized relation. All task nodes are defined in the specialized relation tree (left side) and some task nodes are associated with achieved relation (right side).

3.3 Semantic Description of Task Knowledge with OWL-S

For meeting the requirements in 3.2, we designed a description framework of task knowledge using OWL-S. OWL-S is an OWL [9] based Web service ontology for describing the properties and capabilities of Web services. OWL-S also includes process ontology for describing generic process.

We describe the achieved relation by using the Process model and the control constructs defined in OWL-S, and define the specialized relation as an object property called "specializedBy". In addition, we define a "View" class for describing the viewpoint of specialization. The value of the "view" property is either 1) WHAT; specialization of object, 2) WHERE; specialization of location, or 3) HOW; specialization of method.

Furthermore, we define a "Role" class for describing the role of a lower-level task with respect to an upper-level task in achieved relations. The "role" property can be either, 1) PLAN; the activity of planning to achieve upper-level task (e.g. decide a destination), 2) PREPARE; the activity of preparation before performing concrete action (e.g. collect information of destination in advance), 3) ACTION; the concrete activity to achieve upper-level task (e.g. move to destination), or 4) CONFIRM; the activity of checking the current status of situation (e.g. check traffic jam). Each task node is described as a Service class of OWL-S, and the context information that indicates the applicable condition of the task node is described by using the ServiceProfile.

For describing service knowledge that associates task node with not only Web services but also HTML-based Web content, we define an original class named "BookmarkAtomicProcessGrounding" (BAPG). BAPG has features that can associate multiple Web content with a single task node, and can handle service names and URIs.

3.4 Task Knowledge Modeling Environment

We developed a task knowledge modeling environment, named TEdit, to develop and manage the described task model. Fig. 4 shows the user interface of TEdit. TEdit is implemented in Java and has an SQL Database interface via JDBC. TEdit provides several functions, 1) Create task node and edit specialized relations, 2) Define and edit achieved relations, 3) Define control constructs in achieved relations, 4) Register services and edit association of services with task node, and so on. Furthermore, TEdit provides the feature of automatic creation of OWL-S codes.

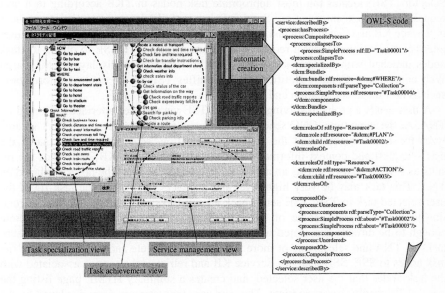

Fig. 4. User Interface of task knowledge modeling environment named TEdit

The left side of the user interface provides a specialization view in which the user can define each task node hierarchically. The viewpoint of specialization can be set by selecting the appropriate view such as WHAT, WHERE and HOW on a context menu shown by clicking on a task node. The selected viewpoint is shown as a special node. The right-upper side of the user interface provides an achievement view in which the user can define the achieved relations between task nodes. The role of achieved relations can also be assigned by selecting appropriate sub-task roles such as PLAN, PREPARE, ACTION, and CONFIRM. The control construct of the set of sub tasks such as Exclusive, Sequence, or IF-then-else, and the context information which indicates applicable condition of the task can also be set in the achievement view.

4 Designing Service Retrieval Framework

We designed and implemented the service retrieval framework based on task knowledge that consists of server module and client module. The client module can run on commercial mobile handsets as a Java program specially designed for mobile handsets. We show the system architecture and the user interface in detail below.

4.1 System Architecture and Execution Sequence

Fig. 5 shows the system architecture of Service Retrieval Framework (SRF) based on task knowledge. The system is composed of several parts: Task Knowledge Base (Task KB) stores description for task nodes and the relationships between task nodes as Semantic Task Descriptions; Service Knowledge Base (Service KB) stores descriptions about the associations between a service (URI, service name and service explanation) with a proper task node in Task KB as Semantic Service Descriptions; Task Selector (TSE) locates the most appropriate task nodes in TKB according to a user request and context information; Service Selector (SSE) locates appropriate services in Service KB associated with task node IDs; Task Navigator (TNA) provides the user interface to let a user input a request and communicates with TSE to obtain the task nodes matched with the user's request; Web browser, which displays HTML-based Web content and Context Notifier (CNO) notifies TSE of the context information, such as user's current location and time.

A user sends a problem-solving request to TSE via the user interface presented by TNA. At the same time, CNO sends the user's context information to TSE. TSE analyzes the user's request and the context information, selects tasks that match the user's request and context information by searching the Task KB, and sends the results to TNA. The user selects an appropriate task from a list of the tasks displayed on TNA. This task may be very high level and abstract. TNA sends the task ID of the user selected task to TSE. TSE sends back all sub-tasks related via the achieved relation to the task. Here, some of the sub-tasks may be very detailed and concrete enough to be directly associated with concrete services. The user can brows all sub-tasks on TNA and selects one or more task nodes to execute and sends the IDs of the task nodes to SSE. SSE searches Service KB and retrieves the service associated with the task nodes that the user selected, and creates a summary HTML page listing the services deemed to be appropriate. The user uses the summary page displayed by the web browser to access the services.

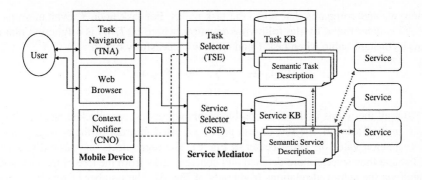

Fig. 5. The system architecture of Service Retrieval Framework (SRF). SRF consists of two parts; 1) Service Mediator, which provides the server module running as Servlet, and 2) Mobile Device, which provides the client module running on the mobile handset.

4.2 Implementation

Fig. 6 shows the user interface of the prototype system. TNA, which runs on a mobile device, was implemented as a Java application running on a mobile device. TSE and SSE were implemented as Servlet running on an application server. The current implementation does not support context-related features such as a Context Notifier.

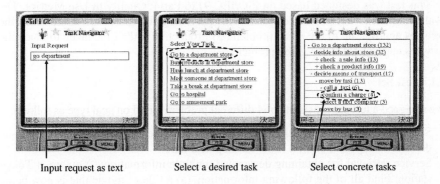

      Input request as text   Select a desired task   Select concrete tasks

Fig. 6. User interface for the execution of task knowledge based service retrieval. Service selection procedure consists of 3 steps; 1) request input, 2) abstract task selection, 3) concrete task selection.

    The user enters a problem-solving request in a text box on TNA (left side of Fig. 6). To respond to the user's problem-solving request, a task node that can solve that request must be selected from the Task KB and presented to the user. This mechanism considers that the input is from a small portable terminal and assumes that the problem-solving request is expressed as a short text message. For this reason, task node selection actually presents not one but a set of task nodes which are associated with achieved relations. For each word in the user's problem-solving request that is in the thesaurus, the mechanism creates word set W consisting of that word and its synonyms and compares that set to the task nodes. For task node T, evaluation value $val(T)$ is determined by the following equation, where $p(T, w)$ is a function that returns a constant value when task T and word w successfully match.

$$val(T) = \sum_{w \in W} p(T, w) \tag{1}$$

After all the words in the user's problem-solving request are checked against all task nodes in the Task KB, the sets of task nodes are listed in order of the average score of the evaluation value on TNA (center of Fig. 6). The user selects one desired task from the list and then selects more detailed and concrete tasks from the tree of the task nodes related via the achieved relations (right side of Fig. 6). The number of services associated with each task node is displayed on the right side of the task nodes.

5 Evaluations

We conducted a user test with 9 adult subjects to confirm the effectiveness of the proposed system. The purpose of this user test was to evaluate the process up to finding services for problem-solving purposes in terms of process functionality. Subjects were asked to retrieve appropriate services to given problem by using the proposed system, a keyword-type full-text search system developed by ourselves, and a major commercial directory-type search system [11].

This test was designed based on ISO/IEC 9126 Part4: Quality In Use Metrics. The evaluation items were 1) Effectiveness: the percentage of users who could reach the services appropriate to the given problem, 2) Productivity: the time taken to reach the services appropriate to the given problem.

5.1 Test Set

We designed a test set consisting of 4 different problem based on goal type as follows.

1. Service retrieval from a designated Web site: "You are at Tokyo station: Find a site that shows the location of a Karaoke shop near here."
2. Service retrieval for obtaining designated multiple information: "You are at Tokyo station: Find all of the following information, (a) a title of movie that is now being shown, (b)movie ranking of the title, (c) the location of a theater that is showing the movie near here, (d) the starting time of the movie."
3. Service retrieval for proper information to perform designated activity: "You are at Tokyo station and have a lot of luggage. Find a proper way to send it to your friend."
4. Service retrieval for proper information to help user to plan and perform activity in the real world to achieve a designated goal: "You are at Tokyo station at midnight. Find a good way to spend the time until tomorrow morning."

5.2 Test Environment

The test environment consisted of 3 different search systems, 1) S1: keyword-type full-text search system, 2) S2: directory-type search system, 3) S3: task knowledge based service retrieval system (proposed system). The target page set to be searched was the same for each system and the number of the page set was about 15,000. Subjects were divided into 3 groups according to their experience of mobile Internet service. 1) U1: subjects using mobile Internet service everyday, 2) U2: subjects using mobile Internet service a few days a week, 3) U3: subjects who have no experience in using mobile Internet service.

5.3 Test Results

Figures 7, 8, 9, and 10 show a test result. The horizontal axis shows the time taken (in seconds) to solve a given problem while the vertical axis shows the number of subjects who solved a given problem at the time. The right end of the horizontal axis, labeled 900, shows the number of subjects who could not solve the given problem.

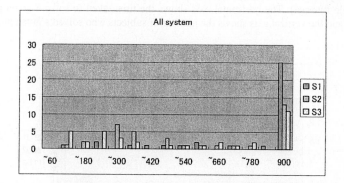

Fig. 7. Test results of all systems (*S1*: Keyword-type search system, *S2*: Directory-type search system, *S3:* Proposed system). The horizontal axis shows the time taken to solve a given problem by the second and the vertical axis shows the number of subjects who solved the problem.

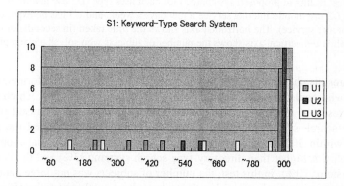

Fig. 8. Test results of Keyword-type search system (*S1*) for each user type (*U1* use mobile Internet everyday, *U2* use mobile Internet a few days a week, and *U3* has no experience in using mobile Internet). The horizontal axis shows the time taken (in seconds) to solve a given problem while the vertical axis shows the number of subjects who solved a given problem.

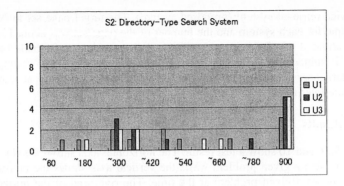

Fig. 9. Test results of Directory-type search system (*S2*) for each user type (*U1* use mobile Internet everyday, *U2* use mobile Internet a few days a week, and *U3* has no experience in using mobile Internet). The horizontal axis shows the time taken to solve a given problem by the second and the vertical axis shows the number of subjects who solved a given problem.

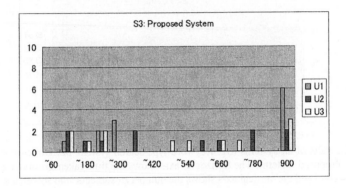

Fig. 10. Test results of proposed system (*S3*) for each user type (*U1* use mobile Internet service everyday, *U2* use mobile Internet service a few days a week, and *U3* has no experience in using mobile Internet service). The horizontal axis shows the time taken (in seconds) to solve a given problem while the vertical axis shows the number of subjects who solved a given problem.

The test results show that the proposed system offers superior performance. The rate of users who could reach the appropriate services was about 63%, which was higher than the result of the keyword-type search system (16%) and the result of the directory-type search system (56%). In particular, 50% subjects reached the appropriate services within 300 seconds which is an acceptable value in actual mobile Internet use, which was higher than directory-type search system (33%) and the keyword-type search system (10%). In this test, the number of subjects was not large enough and the test set was not comprehensive, but the test results actually show the effectiveness of our approach in an actual mobile Internet environment.

With regard to the test results analyzed by user type, only the proposed system allowed non-expert users grouped as U2 and U1 to achieve the same level of success as experienced users, U1. One observed drawback of the proposed system was that performance of U1 was not enhanced much by our system. We imagine the reason is that users in U1 were accustomed to conventional search systems and did not have enough time to get accustomed to the different search strategy of the proposed system. To resolve the above problem, we will consider the idea of changing the search system automatically according to the user's response.

6 Related Work

Task Computing Environment (TCE) [6] is a DAML-S [5] based service discovery and composition framework for pervasive computing environments. TCE can reduce the cost of performing a task by displaying the tasks that could be performed by executing pervasive services located around the user. However, TCE can not associate a user's task with services on the Internet that are not physically adjacent to the user, and does not support abstract tasks that are not solved directly by using those services, because the support range of TCE is limited to just those tasks that are solved directly by pervasive services.

The process-based service retrieval approach [17] is a sophisticated service retrieval method that offers better precision and recall than the conventional service retrieval method. In this research, service models are indexed into a process ontology, such as MIT Process Handbook [14], and the process query language called PQL is introduced. A preliminary evaluation showed that the process-based service retrieval approach offers qualitatively higher retrieval precision than any other existing approach.

Other research has considered the use of a knowledge base to infer what the user really wants to do. The GOOSE system [7], for example, employs a large amount of knowledge (common sense knowledge) collected from general Internet users to infer the user's search goal and to present search results that achieve that goal. This system, though, requires relatively long text input because it applies natural language processing technology to infer the search goal. It would not be easy to apply such a system to an environment where text input is cumbersome as is the case with mobile terminals.

7 Conclusion and Future Work

This paper proposed a task knowledge based service retrieval framework for non-expert mobile users that makes it easy to retrieve services appropriate for tackling the user's problem in the real world. The system features a task knowledge base that contains knowledge about which services will solve the problems that a user faces in daily life. Details of the prototype system including knowledge modeling framework were described. While the prototype system has only limited coverage, the results of a user test confirmed that it lowers the difficulty of service access. In addition, the system allows the user to recognize ancillary tasks that were not initially thought of by the user since the system shows tasks related to the task of solving the problem directly extracted from the user's initial request.

The next step in our research is to consider and develop a task-ontology-based knowledge modelling environment. Task ontology provides a common vocabulary and common viewpoint for describing task knowledge, and enables knowledge authors to create reusable knowledge models. Furthermore, we will extend the scope of the knowledge to be able to describe relationships between obstructive events, such as "missing route" or "no vacant spaces", and the task for preventing and resolving those obstructive events.

We also plan on improving the user interface on the mobile handset. The current prototype system provides just one text box interface to input the user's request. This interface is simple but some users are not certain about what kinds of request can be interpreted. Actually, some users input long sentences into the text box such as "find restaurant now available" or "find hotel near Tokyo station" in our test, but the current prototype system can not interpret conditions that contain time or location information. We will consider more functionality to help the user input his request with minimal load.

Acknowledgement

We would like to acknowledge Prof. Riichiro Mizoguchi, Prof. Yoshinobu Kitamura, and Dr. Munehiko Sasajima at Osaka University for their useful discussions and comments on this work.

References

1. NTT DoCoMo web site.: http://www.nttdocomo.com/
2. Ministry of Public Management, Home Affairs, Posts and Telecommunications, Japan.: Information and communications in Japan, Chapter2, Section5. (2004)
3. Hiramatsu, K., Akahani, J., Satoh, T.: Querying Real World Services Through the Semantic Web. In: Proceedings of The Third International Semantic Web Conference (ISWC 2004) (2004) 741-751
4. Naganuma, T., Kurakake, S.: A task oriented approach to service retrieval in mobile computing environment. In: Proceedings of IASTED International Conference on Artificial Intelligence and Applications (AIA 2005) (2005)
5. The DAML Services Coalition (Anupriya Ankolenkar, et al).: DAML-S: Web Service Description for the Semantic Web. In: Proceedings of The First International Semantic Web Conf. (ISWC), Sardinia, Italy (2002) 348-363
6. Masuoka, R., Parsia, B., Labrou, Y.: Task Computing - the Semantic Web meets Pervasive Computing -. In: Proceedings of The Third International Semantic Web Conference (ISWC 2003) (2003) 865-881.
7. Hugo Liu, Henry Lieberman, and Ted Selker.: GOOSE: A Goal-Oriented Search Engine With Commonsense. In: Proceedings of Adaptive Hypermedia and Adaptive Web-Based Systems Second International Conf., Malaga, Spain (2002) 253-263.
8. Bandula, A.: Self–regulation of motivation and action through internal standards and goal systems, Goal Concepts in Personality and Social Psychology (Hillsdale, NJ: A.P.Lawrence). (1989) 19-85.
9. Web Ontology Language (OWL).: http://www.w3.org/2004/OWL/
10. OWL-S 1.0 Release.: http://www.daml.org/services/owl-s/1.0/
11. Yahoo Mobile web site.: http://mobile.yahoo.co.jp/index.html
12. Kitamura, Y., Kashiwase, M., Fuse, M. Mizoguchi, R.: Deployment of an ontological framework of functional design knowledge. Advanced Engineering Informatics, 18(2), (2004) 115-127

13. Horváth I, Vergeest JSM, Kuczogi G. Development and Application of Design Concept Ontologies for Contextual Conceptualization. In: Proceedings of 1998 ASME Design Engineering Technical Conferences DETC (1998)
14. Herman, G. A., Malone, T. W.: What is in the process handbook?, Organizing Business Knowledge: The MIT Process Handbook, MIT Press (2003) 221-258
15. Mizoguchi, R., Ikeda, M., Seta, K., and Vanwelkenhuysen, J.: Ontology for Modeling the World from Problem Solving Perspectives, in IJCAI Workshop on Basic Ontological Issues in Knowledge Sharing (1995)
16. Schreiber, G., Akkermans, H., Anjewierden, A., de Hoog, R., Shadbolt, N., Van de Velde, W. and Wielinga, B.: Knowledge Engineering and Management - The Common-KADS Methodology, The MIT Press, Cambridge, MA (2000)
17. Bernstein, A., Klein, M. Towards High-Precision Service Retrieval, In: Proceedings of The First International Semantic Web Conf. (ISWC), Sardinia, Italy (2002)

Supporting Rule System Interoperability
on the Semantic Web with SWRL

Martin O'Connor[1], Holger Knublauch[1], Samson Tu[1], Benjamin Grosof[2],
Mike Dean[3], William Grosso[4], and Mark Musen[1]

[1] Stanford Medical Informatics,
Stanford University School of Medicine, Stanford, CA 94305
musen@smi.stanford.edu
[2] Sloan School of Management, MIT, Cambridge, MA 02142
bgrossof@mit.edu
[3] BBN Technologies, Ann Arbor, MI 48103
mdean@bbn.com
[4] Echopass Corp., San Francisco, CA 95105
wgrosso@echopass.com

Abstract. Rule languages and rule systems are widely used in business applications including computer-aided training, diagnostic fact finding, compliance monitoring, and process control. However, there is little interoperability between current rule-based systems. Interoperation is one of the main goals of the Semantic Web, and developing a language for sharing rules is often seen as a key step in reaching this goal. The Semantic Web Rule Language (SWRL) is an important first step in defining such a rule language. This paper describes the development of a configurable interoperation environment for SWRL built in Protégé-OWL, the most widely-used OWL development platform. This environment supports both a highly-interactive, full-featured editor for SWRL and a plugin mechanism for integrating third party rule engines. We have integrated the popular Jess rule engine into this environment, thus providing one of the first steps on the path to rule integration on the Web.

1 Introduction

Many business processes, such as workflow management, computer aided training, compliance monitoring, diagnostic fact finding, and process control, are often best modeled using a declarative approach, leading to a very active commercial interest in rule-based systems. However, interoperability among the multitude of current rule-based systems is limited. Given that interoperability is one of the primary goals of the Semantic Web and that rules are a key part of those goals, there has been significant recent interest in standardization.[1] The goal of sharing rule bases and processing them with different rule engines has resulted in RuleML, SWRL, Metalog, and ISO Prolog, and other standardization efforts.

One of the key steps to rule interoperation on the Web is SWRL[2] which was designed to be the rule language of the Semantic Web. SWRL is based on a combination of the

Y. Gil et al. (Eds.): ISWC 2005, LNCS 3729, pp. 974–986, 2005.

OWL DL and OWL Lite sublanguages of the OWL Web Ontology Language[3] the Unary/Binary Datalog[4] sublanguages of the Rule Markup Language. SWRL allows users to write Horn-like rules expressed in terms of OWL concepts to reason about OWL individuals. The rules can be used to infer new knowledge from existing OWL knowledge bases.

The SWRL Specification[5] does not impose restrictions on how reasoning should be performed with SWRL rules. Thus, investigators are free to use a variety of rule engines to reason with the SWRL rules stored in an OWL knowledge base. They are also free to implement their own editing facilities to create SWRL rules. In this way, SWRL provides a convenient starting point for integrating rule systems to work with the Semantic Web.

To this end, we have developed the Protégé SWRL Editor, a full-featured highly interactive open-source rule editor for SWRL. This editor operates within Protégé-OWL[6] and is tightly integrated with it. It adopts the look-and-feel of Protégé-OWL and allows users to seamlessly switch between SWRL rule editing and normal OWL editing of OWL entities. Users can also easily incorporate OWL entities into rules they are authoring.

One of the main goals of the SWRL Editor is to permit interoperability between SWRL and existing rule engines. An important component of this interoperability is the editor's mechanism for supporting tight integration with rule engines. This mechanism is supported by a subsystem called the Protégé SWRL Factory. The SWRL Factory supports a rule engine plugin mechanism that permits API-level interoperation with existing rule engines. It also allows developers to access real estate on the SWRL Editor tab, which allows the interface for the rule engine to coexist with the SWRL Editor. Developers integrating an existing rule engine with the SWRL Editor have full control of the area inside the panel.

Of course, a looser form of interoperation can also occur at the OWL knowledge base level. Investigators are free to use the SWRL rules created by the editor and stored in OWL files as input to their rule engines. Researchers in the SweetRules[7]project, for example, have already used rules created by the SWRL Editor to perform inference using a Jena 2-based[8]rule engine.

We used the SWRL Factory mechanism to integrate the Jess rule engine with the SWRL Editor. With Jess, users can run SWRL rules interactively to create new OWL concepts and then insert them into an OWL knowledge base. SWRL, coupled with Jess, can provide a rich rule-based reasoning facility for the Semantic Web and can serve as a starting point for further rule integration efforts.

2   Semantic Web Rule Language

In common with many other rule languages, SWRL rules are written as antecedent-consequent pairs. In SWRL terminology, the antecedent is referred to as the rule *body* and the consequent is referred to as the *head*. The head and body consist of a conjunction of one or more *atoms*. At present, SWRL does not support more complex logical combinations of atoms.

SWRL rules reason about OWL individuals, primarily in terms of OWL classes and properties. For example, a SWRL rule expressing that a person with a male sibling has a brother would require capturing the concepts of 'person', 'male', 'sibling' and 'brother' in OWL. Intuitively, the concept of person and male can be captured using an OWL class called Person with a subclass Man; the sibling and brother relationships can be expressed using OWL properties hasSibling and hasBrother, which are attached to Person. The rule in SWRL would then be:

```
Person (?x1) ^ hasSibling(?x1,?x2) ^ Man(?x2) →
hasBrother(?x1,?x2)
```

Executing this rule would have the effect of setting the hasBrother property to x2 in the individual that satisfies the rule, named x1.

SWRL rules can also refer explicitly to OWL individuals. For example, the following example is a variant of the above rule, inferring that a particular individual Fred has a brother:

```
Person(Fred) ^ hasSibling(Fred,?x2) ^ Man(?x2) →
hasBrother(Fred,?x2)
```

In this case Fred is the name of an OWL individual.

SWRL also supports data literals. For example, assuming an individual has a hasAge property, it is possible to ask if Fred has a 40 year-old brother:

```
Person(Fred) ^ hasSibling(Fred,?x2) ^ Man(?x2) ^
hasAge(?x2,40) → has40YearOldBrother(Fred,?x2)
```

String literals — which are enclosed in single quotes — are also supported.

SWRL also supports the common same-as and different-from concepts. For example, the SWRL sameAs atom can determine if two OWL individuals Fred and Frederick are the same individual:

```
sameAs(Fred, Frederick)
```

Similarly, the differentFrom atom can be used to express that two OWL individuals are not the same.

SWRL also has an atom to determine if an individual, property, or variable is of a particular type. For example, the following example determines if variable x is of type unsigned integer:

```
xsd:unsignedInt(?x)
```

These atoms — which are called data range atoms in SWRL — must be preceded by the 'xsd:' namespace qualifier. The type specified must be an XML Schema data type.

A second form of a data range atom can be used to express one-of relationships in SWRL. For example, the following SWRL atom indicates that variable x must be one of 3, 4 or 5:

```
[3, 4, 5](?x)
```

SWRL also supports a range of built-in predicates, which greatly expand its expressive power. SWRL built-ins are predicates that accept several arguments. They are described in detail in the SWRL Built-in Specification[9]. The simplest built-ins are comparison operations. For example, the greaterThan built-in determines if an individual has an older brother.

```
hasBrother(?x1,?x2) ^ hasAge(?x1,?age1) ^
hasAge(?x2,?age2) ^ swrlb:greaterThan(?age2,?age1) →
hasOlderBrother(?x1,?x2)
```

All built-ins in SWRL must be preceded by the namespace qualifier 'swrlb:'.

Finally, SWRL supports more complex mathematical built-ins. For example, the following rule determines if an individual has a brother who is exactly 10 years older:

```
hasBrother(?x1,?x2) ^ hasAge(?x1,?age1) ^
hasAge(?x2,?age2) ^ swrlb:subtract(10,?age2,?age1) →
hasDecadeOlderBrother(?x1,?x2)
```

The SWRL Built-in Ontology[10] describes the range of built-ins supported by SWRL. In addition to mathematical built-ins, there are built-ins for strings, dates, and lists. Additions may be made to this namespace in the future so the range of built-ins supported by SWRL can grow.

3   The Protégé SWRL Editor

The Protégé SWRL Editor is an extension to Protégé-OWL that permits interactive editing of SWRL rules. Users can create, edit, and read/write SWRL rules. With the exception of arbitrary OWL expressions (see Section 6), the SWRL Editor supports the full set of language features outlined in the current SWRL Specification. It is tightly integrated with Protégé-OWL and is primarily accessible through a tab within it. When editing rules, users can directly refer to OWL classes, properties, and individuals within an OWL knowledge base. They also have direct access to the full

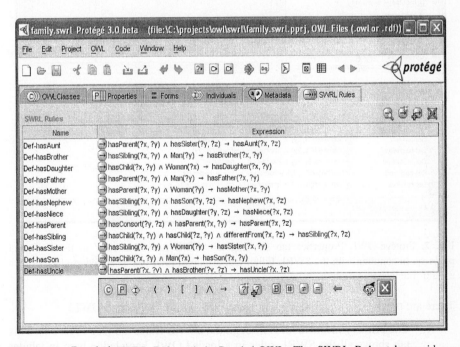

Fig. 1. The Protégé SWRL Rules tab in Protégé-OWL. The SWRL Rules tab provides a tabular listing of all SWRL rules in an OWL knowledge base. These rules can be edited in place or with a multi-line interactive editor, which can be popped up.

set of built-ins described in the SWRL Built-in Ontology and to the full range of XML Schema data types. Figure 1 shows a screenshot of the Protégé SWRL Rules tab. The SWRL Editor also supports inference with SWRL rules using the Jess[11] rule engine (see Section 5). Documentation for the editor is available in the Protégé SWRL Editor FAQ[12].

The SWRL Editor is automatically enabled in Protégé-OWL when loading any OWL knowledge base that imports the SWRL Ontology[13]. It is disabled by default if a loaded knowledge base does not import this ontology. A user can use Protégé-OWL's configuration menu to enable this tab for a knowledge base that does not import the SWRL Ontology; he will then be given an option to import this ontology so that all future loads of the knowledge base will activate the SWRL Editor.

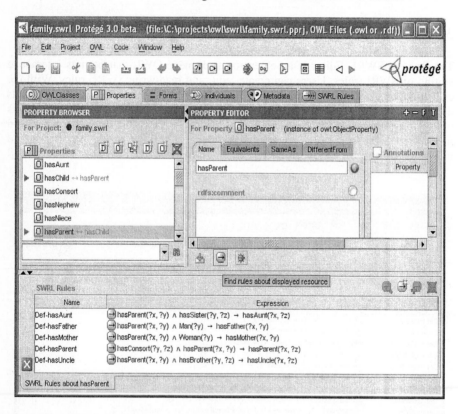

Fig. 2. Protégé-OWL Properties tab showing all SWRL rules that refer to the hasParent property. In common with the SWRL Editor tab, displayed rules can be edited in place or with a multi-line interactive editor.

There are two ways of interacting with the SWRL Editor in Protégé-OWL:

1. The primary mechanism is through the SWRL Rules tab (see Figure 1). This tab shows all the SWRL rules in a loaded OWL knowledge base in tabular form.

2. A second mechanism allows users to find rules relating to a selected OWL class, property, or individual in the respective Protégé-OWL tabs for those entities. For example, if a user is examining a class using the OWL Classes tab, he can display a list of SWRL rules referring to that class. The same mechanism applies in the properties and individuals tabs. Figure 2 shows a Protégé-OWL Properties tab displaying all SWRL rules that refer to a selected property, hasParent.

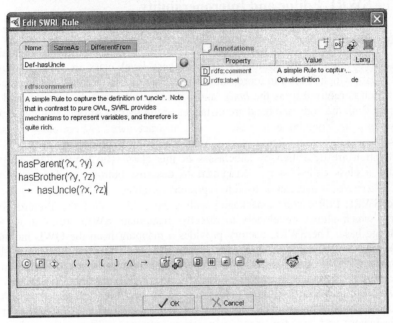

Fig. 3. SWRL Multi-Line Editor Dialog. The icon panel provides selection dialog boxes to select things including OWL classes, properties, and individuals. It also includes shortcuts and selection dialog boxes for various other entities.

There are two editing modes for rules. Users can edit them in place in the table containing them, or they can pop up a multi-line editor (see Figure 3). The difference between the two modes is primarily visual. The same interaction mechanisms apply in both modes, though the multi-line editor has some additional options.

The SWRL Editor allows users to enter rules completely as text. However, it also allows users to select OWL entities from a currently loaded knowledge base and insert them into the rule being edited. This task is performed via an icon panel. The icon panel provides access to selection dialog boxes, select OWL classes, properties, and individuals. It also includes selection dialog boxes for SWRL built-ins, XML Schema data types, and shortcuts for various other entities.

The SWRL Editor performs syntactic and semantic checking as a rule is being entered. It ensures that each rule is syntactically correct and also ensures that any references to OWL entities are valid. It will also ensure that any variables referred to in a rule consequent are present in the head. If a user makes a mistake while entering a rule, the rule text entry box grays out and a textual explanation of the error is presented. A user can continue typing and immediately fix the error or fix it later. The editor does not allow users to save incomplete or erroneous rules.

The editor also has convenience features such as auto-completion. Pressing the tab key while editing an OWL entity, built-in, or XML Schema data type name auto-completes a name if it has a unique expansion. If the name is not unique, the software brings up a selection box containing a list of possible completions.

4   The SWRL Editor and Interoperability

SWRL rules are stored as OWL individuals with their associated knowledge base when an open OWL project is saved. The classes that describe these individuals are described by the SWRL Ontology. The highest level class in this Ontology is `swrl:Imp`, which is used to represent a single SWRL rule. It contains an antecedent part, which is referred to as the *body*, and a consequent part, which is referred to as the *head*. Both the body and head are instances of the `swrl:AtomList` class, which represents a list containing rule atoms. The abstract `swrl:Atom` class is used to represent a rule atom. The various types of atoms described in the SWRL Specification are described by subclasses of this class. The SWRL Ontology also includes a class called `swrl:Builtin` to describe built-ins and a class called `swrl:Variable` that can be used to represent variables.

The SWRL Editor comes packaged with a Java API called the Protégé SWRL Factory, which allows developers to directly manipulate SWRL rules in an OWL knowledge base. The SWRL Factory provides a mapping from the OWL individuals representing SWRL rules to analogous Java instances. It also provides Java classes representing SWRL classes in the SWRL Ontology and mechanisms to create run-time instances of classes that mirror individuals in an OWL knowledge base. It is used internally by the SWRL Editor. However, it is accessible to all Protégé-OWL developers. SWRL Plugin developers can base their work directly on the classes created by this factory and can, for example, use it to integrate existing rule engines with Protégé-OWL. Indeed, this API could also be used to create new SWRL rule editors.

Each class described in the SWRL Ontology has a direct Java equivalent SWRL Factory class to represent it. The factory has utility functions to create Java instances of all these classes. When one Java instance is created, an equivalent OWL individual is also created in the knowledge base. Java instances mirroring existing OWL individuals can also be created. For example, the factory provides methods to create `SWRLImp` and `SWRLAtomList` Java classes that can be used to represent instances of the equivalent `swrl:imp` and `swrl:AtomList` OWL classes. Documentation of the SWRL Factory API is outlined in the Protégé SWRL Factory FAQ[14].

The SWRL Editor itself has no inference capabilities. It simply allows users to edit SWRL rules and save and load them to and from OWL knowledge bases. However, the SWRL Factory supports a rule engine plugin mechanism that permits API-level interoperation with existing rule engines. It also allows developers to access real estate on the SWRL Editor tab, which allows the interface for the rule engine to coexist with the SWRL Editor. Developers integrating an existing rule engine with the SWRL Editor have full control of the area inside the panel.

The SWRL Factory provides this functionality in a class called `SWRLRuleEngineAdapter`. The primary call provided by this class is `getSWRLTabRealEstate`, which returns a Java `JPanel` Swing object representing an area of the screen in the SWRL tab. This class also provides a method called `setRuleEngineIcon` that allows users to access the rule engine interactively. This icon is displayed on the top right of the rule table in the SWRL tab and can be used to toggle the screen real estate of the associated rule engine. If several rule engines are available, multiple icons are displayed. However, only one rule engine can be active at a time.

The SWRL Factory also provides a listening mechanism that allows users to register for rule creation, modification, and deletion events. Thus, when a SWRL rule is modified, a loaded rule engine can maintain an up-to-date image of the SWRL rule base automatically. Rule engine developers also have access to the Protégé event mechanism so that they can be immediately informed of modifications to a loaded OWL knowledge base. Thus, users can configure a rule engine so that it is synchronized with the SWRL rule base and the OWL knowledge base, and so that it performs immediate inference when changes are made to them. This approach has been used successfully in the Protégé environment for both the Jess[15] and Algernon[16] rule engines. These characteristics allow the SWRL factory to provide a bridge for third-party rule engines to interact with the SWRL Editor at run time, allowing users of these engines to experience seamless interaction between the SWRL Editor and the rule engine.

Of course, developers of rule engines may prefer a less dynamic relationship between the knowledge base and the rule engine. For example, instead of continually updating rule engine state in response to modifications to the associated SWRL rules or the loaded OWL knowledge base, a more user-controlled interaction may be desired.

In this regard, users can choose step-by-step control of the inference process. Thus, a user can incrementally control loading of SWRL rules and OWL knowledge into a rule engine, execution of those rules on the knowledge, the review of the results, and storing concluded results back into the OWL knowledge base. This approach may be preferable during early development and testing of a set of rules when the consequences of rules firing may not be obvious. Erroneous rules could easily create hundreds or more incorrect relationships between OWL entities.

5   Integrating the SWRL Editor and the Jess Rule Engine

A large number of rule engines work well with Java[17], and many are available as open source software. Some of the most popular engines include Jess, Algernon[18] and SweetRules. We chose Jess as the first integration candidate for the SWRL Editor because it works seamlessly with Java, has an extensive user base, is well documented, and is very easy to use and configure. Several research teams have also demonstrated that mappings between SWRL and Jess[19,20,21] and between RuleML and Jess[22] are possible. Jess provides both an interactive command line interface and a Java-based API to its rule engine. This engine can be embedded in Java applications and provides a flexible two-way run-time communication between Jess rules and Java. It is not open source but can be downloaded free for a 30-day evaluation period and is available free to academic users.

The Jess system consists of a rule base, a fact base, and an execution engine. The execution engine matches facts in the fact base with rules in the rule base. These rules can assert new facts and put them in the fact base or execute Java functions.

SWRL rules reason about OWL individuals, primarily in terms of OWL classes and properties. When a SWRL rule is fired, it can create new classifications for existing individuals. For example, if a rule consequent asserts that an individual is to be classified as a member of a particular class, that individual must be made a member of that class within OWL when the rule fires. Similarly, if a SWRL rule asserts that two individuals are related via a particular property, then that property must be associated with each individual that satisfies the rule.

Thus, four main tasks must be performed to allow Jess to interoperate with the SWRL Editor: (1) represent relevant knowledge about OWL individuals as Jess facts; (2) represent SWRL rules as Jess rules; (3) perform inference using those rules and reflect the results of that inference in an OWL knowledge base; and (4) control this interaction from a graphical interface.

5.1 Representing OWL Concepts as Jess Knowledge

Relevant knowledge about OWL individuals must be represented as Jess knowledge. The two primary properties that must be represented are 1) the classes to which an individual belongs and 2) the properties the individual possesses. Same-as and different-from information about these individuals must also be captured.

The Jess template facility provides a mechanism for representing an OWL class hierarchy. A Jess template hierarchy can be used to model an OWL class hierarchy using a Jess slot to hold the name of the individual belonging to the hierarchy. Thus, for example, a user must define a Jess template to represent the owl:Thing class:

```
(deftemplate OWLThing (slot name))
```

A hierarchy representing a class Man that subclasses a direct subclass of owl:Thing called Person could then be represented as follows in Jess:

```
(deftemplate Person extends OWLThing)[1]
(deftemplate Man extends Person)
```

Using this template definition, the OWL individual can be asserted as a member of the class Man:

```
(assert (Man (name Fred)))
```

OWL property information can be directly represented as Jess facts. For example, the information that an individual Fred is related to individual Joe through the hasUncle property can be directly asserted using:

```
(assert (hasUncle Fred Joe))
```

Similarly, OWL's same-as and different-from relationships between individuals can be directly represented in Jess. For example, the information that Fred and Frederick are the same OWL individual can be expressed:

```
(assert (sameAs Fred Frederick))
```

---

[1] In practice, a fully qualified namespace would precede each entity name, but we have omitted it here for clarity.

XML Schema data types can be represented using the same approach. For example, the information that individual x is an unsigned integer can be written:

```
(assert (xsd:unsignedInt ?x))
```

Finally, built-ins can be represented using the Jess 'test' mechanism. For example, the SWRL built-in greaterThan applied to two integers can be written:

```
(test (> 10 34))
```

5.2 Representing SWRL Rules as Jess Rules

The representation of SWRL rules in Jess using these facts is relatively straightforward. For example, take the following SWRL rule:

```
Person(?x) ^ Man(?y) ^ hasSibling(?x,?y) ^
hasAge(?x,?age1) ^ hasAge(?y,?age2) ^
swrlb:greaterThan(?age2,?age1) ->
hasOlderBrother(?x,?y)
```

This rule can be represented in Jess — using the representation of individuals outlined above — as:

```
(defrule aRule (Person (name ?x))(Man (name ?y))
                (hasSibling ?x ?y)(hasAge ?x ?age1)
                (hasAge ?y ?age2)(test (> ?age2 ?age1))
   => (assert (hasOlderBrother ?x ?y))
```

5.3 Executing Jess Rules and Updating an OWL Knowledge Base

Once the relevant OWL concepts and SWRL rules have been represented in Jess, the Jess execution engine can perform inference. As rules fire, new Jess facts are inserted into the fact base. Those facts are then used in further inference. When the inference process completes, these facts can then be transformed into OWL knowledge, a process that is the inverse of the mapping mechanism outlined in Section 5.1.

5.4 Visual Interface to the Jess Rule Engine

Interaction between the SWRL Editor and the Jess rule engine is user-driven. The user controls when OWL knowledge and SWRL rules are transferred to Jess, when inference is performed using those knowledge and rules, and when the resulting Jess facts are transferred back to Protégé-OWL as OWL knowledge.

Five tabs in the Jess rule panel control this interaction: (1) *a Jess Control tab*, which is used to initiate fact and rule transfer and perform inference; (2) *a Source Facts tab*, which presents Jess facts that have been transferred from an OWL knowledge base (see Figure 4); (3) *a Rules tab*, which shows the Jess representation of SWRL rules (see Figure 5), (4) *an Asserted Facts tab* showing facts resulting from Jess inference, and (5) *a Configuration tab* that can be used to set Jess operating parameters.

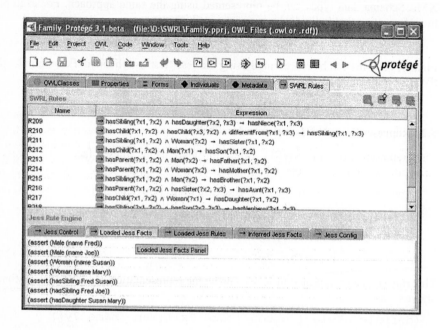

Fig. 4. Jess Loaded Facts Tab in the Protégé SWRL Editor. This tab shows the Jess representation of relevant OWL individuals that will be used by Jess to perform inference.

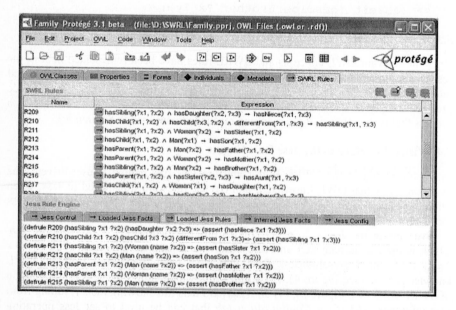

Fig. 5. Jess Rules Tab in the Protégé SWRL Editor. This tab shows the Jess representation of SWRL rules.

6 Discussion

With the exception of allowing arbitrary OWL expressions in SWRL rules, the Protégé SWRL Editor supports all language features in the current SWRL Specification. The inability to use arbitrary OWL expressions is easy to work around by creating a named OWL class that models an expression and using it in the rule.

One limitation of our inference support is that it is not integrated with an OWL classifier. Conflicts can arise in an OWL knowledge base between new information asserted by Jess and inserted into an OWL knowledge base and existing OWL restrictions. For example, a hasUncle property may be asserted for an individual as a result of firing a SWRL rule, but a class level restriction in OWL may forbid this property from belonging to that individual. As present, these conflicts are not detected automatically, and resolving the conflict—which is essentially between a SWRL rule and an OWL restriction and has nothing to do with Jess—is left to the user. Conflicts can be identified by running an OWL classifier on the knowledge base that has been populated by additional Jess-inferred knowledge.

To resolve these conflicts automatically, all OWL restrictions relating to classes and properties operated on by Jess would have to be captured as Jess knowledge. Jess rules would be needed to replicate the functionality of both a classifier and rule integrity checker. An additional issue is that a conflict-free execution of the classifier may also infer new knowledge that may in turn produce information that may benefit from further SWRL inference, a process that may require several iterations before no new knowledge is generated. Clearly, having this classification and inference functionality in a single module would be desirable.

The SWRL Editor has been available as part of Protégé-OWL since late 2004. User response has been very positive. Our hope now is that other investigators will use the Protégé SWRL Factory mechanism to integrate other rule engines with the SWRL Editor, eventually providing a range of rule engine choices. Jess, for example, has a very good implementation of a forward chaining rule engine but has weak backward chaining support. Consequently, a rule engine like Algernon may be more appropriate for users needing this support. Developers working within the Jena 2 environment would probably prefer the inference capabilities available in that environment. As more rule engines become available for SWRL, it should rapidly become a conduit for rule integration on the Semantic Web.

Acknowledgements

Funding for the Protégé SWRL Editor was provided by the DARPA Agent Markup Language Program. We thank Valerie Natale for her valuable editorial assistance.

References

1. W3C Workshop for Rule Languages for Interoperability: http://www.w3.org/2004/12/rules-ws/cfp
2. SWRL: http://www.daml.org/rules/proposal/
3. OWL Web Ontology Language: http://www.w3.org/TR/owl-features/

4. RuleML: http://www.ruleml.org/
5. SWRL Specification: http://www.w3.org/Submission/SWRL/
6. H. Knublauch, R. W. Fergerson, N. F. Noy, M. A. Musen. The Protégé OWL Plugin: An Open Development Environment for Semantic Web Applications. Third International Semantic Web Conference (2004)
7. SweetRules: http://sweetrules.projects.semwebcentral.org/
8. Jena-2: http://www.hpl.hp.com/semweb/jena.htm
9. SWRL Built-in Specification: http://www.daml.org/rules/proposal/builtins.html
10. SWRL Built-in Ontology: http://www.w3.org/2003/11/swrlb.owl
11. Jess Rule Engine: http://herzberg.ca.sandia.gov/jess/
12. Protégé SWRL Editor FAQ: http://protege.stanford.edu/plugins/owl/swrl/
13. SWRL Ontology: http://www.daml.org/rules/proposal/swrl.owl
14. Protégé SWRL Factory FAQ:
     http://protege.stanford.edu/plugins/owl/swrl/SWRLFactory.html
15. Jess Protégé Tab: http://www.ida.liu.se/~her/JessTab/JessTab.ppt
16. Algernon Protégé Tab: http://algernon-j.sourceforge.net/doc/algernon-protege.html
17. Java-based Rule Engines: http://www.manageability.org/blog/stuff/rule_engines/view
18. Algernon: http://www.cs.utexas.edu/users/qr/algy/
19. Kuan M. Using SWRL and OWL DL to Develop an Inference System for Course Scheduling. Masters Thesis, Chung Yuan Christian University, Taiwan, R.O.C. (2004)
20. Mei J., Bontas EP. Reasoning Paradigms for SWRL-Enabled Ontologies Protégé With Rules Workshop held at the 8th International Protégé Conference, Madrid Spain (2005)
21. Golbreich, C., Imai, A. Combining SWRL rules and OWL ontologies with Protégé OWL Plugin, Jess, and Racer. 7th International Protégé Conference, Bethesda, MD (2004)
22. Grosof B., Gandhe, M., Finin, T. SweetJess: Translating DamlRuleML to Jess. International Workshop on Rule Markup Languages for Business Rules on the Semantic Web. First International Semantic Web Conference (2002)

Automated Business-to-Business Integration of a Logistics Supply Chain Using Semantic Web Services Technology

Chris Preist[1], Javier Esplugas-Cuadrado[2], Steven A. Battle[1],
Stephan Grimm[3], and Stuart K.Williams[1]

[1] Hewlett-Packard Laboratories, Filton Road, Stoke Gifford, Bristol, BS34 8QZ, UK
{chris.preist, steve.battle, skw}@hp.com
[2] Hewlett-Packard Espanola SL, Jose Echegaray n°8, La Rozas, Spain. 28230
javier.esplugas.cuadrado@hp.com
[3] Forschungszentrum Informatik(FZI), Haid-und-Neu-Strasse 10-14,
76131 Karlsruhe, Germany
grimm@fzi.de

Abstract. In this paper, we present a demonstrator system which applies semantic web services technology to business-to-business integration, focussing specifically on a logistics supply chain. The system is able to handle all stages of the service lifecycle – discovery, service selection and service execution. One unique feature of the system is its approach to protocol mediation, allowing a service requestor to dynamically modify the way it communicates with aprovider, based on a description of the provider's protocol. We present the architecture of the system, together with an overview of the key components (discovery and mediation) and the implementation.

1 Introduction

The demonstrator system presented in this paper uses semantic web services technology to tackle the problem of business-to-business integration (B2Bi). It was developed as one of four case studies used in the European Union Semantic Web-enabled Web Services (SWWS) project. Increasingly, when two companies wish to do business with each other, they establish a means of exchanging messages via the internet. This connection can be used for a variety of purposes – placing orders, invoicing, making payments, initiating and tracking shipment of goods and providing customer service information, among many others. The aim of such a connection is to allow automated or semi-automated processing of many of the transactions which take place between the two companies, and thus reduce costs and increase speed.

However, to set up such a relationship requires a large initial investment of time and money. A team of developers need to reconcile the business processes of the two organizations and design a set of messages and permissible message sequences that can flow between them. This can be a formidable task. To ease this, standards bodies have developed standard sets of messages and guidelines for how they should be used. Three key standards in the world of B2Bi are EDIFACT, AnsiX12 and Roset-

Y. Gil et al. (Eds.): ISWC 2005, LNCS 3729, pp. 987–1001, 2005.

taNet. By agreeing on one such standard, two organizations can ease the integration task. However, these standards have reasonable flexibility in them, both in terms of message content and message sequencing. This means that even having agreed a standard, significant effort is required to agree and implement exactly how it is used. As a result of this, even a standards-based B2Bi connection can take six months to set up.

Semantic Web Services technology [1, 2] uses the tools of the semantic web to describe both the purpose of a service and the behaviour of its provider during service execution. This has the potential to significantly speed up this integration process; If one business partner gives a description of how to interact with it, it is possible to use mediation technology [3] to adapt the interaction of the other business partner so as to be compatible. Ideally, this would be fully automated, reducing integration time from months to minutes.

Prior to integration, the selection of a business partner can also be time consuming. By providing semantic descriptions of the services a business offers, then discovery techniques [4, 5, 6] can support this process. This is particularly important when selection is needed rapidly, such as the emergency replacement of a link in a supply chain. Our system supports automated discovery and selection of a service provider, and description-driven mediation which allows automated integration. The paper is structured as follows. In section 2, we introduce a motivating example, in the domain of logistics, and show how semantic web technology can be used to support it. In section 3, we present the architecture of the system we have developed, and show how it is used in the logistics domain. In section 4, we present the discovery module, and in section 5 we present the mediation modules. In section 6, we discuss the implementation. In section 7 we discuss limitations of the current implementation, lessons learned and related work. We then present the business value of the system, and conclude.

2 The Logistics Example

To motivate this work, we use an example scenario. We consider a manufacturing company in Bristol, UK which needs to distribute its goods internationally. It does not maintain its own transportation capability, but instead outsources this to other companies, which we refer to as *Freight Forwarders*. These companies provide a service to the manufacturing company – they transport crates on its behalf. However, the manufacturing company still needs to manage relationships with these service providers. One role within this company, which we refer to as the *Logistics Coordinator*, is responsible for doing this. Specifically, it carries out the following tasks;

1. Commissioning new service providers, and agreeing the nature of the service they will provide. (E.g. locating a new freight forwarder in Poland, and agreeing that it will regularly transport crates from Gdansk to Warsaw.)
2. Communicating with service providers to initiate, monitor and control shipments. (E.g. informing the Polish freight forwarder that a crate is about to arrive at Gdansk; receiving a message from them that it has been delivered in Warsaw, and they want payment.) This is done using one of the messaging standards, EDIFACT.

3. Coordinating the activity of service providers to ensure that they link seamlessly to provide an end-to-end service. (E.g. making sure the shipping company plans to deliver the crate to Gdansk when the Polish transport company is expecting it. Informing the Polish company when the shipping company is about to drop it off.)
4. Communicating with other roles in the company to coordinate logistics with other corporate functions. (E.g. sales to know what to dispatch; financial to ensure payment of freight forwarders.)

In our scenario, we consider a specific logistics supply chain from Bristol, UK to Warsaw, Poland (Fig 1). It consists of three freight forwarders: The first is a trucking company, responsible for transporting crates from the manufacturing plant in Bristol to the port of Portsmouth, UK. The second is a shipping company, responsible for shipping crates from Portsmouth to the Polish port of Gdansk. The third is another trucking company, which transports crates to the distribution warehouse in Warsaw. We assume that the Logistics Provider communicates with the Freight Forwarders using the EDIFACT standard, and is already successfully using this logistics chain.

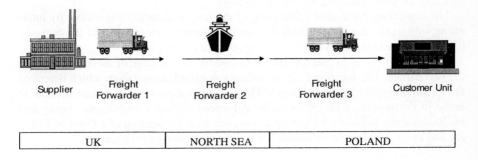

Fig. 1. Example Logistics Supply Chain

However, at some point a problem arises; the shipping company is temporarily unavailable and a new freight forwarder must be used for one shipment. At this point the Logistics Coordinator must;

1. Locate a new shipping service provider able to meet its needs.
2. Agree a service definition with it as to what exactly it should do. (When the crate will be transported, to where, how much it will cost, etc.)
3. Perform B2B integration with the provider, to ensure messages can flow between them. We assume the new provider communicates using RosettaNet.
4. Initiate and monitor the shipment via the logistics supply chain.
5. Coordinate the three freight forwarders to ensure a seamless end-to-end service, resulting in the crate being shipped from Bristol to Warsaw.

Semantic Web Services technology can be deployed throughout this lifecycle to automate or semi-automate what currently takes significant time and effort.

1. Service Discovery can be used to locate potential service providers, based on them advertising descriptions of their service capabilities.

2. Service Definition allows the refining of a service description to specify exactly what the provider and requestor agree the service should do.
3. Message and Protocol Mediation allow a new provider to be integrated and communicated with, even though it uses a different messaging standard.

We now describe how our scenario can be automated using semantic web services. A software agent acting on behalf of the company has detailed information about the transportation task which must be carried out. It contacts a discovery agent which has access to descriptions of services various organisations can provide, and asks for providers able to ship between Portsmouth and Gdansk. The discovery agent responds with a list of possible freight forwarders likely to be able to meet these requirements.

The software agent then selects one or more of the possible freight forwarders, and sends a more detailed description of the task it requires to be performed, including the date the shipment will arrive at Portsmouth, and the date it must reach Gdansk. The freight forwarders respond with lists of services they can offer which meet these requirements. For example, one forwarder may say that it has a ship leaving Portsmouth on the required day which will arrive in Gdansk the day before the deadline. It will also give the cost of placing a crate on that ship.

The requesting agent then selects one of the proposed services (possibly by interacting with a user to make the final decision) and informs the provider of the decision. Effectively, the two parties enter into an agreement at this point.

As the shipment takes place, it is coordinated by an exchange of messages between the two parties. The messages use an industry standard, RosettaNet, which describes the format and order of the messages. The exchange starts when the crate is about to arrive in Portsmouth, with a RosettaNet Advanced Shipment Notification being sent by the requestor to freight forwarder 2, and ends with the sending of a Proof of Delivery and Invoice by freight forwarder 2 when the crate arrives in Gdansk.

3 Overall System Architecture

The overall system architecture used in the demonstrator system is provided by the generic SWWS Technical Architecture. The underlying conceptual model is provided by the SWWS Conceptual Architecture [7]. Here, we summarise the technical architecture and relate it to the specific actors in our B2B scenario.

In Agent Technology research, a distinction is made between a *micro-architecture* and a *macro-architecture*. A micro-architecture is the internal component-based architecture of an individual entity within a community. A macro-architecture is the structure of the overall community, considering each entity within it as a black box. It is also helpful to consider this distinction in semantic web services. Initially, we will present the macro-architecture for our community. There are three possible roles that a software entity can have; service requestor agent, service provider agent and discovery provider agent.

A service requestor agent acts on behalf of an individual or organisation to procure a service. It receives a service requirement description from its owner, and interacts with other agents in an attempt to fulfil the requirement it has been given. It has some model, in an ontology, of the domain of the service and also has some model of the kind of actions that can be taken (through message exchange) in this domain. In our scenario, the Logistics Coordinator takes the role of service requestor agent in relationship with each of the Freight Forwarders.

A service provider agent is able to provide a service on behalf of an organisation. In our scenario, service provider agents represent the three freight forwarder companies used, as well as additional companies which could potentially be used by the logistics provider. It has a service offer description in some domain ontology (ideally, the same as the requestor agent), which gives an abstract description of services it can provide. In our scenario, for example, this would state that a company can ship crates from UK ports to Baltic ports. It also has a means to generate more concrete descriptions of the precise services it can deliver. (For example, a specific shipment of crate42 from Portsmouth to Gdansk on 25/03/05.) Furthermore, it has a formal description of the message protocol used to deliver the service. This includes mappings from the content of messages into concepts within the domain ontology. It also includes mappings from message exchange sequences into actions. In our scenario, a field in the initial Advance Shipment Notification (ASN) message might map onto the 'weight' attribute of the 'crate' concept within the domain. The sequence consisting of one party sending the ASN and the other party acknowledging receipt may correspond to a 'notify shipment' action in the domain ontology.

A discovery provider agent contains descriptions of service offers, together with references to provider agents able to provide these services. These service offer descriptions are all expressed in some domain ontology associated with the discovery provider agent. Within this ontology is a 'service description' concept which effectively acts as a template for the descriptions of services that the discovery provider can contain. In our scenario, the ontology defines concepts relevant to logistics and transportation, and the descriptions the discovery provider contains are descriptions of transportation services the freight forwarders are able to offer.

We illustrate the macro-architecture by describing the interactions which can take place between the different agents. These interactions are roughly in order of the service lifecycle progression [8] adopted by the conceptual architecture.

1.   Provider agent registering a capability with the discovery provider.
Initially, any service provider agent must register its service offer descriptions with the discovery provider using a simple message exchange protocol. It does this in terms of the ontology used by the discovery provider, and hence may require ontology mediation. In our scenario, each Freight Forwarder will register abstract descriptions of the services it can provide.

2.   Requestor agent finding possible providers.
Discovery takes place through a simple message exchange protocol between a service requestor agent and a discovery agent. The requestor agent sends a message containing a service requirement description, and the discovery agent responds with a message containing a list of URIs of service provider agents. These correspond to those provider agents with offer descriptions which match the service requirement description, according to the discovery agent's algorithm. In our scenario, the Logistics Coordinator will send a description of the shipment it requires – that it is from Portsmouth to Gdansk, it must arrive by 27th March, etc. It will receive back a list of all freight forwarders which have advertised a service capability compatible with these requirements, as e.g. one that covers all the Baltic Sea area with its shipping services.

3. Requestor and Provider agents define service.

Following discovery, the requestor agent exchanges messages with one or more provider agents to define the service it will receive, and to select which provider agent to use. In our architecture, we assume a single simple service definition protocol is used by all requestor and provider agents. Our simple protocol consists of two rounds of message exchange. Initially, the service requestor agent sends a service requirement description to each provider agent it is considering using. The provider agent replies with a list of (almost) concrete service descriptions of the services it is able to provide which meet the needs of the requestor. The requestor can select one of these, with the provider confirming the selection to the requestor. The confirm message contains a URI reference where the description of the choreographies, which will be used during service delivery, can be found. If the requestor does not select one within a certain time window, sending no response to the provider, this is taken as cancelling.

In our scenario, the Logistics Coordinator sends a description of the shipment it requires to one or more of the Freight Forwarders located at the previous stage. They respond with specific detailed descriptions of relevant shipment services – for example, one may state that the crate can be carried on a ship departing on 24th March at 3pm, with a cost of 30 euros. A given freight forwarder may provide several options at this stage. The Logistics Coordinator reviews these, and makes a selection (either automatically using stored preference information or, more likely, by providing the best options to a user who makes the final decision.)

4. Service Delivery

Service delivery starts when one party (depending on the choreography used) sends an initiating message. The choreography used at this stage will correspond to the sequence of messages specified by the RosettaNet or EDIFACT standard. Each service provider has a description of the service delivery choreography associated with each service it can provide. At the end of the service definition protocol, as a parameter of the *confirm* message, it informs the requestor of a URI which references this description. The requestor is then responsible for accessing this description, interpreting it and engaging in a message exchange with the provider which satisfies the requirements of the choreography described. Exactly how this is done will be described in section 5.

Having described the macro-architecture, we now turn to the micro-architecture. We look at two of the three roles that software entities can have – requestor agent and provider agent – and present a micro architecture for each. The micro architecture of the discovery service provider agent will be covered in section 4. Figure 2 illustrates our architecture for the service requestor agent. The application logic is responsible for decision making with regard to which service to select and how to make use of it. Normally, this will be integrated with back-end systems within the organisation which the service requestor agent represents. In our demonstrator, we provide a user interface to allow a user to make the decisions that would be made by such a system.

The first role of the application logic is to define a service requirement description for the service it needs. When this has been done, it passes the description to the discovery and definition component, which exchanges appropriate messages to do this. The message format and contents are prepared and passed to the transport routines for transmission via an appropriate transportation protocol. At points where a decision is required – namely, when one or more provider is chosen after discovery and when a service is selected – it is made by the application logic.

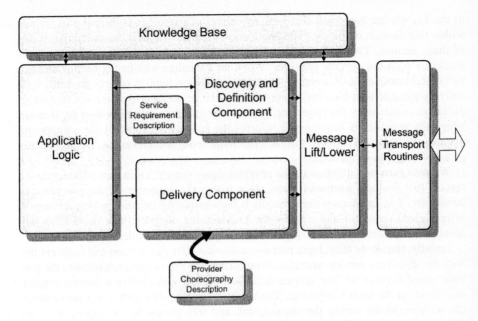

Fig. 2. Service Requestor Agent Micro-Architecture

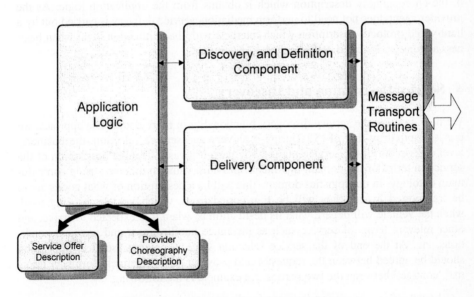

Fig. 3. Service Provider Agent Micro Architecture

When a service has been defined, the application logic initiates the delivery process by using the delivery module. The delivery module is able to carry out protocol mediation. It accesses the description of the choreography given by the service provider. This shows how message contents map into the domain ontology of the knowledge base, and also how sequences of messages correspond to actions within this domain ontology. The application logic can request the execution of one of these actions. This will result in the delivery module initiating an exchange of messages with the service provider. When an exchange terminates (either through successful completion or some failure) the application logic is informed of this. The delivery module also handles messages from the provider which are not part of an exchange initiated by the requestor. These correspond to actions within the domain which the provider is initiating. It informs the application logic of the actions and updates the knowledge base with relevant data from the messages. Details of this process are given in section 5.

We now turn our attention to the provider agent (figure 3). In our architecture we assume that protocol mediation takes place within the requestor, so the provider can be simpler. The application logic module is responsible for deciding which services to offer a given requestor and also for the provisioning of the service itself. This will usually be provided by back-end systems belonging to the provider's organisation.

Initially, the application logic prepares a service offer description and registers this with the discovery service provider. From that point on, in our architecture, the provider agent is reactive. The service definition module can receive a service requirement description from a requestor. The application logic then prepares a set of possible services which satisfy the requirement, and this is sent to the requestor. If the definition module receives a selection message from the requestor, it returns the URI of the choreography description which it obtains from the application logic. As the provider agent does not need to perform mediation, service delivery is carried out by a hard-wired protocol description which interacts with the application logic when business actions are required.

4 Service Description and Discovery

We now describe the service discovery functionality in more detail. The approach we use is inspired by that of [5]. During discovery and service selection, the business-level description of the service plays a key part. It gives a detailed description of the service in terms of the domain in which it provides value to the user, using some domain ontology. In our logistics domain, this will be a description of what goods are to be transported, where they will be transported from, which vehicle is being used, when the vehicle will depart, what its destination is, when it is expected to arrive, and other relevant terms of service such as insurance liability, cost and payment conditions, etc. At the end of the service selection stage, a concrete service description should be agreed between the requestor and provider, and effectively forms an informal 'contract' between the two parties. An example is the following:

$Contract \equiv$
  $Shipping \sqcap \exists startLocation.\{Portsmouth\} \sqcap \exists endLocation.\{Gdansk\} \sqcap$
  $\exists dateOfDeparture. =_{2005\text{-}03\text{-}24} \sqcap \exists dateOfArrival. =_{2005\text{-}03\text{-}26} \sqcap$
  $\exists item.\{SmallCargo\#typeA\} \sqcap \exists vehicle.\{CargoShip\#34\} \sqcap \exists price. =_{90} \sqcap$
  $\exists currency.\{Euro\} \sqcap \exists meansOfPayment.\{EuroCreditTransfer\}$

This concrete service description states that an item of small cargo will be carried on cargo ship 34 from Portsmouth to Gdansk, leaving on the 24th March and arriving on the 26th, and payment of 90 € will be made by credit transfer. It is expressed as an OWL-DL concept whose properties are restricted to specific values, allowing a unique configuration of the service. The terms used in this description are defined in a logistics domain ontology and in more generic ontologies for geography and vehicles.

As it stands, such a concrete description of a service is clearly inappropriate for advertising or discovery, as requests and adverts would have to include many such classes covering all acceptable service parameter configurations. Instead, requestors and providers abstract from concrete parameter information, switching to less specific class descriptions. In such abstract service descriptions they specify the set of concrete services that they are willing to accept. For example, a freight forwarder may advertise the following capability, using an OWL-DL based description approach for abstract service descriptions explained in [6].

$$S_p \equiv Shipping \sqcap \exists\, startLocation.EUPort \sqcap \exists\, endLocation.BalticPort \sqcap$$
$$\forall\, item.Container \sqcap \forall\, vehicle.Ship \sqcap$$
$$\exists\, meansOfPayment.(Cheque \sqcup BankTransfer)$$

This states that the service provider offers shipping services from EU ports to Baltic ports, can carry containers, and can accept payments by cheque or bank transfer. By using concepts and subconcepts to restrict the description appropriately, the service provider can give a precise view of the service it offers. It registers this with the discovery agent. Similarly, a requestor can describe the kind of service it needs;

$$S_r \equiv Shipping \sqcap \exists\, startLocation.\{Portsmouth\} \sqcap$$
$$\exists\, endLocation.\{Gdansk\} \sqcap \exists\, dateOfArrival. \leq_{2005\text{-}03\text{-}27} \sqcap$$
$$\exists\, item.CargoContainer \sqcap$$
$$\forall\, meansOfPayment.(CreditCard \sqcup BankTransfer)$$

This requests the shipping of a cargo container from Portsmouth to Gdansk, to arrive by the 27th March at the latest. Payment can be made by credit card or bank transfer. Hence, by using OWL-DL concepts, we can give descriptions of various granularities, from abstract service requests/offers to specific agreed parameter values in contracts.

When the discovery agent receives a service request, it returns the set of all service advertisements which intersect with the request. An advert and a request intersect if they specify at least one common concrete service. The discovery agent uses an internal DL reasoner (RACER [9]) to check for intersection. Full details of the inferencing mechanism are given in [6]. The list of services returned includes URIs referencing the service providers, allowing the requestor to make direct contact. A requestor then makes contact with one or more of them to select and agree a concrete service. In some domains, negotiation of parameters may be necessary at this stage [10]. However, in our domain it is adequate for a provider to offer a list of relevant concrete services to the requestor, and allow them to select one. Again, this functionality can be provided by using a DL reasoner, this time internally to the service provider.

5 Mediation During Service Execution

Mediation is essential in our scenario to allow the rapid integration of a new freight forwarder into a logistics chain. We now present an overview of the approach taken. For a detailed description, see [11]. Communication is required during the execution of the service, as the shipment is initiated and progresses, to coordinate the behaviour of the service requestor and provider. In our scenario, we assume that the logistics coordinator usually communicates with freight forwarders using EDIFACT, but must now use RosettaNet with its new provider.

Our approach to mediation is based around the insight that, even though there may be several different communications protocols used to communicate about a given task, it is often the case that the underlying models of the task that are implicit in these protocols are very similar to each other. In the case of the logistics domain, analysis of the EDIFACT, ANSI X12 and RosettaNet protocols found that the set of actions carried out to execute the task, and the sequencing constraints on them, are identical. Hence, an *abstract protocol* can be identified and abstracted from the specific communications protocols [12]. In our system, the application logic communicates with the mediation component in terms of the actions within the abstract protocol – it informs the mediation component when it wishes to initiate such an action, and is informed by the mediation component when the other party carries out an action. The abstract protocol is represented as concurrent processes described by finite state machines, which can be used by the mediation component to determine what actions are permitted at any given stage in the process. The actions used are given in Table 1.

Each action in the abstract protocol maps to some exchange of messages in a specific standard such as RosettaNet or EDIFACT. This mapping will vary from standard to standard. We refer to this mapping as a *concrete protocol* relating to a specific standard. For example, in RosettaNet, the informReadyForCollection action maps to a sequence consisting in the Logistics Coordinator sending an Advanced Shipment Notification message (with up to 3 re-sends if no response within half an hour), followed by it receiving a response from the Freight Forwarder. In EDIFACT, however, it maps to a three-way exchange consisting of a DESADV message, responded to by an EDIFACT::ACK, followed by a re-send of the DESADV message. A concrete protocol is represented as concurrent processes described by finite state machines, which are used by the mediation component to manage the exchange of messages when an action takes place. The finite state machines are encoded in RDF, with transitions between states encoded procedurally in JavaScript.

When the application logic wishes to initiate an action, it informs the mediation component. The mediation component checks that this action is permissible in the current state of the abstract protocol, and if it is, it executes the appropriate state machine within the concrete protocol. This will result in the sending and receiving of messages. On termination, the mediation component informs the application logic of the success or otherwise of the action. When the mediation component receives a message from the other party which does not correspond to an action it has initiated, it pattern-matches against the action mappings in the concrete protocol to identify which action the other party is initiating. (If the protocol is well-designed, this should be unique.) It then executes the appropriate concrete protocol to respond to this action, and informs the application logic to allow the service requestor to respond.

Table 1. Communicative acts involved in the execution of a logistics service

Communicative Act	Direc-tion	Communicative intent
informReadyForCollec-tion	LC to FF	Inform the FF that the shipment is available for collection.
requestShipmentStatus	LC to FF	Request an update of the shipment status from the FF.
informShipmentStatus	FF to LC	Inform the LC of the shipment status
informReadyToDeliver	FF to LC	Inform the LC that the FF is ready to deliver the shipment.
informShipmentDeliv-ered	FF to LC	Inform the LC (and provide proof) that the FF has infact delivered the shipment.
requestPayment	FF to LC	Request payment for delivering the shipment from the LC.

In addition to dealing with the message sequencing, the concrete protocol also contains data mappings for the syntax of the messages, showing how the different fields in the message correspond to different concepts in the domain ontology. When a message is received, content within that message is 'lifted' into an RDF knowledge base to become an instance of a concept in the logistics ontology. The application logic is able to read and assert information in this knowledge base as necessary. When a message needs to be transmitted by the mediation component, it 'lowers' appropriate concept instances within this knowledge base into an XML syntax appropriate to the chosen standard. The technology used to do this is described in [13]. Using this mediation technology, a requestor can communicate with different providers using different standards, while allowing the application logic to be encoded in terms of business actions. All it need do is insert the appropriate concrete protocol into its mediation component. Because we assume that the requestor is 'semantically enabled' (i.e. its internal logic uses RDF) the mediation component can be part of it. If it were not, mediation could take place as a semantically enabled intermediary agent using similar techniques. These alternative design decisions are discussed in [11].

During service execution, the freight forwarders' behaviour must be coordinated. For example, when the first is about to deliver the crate to Portsmouth docks, the second freight forwarder must be informed. This is achieved through a combination of the business logic and the mediation component. The actions involved are straightforward, and can be encoded as part of the business workflow. However, the messages involved are in different protocols, so require mediation. The first trucking company sends notification in EDIFACT. The mediation system recognizes that this message corresponds to an 'informReadyToDeliver' action, which the workflow identifies as requiring an 'informReadyForCollection' exchange with the shipment company. This is initiated, and the mediation component generates the appropriate RosettaNet messages. Specific data, such as the estimated time of delivery, are transferred from one message to the other through a process of lifting/lowering to/from the RDF database.

6 Implementation

The demonstrator system is implemented primarily in JAVA, as a distributed system with each requestor or provider agent as an independent entity. Different components internal to each agent access each other via Java RMI, to ease re-use of components beyond the demonstrator. Communication between agents takes place primarily through web service technology. To facilitate this, the agents are deployed on a web server platform consisting of Tomcat servlet container and Axis SOAP engine.

The Discovery Service is a self-contained web service that can be deployed remotely and accessed via a standard web service interface. The generic discovery service is linked to a repository containing OWL-DL service descriptions compliant to an early form of WSMO (http://www.wsmo.org/). Reasoning is performed by the RACER DL reasoner. The Freight Forwarders provide web service interfaces for the exchange of messages involved in service specification. Service execution requires the exchange of EDIFACT or RosettaNet messages, which takes place over a standard http port, as specified by either the EDIFACT or RosettaNet standard. The logistics coordinator interacts with the discovery service via its web service interface, and the freight forwarders both for service specification, via their web service interfaces, and service execution, via a standard http port using RosettaNet or EDIFACT messages in XML. The components within the logistics coordinator are implemented in JAVA, with the RDF knowledge base provided by HP's JENA semantic web application framework (http://jena.sourceforge.net/). Transformation of XML messages into RDF, and vice-versa, was carried out using a combination of XML Schema and the JENA rules engine. As noted above, the application logic is provided by a user interface allowing the user to make decisions the application logic would. If the system were used in a real environment, this functionality would be provided by a business workflow system integrated with the corporate IT systems.

7 Analysis and Related Work

The system presented in this paper is a demonstrator, not a deployed application. For this reason, certain simplifications have been made which need to be revisited. The first issue is that of representation; OWL does not have sufficient support for concrete domain predicates so that date ranges cannot properly be expressed and reasoned with. However RACER does support this feature and extensions to OWL such as OWL-E [14] provide a solution to this problem. Secondly, the system is not as secure as is necessary. The use of JavaScript in the choreography descriptions provides a security loophole; the system should provide a restricted JavaScript environment with a limited set of methods and reduced functionality. The messages sent during service execution should be packaged using S/MIME, to ensure non-repudiation. Thirdly, the system is not as robust as required – for example, conversations are not currently persistent objects, and hence will be lost if either party crashes. These issues require enhancements of the system, but do not invalidate the underlying design, and we are confident that they can be carried out straightforwardly.

If the system is to be deployed, it needs to be integrated with the internal workflow and decision support systems of the various service requestors and providers. Currently, these decisions are made by the user, using a bespoke user interface geared around the specific scenario described in this paper. The ideal approach to integration would be to have all internal systems re-engineered to communicate with each other (and the SWS components) using RDF data in a shared enterprise knowledge base – however, this is unlikely to be acceptable in the short term! Bespoke translation of relevant data into/out of RDF using the lifting tool would be more straightforward.

The approach followed for discovery based on semantic service descriptions works in a relatively small and closed environment, where parties refer to well defined and settled domain ontologies when specifying their service descriptions. However, it does not scale to an open environment in which parties use arbitrary ontological vocabularies that are not connected. This would require ontology mediation during discovery.

The approach adopted in this demonstrator is strongly influenced by architectural work in multi agent systems. Adept [15] was one of the first multi-agent systems to use a service agreement between provider and requestor. The role of contracts between requestors and providers has been incorporated in a semantic-web framework in the SweetDeal system [16]. Our approach to representing contracts is not as expressive as that used in SweetDeal, and it appears that the non-monotonicity they provide is not required in our domain. Trastour et. al. [8] describe the B2B lifecycle in terms of transformations of a DL contract, which has strongly influenced our approach.

Trastour et. al. [17] augment RosettaNet PIPs with partner-specific OWL constraints to determine if parties have compatible processes, and automatically propose modifications if not. This is a simple application of semantic web technology which can ease, but not automate, the linking of two business partners using RosettaNet.

Work on semantic web services provides approaches to service discovery (e.g. [4]) and generation and execution of composite services (e.g. [18]), however the majority of this work focuses on one specific part of the service lifecycle and so does not provide an integrated solution which can be applied to real problems. WSMX [19] is an exception to this, in that it provides an execution framework for semantic web services throughout the lifecycle. While promising, it does not yet provide protocol mediation capabilities or rich business-level descriptions. IRS-II [20] also supports a service lifecycle, but focuses on the composition of simple web services rather than choreography of complex business services.

8 Business Value of the System and Conclusions

If the system, enhanced as described above, were deployed in a business context it would have significant benefits. Specifically;

- By performing service discovery using detailed descriptions of capabilities, it is possible to rapidly locate many freight forwarders able to offer the service required. Because the service description is structured and detailed, it eliminates the many 'false positives' that a yellow-pages style service (or UDDI) would give. This will save a substantial amount of time, and therefore money, during the search for providers. Furthermore, it will increase the visibility of each provider, so will benefit them provided they offer a competitive service.

- By providing semi-automated assistance during the service selection phase, the system replaces a large number of phone calls with a simple selection of contract by the user. This again reduces time. Because it significantly reduces the effort needed to check out each possible freight forwarder, it allows a user to make a wider search of the options and therefore is likely to result in a better final choice.

- By allowing the service requestor to adapt its protocol to communicate with the service provider, the system dramatically reduces the time and effort required to integrate the two parties. Since integration can take months currently, this results in a very substantial cost saving. Furthermore, it means that the choice of service provider becomes far more flexible, as the time and effort of integration no longer results in lock in. This makes it easier to open up logistics chains to competitive tender where appropriate, with the resultant possibility of reducing costs further.

While the demonstrator is focussed around logistics, and so is equipped with ontologies appropriate to this domain, the software developed could be applied to other domains of B2B interaction and integration if given the appropriate ontologies and knowledge. For example, it can be used in purchasing, order management, billing and other areas of supply chain management. The protocol mediation, data mediation and discovery components are designed to be used independently of each other, and can be applied outside the domain of B2B in other semantic web service applications, providing further potential value.

In this paper, we have presented a demonstrator system using semantic web services technology which allows a requestor to discover logistics service providers, select appropriate logistics services, coordinate the services to form a composite service chain, and communicate with the service providers using arbitrary protocols through dynamic mediation. As far as we are aware, this is the first system implemented which manages the full service lifecycle of a realistic business example. The demonstrator itself is not of product quality, and needs augmenting to be more secure and robust before deployment. However, we believe our results demonstrate the feasibility of this approach to B2Bi problems in general, and expect the use of dynamic integration via semantic descriptions to become an important industrial technique in the near future.

Acknowledgements. Thanks to Zlaty Marinova, Dan Twining, Peter Radokov, Silvestre Losada, Oscar Corcho, Jorge Pérez Bolaño and Juan Miguel Gomez for work on the system implementation, and all on the SWWS project for stimulating discussions.

References

1. McIlraith, S. and Martin, D.: Bringing Semantics to Web Services. IEEE Intelligent Systems, 18(1) (2003) 90-93
2. Paolucci, M. and Sycara, K.: Autonomous Semantic Web Services. IEEE Internet Computing, (September 2003) 34-41
3. Fensel, D. and Bussler, C.: The Web Service Modeling Framework WSMF. Electronic Commerce: Research and Applications, 1 (2002) 113-117
4. Paolucci, M., Kawamura, T., Payne, T.R. and Sycara, K: Semantic Matching of Web Service Capabilities. Proc. International Semantic Web Conference (2002) 333-347

5. Trastour, D., Bartolini, C. and Gonzalez-Castillo,J.: A Semantic Web Approach to Service Description for Matchmaking of Services. In Proceedings of the Semantic Web Working Symposium, Stanford, CA, USA, July 30 - August 1, 2001
6. Grimm, S., Motik, B. and Preist, C.: Variance in eBusiness Service Discovery. Proc. of the ISWC Workshop on Semantic Web Services, 2004.
7. Preist, C.: A Conceptual Architecture for Semantic Web Services. Proc. 3rd International Semantic Web Conference (2004) 395-409
8. Trastour, D., Bartolini, C. and Preist, C.: Semantic Web Support for the B2B E-commerce pre-contractual lifecycle. Computer Networks 42(5) (August 2003) 661-673
9. Haarslev,V. and Moller, R.: Description of the RACER System and its Applications. Proc. International Workshop on Description Logics (DL-2001), Stanford, USA, 2001.
10. He, M., Jennings, N.R. and Leung, H: On Agent Mediated Electronic Commerce. IEEE Transactions on Knowledge and Data Engineering 15(4) (2003) 985-1003
11. Williams, S.K., Battle, S.A. and Esplugas Cuadrado, J.: Protocol Mediation for Adaptation in Semantic Web Services. HP Labs Technical Report HPL-2005-78
12. Esplugas Cuadrado, J., Preist, C. and Williams, S.: Integration of B2B Logistics using Semantic Web Services. Proc. Artificial Intelligence: Methodology, Systems, and Applications, 11th International Conference, (2004)
13. Battle, S.A.: Round Tripping between XML and RDF. Poster Proc. of ISWC 2004.
14. Jeff Z. Pan and Ian Horrocks. OWL-E: Extending OWL with Expressive Datatype Expressions. IMG Technical Report, School of Computer Science, the University of Manchester, April 2004
15. Jennings, N.R., Faratin, P.,Johnson,M.J., O'Brien,P. and Wiegand, M.E.: Using Intelligent Agents to Manage Business Processes. Proceedings of the First Int. Conference on the Practical Application of Intelligent Agents and Multi-Agent Technology (1996) 345-360
16. Grosof, B. and Poon, T.: SweetDeal: Representing Agent Contracts with Exceptions using Semantic Web Rules, Ontologies and Process Descriptions. International Journal of Electronic Commerce 8(4):61-98 (2004)
17. Trastour, D., Preist, C. and Coleman, D.: Using Semantic Web Technology to Enhance Current Business-to-Business Integration Approaches. Proc. 7th Enterprise Distributed Object Computing Conference, 2003, p222-231
18. McIlraith, S. and Son, T.C.: Adapting Golog for Composition of Semantic Web Services. Proc. 8th International Conference on Knowledge Representation and Reasoning, 2002, p482-493
19. Oren, E., Wahler, A., Schreder, B., Balaban, A., Zaremba, M., and Zaremba, M.: Demonstrating WSMX – Least Cost Supply Management. Proc. Workshop on WSMO Implementations, 2004.
20. Motta, E., Domingue, J., Cabral, L., and Gaspari, M.: IRS-II: A Framework and Infrastructure for Semantic Web Services. Proc. 2nd International Semantic Web Conference, 2003, p306-318

A Semantic Search Engine for the International Relation Sector

L. Rodrigo[1], V.R. Benjamins[1], J. Contreras[1], D. Patón[1], D. Navarro[1], R. Salla[1],
M. Blázquez[1], P. Tena[2], and I. Martos[2]

[1] Intelligent Software Components, S.A.
{lrodrigo, rbenjamins, jcontreras,
dpaton, dnavarro, rsalla}@isoco.com
www.isoco.com
[2] Real Instituto Elcano
{pilar.tena, isabelmartos}@r-i-elcano.org
www.realinstitutoelcano.org

Abstract The Royal Institute Elcano[1] (Real Instituto Elcano) in Spain is a prestigious independent political institute whose mission is to comment on the political situation in the world focusing on its relation to Spain. As part of its dissemination strategy it operates a public website. In this paper we present and evaluate the application of a *semantic* search engine to improve access to the Institute's content: instead of retrieving documents based on user queries of keywords, the system accepts queries in natural language and returns answers rather than links to documents. Topics that will be discussed include ontology construction, automatic ontology population, semantic access through a natural language interface and a failure analysis.

1 Introduction

Worldwide there are several prestigious institutes that comment on the political situation in the world, such as the UK's *Royal Institute for International Affairs* (www.riia.org), or the Dutch *Institute for International Relations* (www.clingendael.nl). In Spain, the *Real Instituto Elcano* (Royal Institute Elcano, www.realinstitutoelcano.org) is fulfilling this role. The institute provides several types of written reports where they discuss the political situation in the world, with a focus on events relevant for Spain. The reports are organized in different categories, such as Economy, Defense, Society, Middle East, etc. In a special periodic report - the "Barometer of the Royal Institute Elcano" - the Institute comments on how the rest of the world views Spain in the political arena. Access to the content is provided by categorical navigation and a traditional full text search engine. While full text search engines are helpful instruments for information retrieval, in domains where relations are important, those techniques fall short. For instance, a keyword-based search engine will have a hard time to find the answer to a question such as: "Governments of which countries have a favorable attitude toward the US-led armed intervention in Iraq?" since the crux of answering this question resides in "understanding" the relation "has-favourable-attitude-toward".

---

[1] Juan Sebastián Elcano was a Spanish explorer, who commanded back home the first successful expedition to circumnavigate the globe in 1522.

Y. Gil et al. (Eds.): ISWC 2005, LNCS 3729 , pp. 1002–1015, 2005.

In this paper we present and evaluate a semantic search engine that accepts natural language questions to access content produced by the Institute.

In Section 2, we briefly describe the ontology of the International Relations domain. Section 3 details how we automatically populate the ontology with instances. Then, in Section 4, present the semantic search engine, and how we automatically establish relations between the Institute documents and the (instances of the) ontology. In Section 5, we provide a failure analysis of the system based on a test with unknown users. Finally, in Section 6 we provide conclusions.

2   An Ontology of International Affairs

When searching for a particular data, looking for a concrete answer to a precise question, a standard search engine that retrieves documents based on matching keywords falls short. First of all, it does not satisfy the primary need of the user, which is finding a well-defined data, and provides a collection of documents that the user must traverse, looking for the desired information. Besides, not all of the retrieved documents may contain the appropriate answer, and some of the documents that do contain it, may not be included in the collection. These drawbacks seem to suggest a change in the search paradigm, evolving from the extraction of whole documents, to the information contained in those documents. This approach, however, is not feasible in all conditions. It is not affordable to build such a search engine for general purpose, but only for limited, well-defined domains. This is the case of the semantic search engine developed for the Real Instituto Elcano, which focuses on the topics covered by the reports written by the institute analysts, this is, international politics.

In order to be able to analyse the documents, and reach the sufficient "understanding" of them to be able to answer the users questions, the system relies on a representation of the main concepts, their properties and the relations among them in the form of an ontology. This ontology provides the system with the necessary knowledge to understand the questions of the users, provide the answers, and associate it a set of documents that mention the concept of the answer. Based on the ontology, each document gets its relevant concepts annotated and linked to the representing concept or instance in the ontology, allowing a user to browse from a document to the information of a concept he is interested in, and backwards, from the ontology to any of the reports that mention that concept.

2.1   Ontology Design

An ontology is a shared and common understanding of some domain that can be communicated across people and computers [6, 7, 3, and 8]. Ontologies can therefore be shared and reused among different applications [5]. An ontology can be defined as a formal, explicit specification of a shared conceptualization [6, 3]. "Conceptualization" refers to an abstract model of some phenomenon in the world by having identified the relevant concepts of that phenomenon. "Explicit" means that the type of concepts used, and the constraints on their use are explicitly defined. "Formal" refers to the fact that the ontology should be machine-readable. "Shared" reflects the notion that an ontology captures consensual knowledge, that is, it is not private to some individual, but accepted by a group. An ontology describes the subject matter using the notions of concepts, instances, relations, functions, and axioms. Concepts in the ontology are organized in taxonomies through which inheritance mechanisms can be applied. It is our experience that especially the social part for building a commonly agreed ontology is not easy [2].

Based on interviews with experts of the Elcano Institute, we used the CIA world factbook (http://www.cia.gov/cia/publications/factbook/) as the basis for the design of the ontology of International Affairs. The CIA fact book is a large online repository with actual information on most countries of the world, along with relevant information in the fields of geography, politics, society, economics, etc.

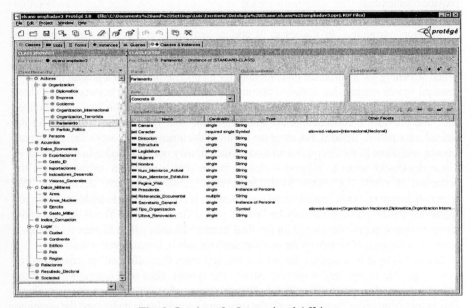

Fig. 1. Ontology for International Affairs

We have used the competency questions approach [10] to determine the scope and granularity of the domain ontology. The ontology consists of several top level classes, some of which are *"Place"* (representing geographical places such as countries, cities, buildings, etc.), *"Agent"* (extracted from WordNet [11], representing entities that can execute actions modifying the domain such as persons or organizations), *"Events"* (time expressions and events), and *"Relations"* (common class for any kind of relations between concepts).

Without instances information, the ontology contains about 85 concepts and 335 attributes (slots, properties). The ontology has been constructed using Protégé [9]. Fig. 1 shows a fragment of the ontology in Protégé.

3 Automatic Annotation

One of the challenges for the success of the Semantic Web is the availability of a critical mass of semantic content [17]. Semantic annotation tools play a crucial role at upgrading the actual web content into semantic content, that can be exploited by semantic applications. In this context we developed the Knowledge Parser ®, a system able to extract data from online sources populating specific domain ontologies, adding new or modifying existing knowledge facts or instances. The Semantic Web community often calls this process as semantic annotation (or just annotation).

The Knowledge Parser ® offers a software platform that combines different technologies for information extraction, driven by extraction strategies that allow the optimal technology combination application to each source type based on the domain ontology definition.

Ontology population from unstructured sources can be considered as the problem of extracting information from the source, its assignation to the appropriate location in the ontology, and finally, its coherent insertion in the ontology. The first part deals with the information extraction and document interpretation issues. The second part deals with the information annotation, in the sense of adding semantics to the extracted information, according to domain information and pre-existing strategies. The last part is in charge of populating, i.e., inserting and consolidating the extracted knowledge into the domain ontology. The three phases can be seen in the architecture of the system, illustrated in Fig. 2.

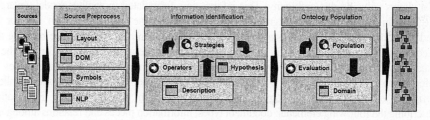

Fig. 2. Overview of the extraction and population process

3.1 Information Extraction

The KP system at present handles HTML pages, and there are plans to extend it to handle also PDF, RTF, and some other popular formats.

To be able to capture as much information as possible from the source document, KP analyzes it using four different processors, each one focusing on different aspects: the plain text processor, the layout processor, the HTML source processor an the natural language processor.

The plain text source interpretation supports the usage of regular expressions matching techniques. The usage of these kind of expressions constitutes an easy way of retrieving data in the case of stable, well known pages. If the page suffers frequent changes the regular expression becomes useless.

It is very common that even if documents of the same domain have very similar visual aspect they have a completely different internal code structure. Most of the online banks offer a position page where all the personal accounts and their balance are shown. These pages have very similar visual aspect, but their source code is completely different. The KP system includes layout interpretation of HTML sources, which allows to determine if certain pieces of information are visually located above or under, right or left, in column or in row, etc. of another piece of information.

In addition to HTML renderization of the source code in a visual model, the KP system needs to process the HTML elements in order to browse through the sources. The source description may include a statement that some information is a valid HTML link (e.g., a country name in a geopolitical portal), and when activated it drives to another document (a country description).

Finally, the fourth model tries to retrieve information from the texts present in the HTML pages. To do that, the user describes the pieces he is interested in in terms of linguistic properties and the relations among them (verbal or nominal phrases, coordinations, conjunctions, appositions, etc.)

3.2 Information Annotation

Once the document is parsed using different and complementary paradigms, there appears the challenge of assigning the extracted information piece to the correct place in the domain ontology. This task is called annotation, since it is equivalent to wrap up the information piece with the corresponding tag from the ontology schema.

The annotation of information is not direct in most of the cases. For instance, a numeric data extracted from the description of a country can be catalogued as the country population, the land area, or its number of unemployed people. It is necessary to have some extra information that allows reducing this ambiguity. This information, formulated in another model, enlarges the domain ontology with background knowledge, the same way the human use for its understanding. The extraction system needs to know, for example, that in online banking the account balance usually appears in the same visual row as the account number, or that the is usually followed by a currency symbol. This kind of information describing the pieces of information expected in the source and the relations among them is formalized in a, so called, *wrapping ontology*. This ontology supports the annotation process holding information describing the following elements: document types, information pieces and relations among the pieces (any kind of relation detectable by the text, layout, html or nlp models).

According to the domain ontology and the background information added, the system should construct possible assignments from the information extracted to the ontology schema. The result of this process is a set of hypotheses about data included in the source and their correspondence with the concepts, properties and relations in the domain ontology. During the construction process the system can evaluate how much the extracted information fits the information description.

The different ways in which hypothesis can be generated and evaluated are called strategies. Strategies are pluggable modules that according to the source description invoke operators. In the current version of the system there are two possible strategies available. For system usages where the response time is critical we use the greedy strategy. This strategy produces only one hypothesis per processed document using heuristics to solve possible ambiguities in data identification. On the other hand when quality of annotation is a priority and requirements on response time are less important we use a backtracking strategy. This strategy produces a whole set of hypothesis to be evaluated and populated into the domain ontology.

3.3 Ontology Population

The task of automatically filling a database or an ontological semantic model is non trivial, especially when the information comes from unstructured sources, where it may happen that the same information is repeated, spread over different places, or even inconsistent. For automatic ontology population, there is a need for a specialized module performing intelligent information integration tasks. In our architecture it is called IPO (Intelligent Population of Ontologies).

When the system has selected an information to be included in the ontology, there are different possible actions to take, which are: create a new instance with the information; insert found data into an existing instance; overwrite a value in an existing instance or, finally, relate two existing instances.

At this point, there is a key decision which affects the action to be taken: is the data found already present in the ontology, even under a different name? For that purposes, we have developed a library, SmartMatching, that decides whether two names refer to the same entity, and whether two instances in the ontology refer to the same concept in the real world. For example, it can decide that George W. Bush, Mr. Bush and Bush, G., all refer to the same person, and at the entity level, it can decide whether two entities holding economical data may be similar enough to suspect that they may belong to the same country (and therefore need to be unified into one single instance) or not.

The IPO module has to decide what hypothesis to insert into the domain ontology. Even if the input hypothesis is ordered from the most (the one that fulfils the source description with the highest degree) to the least probable, it does not take into account yet the consequences that introducing the data in the ontology may have. The best hypothesis may cause inconsistencies or may require many changes in the domain ontology. So there is a final decision step, in which one of the hypotheses generated in the previous step is populated in the ontology. For that reason the IPO makes simulations of the best ranked hypotheses and evaluates their suitability for final population according to their population cost. The population cost is calculated as the amount of changes needed in the domain ontology when filling new hypothesis. It means that hypothesis that contradicts and makes inconsistent the domain ontology has higher cost that the hypothesis that fits directly.

This way of disambiguation assumes that the information that is stored in the source intents to communicate something consistent and coherent with the information already stored in the domain ontology. On the base of the Shannon's information theory [Shannon] we understand that the online sources encode information looking to its easy understanding by the reader. The domain and the wrapping (description) ontology together try to reconstruct the possible mental model of the reader and guide the KP system in the task of its understanding. If the mental model is correct we assume that the cheapest interpretation (the one that require the smallest amount processing effort) is the correct one. We find here an application of the Occam's razor principle.

3.4 International Affairs Ontology Population

Using the Knowledge Parser system, we populated the ontology of international affairs, designed as described in Section 2.1. The domain experts selected four sources where they could find most of the information that they used on their daily basis. These four sources are:

· CIA World Factbook (http://www.cia.gov/cia/publications/factbook/).
· Nationmaster (http://www.nationmaster.com)
· Cidob (http://www.cidob.org/bios/castellano/indices/indices.htm).
· International Policy Institute for Counter-Terrorism (http://www.ict.org.il).

The set of sources is, of course, not exhaustive, but tries to follow the 80-20 rule, where a few sites cover most of the knowledge needed by the users of the system.

For each of the sites, a wrapping ontology was developed, describing the data contained in it, the way to detect it and the relations among them. The development of these kind of descriptive ontologies is at present done by experienced knowledge engineers considerably fast, but it is in the plans for future advances to develop some kind of tools that will allow the domain experts to describe a new source and populate the ontology with its contents themselves. As a result of this process, we evolved from an empty ontology to an ontology with more than 60.000 facts.

4   The International Relations Portal

Modeling the domain in the form of an ontology is one of the most difficult and time consuming tasks in developing a semantic application, but an ontology itself is just a way of representing information and provides no added value for the user. What becomes really interesting for the user is the kind of applications (or features inside an application) that an ontology allows.

Following, we will present how we have exploited the semantic domain description, in the form of enhanced browsing of the already existing reports, and a semantic search engine integrated in the international relations portal, interconnected between them.

4.1   Establishing Links Between Ontology Instances and Elcano Documents

The portal holds two different representations for the same knowledge, the written reports from the institute analysts and the domain ontology, which are mutually independent. However, one representation can enrich the other, and vice versa. For example, an analyst looking for the GDP of a certain country may also be interested in reading some of the reports where this figure is mentioned, and, in the same way, someone who is reading an analysis about the situation in Latin America may want to find out the political parties present in the countries of the region.

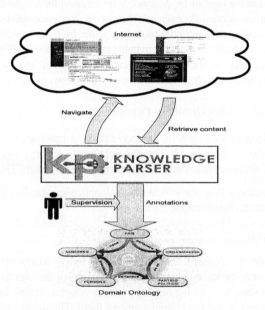

Fig. 3. Domain ontology population process

Trying to satisfy these interests, we inserted links between the instances in the ontology and the documents of the Institute. The links are established in both directions. Each concept in the ontology has links (references) to the documents where it is mentioned, and, viceversa, each document has links that connect every concept mentioned in the article with the corresponding concept in the ontology. This way, the user can make a question, for example, *"¿Quién es el presidente de EEUU?"* (*"Who is the USA president?"*), and gets the information of the instance in the ontology corresponding to George Bush. From this screen, he can follow the links to any of the instances appearing in the text, George Bush being one of them. This process can be seen in Figure 4, where the information about George Bush in the ontology contains a set of links, and the document seen can be reached following one of them.

To generate these links a batch process is launched, that generates at the same time both the links in the ontology and the links in the articles.

At present, the process of adding links is a batch process that opens a document, and looks for appearances of the name of any of the instances of the ontology in that text. For any matching, it adds a link in the text that takes to the instance in the ontology and link in the ontology with a pointer to the text. To evaluate the matching, not only the exact name of the instance is used, but also the possible synonyms, contained in an external thesaurus, which can be easily extended by any user, i.e., the domain expert.

Future plans include the automation of this task, so that any new document in the system (the institute produces new reports on a daily basis) is processed automatically by the link generator tool and the new links are transparently included in the system.

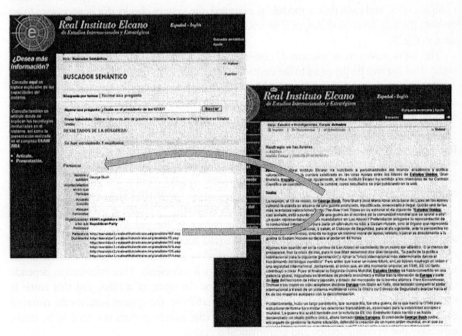

Fig. 4. Links between the instances and the documents

4.2 The Semantic Search Engine

With the objective of making available to the users the knowledge contained in the ontology in a comfortable, easy to use fashion, we also designed a semantic search engine. Using this engine, users can ask in natural language (Spanish, in this case) for a concrete data, and the system retrieves the data from the ontology and presents the results to the user.

The general steps that the system carries out with every query are the following:

· First of all, the user question is interpreted, extracting the relevant concepts from the sentence.

· Second, that set of concepts is used to build a query that is launched against the ontology.

· Finally, the results are presented to the user.

Each of these steps will further detailed in the following sections.

4.2.1 Sentence Analysis

When users go to the web searching for data, they expect a fast, almost immediate answer. If the process takes too long, the system just gives an impression of being unusable and the user will try with an alternative search engine. This is a serious drawback for these kind of systems that require heavy processing before being able to offer an answer to the user. Therefore, the process of obtaining an interpretation of the sentence of the user is optimized trying to provide an answer as fast as possible, sacrificing somehow the depth of the processing.

The module is organized as a cascade of modules, from the most simple to the most complex ones, and each time a module is executed, the system checks if it is necessary to go on with the following modules, or if an answer can be already delivered. This process can be seen in Fig. 5.

The input sentence is tokenized, obtaining a list of words, numbers, and punctuation signs. This list will be the input to the cascade of modules.

The first module detects and marks the words that do not contribute any relevant meaning to the sentence (known as *stopwords*), so that from the very first moment those words are ignored by the rest of the modules.

After every module execution, the system checks if the information collected is enough to provide an answer. To take this decision, the system checks if every token in the sentence is either marked as a stopword, as a punctuation sign or has any semantic information attached. If any of the tokens of the sentence is not annotated, the processing continues with the next module.

The second module, the first one that attaches semantic information, uses the ontology as a gazetteer. Basically, it goes through all the names in the ontology (names of classes, attributes, symbols and instances), taking also into account the synonyms files that were afore mentioned, and checks if any of them appear in the sentence. If so, it attaches to the word the information of the element of the ontology it represents. This information depends on which kind of element was recognized. If it was the name of a class, just that name is enough, while if the word matched the value of an attribute, the system attaches the name of the class, attribute and exact value in the ontology (the matching does not need to be exact, especially due to capitalization and grammatical accents).

The next module uses some shallow linguistic techniques to broaden the detection possibilities. The first thing that the system checks is if any of the words are operators that need to be included in the query. At this moment, only negative (*no*) and comparative operators (*mayor que*, *menor que*, *igual*) are implemented, but future plans include temporal operators also. If this does not complete the sentence analysis, the system verifies if any of the tokens that could not be analyzed is a number, and if so, marks it as such. In the last step of this module, as the word in the sentence that could not be recognized does not match any of the terms contained in the ontology (it was checked in the previous step), the system looks for variations of the word. First of all, it tries with the lemmas of the words in the sentence. This is of special interest in a highly flexible language as Spanish when dealing with verbal forms. Finally, the last step is to check if any of the words that still have not been understood may have been misspelled. For this purpose, we have adapted a spelling corrector, *ispell* [20], adding to the corrector dictionary all the vocabulary contained in the ontology, so that it is optimized for the application domain. The corrections suggested by ispell are checked by the second module, to see if they appear in the ontology and, if so, the word is considered misspelled and the appropriate information is attached.

Finally, if there is still some token that has no information one last "desperate" process is launched that, using regular expressions, checks if the word is part of the name of any element of the ontology. This is quite helpful, as names in the ontology (particularly proper names) are written in their full form, while they are usually referred in a shorter way, for example, users will tipically write "Washington" while the name of the city in the ontology is "Washington D.C.".

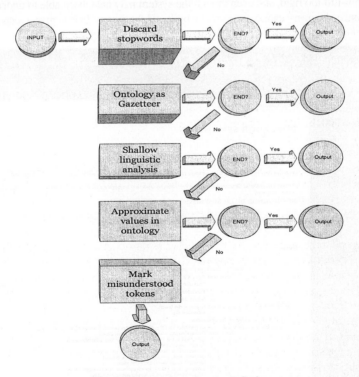

Fig. 5. Steps in the sentence analysis

If all the modules have been executed and any token remains unannotated, the token is marked as misunderstood, and the analysis finishes, returning the tokenized sentence with the corresponding information attached. Every token in the user question, therefore, will have some kind of information attached, which may range from a "Stopword" tag, a "Not understood" tag, or (hopefully) the semantic information that the system could build for it.

4.2.2 Quezry Construction

While human language is ambiguous most of the times, not mentioning facts that the speaker and the listener share, an ontology query language needs to explicitly mention all the facts that take part in the query. From the sentence analysis phase, the system gets a set of spots in the ontology, some classes, attributes and instances that the user has mentioned, but that is not enough to build a query. It is necessary to guess what kind of relations hold between those elements (that the speaker did not mention), so that the query can be well constructed. To achieve this, the system looks for the paths inside the ontology that connect all the elements mentioned in the sentence. Once a full path is found, a query can be constructed.

The process that is carried out at present to calculate the path does not consider possible permutations in the order of the tokens in the sentence, and calculates the minimum distance from one element to the next, not taking into account minimum global paths. This is not the optimal algorithm, but once again efficiency has been preferred to efficacy. Nevertheless, improvement plans include this module as one of the main options, as sometimes the algorithm is just too rigid, and even though the system may have been able to understand the user sentence, the query cannot be correctly built and the system fails to give a response.

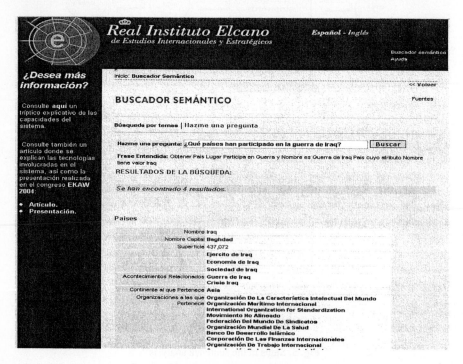

Fig. 6. Results presentation

4.2.3 Results Presentation

Once the system has got one or more URIs that represent the result to the question, the information contained by these URIs is presented to the user as tables with the information contained in the ontology. An example of a visualization of results can be seen in Fig. 6.

5 Failure Analysis

The system has been tested during one month in the context of the W3C Spanish standards tour[2]. The scenario for this external evaluation was the following. Users were given a brief introduction to the system capabilities and functions, and then they could freely interact with it. One hundred utterances were collected from unknown, spontaneous users.

Summarizing the general processing of the system, depicted in Section 4, the system first tries to understand the natural language, translating it to an internal representation based on the ontology, and then tries to build a query that retrieves the instances from the ontology that satisfy the user question. These instances are finally presented to the user as an answer. If the system is not able to complete any of these two steps, it will not be able to offer a response. If this happens, the user will be given the option to redirect the search to an standard search engine, and, moreover, if the system detects that some words were not properly understood it also notifies the user about the problem and gives him the possibility to rephrase the sentence with new words.

The two possible sources for preventing the system from giving an answer have been explicitly identified in the results table, to be able to point out the one that is responsible for a greater number of errors.

Finally, answers classified as "Wrong result" denote an error in the system. It has been able to process the question and thinks that it is providing a sensible answer, but the answer does not correspond to the question. This kind of malfunctioning comes from design or implementation bugs which can be located at any level, in the ontology, in the sentence analysis, or in the query construction and should be studied individually to uncover the reasons.

Table 1. Evaluation figures

| | Correct | No result | | Wrong result | TOTAL |
		NL error	Query generation error		
All Sentences	46	24	21	9	100
Domain sentences	46 (63.01%)	3 (4.11%)	17 (23.28%)	7 (9.59%)	73

From the figures in Table 1, we can conclude two main points. The search engine is clearly domain specific, and only if users understand the implications of this fact will they be able to use the system successfully. This is suggested by the dramatic decrease of errors (specially in the NL) when only domain specific sentences are

---

[2] http://www.w3c.es/gira/info/intro.html.en

considered. Additionally, this decrease suggest that the sources for data acquisition, that implicitly define the domain of the engine, should be chosen with great care and in agreement with the domain experts. The more sources that can be added, the more robust the system will behave.

We can also conclude that the second phase of the analysis, the query construction is at present the weakest link in the chain as it is not flexible enough to ensure that every well understood question will be correctly converted to the appropriate query. This point constitutes one of the future lines of improvements, and we will focus on it in the short term.

6 Related Work

Our Knowledge Parser is related to several other initiatives in the area of automatic annotation for the Semantic Web, including KIM [12], which is based on GATE [13], Annotea [14] of W3C., Amilcare [15] of Sheffield University, and AeroDAML [16]. For an overview of those approaches and others, see [4]. All approaches use NLP as an important factor to extract semantic information. Our approach is innovative in the sense that it combines four different techniques for Information Extraction in a generic, scalable and open architecture. The state of the art of most of these approaches is still not mature enough (few commercial deployments) to provide concrete comparison in terms of performance and memory requirements.

7 Conclusions

A semantic search engine for a closed domain was presented. The figures of the evaluation are promising, as more than 60% of the spontaneous questions are understood and correctly answered when these belong to the application domain. However, there are still some things to improve, such as the automatic link generation, a more flexible mechanism for building queries, an automated process to generate complete synonym files from linguistic resources, just to mention a few of them. It would also be of a high interest to completely decouple the search engine from the domain information, which are now lightly connected, in order to be able to apply the semantic search engine to a new domain just by replacing the domain ontology and the synonyms files.

The semantic search engine is, at the same time, a proof of the utility and applicability of the Knowledge Parser ® which will also be further developed in future projects.

Acknowledgements

Part of this work has been funded by the European Commission in the context of the project Esperonto Services IST-2001-34373, SWWS IST-2001-37134, SEKT IST-2003-506826 and by the Spanish government in the scope of the project: Buscador Semántico, Real Instituto Elcano (PROFIT 2003, TIC). The natural language software used in this application is licensed from Bitext (www.bitext.com). For ontology management we use JENA libraries from HP Labs (http://www.hpl.hp.com/semweb) and Sesame (http://www.openrdf.org/).

References

1. Gómez-Pérez A, et al (2003) Ontological Engineering. Springer-Verlag. London, UK.
2. V. R. Benjamins, et al. (KA)2: Building ontologies for the internet: a mid term report. International Journal of Human-Computer Studies, 51(3):687–712, 1999.
3. W. N. Borst. Construction of Engineering Ontologies. PhD thesis, University of Twente, 1997.
4. Contreras et al. D31: Annotation Tools and Services, Esperonto Project: www.esperonto.net
5. A. Farquhar, et al. The ontolingua server: a tool for collaborative ontology construction. International Journal of Human-Computer Studies, 46(6):707–728, June 1997.
6. T. R. Gruber. A translation approach to portable ontology specifications. Knowledge Acquisition, 5:199–220, 1993.
7. N. Guarino. Formal ontology, conceptual analysis and knowledge representation. International Journal of Human-Computer Studies, 43(5/6):625–640, 1995. Special issue on The Role of Formal Ontology in the Information Technology.
8. G. van Heijst, et al. Using explicit ontologies in KBS development. International Journal of Human-Computer Studies, 46(2/3):183–292, 1997.
9. Protege 2000 tool: http://protege.stanford.edu
10. M. Uschold and M. Gruninger. Ontologies: principles, methods, and applications. Knowledge Engineering Review, 11(2):93–155, 1996.
11. WordNet: http://www.cogsci.princeton.edu/~wn/
12. Atanas Kiryakov, et al. Semantic Annotation, Indexing, and Retrieval 2nd International Semantic Web Conference (ISWC2003), 20-23 October 2003, Florida, USA. LNAI Vol. 2870, pp. 484-499, Springer-Verlag Berlin Heidelberg 2003
13. H. Cunningham, et al. GATE: A Framework and Graphical Development Environment for Robust NLP Tools and Applications. Proceedings of the 40th Anniversary Meeting of the Association for Computational Linguistics (ACL'02). Philadelphia, July 2002
14. José Kahan, et al, Annotea: An Open RDF Infrastructure for Shared Web Annotations, in Proc. of the WWW10 International Conference, Hong Kong, May 2001.
15. Fabio Ciravegna: "(LP)2, an Adaptive Algorithm for Information Extraction from Web-related Texts" in Proceedings of the IJCAI-2001 Workshop on Adaptive Text Extraction and Mining, held in conjunction with the 17th International Conference on Artificial Intelligence (IJCAI-01), Seattle, August, 2001
16. P. Kogut and W. Holmes, "AeroDAML: Applying Information Extraction to Generate DAML Annotations from Web Pages", in Proceedings of the First International Conference on Knowledge Capture (K-CAP 2001).
17. Benjamins, V., et al. Six Challenges for the Semantic Web. White Paper, April 2002.

Gnowsis Adapter Framework: Treating Structured Data Sources as Virtual RDF Graphs

Leo Sauermann and Sven Schwarz

Knowledge Management Department,
German Research Center for Artificial Intelligence DFKI GmbH,
Kaiserslautern, Germany
Knowledge-Based Systems Group, Department of Computer Science,
University of Kaiserslautern, Germany
{leo.sauermann, sven.schwarz}@dfki.de

Abstract. The integration of heterogenous data sources is a crucial step for the upcoming semantic web – if existing information is not integrated, where will the data come from that the semantic web builds on? In this paper we present the gnowsis adapter framework, an implementation of an RDF graph system that can be used to integrate structured data sources, together with a set of already implemented adapters that can be used in own applications or extended for new situations. We will give an overview of the architecture and implementation details together with a description of the common problems in this field and our solutions, leading to an outlook on the future developments we expect. Using our presented results, researchers can generate test data for experiments and practitioners can access their desktop data sources as RDF graph.[1]

1 Introduction

Semantic Web applications have a need for data to work on, and to access existing data sources like file systems, relational databases or legacy applications to extract information and represent it in RDF. For this task, common systems like Aduna Metadata Server, Joseki, Kowari or RDF Gateway use adapter interfaces and implementations. Or developers take existing adapter projects that need some glue code to be deployed. The problem is, that all these adapters conform to the special interfaces of the system and a Kowari adapter cannot be used in Aduna or RDF Gateway. Also, the administrators of the systems have all the same design decisions to make regarding their interfaces and approach to the problem. As they all base on RDF and have similar use cases, a generic adapter infrastructure that converts legacy data to RDF would be a goal. Then adapters would generate RDF and not an implementation of system X, Y or Z. The tedious task of writing adapters would be eased and existing adapters could be reused in the Semantic Web community.

---

[1] This work was supported by the German Federal Ministry of Education, Science, Research and Technology (bmb+f), (Grant 01 IW C01, Project EPOS: Evolving Personal to Organizational Memories).

Y. Gil et al. (Eds.): ISWC 2005, LNCS 3729, pp. 1016–1028, 2005.

The gnowsis adapter framework offers an architecture for adapters that do the task of RDF extraction in different ways. We experimented with approaches that differ in implementation effort and interfaces and evaluated, which interfaces are easy to implement and The framework consists of three parts, first an abstract implementation of adapters that build a skeleton for concrete adapters, second a middleware to integrate multiple adapters into a single, queryable data source and third a set of reference implementations that show how to build adapters that can be used off the shelf. Using this framework, application developers can extract information from heterogenous data sources based on the existing off-the-shelf-adapters or own implementations. The main features of the framework are:

- Interfaces and abstract implementations of adapters
- Existing adapter implementations to access the local filesystem, IMAP email servers, Microsoft Outlook, relational databases, and the Mozilla address book as RDF graphs
- A framework to configure, start and integrate several adapters
- Instructions and Examples to build custom adapters

The gnowsis adapter framework is based on the Jena RDF framework[11] and extends the existing graph API. Each adapter implements either the graph API or a method to create concise bounded descriptions (CBDs), a data exchange format defined by Patrick Stickler in the URIQA web service [15]. In the latter case these CBDs will implement the graph API indirectly. This means arbitrary graph handling can take place nevertheless. Other more specialized third-party adapters have also been integrated into the framework.

The functionality of the framework is restricted to extract information, changes on the underlying data are not supported. There is no clear specification how to express changes and send them to the adapter, especially facing blank nodes, as our focus lies on generating data for the semantic web we decided to start with an extraction framework and continue our work when the SPARQL [7] specification contains a methodology for updates and after reference implementations exist.

In this paper we will describe the implementation and use of the system, together with references to related projects. We will show the necessary steps to create, deploy and use the adapters. The main benefits of using such adapters together with the underlying framework will also be explained. An evaluation has been made regarding (a) the *implementation cost* of adapters (by measuring the time a person takes to write an adapter) and (b) the *performance* of the different adapters, using different query methods and different data sources.

2   Structured Data Sources

For our work we focus on RDF extraction from structured data sources, with a distinction between *files, applications and RDF repositories*. We need these later, when deciding what kind of adapter to implement with what functionality.

2.1 File Data Sources

There exist many popular, standardized file formats, that contain valuable structured data for the semantic web. Usually there also exist tools, which extract the structured information and convert it into RDF conforming to some popular RDF schema(s). Examples of some interesting file formats are:

- *iCalendar* [6] is a popular text format for calendars and consequently used by the MacOs calendar and popular open source calendaring tools. It is an exchange format between calendar applications, and converters for RDF exist as a result of the RDF Calendar Workspace².
- *JPEG Images* are the default file format used by digital cameras and are also popular on the WWW. The format allows embedded meta-data in the EXIF format [3]. There exist several tools [1] to extract EXIF from image files and already represent the result as RDF according to a RDF-Schema [10].
- *HTML files* contain meta-information in the head of the document, structured meta-data about author, keywords, etc.

We concentrate on files that have characteristics of documents, not large storage files like relational database files or excel sheets.

2.2 Application Data Sources

These are systems that hold structured data in a known format and are accessible from outside to extract the data. Some are in popular use and can be easily integrated into the RDF.

- *Relational Databases* that implement the SQL standard are a typical example. For these, bindings in all common programming languages exist and different implementations offer the same behavior. Many web applications use MySQL to store their information, offering a vast pool of information that can be transformed. D2RQ [5] by Chris Bizer, Andy Seaborne and Richard Cyganiak is a generic tool that represents relational data as RDF graph, by transforming RDF queries into SQL statements and then converting the query result to RDF. We used this tool as an example of how to write adapters, our results are written below in the evaluation section.
- *IMAP email servers* are a common way to store emails and access them using different email clients. The protocol is defined as RFC and many existing APIs allow access to the servers. Emails are an important factor in today's knowledge work.
- *Microsoft Outlook* and the corresponding Exchange Server are a common collaboration tool in business environments. The interfaces to the Outlook client are well defined and many applications integrate with Outlook. An RDF adapter for Outlook was already described in [13] and will serve as an example.

---

² http://www.w3.org/2002/12/cal/

For these and other application data sources, generic adapters would be useful to access them through RDF. The cost of implementing an adapter is justified by the possible reuse in many scenarios.

2.3   RDF Repositories and Web-Services

Finally, existing RDF data sources published through proprietary or web interfaces are very interesting, as they already implement the RDF framework. Typical representations are Sesame [4], or kowari[3]. Integration of these has already been discussed in [9] but has to be reviewed again in the current situation of the upcoming SPARQL protocol and the integration with other data sources.

3   Gnowsis Adapter Types

Definition 1. *We define* adapters *as a software tool that can, on request, extract data from existing structured data sources and represent them as RDF.*

The principle of adapters is well known in software architecture, as a design pattern described in [8] and as a data extraction component in many applications areas, ie search engines. To access data sources, we can differ between three basic approaches, each suiting a certain purpose and having advantages and drawbacks. We identified the following approaches to build an adapter:

3.1   Graph and Query Adapters

An adapter that implements the interface of an RDF graph or a sophisticated query language like RDQL, SPARQL or TRIPLE. Typically, these interfaces are based on querying the graph with a method that can be described with a *find (Subject Predicate Object)* interface. The adapter has to answer to queries, each query consists of a pattern matching the graph. The output of such an adapter would be a list of statements that match the query. Both the SAIL API of Sesame and the Jena Graph API offer a comparable architecture to a *graph adapter*.

3.2   Concise Bounded Description (CBD) Adapters

This adapter can return a small subgraph that describes exactly one resource in detail. The exact definition of the result is given as part of the URIQA specification. There, a *Concise Bounded Description* (CBD)[15] is the basis for communication to web services. The interface such an adapter implements would be: *get the CBD of resource with URI X.* The source on which it works could be any application data source or the files stored on a web server. CBD adapters do not depend on a complicated query framework neither can they answer any other request, but they serve as bootstrapping interfaces to quickly retrieve information about a single resource.

---

[3] http://www.kowari.org/

3.3   File Extractors

Finally, extraction of meta-data stored in files requires special handling. Typically, a file extractor is a tool that reads files, parses them and returns some meta-data that was extracted from the data stream. An example would be an EXIF extractor that reads JPEG files and returns an RDF description of the metadata. A typical use case for a file extractors would be a search engine that builds and index over the metadata of files, another example is a Semantic Web browser that can show the content of a file together with the metadata. These usage scenarios require that file extractors have to be lightweight, easy to program and have a fast execution time.

For above approaches we have to discuss the benefits and drawbacks, you will find these below in the evaluation section.

4   How to Build Gnowsis Adapters

Writing an adapter requires a series of important tasks. Aiming at a complete methodology we successively collected information from our own experience and by observing the RDF-Calendar working group of the W3C. The overall task of building an adapter works according to the following main top-level tasks:

1. Analyze the data source
2. Choose an appropriate RDF representation
3. Choose an appropriate adapter type
4. Implement the adapter

Finally, different adapters can be integrated in a *middleware* architecture [9] for RDF repositories, so some additional configuration and deployment tasks have to be done. We implemented a specialized architecture for the integration of desktop data sources. All the above mentioned tasks will now be explained in detail.

4.1   Analyzing the Data Source

First, as a preparation, the data source in question has to be analyzed. You have to find some test data for development of an adapter. A documentation of the file format is needed or a documentation of the API how to access the data source, if it is an IMAP server or a database. Normally, existing tools can be examined that already implement the extraction mechanism and, sometimes, a tool exists that already returns the structured data as RDF.

- Formal Description of the data source. For IMAP this would be the RFC, for Microsoft Outlook it is the Programmer Reference, for iCal it is the RFC.
- Example Source Data. Valid data that has been generated by common applications.
- Search for an existing implementation to extract the information from the data source, preferably one that returns RDF.

4.2   Formal RDF Representation

If two adapters extract the same information but return different RDF representations, or use different identification schemes for resources, the usability suffers.

For most data sources, no formal representation of the data in RDF exists. In 2004 we did a survey on www.schemaweb.info and found only one public data format for representing Emails using RDF-Schema, and it was not in popular use. So, first is the search for an existing RDF-Schema that can represent the data. When an RDF-Schema formalization of the data exists, it should be used. If two exist, take the more popular scheme, we recommend the comparison of search results on google (www.googlefight.com), using the namespace identifier of the vocabulary as a search term. From our experience, it is always better to extend existing schemas to represent additional statements, than to build a new vocabulary from scratch. The FOAF project is a good example how a simple vocabulary can be extended for special needs.

Then, a solution for the *identification of resources* has to be found. Ideally, the data source already uses URIs to identify resources or a specification exists that explains how to identify resources. For our IMAP adapter the RFC [12] gives such a specification. For relational databases, D2RQ defines a way how to use primary keys to create meaningful URIs. Additionally, you have to regard scheme specific requirements, e.g., for the popular FOAF vocabulary, it is best practice to identify human persons by using the email address as inverse functional property. The resulting data should be compatible to already existing RDF representations, so common practice is as valuable as the formal definitions.

When the formal representation in RDF-Schema or OWL is found and the approach to identification is known, *test data* in RDF representation has to be authored. Again, using examples that are in public use will help standardization.

4.3   Adapter Architecture Decision

Based on the nature of the data source, the intended usage scenario and other facts like programming experience or the existing software architecture, an architecture for the implementation can be chosen.

In the web we find a vast scenery of existing adapters, beginning at command line tools written in scripting languages that take input on stdin and return output on stdout to servers that specify their own protocols. We hope that above classification into three adapter types helps picking a suitable implementation path and making adapters reusable.

In table 1 we give an overview of architectures and facts that influence the decision.

4.4   Implementation of an Adapter

Each adapter type requires a different approach to the implementation. While graph adapters can benefit by integration into an existing RDF framework, a file extractor can be implemented only returning an RDF text serialization. During

Table 1. A comparison of the different adapter types

	graph adapter	CBD adapter	file extractor
usage	RDQL, find(spo)	getCBD(uri)	getGraph(file)
data sources	application	application, file	metadata from files
implementation	based on existing API (Jena, SPARQL)	independent	independent
implementation cost	high	low	low
full RDQL support	yes	no	no
CBD support	yes	yes	yes

implementation we recommend to continually test against the data sources and an example RDF file. *Testing against sample data* is especially helpful when working in a distributed team or when the implementation is delegated to untrained personnel.

Graph Adapters. The gnowsis framework offers an abstract implementation of graph adapters. The concrete adapter class is then a subclass implementing the skeleton. Three abstract classes have to be implemented, the adapter itself, a set of resource wrappers and a set of property wrappers. For each resource type in the data source, a wrapping class is needed that represents the resource (and should buffer the source object). For each property, a property wrapper has to be implemented, with the functionality to generate triples. At this point we need the RDF-Schema or OWL formalization of the source's data format. This ontology is mapped to the wrapping Java classes.

The exact functionality of the graph adapters is described in [13,2], together with more instructions on the implementation details, the existing adapters serve can serve as examples. Our approach to wrapping data sources using a mapping file from an ontology to java implementations is similar to the approach by Bizer et al [5].

CBD Adapters. The main function of a CBD adapter is to return a subgraph around a named resource; a call to such an adapter will usually contain the URI of the resource and some parameters. The exact parameters are defined in [16], the gnowsis system only supports a subset of them, more information can be found in the documentation. The results returned by a CBD adapter in gnowsis are Jena Models, generated and filled by the adapter. In the result is the resource of the request together with the statements describing the resource.

The implementation is simpler compared to a graph adapter, it consists of parsing the URL, deciding how to generate the concise bounded description, generating it and returning it. It does not involve dependencies to other parts of gnowsis nor does the implementation require a deeper understanding of the framework. An example for a simple CBD adapter can be found in the IMAP adapter implemented by Shen Jianping (it is part of the gnowsis distribution).

When adapting the data stored inside a third party application data source like the Mozilla Email client Thunderbird, there is another possibility to implement a CBD adapter. The adapter can be embedded into the application itself, generating the RDF representation in the serialized form (RDF/XML or N3) and returning it through an inter-process-communication interface like XML/RPC or activeX. The rather simple CBD interface and the URIQA protocol are easier to implement compared to a full RDF query language. We created such an adapter for Mozilla Thunderbird, it allows the access to data stored inside Thunderbird's address book through a CBD interface. The adapter was implemented mainly in Javascript as a Thunderbird plugin and is contacted by gnowsis.

File Extractors. Similiar to CBD adapters, a file extractor returns the metadata of a single file as RDF. At the moment, we use an adapted CBD interface for file extractors: the call contains the file in question and the URI with which the file is identified. The extractor then uses the passed URI to generate the RDF representation of the file's meta-data.

We implemented an adapter that extracts the ID3 tags from MP3 files, they contain information about title, album, artist, ... Implementation of such adapters is straightforward and we do not need to describe the details here. The interesting question is, how to reuse existing file extractors implementations. For example, the iCalendar converters `fromIcal.py` and `ical2rdf.pl` created by Dan Connolly, Libby Miller, and Tim Berners-Lee provide simple and effective means to convert text files to RDF. They can be called from other applications as they take their input from stdin and return the RDF serialization on stdout. Many such converters and extractors exist for different file types, and as they implement similar interfaces, can be integrated to frameworks such as gnowsis. We hope that the interfaces defined by gnowsis are an aid for others.

4.5   Usage of Adapters

Typical usage of an adapter are requests for concise bounded descriptions (CBDs) or find(subject, predicate, object) calls. More complex query formats can also be implemented in adapters, but this would raise implementation cost and complex queries can be fractionated into several find calls, as it is done in the actual Jena implementation.

Jena (and other popular RDF APIs) require a find(spo) implementation. In complex queries (RDQL, SPARQL) including graph matching, the approach to query execution by the adapter could:

- parse the whole query in its native form (RDQL) and execute it. The adapter therefore has to implement a query parser and an execution engine.
- only implement the find(spo) interface. The query parsing is done by another framework (for example Jena) and fractionated into several find(spo) calls. The result of the calls are aggregated by Jena. This works satisfyingly for most cases, if the client knows the structure of the graph and asks only find(spo) questions that will return an answer. In any case, a query reordering helps the execution engine. We implemented a basic query reordering algorithm in Gnowsis, extending the standard RDQL query engine of Jena.

– buffer all graph information in an RDF Repository. The framework has to crawl all adapters and store the crawled graph into one big database. We recommend using a Quad-Store or named graph store for this and chose the context id (the fourth resource in the quad or the name of the graph) the same as the CBD URI. Then, updates are on CBD identifier level.

4.6   Integration of Heterogenous Data Sources

Faced with several data sources, they have to be integrated to a hub architecture. [9]. In the gnowsis architecture we facilitated a registration of adapters and then a use of these adapters based on the registration information. Configuration of an adapter includes basic information about the implementation class (a Java class implementing an adapter type), human readable data source identifier, an ontology of the adapter and URI patterns that describe what URIs can be found inside the graph of the adapter. This configuration is, of course, stored in an RDF graph.

For crawling, each adapter has to define *root URIs*, one ore more URIs of a resource that is queried first from the adapter, the resulting resources of such querying (either by find(spo) or by CBD) can then be crawled further. The concept of root URIs can also be employed in user interfaces: the information content of the adapter can be explored starting at the root URI.

5   Benefits of the Framework

Reusable adapters help to avoid reinventing the wheel every time some RDF data is needed. The obvious benefit of using standardized adapters is the reduced implementation effort in Semantic Web projects. The time to create and test custom implementations is higher compared to the time needed to integrate an existing adapter. If the existing adapter does not comply to performance requirements or functionality, it can be extended or used as a prototype.

The second, from our perspective far more important benefit, is the standardization process that happens when the data is transformed to RDF. If two distinct applications use different implementations to access the same data source, the two resulting RDF graphs may be different. We observed two main problems in data transformation, the used ontology and the resulting URIs.

The *ontology problem* can be illustrated by looking at the history of the W3C RDF-Calendar working group. A vocabulary to represent iCalendar event information in RDF was authored by Dan Connoly and others[4]. The vocabulary was changed and different implementations either implemented the old or the new version Another case would be, when the same data is transformed into two different ontologies, e.g., information about people can be expressed either in FOAF or in vCARD[5].

---

[4] http://www.w3.org/2002/12/cal/ical
[5] http://www.w3.org/TR/vcard-rdf

The *URI problem* is similar. By what URIs should resources be identified? We request that the same resource should be identified by the same URI. However, even for a simple resource like a local file this is not straightforward. For instance, Mozilla and Internet Explorer use different URIs for the same local files when browsing.

Both problems can be avoided by always using the same adapter. Although automatic matching of ontologies is possible, it could be avoided when using the same extraction algorithm and ontology in the first place.

5.1 Deployment and Use of Adapters

The resulting adapters can be used in concrete applications or embedded in the gnowsis Semantic Desktop framework [14]. In the embedded scenario, the adapter will be packaged as gnowsis service in form of a WAR file (the standard servlet container format, extended by gnowsis). The WAR file is included into an installed gnowsis system and then configured using the options menu of gnowsis, resulting in the integration of the data source into the data sources that will be queried by gnowsis on browsing or searching features. The exact way of deploying an adapter and using it is described in the according tutorials on the project website [2].

Adapters can also be used independent of gnowsis, in any java application. For this, the gnowsis adapter framework has to be included as a dependency together with the complete Jena dependencies. To start and use an adapter, an RDF graph containing the configuration information for the adapter has to be passed during instantiation. Again, details on this can be found on the website. Altogether, using and deploying adapters inside and outside gnowsis is comparable (on the effort level) to other Semantic Web frameworks.

6 Evaluation

6.1 Implementation Cost

The task of implementing an IMAP adapter was delegated to one student. This student was an average skilled developer, who was new to gnowsis and RDF. He had to read and test the standard IMAP protocol, as well as, to read about and get into the gnowsis framework. During his work the student had to write down the amount of time needed for each subtask (reading, coding, testing, etc.). Understanding and implementing for the gnowsis framework, as well as, familiarizing with the adapter architecture took him about six hours. Getting around with the IMAP protocol was already done in about three hours.

The student had to realize two types of adapters: He started with implementing a graph based adapter. It took him 24 working hours of implementation plus 16 working hours of debugging. As a second task, a CBD based adapter has to be implemented, too. In contrast to the graph adapter, it took him only about 8 hours to implement the CBD adapter, debugging included.

Table 2. A comparison of the implementation cost for different adapter types

implementation cost in hours	graph adapter	CBD adapter
familiarize with adapter architecture	2	2
familiarize with gnowsis framework	4	–
reading and testing native data interface	3	3
implementation	24	7
debugging	16	1
deploy adapter	1	1
sum	50	14

The CBD adapter was not only easier to implement, but also easier to test (particularly less debugging time): A CBD of some URI can be tested without any RDF API or framework running. Besides, the CBD adapter can be implemented in any language and the RDF/XML representation of the CBD can be created by simple text concatenation. This was exactly the case for the Mozilla address book plugin: an installable extension (XPI-file) integrates some corresponding Java Script code into the native application (Mozilla Firefox) and answers CBD queries via simple XML-RPC calls.

If existing graph implementations can be reused, the cost of developing a wrapping gnowsis adapter is minimal. On 23th of April 2005, Richard Cyganiak created a wrapper for the D2RQ project [5] in about six hours of programming time. The existing D2RQ project is functional and tested, a stable basis for a gnowsis adapter. It was wrapped in a Java project, and the needed glue code has been written, including the formal RDF description of the adapter and a graphical component to configure the adapter.

6.2   Performance of the Adapters

As displayed in table 1 a graph adapter provides full query support (e.g. RDQL), because all triples in the graph are accessible and can be searched very efficiently. In contrast, the CBD adapter provides "jigsaw pieces" around given URIs. Using and combining these, some RDQL queries can be executed, too (searching for subjects is not possible without crawling).

For such RDQL queries the retrieval and combining of the relevant CBDs costs, of course, more time than directly accessing a graph adapter. On the other hand, if (all) information about a resource shall be retrieved, the CBD provides exactly what is needed, and therefore is as efficient as the graph adapter.

As an example we queried metadata about appointments stored in Microsoft Outlook in form of different queries: (1) the timestamp of one specific appointment, then (2) *all* properties of that appointment, after that (3) the timestamps of 1000 appointments, and finally (4) *all* properties of 1000 appointments. All four queries have been tested on both the graph adapter and the CBD adapter. Table 3 shows, that the graph adapter is, of course, faster on the retrieval of a single property, whereas the CBD adapter needs even less time for the retrieval of *all* properties of a resource.

Table 3. Comparison of the runtimes of queries performed by the graph adapter and by the CBD adapter

runtime in milli seconds	graph adapter	CBD adapter
one appointment, one property	20-30	20-30
one appointment, all properties	20-30	20-30
1000 appointments, one property	16924	26378
1000 appointments, all properties	30644	26378

7 Conclusions and Future Plans

The gnowsis adapter framework is published as an open source project and has been used already by both interested individuals and research institutions. Using the presented adapters, it is possible to connect to a variety of data sources and crawl vast RDF graphs. By extracting real-life data sources, gnowsis adapters eventually allow working on big, real RDF data instead of small, irrelevant sample graphs.

In consequence of the latest developments in the Data Access Working Group of the W3C, and the resulting SPARQL framework, we will concentrate on taking the gnowsis adapter framework in the suggested direction: Each adapter should be represented as a named graph in a graph-set. A single adapter, as well as, the graphset should be published using the SPARQL query language and the according protocol. Then, contacting the framework and relying on this stable protocol, applications can be implemented without any deeper knowledge about adapters or the framework as such.

During the upcoming NEPOMUK EU project (lead by the DFKI) we will take our experience with gnowsis and formulate generic interfaces for adapters that could be used by the major RDF frameworks (Aduna Metadata Server, Kowari, Jena, etc.). For this, we are already in discussion with other developers of Jena and Aduna.

References

1. Exif2RDF by Masahide Kanzaki, http://www.kanzaki.com/test/exif2rdf JpegRDF by Norman Walsh http://nwalsh.com/java/jpegrdf/jpegrdf.html.
2. the gnowsis semantic desktop project website http://www.gnowsis.org.
3. Digital still camera image file format standard (exchangeable image file format for digital still cameras: Exif) version 2.1. Technical report, Japan Electronic Industry Development Association (JEIDA), June 1998.
4. Jeen Broekstra, Arjohn Kampman, and Frank van Harmelen. Sesame: A generic architecture for storing and querying rdf and rdf schema. In *Proc. of the International Semantic Web Conference 2002*, 2002.
5. A. Seaborne C. Bizer. D2rq treating non-rdf databases as virtual rdf graphs. In *Proceedings of the 3rd International Semantic Web Conference (ISWC2004)*, 2004.
6. F. Dawson and D. Stenerson. Rfc 2445: Internet calendaring and scheduling core object specification (icalendar), November 1998.

1028   L. Sauermann and S. Schwarz

7. Andy Seaborne (edts) Eric Prud'hommeaux. Sparql query language for rdf. W3c working draft, W3C, 2005. http://www.w3.org/TR/rdf-sparql-query/.
8. Erich Gamma, Richard Helm, Ralph Johnson, and John Vlissides. *Design Patterns*. Addison-Wesley, 1995.
9. A. Harth. Seco: mediation services for semantic web data. *Intelligent Systems, IEEE*, Volume 19(Issue 3):66 – 71, May-June 2004.
10. Masahide Kanzaki. Exif vocabulary workspace - rdf schema. Technical report, RDF Interest Group, 2004.
11. Brian McBride. Jena: Implementing the rdf model and syntax specification. In *Proc. of the Semantic Web Workshop WWW2001*, 2001.
12. C. Newman. Rfc 2192: Imap url scheme, September 1997.
13. Leo Sauermann. The gnowsis-using semantic web technologies to build a semantic desktop. Diploma thesis, Technical University of Vienna, 2003.
14. Leo Sauermann and Sven Schwarz. Introducing the gnowsis semantic desktop. In *Proceedings of the International Semantic Web Conference 2004*, 2004.
15. Patrick Stickler. Cbd - concise bounded description. Technical report, NOKIA, 2004. http://sw.nokia.com/uriqa/CBD.html.
16. Patrick Stickler. The uri query agent model - a semantic web enabler. Technical report, NOKIA, 2004. http://sw.nokia.com/uriqa/URIQA.html.

Do Not Use This Gear with a Switching Lever!
Automotive Industry Experience with Semantic Guides

Hans-Peter Schnurr and Jürgen Angele

ontoprise GmbH, Amalienbadstr. 36, 76227 Karlsruhe, Germany
{schnurr, angele}@ontoprise.de
http://www.ontoprise.de

Abstract. Besides the reduction of time to market, there may be observed another trend in the automotive industry: built-to-order. Built-to-order reduces the mass production of cars to a limited-lot-production. Emphasis for optimization issues moves then from the production step to earlier steps as the collaboration of suppliers and manufacturer in development and delivering. Thus knowledge has to be shared between different organizations and departments in early development processes. In this paper we describe a project in the automotive industry where ontologies have two main purposes: (i) representing and sharing knowledge to optimize business processes for the testing of cars and (ii) integration of life data into this optimization process. A test car configuration assistant (semantic guide) is built on top of an inference engine equipped with an ontology containing information about parts and configuration rules. The ontology is attached to the legacy systems of the manufacturer and thus accesses and integrates up-to-date information. This semantic guide accelerates the configuration of test cars and thus reduces time to market.

1 Introduction

Having a look at the shares of vehicle sales in US from 1970 – 2001 (see figure 1) we observe that the big three automobile vendors (Chrysler, Ford, General Motors) considerably lost market shares in that time period. One of the reasons was that before the early nineties the poor quality of their cars compared to the competitor's cars has been responsible for this loss. Then the big three started a quality offensive which resulted in a slight market gain until 1994. But after 1994 the big three again lost market shares. The reason for the second loss which lasts until today is the slow innovation in automotive industry in US. The competitors in Asia and Europe have been able to strongly reduce the time for developing new cars. As a consequence time-to-market is one of the main optimization goals in the automotive industry.

Another very important trend in consumer oriented production industry is built-to-order. Built-to-order means that a product is immediately produced and delivered after the consumer configured the product according to his whishes. With this strategy Dell edged out a lot of its competitors on the PC market. In contrast to that in automotive industry cars are first developed and then manufactured in large amounts with a high degree of optimization. Very often the results are huge amounts of cars which cannot be sold and thus produce costs for the investment and for storing them. Finally these cars must be sold with large sales discounts which again reduce the profit of the

Y. Gil et al. (Eds.): ISWC 2005, LNCS 3729, pp. 1029 – 1040, 2005.

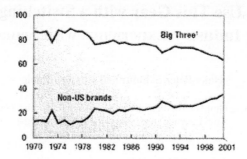

Fig. 1. Market shares of vehicle sales (source: Wards automotive yearbook)

manufacturer. Built-to-order avoids all these problems but has a severe change of logistic processes and business processes as consequence. Built-to-order reduces the mass production of cars to a limited-lot-production. Emphasis for optimization issues moves then from the production step to earlier steps as the collaboration between suppliers and manufacturers in development and delivering. Thus knowledge has to be shared between different organizations and departments. Therefore, the main emphasis has to be put on optimizing these business processes.

In this paper we describe a project in the automotive industry where ontologies have two main purposes: (i) representing and sharing knowledge to optimize business processes for testing of cars and (ii) integration of life data into this optimization process.

The scenario for this process was given by the business processes around the testing of cars. Our client has a fleet of test cars. These test cars are continuously reconfigured and then tested with this new configuration. Reconfiguration means changing the engine, changing the gear, changing the electric, i.e. changing all kinds of parts. For changing parts a lot of dependencies between these parts have to be taken into account. In many cases these dependencies are only known by certain human experts and thus require a lot of communication effort between different departments of the manufacturer, between the manufacturer and suppliers and between suppliers. Very often test cars have been configured which did not work or which hampered the measurement of the desired parameters. So making such dependencies exploitable by computers allows for reducing the error rate in configuring test cars with a lower communication effort. This in turn accelerates the development of new cars and enhances the collaboration between manufacturer and suppliers. Thus it reduces time-to-market and supports the built-to-order process.

2 Knowledge Representation in Automotive

2.1 The Representation Language F-Logic

Conceptual (or Ontology) modeling deals with the question of how to describe in a declarative and abstract way the domain information of an application, its relevant vocabulary, and how to constrain the use of the data, by understanding what can be drawn from it. Corresponding abstract representation languages support the understanding of such descriptions, their rapid development, their maintenance and their reuse.

Representing our domain in our representation language F-logic [1] provides a lot of advantages:

- F-Logic represents knowledge on a high level of abstraction in an explicit way. Thus knowledge is represented in well understandable independent knowledge chunks. It is not hidden in lower levels like SQL programs or even in computer programs.
- The abstraction level of F-Logic supports the rapid development of such models and the maintenance. Both aspects are very important in this domain since new dependencies arise with every new car model. This allows also to directly communicate F-Logic models between the users (in our case the engineers) and thus allow users to evaluate these models.
- The model is immediately executable. This means that as soon as the development of the model has started it could be automatically exploited by queries. Thus it immediately gives a value-add for the user. This distinguishes F-Logic also from other conceptual modeling languages like UML etc. which are not expressive enough to describe the entire system in detail to provide an executable prototype.
- F-Logic provides a clear and well-documented semantics (well-founded semantics cf. [2]). This means that the knowledge models, i.e. the ontologies are interpretable and understandable in an inambigious way independently from an explicit implementation of a reasoning system (which is often the case for other business rules systems).

Basic concepts in the specific are represented as concepts in F-Logic and are arranged in an isa-hierarchy. Concepts may be described by attributes and relationships to other concepts.

```
//schema
component:: DEFAULT_ROOT_CONCEPT.
component[  has_part=>>Component;
            is_part=>> Component].
motor::component[
            maximum_power=>INTEGER].

// instances and relations
tdi_engine: motor.
valve2:     component.
pump3:      component.
tdi_engine[ has_part->>valve2;
            has_part->>pump3;horsepower->340].

//rules
FORALL X,Y Y[is_part->>X] <- X [has_part->>Y].

//queries
FORALL X <- X:component.
```

In this example we have defined a *component* as a basic concept (below the root concept). A component has a relationship *has_part* to another component and an attribute *maximum_horsepower*. A *motor* is a special component. Then we create an instantiation of a component *tdi_engine* being a specific motor. Concrete instances *valve2*, *pump3* are given for concept *component*. A rule is used to describe the inversity of *has_part* and *is_part*. With a query we ask for all components in the model.

OntoBroker, our reasoning system, provides means for efficient reasoning in F-Logic [3]. OntoBroker performs a mixture of forward and backward chaining based on the dynamic filtering algorithm [4] to compute (the smallest possible) subset of the model for answering the query. During forward chaining not only single tuples of variable instantiations but sets of such tuples are processed. It is well-known that set-oriented evaluation strategies are much more efficient than tuple oriented ones. The semantics for a set of F-Logic statements is then defined by a transformation process of F-Logic into normal logic (Horn logic with negation) and the well-founded semantics [2] for the resulting set of facts and rules and axioms in normal logic.

2.2 Answer Justification with F-Logic

There are many reasons that users and applications need to understand the provenance of the information they get back from applications. One major motivating factor is trust. Trust and reuse of retrieval and deduction processes are facilitated when explanations are available. Ultimately, if users and/or applications are expected to trust, use and reuse application results, potentially in combination with other information or other application results, users and agents may need to understand where the derived and source information came from at varying degrees of detail. This information, sometimes called provenance, may be viewed as meta information about information told. Provenance information may include source name, date and author(s) of last update, authoritativeness of the source, degree of belief, degree of completeness, etc.

Our approach for answer justification is based on meta-inferencing. While processing a query the inference engine is producing a log-file of the proof tree for any given answer. This proof tree itself is represented in F-Logic. It contains the instantiated rules that were successfully applied to derive an answer. This file acts as input for a second inference run, where answers are produced, that are explaining the proof tree in natural language and by that how the answer to the original query was inferred.

Rules which are important for justifying results were explicitly named. For these rules certain explain rules are formulated which will be applied in the second, the meta-inference run. Frequently the named rules corresponded to important scientific laws (like load transmission), while less important rules were typically required for technical reasons, e.g. in order to translate between two alternative representations of the same content, but were not important for the human to understand the solution proposed by the system.

3 Business Logic Enhancements

The setting here is the configuration of test cars. These test cars are continuously reconfigured and then tested with this new configuration. Reconfiguration means that according to orders of the test engineers parts have to be replaced by other parts, parts have to be dismantled or have to be built into the test cars. These test cars are then used to test for specific characteristics and to gain series of measurements either in house or in test drives. For changing parts a lot of dependencies between these parts have to be taken into account. In many cases this knowledge about these dependencies is available by experts only. These experts need a lot of time for communication and often enough test cars have been wrongly configured due to inefficiencies in communication.

Besides describing the knowledge about a domain, ontologies serve as mediators between data sources [5]. By this way up-to-date data about parts etc. from the legacy systems of the manufacturer are available. This integration aspect is handled in more detail in the next section.

This ontology will be used in two different ways. In a first step it will be integrated into a software assistant which helps the engineer in configuring test cars. The engineer asks the assistant for a reconfiguration and the system answers with the dependencies which have to be taken into account and the contact information for experts in this case. Additionally to these answers the assistant will provide explanations which help the engineer to understand and validate the decision of the assistant.

3.1 Ontology

The base ontology very strongly relies on parts which are arranged in a part-of hierarchy and their properties. The instances, i.e. concrete values are most often gained from parts list in the legacy systems.

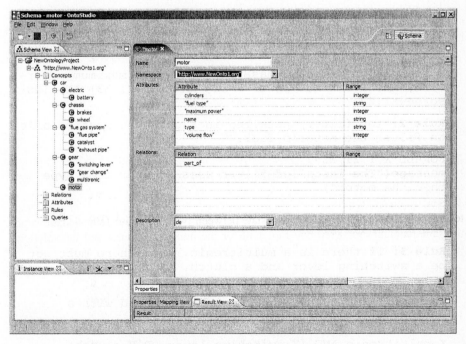

Fig. 2. An excerpt of the automotive ontology in OntoStudio™

In figure 2, an excerpt of that ontology is shown in a part-of view. It shows that e.g. a *gear* is part of a *car* and the *switching lever* is a part of the *gear*. For *motor* some attributes like *maximum power, type* etc. are shown.

An ontology without rules describes only simple relationships between concepts like a part is a part of another part, a part is connected to another part etc. More complex relationships have to be described by rules and constraints. It is this more complex knowledge which has to be captured by the ontology to help configuring test cars. In the following such constraints are presented:

Constraint 1: The maximum power of the motor must not exceed the one of the brakes.
$$Pmotor < | Pbrakes |$$

Constraint 2: The filter installed in a catalyst must be able to filter the motor's fuel.

Constraint 3: If there is a multitronic, then there must not be a switching lever and a clutch.

These constraints are then added to the ontology by using rules:

Rule 1: The maximum power of the motor must not exceed the one of the brakes: Pmotor < | Pbrakes |

```
FORALL X,Y,Z,Z1,Z2,Z3
message("The motor's maximum power exceeds the one of
the brakes.")
<-
X:testcar[hasMotor->Y;hasBrake->Z] and Y[maximum_power-
>>Z1] AND Z[maximum_power->>Z2] AND abs(Z1,Z3) AND les-
sorequal(Z2,Z3).
```

Rule 2: The filter installed in a catalyst must be able to filter the motor's fuel.

```
FORALL X,Y,Z1,Z2
message("The installed filter uses another fuel type
than the motor")
<-
X:motor[fuel_type->>Z1] AND Y:filter[fuel_type->>Z2]
AND not equal(Z1,Z2).
```

Rule 3: If there is a multitronic, then there must not be a switching lever and a clutch.

```
FORALL X,Y
message("A multitronic can not be combined with a
switching lever or a clutch.")
<-
X:multitronic AND (Y:switching_lever OR Y:clutch).
```

It is clear that these single constraints look very simple. In most cases it is not the complexity of such a single relationship which creates the complexity of the task but the overwhelming amount of such rules and constraints which all interfere with a lot of others and thus make the task to configure a correct test car so complex and error prone. On the other hand the simplicity of the single rules gives us the hope that they can be created and maintained by the engineers themselves [6]. With its rules F-Logic is a very powerful language able to express arbitrary complex relationships. Other languages like OWL are much more restrictive. E.g. OWL does not allow to express conditions where variables are chained over different conditions like in rule 1.

3.2 Inferencing

Inferences are facts, derived by means of logical conclusions. Inferencing engines like SiLRI [7] or OntoBroker [3] use a formal logic calculus to generate new facts out of input facts and rules. By that way our ontology with the rules is immediately executable after being loaded into OntoBroker. This means that queries could be posed to OntoBroker which in turn draws logical conclusions by evaluating the rules and produces answers to the queries.

In an inferencing process the rules are applied to the given facts and extend the knowledge base by the newly created facts. Figure 3 visualizes this process.

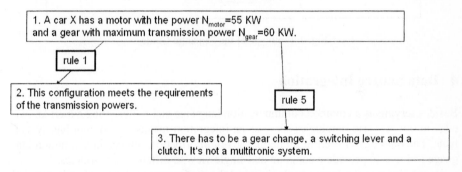

Fig. 3. The inferencing process

3.3 Semantic Guide for Test Car Configuration

On top of OntoBroker equipped with our ontology, a first prototype of a web-based user interface for the semantic guide has been developed (see fig. 4). In the left frame the user navigates within a part-of hierarchy of the components. This view may be switched to an is-a hierarchy. The attribute values of a selected component are editable in a form in the middle frame. The current configuration with all its components is shown in the right frame. If a configuration contains inconsistent components which is checked by applying consistency rules, appropriate error and warning messages are immediately given and alternatives for a selected component are presented to the user which make the configuration consistent. In our screenshot a special motor is selected and presented together with its attribute values.

The current configuration contains two incompatible components: gear 0815 and a switching lever must not be used together. This is indicated by the error message at the bottom. If the system knows about options which make the configuration consistent, these options are shown in the right window. A user can now exchange a component by the suggested option. It is clear that configuration on this way is a mixed-initiative approach between the computer and the user. This is in contrast to problem-solving methods for configuration like [13].

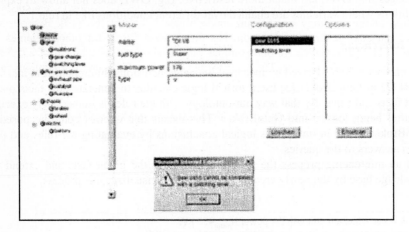

Fig. 4. Prototype of the Semantic Guide

4   Data Source Integration

Besides serving as a common communication language and representing expert knowledge in our scenario ontologies serve as an integration means of different legacy systems. The ontology is used to reinterpret given information sources in a common language and thus to provide a common and single view to different data sources.

In our scenario the components data and the configuration data is already handled widespread in different departments and in different information sources like CAD-, CAE- or CAT-systems or ERP/PPS-applications, databases etc. All these IT systems accompany the whole PLM-process [8], beginning with the product design and ending with the product release. Our test configuration system, and thus our ontology system must access this live information to be up-to-date, to avoid inconsistent data and to avoid additional effort.

An ontology could now catch up these different sources and integrate them in a common logical model. This goes much beyond building just connectors [9] between applications. The goal of integration is to consolidate distributed information intelligently, free of redundancy and providing users and applications a simple access to information without considering the underlying data structure or system.

In our case we already have such a commonly accepted logical model: the automotive ontology. This ontology describes schema information and is not yet populated by instances. This means e.g. that there exists a concept *motor* with attributes *name*, *cylinders, type* etc. But there is no information about concrete *motors* like *TDI V6*, with 6 *cylinders, fuel type super* etc. available. This is achieved by attaching the on-tology to one or more of the existing information sources. In the following we exem-plify the mapping to a relational database.

4.1 Database Schema Import

The first step to connect an ontology to a database is importing the database schema and visualize it in our ontology management environment OntoStudio, the successor version of the ontology engineering environment OntoEdit [6], [10]. Beneath rela-tional database schemas OntoStudio has also import filters for other schemas like RDF [11], [12] or OWL. In our example we will show the attachment of a database table *motor* to our ontology. The database table is given in figure 5. It contains infor-mation about motors like the *fuel type, power* etc.

id	absolute power	fuel	volume flow	engine type
tdi v6	176	super	124	v
cdi 170	83	diesel	105	v
cdi 160	75	diesel	101	v
boxer	32	normal	80	boxer
stern	450	normal	240	stern

Fig. 5. Database table engine

4.2 Database Mappings

After having imported the database schema the ontology and the schema have to be connected appropriately. OntoMap – a mapping tool included in OntoStudio – sup-ports the fundamental mapping types (i) table-to-concept mapping, (ii) attribute-to-attribute mapping and (iii) attribute-to-concept mapping.

In fig. 6 a table-to-concept mapping connects the table engine to the concept motor and additionally an attribute-to-attribute mapping from id in the database to name in the ontology. This means that every row in the database corresponds to one object in the ontology. OntoStudio automatically creates a connection to the database by the *dbaccessuserid*-connector (there are various connectors to information sources avail-able). This built-in automatically creates a unique object ID. It is used in a rule which defines the access and the mapping to our ontology:

```
FORALL X, NAME, MAXIMUM_POWER, VOLUME_FLOW, FUEL_TYPE
X:motor[name->>NAME; maximum_power->>MAXIMUM_POWER;
volume_flow->>VOLUME_FLOW; fuel_type->>FUEL_TYPE]
<-
dbaccessuserid("engine",
X, F( "id", NAME, "absolute power", MAXIMUM_POWER,
"volume_flow", VOLUME_FLOW, "fuel", FUEL_TYPE),
"mssqlserver2000",
"database_motor","server_motordata:1433").
```

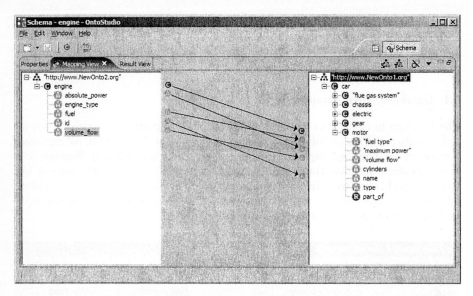

Fig. 6. Database Mapping

Another important mapping type is the mapping of attributes to concepts. This has the consequence that the attribute value is used as unique ID for an ontology instance. E.g. mapping the ID of *engine* to the concept *motor* creates an object for every different ID in the database. By that way information about one and the same object which is spread in different rows and is always identified by the same ID can be linked together. This was the case in our project for part lists.

4.3 Querying the Integration Ontology

Mappings as described in section 4.2 can be defined to different RDBMS and additionally to web services at the same time. A query to the integration ontology is thus at real-time translated (via the mapping rules) into calls for appropriate access builtins which in turn access the data sources (in case of an RDBMS via SQL queries) and translate the answers back into F-Logic. Thus a user or an application on top of the ontology needs only this single ontology view and with it single vocabulary to retrieve all necessary information. In our scenario different information sources contribute to the same ontology. E.g. information about electronic parts are stored in other databases than information about mechanical parts. Information about the 3-D geometry of objects is separated from their mechanical properties etc.

4.4 How to Handle Inconsistencies

It is clear that in practice the different information sources contain redundant ore even inconsistent information. For instance in our scenario car types have not been represented in a unique way. The assignment of properties to car types has been described with different keys for one and the same car type. E.g. Keys like *A3/A4* have been used to describe common properties of two car types while unique properties have been assigned to the car type by a key *A3*. We again use rules and thus inferencing to solve such problems.

```
FORALL X, Part, Type
X:Car[carType->>Type; has_part->>Part]
<-
dbaccessuserid("car", X, F( "id", T, "part", Part),

"mssqlserver2000", "car database","server:1433") and
T is substring(T,0,indexof("/")).
```

5 Conclusion

In a real-life industrial project, viz. in the automotive industry at a car manufacturer, we have shown that ontologies may very well be used to enhance business processes and to integrate different information sources. In our case the ontology represents knowledge about (complex) relationships between different parts which may automatically be exploited in configuring test cars. This reduces the communication effort between the mechanical engineers, and reduces the error rate in configuring test cars. For this task the ontology is attached to the legacy systems of the manufacturer and thus accesses up-to-date information about parts and configurations. We have shown that our ontology engineering environment OntoStudio supports not only the comfortable development of ontologies but with the integrated mapping tool OntoMap also an easy to learn tool to attach ontologies to different information sources. Our semantic guide is based on our ontology run-time environment and inference engine OntoBroker which is based on F-Logic. This semantic guide is a prototype which is currently evaluated at our customer. It has been shown that it accelerates the configuration of test cars at our customer and thus accelerates the development of new cars as well. This will reduce time-to-market in the end.

References

1. M. Kifer, G. Lausen, and J.Wu. Logical foundations of object-oriented and framebased languages. *Journal of the ACM*, 42; (1995) 741–843
2. A. Van Gelder, K. A. Ross, and J. S. Schlipf. The well-founded semantics for general logic programs. *Journal of the ACM*, 38(3); July (1991) 620–650
3. S. Decker, M. Erdmann, D. Fensel, and R. Studer. OntoBroker™: Ontology based access to distributed and semi-structured information. In R. Meersman et al., editor, *Database Semantics: Semantic Issues in Multimedia Systems*. Kluwer Academic, (1999)
4. M. Kifer and E. Lozinskii. A framework for an efficient implementation of deductive databases. In Proceedings of the 6th Advanced Database Symposium, Tokyo, August (1986) 109–116
5. Andreas Maier, Mike Ullrich, and Hans-Peter Schnurr. Ontology-based Information Integration in the Automotive Industry. Technical report, ontoprise whitepaper series, (2003)

6. Y. Sure, M. Erdmann, J. Angele, S. Staab, R. Studer, and D. Wenke. OntoEdit: Collaborative ontology development for the semantic web. In Horrocks and Hendler [HH02], (2002) 221-235.
7. S. Decker, D. Brickley, J. Saarela und J. Angele: A Query and Inference Service for RDF. In *Proceedings of the W3C Query Language Workshop (QL-98)*, Boston, MA, 3.-4. Dezember, (1998)
8. T. Bernold. Product life: from design to disposal : life-cycle engineering: the key to risk management, safer products and industrial environmental strategies. In International Conference on Industrial Risk Management, Elsevier,.Zürich, (1990)
9. D. Kreuz. Formale Semantik von Konnektoren. PhD thesis, Technische Universitaet Hamburg (1999)
10. Y. Sure, S. Staab, J. Angele. OntoEdit: Guiding Ontology Development by Methodology and Inferencing. In: R. Meersman, Z. Tari et al. (eds.). Proceedings of the Confederated International Conferences CoopIS, DOA and ODBASE 2002, October 28th - November 1st, 2002, University of California, Irvine, USA, Springer, LNCS 2519 , (2002)1205-1222.
11. Richard Fikes. Ressource Description Framework (RDF). http://www.stanford.edu/class/cs222/slides2/RDF.PDF. (2002)
12. Steffen Staab, Michael Erdmann, Alexander Mädche, Stefan Decker. An extensible approach for Modeling Ontologies in RDF(S). In *Knowledge Media in Healthcare: Opportunities and Challenges*. Rolf Grütter (ed.). Idea Group Publishing, Hershey USA / London, UK. December (2001)
13. Mittal, S., Frayman, F. Towards a generic model of configuration tasks. In *Proceedings of IJCAI'89*, (1989).

The Concept Object Web
for Knowledge Management

James Starz, Brian Kettler, Peter Haglich, Jason Losco,
Gary Edwards, and Mark Hoffman

ISX Corporation, 4301 N. Fairfax Dr. Suite 370,
Arlington, VA 22203, USA
{jstarz, bkettler, phaglich, jlosco,
gedwards, mhoffman}@isx.com

Abstract. The Semantic Web is a difficult concept for typical end-users to
comprehend. There is a lack of widespread understanding on how the Semantic
Web could be used in day-to-day applications. While there are now practical
applications that have appeared supporting back-end functions such as data integration, there is only a handful of Semantic Web applications that the average
Google user would want to use on a regular basis. The Concept Object Web[1] is
a prototype application for knowledge/intelligence management that aggregates
data from text documents, XML files, and databases so that end-users can visually discover and learn about knowledge object (entities) without reading
documents. The application addresses limitations with current knowl-
edge/intelligence management tools giving end-users the power of the Semantic
Web without the perceived burden and complexity of the Semantic Web.

1   Introduction

Since the creation of the Semantic Web there have been a large number of tools created that have proven its theoretical use and provided the infrastructure for application
development. However, there have been very few Semantic Web applications that
would be acceptable to most end users. There are many reasons this is the case as the
technology is still emerging, but the foremost reason is that is currently difficult to do.
Only recently have the underlying infrastructure tools matured to be used in real applications. Additionally, almost no end user will ever want to see OWL, URIs, ontologies, and the rest of the backbone of the Semantic Web.

Our experience with building and integrating Semantic Web applications has
shown us the difficulties of providing functionality to users that do not care that the
application uses the Semantic Web. The Concept Object Web, built on top of ISX's
Semantic Object Web™ [6], is a prototype application for knowledge/intelligence
management that tries to address many of the challenges of making a user friendly
and useful Semantic Web application. The Semantic Object Web approach extends
the Semantic Web by focusing on how users and software agents can more easily

---

[1] Demo available at http://semanticobjectweb.isx.com

Y. Gil et al. (Eds.): ISWC 2005, LNCS 3729 , pp. 1041 – 1049, 2005.

access and exploit information about specific entities in the world – people, places, events, etc. – that is semantically integrated from multiple distributed, heterogeneous sources. The underlying framework is used by a number of deployed applications. The Concept Object Web is based on a hybrid of features from these deployed applications using the Semantic Web.

This paper describes the basic functionality of the Concept Object Web and how it leverages the power of the Semantic Web. We discuss a number of features of the system and describe our lessons learned from implementing them. Of particular interest is how users can use the Semantic Web to manage knowledge. The system addresses issues with resolving co-references of entities across data sources. It takes into account tradeoffs for generating indices of disparate data stores for fast retrieval and inference. The paper includes Semantic Web tradeoffs on the process of gathering semantically-grounded content, indexing information, performing searches, visualizing results, discovering and browsing information, and tracking data pedigree.

2 Motivation and Requirements

Though there are many great tools for doing search and discovery, they often place a heavy burden on users to eventually read documents or view database records. Users have become quite willing to accept these limitations because in most cases they are not required to read more than a few documents to find the information they are looking for. Google™ works very well for the majority of users because of this assumption. In many real applications, such as business intelligence, the assumption simply does not hold. There do exist tools, such as Endeca®[2] and Siderean™[3], that do a very good job of providing typical users with the ability to perform guided searches. These may provide a better way to navigate to a smaller set of documents that would be required for an end user to read. In all of these cases, if the user wants to know all the details about an object in the document they have no choice but to read all of the documents, even if the documents themselves are mostly repetitive.

The Concept Object Web approach is to gather information from documents using automated, and when possible human, extraction of entities and facts. Additional information can come from other heterogonous sources such as databases. This information can then be represented semantically and many extraction tools are now supporting this functionality out of the box. In this setting, common URI identifiers will not automatically be given to entities, so similar object must be resolved, best they can, into a single view using existing lexical and graph matching algorithms. At this point in the process all of the information has uniform identification, as well as mappings to ontologies. This information can now be stored in a knowledge base. All of the information in the populated knowledge base can now be shown to the user for a specific knowledge object, an instance of an ontological class. Instead of reading 10 documents about a person, a user could view the aggregated information from these 10 documents in a single view. The end user can essentially read all of the

---

[2] http://www.endeca.com
[3] http://www.siderean.com

documents about an entity without reading all the documents[4]. The source material is retained for reference and duplicate information is rolled up. This approach has obvious advantages over other search techniques, but end users are more accustomed to reading documents and simple searching techniques. The next section describes how we bridge the gap to allow keyword search users to utilize a Semantic Web application for knowledge/intelligence management.

3 The Concept Object Web Application

To motivate how the Concept Object Web is relevant to knowledge/intelligence management, we present a thread of a user that highlights the functionalities of the system. This example is followed by the technical approach involved highlighting the differences between other applications and the lessons learned during development.

3.1 Example

Consider an analyst who is researching some suspicious activities in the Ukraine. When the analyst starts using the Concept Object Web they are presented with a sparse page with a familiar keyword search box. In this example the user makes a query for "political murders Ukraine".

The result of the keyword based search, shown in Figure 1, is a display of document metadata relevant for that query and a series of entities that are mentioned in the document collection for the query results. For the keyword query, 36 documents were returned. Along with the summary of each document, the user may view the knowledge objects, class instances, that appear in each document. The knowledge objects from the individual documents in the result set form the knowledge object display at the bottom of the screen. These entities were grouped into three customizable categories which correspond to classes in an ontology. The knowledge object portion of the display shows the occurrence count of knowledge objects that appear in the result set. In this example, the *Ukraine Parliament* occurs 6 times in our initial result set. This is somewhat interesting given our initial keyword key word query was "political murders Ukraine" and that *parliament* is one of the most frequent occurring organization in the set.

The initial query can be refined by clicking on the occurrence count for *parliament* from the previous figure. The query now consists of a keyword query and a semantic query that requires a certain entity, *parliament* in this case, to appear in the result set. The result of this refined query is a set of 6 documents that have document metadata and knowledge objects as before. The user could read those six documents, but COW provides other capabilities for exploring the information space. As was the case with the initial query, *Leonid Kuchma* is the most occurring Person in the document set. It may be of interest to find out more about *Kuchma* before proceeding. This can be done by clicking on the knowledge object link. The figure below shows the information known about *Leonid Kuchma*.

---

[4] The work in this paper was based on this concept introduced by Joseph Rockmore of Cyladian Technological Consulting.

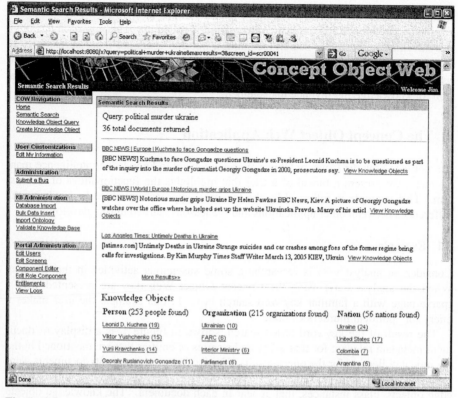

Fig. 1. This screen shows results for a keyword query. It includes document metadata, constrained to show three results for this picture, and knowledge objects for faceted search. The user can refine the queries using these facets or navigate to the knowledge objects themselves. The column on the left shows functions for regular users at the top and for an administrator of the system at the bottom.

This knowledge object aggregates all of the semantic information about this entity and represents it with pointers back to the source document as well as providing information about when and how each fact was obtained. Most of the assertions composing this object were created via natural language processing over the document corpus. As these assertions are just Semantic Web statements, they may come from other sources such as markup tools or relational databases.

At this point users can navigate among knowledge objects to discover new information. Additional visualizations are available supporting graph-oriented views. The application also supports a number of common Semantic Web capabilities, such as graph-based searching and pattern detection agents. For the example, the user simply navigates among related knowledge objects. The user quickly finds that *Kuchma* is accused of being involved in multiple murders. Both murders are accused by *Mykola Melnychenko* with the evidence being secret audio records. With further investigation, the accuser is a relative with *Kuchma's* rival *Victor Yanukovych* and associated with a *Russian FSB agent*. An analyst will be able to determine that *Kuchma* is being framed for these two events

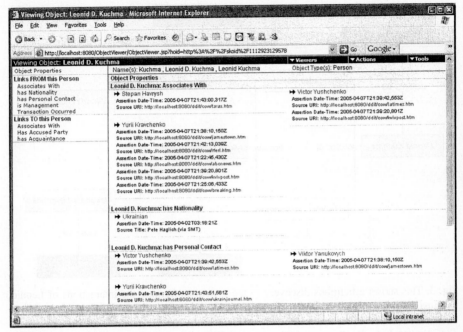

Fig. 2. This knowledge object displays relations and attributes for the entity. Each of the assertions displayed has metadata, which can be hidden, describing the source of the information. In this display, assertions have come from multiple sources and tools. The assertions from different sources may confirm or refute each other. The viewers tab is used for other graphical representation of the information. The actions tab allows users to edit and create knowledge objects. The tools tab is used to launch agents to look for predetermined patterns.

From our initial query concerning "political murders Ukraine" the Concept Object Web lets you refine the query with facets until you arrive at documents and knowledge objects of interest. The example discovery involves only a few hops. In the case above the human is critical in the loop to correlate information about two recordings, described textually. This could not be determined solely by a Semantic Web reasoning system. One of the key components of the Concept Object Web is to use semantics when possible, but fall back on the expertise of the user when necessary. Pointers are always available back to the source documents so users can read the original documents if they need to.

3.2 Technical Approach

This section describes the technical details of the system and how we dealt with the tradeoffs of Semantic Web capabilities in a knowledge/intelligent management domain.

3.2.1 System Architecture
The architecture leverages tools that generate semantic markup to feed text and semantic indexing repositories. ISX's SPARKAL was used for the Semantic Web

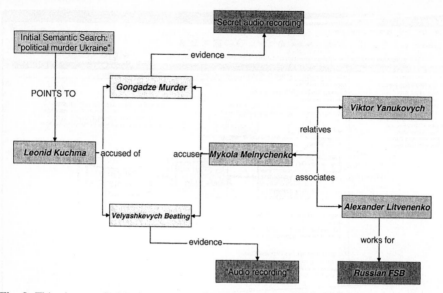

Fig. 3. This shows a fictitious discovery in the system concerning the interactions of Leonid Kuchma and Mykola Melnychenko. The keyword search leads to knowledge objects that help the human correlate information about the entities. In the above figure, the textual evidence is critical to the human's discovery. These types of situations cannot easily be solved by using Semantic Web technologies in isolation.

knowledge base portion and Apache's Lucene [1] was used to incorporate keyword and faceted search. As documents or databases are ingested, the Lucene index must be populated with the semantically-grounded information that results from inference in the knowledge base [4]. We chose arbitrary fields to populate for faceted search based on our ontologies, but you could conceivably take a more dynamic approach.

3.2.2 Search and Discovery
Over the years we have found that most users are simply not comfortable with Semantic Web style queries. This could probably be said about relational databases as well, but they are generally much more restrictive in terms of numbers of tables and fields versus ontology classes and properties. For usability, it seemed the text box was a better alternative. At that point, we could have let users search directly for knowledge objects rather than documents. We feel the use of facets, useful in their own regard, provides a conceptual jumping off point to viewing knowledge objects. The use of the facets allows the users to see how the document metadata could be leveraged.

3.2.3 Navigation and Visualization
Showing knowledge objects creates a number of difficulties. The most prominent of these is determining which information should be displayed to the end user. The current Concept Object Web displays all recent assertions, but other strategies are valuable. Of particular interest is aggregating data into higher abstraction levels allowing the users the ability to drill down on the information they care about while still

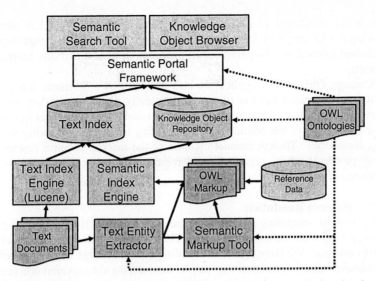

Fig. 4. This is the high-level architecture for COW. Text documents are indexed and processed by an entity extractor for semantic index. The portal framework provides multiple strategies for searching and discovering information.

seeing a comprehensive view of the information. There are many commercial products and research efforts that can be leveraged for visualizing graphs and networks.

The Concept Object Web primarily uses a simple web based display. Our techniques try to ensure objects have names. The first name asserted for that object will be used as the visual handle for that label. This consistency of names has been found to be extremely important. Though many objects do not have easily determined names, such as events, these unnamed objects are not terribly useful in this type of application and are usually hidden from users. To help guide navigation in the web-based view we have chosen ontological information to show in tool tip form. This has proven to help users learn information about objects within their results set without necessarily refining their query. For other navigation and visualization Inxight's StarTree™ and Graphviz are used.

3.2.4 Markup Generation
Markup can come from databases, XML, and text. There are increasing numbers of tools for managing relational databases as though they were semantically-grounded. Additionally, techniques are prevalent for turning XML into RDF/OWL. Text is particularly difficult to obtain markup for. Automated entity/fact extractors can provide a partial set of entities and facts, but it will miss and misclassify many entities and relations. There are a number of research-oriented tools for allowing humans to author semantic markup. These tools are good for advanced users who need to create small amounts of markup, but they can be difficult to use.

The Concept Object Web can leverage all of these types of markup despite the fact that the automated extraction may be errorful. In this application, our ontologies were developed to constrain the amount of inference that is performed. The intention is to limit the propagation of faulty data through inference. We also attempted to build our application around classes of objects that the entity extractor is good at extracting. For the Concept Object Web, Lockheed Martin's Aeroswarm [8] was used to perform the automated extraction. To perform full exploitation of text markup, manual tools are required.

The Concept Object Web application also utilizes ISX's Semantic Markup Tool [7]. This tool leverages the use of the automatically generated markup as well as templates to aid the user. These templates act as ontological views that quickly constrain the complexity of the ontology while providing users with the ability to quickly mark up documents. Though manual creation of the markup requires resources, we have seen problems where organizations have decided the benefits were worth the cost of human effort.

3.2.5 Co-reference Resolution

One of the keys to integrating information across data sources is the ability to perform co-reference resolutions across the sources. This is a very challenging problem that is not easy to address. We have found that seeding our knowledge bases with reference data containing basic information that can be used during the co-reference process is helpful.

In the Concept Object Web we seeded our system with names of popular figures for our data corpus. This data set included entity aliases and some basic information that could be used to determine identical objects. Our co-reference algorithm primarily depended on entity name matching using syntactic and phonetic cues. We used the assumption that most entities have unique names. More sophisticated graph matching could have provided better resolution performance, but for our corpus the simplifying assumptions worked sufficiently. Due to our use of automated markup generation, most entities being co-referenced had very few properties and relationships making sophisticated algorithms ineffective.

Co-reference resolution is an active area of research that cannot be covered here. Our experiences have shown us that generic algorithms for graph matching need to be supported with custom algorithms for entity types. For instance, there may be completely different algorithms for co-referencing entities and people. Syntactic similarity algorithms may work well for co-referencing people, but will lead to many false positives in co-referencing dates. We have found that each algorithm beyond name matching provides a diminishing return. Semantic Web application developers should take into account the characteristics of the data set and the required correctness for resolving duplicate entities.

4   Related Work

Since there are too many tools supporting knowledge/intelligence management to mention in this space, I will only refer to those that are using the Semantic Web. Most Semantic Web applications or components could easily fit into the knowledge/intelligence management framework described in the Concept Object Web. In fact, it shares many similarities to components from EU-funded research projects, such as the Information Society Technologies program, and DARPA's DAML project

[3]. It also leverages popular tools such as Jena [9] and Sesame [2] that were developed under research programs.

In terms of some popular Semantic Web knowledge management applications, there are a number of interesting applications that cover different portions of the space. SWAD-Europe [11] has produced a number of interesting Semantic Web Portal applications. They have similarities to our work, but we focus on the notion of viewing integrated knowledge objects, particularly from text data sources. Haystack [10] is comparable but leans more towards allowing clients manage their own information spaces. In our opinion tools similar to Haystack are complementary to the Concept Object Web. Semantic Search [5] does a nice job of describing integrating Semantic Web with regular search, but doesn't discuss some of the details mentioned in our work.

5 Conclusions

Though the Semantic Web is still emerging it is now clear that some of the barriers are being broken down to support everyday application. The Concept Object Web is an example of a new paradigm of knowledge/intelligence management tools that leverage the powers of the Semantic Web complementing the human to perform their knowledge management tasks. In this application, we believe there is added value in using the semantics to help aggregate the information and present the integrated view to users.

References

1. Apache Lucene. http://lucene.apache.org.
2. Broekstra, J., Kampman, A., and van Harmelen, F. Sesame: A Generic Architecture for Storing and Querying RDF. Published at the International Semantic Web Conference 2002, Sardinia, Italy.
3. The DARPA Agent Markup Language, http://www.daml.org.
4. Finin, T., Mayfield J., Fink, C., Joshi, A., and Cost R. Information Retrieval and the Semantic Web. Proceedings of the 38th International Conference on System Sciences (2005).
5. Guha, R., McCool, R., Miller, E., Semantic Search. WWW2003, Budapest, Hungary.
6. Kettler, B. *et al.* The Semantic Object Web: An Object-Centric Approach to Knowledge Management and Exploitation on the Semantic Web. ISX Corporation Whitepaper. Presented as a poster at the 2nd International Semantic Web Conference (ISWC 2003). http://www.semanticobjectweb.isx.com.
7. Kettler, B., Starz, J., Miller, W., Haglich, P. A Template-based Markup Tool for Semantic Web Content. Submitted to the 4th International Semantic Web Conference (ISWC 2005).
8. Lockheed Martin 2005. Lockheed Martin AeroSWARM tool. http://ubot.lockheedmartin.com/ubot/hotdaml/aeroswarm.html.
9. McBride, B. Jena: Implementing the RDF Model and Syntax Specification. Semantic Web Workshop, WWW2001.
10. Quan, D., Huynh D., and Karger, D. Haystack: A Platform for Authoring End User Semantic Web Applications in ISWC 2003.
11. SWAD-Europe, http://www.w3.org/2001/sw/Europe/.

The Personal Publication Reader

Fabian Abel[1], Robert Baumgartner[2,3], Adrian Brooks[3], Christian Enzi[2],
Georg Gottlob[2,3], Nicola Henze[1], Marcus Herzog[2,3], Matthias Kriesell[4],
Wolfgang Nejdl[1], and Kai Tomaschewski[1]

[1] Research Center L3S & Information Systems Institute, University of Hannover
{abel, henze, nejdl, tomaschewski}@kbs.uni-hannover.de
[2] DBAI, Institute of Information Systems, Vienna University of Technology
{baumgart, enzi, gottlob, herzog}@dbai.tuwien.ac.at
[3] Lixto Software GmbH, Donau-City-Strasse 1/Gate 1, 1220 Vienna, Austria
{baumgartner, brooks, gottlob, herzog}@lixto.com
[4] Inst. f. Math. (A), University of Hannover
kriesell@math.uni-hannover.de

Abstract. This application demonstrates how to provide personalized,
syndicated views on distributed web data using Semantic Web technologies. The application comprises four steps: The **information gathering step**, in which information from distributed, heterogenous sources
is extracted and enriched with machine-readable semantics, the **operation step** for timely and up-to-date extractions, the **reasoning step**
in which rules reason about the created semantic descriptions and additional knowledge-bases like ontologies and user profile information, and
the **user interface creation step** in which the RDF-descriptions resulting from the reasoning step are interpreted and translated into an appropriate, personalized user interface. We have developed this application for
solving the following real-world problem: We provide personalized, syndicated views on the publications of a large European research project
with more than twenty geographically distributed partners and embed
this information with contextual information on the project, its working
groups, information about the authors, related publications, etc.[1]

Keywords: web data extraction, web data syndication, personalized
views.

1 Introduction

In today's information society, the World Wide Web plays a prominent role for
disseminating and retrieving information: lots of useful information can be found
in the web, from train departure tables to consultation hours, from scientific
data to online auctions, and so on. While this information is already available
for consumption by human users, we lack applications that can collect, evaluate,

---

[1] This research has partially been supported by REWERSE - Reasoning on the Web
(www.rewerse.net), Network of Excellence, 6th European Framework Program.

Y. Gil et al. (Eds.): ISWC 2005, LNCS 3729, pp. 1050–1053, 2005.

combine, and re-evaluate this information. Currently, users retrieve online content in separate steps, one step for each information request, and evaluate the information chunks afterwards according to their needs: e.g. the user compares the train arrival time with the starting time of the meeting he is requested to participate in, etc. Another common scenario for researchers is that a user reads some scientific publication, gets curious about the authors, other work of the authors, on related work targeting on similar research questions, etc. Linking these information chunks together is a task that can currently not be performed by machines. In our application, we show how to solve this information integration problem for the latter mentioned "researcher scenario". We show, how to

1. extract information from distributed and inhomogeneous sites, and create semantic descriptions of the extracted information chunks,
2. maintain the web data extraction to ensure up-to-date information,
3. reason about the created semantic descriptions and ontological knowledge,
4. and create syndicated, personalized views on web information.

The Personal Publication Reader (PPR) extends the idea of Semantic Portals like e.g. SEAL [4] or others with the capability of extracting and syndicating web data from various, distributed sites or portals which do not belong to the ownership of the application itself.

2   Extraction and Annotation with Semantic Descriptions

In our application, the web pages from which we extract the information are maintained by partners of the research project REWERSE, thus the sources of the information are distributed and belong to different owners which provide their information in various ways and formats (HTML, Java-script, PHP-generated pages, etc.). Moreover, in each list, authors, titles and other entities are potentially characterized in a different way, and different order criteria are enforced (e.g. by year or by name). Such a web presentation is well suited for human consumption, but hardly usable for automatic processing. Nevertheless, the web is the most valuable information resource in this scenario. In order to access and understand these heterogeneous information sources one has to apply web extraction techniques. The idea of our application is to "wrap" these heterogeneous sources into a formal representation based on Semantic Web standards. In this way, each institution can still maintain their own publication list and at the same way we can offer an integrated and personalized view on this data by regularly extracting web data from all member sites.

This application is open in the sense that it can be extended in an easy way, i.e. by connecting additional web sources. For instance, abstracts from www.researchindex.com can be queried for each publication lacking this information and joined to each entry. Moreover, using text categorization tools one can rate and classify the contents of the abstracts. Another possibility is to extract organization and person data from the institution's web pages to inform the ontology to which class in the taxonomy an author belongs (such as full professor). Web extraction and annotation in the PPR is performed by the *Lixto Suite*. Web data extraction is a hot topic – for an extensive overview of methods and tools refer to [3]. First, with the *Lixto Visual Wrapper* [1] for each type of web site a so-called wrapper is created; the application designer visually and semi-automatically defines the characteristics of publication elements on particular web sites based on characteristics of the particular HTML presentation and some possible domain knowledge. After a wrapper has been generated it can be applied to a given web site (e.g. publications of University of Munich) to generate an "XML companion" that contains the relevant information stored in XML using (in this application context meaningful) XML tags.

3   Extraction Maintenance

In the next step, in the *Lixto Transformation Server* application designer visually composes the information flow from web sources to an RDF presentation that is handed over to the PPR once a week. Then the application designer defines a schedule how often which web source is queried and how often the information flow is executed. Additionally, deep web navigation macros possibly containing logins, cookies and web forms as well as iteration over forms are created. As a next step in the data flow, the data is harmonized to fit into a common structure, and e.g. an attribute "origin" is added containing the institution's name, and author names are harmonized by being mapped to a list of names known by the system. Finally, the XML data structure is mapped to a pre-defined RDF schema structure. Once the wrappers are in place, the complete application runs without further human interference, and takes care of publication updates. In case future extractions fail the application designers will receive a notification.

4   Reasoning for Syndicated and Personalized Views on Distributed Web Data

In addition to the extracted dynamic information, we maintain data about the members of the research project from the member's corner of the REWERSE project web site. We have constructed an ontology for describing researchers and their involvement in scientific projects like REWERSE, which extends the known Semantic Web Research Community Ontology (http://ontobroker. semanticweb.org/ontos/swrc.html) with some project-specific aspects.

Personalization rules reason about all this dynamic and static data in order to create syndicated and personalized views. As an example, the following rule (using the TRIPLE[5] syntax) determines all authors of a publication:

```
FORALL A, P authors(A, P) <- P[dc:creator -> A]@'http:..':publications.
```

In this rule, @'http:..':publications is the name of the model which contains the RDF-descriptions of the extracted publication informations. Further rules combine information on these authors from the researcher ontology with the author information. E.g. the following rule determines the employer of a project member, which might be a company, or a university, or, in general, some instance of a subclass of an organization (see line three below: here, we query for some subclass (direct or inferred) of the class "Organization"):

```
FORALL A,I works_at(A, I) <- EXISTS A_id,X (name(A_id,A)
  AND ont:A_id[ont:involvedIn -> ont:I]@'http:...#':researcher
  AND ont:X[rdfs:subClassOf -> ont:Organization]@rdfschema('..':researcher)
  AND ont:I[rdf:type -> ont:X]@'http:...#':researcher).
```

Disambiguation of results – here especially resource identification problems caused by varying author names – is achieved by an additional name identification step. For a user with specific interests, for example "interest in personalized information systems", information on respective research groups in the project, on persons working in this field, on their publications, etc., is syndicated.

5   User Interface Provision

We run the PPR within our Personal Reader framework for designing, implementing and maintaining personal Web Content Readers [2]. These personal Web Content Readers allow a user to browse information (the *Reader* part), and to access personal recommendations and contextual information on the currently regarded web resource (the *Personal* part). For the PPR, we instantiated a personalization Web service in our Personal Reader framework which holds the above mentioned rules. An appropriate visualization Web service for displaying the results of the reasoning step (which are provided as RDF documents and refer to an ontology of personalization functionality) has been implemented.

Availability of the Personal Publication Reader

The concept of the Personal Publication Reader and its functionality are summarized in a video, and so are the web data extraction and maintenance tasks. All demonstration videos and access to the application itself are available via http://www.personal-reader.de/semwebchallenge/sw-challenge.html.

References

1. R. Baumgartner, S. Flesca, and G. Gottlob. Visual Web Information Extraction with Lixto. In *Proc. of VLDB*, 2001.
2. N. Henze and M. Kriesell. Personalization Functionality for the Semantic Web: Architectural Outline and First Sample Implementation. In *1st Int. Workshop on Engineering the Adaptive Web (EAW 2004)*, Eindhoven, The Netherlands, 2004.
3. S. Kuhlins and R. Tredwell. Toolkits for generating wrappers. In *Net.ObjectDays*, 2002.
4. A. Maedche, S. Staab, N. Stojanovice, and R.Studer. Semantic portal - the seal approach. In D. Fensel, J. Hendler, H. Lieberman, and W. Wahlster, editors, *Spinning the Semantic Web*, pages 317–359. MIT-Press, 2003.
5. M. Sintek and S. Decker. TRIPLE - an RDF Query, Inference, and Transformation Language. In *International Semantic Web Conference (ISWC)*, Sardinia, Italy, 2002.

DynamicView: Distribution, Evolution and Visualization of Research Areas in Computer Science

Zhiqiang Gao, Yuzhong Qu, Yuqing Zhai, and Jianming Deng

Department of Computer Science and Engineering, Southeast University, China
{zqgao, yzqu, yqzhai, jmdeng}@seu.edu.cn

Abstract. It is tedious and error-prone to query search engines manually in order to accumulate a large body of factual information. Search engines retrieve and rank potentially relevant documents for human perusal, but do not extract facts, or fuse information from multiple documents. This paper introduces *DynamicView*, a Semantic Web application for researchers to query, browse and visualize distribution and evolution of research areas in computer science. Present and historical web pages of top 20 universities in USA and China are analyzed, and research areas of faculties in computer science are extracted automatically by segmentation based algorithm. Different ontologies of ACM and MST classification systems are combined by SKOS vocabularies, and the classification of research areas is learned from the ACM Digital Library. Query results including numbers of researchers and their locations are visualized in SVG map and animation. Interestingly, great differences of hot topics do exist between the two countries, and the number of researchers in certain areas changed greatly from the year 2000 to 2005.

1 Introduction

The web is increasingly becoming the primary source of research areas to modern researchers. With millions of pages available from thousands of web sites, finding the distribution and evolution of research areas in different countries and regions is a problematic task. Imagine that a young Chinese researcher, who has just received his PH. D degree in *artificial intelligence*, is planning his future research. He may want to know how many people are doing relative researches, such as *machine learning, multi-agent system, knowledge representation*, etc. He may also want to examine history and prognosticate tendency of *machine learning*. Additionally, if he intends to be a visiting scholar in USA in the near future, finding differences of hot topics between the two countries is rather helpful. However, browsing web sites, extracting related information and analyzing this information is too time consuming for individuals. Therefore, we develop *DynamicView* to tackle this challenge.

In the following of the paper, we begin with the introduction of major components of *DynamicView* in Section 2. In Section 3, we describe key services. Related works are discussed briefly in Section 4. Lastly, conclusions and ongoing works are summarized in Section 5.

Y. Gil et al. (Eds.): ISWC 2005, LNCS 3729, pp. 1054–1058, 2005.

2   Major Components

Crawler. Hub pages (faculty lists) are found by human intervention, and the *Crawler* searches and stores the homepage of each faculty by link analysis. Top 20 universities in USA are chosen mainly according to the ranking of US News [1], but not the exactly same. Top 20 universities in China are selected in accordance with the ranking of Ministry of Education of China [2], with a few universities excluded whose web pages could not be accessed (May, 2005). Historical web pages of top 20 universities in USA are downloaded from the Web Archive [3].

Extraction Engine. English pages are processed automatically, while Chinese ones by hand due to its complexity. Extraction results of research areas, names of researchers and universities are stored into relational databases. Web pages of top 10 universities are browsed manually and 65 *cue phrases* indicating *start* positions for information extraction are obtained, such as *research areas, research interests*, etc. *End* positions may be character '.', html tag <p>, end of file, or the position where the window size exceeds 300. Meanwhile, 1274 *pattern phrases* used for KMP algorithm are obtained. Combining *cue phrases* and KMP algorithm with segmentation of pages for each faculty, the average performance of our algorithm reaches 68.00% recall and 73.11% precision.

Ontology Learner. The ACM digital library [4] is utilized to learn classification of research areas. Each research area is input as a keyword, and top 60 papers returned with primary and additional classifications are used as training samples. Three cases of classification distribution may occur. 1) If one peak exists, the peak classification is the answer. 2) If more than one peak exist, and they belong to the same super classification, the super classification is the answer. 3) If more than one peak exists but they belong to different super classifications, or there is no peak, the classification is specified by human interaction. For each research area, the following relations are defined in SKOS (Simple Knowledge Organisation System) [5] vocabularies: *skos:prefLabelENG, skos:prefLableCHN, skos:altLabelENG, skos:altLabelCHN, skos:narrowerACM, skos:narrowerMST, skos:broaderACM* and *skos:broaderMST*. ENG means the label is expressed in English, and CHN in Chinese. ACM refers to the ACM Computing Classification System (1998)[6], with MST to classification and code of disciplines GB/T 13745/92 by Ministry of Science and Technology, China.

Query Processor. Users may query by country (USA or China), ontology (ACM or MST), hot topics and history. Note, users have to install SVG Viewers [7] to see SVG (Scalable Vector Graphics)[8] maps and animation.

---

[1] http://www.usnews.com

[2] http://www.cdgdc.edu.cn/zhxx/index.jsp

[3] http://www. archive.org

[4] http://portal.acm.org/dl.cfm

[5] http://www.w3.org/TR/swbp-skos-core-guide/

[6] http://www.acm.org/class/1998/ccs98.html

[7] http://www.adobe.com/svg/viewer/install/main.html

[8] http://www.w3.org/Graphics/SVG/

3   Key Services

Distribution of researchers in different countries and areas based on different ontologies. Given as an example, the number of researchers in *artificial intelligence* is shown in Fig.1, which are 327 (USA, ACM), 315 (USA, MST), 125 (China, ACM) and 169 (China, MST), respectively.

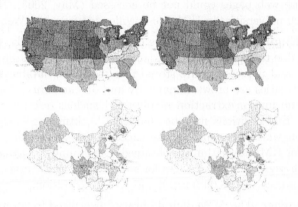

Fig. 1. Distribution of researchers in *artificial intelligence* according to ACM (left) and MST (right) ontologies in USA (top) and China (bottom)

Distribution of hot topics in different countries. Top 10 hot topics are deduced from original research areas with synonym relations, as depicted in Fig. 2 (top). Grey color refers to USA and pink color China. Surprisingly, the 1st

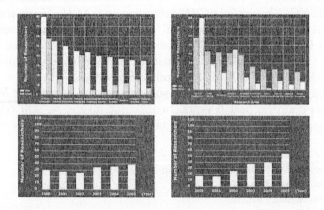

Fig. 2. Distribution of researchers in top 10 hot topics (top) in USA (left) and China (right), as well as evolution of hot topics (bottom) of *operating system* (left) and *machine learning* (right)

and 4th hot topics in two countries are the same: *artificial intelligence* and *software engineering*. But the other 8 hot topics are totally different. It seems that researchers in USA prefer theory and foundation, including *machine learning*, *computer architecture*, *programming languages*, *distributed systems* , *operating systems*, *robotics*, *computer graphics* and *computer vision*. By contrast, Chinese researchers emphasize application, including *data mining*, *databases*, *computer networks* , *information security*, *data warehousing*, *pattern recognition*, *network security* and *image processing*.

Evolution of hot topics from the year 2000 to 2005. The number of researchers in some research areas does not change significantly such as *operating systems*. Meanwhile, The number of researchers in other areas such as *machine learning* has increased nearly 2 times, as demonstrated in Fig. 2 (bottom).

4   Related Works

CS AKTive Space [1] provides a way to explore the UK computer science research domain across multiple dimensions for multiple stakeholders, from funding agencies to individual researchers. *Flink* system [2] extracts, aggregates and visualizes online social networks from a number of information sources including web pages, emails, publication archives and FOAF profiles. However, *D*ynamicView faces a much larger challenge, namely to extract and demonstrate research areas of computer science in different countries, languages, ontologies and over time. To the best of our knowledge there is no well-established approach for this task.

5   Conclusions and Ongoing Works

*D*ynamicView is designed for researchers of computer science to visualize the distribution and evolution of research areas in top 20 universities of USA and China. Research areas are extracted automatically by segmentation based algorithm with the performance of 68.00% recall and 73.11% precision. In order to combine different ontologies of ACM and MST, SKOS vocabularies are extended. Classifications of research areas are learned from the ACM Digital Library by analyzing the peaks of classification distribution. Except for *artificial intelligence* and *software engineering*, the other 8 hot topics in the two countries are different. The number of researchers in some areas such as *machine learning* has changed greatly in the past 6 years. In the near future, we will design a link grammar based information extraction algorithm to detect new areas[9].

Acknowledgments

This work is supported in part by National Key Basic Research and Development Program of China under Grant 2003CB317004, the NSF of Jiangsu Province, China, under Grant BK2003001, Hwa-Ying Culture and Education Foundation as well as Ministry of Education of China under Grant 6809001001.

---

[9] http://xobjects.seu.edu.cn/DynamicView/index.html

References

1. Nigel R. Shadbolt, Nicholas Gibbins, Hugh Glaser, et al.: Walking Through CS AK-Tive Space: A demonstration of an integrated Semantic Web Application. Journal of Web Semantics, volume 1, issue 4. 2004
2. Peter Mika: Flink: Semantic Web Technology for the Extraction and Analysis of Social Networks. Journal of Web Semantics, volume 3, issue 2. 2005

Oyster - Sharing and Re-using Ontologies in a Peer-to-Peer Community

Raúl Palma[1] and Peter Haase[2]

[1] Ontology Engineering Group, Laboratorio de Inteligencia Artificial, Facultad de Informática,
Universidad Politécnica de Madrid, Spain
[2] Institute AIFB, University of Karlsruhe, Germany

Abstract. This paper presents Oyster, a Peer-to-Peer system for exchanging ontology metadata among communities in the Semantic Web. We describe how Oyster assists researchers in re-using existing ontologies, and how Oyster exploits semantic web techniques in data representation, query formulation, query result presentation to provide an online solution to share ontologies.

1 Introduction

Currently, ontology re-use is rather difficult, as it is hard to find and share ontologies available among the community. This leads to the problem of having many isolated ontologies created by many different parties. Besides the costs of the duplicate efforts this also hampers interoperability between ontology-based applications. Oyster[1] is a Peer-to-Peer application that exploits semantic web techniques in order to provide a solution for exchanging and re-using ontologies. To achieve this, Oyster implements a proposal for a metadata standard, so called Ontology Metadata Vocabulary (OMV)[2] [4] which is based on discussions and agreement in the EU IST thematic network of excellence Knowledge Web[3] as the way to describe ontologies. Exchanging ontology metadata is an interesting use case for a Peer-to-Peer application on the Semantic Web application for the following reasons: The information sources (ontologies) are geographically distributed among the community, and developers are willing to share the information about the ontologies they created provided they do not have to invest much work in doing so, while at the same time they are able to mantain the ownership of their ontologies. As a Peer-to-Peer system, Oyster further benefits from the following characteristics: no need for a centralized server (thus avoiding a bottleneck for both computational performance and information update), robustness against failure of any single component, and scalability both in data volumes and the number of connected parties.

Finally, since ontologies can be represented in different languages (such as OWL[5], DAML+OIL[1], RDF-S[2]), Oyster provides the possibility to exchange heterogeneous information through the use of the metadata standard.

---

[1] Oyster is freely available for download under http://oyster.ontoware.org/
[2] The OMV ontology is available at http://ontoware.org/projects/omv
[3] http://knowledgeweb.semanticweb.org/

Y. Gil et al. (Eds.): ISWC 2005, LNCS 3729, pp. 1059–1062, 2005.

2   Oyster

Oyster provides an innovative solution for sharing and re-using knowledge (i.e. ontologies) which is a crucial step to enable Semantic Web.

The Oyster system has been implemented as an instance of the Swapster system architecture[4]. In Oyster, ontologies are used extensively in order to provide its main functions (importing data, formulating queries, routing queries and processing answers).

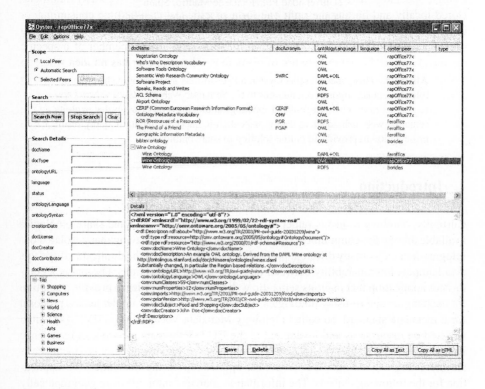

Fig. 1. Oyster screenshot

Creating and Importing Metadata: Oyster enables users to create metadata about ontologies manually, as well as to import ontology files and to automatically extract the ontology metadata available, letting the user to fill in missing values. For the automatic extraction, Oyster supports the OWL, DAML+OIL and RDF-S ontology languages. The ontology metadata entries are aligned and formally represented according to two ontologies: (1) the proposal for a metadata standard OMV which describes the properties of the ontology, (2) a topic hierarchy (i.e. DMOZ topic hierarchy), which describes specific categories of subjects to define the domain of the ontology.

---

[4] http://swap.semanticweb.org/

Formulating Queries: As shown in the left pane of the screenshot, the user can search for ontologies using simple keyword searches, or using more advanced, semantic searches. Here, queries are formulated in terms of these two ontologies. This means queries can refer to fields like name, acronym, ontology language, etc. (using the ontology document metadata ontology) or queries may refer to specific topic terms (using the topic hierarchy i.e. DMOZ).

Routing Queries: As shown in the upper left pane of the screenshot, the user may query a single specific peer (e.g. their own computer, because they can have many ontologies stored locally and finding the right one for a specific task can be time consuming, or users may want to query another peer in particular because this peer is a known big provider of information), or a specific set of peers (e.g. all the member of a specific organization), or the entire network of peers (e.g. when the user has no idea where to search), in which case queries are routed automatically in the network. In the latter case, queries are routed through the network depending on the expertise of the peers, describing which topic of the topic hierarchy (i.e. DMOZ) a peer is knowledgeable about. In order to achieve this expertise based routing, a matching function determines how closely the semantic content of a query matches the expertise of a peer [3].

Processing Results: Finally, the results matching query are presented in a result list (c.f. upper right pane in the screenshot). The answer of a query might be very large, and contain many duplicates due to the distributed nature and potentially large size of the Peer to Peer network. Such duplicates might not be exactly copies because the semi structured nature of the metadata, so the ontologies are used again to measure the semantic similarity between different answers and to remove apparent duplicates. Then a merged representation that combines the knowledge from the individual and potentially incomplete items is presented to the user. The details of particular results are shown in the lower right of the screenshot. The user can integrate results of a query into their local repository for future use. This information may in turn be used later to answer queries by other peers. Also, as proposed by OMV, all the specific realizations of an ontology can be grouped by the same base ontology to organize the answer.

3   Ontology Metadata Vocabulary in Oyster

Oyster applies semantic web technologies in order to build an online application for exchanging information that will assist users in building applications faster. In particular, it targets to re-using existing ontologies. In order to achieve this objective, Oyster provides an infrastructure for storing, sharing and finding ontologies making use of the proposal for a metadata standard OMV.

OMV distinguishes between an ontology base and an ontology document. This separation is based on the observation that any existing ontology document has some kind of core idea (conceptualisation) behind. From an ontology engineering perspective, initially a person develops such core idea of what should be modeled (and maybe how) in his mind. Further, this initial conceptualisation might be discussed with other persons and after all, an ontology will be realised using an ontology editor and stored in a specific format. Over time, there might be created several realisations of this initial conceptualisation in many different formats, e.g. in RDF-S[2] or OWL[5]. Therefore, an Ontology Base (OB) represents the abstract or core idea of an ontology, so called conceptualisation, and it describes the core properties of an ontology, independent from any implementation details. While an Ontology Document (OD) represents a specific realization of an ontology base, describing properties of an ontology that are related to the realization or implementation.

The distinction between an OB and OD leads to an efficient mechanism, e.g. for tracking several versions and evolvements of ontologies as well as for different representations of one knowledge model (conceptualisation) in different languages.

OMV also models additional classes required to represent and support the reuse of ontologies by such metadata vocabulary, especially in the context of the Semantic Web. Hence, OMV further models classes and properties representing environmental information and relations such as Person, Organisation, Party, OntologyEngineeringTool, OntologySyntax, OntologyLanguage, OntologyType. For a description of the complete OMV ontology we refer the reader to [4].

4   Conclusion

Sharing an re-using ontologies within communities is a critical task, which previously was rather difficult because of the heterogeneity, distribution and diverse ownership of the ontologies as well as the lack of sufficient metadata. In this paper, we have summarized the implementation of Oyster, a semantics-based Peer-to-Peer system for the exchange of ontology metadata, that exactly addresses these challenges. Oyster exploits semantic web technologies to provide a solution for re-using ontologies. It builds on a proposed standard for metadata for describing ontologies. Oyster is already being applied in the Knowledge Web project with partner across the european union.

For more information about Oyster, we refer the reader to http://oyster.ontoware.org/.

Acknowledgments. Research reported in this paper has been partially financed by the Knowledge Web project FP6-507482. We would like to thank our colleagues for fruitful discussions.

References

1. DAML+OIL (March 2001) reference description, 2001.   W3C Note, available at http://www.w3.org/TR/daml+oil-reference.
2. D. Brickley and R. V. Guha. RDF Vocabulary Description Language 1.0: RDF Schema. W3C Rec. 10 February 2004, 2004. available at http://www.w3.org/TR/rdf-schema/.
3. P. Haase, R. Siebes, and F. van Harmelen. Peer selection in peer-to-peer networks with semantic topologies. In *Proceedings of the International Conference on Semantics in a Networked World (ICNSW'04)*, Paris, June 2004.
4. J. Hartmann, R. Palma, Y. Sure, M. Suarez-Figueroa, P. Haase, A. Gomez-Perez, and R. Studer. Ontology metadata vocabulary and applications. In *Proc. of the Workshop on Web Semantics (SWWS'05), First IFIP WG 2.12 and WG 12.4 Agia Napa, Cyprus*, 2005.
5. M. K. Smith, C. Welty, and D. McGuinness. OWL Web Ontology Language Guide, 2004. W3C Rec. 10 February 2004, available at http://www.w3.org/TR/owl-guide/.

The FungalWeb Ontology: Semantic Web Challenges in Bioinformatics and Genomics

Arash Shaban-Nejad, Christopher J.O. Baker, Volker Haarslev, and Greg Butler

Dept. of Comp. Sci. and Software Eng., Concordia University, H3G1M8 Montreal, Canada
{arash_sh, baker, haarslev, gregb}@cs.concordia.ca

1 Introduction

Bioinformatics and genomics cover a wide range of different data formats (i.e. annotations, pathways, structures, sequences) derived from experimental and in-silico biological analysis which are stored, used, and manipulated by scientists and machines. The volume of this data is huge and usually distributed in different locations, and often frequently being updated.

FungalWeb is the first project of its kind in Canada to focus on bringing semantic web technology to genomics. It aimed to bring together available expertise in ontologies, multi-agent systems, machine learning and natural language processing to build a tailored knowledgebase and semantic systems of direct use to the scientific discovery process in the domain of fungal genomics [1].

We describe the FungalWeb Ontology which is a large-scale integrated bio-ontology in the domain of fungal genomics using state-of-the-art semantic technologies. The ontology provides simplified access to units of intersecting information from different biological databases and existing bio-ontologies. In particular, the FungalWeb ontology is being used as a core for a semantic web system. This system can be used by human, bioinformatics applications or some intelligent systems for ontology-based information retrieval to provide extended interpretations and annotations. [2]

2 The FungalWeb Ontology Design and Evaluation

The FungalWeb Ontology [2] is the result of integrating numerous biological database schemas, web accessible textual resources and interviews with domain experts and reusing some existing bio-ontologies. The Ontology is designed with a high level of granularity and implemented in OWL-DL language to take advantage of the combination of a frame representation of OWL framework and expressive Description Logics (DL). The majority of the terms in the FungalWeb Ontology come from following sources:

- NCBI taxonomy database [3]: contains the names of all organisms including fungi.
- NEWT: is the taxonomy database maintained by the Swiss-Prot [4].
- BRENDA [5]: a database of enzymes which provides a representative overview of enzyme nomenclature, enzyme features and actual properties.
- SwissProt [6]: a protein sequence database providing highly curated annotations, a minimal level of redundancy and a high level of integration with other databases.
- Commercial Enzyme Vendors: Companies that retail enzymes provide detailed descriptions of the properties and benefits of their products on their websites.

Y. Gil et al. (Eds.): ISWC 2005, LNCS 3729 , pp. 1063–1066, 2005.
© Springer-Verlag Berlin Heidelberg 2005

The FungalWeb Ontology also reuses existing domain specific bio-ontologies such as Gene Ontology (GO) [7] and TAMBIS [8]. This is done by merging, mapping, sharing common concepts and partially importing instances. By reusing concepts from other generic ontologies, a set of well defined concepts is obtained.

The integration is done at two levels: Data and Semantic Integration. Data integration is done by normalizing extracted data into a consistent representation. In order to perform semantic integration these we manually identified the relevant data items and the semantic commonality to bring them in a unified frame of reference.

Currently the Ontology contains 3667 concepts, 12686 instances and 157 Properties. Efforts to expand the conceptualization are continuing. Inclusion of more instance data in the knowledgebase allows us to pose richer and more complex queries.

Different associative properties were defined to relate individuals of concepts. For example the property "has been reported to be found in" relates an enzyme individual to a corresponding fungal species.

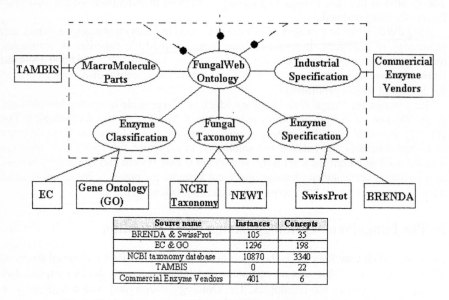

Fig. 1. The major resources included within the FungalWeb Ontology

As shown in Fig.1 most of terminology in the ontology is fungal organisms and fungal enzymes. The classification of fungi presented in the ontology is based on phylum, class, order, family, genus and species. Species are considered as the fungi instances. Enzymes are classified based on catalyzed reactions recommended by the International Union of Biochemistry and Molecular Biology (IUBMB). Enzyme names are defined as the enzyme instances.

The evaluation of the ontology is done pragmatically, by assessing the ontology to satisfy the requirements of our application, including determining the logical and semantic consistency. Logical consistency is checked automatically by KR editors and semantic consistency is assisted by the DL reasoner in the identification of correct or miss-classification. Although we sought to validate the biological data and relations by citing their origin (database or literature) or by checking consistency, validation by the domain expert was also necessary.

We use RACER [15] as a DL reasoning system with support for T-Box (axioms about class definitions) and A-Box (assertions about individuals) for reasoning on the FungalWeb Ontology and Checking the A-Box and T-Box consistency. On average, Racer solves the posed subsumption problems within fraction of a second. The performance of Racer is highly dependent on the number of individuals and response time grows with the number of individuals. The number of properties does not have an important affect on the response time, but, the number of property fillers has strongest influence on the performance with respect to instance retrieval.

3 Application Scenarios and Semantic Querying

We describe real world application scenarios to demonstrate what a bioinformatics application can gain from using ontology-based technologies. We argue for the commercial usage and business feasibility of the ontology by presenting scenarios that show how the diverse needs of the fungal biotechnology manager can be accommodated by semantic querying of an integrated set of data in the ontology. FungalWeb Ontology currently accommodates the application scenarios below [10].

- Identification of enzymes acting on substrates
- Identification of enzyme provenance and common taxonomic lineage
- Identification of commercial enzyme products for enzyme benchmark testing
- Identifying enzymes with unique properties suited for industrial application

These scenarios are illustrated [10] by posing semantic queries to the FungalWeb knowledgebase using a description logics based query language called nRQL (new Racer Query Language) [11]. nRQL is implemented in Racer with its applicability to OWL Semantic Web repositories to retrieve A-box individuals under specific conditions. nRQL is more expressive than traditional concept-based retrieval languages offered by previous DLs reasoning systems.

An example query made to the Ontology: This query retrieves the individuals of vendor name for vendors that sell products containing xylanase enzymes.
(RETRIEVE (?x) (AND (?x ?y |http://a.com/ontology#Sells|)
    (?y ?z |http://a.com/ontology#Contains|) (?z |http://a.com/ontology#Xylanase|)))
Also we use nRQL to retrieve values of annotation properties used to annotate ontological resources. These annotations represent metadata (i.e. comments, creator, date, identifier, source name, source URL, version, etc.) but can not be used for reasoning. This capability can be very useful for the ontology maintenance, versioning and providing proof and trust in a semantic web system.

For example the following query retrieves the source(s) for "Enzyme".

(RETRIEVE (|http://a.com/ontology#Enzyme|
    (TOLD-VALUE (|http://a.com/ontology#Source| |http://a.com/ontology#Enzyme|)))
    (BIND-INDIVIDUAL |http://a.com/ontology#Enzyme|))

4 Challenges

In the process of employing semantic web technology to develop ontology and a large knowledgebase in the domain of fungal biotechnology, we had to deal with variety of different challenges. Some of the major challenges included; working with highly heterogeneous and volatile data, the integration of ontologies implemented in different languages, with different semantic tools and platforms, and the lack of trustable tools for this purpose.

Our ongoing research involves improvement of querying capabilities and using Natural Language Processing (NLP) techniques for ontology update and change management. The project FungalWeb: "Ontology, the Semantic Web and Intelligent Systems for Genomics" is funded by Génome Québec.

References

1. Baker C. J. O., Butler G., and Haarslev V. Ontologies, Semantic web and Intelligent Systems for Genomics. 1st Canadian Semantic Web Interest Group Meeting (SWIG'04) , Montreal, Quebec, Canada (2004).
2. Shaban-Nejad A., Baker C. J. O., Butler G. Haarslev V. The FungalWeb Ontology: Semantic Web Application for Fungal Genomic. 1st Canadian Semantic Web Interest Group Meeting (SWIG'04) , Montreal, Quebec, Canada (2004).
3. National Centre for Biotechnology Information (NCBI) (http://www.ncbi.nlm.nih.gov/).
4. NEWT, UniProt taxonomy browser (http://www.ebi.ac.uk/newt/index.html).
5. Brenda Enzyme Database (http://www.brenda.uni-koeln.de/).
6. SwissProt protein sequence database (http://ca.expasy.org/sprot/).
7. Gene Ontology documentation, (http://www.geneontology.org/doc/GO.doc.html).
8. P.G. Baker, A. Brass, S. Bechhofer, C. Goble, N. Paton, and R. Stevens. TAMBIS: Transparent Access to Multiple Bioinformatics Information Sources. An Overview.In Proceedings of the Sixth International Conference on Intelligent Systems for Molecular Biology (ISMB'98), pages 25-34, California, June 1998.
9. Volker Haarslev, Ralf Möller. RACER System Description. Proceedings of International Joint Conference on Automated Reasoning, IJCAR'2001, R. Goré, A.Leitsch, T. Nipkow (Eds.), June 18-23, 2001, Siena, Italy, Springer-Verlag, Berlin,pp. 701-705.
10. Baker C. J. O., Witte R., Shaban-Nejad A., Butler G., and Haarslev V. The FungalWeb Ontology: Application Scenarios. Eighth Annual Bio-Ontologies Meeting, co-located with ISMB 2005, Detroit, Michigan, USA (2005).
11. M. Wessel, R. Möller. A High Performance Semantic Web Query Answering Engine. International Workshop on Description Logics (DL2005), Edinburgh, Scotland, UK, 2005.

CONFOTO: A Semantic Browsing and Annotation Service for Conference Photos

Benjamin Nowack

appmosphere web applications, Essen, Germany
bnowack@appmosphere.com

Abstract. CONFOTO[1] is a semantic browsing and annotation service for conference photos. It combines recent Web trends with the advantages of Semantic Web platforms. The service offers several tools to upload, link, browse and annotate pictures. Simple forms can be used to create multilingual titles, tags, or descriptions, while more advanced forms allow the relation of pictures to events, persons, ratings, and copyright information. CONFOTO provides tailored and interlinked browsers for photos, people, events, and documents. Remotely maintained photo descriptions can be added to the local knowledge base, data re-use is made possible via customizable syndication functions and a query interface.

1 Introduction

CONFOTO is a browsing and annotation service for conference photos. It combines the flexibility of the Resource Description Framework (RDF)[1] with recent Web trends such as keyword-based classification (so-called "folksonomies"[2]), interactive user interfaces[3][4], and syndication of news feeds. The main advantage of utilizing folksonomies is the ease of metadata creation. Online services such as Flickr[2] were able to attract a large number of users in a relatively short amount of time. However, simple tagging has its limits, as the retrieval of precise or implicit information is not possible. Additionally, a standardized way to directly re-use data does not exist. RDF, on the other hand, is a framework to create fine-grained annotations, but doesn't enjoy a good reputation in terms of simplicity.

CONFOTO is one of the first applications that provides both an end-user-oriented browsing and editing front-end for rich annotations and also a W3C-compliant[3] interface[5] to an RDF-based data store. It supports the Semantic Web[4] idea by allowing resource descriptions to be imported, created, annotated, combined, exported, and re-purposed.

2 Tools and Features

CONFOTO uses a set of wrappers to enable photo and conference data import from several different input formats, e.g. RSS 2.0 feeds from w3photo[6], Atom feeds from

---

[1] http://www.confoto.org/
[2] http://flickr.com/
[3] http://www.w3.org/2001/sw/DataAccess/
[4] http://www.w3.org/2001/sw

Y. Gil et al. (Eds.): ISWC 2005, LNCS 3729, pp. 1067–1070, 2005.

Flickr, or proprietary XML documents from events such ESWC 2005[5] and XTech 2005[6]. The system can generate and enhance RDF data for uploaded pictures, for image files linked via Web-accessible URLs, and also for photos described in external RDF/XML[7] documents.

Semantically, CONFOTO is optimized for information about conferences and photos. However, the RDF model allows any resource description to be freely combined with related objects (e.g. a FOAF[8] file or a list of publications could be associated with a person depicted in a photo).

The sections below give an overview of the tools and features currently available at *confoto.org*.

2.1 Image Upload or Linking

Image files can be uploaded via a simple HTML form. A group of uploaded photos can be annotated with associated date, conference, license, copyright, and/or subject information. The system automatically creates image thumbnails and a scaled image for the photo browser.

Another option is to not copy already published pictures to the server but to simply add photo URLs to the local RDF store. This is done through CONFOTO's "Link remote images" form which accepts a list of Web locations and allows group-annotations as well.

For images which have been described in RDF, the service provides an "Add RDF/XML" form that can be used to import remotely maintained resource descriptions. Again, thumbnails will be created automatically.

2.2 Photo Browser

The photo browser is based on a generic RDF viewer which has been adjusted to generate galleries of clickable thumbnails. Several filters can be used to create custom photo sets. Selecting an image opens a details view which shows a larger version of the image and a list of annotations from the RDF store. In case of non-literal annotations that point to related resources (e.g. persons depicted in the selected photo), the browsers provides a list of labels (e.g. titles of publications, or names of persons) and links to other tools such as a person, event, or document browser when available. This functionality is implemented by utilizing inference capabilities of an underlying OWL[9] toolkit[10].

2.3 Annotators

The main difference between CONFOTO and most existing Semantic Web applications is the availability of browser-based annotation forms. Depending on the type of a selected resource, a list of potential relations and attributes is offered to the user. Where possible, the tools support the annotation creation process by interactively suggesting matching resources as shown in Figure 1. This mechanism allows the seamless re-use of data already existing in the RDF store.

---

[5] http://www.eswc2005.org/
[6] http://www.xtech-conference.org/2005/

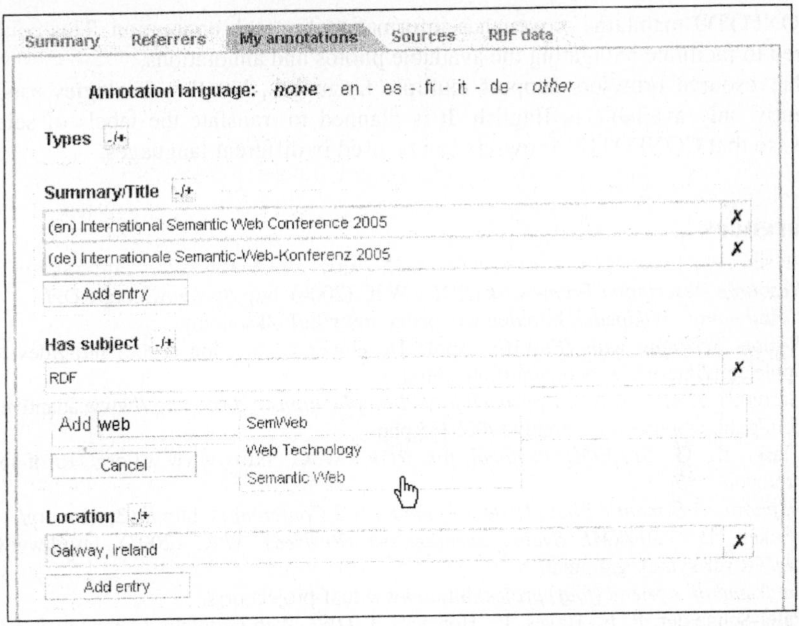

Fig. 1. Annotator with Suggest-as-you-Type Feature

Annotations can directly be added to the RDF store, whereupon the system's inference scripts are executed, iteratively improving the browsing experience. Annotators are rewarded with enhanced results when they switch back to browsing mode.

2.4 Data Export for Re-use

CONFOTO features multiple possibilities to export local data: Each page provides a link to an RDF/XML version of the currently displayed resource(s). Apart from that, machine-readable resource descriptions can be obtained by URIQA[11] requests, and also via a basic SPARQL[12] interface. Finally, as the number of URIQA- or SPARQL-enabled tools is still small, custom photo galleries can be exported as simple RSS 1.0[13] news feeds.

3 Conclusion and Possible Future Work

CONFOTO demonstrates the advantages of an RDF-based infrastructure and shows, that end-user-oriented, Web-based annotation tools don't have to be limited to simple tagging, but can also be used to create and augment rich annotations. However, the system is still in an early stage and a lot of things could be improved:

To better demonstrate the possibilities of RDF and SPARQL, the browsers need to be extended to offer means for context-specific views such as "all photos taken by this person", or "all events attended by this person".

CONFOTO maintains provenance information for each annotation. This could be utilized to facilitate navigating the available photos and annotations.

The resource browsers support multiple languages, but the ontologies used are currently only available in English. It is planned to translate the labels of selected terms, so that CONFOTO's browsers can be used in different languages.

References

1. *Resource Description Framework (RDF)*. W3C (2004). http://www.w3.org/RDF/
2. *Folksonomy - Wikipedia*. http://en.wikipedia.org/wiki/Folksonomy
3. *Remote Scripting with IFRAME*. Apple Developer Connection (2002) http://developer.apple.com/internet/webcontent/iframe.html
4. Garrett, J. J. *Ajax: A New Approach to Web Applications*. (2005) http://www.adaptivepath.com/publications/essays/archives/000385.php
5. Clark, K. G. *SPARQL Protocol for RDF*. W3C. http://www.w3.org/TR/rdf-sparql-protocol/
6. *w3photo - A Semantic Photo History of the IW3C2 Conferences*. http://w3photo.org/
7. Beckett, D. *RDF/XML Syntax Specification (Revised)*. W3C (2004). http://www.w3.org/TR/rdf-syntax-grammar/
8. *the friend of a friend (foaf) project* http://www.foaf-project.org/
9. Patel-Schneider, P. F., Hayes, P., Horrocks, I. *OWL Web Ontology Language Semantics and Abstract Syntax*. W3C (2004). http://www.w3.org/TR/owl-semantics/
10. Nowack, B. *OWLCHESTRA: Facilitating the Development and Publishing of Small-Scale Web Ontologies*. (2004). http://www.appmosphere.com/prod/media/owlchestra_demo_esws2004.pdf
11. Stickler, P. *URIQA: The Nokia URI Query Agent Model*. (2003) http://sw.nokia.com/uriqa/URIQA.html
12. Prud'hommeaux, E., Seaborne, A.: *SPARQL Query Language for RDF*. W3C (2005). http://www.w3.org/TR/rdf-sparql-query/
13. *RDF Site Summary (RSS) 1.0*. http://web.resource.org/rss/1.0/spec

Author Index

Lecture Notes in Computer Science

For information about Vols. 1–3680

please contact your bookseller or Springer

Vol. 3724: P. Fraigniaud (Ed.), Distributed Computing. XIV, 520 pages. 2005.

Vol. 3723: W. Zhao, S. Gong, X. Tang (Eds.), Analysis and Modelling of Faces and Gestures. XI, 4234 pages. 2005.

Vol. 3722: D. Van Hung, M. Wirsing (Eds.), Theoretical Aspects of Computing – ICTAC 2005. XIV, 614 pages. 2005.

Vol. 3721: A. Jorge, L. Torgo, P. Brazdil, R. Camacho, J. Gama (Eds.), Knowledge Discovery in Databases: PKDD 2005. XXIII, 719 pages. 2005. (Subseries LNAI).

Vol. 3720: J. Gama, R. Camacho, P. Brazdil, A. Jorge, L. Torgo (Eds.), Machine Learning: ECML 2005. XXIII, 769 pages. 2005. (Subseries LNAI).

Vol. 3719: M. Hobbs, A.M. Goscinski, W. Zhou (Eds.), Distributed and Parallel Computing. XI, 448 pages. 2005.

Vol. 3718: V.G. Ganzha, E.W. Mayr, E.V. Vorozhtsov (Eds.), Computer Algebra in Scientific Computing. XII, 502 pages. 2005.

Vol. 3717: B. Gramlich (Ed.), Frontiers of Combining Systems. X, 321 pages. 2005. (Subseries LNAI).

Vol. 3716: L. Delcambre, C. Kop, H.C. Mayr, J. Mylopoulos, O. Pastor (Eds.), Conceptual Modeling – ER 2005. XVI, 498 pages. 2005.

Vol. 3715: E. Dawson, S. Vaudenay (Eds.), Progress in Cryptology – Mycrypt 2005. XI, 329 pages. 2005.

Vol. 3714: H. Obbink, K. Pohl (Eds.), Software Product Lines. XIII, 235 pages. 2005.

Vol. 3713: L. Briand, C. Williams (Eds.), Model Driven Engineering Languages and Systems. XV, 722 pages. 2005.

Vol. 3712: R. Reussner, J. Mayer, J.A. Stafford, S. Overhage, S. Becker, P.J. Schroeder (Eds.), Quality of Software Architectures and Software Quality. XIII, 289 pages. 2005.

Vol. 3711: F. Kishino, Y. Kitamura, H. Kato, N. Nagata (Eds.), Entertainment Computing - ICEC 2005. XXIV, 540 pages. 2005.

Vol. 3710: M. Barni, I. Cox, T. Kalker, H.J. Kim (Eds.), Digital Watermarking. XII, 485 pages. 2005.

Vol. 3709: P. van Beek (Ed.), Principles and Practice of Constraint Programming - CP 2005. XX, 887 pages. 2005.

Vol. 3708: J. Blanc-Talon, W. Philips, D.C. Popescu, P. Scheunders (Eds.), Advanced Concepts for Intelligent Vision Systems. XXII, 725 pages. 2005.

Vol. 3707: D.A. Peled, Y.-K. Tsay (Eds.), Automated Technology for Verification and Analysis. XII, 506 pages. 2005.

Vol. 3706: H. Fuks, S. Lukosch, A.C. Salgado (Eds.), Groupware: Design, Implementation, and Use. XII, 378 pages. 2005.

Vol. 3704: M. De Gregorio, V. Di Maio, M. Frucci, C. Musio (Eds.), Brain, Vision, and Artificial Intelligence. XV, 556 pages. 2005.

Vol. 3703: F. Fages, S. Soliman (Eds.), Principles and Practice of Semantic Web Reasoning. VIII, 163 pages. 2005.

Vol. 3702: B. Beckert (Ed.), Automated Reasoning with Analytic Tableaux and Related Methods. XIII, 343 pages. 2005. (Subseries LNAI).

Vol. 3701: M. Coppo, E. Lodi, G. M. Pinna (Eds.), Theoretical Computer Science. XI, 411 pages. 2005.

Vol. 3699: C.S. Calude, M.J. Dinneen, G. Păun, M. J. Pérez-Jiménez, G. Rozenberg (Eds.), Unconventional Computation. XI, 267 pages. 2005.

Vol. 3698: U. Furbach (Ed.), KI 2005: Advances in Artificial Intelligence. XIII, 409 pages. 2005. (Subseries LNAI).

Vol. 3697: W. Duch, J. Kacprzyk, E. Oja, S. Zadrożny (Eds.), Artificial Neural Networks: Formal Models and Their Applications – ICANN 2005, Part II. XXXII, 1045 pages. 2005.

Vol. 3696: W. Duch, J. Kacprzyk, E. Oja, S. Zadrożny (Eds.), Artificial Neural Networks: Biological Inspirations – ICANN 2005, Part I. XXXI, 703 pages. 2005.

Vol. 3695: M.R. Berthold, R. Glen, K. Diederichs, O. Kohlbacher, I. Fischer (Eds.), Computational Life Sciences. XI, 277 pages. 2005. (Subseries LNBI).

Vol. 3694: M. Malek, E. Nett, N. Suri (Eds.), Service Availability. VIII, 213 pages. 2005.

Vol. 3693: A.G. Cohn, D.M. Mark (Eds.), Spatial Information Theory. XII, 493 pages. 2005.

Vol. 3692: R. Casadio, G. Myers (Eds.), Algorithms in Bioinformatics. X, 436 pages. 2005. (Subseries LNBI).

Vol. 3691: A. Gagalowicz, W. Philips (Eds.), Computer Analysis of Images and Patterns. XIX, 865 pages. 2005.

Vol. 3690: M. Pěchouček, P. Petta, L.Z. Varga (Eds.), Multi-Agent Systems and Applications IV. XVII, 667 pages. 2005. (Subseries LNAI).

Vol. 3689: G.G. Lee, A. Yamada, H. Meng, S.H. Myaeng (Eds.), Information Retrieval Technology. XVII, 735 pages. 2005.

Vol. 3688: R. Winther, B.A. Gran, G. Dahll (Eds.), Computer Safety, Reliability, and Security. XI, 405 pages. 2005.

Vol. 3687: S. Singh, M. Singh, C. Apte, P. Perner (Eds.), Pattern Recognition and Image Analysis, Part II. XXV, 809 pages. 2005.

Vol. 3686: S. Singh, M. Singh, C. Apte, P. Perner (Eds.), Pattern Recognition and Data Mining, Part I. XXVI, 689 pages. 2005.

Vol. 3685: V. Gorodetsky, I. Kotenko, V. Skormin (Eds.), Computer Network Security. XIV, 480 pages. 2005.

Vol. 3684: R. Khosla, R.J. Howlett, L.C. Jain (Eds.), Knowledge-Based Intelligent Information and Engineering Systems, Part IV. LXXIX, 933 pages. 2005. (Subseries LNAI).

Vol. 3683: R. Khosla, R.J. Howlett, L.C. Jain (Eds.), Knowledge-Based Intelligent Information and Engineering Systems, Part III. LXXX, 1397 pages. 2005. (Subseries LNAI).

Vol. 3682: R. Khosla, R.J. Howlett, L.C. Jain (Eds.), Knowledge-Based Intelligent Information and Engineering Systems, Part II. LXXIX, 1371 pages. 2005. (Subseries LNAI).

Vol. 3681: R. Khosla, R.J. Howlett, L.C. Jain (Eds.), Knowledge-Based Intelligent Information and Engineering Systems, Part I. LXXX, 1319 pages. 2005. (Subseries LNAI).